A Dictionary of Moroccan Arabic

Moroccan-English

Edited by
Richard S. Harrell

Compiled by
Thomas Fox and Mohammed Abu-Talib

With the assistance of
Ahmed Ben Thami, Allal Chreibi, Habiba Kanouni,
Ernest Ligon, and Mohammed Mekaoui

English-Moroccan

Edited by
Harvey Sobelman
and Richard S. Harrell

Compiled by
Thomas Fox, Alan McAninch, Allal Chreibi,
Majid Soussane, and Mohamed Neheiri

Georgetown University Press
Washington, D.C.

THE RICHARD SLADE HARRELL ARABIC SERIES

As an adjunct to its teaching and research program in the field of modern Arabic studies, Georgetown University's Institute of Languages and Linguistics inaugurated a publication series in Arabic studies in 1962. The Arabic Series is dedicated to the memory of its originator and first general editor Richard Slade Harrell, professor of linguistics, head of the Arabic Division, and director of the Arabic Research Program at Georgetown University.

The research reported herein was performed pursuant to a contract with the United States Office of Education, Department of Health, Education, and Welfare.

Many of the publications in this series, including the present volume, are still available along with their accompanying audiocassettes. A number of subsequent books for the study of the Arabic language have been published by Georgetown University Press and are also accompanied by audio (and in some cases video) materials. A list of Arabic publications may be found on the Georgetown University Press web site at www.georgetown.edu/publications/gup.

Georgetown University Press, Washington, D.C. 20007

Printed in the United States of America

ISBN 0-87840-007-9

A Dictionary of Moroccan Arabic

Moroccan-English

Edited by
Richard S. Harrell

Compiled by
Thomas Fox and Mohammed Abu-Talib

With the assistance of
Ahmed Ben Thami, Allal Chreibi, Habiba Kanouni,
Ernest Ligon, and Mohammed Mekaoui

THE ARABIC RESEARCH PROGRAM
INSTITUTE OF LANGUAGES AND LINGUISTICS
GEORGETOWN UNIVERSITY

The Arabic Research Program was established in June of 1960 as a contract between Georgetown University and the United States Office of Education under the provisions of the Language Development Program of the National Defense Education Act.

The first two years of the research program, 1960-62 (Contract number SAE-8706), were devoted to the production of six books, a reference grammar and a conversational English-Arabic dictionary in the cultivated spoken forms of Moroccan, Syrian, and Iraqi Arabic. The second two years of the research program, 1962-64 (Contract number OE-2-14-029), have been devoted to the further production of Arabic-English dictionaries in each of the three varieties of Arabic mentioned above, as well as comprehensive basic courses in the Moroccan and Iraqi varieties.

The eleven books of this series, of which the present volume is one, are designed to serve as practical tools for the increasing number of Americans whose lives bring them into contact with the Arab world. The dictionaries, the reference grammars, and the basic courses are oriented toward the educated American who is a layman in linguistic matters. Although it is hoped that the scientific linguist and the specialist in Arabic dialectology will find these books both of interest and of use, matters of purely scientific and theoretical importance have not been directly treated as such, and specialized scientific terminology has been avoided as much as possible.

As is usual, the authors or editors of the individual books bear final scholarly responsibility for the contents, but there has been a large amount of informal cooperation in our work. Criticism, consultation, and discussion have gone on constantly among the senior professional members of the staff. The contribution of more junior research assistants, both Arab and American, is also not to be underestimated. Their painstaking assembling and ordering of raw data, often in manners requiring considerable creative intelligence, has been the necessary prerequisite for further progress.

In most cases the books prepared by the Arabic Research Program are the first of their kind in English, and in some cases the first in any language. The preparation of them has been a rewarding experience. It is hoped that the public use of them will be equally so. The undersigned, on behalf of the entire staff, would like to ask the same indulgence of the reader as Samuel Johnson requested in his first English dictionary: To remember that although much has been left out, much has been included.

Richard S. Harrell
Professor of Linguistics
Georgetown University

Director,
Arabic Research Program

Before his death in late 1964, Dr. Harrell had done the major part of the work of general editor for the last five books of the Arabic Series, and to him is due the credit for all that may be found of value in that work. It remained for me only to make some minor editing decisions, and to see these books through the process of proofreading and printing; for any errors or inadequacies in the final editing, the responsibility is mine alone.

Wallace M. Erwin
Assistant Professor of
Linguistics and Arabic
Georgetown University

INTRODUCTION

This dictionary is designed to serve the practical needs of Americans whose lives bring them into contact with Morocco and Moroccans. The aim of the compilers has been to present the core vocabulary of everyday life. No attempt has been made to cover dialect variations or specialized vocabularies, as for example the detailed terminology of the various handicrafts, of commerce, or of industry. The average Moroccan is no more familiar with such terms himself than is the average American with similar terms in English. The entries are based on the speech of educated Moroccans from the cities of Fez, Rabat, and Casablanca. Except for minor variations, their usage may be taken as typical of urban speech in general. This standard urban usage is understood throughout Morocco, including the villages and the countryside.

Although a variety of reference works were consulted in the compilation of this dictionary, the material presented is wholly primary.* No single entry is a simple reworking or translation of previously published material. Every entry is a critically evaluated reflection of a native Moroccan's judgment as to the meaning of his own speech. In a few rare cases secondary reference works have been relied on for limited terminological purposes. An example is the entry *argan,* which is translated as 'argan tree'. The Moroccan members of our staff were familiar with the word *argan* as well as the plant which it represents, but none of them knew the English equivalent. None of the American members of our staff were familiar with the plant. A comparison of various French and English dictionaries convinced the editor that 'argan tree' was the proper entry. No other use has been made of secondary sources.

The word list of Ferré's *Lexique Marocain-Français* ** was taken as a point of departure. Entries not directly familiar to our Moroccan staff members were deleted and various additions were made from their own knowledge. In no case were Ferré's

*Constantly in use for matters of detail were such standard works as: *Webster's Third New International Dictionary* (Springfield: G. and C. Merriam Company, 1961), *Le Petit Larousse* (Paris: Librairie Larousse, 1959), J. E. Mansion, ed., *Mansion's Shorter French and English Dictionary* (D. C. Heath and Company, no date). The French reference works were indispensable in view of the French education of our Moroccan staff members and the consultation of various French language works on Moroccan Arabic. Particularly useful among the latter were: Louis Brunot, *Textes arabes de Rabat* (Paris: Librairie Orientaliste Paul Geuthner, Vol. I *Textes* 1931, Vol. II *Glossaire* 1952); Daniel Ferré, *Lexique Marocain-Français* and *Lexique Français-Marocain* (Editions Nejma, Imprimerie de Fédala, Maroc, no date or place); Henry Mercier, *Dictionnaire Arabe-Français* (Rabat: Les éditions la porte, 1951) and *Dictionnaire Français-Arabe* (Rabat: Les éditions la porte, 1959).

* Cf. the preceding footnote.

definitions used otherwise than as a stimulus for arriving at our own definitions. In the process of criticism and revision each of the entries finally arrived at has been read at least four times.

The use of the dictionary presupposes a familiarity with the basic grammatical structure of Moroccan Arabic.* Except for a sprinkling of illustrative items, regularly predictable forms have been omitted. For example, it was considered unnecessary to enter regular diminutives such as *ktiyyeb* from *ktab* 'book' or regular participles such as *meṣnuɛ* from *ṣnăɛ* 'to make, to manufacture'. Participles, diminutives, and other such derived words are, however, entered if they are irregular in form or specialized in meaning. Entered participles are listed alphabetically but referred back to the parent verb for definition. For example, *ṣaneɛ* is regular both in form and meaning as the active participle of *ṣnăɛ*, but it has the additional specialized meaning 'craftsman, artisan'. The information 'a.p. of *ṣnăɛ*' given for the alphabetically entered *ṣaneɛ* is a signal that the word should be looked up as a sub-entry under the parent verb *ṣnăɛ*. The same is true of the participles beginning with *m-*, irregular diminutives, and in general all other semantically or formally irregular or unpredictable items.

A large number of *FeɛɛaL* pattern adjectives and nouns as well as medio-passive verbs (i.e. Measures Ia, IIa(V), IIIa(VI), and the derived quadriliteral measure) were found to be fully predictable in meaning and have been cross referenced rather than translated independently. For example, the entry for *wezzaɛ* is simply 'ag. n. of *wezzăɛ*' since its meaning is totally predictable from the meaning of *wezzăɛ* 'to distribute, to hand out'. For similar reasons *nebbaḥ* is entered as 'ag. n. and adj. of *nbeḥ*', *ttekteb* is entered as 'm.p. of *kteb*', etc.

Necessary grammatical information (e.g. irregular plurals) is given with the entries. Verbs are entered in the third person singular masculine of the perfect. The imperfect form is written immediately after the perfect form for those verbs which are irregular or which have an unpredictable imperfect vowel. The verbal noun is given for Measure I verbs and elsewhere if irregular. In idioms and expressions which require a variable pronoun (cf. 'I—my', 'he—his', etc. in 'I ate my fill', 'He ate his fill', etc.), the pronoun, like the verb, has been entered in the third person singular masculine with the symbol ϕ after it to indicate that the pronoun varies according to meaning. For example, the entry *fda deqqtuϕ* 'to get revenge' is conjugated *fdit deqqti* 'I got (my) revenge', *fditi deqqtek* 'you got (your) revenge', etc. The symbol ∼ after a pronoun indicates it is invariable, e.g. *bih∼ fih∼* 'immediately'.

---

*Cf. Richard S. Harrell, *A Short Reference Grammar of Moroccan Arabic* (Washington: Georgetown University Press, 1962), *A Basic Course in Moroccan Arabic* (Washington: Georgetown University Press, 1965), and Harvey Sobelman, ed., *A Dictionary of Moroccan Arabic: English-Moroccan* (Washington: Georgetown University Press, 1963).

There are numerous cases where Moroccan and English meanings correspond precisely but with differing constructions in the two languages. This circumstance is indicated by the symbol ≠ placed directly after the English definition, followed by an example which shows the construction. For example, under *mša* 'to go', the sub-entry *mša l-* is translated 'to lose≠', with the illustration *mša-li ṣebbaṭi* 'I lost my shoes'. The illustration shows that the thing lost is the subject of the verb in Moroccan while the person losing the object in question is placed as the object of the preposition *l-*.

In those cases where the Moroccan usage or structure is not immediately clear from the English definition, supplementary information such as 'v.i.' for 'intransitive verb' or 'v.t.' for 'transitive verb' is given. An indented paragraph mark, ¶, is used to set off sub-entries, e.g. the sub-entry *mša f-ḥaluφ* 'to go away' under the main entry *mša* 'to go'. An indented double asterisk, **, preceding a sentence or a group of sentences at the end of an entry or a sub-entry indicates idiomatic uses, e.g. under *ṛaṣ* 'head' the sentence *ɛad faq b-ṛaṣu* 'He's finally realized what's going on'.

In order to be as clear as possible and to give a wider range of information about the entries, numerous illustrative sentences have been included. For example, one of the equivalents given for the verb *bqa* is 'to keep on, to continue, to remain, to persevere (in)', which is then clarified by the appended illustrative sentence *bqa ka-ikteb-lu modda twila* 'He kept on writing him (regularly) for quite a while'.

The transcription differs in only two respects from that given in the works cited in the footnote referred to immediately above. The *e* and the short *ă* are consistently distinguished, and a new symbol, the short ĭ, has been added. There is considerable variation between *e* and *ă* from speaker to speaker. Some speakers almost exclusively have *ă* rather than *e* in the neighborhood of ḥ and ɛ. Other speakers reverse this pattern. Other speakers have *ă* in some words and *e* in others in the neighborhood of ḥ and ɛ. The transcription adopted represents an attempted consensus of our Moroccan staff. In the final analysis, however, there is no escaping the fact that some speakers say *ḥefla* while others say *ḥăfla* 'ceremony, party', and as might be expected each speaker prefers his own pronunciation.

The symbol *ĭ* represents a shorter version of the *i*, which represents a sound similar to the 'i' of English 'machine'. The short *ĭ* occurs in relatively few words, mostly classicisms. Less well educated people usually use *i* instead of *ĭ*, but there are a few words in which *ĭ* is apparently the only acceptable educated usage, e.g. *ɛamĭl* 'governor'.

The entries are arranged alphabetically according to the following sequence:

a b(ḅ) d ḍ f g ġ h i k l(ḷ) m(ṃ) n q r(ṛ) s ṣ š t ṭ u w x y z(ẓ) ž ḥ ɛ
Because of the limited and variable role they play in word formation, the glottal stop, *ʔ*, and the variable vowels *ă, e, ĭ,* and *o* have been disregarded in the alpha-

betization. Thus such a word as *xobz* 'bread' is alphabetized as *x-b-z,* *ع*ă*wd* 'horse' is alphabetized as *ع-w-d,* and *ʔeddeb* 'to educate' is alphabetized as *d-d-b,* etc. The secondary emphatic consonants *ḅ, ḷ, ṃ, ṛ,* and *ẓ* have likewise been disregarded for purposes of alphabetization, for similar reasons. This scheme of arrangement is essentially that of Ferré, and familiarity has convinced the editor of its practical usefulness.

In those cases where differing pronunciations of a word require different alphabetizations, both have been listed, usually with a cross reference. There are five generalized variations which require attention:

(1) The alternation between *q* and *g*. In various dialects of Moroccan, the *q* is regularly replaced by *g*. For example, many speakers say *gal* instead of *qal* 'to say'. For words in which *q* is the standard pronunciation, the alternatives with *g* have not been listed. For words where the alternate with *g* is the more widely accepted pronunciation, the word is entered twice, the translation under the form with *g* and a cross reference under the form with *q*. For example, under the entry *bqeṛ* one finds the note 'same as *bgeṛ',* and under the entry *bgeṛ* the translation 'cattle' is given .

(2) The change of initial *s* (or *ṣ*) to *š* under the influence of a *š* or *ž* further on in the word. The procedure has been to list both forms with cross references. For example, entry *šeṛžem* gives the information 'same as *seṛžem',* and the entry *seṛžem* gives the meaning 'window'.

(3) The change of initial *z* to *ž,* parallel to the alternation between *s* and *š* discussed in (2) above. The alternation is handled similarly, e.g. *žellež* is entered 'same as *zellež',* and *zellež* is translated 'to cover with mosaic'.

(4) The variation between *ăy* and *i* after ح and ع. Where this variation occurs the meaning is usually given under the form with *i* and a cross reference is given under the form with *ăy*. For example, the entry under *ح*ă*yṭ* is 'same as *ح*i*ṭ'* and the entry under *ح*i*ṭ* is 'wall'.

(5) The variation between *ăw* and *u* after ح and ع. The variation is exactly parallel to the variation between *ăy* and *i* discussed in (4) above, e.g. *ح*ă*wma* 'same as*ح*u*ma'* and *ح*u*ma* 'quarter, section (of a city)'.

In closing the editor would like to express his gratitude and warm feelings to all those who participated in the production of this dictionary. Ernest Ligon deserves a final salute for undertaking the proofreading.

Richard S. Harrell
Washington, D. C.
August, 1964

PRONUNCIATION

1. Table of Sounds: Moroccan Arabic has thirty-one consonants and six vowels.* The symbols for them are listed in the table below. Most of the consonants are classified according to the kinds of movements and positions of the lips, tongue, throat, and nasal passages which produce them.

CONSONANTS						
	Labial	*Dental*	*Palatal*	*Velar*	*Pharyngeal*	*Glottal*
Stops	*b ḅ*	*t ṭ d ḍ*		*k g q*		*ʔ*
Fricatives	*f*	*s ṣ z ẓ*	*š ž*	*x ġ*	ح ع	*h*
Nasals	*m ṃ*	*n*				
Resonants	*l ḷ r ṛ w y*					
VOWELS						
a ă e i o u						

Stops are those sounds which involve, momentarily, a complete blocking of the air stream in speech. For example, notice the complete closure of the lips in the pronunciation of the 'b' in English 'bed'. A fricative is a sound in which the air stream is partly blocked but not completely stopped, with a resulting noisy effect. For example, in the 'f' of English 'foot' note the way the air stream escapes through the partial closure of the lower lip against the upper front teeth. Nasals are sounds which involve a flow of air through the nasal passage, e.g. 'm' as in 'mad'.

The terms 'labial', 'dental', 'palatal', 'velar', 'pharyngeal', and 'glottal' refer, in going from front to back, to the parts of the mouth in which sounds are formed.

'Labial' refers to sounds which involve the lips, e.g. *m*.

'Dental' refers to sounds which involve the tip of the tongue in the area around the back of the upper front teeth, e.g., *d*.

---

* No account is taken of the vowel *ĭ* in this description.

'Palatal' refers to sounds formed with the upper surface of the tongue against the roof of the mouth, e.g. *š*.

'Velar' refers to sounds involving the rear part of the tongue against the rear portions of the roof of the mouth, e.g. *ġ*.

'Pharyngeal' refers to sounds formed in the area of the throat above the larynx ('adam's apple'), e.g. ح.

'Glottal' refers to sounds formed in the larynx, e.g. ʔ.

For practical teaching and learning purposes, the sounds listed as 'resonants' are not usefully classifiable according to the system described above. The sounds represented by letters with dots under them, e.g. *ṭ*, are referred to as 'emphatics'. They are discussed below.

There are six vowels, represented by the symbols *a, ă, e, i, o,* and *u*. Each one of these vowels has various pronunciations depending on the consonants they occur with. There is no single isolated pronunciation which can be learned for them. They are discussed individually in relation to the consonants in the following sections.

2. *Consonants Similar to English:* Fifteen of the thirty-one Moroccan consonants are, for practical purposes, identical with consonants which occur in English. These are *b, f, m, t, d, s, z, n, š* (like the 'sh' in 'ship'), *ž* (like the 's' in 'pleasure'), *k, g, w, y,* and *h*.

For the student who wishes to be fully accurate, there is a small difference of detail to be noted between the Moroccan *t, d,* and *n* as opposed to the corresponding English sounds. In Moroccan these sounds are formed with the tip of the tongue against the back of the upper front teeth instead of against the gum ridge immediately above them. Note the tip of the tongue against the gum ridge above the teeth for English 't', 'd', and 'n', as in 'tea', 'day', 'no'.

A word about *w* and *y* is also necessary. The English speaker is familiar with them before vowels, as in words like 'well' and 'yes'. Moroccan *w* and *y* occur after vowels as well as before them. After vowels, the Moroccan *w* sounds to the English speaker somewhat like the vowel in 'who' and the *y* sounds somewhat like the vowel in 'he'. The occurrence of *h* in the middle and at the end of words may also cause the student some difficulty.

3. *Vowel Sounds with Familiar Consonants:* This section has to do with the pronunciation of some of the Moroccan vowels in combination with the consonants listed in *2* above. The descriptions below are accurate only for the vowels in combination with those Moroccan consonants which are similar to English. Elsewhere the vowels are pronounced differently.

(1) The *e:* Like the 'e' in English 'glasses', but always very short.

(2) The *o:* Like the 'u' in English 'put', but always very short.

(3) The *a:* Like the 'a' in English 'mad' except at the end of words. At the end of words, Moroccan *a* is pronounced about half-way between the 'a' of 'mad' and the 'a' of 'father'.

(4) The *i:* Similar to the vowel of 'be' but without any gliding effect. By listening carefully the English speaker will note that from the beginning to the end of the vowel of 'be' there is a sort of gliding change in vowel quality. This gliding effect must be avoided in Moroccan. For the student who knows French, Italian, or Spanish, it may be helpful to point out that the 'i' in these languages is exactly equivalent to the Moroccan *i,* as in French *vite* 'quickly', Spanish *mi* 'my', or Italian *vino* 'wine'.

(5) The *u:* Similar to the vowel of 'do' but without any gliding effect. Compare the discussion of the *i* immediately above. The Moroccan *u* is like the French 'ou', as in *fou* 'insane', or Spanish and Italian 'u', as in Spanish *luna* 'moon', Italian *luce* 'light'.

4. The Emphatic Consonants: The easiest way for the English speaker to distinguish the emphatic consonants from the corresponding non-emphatic consonants is by the great difference in the sound of the vowels when they occur next to these consonants (see the discussion of the emphatic vowels below). By paying careful attention to the vowel differences, which he hears relatively easily, the English speaker will arrive at an acceptable pronunciation of the difference between the plain and emphatic consonants, even if he feels that he can hear no difference between them.

The emphatic consonants are written with a subscript dot under the symbol for the corresponding plain consonants. There are eight emphatic consonants, *ḅ, ṃ, ṭ, ḍ, ṣ, ẓ, ḷ,* and *ṛ*. The first seven are discussed here, while the *ṛ* is considered in section *6* below. These sounds are lower in pitch than their non-emphatic counterparts. They are pronounced with greater muscular tension in the mouth and throat and with a raising of the back and root of the tongue toward the roof of the mouth. The English speaker can notice this contraction of the throat very easily by prolonging the 'l' in 'full', since this English 'l' is exactly like the Moroccan *ḷ* except that in the Moroccan sound the tip of the tongue is against the back of the upper front teeth instead of against the gum ridge above the teeth. After having acquired conscious control of the movement of the back and root of the tongue with *ḷ,* the English speaker can proceed to practice combining it with the other articulatory features of *ḅ, ṃ, ṭ, ḍ, ṣ, ẓ,* and *ṛ*. In addition to lower pitch and the contraction of the throat, *ṭ* differs from *t* by being released without any friction noise whereas the *t* usually has some, as in English.

The emphatics *ṭ, ḍ,* and *ṣ* are quite common, with or without other emphatic consonants in the words in which they occur. The *ṛ* also occurs widely in words without the presence of any other emphatic consonants, but it is limited to the neighborhood of the vowels *e* and *a* unless a *ṭ, ḍ,* or *ṣ* also occurs in the word. The occurrence of *ḅ, ṃ, ẓ,* or *ḷ* in words where no *ṭ, ḍ, ṣ,* or *ṛ* occurs is quite rare. Contrariwise, there is no occurrence of a plain *b* or *m* in a word in which one of the other emphatics occurs. In order to avoid the repetition of subscript dots, the transcription employed here is to write *ḅ* and *ṃ* only if no other emphatic occurs in the word. Otherwise only *b* and *m* are written although they are to be interpreted as *ḅ* and *ṃ* if another emphatic consonant occurs in the word where they are found.

5. *The Emphatic Vowels:* The Moroccan vowels have special pronunciations in the neighborhood of the emphatic consonants. The emphatic pronunciations are:

(1) The *e:* Like the 'u' in English 'nut', but always very short.

(2) The *a:* Like the 'a' in 'father'.

(3) The *i:* Similar to the vowel of 'they', but without any gliding effect.

(4) The *u:* Similar to the vowel of 'blow', but without any gliding effect.

(5) The *o:* Like the emphatic *u,* but always very short.

6. *The Sounds l, r, and ṛ:* A minor difference between English 'l' and Moroccan *l* is that, like the other Moroccan dentals, it is pronounced with the tip of the tongue against the upper front teeth instead of against the gum ridge above them. A more serious difference is that the usual American English 'l' is like the Moroccan emphatic *ḷ*. The Moroccan plain *l* is like the French, Spanish, or Italian *l* in that it is pronounced with the tongue further forward in the mouth and without the back part of the tongue being raised toward the roof of the mouth.

The plain *r* is a flap of the tongue past the gum ridge above the upper front teeth, like the 'r' in Spanish *para* 'for' or the 't' in the usual American pronunciation of such words as 'water' and 'butter'. Emphatic *ṛ* bears exactly the same relation to plain *r* as the other emphatic consonants to the corresponding plain consonants. See the discussion of the emphatic consonants above.

The vowels next to *ṛ* are pronounced the same as around the other emphatic consonants. Around plain *l* and *r* the vowels are pronounced the same as in the neighborhood of the various consonants which are similar to English, such as *m, f,* etc.

7. *The Consonants q, x,* and *ġ:* The *q* is similar to the *k* but is pronounced further back in the mouth. English 'k' ranges over a fairly wide area in the back

of the mouth, and the English speaker must be careful to keep *k* more to the front part and *q* more to the back part of the rear of the mouth in order not to confuse them and pronounce *q* when he means *k* or vice versa.

The *x* and *ġ* are fricatives pronounced in approximately the same position as the *q*, with the rear of the tongue raised toward the roof of the mouth in the neighborhood of the uvula. The *ġ* is similar to the French 'r' and the *x* is the same sound as the 'ch' of German *Bach* or Scotch *loch*. If these sounds seem difficult to the English speaker he can approximate them by gargling gently. The *ġ* is similar to a light gargle accompanied by a musical buzz from the adam's apple ('voice' is the technical term for this musical buzz) whereas the *x* is the same sound without the musical buzz.

The vowels in the neighborhood of the consonants *q*, *x*, and *ġ* are pronounced approximately the same as the vowels in the neighborhood of the emphatic consonants. This equivalence is only approximate, and the student's prime concern should be with exact imitation of native speakers of Moroccan Arabic.

8. The consonants ح *and* ع*:* The ح and ع are different from anything in English. Careful practice with a native speaker or with recordings is necessary for the English speaker to acquire a proper pronunciation of these consonants. These sounds are articulated by a simultaneous raising of the larynx and a movement of the root of the tongue toward the back wall of the throat. The compression of the throat in this way gives rise to the particular sound quality of these two consonants.

The ح is somewhat similar to an English 'h' pronounced in a loud stage whisper, as opposed to Moroccan *h*, which is more like an English 'h' in ordinary conversation. The English speaker must exercise extreme care in learning to distinguish *h* and ح from each other, both in hearing and in pronunciation.

The ع is unlike any English sound, and a proper pronunciation of it can be acquired only by careful imitation. A useful articulatory description of the way to pronounce ع is difficult to give briefly in simple terms. The student may approximate it by practicing a loud, prolonged stage whisper English 'h', as for ح. He should note the tension in his throat and the exact position of the adam's apple during the stage whisper 'h'. Then, with his adam's apple and throat in the exact position as for the stage whisper 'h', the student should try pronouncing the 'a' of 'father'. The result should be an acceptable approximation of ع. The student may contrast it with the normal pronunciation of the 'a' in 'father'.

9. The Vowels with ح *and* ع*:* In the neighborhood of ح and ع, the vowels *a*, *i*, *u*, and *o* are approximately the same as in the neighborhood of the emphatic consonants. The vowel *ă* is almost never found anywhere except next to ح or ع.

It is pronounced about halfway between the 'a' of 'mad' and the 'a' of 'father', but always very short. It is especially important to note the shortness of *ă*. If it is lengthened, it will be confused with *a*. The only difference between *a* and *ă* is that *a* is held longer than *ă*. The vowel e next to ح and ع is similar to the 'e' of English 'bet'.

10. The Glottal Stop: The glottal stop is represented by the symbol ʔ. This sound is as rare in Moroccan as it is in English. It is the break between vowels as heard in the exclamation 'uh oh'. The 'tt' in such a word as 'bottle' is also commonly pronounced as a glottal stop in some varieties of New York English ('Brooklynese') or Scotch English. This sound offers no difficulties for the English speaker. The vowels around the glottal stop are pronounced the same as in the neighborhood of such plain consonants as *f, š, n,* etc.

11. The Diphthongs ăy and ăw: These two diphthongs occur almost exclusively after ح or ع. The English speaker's principal difficulty in pronouncing them is to remember that they are always very short. Except for being pronounced much more quickly, the *ăy* is similar to the 'i' in English 'night' and the *ăw* is similar to the 'ou' in English 'about'.

12. The Sequences ay and aw: The *a* in these sequences is pronounced as usual, i.e. similar to the 'a' of 'father' after the emphatics and the consonants *q, x, ġ,* ح, and ع, and similar to the 'a' of 'mad' after other consonants. In these sequences, the *y* is similar to the 'ee' of 'feed' and the *w* is similar to the 'oo' of 'food'. The sequences *aye* and *awe,* i.e. with an *e* after the *ay* and *aw,* are very common. The pronunciation of the *e* in these sequences is very fleeting, similar to the 'e' of 'towel' or the 'a' of 'trial'. An exception is that before ح or ع the *e* is fully pronounced.

13. Double Consonants: Double consonants are an important feature of Moroccan pronunciation. In English the double writing of a consonant, as the 'dd' in 'middle', is simply a meaningless piece of spelling. In Moroccan, such a writing as *mm* as opposed to *m* or *dd* as opposed to *d* indicates an important difference in pronunciation. The writing of a consonant symbol twice indicates that the consonant is to be held twice as long as a single consonant. Genuine double consonants never occur in English in the middle of words, but they are very common from the end of one word to the beginning of another. Compare the difference between the single 'd' in 'lay down' and the double "dd' in 'laid down'. Many similar examples for other consonants can be found in English.

Medial double consonants are not particularly difficult for the English speaking student. More difficult is the occurrence of double consonants both at the beginning and the end of words. Careful attention and practice are necessary for the mastery of initial and final double consonants.

14. Triple Consonants: Double consonants are held twice as long as single consonants. There are also cases of triple consonants, which are held even longer than double consonants. If the student has exercised the pronunciation of double consonants properly, learning to contrast them with triple consonants should not be difficult.

15. Sequences and Clusters: The preceding sections have discussed the various consonant and vowel sounds of Moroccan Arabic. Some of them are very similar to sounds which occur in English, others are quite different. Mastering the new sounds is only a first step for the student. There remains the task of learning to pronounce unfamiliar sequences. Sequences such at *bt-* at the beginning of of a word or *-hd* at the end of a word strike the English speaking student as quite strange. Moroccan has a large number of such clusters, and the student must be prepared to deal with them, especially at the beginning and in the middle of words. Such sequences are actually not at all difficult, and they are easily mastered with attention and practice. As a matter of fact, similar clusters occur in rapid conversational English, for example the 'gb' in rapid pronunciations of 'good-bye'; the spelling 'g'bye' is sometimes used to represent this initial cluster in writing. A further example is the initial cluster 'tm' in casual pronunciations of 'tomorrow.' A close examination of spoken English at ordinary conversational speed reveals many such clusters. These can serve as a basis on which the student can build in mastering the pronunciation of seemingly unfamiliar Moroccan clusters.

ABBREVIATIONS AND SYMBOLS

adj.	adjective
adv.	adverb
ag. adj.	agentive adjective
ag. n.	agentive noun
a.p.	active participle
art.	(the definite) article
coll.	collective
comp.	comparative
conj.	conjunction
cons.	construct (form, state)
cpl.	collective plural
def. art.	definite article
dept.	department
dim.	diminutive
du.	dual
e.g.	for example
esp.	especially
etc.	et cetera
expr.	expression(s)
f.	feminine
gm.	gram
i.e.	that is
impf.	imperfect
impv.	imperative
inh. pos.	inherently possessed
lit.	literal(ly)
m.	masculine
math.	mathematics
min.	minute(s)
m.p.	medio-passive
n.	noun
n.i.	noun of instance
n.u.	noun of unity
part.	participle
pl.	plural
p.p.	passive participle
prep.	preposition
pron.	pronoun
sg.	singular

s.o.	someone
s.th.	something
U.S.	United States
usu.	usual(ly)
v.	verb
v.i.	intransitive verb
v.n.	verbal noun
v.t.	transitive verb
ϕ	Indicates a variable pronoun ending.
~	Indicates an invariable pronoun ending.
≠	Signals a structural difference between Moroccan and English.
¶	Indicates a sub-entry.
**	Indicates idiomatic usage.

The above symbols are explained further in the Introduction.

A

a vocative particle *fayn ġadi a ʕăbbas?* Where are you going, Abbas? —*mse-l-xir, a sidi.* Good evening, sir. —*a lalla!* Madam! Lady! —*a d-drari, sektu!* Children, be quiet! —*a had l-wld xḷaṣ u-ma tbessel ʕliya.* Stop pestering me, boy!
ʔab pl. *ʔabaʔ* (classicism but fairly common; does not usually take pron. endings) father
ʔabaʔ pl. of *ʔab*
ʔabadan never, not at all
ʔabăd (usually with art.) eternity
¶ *l-l-ʔabăd* forever, eternally
abluʕ *n.u.* -*a* unripe date (at yellow stage)
abraz see *braz*
ʔabril April
ʔabu-l-hăwl (the) Sphinx
ʔabʕat pl. of *beʕt*
ʔada v.t. (v.n. *mʔadya*) to hurt, to harm *ma-baġi-ši idir ši-ʕaža lli tʔadiha.* He doesn't want to do anything to hurt her.
ʔadaʔ 1. v.n. of *ʔedda* 2. pl. -*at* payment
ʔadam Adam (biblical first man)
¶ *bani ʔadam* the human race
ʔadami pl. -*yen* 1. human being 2. courteous, well-mannered
ʔadăb 1. (no pl.) politeness, courtesy 2. pl. *ʔadab* literature *waš ka-iʕăžbek l-ʔadăb l-muʕaṣiṛ?* Do you like contemporary literature?
ʔadilla pl. of *dalil*
ʔadiya pl. -*t* 1. evil, harm *ma-imken-lek-ši ttṣuwweṛ l-ʔadiya f-aš žra l-žiranu.* You have no idea how much harm he caused his neighbors. 2. nuisance *walayenni ʔadiya dak l-bent!* What a nuisance that girl is!
ʔaden b-(s.th.) *l-*(s.o.) to allow, to permit *škun lli ʔaden-lek b-le-mši?* Who permitted you to go?
ʔaden (no pl.) permission
ʔadwiya pl. of *dwa*
ʔadyan pl. of *din*
ʔaḍwaṛ pl. of *ḍuṛ*
ʔafat pl. -*at* accident
¶ *qṛib l-l-ʔafat* fragile
ʔafkaṛ pl. of *fekra* and *fikr*
afrag pl. -*at* partition
agwal pl. -*at* kind of long, large drum, open at one end
ʔaġbiyaʔ pl. of *ġabiy*
aġlal same as *ġlal*
ʔaġlaṭ pl. of *ġalăṭ* and *ġelṭa*
ʔaġniya pl. of *ġani* (a.p. of *ġna*)
ʔahali pl. of *ʔahl*
ʔahl (used as pl.) pl. *ʔahali, ʔahliya* 1. parents 2. family 3. relatives
¶ *ʔahl le-blad* natives (of some city, country)
ʔahliya 1. pl. of *ʔahl* 2. pl. -*t* aptitude, qualification
ʔahlen wa-sehlen, ʔahlăn wa-sahlăn welcome (interjectional usage)
ʔahemmiya pl. -*t* importance
ʔala pl. -*t* 1. musical instrument (any kind) 2. Moroccan Andalusian music 3. machine
ʔalaf pl. of *ʔalef*
ʔalef du. *ʔalfayn* pl. *ʔalaf, ʔuluf, ʔulufat* thousand
ʔalfaḍ pl. of *lefḍa*
ʔalġam pl. of *leġm, loġm*
ʔali musician, instrumentalist
ʔalif-el-ba the abc's, alphabet
ʔaliha pl. of *ʔilah*
aḷḷah same as *ḷḷah*
aḷḷah
¶ *aḷḷahu ʔekbeṛ* God is great (religious formula used in prayers and as an interjection in various social circumstances).
ʔalʕan pl. of *lăʕn*
ama, ʔama what, which *ama ʕsen-lek?* What do you prefer? —*ama huwa?* Which one?
ʔamakin pl. of *makan*
ʔamal (no pl.) hope, wish, desire *ʕăndi ʔamal baš nešri ši-siyaṛa l-ʕam l-maži.* I hope to buy a car next year.
amalus, ʔamalus mud, mire (e.g., in a river when water is low)
aman, ʔaman 1. peace, security 2. trust, confidence
** *ʕlik l-aman!* You don't have to be afraid! You're perfectly safe!
¶ *fihφ l-aman* to be trustworthy ≠
¶ *ma-fihφ aman* to be dishonest, untrustworthy ≠
¶ *ṭleb l-aman* 1. to capitulate, to surrender 2. to request asylum
¶ *ʕmel* (or *dar*) *l-aman f-* to trust (s.o.)
amana, ʔamana pl. -*t, amayen* s.th. delivered (to s.o.) in trust, s.th. entrusted (to s.o.)
amayen pl. of *amana*
ʔamin so be it, amen
amin, ʔamin 1. pl. *ʔumana* administrator, executor (court-appointed) 2. pl. -*at* syndic (agent of a corporation)
¶ *ʔamin ṣ-ṣenduq* treasurer
¶ *ṛažel ʔamin* trustworthy man
amir pl. *ʔumaṛa* emir, prince
¶ *amir l-muminin* Leader of the Faithful (title applied to the king in Muslim countries)
ʔamiṛal pl. -*at* admiral
ʔamkina pl. of *makan*

ʔamma, wa-ʔamma as for *ʔamma ḍ-ḍirasa dyalu ma-bqa-ši ihtemm biha.* As for his studies, he doesn't care about them any longer.

¶ *ʔamma-ma kan men* as for *ʔamma-ma kan men ɛămmtek ma-zal ka-dži tšufna.* As for your aunt, she still comes to visit us.

ʔamn same as *aman* 1

ʔamen b- 1. to believe in *b-aš ka-tʔamen?* What do you believe in? 2. to trust *ma-bqa-li ma-nʔamen biha.* I can't trust her anymore.

ʔamṛ 1. pl. *ʔumuṛ, ʔumuṛat* thing, question, matter 2. pl. *ʔawamir* order, command

¶ *teḥt ʔamṛ* at (s.o.'s) disposal *ana teḥt ʔamṛek.* I'm at your disposal.

ʔameṛ v.t. 1. to order, to command, to give (an) order to *ʔamṛuh baš ixwi le-blad.* They ordered him to leave the country. 2. to allow, to give permission to *ʔameṛha ṛ-ṛaʔis dyalha baš taxod l-ɛoṭla.* Her boss has given her the permission to take a vacation.

amred (coll.) crickets

ʔamṛaḍ pl. of *meṛḍ*

a-meṣṣab see *meṣṣab*

ana (sg. disjunctive pron.) 1. I *ana ktebt le-bṛa.* I wrote the letter. 2. me *ža išufni ana.* He came to see me (not you).

ʔanašid pl. of *našid*

ʔanbiya pl. of *nbi*

ʔandalus (with art.) Andalusia

ʔandalusi pl. *-yen* Andalusian

ʔanḍima pl. of *niḍam*

ʔanisa pl. *-t, ʔawanis* 1. Miss *l-ʔanisa bahiya ma-zala ka-teqṛa.* Miss Bahia is still studying. 2. young lady *šeftu mɛa waḥed l-ʔanisa mziwna.* I saw him with a beautiful young lady.

ʔaqaṛib pl. of *qṛib* (relative)

ʔaqell less

¶ *ʔaqell men* less than

¶ *be-l-ʔaqell, ɛăl l-ʔaqell* at least

ʔaqelliya pl. *-t* minority

aqṛab same as *qṛab*

aṛa pl. *aṛaw* (impv.) give, pass, hand over *aṛa-li dak le-ktab ḷḷah ixellik.* Give me that book, please.

¶ *aṛa-lna* (*daba*) 1. as for (to indicate a change of topic in discourse) *aṛa-lna daba ṛ-ṛažel l-axoṛ, melli ḥṛeb ma-wella.* Now as for the other man, he's never come back since he ran away. 2. suppose that (followed with *ila* or *kun*) *aṛa-lna ila mša ḥetta ža ɛla ġefla, še-ndiru?* Suppose he should come unexpectedly. What would we do? —*aṛa kun ma-kanu-š ɛăndu le-flus, ma-ka-ḍḍenn-ši u-kan ža ɛăndek tsellfu?* Suppose he didn't have the money, don't you think he would've come to you to lend him some?

ʔaṛaʔ pl. of *ṛeyy* 2

ʔaṛaḍi pl. of *ʔaṛḍ, ʔeṛḍ, leṛḍ*

aṛbăɛ (with art.) Wednesday *waš ġedda l-aṛbăɛ?* Is tomorrow Wednesday?

¶ *nhaṛ l-aṛbăɛ* (on) Wednesday

aṛbɛa four (less common than *ṛebɛa*)

aṛbɛin forty (less common than *ṛebɛin*)

ʔaṛḍ same as *eṛḍ*

argan argan tree

ʔaṛkan pl. of *ṛukn*

aṛz n.u. *eṛza* cedar (tree or wood)

asami pl. of *ʔasem, ʔism,* and *sem*

ʔasatida pl. of *ʔustad*

ʔasbaɛ pl. of *subuɛ*

ʔasdas pl. of *sudus*

ʔasăf regret *ɛăbbṛet-lu ɛăl l-ʔasăf dyalha ɛăl l-ḥadita lli wegɛet-lu.* She expressed her regret to him about the accident he had.

¶ *be-l-ʔasăf, mɛa l-ʔasăf* unfortunately *be-l-ʔasăf ma-ža-š.* Unfortunately he didn't come. It's a pity he didn't come.

** *be-l-ʔasăf!* That's too bad!

asfi Safi (Moroccan city)

ʔasʔila pl. of *suʔal*

ʔasem pl. *asami* name

¶ *ʔasem* (plus pron. ending or n.) what's . . . name? ≠ *ʔasmek?* What's your name? —*ʔasem ḅḅak?* What's your father's name?

ʔasmaʔ pl. of *ʔism, ism*

ʔasɛar, ʔasɛaṛ pl. of *sɛăṛ, săɛṛ*

aṣdiqa, ʔaṣdiqaʔ pl. of *ṣdiq*

ʔaṣfaṛ pl. of *ṣafăṛ* 1

ʔaṣili pure, of good quality *had l-keswa le-ḥrir dyalha ʔaṣili.* This dress is of pure silk.

ʔaṣel pl. *ʔuṣul* origin, lineage

¶ *ʔaṣlu≠ men* to be originally from ≠, to originate from ≠ *ʔaṣlu men tunes.* He is originally from Tunis.

ʔaṣli pl. *-yen* original *xellit n-nosxa l-ʔaṣḷiya ɛăndi.* I kept the original copy.

ʔaṣnam pl. of *ṣanam*

aš (often abbreviated to *š-*) 1. what *aš ka-ikteb?* What is he writing? —*b-aš ġeṭṭat le-ġṭaṛ?* What did she cover the dish with? 2. relative pron. used with other particles (usually prepositional) *l-mus b-aš qeṭṭăɛt l-lḥăm maḍi.* The knife I cut the meat with is sharp (i.e., with which I cut . . .). —*l-uṭil f-aš betna ma-ši ġali.* The hotel where we spent the night is not expensive. —*nsa ṣ-ṣoxṛa l-aš ṣafṭettu.* He forgot the errand she sent him for. —*ha š-šelya ɛla-š kanet galsa.* Here's the chair she was sitting on. —*le-blad l-aš ṣafṭuh ɛažbah.* He likes the country where they sent him.

¶ *aš-emma* anything, whatever *aš-emma daret dayez.* Anything she does is all right. —*biʕha b-aš-emma kan.* Sell it for whatever you can get. —*qḍa b-aš-emma ṣab.* He managed with what he could find.

¶ *aš-men* which, what *aš-men ḍar kritiw?* Which house did you rent? —*f-aš-men baxiṛa žitiw?* What ship did you come on?

¶ *l-aš* why, what for *l-aš qolti-lha dak š-ši?* What did you tell her that for?

** *ma-kayen l-aš.* There is no use. It's not necessary.

¶ *w-aš* what . . . then *w-aš ġad-yăʕmel?* What's he going to do then?

ašbar pl. *-at* battlement

ašnu same as *šnu*

aštaṭṭu same as *šṭaṭṭu*

ʔatar pl. *-at* **1.** trace, evidence *ma-bqa ʕetta ʔatar de-d-demm.* No trace of blood was left. **2.** historical monument

¶ *ḍar l-ʔatar* museum

ʔatat (coll., no n.u., no pl.) furniture

atay (no art.) tea

ʔati pl. *-yen* (often f. sg. with pl. n.) **1.** next, coming (year, week, etc.) **2.** following *ketbu l-kelmat l-ʔatiya.* Write the following words.

ʔatṛak pl. of *torki* **2**

aṭleṣ, ʔaṭleṣ (with art.) the Atlas (mountains)

aw or

ʔawamir pl. of *ʔamṛ* **2**

ʔawan used in the expr. *f-had l-ʔawan* at present, at this time, right now

aw-la (also *u-la*) **1.** or *nʕăyyeṭ-lu aw-la nemši ʕăndu?* Shall I call him or go and see him? —*xrož aw-la nšedd ʕlik.* Come out or I'll lock you in. **2.** (also *aw-la-la, u-la-la*) or not *šriti dik s-siyaṛa aw-la?* Did you buy that car or not?

awla, ʔawla same as *wla*

ʔawliya pl. of *wali*

aweq pl. of *wqiya*

ʔawṣiya pl. of *waṣi*

ʔawwalan **1.** first, firstly *awwalan ža mʕăṭṭel, taniyen ma-kan-š ʕafeḍ ḍ-ḍeṛṣ.* First, he came late; second, he didn't know the lesson. **2.** first of all, above all *ʔawwalan xeṣṣek tšuf l-mudir.* First of all, you should see the director.

ʔaxir, ʔaxiṛ **1.** pl. *-in* last *ġedda l-lila l-ʔaxira dyalu hna.* Tomorrow is his last night here. **2.** (no pl.) end *hada ʔaxir ṭ-ṭriq.* This is the end of the road.

¶ *l-ʔaxira* the other world, life after death

ʔaxiren finally, ultimately, in the end

ʔaxlaq (f.) morals, ethics

axoṛ f. *xṛa* pl. *xṛin* **1.** other, another. *ʕṭini ktab axoṛ.* Give me another book. —*xellini nšufek ši-nhaṛ axoṛ.* Let me see you some other day. —*fayn l-weld l-axoṛ?* Where is the other boy? **2.** next, another *imken nebqa hna ʕam axoṛ.* I may stay here next year. **3.** last *l-ʕam l-axoṛ ma-ṣafeṛt-š.* I didn't take any trips last year. **4.** used to emphasize pejorative expr. *dak ben le-ʕmeq l-axoṛ!* That damned fool!

ʔaxeṣṣ used in expr. *be-l-ʔaxeṣṣ* especially, mainly

axuṛ same as *axoṛ*

ʔaya pl. *-t* **1.** verse (Koran) **2.** miracle, wonder

¶ *ʔaya men l-ʔayat* wonderful, excellent, out of this world

ʔayḍan also, too, as well *huwa ʕăndu siyaṛa, u-wladu ʔayḍan ʕăndhom siyaṛa l-l-waʕed.* He has a car, and his sons also each have a car.

ayna (see *ina*) which *ayna bab?* Which door?

azaglu (no art.) pl. *-wat, -yat* yoke

ʔazaliya pl. *-t* legend, story

azfel pl. *zfula* whip, cat-o'-nine-tails

¶ *ʕṭa azfel* to whip, to lash

¶ *kla azfel* to be lashed, to be flogged

azlag see *zlag*

ʔažanib pl. of *ʔažnabi* **2**

ʔažaṛakom ḷḷah expr. of condolence, said upon s.o.'s death

aži pl. *ažiw* impv. of *ža*

ʔažăl (period of) time *šʕal de-l-ʔažăl ʕṭawek?* How much time were you allowed?

¶ *ʔaxiṛ ʔažăl* deadline

¶ *wfa ʔažăluφ* **1.** to expire ≠ *had t-teʔšira ġad-iwfa ʔažălha ġedda.* This visa will expire tomorrow. **2.** to pass away ≠ *ʕămmu wfa ʔažălu had ṣ-ṣbaʕ.* His uncle passed away this morning.

ʔažnabi **1.** pl. *-yen foreign* **2.** pl. *ʔažanib* foreigner

ažeṛ compensation, reward (spiritual)

** *ḷḷah iʕăddem l-ažeṛ.* said to express one's condolences

ʔaʕadit pl. of *ʕadit* and *ʕdit*

ʔaʕfir pl. *-at* ditch

aʕudu-bi-llah God forbid!; also used with *men,* e.g., *aʕudu-bi-llah men dak ṛ-ṛažel!* God preserve us from that man!

ʔaʕwam (rare use) pl. of *ʕam*

B

b (*be-* before consonant clusters, *bi-* before pron. endings) **1.** with *waš tebġi takol l-lɛăm be-s-sferžel?* Would you like meat with quince? —*dbeɛt d-džaža be-l-mus.* I killed the chicken with a knife. —*mwellef ka-nakol b-yeddi.* I usually eat with my hands. —*mša ka-ižri le-ẓ-ẓenqa be-mkɛăltu.* He ran into the street with his rifle. **2.** by *tṣaffu žuž b-žuž.* They lined up two by two. —*xti faytani b-telt snin.* My sister is older than I am by three years. —*saken b-weɛdu.* He lives by himself. —*had š-ši mṣaweb be-l-yedd.* This was made by hand. **3.** for *šritha b-žuž derhem.* I bought it for two dirhams. —*ka-nexdem hna b-walu.* I'm working here for nothing. —*beddlu b-waɛed axoṛ!* Change it for another one! **4.** on *nemši mɛak walayenni b-šeṛṭ waɛed.* I'll go with you on one condition.

** *beɛthom tlata be-tlata.* I sold them three at a time. —*žit qbel š-šuṛuq b-saɛa.* I arrived one hour before sunrise. —*koll žamăɛ be-ṣmăɛtu.* Every mosque has a minaret. —*ɛekmu ɛlih b-ɛam de-l-ɛăbs.* He was sentenced to one year in prison.

¶ *bih~fih~* immediately, at once *mša bih fih.* He left immediately.

¶ *b-žuž* both, together *žaw b-žuž.* They came together.

¶ *b-xemsa, b-setta,* etc. all five, the five of them; all six, the six of them, etc. *žaw b-xemsa.* All five of them came.

¶ *biha baš* that's why, that's the reason (that) *biha baš ma-ža-š.* That's why he didn't come.

bab **1.** (m. or f.) pl. *biban* (dim. *bwiba*) door, gate **2.** (m.) pl. *bwab* chapter (book)

¶ *bab ḍ-ḍaṛ* pl. *biban ḍ-ḍyuṛ* (front) door of a house, main entrance (house)

¶ *bab le-fṣil* door between the vestibule and the inside of a house

baba (inh. pos.) (my) father, daddy (when used as first term of cons. state it reverts to forms of *ḅḅa,* which see)

** *bezzaf ɛla babak tăɛṭini bunya!* The hell you're going to hit me! —*weḷḷah ya babak u-nqebṭek!* There'll be hell to pay if I catch you! —*hada ɛmeq, ddiw babah!* This guy's nuts, take him away!

babbuṛ pl. *-at, bwabeṛ* (dim. *bwibeṛ*) **1.** (steam)ship, (steam)boat **2.** samovar

ḅaḅġiyu pl. *-yat* parrot

babnuz kind of herb which is prepared as a tea and drunk for upset stomach

babuṛ same as *babbuṛ*

badan pl. *bdan* (human) body (relatively uncommon synonym of *dat*)

badawi pl. *-yen* n. pl. *badw* rural, rustic, from the country

baddaz kind of couscous made from corn meal

badiya pl. *-at, bawadi* country *ana ɛayeš fe-l-badiya.* I live in the country (not the city).

badeṛ b- to start doing (s.th.) immediately (not used with v.) *badeṛ be-l-makla!* Start eating right now!

badw n. pl. of *badawi*

baḍ ibiḍ same as *biyyeḍ* **2**

baġbaġ n.u. *-a* catfish (considered inedible)

baġi a.p. of *bġa*

baġi pl. *buġat* **1.** pervert, debauchee, one who is dissolute **2.** one who exercises unjust dominion over others, oppressor

baġiya pl. *-t* prostitute

bahi f. *bahya* pl. *bahyen* beautiful, pretty, magnificent

baher v.t. (v.n. *mbahra*) to contradict, to refute (s.o.)

bakit pl. *-at, bwaket* (dim. *bwiket*) package, parcel, pack (cigarettes)

bakuṛ n.u. *-a* first fig of the season

bal ibul v.i. (v.n. *bul*) to urinate

bal used primarily in certain expr. with the meaning of idea, mind, attention, etc.

¶ *balak* pl. *balaku* **1.** type of interjection: Watch out! Look out! **2.** about, approximately *balak men daba yumayn nži.* I'll come in about two days.

¶ *f-baluᶲ* to think ≠, to be in one's way of thinking ≠ *f-bali hiya ġzala bezzaf.* I think she's quite pretty.

¶ *ɛla bal* alert, on one's toes, attentive

¶ *lahu* (*laha, lak, etc.*) *bal* to be important, esteemed ≠ *ɛămmu lahu bal ɛănd l-ɛukuma.* His uncle is esteemed by the government.

¶ *ṛedd baluᶲ* to pay attention, to be careful *ṛedd balek!* Be careful!

¶ *ɛla bal men* aware of *huwa ɛla bal men dak š-ši.* He's aware of that.

bala v.t. to wear out *balat ksewtha băɛda.* She has already worn her dress out.

¶ *bala b-* to pay attention to *hiya ma-ka-tbali b-ɛădd.* She pays attention to no one.

bala pl. *-wat* ace, whiz (at some job or activity) *walayenni bala hada!* This guy is really a whiz!

baḷa pl. *-t* **1.** spade, shovel **2.** bale (cotton, hay, etc.), large shipping package

baladiya pl. *-t* **1.** municipal administrator and services, municipality **2.** city hall
balaġ pl. *-at* (special) announcement, notice, (press) release, (news) dispatch, bulletin, communiqué
balak see *bal* (n.)
baleġ f- to exaggerate *baleġti bezzaf f-dak le-ɛkaya.* You sure exaggerated that story.
baleġ a.p. of *bleġ*
bali f. *balya* pl. *balyen* **1.** used, worn (out), old (things) *siyyeb ɛwayžu l-balyen.* He threw out his old clothes. **2.** second-hand, used *šra siyaṛa balya.* He bought a second-hand car.
baliza pl. *-t* suitcase
ban iban v.i. (no v.n.) **1.** to look, to appear, to seem *konti bayen mṛiḍ l-bareɛ.* You looked sick yesterday. **2.** (*l-*) to seem (to s.o.), to think ≠ *ban-li bin konti mṛiḍ l-bareɛ.* I thought you were sick yesterday (when I saw you). **3.** to appear, to show up, to come, to arrive *ma-zal ma-ban-š.* He hasn't shown up yet.
bandira pl. *-t* flag, banner, standard
banefsež same as *bellefžuž*
ḅanka pl. *-t* bank *mša xerrež le-flus men l-ḅanka.* He went and got the money from the bank.
ḅanyu pl. *-yat, -wat* bathtub
baqa pl. *-t* bouquet (flowers)
baqaʔ used in the expr. *baqaʔu li-llah* said interjectionally upon hearing of the death of s.o. (implying a "that's-the-way-it-goes" idea)
baqi a.p. of *bqa*
baqiya pl. *-t* rest, remainder
baṛ ibuṛ v.i. **1.** to be left over *had s-selɛa baṛet-lna.* We have this merchandise left over. **2.** to be or become an old maid *dak l-bent ġadi tbuṛ ṭul ɛayatha.* That girl is going to be an old maid all her life.
¶ *ɛateq bayṛa* pl. *ɛwateq bayṛin* spinster
baṛaka pl. *-t* **1.** blessing, beneficial effect (from a religious viewpoint) *had-l-ma fih l-baṛaka.* This water is blessed. **2.** monetary gift, tip (said when donor does not wish to divulge amount given)
** *baṛaka!* Enough! That's enough! —*baṛaka men l-makla.* Stop eating!
¶ *baṛaka ɛla* (to be) enough for *baṛaka ɛliya had ṭ-ṭerf de-l-xobz.* This piece of bread is enough for me.
¶ *ši-baṛaka* (*d-*) a little (bit) (of) *ɛṭini ši-baṛaka d-le-flus.* Give me a little money.
baṛamiž pl. of *beṛnamež*
baṛba (sg. and coll.) pl. *-t* beet
bared pl. *-in* (comp. *bred*) **1.** cool, fresh (air) *had l-ma bared.* This water is cool. **2.** cold *ʔah, yeddik bardin!* My, your hands are cold! **3.** calm-natured, composed **4.** indifferent, unconcerned **5.** cold, frigid (woman), impotent (man)
barda (with art.) fever (with chills or ague) *fih l-barda.* He has a fever.
ḅari pl. *baryen* innocent *ana bari, ma-qteltu-šay!* I'm innocent, I didn't kill him!
** *ana bari mennek.* I won't have anything to do with it (and you better not either); I'll take no responsibility (if you do that).
baṛixa pl. *-t* fishing boat
barek (with *ṛ* rather than *r* in certain expr. and forms, as listed) v.i. **1.** (*f-*) to bless, to favor (mostly used in set expr.) *ḷḷah ibarek fik!* God bless you! Thank you! **2.** (*l-*) to present one's good wishes or compliments, to congratulate *barek-lu fe-l-ɛid.* He wished him a happy holiday.
** *baṛek ḷḷahu fik!* **1.** Thank you! **2.** please . . .
¶ *ḷḷah ibarek fik* please *ḷḷah ibarek fik sellefni ktabek.* Please lend me your book.
¶ p.p. *mbaṛek* used in the set expr. *mbaṛek mesɛud!* Congratulations! —*mbaṛek l-ɛid* or *ɛidek mbaṛek mesɛud!* Happy Holiday!
baruḍ pl. *bwaṛeḍ* (pl. of intensity) **1.** gunpowder **2.** war (local), combat **3.** fusillade
bareɛ (with art.) yesterday
¶ *wel-l-bareɛ* day before yesterday
¶ *wel-l-barɛayn* three days ago
bas ibus v.t. (v.n. *bus, busan*) to kiss, to give a kiss to
bas harm, evil (limited mostly to set expr.)
** *ma-fiha bas.* It's all right (with me); sure, why not; I have no objection; that's all right (in response to an apology). —*ma-ikun bas.* Don't worry; everything will be all right. —*ma-mša mɛakom bas.* said by s.o. who has just lost s.o. in death to the person offering condolences
¶ *la-bas* (I'm he's, etc.) fine, all right *kif-en hiya m̃m̃ek?* —*la-bas.* How's your mother?—Fine. —*la-bas ɛlih.* I hope he gets better; he's all right (health); he's well-to-do, rich. —*yak la-bas?* Is everything all right? Is anything wrong?
basel pl. *-in* **1.** flat, insipid, tasteless (food) **2.** flat, not funny (jokes) **3.** pestering, irksome, vexatious
baṣaṛ (eye)sight *dak ṛ-ṛažel fqed l-baṣaṛ dyalu.* That man has lost his sight.
¶ *ɛla medd l-baṣaṛ* as far as the eye can (could) see
baṣiṛa same as *bṣiṛa*
baṣeṭ pl. *bwaṣeṭ* counter *ɛeṭṭ le-flus ɛăl l-baṣeṭ u-mša.* He put the money on the counter and left.
baš **1.** in order to, in order that *ka-nexdem*

baš nɛiš. I work in order to live (in order that I may live). **2.** since (time expr.) *šḥal hadi baš ža?* How long has it been since he came?

baša (m.) pl. *-wat* pasha, type of town mayor

bašaṛ human being(s), mankind *ana bašaṛ ma-ši malak!* I'm only human (and not an angel)! —*xeṣṣna kollna nxedmu l-meṣlaḥt l-bašaṛ.* We should all work for the benefit of mankind.

bašaša geniality, affability *qabelna b-waḥed l-bašaša kbira.* He welcomed us with great geniality.

bašir same as *beššaṛ*

bašeṛ v.t. **1.** to take care of with patience and understanding (as a sick person) **2.** to take it easy with, to take care of (as one's car)
¶ *bašeṛ b-* (or *mɛa*) same as *bašeṛ*

bat ibat v.i. (v.n. *mbata*) to spend the night, to pass the night, to stay overnight
** *batet š-šta xeddama.* It rained all night long.
¶ a.p. *bayet* pl. *-in* stale (bread, cake), leftover

baṭ pl. *biṭan* armpit

baṭaṭa (sg. and coll.) pl. *-t* same as *bṭaṭa*

baṭel **1.** free (of charge), gratis, for nothing *l-bareḥ dxelt baṭel le-s-sinima.* I got into the movies free yesterday. **2.** injustice, false accusation **3.** groundless *klamek baṭel.* Your statement is groundless.
¶ *be-l-baṭel* unjustly, unfairly *ḥkem ɛlina be-l-baṭel.* He judged us unfairly.
¶ *ṭiyyeḥ* (or *nezzel*) *l-baṭel ɛla* to accuse unjustly, to bring false accusation against

ḅaxennu n.u. *ḅaxennuya* arbutus berry

bayan pl. *-at* **1.** public announcement **2.** clarity, clearness, lucidity

bayn same as *bin* (prep.)

bayṛa f.a.p. of *baṛ*

bayet see *bat*

bayta flannel (cotton)

bayeɛ l- (v.n. *biɛa, mbayɛa*) **1.** to greet or salute with a bow (e.g., a king) **2.** to pledge allegiance to, to recognize the authority of

baz pl. *bizan* **1.** falcon, hawk, buzzard **2.** large bowl (of china or metal)

baẓ **1.** expr. of amazement and approval: Amazing! Marvelous! **2.** expr. of disbelief: Ah, go on! Come off it! You expect me to believe that!
** *baẓ-lek!* How could you! You ought to be ashamed of yourself. (expr. of disapproval)

bazaṛ pl. *-at* bazaar, shop of native handicraft

baḥ ibuḥ b- to disclose, to reveal *baḥu-lu be-s-serr dyalu.* They disclosed his secret.

baɛ ibiɛ v.t. (v.n. *biɛ*) to sell
¶ *baɛ b-* to denounce, to report, to inform against, to turn in (has a rather derogatory connotation) *žaṛu baɛ bih le-š-šorṭa.* His neighbor reported him to the police.
¶ *baɛ u-šra* (impf. *ibiɛ u-išri*) to do business

baɛ (no pl.) arch (of the foot)

baɛir (coll. dim. *bɛiyyeṛ*) young camel

ḅḅa (inh. pos.) pl. *ḅḅawat* (my) father *fayn ḅḅaha l-faṭima* Where's Fatima's father?
** *ḍaṛbu ẓ-ẓelṭ u-ḅḅa ɛăllal.* He hasn't a penny to his name.
¶ *ḅḅahφ siduφ* (first pers. *ḅḅa,* inh. pos.), or *ḅḅa siduφ* (his) grandfather

ḅḅandi, ḅwandi pl. *ḅḅandiya* bandit, highwayman

ḅḅandiya pl. of *ḅḅandi*

ḅḅaxennu same as *ḅaxennu*

bebbuš n.u. *-a, bibuša* snail

bda ibda v.t. or v.i. (v.n. *bidaya, bdu*) to begin, to start, (usually used with other verbs) *men-băɛd-ma xrež bdat š-šta ṭṭiḥ.* After he went out it started to rain.

bdan pl. of *badan, bden,* and *bdin*

bdaɛi pl. of *bedɛiya*

bdaɛiya same as *bedɛiya*

bedda, bodda (used only in set expr.)
¶ *la-bedda, la-bodda,* or *wa-la-bodda* it is (absolutely) necessary (that), without fail, to definitely have to (do s.th.) *wa-la-bodda nšufu ġedda.* I definitely have to see him tomorrow.
** *wa-la-bodda men xlaṣ ḍ-ḍaṛiba.* There's no way of getting out of paying taxes.

beddaṛ adj. pl. *-in* n. pl. *-a* spendthrift, improvident spender

beddel v.t. **1.** to change *ila tbeddel ṛaʔyek qulha-li.* If you change your mind, tell me. **2.** to change (for), to exchange, to replace *beddel had ṭ-ṭebḷa b-ṭebḷa ḥsen mennha.* Change this table for a better one. —*beddel ḥwayžu b-sebġa u-mša l-l-ḥefla.* He quickly changed his clothes and left for the party.
¶ p.p. *mbeddel* pl. *-in* drawn, distorted (one's face with pain, emotion)

beddeṛ v.t. to waste, squander, or throw away (money, time)

bdin pl. *bdan* (comp. *bden*) fat, corpulent, stout

bdiɛ v.n. of *bdăɛ*

bdiɛ pl. *-in, bdaɛ* (comp. *bdăɛ*) beautifully made or done, beautiful, splendid *ṭ-ṭabiɛa f-ʔeyyam ṛ-ṛbiɛ ka-tkun bdiɛa.* In the spring, nature is quite beautiful.

bden comp. of *bdin*

bden pl. *bdan* (human) body *bdenha bšiʕ.* Her body is hideous.
bdenžal n.u. *-a* eggplant
bdu (no pl.) **1.** beginning *hada ġir le-bdu.* That's only the beginning. **2.** v.n. of *bda*
bedwi pl. *-yen* bedouin, peasant
bdăʕ v.i. (v.n. *bdiʕ*) to innovate, to come out with a new style
¶ *bdăʕ f-* to assault (no sexual connotation) *ḥetta bdăʕ fiha ʕad qebṭuh.* They arrested him only after he assaulted her.
bdăʕ comp. of *bdiʕ*
bedʕa pl. *-t* **1.** n.i. of *bdăʕ* **2.** something contrary to the traditions of the Prophet (*sonna*) but not necessarily against the Koran.
bedʕiya pl. *-t, bdaʕi* bolero (loose, waist-length jacket open at the front)
bḍaʕi pl. of *beḍʕa*
beḍʕa pl. *-t, bḍaʕi* **1.** flesh (of fruit), pulp **2.** soft part of bread or cake (as opposed to crust) **3.** harmless, quiet person of weak body; weakling (also adj. usage)
beggaṛ pl. *-a* cattle raiser, cattleman
bgiṛa dim. of *begṛa* (n.u. of *bgeṛ*)
bgeṛ n.u. *begṛa* (dim. *bgiyṛa, bgiṛa*) cattle, cow (as n.u.)
begṛa n.u. of *bgeṛ*
begri **1.** beef (meat) *ka-nfeḍḍel l-begri ʕăl l-ġenmi.* I prefer beef to mutton. **2.** cattle
bġa ibġi v.t. **1.** to want, to desire, to feel like *bġit nešri ši-keswa.* I want to buy a suit. **2.** to like *had ṛ-ṛažel ka-ibġiweh n-nas bezzaf.* People like this man very much. **3.** to try (to do s.th.), to attempt, to make an attempt *bġaw iqetluni.* They tried to kill me. **4.** to be about to, to be on the point of, to be going to, to almost (have done s.th.) *bġa iṭiḥ!* He's going to fall! —*dfăʕni ḥetta bġit nṭiḥ.* He pushed me until I almost fell.
** *bġit mne-ḷḷah u-mennek tsaʕedni f-had l-qaḍiya.* I'd be (very much) obliged if you'd help in this matter. —*lli bġiti,* or *lli bġa xaṭṛek.* As you wish, whatever you say.
¶ a.p. *baġi* pl. *baġyen* (I, he, etc.) would like (to) *baġi nšufha.* I'd like to see her (now).
bġal pl. of *bġel*
bġeḍ v.t. (v.n. *boġḍ*) to hate, to loathe, to detest
boġḍ **1.** v.n. of *bġeḍ* **2.** hatred, aversion, animosity *ma-bqa binothom boġḍ.* There's no more hatred between them.
bġel pl. *bġal* **1.** (he-) mule **2.** strong, husky man with few brains, "big ox"
beġla pl. *-t* (she-) mule
beġli mortar (masonry)
beġrir n.u. *-a* kind of pancake
beġta in the expr. *ʕla beġta* suddenly, unexpectedly, without warning
bha (m.) beauty
bhawat pl. of *bhu*
bhayem pl. of *bhima*
behdel b- to degrade, to debase, to humiliate, to make fun of *behdlu bih ṣḥabu ʕla-lli ža b-serwalu metqub.* His friends humiliated him because he came with a hole in his pants.
bheḍ v.t. (v.n. *bhiḍ*) to amaze, to astound, to astonish
behhat adj. pl. *-in,* n. pl. *-a* **1.** teller of barefaced lies **2.** sly, tricky person
bhiḍ v.n. of *bheḍ*
bhima pl. *-t, bhayem* (dim. *bhiyyma*) **1.** pack animal, beast of burden (usually horse, donkey, mule), mule **2.** stupid or doltish person
bhel f. *behla* pl. *buhel* innocent, naïve, guileless, simple-minded
behlan stupidity, simple-mindedness, idiocy, moronity
behlul pl. *buhala* same as *bhel*
bhet v.i. (v.n. *bhut*) to speak ill (of), to say nasty things (about) *ma-tebqa-š tebhet fe-n-nas!* Stop saying nasty things about people!
bhu pl. *bhawat* alcove of a large room or off a patio
bhut v.n. of *bhet*
bi classicization of *b-* used in such fixed expr. as *bi-xir!* (I'm) fine!
biban pl. of *bab* **1**
bibbuš same as *bebbuš*
bibi (no art.) sg. and coll. f. *-ya,* pl. *-yat* turkey
bidaya v.n. of *bda*
bid-ma, bid-emma bid-man, bid-manat until *qṛa had le-ktab bid-manat iṛžăʕ.* Read this book until he returns.
bidu pl. *-yat, -wat* type of can with a handle used to transport oil, gasoline, water, etc. (especially in military service); jerry-can
bidun pl. *-at, byaden* see *bidu*
biḍ n.u. *-a* (dim. *bwiḍa*) egg
biḍa **1.** f. of *byeḍ* **2.** n.u. of *biḍ*
biḍawa n. pl. of *biḍawi*
biḍawi adj. pl. *-yen* n. pl. *biḍawa* native of Casablanca
biḍeq pl. *byaḍeq* **1.** one of the pieces or "men" used in checkers **2.** nimble person
biha baš see *b-*
bin that *qalu-lu bin ma-imken-lu-š ibqa f-had le-blad.* They told him that he couldn't stay in this country.
bin between (used with both elements if at least one is a pronoun ending) *weqqef ṭ-ṭumubil dyalu bin s-sinima we-l-banka.* He parked his car between the theater and

the bank. —*ma-binu u-bin l-ḥămmam ġiṛ l-ḥăyṭ* There's nothing between him and the bath (place) but the wall.

** *ṭaḥu bin režlih.* They fell at his feet (in supplication, etc.). —*ma-bini u-binhom šay.* I have nothing to do with them. —*š-binek u-bin had š-ši?* It's not your place to do that. What business is this of yours?

¶ *binat* same as *bin* (used with pl. pron. endings) *feṛquha binatkom!* Divide it among yourselves!

** *binatkom.* That's your (pl.) problem, figure it out for yourselves.

¶ *bin u-bin* so-so, fair(ly), mediocre *kif-en huwa had t-tub?—bin u-bin.* How's this material?—So-so.

¶ *bin le-ɛyad* eleventh month of the Muslim lunar year

¶ *ma-bin, men-bin* between (same as *bin*)

bina? pl. *-at* building, structure, edifice

binat see *bin* (prep.)

bir pl. *byar* (dim. *bwiyyer*) well (water, oil)

bisklit pl. *-at* bicycle

biṣaṛ, biṣaṛa dish of mashed fava beans or potatoes served with olive oil, cumin, and paprika

bišklit same as *bisklit*

bit 1. pl. *byut* (dim. *bwiyyet*) room, chamber, compartment (train) 2. square on a checker board 3. pl. *byat* line (of poetry)

¶ *bit ḍ-ḍyaf* guest room

¶ *bit ḷḷah l-ḥaṛam* the Kaada (in Mecca)

¶ *bit l-ma* bathroom (toilet only), rest room, water-closet

¶ *bit l-mal* (public) treasury (building and dept.)

¶ *bit l-makla* dining room

¶ *bit n-naṛ* chamber of a baker's oven

¶ *bit n-nɛas* bedroom

¶ *bit ṣ-ṣabun* laundry room

biṭala same as *bṭala*

biṭan pl. of *baṭ*

biṭaṛ, biṭaṛi pl. *-yen* veterinary, veterinarian

biyyaḍ pl. *-a* 1. egg seller 2. whitewasher

biyyaḍa pl. *-t* 1. f. of *biyyaḍ* 2. a good layer (hen)

biyyar pl. *-a* well-digger

biyyat pl. *-a* night watchman

biyyaɛ pl. *-a* 1. informer, "stool-pigeon" 2. spy

¶ *biyyaɛ šerray* pl. *biyyaɛa šerraya* merchant, businessman

biyyeḍ 1. v.t., to whitewash, to make white 2. v.i., to lay eggs

biyyen v.t. or v.i. 1. to show, to expose, to make manifest 2. to prove, to show *ana ġadi nbiyyen-lkom belli had š-ši lli ka-nqul-lkom ṣḥiḥ.* I'm going to prove to you that what I'm telling you is true.

** *had ž-žaž ma-ka-ibiyyen-š.* You can't see through this glass.

¶ *biyyen ṛaṣu* to make oneself known *dak l-bent ɛăndha ṣewt mezyan, xeṣṣha tbiyyen ṛaṣha.* That girl has a beautiful voice, she should make herself known.

biyyna pl. *-t* proof *ɛăndhom ši-biyyna ɛăl l-xiyana dyalu?* Do they have any proof of his treason?

biyyet v.t. to have or make spend the night, to put up (for the night), to lodge (for the night) *biyyet ṣaḥbu ɛăndu.* He had his friend spend the night with him.

bizagṛa pl. *-t* hinge

bizan pl. of *baz*

biɛ 1. v.n. of *baɛ* 2. sale, selling

¶ *l-biɛ u-š-šra* business, commerce

biɛa pl. *-t* 1. n.i. of *baɛ* 2. v.n. of *bayeɛ* 3. (act of) informing (against s.o.) *l-bareḥ weṣletna bih l-biɛa.* We received information against him yesterday. 4. recognition of superior authority (as a King)

¶ *biɛa de-š-šġal* a specific number or lot of one item of manufacture (by hand) by which the craftsman is paid.

¶ *biɛa u-šerya* (both words take art. and pl.) (business) deal, transaction

¶ *ɛṭa l-biɛa l-* to pledge allegiance to, to proclaim (i.e., announce publicly the accession of a sovereign)

bka ibki v.i. (v.n. *bka*) to cry, to weep, to sob

bka 1. v.n. of *bka* 2. crying, weeping, sobbing

bekka v.t. to make or cause to cry, to move to tears *ḍṛeb xah ṣ-ṣġir u-bekkah.* He hit his little brother and made him cry. —*dak l-qiṣṣa ?etteṛ ɛliha ḥetta bekkaha.* That story impressed her to the point of moving her to tears.

bekkay adj. pl. *-in,* n. pl. *-a* one who cries frequently and with little provocation, a "cry baby"

bekker v.i. to get up early (in the morning)

** *bekkret b-weld.* Her first child was a boy.

bkem f. *bekma* pl. *bukem* mute, unable to speak

bker f. *bekra* pl. *bkura* first-born

bekra pl. *-t* virgin (still in possession of the hymen)

bekri 1. early *ka-nnuḍ dima bekri.* I always get up early. 2. a long time ago, in days gone by, in the old days, in days past, formerly *bekri kanu n-nas mdiyynin kteṛ men l-yum.* In the old days there were more religious people than there are today.

bkura pl. of *bker*

bla ibla v.i. to get old (things), to become used, to wear out *mnin ka-iblaw ḥwayži ka-nešri ḥwayež ždad.* When my clothes wear out I buy new clothes.

bla ibli v.t. (v.n. *belya, bliya*) to teach, show, cause, or allow s.o. to take up bad habits or vices; to corrupt *la-txaḷeṭ-š le-bla la-iblik.* Stay away from vice so that it won't corrupt you.

** *lli bla yăعfu.* may he who has allowed all this (some vice) have mercy (expr. showing pity for s.o. who is victim of some vice or bad habit)

¶ *bla b-* to teach (s.o.) (some vice) *blatni b-le-عgez.* She taught me lazy habits.

bla (m.) calamity, misfortune, catastrophe

** *عăndu waحed l-weld bla.* He has a son that's a little devil.

bla (*bla b-* before personal pron. endings) **1.** without *ṣafeṭ le-bṛa bla tenber.* He sent the letter without a stamp —*mša bla-biya.* He went without me.

¶ *bla-ma* (conj.) without *bqa gales bla-ma yăعmel حetta ši-حaža.* He sat there without doing a thing.

¶ *bla-š* **1.** for nothing, free, gratis *waš bġiti năعṭih-lek bla-š?* Do you want me to give it to you for nothing? **2.** without (it) *ža be-ṭ-ṭeṛbuš wella bla-š?* Did he come with or without his hat (fez)?

blabel pl. of *belbula*

blabez pl. of *belbuza*

blad (f.) pl. *-at, beldan, boldan* **1.** country *mn-ana blad nta?* What country are you from? **2.** country *ža men le-blad baš iḍuwweṛ عăl l-xedma f-le-mdina.* He came from the country to find work in the city. **3.** region, area, locality *blad ṛ-rif kollha žbal.* The region of the Rif is all mountains. **4.** city, town *ḍ-ḍaṛ l-biḍa blad wasعa u-عṛiḍa.* Casablanca is an expansive, sprawling city.

¶ *mul le-blad* pl. *mwalin le-blad* **1.** landowner **2.** (pl.) native people, people of a country or city in which one happens to be

¶ *riح le-blad* homesickness *qaṣu riح le-blad.* He's homesick (i.e., touched by homesickness)

¶ *weld le-blad* fellow citizen, compatriot

blaġi pl. of *belġa*

bḷaṭi pl. *-ya* **1.** carpenter **2.** drunkard

bḷan pl. *-at* **1.** plan, blueprint **2.** plan, project

bḷaṣa pl. *-t, bḷayeṣ* **1.** place, spot, location, site **2.** room, space, area **3.** position, post (as in the government) **4.** seat (theater, bus, etc.)

bla-š see *bla*

bḷaya pl. *-t* beach

bḷayeṣ pl. of *bḷaṣa*

blayeẓ pl. of *bluẓa*

belbel v.i. to prattle, to speak unintelligibly

belbel fluently *ka-ihḍeṛ l-عăṛbiya belbel.* He speaks (Moroccan) Arabic fluently.

beḷbeḷ v.i. **1.** to mumble, to mutter, to chatter (in some foreign language) **2.** to bleat (goat)

belbula pl. *blabel* couscous with buttermilk

belbuza pl. *-t, blabez* eyeball

beldan, boldan pl. of *blad*

beldi pl. *-yen* **1.** native, indigenous, homegrown *waš had t-teffaح ṛumi wella beldi?* Are these apples imported or homegrown? **2.** unsophisticated, naïve **3.** unprogressive, old-fashioned

bleġ (v.n. *bluġ, buluġ*) **1.** v.t. to attain, to reach, to arrive at *bleġ l-muṛaḍ dyalu.* He attained his goal. **2.** v.i. to reach puberty, to become marriageable

¶ a.p. *baleġ* pl. *-in* marriageable, pubescent

belġa pl. *-t, blaġi* (dim. *bliġa*) a pair of a type of North African slippers used as general footwear (one slipper: *ferda de-l-belġa*)

bliġa dim. of *belġa*

bḷiḷṭa dim. of *beḷḷuṭa* (n.u. of *beḷḷuṭ*)

bliya pl. *-t* **1.** v.n. of *bla* **2.** bad habit, vice

bliẓ v.n. of *bleẓ*

bliع v.n. of *blăع*

bell v.t. (v.n. *bellan*) to wet, to get wet

bellan v.n. of *bell*

beḷḷaṛ **1.** crystal *l-beḷḷaṛ kollu lli kan fuq ṭ-ṭebla ṭaح u-therres.* The (whole set of) crystal which was on the table fell off and broke. **2.** crystal *had l-kas mṣuwweb men l-beḷḷaṛ* This glass is made of crystal.

bellarež (no art., sg. and coll.) f. *bellarža* stork

bellati **1.** slowly *men-lli qeṛṛeb le-ḍ-ḍaṛ bda ixellef bellati.* As he neared the house he began to walk slowly. **2.** low, in a low voice, in an aside

** *bellati!* Wait a minute! Just a minute!

bellaع l-biḍ (sg. and pl.) white jellyfish

bellefžuž (no art.) n.u. *-a* violet

belleġ *v.t.* to deliver, to take

¶ *belleġ s-slam* to say hello *belleġ-li s-slam l-عămmek!* Say hello to your uncle for me.

belli that *qolt-lu belli ma-عăndi flus.* I told him that I don't have any money.

beḷḷina pl. *-t* whale

bellel same as *bell*

beḷḷeṭ **1.** v.t. to mess up, to smear *beḷḷeṭi حwayžek be-ṣ-ṣbaġa.* You've smeared your clothes with paint. **2.** v.i. to get drunk

beḷḷuṭ n.u. *-a* (dim. *bḷiḷṭa*) acorn(s)

¶ *beḷḷuṭa* pl. *-t* **1.** tassel (of the *selham*) **2.** eyeball

beḷḷeẓ f-, beḷḷeẓ عăynih∅ f- to stare at

bellăعman (no art.) n.u. *-a* poppy

bleq f. *belqa* pl. *buleq* **1.** very white (skin) **2.** piebald (horse, cow)

¶ *bꜥal tuṛ bleq* sticking out like a sore thumb
bluġ **1.** v.n. of *bleġ* **2.** puberty, marriageability
blul gravy for couscous
bluza pl. *-t, blayez* blouse
belya v.n. of *bla*
bleẓ v.t. and v.i. (v.n. *bliẓ*) to make a faux pas, to botch
belẓa pl. *-t* faux pas, blunder
belꜥuꜥa pl. *-t* Adam's apple
blăʕ v.t. (v.n. *bliʕ*) **1.** to swallow, to swallow up (also metaphorical) **2.** to absorb (as a sponge)
belʕa **1.** n.i. of *blăʕ* **2.** many, a lot, quite a few *belʕa d-le-flus mšaw-lu.* He lost a lot of money.
ben pl. *bni* **1.** son (used in names) *waš ka-tăʕref muꜥămmed ben ʕli?* Do you know Mohammed Ben Ali? **2.** pl. *bnayn* term used in insulting expr. and epithets *ma-ʕămmṛi nelʕăb mʕak l-kaṛṭa a ben l-ġeššaš l-axoṛ!* I'll never play cards with you again, you damn cheat!
¶ *ben ʕămmu*ᶲ (one's) m. cousin
bna ibni v.t. (v.n. *bni*) to build, to construct, to erect (also metaphorical)
bnadem (no art. or pl.) human being(s), people *ʕămmṛek šefti ši-bnadem bꜥal dak xiyyi?* Have you ever seen anyone (a human being) like that guy? —*kan bnadem bezzaf fe-l-ꜥefla.* There were a lot of people at the party.
bnader pl. of *bendir*
bnadri pl. *-ya* **1.** player of the *bendir* **2.** maker of the *bendir*
ḅnak pl. of *ḅenk* (same as *ḅanka*)
bnan pl. of *bnin* and *benna*
bnat pl. of *bent*
bnayn pl. of *ben* **2**
bnayeq pl. of *bniqa*
bendir pl. *bnader* a flat, round North African drum with one head
bendira same as *bandira*
bender v.i. to play the *bendir*
benḍeq l- to greet with a bow, to bow respectfully before
bni (no pl.) **1.** v.n. of *bna* **2.** pl. of *ben* **1** **3.** building, structure, edifice **4.** construction (work), (action of) building
bnin pl. *-in, bnan* delicious
bniqa pl. *-t, bnayeq* **1.** closet (clothes, linen), cupboard **2.** cell (jail) **3.** cabin (ship)
bnita, bniya dim. of *bent*
ḅenk pl. *ḅnak* same as *ḅanka*
benna pl. *-t, bnan* toe (foot)
bennaṛa pl. *-t* comb (fleshy crest on the head of certain kinds of fowl)
bennay pl. *-a* mason, bricklayer
bennefžuž same as *bellefžuž*
bennež v.t. **1.** to drug, to administer a drug to (s.o.) (said only of sleep inducing drugs) **2.** to anesthetize
bent pl. *bnat* (dim. *bnita, bniya*) **1.** girl, daughter **2.** term used in insulting expr. and epithets *a bent l-ꜥămqa l-oxṛa!* You're (f.) out of your mind!
¶ *bent ʕămmu*ᶲ (one's) f. cousin
¶ *bent n-nas* girl of good stock, of fine family background
benter v.t. to paint (houses, tables, etc.)
bnu pl. *-wat* tire (automobile, etc.)
benyan (no pl.) building, structure, edifice
benž anesthetic (e.g. ether, chloroform)
bqa ibqa v.i. **1.** to stay, to remain *bqat be-wꜥădha fe-ḍ-ḍaṛ.* She stayed home alone. **2.** to keep on, to continue, to remain, to persevere (in) *bqa ka-ikteb-lu modda ṭwila.* He kept on writing him (regularly) for quite a while. —*bqat ka-tbessel ʕliya ꜥetta ṭaṛ-li.* She kept bothering me until I got mad.
** *bqa f-qelbi,* or *bqa fiya.* I feel sorry for him.
** *tebqa ʕla xir.* Good-bye (take care of yourself)!
¶ *bqa-lu*ᶲ to have left ≠, to still have ≠ *bqaw-lu žuž de-l-gaṛṛuwat.* He has two cigarettes left.
¶ *bqa ʕla* to prevail upon, to work on (s.o.) *bqit ʕlih ꜥetta ʕṭani ʕăšṛ iyyam de-ṛ-ṛaꜥa.* I worked on him until he gave me ten days' vacation.
¶ *ma-bqa-lu*ᶲ *ġir* **1.** to be about to ≠ *ma-bqa-lu ġir iži.* He's about to come. **2.** to have only . . . left ≠ *ma-bqa-li ġir žuž ryal.* I only have two ryals left.
¶ *ma-bqa-š* to not . . . any more *ma-bqa-š iži.* He doesn't come any more.
¶ *ma-bqa ʕlaš* (plus impf.) to no longer have any reason for or to ≠ *ma-bqa ʕlaš tebki.* You no longer have any reason to cry.
¶ *baqi,* f. *baqya, baqa,* pl. *baqyen, baqin* still, yet *baqya š-šems ma-ṭelʕet.* The sun hasn't come out yet.
bqarež pl. of *beqrež, beqraž*
bqaʕi pl. of *beqʕa, boqʕa*
beqbeq v.i. to gurgle (as water poured from a jug)
beqq n.u. *-a* bed-bug(s)
beqqal pl. *-a* grocer (except meat, vegetables)
beqqaš pl. *-in* inquisitive, prying, curious
beqqeš v.i. to look for s.th. or s.o. (from curiosity), to rummage around (looking into things that do not concern one), to snoop around *baṛaka ma-tbeqqeš-š fe-ꜥwayži!* Quit snooping around in my clothes!
beqqula (coll.) kind of round-leafed plant (used as a food)
bqeṛ same as *bgeṛ*

beqṛa same as *begṛa* (n.u. of *bgeṛ*)
beqraž, beqrež pl. *bqarež* (tea)kettle
beqɛa, boqɛa pl. *-t, bqaɛi* piece, lot, section (of land)
bṛa ibṛa v.i. (v.n. *beṛyan*) to recover (from an illness), to get well
bra ibri v.i. to glitter, to spɔrkle
bṛa pl. *-wat* (cons. *bṛat,* dim. *bṛiya*) letter, written message
braber pl. of *berbri*
bradeɛ pl. of *berdɛa*
bradɛi pl. *-ya* manufacturer of pack saddles
braga pl. of *bergi*
bramel pl. of *bermil*
bramli pl. *-ya* barrel-maker
bṛaniya eggplant
bṛaneṣ pl. of *beṛnuṣ*
brared pl. of *berrad*
brarek pl. of *berraka*
brarem pl. of *berrima*
bṛat cons. of *bṛa*
bṛaṭel pl. of *beṛṭal*
bṛaweṭ pl. of *beṛwiṭa*
bṛayeq pl. of *bṛiq* 2
braz ceremony in which the bride is exhibited to the wedding guests who have come to congratulate her and bring her presents
bṛaž pl. of *beṛž*
braɛed pl. of *berɛud*
berbri pl. *braber* Berber (person)
bred v.i. (v.n. *bruda*) 1. to become or get cold or cool, to cool off *men-lli ka-tebred l-qehwa ma-ka-nqedd-š nešṛobha.* I can't drink coffee when it gets cold. 2. to become discouraged, to give up *bred mnin ma-staṭeɛ-š iḥeṣṣel ɛăl š-šahada.* He became discouraged when he couldn't get his diploma.
** *bred-lu l-ma fe-rkabih.* He was paralyzed (with fear). —*berdu ktafu.* He got discouraged.
bred comp. of *bared*
berd 1. cold(ness) *matu be-l-berd.* They died from the cold. 2. wind *bda iṣuṭ l-berd.* It's getting windy. 3. used for various illnesses attributed to the cold, e.g., colds, flu, bronchitis, etc.
** *ġad ikun l-berd had l-lila.* It's going to be cold tonight. —*žani l-berd.* I'm cold.
¶ *berd le-mfaṣel* arthritis, rheumatism (of joints)
¶ *ḍreb l-berd* to catch cold ≠ *ḍrebni l-berd.* I've caught cold.
berda v.t. to leak, to lose (as air from a tire)
berdan pl. *-in* cold (persons) *ana berdan!* I'm cold!
berdăɛ v.t. to put the packsaddle (*berdɛa*) on an animal
berdɛa pl. *bradeɛ* (dim. *bridɛa*) packsaddle
bṛeḍ v.t. (v.n. *bṛiḍ*) to file (with a file)
bergi adj. pl. *-yen,* n. pl. *braga* brown, brown-skinned (person)
bergem v.t. 1. to mumble, to mutter 2. to speak like a negro (i.e., with a typical accent)
berġaz pl. *-a* secondhand peddler (mostly clothes, but possibly anything)
bridɛa dim. of *berdɛa*
bṛiḍ v.n. of *bṛeḍ*
brik v.n. of *brek*
bṛim v.n. of *bṛem*
bṛiq 1. v.n. of *bṛeq* 2. pl. *bṛayeq* coffeepot
bṛiqqa dim. of *beṛquq*
brirda dim. of *berrada*
bṛiwa pl. *-t* a pastry made of almond paste wrapped in a thin crust and dipped in honey
bṛiya dim. of *bṛa*
briḥ 1. v.n. of *berreḥ* 2. announcement (of the *berraḥ*)
¶ *ṭleq le-briḥ* 1. to make an announcement (the *berraḥ*) 2. to hire a town crier (to make an announcement)
brek v.i. (v.n. *brik*) 1. to sit (down), to squat (down) 2. to stay, to remain (in one place) *brek hna ḥetta nži!* Stay here until I come back.
¶ *brek f-* to attack (physically)
¶ *brek ɛla* 1. to exert pressure on or against 2. to push (a switch or button)
bṛek n.u. *beṛka* duck
berka slave market or stand
berkukeš a dish made of sweetened hominy grits with milk
bṛem v.t. (v.n. *bṛim*) to cord, to braid (hair, rope), to twist together (as two pieces of string)
bṛem pl. of *beṛma*
beṛma pl. *-t, bṛem* 1. hot water storage receptacle for the public bath 2. water heater
bermil pl. *bramel* barrel
beṛnamež pl. *baṛamiž* 1. schedule (radio), program (entertainment) 2. plan *ɛmelti ši-beṛnamež l-had l-lila?* Have you made any plans for tonight?
berniz varnish
beṛnuṣ pl. *bṛaneṣ* burnoose
bernez v.t. to varnish
bṛeq v.i. (v.n. *-bṛiq, bṛuq*) to shine (sun, moon, etc.), to glitter, to sparkle, to scintillate
beṛqeq v.t. to bruise with a blow and cause a bump or swelling
¶ *beṛqeq f-* to stare at, to gawk at
beṛquq n.u. *-a* (dim. *bṛiqqa*) plum, prune
¶ *beṛquqa* pl. *-t* swelling, lump, bump (as from a blow)
berr land (in contrast to sea)
beṛṛ b- to have pity or mercy on, to help
berra v.t. to acquit (of guilt)
¶ *berra f-* to disown (as a son)

beṛṛa v.t. to cure, to heal

beṛṛa (no art.) **1.** country (in contrast to city) *ana mṣafeṛ l-beṛṛa.* I'm going to the country. **2.** outside *galsin beṛṛa.* They're sitting outside.

¶ *beṛṛa men* outside (of) *galsin beṛṛa men ḍ-ḍaṛ.* They're sitting outside (of) the house.

¶ *ɛla beṛṛa* same as *beṛṛa* 2

berrad pl. *brared* (dim. *brired*) teapot

berrada pl. *-t* (dim. *brirda*) small jug of porous, unglazed clay used for cooling water

berraka pl. *brarek* **1.** barracks **2.** hovel, hut (e.g. in a slum) **3.** cabin (beach, etc.)

beṛṛani pl. *-yen* **1.** stranger **2.** strange, not from the local area **3.** foreigner **4.** outside, outer *nsiti tšedd l-bab l-beṛṛaniya.* You forgot to close the outside door.

¶ *l-beṛṛani* the first room one encounters on entering the public bath

berraḥ pl. *-a* town crier

¶ *ṭḷeq l-berraḥ* to hire a public crier (to make some announcement)

berred **1.** v.t. to cool (off), to let cool (off) **2.** v.i. to refresh oneself (as with a cool drink) **3.** v.t. to calm (down) *berredtu b-žuž de-l-kelmat.* I calmed him down with a few words. **4.** v.t. to discourage, to dishearten **5.** v.t. to hush up (an affair), to keep quiet

** *berred ɛliya šwiyeš!* Lay off me (for a while)! —*berred qelbu fiha* (or *le-ġdayed fiha*). He got his revenge on her. —*le-xbaṛ berred-li l-ma fe-rkabiya.* The news scared me to death (paralyzed me with fear, etc.). —*ka-iberred ɛla qelbu.* He's just making excuses (for his failure in doing s.th.).

berri pl. *-yen* pertaining to land (in contrast to sea)

berrima pl. *-t, brarem* **1.** pencil sharpener **2.** brace and bit (carpenter)

berrek v.t. to make sit down (animals)

berriw dung

beṛṛem v.t. to move (over), to pull over *beṛṛem siyaṛtek l-had ž-žih.* Pull your car over to this side. —*beṛṛem ṭ-ṭebḷa l-dak l-qent.* Move the table to that corner.

berren by land (in contrast to sea)

beṛṛeq v.t. to prove false, to give the lie to, to belie, to refute (person or thing)

¶ *beṛṛeq f-* to stare at

¶ *beṛṛeq l-ɛăynin* to stare, to gawk

berrez v.t. (v.n. *briḥ*) to exhibit the bride in the *braz*

berreḥ v.i. to make announcements in public (in streets, etc.)

¶ *berreḥ b-* to spread (around) or divulge (s.th. that should not be told), to blab

beṛṣ, bṛeṣ white blotches on the skin, vitiligo

beṛṣlana cement, mortar

beṛšem v.t. to ornament the edge or fringe of, to decorate with a fringe or border (a garment)

beṛšman fringe or edge of a garment

beṛṭal pl. *bṛaṭel* **1.** bird (small, e.g. a robin) **2.** sparrow **3.** alcove off the patio of a Moroccan house

bruda, brudiya **1.** v.n. of *bred* **2.** cold(ness), cool(ness) (also as a personal trait) **3.** humidity, dampness **4.** lack of vigor, slackness, laziness **5.** banality, platitude

bruk **1.** v.n. of *brek* **2.** fight(ing) *baṛaka men le-bruk!* Stop fighting!

bṛuq v.n. of *bṛeq*

bṛuž, bṛuža pl. of *beṛž, boṛž*

berwag (coll. and n.u.) asphodel

beṛwiṭa pl. *bṛaweṭ* **1.** wheelbarrow **2.** a very old car

beṛyan **1.** v.n. of *bṛa* **2.** pl. *-in* healthy, in good health

brez v.i. **1.** to protrude, to stick out **2.** to participate in the *braz*

beṛž, boṛž pl. *bṛuž, bṛuža, bṛaž* fort, citadel

berɛăd v.t. to roll, to give (s.th.) the shape of a roll (e.g., cake)

berɛud pl. *braɛed* roll (of dough)

bsal v.i. (v.n. *bsala*) **1.** to become flat or tasteless (food) **2.** to become a nuisance or obnoxious

bsala pl. *-t* **1.** v.n. of *bessel* and *bsal* **2.** dullness, vapidity, insipidity (figurative sense) **3.** stupidity, nonsense

besbas fennel

bsibsa mace (spice)

besmala v.n. of *besmel*

besmel v.i. (v.n. *besmala*) to say *be-sme-llah*

bessel v.i. (v.n. *bsala*) **1.** to say silly things, to talk nonsense

¶ *bessel ɛla* to annoy, to bother

bessem v.t. to make or cause to smile

bessăɛ men to get or go away from *bessăɛ menni!* Go away (from me)!

bṣaṛ adj. pl. of *bṣiṛ*

bṣaṣeṭ pl. of *beṣṣiṭa*

bṣaṭ pl. *-at* **1.** large rectangular room on any floor above the first **2.** big paper lantern carried in the *ɛašuṛa* procession, especially in Salé

bṣaṭel pl. of *beṣṭila*

bṣila dim. of *bṣel, beṣla*

bṣiṛ adj. pl. *bṣaṛ* n. pl. *beṣṛa* blind, blind man

bṣiṛa perspicacity

bṣiṭ **1.** pl. *-in* simple, easy **2.** (no pl.) one of the different rhythms of Moroccan Andalusian music

bṣel, beṣla n.u. *beṣla* (dim. *bṣila*) onion

beṣṛa n. pl. of *bṣiṛ*

beṣṣila pl. *-t* **1.** leek **2.** wild onion (for animal consumption)

beṣṣiṭa pl. *-t, bṣaṣeṭ* peseta (Spanish money)
beṣṣeṭ v.t. **1.** to flatten, to squash **2.** to amuse
bṣeṭ (v.n. *beṣṭ*) **1.** v.i. to joke *ġir ka-nebṣeṭ mʕak.* I'm only joking with you. **2.** v.i. to have a good time, to enjoy oneself
¶ p.p. *mebṣuṭ* pl. *-in* gay, jovial
beṣṭ **1.** v.n. of *bṣeṭ* **2.** joke
beṣṭila pl. *-t, bṣaṭel* a pastry made with almond paste and chicken or pigeon giblet baked in a thin crust
bṣuṭi adj. pl. *-yen* jolly, having a sense of humor
bšaṛa **1.** gift given to the mother of a newborn baby **2.** reward (e.g., for finding s.o.'s lost object) **3.** good news
bšaʕ pl. of *bšiʕ*
bšaʕa **1.** meanness, rudeness, despicableness **2.** ugliness (appearance)
bšir v.n. of *bšer*
bšiʕ pl. *-in, bšaʕ* **1.** rude, mean, despicable **2.** ugly (appearance)
bešnixa kind of plant whose flower is composed of various needle-like parts which, when dried, are used as toothpicks; also, toothpick of this type
bšer v.t. (v.n. *bšir*) **1.** to rub (as with sandpaper) **2.** to scale (fish)
bešṛa pl. *-t* look, countenance
** *bšeṛtu meṭluqa.* He's affable (i.e., always smiling).
beššaṛ pl. *-a* bearer of good news or tidings
¶ *beššaṛ l-xir* butterfly
beššeṛ v.t. to announce (good news or tidings)
¶ *beššeṛ b-* (s.th.) *ʕla* (s.o.) to make a present of (s.th.) to (s.o.) (specifically to the mother of a newborn baby)
bṭiṛ v.n. of *bṭeṛ*
bṭeṛ v.t. (v.n. *bṭiṛ*) **1.** to omit, to leave out **2.** to cancel
¶ *bṭeṛ men l-bal* to forget about, to not think about *bṭeṛ had š-ši men balek!* Don't think about it!
beṭṭix n.u. *-a* melon (except watermelon)
bṭa ibṭa v.i. (v.n. *bṭu, beṭyan*) to be late, to take a long time
¶ *bṭa ʕla* to make wait, to let wait *ʕlaš bṭiti ʕliya.* Why did you make me wait (for you)?
bṭala **1.** unemployment **2.** absence (from work, school) **3.** v.n. of *bṭel*
¶ *bla bṭala* unceasingly
bṭana pl. *bṭayen* (dim. *bṭiyyna*) sheepskin
** *ntef-lek bṭantek.* He spoke ill of you.
bṭaqa pl. *-t, bṭayeq* **1.** ticket (admission, travel) **2.** card (filing, etc.) **3.** bond, coupon
¶ *bṭaqa de-ṭ-ṭbib* prescription (medicine)
bṭaṭa (sg. and coll.) *potato*
¶ *bṭaṭa qeṣbiya* Jerusalem artichoke
¶ *bṭaṭa ṛumiya* potato (usual meaning)
¶ *bṭaṭa ḥluwa* sweet potato
bṭayen pl. of *bṭana*
bṭayni pl. *-ya* **1.** seller of sheepskin **2.** backbiter, slanderer
bṭayeq pl. of *bṭaqa*
bṭayḥi Andalusian meter or time used in Moroccan music
beṭbeṭha~ to stuff oneself, to gorge oneself with food)
bṭel (v.n. *beṭlan, bṭul, bṭala*) **1.** to be called off, to be cancelled **2.** to be omitted, to be left out **3.** to expire, to become invalid
beṭlan v.n. of *bṭel*
bṭen pl. *bṭuna* belly, abdomen
beṭniya bellyful
¶ *ḍreb beṭniya* to stuff or gorge oneself (with food)
bṭeṛ v.i. (v.n. *bṭeṛ*) to hurry (up), to hasten
** *bṭeṛ bih!* Make it fast!
bṭeṛ **1.** v.n. of *bṭeṛ* **2.** rapidity, swiftness, hurry
¶ *b-le-bṭeṛ* quickly, rapidly, fast, in a hurry
beṭṭa v.t. **1.** to make late, to keep (s.o.), to delay **2.** to drag out, to make drag on
¶ *beṭṭa b-* same as *beṭṭa*
beṭṭa pl. *-t, bṭeṭ* **1.** large bottle, usually covered with a reed matting or sack cloth and with one or two handles **2.** oil can (i.e., used in oiling machinery)
beṭṭal adj. pl. *-in* n. pl. *-a* (person) out of work, without employment
beṭṭaniya pl. *-t* blanket, cover (bedclothes)
beṭṭix same as *bettix*
beṭṭel v.t. **1.** to be absent from, to not go to or report for *beṭṭel l-xedma.* He didn't go to work. **2.** to cancel, to call off **3.** to leave out, to omit **4.** v.i. to change one's mind *la, beṭṭelt, ma-maši-š.* No, I've changed my mind, I'm not going.
beṭṭen v.t. **1.** to line, to put lining in (clothing) **2.** to beat (rug, blanket) **3.** to beat up, to give a beating to (s.o.)
bṭu v.n. of *bṭa*
bṭul v.n. of *bṭel*
bṭuna pl. of *bṭen*
beṭyan v.n. of *bṭa*
beṭʕa same as *beḍʕa*
bu pl. *-wat* father (usually used to emphasize certain expr. and threats) *wellah ya buh!* Let him try it! I dare him!
bubal (no pl.) top part of either the ferula or fennel plant before it blooms, used in making a dish similar to couscous.
bubbuš same as *bebbuš*
bubbuʕ (no pl., no art.) expr. used to frighten or intimidate small children, similar to English "bogey man"
bu-bṛiṣ (sg. and coll., no art.) gecko (small lizard)

budi pl. *-yen* Buddhist
bu-denžal same as *bdenžal*
bu-drăɛ rancid (butter)
bu-deḥḥas (no art.) whitlow
bu-ḍeḷfa (no pl., no art.) cobra
bu-feṛṭiṭu pl. *-yat* (no art.) butterfly
bu-fessiw pl. *-at* (no art.) **1.** golden-crested or fire-crested wren **2.** one who speaks queerly, indistinctly **3.** child who goes around yelling and shouting
bugadu pl. *-wat, -yat* lawyer
bu-glib (no art.) cholera
buġat pl. of *baġi*
buġaz pl. *-at* **1.** narrow passage, strait **2.** isthmus
buhala pl. of *behlul* and *buhali*
buhali pl. *-yen, buhala* simple-minded (person), idiot
buhel pl. of *bhel*
bu-herras, bu-herrus (no art.) that which seems to make one break things (especially dishes) *yeddih fihom bu-herrus.* He breaks everything.
buhtan **1.** sarcasm **2.** hypocrisy (often connoting a betrayal of confidence)
bu-hezhaz, bu-hezzaz (no art.) (the) shakes, Parkinson's disease
bu-kebbaṛ pl. *-at* (no art.) a swelling in the armpit or groin
bukem pl. of *bkem*
bu-kṛaɛ, bu-kṛăɛ (no art.) one-legged man
bul **1.** v.n. of *bal* **2.** urine
bula **1.** n.i. of *bal* **2.** urine
ḅuḷa pl. *-t* light bulb
bu-lfaf (no pl., no art.) a type of shish kebab made of liver wrapped in caul
bulis **1.** pl. of *bulisi* **2.** police (force)
bulisi pl. *bulis, bwales* policeman
buleq pl. of *bleq*
buluġ v.n. of *bleġ*
ḅuḷun, buḷun pl. *-at* bolt (for fastening together)
bu-le-žlayeb same as *bu-žlayeb*
ḅumḅa pl. *-t* **1.** pump (oil, water, etc.) **2.** (fly) sprayer **3.** bomb (explosive)
ḅumbi pl. *-ya* fireman, fire-fighter
bu-menqaš (sg. and coll., no art.) snipe (bird)
bu-mqiyyeṣ, bu-mqeṣ, pl. *bu-mquṣat* earwig
bu-mquṣa pl. *-t* (no art.) lobster
bu-mwaret (no pl., no art.,) trustee or administrator of vacant successions
bu-mexyeṭ (sg. and coll., no art.) oyster-catcher (bird)
bu-meẓwi (no pl., no art.) sharp stomach-ache
ḅun pl. *-at, ḅwan* **1.** voucher **2.** coupon (e.g. in rationing food)
bunta pl.*-t* (dim. *bwinta*) cigaret butt
bunya pl. *-t* **1.** fist **2.** blow with the fist **3.** fight involving fisticuffs

buq pl. *bwaq* **1.** loudspeaker **2.** megaphone ¶ *dar l-buq b-* to tell everyone about
buqal pl. *bwaqel* **1.** one of the scoops or buckets on a water wheel **2.** (person) with an oblong head
buqala pl. *-t* wen (on the head)
buṛbu powder (face, baby, etc.)
buṛda poem or hymn in honor of the Prophet
buṛḍu pl. *-wat* cane with a metal head
bu-rgiba (coll., no art.) type of pear
buri used in the expr. *ḥut buri* n.u. *ḥuta buriya* gray mullet
bu-rkabi (no pl., no art.) **1.** large, clumsy person; blockhead, bumpkin **2.** ruffian, roughneck
buṛeš v.i. to shiver
** *leḥmu ka-ibureš.* He's got goose pimples.
bus v.n. of *bas*
busa pl. *-t* (dim. *bwisa*) kiss
busan v.n. of *bas*
bu-sekka (no pl., no art.) rattlesnake
bu-ṣeḷḷaṭ (no art.) elephantiasis
buṣ indolence, sloth
buṣ-ḍ-ḍaṛ pl. *-at* patio, court
bu-ṣeffaṛ, bu-ṣeffiṛ (no art.) (yellow) jaundice
bu-ṣiyyaṛ pl. *-at* (art. possible) large sieve with big holes (for seeds)
bu-ṣiḥa (no pl., no art.) tarantula
buṣla pl. *-t* compass (magnetic directional)
buṣṭa pl. *-t* post office (building and department)
buš pl. *bwaš* **1.** marble (as used in a game of marbles) **2.** type of (water) jug
bu-šfeṛ (no pl., no art.) a muzzle-loading musket
** *had š-ši d-bu-šfeṛ.* This (thing) is of bad quality.
bu-šeqṛaq (sg. and coll., no art.) jay
bušra pl. *-t* (item of) good news
bu-šwika (no art.) scarlet fever
bu-teftaf palsy (as commonly accompanying senility) *ḅḅah sidu fih bu-teftaf.* His grandfather has palsy.
butika pl. *-t* pharmacy (store)
bu-tellis (no pl., no art.) nightmare
buṭ (sg. and pl.) pair of boots (sg. *ferda de-l-buṭ*)
buṭa pl. *-t, bweṭ* **1.** metal barrel, drum **2.** bottle (for gas, e.g. butane)
buṭel *ɛla* to be unjust toward (s.o.), to make false accusations against (s.o.)
buwwab pl. *-a* doorman, doorkeeper
buwwaq pl. *-a* one who spreads news or reveals secrets
buwwaḥ pl. *-in* not able to keep secrets.
buwwel v.t. or v.i. to make or cause to urinate, to be diuretic

buwweq b- to spread news about, to disclose a secret about
buwweṣ v.t. **1.** to give (s.o.) the cold shoulder, to ignore (s.o.) **2.** to fire (an employe)
¶ part. *mbuwweṣ* pl. *-in* lazy, indolent
buwwex v.i. to puff, to blow smoke from the mouth (often in a showy manner)
buxala pl. of *bxil* **2**
buxaṛa pl. of *buxaṛi*
buyeḍ pl. of *byeḍ*
bu-zekri used in the expr. *tmeṛ bu-zekri* variety of dry dates
¶ *muẓunt bu-zekri* sequin, spangle, paillette
bu-ẓăɛṛan (no pl., no art.) tumblebug
bužada pl. of *bužadi*
bužadi adj. pl. *-yen* n. pl. *bužada, bwažda* inexperienced, ignorant
buži pl. *-yat, bwaža* **1.** crane (machine) **2.** spark plug
bu-žlayeb (no art.) eleventh month of the Muslim lunar calendar
bu-žniba pl. *-t* (no art.) crab
bu-žăɛṛan same as *bu-ẓăɛṛan*
bu-ḥbel (no pl., no art.) windpipe, trachea
bu-ḥefṛa (no pl., no art.) a kind of musket
bu-ḥămṛun (no art.) measles
bu-ḥšiša pl. *-t* (no art.) gullet, esophagus
buḥut pl. of *beḥt*
bu-ɛbula same as *băɛbula,* n.u. of *băɛbul*
bu-ɛmira pl. *-t* (no art.) sparrow hawk, kestrel
bu-ɛăṭṭu (no pl., no art.) grasshopper (small variety)
bu-ɛwida (sg. and coll., no pl., no art) **1.** pear **2.** pear tree
bwab pl. of *bab* **2**
bwabeṛ pl. of *babbuṛ*
bwaket pl. of *bakit*
bwales pl. of *bulisi*
ḅwan pl. of *ḅun*
ḅwandi same as *ḅḅandi*
bwaq pl. of *buq*
bwaqel pl. of *buqal*
bwaṛeḍ pl. of *baṛuḍ*
bwaser (pl.) hemorrhoids
bwaṣeṭ pl. of *baṣeṭ*
bwaš pl. of *buš*
bwax **1.** vapor (usually steam) **2.** smoke
bwaža pl. of *buži*
bwažda pl. of *bužadi*
bwiba dim. of *bab*
bwibeṛ dim. of *babbuṛ, babuṛ*
bwiḍa dim. of *biḍa* (n.u. of *biḍ*)
bwiket dim. of *bakit*
bwinta dim. of *bunta*
bwisa dim. of *busa*
bweṭ pl. of *buṭa*
bxal pl. of *bxil* **1**
bexbex v.i. to foam at the mouth (as a dying man)
bxil **1.** pl. *-in, bxal* stingy, miserly **2.** pl. *buxala* miser, stingy person, skinflint
bxis pl. *-in* dirt cheap, very inexpensive
bxel v.i. (v.n. *boxl, bxel*) to be or act stingy *ma-tebxel-š ɛliya!* Don't be so stingy (with me)!
boxl, bxel **1.** v.n. of *bxel* **2.** stinginess, miserliness
bxes, bxeṣ v.i. to become cheap (in price)
bxuṛ pl. *-at* incense
bexx v.i. to sprinkle *(š-šta) ka-tbexx.* It's sprinkling.
¶ *bexx ɛla* to sprinkle with water (by spraying from the mouth, as Moroccan shoemakers softening leather)
bexxeṛ **1.** v.t. to steam (s.th.) *waš ma-zal ma-bexxeṛti seksu?* Haven't you steamed the couscous yet? **2.** v.t. to perfume (with incense, etc.) **3.** v.t. to fumigate **4.** v.i. to steam, to give off steam or vapors (often used in perfect) *ṭ-ṭenžṛa bexxṛet.* The pot's steaming.
bexxuš n.u. *-a* bug, beetle (especially those found in grain, beans, etc.)
byaden pl. of *bidun*
byaḍ v.i. to get or become white
byaḍ **1.** whiteness **2.** the white spot(s) on the cornea of the eye (characteristic of a certain eye disease)
¶ *byaḍ le-wžeh* whiting (powder)
¶ *byaḍ l-ɛăyn* white of the eye
byaḍeq pl. of *biḍeq*
byar pl. of *bir*
byanu pl. *-wat* piano, pianoforte
byat pl. of *bit* **3**
byeḍ f. *biḍa* pl. *buyeḍ* white
byuḍa whiteness
byut pl. of *bit* **1** and **2**
beyyina pl. *-t* proof, evidence
bzabez pl. of *bezbuz*
bzaq v.n. of *bzeq*
bzaṛ same as *ibzaṛ*
bẓaṭem pl. of *beẓṭam*
bzayem pl. of *bzim*
bzazel pl. of *bezzula*
bezbuz pl. *bzabez* faucet, tap
beẓbeẓ v.i. to be amazed (with or without expressing it) *mnin šeftu hezz myatayn kilu, bqit ġir ka-nbeẓbeẓ.* When he lifted two hundred kilos I was amazed.
bezgel v.t. **1.** to neglect **2.** to botch
bzim pl. *bzayem* buckle (as on a belt)
bziq v.n. of *bzeq*
bẓiẓ (sg. and coll.) cricket (insect)
bzeq v.i. (v.n. *bzaq, bziq, bzeq*) **1.** to spit **2.** to void excrement (birds)
bzeq **1.** v.n. of *bzeq* **2.** n.u. *bezqa* spit, saliva
beẓṭam pl. *bẓaṭem* wallet, billfold, pocketbook

bezzaf **1.** much, a lot, a great deal, too much, very much; many, too many, very many, numerous. *had ṛ-ṛažel ka-imlek bezzaf d-le-ḥwanet.* That man has many (too many, numerous) stores. **2.** very *ɛăndha bent mezyana bezzaf.* She has a very pretty girl. —*huwa mṛiḍ bezzaf.* He's seriously ill. **3.** too *had l-kas d-atay sxun bezzaf.* This glass of tea is too hot. **4.** much, many, a lot of *kayn l-ḥut bezzaf f-had l-wad.* There are a lot of fish in this river. **5.** very much, a lot *ka-nḥebbek bezzaf.* I love you very much.

** *had š-ši bezzaf ɛlih.* It's too much for him; he's incapable of doing it.

¶ *bezzaf d-* much, many, a lot of *kaynin bezzaf de-n-nas fe-ẓ-ẓenqa.* There are a lot of people in the street.

bezz men in spite of, unwillingly ≠, against the wishes of *d-drari bqaw fe-ḍ-ḍaṛ bezz mennhom.* The children stayed home unwillingly.

bezzeṛ v.t. **1.** to season with *ibzaṛ* **2.** to give color to (a story, a tale)

bezzula pl. *bzazel* breast, teat

bezzez (*be-z-zez*) by force

¶ *bezzez men* same as *bezz men*

bezzez ɛla v.t. to force (s.o.), to oblige (s.o.) *ma-tbezzez-š ɛliya!* Don't force me!

bžeġ v.t. (v.n. *bžiġ*) to crush, to mash, to squash

bžiġ v.n. of *bžeġ*

bežġeṭ v.i. to babble, to prattle, to chatter senselessly (as a baby attempting to talk; also some metaphorical use in speaking of adults)

bežmaṭ n.u. *-a* **1.** small, sweet, hard cake(s), resembling a biscuit in consistency **2.** long, narrow tile(s) used for flooring

bežmeṭ v.t. to toast until hard (the *bežmaṭ*)

bḥal **1.** like, as, similar to, the same as *ɛăndi keswa bḥal dyalek.* I have a suit like yours. —*ḥetta waḥed ma-ka-yăɛṛef iḍṛeb l-ɛud bḥalu.* No one knows how to play the lute like him. **2.** such as *ka-yăɛmel ši-ʔumuṛ qbiḥa, bḥal d-dbaz mɛa ž-žiran.* He has some bad faults, such as his fighting with the neighbors.

** *bḥali bḥalu.* We're (he and I are) both in the same situation; He and I are the same. —*bḥalu bḥal bbah.* He's a chip off the old block (just like his father). —*bḥalu bḥal l-bermil.* He looks just like a barrel.

¶ *bḥal bḥal* **1.** alike *huma bḥal bḥal* They're (very much) alike. **2.** it's all the same (to me), it doesn't make any difference *waš takol daba wella ttsenna ḥetta iži?—bḥal bḥal!* Do you want to eat now or wait until he comes?—It's all the same to me.

¶ *bḥal-lli* as though, as if *ban-li bḥal-lli ma-ɛăndu ġaṛaḍ imši ixdem.* It seemed as though he didn't want to go to work.

¶ *tamam* or *tamamen bḥal, bḥal . . . tamam* or *tamamen* just like *had l-kebbuṭ bḥal dyali tamamen.* This coat is just like mine.

¶ *u-bḥal had š-ši* and so forth, and so on, and the like

bḥaṛ pl. of *bḥăṛ*

bḥayer pl. of *bḥira*

bḥayri pl. *-ya* truck farmer, one who takes care of a truck garden

beḥbeḥ v.t. to make hoarse or husky (voice)

bḥira pl. *bḥayer* (dim. *bḥiyyra*) vegetable garden

beḥlet same as *beḥṣeṣ*

bḥăṛ pl. *bḥuṛ, bḥuṛa, bḥaṛ* (dim. *bḥiyyeṛ*) ocean, sea

¶ *šra l-ḥut f-qaɛ le-bḥăṛ* to buy a pig in a poke

be-ḥṛa **1.** just *be-ḥṛa ža.* He just arrived. **2.** hardly, barely *be-ḥṛa ṣab l-weqt baš išiyyeṭ snanu.* He hardly had time to brush his teeth. **3.** so (that) *xeṣṣna nṛežɛu bekri be-ḥṛa ntṣuwwqu.* We've got to get back early so we can go shopping.

beḥṛaṛ n.u. *-a* (sea)shell *mšaw d-drari l-le-bḥăṛ ileqqṭu l-beḥṛaṛ.* The children have gone to the ocean to pick up some shells.

beḥri **1.** pl. *-yen* maritime, sea-going, of the sea **2.** pl.*-ya* sailor, seaman, mariner

beḥṣeṣ (*f-*) to stare (at), to gaze fixedly (at)

bḥet f- (v.n. *beḥt*) to investigate, to look into, to inquire into *bdina nbeḥtu f-had l-qaḍiya ž-žemɛa lli fatet.* We began investigating this case last week.

¶ *bḥet ɛla* to search for, to look for

beḥt pl. *abḥat, buḥut* **1.** v.n. of *bḥet* **2.** investigation, inquest **3.** research

bḥuṛ, bḥuṛa pl. of *bḥăṛ*

bɛad v.i. to become or get farther (away) *s-siyaṛa bqat tebɛad tebɛad ḥetta ġabet ɛla ɛăyniya.* The car got further and further away until it disappeared from sight.

bɛad pl. of *bɛid*

băɛbul n.u. *-a* **1.** slug (gastropod) **2.** (adj.) very fat, obese (person)

băɛbăɛ v.i. to bleat (sheep)

băɛd after *băɛd le-žtimaɛ ġadi tkun waḥed l-ḥefla.* After the meeting there will be a reception. —*băɛd naklu nemšiw le-s-sinima.* After we eat we're going to the show.

¶ *men băɛd* **1.** after (as *băɛd*) **2.** afterwards, later *ġad nekteb-lu men băɛd.* I'll write him later. 3. then *aži naklu daba u-men băɛd nemšiw le-s-sinima.* Let's eat now and then go to the show.

¶ *băɛd-ma* after (conj.) *băɛd-ma naklu năɛmel-lu tilifun.* After we eat I'll call him.

¶ *băɛd-emma, băɛd-ella* although, even though *băɛd-emma ɛăyyan ža l-l-xedma.* Even though he's sick, he came to work.

bɛăd comp. of *bɛid*

boɛd distance, state of being far (away) *šḥal de-l-boɛd (kayen) ma-bin fas u-ṛ-ṛbaṭ?* What's the distance between Fez and Rabat?

¶ *bla boɛd* not long ago, very recently

¶ *men l-boɛd* from afar, a long way off, from a distance *šeftu men l-boɛd.* I saw him from a distance.

¶ *ɛla boɛd* at a distance of *žat meknas ɛla boɛd settin kilumiṭṛ men fas.* Meknes lies at a distance of sixty kilometers from Fez.

băɛda 1. already *mša băɛda.* He's already left. 2. first *aži naklu băɛda, ɛad nšeṛbu atay.* Let's eat first then have some tea. 3. at least *qul-lna băɛda ġir šnu ɛmelti l-bareḥ.* Tell us at least what you did yesterday. —*u-kan ġir qalha-li băɛda.* He could at least have told me. 4. as for *băɛda hiya ɛămmeṛha ma-kanet hna.* As for her, she's never been here.

băɛḍ some *băɛḍ le-mġaṛba ka-teɛžebhom l-qehwa.* Some Moroccans like coffee.

¶ *băɛḍhom*$^{\phi}$ *băɛḍ* (pl.) each other, one another *ḍḍaṛbu băɛḍhom băɛḍ.* They fought one another.

¶ *băɛḍ l-meṛṛat* sometimes

¶ *l-băɛḍ f-* (or *men*) some of *l-băɛḍ fe-ṭ-ṭalaba labsin ḥmeṛ.* Some of the students are wearing red.

băɛḍiyat (with pl. pron. endings) each other, one another *ma-qeṣṣṛu ɛla băɛḍiyathom be-ḍ-ḍeṛb.* They didn't spare the blows with each other. —*tġamzu băɛḍiyathom.* They winked at each other.

bɛid pl. *bɛad* (comp. *bɛăd*) far, distant, a long way (from) *l-busṭa bɛida men* (or *ɛla*) *had l-maḥăll.* The post office is a long way from this place.

** *bɛid baš ikun ṛžeɛ men ḍ-ḍaṛ l-biḍa l-bareḥ, ɛla-ḥeqq-aš ɛămmṛu ma-mša-lha.* It's quite impossible that he returned yesterday from Casablanca, because he's never been there. —*ma-ši bɛid.* It's quite possible.

bɛir camels (in general)

bɛăṛ v.i. to defecate, to void excrement (animals)

bɛăṛ n.u. *bɛṛă* dung, droppings (excrement)

bɛăt v.t. 1. (no v.n.) to send 2. (v.n. *băɛt*) to resurrect

băɛt 1. v.n. of *bɛăt* 2 2. resurrection

¶ *yum l-băɛt* final Judgment Day

bɛăž v.t. 1. to beat, to give a beating to *băɛžuh u-men băɛd ddaw-lu flusu.* They gave him a beating and then took his money away from him. 2. to castrate (domestic fowl)

băɛɛăd 1. v.t., to get, take, or move away *băɛɛăd dik l-buṭa men l-ɛafya!* Get that (oil, gas) drum away from the fire! 2. v.i., to get or move away *băɛɛăd menni!* Get away from me!

¶ *băɛɛăd men* to avoid

D

d- (*de-* before consonant cluster) 1. of *ɛṭini ṣenduq d-le-wqid.* Give me a box of matches. —*tebġi ši-kas de-l-ma?* Would you like a glass of water? —*kanu bezzaf de-n-nas fe-l-ḥefla.* There were a lot of people at the party. —*nsit l-ɛonwan d-dak le-ktab.* I forgot the title of that book. 2. used to indicate possessive *s-siyaṛa l-ɛămmi ma-zala ždida.* My uncle's car is still new. 3. used in counting with certain numbers (especially three through ten) *ɛăndu tlata d-le-wlad u-ṛebɛa d-le-bnat.* He has three sons and four daughters.

¶ *šḥal d-* how much, how many *šḥal d-atay ka-tešṛob?* How much tea do you drink?

da used in the set expr.: *men da u-ždid* anew, all over again

¶ *ma da bih*$^{\phi}$ 1. to like (very much) to ≠ *ma da biya nešriha mennek be-l-ḥăqq daba ma-imken-li-š.* I would like very much to buy it from you but I can't now. 2. indicates the appropriateness or necessity of s.o.'s action *ma da bik temši daba.* You'd better go now.

dab idub v.i. (v.n. *duban*) to melt, to dissolve

daba 1. now, at the present time 2. used as a particle before verbs to express the (immediate) future *daba nqulha-lu mnayn iži.* I'll tell him when he comes.

¶ *daba daba* immediately

¶ *daba ɛad* just *daba ɛad mšat.* She has just left.

¶ *men daba* in *men daba ʕamayn iržăʕ.* He will return in two years.

¶ *men daba l-fuq, men daba l-qoddam* from now on

dabed pl. *dwabed* compasses, dividers

dada (no art.; inh. poss.) nurse, nanny

dafuniya pl. *-t* punch or blow with the fist

dafeʕ ʕla (v.n. *difaʕ*) to defend

dağur pl. *-in* one who lacks the normal ability to use his deductive powers or to learn easily (pejorative)

daʔimăn same as *daymăn*

dak m. (often f.) f. *dik* pl. *duk* that *dak l-weld ṛaṣu qaṣeʕ, ma-bğa-š ittesmăʕ.* That boy is stubborn, he won't listen. —*be-šʕal šriti dak l-magana?* How much did you pay for that watch?

¶ *f-dak l-weqt, f-dak s-saʕa* at that time, then

dakăṛ pl. *dkuṛa* penis

dala pl. *-t* surf

dalil pl. *ʔadilla* 1. guide (person) 2. guide-book 3. proof, evidence 4. v.n. of *dell*

dalya pl. *-t, dwali* grapevine

dam idum v.i. (v.n. *mdawma, dwam*) to last, to continue *ʕetta ʕaža ma-ka-ddum f-had d-dunya.* Nothing lasts in this world.

¶ *ma-dam* as long as ≠ *ma-demti ka-teqṛa mezyan, ma-ʕăndek mn-aš txaf.* As long as you keep studying hard, you'll be all right.

damawi pl. *-yen* gay, jovial (characteristic of personality)

damim pl. *-in* contemptible, despicable

daq iduq v.t. (v.n. *duqan*) to taste *ʕămmṛi ma-deqt makelthom.* I've never tasted their food.

dar idir v.t. (v.n. *diran*) 1. to do *aš kan ka-idir temma?* What was he doing there? 2. to put *derti ʕwayžek fe-š-šanṭa?* Did you put your things in the suitcase?

** *kif dayrin* (a.p.) *xutek?* How are your brothers?

¶ *dar bʕal* to be or act like, to resemble

¶ *dar f-* to settle *aš derti f-dak l-qaḍiya mʕa žaṛek?* How did you settle that matter with your neighbor?

¶ *darha~ b-* to trick, to play a trick on *daruha bih ʕawed.* They tricked him again.

daṛaža pl. *-t* (dim. *dṛiža*) 1. rank, position *ʕṭaweh daṛaža d-safir.* He was given the rank of ambassador. 2. degree *l-ʕaṛaṛa ṭelʕet žuž de-d-daṛažat.* The temperature has gone up two degrees.

¶ *men d-daṛaža l-luwwla* first-rate, first-class *had atay men d-daṛaža l-luwwla.* This is first-rate tea.

¶ *dṛiža be-dṛiža* (dim.) little by little, step by step

dariž, dariži used in the expr.:

¶ *l-lisan d-dariž* or *l-luğa d-dariža* the spoken language (i.e., colloquial as opposed to Modern Standard Arabic)

¶ (*l-ʕăṛbiya*) *d-dariža* colloquial (Moroccan) Arabic (as opposed to Modern Standard Arabic)

dasayes pl. of *dasisa*

dasisa pl. *-t, dasayes, dsayes* conspiracy, intrigue

daseṛ a.p. of *dseṛ* (same as *dṣeṛ*)

dat (f., no pl.) (human) body

¶ *be-d-dat, b-datuφ* exactly *dak š-ši lli qal-lek be-d-dat.* That's exactly what he told you.

dawa v.t. to cure, to heal, to remedy

dawam same as *dwam*

dawawin pl. of *diwan*

dawem v.t. 1. to perpetuate, to bestow perpetually, to do (s.th.) forever *ḷḷah idawem ʕlik ṣ-ṣeʕʕa!* May you always enjoy good health! 2. to do (s.th.) steadily, regularly *kollna dawemna l-xedma ʕam luwwel.* We all worked regularly last year.

¶ part. *mdawem* pl. *-in* 1. persistent *huwa ṛažel mdawem ʕăl ṣ-ṣḷa.* He's persistent in his praying. 2. permanent, perpetual *ṣ-ṣyam ma-ši mdawem.* The Fast isn't a perpetual thing.

dax idux v.i. (v.n. *duxa*) to get dizzy, to get seasick *daxet b-quwt š-šṭiʕ u-ṭaʕet.* She got dizzy from all the dancing and fell down.

daxili pl. *-yen* 1. internal 2. boarder (in a school)

daxel l- or *ʕla* (s.o.) *b-* (s.th.) to beg or beseech (s.o.) for the sake of (s.th.) *daxelt ʕlik be-ṣ-ṣeʕba lli binatna ila ma tebqa mʕana.* For the sake of our friendship I beg you to stay with us.

daxel 1. inside, inner part 2. (pl. *dwaxel*) intimate and secret matters

¶ *l-daxel* inside, within

daxlani same as *dexlani*

daymăn always, forever

dayra pl. *-t, dwayer* 1. circle 2. surroundings 3. entourage

¶ *dwayer* (pl.) *z-zman* ups and downs, vicissitudes

dayt used in the expr. *men daytuφ l-ṛaṣuφ* on one's own (responsibility), without asking permission or consulting anyone

daz iduz (v.n. *dwaz*) 1. v.t. and v.i. to pass (by), to go by *ʕad dazet* (*men hna*). She just passed by. —*dak s-siyaṛa dazetna b-soṛʕa kbira.* That car passed us at great speed. 2. v.i. to pass *dezti f-le-mtiʕan dyalek?* Did you pass your exam?

** *dezna ʕlihom.* We went by for them —*dazet!* Agreed! O.K.

¶ *dayzu~* (a.p.) *le-klam* excellent, perfect
daḥes same as *dḥes*
daع idiع v.i. (v.n. *diعa*) 1. to spread *le-xbaṛ bda idiع f-le-mdina.* The news has begun to spread through the town. 2. to wander, to roam
daعama pl. *-t* support, prop (also metaphorical)
dbab n.u. *-a* horsefly
dbaben pl. of *debban*
dbabez pl. of *debbuz*
dbal v.i. 1. to fade *l-werḍa lli عṭaha bdat tedbal.* The flower he gave her is fading. 2. to turn pale, to become pale *wežhu dbal men qellt š-šems.* His face has become pale from lack of sun.
dbali pl. of *debla*
dbalež pl. of *debliž*
dbaṛi pl. of *debṛa*
dbayeḥ pl. of *dbiḥa*
dbaz pl. *-at* quarrel, dispute
debbaġ pl. *-a* tanner
debban n.u. *-a* cpl. *dbaben* fly
debbaṛ adj. pl. *-in* n. pl. *-a* resourceful, knowing how to get what one wants
debbeb to walk with pain or laborious difficulty, to drag along *عad naḍ men l-meṛḍa dyalu u-daba ṛah ka-idebbeb.* He's just gotten up from being sick and now he's just dragging along.
debbel v.i. to fade *l-werḍ bda idebbel.* The flowers are fading.
debbeṛ f- to find, to (manage to) get *băعda debbṛet f-ši-ḥaža ma tăعmel.* At least she's found something to do.
¶ *debbeṛ l-ṛaṣuφ* to shift for oneself
¶ *debbeṛ mعa* to handle (s.th. or s.o.) oneself, to take care of *ana ġad-ndebbeṛ mعa had l-weld.* I'm going to handle this boy myself.
debbuz pl. *dbabez* cudgel, club
debbez v.t. 1. to give a beating to (s.o.) 2. to botch
¶ *debbez f-* same as *debbez* above
dbir v.n. of *dbeṛ* (same as *ḍbeṛ*)
dbiz v.n. of *dbez*
dbiḥ v.n. of *dbeḥ*
dbiḥa pl. *-t, dbayeḥ* 1. v.n. of *dbeḥ* 2. slaughter 3. slaughtered animal 4. sacrificial sheep of Greater Bairam
debla pl. *-t, dbali* 1. gnat 2. the part of the wick exposed for burning (candle, lamp)
debliž pl. *dbalež* bracelet
dbeṛ same as *ḍbeṛ*
dbez (v.n. *dbiz*) 1. v.t. (v.n. also *debz*) to botch 2. v.i. to talk nonsense 3. v.t. to cram, to fill to repletion, to crowd
¶ *dbez f-* to give a beating to
debz v.n. of *dbez* 1

debza pl. *-t* 1. n.i. of *dbez* 2. blow of the fist 3. brawl
dbeḥ v.t. (v.n. *dbiḥ, dbiḥa*) to slaughter
debḥa 1. n.i. of *dbeḥ* 2. pl. *-t* slaughter
dda (a.p. *meddi, dday*) 1. to take, to carry *flusha kollhom ddathom mعaha.* She took all her money with her.—*ddina ṣ-ṣnadeq عăl le-bhayem.* We carried the boxes on the mules. 2. to take (time) *had l-xedma ġad-teddi bezzaf de-l-weqt.* This work is going to take a lot of time. 3. to take (away) *šḥal d-le-flus dda-lek dak š-šeffaṛ?* How much money did that thief take from you? —*weld عămmi dda-li l-makina de-t-teṣwiṛ dyali.* My cousin took my camera away from me. 4. to take, to buy *ma-ddit ḥetta ḥaža men dak l-ḥanut.* I didn't buy anything from that shop. 5. to receive, to get, to obtain *xti ddat l-žaˀiza l-luwwla.* My sister received the first prize. 6. to gain, to get, to benefit *šnu dditi men dak l-biعa u-šerya?* What did you get out of that deal?
¶ *dda(ha~) f-* to pay attention to *عămmṛi ma-dditha fe-klamu.* I never paid any attention to what he said.
¶ *ddahφ n-nعas* to fall asleep ≠ *bda iddih n-nعas.* He's falling asleep.
¶ *dda عla* to pay attention to *ila ddina عliha عămmeṛna la-mšina men hna.* If we pay attention to her we'll never leave here.
ˀedda v.t. (v.n. *ˀadaˀ*) 1. to pay (s.th. or s.o.) 2. to pay for (s.th.) 3. to carry out, to fulfil (duty, obligation)
ddabez v.i. to fight, to have a fight (verbal or physical)
ddakeṛ v.i. to have a discussion, to talk things over
ddar same as *tdar* (m.p. of *dar*)
ddawa v.i. 1. (in impf. tense) to be treated (for illness) 2. (in perfect tense) to be cured (of illness) 3. to be curable (disease) 4. to be solvable (problem)
ddaxel (*f-*) 1. to get involved (in) (willingly or otherwise) 2. to interfere (in, with), to stick one's nose (into)
ddaxeṛ same as *dexxeṛ*
dday a.p. of *dda*
ddaḥes v.i. to jostle or crowd one another
¶ *ddaḥes mعa* to jostle, to crowd (s.o.)
ddaعa v.i. 1. to sue one another, to bring suit against each other 2. to claim *ka-iddaعiw bin hiya benthom.* They claim she's their daughter.
¶ *ddaعa mعa* (same as *ddaعa*) *ddaعa mعaha.* He and she have brought suit against each other.
ˀeddeb v.t. 1. to bring up, to educate *waldih ma-عăṛfu-š iˀeddbuh.* His parents didn't know how to bring him up. 2. to correct

ma-tᵓeddbu ġiṛ l-quwwa. Only force can correct him.
¶ part. *mᵓeddeb* pl. *-in* polite, courteous, well-bred
ddfu same as *ttfu*
ddegdeg v.i. to break into (many) pieces
ddegg same as *tdegg* (m.p. of *degg*)
ddekk same as *tdekk* (m.p. of *dekk*)
ddell same as *tdell* (m.p. of *dell*)
ddellel m.p. of *dellel*
dden, ᵓedden **1.** v.t. to announce (prayer), to make the call to (prayer) *le-mwedden ᵓedden le-fžer.* The muezzin has made the call to the dawn prayer. **2.** v.i. to be called (prayer) *dden ḍ-ḍhuṛ aw ma-zal?* Has the noon prayer been called yet?
ddeqq same as *tdeqq* (m.p. of *deqq*)
dderbel v.i. to get old or worn out (clothes)
dderdeb v.i. to roll (as a ball; usually down a grade)
dderra m.p. of *derra*
ddeṛṛeq same as *ḍdeṛṛeq*
dduwwez m.p. of *duwwez*
ddexxem v.i. to live high, to live in luxury and pleasure
¶ *ddexxem b-* to get the most advantage, use, or profit from or out of (usually money)
ddezz same as *tdezz* (m.p. of *dezz*)
dfa idfa v.i. (v.n. *dfawa*) to get warm (water, weather) *l-ḥal bda idfa.* It's getting warm.
dfal **1.** v.n. of *dfel* **2.** spit, saliva
dfali pl. of *defla*
dfawa **1.** v.n. of *dfa* **2.** warmth
dfayen pl. of *dfina*
deff pl. *dfuf* kind of square tambourine without jingles
dfef pl. of *deffa*
deffa pl. *-t, dfef* leaf of a double door
¶ *deffa de-š-šeṛžem* (window) shutter
deffeg v.t. to spill (liquids only)
deffen v.i. to give a beating *bqaw ideffnu-lu ḥetta ɛlayen mat.* They gave him such a beating he nearly died.
dfin v.n. of *dfen*
dfina pl. *-t, dfayen* over-garment of thin material worn by women
dfiɛ v.n. of *dfăɛ*
dfel (v.n. *dfal*) **1.** v.t. to spit out **2.** v.i. to spit
defla pl. *-t, dfali* **1.** n.i. of *dfel* **2.** spit, saliva
dfen v.t. (v.n. *dfin*) to bury
dfuf pl. of *deff*
dfuɛ v.n. of *dfăɛ*
dfăɛ v.t. (v.n. *dfiɛ, dfuɛ*) **1.** to push *ila ma-bġat-ši temši had s-siyaṛa ndefɛuha.* If this car won't start we'll push it. **2.** to spend *le-flus lli kanu ɛăndha kollhom defɛăthom.* She spent all the money she had. **3.** to give, to deliver *ma-zal ma-defɛu-li s-selɛa lli žat.* They still haven't delivered to me the merchandise which has arrived **4.** to pay *dfăɛt-lu lli kan ka-isalni.* I paid him what I owed him.
** *ka-iɛežbu idfăɛ sidi ɛăzzuz.* He likes to be coaxed.
¶ *dfăɛ le-kdub* to tell lies
defɛa **1.** n.i. of *dfăɛ* **2.** payment *ṣafṭet-lu d-defɛa l-luwwla.* She sent him the first payment.
degdeg v.t. **1.** to smash *degdgu-lu z-zaža de-s-siyaṛa.* They smashed his car window. **2.** to crush, to reduce to fine particles, to pulverize
¶ *degdeg ɛla* (or *fuq*) to stamp on, to trample (on)
degg idogg v.t. (v.n. *deggan*) **1.** to crush, to pulverize **2.** to drive (nail, peg)
** *baqi ka-idegg w-idegdeg.* He is still vigorous.
degg cpl. *dgug, dgugat* jewelry
deggag pl. *-a* jeweler
deggan v.n. of *degg*
dgig flour (wheat)
dgug, dgugat cpl. of *degg*
deġdeġ v.t. to tickle (usually a baby)
deġdeġ (no pl.) used in the expr. *ɛmel deġdeġ l-* to tickle
doġri pl. *-yen* **1.** serious-minded **2.** industrious **3.** straight *ɛăndak tewqef f-ši-maḥăll, sir doġri le-ḍ-ḍaṛ!* Don't stop anywhere, go straight home!
deġya quickly, immediately, rapidly
dha idhi v.t. (v.n. *mdahya*) to distract
¶ p.p. *medhi* pl. *-yen* **1.** busy, occupied (person) **2.** distracted, day-dreaming
dhales pl. of *dehlis*
dhani pl. of *dhen* and *dehna*
dhaz pl. *-at* trousseau
dheb gold
dehbi golden
dehḍenni (no pl.) heavy, obese, fat (implies slow, difficult movements; no insult implied)
dehhab pl. *-a* gilder, one who gilds
dehheb v.t. to gild
dehhen v.t. **1.** to stroke, to pet (animal, child) **2.** to put grease or oil on (hair, chicken to be cooked)
¶ *dehhen ɛla* to bribe, to grease the palm of
dehheš v.t. to astonish
dhin v.n. of *dhen*
dhiš v.n. of *dheš*
dehlis pl. *dhales* **1.** basement, cellar **2.** labyrinth
dhem f. *dehma* pl. *duhem* pitch-black (horse)
dhen v.t. (v.n. *dhin*) to grease, to anoint
¶ *dhen l-ḥălq l-* to bribe *dehnet-lhom ḥălqhom.* She bribed them.

dhen pl. *dhani* greasy substance

dehna pl. *-t, dhani* any greasy or oily substance (lubricating oil, grease, ointment, etc.)

¶ *dehna de-ṛ-ṛaṣ* hair oil

dehri pl. *-yen* atheist

dheš v.i. (v.n. *dhiš*) **1.** to be astonished, to be amazed *dehšu melli šafuh neqqez ɛla ṣ-ṣuṛ u-ma-wqăɛ-lu-šay.* They were amazed to see him jump over the wall without getting hurt. **2.** to hesitate, to be afraid to *ka-idheš itkellem mɛa bḅah f-had l-muwḍuɛ.* He hesitates to talk with his father on this subject.

dehša n.i. of *dheš*

dehšan pl. *-in* **1.** frightened **2.** amazed **3.** hesitant

di same as *lli*

dib pl. *dyab, dyuba* wolf

didban (no art.) large piles or stacks of s.th. (emphatic; also metaphorical; often more emphatic with adj. *kḥăl*) *ɛăndu didban le-kḥăl d-le-flus!* He's filthy rich!

didi pl. *-yen* purplish

difaɛ **1.** v.n. of *dafeɛ* **2.** defense

dik pl. *dyuk, dyuka* rooster

dik f. of *dak*

dikr v.n. of *dker*

diktatur pl. *-iyen* dictator

diktaturi pl. *-yen* dictatorial

dil pl. *dyul, dyula* **1.** tail **2.** end, extremity

dima always, constantly

¶ *men dima* all the time

dimašq Damascus

dimuqṛaṭi pl. *-yen* **1.** democratic **2.** Democratic (American political party)

dimuqṛaṭiya democracy

din pl. *dyan, ʔadyan* religion

¶ *qlil d-din* pl. *qlalin d-din* **1.** irreligious **2.** morally untrustworthy, rascal

din pl. *dyun, dyunat* debt

¶ *be-d-din* on credit *koll-ši šraweh be-d-din.* They bought everything on credit.

¶ *be-d-din, be-d-dyunat* in debt *ṛah ġaṛeq be-d-din.* He's up to his ears in debt.

¶ *mul d-din* pl. *mwalin d-din* creditor

¶ *ɛlihφ d-din* to be in debt $\neq$

dini pl. *-yen* religious

diqn pl. *ʔedqan* same as *dqen*

diṛaya pl. *-t* knowledge, know-how

dis n.u. *-a* rush *had le-eṛḍ ɛamṛa be-d-dis.* This field is full of rushes.

diwan pl. *dawawin* **1.** council, cabinet **2.** collection of poems

diwana **1.** (no pl.) customs, import duties *xelleṣt d-diwana fe-l-meṛṣa.* I paid the customs at the harbor. **2.** pl. *-t* customs-house

diwani pl. *-yen* customs officer

diya pl. *-t* **1.** amount of money paid to the family or relatives of a dead or injured person by the one who has caused the death or injury **2.** imprisonment or other sentence suffered for the crime described in **1** above

diyana pl. *-t* **1.** piety **2.** religious doctrine

diyyen pl. *-in* religious, pious

diyyăɛ v.t. **1.** to spread (news) **2.** to broadcast (radio)

dižla used in the expr. *năhṛ dižla* the Tigris River

diɛa v.n. of *daɛ*

diɛaya pl. *-t* **1.** (bit of) propaganda **2.** advertisement (of a product) **3.** rumor

dkaken pl. of *dokkana*

dekk (v.n. *dekkan*) **1.** v.t. to tamp down **2.** v.t. to fill up, to stuff **3.** v.i. to take a sip of tea (while smoking) *ma-ka-yăɛṛef-š ikmi bla-ma idekk.* He can't smoke without taking a sip of tea.

¶ p.p. *medkuk* pl. *-in* small and young-looking (for one's age)

dekka **1.** n.i. of *dekk* **2.** pl. *-t* sip or quantity of tea (taken while smoking)

dekkan v.n. of *dekk*

dokkana pl. *-t, dkaken* stone bench

dokkima pl. *-t* blow of the fist

dekken v.t. to stuff *ma-kan ɛlaš ddekken ṣ-ṣenḍuq b-had l-belɛa d-le-ḥwayež.* You didn't have to stuff the box with so many things.

¶ *dekkenha~* to stuff oneself with food

¶ *dekken l-* to give a beating to

¶ *dekken ɛla* to stamp on (e.g., ground)

dekker v.i. to chant prayers or religious poetry, either formally or informally

dekkeṛ v.t. **1.** to pollenize, to fecundate, to fertilize **2.** (*f-*) to remind (of) *daba nḥawel ndekkṛu fiha.* I'll try to remind him of it.

dekkes v.t. **1.** to press, to tamp **2.** to stuff *dekkset-li š-šanṭa b-le-ḥwayež l-balyen.* She stuffed my suitcase with old clothes.

dker v.t. (v.n. *dikr*) to mention, to cite *dker-li had l-qaḍiya be-l-ḥăqq ma-fesserha-li-š.* He mentioned the matter to me but he didn't explain it.

¶ *dker ḷḷah* to praise God, to say liturgical prayers

dkeṛ pl. *dkuṛa* **1.** male *had l-beṛṭal dkeṛ wella nta?* Is this bird a male or a female? **2.** penis

dkuṛa pl. of *dakăṛ* and *dkeṛ*

dlal pl. of *dlil*

dlala pl. *-t* **1.** v.n. of *dellel* **2.** auction

¶ *xerrež le-d-dlala* to put up for auction

dlaleḥ cpl. of *dellaḥ*

dlaqem pl. of *delqum*

dlawi pl. of *dlu*

delga pl. *-t* **1.** minor scandal, flap **2.** predicament, tight spot

dlik v.n. of *dlek*
dlil pl. *-in, dlal* (comp. *dell*) **1.** vile, base **2.** cowardly **3.** lazy
dlek v.t. (v.n. *dlik*) to rub, to massage *mnayn temši l-l-ẓämmam qul l-l-kiyyas idlek-lek ḍehṛek.* When you go to the (public) bath ask the masseur to rub your back. **2.** to knead (dough)
dell v.i. (v.n. *dellan*) **1.** to mean, to indicate, to show *had š-ši ka-idell bi-ʔennahom ma-ġad-iqeblu-š.* This shows that they won't accept. **2.** to humiliate
¶ *dell b-* (v.n. *doll, dell*) to humiliate
¶ *dell ʕla* (v.n. *dalil, dellan*) to prove, to show, to indicate, to demonstrate
dell, doll v.n. of *dell* (in *dell b-*)
dell comp. of *dlil*
della v.t. **1.** to hang, to suspend **2.** to stick out (arm, head, etc.)
della v.n. of *ndell*
dellal pl. *-a* auctioneer
dellan v.n. of *dell*
dellas pl. *-a, -in* fraudulent, deceitful (person)
dellaẓ n.u. *-a* cpl. *dlaleẓ* watermelon
dellaʕ same as *dellaẓ*
dellel (v.n. *dlala*) **1.** v.t. to sell at auction, to auction off **2.** v.i. to be an auctioneer
delles v.i. to cheat, to use fraud
delqima pl. *-t* uppercut (blow of the fist)
delqem v.t. **1.** to strike with an uppercut **2.** to rein in (horse)
delqum pl. *dlaqem* muzzle, snout (animal)
dlu pl. *delwan, dlawi* leather bucket (for drawing water)
delwan pl. of *dlu*
dmaġ pl. *-at* brain, mind
¶ *dmaġuᶲ tqil.* to be slow-minded, dense ≠
¶ *dmaġuᶲ xfif.* to be quick-minded ≠
dmalež pl. of *demliž*
dmamel pl. of *demmala*
dman pl. *-at* **1.** rudder **2.** steering wheel
dmanži pl. *-ya* **1.** quartermaster **2.** helmsman, steersman
dmayat pl. of *demm*
demġi mental, done in the head (said of calculations) *hada ġiṛ ẓsab demġi.* I just figured it out in my head.
dmingu f. *-ya* pl. *-yat* little man, peewee
dmir v.n. of *dmer*
demliž pl. *dmalež* bracelet
demm f- (v.n. *demman*) to slander, to backbite
demm pl. *dmayat* (of intensity) blood *ġir huwa duwwez ʕäl l-kebš u-d-dmayat bdat ka-tsil.* As soon as he cut the lamb's throat, the blood began to flow
** *šarkin d-demm.* They are related by blood.
¶ *binathomᶲ* (pl.) *d-demm* (to be) blood relatives ≠
¶ *demm le-wžeh* honor, dignity
¶ *demm s-snan* pet aversion
¶ *ġla d-demm f-* to be extremely angry ≠, to seethe with anger ≠ *ġla fiha d-demm.* She was mad as a hornet.
¶ *xerrež d-demm, zuwwel d-demm* to have blood let, to bleed *qlal n-nas lli ma-zalin ka-ixerržu d-demm fe-l-meġṛib.* In Morocco, very few people still have their blood let.
demma ʕla to accuse (s.o.) of being ressponsible for a mishap or some damage
demma pl. *-t* **1.** protection *huwa teẓt d-demma dyali.* He is under my protection. **2.** responsibility *dak š-ši f-demmtu.* That's his responsibility.
demmala pl. *-t, dmamel* abscess, boil
demman v.n. of *demm*
demmiya pl. *-t* responsibility *qal-lek dak š-ši f-demmiytu.* He says that's his responsibility.
demmäʕ v.i. to snivel
dmer v.i. (v.n. *dmir*) to rush, to hurry *ma-kayen ʕlaš ddmer, ma-zal l-ẓal.* You don't need to rush, you still have time.
dmeṣ same as *ḍmeṣ*
dmuʕ pl. of *demʕa*
demʕa pl. *-t, dmuʕ* tear (from eyes)
ʔden same as *ʔidn*
dnaden pl. of *dendna*
dnadni pl. *-ya* musician
dnafel pl. of *denfil*
dnaya same as *ḍnaya*
denb pl. *dnub* sin
¶ *dar d-dnub* to sin
¶ *dda d-dnub* to commit sins
denba tail (of small animals)
** *šafet fiya be-d-denba d-ʕäyniha.* She looked at me out of the corner of her eye.
¶ *denba de-l-gaṛṛu* cigaret butt
denden v.i. to play a musical instrument (casually or informally) *ka-idenden ʕäl l-ʕud dyalu.* He's strumming on his lute.
dendna pl. *-t, dnaden* music
dendul pl. *dnadel* pendulum
denfil pl. *dnafel* porpoise
dnub pl. of *denb*
denya, donya pl. *-t* **1.** world, universe **2.** life *d-denya hadi.* That's life. **3.** wealth, fortune
** *ṭelʕet-lha d-denya f-ṛaṣha.* She is sick and tired of living.
denžal same as *bdenžal*
dqayeq pl. of *dqiqa*
dqiq **1.** (no pl.) flour **2.** pl. *-in* (comp. *deqq*) fine, minute
dqiqa pl. *-t, dqayeq* minute (of time)
dqen pl. *dqun* chin
deqq v.t. or v.i. (v.n. *deqq, doqq, deqqan*)

1. to knock *ši-waɛed ka-ideqq fe-l-bab.* Somebody is knocking at the door. 2. to crush, to pound, to pulverize 3. to grind up, to hash (meat for *kefta*) 4. to drive (nail)
¶ *deqq ɛla* to call at (s.o.'s) door by knocking *deqqina ɛliha l-bareɛ u-ma-lqinaha-š.* We knocked on her door yesterday, but we didn't find her.
deqq, doqq v.n. of *deqq*
¶ *ɛṭa d-deqq* 1. to work unceasingly 2. to eat a great deal
deqq comp. of *dqiq*
deqqa pl. *-t* 1. blow, knock 2. beat *d-deqqa de-ṭ-ṭbeḷ ma-ši bɛal de-ṭ-ṭeṛṛ.* The beat of the drum is different from that of the tambourine.
¶ *fda deqqtu*$^{\phi}$ to avenge oneself, to get revenge
deqqan v.n. of *deqq*
deqqaq pl. *-a* 1. one who hashes meat with a hatchet 2. a man who awakens the people during Ramadan for the dawn meal, by knocking on their doors with a hammer.
deqqeq v.t. to specify
dra rust
drabek pl. of *derbuka*
drabki pl. *-ya derbuka* player
drabel pl. of *derbala*
drahem, dṛahem pl. of *derhem, deṛhem*
drari pl. of *derri*
dras v.n. of *dres*
draweš pl. of *derwiš*
draz pl. *-at* workshop (shoemaker and weaver)
draɛ same as *drăɛ*
derb pl. *druba* (dim. *driba, driyyeb*) alley, small street
derbala pl. *-t, drabel* old, worn-out piece of clothing
derba 1. aptitude, skill 2. experience, training
derbuka pl. *-t, drabek* oblong tambourine without jingles
derd coarse sediment
derdar (no pl.) ash (tree)
derdeb v.t. to cause to tumble down, to cause to roll down
¶ p.p. *mderdeb* pl. *-in* rough, rugged (terrain, road)
derder ɛla to powder, to dust *derderti s-sokkaṛ ɛăl l-ɛălwa?* Did you powder the cake with sugar?
dreg n.u. *derga* cactus
derhem, deṛhem pl. *drahem, dṛahem* dirham (basic unit of Moroccan currency)
driba dim. of *derb*
drik v.n. of *drek*
driri dim. of *derri*
dris v.n. of *dres*
drisi pl. *-yen* descendant of Moulay Idris
dṛiža dim. of *daṛaža*
drek v.t. (v.n. *drik*) 1. to obtain, to get *ila ɛmelti žehdek kollu, lli bġitiha ddrekha.* If you put forth all your efforts, you'll get anything you want. 2. to reach, to arrive at *l-muṛaḍ dyalha derkettu.* She reached her goal.
drer pl. of *derra*
derra 1. v.i. to rust 2. v.t. to winnow 3. v.t. to sprinkle (powder)
derra pl. *-t, drer* handkerchief
¶ *derra de-l-ɛănq* shawl, cashmere
¶ *derra de-ṛ-ṛaṣ* scarf
deṛṛaqa same as *ḍeṛṛaqa*
derras pl. *-a* thresher (person)
derrasa pl. *-t* threshing-machine
derraz pl. *-a* weaver (usually of blankets)
derraɛ pl. *-a* good swimmer
derreb ɛla or *f-* to train
deṛṛeg same as *ḍeṛṛeg*
derri pl. *drari, derriya* (dim. *driri*) little boy
derriya 1. pl. *-t* little girl 2. pl. of *derri*
dorriya pl. *-t* offspring, posterity
derrem f- to run into *derrem fiya be-l-bišklita dyalu.* He ran into me with his bicycle.
deṛṛeq same as *ḍeṛṛeg*
derres v.t. to teach (s.o. s.th.), to instruct (s.o.) in (s.th.)
derrăɛ 1. v.t. to embrace, to take in one's arms 2. to take (s.th.) by the armful 3. v.i. to swim with a breast stroke
dres v.t. (v.n. *dras, dris*) to thresh
druba pl. of *derb*
dṛuk now
druɛ pl. of *drăɛ* 2 and 3
druɛa pl. of *drăɛ* 3
derwa pl. *-t* hump (camel)
derwiš pl. *draweš* 1. poor, needy 2. harmless (person)
drăɛ 1. pl. *derɛan* forearm 2. pl. *druɛ, derɛan* beam of a pair of scales 3. du. *derɛayn* pl. *druɛ, druɛa* cubit
¶ *be-d-drăɛ* by force
derɛan pl. of *drăɛ* 1 and 2
derɛi n.u. *-ya* sea perch
dsam grease (machinery)
dsaṛa same as *dṣaṛa*
dsayes pl. of *dasisa*
dessem v.t. to smear (with a greasy substance)
desseṛ same as *ḍesseṛ*
desses v.i. to grope *hebṭet ka-ddesses fe-d-dṛuž.* She groped her way down the stairs.
dṣaṛa pl. *-t* 1. v.n. of *dṣeṛ* 2. impertinence, effrontery
dṣeṛ (*ɛla*) v.i. (v.n. *dṣaṛa*) to be impertinent (toward) *dak l-weld bda idṣeṛ ɛla waldih.* That boy is becoming impertinent toward his parents.
dṣuṛi pl. *-yen* impertinent, insolent

dšiš, dšiša wheat partly ground, used for a kind of soup
dšeṛ pl. *dšuṛ, dšuṛa* village
deššen v.t. to inaugurate, to open *wazir t-tăɛlim deššen tlata de-l-madaris l-bareḥ.* The Minister of Education inaugurated three schools yesterday.
dšuṛ, dšuṛa pl. of *dšeṛ*
duban v.n. of *dab*
dubuṛ anus (often extended to include the buttocks)
dud n.u. *-a* worm
duda **1.** n.u. of *dud* **2.** passion, great appetite, great desire *fih duda kbira de-l-kuṛa.* He has a great passion for football.
duhem pl. of *dhem*
dula **1.** pl. *-t, dwel* herd, flock **2.** pl. *duwwăl* nation **3.** government *ruʔasaʔ d-duwwăl kollhom ġad-idžemɛu ž-žemɛa ž-žayya.* All government heads are going to convene next week.
du-l-qăɛda eleventh month of the Muslim lunar calendar
du-l-ḥižža twelfth month of the Muslim lunar calendar
dum n.u. *-a* **1.** dwarf palm-tree **2.** bunch of leaves of a dwarf palm-tree
dumali pl. *-yen* rich
duminu dominoes (game)
dun without (prep.)
  ** *ma-ġad-ndir-ši men dun dak š-ši dun.* That's all I'm going to busy myself with.
  ¶ *b-dun* without (prep.)
  ¶ *b-dun-ma* without (conj.)
  ¶ *dun-ma* without (conj.) *mša dun-ma iṭḷeb t-tesriḥ.* He left without asking permission.
  ¶ *men-dun* besides *škun kan temma men dun ḅḅak?* Who was there besides your father?
  ¶ *men dun-ma* without (conj.)
duni pl. *-yen* **1.** vile **2.** of inferior quality
dunya same as *denya*
duq pl. *dwaq, ʔedwaq* **1.** taste, savor **2.** taste, inclination
duqan v.n. of *daq*
duwla same as *dula*
duwwa v.t. **1.** to speak to *hadi šḥal ma-duwwatu ḥit ṭiyyṛu-lha dak n-nhaṛ.* She hasn't spoken to him for some time because he offended her the other day. **2.** to make talk *ma-qḍeṛ ḥădd iduwwi had ḅaḅġiyu.* Nobody could make this parrot talk.
duwway pl. *-a* talkative
duwweb v.t. **1.** to melt **2.** to liquefy
duwwed **1.** to get wormy, to be full of worms **2.** to rot, to decay
duwwăl pl. of *dula* **2** and **3**
duwwem v.t. to prolong, to perpetuate
duwwex v.t. to make dizzy
duwwez **1.** to accept *bġana nduwwzu-lu š-šuṛuṭ kollha.* He wants us to accept all his conditions. **2.** to pass *ma-duwwzuha-š ḥit ma-kanu-š ɛăndha n-nuqaṭ mezyanin.* They didn't pass her because she didn't have good grades. —*duwwzu-lu ṭ-ṭwal ɛla ɛănqu.* They passed the rope around his neck. —*l-mežlis duwwez l-multamas lli qeddem ṛaʔis l-ḥukuma.* The Council passed the motion made by the Premier. **3.** to let pass, to allow *ma-ka-iduwwzu-š l-ɛăfyun fe-d-diwana.* They don't let opium pass at the customs. **4.** to consume (a main beverage or food, with s.th. else) *žul l-ʔuṛubbiyen ka-iduwwzu makelthom be-š-šṛab.* Most Europeans drink wine with their meals. —*duwwezna ʔatay be-n-nwa meqli.* We had toasted almonds with tea. **5.** to take (an examination)
  ¶ *duwwez ɛla* **1.** to review *ġad-nduwwez ɛăl ḍ-ḍuṛuṣ dyali qbel le-mtiḥan.* I'm going to review my lessons before the exam. **2.** to slaughter, to slit the throat of (sheep, etc.)
duwwăɛ (*f-*) to stare (at)
duxa v.n. of *dax*
duza **1.** n.i. of *daz* **2.** stroke *l-gezzar daz ɛăl l-kebš duza weḥda be-ž-ženwi.* The butcher slaughtered the sheep with a single stroke of the knife.
  ** *žabettu d-duza dak n-nhaṛ u-ɛṛeḍt ɛlih itġedda mɛaya.* He happened to pass by the other day, and I invited him to have lunch with me.
duzan pl. *-at* set of tools
dužanbir December
duḥ pl. *dwaḥ* bower, arbor
duɛa pl. *-t* **1.** prayer **2.** wish
dwa idwi v.i. **1.** to talk, to chatter **2.** to reverberate
  ¶ *dwa f-* to slander
dwa (m.) pl. *-yat, ʔadwiya, ʔedwiya* **1.** medicine (drug) **2.** remedy, cure
dwabed pl. of *dabed*
dwali pl. of *dalya*
dwam **1.** v.n. of *dam* **2.** perseverance *l-xedma ṣ-ṣɛiba ma-ka-ttṣuwweb ġir be-ṣ-ṣbeṛ u-d-dwam.* Hard work is completed only through patience and perseverance. **3.** eternity
  ¶ *ḍaṛ d-dwam* the other world
  ¶ *ɛăl d-dwam* constantly, always, forever
dwaq, ʔedwaq pl. of *duq*
dwaxel pl. of *daxel* **2**
dwaya pl. *-t* ink-well
dwayer pl. of *dayra*
dwaz **1.** v.n. of *daz* **2.** anything, such as food or drink, served with bread

dwaɛ pl. of *duɛ*
dwida pl. *-t* **1.** passion (sexual) **2.** vermicelli
dwira pl. *-t* **1.** small house, cottage **2.** apartment
dwiriya pl. *-t* **1.** small apartment **2.** kitchen in a large house
ʔedwiya pl. of *dwa*
dwel pl. of *dula* **1**
dxali pl. of *dexla*
dxašeš pl. of *dexšuša*
dxaxen pl. of *doxxan*
dxayeṛ pl. of *dxiṛa*
dxiṛa pl. *-t, dxayeṛ* **1.** reserve, stock, supply *tṣabet ɛăndhom dxiṛa kbira d-le-mwakel.* They happened to have a good supply of food. **2.** treasure *had l-metḥef ɛameṛ be-d-dxayeṛ.* This museum is full of treasures.
dxel idxol v.i. (v.n. *dxul*) **1.** to enter (go in, come in) **2.** to go back *dxel l-l-meġṛib.* He's gone back to Morocco. **3.** to get married
 ** *dxol ṣuq ṛaṣek!* Mind your own business!
 ¶ *dxel bin* to mediate, to intervene *škun dxel binatkom?* Who intervened between you?
 ¶ *dxel f-* to intervene *ḥetta waḥed ma-dxel f-qaḍiythom.* Nobody intervened in their affair.
 dxel l- to enter (to go or come into) *hadi šḥal ma-dxelt l-dak l-bit.* I haven't gone into that room for some time.
 ¶ *dxel u-xrež fe-l-hedṛa* to wander (in talking), to talk inconsistently or incoherently
dexla **1.** n.i. of *dxel* **2.** pl. *-t, dxali* entry **3.** pl. *-t, dxali* reception or dinner given in honor of s.o. returning from a long journey
dexlani pl. *-yen* **1.** inner part, that which is inside **2.** internal
dexšuša pl. *-t, dxašeš* bride's chamber
dxul v.n. of *dxel*
 ¶ *lilt d-dxul* wedding day
doxxan pl. *dxaxen* **1.** smoke **2.** cigarets
dexxel v.t. **1.** to include, to enter *dak š-ši lli dfăɛti dexxlu mɛa ṣ-ṣayeṛ le-kbir.* Enter whatever you spend under general expenses. **2.** to take in, to get in *dexxelti t-teṣbin?* Did you take the laundry in? **3.** to bring in, to yield *l-molk dyalu ka-idexxel-lu xems alaf derhem fe-š-šheṛ.* His property brings in 5,000 dirhams a month for him.
 ** *aš dexxlu fiha?* Why is he meddling in her affairs?
 ¶ *dexxel ṛaṣuᶲ f-* to stick one's nose in (to)
dexxen v.i. to smoke (tobacco)
dexxeṛ v.t. to accumulate (goods, money)
dyab pl. of *dib*
dyal f. *dyalt* pl. *dyawel* (f. and pl. not standard among some urban speakers) **1.** shows possessive relationship *s-siyaṛa dyal ɛămmi ma-zala ždida.* My uncle's car is still new. —*herres le-kräɛ dyal š-šelya.* He broke the leg of the table. **2.** possessive adj. (with pron. endings) *le-ktuba dyalek kollhom žebthom.* I brought all your books. **3.** possessive pron. *had š-ši dyalek wella dyalhom?* Is this yours or theirs? **4.** introduces constitutive terms *dyal-aš had l-xatem?* What is this ring made of? —*ka-ibiɛ d-dmalež dyal d-dheb u-dyal n-neqṛa.* He sells gold and silver bracelets. **5.** that of *le-mtiḥan had l-ɛam kan ṣɛăb men dyal dak l-ɛam.* This year's exam was more difficult than that of last year.
 ¶ *be-dyaluᶲ* well-off ≠
 ¶ *dyal men* whose *dyal men had ḍ-ḍaṛ?* Whose house is this?
 ¶ *dyal ṛaṣuᶲ* **1.** independent, working independently *huma dyal ṛaṣhom.* They work independently. **2.** bachelor *ma-zal gales dyal ṛaṣu.* He is still a bachelor.
dyan pl. of *din*
dyawel pl. of *dyal*
dyuba pl. of *dib*
dyuk, dyuka pl. of *dik*
dyul, dyula pl. of *dil*
dyun, dyunat pl. of *din*
dzad v.i. **1.** m.p. of *zad* **2.** to be born *f-ayna ɛam dzadet bentek?* What year was your daughter born? **3.** to increase
 ¶ *dzad l-ḥal ɛlihᶲ* to get worse (health) ≠
dzagel v.i. **1.** to miss each other (trying to meet, shooting at each other, etc.) **2.** to forgive one another, to not hold a grudge **3.** to get or become loose (s.th. that should be tight) **4.** to lose one's mind, to crack up
dzayed v.i. **1.** to bid higher (and higher) **2.** to rise, to go higher (price)
 ** *dzaydu fe-l-hedṛa* (or *f-le-klam*). They had a heated discussion.
dzayer pl. of *dzira*
dzayer (no art.) Algeria
dzaḥem v.i. **1.** to crowd, to crowd together **2.** to shove and elbow one's way (in a crowd)
dzefzif v.n. of *zefzef*
dzeġnin **1.** v.n. of *zeġnen* **2.** monotonous noise
dzeġṛit v.n. of *zeġṛet*
dzehza v.i. **1.** to wait *imken-lek ddzehza šwiya? daba u-huwa ṛžăɛ.* Can you wait a little while? He'll be right back. **2.** to procrastinate, to put things off
dzira pl. *-t, dzayer* **1.** island **2.** peninsula
dziri pl. *-yen* Algerian, native of Algiers
dẓiẓin v.n. of *dẓiẓen*
dẓiẓen v.i. to become mute, speechless
dzellef m.p. of *zellef*
dzellăɛ m.p. of *zellăɛ*

dzenzin **1.** v.n. of *zenzen* **2.** buzz, buzzing sound
dẓeṛwiṭ v.n. of *ẓeṛweṭ*
dzuwwed m.p. of *zuwwed*
dzuwwel m.p. of *zuwwel*
dzuwweq m.p. of *zuwweq*
dẓuwweṛ m.p. of *ẓuwweṛ*
dzuwwež (*b-*) to get married (to)
dezz v.t. (v.n. *dezzan*) to shear (sheep)
dzez pl. of *dezza*
dezza pl. *-t, dzez* fleece
dezzan v.n. of *dezz*
dezzaz pl. *-a* shearer
dẓăɛṛiṭ v.n. of *ẓăɛṛeṭ*
dẓăɛṛiṭa caper, gambol
dzăɛziɛ v.n. of *zăɛzăɛ*
dzăɛzăɛ m.p. of *zăɛzăɛ*
džadel v.i. to argue, to have a heated discussion (usually with some purpose)
džaṛ pl. of *tažer* **1**
džara v.i. to race, to have a race (foot, car, political campaign, etc.)
džaṛa same as *tižaṛa*
džaweb v.i. **1.** to answer each other (by letter, i.e., when one writes the other always answers) **2.** to have a mutual understanding or rapport
džaweṛ v.i. to be neighbors
džayži pl. *-ya* poulterer, poultry dealer
džaž coll. **1.** chicken *tġeddina be-d-džaž l-yum.* We had chicken for dinner today. **2.** chickens *šḥal de-d-džaž šriti l-l-ḥefla?* How many chickens did you buy for the party?
džaža pl. *-t* (dim. *džiyža*) hen
¶ *džaža ḥabašiya* guinea hen
džaḥed v.i. to argue, to dispute (often for the sake of argument)
džebbed v.i. **1.** m.p. of *žebbed* **2.** to stretch (relaxing the muscles) **3.** to stretch out (as on a bed) **4.** to become sophisticated (person)
džebbeṛ m.p. of *žebbeṛ*
¶ *džebbeṛ ɛla* to oppress, to tyrannize
džehhed m.p. of *žehhed*
džiyfa pl. *-t* n.i. of *žiyyef*
džiyža dim. of *džaža*
dželled m.p. of *želled*
džemmel ɛla to remind (s.o.) boastfully that one has done him a favor or service *sellef-li ši-flus u-bda ka-idžemmel ɛliya.* He lent me some money, and he made sure I knew where it came from.
džemmeṛ v.i. **1.** m.p. of *žemmeṛ* **2.** to suffer from grief and mental anguish
džemmăɛ same as *žemmăɛ*
dženneb v.t. to avoid, to stay away from (s.o., s.th.)
džennen v.i. to get angry, furious
džennes v.i. to become naturalized
džeṛṛ same as *ttžeṛṛ* (m.p. of *žeṛṛ*)
džeṛžeṛ m.p. of *žeṛžeṛ*
džuwweq to gather together, to form a crowd (people)
džuwwež same as *dzuwwež*
dḥa idḥi v.t. (v.n. *dḥi, deḥyan*) **1.** to dismiss, to fire **2.** to put in(to) *ɛlaš dima ka-idḥi yeddih fe-žyabu.* Why does he always put his hands in his pockets? **3.** to drive (nail)
dḥadeḥ pl. of *deḥduḥ*
dḥas v.n. of *dḥes* and *daḥes*
deḥduḥ pl. *dḥadeḥ* person of small physical stature (adult) (not pejorative)
dḥi v.n. of *dḥa*
dḥes v.t. (v.n. *dḥas, madaḥsa*) to jostle
deḥš pl. *dḥuša* young donkey
dḥuša pl. of *deḥš*
deḥyan v.n. of *dḥa*
dɛa idɛi v.t. (v.n. *dăɛwa, mdaɛya*) to prosecute, to file suit against
¶ *dɛa f-* to slander
¶ *dɛa mɛa, dɛa be-l-xir l-* to pray for
dɛadeɛ pl. of *dăɛduɛ*
dɛawi pl. of *dăɛwa*
dăɛduɛ pl. *dɛadeɛ* kind of large tambourine without jingles
dɛiṛa same as *ḍɛiṛa*
dăɛwa pl. *-t, dɛawi* **1.** v.n. and n.i. of *dɛa* **2.** lawsuit **3.** prayer, invocation **4.** benediction, blessing **5.** curse, malediction
¶*dɛa be-dɛăwt l-xir l-* to wish (s.o.) well
¶ *mul d-dăɛwa* pl. *mwalin d-dăɛwa* or *mwalin d-dɛawi* plaintiff
¶ *qeyyed dăɛwa ɛla* or *b-* to file suit against
¶ *ṣaḥeb d-dăɛwa* pl. *ṣḥab d-dăɛwa* or *ṣḥab d-dɛawi* same as *mul d-dăɛwa*
dăɛɛăm v.t. **1.** to support *ma-žbeṛ ḥădd lli idăɛɛmu fe-ṛ-ṛăʔy dyalu.* He couldn't find anybody to support him in his opinion. **2.** to wedge, to prop

Ḍ

ḍaḍeḍ, ḍaḍḍ v.t. **1.** to oppose **2.** to compete with
daduṣ pl. *-at, ḍwadeṣ* die (pl. dice)
ḍahir pl. *ḍwaheṛ, ḍawahir* decree (royal)
ḍala b- **1.** to start doing (s.th.) (persistently) *ġir šafuh ḍalaw ɛlih be-l-lhib ḥetta beddel*

ṛeʔyu. As soon as they saw him they started flattering him till he changed his mind. 2. (also *ɛla*) to indulge in *šeftha ḍalat ɛăl le-kdub had l-iyyam.* I notice she's been indulging in telling lies recently.

ḍalem a.p. of *ḍlem*

ḍama pl. *-t* 1. checkers 2. checkerboard

ḍamana same as *ḍmana* (v.n. of *ḍmen*)

ḍamen a.p. of *ḍmen*

ḍaq iḍiq v.i. (v.n. *ḍiq*) to get bored, to become restless *fuq-emma ka-ikun mɛahom ka-ibği imši f-ḥalu ḥit ka-iḍiq.* Whenever he is with them he wants to leave because he gets bored.

¶ *ḍaq bih*$^{\phi}$ *l-ḥal* 1. to be in a bad condition *le-mṛiḍ ḍaq bih l-ḥal bezzaf.* The patient is in a very bad condition. 2. to be in difficulty (e.g. financial)

ḍaṛ iḍuṛ v.i. (v.n. *ḍuṛan*) 1. to turn *sir ṭul u-ḍuṛ ɛăl l-imin.* Go straight ahead and then turn right. —*le-mwara de-l-magana de-s-sersar ma-bqaw-š iḍuṛu.* The hands of the alarm clock stopped turning. 2. to take a walk, to go for a walk *dima ka-nexṛož nḍuṛ šwiya men băɛd le-ɛša.* I always go out for a little walk after supper. 3. to take a ride, to go for a ride *mšaw mɛah iḍuṛu fe-s-siyaṛa dyalu.* They've gone out with him for a ride in his car. 4. to wander, to roam *n-nhaṛ kollu u-huwa ka-iḍuṛ fe-l-ğaba.* He's been wandering all day long through the forest.

¶ *ḍaṛ b-* to surround

¶ *ḍaṛ f-* to turn to *ḍaṛet fiya u-qalt-li. .* She turned to me and said . . .

¶ *ḍaṛ ɛla* 1. to look for 2. to turn against, to betray

¶ a.p. *ḍayeṛ* pl. *-in* 1. round 2. circular

¶ *ḍayṛa bih*$^{\phi}$ *t-tekmila* to be in financial straits

ḍaṛ pl. *ḍyaṛ, ḍyuṛ* 1. house *had ḍ-ḍaṛ xawya.* This house is vacant. 2. home, residence *ila ma-lqitih-š fe-l-mekteb ɛăyyeṭ-lu le-ḍ-ḍaṛ.* If you don't find him in the office call him at his home. 3. (often pl. force in sg.) wife (polite euphemism) *ḍ-ḍaṛ dyalek qalu-li ma-mažī-š.* Your wife told me you're not coming. —*ma-žabu-š ḍaṛhom mɛahom l-l-ḥefla.* They didn't bring their wives along to the party. 4. firm (business) 5. square (of a checkerboard)

** *daba džibu ḍ-ḍaṛ u-nefdiwha fih.* We'll run into him some day and get even with him.

¶ *ḍaṛ ḍ-ḍbeğ* tannery

¶ *ḍ-ḍaṛ l-biḍa* Casablanca

¶ *ḍaṛ l-mexzen* seat of the Moroccan government, royal palace

¶ *ḍaṛ le-wḍu* toilet

¶ *ḍaṛ mɛăllma* workshop (in a private home) for little girls

¶ *ḍaṛ ɛrifa* detention home (for women)

¶ *mul ḍ-ḍaṛ* pl. *mwalin ḍ-ḍaṛ* 1. head of the house(hold) 2. landlord

¶ *mulat ḍ-ḍaṛ* pl. *mwalin ḍ-ḍaṛ* 1. mistress of the house(hold) 2. landlady

¶ *mwalin ḍ-ḍaṛ* wife *kif kanu mwalin ḍ-ḍaṛ?* How is your wife feeling?

ḍaṛa pl. *-t* 1. circle *seṭṭeṛ waḥed ḍ-ḍaṛa ṣğiṛa b-le-qlam le-ḥmeṛ ɛăl l-weṛqa.* Draw a small circle on the paper with the red pencil. 2. circumference, periphery 3. disc 4. halo

¶ *ḍṛeb ḍ-ḍaṛa* to form a circle

ḍaṛaṛ 1. v.n. of *ḍeṛṛ* 2. harm *yak ma-kayen ḍaṛar ila selleftha men ɛăndek?* Will there be any harm if I borrow it from you? 3. damage *ma-imken-lek-ši ttṣuwweṛ ḍ-ḍaṛar lli xella ž-žṛad.* You can't imagine the damage caused by the locusts. 4. pain 5. inconvenience

ḍaṛayeb pl. of *ḍariba*

ḍaṛeb v.i. to fight *l-ɛăskeṛ mšaw iḍaṛbu.* The soldiers have gone to fight.

¶ *ḍaṛeb ɛla* 1. to stand up for, to defend *xeṣṣu iḍaṛeb ɛăl l-ḥuquq dyalu.* He'll have to stand up for his rights. 2. to fight for *lli ḍaṛbu ɛăl l-istiqlal de-bladhom kollhom banu.* All those who fought for the independence of their country have been recognized.

ḍaṛi usually

¶ *kif ḍaṛi* as is the custom

ḍaṛiba pl. *-t, ḍaṛayeb* tax

ḍaṛiṛ pl. *-in* blind, sightless (in both eyes, partially or completely)

ḍaṛiḥ pl. *ḍṛayeḥ* mausoleum

ḍaṛuṛa pl. *-t* necessity

ḍaṛuṛi pl. *-yen* necessary

ḍawahir pl. of *ḍahir*

ḍawi pl. *-yen* bright, shiny

ḍaxama pl. *-t* monstrous or huge object or person (usually substituted for actual object in question) *waḥed t-tlata de-ḍ-ḍaxama žaw l-l-mekteb l-bareḥ.* Three enormous fellows came to the office yesterday.

ḍaya pl. *-t* 1. lake 2. pond

ḍayef v.t. (v.n. *ḍyafa*) to offer hospitality to

ḍayeṛ a.p. of *ḍaṛ*

ḍayṛa pl. *-t* 1. circle *ɛămlu ḍayṛa f-qelb ḍayṛa u-bdaw išeṭḥu.* They formed one circle within the other and started dancing. 2. perimeter *ḍ-ḍayṛa d-had s-sehriž fiha xemsa u-ṛebɛin miter.* The perimeter of this pool is forty-five meters. 3. circumference *šḥal fe-ḍ-ḍayṛa d-dak n-naɛuṛa?* What's the circumference of that noria? 4. frame (door, window, etc.) 5. entourage

ḍaɛ iḍiɛ v.i. (v.n. *ḍiɛa*) to be lost, to be wasted *ġad-iḍiɛ-lhom bezzaf de-l-weqt.* They are going to lose a lot of time.
¶ *ḍaɛ f-* to lose *ḍeɛti f-waḥed l-forṣa ɛažiba.* You lost a wonderful opportunity.
ḍaɛif pl. *ḍuɛafa* poor
ḍbab n.u. *ḍbaba* mist
ḍbaṛi pl. of *ḍebṛa*
ḍobb pl. *ḍbuba* bear
ḍebbeb v.i. to get misty
ḍebbeṛ same as *debbeṛ*
ḍbeġ v.t. (v.n. *ḍbiġ, ḍbeġ*) to tan
ḍbeġ v.n. of *ḍbeġ*
¶ *ḍaṛ ḍ-ḍbeġ* pl. *ḍyuṛ ḍ-ḍbeġ* tannery
ḍbiġ v.n. of *ḍbeġ*
ḍbiṛ v.n. of *ḍbeṛ*
ḍbiṭ v.n. of *ḍbeṭ*
ḍbeṛ v.t. (v.n. *ḍbiṛ*) to rub raw, to abrade, to bruise
ḍebṛa **1.** n.i. of *ḍbeṛ* **2.** pl. *-t ḍbaṛi* bruise
ḍbeṭ v.t. (v.n. *ḍebṭ, ḍbiṭ*) **1.** to organize **2.** to specify, to say or do (s.th.) precisely **3.** to vocalize (text)
ḍebṭ v.n. of *ḍbeṭ*
¶ *be-ḍ-ḍebṭ* precisely, exactly *dak š-ši lli bġit nqul-lu be-ḍ-ḍebṭ.* That's precisely what I wanted to tell him.
ḍbuba pl. of *ḍobb*
ḍbuɛa pl. of *ḍbăɛ*
ḍbăɛ pl. *ḍbuɛa* hyena
ḍḍaḍ pl. of *ḍeḍḍ*
ḍḍamen v.i. to unite, to join forces
ḍḍaṛeb v.i. to fight, to have a fight (fisticuffs)
ḍḍayef v.i. to be a guest, to be received as a guest (usually for a few days)
ḍḍaḥek v.i. to laugh (as when having a good time)
ḍḍebbeb v.i. to become misty, foggy
ḍeḍḍ against
ḍeḍḍ pl. *ḍḍaḍ* contrariness
¶ *rfed ḍ-ḍeḍḍ mɛa, ɛmel ḍ-ḍeḍḍ mɛa, dar ḍ-ḍeḍḍ mɛa* to have s.th. against (s.o.)
ḍḍellel v.i. to be or get in the shade
ḍḍellem v.i. to get dark (a room)
ḍḍeṛṛ m.p. of *ḍeṛṛ*
ḍḍeṛṛeq v.i. **1.** to take shelter (as from rain) **2.** to hide
ḍḍeṛṛăɛ v.i. to moan, to groan (from pain)
¶ *ḍḍeṛṛăɛ l-* to ask mercy of (s.o.) (playing heavily on s.o.'s sentimentality)
ḍḍuwweṛ m.p. of *ḍuwweṛ*
ḍḍăɛḍăɛ v.i. **1.** to become loose or less solid (fence post, etc.) **2.** to become less strong, to weaken (also metaphorical)
ḍḍăɛɛăf m.p. of *ḍăɛɛăf*
ḍḍăɛɛăṛ m.p. of *ḍăɛɛăṛ*
ḍfaṛ pl. of *ḍfeṛ*
ḍfayeṛ pl. of *ḍfiṛa*
ḍfiṛ v.n. of *ḍfeṛ*
ḍfiṛa pl. *-t, ḍfayeṛ* plait, braid
ḍfeṛ v.t. (v.n. *ḍfiṛ*) to plait
¶ *ḍfeṛ b-* to obtain, to succeed in getting
ḍfeṛ pl. *ḍfaṛ, ḍfuṛa* (pejorative) **1.** nail (finger, toe) **2.** claw
ḍefṛa same as *ḍfiṛa*
ḍfuṛa pl. of *ḍfeṛ*
ḍġiṭ v.n. of *ḍġeṭ*
ḍoġṛi same as *doġṛi*
ḍġeṭ ɛla (v.n. *ḍeġṭ, ḍġiṭ*) to make, to compel, to exert pressure on *ḍeġṭet ɛlih baš yăɛṭiha le-flus kollhom.* She compelled him to give her all the money.
ḍeġṭ **1.** v.n. of *ḍġeṭ* **2.** pressure
ḍehheṛ v.t. **1.** to show, to manifest, to reveal *ka-iḍehheṛ-lha waḥed l-maḥibba kbira.* He manifests a great affection toward her. **2.** to prove, to show *ġad-nḍehheṛ-lha bi-ʔennaha kanet ġalṭa.* I'm going to prove to her that she was wrong. **3.** to issue *wiẓaṛt l-barid ḍehhṛet ɛadad de-t-tnaber ždad.* The Post Office Department has issued many new stamps.
dheṛ v.i. (v.n. *ḍhuṛ*) **1.** to seem *ka-iḍheṛ(-li) ma-ġad-iži-š.* It seems (to me) he is not coming. **2.** to appear, to show up *melli xwa le-blad ma-ɛawed ḍheṛ.* He left the country and hasn't shown up since. **3.** to come into season *d-dellaḥ ma-zal ma-ḍheṛ.* Watermelon hasn't come into season yet.
ḍheṛ pl. *ḍhuṛ, ḍhuṛa* back
¶ *ɛṭa be-ḍ-ḍheṛ* to turn one's back on *ḥna glesna ḥdaha u-hiya ɛṭatna be-ḍ-ḍheṛ.* She turned her back on us as we sat near her.
ḍhuṛ **1.** v.n. of *ḍheṛ* **2.** pl. *-a* noon prayer **3.** pl. *-a* time of the noon prayer **4.** pl. of *ḍheṛ*
ḍhuṛa pl. of *ḍheṛ*
ḍif pl. *ḍyaf, ḍifan* guest
¶ *ṭleb ḍif ḷḷah* to ask to be taken in as a guest
ḍifan pl. of *ḍif*
ḍileq v.i. to wander around, to roam about
ḍim **1.** worry, worries *ma-ġad-nxelli ḥetta ḥaža ddir-lek ḍ-ḍim.* I won't let anything bring you worries. **2.** oppression, injustice *ma-imken-š itṣuwweṛ l-waḥed ḍ-ḍim lli šafet dak le-blad teḥt le-stiɛmaṛ.* One can't imagine the oppression suffered by that country under colonialism.
** *ṭaḥ ɛlih ši-ḍim.* Some misfortune happened to him.
ḍiq **1.** v.n. of *ḍaq* **2.** v.n. of *ḍyaq* **3.** narrowness **4.** distress
¶ *fe-ḍ-ḍiq* in financial straits
ḍiqa n.i. of *ḍaq*
ḍiyy daylight
ḍiyyeq v.t. to make narrow
¶ *ḍiyyeq l-xaṭeṛ l-* to annoy, to irritate

¶ part. *mḍiyyeq* pl. *-in* low on funds, in financial straits

¶ *mḍiyyeq l-xaṭeṛ* annoyed, irritated

ḍiyyeq pl. *-in* (comp. *ḍyeq*) **1.** narrow *dak ẓ-ẓenqa ḍiyyqa, ma-nqeḍṛu-š nduzu fiha be-s-siyaṛa.* That street is narrow, we can't get through it with the car. —*ɛămmṛi ma-šeft ši-waḥed fekṛu ḍiyyeq bḥal xaha.* I've never seen such a narrow-minded person as her brother. **2.** tight, close-fitting *had ṣ-ṣebbaṭ ḍiyyeq bezzaf ɛliya.* These shoes are too tight for me. **3.** difficult, delicate situation, position) **4.** short, limited (time)

¶ *ḍiyyeq l-xaṭeṛ* irritable, bad-tempered

ḍiyyăɛ v.t. **1.** to lose **2.** to waste

ḍiɛa v.n. of *ḍaɛ*

ḍḷam v.i. to be dark, to become dark *ẓ-ẓenqa dyalna ḍḷamet, xeṣṣha ḍ-ḍuw.* Our street is dark, it needs a light.

¶ *ḍḷam l-ḥal* to get dark *bda iḍḷam l-ḥal băɛda.* It's getting dark already.

ḍlim v.n. of *ḍḷem*

ḍlef pl. of *ḍelfa*

ḍelfa pl. *-t, ḍlef* cactus leaf

ḍliɛa dim. of *ḍelɛa*

ḍeḷḷ (v.n. *ḍeḷḷan*) **1.** v.i. to spend the day *l-ḥădd lli fat ḍeḷḷina f-le-ɛzib d-ɛămmi, u-fe-l-lil ṛžăɛna le-ḍ-ḍaṛ.* Last Sunday we spent the day on my uncle's farm, then we returned home in the evening. **2.** v.t. to stay, to spend (time) *mnayn kanu hna ḍeḷḷu ɛăndna telt iyyam.* When they were here they stayed three days at our house.

ḍell pl. *ḍlul* **1.** shadow **2.** shade

ḍoḷḷam pl. of *ḍalem* (a.p. of *ḍḷem*)

ḍeḷḷan v.n. of *ḍeḷḷ*

ḍeḷḷel v.t. to shade *ḍeḷḷelna maḥăll n-nzaha b-waḥed ṭ-ṭeṛf d-le-qlăɛ kbir.* We shaded our picnic place with a large piece of canvas. —*ḍeḷḷelt ɛla ɛăyniya be-l-žarida.* I shaded my eyes with the newspaper.

ḍeḷḷem v.t. to darken, to make dark *la-tšedd-ši s-sṛažeb kollhom, daba ḍḍeḷḷem l-bit.* Don't close all the windows, that'll darken the room.

ḍḷem v.t. (v.n. *ḍlim, ḍolm*) **1.** to oppress **2.** to be unjust to

¶ a.p. *ḍalem* **1.** pl. *-in* unjust, oppressive **2.** pl. *ḍoḷḷam* oppressor, tyrant

ḍolm v.n. of *ḍḷem*

ḍḷem pl. (of intensity) *ḍḷumat* darkness

ḍelma pl. *-t* darkness

ḍlul pl. of *ḍell*

ḍḷumat pl. of *ḍḷem*

ḍluɛ pl. of *ḍelɛa*

ḍelɛa pl. *-t, ḍluɛ* (dim. *ḍliɛa*) rib

ḍmana v.n. of *ḍmen*

ḍmin v.n. of *ḍmen*

ḍmiṣ v.n. of *ḍmeṣ*

** *mšat ɛla ɛăynu ḍmiṣ.* He's been thwarted.

ḍemm v.t. (v.n. *ḍemm*) to hug, to embrace

ḍemm v.n. of *ḍemm*

ḍomman pl. of *ḍamen* (a.p. of *ḍmen*)

ḍmen v.t. (v.n. *ḍmin, ḍmana*) to guarantee, to promise *ma-neqḍeṛ-ši nḍmen-lek ʔožṛa kteṛ men hadi.* I can't guarantee you a higher salary. —*qalu-li huma ġad-iḍemnuh ḥetta iṛedd-li flusi lli selleftu.* They told me they would guarantee that he'd return the money I lent him. —*ḥna nḍemnuh ḥetta iṛedd-lek le-flus.* We can guarantee that he'll give the money back to you.

¶ a.p. *ḍamen* bail, bond

¶ *ḍamen le-wžeh* pl. *ḍomman le-wžeh* guarantor, bondsman

¶ *ɛṭa ḍ-ḍamen* **1.** to provide bail for oneself, to have s.o. go bail for oneself *l-meḥkama imken-lha ṭṭelqu ila ɛṭa ḍ-ḍamen.* The court may let him go if he has someone go bail for him. **2.** to give a reference *mul ḍ-ḍaṛ ṭḷeb mennhom yăɛṭiw ḍ-ḍamen baš ikri-lhom l-maḥăll.* The landlord asked them for a reference in order to rent them the place. **3.** to have or provide a guarantor *ma-bġaw isellfuh le-flus ḥetta ɛṭahom ḍ-ḍamen.* They didn't want to lend him the money until he had someone serve as a guarantor (that he will return it).

ḍmeṣ v.t. (v.n. *ḍmiṣ*) to shuffle (cards)

ḍnaya pl. *-t* offspring, progeny

ḍenn v.i. (v.n. *ḍenn*) to believe, to think, to suppose *ma-ka-nḍenn-š imken-lu išriha.* I don't think he can buy it.

¶ p.p. *meḍnun* s.th. thought or supposed *ma-kan-š l-meḍnun fik ġadi tăɛmel had š-ši.* I don't think you'd do that.

ḍenn **1.** v.n. of *ḍenn* **2.** pl. *ḍnun* opinion, idea, supposition

ḍnun pl. of *ḍenn* **2**

ḍṛa corn, maize

¶ *ḍṛa biḍa* sorghum

¶ *ḍṛa ḥămṛa* corn, maize

ḍṛaben cpl. of *ḍeṛban*

ḍṛabez pl. of *ḍeṛbuz*

ḍṛaf pl. of *ḍṛif*

ḍṛafa gentleness, affability

ḍṛahem (pl.) money *fayn ḍ-ḍṛahem lli kanu f-le-mžeṛ?* Where's the money which was in the drawer?

ḍṛaṛeq pl. of *ḍeṛṛaqa*

ḍṛaṛež pl. of *ḍeṛṛaža*

ḍṛaṣ pl. of *ḍeṛṣa*

ḍṛawa n.pl. of *ḍṛawi*

ḍṛawi adj. pl. *-yen,* n.pl. *ḍṛawa* native to the Dra River area

ḍṛayeṛ pl. of *ḍeṛṛa*

ḍṛayeḥ pl. of *ḍariḥ*

ḍṛaɛ pl. *ḍṛuɛ, ḍṛuɛa* udder (of cow)

ḍṛeb (v.n. *ḍeṛb, ḍṛib*) **1.** v.t. to hit, to strike, to beat *علaš ka-ḍḍṛeb l-kuṛa mعa l-bab?* Why are you hitting the ball against the door? —*ṛ-ana ġad-nḍṛeb dak l-weld ila ma-hden-š.* I'm going to hit that boy if he doesn't keep quiet. **2.** v.t. to ring *ġad-iḍṛeb n-naquṣ l-le-ġda.* He's going to ring the lunch bell. **3.** v.t. to play *ka-yăعṛef iḍṛeb kamanža.* He knows how to play the violin. —*عămmṛi ma-ḍṛebt had l-qiṭعa.* I've never played this piece (of music). **4.** v.t. to shoot *ḍeṛbuh be-mkoحla.* They shot him with a rifle. **5.** v.t. to coin, to mint (money) **6.** v.t. to multiply *ḍṛeb had l-عadad fe-tmenya.* Multiply this number by eight. **7.** v.i. to ring *s-sersar d-bab ḍ-ḍaṛ ka-iḍṛeb.* The doorbell is ringing. **8.** v.i. to beat (heart)

¶ *ḍṛeb l-عănd* to drop by *qul-lu iḍṛeb l-عăndi ġedda.* Tell him to drop by my place tomorrow.

¶ *ḍṛeb năعsa, ḍṛebha~ b-năعsa* to fall sound asleep

¶ *ḍeṛbettuϕ l-fiqa* to wake up ≠ *ma-ḍeṛbethom l-fiqa حetta l-l-عăšṛa.* They didn't wake up until ten o'clock.

¶ *ḍṛeb ṭ-ṭṛiq* to tramp, to walk a long distance

¶ *ḍeṛbuϕ l-berd, ḍeṛbuϕ ṛ-ṛwaح* to catch cold ≠

¶ *ḍeṛbuϕ ḷḷah* to become ill-fated or unlucky ≠

¶ *ḍṛeb yedduϕ l-žibuϕ* to reach into one's pocket

¶ *ḍṛeb عla* **1.** to stand up for, to defend, to fight for *la-bodd iḍṛeb عla حăqqu.* He has to stand up for his rights. **2.** to remove, to cross out *ġir iḍṛeb عla dak š-ši daba.* He can just cross that out now. **3.** to play (an instrument)

¶ p.p. *meḍṛub* pl. *-in* full *عṭani waحed l-xabya meḍṛuba b-le-عsel.* He gave me a jar full of honey.

** *عăndu waحed l-weld meḍṛub عăl l-makla.* He has a boy that's just crazy about food. —*huwa meḍṛub f-عăqlu.* He's touched in the head.

ḍeṛb v.n. of *ḍṛeb*

ḍeṛba pl. *-t* (dim. *ḍṛiba*) **1.** n.i. of *ḍṛeb* **2.** blow, hit, lash, etc. *عṭah tlata de-ḍ-ḍeṛbat b-le-mṣuṭa.* He gave him three lashes with the whip. **3.** shot *ġir ḍeṛba weحda u-huwa iṭiyyeح l-حăžla.* It took him only one shot to bring the partridge down.

¶ *ḍeṛbet l-عăyn* hex

ḍeṛban (sg. and coll.) cpl. *ḍṛaben* porcupine

ḍeṛbuz pl. *ḍṛabez* railing, balustrade

ḍṛeg n.u. *ḍeṛga* cactus

ḍṛib v.n. of *ḍṛeb*

ḍṛiba dim. of *ḍeṛba*

ḍṛif pl. *ḍṛaf* **1.** gentle, affable **2.** courteous

ḍṛiž v.n. of *ḍṛež*

ḍṛuža dim. of *ḍeṛža*

ḍeṛqawa n.pl. of *ḍeṛqawi*

ḍeṛqawi adj. pl. *-yen* n.pl. *ḍeṛqawa* member of a certain Moroccan religious fraternity

ḍeṛṛ v.t. (v.n. *ḍaṛaṛ, maḍeṛṛa*) **1.** to hurt, to cause pain to *ṛaṣi ka-iḍeṛṛni.* I have a headache. **2.** to cause harm or damage to *l-حămla ḍeṛṛet ṣ-ṣaba bezzaf.* The storm has caused a lot of harm to the crops. **3.** to inconvenience *ila kan had š-ši ġad-iḍeṛṛek la-tعămlu-š.* Don't do it if it's going to inconvenience you

ḍeṛṛ, ḍoṛṛ **1.** illness **2.** pain (physical)

¶ *ḍ-ḍeṛṛ le-qbiح* tuberculosis

ḍeṛṛa pl. *-t, ḍṛayeṛ* n.i. of *ḍeṛṛ*

ḍeṛṛaqa pl. *-t, ḍṛaṛeq* **1.** curtain **2.** shield **3.** porch roof

ḍeṛṛaža pl. *-t, ḍṛaṛež* **1.** bicycle **2.** hoop (toy)

¶ *ḍeṛṛaža nariya* motor bike

ḍeṛṛef v.t. **1.** to trim, to clip (hedge, tree, fingernails, etc.) **2.** to shave

ḍeṛṛeg, ḍeṛṛeq, v.t. **1.** to hide, to put away *kif semعet d-drari ḍeṛṛqet l-حălwa.* As soon as she heard the children she hid the cake. **2.** to give shelter to

ḍeṛṛež to show, to display *lemma kan hna l-mufettiš s-selعa kollha ḍeṛṛežnaha qbaltu.* When the inspector was here we showed him all the merchandise.

ḍeṛṣ pl. *ḍuṛuṣ* **1.** lesson *ma-zalin ma-حefḍu ḍ-ḍuṛuṣ dyalhom.* They haven't learned their lessons yet. **2.** course *sqeṭ fe-tlata de-ḍ-ḍuṛuṣ عam iuwwel.* He failed three courses last year.

ḍeṛṣa pl. *-t, ḍṛaṣ* molar (tooth)

¶ *fihϕ ḍ-ḍeṛṣa, fihϕ حriq ḍ-ḍeṛṣa* to have a toothache ≠

¶ *ḍeṛṣa d-le-عqel* wisdom tooth

ḍṛuba pl. *-t* heifer

ḍṛuṛa pl. *-t* same as *ḍeṛṛ*

ḍṛuž **1.** pl. of *ḍeṛža* **2.** (pl.) staircase, stairs

ḍṛuع, ḍṛuعa pl. of *ḍṛaع*

ḍṛež v.i. (v.n. *ḍṛiž*) **1.** to walk *nḍṛež mعak waحed š-šwiya l-le-mdina.* I'll walk with you a while toward town. **2.** to step out, to leave *ġir hiya ḍeṛžet men ḍ-ḍaṛ u-ṛaželha ža.* Her husband arrived just as she stepped out of the house.

ḍeṛža pl. *-t, ḍṛuž* (dim. *ḍṛiža*) **1.** step (stair, ladder) **2.** rank, degree, classification

ḍṣaṛa same as *ḍṣaṛa*

ḍṣeṛ same as *ḍṣeṛ*

ḍeṣṣ **1.** mortar **2.** pavement

ḍeṣṣaṣ pl. *-a* rammer, ramming instrument

ḍeṣṣeṛ v.t. to let (s.o.) get out of hand

ḍeṣṣeṣ v.t. **1.** to ram (earth) **2.** to pave (road)

ḍṣuṛi same as *ḍṣuṛi*

ḍuṛ pl. *ḍwaṛ, ᵉeḍwaṛ* (dim. *ḍwiyyeṛ*)
1. band, ring (finger) 2. hoop 3. turn
fe-mmen ḍ-ḍuṛ de-ġsil le-mwaεen l-yum?
Whose turn is it to do the dishes today?
4. frame *ḍ-ḍuṛ de-nḍaḍri therres.* The
frame of my glasses is broken. 5. role, part
šҁal de-l-ᵉeḍwaṛ kaynin f-had r-riwaya?
How many roles are there in this play?
6. cycle *l-gemṛa kemmlet ḍ-ḍuṛ dyalha.*
The moon has completed its cycle.
¶ *lεăb ḍuṛ εla, εmel* (or *dar*) *ḍuṛ l-* to
play a trick on (s.o.)

ḍuṛa 1. n.i. of *ḍaṛ, ḍuwwer* 2. pl. *-t* (dim.
ḍwiṛa) turn *xellik ġadi ṭul ҁetta tuwṣel
le-ḍ-ḍuṛa t-tanya εăl l-imin.* Keep going
straight till you get to the second turn on
the right. 3. tour *ġedda ġad-nεămlu
ši-ḍuṛa f-le-mdina.* Tomorrow we're going
to take a tour of the city. 4. rotation
5. curve, bend (road) 6. round(s) *l-εăssas
ka-ibda ḍ-ḍuṛa dyalu fe-ṭ-ṭnaš de-l-lil.* The
watchman begins making his rounds at
midnight.

ḍuṛan v.n. of *ḍaṛ*

ḍuṛuṣ pl. of *ḍeṛṣ*

ḍuw pl. *ḍwaw* (dim. *ḍwiyyew*) 1. light
2. electricity

ḍuwwa v.t. to illuminate
¶ *ḍuwwa εla* to give light to *zid ḍuwwi
εliya šwiyeš l-had ž-žih.* Give me some
more light over here.
¶ *ḍuwwa εăl ṣ-ṣalīҁ* to light a candle
on the tomb of a saint

ḍuwwaṛ pl. *ḍwaweṛ* village

ḍuwwaṛa pl.*-t, ḍwaweṛ* 1. circle *kayna
waҁed ḍ-ḍuwwaṛa kbira εăl l-giṭun.*
There's a big circle around the tent. 2. circumference, periphery 3. tripe (either
organs or a dish)

ḍuwwaya pl. *-t* skylight

ḍuwweṛ 1. to turn *la-ḍḍuwweṛ-ši ṣ-ṣefҁa
daba.* Don't turn the page yet. 2. to round,
to make round 3. to cause to rotate, to turn
around
¶ *ḍuwweṛ b-* to surround
¶ *ḍuwweṛ n-naεuṛa εla* to cheat, to
deceive
¶ *ḍuwweṛ εla* to look for *εla-š kanu
ka-iduwwṛu?* What were they looking for?

duεafa pl. of *daεif*

ḍwa iḍwi v.i. 1. to shine 2. to get bright, light
ḍwa l-bit men băεd ҁăllet š-šṛažeb. The
room got light after she opened the windows.

ḍwadeṣ pl. of *ḍaduṣ*

ḍwaḍṣi adj. pl. *-yen* n.pl. *-ya* 1. dice player
2. crook

ḍwaheṛ pl. of *ḍahiṛ*

ḍwaṛ pl. of *ḍuṛ*

ḍwaw pl. of *ḍuw*

ḍwaweṛ pl. of *ḍuwwaṛa* and *ḍuwwaṛ*

ḍwiṛa dim. of *ḍuṛa*

ḍwiyyef dim. of *ḍif*

ḍwiyyeq pl. *-in* (dim. of *ḍiyyeq*) very narrow

ḍwiyyew dim. of *ḍuw*

ḍewṛ same as *ḍuṛ*

ḍya (m.) daylight

ḍyaf pl. of *ḍif*

ḍyafa pl. *-t* 1. v.n. of *ḍayef* 2. hospitality,
hospitable treatment (including food and
lodging)

ḍyaq v.i. (v.n. *ḍiq*) to become narrow

ḍyar pl. of *ḍar*

ḍyeq comp. of *ḍiyyeq*

ḍyuṛ pl. of *ḍar*

ḍҁa time of the morning when the sun is
already high above the horizon (about
10 a.m.)

ḍҁayek pl. of *ḍeҁka*

ḍҁika dim. of *ḍeҁka*

ḍҁiya pl. *-t* 1. v.n. of *ḍeҁҁa* 1 2. blood
sacrifice 3. victim, prey 4. sacrificial lamb
of *l-εid le-kbir* (see *εid*)

ḍҁăk v.i. (v.n. *ḍeҁk*) to laugh
¶ *ḍҁăk εla* 1. to laugh at 2. to trick, to
lead astray

ḍeҁk 1. v.n. of *ḍҁek* 2. laughter 3. amusement

ḍeҁka pl. *-t, ḍҁayek* (dim. *ḍҁika*) 1. laugh
2. joke
¶ *redd . . . ḍeҁka* to ridicule, to make a
fool of *reddet ṛaželha ḍeҁka.* She made a
fool of her husband.

ḍeҁҁa 1. (v.n. *ḍҁiya*) to sacrifice (animal)
2. (v.n. *teḍҁiya*) to sacrifice, to give up
qbel ideҁҁi b-εămṛu εla ᵉžel wladu. He
accepted to sacrifice his life for his children.

ḍeҁҁăk v.t. to amuse, to make laugh

ḍeҁҁuki pl. *-yen* jovial, gay, amusing

ḍεaf v.i. (v.n. *doεf*) 1. to become weak 2. to
lose weight 3. to become poor

ḍεaf pl. of *ḍεif*

ḍεayer pl. of *ḍεira*

ḍăεdiε v.n. of *ḍḍăεḍăε*

ḍoεf v.n. of *ḍεaf*

ḍεăf comp. of *ḍεif*

ḍεif pl. *ḍεaf* (comp. *ḍεăf*) 1. weak, feeble
2. poor

ḍεira pl. *-t, ḍεayer* fine, penalty

ḍăεεăf v.t. to weaken

F

f- (*fe-* before consonant clusters; *fi-* before pron. endings) **1.** in *ɛetta r-riša ṛaha f-le-mžeṛ.* The pen is in the drawer too. —*kemmlet xdemtha f-saɛtayn.* She finished her work in two hours. —*lexxeṣt-lu l-muwqif dyali f-neṣṣ ṣefɛa.* I outlined my position for him in half a page. —*fe-šmen ṭiyaṛa rkebtiw?* Which plane did you take (i.e., in which plane . . .) ? **2.** into, in *ɛmel had le-flus f-žibek.* Put this money in your pocket. **3.** at *xay ma-zal fe-l-meḍṛaṣa.* My brother is still at school. —*ġad-nemšiw fe-t-tlata.* We are going to leave at three. —*šefthom f-waɛed l-ɛefla dak n-nhaṛ.* I saw them at a party the other day. **4.** on *ka-iseknu f-waɛed ẓ-ẓenqa mešhuṛa.* They live on a famous street. —*š-kayen fe-l-beṛnamež had l-lila?* What's on the program tonight? **5.** among *had le-wlad fihom ši-tlamed mezyanin.* There are some good pupils among these boys. **6.** about, on *tkellemt mɛah f-muškiltek.* I've talked to him about your problem. **7.** by, by means of *mša l-bariz fe-ṭ-ṭiyaṛa.* He went to Paris by plane. —*f-aš ṣafeṛtiw ɛam l-uwwel?* By what means did you travel last year? **8.** by (multiplication) *ḍṛebna l-žamiɛ f-xemsa.* We multiplied the total by five. **9.** used immediately between a verb and its direct object to denote excess, persistence *u-bda ka-yakol fe-l-xobz.* Then he began to eat bread (greedily). —*bqa ižbed fiya ɛetta fe-t-tali hṛebt mennu.* He kept provoking me until I finally ran away from him.

** *ma-fih ma imši.* He doesn't feel like going. —*had ṣ-ṣebbaṭ ma-bqa fih ma ittelbes.* These shoes can't be worn anymore. —*ḍ-ḍaṛ ma-bqa-ši fiha ma ikun.* The house is in a terrible condition.

¶ *f-aš-ma* wherever *f-aš-ma ɛmel flusu ka-inžeɛ.* Wherever he invests his money he succeeds.

¶ *fihφ* . . . (plus n.) to be . . . ≠ (common construction representing English adj. usage) *fiya n-nɛas.* I'm sleepy.

fabrika pl. *-t* factory

fabuṛ pl. *-at* **1.** favor *ɛămmṛu ma-insa l-fabuṛ lli ɛmelti fih.* He'll never forget the favor you did him. **2.** tip, gratuity **3.** gratis, free *xellitu yaxod ṛ-ṛadyu ṣ-ṣġiṛ fabuṛ.* I let him have the small radio gratis.

fad ifid v.t. (v.n. *fayda*) **1.** to be useful to, to help *had s-sefṛa ġad-tfidu bezzaf.* This trip is going to help him a lot. **2.** to transmit (information) to, to give information to

faḍ ifiḍ v.i. (v.n. *fiḍan*) **1.** to overflow (river, etc.) **2.** to boil (water) **3.** to grow up fast (as a person in height)

¶ *faḍ ɛla* to flood (also metaphorical) *faḍu ɛliha le-hdiyat.* She was flooded with gifts.

faḍă? same as *fḍa*

faḍila same as *fḍila*

faḍel pl. *-in* polite, respectful

faged v.t. (v.n. *fged, mfagda*) to remind

fagu pl. *-wat* car (train)

faharis pl. of *fihris, fihrisa*

fahi pl. *fahyen* astonished, (looking) bewildered

fakya dried fruits (such as dates, figs, raisins; includes walnuts)

fal omen

¶ *ḍṛeb l-fal l-* **1.** to tell (s.o.'s) fortune *hadik le-mṛa lli ḍeṛbet-lu l-fal.* That's the woman who told him his fortune. **2.** to have one's fortune told *mšat teḍṛeb l-fal ɛănd dak l-hindiya.* She's gone to that Indian woman to have her fortune told.

¶ *ḍṛib l-fal* fortune-telling, divination

¶ *ḍeṛṛab l-fal* f. *ḍeṛṛabt l-fal* fortune-teller

falaqa pl. *-t* **1.** stick with a loop of rope used for binding together the ankles of s.o. who is to be punished by being beaten on the soles of his feet **2.** bastinado, the punishment of being beaten on the soles of the feet

¶*ɛṭa falaqa l-* **1.** to administer a bastinado to **2.** to reprimand, to reprove

falas **1.** v.n. of *fles* **2.** ruin, bankruptcy **3.** inferior quality *nezzlu-lna makla de-l-falas.* They served us a food of inferior quality. —*kif kanet l-muɛaḍaṛa?—l-falas!* How was the lecture?—Terrible!

faleṭ v.i. to make a blunder, to make a mistake

falṭa pl. *-t* fault, mistake, malapropism

fanid n.u. *fanida* (dim. *fwinda*) **1.** candy (chocolate, nut, fruit, etc.) **2.** pill (medicine)

fanidi pl. *-yen* pink

faq ifiq v.i. (v.n. *fyaq, fyaqa*) **1.** to wake up **2.** to come to

** *faq ɛlih weɛš bladu.* He's homesick.

¶ *faq b-* to become aware of, to notice, to realize *ɛad faqu be-l-xiyana dyalu.* They've just become aware of his treason. —*deġya faqu bih bġa ihṛeb.* They suddenly became aware that he wanted to run away.

¶ a.p. *fayeq* pl. *-in* alert

¶ *fayeq ɛayeq* shrewd

faqiṛ pl. *fuqaṛa* **1.** poor, miserable, indigent **2.** poor elderly man

faṛ ifuṛ v.i. (v.n. *fwaṛ*) **1.** to boil **2.** to steam **3.** to spring up (jet of water)

faṛ pl. *firan* (dim. *fwiyyeṛ*) 1. mouse 2. rat
¶ *faṛ bḷiḷṭi* pl. *firan bḷiḷṭiyen* mouse
¶ *faṛ d-ɛăṭṭaṛa* rat
faṛaˀiḍ, faṛayeḍ pl. of *faṛiḍa*
faṛaž relief, succor (after some ordeal)
faṛažiya pl. *-t, fwaṛež* long tunic of lightweight material worn by men
farid pl. *-in, frad* unique, unlike anything (or anybody) else
faṛiḍa pl. *-t, faṛaˀiḍ, faṛayeḍ* obligation, duty (religious)
farina 1. wheat 2. (wheat) flour
farisi adj. pl. *-yen* n. pl. *foṛs* Persian
faṛeq v.t. (v.n. *fṛaq, mfaṛqa*) to leave, to stay away from
fares pl. *foṛsan* horseman
faṛăẓ joy, pleasure
¶ *bi-kolli faṛăẓ* gladly, with pleasure
fas pl. *fisan* pickaxe
fas Fez
fasi pl. *-yen* native of Fez
faseq a.p. of *fseq*
faṣaẓa eloquence
faṣiẓ adj. pl. *-in* n. pl. *fuṣaẓa* eloquent
¶ *be-l-lsan l-faṣiẓ* explicitly
faṣel (*bin*) (v.n. *fṣal, mfaṣla*) to settle an affair or mediate (between)
faṣma pl. *-t* bandage
faṣux kind of fumigating substance
fašal 1. v.n. of *fšel* 2. failure (as opposed to success)
fat ifut to pass *l-weqt ka-ifut.* Time is passing. —*ɛad fetnah fe-ṭṛiqna le-ḍ-ḍaṛ.* We just passed him on our way home. —*fatet f-le-mtiẓanat kollha.* She passed all her exams.
** *fat l-ẓal,* or *fat l-weqt.* It's late. —*fat l-fut.* It's too late.
¶ *fat ɛla* to pass by *l-bareẓ fatu ɛla ḍaṛna u-ma-weqfu-š išufuna.* They passed by our house yesterday but didn't stop to see us.
¶ a.p. *fayet* pl. *-in* last, past *l-ɛam l-fayet kanu hna.* They were here last year.
** *faytani b-ɛamayn.* She's two years older than me.
fatan v.n. of *ften*
fatiẓ 1. pl. *-in* conquerer 2. first (of the month)
fatiẓa (with art.) first chapter (*ṣura*) of the Koran
fatẓa pl. *-t, fwateẓ* 1. prayer said with palms up 2. pl. *-t* bethrothal ceremony
¶ *rfed fatẓa* to say prayers with palms up
¶ *reffad fatẓa* pl. *reffadin fatẓa* yes-man
faṭen a.p. of *fṭen*
fawaˀid pl. of *fayda*
fayda pl. *-t, fawaˀid* 1. v.n. of *fad* 2. use, usefulness *šni hiya l-fayda d-le-mši dyalha mɛahom?* What's the use of her going with them? —*dak s-siyaṛa ma-qdat-lna ẓetta ši-fayda.* That car wasn't of any use to us. 3. result *duwwez xems snin fe-l-xariž u-ṛžăɛ bla fayda.* He spent five years abroad and returned without any result. 4. idea, inspiration *xdit fawaˀid ktira men dak le-ktab.* I got many ideas from that book. 5. conclusion, inference, understanding *men l-fayda d-le-klam dyalu ḍheṛ-li ma-baġi ixdem-šay.* From (the conclusion of) what he said I don't think he wants to work.
fayel ɛla to say or do s.th. engendering an evil portent for
fayn 1. where *fayn mšat l-bareẓ?* Where did she go yesterday? —*ḍ-ḍaṛ fayn kanu saknin ttbaɛet.* The house where they used to live has been sold. 2. some place, a place *ġad-nšuf-lu fayn ibat.* I'll find him a place to stay overnight. 3. any place, no place, anywhere, nowhere *ma-ṣabet fayn tegles.* She couldn't find any place to sit. —*ma-ġad-nemšiw fayn.* We're not going anywhere.
** *faynek u-fayn ḍ-ḍaṛ!* You're a long way from home.
¶ *faynek ɛla* as for, meanwhile (transitional expr. used in telling a story or reporting an event) *faynek ɛla weld le-wzir . . .* As for the minister's son . . .
¶ *fayn-ma, fayn-emma* wherever, anywhere *fayn-ma mšat ka-itbăɛha.* Wherever she goes he follows her. —*ġir gles fayn-emma kan.* Just sit anywhere.
¶ *ṛa-fayn* right there, over there *qolt-lek ttsennani ṛa-fayn.* I told you to wait for me right there.
¶*ṛahφ fayn* to be over there ≠ *ṛahom fayn.* They're over there.
fayeq a.p. of *faq*
fayet a.p. of *fat*
fayez a.p. of *faz*
faxeṛ n.u. *faxṛa* charcoal
faxeṛ pl. *-in* (comp. *fxeṛ*) big and healthy-looking
faz ifuz (v.n. *fuzan*) to succeed, to pass *šẓal de-d-drari fazu f-le-mtiẓan?* How many boys passed (in) the examination?
¶ *faz b-* to take advantage of *u-kan kont mennek u-kan nfuz băɛda b-had l-foṛṣa.* If I were you I would first take advantage of this opportunity.
¶ a.p. *fayez* pl. *-in* excellent, superior
fazeg a.p. of *fzeg*
faža ɛla to console, to comfort
fažiṛa pl. *-t* prostitute
faẓ ifuẓ v.i. (v.n. *fuẓan*) 1. to spread, to diffuse *ġir hiya dexlet l-l-bit u-riẓt le-ɛteṛ dyalha faẓet.* As soon as she stepped into

the room the odor of her perfume spread around. —*le-xbaṛ d-le-mži dyalha kan bda ifuḥ* The news about her coming had begun to spread. **2.** to boast, to brag

fda ifdi v.t. (v.n. *fedya*) **1.** to replace, to give in compensation for, to make (s.th.) up (to s.o.) **2.** to pay a ransom for (s.o.) *fdaw weldhom be-myat ʔalef derhem.* They paid a ten thousand dirham ransom for their son.

** *xeṣṣek tefdi-lna had l-mežya.* You'll have to come and see us again. —*daba nefdi fih ḥayel u-ždid.* I'll get even with him once and for all.

¶ *fdaha~ f-* (or *men*) to take revenge on, to get even with

¶ *fda t-taṛ, fda taṛuφ, fda deqqtuφ* to get revenge, to revenge oneself

¶ *fda t-taṛ l-* to avenge *fdaw t-taṛ le-ḅḅahom.* They avenged their father.

fdaden pl. of *feddan*

fdawi pl. *-ya* public storyteller who gathers people around him and expects remuneration

fdawiya pl. *-t* folktale, fable, yarn

fdaweš vermicelli

feddan pl. *fdaden* field, farm land *had l-ɛam ġad-iḥeṛtu had l-feddan.* They are going to cultivate this field this year.

fdiɛ v.n. of *fdăɛ*

fedya v.n. of *fda*

fdăɛ v.t. (v.n. *fdăɛ, fdiɛ*) to dislocate (joint)

fdăɛ v.n. of *fdăɛ*

fḍa ifḍa v.i. **1.** (v.n. *fḍa*) to be vacated, to be vacant *ġir ifḍa had l-maḥăll, xudu.* As soon as this seat is vacant, you may have it. —*bdat tɛum ḥetta fḍa s-sehriž.* She started swimming only when the pool was not so crowded. **2.** (v.n. *fedya*) to finish *dima ka-ifḍa bekri.* He always finishes early. **3.** (v.n. *tfeḍya*) to be settled *qaḍiytu fḍat had ṣ-ṣbăḥ fe-l-meḥkama.* His case was settled this morning in court.

fḍa **1.** v.n. of *fḍa* **1** **2.** (no pl.) empty space

fḍal pl. of *fḍil*

fḍayel pl. of *fḍila*

fḍayeḥ pl. of *fḍiḥa*

feḍḍa v.t. (v.n. *tfeḍya*) to finish, to complete

¶ *feḍḍa mɛa* **1.** to settle (s.th.) with (s.o.), to be through with *ma-xrežt ḥetta feḍḍit mɛah le-ḥsabat kollhom.* I didn't leave until I settled all the accounts with him. —*smăɛt feḍḍa mɛa mṛatu.* I hear he's through with his wife. **2.** to kill *š-šṛab ġad-ifeḍḍi mɛah.* Drinking is going to kill him.

feḍḍa silver (metal)

feḍḍaḥ adj. pl. *-in* n. pl. *-a* one who talks too much and cannot keep a secret

feḍḍeḍ v.t. to silver

feḍḍel v.t. to prefer

feḍfeḍ v.t. and v.i. **1.** to beat *l-fellus bda ifeḍfeḍ (žwanḥu).* The young bird started beating its wings. **2.** to flounder

fḍil pl. *fḍal* (comp. *fḍel*) **1.** distinguished, highly regarded *ḅḅah sidu kan waḥed ṛ-ṛažel fḍil.* His grandfather was a highly regarded man. **2.** holy (saint, place, period)

fḍila pl. *fḍayel* virtue, moral quality

fḍiḥ v.n. of *fḍeḥ*

fḍiḥa pl. *-t, fḍayeḥ* **1.** n.i. of *fḍeḥ* **2.** scandalous behavior **3.** infamy, public disgrace

fḍel (no pl.) **1.** profit, gain *šḥal d-le-fḍel ṭlăɛ-lu men dak l-xedma?* How much profit did he make from that job? **2.** extra, in addition *xeḷḷṣu-lu s-sfeṛ u-wekkluh u-sekknuh u-ɛṭaweh xems myat derhem fḍel.* They paid his transportation, gave him room and board and five hundred dirhams extra. **3.** left, left over *tsara ʔuṛubba kollha u-šra ɛadad de-le-ḥwayež u-bqat-lu telt myat derhem fḍel.* He traveled all over Europe, bought a lot of things, and had three hundred dirhams left.

¶ *be-fḍel* thanks to *ma-huwa hna ġir be-fḍel l-mežhud dyalek.* He's here thanks only to your effort.

¶ *fḍel ḷḷah* **1.** God's grace, divine assistance *žmăɛna le-flus lli xeṣṣuna baš nebniw l-medṛaṣa be-fḍel ḷḷah.* We collected the necessary funds to build the school with God's grace. **2.** much, many, a great deal *ɛăndu fḍel ḷḷah d-le-ḥwanet* He owns many shops. **3.** a long time, quite a while, quite some time *fḍel ḷḷah hadi u-ḥna hna.* We've been here for quite some time.

¶ *men feḍlek, b-le-fḍel mennek* please, would you please . . .

fḍel (comp. of *fḍil*) **1.** better, preferable *ḍ-ḍaṛ fḍel men s-siyaṛa.* A house is better (more important) than a car. —*ɛadad de-n-nas ka-iqulu bin ʔalat ʔaḷmanya fḍel men ʔalat ʔiṭalya.* Many people think that German machines are preferable to Italian ones. **2.** it's better (to), had better *fḍel-lek tebqa mɛah, ṛah isaɛdek.* It's better for you to stay with him, he'll help you.

fḍul prying, indiscretion, meddling

fḍuli pl. *-yen* **1.** nosy, very inquisitive **2.** eager beaver

fedya v.n. of *fḍa* **2**

fḍeḥ v.t. (v.n. *fḍiḥ, fḍiḥa*) **1.** to reveal, to divulge **2.** to inform on, to turn in *ma-ɛăṛfu-ši škun lli fḍeḥhom l-l-bulis.* They don't know who turned them in to the police. **3.** to harass *fḍeḥni be-t-tilifunat u-b-le-bṛawat.* He harassed me with telephone calls and letters.

¶ *fḍeḥ b-* to denounce, to turn in

¶ p.p. *mefḍuɛ* pl. *-in* open to view (as a glass house)
ffad same as *fwad*
fged v.n. of *faged*
fged used in the expr. *ḍreb le-fged f-* **1.** to watch over, to take care of, to look after *ž-žiran kanu ka-iḍeṛbu-lna le-fged fe-d-drari mnayn konna mṣafṛin.* The neighbors looked after the children for us while we were away. —*magantek ma-fesdet ġir ɛit ma-ka-ḍḍṛeb fiha fged.* Your watch stopped working only because you don't take any care of it. **2.** to inspect *saɛa saɛa kan l-mudir ka-iḍṛeb le-fged fe-l-ʔasatida.* The principal used to inspect the teachers every once in a while. **3.** to find out about, to inquire about *hadi šehṛayn u-huwa mṛiḍ u-ma-ḍṛeb fih ɛădd le-fged.* He's been sick for two months and nobody's inquired about him. **4.** (with *qal*) to remind (s.o.) *xeṣṣ lli iḍṛeb fiha le-fged w-iqul-lha fuq-aš ġad-nemšiw.* Someone must remind her when we are supposed to leave.
foggaɛ, foggiɛ n.u. *-a* mushroom
¶ *foggiɛa nabta bla šta* lit., a mushroom which has sprung up without rain (used in reference to a nosy person)
fegged v.t. to remind *ma-ɛtažet lli ifeggedha f-dak š-ši* She didn't need to be reminded of that.
foggiɛ same as *foggaɛ*
feggus n.u. *-a* variety of cucumber
fgis v.n. of *fges*
fgiɛ v.n. of *fgăɛ*
fges v.t. (v.n. *fgis*) **1.** to break (an egg) **2.** to open up, to lance (e.g. a boil)
fgăɛ v.t. (v.n. *fgiɛ*) **1.** to afflict, to cause pain or sadness **2.** to irritate, to make angry, to excite
fegɛa n.i. of *fgăɛ*
fhama pl. *-t, fhayem* **1.** v.n. of *fhem* **2.** understanding, comprehension, quick-wittedness **3.** presumption, effrontery, overconfidence
fhayem pl. of *fhama*
fehd pl. *fhud* leopard
fehhem v.t. to explain, to make understand, to demonstrate *le-fqi ɛmel žehdu kollu baš ifehhem-lna ḍ-ḍeṛṣ.* The teacher did all he could to explain the lesson to us.
fhim v.n. of *fhem*
fhem v.t. (v.n. *fhim, fhama, fehm*) to understand
¶ p.p. *mefhum* significance, meaning
fehm v.n. of *fhem*
fhud pl. of *fehd*
fidaɛa pl. *-t* slut, slattern
fiḍa n.i. of *faḍ*
fiḍan v.n. of *faḍ*
fihris, fihrisa pl. *faharis* table of contents
fikr pl. *ʔafkaṛ* mind
fikra same as *fekra*
fil f. *-a* pl. *fyal* elephant
filala n. pl. of *filali*
filali adj. pl. *-yen* n.pl. *filala* native of Tafilalet
filaɛa same as *flaɛa*
filaɛi pl. *-yen* **1.** agricultural **2.** farmer
filil, filila pl. *-at, fyalel* safety-pin
fileṣṭin Palestine
fileṣṭini pl. *-yen* Palestinian
fin same as *fayn*
finu (invariable) excellent, of superior quality
fiqa n.i. of *faq*
¶ *ḍeṛbettuᶲ l-fiqa* **1.** to wake up ≠, to get up ≠ *ma-ḍeṛbettu l-fiqa ɛetta le-t-tlata d-le-ɛšiya.* He didn't wake up until three in the afternoon. **2.** to wake up to (s.th.), to realize *men băɛd sinin ɛad ḍeṛbethom l-fiqa bin-la kanu mestăɛmṛin.* It took them years to realize that they were victims of colonialism.
fiqh **1.** jurisprudence **2.** Muslim law
¶ *fiqh l-luġa* philology
fiqhi pl. *-yen* related to Muslim law
firan pl. of *faṛ*
firma pl. *-t* farm
firɛăwn pl. *fraɛna* pharoah
fisan pl. of *fas*
fisaɛ immediately, right away
fiš boastfulness
fišṭa pl. *-t* festivity
fituṛ sediment remaining from olive oil
fituṛa pl. *-t, fyateṛ* bill *weṣluni tlata d-le-fyateṛ men ɛănd š-šarika had ṣ-ṣbăɛ.* I got three bills from the firm this morning.
fiweq when *fiweq žaw?* When did they come?
¶ *fiweq-mma* whenever
fiyyeḍ v.t. to make or cause to overflow or flood (river, etc.)
fiyyeq v.t. **1.** to wake up, to awaken (s.o.) **2.** to revive (as from a faint)
fiyyeš v.i. to boast
fižel n.u. *fižla* rue (plant)
fiɛl pl. *ʔefɛal* verb
¶ *be-l-fiɛl* in fact, really
fiɛlen in fact, really
fkak **1.** v.n. of *fekk* **2.** pl. of *fekk* **2**
fkaka pl. *-t* n.i. of *fekk*
fkaren, fkaṛen pl. of *fekrun, fekṛun*
fkiṛ v.n. of *fkeṛ*
fekk v.t. (v.n. *fekk, fekkan, fkak*) **1.** to untie **2.** to unravel, to separate the threads of **3.** to decipher, to decode **4.** to solve (problem, puzzle) **5.** (v.n. *fekk*) to sprain, to dislocate **6.** to liberate, to free *huwa ṛ-ṛaʔis lli fekk le-ɛbid.* He is the president who freed the slaves. **7.** to get out, to bail out (of a difficult situation) *ṣɛabu džemɛu*

u-bġaw ifekkuh men l-ḥăbs. His friends got together and tried to bail him out of jail. **8.** to get rid of ≠ *bġa ibiɛ s-siyaṛa u-ma-ṣab-ši lli ifekku mennha.* He wants to sell his car but he can't get rid of it. **9.** to stop from, to make stop (fight, argument) *kanu ka-iddabzu u-ma-bġa ḥădd ifekkhom.* They were fighting and no one cared to make them stop.

fekk **1.** v.n. of *fekk* **2.** jaw (lower)

fekkan v.n. of *fekk*

fekkeṛ **1.** (*f-*) (v.n. *tefkir*) to think (about), to meditate (on) *f-aš ka-ifekkeṛ?* What is he thinking about? **2.** v.t. (v.n. *tefkaṛ*) to remind

fkeṛ f- (v.n. *fkiṛ*) to devise, to conceive

¶ *fkeṛ* (s.th.) (or *fkeṛ f-*) *ɛla* (s.o.) to help (s.o.) get (s.th.), to help (s.o.) obtain (s.th.)

fekra pl. *-t, ʔafkaṛ* **1.** idea, thought **2.** suggestion

fekrun, fekṛun pl. *fkaren, fkaṛen* turtle

fla ifli v.t. (v.n. *fli*) **1.** to delouse **2.** to scrutinize, to peruse

flafel pl. of *felfel, felfla*

flales pl. of *fellus*

flan f. *-a* so-and-so *nfeṛḍu ʔenna weld flan ža ɛăndek.* Let's suppose that so-and-so's son came to see you.

flani used in the expr. *flan le-flani* so-and-so (people)

flayek pl. of *fluka*

flayki pl. *-ya* boatman, ferryman

flayel pl. of *flil*

flaysi pl. *-ya, -yen* venal

flaḥa **1.** v.n. of *felleḥ* 2 **2.** agriculture

flaḥi pl. of *felḥa*

felfel v.t. **1.** to season with red pepper **2.** to add color to (e.g., story)

felfel (f.), *felfla* (coll. and sg.) pl. *felflat, flafel* (dim. *flifla*) red pepper

¶ *felfel xeḍṛa* green pepper

¶ *felfel ḥaṛṛa, felfel sudaniya* hot pepper

¶ *felfel ḥămṛa, felfel ḥluwa* paprika

fli v.n. of *fla*

flifla dim. of *felfel, felfla*

flil pl. *flayel* safety pin

flilles dim. of *fellus*

flisat, fliysat (pl. of *fliyyes*) money

flit v.n. of *flet*

fliyya pennyroyal (type of wild mint)

fellaḥ pl. *-a* farmer, peasant

fellel v.t. to pin, to fasten with a pin

felleq v.t. to hit or injure the head (with a blow)

felles v.t. **1.** to ruin (financially), to make or cause to become poor, to impoverish **2.** to corrupt (morally) **3.** to ruin, to destroy **4.** v.i. to collect things from a junk yard, dump, etc. to sell to others, i.e., to scavenge

¶ part. *mfelles* pl. *-in* **1.** bad, no good, stupid *dak l-film lli šeft mfelles.* That movie I saw was no good. —*huwa ṭalĭb mfelles.* He's a very bad student. **2.** good for nothing, ne'er-do-well **3.** unfortunate, unlucky, jinxed

fellet v.t. **1.** to let escape or get away (opportunity, prisoner, etc.) **2.** to help escape or get away, to save **3.** to make or cause to lose or miss out on *had ṣaḥbi fellet-li waḥed l-biɛa u-šerya mezyana.* This friend of mine made me lose out on a good business deal.

fellus pl. *flales* (dim. *flilles*) chick

felleḥ **1.** v.t., (v.n. *teflaḥ*) to cut, to slash **2.** v.i. (v.n. *flaḥa*) to farm

felq pl. *flaq, fluqa* piece of cut material to be sewn into some piece of clothing (refers only to one of symmetrical right or left pieces)

fles v.i. (v. n. *falas*) to become ruined (financially), to go bankrupt (person or company)

fels pl. *flus* (dim. *fliyyes* pl. *flisat, fliysat*) penny, sou, *ma-ɛăndi ḥetta fels.* I haven't a penny (to my name).

felsa pl. *-t* ruin, bankruptcy (of person or organization)

flet v.i. (v.n. *flit*) **1.** to escape (jail, injury, etc.) **2.** to run or get away

** *flet b-xemsa de-ḍ-ḍulaṛ.* He at least got five dollars out of it.

¶ *falet-luφ* (a.p.) *ɛăqluφ, falet-luφ s-selk, falta-luφ n-neqša* to have a screw loose ≠, to be off one's rocker ≠

felta pl. *-t* n.i. of *flet*

fluka pl. *flayek* rowboat, motor boat, launch

flus (pl.) money

** *flan be-flusu.* so-and-so has money, is rich

¶ *flus ṛqaq* change (money returned)

felža pl. *-t* space (between front teeth)

felḥa pl. *-t, flaḥi* cut, slash, gash

felɛăṣ v.t. to twist (e.g. s.o.'s arm, leg; may also take person as object)

fmaṃ pl. of *fomm*

fṃ̂iyyem dim. of *fomm*

fomm pl. *fmaṃ* (dim. *fṃ̂iyyem*) **1.** mouth (bottle, well, cannon, river, person, etc.) **2.** spout (teakettle)

¶ *fomm ṛumi* false teeth

¶ *ḥetta l-l-fomm* to the top (glass, bottle), to capacity (room) *kanet s-sinima ɛamṛa ḥetta l-l-fomm.* The theater was filled to capacity.

fna ifna v.i. (v.n. *fna*) **1.** to come to an end, to perish, to be destroyed (nation, people) **2.** to have just about had it, to be about "shot" (person, machine)

fna ifni v.t. (v.n. *fna*) to destroy, to make perish, to exterminate (nation, people)
fna (m.) v.n. of *fna*
fnaḍeq pl. of *fenḍeq*
fnaḍqi pl. *-ya* manager of a *fenḍeq*
fnaneš pl. of *fennuš*
fnaṛ pl. *-at, fnayeṛ* 1. flashlight 2. lamp (oil, gas)
fnayeq pl. of *fniq*
fnayeṛ pl. of *fnaṛ*
fenḍeq pl. *fnaḍeq* 1. combination of a livery stable and a place to stay overnight 2. warehouse, building for storage
fniq pl. *fnayeq* kind of metal container for sugar, usually with an accompanying plate on which it rests
fnita dim. of *fent*
fenn pl. *funun* 1. field of study 2. art 3. technique, skill
¶ *fe-l-fenn* just right, expertly, perfectly
fennan adj. pl. *-in* n.pl. *-a* artist (of any of the arts)
fenned v.t. to cover with sugar (pastry), to ice
fenni pl. *-yen* of or pertaining to art
fenniš same as *fennuš*
fennet v.t. to pin, to fasten with a pin
fennuš pl. *fnaneš* hinny (hybrid between a stallion and a she-ass)
fneš f. *fenša* pl. *fenšin, funeš* flat-nosed
fenṭaẓiya 1. part of a celebration in which a number of men ride horses at great speed and fire long-rifles into the air simultaneously 2. airs *had ṛ-ṛažel fih l-fenṭaẓiya bezzaf.* That man puts on airs a lot.
fqayeṣ pl. of *feqṣa*
fqed v.t. (v.n. *fqid*) to lose *fqed* ع*äqlu.* He's lost his mind (gone insane).
feqda n.i. of *fqed*
fqi pl. *feqya, foqya, fuqaha* 1. teacher (in general) 2. adviser or expert in Islamic law 3. learned, erudite
fqid v.n. of *fqed*
fqih same as *fqi*
fqiha pl. *-t* f. of *fqi* in 1 and 2
¶ *ḍaṛ fqiha* Koranic school for little girls
fqiṛ pl. *foqṛa, fuqaṛa* (comp. *fqeṛ*) poor
fqiṣ v.n. of *fqeṣ*
feqqaṣ n.u. *-a* small, elliptical, thin, toasted biscuit made of flour, sesame seeds, and sugar
feqqed v.t. to make or cause to disappear
feqqeh v.t. to teach, to instruct, to explain (usually about the things of life rather than scholarly subjects)
feqqeṛ v.t. to impoverish, to reduce to poverty, to take everything away from (personal subject)
feqqeṣ 1. v.t. to break open (egg) 2. v.t. to lay (eggs) (grasshopper) 3. v.t. to open, to lance (abscess) 4. v.i. to hatch
feqqus same as *feggus*
feqṛ poverty, misery
fqeṛ comp. of *faqiṛ, fqiṛ*
foqṛa pl. of *fqiṛ*
fqeṣ v.t. (v.n. *fqiṣ*) 1. to cause to worry or despair 2. to irritate, to bother
feqṣa pl. *fqayeṣ* sorrow, grief, affliction
** *ka-imut b-le-fqayeṣ u-le-ġdayed.* He's getting extremely irritated.
feqya, foqya pl. of *fqi*
fra ifra v.i. to be or become settled or decided *frat l-qaḍiya.* The matter's been settled.
fra ifri v.t. to settle, to decide
frad pl. of *frid, farid*
frada pl. of *ferdi* 2
fradi pl. of *ferda*
fraḍ pl. of *ferḍ* 5
frafer pl. of *ferfar* and *ferfara*
frag pl. of *ferg*
fraget pl. of *fergaṭa*
fraġ used in the expr. *weqt le-fraġ* leisure time
frami pl. of *ferma*
fran pl. *-at* brake (refers to the pedal or lever as well as the mechanism in the wheel).
fṛanṣa France
fṛanṣawi pl. *-yen* 1. French 2. Frenchman
fṛanṣiṣ (coll.) (the) French
fṛaq 1. v.n. of *faṛeq* and *fṛeq* 2. separation, state of being separated *le-fṛaq ṣ*ع*ib.* Being separated is hard (to take).
fṛaqeš pl. of *feṛqeš, feṛquš*
frara pl. *-t* milk scum
fṛaṛen pl. of *feṛṛan*
fṛaṛni pl. *-ya* one who runs the public ovens for baking
fṛaṛeš pl. of *feṛṛaša*
fṛaṛež pl. of *feṛṛuž*
fṛaṣed pl. of *feṛṣaḍa*
fṛaš pl. *-at* bed (i.e., s.th. to sleep on)
fṛašeṭ pl. of *feṛšiṭa*
fratel pl. of *fertala*
fratet pl. of *fertuta*
fṛaṭeṣ pl. of *feṛṭaṣ*
fṛax pl. of *feṛx*
fṛaxi pl. of *feṛxa*
frayed pl. of *friḍa*
frayes pl. of *frisa*
fṛayež pl. of *fṛaža*
fṛaža pl. *-t, fṛayež* show, spectacle, entertainment (quite general)
fraح, fraحat pl. of *ferح* 2.
fraعna pl. of *fir*ع*äwn*
ferd f. *ferdiya* one (of a pair, as pigeons)
¶ *ferd aw žuž* odd or even
ferda pl. *-t, fradi* one (of a pair of things),

unit *fayn l-ferda l-oxṛa de-ṣ-ṣebbaṭ dyali?* Where's my other shoe?

ferdi 1. pl. *-yen* alone, solitary (i.e., without its mate) 2. pl. *frada* revolver, pistol

¶ *ferdi men ʕăyn* pl. *ferdiyen men ʕăyn* one-eyed

ferdiya f. of *ferd*

fṛeḍ v.i. (v.n. *feṛḍ*) to suppose, to imagine *fṛeḍ ʔennana šrina had l-ḥanut daba, ma-ġad-ibqaw-lna-š le-flus baš nbiʕu u-nešriw.* Suppose we buy the store now; then we won't have the money for doing business.

¶ *fṛeḍ ʕla* to impose upon *ma-tefṛeḍ-š ʕliya ʔiṛadtek!* Don't impose your will on me!

feṛḍ pl. *fṛuḍ, fuṛuḍ* 1. v.n. of *fṛeḍ* 2. obligation, duty (religious) 3. alimony (divorce cases) 4. supposition, hypothesis 5. pl. *fṛuḍa, fṛaḍ* beam, rafter

ferfar pl. *frafer* propeller (airplane)

ferfara pl. *-t, frafer* (dim. *frifra*) pinwheel

ferfer v.i. 1. to flap wings (repetitive) 2. to flutter (as a butterfly) 3. to flit, to fly (as a bird from tree to tree) 4. to take off (bird) 5. to flap, to wave (as a flag) 6. to rustle (leaves, cloth), to swish (cloth)

¶ *ferfer be-ḍ-ḍeḥk* to giggle

feṛfeṭ v.t. and v.i. to flap, to flutter (e.g., bird, butterfly, etc.)

ferg pl. *frag* 1. flock (birds) 2. herd (horses) 3. swarm (bees)

feṛgaṭa pl. *-t, fṛageṭ* warship, naval vessel

feṛgăʕ v.t. 1. to detonate, to explode, to set off (bomb, etc.) 2. to cause to burst (as a balloon)

fṛeġ (v.n. *fṛiġ*) 1. v.t. to empty 2. v.i. to become empty

frid pl. *frad* 1. same as *farid* 2. alone, solitary (without a mate)

¶ *frid f-nuʕu* (the) only one of its kind

fṛiḍa pl. *fṛayeḍ* 1. obligation, duty (religious) 2. alimony (divorce cases)

frifra dim. of *ferfara*

fṛiġ v.n. of *fṛeġ*

frik 1. v.n. of *frek* 2. n.u. *-a* small, green, sour fruit

frim v.n. of *frem*

fṛina pl. *-t* kiln

fris v.n. of *fres*

frisa pl. *frayes* 1. prey, quarry (already caught) 2. carrion

frišk fresh (perishable foods)

frizi a haircut or hairdo in the European style

friž pl. *-in* in pleasant surroundings, with a beautiful view, beautifully situated (e.g. a cottage)

friʕ v.n. of *frăʕ*

frek v.t. (v.n. *frik*) to rub or scrub (clothes by hand)

ferkel v.i. 1. to struggle or squirm (in an effort to escape) 2. to twitch or jerk (as in the throes of death, or a fit)

ferket v.t. 1. to crumble (up) (bread, etc.) 2. to tear or make into little pieces (paper, etc.)

frem v.t. (v.n. *frim*) 1. to notch, to chip (glass, wood) 2. to snag (cloth)

ferma pl. *-t, frami* 1. lump (sugar) 2. cut, notch, chipped place (in wood, porcelain, etc.) 3. harelip

feṛmasyan pl. *-at* pharmacist

fermli pl. *-ya,* f. *fermliya* pl. *-t* nurse (medical)

feṛnatši 1. place where water is heated for the public bath 2. pl. *-ya* one who tends the *feṛnatši,* 1 above

fṛenk pl. *-at* (pl. used to denote the coins) 1. franc 2. one-hundredth of a *derhem*

fernes v.i. to grin

fṛeq (v.n. *fṛaq*) 1. v.t. to separate 2. v.t. to share 3. to change, to give change for (e.g. a ten-dollar bill for ones)

¶ *fṛeq bin* 1. to distinguish between 2. to decide (s.th. for two parties) *ṭḷeb men ḅḅah ifṛeq ma binu u-bin xah.* He asked his father to decide the issue between him and his brother.

feṛq difference, distinction *šnuwa l-feṛq ma bin had ž-žuž de-ṣ-ṣiniyat?* What's the difference between these two trays?

feṛqa pl. *-t* 1. team (sports) 2. gang (work) 3. group (people) 4. detachment (military) 5. part (hair) 6. troupe, cast (actors)

feṛqeš, feṛquš pl. *fṛaqeš* hoof

ferradi pl. *-yen* alone, solitary (without its mate)

¶ *be-l-ferradi* retail *ka-ibiʕ be-l-žumla u-be-l-ferradi.* He sells wholesale and retail.

feṛṛan pl. *fṛaṛen* 1. public oven where people bring their bread to be baked 2. oven

feṛṛaq pl. *-a* ag. n. of *feṛṛeq*

¶ *feṛṛaq le-bṛawat* postman

feṛṛaša pl. *-t, fṛaṛeš* insole (shoe)

ferred v.t. to change (money) *ferred-li had l-ʕăšṛa de-d-drahem, baṛek ḷḷahu fik.* Please change this ten-dirham bill for me.

¶ p.p. *mferred* alone, by oneself

feṛṛeġ v.t. 1. to empty, to take everything out of 2. to pour (s.th.)

ferrek v.t. to shell (peas)

feṛṛeq v.t. 1. to spread (apart) 2. to distribute, to hand out 3. to divide (up) 4. to break up, to disperse, to scatter (as a crowd) 5. to distinguish (between), to separate (mentally) *ma-neqḍeṛ-š nfeṛṛeqhom* (or *nfeṛṛeq binathom*). I can't separate them (in my mind) ; I can't distinguish between them. 6. to change, to give change for (as a ten-dollar bill for ones)

  ** *feṛṛqu had l-musem!* All right, break it up !

feṛṛeš 1. to furnish (a room) 2. to lay down, to spread out (s.th. to sit or sleep on) 3. to make the bed

  ¶ *feṛṛeš* (s.th.) *b-* to pave (s.th.) with, to lay (s.th.) with

feṛṛeṭ f- to neglect

feṛṛuž pl. *fṛaṛež* rooster, cock

feṛṛex v.i. 1. to hatch 2. to have or hatch young

feṛṛez v.t. 1. to make out, to distinguish (as handwriting) 2. to explain, to clarify

  ¶ *ferrez bin* to distinguish between

feṛṛež v.t. to entertain, to give a show for

  ¶ *feṛṛež Ɛla* to relieve (of pain, etc.) *had d-dwa feṛṛež Ɛliya men le-ʒṛiq lli kan fiya.* This medicine relieved me of my pain.

  ** *llah iferṛež Ɛlik!* I hope things get better soon (for you). —*ṛebbi iferṛež Ɛlih men l-ʒābs.* I hope he gets out of prison.

feṛṛeʒ v.t. to cheer up, to make happy

fres v.t. (v.n. *fris*) to devour (animal or like an animal)

foṛs n.pl. of *farisi*

  ¶ *blad l-foṛs* Persia

foṛsan pl. of *fares*

feṛṣada pl. *-t, fṛaṣed* 1. front, façade (of a building) 2. blanket (as a wool army blanket)

feṛša pl. *-t* layer (of mortar, tile, bricks, eggs, etc.)

ferši cork (material)

feršiṭa pl. *-t, fṛašeṭ* (table) fork

feršiya pl. *-t* cork (bottle, etc.)

feršex v.t. 1. to break up or crush with blows 2. to give a beating to

fertala pl. *-t, fratel* round cushion made of esparto, used as a seat

ferteq v.t. to rip apart at the seams, to unseam forcefully (clothing)

fertšex same as *feršex*

fertuta pl. *fratet* 1. crumb (bread, etc.) 2. small piece (of food)

ferṭaṣ pl. *fṛaṭeṣ* (adj. and n.) 1.(one) with the sides of his head shaven 2. having no horns (sheep, goat, etc.)

  ** *huwa qṛăƐ ferṭaṣ.* He's infested with ringworm (or similar disease of the scalp).

ferṭiṭu pl. *-yat* butterfly

fertet v.i. 1. to struggle and flutter (as a butterfly trying to escape captivity) 2. to shake itself (as a dog drying itself)

fṛud pl. of *ferḍ*

fṛuḍa pl. of *ferḍ* 5

fṛuxa pl. of *ferx*

fṛuž, fṛuža pl. of *ferž*

fṛuʒ pl. of *ferʒ* 1

ferx f. *ferxa* pl. *fṛax, fṛuxa* 1. young of an animal or fowl 2. young man, adolescent 3. type of round, tall basket used in carrying figs, mulberries, etc.

ferxa pl. *-t, fraxi* 1. lock (door) 2. young girl (implies strong and healthy)

frez v.t. 1. (*bin*) to distinguish (between), to tell (apart) 2. to sort (out)

ferz used in the expr. *Ɛmel l-ferz, fihɸ l-ferz* to be partial (≠ latter)

ferziya pl. *-t* same as *ferz*

ferž pl. *fṛuž, fṛuža* female genitals (external)

freʒ v.i. (v.n. *ferʒ*) to be happy, content, or glad

  ¶ *freʒ b-* 1. to be happy or glad about (s.th.) 2. to give a warm welcome to, to receive warmly 3. to show happiness on seeing (s.o.) 4. to play with (as with a baby)

ferʒ 1. v.n. of *freʒ* 2. joy, cheerfulness 3. pl. *fṛaʒ, fṛaʒat* celebration (usually family)

ferʒa n.i. of *freʒ*

  ¶ *be-l-ferʒa* gladly, willingly

ferʒan pl. *-in* happy, glad, content *ana ferʒan bezzaf b-ḍaṛi ž-ždida.* I'm quite happy with my new house.

fṛăƐ v.t. (v.n. *friƐ*) to smash, to break up or in (box, door, etc.)

ferƐ 1. pl. *fṛuƐ* branch (tree) 2. pl. *fuṛuƐ* branch (bank, agency)

  ¶ *ṭḷeq le-fṛuƐ* (or *l-fuṛuƐ*) to branch out (tree, agency, etc.)

fsa ifsi v.i. (v.n. *fsu*) to break wind noiselessly

fsad v.n. of *fsed*

fsed (v.n. *fsad*) 1. v.t. to spoil, to ruin (machine, business, relations, etc.) 2. v.t. to corrupt, to pervert, to debase 3. v.i. to break down (car, business, etc.) 4. v.i. to spoil, to rot (food)

  ¶ *fsed f-* to have sexual intercourse with (a girl)

  ¶ f. a.p. *fasda* pl. *-t* prostitute

fsix v.n. of *fsex*

fseq v.i. (v.n. *fsuq*) to lead a sensual, debauched life

  ¶ a.p. *faseq* adj. pl. *-in* n.pl. *fossaq* depraved

fesser v.t. 1. to explain 2. to define

festeq n.u. *-a* pistachio (nut or plant)

fsu v.n. of *fsa*

fsuq v.n. of *fseq*

fsuxa pl. of *fsex*

fsex v.t. (v.n. *fesx, fsix*) 1. to untie, to undo 2. to annul, to make void (contract) 3. to repeal, to revoke (law) 4. to skin (an animal)

fesx 1. v.n. of *fsex* 2. annulment, revocation

fsex pl. *fsuxa* snake skin (shed)
fesya pl. *-t* n.i. of *fsa*
fesyan pl. *-at* **1.** lieutenant (rank) **2.** officer (military)
fṣal v.n. of *faṣel* and *fṣel* **1.** v.n. of *fèṣṣel* **2.** pl. *-t, fṣayel* plan (architecture) **3.** pl. *-t, fṣayel* form, shape
¶*bla fṣala* poorly designed, in bad taste
fṣayel pl. of *fṣala* 2 and 3
fṣiḥ pl. *-in* (comp. *fṣeḥ*) eloquent
fṣel v.t. (v.n. *fṣal*) to separate, to take apart
¶ *fṣel* (s.th.) *bin* to settle (s.th.) between (as an argument)
feṣl, fṣel pl. *fṣul* **1.** season (yearly, hunting, etc.) **2.** article (e.g., in a written constitution) **3.** chapter (book) **4.** act (play)
feṣṣ pl. *fṣuṣ* yolk (egg)
feṣṣa alfalfa, lucern
feṣṣel v.t. (v.n. *fṣala*) **1.** to cut (out) (e.g. material for a dress) **2.** to cut up, to divide into sections (meat by a butcher)
fṣul pl. of *feṣl, fṣel*
fṣuṣ pl. of *feṣṣ*
fṣeḥ comp. of *fṣiḥ*
fosḥa (with art.) classical Arabic
fšil v.n. of *fšel*
fšel v.i. (v.n. *fašal, fšil*) **1.** to fail, to be a failure, to not succeed **2.** to become disheartened or discouraged
fešš v.t. (v.n. *feššan*) **1.** to deflate (e.g. a balloon) **2.** to relieve (s.o. of some anxiety)
feššan v.n. of *fešš*
feššel v.t. to dishearten, to discourage
feššeš v.t. (v.n. *fšuš*) to spoil, to pamper
fšuš v.n. of *feššeš*
¶ *fihφ le-fšuš* to be spoiled ≠ (s.o.)
fta ifta v.i. (v.n. *ftawa*) to become tender (food)
fta ifti v.t. (v.n. *ftu, fetyan*) to dictate (as a letter)
¶ *fta ṛeyy ɛla* to advise, to give counsel to
¶ *fta ɛla* to judge between, to render a judgment between *mšaw ɛănd l-qaḍi ifti ɛlihom.* They went to receive the judge's opinion.
fta comp. of *fti*
ftaqi pl. of *fetqiya*
ftata pl. *-t, ftayet* crumb (bread, cake)
ftawa v.n. of *fta*
ftawi pl. of *fetwa*
ftaxeṛ (*b-*) to be proud (of), to have pride (in)
ftayel pl. of *ftila*
ftayen pl. of *fetna*
ftayet pl. of *ftata*
fti pl. *-yen* (comp. *fta*) **1.** tender (meat, bread) **2.** reasonable in selling, giving a good deal (to buyers)
ftil v.n. of *ftel*
ftila pl. *ftayel* wick (candle, etc.)
ftin v.n. of *ften*
ftiq v.n. of *fteq*
ftiḥ v.n. of *fteḥ*
ftel v.t. (v.n. *ftil*) **1.** to roll (e.g. a cigaret, small piece of dough for *seksu,* etc.) **2.** to braid, to plait, to cord (string, thread)
ften v.t. (v.n. *fatăn, ftin*) **1.** to pester, to bother, to disturb **2.** to incite, to agitate (to riot, revolt, etc.) **3.** to bewitch, to dazzle (as one's beauty) *l-žamal dyalha ka-iften ɛibad ḷḷah.* Her beauty has dazzled everyone.
fetna pl. *-t, ftayen* **1.** n.i. of *ften* **2.** state of agitation, rioting **3.** brawl, free-for-all **4.** revolution, revolt
¶ *nuwweḍ fetna* to raise a commotion, "to raise the roof"
¶ *nuwweḍ l-fetna* **1.** to agitate, to incite a riot **2.** to incite or foment revolt
fteq v.t. (v.n. *ftiq*) to unsew, to unseam, to rip apart at the seam
fteq hernia
fetqiya pl. *-t, ftaqi* **1.** s.th. used to patch a hole (usually wooden) **2.** board used in boarding up a door (permanently)
fteṛ v.i. (v.n. *fetṛan*) to stop (rain)
fter pl. *ftura* measurement from the tip of the index finger to tip of the thumb of the open hand
fetṛan v.n. of *fteṛ*
fettaḥ used in the expr. *ya-fettaḥ* said at the beginning of some action to invoke the help of God
fetteš v.t. to search, to make a search of, to inspect
¶ *fetteš f-* same as *fetteš* above
¶ *fetteš ɛla* to look for, to be in search of
fettet v.t. to crumb, to break into tiny pieces (bread)
fetteḥ v.i. **1.** to recite the *fatiḥa* **2.** to blossom, to bloom (flowers)
ftu v.n. of *fta ifti*
ftura pl. of *fter*
ftuḥ pl. *-at* **1.** kind of down payment given to a *fqi* for providing a *ḥerz*
** *hada ġir le-ftuḥ!* This is only the beginning!
fetwa pl. *-t, ftawi* **1.** authoritative opinion or decision on matters judicial or religious
fetya n.i. of *fta* (in *fta ɛla;* see *fta ifti*)
fetyan v.n. of *fta ifti*
fteḥ (v.n. *ftiḥ*) **1.** v.t. to open (usually when what is opened is connected as a door) **2.** v.i. to open (as a flower) **3.** v.t. to start, to open, to go into (business, etc.) **4.** v.t. to start, to initiate (ceremony) *fteḥ l-ḥefla b-waḥed l-xoṭba.* He opened the proceedings with a speech. **5.** v.t. to operate on

(surgery) **6.** v.t. to conquer (country, city, etc.) **7.** v.i. to recite the *fatiḥa*

** *l-beqrež fteḥ.* The kettle's boiling. —*fteḥ ɛlih llah* He's had some good luck (after having bad luck).

¶ p.p. *meftuḥ* pl. *-in* light (in color)

fetḥa pl. *-t* **1.** n.i. of *fteḥ* **2.** opening, hole (e.g. in a wall, fence, armhole in a robe)

fṭa used in the expr. *bin fṭa u-hwa* in the air, in mid-air

fṭana intelligence, quick-wittedness

fṭaṛ pl. of *fṭiṛ*

feṭfeṭ same as *feṛfeṭ*

fṭim v.n. of *fṭem*

fṭin v.n. of *fṭen*

fṭiṛ pl. *fṭaṛ* said of bread that has not risen in the baking for some reason or other

fṭem (v.n. *fṭim*) to wean

fṭen b- (v.n. *fṭin*) to find out about, to learn of, to become aware of

¶ a.p. *faṭen* pl. *-in* intelligent, alert

fṭeṛ v.i. (v.n. *fṭuṛ*) **1.** to break (the) fast **2.** to have breakfast, to breakfast

feṭṛa alms of grain distributed to the poor on *l-ɛid ṣ-ṣġiṛ*

feṭṭeṛ v.t. **1.** to feed or give (s.o.) breakfast **2.** to cause to break *ṣ-ṣyam*

fṭuṛ **1.** v.n. of *fṭeṛ* **2.** pl. *-at* breakfast

ful n.u. *-a* fava bean, horsebean

funun pl. of *fenn*

funeš pl. of *fneš*

fuq **1.** on, upon *ḥeṭṭ had ṣ-ṣenduq fuq ṭ-ṭebla!* Put this box on the table! —*fayn konnaši?* —*fuq l-meṛfăɛ.* Where's my notebook?— On the shelf. **2.** above, over *l-qeṛṭaṣa dazet fuq ṛaṣi.* The bullet passed over my head. —*ɛălleq z-zaža fuq ṭ-ṭebla!* Hang the lamp over the table!

¶ *fuq-aš* when (interrogative), at what time

¶ *fuq-aš-emma* every time (that), each time (that), whenever

¶ *fuq men* over, above (especially with verbs of motion)

¶ *l-fuq* **1.** upstairs *ṛah l-fuq.* He's up stairs. **2.** on top, at the top

¶ *men fuq* from, off *rfedt le-ktab men fuq ṭ-ṭebla.* I took the book off the table.

¶ *men fuq had š-ši* moreover, besides

¶ *men l-fuq* **1.** from above **2.** in addition to

fuqaha pl. of *fqi*

fuqani pl. *-yen* upper (room, etc.)

fuqaṛa pl. of *faqiṛ, fqiṛ*

fuqi **1.** pl. *fwaqa* second floor (building) **2.** pl. *-yen* upper (room, etc.)

fuqiya pl. *-t* a sheer, usually white, over-garment

fuṛat (with art.) Euphrates (river)

fuṛuḍ pl. of *feṛḍ*

fuṛusiya horseback riding, equitation

fuṛuɛ pl. of *feṛɛ* **2**

furyan pl. *-at* pound (dog, etc.)

fuṣaḥa n.pl. of *faṣiḥ*

fuṭa pl. *-t, fweṭ* towel (often used as napkin)

fuwwaqa (coll. and sg.) pl. *-t* hiccup(s) *žatu l-fuwwaqa.* He has the hiccups.

fuwwaṛa pl. *-t* geyser (natural)

fuwweḍ v.t. to delegate (authority, power)

fuwweh v.t. to cause or make yawn

fuwweṛ **1.** v.t. to steam (food) **2.** v.i. to steam, to give off steam or vapor

fuwwež v.i. to relax, to divert oneself (by taking a walk, etc.)

¶ *fuwwež ɛla* to entertain, to amuse, to divert (s.o.)

fuyaq when, at what time (rare usage)

fuzan v.n. of *faz*

fužuṛ dissoluteness

fuḥan v.n. of *faḥ*

fwad viscera

fwaqa pl. of *fuqi* **1**

fwaṛ **1.** v.n. of *faṛ* **2.** steam, vapor

fwaṛež pl. of *faṛažiya*

fwateḥ pl. of *fatḥa*

fwinda dim. of *fanida* (n.u. of *fanid*)

fwiyyeṛ dim. of *faṛ*

fweṭ pl. of *fuṭa*

fxaḍ pl. of *fexḍ*

fxax pl. of *fexx*

fexḍ pl. *fxaḍ* thigh

fxeṛ v.i. (v.n. *fexṛ*) to boast, to brag

fxeṛ comp. of *faxeṛ*

fexṛ v.n. of *fxeṛ*

fexx pl. *fxax* **1.** trap **2.** ambush

fexxaṛ **1.** (no pl.) ceramic ware, pottery **2.** pl. *-a* potter

fexxem v.t. to velarize, to render emphatic (i.e., pronounce *t* as *ṭ*, *s* as *ṣ*, etc.)

fyal pl. of *fil*

fyalel pl. of *filil, filila*

fyaq **1.** v.n. of *faq* **2.** wakefulness

fyaqa **1.** v.n. of *faq* **2.** intelligence, quick-wittedness

fyateṛ pl. of *fituṛa*

fzag wetness, dampness

fzeg v.i. (v.n. *fzig*) to get or be wet, damp

¶ a.p. *fazeg* pl. *-in* wet, damp

fzig v.n. of *fzeg*

fziɛ v.n. of *fzăɛ*

fezzeg v.t. to wet, to dampen

fzăɛ v.t. (v.n. *fziɛ*) to frighten, to scare

fezɛa n.i. of *fzăɛ*

fžiṛ v.n. of *fžeṛ*

fžel n.u. *fežla* cpl. *fžulat* radish

¶ *fžel le-xla* horse-radish

¶ *klam le-fžel* **1.** sarcastic remark **2.** flattery, soft-soap *fžeṛ* v.i. (v.n. *fžiṛ*) **1.** to open up, to burst open *d-demmala fežṛet.* The boil has opened up. **2.** to corrupt, to become corrupt (morally)

fžer **1.** dawn **2.** dawn prayer

¶ *ṣlat le-fžer* dawn prayer

fžulat cpl. of *fžel*

fežwa pl. *-t* patch or area of blue sky (sometimes extended to the entire unclouded sky)

fežžel l- **1.** to make sarcastic remarks to **2.** to flatter, to soft-soap

fežžeṛ v.t. **1.** to open, to lance (boil, blister) **2.** to detonate (bomb, dynamite charge, etc.)

fežžež v.t. to take for a walk or on a tour, to show around, to take for a ride *ġedda ġad-nfežžež ḍ-ḍyaf dyali f-le-mdina ḥit ma-xeddam-š.* Tomorrow I'll take my guests around town since I'm not going to be working.

¶ part. *mfežžež* pl. *-in* having a nice view *had l-maḥăll mfežžež.* This place has a nice view.

f-ḥal see *ḥal*

fḥăl pl. *fḥul, fḥula* **1.** stallion **2.** vigorous

fḥăm n.u. *feḥma* cpl. *fḥumat* charcoal

foḥš immorality, debauchery

fḥul, fḥula pl. of *fḥăl*

fḥula, fḥuliya virility, manly vigor

fḥumat cpl. of *fḥăm*

feḥḥam pl. *-a* coal-merchant

fɛal pl. of *făɛl*

ˀefɛal pl. of *fiɛl*

fɛayel pl. of *făɛla*

fɛăl used in the expr.:

¶ *fɛăl f-* to rape, to molest sexually

¶ *fɛăl u-trek* to do great harm

¶ *faɛel* (a.p.) *tarek* pl. *faɛlin tarkin* excellent, first-class, tops

făɛl pl. *fɛal* **1.** action, act **2.** (in pl.) conduct, behavior

** *daba ilqa făɛlu.* He'll get his just deserts.

făɛla pl. *fɛayel* foul act or action, dirty trick

făɛfăɛ v.t. to shake, to jiggle (e.g., a table)

G

gabel v.t. **1.** to take care of, to take or be in charge of, to attend, to tend to *gabel ḍ-ḍyaf!* Take care of the guests. **2.** to face, to be in front of *ḍaṛna mgabla ž-žameɛ.* Our house faces the mosque.

gabel (with art.) refers to the next or coming Ramadan

gadd pl. *-in* capable, able, resourceful

¶ *gadd b-ṛaṣu*$^{\phi}$ capable or able to take care of oneself

gadum pl. *gwadem* same as *qadum*

gafla pl. *-t, gwafel* caravan

gal same as *qal*

gala same as *qala*

gales a.p. of *gles*

gama same as *qama*

gamila pl. *-t, gwamel* **1.** small sauce pan **2.** mess kit, mess tin (military)

gamus pl. *gwames* (water) buffalo

gana patience, good humor *ma-ɛăndu gana mɛa d-drari.* He has no patience with children.

¶ *ɛla gantu*$^{\phi}$ in a good mood or humor *l-yum huwa ɛla gantu.* He's in a good mood today.

** *kollha u-gantu.* To each his own (way, manner, disposition). Everybody to his own taste.

gaṛa pl. *-t* large vacant area or yard, esplanade

gaṛanṭiya pl. *-t* guarantee (commercial)

gaṛaž pl. *-at* garage (parking and repair)

gaṛfu pl. *-wat* (table) fork

gaṛṛu pl. *-wat, -yat* cigaret

gaṛṣun pl. *gṛaṣen* **1.** waiter **2.** shorts (underwear)

gaṛṣuna pl. *-t* waitress

gareḥ pl. *-in* (dim. *gwireḥ*) decrepit, old and infirm

gaṭeɛ pl. *-in* adult (sheep)

gayla **1.** burning noontime sun (summer) **2.** siesta time **3.** same as *qayla*

gayza pl. *-t, gwayez* beam (construction), timber, (sometimes a kind of supporting plank)

gaz same as *daz*

gaz **1.** (also *zit l-gaz*) kerosene **2.** gas (e.g., natural gas)

gazița pl. *-t, gwazeț* newspaper

gazuza pl. *-t* soft drink (carbonated)

gaža f- to join, to sign up for (army) *gaža fe-l-ɛăskeṛ.* He joined the army.

gaɛ **1.** all *gaɛ le-ḥwayež lli ɛăndi balyen.* All my clothes are worn out. **2.** at all (with negative phrase) *gaɛ ma-ka-nebġih.* I don't like him at all.

¶ *gaɛ lli* all (those) who, everyone who, anybody that, whoever *gaɛ lli žaw fe-l-mašina weṣḷu mɛăṭṭḷin.* All those who came on the train arrived late.

¶ *gaɛ waḥed* the same, alike *huma gaɛ waḥed.* They're alike.

** *gaɛ waḥed!* It's all the same (to me).

gaḥa pl. *-t, gyăḥ* threshing area (wheat)

gbaḍi pl. of *gebḍa*
gbala same as *qbala*
gebbaṣ pl. *-a* plasterer
gebbaعi, gobbaعi (no *pl.*) **1.** a rhythmic clapping of the hands **2.** a volley of oaths
gebbel *عla* to appear before, to come near, to come to (generally used in statements of warning) *ila عawed gebblet عliya ṛ-ana nxerrežha.* If she come to me again I'll throw her out.
gebbeṣ v.t. to plaster
gbeḍ same as *qbeḍ*
gebḍa same as *qebḍa*
gbila same as *qbayla*
gebṣ pl. *gbuṣat* (pl. of intensity) **1.** plaster **2.** chalk, gypsum
gbuṣat pl. of *gebṣ*
gda igdi v.i. (v.n. *gdi*) **1.** to become incandescent from burning (as coal) **2.** v.t. to light (a fire)
gdam pl. of *gdem*
gdawer pl. of *gedwar*
gedd same as *qedd*
gedd shallow place or spot (as in a river) that can be crossed on foot; ford
goddam, geddam same as *qoddam*
goddami pl. *-yen* foreword, placed in front
gedded v.t. **1.** to cut into strips (meat) **2.** to prepare *geddid* **3.** to gnaw on (as a bone)
geddid a type of meat preserves in strips, smoked meat
geddem v.t. **1.** to step on, to stomp **2.** to run over (car, bicycle, etc.)
gdi v.n. of *gda*
gdem pl. *gdam* heel (shoe and foot)
gedmiya pl. *-t* heel (shoe)
gedra pl. *-t, gdur* **1.** type of clay pot used in cooking **2.** folk dance of southern Morocco
gdur pl. of *gedra*
gedwar pl. *gdawer* old piece of cloth, rag
gfa same as *qfa*
geffeṭ v.t. to roll up (sleeves, etc.)
ghim v.n. of *ghem*
ghem v.t. (v.n. *ghim*) to fill (up), to cloy, to surfeit, to take away the appetite (e.g., rich food)
gid pl. *gyad* guide (tourist)
gidun pl. *-at* **1.** handle bar (bicycle, motorcycle, etc.) **2.** handle, grip (e.g., lawn mower, bicycle)
giṭun pl. *-at, gyaṭen* tent
giyyed v.t. to lure, to entice (with some deception as to purpose)
giyyel v.i. to rest or nap during hottest time of day (country folk)
giyyeع same as *qiyyeع*
giع same as *qiع*
gla same as *qla*
glales pl. of *gellas* 2
glas **1.** v.n. of *gles* **2.** idleness
glasi pl. of *gelsa*
glati pl. of *gelta*
gleb v.t. (v.n. *glib*) **1.** same as *qleb* **2.** to turn over, to upset, to turn upside down **3.** to loosen, to break up (the ground)
  ** *leh-la igleb bik!* I couldn't care less (what you do); To hell with you then!; I wash my hands of the whole thing (expr. used after attempting to give help or advice to s.o. who refuses it).
gelb pl. *glub* same as *qelb*
gelba **1.** n.i. of *gleb*
  ¶ *faq men l-gelba* to wake up, to become aware
gelgel v.t. to gargle with
glib v.n. of *gleb*
gliع v.n. of *glăع* (same as *gellăع*) and *gellăع*
glel pl. of *golla* (same as *qolla*)
golla pl. *glel* same as *qolla*
gellas **1.** pl. *-a* manager or superintendent of a public bath (for men) **2.** pl. *glales* chamber pot
gellasa pl. *-t* manager or superintendent (f.) of a public bath (for women).
gellasiya pl. *-t* kind of clay jug
gellay adj. pl. *-in* n.pl. *-a* ag. adj. and n. of *gla*
gelleb same as *qleb*
gelles v.t. **1.** to cause or make to sit **2.** to show to a seat, to have (s.o.) sit **3.** to have or make stay *gellesnah عăndna ṛebع iyyam.* We had him stay with us for four days. **4.** to have or make sit up (in bed, etc.) **5.** to straighten up, to set up straight, to put on end
gellet v.i. to stagnate (water)
gellăع v.t. (v.n. *gliع*) to pull out, to extricate, to uproot (same as *qellăع*)
gles v.i. (v.n. *glas*) **1.** to sit (down) **2.** to stay *gles عăndi telt iyyam.* He stayed three days with me.
  ¶ a.p. *gales* pl. *-in* **1.** living, staying *hadi sebع iyyam w-ana gales عănd عămmi.* I've been staying with my uncle for a week now. **2.** idle, out of work
gelsa, golsa pl. *-t, glasi* **1.** n.i. of *gles* **2.** dressing room of the public bath **3.** session (court, conference, etc.) **4.** sitting posture or position **5.** kind of cushion used as a seat
gelta pl. *-t, glati* pond, puddle (usually of rain water)
glub pl. of *gelb* (same as *qelb*)
gelya same as *qelya*
glăع (v.n. *gliع*) same as *qellăع*
gmagem pl. of *gemgum, gemguma*
gmaṛi pl. of *gemṛa*
gmaṭ pl. *gmayeṭ* diaper

gmayeṭ pl. of *gmaṭ*
gemgam pl. *-in* one who grumbles, complains
gemgem **1.** v.i., to grumble, to complain **2.** v.t., to mumble (s.th.) **3.** v.t. and v.i. to stutter
gemgum, gemguma pl. *gmagem* snout, muzzle, nose
gmim lead (metal)
gmiṛa dim. of *gemṛa*
gmel same as *qmel*
gemmel v.i. to become infested or covered with lice (same as *qemmel*)
gemmeṭ v.t. to put diapers on, to wrap in swaddling clothes
gomna pl. *-t* cable
gemṛa pl. *gmaṛi* (dim. *gmiṛa*) **1.** moon **2.** moonlight
** *gmaṛi hadi!* What beautiful moonlight! —*le-gmaṛi našṛa fe-z-znaqi.* Moonlight is flooding the streets.
gemḥ wheat
gnaber pl. of *genbri* and *genbura*
gnafed pl. of *genfud*
gnaṭeṛ pl. of *genṭṛa* (same as *qenṭṛa*)
gnawa pl. of *gnawi*
gnawi pl. *gnawa* **1.** member (negro) of the *gnawa* brotherhood **2.** used in describing one in a rage or temper tantrum.
¶ *ful gnawa* black-eyed peas
gnayez pl. of *gnaza*
gnaza pl. *gnayez* funeral
genbri pl. *gnaber* small, banjo-like instrument of two and sometimes three strings
genbura pl. *-t, gnaber* jug
gondaya pl. *-t* **1.** crest or tuft of hair **2.** crest (of rooster)
gnef v.i. (v.n. *gnif*) to get angry, to get upset *gnef ɛliya ɛla ḥeqq-aš ma-xdemt-š l-bareḥ.* He got angry with me because I didn't work yesterday.
genfud pl. *gnafed* hedgehog (Erinaceus)
¶ *genfud le-bḥăṛ* sea urchin, sea hedgehog
geng pl. *gnug, gnuga* blow with the head, butt
gnif v.n. of *gnef*
gniṭṛa same as *qniṭṛa*
gnen pl. of *gonna*
gonna pl. *-t, gnen* **1.** summit (mountain) **2.** crown of the head
gennef v.t. to provoke, to pester
gens pl. *gnus* **1.** race, people, nation **2.** breed (animal)
genṭṛa pl. *gnaṭeṛ* same as *qenṭṛa*
gnug, gnuga pl. of *geng*
gnus pl. of *gens*
gṛaḍi pl. of *geṛḍa*
gṛam pl. *-at* gram
gṛameṭ pl. of *geṛmaṭ* and *geṛmaṭa*
gṛan pl. of *gṛin*
gṛaṣen pl. of *gaṛṣun*
gṛaṭeṭ pl. of *geṛṭiṭ*
gṛaweṭ pl. of *geṛwaṭ*
gṛayeḥ pl. of *gṛiḥa* (same as *qṛiḥa*)
gṛayḥi pl. *-ya* type of singer of simple tunes, often extemporaneously invented
gražem pl. of *geržuma*
gṛažeṭ pl. of *geṛžuṭa* (same as *geržuma*)
greb pl. of *gerba*
gerba pl. *-t, greb* goatskin for carrying water
gerdăɛ v.t. to knock down (s.o.)
goṛḍ kind of pasture grass
geṛḍa pl. *-t, gṛaḍi* **1.** chopping block (butcher) **2.** piece (bread, meat, cloth, etc.)
gergaɛ n.u. *-a* **1.** walnut **2.** walnut tree
gergef v.t. to guzzle down all in one draught
grig n.pl. of *grigi*
grigi adj. pl. *-yen* n.pl. *grig* Greek
¶ *blad le-grig* Greece
gṛiḥa pl. *gṛayeḥ* same as *qṛiḥa*
gṛin v.n. of *gṛen*
gṛiṣa (dim. of *geṛṣa*) pl. *-t* **1.** small loaf of bread (about the size of a bun)
¶ *gṛiṣa de-l-ḥălwa* piece or tablet of candy (as a mint)
geṛmaṭ pl. *gṛameṭ* short-eared
geṛmaṭa pl. *-t, gṛameṭ* wooden or metal basin for mortar or plaster
germel v.t. to make crisp, to brown (as in an oven, frying pan, etc.)
geṛmeṭ v.t. to shorten, to cut off
gṛen v.t. (v.n. *gṛin*) to join, to attach *gṛen hada mɛa hadak.* Attach this to that.
¶ *gṛen ɛăynuφ f-* to stare at
geṛn pl. *gṛun* **1.** horn (cow, antelope, etc.) **2.** powder horn **3.** tuft of hair left after shaving part of the head (custom of certain North African country people) **4.** tress which hangs down on the bosom (women)
gorna pl. *-t* slaughterhouse
gernin n.u. *-a* thistle
gerr v.i. (v.n. *gerran*) to confess, to admit guilt
¶ *gerr be-l-xir* to be grateful
gerrab pl. *-a* one who carries and sells water (in a *gerba*) in the street to passers-by, and also to houses
gerran v.n. of *gerr*
¶ *gerran be-l-xir* gratitude
geṛṛeḍ v.t. to cut into pieces
geṛṛeṣ v.t. to flatten (as bread before baking)
gerrež v.t. to cut a little off, to shorten (e.g. a sleeve)
** *gerržu-lu debḥa.* They slit his throat.
gerrăɛ v.t. to cause to belch (food, drink)
geṛṣ, goṛṣ, n.u. *geṛṣa, goṛṣa* small loaf of bread
gerš pl. *gruš, grušat* old coin worth one-quarter franc

geṛtiṭ pl. *gṛaṭeṭ* (n. and adj.) animal whose tail has been cut off
geṛṭeṭ v.t. to cut off, to lop off, to shorten (e.g. sleeves, hair, animal's tail)
gṛun pl. of *geṛn*
gruš, grušat pl. of *gerš*
geṛwaṭ pl. *gṛaweṭ* (n. and adj.) one with a speech defect
gerwaža pl. *-t* sheep's ear (from the gastronomic viewpoint)
geṛweṭ v.i. to speak with some impediment
gorža, be-l-gorža wholesale *šritha be-l-gorža.* I bought it wholesale.
geržuma pl. *gražem* **1.** throat (internal and external aspect) **2.** Adam's apple
geṛžuṭa pl. *gṛažeṭ* same as *geržuma*
gṛăƐ n.u. *geṛƐa* squash (including pumpkin)
¶ *gṛăƐ slawi* kind of long, green squash
¶ *gṛăƐ tixṛifin* (or *taxṛifin*) zucchini squash
¶ *gṛăƐ Ɛămṛa* pumpkin
gṣaƐi pl. of *geṣƐa*
gṣeb, geṣba same as *qṣeb, qeṣba*
geṣṣ pl. *gṣuṣ* floor of tamped earth or concrete
geṣṣaṣ pl. *-a* ag. n. of *geṣṣeṣ*
geṣṣaṣa pl. *-t* tool or machine for tamping earth
geṣṣeṣ v.t. **1.** to make flat or level by tamping (in preparation for laying a floor) **2.** to lay (a concrete floor), to pave (with concrete or asphalt)
gṣuṣ pl. of *geṣṣ*
geṣƐa pl. *-t, gṣaƐi* large bowl or dish in which couscous is served and often eaten
gešgaš twigs, branches and dried cow dung used for lighting fires
gṭaṭi pl. of *geṭṭaya*
gṭaƐi pl. of *geṭƐa*
geṭran tar, pitch
geṭṭaya pl. *-t, gṭaṭi* tuft of hair on the crown of the head (custom of some Northwest African country folk)
geṭƐa pl. *-t, gṭaƐi* same as *qeṭƐa*
gud straight (ahead) *sir gud!* Go straight ahead! —*aži gud le-ḍ-ḍaṛ!* Come straight home!
guma pl. *-t* eraser (rubber)
guṛaṛa pl. *-t* stain, spot
guses v.i. to spy, to engage in espionage
¶ *guses Ɛla* to spy on
guwwad pl. *-a* guide (tourist, expedition, etc.)
guwwed v.t. **1.** to lead, to conduct, to show (s.o. to some place), to take (somewhere) **2.** to drive (cattle, sheep, etc.)
guwwez same as *duwwez*
guz n.u. *-a* **1.** walnut **2.** walnut tree
¶ *guza de-t-tenfiƐa* snuff container (pear-shaped)
gwadem pl. of *gadum* (same as *qadum*)
gwafel pl. of *gafla*
gwamel pl. of *gamila*
gwames pl. of *gamus*
gwayez pl. of *gayza*
gwazeṭ pl. of *gazịṭa*
gwireƐ dim. of *gareƐ*
gyad pl. of *gid*
gyaṭen pl. of *giṭun*
gyăƐ pl. of *gaƐa*
gzami pl. of *gezma*
gezz v.t. (v.n. *gezzan*) to shear (sheep)
gezzan v.n. of *gezz*
gezzar pl. *-a* butcher
gezzer v.t. to cut (up) (as does a butcher in preparing meat)
gežder used in expr. e.g., *aš ka-tgežder?* What the hell are you doing? —*aš gežderti l-yum?* What have you done today? (implying nothing worthwhile was done)
gežgež v.i. to swarm (insects)
gƐad **1.** v.n. of *gƐăd* **2.** idleness, inaction
gƐadi pl. of *găƐda* **2**
gƐăd v.i. (v.n. *gƐad*) **1.** to sit (down) **2.** to stay *găƐdet Ɛăndna telt iyyam.* She stayed with us three days. **3.** to stop work(ing), to retire, to be retired **4.** to be unemployed or out of work
găƐda **1.** n.i. of *gƐăd* **2.** pl. *-t, gƐadi* sitting position
găƐgăƐ v.i. to make the sound of a camel
gƐiṛ v.n. of *gƐăṛ*
gƐăṛ v.t. (v.n. *gƐiṛ*) to throw violently (so as to break or smash)
găƐƐăd v.t. **1.** to raise (the head from a bowed position) **2.** to cause or make sit (down), to seat **3.** to cause or make sit up (as in bed) **4.** to set up, to straighten (up) (s.th. that has been overturned or knocked down) **5.** to make or have stay (as overnight) **6.** to retire (s.o.) **7.** to support, to back (up)
** *ḷḷah igăƐƐăd milu.* I hope everything works out for him.

Ġ

ġa abbreviation of *ġadi* (as auxiliary before the imperfect)
ġab iġib v.i. (v.n. *ġiba*) **1.** to be away, to be absent **2.** to disappear *ġabet š-šemš.* The sun's disappeared (e.g., behind a cloud). **3.** to set (sun)

¶ ġab ʿla ʿăqluφ to faint, to pass out
¶ a.p. ġayeb pl. -in absent
¶ ġayeb ʿla ʿăqluφ (to be) unconscious, to be out
ġaba pl. -t, ġyeb forest, woods
¶ ġaba de-z-zitun olive grove, orchard
¶ mul l-ġaba, bu-ġaba forester, forest ranger
ġabawa 1. stupidity, denseness 2. stubbornness
ġabiy pl. ʔaġbiyaʔ 1. stupid, dense 2. stubborn
ġadi f. ġadya or ġada pl. ġadyen going fayn ġadi? Where are you going? —(ana) ġadi le-ḍ-ḍaṛ. I'm going home.
¶ ġadi, ġad, ġa (invariable) auxiliary used before the imperfect to indicate future time ġad-ṭṭiʿ š-šta. It's going to rain. —ġa-nšufha ġedda. I'm going to see her tomorrow.
ġaḍ iġiḍ v.t. (v.n., ġiḍ) to offend, to hurt ġaḍni dak š-ši lli qolti had ṣ-ṣbaʿ. What you said this morning offended me.
** ġaḍu l-ʿal. He's angry, peeved.
ġaḍab wrath, anger
ġafel a.p. of ġfel
ġalĭb used in the expr. fe-l-ġalĭb, ġalĭb š-ši 1. most of the time, in general f-fas ka-ikun l-ʿal fe-ṣ-ṣif sxun fe-l-ġalĭb. In Fez the weather is hot most of the summer. 2. most likely, probably fe-l-ġalĭb ṭṭiʿ š-šta had l-lila. It'll most likely rain tonight.
ġali a.p. of ġla iġla
ġalăṭ pl. ʔaġlaṭ 1. v.n. of ġleṭ 2. mistake, error
ġaleṭ a.p. of ġleṭ
ġameq pl. -in profound, hard to understand
ġameṛ v.i. to venture forth (to seek adventure)
ġanayim pl. of ġanima (same as ġnima)
ġani a.p. of ġna
ġanima pl. ġanayim same as ġnima
ġanen v.t. (v.n. ġnan) to contradict, to disagree with (s.o.)
ġanžu f. -ya pl. ġwanež gullible, easily duped (rather slangy)
ġaṛ iġir (men) (v.n. ġiṛa) to be jealous (of)
¶ ġaṛ ʿla to defend, to take the side of, to back up (s.o., as in an argument)
ġaṛ pl. ġiṛan 1. cave, cavern 2. hole (mouse, rabbit, ant, etc.) 3. tunnel
ġaṛa pl. -t act of aggression, attack (military)
ġaṛad, ġaṛaḍ aim, goal, desire
¶ ʿănduφ l-ġaṛaḍ b- to need ʿăndi l-ġaṛaḍ bik. I need you (to help me). —ʿăndi l-ġaṛaḍ b-ši-šwiya d-le-flus. I need a little money.
ġaṛaʔib pl. of ġriba
ġaṛama pl. -t ġaṛayim same as ġṛama
ġaṛayim pl. of ġaṛama (same as ġṛama)
ġareb pl. ġwareb corner where three sides come together
ġariba same as ġriba
ġaṛăq 1. v.n. of ġṛaq 2. flood, deluge (extended to a heavy rain)
ġaṛeq a.p. of ġṛeq
ġasul fuller's earth (used for shampooing the hair)
ġaṣ iġiṣ v.i. to submerge, to go under
** huwa ġayeṣ f-demmu. He's lying in a puddle of (his) blood.
ġaša v.t. to cause to be oblivious to what is going on, (e.g. by plying with liquor to gain some advantage)
ġaši (with art.) somebody, something (vague) smăʿt l-ġaši l-fuq. I heard somebody (i.e., a noise) upstairs.
ġat iġit v.t. (v.n. ġit, iġata) to come to the aid of, to save (especially from impending death)
ġaya goal, aim
¶ fe-l-ġaya, fe-l-ġaya u-n-nihaya, fi-ġayati ma yakun very good, excellent, perfect
¶ ġaytu~ in short, in a word
ġayeb a.p. of ġab
ġayel v.i. (v.n. ġil, ġyal) to nurse (suckle) one's child during a succeeding pregnancy (considered unhealthy for the unborn child)
ġazw v.n. of ġza
ġbabeṛ pl. of ġobṛa
ġbaṛ manure
ġbayen pl. of ġbina
ġebbaṛ pl. -a one who collects the combustible materials used in heating water for the public bath
ġebben v.t. to make sad or disconsolate, to grieve
ġebbeṛ v.t. to hide (s.th.)
ġebbeṛ v.t. 1. to get dust on or all over (s.th.) 2. to spread or dust (e.g., sugar or cinnamon on a cake) 3. to powder (e.g., one's face) 4. to spread fertilizer on or over (a field)
ġbina pl. ġbayen disconsolation, dejection, sadness žatha le-ġbina. She's down in the mouth (i.e., sadness came to her).
ġben gloominess, moroseness nzel ʿliha le-ġben. She's become gloomy.
ġber v.i. to disappear (with whereabouts unknown)
ġebra pl. -t, ġbuṛ n.i. of ġber
ġobṛa pl. ġbabeṛ (pl. of intensity) 1. dust 2. (pl.) clouds of dust (as on a windy day) 3. powder (general term)
ġbuṛ pl. of ġebra
ġda pl. -wat lunch, dinner (just after the noon hour)
ġdayed pl. of ġodda, ġedda

ġdayer pl. of *ġdir*
ġedd anger, fury *ṭlăɛ fih l-ġedd.* He became furious.
¶ *ġedd lih~* the day after (some previously mentioned day)
ġedda tomorrow
¶ *băɛd ġedda* (the) day after tomorrow
¶ *ġedda men ġedda* one of these days, some day
¶ *lla ġedda* the next day, the following day *ṛžăɛt men l-ɛoṭla u-lla ġedda ṣbeɛt nexdem.* I came back from my vacation and the following day I started back to work.
ġodda, ġedda pl. *ġdayed* **1.** grief, sorrow **2.** resentment *ma-berdet-lu-š dik l-ġodda.* He's still resentful (and is planning to get even).
** *a ġdayed qelbi!,* or *a ġdaydi!* Oh, I wish I'd never been born! Oh, woe is me!
¶ *berred le-ġdayed f-* to take out one's anger on, to cool off by venting one's spleen on
ġedded v.t. to irritate (by pestering)
ġdir pl. *ġdayer* stream, rill (small enough to be jumped)
ġedwa same as *ġedda*
ġḍeb v.i. (v.n. *ġḍib*) to get angry, to get mad
ġeḍba n.i. of *ġḍeb*
ġeḍban pl. *-in* **1.** angry **2.** in a bad mood or humor
ġeḍḍab pl. *-in* irascible, touchy, cross (character trait)
ġeḍḍaṛ **1.** pl. *-in* deceitful, unfaithful **2.** pl. *-in* misleading, fraudulent **3.** pl. *-a* deceiver, unfaithful person
ġeḍḍeb v.t. to make angry or mad
ġḍib v.n. of *ġḍeb*
ġḍeṛ v.t. (v.n. *ġḍeṛ*) **1.** to deceive, to mislead **2.** to be unfaithful to, to betray
ġḍeṛ v.n. of *ġḍeṛ*
¶ *b-le-ġḍeṛ* with intentions of deceiving or betraying
ġeffel v.t. to wait for (s.o., in order to take advantage of his inattention or absence in order to do s.th. that cannot be done in his presence) *ġeffeltu ɛetta ḍuwweṛ wežhu u-xdit fanida xṛa.* I waited until he turned his head, then I took another piece of candy.
ġfil v.n. of *ġfel*
ġfir (no pl., no comp.) used in the expr. *ḷḷah ġfir.* God is forgiving.
ġfiṛ v.n. of *ġfeṛ*
ġfel ɛla (v.n. *ġfil*) **1.** not to give due attention to, to neglect (things) **2.** to have patience with, to wait for or on *ġfel ɛliya waɛed š-šwiya.* Wait a little while (e.g., and I'll pay you).
¶ a.p. *ġafel* pl. *-in* **1.** inattentive, distracted **2.** careless, negligent
ġefla n.i. of *ġfel*
¶ *ɛla ġefla* all of a sudden, suddenly, without warning, unexpectedly
ġfeṛ l- (v.n. *ġofṛan, ġfiṛ, meġfaṛa*) to forgive (religious sense)
ġofṛan **1.** v.n. of *ġfeṛ* **2.** remission of sin(s)
ġib used in the expr. *fe-l-ġib* not known, secret *kif kan le-mtiɛan dyalek?—fe-l-ġib.* How did you come out in the exam?—I don't know.
ġiba pl. *-t, ġwayeb, ġyub* **1.** v.n. of *ġab* **2.** absence *hedṛu ɛlih f-ġibtu.* They talked about him in his absence.
** *fayn had le-ġwayed?* or *fayn ġyubek?* Where have you been (all this time)?
ġibṭa joy, gladness, elation
ġiḍ v.n. of *ġaḍ*
ġil v.n. of *ġayel*
ġina riches, wealth
ġir **1.** only, nothing but, just (often with *ma-* preceding the verb) *ka-nšuf ġir ḍ-ḍḷem* or *ma-ka-nšuf ġir ḍ-ḍḷem.* I see only darkness. **2.** minus, less (implied in telling time) *hadi z-zuž ġir tulut.* It's twenty to (before, of) two. **3.** as soon as, when *ġir iži qulha-li.* As soon as he comes, tell me. **4.** other than, (an)other, others, (used with pron. endings) *taxod had le-ktab? la, ɛṭini ġiru.* Do you want (to take) this book? No, give me another (a different) one. —*telleft flusek u-flus ġirek.* I lost your money as well as the others'. **5.** used with impv. to show lack of objection to the act *ġir sir!* Go ahead and go! You can go (if you want). —*ġir kul!* Go ahead and eat!
** *la-hada wa-la ġiru wa-la ġiru!* Not this (one) or any other (one)!
¶ *ġir kif* as soon as, when *ġir kif tuwṣeḷ aži šufni.* As soon as you arrive come and see me.
¶ *men ġir* (with *ma-* before verbs) **1.** instead of, other than, besides *ṣifeṭ ši-waɛed men ġiru.* Send someone instead of him. **2.** without *sir men ġir xewf* (or *men ġir-ma txaf*) Go and don't be afraid! **3.** except *šefthom kollhom men ġir xak.* I saw all of them except your brother.
¶ *l-ġir* other people, others *ka-ixelli šġalu baš iɛawen l-ġir.* He leaves his own work to help others.
ġiṛa **1.** v.n. of *ġaṛ* **2.** jealousy, envy **3.** indignation *žatu l-ġiṛa ɛla xtu.* He's really riled about his sister (her being treated improperly, etc.)
ġiṛan pl. of *ġaṛ*
ġit **1.** v.n. of *ġat* **2.** rain (as a relief from

drought) *mšaw iṭelbu l-ġit.* They went (to the mosque) to pray for rain.

ġiṭa pl. *-t, ġyeṭ* type of Moroccan oboe with holes in place of keys

** *ɛălqha ṛqiq bɛal l-ġiṭa.* She has a shrill, piercing voice. —*ža be-ṭ-ṭbel u-l-ġiṭa.* He arrived with a great display of pomp.

ġiyabiyen in absentia *ɛekmu ɛlih ġiyabiyen.* They sentenced him in absentia.

ġiyyaṭ pl. *-a* one who plays the *ġiṭa*

ġiyyeb **1.** v.i. to be away for a long time **2.** v.t., to cause to be absent, away

** *la-tġiyyeb-š b-le-bṛa ɛlina.* Don't wait forever to write us.

ġiyyeḍ v.t. **1.** to hurt (i.e., one's feelings) **2.** to anger, to make indignant

ġiyyem v.i. to get cloudy, overcast *l-ɛal bda ka-iġiyyem.* It began to get cloudy.

ġiyyeṛ v.t. **1.** to change, to alter, to modify **2.** to transform **3.** to anger, to upset

ġiyyeṣ v.t. **1.** to get muddy, to muddy, to get mud on **2.** to make muddy, to cause (the ground) to get muddy

ġla iġla v.i. (v.n. *ġla*) to become expensive, to go up (in price)

¶ a.p. *ġali* f. *ġalya* pl. *ġalyen* (comp. *ġla*) expensive, high (price)

ġla iġli v.i. (v.n. *ġli*) **1.** to boil **2.** to crowd, to throng *s-saɛa de-s-suq kanet ka-teġli b-le-ġnem.* The market place was crowded with sheep. **3.** to swarm (bees, flies, etc)

** *ġla d-demm f-ṛaṣu.* He became furious.

ġla (m.) v.n. of *ġla iġla*

¶ *b-le-ġla* high, at a high price *ka-ibiɛu b-le-ġla w-išriw b-le-ġla.* They sell at a high price as well as buy at a high price.

ġla comp. of *ġali* (a.p. of *ġla iġla*)

ġḷaḍ v.i. (v.n. *ġeḷḍ, ġoḷḍ*) **1.** to get fat (person, animal) **2.** to become blunted (as a sharp point)

ġlaf pl. *-at* **1.** scabbard, sheath **2.** case (eyeglasses, camera, etc.) **3.** envelope **4.** cover (book) **5.** pod, shell (pea, bean)

ġlal n.u. *-a* snail

ġlaleq pl. of *ġellaqa*

ġlaq, ġlaqa pl. *ġlaqat* wooden or metal blind used to close the front of a shop or store

ġḷaṭ pl. of *ġeḷṭa*

ġlayli pl. *-ya* fruit and vegetable wholesale dealer

ġleb v.t. (v.n. *ġolb*) to beat, to be victorious over

¶ *ġleb ɛla* **1.** to harm (sadistically) **2.** to overpower, to overcome *ġleb ɛlih t-tqel.* The weight overpowered him.

ġolb v.n. of *ġleb*

gelba pl. *-t* **1.** n.i. of *ġleb* **2.** victory

ġeḷḍ, ġoḷḍ **1.** v.n. of *ġḷaḍ* **2.** thickness **3.** fatness, obesity

ġḷeḍ comp. of *ġḷiḍ*

ġli v.n. of *ġla iġli*

ġḷiḍ pl. *ġḷaḍ* (comp. *ġḷeḍ*) **1.** thick (not liquids) **2.** dull, blunt (a point) **3.** fat, obese, heavy **4.** deep and gruff (voice)

gliq v.n. of *ġleq*

ġoll, ġell rancor, resentment

ġlel pl. of *ġella*

ġella v.t. **1.** to boil (water) **2.** to raise the price of **3.** to sell at a high price, to charge a lot for

ġella pl. *-t, ġlel* **1.** crop, harvest **2.** fruit

ġellal pl. *-a* seller of fruit

ġellaqa pl. *-t, ġlaleq* bottle-stopper (includes caps, corks, etc.)

ġellay pl. *-a* tea-kettle

ġelleb ɛla to help, cause, or make (s.o.) win (over s.o. else) *ġellbuh ɛliha.* They helped him beat her (in the contest, etc.)

ġeḷḷeḍ v.t. **1.** to thicken, to make thick(er) (as a wall) **2.** to cause to put on weight, to make fat(ter) **3.** to make deep(er) and gruff(er) (voice)

ġellef v.t. **1.** to cover (book, wall) **2.** to wrap (package)

geḷḷeq v.t. to darken (color)

¶ *ġeḷḷeqha~* or *ġeḷḷeq babaha~* to gorge oneself (with food)

ġelles v.i. to do (derogatory usage) *aš ka-tġelles?* What the hell are you doing?

geḷḷeṭ v.t. to cause or make (s.o.) commit an error *xḷaṣ, ġeḷḷeṭtini!* Blast it, you made me make a mistake!

ġlem (f., coll.) sheep

ġelmi mutton, lamb (meat)

ġleq v.t. (v.n. *ġliq*) to close or shut (door, room, etc.)

** *ġelquha.* They stuffed themselves (with food)

¶ *ġleq ɛla* **1.** to shut in, to lock in *ġelqu ɛlih.* They locked him in. **2.** to talk over the head of (s.o.) **3.** to tell tall stories to

ġelqa pl. *-t* n.i. of *ġleq*

** *ḍeṛbuha b-ġelqa.* They stuffed themselves (with food).

ġḷeṭ v.i. (v.n. *ġaḷăṭ*) to make a mistake, to err

¶ a.p. *ġaḷeṭ* pl. *-in* wrong, mistaken *nta ġaḷeṭ.* You're mistaken.

ġeḷṭa pl. *-t, ġlaṭ, ʔaġlaṭ* mistake, error

ġḷuḍiya **1.** thickness **2.** fatness, obesity

ġelya n.i. of *ġla*

**ɛ*la ġelya ka-itib.* It only takes a minute to cook.

ġelyan pl. *-in* (adj.) boiling

ġmal **1.** v.n. of *ġmel* **2.** mold (e.g. on bread)

ġmam n.u. *-a* dark, low clouds

ġmameḍ pl. of *ġommaḍa*

ġmaq v.i. **1.** to deepen, to become deep **2.** to go deep(er) (e.g. s.o. digging)

ġmayem pl. of *ġemm*
ġemḍa pl. *-t* (dim. *ġmiḍa*) nap, snooze, light sleep
¶ *ɛmel ġemḍa* to take a nap or snooze
ġmiḍa dim. of *ġemḍa*
ġmiz v.n. of *ġmez*
ġmel v.i. (v.n. *ġmel, ġmal*) to get moldy
ġmel v.n. of *ġmel*
ġemm v.t. to smother, to asphyxiate (other than by gas; not necessarily fatal)
¶ pp. *meġmum* pl. *-in* sad, low (in spirit)
ġemm pl. *ġmum, ġmayem* (pl. of intensity) dejection, despondency
ġemma **1.** n.i. of *ġemm* **2.** same as *ġemm* pl. *ġmum, ġmayem*
ġommaḍa pl. *-t, ġmameḍ* blinder (for horse's bridle)
ġommayḍa hide-and-seek (children's game)
ġemmed v.t. to sheathe (sword, knife)
ġemmeḍ v.t. **1.** to close (the eyes) **2.** to cover the eyes of, to blindfold *ġemmeḍ-lu ɛăynih ɛetta nexrož!* Cover his eyes until I leave!
¶ *ġemmeḍ waɛed t-teġmiḍa* to take a (little) nap, to snooze (a while)
ġemmem v.i. to become overcast, to cloud up *ġemmmet s-sma.* The sky's clouded up.
ġemmeq v.t. **1.** to hide, to conceal (by removing the object rather than covering it with s.th. else). **2.** to make deep(er) (as a hole)
ġemmes v.t. to dip (in a sauce, as a piece of bread)
ġomq depth, deepness (physical quality)
ġmum pl. of *ġemm*
ġmez v.t. (v.n. *ġmiz*) to wink at
ġna iġni v.t. (v.n. *ġna*) to make rich or wealthy
** *ġnah ḷḷah ɛla ġiru.* He's pretty well off (and needs no financial help).
¶ a.p. *ġani* f. *-ya* pl. *aġniya* **1.** rich, wealthy **2.** self-sufficient (financially)
ġna comp. of *ġani* (see *ġna*)
ġna (m.) v.n. of *ġna*
ġnabeṛ pl. of *ġenbuṛ*
ġnabež pl. of *ġenbaž*
ġnan **1.** v.n. of *ġanen* and *tġanen* **2.** contrariness
ġnayem pl. of *ġnima*
ġenbaž, ġonbaž pl. *ġnabež* kind of *žellaba* worn by mountain folk.
ġenber v.i. to pull a hood (e.g., of the *žellaba*) over the head in such a way as to hide the face
ġenbuṛ pl. *ġnabeṛ* type of veil, used mostly by country women, which encircles the head as well as the face
ġnima pl. *-t, ġnayem* **1.** trophy (war) **2.** (pl.) booty, spoil **3.** game (i.e., animals taken in hunting)
ġnem v.t. **1.** to take advantage of, to profit by (opportunity) **2.** to get (s.th. out of s.o.) *sir u-šuf kan teġnem ši-ɛăšra de-d-drahem mennu.* Go and see if you can get ten dirhams or so out of him.
ġnem (f., coll.) sheep
¶ *qeṭɛa d-le-ġnem* flock of sheep
ġenmi same as *ġelmi*
ġenna v.t. and v.i. **1.** to sing **2.** to repeat or say again and again (insistently) *bqa ka-tġenni temmaya!* You can keep repeating that until doomsday (I'm not changing my mind)!
ġonya pl. *-t* (a) song
ġṛa paste, glue
ġṛab pl. of *ġrib* 1 and 2
ġṛab pl. *-at, ġoṛban, ġṛobba* crow, raven
ġṛabi pl. *-yen* raven black, pitch black
ġrabel pl. of *ġerbal, ġorbal*
ġrabli pl. *-ya* one who makes and sells the *ġerbal*
ġṛafi pl. of *ġoṛfa*
ġṛama pl. *-t, ġṛayem* **1.** v.n. of *ġṛem* **2.** gift, usually money, given to the bride by relatives and friends **3.** security, collateral *ila bġiti le-flus ɛṭini ši-ġṛama.* If you want the loan give me some security. **4.** compensation, remuneration (for some loss)
ġṛaq v.i. (v.n. *ġoṛq, ġaṛăq*) **1.** to go under, to sink (but not quite drown) **2.** to drown **3.** to sink, to founder (ship) **4.** to get deeper (as a well)
ġṛaṛef pl. of *ġoṛraf*
ġṛaṣi pl. of *ġeṛṣa*
ġrayeb pl. of *ġriba*
ġṛayem pl. of *ġṛama*
ġraz pl. of *ġerza, ġorza*
ġrazi pl. of *ġerza*
ġṛeb (v.n. *ġṛub, ġurub*) to set, to go down (sun)
ġeṛb **1.** west **2.** (with art.) name of a fertile valley on the *sbu* river
ġoṛba pl. of *ġrib* 3
ġoṛba **1.** state of feeling out of place, loneliness **2.** homesickness
** *ka-iɛiš hna f-ġoṛba.* He feels all alone living here.
ġerbal, ġorbal pl. *ġrabel* kind of sieve or sifter used in grading sand and wheat
ġoṛban pl. of *ġṛab*
ġeṛbawa pl. of *ġeṛbawi*
ġeṛbawi pl. *ġeṛbawa* inhabitant of *l-ġeṛb* (see *ġeṛb* 2)
ġṛobba pl. of *ġṛab*
ġeṛbi **1.** pl. *-yen* western, occidental **2.** cool breeze from the west
ġerbel v.t. to sift (flour, sand)
ġṛef to dip, to serve with a spoon
ġṛef pl. of *ġoṛfa*

ġoṛfa pl. *-t, ġṛafi, ġṛef* **1.** n.i. of *ġṛef* **2.** room above the ground floor

¶ *ġoṛfa de-l-ʕăwla* pantry

¶ *l-ġoṛfa l-filaʕiya* Chamber of Agriculture

¶ *l-ġoṛfa t-tižariya* Chamber of Commerce

ġeṛġeṛ v.t. to gargle with *xeṣṣek tġeṛġeṛ l-ma šwiya.* You should gargle a little bit with some water.

ġrib **1.** pl. *ġṛab* strange, weird, odd **2.** pl. *ġṛab* marvelous, amazing **3.** pl. *ġoṛba* one away from home (and somewhat alone), stranger

ġriba pl. *ġṛayeb, ġaṛaʔib* very unusual thing; s.th. very much out of the ordinary

ġṛim v.n. of *ġṛem*

ġris v.n. of *ġres*

ġṛiyba pl. *-t* type of teacake made of semolina or flour, sugar, and butter

ġṛiz v.n. of *ġṛez*

ġṛem v.t. (v.n. *ġṛim, ġṛama*) **1.** to give *ġṛama* to (the bride) **2.** to make restitution or compensation for, to pay (back) for *xeṣṣek teġṛem-li ktabi.* You've got to pay me back for my book.

ġeṛnaṭa Granada (Spain)

ġṛeq same as *ġṛaq*

¶ a.p. *ġaṛeq* pl. *-in* (comp. *ġṛeq*) **1.** deep (as a well, hole, dish, etc.) **2.** sunk, submerged (as a ship)

¶ *ġaṛeq fe-d-din* deep in debt

¶ *ġaṛeq fe-n-nʕas* fast asleep

ġṛeq comp. of *ġaṛeq* (a.p. of *ġṛeq*)

ġoṛq **1.** v.n. of *ġṛaq* **2.** depth, deepness **3.** deep place (as in a river)

ġeṛqa **1.** n.i. of *ġṛaq* **2.** complete failure, fiasco (business project)

ġeṛṛ v.t. (v.n. *ġṛuṛ, ġuṛuṛ, ġeṛṛan* **1.** (sometimes with *b-*) to tempt (to do wrong), to lead into error or astray **2.** to lead (s.o.) on, to deceive

ġeṛṛa v.t. to apply *ġṛa* to (for gluing purposes)

ġerrada used in the expr. *ʕla ġerrada* without warning, unexpectedly

ġoṛṛaf pl. *ġṛaṛef* **1.** type of clay jar for storing drinking water **2.** Kind of clay drinking mug **3.** pitcher

ġeṛṛan v.n. of *ġeṛṛ*

ġeṛṛaṛ pl. *-a* tempter, one who leads astray

ġerreb v.t. **1.** to exile, to banish **2.** to make (s.th.) face west (as in building a house) **3.** v.i. to go or bear west

¶ part. *mġerreb* pl. *-in* away from one's own country, in a foreign land

ġerred v.i. to chirp, to warble (bird)

ġeṛṛem v.t. to make pay for, to make (s.o.) make restitution or compensation for

ġeṛṛeq v.t. **1.** to drive deep (as a nail, drill) **2.** to dunk (s.o.), to drown or almost drown **3.** to submerge, to immerse (s.th.) **4.** to sink, to scuttle (ship) **5.** to make deep(er) (as a hole) **6.** to prosecute

¶ *ġeṛṛeq fe-d-din* to cause or make go into debt

ġeṛṛeṣ v.t. to make go deep, to drive in deep

ġerrez v.t. **1.** to baste, to tack **2.** to stitch (surgery)

ġres, ġṛeṣ v.t. (v.n. *ġris, ġṛeṣ, ġeṛṣ*) to plant (a plant or area)

ġṛeṣ v.n. of *ġres, ġṛeṣ*

ġeṛṣ (no pl.) **1.** garden (vegetable, flower) **2.** group of potted plants **3.** v.n. of *ġṛeṣ*

ġeṛṣa n.i. of *ġres, ġṛeṣ*

ġṛub v.n. of *ġṛeb*

ġṛuṛ v.n. of *ġeṛṛ*

ġṛez (v.n. *ġṛiz*) same as *ġerrez*

ġorza pl. *-t, ġraz, ġrazi* stitch (sewing, surgery)

ġsil v.n. of *ġsel*

ġsel v.t. and v.i. (v.n. *ġsil*) to wash (up), to clean (up) (usually with water)

ġesla pl. *-t* n.i. of *ġsel*

ġessal pl. *-a* kind of mortician who washes and wraps the dead before burial

ġessel v.t. to wash and wrap (the dead before burial)

ġṣan pl. of *ġṣen*

ġṣeb v.t. (v.n. *ġṣib, ġṣeb, ġeṣb*) **1.** to pick (fruit, etc.) before ripening **2.** to deprive (of s.th. due) *ḅḅah ġeṣbu fe-qṛaytu.* His father took him out of school (deprived him of his studies). **3.** to take away (by force or intimidation) *ġṣebni f-flusi.* He took my money away. —*ġeṣbuha f-ʕayatha.* They took away her life (implies in one's prime).

ġṣeb, ġeṣb v.n. of *ġṣeb*

ġṣib v.n. of *ġṣeb*

ġṣen pl. *ġṣan* branch (tree)

ġeṣṣab pl. *-a* ag.n. of *ġṣeb*

ġša (cons. *ġšat*) pl. *-wat, ġši* **1.** envelope (letter) **2.** case, cover (as for a pillow)

ġšam pl. of *ġšim*

ġšat cons. of *ġša*

ġši pl. of *ġša*

ġšim pl. *ġšam* **1.** inexperienced, naive, rustic **2.** beginner, tyro, novice

** *kont ġšim fik!* I didn't know you could do that, or were like that (favorable surprise); I didn't think you'd ever do a thing like that (disappointment).

ġešš v.t. (v.n. *ġešš*) to cheat, to deceive (e.g. in a game, sale)

** *ka-tġešš ṛaṣek.* You can do better than that (i.e., you're not matching up to your potential).

ġešš v.n. of *ġešš*

¶ *be-l-ġešš* fraudulently, through deception

ġešša same as *ġellef*
ġeššaš pl. *-a* cheat (person)
** *nta ġeššaš!* You know you can do better! (i.e., have greater potential)
ġeššem v.t. to take advantage of (an ingenuous and naive person), to dupe
ġošt August (month)
ġṭari pl. of *ġeṭra*
ġṭir v.n. of *ġṭer*
ġṭer v.i. (v.n. *ġṭir*) to go away (somewhere) and not return at the expected time *ġṭerti ʕliya!* Where have you been! (i.e., you went out and didn't come back when you were supposed to)
ġeṭra pl. *-t, ġṭari* n.i. of *ġṭer*
ġeṭṭer v.t. to hide (by removal of the object rather than covering it up)
ġṭa pl. *-wat ġṭi* (dim. *ġṭiya*) **1.** blanket, cover (bed) **2.** lid (box, pot, jar, etc.)
ġṭaṛ pl. *ġoṭṛan* (said mainly in Fez) plate, dish
ġṭi pl. of *ġṭa*
ġṭiṣ v.n. of *ġṭeṣ*
ġṭiya dim. of *ġṭa*
ġoṭṛan pl. of *ġṭaṛ*
ġṭeṣ (v.n. *ġṭiṣ*) **1.** v.t. to put under, to immerse (as in water) **2.** v.i. to go under, to submerge (voluntarily) **3.** v.i. to disappear *fayn ġṭeṣ ḥmed?* Where did Ahmed disappear to?
¶ *ġṭeṣ ʕla* to make (s.o.) wait, to be away from (s.o. who is waiting) *yak, ma-ġṭeṣna ʕlik?* Well, we were gone (from you) quite a while, weren't we?
ġeṭṣa pl. *-t* n.i. of *ġṭeṣ*
ġeṭṭ muggy weather; heavy, close atmosphere
ġeṭṭa v.t. to cover (with a blanket, lid, etc.)
ġeṭṭaya, ġoṭṭaya pl. *-t* lid, top
ġeṭṭeṣ v.t. to immerse, to put under (water, etc.)
ġubaša frown, scowl
¶*qbeṭ ġubaša* to frown, to scowl
ġubeš v.i. to frown, to scowl
ġubeš f- to give a dirty or mean look to
ġufala mop (of hair), long hair (in need of cutting) *šuf ʕla ġufala ʕăndu!* He sure needs a haircut!
ġufel v.i. to let the hair grow (until it needs cutting) *ġufelti!* You need a hair cut! (i.e., you've let it get too long)
ġul pl. *ġwal,* f. *ġula* pl. *-t* **1.** imaginary evil being, as an ogre, that eats people, etc. **2.** glutton, "pig"
** *f-keršu l-ġula.* He eats like a horse.
ġuṛub **1.** v.n. of *ġṛeb* **2.** sunset
ġuṛuṛ **1.** v.n. of *ġeṛṛ* **2.** delusion (of grandeur, etc.)

ġus "little language" known and used by only a few (e.g., pig latin)
ġuta pl. *-t* **1.** scream, cry (either of pain or happiness) **2.** heated argument, dispute
ġuwwat pl. *-a* one given to shouting or vociferousness
ġuwweġ ʕla to attack (by surprise)
ġuwwet v.i. to shout, to yell, to scream
¶ *ġuwwet ʕla* **1.** to scold, to reprimand **2.** to call (e.g. with a shout)
ġwa iġwi v.t. (v.n. *ġwa*) **1.** to tempt, to (try to) induce (s.o. to do s.th.) *ġwatu baš yăʕmelha.* She tempted him to do it. **2.** to lead astray
ġwa (m.) v.n. of *ġwa*
ġwal pl. of *ġul*
ġwanež pl. of *ġanžu*
ġwareb pl. of *ġareb*
ġwat **1.** shouting, yelling, screaming **2.** noisy conversation or talk **3.** dispute, heated argument
ġwayeb pl. of *ġiba*
ġews same as *ġus*
ġewt same as *ġut*
ġewwaṣa pl. *-t* submarine, sub
ġyal v.n. of *ġayel*
ġyam (coll.) clouds
ġyaṛ **1.** misunderstanding, quarrel **2.** grief, distress
ġyeb pl. of *ġaba*
ġeyṣ pl. *ġyuṣat* (of intensity) mud
ġeyṣa pl. *-t* muddy place, mire
ġyeṭ pl. of *ġiṭa*
ġyub pl. of *ġiba*
ġyuṣat pl. of *ġeyṣ*
ġza iġzi v.t. (v.n. *ġazw*) to conquer (a country)
ġzal pl. *ġezlan, ġozlan;* f. *ġzala* pl. *-t* **1.** gazelle **2.** (m.) handsome boy; nice, congenial boy **3.** (f.) pretty, beautiful girl
¶ *ġezlan l-lil* thieves, burglars
ġzil v.n. of *ġzel*
ġzir (no pl.) abundant, plentiful (e.g., rain, wheat)
gzel (v.n. *ġzil*) **1.** v.t. to spin (wool, cotton, and silk into thread) **2.** v.i. to shiver, to shake, to tremble (from cold, fear)
ġezlan, ġozlan pl. of *ġzal*
ġezwa pl. *-t* military expedition (especially as carried out by the Prophet Mohammed)
ġezzala pl. *-t* woman who spins (wool, silk, and cotton into thread)
ġeẓẓeẓ v.t. **1.** to gnaw on **2.** to bite, to crack (with the teeth) **3.** to nibble on
¶ *ġeẓẓeẓ s-snan* to gnash or grind the teeth

H

ha here, here is, here are (used before n. and pron. as an interjection and demonstrative) *ha-l-baxiṛa f-aš ġad-nrekbu!* Here's the ship we're going on! —*ha-le-ktub lli šrit mennu!* Here are the books I bought from him! —*ha-ʕămmek, ha-huwa!* Here's your uncle, here he is! —*ha-huma žaw!* Here they are! Here they come! —*ha-ḥna mašyen nšufuhom.* We are going to see them. —*h-ana ġad-nekteb-lu daba.* I'm going to write him now. —*ha-lli qolt-lek qbel-ma nxeržu!* Here's what I told you before we left! (Do you see?)

had (invariable) **1.** demonstrative adj. denoting nearness, proximity (art. required before following n. if admissible) *had l-weld dki.* This boy is clever. —*had le-bṛa ʕad weṣlet had ṣ-ṣbaḥ.* This letter has just arrived this morning. —*had n-nas kollhom ka-iqellbu ʕăl l-xedma.* All these people are looking for work. —*had atay sxun ʕliya bezzaf.* This tea is too hot for me. **2.** used in certain exclamatory remarks *a had le-fḍuli, dxol ṣuq ṛaṣek!* Hey nosey, why don't you mind your own business?

hada f. *hadi* pl. *hadu* (near demonstrative pron.) this, this one, the one *hada l-meṭʕăm lli qolt-lek ʕlih.* This is the restaurant I told you about. —*hadi hiya le-mṛa lli qalt-li xrežti.* This is the woman who told me you'd gone out. —*hada ġir le-bdu.* This is just the beginning. —*hada be-ḍ-ḍebṭ lli fekkeṛt fih ḥett-ana.* It's exactly what I thought, too. —*hada ġad-ibiʕuh ġedda.* They're going to sell this one tomorrow. —*hadu ʕămmeṛhom ma-kanu ʕăndna fe-ḍ-ḍaṛ.* These people have never been at our house. —*u-dyal men hadi?* And who does this belong to?

** *hada ma kan.* That's all (there is). —*fḍiḥa hadi ʕămlu!* What a riot they've caused! —*walayenni seṛṛaqa hadu!* Why, these people are thieves!

¶ *hadi . . . baš* it has been . . . since, . . . ago *hadi sett snin baš matet.* She died six years ago.

¶ *hadi . . . u . . .* (time expr.) . . . for . . . *hadi ʕamayn u-huwa ġiyyab.* He's been away for two years.

** *šḥal hadi (fe-s-saʕa)?* What time is it? —*hadi l-xemsa u-neṣṣ.* It's half past five.

¶ *hadi xir ṛebbi, hadi xir ḷḷah, xiṛ ṛebbi hadi, xiṛ ḷḷah hadi, hadi šḥal, šḥal hadi* a long time ago, for quite some time *hadi šḥal ma-šefthom.* I haven't seen them for a long time.

hadaf pl. *ʔehdaf* **1.** goal, aim, purpose **2.** goal (e.g., in soccer)

hadak f. *hadik* pl. *haduk* demonstrative pron. and adj. (as adj., art. required before following n. if admissible) referring to remote persons, objects, ideas, etc.; (*ha-* usu. omitted as adj.; see *dak.*) *hadik hiya l-bent lli šeft.* That's the girl I saw. —*tebġi haduk?* Would you like those (ones)?

** *huwa hadak.* It's the same. (It makes no difference.) —*dak ṣ-ṣebbaṭ žaha huwa hadak.* The shoes fit her just right. —*hadak nta!* Perfect! Just right!

hadana tranquility, calmness

hadi f. of *hada*

hadik f. of *hadak*

hadu pl. of *hada*

haduk pl. of *hadak*

haʔil pl. *-in* excellent, splendid, marvelous

hak pl. *haku* here, take (when handing s.th. to s.o.) *hak had le-flus!* Take this money! —*hak!* Here (it is, take it)!

hakda like this, this is the way, this way, in this manner, this is how *hakda kanet ka-txeyyeṭ ksawiha.* This is the way she used to have her dresses made (sewn). —*ma-ši hakda bġat had l-bit mʔettet.* This is not how she wants this room furnished. —*sir hakda u-lwi ʕăl š-šmal.* Go this way and make a left turn.

hakdak **1.** like that, that's the way, in that manner, that's how **2.** about, approximately *ġad-nebqa hna ši-šheṛ hakdak.* I'm going to stay here about a month.

** *hakdak!* That's the way!

hakka same as *hakda*

hakkak same as *hakdak*

haku pl. of *hak*

halak catastrophe, disaster

ham ihim v.i. (v.n. *himan*) to wander, to walk aimlessly

hamaži adj. pl. *-yen* n.pl. *himaž* savage, barbarian

hamažiya savagery, barbarism

han ihin v.t. to despise, to have a low opinion of

haṛaž (no pl.) noise, uproar

hayažan v.n. of *haž*

hayhay interjection expressing doubt, unlikelihood, and astonishment *hayhay waš imši mʕana!* I doubt if he'd go with us. —*hayhay! u-ka-ḍḍenn ma-iʕămluha-š!* Well, you think they wouldn't do it!

hayet v.i. (v.n. *hyat*) to yell, to shout
¶ *hayet ʕla* to call, to yell at (s.o.)
haž ihiž v.i. (v.n. *hižan, hayažan*) **1.** to be agitated, to be troubled *hada l-weqt f-aš ka-ihiž le-bḥăṛ.* This is the time when the sea is agitated. **2.** to get excited, to become furious **3.** to show sexual excitement
hažeṛ v.t. or v.i. (v.n. *hižṛa, hežṛan*) **1.** to emigrate *ʕadad de-l-lubnaniyen hažṛu bladhom baš igelsu f-ʔamirika.* Many Lebanese emigrated from their country to settle in America. **2.** to immigrate *—lli ka-ihažṛu l-had le-blad kollhom ka-iṣʕab ʕlihom ittsansu biha.* All those who immigrate to this country find it hard to get adjusted. **3.** to leave, to go (be) away from *hadi telt snin baš hažṛu ḥbabhom.* They've been away from their families for three years. **4.** to flee *n-nbi, ṣelle-ḷḷah ʕlih wa-sellem, hažeṛ men mekka l-l-madina.* The Prophet (may God's blessing be upon him) fled from Mecca to Medina.
hbal **1.** v.n. of *hbel* **2.** madness, folly (lack of critical judgment)
hebb v.i. (v.n. *hebban*) to blow (wind)
hebbal, hobbal pl. of *hbil*
hebban v.n. of *hebb*
hebbaz pl. *-in, -a,* ag. adj. and n. of *hbez*
hebbel v.t. to madden, to make angry or crazy
hebbeṭ v.t. to lower; to put, take, or bring down *ka-nḥăyyiw ṛ-ṛaya mnayn ka-nṭellʕuha aw nhebbṭuha.* We salute the flag when raising or lowering it. *—la-bodda neṛžăʕ le-ḍ-ḍaṛ ḥit nsit ma-hebbeṭt-š le-ġlaqat.* I have to go back home because I forgot to put the blinds down. *—men băʕd ṣ-ṣif l-uṭilat le-kbaṛ ka-ihebbṭu l-ʔatmina dyalhom.* After summer the big hotels lower their rates.
¶ *hebbeṭ b-* to degrade, to humiliate
hbil pl. *hebbal, hobbal* fool, idiot (lacking critical judgment)
hbiš v.n. of *hbeš*
hbiṭ v.n. of *hbeṭ*
hbiz v.n. of *hbez*
hbel v.i. (v.n. *hbal*) to go mad, to lose one's mind
hbeṛ pl. of *hebṛa*
hebṛa pl. *-t, hbeṛ* boneless meat
hbeš v.t. (v.n. *hbiš*) to dig up (e.g. ground)
hbeṭ v.i. (v.n. *hbuṭ, hbiṭ*) to come down, to go down, to descend
¶ *hbeṭ ʕla* to assault, to attack *mnayn kanu ṛažʕin hebṭu ʕlihom qeṭṭaʕin ṭ-ṭṛiq.* On their way back they were attacked by highwaymen.
hebṭa **1.** n.i. of *hbeṭ* **2.** pl. *-t* width
hbuṭ v.n. of *hbeṭ*
hbez v.i. (v.n. *hbiz*) to digress, to talk nonsense
hda ihda v.i. to be quiet *qul le-d-drari ihdaw be-l-ḥăqq la-ḍḍṛebhom-š.* Tell the kids to be quiet, but don't hit them.
hda ihdi v.t. **1.** (v.n. *hdiya*) to give (as a present) *hdaw-lu ʔala de-t-tesžil.* They gave him a tape recorder. **2.** (v.n. *hidaya*) to show the right way to, to guide (God)
ʔehdaf pl. of *hadaf*
hdana same as *hadana*
hedba pl. *-t, hdub* fringe (dress)
hedd v.t. (v.n. *heddan*) to tire out
heddam ag. n. of *heddem*
heddan v.n. of *hedd*
heddawa n.pl. of *heddawi*
heddawi adj. pl. *-yen* n.pl. *heddawa* member of a religious group called Heddawa
heddeb v.t. to teach proper behavior or good manners to (s.o.)
hedded v.t. to menace, to threaten (s.o.)
heddem v.t. to destroy, to demolish
hedden v.t. to calm, to appease, to quiet
hdef ʕla (v.n. *hdif*) to see or pay a visit to (s.o.) unexpectedly *ž-žemʕa lli dazet hedfu ʕlina bezzaf de-ḍ-ḍyaf.* Last week we had many unexpected visitors.
hedhud (sg. and coll.) hoopoe
hdif v.n. of *hdef*
hdim v.n. of *hdem*
hdin v.n. of *hden*
hdir v.n. of *hder*
hdiya **1.** v.n. of *hda* **1** **2.** pl. *-t* present, gift
hdem v.t. (v.n. *hdim*) to destroy, to demolish
hden v.i. (v.n. *hdin*) to calm down, to cease, to stop, to end *ma-qḍeṛ inʕăs ḥetta hden le-ḥṛiq.* He couldn't sleep until the pain stopped. *—f-ayna blad konti men băʕd-ma hednet l-ḥăṛb?* What country were you in after the war ended?
hedna, hodna **1.** n.i. of *hden* **2.** pl. *-t* truce
hder v.i. (v.n. *hdir*) **1.** to rattle on, to speak continuously and incoherently **2.** to coo (dove, etc.)
hedref v.i. to talk nonsense, to wander, to babble
hedrez v.i. **1.** to talk nonsense, to wander, to babble **2.** to roar (sea)
hdub pl. of *hedba*
hḍaḍeṛ pl. of *hḍuṛ* **3**
hḍaṛi pl. of *hedṛa*
heḍḍaṛ pl. *-a* **1.** talkative **2.** boastful
heḍḍeṛ v.t. **1.** to make talk, to cause to talk *l-bulis xeddmu žmiʕ l-wasaʔil baš iheḍḍṛuh.* The police used all methods to make him talk. **2.** to talk to, to speak to (contemptuously)
hḍim v.n. of *hḍem*
hḍem v.t. (v.n. *hḍim, heḍm*) to digest
heḍm v.n. of *hḍem*
hḍeṛ (v.n. *hḍuṛ*) **1.** v.i. to talk, to chat *l-bareḥ u-hiya ka-tehḍeṛ mʕah fe-t-tilifun.*

She was talking to him on the phone only yesterday. —*n-nas kollhom kanu ihedṛu ʕliha.* Everybody was talking about her. **2.** v.t. to speak *ka-ihdeṛ belʕa de-l-luġat.* He speaks several languages.

¶ *hdeṛ f-* to slander

hedṛa pl. *-t, hdaṛi, hduṛ* **1.** talk, chat, conversation **2.** language, speech

** *walayenni šʕal fih de-l-hedṛa!* He's such a talkative person!

¶ *dxel u-xrež fe-l-hedṛa.* **1.** to talk incoherently, to wander **2.** to contradict oneself

hduṛ **1.** pl. of *hedṛa* **2.** v.n. of *hdeṛ* **3.** pl. *hdadeṛ* gossip, chatter

hiʔa pl. *-t* **1.** shape *l-hiʔa d-had le-bni ma-ʕažbani-š.* I don't like the shape of this building. **2.** appearance (physical, dress) **3.** body, corps, bureau (government, military, diplomatic, etc.)

hiba dignified appearance (inspiring fear and respect)

¶ *fihᶲ l-hiba, ʕlihᶲ l-hiba* to look imposing, dignified ≠; to inspire fear and respect ≠

hidaya v.n. of *hda* **2**

hiduṛa pl. *-t, hyadeṛ* sheepskin (with the fleece)

hif **1.** starvation *l-ʔuluf de-n-nas qtelhom l-hif.* Thousands of people died from starvation. **2.** voracious appetite, gluttony *kan fih waʕed l-hif dyal lli modda ma-kla.* He showed a voracious appetite as if he hadn't eaten for some time. **3.** greediness, cupidity

hilal same as *hlal*

himan v.n. of *ham*

himaž pl. of *hamaži*

hiša pl. *-t, hyuš, hwayeš* animal, beast

¶ *fihᶲ le-hwayeš* to be epileptic ≠, to have epilepsy ≠

¶ *hiša d-le-bʕăṛ* whale

¶ *hiša d-le-xla* wild animal, beast

¶ *le-hwayeš* epilepsy

hiya (f. sg. disjunctive pron.) **1.** she *ʕna xrežna u-hiya bqat fe-ḍ-ḍaṛ.* We went out while she stayed home. **2.** it *fayn ksuwtek?—ha-hiya.* Where is your dress?—Here it is. **3.** so, that means (used in connected discourse) *hiya bqit ka-nsalek settin derhem.* So you still owe me fifty dirhams. **4.** used as question marker (see *huwa*) *hiya mšat mʕakom?* Did she go with you? —*škun hiya dak le-mṛa?* Who's that woman? —*fayn hiya l-magana lli šra-lek ḅḅak?* Where's the watch your father bought you?

¶ *hiya lli* she, it (emphatic), she's the one who (see *huwa lli*)

¶ *hiya daba* so, that means *hiya daba imken iwelliw ḍeḍḍu.* That means they might turn against him.

** *hiya hadik* (see *huwa hadak*). That's her (That's the one); That's it (That's the one); It comes out the same.

hiyyen pl. *-in* easy, simple

hiyyež v.t. to excite, to arouse

hiža n.i. of *haž*

hižaʔ v.n. of *hža*

hižan v.n. of *haž*

hižṛa **1.** v.n. of *hažeṛ* **2.** Hegira

hižri pl. *-yen* of or pertaining to the *hižṛa*

hel (used in combination with other n.) **1.** family, relatives *hel le-mṛa dyalu mažyen ġedda.* His wife's family is coming tomorrow. **2.** people, inhabitants, natives (of city, etc.) e.g. *hel fas* the people of Fez

¶ *hel l-ʕărfa, hel ṣ-ṣenʕa* experts

hlak v.n. of *hlek*

hlal pl. *-at* crescent (moon)

hlika v.n. of *hlek*

hliya same as *ʔahliya*

hlek v.t. (v.n. *hlak, hlika*) **1.** to cause much harm to **2.** to endanger **3.** to ruin, to reduce to nothing

¶ *hlek ṛaṣuᶲ* to put oneself in a dangerous situation

hellel v.i. **1.** to recite litanies containing the formula *la-ʔilaha ʔilla ḷḷah* **2.** to talk nonsense

hmameṣ pl. of *hemṣa* **2**

hmed v.i. (v.n. *hmid*) to calm down (e.g., pain)

hemda n.i. of *hmed*

hmid v.n. of *hmed*

hmiz v.n. of *hmez*

hmel v.t. (v.n. *ʔihmal*) **1.** to neglect **2.** to give the cold shoulder to

hemm v.t. to concern, to involve *smăʕ had š-ši, ṛah ka-ihemmek.* Listen to this, it concerns you. —*š-ka-ihemmni ana f-had š-ši kollu?* What do I care about all this?

hemm pl. *hmum, humum* trouble, worry

hemma pl. *-t* dignity, self-respect, nobility of spirit

¶ *ṭaʕet hemmtuᶲ* to lose prestige ≠, to be disgraced ≠

¶ *ṭiyyeʕ b-hemma* to dishonor, to disgrace *ṭiyyʕu be-l-hemma d-ṛaželha.* They disgraced her husband.

hemmeṣ v.i. to track up a surface by walking on it with dirty feet

hemses v.i. and v.t. to whisper

hemṣa **1.** n.i. of *hemmeṣ* **2.** pl. *-t, hmameṣ* dirty footprint

hmum pl. of *hemm*

hmuz pl. of *hemza* **2**

hmez v.i. (v.n. *hmiz*) **1.** to make a big deal, to make a good haul **2.** to spur (horse)

hemza **1.** n.i. of *hmez* **2.** pl. *-t* letter of the

Arabic alphabet (glottal stop) **3.** pl. *-t, hmuz* big deal, good deal, good haul
hemziya (with art.) elegy on the Prophet composed by the poet *al-buṣiṛi*
hna ihna v.i. (v.n. *hna*) **1.** to become peaceful, to calm down (condition) **2.** to live in peace
hna (m.) **1.** v.n. of *hna* **2.** peace, tranquility *kanu ع ăyyšin f-le-hna qbel ma-iži.* They lived in peace before he came.
hna here *xellik hna ح etta nemšiw žmiع.* Stay here till we can go together.
¶ *hna u-hna* here and there
¶ *le-hna, lle-hna* here, hither *fuq-aš žat lle-hna?* When did she come here?
¶ *ma-hna . . . ha* (*hadi* or *hadu*) expr. used in a statement of disapproval or resentment *ma-hna klam hada qal-lha.* He shouldn't have said that to her (i.e. he shouldn't have talked to her the way he did) —*ma-hna makla hadi.* This is no food. —*ma-hna ktub hadu.* These books aren't worth much.
¶ *men hna l-l-fuq, men hna l-l-qoddam* from now on
hnak there, over there
hnakeṛ pl. of *henkaṛa*
hnaya same as *hna*
hend steel
¶ (*blad*)*l-hend* India
¶ *bح al l-hend* very strong, hard
¶ *ṛaṣ l-hend* pl. *ṛyuṣ l-hend* hardheaded, stubborn *walayenni dak l-weld ṛaṣ l-hend.* That boy is so stubborn.
hendasa **1.** geometry **2.** architecture **3.** engineering (science)
hendi adj. pl. *-yen* n.pl. *hnud* Indian (of India)
hendi, hendiya pl. *hnud* (of intensity) prickly pear (fruit or cactus)
hendez v.t. to scrutinize, to look at very closely
hniya ع*la* **1.** congratulatory expr. addressed to a person to whom a baby has just been born: to the mother, *hniya* ع*lik;* to the father or other relative, *hniya* ع*la* followed by the mother's name or relationship, e.g., *hniya* ع*la lalla faṭma,* or *hniya* ع*la mṛat xak.* **2.** sarcastic remark made about or to s.o. doing s.th. late or arriving late *iwa hniya* ع*lik!* Here you are, at last! (You finally made it!)
henkaṛa pl. *hnakeṛ* old shoe
henna v.t. **1.** to leave alone, to leave in peace *sir weح dek u-hennina.* Go by yourself and leave us alone (i.e. don't bother us any more). —ع*laš had d-duwăl le-kbaṛ ma-ittawaw-š bă*ع*ḍiyathom w-ihenniw d-denya?* Why can't these big nations get along together and leave the world in peace? **2.** to congratulate *henninah be-n-nažaح dyalu.* We congratulated him on his success. **3.** to deliver, to rescue, to save *xeṣṣu ši-ṭbib mezyan lli ġad-ihennih men had l-meṛḍ.* He needs a good doctor to deliver him from this illness. **4.** to save (s.o.) the trouble *ṛak tă*ع*mel fiya xir kbir ila hennitini men s-sfeṛ l-meṛṛakeš.* You'll do me a big favor if you save me the trouble of making a trip to Marrakesh.
** *ḷḷah ihennik!* Good-by!
¶ *henna bal, henna ḍmaġ* to assure, to give confidence to *hennina-lhom balhom u-qolna-lhom šrina ḍ-ḍaṛ.* We assured them that we bought the house. —*ġir henni balek* (or *ḍmaġek*) *men had l-qaḍiya.* Just don't worry about this matter.
henned v.t. to strengthen, to fortify (door, fort, etc.)
hnud **1.** n.pl. of *hendi* **2.** pl. (of intensity) of *hendi, hendiya*
hra ihra v.i. **1.** to be or become overripe **2.** to be or become overcooked **3.** to be or become spoiled (person)
hragem pl. of *hergma*
hrarez pl. of *herrazi*
hrawa pl. *-t* club, cudgel
hṛeb v.i. (v.n. *hṛib, hṛub;* a.p. *haṛeb, heṛban*) **1.** to run away, to flee **2.** to play hooky
heṛba n.i. of *hṛeb*
heṛban **1.** a.p. of *hṛeb* **2.** pl. *-in* fugitive, runaway
hred v.t. (v.n. *hrid*) **1.** to crush **2.** to scrub **3.** to eat a great deal of **4.** to cram (lesson)
¶ *hred n-nab* to chat, to beat one's gums
hergma pl. *-t, hragem* **1.** feet of sheep or cattle **2.** meal of sheep or cattle feet
heṛhuṛi pl. *-yen* **1.** turbulent (of river) **2.** noisy, boisterous
** *duz* ع*ăl l-heṛhuṛi la-dduz* ع*ăl s-sakuti.* saying implying that a person who appears to be quiet and easy-going might turn out to be very hard to handle or deal with
hri pl. *herya, heryan* **1.** storehouse, warehouse **2.** large store **3.** granary
hṛib v.n. of *hṛeb*
hrid v.n. of *hred*
hrim v.n. of *hrem*
hṛiq v.n. of *hṛeq*
hrem v.i. (v.n. *hrim*) to get old, to be broken down by old age (people, things)
hermeš v.t. to partly crush or grind
hernan pl. *-in* grumbler, one who grumbles
hernen v.i. to grumble
heṛneṭ v.i. **1.** to bray (donkey) **2.** to bawl, to scream violently
hṛeq v.t. (v.n. *hṛiq*) to spill (liquid)

¶ *hṛeq l-ma* to urinate

herr v.t. (v.n. *herran*) to tickle *waxxa ka-nherruh ma-ka-iḍɛăk-š.* Even when we tickle him he doesn't laugh.

herr (no pl.) sensitivity to being tickled
¶ *fih*◊ *l-herr* to be ticklish ≠

herra v.t. 1. to overcook 2. to spoil (s.o.)

heṛṛab adj. pl. *-in* n.pl. *-a* 1. deserter, runaway 2. one given to running away 3. one given to playing hooky

herran v.n. of *herr*

heṛṛaqa pl. *-t* urinal

herrazi pl. *-yat, hrarez* cylindrical clay drum open at one end

heṛṛeb v.t. 1. to cause or help to run away, escape *l-ɛăssas b-ṛaṣu lli heṛṛebhom men l-ḥăbs.* It was the guard himself who helped them escape from jail. 2. to cause to stay away, to keep away from *ɛămmeṛha ma-ka-tɛăllem wladha ši-ḥaža lli ġad-theṛṛebhom men l-meḍṛaṣa.* She never teaches her children anything that might keep them away from school. 3. to smuggle out *f-weqt l-ḥăṛb kanu ka-iheṛṛbu s-selɛa le-qlila.* During the war rare goods were smuggled out. 4. to banish, to deport

herrbel kind of sweet gruel made of corn and milk

horrma pl. *-t* obese or very fat person (derisive)

heṛṛeq v.t. to spill (intentionally), to pour (out)

herres v.t. (v.n. *tehras, hers*) 1. to break *škun herres had l-kas?* Who broke this glass? —*ṭaḥet men fuq l-ɛăwd u-herrset rželha.* She fell off the horse and broke her leg. 2. to cut up *herrsu r-rkiza u-gdaw ṭ-ṭṛaf kollhom.* They cut the log up and burned all the pieces. 3. to ruin *dak l-biɛa u-šerya herrsettu.* That business deal ruined him.

herrus see *bu-herrus*

hers v.n. of *herres*

hṛub v.n. of *hṛeb*

herwal pl. *-in* ambler, one that goes at an amble (horse, person)

herwi (sg. and coll.) bull (bovine)

herwel v.i. to go at an amble (horse, person)

herya pl. of *hri*

heryan pl. of *hri*

hšaš v.i. (v.n. *hšaša*) 1. to become tender (e.g., cooked meat) 2. to become crumbly (e.g., construction)

hšaš pl. of *hšiš*

hšaša v.n. of *hšaš*

hšiš pl. *hšaš* 1. tender (e.g., cooked meat) 2. crumbly

htef b- (v.n. *htif*) 1. to acclaim (s.o.) 2. to praise incessantly

htif v.n. of *htef*

htik v.n. of *htek*

htir v.n. of *hter*

htek v.t. (v.n. *htik*) 1. to tear up, to make a hole in (by beating hard on s.th., e.g., a drum) 2. to deflower, to deprive of virginity (pejorative)
¶ *htek l-ḥorma dyal, htek ḥormt* to cast aspersions on the honor of (s.o.), to dishonor, to disgrace

htemm b- 1. to take care of *ɛămmeṛha ma-htemmet b-ṣeḥḥtha.* She never took care of her health. 2. to be interested in, to give importance to, to pay attention to *kan ka-ihtemm be-l-muḥaḍaṛat.* He used to be interested in lectures. 3. to worry about, to be concerned about *ka-ihtemmu bezzaf be-l-musteqbal dyalu.* They are very much concerned about his career.

hter v.i. (v.n. *htir*) 1. to talk nonsense, to wander 2. to get out of hand (as a spoiled child)

hetref v.i. to rave, to talk deliriously

hudhud same as *hedhud*

hul pl. *hwal* calamity, trouble, disaster

huma they (pl. disjunctive pron.)

humum pl. of *hemm*

huwa (m. sg. disjunctive pron.) 1. he *huwa ma-ɛăndu flus.* He has no money. —*ṛa-huwa maži ġedda.* He's coming tomorrow. 2. it *ha le-ktab ɛla-š ka-ḍḍuṛ.* —*fayn huwa?* Here's the book you're looking for.—Where is it? 3. used as a question marker *huwa lli tlaqat?* Was he the one she met? —*škun huwa had l-weld?* Who's this boy? —*fayn huwa ṭ-ṭbib?* Where's the doctor?
¶ *huwa lli* he, it (emphatic), he's the one who *huwa lli bda had d-dbaz.* He's the one who started this fight.
** *huwa hadak.* That's him (That's the one); That's it (That's the one); It's the same (it comes out the same). —*huwa huwa.* It's the same (there's no difference).

huwwa v.t. 1. to air, to ventilate (a place) 2. to make cool 3. to fan

huwwas pl. *-in* bothersome, annoying

huwwed v.i. to go down, to come down, to descend

huwwel v.t. to worry, to alarm *bqit mhuwwel mnin ma-ɛăyyetti-š.* I was worried when you didn't call. —*huwwlu n-nas b-le-xbaṛ lli žabu.* They alarmed the people with the news they brought.

huwwen v.t. to facilitate, to make easy *waldih huwwnu ɛlih koll-ši mnin ɛṭaweh le-flus lli xeṣṣuh.* His parents made everything easy for him by giving him all the money he needed

huwwes v.t. to bother, to annoy

hužum v.n. of *hžem*
hwa ihwa v.t. (v.n. *hwa*) **1.** to love, to fall in love with *ka-ihwa l-musiqa.* He loves music. **2.** to please, to be agreeable to *hwatni ṭ-ṭabiεa d-had le blad.* I like the scenery in this town.
hwa (m.) **1.** v.n. of *hwa* **2.** air *εell s-seržem baš idxolna šwiya d-le-hwa.* Open the window so we can have some air. **3.** climate, weather *le-hwa de-bladkom ṣεib.* Your country has a rough climate. **4.** capriciousness
hwal pl. of *hul*
hwas annoyance, bother
¶ *fihᵠ le-hwas* to be annoying, bothersome ≠ *had d-drari šεal fihom d-le-hwas!* These children are so annoying!
hwayeš pl. of *hiša*
hăwl same as *hul*
hewya pl. *-t* ditch, large hole in the ground
hăyʔa same as *hiʔa*
hyaḍeṛ pl. of *hiḍuṛa*
hyat v.n. of *hayet*
hyuš pl. of *hiša*
hzal pl. of *hzil*
hil pl. *-in, hzal* (comp. *hzel*) thin, skinny, slender, lean *l-begṛat lli εăndu kollhom hzal.* All the cows he has are skinny. —*šrat waεed l-lεăm hzil.* She bought lean meat.
hziza (a) little while *bqa mεana ġir hziza u-mša.* He stayed just a little while with us and then left.
hzel v.i. to become thin, to become skinny
hzel comp. of *hzil*
hezz (v.n. *hezzan*) **1.** to take, to pick up *ṛa-εna hezzina-lkom men makeltkom.* We took some of your food. —*hezz dak le-ktab qbel ma-izḍem εlih ši-waεed.* Pick up that book before somebody steps on it. **2.** to shake, to move *bqa ihezz ṭ-ṭebla εetta therrsu kerεanha.* He shook the table so hard that the legs broke. **3.** to lift *hezz režlik baš nšeṭṭeb teεthom.* Lift your feet so I can sweep under them.
¶ *hezz nifuᵠ εla* to look with disdain upon
hezza pl. *-t* n.i. of *hezz*
¶ *hezza ʔaṛḍiya* earthquake
hezzan v.n. of *hezz*
hža ihži v.t. (v.n. *hižaʔ*) to attack or malign (s.o.) through poetry, to lampoon in poetry
hžažel pl. of *hežžal* and *hežžala*
hžim v.n. of *hžem*
hžem v.i. (v.n. *hžim, hžum, hužum*) to attack, to assault *fayna žäyš lli hžem l-luwwel?* Which army attacked first? —*l-žarida de-l-muεaṛaḍa hežmet bezzaf εla ṛaʔis l-εukuma.* The Prime Minister was bitterly attacked by the opposition newspaper.
hežma **1.** n.i. of *hžem* **2.** pl. *-t* aggressive act
hžeṛ v.t. **1.** to emigrate from **2.** to stop sleeping with (one's wife)
hežṛan v.n. of *hažeṛ*
hžuliya widowhood
hžum v.n. of *hžem*
hežžal pl. *hžažel* widower
hežžala pl. *-t, hžažel* widow
hežžeṛ v.t. to cause to emigrate
¶ *hežžeṛ l-* to make (s.o.) feel sorry or sad after having done s.th. pleasant, to spoil (s.th.) for (s.o.) *qalt-lek ġad-thežžeṛ-lhom nzahthom.* She said she's going to make them feel sorry for (ever) having gone picknicking.
¶ *hežžeṛha~ l-* to change the happiness of (s.o.) into sadness
hežžež v.t. **1.** to disturb *f-neṣṣ l-lil naḍu ka-iddabzu u-hežžžu ž-žiran.* They started fighting in the middle of the night and disturbed the neighbors. **2.** to displace, to force to move *nfaweh u-hežžžu εaʔiltu kollha men ḍaṛhom.* They exiled him and forced all his family to move out of their home.

I

ibari pl. of *ibra*
ibas v.n. of *ibes*
ʔibban (no pl.) **1.** season (of the year, hunting, opera, etc.) **2.** time, epoch, era
ʔibham pl. *-at* **1.** ambiguity, vagueness *ka-tkellem b-ʔibham.* You're speaking ambiguously. **2.** thumb
ʔibĭl (coll.) camel(s) *ka-tewžeb z-zka εetta εăl l-ʔibĭl.* The *zka* must be paid even on camels.
ibis v.n. of *ibes*
ʔiblis (no art.) Satan, the Devil
ibra pl. *-t, ibari* **1.** needle (sewing, hypodermic) **2.** shot (hypodermic)
¶ *ḍṛeb l-ibra l-* to give a shot to
ʔibril same as *ʔabril*
ibes iybes v.i. (1st person impf. sg. *nibes* pl. *nibsu* or *nyebsu,* 3rd person f. sg. impf. *yebsat or yebset,* 3rd person pl. impf. and perfect *yebsu;* v.n. *ibas, ibis, ibus, ibusa*) to dry (out or up) *nšeṛt t-teṣbin baš iybes.* I've hung the wash out to dry. —*had l-xobz ibes men ṣ-ṣbaε l-daba.* This bread has dried out just since this morning.

*** ibest f-maẓălli.* I froze on the spot (from fear.)

¶ a.p. *yabes* pl. *-in* dry

ibus v.n. of *ibes*

ibusa v.n. of *ibes*

ibzaṛ black pepper

ida same as *ila*

idam pl. (of intensity) *idumat* grease (as used in cooking)

idida pl. *-t* dim. of *yedd*

ˀidn (no pl.) authorization, permission

idumat pl. of *idam*

ˀiḍaṛa pl. *-t* 1. administration *l-žamiεa dyalna εăndha ˀiḍaṛa ḍεifa.* Our university has a weak administration. 2. management *l-ˀiḍaṛa d-had l-măεmel žatu ṣεiba bezzaf.* He found the management of this factory very difficult. 3. office *l-ˀiḍaṛat kollhom ka-išeddu f-le-εyad.* All offices are closed during the holidays. 4. principalship, office of principal *hadak ˀustad istaḥeqq ši-ˀiḍaṛa.* He is a teacher fit for principalship.

iġaṛa pl. *-t* (usually with art.) ruckus, big to-do *qiyyem ḥlina l-iġaṛa.* He really raised a ruckus (about it) with us.

iġata 1. v.n. of *ġat* 2. help, assistance, aid *mšaw l-l-iġata dyalu.* They went to his aid.

ˀihmal v.n. of *hmel*

ihud pl. of *ihudi*

ihudi pl. *ihud,* f. *ihudiya* pl. *-t* Jew (person)

ˀiklil (no. pl.) bouquet (of flowers)

ˀikṛam generosity

ila 1. if, in case (that) (not used in contrary-to-fact cases) *ila ṭaḥet š-šta ma-nexṛož-š.* If it rains I won't go out. —*nemši mεak ila ġad-ttεăšša mεana ġedda.* I'll go with you if you have supper with us tomorrow. —*xeṣṣek tebqa hna ḥetta ila ža ižebṛek.* You should stay here so that if he comes he'll find you. 2. used in various expr. *we-ḷḷah ila εăyb εlikom ma-žitiw-š l-εersna.* I'm a little mad at you for not coming to our wedding. —*ḷḷah ixellik ila ma tnub εliya.* Would you please see if you can replace me?

¶ *ila ˀaxirih~* and so forth, et cetera

ˀilah, ilah pl. *-at, ˀaliha* god, deity

*** la-ˀilaha illa ḷḷah, muḥămmed ṛasul ḷḷah.* There is no god but God and Mohammed is the prophet of God.

¶ *l-ˀilah* same as *ḷḷah*

ˀilham inspiration

illa except, but *koll-ši ža illa ḥmed.* Everyone came but Ahmed.

imam, ˀimam pl. *-at* 1. one who leads the prayer in the mosque, imam 2. n.u. *-a* turtle-dove

iman, ˀiman faith, belief (religion)

imaṛa pl. *-t, imayeṛ* 1. trace, sign, clue *š-šeffaṛ ma-xella ḥetta imaṛa fe-ḍ-ḍaṛ.* The thief didn't leave a single clue in the house. 2. track, print (as left by an animal or man) 3. password, countersign 4. proof, evidence *ma-taq biya ḥetta rewwitu l-imaṛa.* He didn't believe me until I showed him proof. 5. description, particulars (for purposes of identification)

imayeṛ pl. of *imaṛa*

ˀimḍaˀ pl. *-at* signature *baš š-šak ikun ṣḥiḥ xeṣṣek tḥeṭṭ fih l-ˀimḍaˀ dyalek.* In order for this check to be valid you'll have to put your signature on it.

imin right, right side *ka-nakol dima b-yeddi d-l-imin.* I always eat with my right hand.

¶ *εăl l-imin* 1. on the right *ḍaṛi εăl l-min.* My house is on the right. 2. right, to the right *sir εăl l-imin!* Go to the right!

¶ *ḥlef b-l-imin* same as *ḥlef b-le-ḥṛam* (see *ḥṛam*)

ˀimkan 1. v.n. of *mken* 2. means, possibility *ṣafeṭ-lhom ˀiεana εla ḥasab l-ˀimkan dyalu.* He sent them a contribution according to his means. —*f-ˀimkanu ixeḷḷeṣ le-qdeṛ kamel.* He can pay all the amount. 2. possibility, ability *f-ˀimkani nṣafeṛ fuq-emma bġit.* I can take the trip any time I want. —*f-ˀimkanek dži had l-lila?* Could you come over tonight?

ˀimma used in the expr. *ˀimma . . . aw,* or *ˀimma . . . wa ˀilla* either . . . or *imken-lek ˀimma tεăyyeṭ-lu aw temši l-εăndu le-ḍ-ḍaṛ.* You can either call him or go to his home.

imen same as *imin*

imni f. *imna, imniya* pl. *-yen* 1. right, on the right 2. right-handed (person)

ˀimta when (interrogative) *ˀimta maži?* When are you coming?

ina which (interrogative) *ina keswa bġiti telbes?* Which dress do you want to put on?

inbaġi used in the expr. *ka-ma inbaġi* suitably, correctly, properly, in due form, right *ka-ixeṣṣek tεameṛ l-weṛqa ka-ma inbaġi.* You must fill out the form correctly. —*ila ma-sketti nṣawbek mεa ṛaṣek ka-ma inbaġi.* If you don't be quiet, I'm going to fix you up right.

ˀindaṛ pl. *-at* ultimatum

ˀinsan, insan 1. man, human (being) *l-ˀinsan siyyed l-ḥayawan.* Man is lord over the animals. 2. pl. *nas* person (pl. people)

¶ *waḥed l-ˀinsan, ši-ˀinsan* somebody, someone

ˀinsaniya mankind, humanity

*** ma-fih ˀinsaniya.* He's cruel, inhuman.

ˀinṣaf fairness, impartiality

intaž v.n. of *ntež*

ˀinžil (usually with art.) 1. gospel (Christian) 2. Bible

iqala v.n. of *qal iqil*
iqama pl. (of intensity) *iqayem* 1. mint (plant) 2. necessary accessories (for doing s.th.) *xeyyeṭti-li l-qeftan?—la, ma-zal, xeṣṣek teŝri-li l-iqama băɛda.* Have you made that caftan for me?—No, not yet; you'll have to buy me the stuff first. 3. ingredients (as in preparing a meal)
¶ *l-iqama de-ṣ-ṣiniya* tea set (i.e., all the necessary utensils for making and serving)
iqayem pl. of *iqama*
ˀiqbal clientele
ˀiqraṛ approval, ratification
irŝadat (pl.) instructions (to be carried out)
ˀislam (with art.) 1. Islam, Muslim religion 2. v.n. of *slem* 2
ˀislami pl. *-yen* Islamic
ˀism, ism pl. *ˀasmaˀ, asami, smiyat* (usually *sem or sm* in cons.) name *smek?* What's your name?
¶ *b-ismi llah,* or *be-sme-llah* 1. in the name of God 2. let's get started (eating, working, etc.)
ˀisṛafil archangel who is to announce the Final Judgment
ˀisṛaˀil Israel
isṛi same as *iṣṛi*
istidɛa same as *stidɛa*
istiġlal same as *stiġlal*
istinaf same as *stinaf*
istiɛmal same as *stiɛmal*
iṣaba pl. *-t* goal, score (soccer, hockey)
iṣaṛ, iṣeṛ left *ka-ikteb b-yeddu d-l-iṣaṛ.* He writes with his left hand.
¶ *ɛăl l-iṣaṛ, ɛăl l-iṣeṛ* 1. left, to the left *ḍuṛ ɛăl l-iṣaṛ hna.* Turn left here. 2. on the left —*ŝritha men l-ḥanut lli ɛăl l-iṣeṛ.* I bought it from the shop which is on the left.
ˀiṣlaḥ pl. *-at* v.n. of *ṣleḥ*
iṣṛi f. *iṣṛa, iṣṛiya* pl. *-yen* 1. left, on the left *žeṛḥet yeddha l-iṣṛiya.* She cut her left hand. 2. left-handed (person)
iŝafi pl. of *iŝfa*
iŝaṛa pl. *-t* 1. signal, sign *ɛṭini l-iŝaṛa mnin tebġini nxerrež le-ɛmaṛa.* Give me the signal when you want me to fire. 2. sign, direction (e.g. street sign) 3. gesture (as with the hand) 4. mark, scar 5. landmark 6. omen, presage, sign 7. target
¶ *ḍreb l-iŝaṛa* to play at throwing rocks (or similar item) at a target (as old cans); to indulge in target-shooting
iŝaɛa pl. *-t* rumor
iŝfa pl. *-t, iŝafi* awl
iŝŝir (pl. *drari*) little boy
itama pl. of *itim*
itbat v.n. of *tbet*
itim pl. *itama,* f. *itima* pl. *-t* orphan (either parent or both dead)
ˀitqan v.n. of *tqen*
¶ *be-l-ˀitqan* to perfection, with great pains
iṭali pl. *-yen* Italian
iṭalya Italy
iṭṛa pl. *-t, iṭaṛi* payment (by installment plan) *ma-zalin-li ṛebɛa d-l-iṭaṛi u-nkemmel le-xlaṣ de-ḍ-ḍaṛ.* I still have four more payments to make on the house.
iṭṛu pl. *-yat, -wat* liter
iwa interjection of various usages *iwa!* Hey! (i.e., you kids be quiet); Well, go on! (i.e., what happened then?). —*iwa sir!* Well, go on! —*iwa, nemŝiw?* Well, shall we go?
i-we-llahi expr. of emphasis *i-we-llahi biɛa u-ŝerya hadi!* My God, what a problem (i.e., situation)!
ixiya bleach
ˀixwan pl. of *xu*
ixx expr. of disgust or repugnance at an offensive odor or filth
iyeh yes
iyyam, iyyamat pl. of *yum*
iyyas same as *yeˀs*
izaṛ pl. *izuṛ* (bed) sheet
izuṛ pl. of *izaṛ*
ižaṛa pl. *-t, ižayeṛ* 1. pay, salary (regular) 2. remuneration
ižayeṛ pl. of *ižaṛa*
ˀižaza pl. *-t* 1. vacation, leave 2. degree, diploma
ˀiḥsan kindness, benevolence
ˀiḥṣaˀ v.n. of *ḥṣa*
ˀiḥtilal v.n. of *ḥtell*
iɛana help, aid, assistance
ˀiɛdam 1. v.n. of *ɛdem* 2. capital punishment
ˀiɛlam pl. *-at* announcement, notice (written or spoken)

K

kabab pieces or cutlets of meat (usually lamb) broiled on a skewer
¶ *kabab meġḍuṛ* dish of lamb cutlets cooked with onions, parsley, spices, and sometimes eggs
kabina pl. *-t* bathroom (usually with toilet only)
kaber v.i. to stick with it, to not give up, to persevere
¶ *kaber mɛa* to be tolerant of (s.o.), to not give up on (s.o.)
kabṛan pl. *-at* 1. corporal 2. foreman
kabus pl. *kwabes* pistol, revolver
kada used in the expr. *kada wa-kada* such

and such *qolt-lu xeḷḷeṣt kada wa-kada.* I told him I paid such an such.

kadalik **1.** too, also *ana kadalik qemt fe-s-setta de-ṣ-ṣbaꜥ.* I got up at six in the morning too. **2.** either (with negative sentence) *kadalik ana ma-ꜥăndi flus.* I don't have any money either. **3.** exactly, right (in affirmative replies) *ma-qolt-lu-ši imken-lu yaxodha?—kadalik.* Didn't I tell him he could have it?—Right.

kadăṛ grief, sadness

kaf pl. *kifan* cave, cavern, grotto

kafa v.t. (v.n. *mkafya*) to reward *kafana ꜥăl l-xedma lli xdemna.* He rewarded us for the work that we did.

kafatira pl. *-t* type of hot-water heater (e.g. used in a café)

kaffa all *le-mġaṛba kaffa ka-ifeḍḍlu atay ꜥăl l-qehwa.* All Moroccans prefer tea to coffee.

kafi a.p. of *kfa*

kafuṛ camphor

kaġiṭ, kaġeṭ pl. *kwaġeṭ* **1.** paper (in general)

kaka v.i. to laugh out loud, to guffaw

kal yakol same as *kla*

kala v.t. **1.** to chock, to wedge (as to immobilize a vehicle or door) **2.** to cause or make stall (an engine)

kala pl. *-t* chock, wedge (for immobilizing s.th.)

kama, ka-ma as, like *ṣeqqem kama qolt-lek!* Do as I told you!

** *xellih kama huwa!* Leave it like it is! —*ṣ-ṣafaṛ kan kama inbaġi.* The trip was just right.

kamal perfection

kamanža pl. *-t* violin

kamanži pl. *-ya* violinist

kamiyu pl. *-yat, -wat* truck *waš kamiyu dyal sebꜥa ṭun iqeddek baš tneqqel s-selꜥa?* Will a seven-ton truck be enough for you to haul the merchandise?

kamel a.p. of *kmel*

kamun cumin

kamuni pl. *-yen* brownish-green (i.e., color of cumin)

kan ikun **1.** to be (not expressed in equational sentences) *l-muḥaḍaṛa kanet muhimma.* The lecture was interesting. —*ma-txelli ḥetta waḥed idxol ꜥăndi waxxa ikun ḅḅa!* Don't let anyone in here, even if it's my father! —*ṣuq ꜥam d-duwăli ka-ikun ꜥadatan fe-ḍ-ḍaṛ l-biḍa.* The Annual International Fair is usually in Casablanca. —*kun ḍṛiyyef!* Be nice! **2.** to exist, there to be *ila ma-kan-š ḷḷah škun xḷeq had l-ꜥalăm?* If God doesn't exist (or, there is no God), who created this world? —*kanu bezzaf d-le-qbayel d-le-hnud f-ʔamirika.* There were many Indian tribes in America. **3.** various auxiliary uses *kanet dima ka-tqul-lu iži bekri.* She always used to tell him to come early. —*ꜥlaš ma-kanet-š ka-tehḍeṛ mꜥah?—kan qal-lha ši-klam qbiḥ.* Why wasn't she talking to him?—He had said something to her she didn't like. —*ġedda f-had l-weqt tkun wṣelti.* By this time tomorrow you will have arrived. —*kun dži bekri koll nhaṛ.* Come early every day.

** *sir tqelleb ꜥlih kan ꜥăl ḷḷah telqah.* Go look for him to see if you can find him. —*w-ila kan!* So what! What of it! —*hada ma kan.* That's all (there is). —*dak š-ši lli kan.* (Do, Say, Give, etc.) whatever you can; something, anything. —*u-kan?* Is that all? No more?

¶ *ikun* maybe, perhaps *ikun ꜥṭaha-lhom.* Maybe he gave it to them.

¶ *u-kan* if *u-kan ma-konti-š ꜥăndi ꜥziza ma-nqul-lek-š had le-klam.* If you weren't such a good friend I wouldn't tell you this.

kanaṛ pl. *-at* canary (bird)

kantina pl. *-t* canteen, cantina, cabaret

kanun pl. *kwanen* type of brazier (for cooking and heat)

kaṛ pl. *-at, kiṛan* bus (cross-country)

kaṛa pl. *-t* trick, wile

kaṛama pl. *-t* s.th. good, good fortune, gift (from God)

kaṛḅun carbide(used in generating acetylene)

kari a.p. of *kra*

karim pl. *kuṛama* generous, beneficent, munificent.

¶ *l-karim* The Beneficent (God)

karem a.p. of *krem*

kaṛăm generosity, munificence

kaṛṭa pl. *-t, kwaṛeṭ* **1.** card (membership, credit, playing, etc.) **2.** (coll., with above pl. as cpl.; sg. *weṛqa de-l-kaṛṭa*) (deck of) cards

karyan pl. *-at* quarry (rock)

kas pl. *kisan* **1.** (drinking) glass **2.** cup (trophy)

kasăl laziness

kasăṛ used in the expr. *ma-ꜥăndi kasăṛ.* I don't care one way or the other.

kašša pl. *-t, kwaš* type of light blanket, cover

kateb v.t. to correspond with, to write to (regularly)

katib pl. *kottab* **1.** secretary **2.** writer (as in a newspaper)

katir same as *ktir*

kaṭṛi pl. *-yat* wooden shelf built just below the ceiling, used for storage, and often a bed.

kawakib pl. of *kewkeb*

kawatšu rubber (especially of tires)

kawkaw n.u. *-a* peanut(s)

kawya pl. *-t, kwawi* **1.** solder **2.** welding metal

kayaṣ **1.** gravel (large gauge) **2.** n.u. *-a* rock, stone (e.g., which one might throw)

kayen, kayn pl. *-in* there is, there are (pl. used mostly with persons) *waš kayen ši-waعed fe-ḍ-ḍaṛ?* Is there anyone at home? —*kaynin ši-nas temma?* Are there any people there?

** *ma-kayen علaš temši l-temma.* There's no reason for you to go there. —*fayn kayna ḍaṛkom?* Where is your house?

kayenn (with pron. endings) as if *ka-tăعṛef l-meġṛib kayennek konti temma.* You know (about) Morocco as if you had been there.

kbabeṭ pl. of *kebbuṭ*

kbad pl. of *kebda*

kbal pl. of *kbel*

kbal n.u. *-a* ear of corn

kbaṛ pl. of *kbir*

kbaš pl. of *kebš*

kbaybi pl. *-ya* one who makes, cooks, and sells *kabab*

kebb ikobb (v.n. *kebban, kobban*) **1.** v.t. to pour (liquids) *kobb-li šwiya d-atay f-had l-kas!* Pour me a little tea in this glass. **2.** v.i. to come unexpectedly in large numbers (e.g., guests)

¶ *kebb عla* **1.** to concentrate on, to take great pains with **2.** to crowd around (s.o. or s.th.) *l-xeddama kollhom kebbu عăl l-mekteb de-l-mudir.* All the workers crowded around the manager's office.

kobba pl. *-t, kbeb* (dim. *kbiba*) ball, skein (of yarn, etc.)

¶ *kobba men šib* (or *d-šib*) area of grey or white hair (on s.o.'s head)

kebban, kobban v.n. of *kebb*

kobbaniya pl. *-t* **1.** company, firm **2.** group (of people)

kebbeb v.t. to twine or roll into a *kobba* (yarn, etc.)

kebbed v.i. (some v.t. use) to coagulate (blood)

kebbel v.t. to fetter, to put handcuffs or shackles on (s.o.'s hands, feet; may extend to rope used in tying s.o.)

kebber v.t. **1.** to grow, to raise (flowers, crops, etc.) **2.** to raise, to rear (child) **3.** to enlarge, to make bigger

¶ *kebber b-* **1.** to do (s.o.) an honor *žiti l-عăndi u-kebberti biya.* You do me an honor by coming to my house. **2.** to receive cordially, warmly **3.** to build up (s.o.)

¶ *kebber keršu*$^{\phi}$ to be or act greedy

kebbeṛ to say the expr. *ʔeḷḷahu ʔekbaṛ*

kebbuṭ pl. *kbabeṭ* **1.** coat, jacket **2.** pullover, sweater **3.** overcoat

kebda pl. *-t, kbad, kbud* (dim. *kbida*) **1.** liver **2.** courage *kbedtu qaṣعa, gaع ma-ka-ixaf.* He has great courage and fears nothing. **3.** love, affection *l-yemm عăndha l-kebda* *عla wladha.* A mother has children.

¶ *ṛebba l-kebda عla* to devel of or fondness for *bubker ṛeι* *عla šṛib l-qehwa.* Bubker has the habit of drinking coffee.

** *aži, ya kbidti!* Come, my dε children)

kbibeṛ pl. *-in* not very old but ol certain others (as a twelve-year-ol seven- or eight-year-olds).

¶ *kbibeṛ عla* a little bigger than

kbida dim. of *kebda*

kbir pl. *kbaṛ* (comp. *kbeṛ*) **1.** big, lar *ṣ-ṣebbaṭ kbir عliya.* These shoes are big for me. **2.** old, aged (person) **3.** serious (matter)

kbel pl. *kbal* leg irons, fetters

kber v.i. **1.** to get big(ger), to enlarge **2.** to get or become old or aged (per **3.** to grow (up) (person, plant, anin

kbeṛ comp. of *kbir*

kboṛ old age (of person)

kebrata pl. *-t* reed basket-like device plac over a brazier, used to dry certain cloth (usually diapers)

kebrit sulfur

kebriti pl. *-yen* light or pale yellow

kebret v.t. to treat with sulfur

kebš pl. *kbaš* male sheep, ram

kbud pl. of *kebda*

kda u- odd *xeḷḷeṣt kda u-عešrin derhem.* I paid twenty-odd dirhams.

kdeb v.i. (v.n. *kdub*) to lie, to tell a lie *علaš kdebti عliya?* Why did you lie to me?

kedba pl. *-t* lie, untruth

keddab adj. pl. *-in* n.pl. *-a* **1.** liar **2.** one who frequently breaks his word

keddeb v.t. **1.** not to believe, to give the lie to (s.o.) **2.** to deny (a fact)

keddeṛ v.t. **1.** to irritate, to peeve **2.** to cause to be saddened or grieved

keddes v.t. **1.** to put into a pile or heap, to pile or heap **2.** to cram, to stuff (s.th. into s.th.)

kdi pl. of *kodya*

kdub v.n. of *kdeb*

¶ *b-le-kdub* used to express the pretending or faking of some action *ġadi nḍeṛbek b-le-kdub.* I'm going to pretend to hit you.

kodya pl. *-t, kdi* **1.** hill, knoll **2.** mound, bump (on the ground)

keḍḍeṛ same as *keddeṛ*

kfa ikfi (v.n. *kfaya*) to be enough, to suffice *عṭitu žuž kilu de-l-limun u-kfaweh.* The two kilos of oranges I gave him were enough (for him).

** *ikfik men le-qṛaya.* You've done enough studying.

¶ a.p. *kafi* pl. *kafyen* enough *waš had š-ši*

lli žebt-lek kafi wella la? Is what I brought you enough (or not)?
kfaf pl. of *kfif*
kfafes pl. of *keffus*
kfaya **1.** v.n. of *kfa* **2.** sufficiency
kfayti pl. *-ya* one who sells hamburger or ground beef, i.e. *kefta* (sometimes cooked)
kfef pl. of *keffa*
keff pl. *kfuf* palm (hand)
keffa pl. *-t, kfef* pan (of balance or scales)
koffaṛ pl. of *kafer* (a.p. of *kfeṛ*)
keffef v.i. **1.** to clap (hands) **2.** to applaud
¶ *keffef ʕla* **1.** to clap for (as in calling a servant) **2.** to applaud for (s.o.)
keffen v.t. to put the shroud or winding sheet on (the dead)
keffes v.t. to ruin, (meal, work, watch, etc.)
keffus pl. *kfafes* **1.** soot, lampblack **2.** hideous, ugly, deformed (expr. used by women)
kfif pl. *-in, kfaf* blind, sightless
kfiṛ v.n. of *kfeṛ*
kfen pl. *kfuna* shroud, winding sheet (for the dead)
kfeṛ v.i. (v.n. *kfiṛ*) **1.** to renounce or apostatize from Islam **2.** to get irritated or furious (as from losing one's patience, or from frustration)
¶ a.p. *kafer* pl. *koffaṛ* unbeliever (in Islam), non-Muslim, infidel
kfes (*men*) worse (than) *huwa kfes menni f-le-ḥsab.* He's worse than me in arithmetic.
kefta ground meat (usually beef)
kfuf pl. of *keff*
kfuna pl. of *kfen*
kehhan pl. *-a* **1.** sorcerer, magician **2.** fortune-teller
kehhen v.i. **1.** to indulge in or practice sorcery **2.** to practice fortune-telling
ki abbreviated form of *kif* (the adv.)
kib pl. *kyab* type of overhanging roof covering a door or window
kidaṛ pl. *kyaḍeṛ* (he-)mule
kif marijuana (prepared for smoking)
kif (usually *ki* before consonants) **1.** how (with *-en* before *hiya, huwa, huma;* often with *-aš* when equivalent to "in what manner") *kif-en huwa ḅḅak?* How's your father? —*kif* (or *kif-aš*) *ka-tḥell had ṣ-ṣenḍuq?* How do you open this box? —*werri-li kif-aš nestăʕmel had l-makina.* Show me how to use this machine. **2.** as, like *ḥmed kif xah.* Ahmed is like his brother. —*ʕmel kif qolt-lek!* Do as I told you! **3.** as soon as, when *kif dxel mša itḥămmem.* As soon as he came in he went to take a bath.
¶ *beḥṛa kif, yaḷḷah kif* just *beḥṛa kif wṣel had ṣ-ṣbaḥ.* He just arrived this morning.
¶ *kif kif* just alike, the same *huma kif kif.* They're just alike.
** *kif kif!* Makes no difference (to me).
¶ *kifu*⌽ *kif* (to be) just like ≠ *kifu kif ḅḅah.* He's just like his father.
¶ *kif-ma, kif-emma* as *kif-emma bġiti.* As you wish.
kifan pl. of *kaf*
kifaya sufficiency
kifayaš same as *kif-aš* (variation of *kif,* how)
kifiya **1.** way, manner *ana ġadi nrewwik l-kifiya baš txeddem had l-ʔala.* I'll show you the way to run this machine. **2.** method, procedure *šniya l-kifiya lli stăʕmelti baš txerrež had l-muškila l-ḥisabiya?* What procedure did you follow to solve this arithmetic problem?
kil pl. *kyal* (amount of) two liters (wet or dry)
kilu pl. *-wat, -yat* kilogram
ki-ma same as *kif-ma* (see *kif,* how)
kimiya **1.** chemistry **2.** s.th. outstanding or marvelous, a wonder
ki-mma same as *kif-ma* (see *kif,* how)
kina quinine
kir pl. *kyar* **1.** bellows **2.** accordion, concertina
kiṛan pl. of *kaṛ*
kis pl. *kyas, kyus* pouch, bag (for money)
¶ *kis de-l-ḥămmam* bag-like mitten used for washing in the bath
kisan pl. of *kas*
kitaba same as *ktaba*
kitabatan by or in writing
kitabi pl. *-yen* written (i.e., not oral)
kitab-ḷḷah the Koran
kiyy n.u. *-a* n.i. of *kwa* **2, 3,** and **4**
** *kiyytek!* Now you're in for it! You'll get hell for doing that! (said by women)
kiyyal pl. *-a* one who measures out cereal grains
¶ *ʕṭa wden l-kiyyal* to pretend not to hear *ʕṭani wden l-kiyyal.* He pretended he didn't hear me.
kiyyas pl. *-a* masseur (in the public bath)
kiyyef v.t. to give (s.o.) *kif* to smoke
kiyyel v.t. to measure (out) (cereal grains)
kiyyes v.t. to wash (s.o.) with the *kis de-l-ḥămmam*
kiyyes pl. *-in* **1.** refined, having finesse (in one's manner) **2.** intelligent
ʔekked v.t. to confirm, to make sure of (information, etc.)
¶ *ʔekked ʕla* to make sure (s.o.) knows or is aware *ʔekked ʕlih baš iži ʕăndna l-yum fe-l-lil.* Make sure he knows he's to come to our house tonight.
kel same as *kla*
kla yakol (impv. *kul* pl. *kulu;* a.p. *wakel;* p.p. *mukul*) **1.** to eat *men ṣ-ṣbaḥ ma-klit.* I haven't eaten since morning. —*le-mselmin*

ma-ka-yaklu-š l-ẓălluf. Muslims don't eat pork. —*l-ʕăwd ma-ka-yakol-š l-lẓăm.* A horse doesn't eat meat. 2. to itch *ḍehṛi ka-yakolni.* My back itches (i.e., is itching me). 3. to take (a trick in cards, or a man in chess)

** *klani f-flusi.* He didn't pay me what he owes me. —*kla le-ʕṣa.* He got a beating, a whipping. —*leẓmek ka-yaklek!* You're asking for it! (a beating or whipping)

¶ a.p. *wakel* pl. *-in*

** *ana ʕayeš wakel šaṛeb, l-ẓămdu-llah.* Thank God I have plenty to eat and drink.

klab pl. of *kelb*

klaleb pl. of *kellab, kollab*

klam 1. what is said or told *klamha dima mezyan.* She always says nice things. —*ka-tqul-lu ši-klam.* She's telling him something. —*ma-ka-ismăʕ-š klam ḅḅah.* He doesn't pay any attention to what his father says. 2. language *ka-ifhem klam ṭ-ṭyuṛ.* He understands the language of birds. —*ka-tăʕṛef le-klam de-š-šluẓ?* Do you know the language of the Berbers? 3. saying, maxim *tṣennet l-had le-klam dyal ʔaflaṭun!* Listen to this saying of Plato's.

kḷaṭa pl. *-t, kḷayeṭ* rifle

klawi pl. of *kelwa*

kḷayeṭ pl. of *kḷaṭa*

kelb pl. *klab* 1. dog (canine) 2. kind of sea-perch

kelfa, kolfa pl. *-t* 1. gift or group of gifts (as at a reception or shower) 2. family get-together, party

keḷfeṭ v.t. 1. to throw down or to the ground 2. to throw *keḷfṭet-lu l-kuṛa.* She threw him the ball.

kell v.i. to get tired, to become exhausted

¶ *kell u-mell (men)* to be fed up (with)

koll 1. every, each *ʕăndak yeẓsabek koll ktab ṛah mezyan.* Don't think that every book is good. 2. all (of) *kla t-teffaẓa kollha.* He ate all (of) the apple. —*ṭ-ṭalaba kollhom hedṛu f-dak l-muẓaḍaṛa.* All the students talked about that lecture. —*had le-klam ṛah metwežžeh lilkom kollkom.* This (i.e., these words) is directed to all of you.

¶ *be-l-koll* at all *be-l-koll ma-ʕămmṛu ža lle-hna.* He never came here at all.

¶ *koll-ma,* or *koll-emma* 1. whenever, every time (that) *koll-emma ža žab mʕah hdiya.* Every time he came he brought a present with him. 2. whatever, everything that, all that *ʕṭaha koll-emma ʕăndu.* He gave her everything he had.

¶ *koll-men* whoever, anyone or anybody who *koll-men xalef l-qanun itʕaqeb.* Anyone who disobeys the law will be punished.

¶ *koll-ši* 1. everything 2. everybody, everyone *koll-ši feṛẓan lli žiti.* Everyone's happy that you came.

¶ *koll waẓed* everybody, everyone

kellab, kollab pl. *klaleb* dental forceps or tongs

kellef v.t. (v.n. *takelluf*) to put in charge, to charge *škun lli kellfek b-had š-šġal?* Who put you in charge of this job? —*škun lli kellfek tăʕmel had š-šġal?* Who put you in charge of doing this work?

¶ *kellef ʕla* to try to constrain or compel (more insisting than forcing) *ma-tkellef-š ʕliya ṛani šbăʕt.* Don't insist (i.e., don't compel me to eat more), I'm full.

kellem v.t. 1. to speak to or with 2. to call, to tell (to come), to summon *kellmu-li!* Tell him to come here (i.e., call him for me)! 3. to shoot, to fire (rifle, cannon, for the loud report) *kellmu le-mdafeʕ d-ṛemḍan.* They have fired the cannons announcing the beginning of Ramadan. 4. to make a sound or noise with *ma-tkellem-š ṣ-ṣebbaṭ!* Don't make any noise with those shoes!

kelma pl. *-t* word *ma-ʕămmṛi smăʕt had l-kelma.* I've never heard this word before. —*ʕṭani l-kelma.* He gave me his word.

** *xellini nqul-lek ġir kelma weẓda.* Let me talk to you for just a second.

kluf nosiness, inordinate curiosity

klufi pl. *-yen* nosy, overly curious

kelwa pl. *-t, klawi* kidney

kelxa used in the expr. *ʕla kelxa!* What a numbskull!

kma ikmi (v.n. *kemyan*) to smoke *šnu ka-tekmi?—ma-ka-nekmi-š.* What do you smoke?—I don't smoke.

kmal, kmala (cons. *kmalt*) 1. completion (v.n. of *kmel*) *f-le-ʕšiya ʕăndna waẓed ḍ-ḍyafa dyal kmalt ḍ-ḍaṛ.* In the evening we're having a reception to celebrate the completion of our house. 2. rest, remainder *fayn le-kmala d-le-flus lli ka-nsalek?* Where's the rest of the money you owe me? 3. end, ending (as of a story)

¶ *kmalt le-ʕṭiya* final answer, with attendant ceremony, of the parents of the girl whose hand has been asked in marriage

¶ *kmalt ṛ-ṛebʕa, le-mya,* etc. the fourth (one), the hundredth (one), etc.

kmam pl. of *kemm, komm*

kmama pl. *-t* muzzle (as used on a dog)

kmamer pl. of *kemmara*

kmanḍaṛ pl. *-at* major (officer)

kmaš 1. (coll.) wrinkles (in cloth, face, etc.) 2. fight (hand to hand)

kmaši pl. of *kemša*

kmel v.i. (v.n. *kmal, kmala*) to end, to come to an end, to be finished

¶ a.p. *kamel* pl. *-in* 1. complete, entire *had l-kaṛṭa ma-kamla-š.* This deck of cards isn't complete. 2. (with art.) God 3. all *ɛṭani le-flus kamlin.* He gave me all the money. —*žaw kamlin.* They all came.

kemm, komm pl. *kmam* sleeve (clothes)

kemma v.t. 1. to make (s.o.) smoke (cigarettes, etc.) *kemmawni l-kif.* They made me smoke marijuana. 2. to give to smoke *kemmini, ḷḷah ixellik!* Give me something to smoke, please!

kemmara pl. *-t, kmamer* face (pejorative; human and animal)

kemmay pl. *-a* habitual smoker, one who smokes a great deal

kemmed v.t. 1. to warm (body, feet, etc., usually with hot water) 2. to press (on), to exert pressure on (a bruise with the hand, compress) 3. to heal, to help heal (an open cut)

** *kemmedha u-sket.* He maintained his composure (through the crisis).

kommiya pl. *-t* kind of curved knife or dagger (worn slung around the shoulder)

kemmel v.t. to finish, to complete

** *kemmel men ṛaṣek!* You can just imagine the rest! —*kemmlu fiha.* They've set the marriage up (i.e., both parents have agreed on the match).

¶ *kemmel b-* to be through with *kemmelti b-had le-ktab?* Are you through with this book?

¶ *kemmel ɛla* to finish off (kill, and also metaphorical sense)

kemmem v.t. 1. to muzzle (dog) 2. to gag (s.o.)

kemmes v.t. to wrap (up) (not necessarily neatly)

kemmeš v.t. 1. to wrinkle (face, cloth, etc.) 2. to grab, to grasp (with a wide-open hand) 3. to double (up) (fist, toes) 4. to pucker, to cause to pucker (mouth)

kemmuša pl. *-t* make-shift bag or sack (as s.th. wadded up in a handkerchief)

kmeš pl. of *kemša*

kemša pl. *-t, kmaši, kmeš* handful

kemya pl. *-t* n.i. of *kma*

kemyan v.n. of *kma*

knaneš pl. of *konnaš, kennaš*

knayes pl. of *knisa*

kniniṛ pl. *-at* colonel

knis v.n. of *knes*

knisa pl. *knayes* church

knisiya pl. *-t* same as *knisa*

kniya pl. *-t* nickname

kniz v.n. of *knez*

kenna v.t. to call, to nickname, to give (s.o.) the nickname (of) *ka-ikenniweh dambu.* They call him *dambu.*

kennas pl. *-a* 1. sweeper, one who sweeps 2. raker, one who rakes (as leaves on a lawn)

kennasa pl. *-t* broom (for sweeping)

konnaš, kennaš pl. *knaneš* 1. notebook 2. writing pad

kenneš v.t. to record (as in a notebook)

knes v.t. (v.n. *knis*) to sweep (floor, etc.)

knuz pl. of *kenz*

kenwa pl. *-t* same as *kniya*

knez v.t. (v.n. *kniz*) to treasure, to hoard (s.th. valuable)

kenz pl. *knuz* treasure, valuable or treasured object

kra ikri (v.n. *kra*) to rent *l-bareḥ kra dak ḍ-ḍaṛ l-xay.* Yesterday he rented that house to my brother. —*krit mennu s-siyaṛa dyalu b-ɛešrin derhem.* I rented his car from him for twenty dirhams.

¶ a.p. *kari* pl. *korray* 1. renter, lessee 2. lessor, landlord

kra 1. v.n. of *kra* 2. pl. *-wat* rent (payment)

kṛafeṣ celery

krakeb pl. of *kerkuba*

kṛakeṛ pl. of *keṛkuṛ*

kṛaṛeṣ pl. of *keṛṛuṣa*

kṛaṛṣi pl. *-ya* one who hires himself and his cart out for various transporting jobs

krasa pl. of *korsi*

kerballu pl. *-yat* sifter, sieve

kerbel v.t. to sift, to strain (with the *kerballu*).

kord n.u. *-a* stone, rock (small enough to throw)

kordas n.u. *-a* tripe (mostly of sheep)

kerdeġ v.t. to crunch, to crumple (s.th. stiff, but ultimately pliable)

kref (v.n. *krif*) 1. v.t. to tighten, to make tight (a knot, belt, etc.) 2. v.i. to shrink

¶ *kref ɛla* to grab, to take hold of (s.o., by the collar, sleeve, belt, etc.)

keṛfa pl. *-t* 1. that which is strained or sifted out 2. s.th. cheap, of poor quality (also used for persons)

keṛfaṣ pl. *-a* one who does things in a slipshod manner

keṛfeṣ v.t. 1. to botch (up), to do in a slipshod manner 2. to maltreat, to beat (s.o.) unnecessarily

keṛfeṭ same as *keḷfeṭ*

kṛeh v.t. (v.n. *kṛih*) to hate, to dislike, to detest

¶ *ma-kṛeh-š* to not mind if, to be glad to *ma-nkṛeh-š nešṛob šwiya d-atay.* I don't mind if I do have some tea.

koṛh, koṛhaniya hate or hatred, dislike, aversion

krif v.n. of *kref*

kṛih v.n. of *kṛeh*

krim 1. v.n. of *krem* 2. same as *karim*
kriša dim. of *kerš*
kerkeb v.t. to roll, to make roll(as a ball, log)
korkdan, kerkdan pl. *-at* rhinoceros
keṛkeṛ 1. to throw together, to pack up (hurriedly) 2. to dump, to unload in a quick, noisy fashion 2. to have a noisy, diarrhetic bowel movement
kerkuba pl. *-t, krakeb* bump (as from a blow)
¶ *kerkuba de-l-ʕăyn* eyeball
keṛkuṛ pl. *kṛakeṛ* pile of rocks, stones
krem v.i. (v.n. *krim*) 1. to get hard and dry (as bread) 2. to freeze, to become frost-bitten
¶ a.p. *karem* pl. *-in* hard and dry
kṛem v.t. 1. to receive and entertain cordially and generously (often for days) 2. to be generous to or with (s.o., as in giving money)
kṛem n.u. *keṛma* fig tree
kṛomb 1. cabbage 2. cauliflower
keṛmuṣ n.u. *-a* fig
¶ *keṛmuṣ n-nṣaṛa* prickly pear (fruit)
koṛniṭa pl. *-a* bugle
koṛṛaṣ type of notebook formed from folded pages accumulatively placed one within another
keṛṛaṭa pl. *-t* rake (type used for leveling or breaking up clods)
kerray pl. *-a* lessor, one who rents (to s.o.)
¶ *kerray ʒănku* nosy, meddlesome person
keṛṛeh v.t. to make or cause to dislike *keṛṛehha f-xaha.* He's caused her to dislike her (own) brother.
keṛṛeṛ v.t. to repeat, to say again
kerrem 1. v.t. to dry (out) and harden (mostly bread) 2. v.i. to squat (down)
keṛṛeṭ v.t. 1. to scratch, to mark by scratching 2. to scrape (off) *keṛṛeṭ ṣ-ṣbaġa men z-zaž!* Scrape the paint off the window pane! 3. to shave (head, face, leg, etc.) 4. to rake *keṛṛeṭ l-ˀeṛḍ men le-ʒžeṛ!* Rake the rocks out of the soil!
keṛṛuṣa pl. *-t, kṛaṛeṣ* 1. cart (usually animal-drawn) 2. baby carriage, perambulator
¶ *keṛṛuṣa d-le-wqid* pack of match boxes (with matches)
kerruš large belly or abdomen, paunch
korsi pl. *krasa* 1. stool (for sitting) 2. bench (for sitting) 3. chair
kerš (f.) pl. *kruš* (dim. *kriša*) stomach, belly, abdomen (area)
** *ma-tkun-š keršek kbira!* Don't be so greedy!
¶ *bu-kerš* pl. *m̄m̄alin le-kruš* man with a paunch
kerša pl. *-t* stomach (organ)
keršawi pl. *-yen* gluttonous, given to eating like a pig
kruš pl. of *kerš*
keṛwila pl. *-t* one-horse carriage
keṛwiya caraway
krăʕ pl. *kerʕan, kerʕin* lower part of a ḥoofed animal's leg
kerʕan, kerʕin pl. of *krăʕ*
ksa iksi v.t. to clothe, to provide with clothes
ksa pl. *-wat, ksi* (dim. *ksiya*) type of over-garment
ksab same as *kseb*
ksad fall-off, slack, slow period (business)
ksakes pl. of *keskas* and *kesksu* (same as *seksu*)
ksari pl. of *kesra*
ksawi pl. of *keswa*
kseb v.t. 1. to get or gain possession of, to acquire *fuq-aš ksebti had le-ġnem?* When did you acquire these sheep? 2. to have, to possess, to own
ksed v.i. to not sell, to become unsalable *had s-selʕa kesdet.* This merchandise won't sell.
kesda pl. *-t* 1. body (human) 2. trunk (of the body), torso
ksi pl. of *ksa*
ksiba livestock (specifically sheep, cattle, and goats)
ksiṛ v.n. of *kseṛ*
ksiwa dim. of *keswa*
ksiya dim. of *ksa*
keskas pl. *ksakes* pot with holes in the bottom used in steaming couscous
keskes v.i. 1. to make couscous 2. to eat couscous
kesksu pl. (intensity) *ksakes* same as *seksu*
keslan pl. *-in* lazy, indolent
kseṛ v.i. (v.n. *ksiṛ*) to relapse, to have a relapse (s.o. ill)
¶ *kseṛ d-denya* to raise Cain
kesṛa pl. *-t, ksaṛi, ksuṛ* piece of bread
kosṛan same as *kusuṛ*
kessab pl. *-a* dealer in livestock (i.e., breeder and seller)
kessal pl. *-a* masseur (at the public bath)
kessel v.t. to massage (as in the public bath)
kesseṛ v.t. to break (in two, into pieces, etc.)
ksuṛ pl. of *kesṛa*
keswa pl. *-t, ksawi* (dim. *ksiwa*) 1. suit (men's or women's) 2. dress (girl's) 3. covering placed over the tomb of a saint
kṣeṛ, keṣṛa, keṣṣeṛ same as *kseṛ, kesra, kesser*
kšafi pl. of *kešfa*
kšakeš pl. of *keškuša*
kšayef pl. of *kešfa*
kšef v.i. (v.n. *kšif*) to fade, to become discolored
kešfa pl. *-t, kšafi, kšayef* 1. difficulty 2. embarrassment, embarrassing situation (pl. used for emphasis). *kanet le-kšafi habṭa*

ɛliya. I was awfully embarrassed (i.e., embarrassment fell on me).
kešfiya scouting (as boy scouts)
kšif v.n. of *kšef*
keškeš **1.** v.t. to scare (off), to drive away, to shoo **2.** v.i., to foam, to become foamy **3.** v.i., to foam at the mouth
keškuša pl. (of intensity) *-t, kšakeš* foam
keššaf pl. *-a* **1.** scout **2.** boy scout
keššef v.t. to make or cause to fade (color)
keššina pl. *-t* kitchen
keššeṭ **1.** v.t. to rob (s.o. of everything, including clothes) **2.** v.i. to dress up, to doll up
¶ *keššeṭ l-* to dress (s.o.) up (in nice, clean clothes)
ktab v.i. to be written (as in the Book of Destiny), to be fated *ktab ɛlih imut f-dak lɛadita.* It was fated that he should die in that accident.
ktab pl. *-at, ktub, ktuba* book (any kind)
ktaba **1.** v.n. of *kteb* **2.** writing *tăɛref teqra had le-ktaba?* Can you read this writing? **3.** s.th. written and used as an amulet
¶ *b-le-ktaba* in writing, by letter
ktaf pl. of *ktef*
ktaṛ pl. of *ktir*
ktatbi pl. *-ya* secretary (also acts as records keeper and accountant)
kteb (v.n. *ktaba*) **1.** v.t. to write (letter, book, music, etc.) **2.** v.i. to get or acquire a written amulet (for protective purposes)
¶ *kteb l-* to leave or bequeath to (by will) *kteb-lu ḍ-ḍaṛ.* He bequeathed the house to him.
ketba pl. *-t* same as *ktaba*
kotbi pl. *-ya* bookseller
ktef pl. *ktaf* shoulder *ketfi ka-ideṛṛni.* My shoulder hurts.
** *h-ana fe-ktafek!* I'll stand ready to help you.
ktir pl. *-in, ktaṛ* (comp. *kteṛ*) much, a lot of (pl. many) *kaynin ši-nas ktaṛ temma?* Are there a lot of people there? *—le-flus lli ɛăndek kteṛ men lli ɛăndu.* You have more money than he does.
¶ *le-ktir* most, the majority *le-ktir fe-n-nas ka-iɛebbu kuṛat l-qadam.* Most people like soccer.
¶ *ktir ši, ktir š-ši* **1.** most of the time, usually *ktir š-ši ka-iži mɛa ṭ-ṭnaš.* Most of the time he comes around twelve. **2.** mostly *ka-yakol ktir š-ši l-xuḍăṛ.* He eats mostly vegetables.
** *ka-nɛebb l-musiqa l-ʔandalusiya. —ktir š-ši ana!* I like Andalusian music.—Not as much as I do!
ktirt used in the expr. *ktirt š-ši* same as *ktir ši* (see *ktir*)
** *ktirtu mṛid* He's sick most of the time.
ktem v.t. to keep (a secret)
kteṛ v.i. **1.** to increase (in numbers, amount) **2.** to multiply, to become (more) abundant
kteṛ comp. of *ktir*
ketṛa **1.** abundance, excessive amount **2.** especially, particularly *f-fas ka-ikun l-berd u-ketṛa mnin ka-dži š-šetwa.* It's cold in Fez, particularly when winter comes.
¶ *be-l-ketṛa* a great deal, a lot *n-nas ka-ižiw be-l-ketṛa l-had s-suq baš išriw d-džaž.* People come to this market a lot to buy chickens.
¶ *l-ketṛa* most, the majority *žaw ɛăndna n-nas le-ḍ-ḍaṛ u-l-ketṛa fihom kanu fṛanṣawiyen.* Some people came to our house, most of whom were French.
¶ *men kteṛt* because of, by dint of *men kteṛt le-ɛṭeš šṛeb l-qeṛɛa kollha.* He was so thirsty he drank the whole bottle. (i.e., because of the thirst . . .)
¶ *men kteṛt lli* to . . . so much that *men kteṛt lli žra ṭaɛ sexfan.* He ran so much he fainted.
kottab pl. of *katĭb*
kettan material, cloth
kettani pl. *-yen* member of a Moroccan religious fraternity (also family name)
ketteb v.t. **1.** to make (s.o.) write *kettbetni dak š-ši.* She made me write that. **2.** to decree, to predestine (God) *ṛebbi ketteb ɛlih dak š-ši.* It was in the cards for that to happen to him.
kettef v.t. to tie up, to truss up (s.o., with a rope, chain, etc.)
ketteṛ, ketteṛ men **1.** to add (more) *ketteṛ šwiya men s-sokkaṛ fe-l-qehwa dyali.* Add a little sugar to my coffee. **2.** to increase *ketteṛ men l-ma!* More water! (i.e., increase the water)
** *ḷḷah iketteṛ xiṛek.* Thank you; Please.
ktub, ktuba pl. of *ktab*
ktabeṛ October
kṭaṛ pl. *-at* hectare
ku same as *kun*
kudši pl. *kwadša* surrey
kufeṛ v.t. to preserve (as in alcohol, formaldehyde)
kufri pl. *kwafer* chest for storing clothes and jewelry (usually with a round top)
kul pl. *kulu* impv. of *kla*
kuliya pl. *-t* (postal) package, parcel
kumir n.u. *-a* French-type bread
kumisir pl. *-at* police chief
kun (also *ku*) if (in contrary to fact phrases; also used in the conclusion) *kun ma-kanet-š š-šta kun xrežt men ḍ-ḍaṛ.* If it wasn't raining I'd leave the house; also: If it hadn't been for the rain I would have left the house. *—kun ža kun mšit ana wiyah.*

If he came we'd go together; also: If he had come we'd have gone together.

¶ *kun ġir* if only *kun ġir qoltiha-li!* If only you had told me!

kunṭraḍa pl. *-t* 1. contract *ɛändi kunṭraḍa dyal xems snin mɛa l-ɛukuma.* I have a five-year contract with the government. 2. franchise (monopolizing type)

kuṛ n.u. *-a* 1. charcoal briquet 2. bomb (aerial) 3. projectile (cannon)

kuṛa pl. *-t, kweṛ* (dim. *kwiṛa*) 1. ball (especially in sports) 2. padlock

kuṛama pl. of *karim, krim*

kuṛba pl. *-t* type of open basket (used especially in the food market)

kuri pl. *-yat* stable (for horses)

kuriya rage, fury

¶ *ṭelɛät l-kuriya fih*φ to become furious ≠, to have a fit of rage ≠

kuša pl. *-t* kiln (pottery)

kutši pl. *kwatša* same as *kudši*

kuwwaṛ n.u. *-a* watermelon

kuwway pl. *-a* one who does soldering

kuwwaya pl. *-t* soldering iron

kuwwen 1. v.t., to create, to make (s.th. from s.th.) 2. v.i., to be quiet, to remain silent, to shut up

** *kuwwen ɛlih ɛetta iṛžäɛ le-d-daṛ.* You just wait and see what I'll do to him when he gets home! (i.e., for revenge)

kuwweṛ v.t. 1. to form into a ball, to make a ball out of 2. to roll, to make roll (as a ball)

kuwyan v.n. of *kwa*

kuzina pl. *-t* kitchen

kuɛel pl. of *kɛäl*

kwa ikwi v.t. (v.n. *kuwyan*) 1. to solder *imken-lek tekwi had r-ržel de-ṣ-ṣiniya?* Can you solder this leg to the tray? 2. to cauterize, to sear 3. to burn (with s.th. hot)

** *kwatni f-qelbi.* I've fallen for her. —*l-mut kwatu f-weldu.* Death has taken his son. —*lsanu ka-ikwi.* He has a sharp tongue.

kwabes pl. of *kabus*

kwadša pl. of *kudši*

kwafer pl. of *kufri*

kwaġeṭ pl. of *kaġiṭ, kaġeṭ*

kwanen pl. of *kanun*

kwaṛeṭ pl. of *kaṛṭa*

kwarṭi pl. *-ya* card player

kwaš pl. of *kašša*

kwatša pl. of *kutši* (same as *kudši*)

kwatši pl. *-ya* driver of a *kudši, kutši*

kwawi pl. of *kawya*

kwayɛi pl. *-ya* one who cooks and sells *kwaɛ*

kwaɛ heart and liver (usually lamb) cutlets cooked on a skewer

kwiṛa dim. of *kuṛa*

kewkeb pl. *kawakib* 1. star (in sky, movie) 2. planet

kewn 1. universe (i.e., everything that exists) 2. outer space

** *kewn mulana hada.* expr. used in remarking about s.o.'s good fortune, or s.th. near perfection

¶ *ɛla kewn* because *ma-imken-lek-š ddzuwwež ɛla kewnek ma-zal ṣġiṛ.* You can't get married because you're still too young.

kweṛ pl. of *kuṛa* (n.u. of *kuṛ*)

kyab pl. of *kib*

kyaḍeṛ pl. of *kiḍaṛ*

kyal pl. of *kil*

kyar pl. of *kir*

kyas pl. of *kis*

kyasa 1. gentleness 2. scrupulousness

¶ *b-le-kyasa* gently *ɛamelha b-le-kyasa!* Treat her gently!

kyus pl. of *kis*

kezz, kezẓ v.i. to become numb (from cold)

** *ka-ikezẓ ɛäl le-flus.* He's an old skinflint.

kḥal v.i. to get or turn black or dark

kḥob ikḥob v.i. (v.n. *kḥib*) to cough

koḥba pl. *-t* cough

keḥfar pl. *-a* ag. n. of *keḥfer*

keḥfer v.i. to walk or wander around a great deal (for fun)

kḥib v.n. of *kḥob*

kḥiz v.n. of *kḥäz*

käḥk n.u. *-a* kind of ring-shaped pastry stuffed with almonds

keḥkeḥ v.i. to cough in a series of relatively weak coughs

kḥäl f. *keḥla* pl. *kuḥel* black

keḥṭ 1. drought 2. famine

kḥul black eye make-up (used by Moroccan women)

kḥula, kḥuliya blackness, black

kḥäz ikḥoz v.i. (v.n. *kḥiz*) to move (usually persons) *kḥoz le-š-šmal!* Move to the left!

** *kḥoz menni!* Leave me alone!

koḥḥ ikoḥḥ (v.n. *koḥḥan*) to cough

koḥḥa pl. *-t* cough

koḥḥan v.n. of *koḥḥ*

keḥḥäl v.t. 1. to blacken, to make black 2. (also v.i.) to apply *kḥul* (a kind of eye make-up) to (eyes)

** *keḥḥäl-lha qelbha ɛliya.* He's turned her against me.

keḥḥäz v.t. to move *keḥḥäz had ṭ-tebla le-š-šmal!* Move this table to the left! —*keḥḥäzha ɛliya!* Move it away from me! —*keḥḥäzha l-ɛändi!* Move it toward me!

kɛab pl. of *käɛba*

kʕaba n. pl. of *koʕbi*

kăʕba pl. *-t, kʕab* **1.** ankle **2.** bad luck *dima fih l-kăʕba.* He always has bad luck.
¶ *rfedha be-l-kăʕba* to take to one's heels, to take off like a scared rabbit
¶ *l-kăʕba* the Kaaba (in Mecca)

kăʕb-oġzal type of crescent-shaped cookie made with almonds

koʕbi adj. pl. *-yen* n.pl. *kʕaba* jinxed, afflicted with constant bad luck

kăʕkăʕ v.i. to laugh loudly, to guffaw

koʕlal n.u. *-a* small clump of dirt attached to the wool of a sheep

kăʕweṛ v.t. **1.** to knock down or over, to upset **2.** to roll, to make roll

L

l- (*le-* before consonant clusters except those beginning with *l;* often *li-* or *lil-* before pron. endings) **1.** to *mšat l-meṛṛakeš š-šheṛ lli daz.* She went to Marrakesh last month. —*ma-gal-li ʕădd šay.* Nobody told me anything. **2.** for *hadi magana šritha le-xti.* This is a watch I bought for my sister. —*had l-ʕanut ṛaha l-l-biʕ.* This store is for sale. —*l-aš ka-teṣlaʕ had l-ʔala?* What's this machine for? —*šrathom-lek.* She bought them for you.

l- (*le-* before consonant clusters except those beginning with *l*) definite art. *ṛa le-mḍeḷḷ ʕda l-bab.* The umbrella's by the door.

la **1.** no *šraha mennek?* —*la.* Did he buy it from you?—No. **2.** negation used with impv. *la-tqulu-lha-š šeftiwni.* Don't tell her you saw me. **3.** negation used in subordinate clauses of the conditional *we-ḷḷah la-ža u-kan ma-kanet l-qaḍiya fiha le-flus.* I swear he wouldn't have come if money weren't involved in this affair. **4.** so that . . . not, before *sir ʕăndhom daba la-iduz l-weqt.* Go and see them now before it's too late. —*ṛbeṭ d-džaža la-temši tehṛeb!* Tie up the chicken so it won't get away!
¶ *la . . . wa-la* **1.** as well as *koll-ši kan temma, la l-ʔasatida wa-la t-tlamed.* Everybody was there, the teachers as well as the students. **2.** neither . . . nor *ma-mšaw ixedmu la le-wlad wa-la le-bnat.* Neither the boys nor the girls went to work.

la-bedda see *bedda*

la-dini pl. *-yen* **1.** atheistic **2.** atheist

lagaṛ pl. *-at* railroad station

laġa ʕla to call *laġi ʕliha, ṛaha fe-l-fuqi.* Call her, she's upstairs.

lakin but, however, yet *ma-weṣḷetha ʕăṛda lakin ġad-temši.* She didn't get any invitation, but she's going.

lalla pl. *lalliyat* **1.** used in addressing a lady *šnu xeṣṣek a-lalla?* What would you like, Madam (or Miss)? **2.** (inh. pos.; used in cons.) grandmother *mšaw išufu lallahom.* They went to see their grandmother.
¶ *lalla u-mali* easy life *kanu galsin ʕla lalla u-mali.* They were leading an easy life.
¶ *ṃṃuᶲ lallahᶲ* (one's) grandmother

lalliyat pl. of *lalla*

lam ilum v.t. (v.n. *luman*) to blame (s.o.) *lamuh ʕla lli ma-kemmel-š xdemtu.* They blamed him for not finishing his work.

laṃḅa pl. *-t* **1.** lamp (oil, kerosene) **2.** bulb (electric)

lamin pl. *-at* **1.** syndic, guild master, head of a corporation of craftsmen or businessmen **2.** (hired) water carrier (same as *gerrab*)

lan ilin v.i. (v.n. *lyana, lyuna*) **1.** to get more lenient, more understanding *l-ʔustad bda ka-ilin mʕa t-tlamed dyalu.* The teacher is getting more lenient with his pupils. **2.** to become more obedient, to cooperate, to give in *bqina mʕahom b-le-klam ʕetta lanu-lna.* We kept talking to them until they agreed to cooperate.

laq iliq b- or *l-* (v.n. *lyaqa*) to suit, to be suitable for *had l-xedma ma-ġad-tliq-š bih.* This work won't be suitable for him.

laqa v.t. **1.** to join, to put together *daba nlaqi ṭ-ṭṛaf kollhom.* I'll put all the pieces together. **2.** to get together, to gather together *kif laqiti had n-nas?* How did you get these people together? **3.** to encounter, to meet with *laqaw ṣuʕubat kbira fe-l-beʕt dyalhom.* They encountered great difficulties in their research.
¶ *laqa s-sluk* (or *s-sluka*) to cause trouble, to cause dissension *dima ka-ilaqi s-sluka bin ṣʕabu.* He's always causing dissension among his friends.

laqab pl. *ʔelqab* nickname (excluding traditional shortened forms of names)

laqiṭ pl. *luqaṭaʔ* foundling

lašuniya Hebrew (language)

laṭef v.t. to treat gently

ḷaṭif good, merciful (God)
** *ya-laṭif!* God help us! (used in a situation of sorrow, disaster)
¶ *ṭḷeb* or (*xerrež*) *ḷ-ḷaṭif* to say prayers containing the formula *ya-ḷaṭif* (in a situation of great danger or disaster)

lawah no *lawah, ma-txellih-š ka-isayen.* No,

don't keep him waiting. —*ka-nḍenn ma-ƹežbu l-ƺal hna.—lawah!* I don't think he likes it here.—No (really?)!

l-axṛa same as *l-ʔaxiṛa* (see *axiṛ*)

layn where (directional) *layn nemšiw?* Where shall we go?

¶ *layn-ma, layn-emma, lay-emma* wherever (directional) *layn-emma mšat ka-itebƹuha.* Wherever she goes they follow her.

¶ *ma-ƹănduφ layn ƹla* (n.) to have to (v.) *ma-ƹăndha layn ƹăl le-xḷaṣ.* She has to pay.

** *waš hiya fe-ḍ-ḍaṛ?—ma-ƹăndha layn.* Is she home?—I don't see how she could be anyplace else.

¶ *ƺetta layn* **1.** very late, quite late, until late *l-bareƺ xedmu ƺetta layn.* Yesterday they worked quite late. **2.** how late *ƺetta layn bqitiw ṣahṛin?* How late did you stay up? —*ma-ƹṛef-ši ƺetta layn bqina fayqin.* He doesn't know how late we stayed up. **3.** very far, quite far *ƺetta layn mšit mƹahom.* I walked quite far with them. **4.** how far *xeṣṣek tšuf ƺetta layn mšina ƹla režlina.* You should see how far we walked. —*ƺetta layn weṣlu?* How far did they get?

lazem v.t. **1.** to be or associate regularly with *xay ma-ka-ilazem ġir d-drari lli qeddu.* My brother is always with kids his age. **2.** to frequent, to be at or go to frequently *ƹam luwwel kanu ka-ilazmu dak l-qehwa.* Last year they used to go to that café all the time. **3.** to do (s.th.) regularly *ƹăndu măƹlumat qwiya ƺit ka-ilazem l-muṭalaƹa.* He's well informed because he reads regularly.

¶ *lazem le-fṛaš* to keep to one's bed

lazem a.p. of *lzem*

lažuṛ same as *yažuṛ*

lažež v.i. to split hairs, to make oversubtle distinctions

laƺ iluƺ v.t. **1.** to throw *laƺet ktubha ƹăl l-feṛš.* She threw her books on the bed. **2.** to throw away or out

laƺeḍ **1.** v.t. to remark, to notice *ma-laƺeḍti-š l-ferq?* Didn't you notice the difference? **2.** v.i. to make remarks *dima ka-ilaƺeḍ ƹăl l-oxṛin.* He's always making remarks about others.

la-ƹălla see *ƹălla*

laƹuq jam, marmalade

lbadi pl. of *lebda*

l-bareƺ see *bareƺ*

lbas **1.** v.n. of *lbes* **2.** dress style **3.** clothing, clothes

lbasi pl. of *lebsa*

lbayex pl. of *lbixa*

lebba v.t. **1.** to answer, to yield to (a request) *ƹămmṛu ma-lebba-lhom ši-ṭalab.* He's never yielded to any of their requests. **2.** to fill (an order) *š-šarika lebbat-lna ṭ-ṭalab.* The company filled our order.

** *lebbayk ḷḷahumma lebbayk!* invocation said by Muslim pilgrims while circling the Kaaba during the Pilgrimage ceremony in Mecca

lebbad pl. *-a* one who deals in felt (material)

lebbas used in the expr. *lebbas le-xwatem* ring finger

lebbeq v.t. **1.** to patch, to darn *ḷḷah ixellik lebbeq-li had t-tqašer.* Would you please patch these socks for me. **2.** to botch, to do (s.th.) clumsily

lebbes v.t. **1.** to make (s.o.) wear *lebbsettu dak ṣ-ṣebbaṭ waxxa ma-ka-ibġih-š.* She made him wear those shoes even though he doesn't like them. **2.** to put (clothes) on (s.o.), to dress (s.o.) with (s.th.) *lebbset-lu le-ƺwayež ž-ždad.* She put the new clothes on him.

lbed v.i. to crouch, to cower (from fright)

lbed pl. of *lebda*

lebda pl. *-t, lbadi, lbed* small felt rug used for praying

lbina dim. of *lben*

lbixa pl. *-t, lbayex* plaster cast *kan ƹamel lbixa ƹla režlu d-l-imin.* He had a plaster cast on his right leg.

lbiya pl. *-t* lioness

lben (dim. *lbina*) buttermilk

lbes v.t. (v.n. *lbas*) **1.** to wear *ƹămmṛi ma-lbest ṛ-ṛezza.* I've never worn a turban. **2.** to put on *kont ka-nelbes ƺwayži mnin ƹăyyeṭti-li.* I was putting on my clothes when you called me.

lebsa pl. *-t, lbasi* **1.** n.i. of *lbes* **2.** dress, gown **3.** complete set of clothes, suit

ldad pl. of *ldid*

ledd v.i. (v.n. *ledda*) to taste good *had l-makla koll-ma berdet ka-tledd.* The colder this food is the better it tastes.

ledd comp. of *ldid*

ledda v.n. of *ledd*

¶ *fih l-ledda* to be delicious ≠ *had l-ƺălwa fiha l-ledda.* This cake is delicious.

ldeġ v.t. (v.n. *ldiġ*) **1.** to sting *ledġettu neƺla.* He's been stung by a bee. **2.** to bite (insects, snakes) *ledġu ƺenš.* He's been bitten by a snake.

ledġa pl. *-t* n.i. of *ldeġ*

ldid pl. *ldad* (comp. *ledd*) **1.** delicious, tasty *l-makla lli ṭiyybet kanet ldida.* The food she prepared was delicious. **2.** pleasant *klamu ldid.* He has a pleasant way of talking.

ldiġ v.n. of *ldeġ*

ldiƹ v.n. of *ldăƹ*

ldăع v.t. (v.n. *ldiع*) to bite (said of a reptile)
ledعa n.i. of *ldăع*
lfati pl. of *lefta*
lfayef pl. of *leffa*
lfaعi pl. of *lefعa*
lefḍa pl. *-t, ʔalfaḍ* word *lefḍa weḥda ma-xerržetha-š.* She didn't utter a single word.
leff v.t. (v.n. *leffan*) to wrap
leffa pl. *-t, lfayef* (dim. *lfifa*) 1. n.i. of *leff* 2. package, parcel 3. turn (of a turban) *leff ṛeẓẓtu xemsa de-l-leffat عla ṛaṣu.* It took him five turns to wrap his turban around his head.
leffan v.n. of *leff*
leffef v.t. to wrap
lfifa pl. *-t* dim. of *leffa*
left n.u. *-a* turnip
lefta pl. *-t, lfati* plug, peg *šeddina l-qaḍuṣ b-waḥed l-lefta.* We stopped the drain with a plug.
lefعa pl. *-t, lfaعi* viper
lga ilga same as *lqa*
legget same as *leqqeṭ*
lġa ilġi v.i. (v.n. *lġa*) 1. to talk, to babble (baby) 2. to chirp

¶ *lġa عla* to call *ṛah fe-l-bit dyalu, lġi عlih!* He's in his room, call him!

** *koll ṭiṛ ka-ilġi lġah.* Every bird sings his (own) song. (proverb indicating that differences of opinion are to be expected among people)

lġa v.n. of *lġa*

¶ *feṛṛeq l-lġa* to chat

leġm, loġm pl. *ʔalġam* mine (explosive)
lha ilhi v.t. 1. to distract, to divert the attention of (s.o.) *dak l-bent ka-telhih عla šġalu.* That girl distracts him from his work. 2. to keep busy, to keep amused, to entertain *lhat t-teṛbya b-le-qšawš baš ma-ibki-š.* She kept the baby busy with the toys so it wouldn't cry.
lheb v.i. (v.n. *lhib*) to blaze

¶ *lheb عla* to flatter, to soft-soap, to curry favor with (s.o.) by being extremely agreeable

lehba n.i. of *lheb*
lehfa 1. gluttony, voracity 2. starvation, act of starving
lehfan pl. *-in* voracious, gluttonous
lehhet v.i. to pant, to gasp (for breath)
lhib v.n. of *lheb*
lhih there, over there
lhit v.n. of *lhet*
lehla used in wishes made to the contrary of what might happen *lehla ižعălhom kif iziw.* I do hope they don't come.

** *lehla irewwik bas* reply of a sick person to *la-bas عlik*

lhem v.t. to inspire, to give inspiration to, to guide (God) *ṛebbi lehmu ḥetta daz men had ž-žih.* God gave him the inspiration to come this way.
lhet v.i. (v.n. *lhit*) to pant, to gasp (for breath)
lehṭa 1. starvation, act of starving 2. gluttony
lehža pl. *-t* 1. dialect *šḥal de-l-lehžat ka-itkellmu fe-bladek?* How many dialects are spoken in your country? 2. accent *ma-zal ka-itkellem l-عăṛbiya b-lehža negliziya.* He still speaks Arabic with an English accent. 3. tone *ma-wažeb-š عlik ttkellem mعaha b-dak l-lehža.* You shouldn't speak to her in such a tone.
li- see *l-*
liga 1. pl. *-t* glove 2. pl. *-t, lyeg* same as *liqa*
lil- see *li-*
lil (no. pl.) night, night-time

¶ *be-l-lil, fe-l-lil* at night, nights *dima ka-iعăyyeṭ-lna be-l-lil.* He always calls us at night. —*ma-zalin ka-ixedmu be-l-lil?* Do they still work nights?

¶ *l-bareḥ fe-l-lil* last night

¶ *l-yum fe-l-lil* tonight

¶ *neṣṣ l-lil* midnight

¶ *ṭiṛ l-lil* bat (mammal)

¶ *ḥmaṛ l-lil* nightmare *ḍṛebha ḥmaṛ l-lil.* She had a nightmare.

lila du. *liltayn* pl. *-t, lyali* (dim. *lwila*) 1. night *bqaw عăndna tlata de-l-lyali.* They spent three nights at our place. 2. eve, night before *mat lilt l-عid le-kbir.* He died on the eve of Greater Bairam. 3. party *men băعd le-mtiḥanat nعămlu ši-lila.* We'll have a party after exams.

¶ *lilt l-qadṛ* the 27th night of Ramadan, celebrated by Muslims as the date of the revelation of the Koran

¶ pl. *l-lyali* the forty-day period from December 24th to February 2nd, generally considered the coldest part of the year

lim n.u. *-a* lime (the citrus fruit)
limun n.u. *-a* 1. lemon 2. orange (in Rabat and environs) 3. lemon tree 4. orange tree (in Rabat and environs)
limuni pl. *-yen* 1. pale yellow 2. orange-colored (around Rabat)
lingaṣ n.u. *-a* pear
liqa pl. *-t, lyeq* 1. tuft or ball (of wool or cotton 2. (snow)flake
liṛa pl. *-t* 1. recorder, type of flute 2. lira (Italian money)
liṣaṛ, liṣeṛ see *iṣaṛ*
liṣṛi see *iṣṛi*
liṭṛa same as *iṭṛa*
liṭṛu same as *iṭṛu*
liyen same as *liyyen* (adj.)

liyyah why *liyyah ma-ʕlemtihom-š?* Why didn't you notify them?
liyyen pl. *-in* 1. soft, flexible 2. lenient
liyyen v.t. to soften, to make flexible
liyyeṛ v.i. to play the flute
ližan pl. of *ležna*
lekk sealing wax
lekkek v.t. to seal, to fasten with sealing wax
ḷḷah (often *ḷḷa* in normal conversation; *llah* after *b-* or *l-*) God *yăʕlem ḷḷah fuq-aš ġad-ixeḷḷṣuna.* God knows when they're going to pay us.
** *be-llah ʕliya ma-kont mʕahom.* I swear I wasn't with them. —*ḷḷa ihennik* (pl. *ihennikom*)*!* Good-by! —*ḷḷa ihennih b-dak š-ši kollu.* Let him have all of that; He can have all of it, I don't need it. —*be-sme-llah!* said as a form of grace before meals, or before performing any act
¶ *be-llah lladi la-ilaha illa huwa, . . .; we-ḷḷah . . .* By God, . . . *we-ḷḷah u-bqa ka-ibeṭṭel l-medṛaṣa ḥetta idḥiweh.* By God, if he keeps skipping classes he'll be expelled.
¶ *ḷḷa* (or *ḷḷah*) *ixellik* (pl. *ixellikom*) please *ḷḷa(h) ixellik tʕăšša mʕana.* Please have supper with us.
¶ *ḷḷahomma* it is preferable, (I, you, he, etc.) would rather *ḷḷahomma nesmăʕha men fommu băʕda.* I'd rather hear it from his own mouth.
¶ *ḷḷahomma . . . wa-la* (I, you, he, etc.) had better . . . rather than *ḷḷahomma temši mʕana wa-la tebqa weḥdek.* You had better come with us rather than stay by yourself.
** *ḷḷahomma hakda wa-la bla-š.* It's better than nothing. —*ḷḷahomma hakdak ḥsen.* It's better that way.
** *ḷḷahomma ila* unless *xeṣṣu iži ixdem koll nhaṛ ḷḷahomma ila kan mṛiḍ.* He has to come to work every day unless he's sick.
¶ *le-llah, l-llah* for God's sake (when asking s.o. a favor)
¶ *l-ḥămdu li-llah* (*or l-llah*), *ḷḷahumma-lak l-ḥămd* see *ḥămd*
¶ *yaḷḷah* pl. *yaḷḷahu* (used affirmatively) 1. Come (on) . . . *yaḷḷah mʕaya le-ḍ-daṛ nwerrik šnu šrit.* Come on home with me and I'll show you what I bought. —*yaḷḷahu mʕana.* Come along with us. 2. Let's . . . *yaḷḷah ntmeššaw šwiya.* Let's go for a little walk. 3. (invariable) only, just *ʕṭatu fiha yaḷḷah sett myat derhem.* She offered him only six hundred dirhams for it. 4. (invariable) shows the immediate past *yaḷḷah kif wṣeḷt hadi ši-šwiya.* I just arrived a little while ago.
¶ *ʕla ḷḷah, ʕăl ḷḷah* expr. of hope, possibility, taking a chance, etc. *ʕăl ḷḷah ibqa l-žuw mezyan l-yum.* I hope the weather will stay fine today. —*šuf kan ʕăl ḷḷah ibġi iži mʕak.* See if he would like to come with you. —*šrit had l-ʔala ġir ʕăl ḷḷah.* I took a chance on buying this machine.
llaṛeb, llaṛob a quarter to ≠ *hadi t-tlata llaṛeb.* It's a quarter to three.
ʔellef v.t. to compose, to write *ʔellfet ṛebʕa de-l-mesṛaḥiyat.* She wrote four plays.
llehla same as *lehla*
lli 1. who, that *n-nas lli kanu hna.* The people who were here. —*hada l-weld lli qolt-lek ʕlih.* This is the boy I told you about. 2. that, which *t-telž lli ṭaḥ kollu dab.* All the snow that fell has melted. —*hadik l-qehwa lli kont ka-nemši-lha.* That's the café (that) I used to go to. —*le-qniya lli ṣiyyeḍ matet.* The rabbit (that) he caught is dead. 3. whoever *lli xalef l-qanun itʕaqeb.* Whoever breaks the law will be punished. 4. whichever (one) *xud lli ʕežbettek fihom.* Take whichever one of them you like. 5. whatever *lli qalt-lkom diruh.* Do whatever she tells you. 6. that (conj.) *ḥsen lli ma-ža-š.* It's better (that) he didn't come. —*ana feṛḥan lli žat.* I'm happy she came.
¶ *men-lli* (or *me-lli*) 1. since, ever since *men-lli mša ma-kteb-lna.* We haven't heard from him since he left. 2. than (before clauses) *wellat kfes men-lli kanet.* She has become worse than she was.
lmayeʕ pl. of *lemʕa*
lmiʕ v.n. of *lmăʕ*
lemm v.t. (v.n. *lemman*) to assemble, to bring together
lemma when *lemma iži qolha-lu.* Tell him when he comes.
lemman v.n. of *lemm*
lemmăʕ v.t. to shine, to make shine
lmăʕ v.i. (v.n. *lmiʕ*) to shine, to glisten
lemʕa pl. *lmayeʕ* n.i. of *lmăʕ*
lqa ilqa v.t. 1. to find *lqiti le-ktab ʕla-š konti ka-tqelleb?* Did you find the book you were looking for? 2. to meet *ġad-nemšiw nelqaweh fe-l-meṛṣa.* We're going to go meet him at the harbor. 3. to see, to encounter *lqithom fe-l-ḥefla.* I saw them at the party. 4. to encounter, to meet with, to find *lqat ṣuʕubat kbira.* She encountered great difficulties. 5. to receive *ma-lqahom-š mezyan.* He didn't receive them well.
¶ *lqa ʕla* to protect *kun ma-lqat-š ʕlih š-šežṛa u-kan ḍeṛbettu l-qeṛṭaṣa.* If he hadn't been protected by the tree the bullet would have struck him.
ʔelqab pl. of *laqab*
lqaqeṭ pl. of *leqqaṭ* 2

lqef v.t. (v.n. *lqif*) to catch (in the air) *huwa siyyeb l-kuṛa w-ana lqeftha.* He threw the ball and I caught it.
leqfa n.i. of *lqef*
lqif v.n. of *lqef*
lqim n.u. *-a* small variety of quince
leqma, loqma pl. *-t* **1.** mouthful *kla koll-ši fe-tlata de-l-leqmat.* He ate everything in three mouthfuls. **2.** bite, s.th. to eat *ɛmelt waḥed l-leqma fe-ḍ-ḍaṛ qbel ma-nži.* I had a bite at home before I came.
leqqa v.t. **1.** to put *leqqi ši-ṣṭel l-l-qeṭṛa lli fe-ṣ-ṣqef.* Put a pail under the leak in the roof. **2.** to put out, to stick out *leqqa-li režlu u-ɛăkkelni.* He stuck his foot out and tripped me.
** *ḷḷah ileqqik l-xir u-r-rbeḥ.* The best of luck to you.
leqqam pl. *-a* ag. n. of *leqqem*
leqqaṭ **1.** pl. *-a* ag. n. of *leqqeṭ* 2 **2.** pl. *lqaqeṭ* pincers, (pair of) pliers
leqqaḥ pl. *-a* ag. n. of *leqqeḥ*
leqqeb v.t. to give a nickname to, to nickname *leqqebnaha le-qniya.* We nicknamed her "Rabbit."
leqqef v.i. **1.** to gasp for breath *ṭeḷɛet ka-džri fe-ḍ-ḍṛuž ḥetta bdat tleqqef.* She ran up the stairs until she began gasping for breath. **2.** to be badly in need of *žbeṛthom ka-ileqqfu ɛla lli ixdem mɛahom.* I found them badly in need of someone to work for them.
leqqem v.t. same as *leqqeḥ* **1** and **2**
¶ *leqqem l-berrad* to add fresh tea, mint leaves, sugar, and boiling water to the teapot in order to prepare another serving of tea
leqqeṭ v.t. **1.** to pick up *leqqṭet ṭ-ṭṛaf de-z-zaž lli kanu fuq l-eṛḍ.* She picked up the pieces of glass that were on the floor. **2.** to glean *ma-zal ma-leqqṭu z-zṛăɛ men l-feddan.* They haven't gleaned the wheat from the field yet.
leqqeḥ **1.** v.t. to graft **2.** v.t. to cross-pollinate **3.** v.i. to blossom (tree)
leṛḍ same as *ʔeṛḍ*
leṛwi wild ram with large, curved horns
lsan pl. *lsun* **1.** tongue **2.** language
** *lsanu mteqqef.* He's tongue-tied. —*lsanu qaṣeḥ.* He's rude (when talking). —*lsanha ṛṭeb mɛa koll-ši.* She talks softly with everybody. —*lsanu ṭwil.* He talks too much. —*sbeqni lsani.* It slipped my tongue. —*dak š-ši ɛla ṭeṛf lsani.* I have it on the tip of my tongue.
¶ *lsan waḥed* all together, unanimously
¶ *tserreḥ lsanu*$^{\phi}$, *nṭḷeq lsanu*$^{\phi}$ **1.** to become fluent ≠ *tserreḥ lsanhom fe-n-negliza.* They've become fluent in English. **2.** to find one's tongue ≠ *tserreḥ-lha l-lsan, ma-bqat-ši ḥeššumiya.* She found her tongue; she's no longer shy.
lsaq same as *lṣaq*
lsas pl. *-at* foundation *bdaw iṭellɛu l-lsas l-le-bni.* They have started laying down the foundation for the building.
lsaɛi pl. of *lesɛa*
lsiɛ v.n. of *lsăɛ*
lseq same as *lṣeq*
lesseq same as *leṣṣeq*
lsun pl. of *lsan*
lsăɛ v.t. (v.n. *lsiɛ*) to sting, to bite *lesɛu waḥed ẓ-ẓenbuṛ.* A wasp stung him.
lesɛa pl. *-t, lsaɛi* n.i. of *lsăɛ*
lṣaq pl. *-at* **1.** glue **2.** cellophane adhesive tape (e.g., Scotch tape)
¶ *kaġiṭ l-lṣaq* masking tape
lṣiq v.n. of *lṣeq*
lṣeq v.i. (v.n. *lṣiq*) **1.** to stick *fezzeg t-tenber baš ilṣeq f-le-ġlaf.* Wet the stamp so it'll stick to the envelope. **2.** to be communicable or contagious *had l-meṛḍ ma-ka-ilṣeq-š.* This disease is not contagious.
¶ *lṣeq f-* to bother, to be obnoxious toward *ana dayez u-huwa lṣeq fiya.* I was just passing by and he started bothering me.
¶ *lṣeq fih*$^{\phi}$ to contract, to get (disease) ≠ *ma-ɛreft fuq-aš lṣeq fiha dak l-meṛḍ.* I don't know when she contracted that disease.
leṣqa n.i. of *lṣeq*
leṣṣeq v.t. to stick, to glue *nta lli leṣṣeqti dak l-ʔiɛlan fe-l-ḥăyṭ?* Did you stick that poster on the wall?
¶ *leṣṣeq f-* to give to, to cause (s.o.) to get (disease) *leṣṣqet fih bu-ḥămṛun.* She gave him the measles.
ltam pl. *-at, ltum* veil *ma-bqat-š texrož be-l-ltam.* She doesn't go out with a veil any more.
letšin n.u. *-a* **1.** orange (fruit) **2.** orange tree
lettem v.t. and v.i. to put on (a veil, i.e. *ltam*)
ltum pl. of *ltam*
lṭaf pl. of *lṭif*
lṭafa gentleness *dima ka-ihḍeṛ mɛaha be-l-lṭafa.* He always talks to her with gentleness.
lṭef b- (v.n. *loṭf*) to be kind and gentle toward
lṭef comp. of *lṭif*
loṭf v.n. of *lṭef*
lṭif pl. *lṭaf* (comp. *lṭef*) gentle, nice *ka-tebġi n-nas ikunu lṭaf mɛaha.* She likes people to be nice to her.
lṭim v.n. of *lṭem*
lṭem v.t. (v.n. *lṭim*) to slap, to strike (s.o.)
leṭma n.i. of *lṭem*

luba pl. *-t* doorknob
lubya kidney bean
luġa pl. *-t* language *ka-itkellem ʕadad de-l-luġat.* He speaks many languages.
luġawi pl. *-yen* 1. linguistic 2. linguist
lu-kan see *kun*
lula pl. *-t* 1. defect *baʕuh-lu ṛxiṣ li-ʔenna kan fih waḥed l-lula.* They sold it to him cheap because it had a defect. 2. bad habit *fiha l-lula d-tafḍulit.* She has a bad habit of being nosy.
luleb pl. *lwaleb* (dim. *lwileb*) screw *rekkebt kerʕan ṭ-ṭebḷa be-l-lwaleb.* I fastened the legs to the table with screws.
lum, luma pl. *-t* blame, reproach *ma-ʕliha luma.* She is not to blame.
luman v.n. of *lam*
lun pl. *lwan, ʔelwan* 1. color *ka-yeʕžebni lun siyaṛtek.* I like the color of your car. *—ġir hiya šafettu u-l-ʔelwan tbeddlu fiha.* The minute she saw him she changed color. 2. complexion *lunha ḥămṛani.* She has a dark complexion.
luqaṭaʔ pl. of *laqiṭ*
ḷuṛ, ḷuṛa (no pl.) back, rear *ḷ-ḷuṛ de-l-bab xeṣṣu itteṣbeġ.* The back of the door needs painting. *—hežmu ʕlihom men ḷ-ḷuṛ.* They attacked them from the rear.
¶ *be-ḷ-ḷuṛ* backwards *dext melli bdit nemši be-ḷ-ḷuṛ.* I got dizzy when I started walking backwards.
¶ *ḷ-ḷuṛ, ḷ-ḷuṛa* 1. in the back, in the rear *huma gelsu l-qeddam u-hiya ḷ-ḷuṛ.* They sat in the front and she sat in the back. 2. behind *wqefna ntsennawhom ḥit kanu ma-zalin ḷ-ḷuṛ.* We stopped and waited for them because they were still behind. 3. backwards *ṭaḥet ḷ-ḷuṛa.* She fell backwards.
luṛani see *wṛani*
ḷuṛi, ḷuṛani pl. *-yen* last, (the one) at the end
¶ *be-ḷ-ḷuṛi* same as *be-ḷ-ḷuṛ* (see *ḷuṛ*)
lus pl. *lwas, lwayes* brother-in-law (husband's brother)
lusa pl. *-t, lwayes* sister-in-law (husband's sister)
luwla f. of *luwli*
luwlani pl. *-yen* same as *luwwel*
luwli f. *luwla* pl. *-yen, lwala* 1. same as *luwwel* 2. midday prayer
luwwa v.t. 1. to roll up *luwwa kmamu u-bda ixdem.* He rolled up his sleeves and started working. 2. to wind *luwwat l-xeyṭ ʕăl l-qennuṭ.* She wound the thread around the spool.
luwwaya pl. *-t* ivy
luwwek v.t. to chew, to chew on (gum, candy)
luwwel 1. (no pl.) beginning *šrawha f-luwwel l-ʕam.* They bought it at the beginning of the year. 2. f. *luwla* pl. *luwlin, lwala* first *semma weldu l-luwwel žamal.* He named his first son Jamal *—men l-luwwel ʕreftu ṛažel mezyan.* From the first, I knew he was a good man.
¶ *ʕam luwlayn* two years ago, year before last
¶ *ʕam luwwel* last year
luwwen v.t. to color in a multicolored fashion
luya pl. *-t* 1. n.i. of *lwa* and *luwwa* 2. turn, turn-off *kayna waḥed l-luya qeddam ḍ-ḍaṛ.* There's a turn by the house. 3. curve (in a road)
luyan v.n. of *lwa*
luz n.u. *-a* (dim. *lwiza*) 1. almond 2. almond tree
¶ *luz mfenned* candied almonds
luzum v.n. of *lzem*
luḥ n.u. *-a* pl. *-t, lweḥ, lwaḥ* (dim. *lwiḥa*) 1. wood 2. board, plank 3. wooden tablet used for writing
lwa ilwa v.i. (v.n. *luyan*) to wither *xeṣṣek tesqi had l-ġeṛs qbel-ma ilwa.* You need to water this plant before it withers.
¶ *lwa be-n-nʕas* to fall asleep
lwa ilwi v.i. (v.n. *luyan*) to turn, to make a turn *telfu ʕlina mnayn lwina ʕăl š-šmal.* We lost them when we turned left.
¶ *lwa ʕla* 1. to arrest *l-bulis lwaw ʕlih kif xrež men ḍaṛu.* The police arrested him just as he left his house. 2. to grab by the collar *ma-ṭṛešha ḥetta lwat ʕlih.* He didn't slap her till she grabbed him by the collar. 3. to take by force *tʕăṛṛḍu-lu tlata de-š-šeffaṛa u-lwaw-lu ʕla šwanṭu.* Three thieves stopped him and took his suitcases by force.
lwala pl. of *luwli* and *luwwel*
lwaleb pl. of *luleb*
lwan, ʔelwan pl. of *lun*
lwani (pl.) dishes, utensils
lwas pl. of *lus*
lwayes pl. of *lus* and *lusa*
lwayez pl. of *lwiz*
lwaḥ pl. of *luḥa* (n.u. of *luḥ*)
lwila dim. of *lila*
lwileb dim. of *luleb*
lwiz pl. *-at, lwayez* gold coin (some romantic attachment, as with English "doubloon")
lwiza 1. dim. of *luza* (n.u. of *luz*) 2. vervain
lwiḥa dim. of *luḥa* (n.u. of *luḥ*)
lewya same as *luya*
lweḥ pl. of *luḥa* (n.u. of *luḥ*)
lexxeṛ pl. *-in* last, last one *l-meṛṛa l-lexxṛa lli šefthom hiya l-bareḥ.* The last time I saw them was yesterday. *—huma l-lexxṛin lli xeržu.* They were the last ones to leave.
¶ *f-lexxeṛ, mʕa lexxeṛ* finally, in the end

lexxṛani pl. *-yen* last, last one *dima ka-dži hiya l-lexxṛaniya.* She's always the last one to come.

lexxeṣ v.t. to sum up, to summarize

lyali pl. of *lila*

lyan v.i. (v.n. *lyana, lyuna*) **1.** to soften, to become softer **2.** to become co-operative

lyan pl. *-at* kind of homemade liquid soap, prepared from ashes, lye, and potassium carbonate

lyana v.n. of *lan* and *lyan*

lyaqa v.n. of *laq*

lyeg pl. of *liga* 2 (same as *liqa*)

lyeq pl. of *liqa*

lyuna v.n. of *lan* and *lyan*

lzaz pl. *-at* **1.** wedge **2.** prop, support

lzem v.t. (v.n. *luzum*) **1.** to owe ≠ *šḥal lezmu ɛla had l-xedma?* How much does he owe for this work? **2.** to have to ≠ *ġad-ilezmek tɛămmeṛ ši-wṛaq.* You'll have to fill out some forms.

¶ a.p. *lazem* (may take pron. endings) denotes obligation, necessity, or incumbency *lazem ḥetta huma ixedmu.* They must work too. —*lazem nqulha le-bḅah.* I have to tell his father. —*kan lazemhom iketbu-lu.* They should have written him.

lezzem v.t. to force *bġaw ilezzmuh (baš) imši mɛahom.* They wanted to force him to go with them. —*ma-lezzem ḥădd ɛliya had l-xedma.* Nobody forced this work on me.

lezzez v.t. **1.** to wedge **2.** to prop (up), to support

lžam pl. *-at* rein(s)

ležna pl. *-t, ližan* committee

ležžem v.t. to bridle, to put a bridle on

lḥaf pl. *lḥuf, lḥufa* same as *lḥifa*

lḥayef pl. of *lḥifa*

leḥd pl. *lḥud, lḥuda* large stone slab placed in a grave over the dead body before it is covered with dirt

lḥeg same as *lḥeq*

lḥi pl. of *leḥya*

lḥifa pl. *-t, lḥayef* long, narrow mattress shaped somewhat like a couch

lḥiq v.n. of *lḥeq*

lḥis v.n. of *lḥes*

lḥiwa dim. of *leḥya*

leḥlaḥ pl. *-a* flatterer

leḥleḥ ɛla to flatter *ma-ɛăndek l-aš tleḥleḥ ɛliha.* There's no need for you to flatter her.

lḥăm pl. (intensity) *lḥum, lḥumat* **1.** meat *had l-lḥăm ma-zal ma-ṭab.* This meat hasn't cooked yet. **2.** flesh *s-sbuɛa ka-iɛišu ɛla makelt l-lḥăm.* Lions are flesh-eating animals.

** *xellaweh b-qamižžtu ɛăl l-lḥăm.* They left him with nothing but his shirt on his back.

¶ *šuwwek l-lḥăm l-* to give goose flesh to

lăḥn pl. *ʔalḥan* tune, (piece of) music (excluding any attendant lyrics)

lḥeq v.t. (v.n. *lḥiq*) **1.** to obtain, to get *ma-qḍeṛ-š ilḥeq ši-xedma ḥsen men hadi.* He wasn't able to get a better job. **2.** to reach *ġir ka-ihezz yeddu ka-ilḥeq s-sqef.* He reaches the ceiling just by lifting his arm. **3.** to catch *xeṣṣek tebṭeṛ baš tleḥqu fe-ḍ-ḍaṛ.* You have to hurry so you can catch him at home. **4.** to catch up with or to *daba ṛahom sabqinna, be-l-ḥăqq ġad-ndiru žehdna baš nleḥquhom.* They're ahead of us now, but we'll try our best to catch up with them.

¶ *lḥeq be-d-dbiḥa* to slaughter (a dying animal) in order to make its flesh acceptable for food according to Muslim law

lḥes v.t. (v.n. *lḥis*) to lick *l-kelb ka-ilḥes-lha yeddha.* The dog is licking her hand.

lḥud, lḥuda pl. of *leḥd*

lḥuf, lḥufa pl. of *lḥaf*

lḥum, lḥumat pl. of intensity of *lḥăm*

leḥya pl. *-t, lḥi* (dim. *lḥiwa*) **1.** chin **2.** beard

leḥḥăf **1.** v.t. to wrap (s.o.) in a *ḥayek* **2.** v.i. to put on a *ḥayek*

leḥḥeq v.t. to take, to carry *škun ġad-ileḥḥeq had le-ktub l-l-xizana?* Who's going to take these books to the library?

¶ *leḥḥeq b-* to make reach, to help attain, to help find *ma-leḥḥeqni ḥădd b-had l-minḥa, žebtha b-mubaṛa.* Nobody helped me obtain this scholarship; I won it in a contest.

lɛaybi pl. *-ya* player *xah lɛaybi de-l-kuṛa mezyan.* His brother is a good ball player.

lɛăb v.t. or v.i. (v.n. *lăɛb*) **1.** to play *lɛăbna ṭeṛḥ de-s-sentṛež qbel ma-tɛăššina.* We played a game of chess before we had supper. —*ka-yăɛṛef ilɛăb l-ɛud.* He knows how to play the lute. **2.** to trifle, to fool or play around, to waste time *ma-dazet-š f-le-mtiḥan li-ʔenna kanet ġir ka-telɛăb.* She didn't pass her exam because she was just fooling around.

¶ *lɛăb b-* (or *ɛla*) to dupe, to mislead, to take advantage of *mnin ṣabuh ma-ka-yăɛṛef-š ḷ-ḷuġa lăɛbu bih.* When they found out he didn't know the language, they took advantage of him.

¶ *lɛăb f-* **1.** to play (around) with, to fool (around) with *ma-txelli-š d-drari ilăɛbu fe-ṭ-ṭumubil.* Don't let the kids fool around with the car. **2.** to misuse, to misappropriate *dɛaw ʔamin ṣ-ṣenḍuq ɛla lli* *kan ka-ilƐăb f-le-flus de-l-muʔessasa.* The treasurer was sued for misappropriating the society's funds.

¶ *lƐăb le-qmeṛ* to gamble, to play for money

lăƐb v.n. of *lƐăb*

¶ *lăƐb l-xil* horse race

¶ *lăƐb l-kuṛa* ball game

lăƐba n.i. of *lƐăb*

lƐin v.n. of *lƐăn*

lƐiq v.n. of *lƐăq*

lƐăn v.t. (v.n. *lƐin*) to curse, to swear at

lăƐna n.i. of *lƐăn*

lƐăq v.t. (v.n. *lƐiq*) to lick *lăƐqet z-zlafa Ɛad ġesletha.* She licked the bowl and then washed it.

¶ p.p. *melƐuq* pl. *mlaƐeq* ill-fated person, one always having bad luck

lăƐq pl. of *lăƐqa* 2

lăƐqa 1. n.i. of *lƐăq* 2. pl. *-t, lăƐq* leech, bloodsucker

lăƐƐab pl. *-a* player *šƨal de-l-lăƐƐaba fe-l-feṛqa dyalkom?* How many players are there in your team?

lăƐƐăb v.t. to make play *lăƐƐbuni l-kaṛṭa bezz menni.* They made me play cards in spite of myself.

M

ma (m.) pl. *myah* 1. water 2. juice (of fruit, vegetables, etc.) 3. sap (plant)

¶ *ma de-z-zheṛ* or *ma zheṛ* orange blossom perfume

¶ *ma wṛeḍ* or *ma de-l-werḍ* rose water

¶ *ma ƨya* a relatively weak alcoholic beverage resembling aquavit or brandy

ma 1. used as a type of relative pron. *ma-Ɛăndi ma nqul.* I have nothing to say. (** What can I do? I'm caught.) —*ma-xellit ma qellebt.* I looked everywhere (i.e., I didn't leave out inspecting anything). —*ma-bqa-li ma nemši.* There's no longer any reason for me to go. —*ma-fiya ma nemši.* I don't feel like going. 2. used with various other words to form a type of compound conj. (often in the form of *-emma*): *băƐd-ma tƐăššina xrežna ntsaraw.* After we ate supper we went to take a walk. —*ma-Ɛăndi suq, aš-emma kanet ġir werriha-li!* I don't care; whatever it is, show it to me! —*fayn-ma ikun Ɛăndek l-weqt, aži šufna.* Whenever you have time, come and see us. —*weqt-emma weždu-lek le-flus Ɛṭini lli ka-nsalek.* Pay me what you owe me whenever you get the money. (see *aš, baš, bƨal, bin, bla, băƐd, f-, fayn, fuq, gaƐ, ġiṛ, ƨit, ƨsen, ƨetta, kif, layn, men, mnayn, qedd, saƐa, šƨal, škun, wa, wayn, weqt, Ɛla, Ɛlaš, Ɛănd*)

ma used in certain interrogative terms with the preposition *l-*: *ma-lek tƐăṭṭelti?* Why were you late? —*ma l-had š-šelya mherrsa?* Why is this chair broken? —*ma-lek?* What's the matter with you? —*aš žabek fiya ma-li?* What do you care what's the matter with me?

ma particle of negation (usually used with *-š* or *-ši*) *l-bareƨ ma-kont-š fe-ḍ-ḍaṛ.* I wasn't home yesterday. —*ma-Ɛăndi ƨetta ƨaža.* I don't have a thing.

¶ *ma-ši* term of negation (in equational sentences) *hiya ma-ši mezyana!* She's not pretty!

ma used to express amazement or admiration: *ma ƨlaha!* How nice she is! —*ma bennu!* How good this tastes! —*ḷḷah Ɛla had l-bent ma zinha!* God, she's a beautiful girl!

mabadiʔ pl. of *mebdeʔ*

ma da bihφ see *da*

madad used in the expr. *madad, ya ṛasul ḷḷah!* prayerful invocation for assistance upon undertaking s.th. that one feels he cannot do without help

madahib pl. of *medheb*

madani pl. *-yen* civil, civilian (in contrast to military)

madaniya civilization

madaq taste *had l-Ɛineb fih waƨed l-madaq moƐtabaṛ.* These grapes have an excellent taste.

madaṛ pl. *-at* orbit (of planet, etc.)

madda 1. pl. *mawadd* element (chemical) 2. pl. *mawadd* field, area (profession, of study) 3. (no pl.) finances, funds 4. pl. *-t* distance (from one point to another)

madina (with art.) Medina (near Mecca)

madiƨ (no pl.) 1. eulogy (especially to a saint or the Prophet) 2. eulogist, panegyrist

madella humiliation, degradation

madriya pl. *-t* beam, timber

mʔadya v.n. of *ʔada*

madi a.p. of *mḍa*

maḍeṛṛa harm, detriment (v.n. of *ḍeṛṛ*) *l-gaṛṛu lli ka-tekmi ṛah fih ġir l-maḍeṛṛa.* Those cigarettes you smoke are nothing but harmful.

magana pl. *-t, mwagen* 1. watch (time-piece) 2. clock

¶ *magana de-ḍ-ḍuw* electric or light meter

¶ *magana de-l-ma* water meter

¶ *magana de-s-sersar* alarm clock
¶ *magana de-ṣ-ṣemṭa* (or *de-l-yedd*) wrist watch
¶ *magana de-š-šems* sun dial
¶ *magana de-š-šun* (or *de-ṭ-ṭuq*) pocket watch
mağul n.pl. of *mağuli*
mağuli adj. pl. *-yen* n.pl. *mağul* Mongolian, Tatar (referring mainly to the savage hordes of the late middle ages)
mahana same as *ʔihana* (v.n. of *han ihin*)
mahaṛa skill, dexterity
maheṛ pl. *-in* skillful, dextrous, adroit
makan pl. *ʔamkina, ʔamakin* classicism for *maḥăll*
makayed pl. of *makida*
makida pl. *makayed* trap, snare (also metaphorical)
¶ *debbeṛ makida l-* to lay or set a trap for (s.o., animal)
makina pl. *-at, mwaken* machine, apparatus
¶ *makina de-ḍ-ḍuw* generator
¶ *makina d-le-ḥsana* razor (electric and safety)
¶ *makina de-le-ḥṣad* harvester, combine
¶ *makina de-ṭ-ṭbaṣel* phonograph, record player
¶ *makina de-ṭ-ṭḥin* grain mill (electric)
¶ *makina d-le-xyaṭa* sewing machine
makla **1.** v.n. of *kla* **2.** pl. *-at, mwakel* food (in general) **3.** pl. *-at, mwakel* meal (dinner, supper, etc.)
makul pl. *-at* food (in general; usually pl.)
mal imil v.i. (v.n. *milan, muyul*) **1.** to lean, to tilt, to be inclined or at an angle *š-šežṛa mayla le-š-šeṛq.* The tree is leaning to the east. —*ka-imil le-š-šuyuɛiya.* He leans toward Communism. **2.** to tend —*lun l-qamižža ka-imil l-le-zṛeq.* The color of the shirt tends toward blue. **3.** to roll, to rock (as a ship)
mal pl. *mwal* money, capital
malak pl. *malayka, mlayka* angel (e.g., Gabriel)
malal **1.** satiety, quality of being fed up **2.** s.th. wrong or amiss *ɛăndu ši-malal f-keršu.* He has something wrong with his stomach.
malayka pl. of *malak*
malĭk pl. *muluk* king, monarch
malika pl. *-t* queen
maliya **1.** same as *mal* **2.** finance (dept.)
¶ *wazir l-maliya* Minister of Finance
¶ *wizaṛt l-maliya* Ministry of Finance
maleḥ pl. *-in* salty
mamat death *men qbel l-mamat dyalu kteb-lha risala.* He wrote her a letter before his death.
mamun pl. *-in* **1.** safe, without danger (place) **2.** loyal, trustworthy
mamuni pl. *-yen* trellis
mamuriya pl. *-t* mission (diplomatic, religious, etc.)
man imun same as *muwwen*
manaḍiṛ pl. of *menḍeṛ*
manafiɛ pl. of *menfaɛa* 2
manakiṛ pl. of *munkăṛ*
manam same as *mnam*
manama same as *mnama*
manasik (treated as f.sg.) used in the expr. *manasik l-ḥăžž* prescribed attire, standard of appearance, rites, etc., to be observed during the pilgrimage at Mecca
manazil pl. of *menzila*
manḍa pl. *-t* salary, pay
manḍulina pl. *-t* mandolin
maniṛa pl. *-t* **1.** manner, way *xeṣṣni nšuf ši-maniṛa baš nḥell had le-qfel.* I have to find some way to open this lock. **2.** trick, ruse *dda le-flus mennu b-waḥed l-maniṛa.* He got the money from him by trickery.
maniɛ pl. *mawaniɛ* obstacle, hindrance
¶ *ma-ɛănduᶲ maniɛ* to have no objection, to be all right with (s.o.)≠
manta type of wild mint
maqadir destiny, fate
maqal pl. *-at* article (magazine, newspaper)
maqala pl. *-t* same as *maqal*
maqam pl. *-at* **1.** tomb of the Prophet Mohammed or a Muslim saint **2.** position, rank, grade
maqama pl. *-t* type of Arabic poetry
maqayis pl. of *meqyas*
maṛakiz pl. of *meṛkez*
maṛăḍ s-sell same as *sell, soll*
maṛiya tide (sea)
** *xellih ḥetta džibu l-maṛiya.* Leave it until a better opportunity comes.
¶ *maṛiya ṭalɛa* high tide
¶ *maṛiya habṭa* low tide
mariyu pl. *-yat, -wat* wardrobe, portable closet
maṛka pl. *-t* brand, make *šmen maṛka ṭ-ṭumubil dyalek?* What make is your car?
maṛṣ March (month)
masafa same as *msafa*
masaʔil pl. of *mesʔala*
masakin pl. of *meskin*
masaḥa pl. *-t* area, surface *l-ma daɛ f-waḥed l-masaḥa kbira.* The water spread over a large area.
masiḥ (with art.) (the) Messiah, (the) Christ
maṣaliḥ pl. of *meṣlaḥa*
maṣeṛ (f.) Egypt
maṣṣa pl. *-t* sledge hammer
maṣṣu pl. *-wat, -yat* **1.** pile (of coins, jewels, gold) **2.** nugget (gold)
ma-ši see *ma* (negation)
maši a.p. of ***mša***

mašina pl. *-t* train *ṣafeṛt l-meṛṛakeš fe-l-mašina.* I went to Marrakesh by train.
mašiya cpl. *mawaši* livestock (pl. implies more emphasis on the various kinds)
mašeqqa pl. *-t* difficulty *ma-wṣelt ġir b-mašeqqa.* I arrived only after some difficulty. —*f-had š-šġol kayna mašeqqa.* This work is difficult to do.
mat imut v.i. to die *l-bareḥ mat ḅḅah ḷḷah iṛeḥmu.* His father died yesterday, God rest his soul. —*ɛṭini nakol, ka-nmut be-ž-žuɛ!* Give me something to eat, I'm dying of hunger.
¶ *mat ɛla* to be crazy or mad about (s.o.) *ka-iḥebb mṛatu u-ka-imut ɛliha.* He's just crazy about his wife.
matabaqi (no art.) the rest, what is left *ana ɛṭiwni ġir had l-xatem, u-matabaqi ḷḷah irebbeḥkom bih.* Just give me this ring and you can have the rest.
matal same as *mtel* 2
matalan for example, for instance, such as
maṭaṛ pl. *-at* airport, air field
maṭiša (coll. and sg) pl. *-t, mwaṭeš* (no art.) 1. tomato 2. swing *kanet ka-telɛăb f-maṭiša u-hiya ṭṭiḥ u-herrset yeddiha.* She was playing on the swing when she fell and broke her arm.
maṭel b- to put (s.o.) off *hadi modda u-nta ka-tmaṭel biya, ɛṭini flusi, ḷḷah ibarek fik!* You've been putting me off long enough, now please give me my money!
maṭăṛ pl. *mṭaṛ, ʔemṭaṛ* rain (pl. for intensity)
mawadd pl. of *madda* 1 and 2
mawaḍiɛ pl. of *muḍuɛ*
mawaši cpl. of *mašiya*
mawi pl. *mawyen* 1. (too) watery, thin *had le-mdad mawi.* This ink is too watery. 2. (extra) juicy (of citrus)
maya pl. *-t* melody, tune *waš ka-tăɛṛef l-maya dyal had l-ġonya?* Do you know the melody of this song?
mayu May (month)
ma-zal see *zal*
mazid used in the expr. *l-ḥămdu li-llahi wa-mazid š-šokr* used to express one's satisfaction as to how s.th. is (e.g., one's business, a good meal)
maẓuẓi pl. *-yen* late (e.g., a crop) *had z-zṛăɛ lli f-had l-menṭaqa kollu maẓuẓi.* The wheat in this region has all come in late.
mazeḥ v.t. 1. to joke or kid around with (s.o.) 2. to play or fool around with, to be playful with (s.o.)
maž imuž v.i. to be wavy, to undulate (sea)
maži a.p. of *ža*
mažella pl. *-t* magazine, journal
mažus pl. of *mažusi*
mažusi pl. *mažus* pagan, heathen (also often said of any non-believer in a one-and-only God)
maḥăll pl. *-at* place *šnu had l-maḥăll?* What's this place (here)? —*aži l-maḥălli had l-lila!* Come over to my place tonight! —*fayn ža maḥăllek de-l-xedma?* Where's your place of business? —*škun lli ɛămlu f-maḥăllu?* Who did they put in his place?
maḥălli pl. *-yen* local, of or pertaining to a particular place
ma-ḥya see *ma*
maɛad-ḷḷah usually in the expr. *ḥaša maɛad-ḷḷah* expresses some disbelief in or unacceptance of s.o.'s remark *šeftu ka-išeffeṛ* —*ḥaša maɛad-ḷḷah!* I've seen him steal.—Impossible!
maɛariḍ pl. of *măɛṛiḍ*
maɛarif pl. of *măɛrifa* 2
meɛida pl. *-t* stomach (organ)
maɛun pl. *mwaɛen* 1. dish (includes pots and pans) *ɛawenni fe-ġsil le-mwaɛen.* Help me wash the dishes. 2. musical instrument 3. tool (of any kind)
mbadla pl. *-t* trade, barter
mbaleġ pl. of *mebleġ*
mbaṛed, mbaṛeḍ pl. of *mebṛed, mebṛeḍ*
mbaṛek part. of *baṛek*
mbarka pl. *-t* n.i. of *barek* and *tbarek*
mbata v.n. of *bat*
mbawsa pl. *-t* n.i. of *tbawes*
mbaxeṛ pl. of *mbexṛa*
mbayɛa pl. *-t* bow, obeisance, curtsy
mebdeʔ pl. *mabadiʔ* principle *huwa ma-ɛăndu ḥetta mebdeʔ.* He has no principles at all.
mbixṛa dim. of *mbexṛa*
mebleġ pl. *mbaleġ* amount, sum *wret men ḅḅah waḥed l-mebleġ dyal le-flus kbir bezzaf.* He inherited a very large sum of money from his father.
mebrad pl. *-in* (one) sensitive to cold
mebṛaṣ pl. *-in* (one) afflicted with vitiligo
mebṛed, mebṛeḍ pl. *mbaṛed, mbaṛeḍ* file, rasp (tool)
mebṛuk usually used in set expr. e.g., *ɛwašrek mebṛuka,* or *ɛidek mebṛuk!* Happy holiday! —*ṣbaḥek mebṛuk!* Good morning! —*hadi saɛa mebṛuka f-aš šefnak.* It's (been) good to see you again.
mbexṛa pl. *mbaxeṛ* (dim. *mbixṛa*) censer, thurible
mebyuɛ p.p. of *baɛ*
mdabez part. of *ddabez*
mdabza pl. *-t* fight, scrap
mdabeḥ pl. of *medbeḥ*
mdad 1. pl. of *modd* 2. ink
mdadi pl. *-yen* blue (basically color of blue ink)
mdadeḥ pl. of *meddaḥ*
mdafeɛ pl. of *medfăɛ*

mdagga pl. *-t* n.i. of *tdagg*
mdaheb pl. of *medheb*
mdahya v.n. of *dha*
mdakk pl. of *mdekka*
mdaker (pl.) testicles
mdaqqa same as *mdagga* (n.i. of *tdagg*)
mdari pl. of *medra*
mdarya v.n. of *dara*
mdawem part. of *dawem*
mdawma v.n. of *dam*
mdawez pl. of *medwez*
mdaxel pl. of *medxel*
mdayni pl. *-ya* creditor
mdayež, mdažž pl. of *mdežža*
mdaḥsa v.n. of *dḥes* and *daḥes*
mdaεya v.n. of *dεa*
medbal pl. *-in* wilted, withered (as a flower; also a person)
medbeḥ pl. *mdabeḥ* part of animal's throat which is cut or slit when it is slaughtered
medd v.t. (v.n. *meddan*) **1.** to hold out, to extend *medd-li yeddik nšuf aš fiha!* Hold out your hand so I can see what's in it! **2.** to pass, to reach, to hand *medd-li hadak le-ktab llah ixellik!* Hand me that book, please! **3.** to lay out or down (s.o.) *hak, medd had l-weld fuq le-fraš.* Here, lay the boy down on the bed.
medd, modd du. *-ayn* pl. *mdud, mdad* container used for measuring grain
modda pl. *-t* **1.** (long) time, a while *fayn had l-ġiba, hadi modda ma-šefnak.* Where have you been, it's been a long time since we've seen you. **2.** period *εṭaha modda dyal εăšṛ iyyam.* He gave her a period of ten days.
¶ *modda madida* a long time, ages
meddan v.n. of *medd*
meddaḥ pl. *-a, mdadeḥ* **1.** kind of street singer, minstrel **2.** kind of public storyteller
mᵊeddeb part. of *ᵊeddeb*
meddi pl. *-yen* a.p. of *dda*
medden v.t. to civilize
medfăε pl. *mdafeε* cannon
¶ *ḍṛeb* (or *ṭleq,* or *kellem*) *medfăε* to fire or discharge a cannon
¶ *teklima* (or *ḍeṛba*) *de-l-medfăε* cannon shot
medheb pl. *mdaheb, madahib* **1.** doctrine, school (of thought) **2.** sect, denomination
medhi p.p. of *dha*
moᵊdi (*l-*) pl. *moᵊdyen* harmful, injurious, noxious (to)
mdina pl. *-t, mdun* city, town (often referring to the old, original city rather than the newer, more modern city next to the old)
mdini pl. *-yen* city-dweller, urbanite
mdiḥ v.n. of *mdeḥ*
mdekka pl. *-t, mdakk* ramrod (for loading guns)
medkuk p.p. of *dekk*
mdeldel pl. *-in* dangling, hanging loose (as shirt tail, loose wires hanging from ceiling, loose vine)
medra pl. *-t, mdari* pitchfork
medṛasa same as *medṛaṣa*
mderbel pl. *-in* ragged, torn and tattered (clothes or person)
mderdeb p.p. of *derdeb*
mdud pl. of *medd, modd*
mdun pl. of *mdina*
mduwwed part. of *duwwed*
medwez pl. *mdawez* **1.** corridor, hallway **2.** passageway, pass **3.** path, trail **4.** aqueduct, ditch
medxel pl. *mdaxel* **1.** way in, entrance **2.** definition (of a word), lexicographical entry **3.** introduction, preface
mdexna pl. *-t* chimney, flue
medxul **1.** income, revenue **2.** pl. *-in* sickly, in bad health
mdexxem pl. *-in* same as *mḍexxem*
medyan pl. *-in* debtor
mdežža pl. *-t, mdažž, mdayež* pearl necklace
mdeḥ v.t. (v.n. *medḥ, mdiḥ*) **1.** to praise in song (the Prophet Mohammed) **2.** to praise, to speak well of (s.o.)
medḥ v.n. of *mdeḥ*
mdeḥḥes pl. *-in* (over)packed, crammed, (over)crowded
mdăεwi pl. *-yen* unfortunate, wretched (person)
mḍa imḍa v.i. **1.** to get or become sharp (knife) **2.** to become mentally keen, to develop one's personality **3.** to get lost *mḍat fe-l-ġaba l-bareḥ.* She got lost in the forest yesterday.
mḍa imḍi **1.** v.t. to sign (object may be signature or the paper) **2.** v.i. to get lost *mḍa-li ṣebbaṭi.* My shoes have gotten lost.
¶ a.p. *maḍi* pl. *maḍyen* (comp. *mḍa*) **1.** sharp, keen *ma-kan-š ka-yeḥsab-li had ž-ženwi maḍya hakda.* I wasn't aware that this knife was so sharp. —*εăndu waḥed l-weld maḍi mεa ṛaṣu.* He has a boy with a sharp mind. **2.** (with art.) the past *fe-l-maḍi le-mġaṛba kanu ka-ilebsu ṭ-ṭṛabeš bezzaf.* In the past, Moroccans wore the fez a great deal.
mḍa comp. of *maḍi* (a.p. of *mḍa*)
mḍabeε pl. of *meḍbuε* (same as *mḍebbăε*)
mḍaḍeġ pl. of *meḍḍaġa*
mḍall pl. of *mḍell*
mḍamm pl. of *mḍemma*
mḍaṛeb pl. of *mḍeṛṛba*
mḍaṛeṣ pl. of *meḍṛaṣa* and *mḍeṛṣa*
mḍawa intelligence, sharpness (of mind)
mḍayeq pl. of *meḍyeq*

mḍebbăɛ pl. *-in* stupid, dense
meḍbuɛ pl. *-in, mḍabeɛ* same as *mḍebbăɛ*
meḍḍa v.t. to sharpen, to hone (a blade)
meḍḍaġa pl. *mḍaḍeġ* temple (of head)
meḍḍay pl. *-a* one who sharpens knives, etc.
mḍeġ v.t. (v.n. *mḍiġ*) to chew, to masticate
¶ *mḍeġ l-heḍṛa* (or *le-klam*) **1.** to swallow one's words, to mumble **2.** to think carefully before speaking, to measure one's words
meḍġa pl. *-t* n.i. of *mḍeġ*
mḍiġ v.n. of *mḍeġ*
mḍiyyeq part. of *ḍiyyeq*
meḍḷam pl. *-in* dark, unlit *had l-bit meḍḷam bezzaf.* This room is too dark.
mḍeḷḷ pl. *mḍaḷḷ, mḍuḷa* **1.** umbrella, parasol **2.** parachute
meḍmeḍ v.t. to rinse (out) (the mouth)
mḍemma pl. *-t, mḍamm* type of embroidered woman's belt (usually of silk)
meḍnun p.p. of *ḍenn*
meḍṛaṣa pl. *-t, mḍaṛeṣ* school *ɛad zadu tlata d-le-byut fe-l-meḍṛaṣa dyalna.* They've just added three rooms to our school.
meḍṛaṣi pl. *-yen* of or pertaining to school
mḍeṛṛba pl. *-t, mḍaṛeb* mattress
mḍeṛṣa pl. *mḍaṛeṣ* kind of student dormitory
meḍṛub p.p. of *ḍṛeb*
mḍuḷa pl. of *mḍeḷḷ*
mḍexxem pl. *-in* excellent, magnificent, outstanding
meḍyeq pl. *mḍayeq* gorge, pass, gap (mountain)
moḍḥika pl. *-t* most anything that causes laughter
mfaṛeq pl. of *mefṛeq*
mfaṣel **1.** a.p. of *tfaṣel* **2.** pl. of *mefṣel*
mfateḥ pl. of *meftaḥ*
mfatel pl. of *meftel*
mfawet pl. *-in* unequal, not the same *had l-xut mfawtin fe-s-senn.* These brothers are not the same age.
mefḍuḥ p.p. of *fḍeḥ*
mefhum p.p. of *fhem*
mfelles part. of *felles* and a.p. of *tfelles*
mefṛeq pl. *mfaṛeq* fork(ing), bifurcation
¶ *mefṛeq ṭ-ṭeṛqan* **1.** junction, fork (road) **2.** intersection (road)
mferred p.p. of *ferred*
mfeṛṛek pl. *-in* knock-kneed
mefṣel pl. *mfaṣel* joint, articulation (bone)
meftaḥ pl. *mfateḥ* key (which opens some lock; also metaphorical)
meftel pl. *mfatel* joint, articulation (bone)
meftuḥ p.p. of *fteḥ*
mfežžež part. of *fežžež*
mgada pl. of *megdi*
mgadd pl. *-in* **1.** straight (i.e., not curved or crooked) **2.** straightforward, frank (person)
mgader pl. of *megder*
mgag pl. of *mogg*
megdi pl. *mgada* type of chisel used on concrete, bricks, etc.
megder pl. *-in, magader* large and strong, big and husky
mogg pl. *mgag* nasal junction of upper and lower eyelids.
mgemmeṛ pl. *-in* **1.** moonlit **2.** glowing, beaming (face; attributed to pious living)
mgezṛa pl. *-t* slaughterhouse
megɛăd same as *meqɛăd*
mġanna pl. *-t* v.n. of *tġanen, tġann*
mġaṛba n.pl. of *mġeṛbi, meġṛibi, meġṛibi*
mġaṛef pl. of *moġṛef, mġeṛfa, mġoṛfa*
mġasel pl. of *meġsel*
mġawta pl. *-t* quarrel, argument
mġazel pl. of *meġzel*
meġbun pl. *-in* **1.** sad, low (in spirit) **2.** depressing, sad (situation, problem)
mġedded pl. *-in* a.p. of *tġedded* and part. of *ġedded*
meġfaṛa v.n. of *ġfeṛ*
meġfira absolution, forgiveness (of God) *l-meġfira ka-tkun ġir men ɛănd ḷḷah.* Forgiveness comes only from God.
meġġeṭ v.t. to lay down (usually a child) *meġġeṭha baš tenɛăs!* Lay her down so she can go to sleep!
meġmum p.p. of *ġemm*
moġṛef, mġeṛfa, mġoṛfa pl. *-t, mġaṛef* **1.** wooden spoon (for eating soup, etc.) **2.** ladle
meġṛib (with art.) Morocco
meġribi, meġṛibi, mġeṛbi adj. pl. *-yen* n.pl. *mġaṛba* Moroccan
mġerreb part. of *ġerreb*
meġsel pl. *mġasel* wooden slab or table with short legs on which the dead are washed
meġṭuṭ muggy (weather)
meġyaṛ pl. *-in* jealous, envious *huwa meġyaṛ men xah.* He's jealous of his brother.
meġzel pl. *mġazel* **1.** spindle (in spinning wool) **2.** axle
mhabel pl. of *mehbul*
mhadd pl. of *mhedd*
mhal pl. of *mhil*
mhara **1.** same as *mahara* **2.** pl. of *mehri*
mharez pl. of *mehraz*
mehbul pl. *-in, mhabel* crazy, mad (literal and loose sense)
mehd pl. *mhud* same as *mhedd*
mhedd pl. *mhadd* cradle (baby)
mehhed v.t. to facilitate, to make easy or easier
mehhel **1.** v.t. to slow down, to take easy or easier (work, speed) **2.** v.i. to slow up or down, to take it easy
¶ *mehhel ɛla* **1.** to give extra time to (s.o.) (as for paying a debt) **2.** to not rush

(s.o.) *mehhel ɛliha!* Don't rush her! **3.** to give a breather or respite to (s.o.)
mhil pl. *mhal* (comp. *mhel*) **1.** slow, not capable of fast action (as a poor runner, worker) **2.** low (flame)
mhel **1.** comp. of *mhil* **2.** patience
¶ *b-le-mhel* patiently
mohl same as *mhel* 2
mehmum pl. *-in* worried, anxious, preoccupied
mehr, mohr dowry
mehrar pl. *-in* ticklish (sensitive to touch)
mehraz pl. *mharez* mortar (and pestle)
mehri pl. *mhara* dromedary, one-humped camel
mhud pl. of *mehd* (same as *mhedd*)
mehyab pl. *-in* **1.** scary, frightening (as a haunted house, cemetery) **2.** inspiring a kind of shy fear, apprehension (as fear of talking to a pretty girl, important personality)
mida pl. *-t, myadi* **1.** board used in transporting unbaked bread to the public oven **2.** table (furniture) **3.** low, round serving table with a raised edge or rim
midum pl. *-in* having fat, fatty (meat)
¶ *luz midum* almonds used for their oil
miḍa pl. *-t, myaḍi* bathroom, rest room, latrine
mikṛub pl. *-at* microbe, germ
mil **1.** taste, penchant *xay ɛăndu mil l-l-musiqa.* My brother has a taste for music. **2.** slope, incline, inclination *l-mil dyal had ḍ-ḍṛuž šġiṛ.* These stairs have (only) a slight slope. **3.** pl. *myal* mile
milad l-masiḥ Christ's birth, the Nativity, Christmas
milan v.n. of *mal*
milud same as *mulud*
miludiya same as *muludiya*
mim the Arabic and Moroccan letter *m*
** *sebbeq l-mim tertaḥ.* Always say "no" and you won't have any problems (i.e., you won't be responsible for anything).
mimun luck, good fortune
mina pl. *-t* mine (explosive)
miqat about, around *nšufek ġedda miqat l-ɛăšṛa de-ṣ-ṣbaḥ.* I'll see you tomorrow about ten in the morning.
miqdaṛ amount, quantity (usually of money)
mirat **1.** inheritance, bequest **2.** succession, inheritance (as to the crown)
miṣṣel same as *myeṣṣel*
mital pl. *ˀemtila* **1.** example **2.** proverb, saying
mitin (country usage) same as *myatayn*
miteṛ, mitru pl. *mitruwat, -yat* meter (metric system)
miyyal pl. *-in* (*l-*) tending (to, toward) *lunu miyyal l-le-ḥmeṛ.* Its color tends toward the red.
** *ana lih miyyal.* I like him; I'm for him; I'm on his side.
miyyaz pl. *-in* observant, perspicacious
miyyel v.t. **1.** to tilt, to incline *ila bġiti tɛămmeṛ s-stilu miyyel d-dwaya!* Tilt the ink bottle if you want to fill the pen. **2.** to get (s.o.) to come over to one's side or way of thinking
miyyeq v.t. to give a dirty look to (s.o.), to grimace at (s.o.) disgustedly or disapprovingly
mˀiyyes pl. *-in* having given up in desperation
miyyet **1.** pl. *in* dead *m̄m̄u miyyta be-l-ḥăqq ḅḅah ma-zal ɛayeš.* His mother is dead but his father is still living. **2.** pl. *-in* sterile, infertile (soil) **3.** pl. *muta* dead person
miyyez v.t. **1.** to distinguish, to discern, to tell (the difference between) *imken-lek tmiyyez le-xḍeṛ men le-zṛeq?* Can you tell green from blue? —*ma-imken-lek-š tmiyyez bin l-beġla u-l-ɛăwd?* Can't you distinguish between a mule and a horse? **2.** to think, to reflect *dima ka-imiyyez qbel-ma idwi.* He always thinks before he speaks.
miz discrimination, differentiation
¶ *be-l-miz* by a rough estimation or guess *ɛmelt z-zit fe-ṭ-ṭawa ġir be-l-miz.* I poured the oil into the pot, merely estimating the amount (and not measuring exactly).
mizan pl. *myazen* **1.** balance, scale(s) **2.** equilibrium, balance (usually involving one side in respect to another) **3.** meter, rhythm **4.** check, proof (as of a mathematical problem)
¶ *mizan l-ma* (carpenter's) level
¶ *mizan l-xiṭ* plumb line
¶ *mizan lḥal* barometer
¶ *mizan l-ḥaṛaṛa* thermometer
mizaniya pl. *-t* budget
mizaž same as *mzaž*
mižuṛ pl. *-in* hired, employed (especially irregularly)
miḥaḍ pl. of *măḥḍ*
miɛad pl. *-at* **1.** date, appointment **2.** at (time expr.) *ġadi nexrož miɛad l-xemsa.* I'm leaving at five o'clock. **3.** correlative of *ġir* taking pron. endings in such expr. as *ġir ža miɛadi xrežt.* As soon as he came I left.
¶ *miɛad ṣ-ṣbaḥ, miɛad ġedda fe-ṣ-ṣbaḥ* (by) tomorrow morning *miɛad ġedda fe-ṣ-ṣbaḥ ɛad neqdeṛ nwežžedha-lek.* I can have it ready for you by tomorrow morning.
¶ *ḥetta l-miɛad* until (time expr.) *ma-imken-lek texrož ḥetta l-miɛad le-ɛša.* You can't leave until evening.
miɛaṛa pl. *-t* Jewish cemetery
mkabb pl. of *mkebb*
mkafya v.n. of *kafa*

mkan pl. *-at* same as *makan*
mkateb pl. of *mekteb* and *mektub*
mkaḥel pl. of *mkeḥla, mkoḥla*
mkebb pl. *mkabb* **1.** reflector for an overhead light bulb **2.** conical lid for a kind of bread basket (for keeping bread)
mekka Mecca
mekkaṛ adj. pl. *-in* n.pl. *-a* subtly evil and malicious
mekken v.t. to make it possible for (s.o.) *mekkenha men l-ḥuṣuḷ ʕăl l-măʕlumat lli bġat.* He made it possible for her to get the information she wanted.
mekkeṛ b- to mistreat, to be mean to, to do evil to
mekmul pl. *-in* perfect, faultless (person)
mken v.i. (v.n. *ʔimkan*) to be possible *imken iži.* It's possible he'll come.
** *imken!* Could be! Maybe!
¶ *mken l-* to be able ≠ *waš mken-lek temši l-dak l-muḥaḍaṛa?* Were you able to go to that lecture? —*imken-lek dži?* Can you come?
mektab f. sg, used as pl., destined, fated *l-mut mektaba ʕlina kollna.* Death is destined for all of us.
mektaba pl. *-t* **1.** library **2.** bookstore
mekteb pl. *mkateb* **1.** office (place of work) *ḍṛeb-li t-tilifun l-l-mekteb dyali.* Call me at my office. **2.** office, bureau, department **3.** desk (as in an office)
mketba pl. *-t* desk
mektub pl. *mkateb* pocket (clothing)
meʔkul same as *makul*
mkeḥla, mkoḥla pl. *mkaḥel* **1.** rifle **2.** container for storing *kḥul*
mkăʕlel pl. *-in* **1.** disheveled, messed up (hair) **2.** full of *koʕlal* (wool)
mla imli v.t. (v.n. *melyan, mli*) to dictate, to read off (so one can write) *aži ḷḷah ixellik mli ʕliya had l-qiṭʕa.* Please dictate this excerpt to me.
mlaġa **1.** v.n. of *tmelleġ* **2.** pl. *-t* joke, jest
mlak engagement (for marriage)
mlak, mlakat pl. of *melk*
mlales pl. of *mellasa*
mḷaḷeṭ pl. of *meḷḷaṭi*
mlaleḥ pl. of *mellaḥ*
mlalḥi pl. *-ya* one who extracts and refines salt (from sea water)
mlas v.i. to get or become smooth, polished (as a sanded piece of wood)
mlasi pl. of *melsa* (same as *mellasa*)
mlaʕeb pl. of *melʕăb*
mlaʕeq pl. of *melʕuq* (pp. of *lʕăq*)
mlaxi pl. of *melxa*
mlayka pl. of *malak*
mlayen pl. of *melyun*
mḷayeṛ pl. of *meḷyaṛ*
mlaḥ v.i. (v.n. *mlaḥa*) to turn out all right, to turn into a good person (said of formerly mischievous or unruly children)
mlaḥ pl. of *mliḥ* **1**
mlaḥa v.n. of *mlaḥ*
melf pl. (intensity) *mluf, mlufa* felt (cloth)
melhuf pl. *-in* gluttonous, voracious
melhut pl. *-in* same as *lahet* (a.p. of *lhet*)
meḷhuṭ pl. *-in* gluttonous, voracious
mli v.n. of *mla*
mlik v.n. of *mlek*
mḷiṣ v.n. of *mḷeṣ*
mliḥ **1.** pl. *mlaḥ* (comp. *mleḥ*) good, excellent **2.** well *ka-năʕṛef nekteb b-l-ingliza mliḥ.* I know how to write well in English.
** *mliḥ!* All right! O.K.!
mlek v.t. (v.n. *mlik, melk* **1.** to possess, to own **2.** to master (language, job) **3.** to conquer (country, etc.)
¶ *mlek nefsuᶲ* to have control of one's emotions, to have a good grip on oneself
¶ p.p. *memluk* pl. *-in* (living) in slavery, in bondage
melk pl. *mlak, mlakat* **1.** v.n. of *mlek* **2.** property, that which is owned
¶ *f-melkuᶲ* in one's possession, belonging to (s.o.) *had s-siyaṛa f-melki.* This car belongs to me.
molk state or office of being king, kingship
melkiya pl. *-t* **1.** deed (to property) **2.** ownership, title *škun lli ʕăndu ʕliha l-melkiya?* Who has (legal) title to it?
mell (v.n. *mellan*) to be tired of, to be fed up with *mellit* (or *mellit men*) *had š-šġol.* I'm fed up with this job.
mella pl. *-t* religious doctrine, religion
mellak pl. *-a* proprietor, owner (usually with landlord implications)
mellan v.n. of *mell*
mellasa pl. *-t, mlales* **1.** plane (tool) **2.** trowel (mortar)
meḷḷaṭi pl. *mḷaḷeṭ* (adj.) bare-back, without a saddle (horse)
mellaḥ pl. *mlaleḥ* Jewish quarter, ghetto
melli contraction of *men-lli*
mellek v.t. to betroth, to affiance, to promise in marriage *mellek weldu b-bent žiranhom.* He betrothed his son to their neighbors' daughter.
mellel v.t. to tire, to cause (s.o.) to get fed up *le-qṛaya dyal had le-ktab melletni.* I'm getting tired of reading this book.
melles v.t. **1.** to make smooth, to give a smooth finish to **2.** to stroke, to pet
melleḥ v.t. (v.n. *mluḥa, mluḥiya*) **1.** to salt, to preserve in salt **2.** to overseason with salt
¶ *melleḥ le-klam* to imbue one's speech with colorful words or phrases

¶ *melleẓ b-le-ɛṣa* to beat (s.o.) (as punishment)

melmel v.t. to shake, to move *baṛaka*
ma-tmelmel ṭ-ṭebla! Stop shaking the table!

melqa (m.) meeting (approximately n.i. of *lqa*)
¶ *melqa* (pl. *mlaqi*) *ṭ-ṭuṛuq* (or *ṭ-ṭoṛqan*) intersection, junction

mles f. *melsa* pl. *mules* smooth, polished (in texture)

melsa pl. *mlasi* same as *mellasa*

mleṣ v.t. (v.n. *mliṣ*) **1.** to unsheathe, to pull off (sheath, gloves, pillow case, etc.) **2.** to wipe or scrape off (e.g., excess cream from hands)

mlu (state of) high tide

mluf, mlufa pl. of *melf*

mluk used in the expr. *ẓăbb le-mluk* n.u. *ẓăbb le-mluka* **1.** cherry **2.** cherry tree

mlusa, mlusiya smoothness, polish (of texture)

mluxiya okra

mluẓa, mluẓiya **1.** v.n. of *melleẓ* **2.** over-saltiness **3.** congeniality (of character)

melxa pl. *mlaxi* **1.** laceration, scrape (skin) **2.** half-sole

melya pl. *-t* (occasion of) high tide

melyan v.n. of *mla*

meḷyaṛ pl. *mḷayeṛ* billion (U.S.) *kaynin ši-tlata d-le-mḷayeṛ de-s-sokkan fe-l-ɛalăm.* There are about three billion inhabitants in the world.

melyun pl. *mlayen* million *fe-l-meġrib kayen ṭnaš-eṛ melyun de-s-sokkan.* There are twelve million inhabitants in Morocco.

melž leg of lamb (meat)

meẓ, mleẓ, melẓa salt
¶ *melẓa de-l-baṛuḍ* saltpeter
¶ *melẓa ẓeyya* rock salt

mleẓ comp. of *mliẓ* **1**

melẓun (no pl.) poetry (of the ballad type) sung in dialect

melɛăb pl. *mlaɛeb* **1.** playground **2.** stadium, arena **3.** court (tennis, basketball) **4.** track (race)

melɛuq p.p. of *lɛăq*

ʔomm (*ṃṃ-* before pron. endings) pl. *ʔommahat, ṃṃawat* (dim. *ṃṃima, mwima, ṃṃima*) **1.** mother **2.** (with first person pron. ending) used with proper name to indicate an elderly woman without regard to kinship *ṃṃi ɛiša ka-tăɛṛef ddawi had l-meṛḍ.* Ma Isha knows how to cure this illness. **3.** polite term of address to elderly woman *a ṃṃi xaduž qalt-lek ṃṃi aži tɛăšša mɛana l-lila.* Mrs. (mother) Khaduj, my mother would like you to have dinner with us this evening.
¶ *ṃṃuᶲ lallahᶲ* (inh. pos.) (one's) grandmother (paternal) *l-yum mariya mšat tšuf ṃṃha lallaha ẓit mṛiḍa.* Today Maria went to see her sick grandmother.
¶ *omm s-swalef* (no pl.) weeping willow tree
¶ *omm š-škawi* (no pl.) carbuncle
¶ *omm ɛziza* (or *le-ɛziza*) grandmother (maternal) *l-ʔomm le-ɛziza ka-tsaɛed fe-t-terbiya dyal d-drari ṣ-ṣġaṛ.* The grandmother helps out in educating little children. —*ṃṃi le-ɛziza ɛăndha tmanin ɛam.* My (maternal) grandmother is eighty years old.

ʔomma pl. *ʔumam* nation, people

ṃṃagni same as *mwagni*

ʔommahat pl. of *ʔomm*

ṃṃalin pl. of *mula*

ṃṃawat pl. of *ʔomm*

ṃṃima, ṃṃima dim. of *ʔomm*

memlaka pl. *-t* kingdom

memluk p.p. of *mlek*

mommu pl. *-yat* **1.** pupil (eye) **2.** small baby, tyke

ʔemmen v.t. to entrust *fuq-emma ka-nṣafṛu ka-nʔemmnu ẓwayežna ɛăndhom.* Whenever we go away we entrust our belongings to them.

mmuṛ, mmuṛa (pron. endings used only with *-a* form) **1.** behind *txebbăɛ mmuṛ l-ẓăyṭ.* He hid behind the wall. **2.** up from behind, up behind *ža mmuṛaha u-šedd-lha ɛăyniha.* He came up behind her and covered her eyes (with his hands). **3.** after *ža mmuṛaya.* He came after me (i.e., either to pick me up, or arrived after I did). —*sir mmuṛ le-ẓlib.* Go after the milk.
¶ *mmuṛa l-axoṛ* one at a time, one after the other *mekkel-li ktab mmuṛa l-axoṛ.* Hand me the books one at a time.
¶ *mmuṛ ḍ-ḍhuṛ* (this) (in the) afternoon *aži ɛăndi mmuṛ ḍ-ḍhuṛ.* Come over to my place this afternoon.

men (*-mmen* after *fe-, be-, le-, de-, mne-*) who, whom (some interrogative and relative pron. use; usu. used only after prep. and as second part of cons.) *le-mmen ɛṭitiha?* Whom did you give it to? —*l-weld l-emmen ɛṭaha ma-zal ṣġiṛ.* The boy to whom he gave her (in marriage) is still quite young. —*weld men hada?* Whose boy is this?
** *benti džuwwžet b-weld men u-ẓfiḍ men.* My daughter has married into high society.
¶ *škun-men kan* anybody, anyone *le-mmen năɛṭi hada?—škun-men kan!* Whom should I give this to?—Anybody!

men (*menn-* before *-ek, -u,* with some speakers also before *-ha, -hom, -kom, -na;* in some contexts *mne-, me-*) **1.** from *ɛad ža men fas had ṣ-ṣbaḥ.* He just came from Fez this morning. —*txebbăɛt mennu baš ma-išufni-š.* I hid from him so he wouldn't see me. —*xditha mennu be-d-drăɛ.* I took it from him by force. **2.** since *men n-nhaṛ lli žiti u-hiya ṭayeṛ-lha.* She's been angry since the day you arrived. **3.** through *dxel men l-bab ḷ-ḷuṛaniya.* He came through the back door. —*ṛ-riḥa lli daxla men š-šeṛžem qbiḥa.* The odor coming through the window is horrible. **4.** by *dazet men hna* (or *menn hna*). She passed by here. **5.** used in certain possessive cases *had l-ġeḷṭa mennek.* This mistake is yours. **6.** than (with comp.) *imken huwa kbeṛ mennha fe-s-senn, be-l-ḥăqq hiya dka mennu.* He may be older than she is, but she's smarter.

** *ma-ḥna mennek ma-nta menna!* We have nothing to do with you, nor do you with us!

¶ *men băɛd* **1.** afterwards **2.** later *xelli had š-ši daba u-ɛămlu men băɛd.* Leave this for now and do it later.

¶ *men qbel* or *me-qbel* before, beforehand

mnabeṛ pl. of *menbeṛ*

mnadeb pl. of *mendba* and *mendub*

mnadel pl. of *mendil*

mnaḍeṛ pl. of *menḍeṛ*

mnafes pl. of *menfes*

mnages pl. of *mengus* (p.p. of *nges*)

mnaġez pl. of *menġaz*

mnahya v.n. of *nha*

mnam **1.** v.n. of *nam* **2.** sleep *f-le-mnam dyali dima ka-neḥlem.* I always dream in my sleep.

mnama pl. *-t, mnayem* dream *ḥlemt waḥed le-mnama qbiḥa l-bareḥ fe-l-lil.* I dreamed a bad dream last night.

mnaqeṛ pl. of *menqaṛ*

mnaqeš pl. of *menqaš*

mnaqša pl. *-t* discussion

mnaṛa pl. *-t* type of oil lamp

mnaseb pl. *-in* **1.** right, appropriate, opportune *xellik ḥetta l-l-weqt le-mnaseb u-ṭlebha-lu.* Wait until the right time to ask him for it. **2.** reasonable *had t-taman mnaseb.* This is a reasonable price.

mnasež pl. of *mensež*

mnaṣeb pl. of *menṣeb*

mnaṣeṛ pl. of *menṣuṛiya*

mnaṣṣ pl. *-in* half-full *had l-kas mnaṣṣ b-atay.* This glass is half-full of tea.

mnašeṛ pl. of *menšaṛ* and *menšeṛ*

mnaxeṛ pl. of *menxaṛ*

mnayem pl. of *mnama*

mnayn, mnin **1.** from where, whence *mnayn maži had ṣ-ṣdăɛ?* Where's that noise coming from? **2.** how (i.e. through where, by what road or path) *mnayn nemši l-l-ḅanka, ḷḷah ixellik?* Please, how do I get to the bank? **3.** when (relative) *mnayn ikun l-ʔinsan mṛiḍ ma-ka-ixeṣṣuš itɛăb ṛaṣu.* When one is sick he shouldn't tire himself. **4.** since, seeing that *mnin nta daba hna xellik ttɛăšša mɛana.* Since you're here now, stay and eat dinner with us.

¶ *mnayn-ma* (from) wherever, everywhere *mnayn-ma ža ixrož ka-ižbeṛ ṭ-ṭṛiq mešduda.* Everywhere he tries to get out he finds the way closed.

mnazeh pl. of *menzeh*

mnazel pl. of *menzil, menzila, menzel,* and *menzla*

mnažel pl. of *menžel*

mnažeṛ pl. of *menžṛa*

mnaḥa v.n. of *naḥ*

mnaḥes pl. of *menḥus*

menbeṛ pl. *mnabeṛ* podium or platform from which the Imam delivers his sermon

men-da u-ždid see *ždid*

mendba pl. *-t, mnadeb* **1.** a lot, a (great) deal, amount *baqya ɛăndi l-mendba l-kăḥla de-l-ʔašġal.* I still have an enormous amount of work. —*ɛăndu l-mendba l-kăḥla d-le-flus.* He has an awful lot of money. **2.** genital area

mendil pl. *mnadel* **1.** towel (made of some material other than terry cloth) **2.** napkin **3.** tablecloth **4.** any good-sized rectangular piece of cloth

mendub pl. *mnadeb* delegate, representative

menḍeṛ pl. *manaḍiṛ, mnaḍeṛ* **1.** view, sight *menḍeṛ hada!* What a view! **2.** appearance, aspect, looks **3.** scene (theater)

¶ *menḍeṛ ṭabiɛi* landscape, scenery

menḍuṛ p.p. of *nḍeṛ*

menfaɛa **1.** v.n. of *nfăɛ* **2.** pl. *manafiɛ* benefit, use, profit

mneffes part. of *neffes*

menfiɛa same as *menfaɛa*

menfes pl. *mnafes* **1.** pore (skin) **2.** place through which air may escape or enter **3.** (air) vent

mengad pl. *-in* having a long, straight nose

mengus p.p. of *nges*

menġaz pl. *mnaġez* **1.** goad, prod (or anything used thus) **2.** spur (for goading horses, etc.)

** *fih le-mnaġez.* He's sitting on pins and needles; also: He's restless, can't stay in one place.

mnin same as *mnayn*

mniɛ v.n. of *mnăɛ*

mnemmeš pl. *-in* **1.** freckled **2.** speckled

menn v.i. to boast, to brag *ɛṭa le-flus l-l-xiriya u-bda ka-imenn ɛăl n-nas.* He gave some money to charity and then bragged to everybody (about it).

mennăɛ v.t. **1.** to save, to rescue, to deliver (from danger, etc.) *ma-qdeṛt-š nmennɛu ɛla-wedd ma-žit newṣel-lu ɛetta ġṛaq.* I couldn't save him because I couldn't manage to get to him until he had (already) drowned. **2.** to miss *mennăɛti waɛed l-ɛefla mezyana.* You missed a great party.

menqaṛ pl. *mnaqeṛ* beak, bill (bird)

menqaš pl. *mnaqeš* kind of tool with sharp-edged head used in tile work and decorative metal stamping (often in a hammer shape)

mensum pl. *-in* **1.** aromatic **2.** flavorful

mensež pl. *mnasež* loom

menṣeb pl. *mnaṣeb* type of makeshift stove, usually made of three stones around a fire

menṣuṛiya pl. *-t, mnaṣeṛ* kind of sheer over-dress worn by women

menšaṛ pl. *mnašeṛ* saw (tool)

menšeṛ pl. *mnašeṛ* place where fruits (e.g., raisins) are dried in the sun

menṭaqa pl. *-t* area, region, zone

menxaṛ pl. *mnaxeṛ* (pl. often used in sg. sense) **1.** nose, snout (person, animal) **2.** any projection or protuberance

menzala same as *menzila*

menzeh pl. *mnazeh* place from which a beautiful or pleasing view may be seen (e.g., a balcony)

menzil, pl. *mnazel* residence, domicile

menzila pl. *-t, manazil, mnazel* (social) position

menzel pl. *mnazel* **1.** same as *menzil* **2.** hotel, inn (for transients)

menzla pl. *-t, mnazel* **1.** same as *menzila* **2.** bad cold, flu-like condition **3.** phase (moon)

menžel pl. *mnažel* sickle

menžṛa pl. *-t, mnažeṛ* **1.** workbench (carpenter) **2.** saw-mill (factory)

menɛus pl. *-in, mnaɛes* **1.** bringing bad luck person), jinx **2.** jinxed, having bad luck

mnăɛ v.i. (v.n. *mniɛ, mnăɛ, menɛ*) **1.** to escape, to get away *bqaw ka-ižriw ɛlih be-l-ɛăqq mnăɛ-lhom.* They chased him but he got away from them. **2.** to be saved, to be spared *koll-ši f-ḍaṛha mṛiḍ be-ṛ-ṛwaɛ illa hiya menɛet.* Everyone in her house has a cold, but she was spared.
** *mnăɛ băɛda b-had le-flus!* Take the money while you can!
¶ *mnăɛ ɛla* to forbid *mnăɛ ɛliha ḅḅaha texrož* (or *ma-texrož-š*) *fe-l-lil.* Her father forbade her to go out at night.

mnăɛ, menɛ v.n. of *mnăɛ*

mqabeḍ pl. of *meqbeḍ* (same as *meqbeṭ*)

mqabeṛ **1.** pl. of *qbuṛ* and *mqebṛa* **2.** (pl.) cemetery

mqabeṭ pl. of *meqbeṭ*

mqadd pl. *-in* same as *mgadd*

mqadef pl. of *meqdaf*

maqaḍiṛ-ḷḷah God's will

mqaḍya v.n. of *qaḍa*

mqal pl. *-at* s.th. spoken, that which is said (less common equivalent of *klam*)
¶ *qeyyed le-mqal ɛla* to lodge a complaint against (s.o.)

mqali pl. of *meqla*

mqaleɛ pl. of *meqlăɛ*

mqam pl. *-at* same as *maqam*

mqanen pl. of *meqnin*

mqaqya v.n. of *qaqa*

mqarež pl. of *meqrež*

mqaṣya v.n. of *qaṣa*

mqatla any fight or battle in which s.o. is, or presumably could be, killed

mqaṭeɛ pl. of *meqṭăɛ*

mqayla v.n. of *qal iqil*

mqaɛed pl. of *meqɛăd*

meqbeḍ same as *meqbeṭ*

mqebṛa pl. *-t, mqabeṛ* **1.** tomb **2.** cemetery

meqbeṭ pl. *mqabeṭ* handle, grip

meqbuḍ, meqbuṭ pp.. of *qbeḍ, qbeṭ*

meqdaf pl. *mqadef* oar

meqdaṛ same as *meqḍaṛ*

mqedda pl. *-t* meat-cleaver

mqeddem part. of *qeddem*

meqdur pl. *-in* filthy, dirty (i.e., soiled)

mqeḍya **1.** v.n. of *qḍa* **2.** pl. *-t* errand (n.i. of *qḍa*)

mqila dim. of *meqla*

meqla pl. *mqali* (dim. *mqila*) frying pan, skillet

meqlub p.p. of *qleb*

meqlăɛ pl. *mqaleɛ* sling (for throwing stones)

meqnaṭ pl. *-in* **1.** boring, uninteresting (person, thing) **2.** easily bored (person)

meqnin pl. *mqanen* small, finch-like songbird

meqqaṣ pl. *-a* one who shears excess wool off handmade rugs to even the nap

meqqeṣ v.t. to cut (with scissors or shears)

meqrež pl. *mqarež* long-spouted pot used for heating water, kind of tea kettle

mqerfed p.p. of *qerfed*

meqṛun pl. *-in* (*ɛla*) obsessed (with)

meqṛuṣ p.p. of *qṛeṣ*

mqeṣ pl. *mquṣa* **1.** scissors, shears **2.** pincers (insect, crab)

meqṣuḍ p.p. of *qṣeḍ*

meqṣum p.p. of *qṣem*

meqṣuṛa pl. *-t* **1.** chamber where the *qaḍi* holds audience **2.** preparation chamber for the *imam*

mqeššeṛ part. of *qeššeṛ*

mqeṭben pl. *-in* **1.** svelte, slender (person) **2.** well-built (man, girl)
meqṭăɛ pl. *mqaṭeɛ* **1.** place where persons are beheaded **2.** joint where s.th. can be easily separated or cut (as an elbow, knee, joint in a twig)
¶ *meqṭăɛ de-l-măɛden* mine (gold, iron ore, etc.)
mquṣa pl. of *mqeṣ*
meqyas pl. *maqayis* (any) standard of measurement
mqezder part. of *qezder*
meqɛăd pl. *mqaɛed* **1.** seat, place to sit **2.** rump, seat (person)
ˀmeṛ same as *ˀamṛ*
mra imri v.i. to shine
mṛa (cons. *mṛat, meṛt*) pl. *-wat, ɛyalat, nsa* **1.** woman **2.** wife
¶ *mṛat ḅḅahφ* (one's) stepmother
¶ *mṛat xahφ* (one's) sister-in-law (brother's wife)
mṛabeɛ pl. of *meṛbuɛ* **2**
mṛaḍ adj. pl. of *mṛiḍ*
mṛafeg, mṛafeq pl. of *meṛfeg, meṛfeq*
mṛafeɛ pl. of *meṛfăɛ*
mrakeb pl. of *merkeb*
mṛakez pl. of *meṛkez*
mṛamm pl. of *mṛemma*
mṛaqi pl. of *meṛq, mṛeq, meṛqa*
mrar v.i. (v.n. *mrura, mṛuṛa, mruriya*) to become bitter (taste)
mṛaṛ pl. *mṛayeṛ* **1.** bile, gall **2.** bitterness (taste) **3.** (especially pl.) troubles and difficulties of life or living
mṛaṣi pl. of *meṛṣa*
mṛašem pl. of *meṛšem*
mṛašš pl. of *mṛešša*
mṛat cons. of *mṛa*
mrawed pl. of *merwed*
mṛaweḥ pl. of *meṛweḥ*
mraya pl. *-t* **1.** mirror, looking-glass
¶ *mraya de-l-hend, mrayt l-hend* binoculars
¶ *ɛṭa le-mraya* to shine (v.i.)
mṛayeṛ pl. of *mṛaṛ*
mṛaḥ pl. *-at, mṛuḥa* kind of yard or court (especially in country dwellings)
mṛaɛi pl. of *meṛɛa*
meṛbuɛ **1.** pl. *-in* medium-built (physique) **2.** pl. *mṛabeɛ* wood chisel
¶ *meṛbuɛ l-qedd* (or *l-qama*) well-proportioned, well-built (male person, animal)
merdeddus (sweet) marjoram
mṛeḍ v.i. (v.n. *meṛḍ*) to get sick, to fall ill
meṛḍ **1.** v.n. of *mṛeḍ* **2.** pl. *ˀamṛaḍ* illness, sickness, disease
¶ *meṛḍ s-sell* (or *r-riya* or *s-sder*), *l-meṛḍ le-qbiḥ* (or *l-xayeb*) tuberculosis
merda **1.** n.i. of *mred* **2.** n.pl. of *mṛiḍ*
meṛḍi pl. *-yen* used in the expr. *meṛḍi l-walidin* (f. *meṛḍiyt l-walidin*) said of s.o. who seems to succeed in all his undertakings (literally, blessed of his parents)
meṛḍiya pl. *-t* joking, playing around (spoken or acted)
meṛfeg, meṛfeq pl. *mṛafeg, mṛafeq* elbow (also as in a water pipe)
meṛfuq pl. *-in* **1.** reasonable (person, price) **2.** of an even disposition, stable (person) **3.** fair, fairly good
meṛfăɛ pl. *mṛafeɛ* shelf (for storing)
mṛiḍ adj. pl. *mṛaḍ* (comp. *mṛeḍ*) n.pl. *meṛḍa* sick, ill
mrina muraena, moray
mṛiṛa dim. of *meṛṛa*
merkeb pl. *mrakeb* ship, vessel
meṛkez pl. *mṛakez, maṛakiz* center (of some figure, area; commercial, industrial, etc.)
¶ *meṛkez raˀisi* headquarters
mermad pl. *-in* tending to get dirty or soiled easily (as a playing child)
meṛmad pl. *-in* afflicted with trachoma
mermed v.t. **1.** to soil, to dirty (as clothes) **2.** to punish by striking, to give a beating to **3.** to mistreat **4.** to roll in a powder (such as fish in flour before frying)
mṛemma pl. *-t, mṛamm* loom (weaving)
meṛq, mṛeq, meṛqa pl. *meṛqat, mṛaqi* gravy, sauce (made from the cooked meat juices)
merr pl. *-in* bitter (taste)
meṛṛa du. *meṛṛtayn* pl. *-t* (dim. *mṛiṛa*) time *mšit l-bariz tlata de-l-meṛṛat.* I've been to Paris three times.
¶ *băɛḍ l-meṛṛat* sometimes *ka-iži băɛḍ l-meṛṛat.* He comes sometimes.
¶ *f-meṛṛa* **1.** once and for all *ma-bqa-š iži f-meṛṛa.* He stopped coming once and for all. **2.** all at once, all at one time **3.** all at once, suddenly, all of a sudden
¶ *meṛṛa fe-xṭa* once in a while, occasionally
¶ *meṛṛa meṛṛa* from time to time
¶ *meṛṛa . . . meṛṛa* sometimes . . . sometimes *meṛṛa ka-iži u-meṛṛa ma-ka-iži-š.* Sometimes he comes, sometimes he doesn't.
¶ *ši-meṛṛa*t occasionally, from time to time
meṛṛakeš Marrakech
meṛṛaṛa gall bladder
meṛṛeḍ v.t. to make or cause to be sick or ill (also figurative) *meṛṛeḍ ṛaṣu be-ktert l-makla.* He made himself sick by eating too much.
meṛṛeġ to roll, to dip (in s.th. for cooking) *meṛṛeġ l-ḥut fe-d-dgig qbel-ma teqlih.* Roll the fish in flour before you fry it.
merriwt, merriwet horehound (plant)
merren v.t. to train, to exercise (s.o.)
merrer, meṛṛeṛ v.t. **1.** to make bitter (taste)

2. to make difficult or cause difficulties to occur in (s.o.'s life)

merret v.t. **1.** to overwork, to make (s.o.) do more than what is due. **2.** to mistreat

meṛṛeḥ v.t. **1.** to stretch out (as one's legs) **2.** to stretch out, to lay out (rug, blanket, etc.)

¶ *meṛṛeḥ ɛla* **1.** to distract, to make (s.o.) forget (his) problems and worries. **2.** to give extra time to (as for paying a debt) **3.** to give a respite or breather to (s.o.)

meṛṣa pl. *-t, mṛaṣi* port, harbor

meṛṣṭan pl. *-at* asylum, mental hospital

merši p.p. of *ṛša*

meṛšem pl. *mṛašem* engraving tool, graver

mṛešša pl. *-t, mṛašš* perfume atomizer or sprayer

meṛt cons. of *mṛa*

meṛtaba, meṛtba pl. *-t* rank, position (military, social, academic, etc.)

mrura, mṛuṛa, mruriya **1.** v.n. of *mrar* **2.** bitterness (taste) **3.** hard times, rough time (in life)

mṛuwwa used in the expr. *ɛmel le-mṛuwwa mɛa* to give a reduction or discount in price to *ɛmel mɛaha le-mṛuwwa f-dak l-keswa.* He gave her a discount on that dress.

mṛuẓiya dish made up of lamb, honey, almonds, cinnamon, saffron, raisins, and onions (esp. at Greater Bairam)

mṛuḥa pl. of *mṛaḥ*

merwed pl. *mrawed* pencil-like applicator for eye make-up

meṛweḥ pl. *mṛaweḥ* (hand) fan

meṛxi p.p. of *ṛxa*

meryag pl. *-in* (adj.) slavering or dribbling from the mouth (as a cow)

meṛẓaq pl. *-in* lucky, favored by fate (person)

merzaya fine cotton fabric, percale (all white)

mrež v.i. to spoil (usually fruit, vegetables)

merža pl. *-t* meadow, grassy area

meṛžan coral

meṛḥaban, meṛḥaben Welcome! (mostly educated usage)

meṛḥeb b- to welcome (a guest)

mṛeḥba Welcome! —*mṛeḥba bik le-ḍ-ḍaṛ!* Welcome to my house!

meṛḥum p.p. of *ṛḥem*

meṛɛa pl. *mṛaɛi* pasture, grazing land

msa used in the expr.

** *msak!* or *mse-l-xir!* Good evening! —*ḷḷah isɛăd msak!* Good night!

msabqa pl. *-t* race (foot, car, horse, missile, etc.)

msafa pl. *-t* distance (between two points)

msaken pl. of *meskin* and *mesken*

mesʔala pl. *masaʔil* something, matter *ɛăndi waḥed l-mesʔala muhimma ġadi nqulha-lek.* I've got something important to tell you.

msali a.p. of *sala*

msalek pl. of *meslek*

msalen pl. of *meslan*

msalet pl. of *meslat*

msaned pl. of *mesned*

msaqṛa fencing, (art of) fighting with the sword

msaqṛi pl. *-ya* swordsman, fencer

msareb pl. of *mesreb*

msareḥ pl. of *mesreḥ*

msaṛeḥ pl. of *mesṛeḥ*

msas pl. of *mess*

msasa insipidity, tastelessness

msasi u-mgasi (or *mqasi*) pl. *msasyen u-mgasyen* (or *mqasyen*) experienced, having learned through life's experiences

msayed pl. of *msid*

msažed pl. of *mesžid*

msažen n.pl. of *mesžun* (p.p. of *sžen*)

msebba pl. *-t* excuse, reason

¶ *ɛla msebba* because of *žit ɛla msebbtek.* I came because of you.

msid pl. *msayed* school where the Koran is taught

msika dim. of *meska*

msix v.n. of *msex*

msiyyeḥ pl. *-in* bohemian, beatnik

msiḥ v.n. of *mseḥ*

mesk musk

meska (coll. and n.u.) pl. *-t* (dim. *msika*) chewing gum

meski pl. *-yen* **1.** muscat grape (usually *ɛineb meski*) **2.** kind of small, savory pear (usually *lingaṣ meski*)

meskin adj. and n.pl. *msaken, masakin* poor, indigent, miserable (also metaphoric) *meskin ṛah mṛiḍ.* The poor fellow is sick. —*dima ka-iṣeḍḍeq flusu ɛăl le-msaken.* He always gives his money to the poor.

** *ṛažel meskin mɛa ṛaṣu.* He's just a simple man who minds his own business.

mesken pl. *msaken* **1.** place of residence, domicile **2.** room *šḥal d-le-msaken f-ḍaṛkom?* How many rooms are there in your house?

meskuf p.p. of *skef*

meskun p.p. of *sken*

meslan pl. *msalen* buttock (i.e., one side of the rump)

meslat pl. *msalet* (butcher's) steel

meslek pl. *msalek* **1.** passage, way (for water, smoke, walking, etc.) **2.** way in, way out

meslem f. *mselma* pl. *mselmin* muslim, moslem

meslut pl. *-in* skinny, thin (animal, person)

mesmum pl. *-in* thin but strong, wiry (person)

mesned pl. *msaned* cushion, throw-pillow (as on a sofa)

msender pl. *-in* buck-toothed

msenn pl. *msuna* whetstone

mseqqem p.p. of *seqqem*
mesrar pl. *-in* cordial, charming
mesreb pl. *msareb* path, trail
mesreɛ pl. *msareɛ* pasture, grazing area
mesṛeɛ pl. *msaṛeɛ* **1.** stage (of a theater) **2.** theater
mess v.t. (v.n. *messan*) to touch *ġir kif messit le-briz u-ḍ-ḍuw iḍṛebni.* Just as I touched the plug I got shocked.
mess pl. *msas* **1.** knife (usually relatively small, as a pocket knife) **2.** razor, razor blade **3.** sharp-witted
messa v.i. to say good evening *messat ɛlina u-gelset.* She said good evening to us and sat down.
** *ḷḷah imessik bi-xir!* Good night!
messan v.n. of *mess*
messaɛa pl. *-t* eraser (rubber and blackboard)
messi used in the expr. *ɛessi messi* furtively, stealthily
messeq f- to stare at, to gawk at
messus pl. *-in* **1.** flat, tasteless, insipid **2.** lacking anything which tends to round out or make more acceptable *had l-meṛṭub baqi messus.* This mortar needs some more lime.
msuden pl. *-in* choleric, irascible
mesᵓul pl. *-in* responsible *ana ma-ši mesᵓul ɛla had š-ši.* I'm not responsible for this.
mesᵓuliya pl. *-t* responsibility *škun lli ɛăndu l-mesᵓuliya dyal had š-ši?* Who has the responsibility for this?
msuna pl. of *msenn*
msex v.t. (v.n. *msix*) to change, to transform (God usually understood as the subject) *mesxu ṛebbi u-ṛeddu qerd.* He was changed and turned into a monkey.
mesxaṛa mockery
meszid pl. *msažed* mosque
meszun p.p. of *sžen*
mseɛ v.t. (v.n. *msiɛ*) **1.** to erase (as with an eraser) **2.** to clean off, to remove *mseɛ wežhek men le-mdad* (or *mseɛ le-mdad men wežhek*). Clean the ink off your face.
mesɛa pl. *-t* n.i. of *mseɛ*
mesɛud p.p. of *sɛăd*
mesɛuṛ same as *meṣɛuṛ*
mṣabeɛ pl. of *mṣebɛiya*
mṣaḍfa pl. *-t* coincidence (almost strictly in the literal simultaneous sense)
mṣaḍma pl. *-t* collision
mṣaleɛ pl. of *meṣḷuɛ* (p.p. of *ṣḷeɛ*) and *mṣelɛa*
mṣameṛ pl. of *meṣmaṛ*
mṣaṛef pl. of *meṣṛuf* (p.p. of *ṣṛef*)
mṣaṛen pl. of *meṣṛan, meṣṛana*
mṣaṛwa n.pl. of *meṣṛi*
mṣaṣeṭ pl. of *meṣṣaṭa*
mṣaṭeṛ pl. of *mṣeṭṛa*
mṣayeb pl. of *muṣiba*
mṣayeḍ pl. of *mṣiḍa*
mṣaɛef pl. of *meṣɛaf*
mṣebɛiya pl. *mṣabeɛ* kind of oil lamp
mṣiba same as *muṣiba*
mṣiḍa pl. *mṣayeḍ* trap, snare
mṣiwṭa dim. of *mṣuṭa* and *meṣwiṭa*
meṣlaɛa pl. *maṣaliɛ* **1.** benefit, profit **2.** interest, profit (monetary) **3.** department, office
mṣeḷḷa pl. *-t* open-air place for prayer (on special occasions)
meṣḷuɛ p.p. of *ṣḷeɛ*
mṣelɛa pl. *-t, mṣaleɛ* kind of whisk broom
meṣmaṛ pl. *mṣameṛ* nail (from tack to spike)
¶ *meṣmaṛ l-kif* corn (on foot)
¶ *meṣmaṛ l-mida* great-grandchild
meṣnan pl. *-in* **1.** having foul breath **2.** exuding a foul underarm odor
meṣṛan n.u. *-a* pl. *mṣaṛen* (pl. same as coll.) intestine(s)
¶ *meṣṛana zayda* (vermiform) appendix
meṣṛi adj. pl. *-yen* n.pl. *mṣaṛwa* Egyptian
meṣṛiya pl. *-t* kind of small room entered only by a ladder or stairway (used for sleeping quarters, etc.)
meṣṛuf p.p. of *ṣṛef*
meṣṛuṛ pl. *-in* happy, glad, content *ana meṣṛuṛ biha bezzaf.* I'm very happy with it (also, about it).
meṣṣ v.t. (v.n. *meṣṣan*) **1.** to suck, to suck on *dima ka-imeṣṣ ṣebɛu le-kbir.* He's always sucking his thumb. **2.** to suck out or up (liquid)
meṣṣab, a-meṣṣab denotes hoping (for s.th.) *meṣṣab teṣṛeq š-šems!* I hope the sun comes out!
meṣṣan v.n. of *meṣṣ*
meṣṣaṣ pl. *-a* person called on to suck venom (orally) from a bite
meṣṣaṣa pl. *-t* **1.** breast pump **2.** suction pump or cup used in pulling venom from a wound
meṣṣaṭa pl. *mṣaṣeṭ* area of the body made up of the upper thigh and lower buttock (referred to in spankings, hypodermic shots, etc.)
mṣeṭṛa pl. *-t, mṣaṭeṛ* **1.** ruler (for measuring, etc.) **2.** shelf (for storing, etc.)
mṣuṭa pl. *-t* (dim. *mṣiwṭa*) whip, lash
meṣwab pl. *-in* polite, courteous *ana ka-nɛăṛfu dima meṣwab mɛa n-nas.* I've always known him to be polite with people.
meṣwiṭa pl. *-t* same as *mṣuṭa*
meṣɛaf pl. *mṣaɛef* Koran, the Holy Book
meṣɛuṛ pl. *-in* **1.** rabid (dog) **2.** mischievous and wild (children)
mša imši (v.n. *mši,* impv. *sir* pl. *siru*) **1.** to go *mšiti tšuf dak l-film lli qolt-lek ɛlih?* Have you gone to see that movie I told you about? —*sir žib l-xobz!* Go get the bread! —*mšat qaletha-lhom l-bareɛ.* She went and told them yesterday. —*mšina nšufuhom*

saƐa ma-lqinahom-š. We went to see them, but we didn't find them. **2.** to leave *waš mša l-qiṭaṛ băƐda?* Has the train already left?

¶ *ma-mša ḥetta* to finally (do s.th.) *ma-mšit ḥetta xdit le-flus dyali.* I finally got my money.

¶ *ma-mša ma-ža* exactly (in comparisons) *bḥal hadi s-siyaṛa lli kanet Ɛăndna ma-mšat ma-žat.* The car we had looks exactly like this one.

¶ *mša f-ḥaluφ* to go away, to leave *sir f-ḥalek!* Go away!

¶ *mša l-* **1.** to lose ≠ *mša-li ṣebbaṭi.* I lost my shoes. **2.** to get away from *mša-li le-bṛiṭeḷ.* The bird got away from me.

¶ *mša Ɛla* **1.** to go away or get away from *sir Ɛliya!* Get away from me! **2.** to leave (s.o.)

¶ a.p. *maši* pl. *mašyen* same as *ġadi*

mšabha pl. *-t* resemblance *binathom ma-kayen ḥetta mšabha.* There's no resemblance between them at all.

mšafeṛ pl. of *mšefṛa*

mšamem pl. of *mešmum* (p.p. of *šemm*)

mšaneq pl. of *mšenqa*

mšaṛeƐ pl. of *mešṛăƐ*

mšaš pl. of *mešš, mošš*

mšaši pl. of *meššaya*

mšati pl. of *mešta*

mšaṭ pl. of *mšeṭ*

mšaṭi pl. of *mešṭa*

mšaweṛ pl. of *mešweṛ*

mšawṛa **1.** v.n. of *tšaweṛ* **2.** consultation

mšawṛi pl. *-ya* kind of usher employed in showing s.o. to the quarters of some official.

mšayex pl. of *mšixa* **2**

mšayxa same as *mšixa*

mšaḥeṭ pl. of *mešḥeṭ*

mšaƐel pl. of *mešƐăl*

mšefṛa pl. *-t, mšafeṛ* trimming tool used in shoeing horses, mules, etc.

mešhuṛ pl. *-in* famous (either renowned or notorious)

mši **1.** v.n. of *mša* **2.** departure

¶ *weṛqa* (pl. *wṛaq*) *de-le-mši u-le-mži, nfula* (pl. *nfayel*) *mši u-mži* round-trip ticket

mšimša dim. of *mešmaša* (also n.u. of *mešmaš*)

mšiša dim. of *mešša*

mšiṭ v.n. of *mšeṭ*

mšixa **1.** coaxing *ma-ža Ɛăndna ġir b-le-mšixa.* He came to our place only after some coaxing. **2.** pl. *-t, mšayex* sheikdom (including the people)

meškak pl. *-in* suspicious, prone to suspect and doubt

mšekwi pl. *-yen* flabby and wrinkled (skin)

mšelgem pl. *-in* big- or thick-lipped (person)

mšellel part. of *šellel*

mešmaš n.u. *-a* (dim. *mšimša*) **1.** apricot **2.** apricot tree

mešmaši pl. *-yen* apricot colored

mšemmăƐ p.p. of *šemmăƐ*

mešmum p.p. of *šemm*

mšenqa pl. *-t, mšaneq* gallows, gibbet

mšenqeṛ pl. *-in* **1.** spiked, having spikes (usually animals, as the porcupine) **2.** having many projecting parts or protuberances (as a rocky beach or path)

mšentef pl. *-in* **1.** unkempt, tousled (hair, and similar things) **2.** full of hanging threads or snagged spots (cloth)

mešnuƐ pl. *-in* well-known, known, (implies of good reputation) *ˀuṃiga, magana mešnuƐa fe-d-denya kollha.* Omega is a well-known watch throughout the world.

mešra (m.) v.n. of *šra*

mešṛiq (usually with art.) **1.** the East, the Orient **2.** east, where the sun rises **3.** pilgrimage region around Mecca and Medina

mšeṛqi pl. *-yen* **1.** oriental, of or pertaining to the Orient **2.** Middle Eastern

mešṛub p.p. of *šṛeb*

mešṛuḥ p.p. of *šṛeḥ*

mešṛăƐ pl. *mšaṛeƐ* ford (river)

¶ *qṭăƐ l-mešṛăƐ* to ford a river

mešš, mošš pl. *mšaš* cat (m.)

mešša pl. *-t,* (dim. *mšiša*) f. of *mešš*

mešša v.t. **1.** to make (s.o.) walk **2.** to walk, to take for a walk (dog, child) **3.** to run, to operate (machine, business, etc.)

meššay adj. pl. *-in* n.pl. *-a* fond of or accustomed to much walking

meššaya pl. *-t, mšaši* **1.** slippers (as worn in the house, usually by women) **2.** walk, footpath (as in a garden)

mešta (m.) pl. *mšati* winter resort or place (cabin, town, etc.)

mšeṭ (v.n. *mšiṭ*) to comb (hair)

mšeṭ pl. *mšaṭ* reed (of a loom)

mešṭa pl. *mšaṭi* comb (hair)

mešˀum pl. *-in* **1.** attended with risk, hazard, or possible danger (person, place, thing)

mšureb pl. *-in* thick-lipped (person)

mešwa pl. *-t* grill (for broiling)

mešwi p.p. of *šwa*

mešweṛ pl. *mšaweṛ* **1.** administration building, containing the offices of the king and his cabinet or advisors **2.** place where the king holds audience (obsolescent)

mešya pl. *-t* **1.** n.i. of *mša* **2.** any of the different gaits (person, horse)

mešḥaḥ pl. *-in* (*Ɛla*) stingy, miserly (toward) (often to the point of self-denial)

mešḥeṭ pl. *mšaḥeṭ* **1.** whip (e.g., quirt, cat-o'-nine-tails, often a switch) **2.** (fly) swatter **3.** (pl.) large or huge hands

mšeḥḥem p.p. of *šeḥḥem*

mešɛăl pl. *mšaɛel* torch (fire)
mšăɛṭeṭ pl. *-in* unkempt, messed up (hair)
mšăɛɛăṛ pl. *-in* hairy, hirsute (usually a person)
mtal pl. of *mtel* 2
mtamna denotes eight, in eights, with eight, in group(s) of eight, etc. *lɛăbna l-kaṛṭa mtamna.* Eight of us played cards.
mtan pl. of *mtin*
mtana strength (of materials)
mtaneɛ v.i. to refuse *ṭeḷbu mennu baš yăɛṭihom r-reyy dyalu u-mtaneɛ.* They asked him to give (them) his opinion, but he refused.
¶ *mtaneɛ ɛla* (with v.n. and n.) to refuse *mtanɛu ɛăl le-klam.* They refused to speak. —*mtaneɛ ɛăl t-teṣwit.* He refused to vote.
mtaqeb pl. of *metqeb*
mtaqel pl. of *metqal*
mtared pl. of *metred*
mtaref pl. of *metruf*
mtawya bargaining, haggling
mtaweɛ pl. of *mtaɛ*
mtayeb pl. *-in* usually used in the expr. *mtayeb l-llah* sorry, repentant
mtayel pl. of *mtil*
mtaḥef pl. of *metḥăf*
mtaḥen v.t. to examine, to give an examination to, to test (in some subject)
mtaɛ f. *mtaɛt* (rare) pl. *mtaweɛ* (rare) same as *dyal*
** *huwa be-mtaɛu.* He's pretty well off (as to necessities of life). —*mtaɛ ḷḷah* (*l-llah*)*!* expr. used by beggars to invoke alms from people.
¶ *mtaɛ d-denya* 1. all one has or owns, one's earthly possessions 2. money, funds *ma-ɛăndi-š mtaɛ d-denya.* I haven't got the money (to do it).
metfawtin (pl.) different, unequal, not the same *huma metfawtin fe-s-senn.* They are of different ages.
metgaṣṣ pl. *-in* flat, level, even (floor, ground)
mtil pl. *mtayel* equal *qlil f-aš tṣib mtayel hadak ṛ-ṛažel.* Rarely do you find people like that man. —*ḍ-ḍaṛ lli šra, ma-ilha mtil.* The house he bought has no equal.
ʔemtila pl. of *mital*
mtin pl. *-in, mtan* (comp. *mten*) strong, tough (materials)
mtissăɛ pl. *-in* same as *waseɛ*
mtiḥan pl. *-at* examination, test (in some subject)
mtel 1. same as *bḥal* 1 2. pl. *mtal* same as *metla*
** *ṛžăɛt ɛla mtel ṭṛiqi.* I came back (went back) by the same route I had gone (come).
¶ *ḍṛeb le-mtel b-* to give or present as an example *dima ka-iḍeṛbu bik le-mtel.* They always give you as an example.
metla pl. *-t* proverb, saying
¶ *ḍṛeb l-metla b-* to give as an example *ḍeṛbet biya l-metla.* She gave me as an example.
mtellet pl. *-in* 1. tripled, triple 2. triangular 3. big and strong, husky
mtellta pl. *-t* kind of long, narrow, backless sofa.
mtemmen pl. *-in* 1. octagonal, octangular 2. consisting of eight parts, sections, etc. 3. eight-fold *ṛeḍḍu-li mtemmen.* He returned it to me eight-fold.
** *ṣbăḥ mtemmen.* He woke up still (somewhat) drunk.
metmuṛ pl. *-in* 1. honest (in one's dealings) 2. serious, conscientious
mten comp. of *mtin*
metqadd pl. *-in* 1. straight, not crooked or bent 2. (pl.) equal, the same
metqal pl. *mtaqel* old coin
metqeb pl. *mtaqeb* 1. kind of star-drill used in making holes in brick or concrete 2. awl
mteqteq pl. *-in* used in expr. *mteqteq be-l-mal* very rich, wealthy
metred pl. *mtared* large clay or earthen plate used in serving *trid*
metruf pl. *mtaref* big and husky boy or man (rural usage)
mtšekka pl. *-t* (table, cooking) fork
mettawya same as *mtawya*
mettel v.t. 1. to play, to act (a part) *škun huwa lli ka-imettel* (*ḍewṛ*) *l-ʔab?* Who's playing the (part of the) father? 2. to represent *ḥmed mša imettel l-meġṛib f-dak le-žtimaɛ d-duwwăli.* Ahmed has gone to represent Morocco at that international meeting. 3. to symbolize, to represent *had ṣ-ṣuṛa ka-tmettel l-quwwa ṭ-ṭabiɛiya.* This picture symbolizes the power of nature.
¶ *mettel b-* to give or cite as an example *dima ka-imettlu be-ḅḅahom.* They always cite their father as an example.
mettăɛ v.t. to give (s.o.) the opportunity of living in luxury and ease (as a rich father may do for his children)
** *mettăɛna ṛaṣna.* We lived high on the hog (for a little while).
mtuni pl. *mtunyen* moth-eaten
metḥabbin (pl.) in love with or loving each other
metḥef pl. *mtaḥef* 1. museum 2. (art) gallery
metḥesseb pl. *-in* same as *mḥetteb*
metɛăllem pl. *-in* 1. servant (domestic) 2. apprentice
metɛăllma pl. *-t* (house) maid

metɛus pl. *-in* unlucky, ill-fated (person)
mṭabeq pl. of *meṭbeq*
mṭabex pl. of *meṭbex*
mṭabeɛ pl. of *mṭebɛa*
mṭafi pl. of *meṭfiya*
mṭaheṛ pl. *-at* rest room, bathroom (toilet only)
mṭaḷeb pl. of *meṭḷeb* (same as *ṭaḷab*)
mṭaleɛ 1. pl. of *meṭḷăɛ* 2. (*ɛla*) well-informed (of), learned (in)
mṭameṛ pl. of *meṭmuṛa*
mṭaṛ, ʔemṭaṛ pl. of *maṭăṛ*
mṭaṛeb pl. of *mṭeṛṛba* (same as *mḍeṛṛba*) and *meṭṛeb*
mṭaṛeq pl. of *mṭeṛqa*
mṭaṛeɛ pl. of *meṭṛeɛ*
mṭawi pl. of *meṭwi*
meṭbeq pl. *mṭabeq* pit, dungeon (usually with a trap door for access)
meṭbex pl. *mṭabex* kitchen
mṭebɛa pl. *mṭabeɛ* 1. printing shop or establishment 2. typewriter
meṭfiya pl. *-t, mṭafi* type of underground reservoir for storing olive oil, water, grain
mṭiṛqa dim. of *mṭeṛqa*
mṭiwi dim. of *meṭwi*
mṭiyyen pl. *-in* muddy, muddied, covered with mud (things, places)
meṭḷaqa pl. *-t* 1. v.n. of *ṭḷeq* 2 2. vacation
meṭḷeb pl. *mṭaḷeb* same as *ṭaḷab*
meṭḷub pl. *-in* in demand *had s-selɛa meṭḷuba.* This merchandise is in demand.
meṭḷuq pl. *-in* 1. sincere, genuine (person) 2. smiling, gay *wežhu meṭḷuq* He has a smiling face.
meṭmuṛa pl. *mṭameṛ* 1. pit or dungeon entered by a trap door (generally used for storing grain) 2. latrine (in ground)
meṭṛeb pl. *mṭaṛeb* 1. bottle (about one liter capacity) 2. strop (for honing razors)
mṭeṛqa pl. *-t, mṭaṛeq* (dim. *mṭiṛqa*) hammer (as for nails)
mṭeṛṛba pl. *mṭaṛeb* same as *mḍeṛṛba*
mṭeṛṛeq a.p. of *ṭeṛṛeq*
meṭṛeɛ pl. *mṭaṛeɛ* 1. peel (large wooden spatula for placing things in and removing things from an oven) 2. small shovel or scoop for transferring or removing hot coals or ashes 3. general term for a small area or place where s.th. is stored temporarily 4. cot (bed)
meṭṭaleɛ same as *mṭaleɛ* 2
mṭuwweṛ pl. *-in* adaptably clever or astute
meṭwi pl. *mṭawi* (dim. *mṭiwi*) tobacco pouch
meṭyaṛ pl. *-in* contemptuous epithet said primarily by mothers to their children; similar to: You miserable brat!
mubalaġa 1. exaggeration 2. excess, abuse *l-mubalaġa fe-s-soṛɛa ka-tʔeddi l-l-halak.* An excess in speed leads to dangerous situations.
mubaṛa pl. *-t* 1. match, contest (usually between two) 2. competitive examination (as for some position)
¶ *ɛmel* (or *duwwez*) *mubaṛa* to take an examination (i.e., 2 above)
mubbeṛ velvet (cloth)
mubeddir pl. *-in* spendthrift, big spender
mudden pl. *-in* same as *mwedden*
mudir pl. *-in* 1. manager, director 2. principal (school)
mudellis pl. *-in* 1. counterfeiter 2. falsifier, forger (documents, etc.)
muderris pl. *-in* teacher, instructor
muḍa 1. fashion, mode 2. fad, passing fancy
¶ *muḍa, de-l-muḍa, mɛa l-muḍa* in fashion, in vogue, in style *had l-keswa muḍa daba.* This dress is in fashion now.
muḍahaṛa pl. *-t* demonstration *l-bareɛ kanet waɛed l-muḍahaṛa ḍeḍḍ s-sifaṛa de-fṛanṣa.* Yesterday there was a demonstration against the French Embassy.
muḍuɛ pl. *mawaḍiɛ* subject, theme
muḍăɛ (m. or f.) *mwaḍeɛ* (f. cons. *muḍăɛt*) place, spot *ɛmel had le-ktab f-dak l-muḍăɛ!* Put this book in that place (over there). —*žbeṛt waɛed l-muḍăɛ mezyan.* I've found a nice place (to live.)
¶ *f-muḍăɛ, f-muḍăɛt* instead of *f-muḍăɛ magana šrit makina de-t-teṣwaṛ.* Instead of a watch I bought a camera.
mufid pl. *-in* 1. useful 2. serious, not joking 3. interesting
¶ *be-l-mufid* seriously, all joking aside
mufti pl. *-yen* mufti, expounder of Islamic law
mufettiš pl. *-in* 1. inspector 2. investigator
muhažir pl. *-in* 1. emigrant 2. one who left Mecca for Medina with the Prophet Mohammed
muhandis pl. *-in* 1. engineer (civil, chemical, electrical, etc.) 2. architect
muhimm pl. *-in* important
muhmal pl. *-in* same as *mehmul* (p.p. of *hmel*)
muka pl. *-t* (no art.) owl
mukul pl. *-in* p.p. of *kla, kal*
mula (*mul* before art.) f. *mulat* pl. *mwalin, m̄m̄alin* (*mwali-, m̄m̄ali-* before pron. endings) 1. owner *škun huwa mul* (or *mula*) *had ḍ-ḍaṛ?* Who's the owner of this house? 2. one who sells or vends *baqi ma-ža mul le-ɛlib.* The milkman hasn't come yet. 3. one who has, one with *waš ka-tăɛref hadak mul ẓ-ẓɛafer?* Do you know that guy with the mustache? 4. one with the age of *hadak mul s-sebɛin ɛam ka-yɛăref ṛebɛa de-l-lsun.* That seventy-year-old (man) knows four languages.

¶ *mulana* **1.** God, Our Lord **2.** The Prophet Mohammed

¶ *mulay* title given to a *šrif,* descendant of the Prophet Mohammed

¶ *mwalin ḍ-ḍaṛ* **1.** (one's) family, folks at home **2.** (one's) wife

¶ *mwalin ḷ-ḷeṛḍ* demons, evil spirits

¶ *mwalin z-zman* well-to-do people

mulaqat (f.sg. and pl.) **1.** meeting, encounter (unexpected) **2.** rendezvous, meeting

¶ *ɛăddef l-mulaqat* to make "sick," to be unable to stand or bear (s.o.) ≠ *ka-tɛăddefni l-mulaqat!* She makes me sick!

mulaqi pl. *-yen* go-between, intermediary

mulaḥaḍa pl. *-t* remark, observation

muˀellif pl. *-in* **1.** author, writer **2.** composer (music, poetry)

mules pl. of *mles*

mulud **1.** p.p. of *wled* —*ana mulud fe-ṛ-ṛbaṭ.* I was born in Rabat. **2.** holiday celebrating the birth of the Prophet, 12th of *rabiɛ l-ˀewwel*

** *dzad ɛăndu waḥed l-mulud had ṣ-ṣbaḥ.* He had a new addition to his family this morning.

¶ *šayeɛ l-mulud* fourth month of the Muslim lunar calendar

muludiya poetry chanted in celebrating the Prophet's birth

muluk pl. of *malĭk*

muluɛ pl. *-in* (*b-*) fond (of), crazy (about) *ana muluɛ be-l-musiqa.* I'm fond of music.

mu-le-ḥsen nightingale

mumaṭala procrastination

mumin, muˀmin, mumen, pl. *-in* believer (in some faith, belief, school of thought)

mumettil pl. *-in,* f. *-a* pl. *-at* **1.** actor (theater, movies, etc.) **2.** representative, one who represents (s.o., company, country, etc.)

muna pl. *-t* allowance, monetary or in kind, sent to s.o. regularly (for sustenance)

munaḍa pl. *-t* generally, any light-colored soft drink

munafiq pl. *-in* hypocrite

munasaba **1.** v.n. of *naseb* **2.** occasion *weṣḷuh bezzaf d-le-hdiyat be-l-munasaba d-ɛid miladu.* He received many gifts on the occasion of his birthday.

munika pl. *-t* doll (child's)

munkăṛ pl. *manakiṛ* evil, sin

muqabala meeting, confrontation (classicized v.n. and n.i. of *qabel*)

muqeddima pl. *-t* **1.** preface, foreword (book) **2.** prologue (play, opera) **3.** introduction (to a speaker)

muqef **1.** place where those who desire employment in odd jobs congregate. **2.** place where animals are kept to be sold or rented

muquf ɛla **1.** in need of *ɛăndi t-tesriḥ baš nebni wa-lakin baqi muquf ɛăl le-flus.* I have the permit to build but I still need the money. **2.** dependent on *had š-ši muquf ɛăl l-qaṛaṛ de-l-ḥukama.* It depends on the decision of the government.

muṛ, muṛa same as *mmuṛ, mmuṛa*

muṛaḍ (no pl.) **1.** goal, aim (long-range) **2.** intention, aim (short-range) **3.** desire, wish

muṛaqaba pl. *-t* **1.** control **2.** inspection (for the control of s.th.) **3.** censorship

muṛaqib pl. *-in* **1.** inspector, one who carries out a *muṛaqaba.* **2.** censor

muṛažaɛa classicized v.n. of *ṛažeɛ*

mured pl. *mwared* watering or drinking trough

muri pl. *mwara* hand, pointer (of watch, gauge, etc.)

** *ɛăndu le-mwara fe-ṭ-ṭnaš.* He's in a real good mood. He's sitting on top of the world. —*had ṣ-ṣbaḥ le-mwara dyalu ma-metqaddin-š.* He's in a foul mood this morning.

muṛut pl. *-in* p.p. of *wṛet*

mus pl. *mwas* same as *mess*

musa Moses

musakin same as *masakin* (pl. of *meskin*)

musamaḥa pl. *-t* **1.** classicized v.n. and n.i. of *sameḥ* **2.** forgiveness

musebbib pl. *-in* same as *sbaybi*

musiqa pl. *-t* music (pl. used in sense of kinds of music)

musiqi pl. *-yen* musician

musem pl. *mwasem* kind of carnival celebrated on the day of some saint

musemmiɛ pl. *-in* member of a kind of chorus which sings songs in honor of the Prophet at various occasions

mussex same as *mwessex*

musteqbal future *musteqbalu mezyan.* His future is promising. —*š-ġadi tăɛmel fe-l-musteqbal?* What are you going to do in the (near) future?

mustexdam pl. *-in* employee, worker

muṣab pl. *-in* unfortunate, plagued with setbacks and difficulties (person, things)

** *l-mumen muṣab.* It is the faithful one who suffers tribulation (said to console s.o. who has been suffering great difficulties or trials).

¶ *muṣab b-* afflicted with (disease, sickness)

muṣafaḥa pl. *-t* classicized v.n. and n.i. of *ṣafeḥ*

muṣaḷaḥa pl. *-t* classicized form of *mṣaḷḥa* v.n. of *ṣaḷeḥ* and *tṣaḷeḥ*

muṣiba pl. *mṣayeb* **1.** misfortune, (bit of) bad

luck 2. disaster, calamity 3. accident (with some calamitous or afflictive result)
muṣewwiṛ pl. *-in* 1. painter, artist 2. photographer
mušawaṛa pl. *-t* 1. classicized v.n. and n.i. of *šaweṛ* 2. consultation 3. deliberation, weighing of alternatives
mušrik pl. *-in* believer in a Godhead rather than a single divine entity; hence, Christians in general
mušum pl. *-in* p.p. of *wšem*
mut (m. or f.) death *l-mut ma-ʕändha dwa.* Death has no cure.
¶ *be-l-mut* at long last, after much difficulty *be-l-mut b-aš xella hadi b-tesʕin derhem.* At long last he let this go for ninety dirhams.
¶ *f-ḥalt l-mut* dying, on the verge of dying, about to die
¶ *mut ḷḷah* natural death *mat mut ḷḷah.* He died a natural death.
muta pl. of *miyyet* 3
muṭuṛ pl. *-at* 1. engine, motor 2. motorcycle, motor scooter
muṭäʕ same as *muḍäʕ*
muwafaqa pl. *-t* classicism for *mwafqa* v.n. of *wafeq*
muwkul same as *mukul* (p.p. of *kla, kal*)
muwellida pl. *-t* midwife
muweqqit pl. *-in* person in charge of regulating the clocks of the mosque and telling the muezzin when to start the call to prayer
muwrut same as *murut* (p.p. of *wret*)
muwšum same as *mušum* (p.p. of *wšem*)
muwwal pl. *mwawel* kind of chant-like Moroccan song similar to Flamenco music
muwweg v.i. to moo, to low (cow)
muwwen v.t. 1. to send *muna* to (s.o.) 2. to provide with funds and/or supplies
muwwet v.t. to kill (chiefly child and feminine usage)
muwxud same as *muxud* (p.p. of *xda*)
muwzun same as *muzun* (p.p. of *wzen*)
muxud pl. *-in* p.p. of *xda*
muxum pl. *-in* close, stuffy (room)
muyul v.n. of *mal*
muzun pl. *-in* p.p. of *wzen*
muẓuna du. *muẓuntayn* pl. *-t* old coin equal to one-fortieth of a *metqal*
** *ma-ka-iksab ḥetta muẓuna.* He's flat broke.
muža pl. *-t, mwaž* wave (sea, radio)
¶ *muža qṣiṛa* (or *qaṣiṛa*) shortwave (radio)
mužahid pl. *-in* same as *mžahed* (a.p. of *žahed*)
mužeb pl. *mwažeb* complaint (as filed with police or in court)
mužniba pl. *-t* crab (generic term)
mužrim pl. *-in* criminal, one guilty of committing a felony, felon
mužud pl. *-in* denotes existence or presence *had s-selʕa ma-mužuda ḥetta f-ši-maḥäll.* This merchandise can't be found anywhere (else). *—l-ma mužud fe-l-bir.* There's water in the well. *—ʕändek le-mdad le-zṛeq?—mužud!* Do you have blue ink? —Yes, I have.
muḥafaḍa 1. v.n. of *ḥafeḍ.* 2. preservation, maintenance (as of order)
¶ *mekteb l-muḥafaḍa* land office
muḥal expresses doubt as to some action *muḥal ṭṭiḥ š-šta had l-lila.* I doubt that it will rain tonight. *—muḥal had š-ši!* Oh, come on! You're kidding!
muḥami pl. *-yen* (trial) lawyer
muḥarib pl. *-in* combatant, warrior
¶ *qudamaʔ l-muḥaribin* veterans (war) *huwa men qudamaʔ l-muḥaribin.* He is a veteran.
muḥaṛṛam first month of Muslim lunar calendar
muḥasaba pl. *-t* classicized v.n. and n.i. of *ḥaseb*
muḥawala classicized v.n. of *ḥawel*
muḥawaṛa pl. *-t* 1. dialogue 2. kind of song in which a dialogue is carried on by two singers
muḥibb pl. *-in* 1. kind of benefactor to the *šuṛfa* (*šoṛfa*) (descendants of the Prophet Mohammed) who are needy 2. fan, admirer
muḥäṛṛam same as *muḥaṛṛam*
muḥsin pl. *-in* 1. philanthropic 2. philanthropist
muʕahada pl. *-t* 1. treaty, agreement (as between nations) 2. pact, (written) agreement (as between persons)
muʕawana 1. v.n. of *ʕan* 2. help, aid, assistance
muʕiḍa pl. *mwaʕeḍ* admonishment, exhortation
muʕin used primarily in the expr. *ḷḷah l-muʕin!* (May) God help you! Good luck!
muʕämmir pl. *-in* colonial settler
muʕžiza pl. *-t* miracle
mwaḍeʕ pl. of *muḍäʕ*
mwafeq a.p. of *wafeq*
mwagen pl. of *magana*
mwagni pl. *-ya* watch and clock repairman
mwakel pl. of *makla* 2 and 3
mwaken pl. of *makina*
mwal pl. of *mal*
mwalin pl. of *mula*
mwara pl. of *muri*
mwared pl. of *mured*
mwas pl. of *mus* (same as *mess*)
mwasem pl. of *musem*

mwaṭi f. *mwaṭya* pl. *mwaṭyen* flat, level
mwaṭeš pl. of *maṭiša*
mwawel pl. of *muwwal*
mwaž pl. of *muža*
mwažeb pl. of *mužeb*
mwaʕeḍ pl. of *muʕiḍa*
mwaʕen pl. of *maʕun*
mwodda pl. *-t* gift, present
mwedden pl. *-in* muezzin
mweddeʕ pl. *-in* containing the grease or yolk (said of wool before being washed for spinning, etc.)
mwiha dim. of *ma*
mwima dim. of *ʔomm*
mwessex, mwossex pl. *-in* dirty, soiled
mweswes p.p. of *weswes*
mweṣṣeṭ pl. *-in* **1.** medium, medium-sized **2.** denotes mediocrity or moderation *waš hiya žmila?—mweṣṣṭa.* Is she pretty?—More or less. *—kif kan le-mtiʕan, ṣʕib?—la, mweṣṣeṭ.* Was the exam hard?—No, not really.
mxadd pl. of *mxedda*
mxafi pl. of *mexfiya*
mxaleb pl. of *mexleb*
mxaṛeṭ pl. of *mxeṛṭa*
mxarež pl. of *mexrež*
mxaṣma pl. *-t* quarrel, dispute
mxaṭef pl. of *mexṭaf*
mxaṭṛa pl. *-t* **1.** v.n. of *xaṭeṛ* and *txaṭeṛ* **2.** bet, wager
mxax pl. of *moxx*
mxayed pl. of *mxedda*
mxayeṭ pl. of *mexyeṭ*
mxazen pl. of *mexzen* 4
mxazni same as *mxezni*
mxazniya pl. of *mxezni*
mxedda pl. *-t, mxadd, mxayed* pillow (for sleeping)
mxeḍ v.t. (v.n. *mxiḍ*) **1.** to churn (milk for butter) **2.** to shake, to agitate (to mix) **3.** to pester *xlaṣ u-ma-temxeḍni b-had l-ʔasʔila lli ma-ʕăndha măʕna.* Stop pestering me with these meaningless questions. **4.** same as *mxeṭ*
mexfiya pl. *-t, mxafi* kind of earthen container of varying shapes buried up to the lid in the ground, used to store oil, water, etc.
mxiḍ v.n. of *mxeḍ*
mxinza kind of minty tea usually used for medicinal purposes
mxiṭ v.n. of *mxeṭ*
mexleb pl. *mxaleb* claw, or a claw-like point
mexluq p.p. of *xleq*
mxelwi pl. *-yen* **1.** a.p. of *txelwa* **2.** isolated, solitary, out-of-the-way
mxenfeṛ pl. *-in* having a large, flat nose (person)
mxennen pl. *-in* snotty, having a runny nose
mexrež pl. *mxarež* **1.** exit, way out **2.** anus **3.** urethra
mxeṛṛqa (usually coll. use) pl. *-t* kind of fried pastry dipped in honey
mxeṛṭa pl. *-t, mxaṛeṭ* lathe
mexruž expenses *l-mexruž d-had š-šheṛ kteṛ men š-šheṛ lli daz.* This month's expenses were more than last month's.
mextalef pl. *-in* (*ʕla* persons, *men* things) **1.** different (from), dissimilar (to) **2.** different, varied *had l-xil kollhom mextalfin fe-l-lun.* All these horses are different in color.
moxtaṛ **1.** (with art.) the Prophet (the Chosen One) **2.** m. proper name
mxeṭ imxoṭ v.t. and v.i. (v.n. *mxiṭ*) to blow (the nose)
mexṭaf pl. *mxaṭef* **1.** hook, s.th. used as a hook (for hanging s.th.) **2.** anchor
mxuxa pl. of *moxx*
moxx pl. *mxax, mxuxa* **1.** brain (organ) **2.** (sg.) brains, intelligence
mexxaḍa pl. *-t* (butter) churn, or anything used for making butter (as a goatskin)
mexyeṭ pl. *mxayeṭ* large needle (from a few inches to one or two feet) used for sewing tents, mattresses, certain trappings for beasts of burden, etc.; also used to goad the beasts.
mxeyyeṛ part. of *xeyyeṛ*
mexzen **1.** government, administration **2.** the reigning and judging authority (as of the town) **3.** authorities **4.** pl. *mxazen* any storage place or area
mxezni pl. *mxazniya* kind of uniformed employee, usually having messenger duties, who works in government service (royal)
mya (*myat* before sg. n.) du. *-tayn* pl. *-wat* (pl. rarely used) hundred *ʕṭini mya de-l-biḍ.* Give me a hundred eggs. *—ʕăndi myat ḍulaṛ.* I have a hundred dollars.
myadi pl. of *mida*
myaḍi pl. of *miḍa*
myah pl. of *ma*
myal pl. of *mil* 3
myatayn du. of *mya*
myazeb pl. of *mizab*
myazen pl. of *mizan*
myeṣṣel pl. *-in* (*men*) original (with), derived (from) *l-kaṛăm myeṣṣel men l-ʕaṛăb.* Generosity is original with the Arabs.
** *huwa keddab myeṣṣel.* He's a real liar.
meyz same as *miz*
mzabel pl. of *mezbala, mzebla*
mzareg pl. of *mezrag*
mzawed pl. of *mezwed*
mzawer pl. of *mezwar*
mzayʕi pl. *-ya* joker, funny person
mzaž mood, disposition *ana ma-ši f-le-mzaž*

d-le-mlaġa (or *baš ntmelleġ*) *daba.* I'm not in the mood for joking right now.
mzaε 1. joking (around), fooling (around) *xḷaṣ men le-mzaε!* Quit fooling around (and get serious)! 2. n.u. *-a* medlar (fruit or tree)
mezbala, mzebla pl. *mzabel* dump, dump-yard
mzebṛa pl. *-t* pruning shears
mezgur n.u. *-a* (ear of) corn
mzeġġeb pl. *-in* hairy, hirsute (person, animal)
mezġub pl. *-in* ill-fated, having bad luck
mzirεa dim. of *mzerεa*
mziwen pl. *-in* (dim. of *mezyan*) 1. cute (girl, little boy) 2. nice *εsana mziwna hadi εmelti!* That's a nice haircut you got!
mziya pl. *-t* favor, service *εmel fiya waεed le-mziya ḷḷah ixellik.* Please do me a favor.
** *mziya fik!* That'll teach you! (as when s.o. does s.th. he was warned not to do for his own good) —*mziya hadi!* expr. of surprise at s.o.'s inability to remember s.th. he should (e.g. a debt)
¶ *mziya lli* it's a good thing that *mziya lli žiti.* It's a good thing you came.
mezḷuṭ pl. *-in* broke, without funds
meẓmut, mezmut pl. *-in* 1. muggy, warm and damp (weather) 2. (warm and) stuffy (room)
mezrag pl. *mzareg* javelin, spear
mezṛaṛ n.u. *-a* gravel
mẓeṛqeṭ pl. *-in* mottled, motley
mẓeṛṛeq pl. *-in* off-color white tending to blue
mezrub pl. *-in* in a hurry *ṛ-ana mezrub u-xeṣṣni nkun fe-ḍ-ḍaṛ qbel-ma iweṣḷu ḍ-ḍyaf.* I'm in a hurry; I have to be home before the guests arrive.
mzerεa pl. *-t* (dim. *mzirεa*) kind of sieve used in sowing seed
mezwar pl. *mzawer* kind of notary or *εadel* for the *šuṛfa,* serving as a special attestant to one's position as a *šrif* and related matters
mezwed pl. *mzawed* 1. bag used for carrying food, money, etc., on a trip 2. idiot, dense person
¶ *nεăs bεal l-mezwed* to sleep like a log
mezyan (dim. *mziwen,* comp. *εsen*) 1. pl. *-in* good *ka-nqelleb εla ši-siyaṛa mezyana.* I'm looking for a good car. 2. pl. *-in* pretty, good-looking 3. well *ka-tġenni mezyan bezzaf.* She sings quite well.
** *mezyan!* O.K.! All right!
mezyud pl. *-in* 1. p.p. of *zad* 2. born
mezzeq v.t. to tear (up) *mezzeq le-bṛa lli žatu.* He tore up the letter he got.
mzeε v.i. to fool (around), to be a pest, to joke
mžadel pl. of *meždul*
mžales pl. of *mežlis*
mžameṛ pl. of *mežmaṛ, mežmeṛ*
mžameε pl. of *mežmăε*
mžaṛi pl. of *mežṛa*
mžarya pl. *-t* race, competition (running)
mžaṛeε pl. of *mežṛuε* (pp. of *žṛeε*)
mžažeṭ pl. of *mežžuṭ*
mžebbed part. of *žebbed*
mžebna large intestine (animal)
mežd glory (usually not of God) *l-mežd dyal ˀamirika ka-itmettel f-le-qtiṣad dyalha.* The glory of America is represented in its economy.
meždam pl. *-in* leprous
meždub pl. *-in* eccentric, odd (person)
meždul pl. *mžadel* kind of knit silk strap, often embroidered (various uses)
mžeffen pl. *-in* hollowed out, concave (in a rounded fashion)
mežhed pl. *-in* 1. strong (of person, light, drink, etc.) 2. heavy (beard)
mežhud pl. *-at* effort
¶ *mežhudu* to be all one can do or give ≠ *mežhudi ġir ˀalef ḍuḷaṛ.* All I can give is a thousand dollars. —*mežhudi năεṭik l-măεlumat, u-nta ḍebbeṛ ṛaṣek.* All I can do is give you the information, and you'll have to take it from there.
¶ *εmel mežhudu* (*baš*) to do one's best, to do all one can (to) *ṭ-ṭbib εmel mežhudu baš inqedha.* The doctor did all he could to save her.
mežhul pl. *-in* used in *tmeṛ mežhul* superior variety of date(s)
mži v.n. of *ža*
mežlis pl. *mžales* 1. assembly 2. council 3. meeting place for 1 and 2 above 4. seminar (university)
¶ *mežlis le-stinaf* appellate court, court of appeals
¶ *mežlis n-nuwwab* chamber of deputies, house of representatives
mežmaṛ, mežmeṛ, pl. *mžameṛ* brazier, coal or charcoal-burner (for cooking, heating)
mežmuε p.p. of *žmăε*
mežmăε pl. *mžameε* 1. gathering, group (in a meeting) 2. meeting, get-together 3. committee 4. kind of rack or tray, usually of ceramic material, with multiple built-in ink wells
mežnun pl. *-in* possessed (of the devil or demons; also figurative)
mžeṛ pl. *mžuṛa* drawer *xebbăεt le-ktab dyalek f-le-mžeṛ.* I hid your book in the drawer.
mežṛa pl. *mžaṛi* any place where water runs or customarily runs (river bed, drain, etc.)
mežṛab pl. *-in* mangy, scabietic
mežṛuε pp. of *žṛeε*

mžura pl. of *mžeṛ*
mežwaɛ pl. *-in* **1.** starved, famished, ravenous (person) **2.** stingy, niggardly
mežya pl. *-t* **1.** n.i. of *ža* **2.** arrival, coming
mežžed v.t. to praise, to extol, to glorify (s.o. other than God)
mežžuṭ pl. *mžažeṭ* person afflicted with tinea (type of ringworm)
mežɛub pl. *-in* hollow (said of long objects, (e.g. pipes)
mḥa imḥi v.t. (v.n. *mḥi*) to erase (also metaphorical)
mḥabeq pl. of *meḥbeq, mḥăbqa*
mḥabes pl. of *meḥbes*
mḥadya v.n. of *ḥada*
mḥadeq pl. of *meḥduq*
mḥaḍeṛ pl. of *meḥḍeṛ*
mḥafeḍ pl. of *mḥăfḍa*
mḥagen pl. of *meḥgen*
mḥakk pl. of *mḥăkka*
mḥamel pl. of *meḥmel*
mḥareb pl. of *meḥrab*
mḥaṛet pl. of *meḥṛat*
mḥaṣeṛ pl. of *meḥṣuṛ* 2
mḥašš pl. of *mḥăšša*
mḥaweṛ pl. of *meḥwaṛ, meḥweṛ*
mḥawet pl. of *meḥwet*
mḥayen pl. of *meḥna*
mḥažeṛ n.pl. of *meḥžuṛ*
mḥažya **1.** v.n. of *ḥaža* **2.** pl. *-t* riddle, conundrum
mḥažž pl. of *mḥăžž*
mḥaḥ pl. of *meḥḥ*
mḥăbba pl. *-t* (mutual) affection, close friendship
  ¶ *b-le-mḥăbba* affectionately
meḥbeq, mḥăbqa pl. *mḥabeq* flower pot
meḥbes pl. *mḥabes* (dim. *mḥibes*) chamber pot
meḥbuk used in the expr. *ġir imma meḥbuk wella metṛuk* said of s.o. who desires s.th. very strongly, but when the opportunity to get it arises he loses interest
meḥbus p.p. of *ḥbes*
meḥduq pl. *-in, mḥadeq* clever, intelligent
măḥḍ pl. *miḥaḍ* (pl. rare) pure, undefiled (milk, gold, ancestry, etc.)
meḥḍeṛ pl. *mḥaḍeṛ* gathering, get-together, meeting
mḥăfḍa pl. *-t, mḥafeḍ* briefcase, portfolio
meḥgad pl. *-in* holding a grudge, rancorous
meḥgen pl. *mḥagen* funnel (used in pouring)
mḥi v.n. of *mḥa*
mḥibes dim. of *meḥbes*
mḥiq v.n. of *mḥeq*
mḥăkka pl. *-t, mḥakk* piece of cork lined with cloth used in bathing or washing
meḥlul p.p. of *ḥăll*
meḥmel pl. *mḥamel* **1.** type of bier **2.** stretcher, litter **3.** group of pilgrims (going to Mecca)
mḥămmeṣ part. of *ḥămmeṣ*
mḥămmṣa food made of small rolled balls or pellets of flour, boiled and eaten as a kind of soup
meḥna pl. *mḥayen* **1.** hardship **2.** difficulty **3.** trial, tribulation
mḥănna **1.** v.n. of *ḥănn* **2.** pl. *-t* compassion
mḥănneš p.p. of *ḥănneš*
mḥănnša pl. *-t* type of spiral-shaped, filled pastry
mḥeq, v.t. (v.n. *mḥiq*) to destroy (totally; peoples, cities, nations)
meḥrab pl. *mḥareb* niche in the mosque wall (facing Mecca) from where the imam leads the prayer
meḥṛat pl. *mḥaṛet* plow (animal-drawn)
meḥsad pl. *-in* jealous, envious
meḥṣuṛ **1.** pl. *-in* needing badly to urinate (from overfull bladder) **2.** pl. *mḥaṣeṛ* kind of long overshirt
meḥšaša pl. *-t* place of congregation for hashish addicts
mḥăšša pl. *-t, mḥašš* sickle
moḥtaḍaṛ pl. *-in* dying, moribund
mḥetteb pl. *-in* type of chief inspector of foods, markets, etc.
mḥăṭṭa pl. *-t* station (radio and train)
meḥwaṛ, meḥweṛ pl. *mḥaweṛ* spit, large skewer (for roasting)
meḥwet pl. *mḥawet* kind of large oval dish for serving fish
meḥya pl. *-t* **1.** n.i. of *mḥa* **2.** in Koranic studies, that portion of the Koran which can be entered on the student's slate
meḥžuṛ adj. pl. *-in* n.pl. *mḥažeṛ* (one) under a tutelage or guardianship, ward
mḥăžž pl. *mḥažž* avenue, boulevard
meḥḥ pl. *mḥaḥ* eggyolk
meḥḥen v.t. to overwork (s.o.), to abuse the service of (s.o.)
mɛa **1.** with (not in instrumental sense) *škun lli ṣafeṛ mɛak?* Who went on the trip with you? —*ḥeṭṭ had le-ktab mɛa l-oxṛin.* Put this book with the others. —*ka-ihḍeṛ mɛa l-ʔustad dyalu.* He's talking with his teacher. **2.** along *mšaw mɛa l-wad ḥetta weṣlu l-le-bḥăṛ.* They went along the river until they reached the sea. **3.** around, about (time expr.) *ža mɛa ṭ-ṭnaš.* He came around twelve o'clock.
mɛabẓa pl. *-t* wrestling (sport)
mɛabẓi pl. *-ya* wrestler
mɛaden pl. of *măɛden*
mɛader pl. of *măɛdur* 2
mɛalef pl. of *măɛlef*
mɛaleq pl. of *mḥălqa* and *măɛleq*
mɛamel pl. of *măɛmel*
mɛani pl. of *măɛna* 2

mɛaṛeḍ pl. of *măɛṛaḍ*
mɛaref pl. of *mɛărfa* and *măɛrifa* 2
mɛaṛef pl. of *măɛṛuf*
mɛaṛek pl. of *mɛăṛka*
mɛaṣi 1. pl. of *măɛṣiya* 2. (f. sg.) emphatic form of *ɛṣa*
mɛaṣem pl. of *măɛṣem*
mɛaṣeṛ pl. of *mɛăṣṛa*
mɛaš living, sustenance *beẓṛa ka-irbeẓ mɛašu.* He barely makes a living (his living).
mɛawen pl. of *măɛwan*
mɛawna pl. -*t* 1. v.n. and n.i. of *ɛawen* 2. aid, help, assistance
mɛayna same as *mɛăyna*
mɛayer pl. of *măɛyar*
măɛda pl. -*t* (dim. *mɛida*) stomach (organ)
măɛdani, măɛdini pl. -*yen* mineral (adj.) *xeṣṣek tešṛob ši-ma măɛdini baš ttehḍem-lek l-makla.* You should drink some mineral water so that your food will digest.
măɛden pl. *mɛaḍen* 1. mine (gold, salt, etc.) 2. metal 3. silver
¶ *măɛden d-le-ẓžeṛ* (rock) quarry
mɛădnus parsley
măɛdum pl. -*in* 1. seriously ill 2. habitually penniless, destitute (usually said of a man with a family)
măɛdur 1. pl. -*in* having an excuse (for not showing up somewhere, etc.) 2. pl. *mɛader* infirm person, cripple
mɛăḍḍem pl. -*in* 1. skin and bones, bony (person) 2. having a large pit or many small pits (fruit, etc.)
mɛăffen, măɛfun pl. -*in* filthy, dirty (has metaphorical use as in English)
măɛgaz pl. -*in* lazy, indolent
mɛăgged same as *mɛăqqed*
mɛida dim. of *măɛda*
mɛik v.n. of *mɛăk*
mɛilqa dim. of *mɛălqa*
mɛis v.n. of *mɛăs*
mɛiṣ v.n. of *mɛăṣ* (same as *mɛăs*)
mɛiša living, life *le-mɛiša ṣɛiba f-dak le-blad.* Life is difficult in that country.
mɛiz pl. of *măɛza*
mɛăk v.t. (v.n. *mɛik*) 1. to mash (foods) 2. to shake (s.o., as to awaken him, or just to be obnoxious) 3. to pester, to annoy (as with questioning)
mɛăkred, mɛăkreš pl. -*in* kinky (hair)
măɛkus pl. -*in* 1. done in a strange or unconventional fashion 2. contrary, opposite
¶ *be-l-măɛkus* contrarily (to the norm), in an unconventional fashion
măɛlal, meɛlal pl. -*in* sickly, feeble
măɛlef pl. *mɛalef* feeding trough (for cattle, etc.)
mɛăllem pl. -*in* 1. master of some field or profession 2. chief, boss 3. knowledgeable and capable (as one who can fix his own car)
mɛăllma pl. -*t* kind of woman foreman, director, or manageress of a weaving, sewing, etc., factory where women make up the force
măɛleq pl. *mɛaleq* hook (for suspending or hanging s.th.)
mɛălqa pl. -*t, mɛaleq* (dim. *mɛilqa*) spoon
măɛluf pl. -*in* fattened, well-fed (animals)
măɛlum of course, naturally *waš ɛăndkom t-telž fe-l-meġrib?—măɛlum!* Do you have snow in Morocco?—Of course (we do)!
măɛlumat (pl. treated as f. sg.) information *waš imken-lek tăɛṭini ši-măɛlumat ɛla tunes?* Can you give me some information on Tunisia?
măɛmi p.p. of *ɛma*
măɛmel pl. *mɛamel* factory, manufacturing establishment
măɛmuṛ (with art.) (the) world
măɛmuṛa (no art.) forest to the east of Rabat
măɛmăɛ v.i. to bleat (goat)
măɛna ɛla to refer to, to allude to, to make allusions to *ṛaha kanet ka-tmăɛni ɛlik mnayn daret dak l-mulaẓaḍat.* She was referring to you when she made those remarks.
măɛna (m. or f.) 1. v.n. of *ɛna yăɛni* 2. pl. -*t, mɛani* meaning, sense, significance *šnu huwa l-măɛna dyal had š-ši lli ka-tqul?* What's the meaning of all this that you're saying?
¶ *ḍṛeb l-măɛna ɛla* to allude to, to make an allusion to, to refer subtly to
măɛnad pl. -*in* obstinate, stubborn (person, mule, etc.)
mɛănni pl. *mɛănnyen* (*b*-) proud (of s.o., because of his ability to help or protect)
mɛăqqed pl. -*in* complicated, knotty (problem, etc.)
măɛquda pl. -*t* omelet
măɛqul pl. -*in* 1. reasonable, acceptable (price, offer, argument, statement) 2. well-balanced, even-tempered (person)
¶ *be-l-măɛqul* seriously *tkellem mɛaya be-l-măɛqul!* Be serious with me!
măɛṛaḍ pl. *mɛaṛeḍ* 1. prop, support (for barricading, holding up a wall, etc.) 2. bar (for barring a door or window) 3. yoke (as used by water carriers) 4. rod used across the *šwari* to prevent the baskets from sagging and spilling the contents.
măɛṛaž (usually with art.) ascension of the Prophet Mohammed into heaven
mɛărfa pl. *mɛaref* 1. relation(ship) *ɛăndi mɛărfa mezyana mɛahom.* I have a good relationship with them. 2. acquaintance

huwa waḥed men le-mɛaref dyali. He's one of my acquaintances.

măɛṛiḍ pl. *maɛaṛiḍ* fair, exposition

măɛrifa 1. v.n. of *ɛṛef* 2. pl. *maɛarif, mɛaref* knowledge, experience

¶ *daˀirăt l-maɛarif* encyclopedia (the complete work)

¶ *hel* (or *rbab*) *l-măɛrifa* the experts, those who are in the know

mɛăṛka pl. *mɛaṛek* fight, battle (physical, verbal)

măɛṛuf pl. *mɛaṛef* good deed, charitable act, favor

mɛăs v.t. (v.n. *mɛis*) 1. to crush, to squash 2. to bruise (s.o.)

mɛăssel p.p. of *ɛăssel*

mɛăṣ same as *mɛăs*

măɛṣiya pl. *-t, mɛaṣi* sin, transgression

măɛṣem pl. *mɛaṣem* wrist

mɛăṣṛa pl. *mɛaṣeṛ* juicer, squeezer (for juicing oranges, etc.)

măɛṣum pl. *-in* constipated (bowels)

măɛṣuṛa (f. adj.) used in the expr. *măɛṣuṛt ž-žlayel* (mentally) sharp woman

măɛšaṛ, măɛšeṛ (no pl.) group, gathering, assemblage

** *ya măɛšeṛ l-ˀislam!* O, ye Muslims!

moɛtabaṛ pl. *-in* excellent, extraordinary, magnificent, remarkable, etc.

măɛtad, meɛtad pl. *-in* (to be) used to, in the habit of, accustomed to *ana măɛtad ka-nersel l-ḍaṛna bṛa koll ˀusbuɛ.* I'm used to sending a letter home every week.

măɛtadel, moɛtadel, meɛtadel pl. *-in* 1. temperate, mild (weather) 2. lukewarm, tepid (liquid) 3. moderate, non-extremist (person)

măɛṭa (no pl.) 1. gift (monetary) 2. donation

mɛuqeb pl. *-in* infirm, cripple

măɛwan, meɛwan pl. *mɛawen* blacksmith's hammer

măɛweq v.i. to mew (cat)

mɛăwwed part. of *ɛăwwed*

mɛăwwež part. of *ɛăwwež*

măɛyar pl. *mɛayer* insult, insulting remark

mɛăyna "by the eye," by estimating or guessing (used when s.th. is not measured exactly)

¶ *b-le-mɛăyna* same as *mɛăyna*

măɛyuf pl. *-in* 1. very unpleasant to the senses, offensive 2. obnoxious, odious (person)

măɛyur same as *măɛyar*

măɛza pl. *-t, mɛiz* 1. she-goat, nanny goat 2. knot (in wood)

măɛzi 1. goat meat 2. goat skin 3. pl. *-yen* goat (adj.)

moɛžiza same as *muɛžiza*

măɛžun a pasty preparation composed of dates, honey, sesame (and sometimes a little opium) taken as a tonic

N

-n, -en particle linking *lli, kif, kif-aš* or *waš* to third person pron. *hadi waḥed l-ḥaža lli-n hiya măɛṛufa.* This is something everyone knows. —*kif-en huwa?* How is he? —*kif-aš-en hiya?* How is she? —*waš-en huma mažyen aw la?* Are they coming or not?

nab inub (*ɛla*) (v.n. *niyaba*) to substitute (for), to do duty (for), to stand in (for) *škun ġad-inub ɛlik mnayn tšedd ṛ-ṛoxṣa dyalek?* Who's going to substitute for you when you take your leave?

¶ a.p. *nayeb* pl. *nuwwab* 1. substitute (person) 2. representative, delegate 3. assistant *ma-žbeṛt-š l-mudir, žit ana hḍeṛt mɛa n-nayeb dyalu.* I didn't find the director, so I talked to his assistant.

¶ *mežlis n-nuwwab* House of Representatives

nab pl. *nyab, niban* 1. canine (tooth) 2. fang 3. tusk

¶ *hred n-nab* to chatter, to gossip

nabat pl. *-at* 1. plant (flora) 2. vegetation

nabi same as *nbi*

nader pl. *nwader* 1. heap, pile (grain, straw) 2. a great deal, a heap *defɛăt nader d-le-flus fe-l-lbas.* She spent a great deal of money on clothes.

naḍ inuḍ v.i. (v.n. *nwaḍ, nuḍan*) 1. to get up, to stand up *naḍ men š-šelya u-gelles s-siyda.* He got up out of the chair and seated the lady. 2. to start *l-muṭuṛ ma-bġa-š inuḍ had ṣ-ṣbaḥ.* The motor wouldn't start this morning. 3. to break out *kanu ṣḥab qbel-ma tnuḍ l-ḥăṛb.* They were friends before the war broke out. —*ɛafya kbira naḍet fe-ḍ-ḍaṛ.* A big fire broke out in the house. —*naḍet binathom waḥed d-debza.* A fight broke out among them. 4. to grow (plant) *bda inuḍ r-rbiɛ fe-l-ɛăṛṣa.* Grass started growing in the garden.

** *nuḍ ɛliya!* Get out of here! Beat it!

¶ *naḍ men n-nɛas* to wake up

naḍi f. *naḍya* pl. *naḍyen* 1. finished, done *l-xedma dyali naḍya.* My work is done. 2. ready *ila kan koll-ši naḍi nemšiw.* If everybody is ready, we'll go. 3. alert, on the ball

naḍïṛ pl. *neḍḍaṛ* official supervisior of the mortmains

naḍeṛ pl. *nwaḍeṛ* **1.** temple (head) **2.** lock of hair growing on the temple

naḍăṛ pl. *-at* view, opinion

nafaqa pl. *-t* **1.** alimony *melli ṭeḷḷeq mṛatu ɛkem ɛlih l-qaḍi b-sett mya de-d-derhem dyal n-nafaqa fe-š-šheṛ.* When he divorced his wife, the judge ruled that he must pay six hundred dirhams a month in alimony. **2.** support (usually financial) *rfed n-nafaqa l-žeddatu.* He undertook the support of his grandmother.

¶ *ɛla nafaqtu*ᶲ at one's expense *xeḷḷeṣ taman ṣ-ṣafaṛ u-š-ši l-axoṛ ɛla nafaqti.* You pay the price of the trip and the rest is at my expense.

nafila pl. *-t, nawafil, nwafel* voluntary supplementary prayer done after a regularly prescribed one

nafeq v.i. (v.n. *nifaq*) to be hypocritical, to act hypocritically

nafex pl. *nwafex* **1.** charcoal burner or brazier made of clay **2.** hot-plate

nafăɛ, nafeɛ fennel seed

naga pl. *-t* female camel

naġeš v.t. and v.i. to cheat *naġšat f-l-imtiɛan.* She cheated on the examination. *naġešni f-ɛăšṛa de-ḍ-ḍuḷaṛ.* He cheated me out of ten dollars.

naġuši pl. *-yen* **1.** trickster, cheater **2.** cheating trick *lɛăb mɛaha be-n-naġuši.* He cheated her.

naka v.t. **1.** to tease *bdat ka-tnakih ɛetta tqelleq.* She teased him until he got upset. **2.** to irritate, to bother, to annoy *la-tnakini had-ṣ-ṣbaɛ, ṛah ṭayṛa liya.* Don't annoy me this morning (because) I'm already mad.

nal inal v.t. to obtain, to reach, to get (goal)

nam inum v.i. (v.n. *mnam*) to sleep)

namaṭ pl. *-at* pattern, design

namsa pl. *-t* **1.** cotton cloth of ordinary quality **2.** (with art.) Austria

namus n.u. *-a* mosquito

namusiya pl. *-t, nwames* bedstead (may refer to whole bed)

nan inin v.i. (v.n. *ninan*) to moan, to groan (from pain)

naqib pl. *nuqaba* official head of a group of Shareefs having the same family name

naqima pl. *-t* dotard, foolish old person

naqma pl. *-t* same as *naqima*

naqeṣ a.p. of *nqeṣ*

naqeš v.t. **1.** to discuss, to talk over *naqešna l-muḍuɛ mežmuɛin.* We discussed the subject together. **2.** to argue with

naquṣ pl. *nwaqeṣ* (dim. *nwiqeṣ*) bell

naṛ (f.) pl. *niran* **1.** fire, flame **2.** (with art.) hell

** *a-naṛi!* or *ya-naṛi!* My goodness! —*n-naṛ šăɛlet binathom.* They had a heated argument.

nas **1.** pl. of *ˀinsan* 2 **2.** people *ġad-ižiw ɛăndna ši-nas l-le-ɛša.* We're having some people for supper. —*n-nas d-had le-mdina mˀeddbin.* People in this town are courteous. —*n-nas ma-iqulu-š had š-ši qeddam d-drari.* People don't say this in front of children.

nasab lineage, ancestral line

naseb v.t. **1.** to suit *ila nasbetni nešriha.* If it suits me I'll buy it. —*inasbek le-xmis fe-l-lil?* Would Thursday evening suit you? **2.** to match *had ṣ-ṣebbaṭ inaseb l-keswa ẓ-ẓeṛqa.* These shoes will match the blue dress.

¶ *naseb mɛa* to match (s.th. or s.o.) with

nasim (no pl.) breeze

naṣaˀiɛ pl. of *naṣiɛa*

naṣib (no pl.) share, portion *baɛet naṣibha fe-l-molk.* She sold her share of the estate. —*ɛṭaweh lli žah fe-n-naṣib.* They gave him whatever his share was. —*dfăɛ naṣib kbir de-t-teṛwa dyalu f-le-ksiba.* He spent a large portion of his fortune on livestock.

naṣiɛa pl. *-at, naṣaˀiɛ* advice *n-naṣiɛa dyali hiya nṣebṛu ɛetta iṛžăɛ.* My advice is we should wait till he comes back.

našaṭ **1.** v.n. of *nšeṭ* **2.** pleasure, enjoyment *qal-lek ma-žbeṛ našaṭ f-dak l-xedma.* He says he didn't find any enjoyment in that work. **3.** enthusiasm, fervor, zeal *f-le-bdu kollhom biyynu našaṭ kbir fe-xdemthom.* In the beginning they all showed great enthusiasm in their work.

našid pl. *ˀanašid* song (for group or community singing)

¶ *našid dini* hymn (religious)

¶ *našid waṭani* **1.** patriotic song **2.** anthem

natiža same as *ntiža*

nawafil pl. of *nafila*

nawaɛi pl. of *naɛiya*

nayeb a.p. of *nab*

nayem pl. *-in* **1.** sleepy, drowsy **2.** asleep

nayeɛ a.p. of *naɛ*

nazeɛ **1.** v.t. to challenge, to dispute **2.** v.t. to compete with **3.** v.i. to pant, to gasp for breath

nažat v.n. of *nža*

nažaɛ v.n. of *nžeɛ*

naɛ inuɛ (*ɛla*) (v.n. *nwaɛ, mnaɛa*) to wail (over), to express sorrow (over) *kanet tnuɛ ɛla ḅḅaha.* She was wailing over her father's death.

¶ a.p. *nayeɛ* pl. *-in* of poor quality, horrible, lousy

naɛiya pl. *-t, nawaɛi* **1.** region, area **2.** neighborhood **3.** aspect, angle *ḍṛest l-muḍuɛ men koll naɛiya.* I studied the

subject from every angle.
naɛuṛa pl. *-t, nwaɛeṛ* (dim. *nwiɛṛa*) **1.** noria (water wheel with buckets) **2.** wheel (as in a watch, clock) **3.** merry-go-round **4.** spinning wheel **5.** sly person, schemer
¶ *ḍuwweṛ naɛuṛa* (*l-*) to play a trick (on) *ḍuwwṛu-lu waḥed n-naɛuṛa.* They played a trick on him.
nbaha ingenuity, ingeniousness, cleverness
nbala pl. *nbayel* bracelet
nbayel pl. of *nbala*
nbayeḥ pl. of *nbeḥ*
nbaɛ m.p. of *baɛ*
nebbar pl. *-a* resourceful
nebbaḥ pl. *-a, -in* ag. n. and adj. of *nbeḥ*
nebbeh v.t. **1.** to guide, to show the right way to, to advise **2.** to remind
¶ *nebbeh ɛla* (or *l-*) to call (s.o.'s) attention to (s.th.), to point out (s.th.) to (s.o.)
nebbel v.t. to tack, to baste
nebbeš same as *nbeš*
nebbet **1.** v.t. to grow, to raise *ka-inebbtu le-mɛădnus fe-žnanhom.* They grow parsley in their garden. **2.** v.t. to set (a piece of jewelry with precious stones) **3.** v.i. to grow *ṛ-ṛbiɛ bda inebbet fe-ṣ-ṣṭaḥ.* Grass began to grow on the roof. **4.** v.i. to be fertile, arable
nebburi dawn
¶ *ɛăl n-nebburi* very early in the morning
nebbăɛ v.i. to spring, to flow (water)
nbeḍ v.i. (v.n. *nbiḍ, nebḍ*) to beat (pulse, heart)
nebḍ **1.** v.n. of *nbeḍ* **2.** pulse (heart beat)
nbeg same as *nbeq*
nbi pl. *ᵓanbiya* prophet
¶ *n-nbi* (*ṣeḷḷa ḷḷahu ɛlih wa-sellem*) the Prophet Mohammed (peace be upon him)
nbiḍ v.n. of *nbeḍ*
nbir v.n. of *nber*
nbiš v.n. of *nbeš*
nbiḥ v.n. of *nbeḥ*
nebla m.p. of *bla*
nbeq n.u. *nebqa* jujube (edible drupaceous fruit of the buckthorn tree)
nber v.i. (v.n. *nbir*) to be resourceful
nbeš v.t. (v.n. *nbiš*) **1.** to scratch or dig with the claws (animal) **2.** to nibble
nbet v.i. to grow (plant)
nbula pl. -t urinary bladder
nbuḥa pl. of *nbeḥ*
nbeḥ v.i. (v.n. *nbiḥ*) to bark
nbeḥ pl. *nbayeḥ, nbuḥa* **1.** veranda **2.** corridor
¶ *ṛaṣ n-nbeḥ* corner of the courtyard of a Moroccan house

nbăɛ same as *nebbăɛ*
nda (m.) **1.** dampness **2.** dew
ndama **1.** v.n. of *ndem* **2.** pl. *ndayem* regret, remorse
*** dak š-ši ṛžăɛ ɛlih be-n-ndama.* He's sorry that he did it.
¶ *ḍaṛet bihᶲ* (or *ɛlihᶲ*) *n-ndama* to feel remorse ≠, to be sorry ≠ *ḍaṛet bih* (or *ɛlih*) *n-ndama ɛla lli ma-ttesmăɛ-š l-waldih.* He's sorry he didn't listen to his parents.
ndayem pl. of *ndama* **2**
ndeb v.t. or v.i. (v.n. *ndib*) to scratch (one's face as a sign of grief)
nedd variety of incense
nedda **1.** v.t. to moisten **2.** v.i. to get damp, to become moist
neddam pl. *-in* remorseful
neddem v.t. to make (s.o.) regret *neddemha lli ɛăṛḍet ɛlih.* He made her regret having invited him.
ndeh (v.n. *ndih*) **1.** v.t. to drive *ka-tăɛṛef tendeh had s-siyaṛa?* Can you drive this car? **2.** v.t. to fly (plane) **3.** v.i. to take off, to beat it
ndib v.n. of *ndeb*
ndih v.n. of *ndeh*
ndell v.i. (v.n. *della*) to debase oneself, to lose one's reputation
ndem v.i. (v.n. *ndama*) to regret, to feel sorry, to feel remorse *nedmet lli ġuwwtet mɛa ḅḅaha.* She feels sorry about having argued with her father.
nḍaḍeṛ (pl.) (eye-)glasses
nḍaf pl. of *nḍif*
nḍafa cleanness, neatness
neḍḍa v.t. to finish, to complete *ġiṛ tneḍḍi šġalek aži šufni.* As soon as you finish your work come and see me.
neḍḍam pl. *-in* rhymester
neḍḍaṛ pl. of *naḍiṛ*
neḍḍaṛat same as *nḍaḍeṛ*
neḍḍef v.t. to clean
neḍḍem v.t. **1.** to put in order *xeṣṣek tneḍḍem le-ktub dyalek.* You need to put your books in order. **2.** to organize *neḍḍemna-lu waḥed l-ḥăfla ṣġiṛa.* We organized a little party for him. *neḍḍemna ṛebɛa de-l-ližan.* We organized four committees. **4.** to compose (poetry, music)
nḍef comp. of *nḍif*
nḍeġ v.t. (v.n. *nḍiġ*) to chew
nḍif pl. *nḍaf* (comp. *nḍef*) clean
nḍiġ v.n. of *nḍeġ*
nḍiṛ similar to, equal to *ɛămmeṛhom ma-ġad-ilqaw nḍiṛ had ḍ-ḍaṛ.* They'll never find a house equal to this one.
nḍeṛ *l-* or *f-* (v.n. *nḍeṛ*) **1.** to look at, to see **2.** to consider, to think about

¶ p.p. *menduṛ* attractive, pleasing to the eye
nḍeṛ **1.** v.n. of *nḍeṛ* **2.** sight, vision
neḍṛa **1.** n.i. of *nḍeṛ* **2.** pl. *-t* impression *šnu kanet n-neḍṛa dyalha ɛlih?* What was her impression of him?
nfa infi v.t. (v.n. *nefyan*) **1.** to exile, to banish **2.** to deny, to disprove
nfad v.n. of *nfed*
¶ *n-nfad ɛla* to be in demand ≠, to be popular ≠ *slăɛthom kollha ɛliha n-nfad.* All their merchandise is in demand.
nfafex pl. of *neffaxa*
nfaq hypocrisy
nfas **1.** pl. of *nfis* **2.** recovery period following childbirth
¶ *iyyam n-nfas* post-natal period of forty days
nfaṭi pl. of *nefṭa*
nfayel pl. of *nfula*
nfayer pl. of *nfir*
nfayes pl. of *nfisa*
nfayɛi pl. *-ya* one who takes snuff, snuffer
nfed v.i. (v.n. *nfad*) to sell, to be in demand *walayenni slăɛthom kif ka-tenfed.* Their merchandise really sells.
nfeḍ (v.n. *nfiḍ*) **1.** v.t. to shake *nfeḍ had le-ġṭa fe-n-nbeɛ.* Shake this blanket in the hall. **2.** v.i. to beat (heart, pulse)
neffaṛ pl. *-a* one who plays the *nfir*
neffaxa pl. *-t, nfafex* balloon
neffed v.t. to execute, to put into effect, (order, law)
neffel v.i. to perform supplementary prayers
neffeṛ f- or *b-* to play (*nfir*)
neffes v.t. **1.** to open slightly, to leave ajar **2.** to open, to lance (boil) **3.** to uncover partially
¶ *neffes ɛla* **1.** to comfort, to soothe **2.** to give a break to, to allow (s.o.) an extension of time
¶ part. *mneffes* roomy, loose, (clothing)
neffex v.t. **1.** to make swell or become swollen **2.** to inflate, to fill with air **3.** to cause (s.o.) to be conceited
neffeɛ v.i. to take snuff
nfiḍ v.n. of *nfeḍ*
nfiq v.n. of *nfeq*
nfir pl. *nfayer* long brass instrument, without slide or pistons, having a tone similar to a trombone
nfiṛ v.n. of *nfeṛ*
nfis pl. *nfas* (comp. *nfes*) **1.** precious (e.g., stone) **2.** rare, of fine quality
nfisa pl. *-t, nfayes* woman in labor, in childbirth
nfix v.n. of *nfex*
nefnaf pl. *-a* one with a nasal twang
nefnef v.i. to speak with a nasal twang
nfeq v.i. (v.n. *nfiq*) to buy food or provisions *nhaṛ s-sebt ka-nnefqu l-l-ʔusbuɛ kamel.* On Saturdays we buy food for the whole week.
¶ *nfeq ɛla* to support (financially)
nefqa n.i. of *nfeq*
nfeṛ f- (v.n. *nfiṛ*) to forsake, to renounce
nfes comp. of *nfis*
nefs (f.) pl. *nfus* **1.** breath **2.** person, soul *nefs weɛda ma-bqat-ši fe-l-meḍṛaṣa.* There wasn't a single soul left at school. —*kteṛ men tlatin nefs kanet f-dak l-bit.* There were more than thirty people in that room. **3.** (no pl.) conscience *nefsu bdat twebbxu.* His conscience began to hurt him. **4.** self-pride **5.** self *qolt mɛa nefsi. . .* I said to myself. . .
¶ *b-nefsuᵠ* **1.** oneself *ɛna b-nefsna qolnaha-lu.* We told him ourselves. **2.** by oneself *ɛmeltha b-nefsi.* I did it by myself.
¶ *fihᵠ n-nefs* **1.** to have self-respect ≠ **2.** to be conscientious ≠
¶ *nefsuᵠ ɛăṛṛa* (to be) energetic, dynamic ≠
¶ *nuwweḍ* (or *ɛmel*) *n-nfes f-* to stimulate the interest or ambition of (s.o.)
¶ *qlil n-nefs* **1.** without self-respect **2.** without conscience, unscrupulous
¶ *qellel n-nefs* to stoop, to condescend
¶ *qṭăɛ n-nefs* **1.** to hold one's breath **2.** to stop talking suddenly, to shut up
¶ *qṭăɛ n-nefs l-* to make (s.o.) shut up
¶ *ṭeḷḷăɛ n-nefs* to breathe
¶ *žatuᵠ n-nefs ɛla* to be on (s.o.'s) side ≠, to defend ≠
¶ *ɛănduᵠ n-nefs* same as *fihᵠ n-nefs*
nefṭa pl. *nfaṭi* boil, carbuncle
nfula pl. *-t, nfayel* ticket *šɛal de-n-nfayel xditi-lna?* How many tickets did you get for us?
nfus pl. of *nefs*
nfex (v.n. *nfix*) **1.** v.t. to pump up, to put air into (tire) **2.** v.i. to blow (wind) **3.** v.i. to be conceited **4.** v.i. to hiss (snake)
nefx (no pl.) **1.** swelling (physiological) **2.** tumor
nefxa **1.** n.i. of *nfex* **2.** pl. *-t* conceited person
¶ *fihᵠ n-nefxa* to be conceited ≠
nefyan v.n. of *nfa*
nefɛa pl. *-t* pinch of snuff
nfăɛ v.t. (v.n. *nfăɛ, menfaɛa, menfiɛa*) to do (s.o.) good, to be useful to *nefɛăk dak d-dwa?* Did that medicine do you any good?
¶ *ma-nefɛuᵠ ġir* (or *ma-ɛada*) to be forced ≠, to not be able to help (but) ≠ *ma-nefɛu ġir* (or *ma-ɛada*) *iži mɛana.* He couldn't do anything but come with us. He couldn't help but come with us.
nfăɛ **1.** v.n. of *nfăɛ* **2.** benefit, profit, use, advantage

¶ *fihφ n-nfăƹ* 1. to be useful ≠ *l-žemƹiya žebṛet n-nfăƹ f-ƹămmek.* The organization found your uncle useful. 2. to be profitable ≠ *ṣ-ṣefṛa kan ƹăndu fiha bezzaf de-n-nfăƹ.* The trip was very profitable for him. 3. to be effective *dak d-dwa ma-fih nfăƹ.* That medicine is not effective.

ngab pl. *-at* veil

ngagef pl. of *neggafa*

ngalza n.pl. of *neglizi*

ngasa v.n. of *nges*

negga same as *neqqa*

neggafa pl. *-t, ngagef* woman hired to attend the bride during the wedding ceremony

neggel v.t. to carry from one place to another (especially water)

neggeṛ v.i. (v.n. *ngiṛ*) 1. to tap, to beat lightly *smăƹt ši-ḥădd ka-ineggeṛ fe-l-bab.* I heard someone tapping at the door. —*ġir huwa bda ineggeṛ ƹăl ṭ-ṭbel u-hiya qamet tešṭeḥ.* As soon as he began to beat lightly on the drum she got up to dance. 2. to have a bite *waxxa ma-kan biya žuƹ neggeṛt mƹahom.* Although I wasn't hungry I had a bite with them. 3. to take a pinch (of) (e.g., spice) *xdat mƹălqa de-l-kamun u-yaḷḷah neggṛet men l-ibzaṛ.* She took a spoonful of cumin and just a pinch of pepper.

¶ *neggeṛ l-* to give a hint to

ngiṛ v.n. of *neggeṛ*

negṛa pl. *-t* 1. very old woman 2. shrew, termagant

negrez v.i. to grumble, to complain

nges v.t. (v.n. *ngasa*) to make unclean

¶ p.p. *mengus* pl. *mnages* "jerk," "slob"

nġaneġ pl. of *neġnaġ*

neġġes v.t. to bother, to pester *neġġesha bezzaf be-l-ˀasˀilat.* He pestered her a lot with questions.

nġima dim. of *neġma*

nġiz v.n. of *nġez*

nġiza 1. dim. of *neġza* 2. pl. *-t* small amount, pinch

neġma pl. *-t* (dim. *nġima*) 1. musical note 2. melody

neġnaġ pl. *nġaneġ* one with a nasal twang

neġneġ v.i. to speak with a nasal twang

nġez, nġeẓ v.t. (v.n. *nġiz*) 1. to prick 2. to spur 3. to arouse, to stir up *n-niqaba neġzet l-xeddama ƹăl l-mudir de-l-măƹmel.* The union aroused the workmen against the plant manager. 4. to accelerate 5. to race (engine) 6. to nudge

neġza pl. *-t* (dim. *nġiza*) n.i. of *nġez*

¶ *berred n-neġza* to satisfy a burning desire

¶ *fihφ n-neġza d-* to have a passion or a special fondness for ≠ (s.th.) *fih n-neġza de-l-ƹăwm.* He has a passion for swimming. —*xetha fiha n-neġza de-l-qehwa.* Her sister has a special fondness for coffee.

nha inhi v.t. (v.n. *nhi, mnahya*) to warn (against s.th.), to advise (not to do s.th.) *ma-ṣab ḥădd lli inhih.* There was no one to advise him. —*koll-ši ka-inhih ƹăl le-xṛuž mƹaha.* Everybody warns him against going out with her.

** *nhih nhih w-ila ƹma xellih.* Do your best advising him, but if he turns a deaf ear, leave him (proverb said in reference to s.o. who disregards everybody's advice).

nhaṛ pl. *-at, nhayeṛ* day *xedmu fe-n-nhaṛ u-fe-l-lil l-bareḥ.* They worked day and night yesterday. —*nhar-aš mšat?* What day did she leave?

¶ *dak n-nhaṛ* the other day *ƹad šefthom dak n-nhaṛ.* I saw them just the other day.

¶ *had n-nhaṛ* today

¶ *nhaṛ l-ḥădd* (on) Sunday (used similarly in connection with all the days of the week, holidays, and feast occasions)

¶ *nhaṛ l-ƹid k-kbir* (on) the day of Greater Bairam

¶ *ši-nhaṛ, waḥed n-nhaṛ* one day, some day

nhaya same as *nihaya*

nhayeṛ pl. of *nhaṛ*

nehd pl. *nhud* (woman's)breast

nheḍ v.i. (v.n. *nhiḍ, nhuḍ*) 1. to shout *nehḍet fiya qbel ḥetta ma-nsellem ƹliha.* She shouted at me before I even greeted her. 2. to become emancipated

¶ *nheḍ b-* to come out with (as a new fashion)

nehḍa pl. *-t* 1. emancipation *ketbet waḥed l-maqal ƹăl n-nehḍa n-niswiya fe-bladha.* She wrote an article about the emancipation of women in her country. 2. renaissance *šeft riwaya ƹăl n-nehḍa l-ˀirḷandiya dak n-nhaṛ.* I saw a play about the Irish Renaissance the other day.

nhi v.n. of *nha*

nhiḍ v.n. of *nheḍ*

nhiq v.n. of *nheq*

nhiž v.n. of *nhež*

nheq v.i. (v.n. *nhiq*) to bray (donkey)

nhud pl. of *nehd*

nhuḍ v.n. of *nheḍ*

nhež v.i. (v.n. *nhiž*) to pant, to breathe with shallow, rapid breaths

nehža n.i. of *nhež*

¶ *fihφ n-nehža* to be out of breath

niban pl. of *nab*

nibru n.u. *weṛqa de-n-nibru* cigaret paper (for rolling one's own cigarets)

niḍam pl. *nuḍum, ˀanḍima* 1. order *l-mudir ṭḷeb men t-tlamed iḥafḍu ƹăl n-niḍam.* The principal asked the students to main-

tain order. **2.** rule, regulation, statute **3.** regime, political system
nif pl. *nyuf* nose (human)
nifaq **1.** same as *nfaq* **2.** v.n. of *nafeq*
nihaʔi pl. *-yen* final *εṭaha ž-žwab n-nihaʔi.* He gave her the final answer.
nihaʔiyăn **1.** completely *had ṛ-ṛažel ḥmeq nihaʔiyăn.* This man is completely crazy. **2.** not . . . at all *ma-qolt-lu-šay men had š-ši nihaʔiyăn.* I haven't told him this at all.
nihaya pl. *-t* **1.** end *hadi n-nihaya de-ṭ-ṭṛiq.* This is the end of the road. **2.** extreme, utmost degree, maximum *weṣṣeḷ le-n-nihaya de-t-tṣaṛa.* He reached the utmost degree of insolence.
¶ *fe-l-ġaya u-n-nihaya* **1.** excellent, perfect **2.** perfectly **3.** neat, shipshape
nila aniline (kind of blue dye)
nili pl. *-yen* indigo
nimiru pl. *-yat, nwamer* number *εṭini n-nimiru de-t-tilifun dyalek.* Give me your telephone number.
¶ *nimiru waḥed* first-rate, excellent
ninan v.n. of *nan*
ninna ininni v.i. to go to sleep (said to little children only)
nira pl. *-t* shuttle (weaving)
niran pl. of *naṛ*
nišan (invariable) **1.** straight *εmel waḥed s-sṭeṛ ikum nišan.* Draw a straight line. —*tbăε dak ṭ-ṭṛiq nišan.* Keep straight on that road. **2.** exactly, sharp *ža fe-t-tlata nišan.* He came exactly at three. **3.** pl. *nyašen* medal
niya pl. *-t* **1.** v.n. of *nwa* **2.** intention *kanet niyti nεăwwnu.* My intention was to help him. **3.** faith, confidence, trust *hadik ma-εamla niya f-ḥădd.* She has faith in nobody. **4.** simple-mindedness **5.** naive, simple, or artless person *hadak ġir weld niya.* He's just a naive boy.
¶ *be-n-niya* (sometimes with pron. endings) really, seriously *be-n-niya ġad-dzuwwež?* Are you really going to get married? —*ṛ-ana ka-ntkellem mεak b-niyti.* I'm talking to you seriously.
¶ *niya u-ḥṛamiya* deceptively naive
¶ *εla niytu* same as *be-n-niya*
niyaba v.n. of *nab*
¶ *be-n-niyaba εla* on behalf of
niyy pl. *-en* **1.** raw *had l-lḥăm ma-zal niyy.* This meat is still raw. **2.** untanned (hide)
nkaya pl. *-t* n.i. of *naka*
nked v.i. (v.n. *nkid*) **1.** to become sad (person) **2.** to fade, to become dim (color, light)
nekda n.i. of *nked*
nkid v.n. of *nked*
nkiṛ v.n. of *nkeṛ*
nkis v.n. of *nkes*
nekkaṛ pl. *-in* ag. adj. of *nkeṛ*
¶ *nekkaṛ l-xir* f. *nekkaṛt l-xir* ungrateful
nekked v.t. to sadden, to grieve
neknak adj. pl. *-in* n.pl. *-a* ag. adj. and n. of *neknek*
neknek v.i. to complain constantly, to voice continually one's dissatisfaction
nkeṛ v.t. (v.n. *nkiṛ, nokṛan*) to deny *ka-inkeṛ l-waqiε.* He denies the truth. —*nekṛettu f-šehṛayn d-le-kra.* She denied she owes him two months' rent.
¶ *nkeṛ l-xir* to show ingratitude
nekṛa pl. *-t* n.i. of *nkeṛ*
¶ *ḍṛeb nekṛa* to deny completely
nokṛan v.n. of *nkeṛ*
¶ *nokṛan l-xir* ingratitude
nkes v.t. (v.n. *nkis*) to sweep (floor)
nmari pl. of *nemra*
nmili variety of green tea (of inferior quality)
nmel n.u. *nemla* ant
nemmam pl. *-in* slanderer
nemmem f- to slander
nemmer v.t. to number, to designate by number
nmer pl. *nmura* tiger
nemra pl. *-t, nmari* number *εăndek n-nemra de-t-tilifun dyalu?* Do you have his telephone number?
nems **1.** pl. *nmusa* (dim. *nmiyysa*) ferret **2.** n.u. *-a* freckle
nmura pl. of *nmer*
nmusa pl. of *nems* **1**
nnit used in indicating precision as to persons, things, places, time, situations, etc. *hiya nnit lli šrathom.* It was she who bought them. —*huma nnit lli qaluha-li.* They told me themselves. —*hadak nnit l-uṭil fayn bett.* That's exactly the hotel where I spent the night.
nqa (m.) **1.** cleanness **2.** comp. of *nqi*
nqabi pl. of *noqba*
nqali pl. of *neqla*
nqaši pl. of *neqša*
nqaṭi pl. of *neqṭa*
nqawa same as *nqa* **1**
nqayeṛ pl. of *nqiṛ*
nqayṛi pl. *-ya* silversmith
nqaz v.n. of *neqqez*
nqeb v.t. (v.n. *nqib*) **1.** to peck at, to eat with the beak **2.** to nibble at, to eat in little bites **3.** to make a hole in (e.g., wall, door)
nqeb pl. of *neqba, noqba*
neqba, noqba pl. *-t, nqabi, nqeb* hole (especially in a wall; perforation rather than cavity)
¶ *ḍṛeb n-nqeb εla* to rob (a building) by breaking through the wall

nqed v.t. (v.n. *nqid, neqdan*) to rescue, to deliver, to save
neqdan v.n. of *nqed*
nqi pl. *-yen* (comp. *nqa*) clean
nqib v.n. of *nqeb*
nqid v.n. of *nqed*
nqil v.n. of *nqel*
nqiṛ pl. *nqayeṛ* **1.** vat for storing oil at an oil-press **2.** box-like brick (or stone) bowl (with drain) constructed at the floor level and directly beneath a tap or faucet
nqiṣ v.n. of *nqeṣ*
nqiš v.n. of *nqeš*
nqiz v.n. of *neqqez*
nqel v.t. (v.n. *nqil, neql*) **1.** to carry (as from one place to another) **2.** to copy, to reproduce
neql v.n. of *nqel*
¶ *šarika de-n-neql* transportation service
neqla, noqla pl. *-t, nqali* **1.** load (carried by a porter, a horse, a cart, a truck, etc.) **2.** shoot (plant)
neqneq v.i. to ferret, to nose around *bqa ka-ineqneq ḥetta lqa s-saṛeq.* He kept nosing around until he found the thief.
neqqa v.t. **1.** to clean **2.** to peel or scrape (vegetables) **3.** to shell, to hull (e.g., beans, peas, etc.) **4.** to clear (earth)
neqqal pl. *-a* carrier, porter
neqqaš pl. *-a* sculptor
neqqaz pl. *-a* ag. n. of *neqqez*
neqqel v.t. **1.** to carry, to remove from one place to another **2.** to transfer
neqqeṛ v.t. to plate with silver, to silver-plate
neqqeš same as *nqeš*
neqqeṭ **1.** v.t. to dot, to mark with dots **2.** v.t. or v.i. to drip **3.** v.i. to play (musical notes)
¶ *neqqeṭ š-šmăɛ* (*ɛla*) to make sarcastic remarks (about)
neqqez v.i. (v.n. *tenqaz, nqaz, nqiz*) **1.** to jump, to leap, to hop *ma-qdeṛ-š ineqqez ɛăl l-ḥăyṭ.* He couldn't jump over the wall. **2.** to dive (swimming)
noqṛa, neqṛa silver *šrat demliž de-n-noqṛa.* She bought a silver bracelet.
nqeṣ (v.n. *nqiṣ, neqṣan, noqṣan, neqṣ*) **1.** v.t. to suppress, to eliminate, to omit, to cut out *neqṣu-lu tlata de-ṣ-ṣefḥat men l-maqal dyalu.* They cut three pages out of his article. **2.** v.t. to subtract, to take away **3.** v.i. to decrease, to diminish *l-begṛa neqṣet fe-t-tqol.* The cow decreased in weight. **4.** v.i. to go down (price) **5.** v.i. to depreciate, to lessen (in value) *ḍ-ḍaṛ neqṣet fe-l-qima.* The house has depreciated in value.
¶ *nqeṣ men* **1.** to cut down, to lower, to reduce *mnayn tuwṣel l-le-mdina nqeṣ men ṣ-ṣoṛɛa.* When you reach town, reduce the speed. **2.** to turn down (radio, motor) **3.** to set back (clock) *nqeṣna saɛtayn men l-magana.* We set the clock back by two hours.
¶ a.p. *naqeṣ* pl. *-in* **1.** incomplete *l-xedma naqṣa.* The work is incomplete. **2.** missing *bezzaf d-le-ḥwayež naqṣin f-had l-bit.* There are a lot of things missing from this room. **3.** incompetent, weak (in performance) *xti ma-zala naqṣa f-le-ḥsab.* My sister is still weak in mathematics.
¶ *dar b-naqeṣ* to change one's mind *kan ġad-iṣafeṛ mɛana u-dar b-naqeṣ.* He was going on the trip with us but he changed his mind.
¶ *dar* (or *ɛmel*) *b-naqeṣ men* to do without *ila šrit ṛadyu ġad-ndir b-naqeṣ men magana ždida.* —If I buy a radio I'll do without a new watch.
¶ *naqeṣ ṭyab* **1.** incompletely cooked **2.** not quite ripe, green
¶ *murekkab neqṣ* inferiority complex
noqṣan, neqṣan **1.** v.n. of *nqeṣ* **2.** defect *ila žbeṛti ši-noqṣan f-had l-ʔala ṛeddha-lna.* If you find any defect in this machine, bring it back to us. **3.** drawback, shortcoming *n-noqṣan le-kbir lli fih huwa ɛămmṛu ma-ka-iḥafeḍ ɛăl l-mawaɛid dyalu.* His big drawback is that he never keeps his appointments.
nqeš v.t. (v.n. *neqš, nqiš*) **1.** to carve (wood, marble, etc. artistically) **2.** to sculpture **3.** to harrow (ground)
neqš v.n. of *nqeš*
neqša pl. *-t, nqaši* **1.** spring (as in a clock) **2.** catch release (on a switchblade knife)
** *feltet-lu n-neqša.* He's gone mad.
neqṭa, noqṭa, pl. *-t, nqaṭi* **1.** drop *ma-bqat-ši neqṭa weḥda de-z-zit.* There is not a single drop of oil left. **2.** stop, period *xeṣṣek noqṭa men băɛd had l-žumla.* You need a period after this sentence. **3.** dot, spot **4.** stroke, apoplexy
neržis n.u. *-a* daffodil
nsa insa v.t. (v.n. *nesyan*) to forget *ɛăndak tensa ma-dži-š!* Don't forget to come!
nsa pl. of *mṛa*
nsab pl. of *nsib*
nsawi pl. *-yen* effeminate
nsaxi pl. of *nesxa*
nseb (*l-*) (v.n. *nsub*) to attribute (to) *l-aš ġad-nnesbu ṣ-ṣuquṭ dyalu?* What can we attribute his failure to?
¶ *nseb ɛla* to charge, to impute to (s.o.) *ka-nḍenn bariʔ men l-žarima lli nesbu ɛlih.* I think he is innocent of the crime imputed to him.
nesba pl. *-t* comparison
¶ *be-n-nesba l-* in comparison to

nsib pl. *nsab* relative by marriage, in-law (usually parents, brothers, and sisters)
nsiba pl. *-t* f. of *nsib*
nsil v.n. of *nsel*
nsim breeze, light wind
nsix v.n. of *nsex*
nsiž v.n. of *nsež*
nsel v.i. (v.n. *nsil*) **1.** to fall out (hair) *šʕăṛha nsel.* Her hair fell out. **2.** to shed skin (snake) *l-ḥenš ka-insel.* The snake sheds (his) skin.
nsel progeny, offspring
¶ *ḥmaṛ le-n-nsel* jackass used for breeding purposes, stud ass
nesma pl. *-t* **1.** very soft wind **2.** slight odor (pleasant or unpleasant)
nser pl. *nsura* vulture
nessa v.t. to make forget *nessatni š-šġal lli kont ġad-ndir.* She made me forget the work I was going to do. —*ḥawel inessiha f-ṛaželha l-luwwel.* He tried to make her forget her first husband.
nessax pl. *-a* copyist, transcriber
nessay pl. *-in* forgetful
nessel v.t. to sire, to beget
nessem v.t. to give flavor to, to flavor
nsub v.n. of *nseb*
nsubiya in-law relationship, relationship by marriage
nsura pl. of *nser*
nsex v.t. (v.n. *nsix*) to copy down (text), to transcribe
nesxa pl. *-t, nsaxi* copy *hadi n-nesxa l-ʔaṣliya.* This is the original copy. —*nṭebʕăt myatayn nesxa.* Two hundred copies were printed.
nesyan v.n. of *nsa*
nsež v.t. (v.n. *nsiž*) to weave
nṣaḷi pl. of *neṣḷa*
nṣaṛa pl. of *neṣṛani*
nṣaṣ pl. of *neṣṣ, noṣṣ*
nṣaḥa **1.** v.n. of *nṣeḥ* **2.** clearness, brightness
nṣeb v.t. (v.n. *nṣib*) **1.** to prepare (food) for cooking **2.** to set (trap)
¶ *neṣbu~ l-* to frame (s.o.), to make (s.o.) the victim of a false charge
neṣba n.i. of *nṣeb*
nṣib v.n. of *nṣeb*
nṣiṛaf pl. *-at* finale (music)
nṣiḥ v.n. of *nṣeḥ*
neṣḷa pl. *-t, nṣaḷi* blade of an old knife (generally used together with a hammer for breaking big lumps of sugar)
nṣeṛ v.t. (v.n. *neṣṛ, nṣeṛ*) **1.** to crown (king) **2.** to make victorious (God as the subject)
nṣeṛ **1.** v.n. of *nṣeṛ* **2.** victory, triumph
neṣṛ v.n. of *nṣeṛ*
neṣṛani pl. *nṣaṛa* Christian (n.)
neṣṣ, noṣṣ pl. *nṣaṣ* **1.** half *ntaḍeṛtu neṣṣ saʕa.* I waited half an hour for him. **2.** middle *bnaw ṣuṛ f-neṣṣ ž-žnan.* They built a wall in the middle of the garden. **3.** light blanket **4.** trick, ruse
¶ *ḍṛeb b-neṣṣ* to trip (s.o.)
neṣṣ pl. *nṣuṣ, nuṣuṣ* text *had ṣ-ṣbăḥ nešṛu neṣṣ l-xiṭab de-ṛ-ṛaʔis.* The text of the President's speech was published this morning.
neṣṣab pl. *-a* crook, swindler
nṣuṣ pl. of *neṣṣ*
nṣuḥiya same as *nṣaḥa*
nṣeḥ (v.n. *nṣiḥ, nṣaḥa*) **1.** v.t. to counsel, to advise *l-ʔustad dyalu neṣḥu idir ṭ-ṭibb.* His teacher advised him to study medicine. **2.** v.i. to shine, to be bright **3.** v.i. to excel *ka-inṣeḥ fe-xdemtu.* He excels in his work.
nšeʔ v.t. (v.n. *nšiʔ*) **1.** to build, to raise *l-ḥukuma nešʔet ʕadad d-le-mḍaṛeṣ had l-ʕam.* The government has built many schools this year. **2.** to start, to launch, to found *xeṣṣna nnešʔu ši-žemʕiya ždida.* We have to start a new organization.
nša (f.) starch
nšabi pl. of *nešba*
nšašef pl. of *neššafa*
nšawi pl. of *nešwa*
nšaywi pl. *-ya* addict (smoking, drinking, etc.)
nešba pl. *-t, nšabi* trap, snare
nšed v.i. (v.n. *nšid*) **1.** to sing (group song, hymn) **2.** to read poetry (musically)
nšef v.i. (v.n. *nšif*) **1.** to dry, to get dry *l-tqašeṛ nešfu deġya.* The socks dried quickly. **2.** to dry up, to go dry *had l-bir ka-inšef fe-ṣ-ṣif.* This well goes dry in summer.
nšiʔ v.n. of *nšeʔ*
nšid v.n. of *nšed*
nšif v.n. of *nšef*
nšiṛ v.n. of *nšeṛ*
nšiṭ v.n. of *nšeṭ*
nešneš v.i. to drizzle
nšeqq m.p. of *šeqq*
nšeṛ v.t. (v.n. *nšiṛ*) **1.** to saw **2.** to hang (linen on the line) **3.** to publish
nešša v.t. to starch, to put starch in (clothes)
neššafa pl. *-t, nšašef* blotter, piece of blotting paper
neššef v.t. **1.** to blot, to dry with a blotter **2.** to wipe, to dry *neššef režlik b-had l-fuṭa.* Dry your feet with this towel. —*ana neġsel l-lwani u-nta neššefhom.* I'll wash the dishes and you dry them.
neššeṭ v.t. to please, to make happy *neššṭetni l-xoṭba dyalu.* His speech pleased me.
nšeṭ v.i. (v.n. *našaṭ, nšiṭ*) **1.** to be glad, to rejoice **2.** to have fun **3.** to be active, energetic

nešwa pl. *-t, nšawi* habit, addiction (e.g., smoking, drinking) *fih n-nešwa de-d-doxxan.* He's addicted to smoking.
nta you (m. sg. disjunctive pron.)
nta pl. *-wat* female *sʕib l-waḥed ifrez ḍ-ḍker men n-nta f-le-bṛaṭel.* It's hard to tell a male from a female among birds.
ntaqel v.i. (v.n. *ntiqal*) **1.** to be promoted or advanced (in rank, position) **2.** to move, transfer (from one place to another)
ntaqem l- to avenge, to get revenge for *kan bġa intaqem l-l-mut de-ḅḅah.* He wanted to avenge his father's death.
¶ *ntaqem men* to get revenge on, to get even with *hadi telt snin u-hiya ka-tḥawel tentaqem mennu.* She's been trying to get revenge on him for three years.
ntaxeb v.t. (v.n. *ntixab*) to elect *ntaxbuh xlif de-ṛ-ṛaʔis.* They elected him vice-president.
ntaya same as *nta* (you m. sg.)
ntayež pl. of *ntiža*
ntaž v.n. of *ntež*
ntaʕ same as *mtaʕ*
ntef v.t. (v.n. ntif) to pluck (fowl, feather)
¶ *ntef bṭant* (pl. *bṭayen*) to backbite, to speak evil of *men ʕadtu ma-ka-intef bṭant ḥădd.* He doesn't usually speak evil of anybody. —*baṛaka u-ma-tentef fe-bṭayen sḥabek!* Stop backbiting your friends.
nti you (f. sg. disjunctive pron.)
ntif v.n. of *ntef*
ntina same as *nta* (you m. sg.) and *nti* (you f. sg.)
ntiqal pl. *-at* **1.** v.n. of *ntaqel* **2.** promotion, advancement (of rank, position) **3.** transfer, move
ntiṛ v.n. of *nteṛ*
ntixab **1.** v.n. of *ntaxeb* **2.** pl. *-at* election
ntiya same as *nti* (you f. sg.)
ntiža pl. *-t, ntayež* **1.** result *kif kanet n-ntiža d-le-mtiḥan?* What was the result of the examination? **2.** profit, use *ma-telʕăt-lu ntiža men ṣ-ṣefṛa dyalu.* His trip was of no use.
ntkel same as *ttkel*
nteṛ v.t. (v.n. *ntiṛ*) **1.** to snatch away, to grab *kont ka-neqṛa u-hiya netṛet-li le-ktab men yeddi.* I was reading when she suddenly snatched the book out of my hand. **2.** to puff on (cigaret)
netṛa pl. *-t* n.i. of *nteṛ*
ntuma you (pl. disjunctive pron.)
netwa pl. *-t* female *had l-beṛṭal ḍkeṛ wella netwa?* Is this bird a male or a female?
ntež v.t. (v.n. *ntaž, intaž*) to produce, to yield *had le-blad ka-tentež-lu le-ṭwan de-l-gemḥ.* This field yields him tons of wheat.
nṭiq v.n. of *nṭeq*
nṭiḥ v.n. of *nṭeḥ*

nṭeq v.i. (v.n. *nṭiq, noṭq*) to pronounce, to articulate *mnayn ka-ikun ka-iqṛa ma-ka-inṭeq-š mezyan.* When he reads he doesn't articulate well.
¶ *nṭeq b-* to utter, to mention *ġir ana nṭeqt be-smiytu u-huwa wqef.* As soon as I mentioned his name, he stood up.
noṭq v.n. of *nṭeq*
nṭeḥ v.t. (v.n. *nṭiḥ*) **1.** to hit with the horns **2.** to give a blow with the head, to butt
neṭḥa pl. *-t* n.i. of *nṭeḥ*
nuba du. *nubtayn* pl. *-t, nweb* (dim. *nwiba*) **1.** time *šḥal men nuba mšaw l-bariz?* How many times did they go to Paris? **2.** turn *nubt men l-yum fe-ġsil l-lwani?* Whose turn is it to wash dishes today? **3.** movement (music)
¶ *be-n-nuba* by turns, alternately
¶ *băʕḍ n-nubat* sometimes
¶ *nuba nuba* every once in a while
¶ *šedd* (or *qbeṭ*) *n-nuba* to line up, to queue up
¶ *ʕmel* (or *dar*) *n-nuba* to take turns *dayrin n-nuba ʕla ġsil le-mwaʕen.* They take turns at washing dishes.
nuder v.t. to stack (e.g., hay)
nuḍa n.i. of *naḍ*
nuḍan v.n. of *naḍ*
nuḍum pl. of *niḍam*
nuġeš same as *naġeš*
nun n.u. *-a* eel
nuqaba pl. of *naqib*
nuṣuṣ pl. of *neṣṣ*
nuwambir, nuwamber November
nuwwab pl. of *nayeb* (a.p. of *nab*)
nuwwala pl. *-t, nwawel, nwayel* thatched hut
nuwwaṛ n.u. *-a* pl. *-t, nwaweṛ* (dim. *nwiwṛa*) flower
¶ *n-nuwwaṛ* syphilis
¶ *nuwwaṛ š-šems* sunflower
nuwwaša pl. *-t, nwaweš* puff, knob (as on a cap)
nuwwaḥ pl. *-in* whiny, given to whining
nuwweb v.t. to appoint as delegate or assistant
nuwweḍ v.t. **1.** to wake up, to rouse (from sleep) **2.** to stir up, to raise *s-siyaṛa nuwwḍet bezzaf de-l-ġobṛa.* The car stirred up a lot of dust. **3.** to start *nta lli nuwweḍti l-muṭuṛ?* Did you start the motor? —*koll ṣbaḥ ka-inuwweḍ debza mʕa l-xeddama.* Every morning he starts a fight with the workers. —*kanu nuwwḍu waḥed l-ʕafya kbira fe-l-ġaba.* They had started a big fire in the forest. **4.** to stage, to mount *l-ʕommal nuwwḍu muḍahaṛa l-bareḥ.* The workers staged a demonstration yesterday.
¶ *nuwweḍ l-qelb* **1.** to make throw up *l-kebda lli klat nuwweḍet-lha qelbha.* The liver she ate made her throw up. **2.** to

nauseate *hdeṛtha ka-tnuwweḍ l-qelb.* The way she talks is nauseating.
nuwwem v.t. **1.** to anesthetize **2.** to hypnotize
nuwweṛ **1.** v.t. to enlighten *dak le-ktab ح aqiqăten nuwweṛ-lu l-fikr dyalu.* That book really enlightened his mind. **2.** v.t. to give more charm and more pleasure to, to honor (a place or a person as a result of one's desired presence, and as a comparison to a flower) *nuwwṛet-lna l-حăfla b-le-mži dyalha.* She made our party more charming by coming. **3.** v.i. to flourish, to blossom
nuwweح v.i. to lament, to wail
nuzha same as *nzaha*
nuع pl. *nwaع, ʔenwaع* kind, sort, variety *šmen nuع de-l-qehwa ka-tešṛob?* What kind of coffee do you drink?
nwa, inwi (v.n. *niya*) **1.** v.t. to think *ma-nwitu-š iži l-yum.* I didn't think he would come today. **2.** v.t. to wish for, to make a wish *lli nwatha ka-tحeṣṣel عliha.* Whatever she wishes for she gets. **3.** v.i. to intend, to plan *ka-inwi išri siyaṛa ždida.* He intends to buy a new car.
nwa n.u. *-ya* almond
nwader pl. of *nader*
nwaḍ v.n. of *naḍ*
nwaḍeṛ pl. of *naḍeṛ*
nwafel pl. of *nafila*
nwafex pl. of *nafex*
nwala same as *nuwwala*
nwamer pl. of *nimiru*
nwames pl. of *namusiya*
nwaqeṣ pl. of *naquṣ*
nwawel pl. of *nuwwala*
nwaweṛ pl. of *nuwwaṛa* (n.u. of *nuwwaṛ*)
nwaweš pl. of *nuwwaša*
nwayel pl. of *nuwwala*
nwaح v.n. of *naح*
nwaع, ʔenwaع pl. of *nuع*
nwaعeṛ pl. of *naعuṛa*
nwaعṛi f. *-ya* pl. *-ya, -yat* cunning, wily
nweb pl. of *nuba*
nwiba dim. of *nuba*
nwiqeṣ dim. of *naquṣ*
nwiwṛa dim. of *nuwwaṛa* (n.u. of *nuwwaṛ*)
nwiعṛa dim. of *naعuṛa*
nxasi pl. of *nexsa*
nxel n.u. *nexla* palm-tree
nexsa pl. *nxasi* side-ache (e.g. from too much running)
nexwa distinguished appearance

¶ *dfăع n-nexwa* to assume a distinguished air

noxxal, noxxala bran

¶ *عṭa n-noxxal* not to pay attention (to s.o.) *عṭih n-noxxal!* Don't pay any attention to him!

nexxel v.t. to give (s.o.) the cold shoulder
nyab pl. of *nab*
nyašen pl. of *nišan*
nyuf pl. of *nif*
nzaha pl. *-t, nzayeh* **1.** v.n. of *nezzeh* **2.** picnic **3.** pleasure *ṣ-ṣfeṛ fe-l-baxiṛa nzaha.* It's a pleasure to travel by ship.
nzali pl. of *nezla*
nzayeh pl. of *nzaha*
nzayhi pl. *ya* party-goer, one who attends or likes parties
nzef v.i. (v.n. *nzif*) to go dry *had ṣ-ṣaqya fe-ṣ-ṣif ka-tenzef.* This creek goes dry in summer.
nzif v.n. of *nzef*
nzel v.i. (v.n. *nzul*) **1.** to fall *nzel bezzaf de-t-telž l-bareح.* A lot of snow fell yesterday. **2.** to land *f-ayna maṭaṛ nezlet ṭiyaṛtkom?* What airport did your plane land at? **3.** to disembark, to go ashore **4.** to get off *ġir l-mašina weqfet w-ana nzelt.* As soon as the train stopped I got off. —*nzel men fuq l-عăwd.* He got off of the horse. **5.** to be served *ma-nezlet le-عša حetta wṣel.* Supper wasn't served until he arrived. **6.** to stay, to stay at *l-lila l-luwwla nzelt f-l-util.* The first night, I stayed at the hotel. —*mnayn kont fe-ḍ-ḍaṛ l-biḍa nzelt عănd عămmi.* When I was in Casablanca I stayed at my uncle's. **7.** to be revealed *l-qoṛʔan nzel fe-š-šheṛ d-ṛemḍan.* The Koran was revealed during the month of Ramadan.

¶ *nzel عla* **1.** to strike, to hit violently *nezlu عlih b-ẓeṛwaṭa le-ṛ-ṛas.* They struck him on the head with a club. **2.** to take by surprise, to visit (s.o.) by surprise (in order to have a meal or stay) **3.** to be sold to (the highest bidder) at auction **4.** to be revealed to, to come as revelation or inspiration to *l-qoṛʔan nzel عăl n-nbi.* The Koran was revealed to the Prophet. **5.** to get (down) off of, to come down from *nzel عăl le-حmaṛ.* He got down off of the donkey. —*nzel عăl l-حiṭ!* Get down off the wall!

nezla pl. *-t, nzali* **1.** n.i. of *nzel* **2.** sudden illness of short duration (e.g., flu)
nzeq pl. *nzuqa* shuttle (in weaving)
nzul v.n. of *nzel*
nzuqa pl. of *nzeq*
nezzeh v.t. (v.n. *nzaha*) **1.** to give a picnic for **2.** to entertain (with amusement)
nezzel v.t. **1.** to put or lay (down) *fayn nezzelti le-ktab lli kan hna?* Where did you put the book that was here? **2.** to serve (food) *fuq-aš ka-tnezzlu le-عša?* When do you serve supper? **3.** to unload (burden)

¶ *nezzel عla* to sell to (the highest bidder, at auction)

nža inža v.i. (v.n. *nažat*) to escape, to come out safe *nža men l-mut.* He escaped (from) death.
nžab pl. of *nžib*
nžaṛa (coll.) wood chips
¶ *ṭeṛf de-n-nžaṛa* chip of wood
nžeb comp. of *nžib*
nžib pl. *-in, nžab* (comp. *nžeb*) **1.** intelligent **2.** studious
nžiṛ v.n. of *nžeṛ*
nežma pl. *-t, nžum* star
¶ *šaf n-nžum* to get dizzy (as a result of a blow), "to see stars"
nžeṛ v.t. (v.n. *nziṛ*) **1.** to plane (wood) **2.** to sharpen (pencil) **3.** to pave (road)
nežṛeḥ v.i. to be wounded *nžeṛḥu ɛadad de-n-nas fe-l-muḍahaṛa.* Many people were wounded in the riot.
nžum pl. of *nežma*
nežža **1.** to free, to liberate *nežža š-šăɛb men l-ɛubudiya.* He freed the people from slavery. **2.** to save, to deliver *nežžat d-drari men l-ɛafya.* She saved the children from the fire. **3.** to protect, to preserve *ḷḷah inežžik!* (May) God preserve you!
nežžaṛ pl. *-a* carpenter
nežžem v.i. to be able *ma-nežžmu-š ixeṛžu l-bareḥ ɛla wedd kanu ɛăndhom ḍ-ḍyaf.* They couldn't go out yesterday because they had guests.
nžeḥ v.i. (v.n. *nažaḥ*) **1.** to succeed *dima ka-inžeḥ fe-t-tižaṛa.* He always succeeds in business. **2.** to pass *xtu ma-nežḥet-š f-le-mtiḥan.* His sister didn't pass the exam.
nḥaf pl. of *nḥif* (same as *nḥil*)
nḥal pl. of *nḥil*
nḥas **1.** copper **2.** bronze
nḥasi pl. *-yen* **1.** made of copper **2.** coppery, copper colored **3.** copper-plated
nḥaysi pl. *-ya* tinsmith
nḥif pl. *-in, nḥaf* same as *nḥil*
nḥil pl. *-in, nḥal* thin, sickly, weak
nḥila dim. of *nḥăl*
nḥiṛ v.n. of *nḥeṛ*
nḥis pl. *-in* ill-fated, unlucky
nḥăl n.u. *neḥla* (dim. *nḥila*) bee
nḥăll same as *tḥăll*
nḥeṛ v.t. (v.n. *nḥiṛ*) to slaughter
năḥwi pl. *-yen* **1.** grammarian **2.** grammatical
neḥḥa v.t. to get rid of completely, to exterminate
neḥḥal pl. *-a* beekeeper, apiarist
nɛal leather for shoe soles
nɛala pl. *-t, nɛayel* (pair of) sandals
nɛam yes (replied when one's name has been called or when answering a request)
** *nɛam-as!* Sir! (used especially by students when addressing a teacher)
nɛam n.u. *-a* ostrich
nɛas **1.** v.n. of *nɛăs* **2.** sleep
¶ *bihφ* (or *fihφ*, or *žahφ*) *n-nɛas* to be sleepy ≠
¶ *ddahφ n-nɛas* to fall asleep ≠ *ddani n-nɛas.* I fell asleep.
nɛaš pl. *-at, nɛuša* stretcher, litter
nɛayel pl. of *nɛala*
nɛayem pl. of *năɛma*
nɛaž pl. of *năɛža*
nɛil v.n. of *nɛăl*
nɛăl v.t. (v.n. *nɛil*) to curse at, to call (s.o.) names
¶ *nɛăl š-šiṭan* **1.** to calm down (from anger) **2.** to become reconciled
năɛnaɛ cpl. *nɛaneɛ* mint (plant, pleaves)
năɛža pl. *-t, nɛaž* ewe
năɛla n.i. of *nɛăl*
năɛma pl. *-t, nɛayem* food (considered as a gift from God and therefore demanding respect) *baṛaka u-ma-ḍḍiyyăɛ nɛămt ḷḷah!* Stop wasting God's food!
nɛăs v.i. (v.n. *nɛas*) **1.** to sleep, to go to sleep **2.** to stop *magantek năɛset.* Your watch has stopped. **3.** to be quiet, motionless
năɛsa n.i. of *nɛăs*
¶ *ḍṛebha b-năɛsa* to sleep soundly *žbeṛtha ḍaṛbaha b-năɛsa.* I found her sleeping soundly.
năɛt **1.** v.n. of *năɛɛăt* **2.** pl. *nɛut* adjective, modifier
nɛuša pl. of *nɛaš*
nɛut pl. of *năɛt 2*
năɛɛăs v.t. to put to sleep,, to put to bed
năɛɛăt v.t. (v.n. *tenɛat, tenɛit, năɛt*) **1.** to point out (with finger), to indicate **2.** to describe, to give description of *waxxa năɛɛăttiha-li ma-ɛqelt-š ɛliha.* Although you described her for me, I couldn't remember her. **3.** to tell about *l-bareḥ mšit l-dak ṣ-ṣuq lli năɛɛătti-li.* Yesterday I went to that market you told me about.

Q

qabeḍ a.p. of *qbeḍ*
qabil Cain (biblical)
qabiliya **1.** attention, consideration *ma-ka-yăɛṭi qabiliya le-wladu.* He doesn't give his children any attention. **2.** energy, effort *ma-zal fiha l-qabiliya l-l-xedma.* She still feels she has enough energy to work.
qabel v.t. (v.n. *mqabla*) **1.** to take care of, to

attend *ɛămmti lli qablet ḅḅa melli kan mṛiḍ.* My aunt took care of my father when he was ill. **2.** to meet, to have an encounter with (as in a contest) **3.** to meet with, to encounter *qablet ṣuɛuba kbira.* She met with great difficulty. **4.** to be in front of, to face **5.** to be the partner of (e.g., card game)

qabla pl. *-t, qwabel* midwife

qabul v.n. of *qbel* 1 and 3

qadd v.t. **1.** to level *xeṣṣhom iqaddu ṭ-ṭṛiq.* They have to level the road. **2.** to compare *ma-ka-imken-lek-ši tqadd telmid mɛa l-ˀustad dyalu.* You can't compare a pupil with his teacher.

qadim used in the expr.

¶ *fe-l-qadim, f-qadim z-zaman* in olden times

qadum pl. *qwadem* hoe

qaḍa v.t. (v.n. *mqaḍya*) **1.** to finish, to be through *qaḍaw xdemthom qbel mennu.* They finished their work before he did. **2.** to use up *le-flus lli ɛṭah xah kollhom qaḍahom.* He used up all the money his brother gave him. —*qaḍaw s-sokkaṛ lli šrit l-bareḥ.* They used up the sugar I bought yesterday.

¶ *qaḍa b-* to finish with, to be through with —*qaḍiti b-le-ktaba?* Are you through writing? —*mnayn iqaḍi b-had r-riša xudha.* You may have this pen when he's through with it.

¶ *qaḍa men* **1.** to stop (doing s.th.) *ma-ka-ibġi-š iqaḍi men l-heḍṛa.* He never wants to stop talking. **2.** to give up *ḅḅa qaḍa men d-doxxam.* My father gave up smoking. **3.** to finish with, to be through with *mnayn nqaḍi men had l-makina ġad-nbiɛha.* When I'm through with this machine I'm going to sell it.

¶ *qaḍa mɛa* **1.** to exhaust, to use up *qaḍaw băɛda mɛa le-flus lli-ɛṭahom ḅḅahom.* They've already used up the money their father gave them. **2.** to exhaust, to tire *ṣ-ṣfeṛ ṭ-ṭwil dima ka-iqaḍi mɛaha.* A long trip always tire her. **3.** to break (up) with *ma-ɛṛeft-ši ɛlaš qaḍa mɛa ṣḥabu kollhom.* I can't understand why he broke with all his friends.

qaḍa, qaḍaˀ **1.** predestination (theological) **2.** calamity, disaster

qaḍi pl. *quḍat* judge (justice)

qaḍiya pl. *-t* **1.** thing, matter *mša išufu ɛla ši-qaḍiya muhimma.* He went to see him about an important matter. **2.** case *qaḍiytu duwwzetha l-meḥkama.* His case has been judged by the court.

qaḍăṛ **1.** destiny **2.** means *ma-ɛăndu qaḍăṛ baš išriha.* He doesn't have the means to buy it. **3.** capability *ma-bqa-lu qaḍăṛ le-rkub l-xeyl melli wqăɛ-lu l-ˀafat.* He's no longer able to ride horses since he had the accident. **4.** authority *qolt-lha temši tšuf l-mudir li-ˀenna ma-ɛăndi-š l-qaḍăṛ baš nxelliha texṛož.* I told her to go and see the director because I don't have the authority to let her go out.

qaḍaṛi pl. *-yen* one who believes in predestination

qaḍus pl. *qwaḍes* **1.** drain **2.** gutter

qafiya pl. *-t, qawafi* rhyme

qahṛa pl. *-t* poverty, misery

¶ *nsa l-qahṛa* to be a parvenu

qaˀima pl. *-t* list, roster

qal iqil v.t. (v.n. *mqayla, iqala*) **1.** to leave alone, to give peace to *qul le-d-drari iqilu l-qeṭṭ ɛlihom.* Tell the children to leave the cat alone. **2.** to grant (s.o.) a cancellation of sale or agreement (if the latter is unsatisfactory) *kanet šrat tlata de-ṛ-ṛadyuyat men ɛăndu u-mnayn ma-ɛăžbuha-š qalha fihom.* She had bought three radios from him, and when she didn't like them he gave her her money back. **3.** to fire, to dismiss *qaluh men l-menṣib dyalu.* They dismissed him from his position.

qal iqul (v.n. *qewl*) **1.** v.t. to say *šnu qalet melli dexlet?* What did she say when she came in? —*kif tqul had š-ši be-n-negliza?* How would you say this in English? **2.** v.t. to tell (the person told s.th. is introduced by the prep. *l-*) *qolt-lu ibqa mɛana.* I told him to stay with us. —*ma-qalu-li-š smiytu.* They didn't tell me his name. **3.** v.i. to think about, to plan to, to intend *ka-iqul ġad-imši l-l-meġrib f-had ṣ-ṣif.* He's thinking about going to Morocco this summer.

¶ *ka-iqulu* they say, it is said *ka-iqulu ka-iṭiḥ t-telž ġedda.* They say it's going to snow tomorrow. —*had š-ši lli ka-iqulu.* That's what they say.

¶ *qal l-* to call *š-ka-tqulu l-hadi be-l-ɛăṛbiya?* What do you call this in Arabic?

¶ *qal-luφ ṛasuφ* (or *ɛăqluφ*) to like, to please ≠ *ma-iɛămlu ġir lli qal-lhom ɛqelhom.* They only do what they please.

¶ *tqul* it seems, it looks like *tqul š-šta ġad-tenzel.* It looks like it's going to rain. —*duk le-wlad ma-tqul-š xut.* Those boys don't look like brothers.

¶ *u-tqul* used to show absolute shortage or absence (uttered with more stress and higher pitch than the remainder of the sentence) *u-tqul bqa-lu derhem waḥed.* He doesn't have a single dirham left. —*žberti ši-waḥed temma?—u-tqul!* Did you find anyone there?—Not a soul.

qala pl. *-t, qyel* cubit

qala (also *qalak*) used in stressing the contrary of a statement or situation *ma-dazet-š f-le-mtiḥan—dazet, qala.* She didn't pass her examination.—Yes, she did! —*ṛak ġad-tuwṣel mɛăṭṭel.—qala ya-weddi.* You're going to be late.—Oh, no, I'm not! —*nɛăyyṭu-lu qala u-nfessru-lu koll-ši.* On the contrary, we should call him and explain everything to him.

qalaba pl. *-t* turbulence, disturbance

¶ *nwwed qalaba* to raise Cain

qalak same as *qala*

qalaq impatience *l-qalaq dyalu ka-iʔeddi bih l-l-mašakil.* His impatience gets him into trouble.

qalayba same as *qalaba*

qaleb pl. *qwaleb* **1.** mold **2.** shoe-tree **3.** sugar loaf (coneshaped)

qales Cadiz

qam iqim v.t. (v.n. *qiman, qyum*) **1.** to prepare, to brew (tea, coffee) **2.** to furnish, to supply

¶ *qam ṣ-ṣla* to announce a prayer (Muslim) at the time of its performance

qam iqum v.i. (v.n. *qyam*) **1.** to get up, to arise *qam men mudɛu u-gelles s-siyda.* He got up from his place and seated the lady. —*qemna bekri had ṣ-ṣbaḥ.* We got up early this morning. **2.** to start, to begin *huwa lli qam ka-isebbhom.* He's the one who started calling them names. **3.** to start, to break out *had š-ši wqăɛ qbel-ma tqum l-ḥăṛb.* This happened before the war started. —*l-ɛafya qamet f-daṛhom.* A fire broke out in their house. —*debza qamet binathom.* A fight broke out between them. **4.** to stage *l-ɛommal qamu b-mudahaṛa l-bareḥ.* The workers staged a demonstration yesterday.

¶ *qam b-* **1.** to take care of *xellih iqum be-ḍ-ḍyaf.* Let him take care of the guests. **2.** to perform, to do, to play *kan f-ʔimkanu iqum b-waḥed ḍ-duṛ muhimm fe-l-muʔtamaṛ.* He could have played an important role at the conference.

** *qamet le-mnaḥa ɛlih.* He was mourned.

qama pl. *-t* stature, height *ḅḅah ṛažel qamtu kbira.* His father is a tall man.

qamižža pl. *-t, qwamež* (dim. *qwimža, qwimižža*) shirt

qamus pl. *qwames* dictionary

qana pl. *-t* ditch, canal

qanabil pl. of *qonbula*

qanal pl. *-at* canal

qanṣa pl. *-t, qwaneṣ* gizzard

qanun pl. *qwanen* **1.** regulation, law **2.** zither

qaqa v.i. (v.n. *mqaqya*) to cackle

qaṛaba (family) relationship *ɛăndek ši-qaṛaba mɛa l-ʔustad dyalek?* Do you have any family relationship with your teacher?

qarabala pl. *-t* racket, hullabaloo, commotion *aš had-l-qarabala lli ka-nesmăɛ fe-z-zenqa?* What's the racket I hear in the street?

qaṛaṛ pl. *-at* **1.** decision **2.** decree

qaṛaṣina pl. of *qoṛṣan*

qaṛi a.p. of *qṛa*

qaṛib same as *qṛib* (relative)

qariḥa pl. *-t* zeal, enthusiasm *ɛăndu qariḥa kbira fe-xdemtu ž-ždida.* He has a lot of enthusiasm for his new work.

qaṛṭaxenna **1.** Carthage **2.** Cartagena (Spain)

** *sir ḥetta l-qaṛṭaxenna!* Go to the devil!

qas iqis v.t. **1.** to touch *ṛasu ka-iqis s-sqef.* His head touches the ceiling. **2.** to stain *qaset ksewtha b-la-mdad.* She stained her dress with ink. **3.** to hurt, to offend *ma-bġa yăɛmel mulaḥaḍa baš ma-iqis ḥădd.* He didn't want to make any remark in order to avoid hurting someone.

qaṣa v.i. (v.n. *mqaṣya*) to suffer, to endure, to go through hardship

qaṣaʔiḍ pl. of *qaṣiḍa*

qaṣeḍ a.p. of *qṣeḍ*

qaṣiḍa pl. *-t, qaṣaʔiḍ* poem (usually lengthy)

qaṣeḥ pl. *-in* (comp. *qṣeḥ*) **1.** thick (liquid) **2.** rugged **3.** harsh, cruel *hadik mṛa qelbha qaṣeḥ.* She is a hard-hearted woman. **4.** rough, severe *l-berd ža qaṣeḥ had l-ɛam.* We've had a rough winter this year. **5.** difficult *le-mtiḥan kan qaṣeḥ.* The examination was difficult.

¶ *ṛaṣuᶲ qaṣeḥ* to be stubborn ≠

qatel v.t. or v.i. (v.n. *qital, mqatla*) to fight, to combat

qaṭeɛ a.p. of *qṭăɛ*

qawafi pl. of *qafiya*

qawaɛid pl. of *qaɛida*

qawel v.t. (v.n. *mqawla*) to promise, to give one's word *qawelt xti baš nddiha le-s-sinima.* I promised my sister I would take her to the movies. —*qawlu ḅḅah b-ṛadyu ždid.* His father promised him a new radio.

qawem v.t. (v.n. *mqawma*) to withstand, to repel, to hold off

qayed pl. *qiyyad, qoyyad* administrative head of a county

¶ *qayed l-mešweṛ* Master of Ceremonies at the Royal Palace

qayla pl. *qwayel* **1.** hottest part of a summer day **2.** blazing summer sun

qayma same as *qaʔima*

qaɛ pl. *qiɛan* **1.** bottom **2.** pedestal **3.** buttocks, rump **4.** sole (foot or shoe)

¶ *qaɛ d-derb* end of a street

¶ *qaɛ le-blad* (the) heart of town

¶ *qaɛ-qolla* cardamom

¶ *weld* (*bent*) *l-qaɛ u-l-baɛ* one who has lived in the city all his life, and who comes from a well-known family

qaɛa pl. *-t* **1.** market for fats and dry fruit **2.** housewarming *ġad-iɛămlu l-qaɛa le-ḍḍaṛ ž-ždida.* They're going to have a housewarming for the new house.

qaɛida pl. *-t, qawaɛid, qwaɛed* **1.** rule *ɛṭini ši-qaɛida ntmešša ɛliha.* Give me a rule I can follow. **2.** principle *men qaɛidti ma-ka-nsellef ḥădd ma-ka-isellefni.* One of my principles is never to lend or borrow. **3.** habit, manner *fiha qaɛida qbiḥa, dima ka-dži mɛăṭṭla.* She has the bad habit of always coming late. —*ɛăwwed-li ɛăl l-qawaɛid de-l-makla fe-bladkom.* Tell me about the table manners in your country. **4.** custom *l-qawaɛid de-z-zwaž bdat ttbeddel fe-l-meġṛib.* Marriage customs are changing in Morocco. **5.** base *l-ḥukuma l-ʔamirikiya ɛăndha ɛadad de-l-qawaɛid ɛăskariya fe-l-xariž.* The U.S. Government has many military bases abroad.

¶ *bla qaɛida* improperly

¶ *be-l-qaɛida, ɛăl l-qaɛida* properly, correctly, (in) the proper way

qbab pl. of *qobb*

qbaḍi pl. of *qebḍa*

qbala **1.** v.n. of *qbel* 2 **2.** well, very well, thoroughly *had l-bit xeṣṣu itneḍḍef qbala.* This room needs to be cleaned thoroughly.

qbalt in front of, facing

qbaqeb pl. of *qebqaba*

qbaṭi pl. of *qebṭa* (same as *qebḍa*)

qbaṭen pl. of *qebṭan*

qbaybi pl. *-ya* same as *qebbab*

qbayel pl. of *qbila*

qbayla a while ago *qbayla wṣelna.* We arrived a while ago

¶ *men qbayla* (for) quite a while *men qbayla u-ḥna nessennaw.* We've been waiting for quite a while.

qbaḥ v.i. (v.n. *qbaḥa*) **1.** to get bad *l-ḥala s-siyasiya bdat teqbaḥ.* The political situation is getting bad. —*sirtu qbaḥet bezzaf.* His conduct got very bad. **2.** to become bad-looking, to look bad or ugly *qbaḥet melli qeṣṣṛet šɛăṛha.* She looks ugly since she had her hair cut short.

qbaḥ pl. of *qbiḥ*

qbaḥa **1.** v.n. of *qbaḥ* **2.** pl. *-t* villainy

qbeb pl. of *qobba*

qobb pl. *qbab* **1.** hood *kebbuṭi de-š-šta ma-fih qobb.* My raincoat doesn't have a hood. **2.** bucket, wooden pail

qobba pl. *-t, qbeb* (dim. *qbiba*) **1.** dome, cupola **2.** the best furnished room of a house, used as a living-room (usually isolated from other rooms and having a domed ceiling) **3.** shrine built around the tomb of a saint

¶ *bna* (or *ɛmel*) *l-qobba l-* to give a big build-up to, to overpraise

¶ *dfăɛ l-qobba* to boast

qebbab pl. *-a* cooper

qebbaḍ pl. *-a* same as *qabeḍ* (a.p. of *qbeḍ*)

qebbeb v.t. to give the shape of a dome to

¶ *qebbeb le-ɛbaṛ* to measure generously (wheat, flour, etc. in a measuring cup)

qebbel **1.** v.t. to kiss **2.** v.i. to face Mecca (e.g., when praying)

qebbeṛ v.t. **1.** to bury **2.** to hide, to conceal

qebbeṭ v.t. to make a bundle of (mint leaves, carrots, etc.)

¶ *qebbeṭ b-* **1.** to make (s.o.) get hold of *škun lli qebbṭek b-had l-makina de-t-teṣwiṛ?* How did you get hold of this camera? **2.** to put into a situation (usually undesirable) *biɛa u-šerya b-aš qebbṭuh!* What a deal they got him into!

¶ *qebbeṭ l-* **1.** to burden, to "stick" with *qebbṭu-lha t-teftiš d-le-myaḍi.* They stuck her with the inspection of the toilets. **2.** to inflict upon *qebbeṭ-lu waḥed ḍ-ḍeṛba qaṣḥa.* He inflicted a heavy blow upon him.

¶ *qebbeṭ le-klam l-* to make sarcastic remarks to

qbeḍ v.t. (v.n. *qbiḍ, qbuḍ, qebḍ*) **1.** to take, to accept *ma-bġa iqbeḍ le-flus men ɛănd ḥădd.* He didn't want to accept money from anyone. **2.** to hold *ḷḷah ixellik qbeḍ-li had ṣ-ṣenduq ɛla-ma năɛmel waḥed t-tilifun.* Would you please hold this box for me while I make a phone call? **3.** to get, to receive *qbeḍti le-xlaṣ de-š-šheṛ lli daz?* Did you get last month's pay? **4.** to collect (rent, tax, etc.) **5.** to catch *qebḍuh ka-isṛeq.* They caught him stealing. **6.** to arrest, to detain *qebḍuh l-bulis l-bareḥ.* The police arrested him yesterday. **7.** to keep, to retain *kont nawi nbat ɛăndhom lila weḥda, saɛa qebḍuni telt iyyam.* I was intending to spend one night with them, but they kept me for three days. **8.** to constipate *ma-ka-takol-š t-teffaḥ ɛla ḥăqq ka-iqbeḍha.* She doesn't eat apples because they constipate her.

¶ *qbeḍ f-* **1.** to hold on to, to hang on to *ṭaḥ ḥit ma-ṣab fayn iqbeḍ.* He fell because he couldn't find anything to hold on to. **2.** to stick to, to keep *meṣṣab ġir iqbeḍ fe-klamu.* I just hope he sticks to his word. **3.** to abide by, to practice *hadak ṛažel ka-iqbeḍ fe-l-mabadiʔ dyalu.* He's a man who abides by his principles.

¶ *qbeḍ l-qeššaba ɛla* to tease, to poke fun at

¶ *qabeḍ* pl. *qobbaḍ* **1.** cashier **2.** collector (rent, tax, etc.)

¶ p.p. *meqbuḍ* **1.** constipated **2.** reserved, reticent

qebḍ v.n. of *qbeḍ*

qebḍa pl. *-t, qbaḍi* **1.** n.i. of *qbeḍ* **2.** handle (hammer, rake, broom, suitcase, etc.) **3.** knob (of door) **4.** bundle, bunch (mint leaves, vegetables)

qbel **1.** v.t. (v.n. *qbul, qabul*) to accept, to admit *qeddmet ṭ-ṭalab be-l-ḥăqq ma-qebluha-š.* She applied but was not accepted. **2.** v.t. (v.n. *qbala*) to midwife, to assist a mother in childbirth **3.** v.i. (v.n. *qbul, qabul*) to consent, to agree

** *qbelt u-ṛḍit.* O.K., I accept.

qbel, qbel men before *weṣlet qbel le-ġda.* She arrived before dinner. —*qaḍat šġalha qbel menni.* She finished her work before me.

¶ *men qbel* previously, before(hand), already *šeft had r-riwaya men qbel.* I've already seen this play.

¶ *qbel-ma, qbel-la* before (conj.) *ġsel yeddik qbel-ma takol.* Wash your hands before you eat. —*ṣellat qbel-ma tenɛăs.* She prayed before she went to sleep. —*ġad-nɛăyyeṭ-lhom qbel-la imšiw.* I'm going to call them before they leave.

¶ *ɛla qbel* because *ma-šeftha-š ɛla qbel xeržet bekri.* I didn't see her because she left early.

qebla direction (toward Mecca) faced when praying

qebqaba pl. *-t, qbaqeb* sandal made of wooden sole and a leather strap

qbeṛ same as *qbuṛ*

qbeṭ same as *qbeḍ*

qebṭa same as *qebḍa*

qebṭan pl. *-at, qbaṭen* captain (military)

qbeḥ comp. of *qbiḥ*

qbiḍ v.n. of *qbeḍ*

qbila pl. *-t, qbayel* tribe

qbiba dim. of *qobba*

qbiḥ pl. *qbaḥ* (comp. *qbeḥ*) bad, unpleasant *had l-lḥăm riḥtu qbiḥa.* This meat smells bad. —*dima ka-tšedd nuqaṭ qbaḥ f-le-ḥsab.* She always gets bad grades in mathematics. —*l-žuw kan qbiḥ dak n-nhaṛ.* The weather was bad that day.

qbuḍ v.n. of *qbeḍ*

qbul **1.** v.n. of *qbel* **2.** charm, amiability

** *ɛlih le-qbul.* He's pleasant-looking.

qbuṛ pl. *-a, mqabeṛ* grave, tomb

qbuṛa pl. of *qbuṛ*

qdam v.i. to get old, used (thing) *ḥwayžu mnayn ka-iqdamu ka-isiyyebhom.* When his clothes get old, he throws them away.

qdam pl. of *qdim* and *qdem* **2** (same as *gdem*)

qedd v.t. **1.** to be enough for, to suffice *l-xobz lli ɛăndna ma-iqedd-š l-le-ġda.* The bread we have won't be enough for lunch. **2.** to be able (physically or morally) *daba tqedd texṛož ḥit bṛat.* Now that she's recovered she can go out.

¶ *qedd ɛla* **1.** to afford *f-had s-saɛa ma-nqedd ġir ɛla siyaṛa neṣṣ lebsa.* For the time being I can only afford a second-hand car. **2.** to be able to bear, stand, or endure *imken tɛăžbek dak le-blad ila tqedd ɛăl ṣ-ṣehḍ dyalha.* You might like that country if you can stand its heat.

qedd **1.** size, stature, height *xtu bent qeddha meṛbuɛ.* His sister is a medium-sized girl. **2.** the size of *ka-inɛăs f-bit qedd ṭ-ṭabaqa dyalna.* He sleeps in a room the size of our classroom. —*wella qedd bḅah fe-ṭ-ṭul.* He became as tall as his father. **3.** the equal of, on a par with (rank, position)

¶ *ža qedd* to fit *šuf kan had l-keswa dži qeddek.* See if this dress fits you.

¶ *qedd qedd* **1.** the same, equal (in age, size, rank, etc.) *hiya u-ṛaželha qedd qedd fe-ṭ-ṭuḷ.* She's as tall as her husband. —*škun lli kbeṛ, huwa wella hiya?—b-zuž qedd qedd.* Who's the older, he or she?—They're both the same age. **2.** exactly *weṣlet fe-s-sebɛa qedd qedd.* She arrived exactly at six. **3.** the same size as, as big (small) as *qeddu qedd ši-tuṛ.* He's as big as an ox.

¶ *qedd-aš, qedd-aš-en* **1.** how big (small, tall, long, etc.) *qedd-aš ḍ-ḍaṛ lli kritiw?* How big is the house you rented? —*qedd-aš t-tisaɛ dyal dak l-bit?* How wide is that room? —*qol-lna qedd-aš kanet l-xoṭba dyalu.* Tell us how long his speech was. —*xeṣṣek tšuf xtu qedd-aš-en hiya fe-ṭ-ṭul.* You should see how tall his sister is. **2.** indicates intensification of an idea *qedd-aš ka-teḥseb f-ṛaṣha.* She thinks a lot of herself. —*qedd-aš-en huwa ɛănd waldih.* His parents think a whole lot of him.

¶ *ɛla qedd* according to (means) *ka-iɛiš ɛla qedd meṣwaṛu.* He lives according to his earnings.

qeddaf pl. *-a* oarsman, rower

qeddam, qoddam **1.** near, beside *ka-iseknu qeddam s-sinima.* They live near the theater. **2.** ahead of, before *ġir sir qeddami le-ḍ-ḍaṛ, ana ġad-nži mɛăṭṭel.* You can go home ahead of me, I'll be coming late. **3.** in front of *kan gales qeddami fe-s-sinima.* He was sitting in front of me at the movies. **4.** in front of, in the presence of, before *ma-ka-ibġi-š ikmi qeddam waldih.* He doesn't like to smoke in front of his parents. **5.** (the) front *qolna-lhom izidu l-goddam.*

We told them to move up to the front. **6.** (up) ahead *ƹṛefti šnu hadak qeddamna?* Do you know what that is up ahead of us? **7.** a movement in Moroccan Andalusian music (e.g., *qoddam le-ġriba*)

qedded v.t. to cut up in small pieces (especially meat before smoking it)

qeddef v.i. to row

qeddid n.u. *-a* meat cut up to be smoked

qeddem v.t. **1.** to introduce *bġiṭ nqeddmek l-waḥed s-siyyed ṣaḥbi ƹad ža men ʔamirika.* I want to introduce you to a friend of mine who has just arrived from America. —*škun ġad-iqeddem l-muḥaḍiṛ.* Who's going to introduce the speaker? **2.** to give precedence to *băƹḍ n-nas ka-iqeddmu le-mlaġa ƹăl l-xedma.* Some people give pleasure precedence over work. **3.** to put in (request, application) *bġat tqeddem ṭ-ṭalab ƹla dak l-xedma.* She wants to put in an application for that work. **4.** to name or appoint as *mqeddem* **5.** to appoint as guardian *men qbel ma-imut qeddem m̄m̄u ƹla wladu.* Before he died, he appointed his mother as guardian over his children.

¶ part. *mqeddem* pl. *-in* **1.** official in charge of one precinct of a city **2.** guardian

qeddeṛ same as *qeḍḍeṛ*

qeddes v.t. to revere, to venerate

qeddeḥ v.t. **1.** to hit (s.o.) on the top of the head with the palm of the hand, or with both hands joined **2.** to humiliate (s.o.) by refuting a statement of his

qdim pl. *qdam* (comp. *qdem*) old, used *ġad-iṭiyyḥu le-bni le-qdim.* They're going to tear down the old building.

qdira dim. of *qedra*

qdem ƹla (v.n. *qdum*) **1.** to drop in on (unexpectedly) **2.** to tackle, to undertake

qdem **1.** comp. of *qdim* **2.** pl. *qdam* same as *gdem*

qdeṛ same as *qḍeṛ*

qedra pl. *-t, qdur* (dim. *qdira*) **1.** clay pot (cooking) **2.** dish of meat or fowl prepared with vegetables and butter or oil

qods in *l-qods š-šarif* and *bit l-qods* Jerusalem

qdum v.n. of *qdem*

qdur pl. of *qedra*

qduḥa pl. of *qdeḥ*

qdeḥ pl. *qduḥa* **1.** small container (old and used, usually of metal) **2.** chamber pot

qedḥiya pl. *-t* n.i. of *qeddeḥ*

qḍa iqḍi (v.n. *mqeḍya, qoḍyan*) **1.** v.t. to accomplish, to achieve *lli bġina kollu qḍinah.* We achieved all that we wanted. —*ši ma-qḍah.* He didn't accomplish a thing. **2.** v.t. to get, to buy *š-xeṣṣna neqḍiw l-le-ġda?* What do we have to buy for lunch? **3.** v.i. to get by *dak š-ši lli rbeḥ ka-iqḍi bih.* Whatever he earns he gets by on.

¶ *qḍa b-* to use *ƹăndek ši-mqeṣ neqḍi bih?* Do you have a pair of scissors I can use?

¶ *qḍa l-* **1.** to do (s.o.) good, to be beneficial to, to be good for *qḍa-lha ši dak d-dwa?* Did that medicine do her any good? **2.** to be enough for, to suffice *imken iqḍiw-lu le-flus lli ƹṭaweh waldih.* The money his parents gave him might be enough for him.

¶ *qḍa ḥaža b-* **1.** to use *qḍat ḥaža be-l-mus u-ṛeddettu.* She used the knife and brought it back. **2.** to take advantage of *ġir qḍaw bih ḥaža u-ṣafṭuh f-ḥalu.* They just took advantage of him and sent him away.

qḍa same as *qaḍa, qaḍaʔ*

qeḍḍeṛ **1.** to decree, to cause to happen (God) *ṛebbi qeḍḍeṛ l-mut ƹla koll-ši.* It's God's will that everyone should die. —*lehla iqeḍḍeṛ ƹlina ši-ḥăṛb ƹawed.* I hope we don't have another war. **2.** to estimate, to make an estimate of *qeḍḍeṛna tlatin alef derhem l-dak ḍ-ḍaṛ.* We estimated that house at 30,000 dirhams. **3.** to esteem, to have respect for *koll-ši ka-iqeḍḍeṛ-lu xdemtu.* Everyone esteems his work.

qḍeṛ v.i. **1.** to be able *ma-qeḍṛu-š ixeṛžu bekri.* They couldn't leave early. —*qalt-lek teqḍeṛ ƹla had l-xedma.* She said she could do this work. **2.** to be able to afford (*ƹla* before n. and pron.) *ma-neqḍeṛ-š nḍiyyăƹ had l-weqt kollu.* I can't afford to waste so much time. —*ila teqḍeṛ ƹla dak ḍ-ḍaṛ, ġir šriha.* If you can afford that house, go ahead and buy it.

qḍeṛ **1.** means, possibility *ma-ƹăndu-š le-qḍeṛ baš išri ḍaṛ xṛa.* He doesn't have the means to buy another house. **2.** amount, sum *žah qḍeṛ kbir d-le-flus men bladu.* He received a large sum of money from his country. **3.** esteem, importance, high regard *koll-ši ka-iƹăḍḍem qḍeṛhom.* Everybody holds them in high regard (because of their social position).

¶ *ṭaḥ qeḍṛu*ᶲ to be held in low regard ≠, to lose the respect of others ≠

¶ *ṭiyyeḥ men qḍeṛ l-* to show disrespect for, to be disrespectful toward (usually in an embarrassing manner) *ṭiyyḥet-lu men qeḍṛu.* She showed disrespect for him.

¶ *ƹla qḍeṛ* according to, in proportion to *koll waḥed ka-irbeḥ ƹla qḍeṛ l-xedma lli ka-yăƹmel.* Each one earns according to the work he performs.

qoḍra **1.** power, authority *ma-ƹăndu-š l-qoḍra baš ixeddem n-nas.* He doesn't have the authority to hire people. **2.** capability, aptitude, competence *ṛ-ṛaʔis ka-iqelleb* ع*la ši-wa*ح*ed* ع*ăndu l-qoḍṛa* ع*la had l-xedma.* The president is looking for someone with the capability for this work. **3.** omnipotence (God)

¶ *žabettu*$^{\phi}$ *l-qoḍṛa* by chance ≠ *ila žabettu l-qoḍṛa dayez . . .* If by any chance he comes by . . .

qeḍya pl. *-t* n.i. of *qḍa*

qoḍyan v.n. of *qḍa*

qfa iqfi v.t. (v.n. *qefyan*) **1.** to interrupt, to stop (s.o.) abruptly in a conversation **2.** to ostracize (children's language)

qfa pl. *-wat, qfi* nape, back of the neck

qfafel pl. of *qeffal*

qfal pl. of *qfel*

qfaṭen pl. of *qefṭan*

qfaz pl. of *qfez*

qfef pl. of *qoffa*

qoffa pl. *qfef* straw basket with two handles

qeffal pl. *qfafel* piece of cloth with which the parts of the double boiler used for making *seksu* are sealed

qeffel v.t. to seal (a double boiler) with a *qeffal*

qefferha~ ع*la* to put (s.o.) in a difficult situation (by denouncing him, accusing him, or taking his possessions away)

qfi pl. of *qfa*

qfil v.n. of *qfel*

qfiz v.n. of *qfez*

qfel v.t. (v.n. *qfil*) **1.** to lock, to put a padlock on **2.** to complete *š-šheṛ l-maži ġad-iqfel* ع*ešrin* ع*am de-l-xedma m*ع*a l-*ح*ukuma.* Next month he'll complete twenty years of work for the government. **3.** v.t. and v.i. to close, to end *ġad-nqeflu l-žem*ع *be-l-kalima dyalu.* We're going to close the meeting with his talk. —*moddt temn snin qeflet.* The eight-year period has ended.

¶ *qfel* ع*la* **1.** to shut in **2.** same as *qeffel*

qfel pl. *qfal, qful, qfula* padlock

qefqafa n.i. of *qefqef*

qefqef v.i. to tremble, to shiver

qefṭan pl. *qfaṭen* caftan, long-sleeved robe with girdle

qful, qfula pl. of *qfel*

qfuza pl. of *qfez*

qefya n.i. of *qfa*

qefyan v.n. of *qfa*

qfez v.i. (v.n. *qfiz*) to start, to jump, to dart

qfez pl. *qfaz, qfuza* cage

qefza pl. *-t* n.i. of *qfez*

qhawi pl. of *qehwa*

qhiṛ v.n. of *qheṛ*

qheṛ v.t. (v.n. *qhiṛ*) **1.** to beat, to overcome *l-feṛqa dyalna qehṛethom fe-l-mubaṛat.* Our team beat them at the tournament. **2.** to oppress, to treat unjustly

qehwa pl. *-t, qhawi* **1.** coffee **2.** café (usually with emphasis on coffee, tea, etc.) **3.** tip (money)

qehwaži pl. *-yen* café owner, café manager

qehwi pl. *-yen* dark brown

qibal see ع*la qibal*

qil used in the expr. *l-qil u-l-qal* gossip

qima pl. *-t* **1.** importance ع*ṭaw qima kbira l-le-ktab dyalu.* They attached great importance to his book. **2.** cost, price *š*ح*al qimt had ḍ-ḍaṛ?* What's the price of this house? **3.** approximately, about *šrina qimt tlata kilu de-l-l*ح*ăm.* We bought about three kilos (weight) of meat.

qiman v.n. of *qam iqim*

qiqlan n.u. *-a* mimosa

qisari pl. *-yen* cloth merchant

qisariya pl. *-t* cloth market

qital v.n. of *qatel*

qiṭan pl. *qyaṭen* silk cord

qiyama **1.** resurrection **2.** commotion, tumult

¶ *yum l-qiyama* Judgment Day

qiyyad pl. of *qayed*

qiyyed v.t. **1.** to register, to put down (as in records) **2.** to appoint as *qayed*

qiyyel v.i. to spend the day, to stay all day *qiyyelt ka-neṣbeġ ḍ-ḍaṛ l-baṛe*ح. I spent the day painting the house yesterday.

qiyyes, qiyyeṣ v.t. **1.** to measure *qiyyeṣ š-šeṛžem qbel-ma tešri l-xamiya.* Measure the window before you buy the curtain. **2.** to try on *qiyyest dak ṣ-ṣebbaṭ sa*ع*a ma-ža-š qeddi.* I tried those shoes on but they didn't fit me.

*qiyye*ح v.i. to suppurate, to fester, to form pus

*qi*ح pl. *qyu*ح*, qyu*ح*at* pus

*qi*ع*an* pl. of *qa*ع

qla iqli v.t. **1.** to fry **2.** to roast (beans, peas, etc.)

qladi pl. of *qelda*

qlal pl. of *qlil*

qlaleš pl. of *qelluš, qellušа*

qlaq same as *qalaq*

qlaqel pl. of *qelqula*

*qla*ع*at* pl. of *qlă*ع

qleb v.t. (v.n. *qlib*) **1.** to turn *bqa ka-iqleb ṣ-ṣef*ح*at bla-ma iqṛahom.* He kept turning the pages without reading them. **2.** to turn over *ka-teqleb le-mṭeṛṛbat meṛṛa fe-š-šheṛ.* She turns the mattresses over once a month. —*qleb le-ṣ-ṣef*ح*a xemsa u-ṛeb*ع*in.* Turn (over) to page 45. **3.** to knock over, to tip over *qelbet ṭ-ṭenžṛa mnayn kanet t*ح*ărrekha.* She knocked the pot over while she was stirring it. **4.** to turn upside down *qlebt ṣ-ṣenḍuq baš nexwih.* I turned the box upside down to empty it. **5.** to put in disorder, to make a mess of **6.** to change, to alter, to misinterpret *l-žarida qelbet-lu* *t-teṣriḥ lli dar.* The newspaper altered the statement he made. 7. to break up (soil)

¶ p.p. *meqlub* pl. *-in* 1. inside out *lbes tqašṛu meqlubin.* He wore his socks inside out. 2. upside down

¶ *be-l-meqlub* backwards, the wrong way *ka-yăɛmel koll-ši be-l-meqlub.* He does everything the wrong way. —*ḥetta huma ka-iketbu be-l-meqlub?* Do they write backwards, too?

qelb pl. *qlub* 1. heart *had le-mṛiḍ qelbu ḍɛif.* This patient has a weak heart. 2. interior, inside *xeṣṣek tšuf qelb dak le-qṣeṛ.* You should see the interior of that palace. —*yaḷḷah ndexlu l-qelb ḍ-ḍaṛ, temma nheḍṛu.* Let's go inside the house, we can talk there.

¶ *be-l-qelb* wholeheartedly

¶ *bqa f-qelbu*$^\phi$*, ɛmel f-qelbu*$^\phi$ to be offended by (or because) *bqa f-qelbha lli ma-ža-š ɛăndha fe-l-ɛid.* She was offended that he didn't come to her house for the celebration.

¶ *men qelb* out of, (out) from inside of

¶ *naḍ-lu*$^\phi$ *qelbu*$^\phi$ to feel nausea $\neq$, to be nauseated $\neq$

¶ *nuwweḍ l-qelb l-* to nauseate

¶ *qelbu*$^\phi$ *kbir* (to be) generous, (to be) bighearted

¶ *qeṭṭăɛ l-qelb l-* to break (s.o.'s) heart

¶ *ɛṭa qelbu l-* to buckle down to, to apply oneself resolutely to

qelda pl. *-t, qladi* height, stature (implies large)

¶ *qelda u-hemma* of fine appearance *ḅḅah ṛažel qelda u-hemma.* His father is a man of fine appearance.

qlib v.n. of *qleb*

qlil rarely, seldom, not very often *ka-temši tɛum?—qlil.* Do you ever go swimming? —Rarely. —*qlil f-aš ka-ixeṛžu mežmuɛin.* They seldom go out together.

qlil pl. *qlal* (comp. *qell*) 1. rare, scarce *t-tlamed l-mezyanin qlal f-had l-medṛaṣa.* Good students are rare in this school. 2. slight, little, insignificant *kayen feṛq qlil fe-t-taman.* There's a slight difference in the price. 3. insufficient, not enough *ɛṭawna l-makla qlila.* They didn't give us enough food.

¶ *qlil* (f. *qlilt*) *l-ˀadăb* (or *ṣ-ṣwab*) impolite, ill-mannered

¶ *qlil l-fayda* good for nothing

¶ *qlil* (f. *qlilt*) *le-ḥya* impudent, saucy

¶ *qlil n-nefs* lacking in self-respect or pride

¶ *qlil ṣ-ṣeḥḥa* weak (physically by nature)

qliɛ v.n. of *qlăɛ*

qell same as *qellel*

qell comp. of *qlil* —*ṭiyybet xizzu qell men baṭaṭa.* She cooked less carrots than potatoes. —*ka-itxeḷḷeṣ qell mennek.* He's paid less than you are.

¶ *qell-emma f-* the worst of

¶ *ɛla qell ḥaža,* or *ɛla qell men hiya ḥaža* for the slightest reason

qlel pl. of *qolla*

qella v.t. to simmer or let simmer

qella lack, shortage

¶ *qellt l-ˀadăb* (or *ṣ-ṣwab*) lack of manners, impoliteness

¶ *qellt l-fayda* uselessness

¶ *be-l-qella* at least

¶ *qellt l-ḥămd* ingratitude (to God)

¶ *qellt le-ḥya* impudence, insolence

¶ *qellt š-ši* indigence

¶ *ɛla qellтha fayda* for a trifle, for no reason

qolla pl. *-t, qlel* measuring can (used especially for oil)

qellan v.n. of *qell* (same as *qellel*)

qelleb v.t. 1. to examine, to give a physical examination to 2. to search (person, place) 3. to try, to try out *nebġi nqelleb dik s-siyaṛa qbel-ma nešriha.* I would like to try that car out before I buy it.

¶ *qelleb ɛla* to look for

qellel men to reduce, to diminish *bġaw iqelllu-lu men lˀožṛa dyalu.* They wanted to reduce his salary. —*mnayn tewṣeḷ l-ši-lewya qellel men ṣ-ṣoṛɛa.* When you reach a curve, reduce the speed.

¶ *qellel le-ḥya ɛla* to become disrespectful toward or with (s.o.)

qelleq v.t. 1. to irritate, to irk 2. to worry, to upset *le-xbaṛ lli wṣeḷni ɛlihom mqelleqni.* The news I received about them is worrying me.

qelluš, qelluša pl. *-t, qlaleš* type of clay pot for keeping water

qellăɛ 1. v.t. to pull up, to extract, to pull out *ṛ-ṛiḥ be-kteṛt ž-žehd dyalu ḥetta qellăɛ š-šežṛa.* The wind was so strong that it pulled up the tree. —*ṭ-ṭbib qellăɛ-li ḍeṛṣa l-bareḥ.* The dentist pulled out one of my teeth yesterday. 2. v.i. to leave (uncommon usage) *xeṣṣna nqellɛu bekri ḥit ġad-nemšiw ɛla režlina.* We have to leave early since we're going to walk. 3. to take off (airplane) *ṭ-ṭiyaṛa ġad-tqellăɛ men daba qṣem.* The plane is going to take off in five minutes.

qlam pl. *qluma* pencil *ka-tekteb b-le-qlam aw be-ṛ-ṛiša?* Are you writing with a pencil or a pen?

¶ *qlam de-l-lwan* coloring pencil

¶ *qlam d-le-xfif* lead pencil

qelqel v.t. to shake, to jerk, to jolt
qelqula pl. *-t, qlaqel* wen, tumor on the scalp
qlub pl. of *qelb*
qluma pl. of *qlam*
qluع pl. of *qlăع*
qelya n.i. of *qla*
qlăع (v.n. *qliع*) **1.** v.t. to copy (e.g., text) **2.** v.i. to cheat *šedduh ka-iqlăع f-le-mtiحan.* He was caught cheating in the examination.
qlăع pl. *qlaعat, qluع* **1.** canvas **2.** sail (of boat)
** *žmăع qluعek!* Beat it! Get out of here!
qmaqem pl. of *qemqum*
qmaš pl. *qmayeš* cloth, material
qmayeṣ pl. of *qmiṣ*
qmayeš pl. of *qmaš*
qmiṣ pl. *qmayeṣ* long shirt with long, broad sleeves
qmel n.u. *qemla* louse
qemmaṛ pl. *-a* **1.** gambler **2.** swindler
qemmel v.i. to become infested with lice
qemmeṛ (v.n. *taqemmaṛt, qmeṛ*) **1.** v.t. to steal, to swipe **2.** v.i. to gamble
qemqum pl. *qmaqem* muzzle, snout
qmeṛ **1.** v.n. of *qemmeṛ* **2.** game of chance, gambling
qemṛun n.u. *-a* shrimp
qmul same as *qmel*
qmežža same as *qamižža*
qemحi pl. *-yen* **1.** wheat colored **2.** golden tan (skin) *lunha qemحi.* She has a golden tan.
qnadel pl. of *qendil*
qnafed pl. of *qenfud*
qnanef pl. of *qennufa*
qnaneṭ pl. of *qennuṭ*
qnaṭeṛ pl. of *qenṭaṛ* and *qenṭṛa*
qnaعa v.n. of *qnăع*
qenbula pl. *qanabil* bomb
qendil pl. *qnadel* oil lamp
qendiša n.i. of *qendeš*
¶ *عayša qendiša* siren, female monster in Moroccan mythology
qendrisa in expr. *serwal qendrisa* Moroccan garment similar to knee pants, very full, without an inseam
qenfud pl. *qnafed* hedgehog
qniṭ v.n. of *qneṭ*
qniṭṛa dim. of *qenṭṛa*
qniya pl. *-t* rabbit
qniع v.n. of *qnăع*
qennariya artichoke stalk (used as vegetable)
qenneb **1.** hemp **2.** n.u. *qennba* pl. *-t, qnaneb* string, cord
qennet v.t. to fold (s.th. e.g., cloth, paper) so as to have pointed corners
qenneṭ v.t. **1.** to bore *dak n-nuع de-l-ʔaflam ka-iqenneṭni.* That kind of movie bores me. **2.** to roll, to give the shape of a roll (e.g. pastry)
qennufa pl. *-t, qnanef* upper lip when thick and turned up
¶ *hezz qennuftuᵠ* to sulk, to pout
qennuṭ pl. *qnaneṭ* **1.** spool (of thread) **2.** roll (e.g. of pastry)
qennăع v.t. to satisfy, to please *dima ka-iqennăعni be-xdemtu.* I'm always pleased with his work.
qent pl. *qnut* corner *melli dxel u-huwa gales f-dak l-qent.* He's been sitting in that corner ever since he came in.
qneṭ v.i. (v.n. *qenṭ, qniṭ* to get bored, to get tired *mnayn ka-tebqa wحedha fe-ḍ-ḍaṛ ka-teqneṭ.* When she stays home by herself she gets bored. —*waš عămmeṛhom ma-ka-iqenṭu bla šġal?* Don't they ever get tired of doing nothing? —*ila qneṭṭi men had l-xedma nšufu-lek weحda ẋṛa.* If you get tired of this job we can find you another one.
qenṭ v.n. of *qneṭ*
qenṭaṛ pl. *qnaṭeṛ* quintal, one hundred kilograms
qenṭṛa pl. *-t, qnaṭeṛ* (dim. *qniṭṛa*) bridge *had l-wad ġad-ibniw عlih tlata d-le-qnaṭeṛ.* They're going to build three bridges across this river.
qnut pl. of *qent*
qnuعi pl. *-yen* contented
qnăع v.i. (v.n. *qniع, qnaعa*) to be satisfied, to feel contented *dak š-ši lli rbeح ka-iqnăع bih.* He feels satisfied with whatever he earns.
qṛa iqṛa v.t. and v.i. (v.n. *qṛaya*) **1.** to read *koll ṣbăح ka-neqṛa l-žarida.* I read the newspaper every morning. **2.** to study, to go to school, to be a student *ka-nḍenn ġad-iqṛa ṭ-ṭibb.* I think he's going to study medicine. —*f-ayna žamiعa baġya xtek teqṛa?* At what university does your sister want to study? —*qal-lek ġad-ibda iqṛa mعana.* He says he's going to start going to school with us. —*kollhom ka-iqṛaw fe-t-tanawi.* They are all high school students.
¶ *qṛa l-ʔaman f-* to have confidence in, to trust *huwa qṛa fiha l-ʔaman be-l-حăqq hiya xedعăttu.* He trusted her, but she failed him.
¶ *qṛa le-حsifa f-* to bear (s.o.) a grudge, to have a grudge against
¶ *qṛa l-عaqiba d-* to foresee the consequences of
¶ *qṛa s-slam l-* (or *عla*) to give regards to *qṛa-li s-slam عla عămmek.* Give my regards to your uncle.
¶ *qṛa xiṛ* to be grateful to, to show gratitude *huwa ka-iqṛa xiṛek.* He's grateful to you.
¶ *qṛa عla* **1.** to study under *qṛit عla nefs le-fqi lli qeṛṛa ḅḅa.* I studied under the

same teacher who taught my father. **2.** to pray for (a deceased person) by reading verses of the Koran (over the grave, at the funeral or any time later for memorial purposes)

¶ a.p. *qaṛi* pl. *qaṛyen* educated, learned

qṛab **1.** pl. of *qṛib* **2.** pl. *-at* creel, wicker basket

qrafed pl. of *qerfada*

qramed pl. of *qermud*

qṛamel pl. of *qoṛmil*

qṛan pl. of *qṛin*

qoṛʔan (with art.) Koran

qṛaqeb pl. of *qeṛqaba*

qṛaṛen pl. of *qeṛṛan*

qṛaṛeṣ pl. of *qeṛṛaṣa*

qṛaṣen pl. of *qoṛṣan*

qṛašel **1.** pl. of *qeṛšal* **2.** n.u. *qeṛšala, qṛišla* type of bread baked with sesame, aniseed and sugar

qṛašli pl. *-ya* carder, one who cards

qṛaṭi pl. of *qeṛṭa*

qṛaṭeṣ pl. of *qoṛṭaṣ* **2**

qṛaya v.n. of *qṛa*

qṛaعi pl. of *qeṛعa*

qṛeb comp. of *qṛib*

qoṛb **1.** v.n. of *qeṛṛeb* **2.** nearness

qoṛb yellowish, brown-banded ocean fish

qoṛba pl. of *qṛib*

qerbla pl. *-t* same as *qarabala*

qerd pl. *qrud, qruda* monkey, small ape

qeṛfa cinnamon

qerfada pl. *-t, qrafed* thick nape, back of the neck (pejorative)

¶ *bu-qerfada* one with a thick back of the neck (pejorative)

¶ *ṛebba l-qerfada* **1.** to get fat **2.** to get rich

qerfed v.t. to hit (s.o.) on the back of the neck

¶ p.p. *mqerfed* having a stout, thick neck (person)

qeṛfi pl. *-yen* cinnamon-colored

qṛib pl. *qṛab* (comp. *qṛeb*) **1.** near, close *l-žamiعa qṛiba men ḍaṛhom.* The university is near their house. **2.** insignificant, negligible, very little *kayen feṛq qṛib fe-t-taman.* There's very little difference in the price. **3.** simple *mesʔala حalha qṛib hadik.* That's a simple matter. **4.** soon *weldna qṛib isali qṛaytu.* Our son will soon finish his studies. **5.** about to *kan qṛib irbeح l-žaʔiza.* He was about to win the prize. **6.** just *qṛib baš xrežna men عăndhom.* We've just left their place.

qṛib pl. *qṛab, qoṛba, quṛaba, ʔaqaṛib* relative *عăṛḍu ġir عăl le-qṛab dyalhom.* They invited just their relatives.

qṛin pl. *qṛan* peer, one of the same age or rank *weldek xeṣṣu ibda ixṛož mعa qṛanu šwiya.* Your son needs to start going out some with kids his own age.

qṛina wrath, violent anger

¶ *ḍeṛbettuʰ le-qṛina عla* (s.o.) to be crazy about ≠

qṛiq v.n. of *qṛeq*

qṛiṣ v.n. of *qṛeṣ*

qṛiṣa dim. of *qeṛṣa*

qṛišla n.u. of *qṛašel* **2**

qṛiṭ v.n. of *qṛeṭ*

qṛiṭa dim. of *qeṛṭa*

qṛiحa same as *qaṛiحa*

qṛiعa dim. of *qeṛعa* (n.u. of *qṛăع*)

qermed v.t. to tile (roof)

qoṛmil pl. *qṛamel* kind of three-legged block with which the shoemaker works

qermud n.u. *-a* pl. *qramed* roofing tile

qeṛn **1.** pl. *qṛun* horn *dak t-tuṛ qṛunu maḍyen.* That bull has sharp horns. **2.** pl. *quṛun* century

¶ *l-quṛun l-wesṭa* the Middle Ages

qṛonfel n.u. *qṛonfla* clove

qṛeq v.t. (v.n. *qṛiq*) to hatch (eggs)

qeṛqaba pl. *-t, qṛaqeb* large metal castanet

qeṛqeb v.t. **1.** to slam *ḷḷah ixellik ma-tعăwwed-š tqeṛqeb l-bab.* Please don't slam the door again. **2.** v.t. or v.i. to jingle, to rattle *l-عătrus ka-iqeṛqeb le-kbel.* The goat is rattling the shackle. —*le-flus ka-iqeṛqbu f-žibu.* The money is jingling in his pocket.

qeṛqeṛ v.i. to croak

qeṛṛ same as *gerr*

qeṛṛa v.t. **1.** to teach, to give lessons in (s.th.) to (s.o.) *had ṣ-ṣbaح le-fqi qeṛṛana ḍeṛṣ ždid.* This morning the teacher taught us a new lesson. **2.** to send to school, to educate *xeṣṣni nweffeṛ le-flus baš nqeṛṛi wladi.* I have to save money so I can send my children to school.

qeṛṛan pl. *-a, qṛaṛen* cuckold

qorraqiya pl. *-t* screwhook

qeṛṛaṣa pl. *-t, qṛaṛeṣ* clothespin

qeṛṛeb v.t. (v.n. *qoṛb*) **1.** to bring closer *qeṛṛeb dak š-šelya u-gles حdaya.* Bring that chair closer and sit near me. **2.** to touch *ma-kayen-ši lli qeṛṛeb-lek حwayžek mnayn konti ġayeb.* Nobody touched your things while you were away. **3.** v.i. to move closer *qeṛṛeb lle-hna baš nsemعek.* Move closer over here so I can hear you.

qerred v.i. **1.** to kneel down **2.** to cower

qeṛṛeṣ same as *geṛṛeṣ*

qeṛṛăع v.t. **1.** to make bald **2.** to shave off (hair of head) **3.** to strip, to make bare by removing removable parts (such as a room)

qṛeṣ v.t. (v.n. *qṛiṣ*) **1.** to pinch, to squeeze (between finger and thumb) **2.** to afflict, to distress **3.** to pull the trigger of

¶ *qṛeṣ ʕănyuᶲ* to close one's eye half-way
¶ p.p. *meqṛuṣ* half-shut, droopy (eye; from physical defect)
qeṛṣ pl. *qṛuṣ, qṛuṣa* trigger
¶ *ḍṛeb l-qeṛṣ* to pull the trigger
qeṛṣa pl. *-t* (dim. *qṛiṣa*) n.i. of *qṛeṣ*
qoṛṣan pl. *qaṛaṣina, qṛaṣen* pirate
qeṛšal pl. *qṛašel* carding brush
qeṛšala n.u. of *qṛašel* 2
qeṛšel v.t. to card (wool, cotton, etc.)
qṛeṭ v.t. (v.n. *qṛiṭ*) to wring (laundry, mop)
¶ *qṛeṭ f-* to slander
qeṛṭa pl. *-t, qṛaṭi* (dim. *qṛiṭa*) 1. chopping board 2. guillotine
qoṛṭaṣ 1. n.u. *-a* bullet, cartridge, shell (also empty) 2. pl. *qṛaṭeṣ* carton (tobacco, candles, etc.)
qeṛṭeṣ v.t. 1. to shoot (s.o.), to riddle with bullets 2. to put into a carton
qeṛṭaxenna same as *qaṛṭaxenna*
qeṛṭuba Cordoba
qrud, qruda pl. of *qerd*
qṛun pl. of *qeṛn* 1
qṛuṣ, qṛuṣa pl. of *qeṛṣ*
qṛuʕa, qṛuʕiya scalp disease
qeṛwiyen (with art.) Mosque and University of Fez
qeṛya pl. *-t* village
qṛăʕ f. *qeṛʕa* pl. *quṛăʕ* 1. one afflicted with scalp disease 2. bare (such as a place from which furniture has been removed)
qṛăʕ n.u. *qeṛʕa* pl. *qṛaʕi* (dim. *qṛiʕa*) 1. gourd 2. bottle (not ink bottle, although dim. may be used for ink cartridge)
¶ *qṛăʕ taxṛifin* (or *tixṛifin*) zucchini squash
¶ *qṛăʕ ḥămṛa* pumpkin
qoṛʕa drawing of lots
¶ *ḍṛeb l-qoṛʕa* to draw lots *ḍeṛbu l-qoṛʕa u-šufu škun lli ġadi ixelleṣ fikom.* Draw lots and see which one of you is going to pay.
qsawa harshness, cruelty
qsem same as *qṣem*
qosṭal n.u. *-a* chestnut
qosṭali, qosṭli pl. *-yen* chestnut (color)
qṣabi pl. of *qeṣba*
qṣam pl. of *qṣem*
qṣami pl. of *qeṣma*
qṣaṛ v.i. to get short(er) *fe-l-berd n-nhaṛ ka-iqṣaṛ.* In winter the day gets shorter.
qṣaṛ pl. of *qṣiṛ*
qṣaṛi pl. of *qeṣṛiya*
qṣayeḍ pl. of *qṣiḍa*
qṣayḍi pl. *-ya* ballad singer, balladeer
qṣayeṣ pl. of *qeṣṣa*
qṣaḥ v.i. (v.n. *qṣuḥa, qṣuḥiya*) 1. to thicken, to get thick *ila qṣaḥet le-ḥrira zidha šwiya de-l-ma.* If the soup gets thick, add some water to it. 2. to become severe, hard *l-mudir bda iqṣaḥ mʕa t-tlamed.* The principal is becoming severe with the pupils.
qṣeb n.u. *qeṣba* reed (plant)
qeṣba pl. *-t, qṣabi* (dim. *qṣiba*) 1. reed (plant) 2. flute made of reed
¶ *qeṣba de-r-ržel* shin
qeṣbiya (also *bṭaṭa qeṣbiya*) Jerusalem artichoke
qeṣbuṛ coriander
qṣeḍ v.t. (v.n. *qeṣḍ*) 1. to turn to, to call on *qeṣḍethom baš iʕawnuha.* She turned to them for help. 2. to mean, to have in mind *š-ka-iqṣeḍ be-ḍ-ḍebṭ?* What does he mean exactly?
¶ a.p. *qaṣeḍ* pl. *-in* straight *mšaw le-ḍ-ḍaṛ qaṣḍin.* They went straight home.
¶ p.p. *meqṣuḍ* pl. *maqaṣiḍ* aim, purpose, goal
¶ *be-l-qeṣḍ* on purpose, intentionally
qṣiba dim. of *qeṣba*
qṣiḍa pl. *qṣayeḍ* ballad
qṣim v.n. of *qṣem*
qṣiṛ pl. *qṣaṛ* (dim. *qṣiweṛ, qṣiṣeṛ;* comp. *qṣeṛ*) 1. short, little *hiya qṣiṛa u-dzuwwžet b-ṛažel ṭwil.* She's short and she married a tall man. 2. low *had l-ḥăyṭ qṣiṛ bezzaf.* This wall is too low.
qṣiṣeṛ, qṣiweṛ dim. of *qṣiṛ*
qṣem v.t. (v.n. *qṣim*) 1. to cut, to cut up *ʕṭini ši-mess baš neqṣem l-xobz.* Give me a knife to cut the bread with. 2. to divide *qeṣmu had le-flus binatkom be-tlata.* Divide this money among the three of you. —*qeṣmet l-ḥălwa kollha ʕăl d-drari.* She divided all the cake among the children.
¶ p.p. *meqṣum* dividend (arithmetic)
¶ *meqṣum ʕlih* divisor (arithmetic)
qṣem du. *qeṣmayn* pl. *qṣam* a period of five minutes *hadi l-xemsa u-qṣem.* It's five past five. —*qeṣmayn w-ana waqef temma.* I stood there for ten minutes.
¶ *qṣiyyem* (dim.) a moment, a minute *imken-li nšufek ši-qṣiyyem?* Could I see you a minute?
qeṣma pl. *-t, qṣami* 1. n.i. of *qṣem* 2. part, portion 3. division (mathematics) 4. part (hair)
qṣeṛ 1. comp. of *qṣiṛ* 2. pl. *qṣuṛ, qṣuṛa* palace, castle
qeṣṛiya pl. *-t, qṣaṛi* large earthenware bowl used for kneading dough
qeṣṣa pl. *-t, qṣayeṣ* 1. story, tale 2. occurrence, incident, affair
qeṣṣem same as *qṣem*
qeṣṣeṛ v.t. or v.i. 1. to shorten, to cut short *qeṣṣṛet ksewtha ḥit kanet ṭwila bezzaf.* She shortened her dress because it was too long. —*ḍteṛṛina nqeṣṣṛu ṣ-ṣfeṛ dyalna.* We had

to cut our trip short. **2.** to sit up, to stay up *l-bareɛ qeṣṣeṛna ɛetta le-t-tlata.* Yesterday we stayed up till three o'clock. **3.** to spend the evening among company (chatting, playing cards, dancing, etc.) **4.** to fall short of, or not match up to expectations (especially in reference to a duty) *qeṣṣeṛ fe-xdemtu.* He didn't match up to expectations in his work.

¶ *ma-qeṣṣeṛ-š* to do one's best *ma-qeṣṣṛu-š mɛana.* They've done their best with us.

¶ *qeṣṣeṛ ṭ-ṭriq* to stop over (on a journey)

qeṣṣeṣ v.t. to chop, to mince *xeṣṣek tqeṣṣeṣ le-mɛădnus.* You have to chop the parsley.

qeṣṣeɛ v.t. **1.** to thicken, to make thick (liquid) **2.** to hurt (physically, s.o.'s feelings, etc.)

qṣuṛ qṣuṛa pl. of *qṣeṛ*

qṣuɛa, qṣuɛiya v.n. of *qṣaɛ*

qṣeɛ comp. of *qaṣeɛ*

qšali pl. of *qešla*

qšaš pl. of *qešš*

qšašeb pl. of *qeššaba*

qšaweš pl. of *qešwaša*

qšiṛa dim. of *qešṛa*

qšiwša dim. of *qešwaša*

qešla pl. *-t, qšali* barracks

qešqaša pl. *qšaqeš* baby rattle

qešṛa pl. *-t, qšuṛ* (dim. *qšiṛa*) **1.** bark **2.** peel, rind **3.** crust **4.** shell, pod (nuts, peas) **5.** scale (fish) **6.** shell, carapace **7.** (flake of) dandruff

qešš pl. *qšaš, qšuš, qšuša* **1.** luggage **2.** furniture **3.** odds and ends

qeššaba pl. *-t, qšašeb* woolen outfit of the *žellaba* type

** *qeššabtu wasɛa.* He's very patient.

¶ *qbeṭ l-qeššaba ɛla* to tease *ġir dxel qbeṭna ɛlih l-qeššaba.* As soon as he came in we began to tease him.

¶ *qeṭṭăɛ qeššabt* (plus n. or pron.) to slander, to backbite

qeššeṛ v.t. **1.** to strip bark off (a tree) **2.** to scale (fish) **3.** to peel **4.** to shell

¶ part. *mqeššeṛ* lacking knowledge (on some subject)

qšuṛ pl. of *qešṛa*

qšuš, qšuša pl. of *qešš*

qešwaša pl. *-t, qšaweš* (dim. *qšiwša*) **1.** any object (such as tool, utensil) used for a specific purpose **2.** toy **3.** (pl.) things *hezzet qšawešha u-mšat.* She took her things and left.

qšăɛ v.t. to see, to glance at

qtil v.n. of *qtel*

¶ *qtil ṛ-ṛuɛ* **1.** murder, killing, slaughter **2.** used in describing a boisterous crowd

qtila pl. *-t* **1.** n.i. of *qtel* **2.** murder *weqɛăt waɛed le-qtila l-bareɛ.* There was a murder last night.

qtel v.t. (v.n. *qtil*) **1.** to kill **2.** to murder, to assassinate **3.** to be deadly *had l-madda ka-teqtel.* This substance is deadly. **4.** to execute *l-bareɛ qetlu lli meɛkumin ɛlihom be-l-ʔiɛdam.* Those sentenced to death were executed yesterday. **5.** to finish, to complete *ma-xrežna ɛetta qtelna ṭ-ṭeṛɛ.* We didn't leave until we finished the game (cards, chess, etc.)

¶ *qtel ṛaṣuᵠ* to commit suicide

qettal adj. pl. *-in* n.pl. *-a* ag. adj. and ag. n. of *qtel*

¶ *qettal ṛ-ṛuɛ* murderer

qṭab pl. of *qoṭb*

qṭaṛi pl. of *qeṭṛa*

qṭaṛni pl. *-ya* tar dealer

qṭaṭɛi pl. *-ya* **1.** swindler **2.** brigand, highwayman

qṭayeb pl. of *qṭib*

qṭaɛi pl. of *qeṭɛa*

qoṭb pl. *qṭab* pole (axial)

¶ *l-qoṭb š-šamali* the North Pole

¶ *l-qoṭb l-žanubi* the South Pole

qeṭban, qoṭban pl. of *qṭib*

qṭib pl. *qeṭban, qoṭban, qṭayeb* **1.** stick, twig **2.** poker, bar (wood or metal) **3.** spit, skewer

qṭiṛ v.n. of *qṭeṛ*

qṭiṭa dim. of *qeṭṭa*

qṭiɛ v.n. of *qṭăɛ*

qṭen, qṭon cotton

qoṭniya dried food (especially beans and peas)

qṭeṛ v.i. (v.n. *qṭiṛ*) **1.** to drip, *l-ma ka-iqṭeṛ men ṣ-ṣqef.* The water is dripping from the ceiling. **2.** to drip dry *xellit ɛwayži iqeṭṛu.* I let my clothes drip dry.

qeṭṛa pl. *-t, qṭaṛi* **1.** drop (liquid) **2.** leak *had l-bit fih l-qeṭṛa.* There is a leak in this room.

qeṭṛan tar, pitch

qeṭṛen v.t. **1.** to tar **2.** to smear, to get very dirty

qeṭṭ pl. *qṭuṭ* tomcat

¶ *qeṭṭ le-xla* wildcat

qeṭṭa pl. *-t* (dim. *qṭiṭa*) cat (f.)

qeṭṭab pl. *-a* ag. n. of *qeṭṭeb*

qeṭṭaṛa pl. *-t* **1.** alembic, apparatus used in distillation **2.** dropper, glass tube with rubber suction cap for doling out liquids (primarily medicines) drop by drop

qeṭṭaɛ pl. *-a* same as *qṭaṭɛi*

qeṭṭeb v.t. beat (s.th., e.g. wool) with a stick

qeṭṭeṛ **1.** v.t. to distil **2.** v.t. to pour or let fall in drops **3.** v.i. to fall in drops, to leak

qeṭṭăɛ v.t. **1.** to cut *ha s-sekkin baš tqeṭṭăɛ l-lɛăm.* Here's a knife you can cut the meat with. 2. to tear, to rip (paper, cloth) 3. to make or help cross *qeṭṭăƹnahom l-wad.* We helped them cross the river. 4. to buy a ticket *qeṭṭăƹt-lhom ṛebƹa d-le-wṛaq le-ṛ-riwaya.* I bought them four tickets for the play.

¶ *qeṭṭăƹ l-qelb l-* to break the heart of (s.o.)

qṭuṭ pl. of *qeṭṭ*

qṭuƹ v.n. of *qṭăƹ*

qṭuƹa, qṭuƹiya acidity, sourness

qṭăƹ v.t. (v.n. *qṭiƹ, qṭuƹ, qeṭƹan*) 1. to break(off) *qṭăƹna l-ƹalaqat d-diblumasiya mƹa dak le-blad.* We've broken diplomatic relations with that country. 2. to abstain from (food, drink, pleasure), to stop, to cut out *mnayn ka-nkun mṛiḍ ka-neqṭăƹ l-makla lli ka-ḍḍeṛṛ.* When I'm sick I abstain from harmful food. —*ṭ-ṭbib qṭăƹ ƹlih d-doxxan.* The doctor told him to stop smoking. 3. to cut off *qeṭƹu-lu ḍ-ḍuw ḥit hadi sett šhuṛ ma-xeḷḷeṣ.* They cut off his electricity because he hasn't paid for six months. —*qeṭƹu-lha yeddha.* They cut her hand off. 5. to cross (road, bridge, river) 6. to go through *qṭăƹna l-ġaba f-neṣṣ l-lil.* We went through the forest in the middle of the night. —*ƹad qeṭƹăt ˀeṣƹăb meṛḥala.* She's just gone through the most difficult stage.

¶ *qṭăƹ l-* to wean (suckling) *had le-wliyyed ƹad qeṭƹăt-lu ṃṃu.* This little boy's mother has just weaned him.

¶ *qṭăƹ ṛ-ṛaṣ l-* to settle (affair, business)

¶ *qṭăƹ ṭ-ṭṛiq ƹla* to rob (said of highwaymen)

¶ a.p. *qaṭeƹ* pl. *-in* (comp. *qṭăƹ*) 1. very sharp (blade) 2. keen, sharp (intellectually) 3. strong, acid (food, drink)

¶ *l-ma l-qaṭeƹ* sulfuric acid

qṭăƹ comp. of *qaṭeƹ* (a.p. of *qṭăƹ*)

qeṭƹa pl. *-t, qṭaƹi* 1. n.i. of *qṭăƹ* 2. piece, fragment 3. flock, herd

¶ *be-l-qeṭƹa* by contract, by the job *l-xeddama f-had l-măƹmel kollhom ka-itxeḷḷṣu be-l-qeṭƹa.* All the workmen in this factory are paid by the job.

qeṭƹan v.n. of *qṭăƹ*

¶ *qeṭƹan ṭ-ṭṛiq* brigandage

qubeƹ n.u. *-a* pl. *-t, qwabeƹ* lark

qudamaˀ (pl.) used in the expr. *qudamaˀ l-muḥaribin* veterans (of military service)

quḍat pl. of *qaḍi*

quleb v.t. to mold

qum pl. *qwam* the masses, people

quma n.i. of *qam*

qunut invocation recited during the morning prayer

quq n.u. *-a* (dim. *qwiqa*) artichoke

quṛaba pl. of *qṛib*

quṛaṛa pl. *-t, qwaṛeṛ* 1. device or receptacle used in bloodletting, cupping glass 2. stain, large spot (blood, grease, etc.) 3. round hole (in cloth)

quṛun pl. of *qeṛn* 2

quṛăƹ pl. of *qṛăƹ*

qut food, sustenance

quwwa pl. *-t* 1. strength, vigor, energy 2. force, power *ddaweh be-l-quwwa.* They took him away by force.

¶ *l-quwwat l-musellaḥa* the Armed Forces

¶ *b-quwwt* 1. so much *ḍaḷa ƹlihom b-quwwt l-xedma ḥetta ma-bqaw-š ixeṛžu.* He gave them so much work that they stopped going out. 2. so many *b-quwwt n-nas lli kanu ma-žbeṛna fayn nweqfu.* There were so many people we couldn't find a place to stand.

¶ *men quwwt* from just *imṛeḍ l-waḥed men quwwt le-glas bla šġal.* One can get sick from just sitting around doing nothing.

qwa iqwa v.i. 1. to get strong(er), (more) powerful *zadu šraw s-slaḥ baš iqwa l-žeyš.* They bought more arms so the army would be stronger. 2. to increase *ƹadadhom ġir ka-iqwa.* They keep increasing in number. 3. to worsen, to get worse *ila qwa ƹliha le-ḥriq ƹăyyeṭ le-ṭ-ṭbib.* If her pain gets worse, call the doctor.

qwa comp. of *qwi*

qwabel pl. of *qabla*

qwabeƹ pl. of *qubƹa* (n.u. of *qubeƹ*)

qwadem pl. of *qadum*

qwaḍes pl. of *qaḍus*

qwaḍsi pl. *-ya* plumber

qwaleb pl. of *qaleb*

qwam pl. of *qum*

qwames pl. of *qamus*

qwamež pl. of *qamižža*

qwanen pl. of *qanun*

qwaneṣ pl. of *qanṣa*

qwaṛeṛ pl. of *quṛaṛa*

qwaṣ, qwaṣat pl. of *qewṣ*

qwawed pl. of *qewwad*

qwayel pl. of *qayla*

qwaƹed pl. of *qaƹida*

qwi pl. *-yen* (comp. *qwa*) 1. strong, powerful 2. energetic 3. large in number 4. high (price)

qwimižža, qwimža dim. of *qamižža*

qwiqa dim. of *quq*

qewl v.n. of *qal iqul*

qewm same as *qum*

qewṣ pl. *qwaṣ, qwaṣat* 1. arch, arcade 2. bow (archery, violin) 3. small room for storing charcoal (usually near the kitchen or in the basement)

¶ *qewṣ n-nbi* rainbow
qewwa v.t. to reinforce, to strengthen
qewwad pl. *-a, qwawed* pander, pimp
qewwam pl. *-a, -in* appraiser
qewwed v.t. and v.i. to solicit, to lure (s.o.) for immoral purposes
qewwem v.t. **1.** to prepare (with the necessary gear) *qewwem ɛăwdek u-yaḷḷah nemšiw.* Get your horse ready and let's go. **2.** to wake up *ila žbeṛtiha naɛsa qewwemha.* If you find her asleep wake her up. **3.** to evaluate, to estimate at **4.** to equip with
qewweṛ v.t. **1.** to cover with stains **2.** to cut round holes in (e.g. cloth) **3.** to cut in round pieces (e.g. dough) **4.** to earn (money)
qewweṣ v.t. to curve, to arch, to give the shape of an arch to
qewwet v.t. to nourish *had l-makla ka-tqewwet.* This food is nourishing.
qyada function of a *qayed*
qyam **1.** v.n. of *qam iqum* **2.** very thin weaving thread of fine quality
qyas, qyaṣ pl. *-at* **1.** measurement *had le-qyaṣat ma-ši huma haduk.* These measurements are not correct. **2.** size *š-men qyaṣ ka-ilbes?* What size does he wear?
¶ *bla qyaṣ* excessively, too much *ka-ibġi l-makla bla qyaṣ.* He likes food too much.
¶ *b-le-qyaṣ* sparingly
¶ *šedd* (or *xda*) *le-qyaṣ* to take measurements *l-xeyyaṭ xda-li le-qyaṣ.* The tailor took my measurements.
qyaṭen pl. of *qiṭan*
qyel pl. of *qala*
qeylula hottest period of the day in summer
qyum v.n. of *qam iqim*
qyuɛ, qyuɛat pl. of *qiɛ*
qeyy vomit
qeyya v.t. **1.** to cause to vomit **2.** to nauseate
qoyyad pl. of *qayed*
qeyyal pl. *-in* ag. adj. of *qeyyel*
qzader pl. of *qezdira*
qzadri pl. *-ya* tinsmith
qezbuṛ same as *qeṣbuṛ*
qezdir n.u. *-a* tin, sheet metal
qezdira pl. *-t, qzader* tin, can (container)
qezder v.t. to tin, to galvanize
¶ part. *mqezder* used in the expr. *wežhuφ mqezder* (to be) nervy, brazen
qezqez v.t. and v.i. to joggle, to bounce up and down
qezzeb v.t. **1.** to shorten, to clip, to trim **2.** to gyp, to swindle
qezziba pl. *-t* tail (especially when short)
qžaymi same as *qežžam* (ag. n. of *qžem*)
qžim v.n. of *qžem*
qžem v.i. (v.n. *qžim*) to joke, to jest
¶ *qžem ɛla* to tease, to make fun of
qežma pl. *-t* n.i. of *qžem*
qžeṛ pl. *qžuṛa* **1.** drawer (of desk, table, etc.) **2.** case (watch, clock, pencils)
qžuṛa pl. of *qžeṛ*
qežž v.t. (v.n. *qežžan*) to strangle
qežža n.i. of *qežž*
qežžam pl. *-a* ag. n. of *qžem*
qežžan v.n. of *qežž*
qẓab pl. of *qeẓba*
qẓeb (taboo) v.i. (v.n. *qẓub*) to prostitute oneself
qeẓba (taboo) pl. *-t, qẓab* prostitute
qeẓṭ same as *keẓṭ*
qẓub v.n. of *qẓeb*
qăɛɛăd v.t. **1.** to cause to stagnate **2.** to sift, to strain (through a *teqɛida*)

R

ṛa iṛa, ra ira v.t. **1.** to see (rare form used mostly by Jews **2.** used in the expr. (in all persons, perfect tense) *ma-šeft ma-ṛit.* I haven't seen anything at all.
ṛa (used with n., pron., and pron. endings) **1.** demonstrative particle used to emphasize or affirm a state or action —*ṛa-huwa ža.* He's come (he's right there). —*ṛa-ḅḅak maži had le-ɛšiya.* Your father is (definitely) coming this evening. **2.** signifies remoteness (in contrast to *ha-*) *ṛa-huwa temma!* He's over there! There he is! **3.** often used with subject of conclusion clause of a conditional sentence *ila ḍḍrebtiha ṛaha ḍḍeṛbek.* If you hit her, she'll hit you. —*ṛak tmut ila neqqezti men dak š-šeṛžem.* You'll get killed (die) if you jump out that window.
¶ *ṛa-fayn* there, right (over) there
rab irib v.i. **1.** to fall or come apart (s.th. constructed, e.g. a house, bridge; implies internal weakness from age, poor materials, etc.) **2.** to be destroyed, demolished (house, bridge, etc.)
ṛab iṛub v.i. to curdle (milk)
¶ a.p. *ṛayeb* curdled milk
ṛabiɛ used in *ṛabiɛ l-luwwel* and *ṛabiɛ t-tani* third and fourth month of the Muslim lunar calendar
ṛabṭa f. a.p. of *ṛbeṭ*
ṛabuz pl. *ṛwabez* bellows (for forcing air)
ṛabeɛ v.t. **1.** to play (a game) with four players **2.** to join (three other players) as the fourth player (in a game)
ṛabeɛ pl. *-in* fourth *hada l-ɛam ṛ-ṛabeɛ*

baš žit l-ˀamirika. This is the fourth year I've been in America.

ṛabɛa pl. *-t* quarter of kilogram (250 gm.)

rad irid v.t. to want, to desire; used in expr. such as: *žah l-kas d-atay kif bġa u-rad.* The glass of tea was just the way he wanted it.

ṛadyu pl. *-wat* radio

ṛaf iṛuf b- to give (money) *ḅḅa dima ka-iṛuf ɛliya b-le-flus.* Father is always giving me money. —*ṛaf ɛăl l-qaḍi b-ši-flisat u-serrɛu.* He gave the judge a little money and he released him.

rafahiya comfort, luxury *ɛumăṛ ka-iɛiš f-rafahiya ɛḍima.* Omar is living in solid comfort.

ṛafeg, ṛafeq v.t. to associate with, to have as companion(s) *weldi ka-iṛafeq wlad mˀeddbin.* My son associates with boys that are well brought up.

ṛaġ iṛuġ v.i. to move or go away, to move out of the way, to step aside *ṛuġ men temma!* Move away from there!

¶ *ṛaġ ɛla* to turn away away from, to avoid by moving aside or turning away *ila šeftih žay-lek, ṛuġ ɛlih!* If you see him coming at you, move aside (from him).

ṛaˀis same as *ṛayes*

rakeb a.p. of *rkeb*

ṛam iṛum v.i. (v.n. *ṛwam*) to give in, to acquiesce *ɛad ṛam u-ɛṭani le-flus.* He finally gave in and gave me the money.

** *ṛum ṭ-ṭṛiq!* Get back on the straight and narrow (morally)!

¶ *ṛam ɛla* to fit *had s-sarut ma-ṛam-š ɛăl l-feṛxa.* This key doesn't fit the lock.

ṛaqaba same as *ṛeqba* 2

ṛaqeb v.t. 1. to control *xeṣṣna nṛaqbu d-dxul u-le-xṛuž dyal l-lažiˀin.* We've got to control the coming and going of refugees. 2. to supervise, to superintend 3. to censor

ṛaqed pl. *ṛwaqed* 1. stone used in pressing olives in the preparation of olive oil 2. axle of the wheel used in an olive press

raqda f. a.p. of *rqed* (same as *rged*)

rara b- to rock (a baby) while singing a lullaby

ṛasul pl. *rusul* 1. messenger 2. prophet

¶ *ṛasul ḷḷah* prophet of God (usually Mohammed)

ṛaṣ pl. *ṛuṣ, ṛyuṣ* (first pl. primarily literal) 1. head (of person, animal, bed, livestock, nail, page, etc.) *ṛaṣu ka-iɛăṛqu.* His head hurts (him). —*ɛăndna geṭɛa d-le-ġnem fiha settin ṛaṣ.* We have a flock of sixty head of sheep. 2. front, head (of a column, caravan, etc.) 3. summit (mountain) 4. peak (mountain, graph) 5. top (tree, pole, tower, etc.) 6. end, extremity *ma-žbeṛ-š ṛaṣ l-xăyṭ.* He hasn't found the end of the string. —*ɛămlu f-ṛaṣ ṭ-ṭebḷa!* Put it at the end of the table! 7. source, head (river) 8. beginning (as of a story) 9. point, sharp end *ṛaṣ l-ibra therres.* The point of the needle has broken. 10. cape (Cod, Good Hope, etc.) 11. ability, knack, "head" *ɛăndu ṛ-ṛaṣ f-le-ɛsab.* He has a head for figures. 12. (good) judgment, "head" *ka-ixxeddem ṛaṣu.* He uses his head.

** *ɛad faq b-ṛaṣu.* He's finally realized what's going on. —*qal mɛa ṛaṣu . . .* He said to himself . . . —*nta tăɛṛef l-ṛaṣek.* You know better than anyone else what you should do. —*kont fe-ḍ-ḍaṛ ġir ṛaṣi ṛaṣ xay.* Just my brother and I were home. —*qulha l-ṛaṣek!* Look who's talking! You should talk! —*had š-ši ġir men ṛaṣi l-ṛaṣek.* This is just between you and me.

¶ *b-ṛaṣu*ᶲ 1. by oneself, alone *koll nhaṛ kan ka-iži huwa u-mṛatu, l-yum ža ġir b-ṛaṣu.* He and his wife used to come every day—today he came by himself.

¶ *dar* (or *ɛmel*) *b-ṛaṣu*ᶲ to play, to act like one is (faking) *ɛmel b-ṛaṣu mṛiḍ.* He played sick.

¶ *dyal ṛaṣu*ᶲ independent, free (to do what one wishes) *kont dyal ṛaṣi u-qemt ka-ndzuwwež.* I used to be free but I went astray and got married.

¶ *fayeq mɛa ṛaṣu*ᶲ sharp, astute, difficult to put s.th. over on

¶ *men ṛaṣu*ᶲ *l-ṛaṣu*ᶲ on one's own, without the aid of others (implies that one should have accepted aid) *ɛămletha men ṛaṣha l-ṛaṣha.* She (went ahead and) did it on her own.

¶ *mɛa ṛaṣu*ᶲ used expletively (often implying "alone") *mša inɛăs mɛa ṛaṣu.* He went to bed (to sleep). —*ṛahom mšaw itsaraw mɛa ṛaṣhom.* They've gone for a stroll.

¶ *ṛaṣu*ᶲ self *qtel ṛaṣu u-huwa ma-zal šabb.* He committed suicide (killed himself) while he was still young.

¶ *ṛaṣ l-mal* same as *ṛaṣmal*

¶ *ṛaṣ l-ɛanut* mixture of various spices used in seasoning foods

¶ *ṛaṣu*ᶲ *tqil* (or *qaṣeɛ*) (to be) dense, slow-witted ≠

¶ *ṛaṣu*ᶲ *xfif* (to be) intelligent, quick-witted ≠

¶ *ṛaṣ l-ɛam* 1. New Year's Day 2. beginning of the new year (first few days)

¶ *rfed ṛ-ṛaṣ mɛa* 1. to give a hard time to *ɛlaš ka-terfed ṛ-ṛaṣ mɛa xak?* Why are you giving your brother such a hard time? 2. to be prejudiced against, to have it in for (s.o.)

¶ *ɛăl ṛ-ṛaṣ u-l-ɛăyn* gladly, with pleasure

ṛaṣmal (no. art.) *ṛaṣ l-mal* 1. capital (financial) *ka-ixeṣṣna nzidu f-ṛaṣ-l-mal.* We need more capital. 2. funds

ṛateb, ṛatib pl. *ṛwateb* salary, pay, wage

ṛawaž v.n. of *ṛaž*

ṛaya pl. *-t* 1. flag, banner, pennant 2. ray (fish)

ṛayeb a.p. of *ṛab*

ṛayes pl. *ṛoyyas, ṛuʔasa* 1. chief, head 2. leader (gang, group, etc.) 3. president 4. captain (ship)

ṛaž iṛuž v.i. (v.n. *ṛawaž*) 1. to sell *had n-nuɛ d-atay ka-iṛuž mezyan.* This kind of tea sells well. 2. to go around, to circulate (news) *waḥed le-xbaṛ ka-iṛuž belli . . .* There's a rumor going around that . . .

ṛaža, ṛažaʔ same as *ṛža*

ṛažăb seventh month of the Muslim lunar calendar

ṛažim used in phrase *š-šiṭan ṛ-ṛažim* (literally, "Satan stoned or having been stoned," the implication being "damned"); in turn usually used in expr. *aɛudu bi-llah men š-šiṭan ṛ-ṛažim!* said upon making an error or flub (similar to "whoops, I mean . . ."), or at s.o.'s rather unusual or surprising act (similar to "My God, what are you doing?" or "What have you done?")

ṛažel pl. *ṛžal, režžala* 1. man (not used in the general sense of "mankind") *dzuwwžet b-waḥed ṛ-ṛažel la-bas ɛlih.* She married a man who's quite well-to-do. 2. husband

¶ *ṛžal* (or *rižal*) *le-blad* national saints, saints peculiar to a country

ṛažla pl. *-t* masculine woman

ṛažeɛ v.t. (v.n. *muṛažaɛa*) 1. to check, to go over again *ṛažeɛ had l-žemɛ u-šuf waš ṣḥiḥ.* Check this addition and see if it's correct. 2. to review, to go over again *ṛažeɛ ḍ-ḍuṛuṣ dyalek!* Review your lessons!

ṛaḥ iṛuḥ (v.n. *ṛwaḥ*) 1. to return, to go (home, as after work, school) *mnin ṛeḥt l-bareḥ le-ḍ-ḍaṛ tɛăššit deġya u-nɛăst.* When I went home yesterday I ate a quick supper and went to bed. 2. to sleep with one's spouse for the first time (wedding night) 3. to set (sun) 4. to fall (night) *l-lil ṛaḥ.* Night has fallen

¶ *ṛaḥ b-* to consummate the marriage with

ṛaḥa pl. *-t* 1. rest, repose 2. tranquillity, peacefulness 3. recess, break 4. time off, vacation, leave 5. improvement (in health)

** *ṛ-ṛaḥa ya-ḷḷah!* Ah, there's nothing like taking it easy (i.e., doing nothing)!

ṛaḥim (no pl.) 1. merciful, having pity (God) 2. generous, charitable 3. kinship, relation *ɛăndu ṛ-ṛaḥim mɛaya.* I'm a relative of his (i.e., he has kinship with me). 4. relative (person) *mša iṣil* (or *yeḥyi*) *ṛ-ṛaḥim.* He's gone to visit (all) his relatives. 5. pl. *ṛḥam* womb

ṛaɛi a.p. of *ṛɛa*

rbab pl. *-at* rebec

ṛbab pl. of *ṛebb*

ṛbaṭ (with art.) 1. Rabat (capital of Morocco) 2. pl. *-at* hobble, fetter (for animals)

ṛbaṭi 1. pl. of *ṛebṭa* 2. pl. *-yen* from, of, or native to Rabat

rbayeb pl. of *rbib* and *rbiba*

rbaybi pl. *-ya* one who plays the rebec

rbayeɛ pl. of *rbaɛa*

ṛbayeɛ pl. of *ṛbiɛa*

ṛbaɛ pl. of *ṛbăɛ*

ṛbaɛa pl. *-t, rbayeɛ* 1. group (people) 2. gang, band (criminal) 3. gang, team (work)

ṛbaɛiya pl. *-t* 1. obsolete coin of fifty centimes 2. kind of four-shot rifle

ṛebb pl. *ṛbab* owner (less common than *mul*)

¶ *ṛbab le-bṣeṛ* (almost always pl.; rare usage) appraisers

¶ *ṛebb ṭ-ṭoṛqa* expert (in his field)

ṛebba v.t. (v.n. *teṛbiya*) 1. to raise, to rear (person, animals) 2. to educate 3. to discipline (person, dog, etc.) 4. to train (animals) 5. to correct, to punish 6. to carry (as a child on one's back) *ḅḅah dima ka-iṛebbih fuq ḍehṛu mnin ka-imšiw itsaraw.* His father always carries him on his back when they go for a walk.

¶ *ṛebba l-welf ɛla* to get used or accustomed to (s.o.)

¶ *ṛebba l-lḥăm* (or *le-hbuṛ*) to gain weight

¶ *ṛebba r-riš* 1. to grow feathers (bird) 2. to get or become rich

ṛobbama perhaps, maybe *ṛobbama nšufuh had le-ɛšiya.* Maybe we'll see him this evening.

ṛebbani pl. *-yen* 1. religious, pious 2. honest, sincere (may imply naïveté)

ṛebbaṭ pl. *-a* guardian of an olive grove

ṛebbaɛ pl. *-a* 1. gardener (flower, vegetable) 2. share-cropper (getting a quarter of crop profits)

rebbi, ṛebbi (usually used with the name of the person) rabbi

ṛebbi (no art., no pl.) God, Lord

¶ *ɛla ṛebbi* for (the love of) God, used as "please" with requests *dir fiya xir ɛla ṛebbi.* Do me a favor, please.

rebbel v.t. **1.** to disturb, to upset (s.o.'s mind) **2.** to put in disorder, to mess up

rebbeẓ v.t. **1.** to cause to win, to let win, to help win *t-teryes huwa lli rebbeẓna had ṭ-ṭeṛẓ.* The trey is what helped us win this (card) game. **2.** to give (s.o.) a grade of *rebbeẓtu ɛešrin ɛla ɛešrin.* I gave him a grade of twenty over twenty (i.e., an "A plus").

** *ḷḷah irebbẓek!* It's a deal!

ṛebbăɛ v.i. **1.** to sit with the legs crossed or interlaced (as in sitting on the ground) **2.** to produce or grow grass, to get green (ground) *had l-ˀeṛḍ bdat ka-tṛebbăɛ.* This ground is starting to grow grass.

rbib pl. *rbayeb* step-son

rbiba pl. *-t, rbayeb* step-daughter

ṛbiṭ v.n. of *ṛbeṭ*

ṛbiṭa dim. of *ṛebṭa*

rbiẓ v.n. of *rbeẓ*

ṛbiɛ **1.** grass (in a field, around the house) **2.** spring (season)

ṛbiɛa pl. *-t, ṛbayeɛ* kind of small container (for sugar, tea, alms, etc.)

ṛbiɛi pl. *-yen* grassy-green

ṛbeṭ v.t. (v.n. *ṛbiṭ*) to tie, to fasten (always involves a knot of some kind) *xeṣṣek teṛbeṭ ṣebbaṭek.* You'd better tie your shoes. —*ṛbeṭ had l-qennba f-dak l-meṣmaṛ.* Tie this string to that nail. —*xeṣṣek teṛbeṭ le-ẓmaṛ dyalek mɛa dik s-sarya.* You'd better tie your donkey to that pillar.

¶ *ṛbeṭ b-žuž* to tie together

¶ f. a.p. *ṛabṭa* pl. *ṛabṭin* in mourning (and enclosed in the house until the period is up; of women only)

ṛebṭa pl. *-t, ṛbaṭi* (dim. *ṛbiṭa*) **1.** n.i. of *ṛbeṭ* **2.** bunch (used as a measure in selling things, e.g., mint)

ṛbuɛa pl. of *ṛbăɛ*

rbeẓ v.t. (v.n. *rbiẓ, rbeẓ*) **1.** to win (money, game, contest, etc.) **2.** to earn (money, fame)

rbeẓ (no pl.) **1.** v.n. of *rbeẓ* **2.** profit, gain (money) **3.** benefit, profit

ṛbăɛ pl. *ṛbaɛ, ṛbuɛa* quarter, fourth *klit ṛbăɛ de-l-xobz.* I ate a quarter loaf of bread.

ṛbăɛ, ṛebɛ, ṛebɛa (first two used with pl. of n. admitting du.) four *ɛăndu yaḷḷah ṛbăɛ snin f-ɛămṛu.* He's just four years old. —*dbeẓna ṛebɛa d-le-ẓwala f-had l-ɛid.* We slaughtered four sheep during this feast (holiday).

ṛobɛi pl. *-yat* measuring cup (for grain)

ṛebɛin **1.** forty **2.** fortieth *ža huwa ṛ-ṛebɛin f-le-mtiẓan.* He came out fortieth in the exam.

ṛbăɛṭaš **1.** fourteen **2.** fourteenth *ɛaš u-mat fe-l-qeṛn ṛ-ṛbăɛṭaš.* He lived and died in the fourteenth century.

rda pl. *rdi* **1.** tunic of thin white material worn by a preacher on Friday **2.** fatty tissue covering the bowels of a lamb

rdadeẓ pl. of *reddaẓa*

rdal pl. of *rdil*

rdala baseness, lowness (moral)

ṛedd v.t. (v.n. *ṛedd, ṛeddan*) **1.** to return (bring, take, or give back) **2.** to restore (to a former state) **3.** to refuse, to turn down *ža iṭḷeb menni le-flus be-l-ẓăqq ṛedditu.* He came to ask me for the money, but I turned him down. **4.** to send away, to make go away (s.o.) **5.** to change to, to alter to, to make *ṛeddit s-siyaṛa dyali ɛămṛa.* I changed my car to red. **6.** to turn into, to change into, to transform into *s-seẓẓar ṛedd le-ẓmama džaža.* The magician turned the pigeon into a chicken. **7.** (also v.i.) to vomit, to regurgitate

** *ṛedd bih ḷḷah.* Things have turned out pretty well for him (after all). —*ṛedditini keddab daba!* So, now I'm a liar! Are you calling me a liar?

¶ *ṛedd l-bal* (or *baluφ*), *ṛedd l-welha* (or *wlehtuφ*) to pay attention *ṛedd l-bal l-l-ˀustad š-ka-iqul!* Pay attention to what the professor is saying!

¶ *ṛedd le-xbaṛ* (*ɛla*) to give an account (of), to tell (about) *sir ṣeqṣih waš ġad iži mɛana u-ṛedd ɛliya le-xbaṛ.* Go ask him if he's coming with us and tell me (what he said).

ṛedd, ṛeddan v.n. of *ṛedd*

reddaẓa pl. *-t, rdadeẓ* flame (fire)

redded v.t. **1.** to repeat *redded had le-klam lli ġadi nqul men băɛdi.* Repeat what I'm going to say after me. **2.** to recite *dima ka-iredded š-šiɛr.* He's always reciting poetry.

reddeẓ v.t. to put some flammable fuel on (a fire to make it burn stronger)

rdi pl. of *rda*

rdil pl. *-in, rdal* low, base (person)

rdim v.n. of *rdem*

rdiẓ v.n. of *rdeẓ*

rdiɛ v.n. of *rdăɛ*

rdem v.t. (v.n. *rdim*) **1.** to raze, to knock down or out (house, wall, either by act of God or purposefully as for improvement) **2.** to break or break off (the point of s.th.) **3.** to bury with debris (e.g., s.o. caught in a collapsing building)

redma pl. *-t* n.i. of *rdem*

rleẓ (v.n. *rdiẓ*) **1.** v.t. to kick (person, animal) **2.** v.i. to beat (heart) **3.** v.i. to boil (water) **4.** v.i. to dance (a kind of tap or stamping dance) *redḥa* pl. *-t* n.i. of *rdeḥ*

rdăɛ v.t. (v.n. *rdiɛ*) **1.** to inhale (smoke, as from a cigarette) **2.** to drive all the way in (nail) **3.** to shock (electricity) **4.** to throw or buck off (as a horse)

redɛa pl. *-t* n.i. of *rdăɛ*

ʔeṛḍ, eṛḍ pl. *ʔaṛaḍi* **1.** ground *l-ʔeṛḍ sebḥet fazga.* The ground is wet this morning. **2.** floor *xeṣṣna nzuwwlu ẓ-ẓeṛbiya baš nḥekku l-eṛḍ.* We have to remove the rug so we can scrub the floor. **3.** land *ḅḅah ka-imlek bezzaf d-l-eṛḍ.* His father owns a lot of land.

ṛḍa iṛḍi v.t. (v.n. *ṛiḍa, ṛḍa*) to satisfy, to content

** *ḷḷah iṛḍi ɛlik!* May God bless you; Thank you (said by an older person to a younger for some reverence given).

¶ *ḷḷah iṛḍi ɛlik* . . . please . . .

ṛḍa iṛḍa b- (v.n. *ṛḍa*) to accept, to be satisfied with (s.th., s.o.) *ma-ṛḍa-š ġir b-xemsin fṛenk.* He would accept (only) fifty francs.

¶ *qbel u-ṛḍa* to really or definitely want *qbelt u-ṛḍit ndzuwwež biha.* I really wanted to marry her.

ṛḍa (m. or f., cons. *ṛḍat*) v.n. of *ṛḍa*

¶ *ṛḍat l-waldin* kind of parental blessing

ṛḍayem pl. of *ṛḍuma*

ṛḍayeɛ pl. of *ṛḍiɛ*

ṛḍaɛa v.n. of *ṛḍăɛ*

¶ *xut mne-ṛ-ṛḍaɛa* brothers by virtue of having been nursed or suckled by the same woman (one of their mothers)

ṛeḍḍ (v.n. *ṛeḍḍ, ṛeḍḍan*) same as *ṛedd*

ṛeḍḍ, ṛeḍḍan v.n. of *ṛeḍḍ* (same as *ṛedd*)

ṛeḍḍaɛa pl. *-t* **1.** wet nurse **2.** feeding bottle (baby)

ṛeḍḍăɛ v.t. to nurse, to breast-feed, to suckle

ṛḍix v.n. of *ṛḍex*

ṛḍiɛ f. *ṛḍiɛa* pl. *ṛḍayeɛ* one having a relationship with others by virtue of having been nursed or suckled by the same woman *ḥmed ṛḍiɛ dyal bṛahim.* Ahmed and Abraham were suckled by the same woman (one of their mothers).

ṛḍuma pl. *ṛḍayem* bottle (usually from about liter-size on up)

ṛḍex v.t. (v.n. *ṛḍix*) **1.** to hurl or throw violently (implies a breakable object) (*ɛla* at) **2.** to push or knock (s.th., s.o.) over or down

ṛḍăɛ v.i. (v.n. *ṛḍaɛa*) to suckle, to nurse, to be breast-fed

ṛfa iṛfi v.t. (v.n. *ṛfi*) to darn, to mend

ṛeʔfa compassion, mercy, clemency

rfafed pl. of *reffada*

ṛfafeṣ pl. of *ṛeffaṣ*

ṛfaga, ṛfaqa (no. pl.) group or those with whom one usually associates

rfed v.t. (v.n. *rfid, rfud*) **1.** to pick up *rfed dak le-qlam lli ṭayeḥ fe-l-ʔeṛḍ!* Pick up that pencil that's fallen on the floor! **2.** to lift, to raise **3.** to lift, to take away, to remove (sickness) *ḷḷah irfed ɛlik had l-meṛḍ.* May God remove this sickness from you. **4.** to (be able to) contain, to hold *had l-ġoṛṛaf ka-irfed žuž liṭṛu de-l-ma.* This pitcher holds two liters of water. **5.** to hold *rfed had š-šanṭa ɛla-ma nšedd ṣebbaṭi.* Hold this suitcase while I tie my shoes. **6.** to carry, to take *rfed had ṣ-ṣenḍuq men hna l-temma!* Take this box from here over to there! **7.** v.i. to stop, to end (rain, plague, etc.)

** *ḷḷah irefdek ɛlina*! Scram! Beat it! Go play in the traffic (to children)! Go jump in the lake! Drop dead (to adults)! —*ma-bqa l-qelbi ma irfed!* I can't stand any more of this!

¶ *rfed ḍ-ḍeḍḍ mɛa* to be prejudiced against, to be against (s.o.)

¶ *rfedha~ b-žerya* to take to one's heels

refda pl. *-t* n.i. of *rfed*

reffad pl. *-a* **1.** carrier, bearer **2.** barber's or weaver's assistant

reffada pl. *-t, rfafed* brassiere, bra

ṛeffaṣ pl. *ṛfafeṣ* **1.** screw, propeller (ship, outboard motor) **2.** rapid, scissor-like kicking of the feet (as used in the swimming crawl)

refqa (no pl.) **1.** escort (on business or friendly basis) **2.** comradeship, friendship

ṛefgan pl. of *ṛfig*

ṛfi v.n. of *ṛfa*

rfid v.n. of *rfed*

ṛfig, ṛfiq pl. *ṛefgan, ṛefqan* comrade, buddy

rfisa pl. *-t* **1.** a sort of pudding, made with bread, milk, and butter **2.** a kind of soup made for dogs from bones, bread, etc. **3.** carcass, remains (of an animal)

¶ *daṛ rfisa f-* to tear (s.o.) to pieces, to make a wreck (out of s.o.) *daru fih rfisa.* They tore him to pieces.

¶ *bnadem rfisa* s.o. who has been seriously beaten (physically), a human wreck (after such a beating)

rfiɛ pl. *-in* (comp. *ṛfăɛ*) **1.** excellent, superior, superb **2.** sharp (-pointed)

ṛfiɛ v.n. of *ṛfăɛ*

ṛfeq b- (v.n. *ṛifq*) **1.** to give a good price to (s.o.) **2.** to help, to be helpful to (s.o.) **3.** to go easy on, to be lenient with (s.o.)

¶ p.p. *meṛfuq* pl. *-in* moderate, reasonable (prices)

ṛefqa same as *refga*

ṛefqan same as *ṛefgan* (pl. of *ṛfig*)

ṛefṛef v.i. **1.** to wave, to flap (as a flag) **2.** to turn, to spin (as a pinwheel)

rfud v.n. of *rfed*
¶ *be-r-rfud u-n-nzul, . . .* After long debate, . . .
ṛfăɛ v.t. (v.n. *ṛfiɛ, ṛefɛ*) **1.** to raise, to lift **2.** to raise, to hoist (flag)
ṛfăɛ comp. of *ṛfiɛ*
ṛefɛ v.n. of *ṛfăɛ*
ṛefɛa pl. *-t* n.i. of *ṛfăɛ*
rgad v.n. of *rged*
rgayel pl. of *rgila*
rgeb ɛla same as *reggeb ɛla*
ṛegba same as *ṛeqba*
rged v.i. (v.n. *rgad*) **1.** to (go to) sleep **2.** to become paralyzed (as a foot going to sleep or with a morbid paralysis) **3.** to die down (wind)
¶ f. a.p. *ragda* (*l-ˀeṛḍ*) fallow, lying fallow (soil)
regda pl. *-t* n.i. of *rged*
reggabiya pl. *-t* collar (clothes)
reggeb ɛla **1.** to observe from above, to look down onto **2.** to look down onto *had š-šeṛžem ka-irreggeb ɛle-ž-žameɛ.* This window looks down onto the mosque. **3.** to look over the shoulder of (s.o.)
regged v.t. **1.** to make or cause to sleep **2.** to prepare for planting (ground) **3.** to let lie fallow (soil) **4.** to do nothing about, to forget about doing (s.th.) *l-muḥami regged l-qaḍiya lli ɛṭinah idafeɛ ɛliha.* The lawyer hasn't done a thing about our case.
ṛgig same as *ṛgiq*
rgila pl. *-t, rgayel* crutch *ka-imši be-r-rgayel.* He walks on crutches.
ṛgiɛ v.n. of *ṛgăɛ*
ṛgăɛ (v.n. *ṛgiɛ*) **1.** v.i. to botch everything, to do everything all wrong **2.** v.i. to talk incoherently or without making any sense **3.** v.t. to hit, to strike (s.o., usually with one's head)
ṛġawi pl. of *ṛeġwa*
ṛġayef pl. of *ṛġifa*
ṛġeb v.t. (v.n. *ṛġib*) to ask, to beg *ṛġebt bḅa baš išri-li ṭumubil.* I begged my father to buy me a car.
ṛeġba pl. *-t* **1.** n.i. of *ṛġeb* **2.** wish, desire
ṛeġġab pl. *-a* ag. n. of *ṛġeb*
ṛġib v.n. of *ṛġeb*
ṛġifa pl. *ṛġayef* variety of pancake
¶ *ṛġayef de-l-feṛṛan* flat tart made of bread dough, stuffed with spiced meat and baked
ṛeġwa pl. *ṛġawi* **1.** foam, froth **2.** suds
rhaf v.i. (v.n. *rhafa*) **1.** to become thin or worn (as cloth) **2.** to get thin(ner) (dimensionally) **3.** to get or become slim (things)
rhaf pl. of *rhif*
rhafa v.n. of *rhaf*
ṛhayen pl. of *ṛhina*
ṛhayṭi pl. *-ya* trouble maker, mischievous person (usually between people)
ṛheb v.t. (v.n. *ṛhib*) to scare, to frighten (to "death")
ṛehba pl. *-t* n.i. of *ṛheb*
ṛehban pl. of *ṛhib* **2**
ṛehheb v.t. to scare, to frighten
ṛehhež v.t. **1.** to overseason with salt **2.** to poison with arsenic
ṛhib **1.** v.n. of *ṛheb* **2.** pl. *ṛehban* priest (Christian)
rhif pl. *rhaf* **1.** thin, light (cloth) **2.** thin, not thick (dimensionally) **3.** slim, slender (things)
ṛhin v.n. of *ṛhen*
ṛhina pl. *ṛhayen* **1.** security, collateral *ḥeṭṭ ṛhina dyal xems alaf ḍulaṛ.* He put up a collateral of five thousand dollars. **2.** mortgage *ḥeṭṭiṭ ṛhina fe-ḍ-ḍaṛ.* I have a mortgage on the house.
ṛhen v.t. (v.n. *ṛhin*) **1.** to put up as security or collateral *neṛhen maganti fe-l-ˀala l-katiba.* I'll put up my watch as security for the typewriter. **2.** to mortgage *ṛhen ḍaṛu f-xems alaf ḍulaṛ.* He mortgaged his house for five thousand dollars.
ṛhen, ṛehniya same as *ṛhina*
ṛeḥṭ pl. *ṛhuṭ, ṛhuṭa* **1.** kind, sort, type (pejorative use) **2.** brand, make (pejorative use) **3.** undesirable person
ṛhuṭ, ṛhuṭa pl. of *ṛeḥṭ*
riba illicit gain or profit (money)
ṛiḍa v.n. of *ṛḍa*
rif pl. *ryaf* area of a slum inhabited by one particular family group
rifi adj. pl. *-yen* n.pl. *rwafa, ryafa* Riff, Riffian
ṛifq v.n. of *ṛfeq*
rig same as *ṛiq*
rim pl. *ryam* **1.** gazelle **2.** pretty girl
rimaya same as *ṛmaya*
ṛiq, rig pl. *ṛyuq, ryug* spittle, saliva
¶ *ɛle-ṛ-ṛiq* without eating, not having eaten (yet)
riš n.u. *-a* feather
ṛiša pl. *-t* **1.** n.u. of *riš* **2.** pen (writing)
¶ *riša de-t-tăɛmaṛ* fountain pen
ritel v.t. (v.n. *tritil*) **1.** to rob, to steal from **2.** to pillage, to loot **3.** to put in disorder, to mess up (a place)
riwaya pl. *-t* **1.** novel, narrative (written or told) **2.** play (theater)
ṛiyaḍa sports, athletics
ṛiyaḍi pl. *-yen* **1.** of or pertaining to sports, athletics **2.** athlete
ṛiyasa **1.** presidency **2.** state of being in charge or command

riyya pl. *-t* lung
riyyaga pl. *-t* bib (child's)
riyyaḥa pl. *-t* fan (electric)
riyyeb v.t. **1.** to demolish (building, etc.) **2.** to dismantle
ṛiyyeb v.t. to curdle (milk)
riyyeg same as *ṛeyyeq*
riyyeš v.t. **1.** to pluck (the) feathers from **2.** to pluck (s.o.) clean
riyyeḥ v.i. **1.** to stink, to reek *had l-lḥăm riyyeḥ, ma-bqa fih ma ittkel.* This meat stinks; it's no longer fit to eat. **2.** to rest, to take a break
rižal classicized pl. of *ṛažel*
  rižal le-blad saints of a particular city (less often, country)
riḥ pl. *ryaḥ* wind *r-riḥ bared had ṣ-ṣbaḥ.* The wind is cold this morning.
  ** *ma-žbeṛt ġir r-riḥ.* I didn't find a thing. —*had š-ši lli ka-iɛăwwed-lek ṛah ġir r-riḥ.* What he's telling you is just so much hot air. —*xellaweh ka-itsenna r-riḥ.* They left him there waiting (for them, but they never showed up).
  ¶ *le-ryaḥ* epilepsy *qebṭuh le-ryaḥ.* He's having an epileptic fit.
  ¶ *ɛăl r-riḥ* in vain, for nothing
riḥa pl. *-t, rwayeḥ* (dim. *rwiḥa*) **1.** odor, smell **2.** perfume
riḥan, ṛiḥan myrtle
riḥiya pl. *-t, rwaḥi* (sg. *ferda de-r-riḥiya*) kind of old-fashioned woman's shoes
rkab pl. *-at* **1.** square (tool) **2.** stirrup (saddle)
rkabi pl. of *rokba*
ṛkani pl. of *ṛokna*
rkayez pl. of *rkiza*
ṛkaɛi pl. of *ṛekɛa*
rkeb ɛla (v.n. *rkub*) **1.** to mount, to get on (horse) **2.** (or *f-*) to get into or onto, to board (train, car, plane, ship) **3.** (or *f-*) to ride, to ride in or on (horse, car, plane, etc.)
  ¶ a.p. *rakeb* pl. *rokkab* **1.** passenger **2.** rider
rokba pl. *rkabi* knee (person, animal)
rokbi pl. *-yen* big and loutish
rokbiya pl. *-t* blow with the knee *ɛṭatu b-waḥed r-rokbiya.* She hit him with her knee.
rkil v.n. of *rkel*
rkina dim. of *rokna*
rkiz v.n. of *rkez*
rkiza pl. *rkayez* **1.** tent pole or support **2.** support, mainstay (metaphorical)
rekkab pl. *-a* rider (e.g. of a horse)
rokkab n.pl. of *rakeb* (a.p. of *rkeb*)
rekkal pl. *-in* ag. adj. of *rkel*
rekkeb v.t. **1.** to make get (in or on), to put (in or on; car, plane, horse, etc.) **2.** to mount, to set (in), to put (in) (as a window pane, light bulb, etc.) **3.** to set up, to put up, to put together (tent, machine, etc.) **4.** to set (trap) **5.** to make, to construct, to compose (as a sentence) *rekkeb ši-žumla b-had l-kelma.* Make a sentence with this word.
ṛekken v.t. to put in a corner (inside)
rekkez v.t. **1.** to concentrate *rekkez l-žuhud dyalek kollha fe-l-xedma baš nsaliw deġya.* Concentrate all your efforts on the work so we can finish it quickly. **2.** to learn well (lesson, subject) **3.** to tamp down (earth, etc., as when paving s.th.)
rkel v.t. (v.n. *rkil*) to kick (person, horse, etc.)
rekla pl. *-t* **1.** n.i. of *rkel* **2.** kick, blow with the foot
rokna pl. *rkani* (dim. *rkina*) corner (inside)
rkub v.n. of *rkeb*
ṛkuɛ v.n. of *ṛkăɛ*
rkez v.t. (v.n. *rkiz*) to stick or drive (in), to implant *ɛlaš rkezti s-sekkin fe-l-leṛḍ?* Why did you stick the knife in the ground?
ṛkăɛ v.i. (v.n. *ṛkuɛ*) to bend over (at the waist, in prayer)
ṛekɛa pl. *-t, ṛkaɛi* du. *ṛkăɛtayn* **1.** n.i. of *ṛkăɛ* **2.** complete set of movements, words, etc., done in a certain prescribed prayer
ṛma iṛmi v.t. (v.n. *ṛmi, ṛemyan*) **1.** to throw, to cast, to toss **2.** to shoot (as an arrow) **3.** (*ɛla*) to throw or put (over) (as a blanket) **4.** to throw (on) *ṛma ɛlih kebbuṭu u-xrež.* He threw on his jacket and left. **5.** to throw away or out
ṛmad **1.** ashes **2.** conjunctivitis, pinkeye
  ṭlăɛ-lu ṛ-ṛmad ɛla ɛăynu. He has conjunctivitis.
ṛmadi, pl. *-yen* gray
ṛmaḍ same as *ṛmad*
ṛmaḍi same as *ṛmadi*
ṛmaya **1.** shooting (for recreation, as in a shooting gallery) **2.** archery
ṛemḍan Ramadan, ninth month of the Muslim lunar calendar
ṛmi v.n. of *ṛma*
ṛmiq v.n. of *ṛmeq*
ṛmiqa dim. of *ṛemqa*
ṛmiš v.n. of *ṛmeš*
rmiz n.u. *-a* trump (cards)
ṛmel sand
  ¶ *ḥăbba de-ṛ-ṛmel* grain of sand
ṛeml re (music)
  ¶ *ṛeml l-maya* rhythm used in Andalusian music
ṛemla same as *ṛmel*
ṛemli pl. *-yen* sandy, full of sand
ṛomman n.u. *-a* pomegranate

ṛemmay pl. *-a* marksman (gun, bow)
ṛemmel v.t. **1.** to put sand into, to add sand to (cement, mortar) **2.** to put sand on, to cover with sand **3.** to get full of sand (shoes, etc.)
ṛemmeš v.t. or v.i. **1.** to blink (eyes) **2.** to wink (one eye)
ṛmeq v.t. (v.n. *ṛmiq*) to leer at, to watch out of the corner of one's eye
ṛemqa pl. *-t* (dim. *ṛmiqa*) n.i. of *ṛmeq*
ṛmeš v.t. and v.i. (v.n. *ṛmiš*) **1.** to blink (eyes) **2.** to wink (one eye)
ṛemša pl. *-t* n.i. of *ṛmeš*
ṛmuk pl. *-at* tugboat
ṛmuz pl. of *ṛemz*
ṛemya pl. *-t* n.i. of *ṛma*
ṛemyan v.n. of *ṛma*
ṛemz pl. *ṛmuz, ṛumuz* symbol
ʔeṛneb, ṛneb pl. *ṛwaneb* hare, rabbit
ṛqa iṛqi v.t. (v.n. *ṛqi;* primarily used by women as a somewhat narrower synonym for *ɛmel* or *dar*) **1.** to make, to prepare (as food, party) **2.** to put, to place *ila žak l-berd f-yeddik ṛqihom fe-žyabek.* If your hands get cold put them in your pockets. **3.** to do *aš ka-teṛqi?* What are you doing?
ṛqab, ṛqabi pl. of *ṛeqba*
ʔeṛqam pl. of *ṛeqm*
ṛqaq v.i. **1.** to become thin (dimensionally) **2.** to become slim or slender (things, person) **3.** to become high(er)-pitched (voice)
ṛqaq pl. of *ṛqiq*
ṛqaqa pl. *-t* matzoth, matzo(s) (for Jewish Passover)
ṛqaqeṣ pl. of *ṛeqqaṣ* **2**
ṛqayqi pl. *-ya* specialist in any fine, artistic work (leathercraft, sculpture, ivory, etc.)
ṛqaɛi pl. of *ṛoqɛa*
ṛeqba pl. *-t, ṛqab, ṛqabi* nape or back of the neck **2.** (also, *ṛaqaba*) human being, person (Koranic usage)

¶ *ɛla* or *fe-ṛqebtu*[ϕ] (to be) the responsibility of, on the head of *ṛaha fe-ṛqebtek ila weqɛăt ši-ḥaža fe-s-siyaṛa.* It's your responsibility if something happens to the car.

** *ɛla ṛqebtek waš ana lli herrest dak lkas?* You know I didn't break that glass!

rqed same as *rged*
ṛqi v.n. of *ṛqa*
ṛqim v.n. of *ṛqem*
ṛqiq pl. *-in, ṛqaq* (dim. *ṛqiweq, ṛqiyyeq;* comp. *ṛeqq*) **1.** thin, not thick (dimensionally) **2.** slim, slender (things, person) **3.** fine, sharp (-pointed) **4.** high-pitched (voice)
ṛqiweq dim. of *ṛqiq*
ṛqem v.t. (v.n. *ṛqim*) to embroider
ṛeqm pl. *ʔeṛqam* number *šnu huwa ṛeqm dik ṭ-ṭumubil?* What's the number of that car?
ṛeqq comp. of *ṛqiq*
ṛeqqa **1.** thinness (dimensional) **2.** slimness, slenderness (things, person) **3.** sharpness (of point)
ṛeqqa v.t. to promote, to advance (s.o.)
ṛeqqama pl. *-t* (female) embroiderer
ṛeqqaṣ **1.** pl. *-a* messenger, courier **2.** pl. *ṛqaqeṣ* pendulum (clock)
ṛeqqaɛ pl. *-a* one who mends or repairs clothing
ṛeqqed v.t. **1.** same as *regged* **2.** to preserve, to put up as preserves (fruit, meat, etc.)
ṛeqqeq v.t. **1.** to make thin, to thin (a solid) **2.** to slim, to make slim or slender (person, things) **3.** to sharpen, to make sharp (-pointed) *ṛeqqeq had r-rkiza.* Sharpen this stake.
ṛeqqăɛ v.t. to mend, to repair (clothing)
ṛoqɛa pl. *-t, ṛqaɛi* patch, patched-up spot (on repaired clothing)
rra interjection used to make a donkey or mule start
ṛsamel pl. of *ṛesmal* (same as *ṛaṣ-l-mal*)
rsil v.n. of *rsel*
rsel v.t. (v.n. *rsil*) to send *rselt l-bareḥ risala l-l-meġrib.* I sent a letter to Morocco yesterday.
ṛesmal pl. *ṛsamel* (dim. *ṛsimel*) same as *ṛaṣ-l-mal*
ṛṣa iṛṣa v.i. (v.n. *ṛeṣyan*) **1.** to be or become solid, fixed (s.th. loose) **2.** to stop, to quit doing s.th. (usually at s.o.'s request) **3.** to dock, to drop anchor

¶ *ṛṣa men* to stop, to quit (some action)

ṛṣaṣ **1.** lead (metal) **2.** n.u. *-a* bullet (either the ball or the complete cartridge)
ṛṣaṣi pl. *-yen* lead gray
ṛṣem pl. *ṛṣum* title, deed
ṛeṣmi pl. *-yen* (adj.) official
ṛeṣṣa **1.** v.t. to immobilize, to make solid or fixed (s.th. loose) **2.** v.t. to hold still, to stop from moving *ṛeṣṣi ṛaṣek!* Hold your head still! **3.** v.t. to settle, to decide about (some matter) **4.** v.i. to dock, to drop anchor
ṛeṣṣef v.t. to pave (road, floor)
ṛeṣṣăɛ v.t. to set (stones, e.g. jeweler)
ṛṣum pl. of *ṛṣem*
ṛeṣyan v.n. of *ṛṣa*
ṛša irša v.i. (v.n. *rešyan, ršawa*) **1.** to get or become old and rotten (wood, clothes, etc.) **2.** to get or become aged or very old (person)
rša irši v.t. (v.n. *rši*) to bribe

¶ p.p. *merši* pl. *-yen* sold on black market or as contraband

ršawa v.n. of *rša irša*
ršawi pl. of *rešwa*
ṛšaḥi pl. of *ṛešḥa*
ṛšed (v.n. *ṛšid, ṛošd*) **1.** v.i. to become or come of age (person) **2.** v.t. to show or indicate

to (s.o.) *ana ġir ka-nebġi nṛešdek le-ṭ-ṭṛiq l-mezyana.* I'm only trying to show you the right way.
ṛošd **1.** v.n. of *ṛšed* **2.** maturity, legal age
ṛšid v.n. of *ṛšed*
ṛšim v.n. of *ṛšem*
ṛšiḥ v.n. of *ṛšeḥ*
ṛšem v.t. (v.n. *ṛšim*) **1.** to mark, to put a mark on (for some identification) **2.** to brand (cattle) **3.** to put a marker in (as a book)
ṛešma pl. *-t* **1.** n.i. of *ṛšem* **2.** mark, brand (for identification)
ṛšeq l- (v.n. *ṛšuq*) to make happy or gay (anything from music to narcotics) *mnin ma-ka-ikmi-š ma-ka-ikun-š ṛašeq-lu.* He's not happy when he's not smoking.
ṛešš v.t. (v.n. *ṛeššan*) **1.** to sprinkle (grass, etc.) **2.** to spatter (s.th., as with paint, etc.)
ṛešš (coll., no n.u.) bullets, ammunition (small arms)
rešša v.t. to make or cause to get old and rotten (wood, clothes, etc.)
ṛešša pl. *-t* n.i. of *ṛešš*
ṛeššam pl. *-a* one who brands (cattle)
ṛeššan v.n. of *ṛešš*
ṛeššaša pl. *-t* machine gun
ṛšuq v.n. of *ṛšeq*
rešwa pl. *-t, ṛšawi* bribe
rešyan v.n. of *rša irša*
ṛšeḥ v.i. (v.n. *ṛšiḥ*) to filter, to be filtered (liquid)

¶ *ṛšeḥ b-* to cheat, to take (s.o., in a deal)

ṛešḥa pl. *-t, ṛšaḥi* n.i. of *ṛšeḥ*
rta irta ɛla (v.n. *retyan*) **1.** to take care of, to care for (not persons) **2.** to be thrifty or frugal with, to use sparingly, to go easy on *rta ɛla atay, ṛa-dak n-nuɛ ma-bqa-š ka-itbaɛ bezzaf.* Go easy on the tea; they don't sell that kind much any more.
rtaḥ v.i. **1.** to rest, to take it easy **2.** to get better, to recuperate

¶ *rtaḥ men* to get rid of *ḷḷah rtaḥina men dak l-kelb lli kan ka-ibiyyetna fayqin be-n-nbiḥ.* Thank heavens, we got rid of that dog that was keeping us awake with its barking.

ṛotba pl. **1.** job, position, function **2.** position (social) **3.** rank (military, etc.)
rtila pl. *-t* spider
rtella pl. *-t* pad placed on the head under a board on which bread is carried
ṛetteb v.t. **1.** to put in order, to arrange **2.** to classify **3.** to arrange, to set up (schedule, etc.)
rettel v.t. to chant (Koran)
retteḥ v.t. **1.** to make or allow to rest **2.** to allow or give time off to (s.o.) **3.** to cause not to worry, to put at ease

¶ *retteḥ ṛaṣuφ men* same as *rtaḥ men*

retyan v.n. of *rta*
ṛṭab v.i. (v.n. *ṛṭuba*) **1.** to get or become smooth **2.** to get or become soft **3.** to get or become tender (meat)
ṛṭal pl. of *ṛṭeḷ*
ṛṭawa **1.** softness (texture) **2.** tenderness (meat) **3.** suppleness (as of body) **4.** springiness, elasticity

¶ *fihφ* (or *ɛănduφ*) *ṛṭawa* to be flexible, adaptable ≠ (person)

ṛṭeb f. *ṛeṭba* pl. *ṛeṭbin, ṛuṭeb* **1.** smooth (surface) **2.** soft (texture) **3.** tender (meat) **4.** easy-going, affable **5.** humid (weather)
ṛṭeḷ pl. *ṛṭal, ṛṭula* pound, half a kilogram
ṛeṭṭa v.t. **1.** to make soft(er), to soften **2.** to make (more) tender (meat)
ṛeṭṭeb v.t. **1.** to smooth, to make smooth **2.** to make soft(er), to soften **3.** to make (more) tender (meat)
ṛṭuba **1.** v.n. of *ṛṭab* **2.** smoothness (surface) **3.** softness (texture) **4.** tenderness (meat, person) **5.** humidity (weather)
ṛṭula pl. of *ṛṭeḷ*
ṛuʔasa pl. of *ṛayes, ṛaʔis*
ṛubuɛ pl. *-at, ṛwabeɛ* quarter, fourth, fourth part
ṛubyu (n.) f. *-ya* pl. *-wat* blond(e)
rudani pl. *-yen* from *tarudanet,* province of Morocco
ṛuḍa pl. *-t* cemetery
ṛukn pl. *ʔaṛkan* fundamental, basic principle
ṛukuɛ classicized v.n. of *ṛkăɛ*
ṛumi **1.** pl. *-yen* (adj.) European (often extended to mean Western as opposed to Oriental) **2.** pl. *ṛwama* (n.) European (person)
ṛumiya pl. *-t, ṛwama* kind of silk scarf or shawl worn by older women
ṛumuz pl. of *ṛemz*
rus same as *ṛuṣ* (n.pl. of *ṛuṣi*)
rusi same as *ṛuṣi* 2
rusul pl. of *ṛasul*
ṛuṣ **1.** pl. of *ṛaṣ* **2.** n.pl. of *ṛuṣi* **2**
ṛuṣi **1.** pl. *-yen* narrow-minded, fanatical **2.** (adj. pl. *yen* n.pl. *ṛuṣ*) Russian
ṛuṣiya pl. *-t* blow (given) with the head, butt
ṛuṭal n.u. *-a* **1.** octopus **2.** squid
ṛuṭeb pl. of *ṛṭeb*
ṛuwwaba pl. *-t* any vessel used to contain milk as it curdles
ṛuwwaṣ pl. *-a* one who prepares and sells sheep heads for consumption
ṛuwwaṣa pl. of *ṛuwwaṣi*
ṛuwwaṣi pl. *ṛuwwaṣa* **1.** celibate, single man **2.** man living alone

ṛuwweb v.t. to make or allow to curdle or become yoghurt
ṛuwweb v.t. to curdle (milk)
ṛuwweġ v.t. to move (s.th.), to move (s.th.) out of the way, to move (s.th.) aside *ṛuwweġ s-siyaṛa men ṭ-ṭṛiq.* Move the car from the street.
ṛuwwem v.t. **1.** to make fit, to fix so as to fit *ṛuwwemt had s-sarut u-ḥällit l-bab.* I fixed this key so that it fitted and opened the door. **2.** to see whether (s.th.) fits, to try (and make fit or match) *ṛuwwem had s-swaret u-šuf waš teqdeṛ tḥell had l-bab.* Try these keys and see if you can open this door.
 ¶ *ṛuwwem l-* to try to get (s.o.) to accept *ṛuwwmu-li w-ana ndebbeṛ mεah.* Try to get him to accept me and I'll do the rest.
ruwwen (*f-*) to fool around (with), to mess around (with)
ruwweḥ v.t. to add oil or butter to (especially couscous)
ṛuwweḥ v.t. **1.** to cause to catch (a) cold **2.** to bring in for the night (sheep, cows, etc.) **3.** to take or bring (the bride to her husband's place for their first night)
 ¶ *ṛuwweḥ εla* to fan *ṛuwweḥ εäl l-εafya b-had l-žarida!* Fan the fire with this newspaper!
ṛuwwäε v.t. to disturb (s.o., still water, the peace, sleep, etc.)
ṛuˀya pl. *-t* dream, vision
ṛuẓ rice
ṛužuε v.n. of *ṛžäε*
 ¶ *bla ṛužuε* irremediab(le, -ly), irrevocab(le, -ly)
ṛuḥ (f.) pl. *ṛwaḥ* **1.** spirit, soul **2.** nature (of person) *ṛuḥu ṭeyyba.* He's good-natured. **3.** person, human being *tmenya d-le-ṛwaḥ matu f-dak l-ḥadita.* Eight people were killed in that accident. 4. self *bġa iqtel ṛuḥu mnin ṣaq le-xbaṛ.* He tried to kill himself when he found out.
 ** *baqya fih ṛ-ṛuḥ.* He's still alive.
 ¶ *b-ṛuḥuφ* **1.** by oneself, alone *εämletha b-ṛuḥha.* She did it by herself. 2. oneself, in person *ža εändi b-ṛuḥu.* He came in person to my place.
 ¶ *dar* (or *εmel*) *ṛuḥuφ* (or *b-ṛuḥuφ*) to act, to act as if one were *ṛa ġir ka-iεämlu b-ṛuḥhom εäyyanin.* They're only acting tired.
ṛuεa disorder, confusion
 ¶ *εmel ṛuεa* to riot
rwa (m.) pl. *rwi* stable (horse, etc.)
ṛwa iṛwa v.i. (v.n. *ṛewyan*) **1.** to be or get watered or irrigated (grass, soil, etc.) **2.** to rain
ṛwa iṛwi v.t. (v.n. *ṛewyan, ṛeyy*) **1.** to water, to irrigate (grass, soil, etc.) **2.** to recite (the *ḥadit*)
ṛwabez pl. of *ṛabuz*
ṛwabzi pl. *-ya* maker and seller of bellows (see *ṛabuz*)
ṛwabeε pl. of *ṛubuε*
ṛwafa n.pl. of *ṛifi*
ṛwam v.n. of *ṛam*
ṛwama **1.** n.pl. of *ṛumi* **2.** pl. of *ṛumiya*
ṛwaneb pl. of *ˀeṛneb, ṛneb*
ṛwaq pl. *-at* kind of doorway curtain
ṛwaqed pl. of *ṛaqed*
ṛwateb pl. of *ṛateb, ṛatīb*
ṛwayeḍ pl. of *ṛwiḍa*
ṛwayeḥ pl. of *riḥa*
ṛwaḥ **1.** pl. of *ṛuḥ* **2.** v.n. of *ṛaḥ* **3.** cold *žani ṛ-ṛwaḥ.* I've got a cold; I've caught cold.
 ¶ *lilt ṛ-ṛwaḥ* first night the bride and groom sleep together
rwaḥi pl. of *riḥiya*
rwi pl. of *rwa*
ṛwiḍa pl. *-t, ṛwayeḍ* wheel
ṛwiyyeḍ dim. of *ṛyaḍ*
rwiḥa dim. of *riḥa*
ṛewyan v.n. of *ṛwa*
ṛxa iṛxi v.t. (v.n. *ṛxi*) to loosen, to relax (s.th. taut)
 ¶ *ṛxa wednuφ* (*εla*) to pay close attention (to), to lend an ear (to)
 ¶ p.p. *meṛxi* pl. *-yen* lazy, indolent
ṛxa (m.) cheapness, inexpensiveness
 ¶ *be-ṛ-ṛxa* cheap (adv.) *slăεtu kollha ka-ibiεha be-ṛ-ṛxa.* He sells all his merchandise cheap.
ṛxam n.u. *-a* marble *had s-saryat kollhom mebniyin be-ṛ-ṛxam.* All these pillars are made of marble.
ṛxama pl. *-t* **1.** n.u. of *ṛxam* **2.** dial, face (watch, clock)
ṛxaṣ v.i. (v.n. *ṛexṣan, ṛexṣ*) to become cheap(er) or (more) inexpensive *l-lḥăm ṛxaṣ had l-iyyam.* Meat has gotten cheaper lately.
ṛxaṣ pl. of *ṛxiṣ*
ṛxawa softness (of yielding texture)
ṛxaymi pl. *-ya* marble worker, stonemason specializing in marble (also one who manufactures the slabs and pieces to be used)
ṛxef v.t. (v.n. *rxif*) to loosen (s.th. taut)
ṛxi v.n. of *ṛxa*
rxif v.n. of *ṛxef*
ṛxiṣ pl. *ṛxaṣ* (comp. *ṛxeṣ*) cheap, inexpensive
ṛxeṣ v.i. (v.n. *ṛexṣ*) same as *ṛxaṣ*
ṛxeṣ comp. of *ṛxiṣ*
ṛexṣ v.n. of *ṛxaṣ* and *ṛxeṣ*
ṛoxṣa pl. *-t* vacation, leave, time off
ṛexṣan v.n. of *ṛxaṣ*
ṛoxx pl. *ṛxax* **1.** roc **2.** rook (chess)

¶ *mulay ṛ-ṛoxx* a dull man, a boring person

ṛexxeṣ v.t. **1.** to lower the price of **2.** to sell inexpensively or at a low price **3.** to cover (a fire) with ashes (in order to keep it alive for future use)

¶ *ṛexxeṣ mƐa* to give a good or low price to (s.o.) *ila ṛexxeṣti mƐaya nešriha.* If you give me a good price I'll buy it.

ṛyaḍ pl. *-at* (dim. *ṛwiyyeḍ*) kind of flower garden (domestic)

ryaf pl. of *rif*

ryafa n.pl. of *rifi*

ryal pl. *-at* coin of five francs (also the amount)

ryam pl. of *rim*

ṛyay pl. of *ṛeyy* **2**

ryaƹ pl. of *riƹ*

ryug, ṛyuq pl. of *rig, ṛiq*

ṛyuṣ pl. of *ṛaṣ*

ṛeyy **1.** v.n. of *ṛwa iṛwi* **2.** pl. *ṛyay, ˀaṛaˀ* opinion, idea, way of thinking

ṛoyyas pl. of *ṛayes*

ṛeyyeḍ v.t. to train, to instruct (person, animal)

ṛeyyeq **1.** v.t. to wet or moisten with saliva **2.** v.i. to breakfast or break one's fast (with s.th. light) *ṛeyyeqt be-šfenža, Ɛad žit.* I breakfasted with a doughnut and came.

ṛeyyes v.t. to elect (s.o.) president, to make (s.o.) leader or head of a group or organization

ṛeyyeƹ v.i. to relax, to sit or lie down to rest

rza irzi v.t. to cause (s.o.) to lose (s.th.) *rzitini f-flusi f-dik l-biƐa-u-šerya.* You made me lose money on that deal.

** (*ḷḷah*) *irzini fik!* I wish I could get rid of you!

rzama pl. *-t* mallet

ṛẓami pl. of *ṛeẓma*

ṛẓan pl. of *ṛẓin*

ṛzana, ṛẓana serious-mindedness

ṛzaq pl. of *ṛezq, ṛzeq*

rzim v.n. of *rzem*

ṛẓin pl. *-in, ṛẓan* serious-minded

ṛẓina pitch, resin

ṛziq v.n. of *ṛzeq*

rziya pl. *-t* serious or grave loss

rzem v.i. (v.n. *rzim*) **1.** to get or become worse (sick person) **2.** to be unable to do any activity, to be helpless (as an aged person)

ṛẓem pl. of *ṛeẓma*

ṛeẓma pl. *-t, ṛẓami, ṛẓem* bundle (of clothes, etc.)

ṛzeq, ṛẓeq v.t. (v.n. *ṛziq*) to give, to grant (subject is usually God) *ḷḷah iṛzeqni ṣ-ṣbeṛ!* God give me patience!

ṛezq, ṛzeq, ṛeẓq, ṛẓeq pl. *ṛzaq* **1.** s.th. earned or deserved, compensation **2.** fortune, possessions

** *huwa-b-ṛezqu.* He's pretty well off (financially).

ṛẓuẓi n.u. *-ya* wasp

ṛẓeẓ pl. of *ṛeẓẓa*

ṛeẓẓa pl. *-t, ṛẓeẓ* turban

ṛezzaq, ṛeẓẓaq (with art.) God, epithet of *ḷḷah*

ṛezzem v.t. to bundle (up), to put in a bundle

ṛeẓẓen v.t. to make or cause to be serious-minded, sober

** *ṛeẓẓen ṛaṣek!* Be serious!

ṛža iṛža (v.n. *ṛža*) to hope *ka-neṛžah* (or *ka-neṛža baš*) *yuṣel fe-l-weqt.* I hope he arrives on time.

ṛža (m.) **1.** v.n. of *ṛža* **2.** hope

ṛžal pl. of *ṛažel*

ṛžali **1.** pl. of *režla* **2.** pl. *-yen* masculine, of or pertaining to a man

ṛžeb seventh month of the Muslim lunar calendar

ržila dim. of *ržel*

ržel (f.) pl. *režlin* (*režli-* before pron. endings; dim. *ržila*) **1.** foot (person, animal) **2.** leg (up to the knee; also of a table) **3.** support, base, piling (as for supporting a bridge) **4.** pedestal, base (of statue)

¶ *b-režluᶲ* in person, oneself *ġir kun hani, daba nemši-lu ana b-režli u-ntkellem mƐah.* Don't worry, I'll go see him myself and talk to him.

¶ *Ɛla režlihᶲ* on foot, walking *mšat Ɛla režliha l-ḍaṛhom.* She went to their house on foot.

režla pl. *-t, ržali* leg of lamb, mutton (sometimes beef, veal, pork)

ṛežla courage, quality of being a man

ṛžuliya same as *ṛežla*

ṛžuƐ v.n. of *ṛžăƐ*

ṛežžala **1.** pl. of *ṛažel* **2.** (no sg.) courageous men

ṛežžel v.t. to give courage to, to encourage

¶ *ṛežžel ṛaṣuᶲ* to be courageous, to encourage oneself to be a man

ṛežžăƐ v.t. **1.** to return (give, send, take, or bring back) **2.** to return or restore to a former state **3.** to make *ṛezzăƐna l-bab ṣġiṛa.* We've made the door small(er). —*l-makla ṛežžƐättu mṛiḍ.* The food made him sick. **4.** to transform into, to change into, to turn into *s-seƹƹar ṛežžăƐ le-ƹmama džaža.* The magician turned the pigeon into a chicken.

ṛžăƐ (v.n. *ṛžuƐ, ṛužuƐ*) **1.** to return, to go back, to come back *mšit le-ḍ-ḍaṛ l-biḍa fe-l-mašina u-ṛžăƐt fe-ṭ-ṭumubil.* I went to Casablanca by train and came back by car. **2.** to become *bqa ka-ixṣeṛ le-flus dyalu* *ḥetta ṛžăʕ faqir.* He squandered his money until he became a poor man. 3. to turn into, to be transformed into *b-ʕăyniya šeftha, le-ḥmama ṛežʕăt džaža.* I saw the pigeon turn into a chicken with my own eyes.

** *ṛžăʕ b-ʕăqlu.* He's regained his sanity.

¶ *ṛžăʕ l-* to be a result of, to be due to *s-suquṭ dyalek ka-iṛžăʕ l-ʕadăm le-žtihad dyalek.* Your failing (in school) is a result of your not having studied.

¶ *ṛžăʕ l-llah* to stop doing s.th., to repent *ṛžăʕ l-ḷḷah, u-baṛaka men ʕmayel š-šiṭan!* Stop that! That's enough of your mischief!

¶ *ṛžăʕ le-ṭ-ṭriq* to turn over a new leaf, to return to the straight and narrow

¶ *ṛžăʕ ʕla klamuɸ* to go back on one's word, to break one's promise

¶ *ṛžăʕ ʕăl ṭ-ṭriq* to backtrack, to go back the way one came (as when getting lost)

ṛežʕa pl. *-t* n.i. of *ṛžăʕ*

ṛḥa pl. *ṛḥi* 1. mill, grinding device or machine (flour, coffee, pepper, etc.) 2. sharpening apparatus (knives, etc.)

ṛḥam 1. (no pl.) womb (also *ṛaḥim* with pl. *ṛḥam*) 2. n.pl. of *ṛḥim* and pl. of *ṛaḥim* 5

ṛḥi pl. of *ṛḥa*

ṛḥil 1. v.n. of *ṛḥel* 2. household furnishings, fixtures, utensils, etc., all taken collectively

ṛḥim adj. pl. *-in* n.pl. *ṛḥam* merciful, compassionate

ṛḥel v.i. (v.n. *ṛḥil*) to move, to change one's place of residence

ṛeḥla pl. *-t* 1. n.i. of *ṛḥel* 2. trip, journey

ṛḥem v.t. (v.n. *ṛeḥma*) 1. to have mercy or pity on 2. to give charity to

** *ḷḷah iṛḥem waldik!* Thank you!

¶ *ḷḷah iṛḥem waldik, . . .* please, . . .

¶ p.p. *meṛḥum* pl. *-in* late, deceased, defunct

ṛeḥma 1. v.n. and n.i. of *ṛḥem* 2. mercy, compassion

ṛeḥman 1. merciful, compassionate (God) 2. God

ṛeḥwi pl. *-ya* miller

ṛeḥḥal pl. *-a* nomad

ṛeḥḥeb b- to welcome or receive (as in one's home)

ṛʕa iṛʕa 1. v.i. to graze (cattle, etc.) 2. v.t. to graze on (grass, etc.)

¶ a.p. *ṛaʕi* pl. *ṛoʕyan* herder, one who tends a flock or herd (sheep, goats, etc.)

ṛʕad n.u. *ṛăʕda* thunder

rʕăd v.i. (v.n. *rʕid*) 1. to shiver, to tremble, to shake (s.o.) 2. to thunder

răʕda pl. *-t* n.i. of *rʕăd*

ṛăʕda pl. *-t* thunderclap (n.u. of *ṛʕad*)

rʕăf v.i. (v.n. *rʕif*) to bleed from the nose

rʕid v.n. of *rʕăd*

rʕif v.n. of *rʕăf*

rʕiyya (coll.) subjects (king's)

ṛʕăš v.i. to shiver, to tremble (s.o.)

ṛăʕša pl. *-t* n.i. of *ṛʕăš*

ṛoʕyan pl. of *ṛaʕi* (a.p. of *ṛʕa*)

răʕʕăd v.t. 1. to shake, to make (s.o. or s.th.) tremble *šeddu men ketfu u-răʕʕdu ḥetta ṭaḥ.* He grabbed him by the shoulder and shook him until he fell down.

—*răʕʕdu l-berd.* The cold made him tremble .

ṛăʕʕăf v.t. 1. to give a bloody nose to 2. to cause or make bleed from the nose (as high altitude)

S

sab isib v.i. (v.n. *siban*) to rebel, to revolt, to mutiny, to rise in rebellion

¶ a.p. *sayeb* pl. *soyyab* rebel, insurgent

sabab pl. *sbab, ʔesbab* reason, cause, motive

sabil used in the expr. *fi-sabil llah* freely, without expecting a return or compensation *bna medṛaṣa fi-sabil llah baš iqṛaw wlad l-fuqaṛa.* He built a school for poor children out of the kindness of his heart.

sabeq v.t. to compete or go up against (usually in some physical sense, as racing)

sabeq a.p. of *sbeq*

sabeʕ pl. *-in* (adj.) seventh

¶ (*nhaṛ*) *s-sabeʕ* seventh day after birth when the child is named

sadat pl. of *sid* and *siyyed*

sades pl. *-in* (adj.) sixth

safali pl. *-yen* coarse, rude (person)

safih same as *sfih*

safăṛ same as *ṣafăṛ* 1

safeṛ same as *ṣafeṛ*

sagya pl. *swagi* same as *saqya*

sahel pl. *-in* (dim. *swihel,* comp. *shel*) 1. easy, simple (to learn, to do, etc.) 2. docile, easy to tame or master 3. (n.) one of the optional afternoon prayers

¶ *sahel mahel* same as *sahel* 1

sakarat l-mut 1. dying, imminent death *žatu sakarat l-mut.* He's dying. 2. death throes

saken a.p. of *sken*

saket a.p. of *sket*

sakuti pl. *-yen* silent, taciturn, quiet

** *duz ʕăl l-heṛhuṛi, la-dduz ʕăl s-sakuti.* Better to be wary of him who does not speak than of him who babbles endlessly.

sal isal v.t. **1.** to reclaim from, to claim back from (s.o.) *ža ka-isal ɛla ktabu.* He came asking for his book. **2.** to owe ≠ *šɛal baqi ka-tsalni?* How much do I still owe you?
** *ma-isal-š.* That's all right. It doesn't matter.

sal isil v.i. (v.n. *sayalan, silan*) **1.** to run, to flow (water, tears, nose) **2.** to leak (out), to drip (out) **3.** to leak, to be leaky (container)

saʔil pl. *soyyal* beggar

sala isali **1.** v.t. to finish, to end *l-bareḥ sala šġalu bekri.* He finished his work early yesterday. **2.** v.i. to end, to terminate, to be over
¶ *sala mɛa* to finish or polish off *b-ḍeṛḅa weḥda sala mɛah.* He finished him off with one blow.
¶ a.p. *msali* pl. *msalyen* free, unoccupied, having nothing to do

salam **1.** peace (as opposed to war) **2.** greeting, salutation
** *u-s-salam!* That's all! Nothing else! —*s-salamu ɛalaykom!* Hello!

salama used in the expr. *maɛa s-salama!* Good-by!

salef pl. *swalef* braid, braided tress (woman's hair)

salăf (no pl.) loan (bank, etc.)

salem a.p. of *slem*

salma (no pl.) sage (plant and spice)

sama isami v.t. to put together, to place next to one another *sami had ṭ-ṭwabel!* Put these tables together!
¶ *sama mɛa* to put or place against, next to *sami had š-šelya mɛa l-ḥăyṭ!* Put this chair against the wall!

sameḥ v.t. to pardon, to forgive (s.o.)
¶ *sameḥ f-* **1.** to not take, to give up (e.g. one's share) **2.** to give up the idea of, to decide against (s.th.) *sameḥt f-meṛṛakeš u-mšit neskon fe-sla.* I decided against (living in) Marrakech and went to live in Salé.
¶ *ḷḷah isameḥ f-* denotes a willingness to forget about s.th. *ɛṭini ġir alfayn fṛenk u-ḷḷah isameḥ-lek fe-t-telt alaf fṛenk l-baqya.* Just give me two thousand francs and we'll forget about the other three thousand.

sana (less commonly used than *ɛam*) pl. *sinin* year (period, particular year)

sanawi pl. *-yen* annual, yearly

sanida granulated or powdered sugar

sanes v.t. to acquaint (s.o.), to get (s.o.) used (to s.th.) *sanesni xay b-ṣugan ṭ-ṭumubil.* My brother got me used to driving a car.

sanuž seeds of the nigella used as a condiment

sanya pl. *swani* kind of vegetable or fruit garden (often watered by a noria)

saq isuq v.t. (v.n. *suqan*) **1.** to drive, to operate (car, bicycle, sailboat, mule, etc.) **2.** to pilot, to fly (plane, ship)
¶ *saq* (*isiq* or *isuq*) *le-xbaṛ* to find out, to hear (about) *ḅḅah saq-lu le-xbaṛ ka-ikmi u-ɛṭah le-ɛṣa.* His father found out he was smoking and gave him a licking.

saq pl. *siqan* calf (leg)

saqṭa pl. *-t, swaqeṭ* latch, bolt, lock (s.th. that locks without a key)

saquṭ **1.** fruit prematurely fallen from the tree **2.** miscarriage, abortion

saqya pl. *swaqi* irrigation ditch or flume

sar isir v.i. (v.n. *sir*) **1.** to go (rare usage, except impv. which is used for the more common *mša*) **2.** to go (and), to begin *ġir qbeḍ le-flus u-sar ka-ixṣeṛ fihom.* As soon as he got hold of the money he began to spend it.
¶ *ka-isir . . .* so, . . . *ka-isir ana daba wellit keddab!* So, now I'm a liar, am I!
¶ *sar ɛla* to beat (s.o., as a punishment)
¶ . . . *u-sir u-sir,* or *u-sir ɛla had š-ši* . . . and so forth, and so on, etc.

sara v.t. to show around, to take on a tour, to show the sights to (s.o.) *sarawni le-mdina.* They showed me around the city.

saṛaṭan cancer

sarga **1.** same as *sargana* **2.** same as *šarga*

sariž pl. *swarež* **1.** reservoir tank (water) **2.** fish bowl, aquarium **3.** pond, pool (fish, swimming, etc.)
¶ *ɛămmeṛ s-swarež* to brag, to boast (implies lying about it)

saṛeq a.p. of *sṛeq*

sarut pl. *swaret* key (of lock, clock, etc.)

sarya pl. *-t, swari* pillar, column

sareḥ a.p. of *sreḥ*

sas isus v.t. (v.n. *susan*) **1.** to shake (to get s.th. out or off) *sus l-xenša men ṭ-ṭḥin!* Shake the bag and get the flour out! **2.** to shake off or out *sus ṭ-ṭḥin men l-xenša!* Shake the flour out of the bag! **3.** to blow (nose)

sas pl. *sisan* foundation, base (building, argument, etc.)

satt, satet same as *sades*

sawa v.t. **1.** to level, to even, to make level or even (ground, chair, etc.) *sawi z-zlafa f-yeddek!* Keep the bowl level with your hand! **2.** to settle, to decide (matter, problem)
¶ *sawa bin . . . u-bin* (or *binat*) to treat equally, impartially, fairly *sawaw bini u-binu.* He treated both of us fairly.

sawa used in the expr. *ɛănduφ sawa* (or

sawa sawa) *ɛăndi kollhom sawa*. I treat (or consider) them all the same.

sawaẓil pl. of *saẓil*

sawem v.t. 1. to bargain over (price) 2. to bargain with (s.o.)

¶ *sawem t-taman d-* to price, to determine the price of (s.th.)

sayalan v.n. of *sal isil*

sayeb a.p. of *sab*

sayen v.t. to wait for, to await

sayer all (often with actual meaning of "most") *had š-ši sayer n-nas ka-iɛărfuh*. Everyone (i.e., all the people) knows that.

sayeẓ a.p. of *saẓ*

saẓ isiẓ v.i. (v.n. *siẓan*) 1. to spread (water on the ground, a stain on s.th., etc.) 2. to go on tour, to travel around

¶ a.p. *sayeẓ* pl. *soyyaẓ* tourist

saẓa pl. *-t* 1. open or vacant area 2. yard (school) 3. field, court (sports) 4. square, plaza

¶ *băɛɛăd men saẓt* to go or get away from, to get out of (one's) sight *băɛɛăd men saẓti wella džibha f-ṛasek!* Get away from me or you'll be sorry!

saẓil pl. *sawaẓil*, *swaẓel* coast, shore

saẓqa pl. *-t* 1. meteor, meteorite 2. sudden, choleric attack (e.g., appendicitis)

saɛa du. *saɛtayn* pl. *-t*, *swayeɛ* (dim. *swiɛa*) hour (60 min., time of day)

** *ṣ̌al hadi fe-s-saɛa?* What time is it?

¶ *f-had s-saɛa* 1. now, at the present time 2. nowadays, these days

¶ *f-saɛtuɸ* 1. right away ≠, immediately ≠, right afterwards ≠ *kla s-sehla u-f-saɛtu dxel l-bit l-ma*. He took the laxative and immediately went to the bathroom. 2. to be able ≠ (usually financially) *ma-ši f-saɛtu išri ṭ-ṭumubil daba*. He can't buy the car right now.

¶ *saɛa saɛa* from time to time, every now and then

¶ *saɛt-aš* (at) what time or hour *saɛt-aš maži?* What time is he coming?

¶ *saɛt-emma* whenever, any time

¶ *s-saɛa* but *ɛyit ma nɛaynu*, *s-saɛa ma-ža-š*. I waited and waited for him, but he didn't come.

saɛada 1. v.n. of *sɛăd* 2. happiness

¶ *saɛadat* Excellency *l-bareẓ tkellemt mɛa saɛadat l-ɛamil*. Yesterday I spoke with His Excellency the Governor.

saɛed v.t. to help, to aid (s.o.)

¶ *saɛed mɛa* to be patient with (s.o.)

¶ *saɛed ɛla* to be favorable to, to help (as rain to crops)

saɛef v.t. 1. to follow *saɛfu l-wad f-le-hbuṭ*. They followed the river downstream. 2. to

listen to, to follow (advice) 3. to listen to, to follow the advice of (s.o.)

saɛi a.p. of *sɛa*

saɛid pl. *suɛada* (comp. *sɛăd*) happy, full of happiness (character trait)

** *sbaẓek saɛid!* Good morning (to you)! —*ɛid mubaṛek saɛid!* Happy holiday! (Islamic holidays)

saɛudi pl. *-yen* 1. Saudi Arabian 2. (no pl.) gold or silver brocaded cloth

sba isbi v.t. (v.n. *sebyan*) to captivate, to charm (often used with *ɛqel*) *dik l-bent sbat-lu ɛăqlu*. That girl has captivated him.

sbab, *ʔesbab* pl. of *sabăb*

sbabel pl. of *sebbala*

sbani pl. of *sebniya*

sbasa pl. of *sebsi*

sbayeb pl. of *sebba* and *sbib*

sbaybi pl. *-ya* one who buys old things, refurbishes them, and resells them

sbayek pl. of *sbika*

sbayel pl. of *sbula*

sbaysi pl. *-ya* Spahi (North African trooper, generally cavalryman from Algeria or Morocco)

sbaɛ pl. of *subuɛ*

sbaɛiya pl. *-t* seven-shot rifle

sebb v.t. (v.n. *sebb, sebban*) to insult, to treat insolently

sebb (no pl.) 1. v.n. of *sebb* 2. insult, insolent remark or act

¶ *sebb sebbut* (no art.) leapfrog (game)

sebba pl. *-t*, *sbayeb* 1. cause, reason 2. pretext, excuse

¶ *b-sebbt* because of, on account of *ana b-sebbtek gaɛ ɛlaš žit*. I came only because of you.

¶ (*ġir*) *ɛla sebba* in a precarious position or condition (about to fall, break, to go off, etc.) *ɛăndak ṛa dik le-mraya ġir ɛla sebba waqfa!* Watch out! That mirror is about to fall and break!

sebbaba pl. *-t* index finger

sebbag adj. pl. *-in* n.pl. *-a* ag. adj. and n. of *sbeg*

sebbala pl. *sbabel* kind of fountain, usually continuously running, where people may get water

sebban v.n. of *sebb*

sebbeb v.t. to cause, to occasion *huwa gaɛ lli sebbeb had ṣ-ṣdaɛ kollu*. He's the one that caused all the ruckus.

sebbel 1. v.t. to sacrifice, to give *sebbel ɛămṛu baš yăɛteqha*. He gave his life to save her. 2. v.t. to donate (as to the poor) 3. v.i. to be boiling or steaming (water) *baqi l-beqṛež ma-sebbel*. The kettle isn't boiling yet. **4.** v.i. to form ears (wheat, in growing)

sebbeq v.t. **1.** to advance, to give in advance (money) *sebbeqt-lu šher dyal le-kra.* I gave him a month's rent in advance. **2.** to do first *ṣ-ṣbaḥ sebbeqt l-ḥămmam ʕăl le-fṭuṛ.* This morning I took a bath before breakfast.

sebbuṛa pl. *-t* blackboard

sebbeḥ v.i. to pronounce any formula, e.g., *sebḥan ḷḷah,* which glorifies God (often in connection with saying the rosary)

sbeg v.i. to run (person, animal)

sbib n.u. *-a* pl. *sbayeb* **1.** lock of hair (as horse's forelock or tail) **2.** fishing line **3.** string (e.g. violin)

sbik v.n. of *sbek*

sbika pl. *sbayek* **1.** nugget (as gold) **2.** ingot, bar (gold, silver) **3.** composite gold bracelet (i.e., many loose rings)

sbil free gift, donation

¶ *le-s-sbil* at one's own expense

¶ *ʕăṛṣa de-s-sbil* public garden or park

sbiq v.n. of *sbeq*

sbiritu alcohol (never for beverage)

¶ *sbiritu de-d-dwa* denatured alcohol, for medicinal antiseptic purposes

¶ *sbiritu de-l-ʕafya* methylated alcohol, cooking alcohol

sbiṭṛi pl. *-ya* one who sells, and may make, shoes (*ṣebbaṭ*)

sbiṭṛiyin (f. sg.) leather goods market or section (of city)

sbek v.t. (v.n. *sbik*) to pour or form into ingots

sebniya pl. *sbani* **1.** handkerchief **2.** scarf (head) **3.** kind of mosaic tile centerpiece (usually in the floors of patios)

sbeq v.t. (v.n. *sbiq*) **1.** to precede, to go before (s.o.), to go (on) ahead of (s.o.) **2.** to arrive before (as in a race) **3.** to get in front of (as when waiting in line) **4.** to pass (as in driving, being promoted over s.o.) **5.** to surpass, to come out ahead of (as in a test)

** *sbeqni lsani.* It just slipped out (what I said).

¶ a.p. *sabeq* pl. *-in* **1.** last, former previous **2.** used in the expr. *s-sabeq* or *fe-s-sabeq* before, previously

sberdila pl. *-t* (sg. *ferda de-s-sberdila*) (pair of) sneakers

sebseb v.i. to depart in shame or embarrassment, to leave in humiliation *ʕayratu u-sebseb bla-ma iwažeb.* She insulted him and he left in embarrassment, without answering.

sebseb pl. *sbaseb* mongoose

sebsi pl. *sbasa* kind of long Moroccan hashish pipe with a clay bowl

sebsub, šebšub pl. *sbaseb, šbašeb* **1.** horse's mane **2.** long, abundant hair on woman's head

sebt (with art.) Saturday

¶ *nhaṛ s-sebt* (on) Saturday

sebta Ceuta

sebti **1.** pl. *-yen* of or pertaining to Ceuta **2.** pl. *sbata* person from Ceuta

sbula pl. *sbayel* **1.** ear of wheat, barley, etc. (not corn) **2.** bayonet

** *l-beqṛež ṭḷeq s-sbula.* The kettle's boiling.

sbuʕ same as (*nhaṛ*) *s-sabeʕ* (see *sabeʕ*)

sbuʕa pl. of *sbăʕ*

sebyan v.n. of *sba*

sebḥan used in the expr. *sebḥan ḷḷah!,* expr. of amazement, surprise, or disbelief *sebḥan ḷḷah! ka-itkellem l-ʕăṛbiya!* I just can't believe it, he speaks (Moroccan) Arabic!

sbăʕ pl. *sbuʕa* lion

sebʕ, sebʕa (former used with n. admitting du.) seven

sebʕin **1.** seventy **2.** seventieth

sbăʕṭaš **1.** seventeen **2.** seventeenth

sda (m.) warp (weaving)

sdader pl. of *seddari*

sdas pl. of *sudus*

sdasi (no pl.) six-shooter (revolver)

sdasiya pl. *-t* six-shot rifle

sedd same as *šedd*

sedd pl. *sdud, sudud* **1.** dam (water) **2.** sluice or ditch gate

sedda v.i. to arrange or form the warp, to warp (before placing the woof)

seddan same as *šeddan* (v.n. of *šedd*)

seddari pl. *sdader* type of wall-to-wall sofa placed so that it faces the entrance to the room

seddaya pl. *-t* woman who forms the warp (before the woof is woven in)

sder, sdeṛ pl. *sdur, sdura* **1.** chest, breast (person, animal) **2.** bust (woman) **3.** wall facing the entrance of a room

sedra pl. *-t* kind of jujube tree or bush

sdud pl. of *sedd*

sdur, sdura pl. of *sder, sdeṛ*

sfa n.u. *-ya* hair-like filament growing from each grain husk of a cereal spike

sfafed pl. of *seffud*

sfaha obscenity, obscene words or actions

sfar pl. of *sfer*

sfayef pl. of *sfifa*

sfayen pl. of *sfina*

seff v.t. (v.n. *seffan*) to suck (up, out, in) (e.g. a liquid)

seffa kind of couscous made with sugar and cinnamon

¶ *seffa merduma* the dish *seffa* with pigeon added
seffan v.n. of *seff*
seffar pl. *-a* bookbinder
seffaž pl. *-a* one who makes and sells a kind of Moroccan doughnut (*šfenž*)
seffed v.t. to place on a skewer or brochette (for cooking)
seffel b- to yell or shout at, to bawl out
seffer v.t. to bind (books)
seffud pl. *sfafed* brochette, skewer, small spit
sfeh comp. of *sfih*
sfifa pl. *-t, sfayef* ornamental border (added to handkerchiefs, dresses, curtains, etc.)
sfih pl. *sufaha* (comp. *sfeh*) obscene, gross (person)
sfina pl. *-t, sfun, sfayn, sufun* ship (passenger, naval)
sfel, ˀesfel used in the expr. *sfel s-safilin* the bottom (of the ladder of success), "low man on the totem pole"
sefli pl. *-yen* ground floor
sefnaž pl. *-a* same as *seffaž*
sfenž n.u. *-a* same as *šfenž*
sfer pl. *sfar, sfura* zero, cipher
sfeṛžel n.u. *-a* 1. quince 2. quince tree
sefsa b- or *ƹla* to fail to keep an appointment or engagement with (s.o.)
sefsawi pl. *-yen* given to not keeping appointments or engagements
sfuf dish made of flour, sugar, and oil, seasoned with sesame
sfun pl. of *sfina*
sfura pl. of *sfer*
sga same as *sqa*
segga v.t. to put a sauce or gravy on (couscous)
segged v.t. to straighten (out) (s.th. crooked, bent, or dented)
seggem same as *seqqem*
segni pl. *sgani* 1. bowl-shaped frame of woven reeds, inverted over a fire to support bedding or clothing to be fumigated with sulphur 2. same sort of frame (covered to retain heat and vapors) inside which one sits for a vapor bath
seġnas pl. *sġanes* 1. butcher's steel, sharpening steel 2. letter opener 3. toothpick 4. any small, pointed tool used for cleaning out a clogged opening or hole
seġnes v.t. to remove dirt or other obstruction from (an opening or a hole) by means of a small pointed tool; to clean out (an opening) *seġnsat l-ƹăyn d-l-ibṛa.* She cleaned out the eye of the needle. —*ka-iseġnes snanu b-seġnas d-le-xšeb.* He's picking his teeth with a wooden toothpick.
sha isha v.i. (v.n. *shu, sehyan*) to get or be distracted

¶ *sha ƹla* to forget, to let slip one's mind *shit ƹliha.* It slipped my mind.
shal v.i. (v.n. *shula, shuliya*) 1. to get or become easy or easier *l-luġa shalet ƹliya men băƹd-ma žit l-ˀamirika.* The language became easier for me after I came to America. 2. to become (more) docile or easy (easier) to tame (e.g., an animal)
sham pl. of *sehm*
sharež pl. of *sehriž*
sehb pl. *shub* (foot)path, trail
sehhel v.t. 1. to facilitate, to make easy or easier (s.th.) 2. to simplify 3. to loosen the bowels of (s.o., as in constipation)
** *ḷḷah isehhel ƹlina u-ƹlik.* expr. said either to a beggar to whom one has no money to give, or as a good-luck wish to s.o. about to undertake s.th.
¶ *sehhel mƹa* to go easy on (s.o.) *ƹăndi z-zheṛ, sehhel mƹaya le-fqi f-le-mtiƹan.* I was lucky; the teacher went easy on me in the exam.
shit v.n. of *shet*
shel same as *shal*
shel comp. of *sahel*
sehla pl. *-t* laxative
sehm pl. *sham* share, portion
** *hada sehmek!* Serves you right! —*ma-hiya-š men sehmek!* She's out of your class! (i.e., socially)
sehma pl. *-t* same as *sehm*
sehriž pl. *sharež* pond, pool (fish, swimming)
shet (v.n. *shit*) 1. v.i. to calm down; to stop groaning, moaning (baby, sick person; often implies going to sleep also) 2. v.t. to exhaust, to wear out (s.o.)
sehta pl. *-t* n.i. of *shet*
shu v.n. of *sha*
shub pl. of *sehb*
shula, shuliya v.n. of *shal*
sehyan v.n. of *sha*
si (with art.) abbreviation of *siyyed,* used similarly to English "Mister", showing some respect; often used with first names among friends
siba anarchy, complete disorder
siban v.n. of *sab*
sid pl. *syad, sadat* 1. master, lord 2. mister (usually with first person sg. ending)
¶ *ḅḅahΦ siduΦ* (one's) grandfather
¶ *sidi ṛebbi* (my) God, Lord
sif pl. *syuf* sword (generic)
¶ *be-s-sif* by force *žaw ƹlih u-ddaweh mƹahom be-s-sif.* They came and took him away by force.
¶ *be-s-sif ƹla* (to be) incumbent on (s.o.), (to be) duty-bound *l-ˀinsan be-s-sif ƹlih ixeḷḷeṣ ḍ-ḍaṛiba.* It's one's duty to pay (his) taxes.

sifa pl. *-t, syef, syuf* face (usually used in describing) *siftu sift l-kelb.* His face looks like a dog's.
sikran, sikṛan henbane
sikuk same as *ṣikuk*
sil pl. *syul* stream made up of melting snow or rain runoff
silan v.n. of *sal*
silun pl. *-at* cell or dungeon for solitary confinement of a prisoner
simana same as *ṣimana*
sinima pl. *-t* **1.** movie house **2.** theater (shows, plays, etc.)
sinin pl. of *sana, sna* and *ʕam*
siniya same as *ṣiniya*
sinta pl. *-t* **1.** film (photographic) **2.** parasitic worm (e.g., tapeworm)
siqan pl. of *saq*
siqelliya Sicily
sir pl. *siru* impv. of *mša* (see *sar*)
sir **1.** v.n. of *sar* **2.** pl. *syur* cord, lace (shoes, corset, etc.)
sira pl. *-t* **1.** walk, gait **2.** behavior, comportment, conduct **3.** biography
sisan pl. of *sas*
sisban n.u. *-a* sweet pea
siwa except, save, but *had n-nas kollhom ka-năʕṛefhom siwa had s-siyyed.* I know everybody except this gentleman.
siwana pl. *-t* kite (as flown on a string)
siya rare colloquial form of *siyyʔa*
siyada **1.** sovereignty **2.** Excellency (title) *siyadet xalifet beġdad!* His Excellency the Caliph of Bagdad!
siyama, la-siyama especially, in particular *dik n-nas kollhom ṭeyybin, siyama bṛahim.* They're all fine people, especially Brahim.
siyaḥa tourism
siyyʔa pl. *-t* sin, transgression
siyyaf pl. *-a* headsman (executioner)
siyyala pl. *-t* tattooed spot or mark on a woman's chin
siyyas pl. *-a* (horse)trainer
siyyasa **1.** politics, political science **2.** diplomacy (international)
siyyasi pl. *-yen* **1.** political **2.** diplomatic (in dealing with others) **3.** (n.) politician
siyyeb v.t. **1.** to throw, to toss, to cast **2.** to throw away or out **3.** to drop, to let fall **4.** to leave, to abandon **5.** to neglect, to not take care of
siyyed v.t. to cause to be considered important, a "somebody" (e.g., money, fame) *we-ḷḷah-ila le-flus siyydu.* Money has really made him a somebody.
siyyed pl. *sadat* **1.** master, lord **2.** (with art. or first person pron. ending) mister **3.** gentleman, man **4.** saint **5.** tomb of a saint
siyyda pl. *-t* (f. of *siyyed*) **1.** more formal title than *lalla* **2.** lady, woman
siyyel v.t. **1.** to leak, to let leak (liquid) **2.** to make run or flow slightly, to let trickle (water, blood, etc.)
siyyeq v.t. to mop (floor)
siyyer v.t. **1.** to direct, to lead (orchestra) **2.** to instruct, to give instruction to
siyyes v.t. to train (animals)
¶ *siyyes mʕa* to have patience with (s.o.)
siyyež v.t. to enclose (with hedges, trees, fence), to fence in
siḥan v.n. of *saḥ*
skaken pl. of *sekkin*
skat **1.** silence, quiet **2.** v.n. of *sket*
¶ *be-s-skat* discreetly, without letting anyone hear, listen, or know
skawel pl. of *sekwila*
skayri pl. *-ya* drunkard
skef v.t. (v.n. *skif*) to suck (blood)
¶ p.p. *meskuf* pl. *-in* skinny, very thin (person)
¶ *meskuf mennuḍ d-demm* (to be) haggard, gaunt
skif v.n. of *skef*
skikku saints preserve us! God help us!
skinžbir ginger (spice)
skek pl. of *sekka*
sekka pl. *-t, skek* **1.** track (railroad) **2.** plowshare (including the moldboard) **3.** coin
¶ *ḍṛeb s-sekka* to mint coin(s)
sekkak pl. *-a* goldsmith
sokkaṛ sugar
¶ *sokkaṛ de-l-qaleb* loaf sugar
¶ *sokkaṛ mqaṛeṭ* lump (i.e., rectangular) sugar
¶ *sokkaṛ sanida* granulated sugar
sekkin pl. *skaken* knife
sekken v.t. **1.** to calm or quiet down (baby, turbulent water, etc.) **2.** to put up, to lodge (s.o.)
sekker v.t. **1.** to get (s.o.) drunk **2.** to drug, to narcotize (less common)
sokkoṛ same as *sokkaṛ*
sekket v.t. to calm or quiet down (s.o.)
sekkum asparagus
sekkuti pl. *-yen* quiet, taciturn
** *duz ʕăl l-wad l-heṛhuṛi la-dduz ʕăl s-sekkuti.* see *sakuti*
sekkež **1.** v.i. to become jammed or stuck (door, lock) **2.** v.t. to abash, to nonplus (s.o.)
sken v.i. **1.** (v.n. *sukun*) to become calm or quiet (baby, water, etc.) **2.** (v.n. *sokna*) to live, to dwell, to reside
¶ a.p. *saken* pl. *sokkan* inhabitant
¶ p.p. *meskun* pl. *-in* **1.** haunted (spirits, devils) **2.** possessed (as by the devil)

sokna **1.** v.n. of *sken* **2** **2.** dwelling, place to live

sker v.i. (v.n. *sekra*) to get drunk, intoxicated

sekra **1.** n.i. and v.n. of *sker* **2.** drunkenness ¶ *dṛebha b-sekra* to get drunk, intoxicated (deliberately)

sekran pl. *-in* drunk, intoxicated

sokri pl. *-yen* light beige

seksu couscous

sket iskot v.i. (v.n. *skat*) **1.** to be or keep quiet, to shut up **2.** to stop (clock, watch, heart) ¶ a.p. *saket* pl. *-in* quiet, silent

sekta n.i. of *sket*
¶ *dṛebha b-sekta* to keep quiet, to shut up
¶ *sekta qelbiya* heart attack

skubbi fibbing, tall tales, "fish stories"

sekwila pl. *-t, skawel* obsolescent term for *medṛaṣa*

sla **1.** Salé (city across the river from Rabat) **2.** mucus **3.** placenta ¶ *tqiyya ġir s-sla* to have the "dry heaves", to retch with an empty stomach

slaf (pl.) ancestors

slag pl. of *slugi*

slahem pl. of *selham*

slaki pl. of *selka*

slala **1.** descent, lineage, line *huwa men slalet muḥămmed.* He's of Mohammed's lineage. **2.** heredity (usually somewhat adj.) *dak l-meṛḍ fihom slala.* Among them that disease is hereditary.

slalem pl. of *sellum*

slam **1.** v.n. of *sellem* **2.** greeting, salutation

slama v.n. of *slem* **1**
** *be-s-slama!* Good-by! —*ṭriq s-slama!* Have a nice trip! —*ع la slamtek!* greeting for s.o. who has been away

slasel pl. of *selsla* (same as *sensla*)

slawi pl. *-yen* of or from Salé ¶ *geṛع a slawiya* kind of long, green squash

slayef pl. of *slif*

slayli pl. *-ya* basket maker

slaḥ (sg. and coll.) pl. *ʔesliḥa* arms, weapons

sleb v.t. (v.n. *selb*) to steal (as from a drunk or sleeping person, or by pickpocketing) *xellaweh ḥetta ddah n-nع as u-selbu-lu le-flus dyalu.* They waited until he was asleep then stole his money.
** *selbet-li ع ăqli.* She's stolen my heart.

selb v.n. of *sleb*

selba pl. *-t* lasso, lariat

selham pl. *slahem* kind of overrobe with a hood and no sleeves

slif pl. *slayef* husband of the wife's sister

slik v.n. of *slek*

sliman same as *šliman*

sliq v.n. of *sleq*

slit v.n. of *slet*

slix v.n. of *slex*

ʔesliḥa pl. of *slaḥ*

slek v.i. (v.n. *slik*) **1.** to save oneself, to escape (from some danger) **2.** to (finally) be sold or gotten rid of (old merchandise) **3.** to finish one's memorization of the Koran (Koranic school)

selk pl. *sluk* **1.** wire (fencing, electrical, etc.) **2.** cable (electrical) **3.** wire spoke (wheel)

selka, solka pl. *-t, slaki* n.i. of *slek* **3**
¶ *xerrež s-selka* same as *slek* **3**

sell v.t. (v.n. *sellan*) **1.** to pick out or off, to remove (as a fly from soup) **2.** to take furtively, to sneak
¶ *sell ṛaṣuφ men* to exclude oneself from, to stay out of (some situation, etc.)

sell, soll, maṛăḍ s-sell tuberculosis

slel pl. of *sella*

sella v.t. **1.** to entertain, to show a good time to **2.** to cheer up, to console

sella pl. *-t, slel* (woven)basket

sellak pl. *-a* savior (uncommon usage)

sellal pl. *-a* same as *slayli*

sellan v.n. of *sell*

sellef v.t. **1.** (*l-*) to lend (to), to loan (to) **2.** (*men*) to borrow (from)

sellek v.t. **1.** to save, to rescue **2.** to liberate, to free **3.** to bring some profit to (s.o.) (upon selling s.th.)

sellem v.t. **1.** to deliver, to hand over **2.** to transmit (s.th. to s.o.) **3.** to convert to Islam
¶ *sellem f-* to resign from (office)
¶ *sellem ṛaṣuφ* to surrender, to give oneself up
¶ *sellem ع la* to greet, to give regards to, to say "hello" to

sellum pl. *slalem* ladder
** *huwa bḥal s-sellum* (or *bḥal sellum baba ṛebbi*). He's a long drink of water (i.e., very tall and thin).

selleḥ v.t. to arm, to equip with weapons

slem v.i. **1.** (v.n. *slama*) to be safe (and sound) **2.** (v.n. *ʔislam*) to be converted to Islam, to embrace Islam
¶ a.p. *salem,* or *salem ġanem* safe and sound

sleq v.t. (v.n. *sliq*) **1.** to boil (eggs, etc.) **2.** to scald

selq chard

selsel same as *sensel*

selsul same as *sensul*

slet v.t. (v.n. *slit*) **1.** to pick off or out, to remove (as a fly from soup) **2.** to take furtively, to sneak

slugi pl. *slag* greyhound

slugiya pl. *-t* f. of *slugi*

sluk pl. of *selk*

sluع pl. of *selع a*

slex v.t. (v.n. *slix*) to skin (animal)
¶ *slex b-le-ʕṣa* to "skin" alive (as in punishing a child)
selʕa pl. *-t, sluʕ* (pl. rare) merchandise, goods
sem, sm pl. *asami, ʔesmaʔ* name *smek?* (What's) your name?
** *be-sme-llah!* In the name of God! (said in beginning some activity, i.e., Let's begin! Let's get started!)
sma pl. *-wat* (pl. rare) sky
ʔesmaʔ pl. of *sem, sm*
sman v.i. to become fat(ter), to gain weight
sman pl. of *smin*
smasṛiya, smasṛiya pl. of *semsaṛ*
smaṭ pl. *smayeṭ* **1.** diaper **2.** swaddling cloth or cover
smaṭi pl. of *semṭa* (same as *ṣemṭa*)
smawat pl. of *sma*
smawi pl. *-yen* **1.** heavenly, celestial **2.** sky blue
smayeṭ pl. of *smaṭ*
smaḥa v.n. of *smeḥ*
smid, smida semolina
smimen pl. *-in* dim. of *smin*
smin pl. *sman* (comp. *smen*) fat (person, animal)
¶ dim. *smimen* nice and fat
smir v.n. of *smer*
smiya pl. *-t* **1.** name *smiytek?* (What's) your name? **2.** ceremony in which a child is named
smiyat pl. of *smiya* and *ʔism, ism*
smiḥ pl. *-in* (comp. *smeḥ*) tolerant, forgiving
smiʕ **1.** v.n. of *smăʕ* **2.** pl. *-in* (no comp.) obedient
¶ *smiʕ muṭiʕ* obedient, submissive
semm pl. *smum* **1.** poison **2.** venom
semma **1.** v.t. to name, to call *aš ka-tsemmiweh?* What do you call it? —*dzad ʕăndhom wliyyed, ma-zal ma-ʕăṛfu šnu ġad-isemmiweh.* They had a baby boy, but they still don't know what they're going to name him. **2.** v.t. to title (book, etc.) **3.** v.t. to name, to appoint **4.** v.i. to say the expr. *be-sme-llah* (see *sem*)
** *aš semmak ḷḷah?* What's your name?
semman pl. *-a* one who sells salted (preserved) butter
semmaʕ pl. *-in* **1.** capable of being heard from a distance **2.** ag. adj. of *semmăʕ*
semmem v.t. to poison
¶ p.p. *mesmum* pl. *-in* belligerent and vindictive
semmen v.t. to fatten (up) (s.o., animal)
semmeṭ v.t. **1.** to wrap or bundle up (child) **2.** to cinch (horse)
semmăʕ v.t. **1.** to let or cause to hear **2.** to sing (s.th.) for *semmăʕna ši-ḥaža!* Sing us something! **3.** to insult *semmăʕ-li l-žedd u-ṭ-ṭayfa.* He insulted my whole family.
smen comp. of *smin*
smen pl. *smuna* salted butter (actually about the same as American store-bought butter, as opposed to freshly made salt-free butter)
¶ *smen bu-draʕ* kind of aged butter
smeq kind of black ink used in Koranic schools
¶ *smeq d-le-wden* earwax, cerumen
smer ʕla (v.n. *smir*) to wait for, to lie in wait for
smeṛ f. *semṛa* pl. *sumeṛ* brown-skinned, tan (either naturally or from sun)
semsaṛ pl. *-a, smasṛiya, smasṛiya* real estate agent or broker
semser v.t. **1.** to separate from the bone, to cut away from the bone (meat) **2.** to pick (s.o.) clean, to get all the money of (s.o.) away from him (gambling, robbing, etc.) **3.** to divest or rob (s.o.) of his clothes
semṭa same as *ṣemṭa*
smum pl. of *semm*
smuna pl. of *smen*
smeḥ l- (v.n. *smaḥa*) **1.** to excuse, to pardon, to allow (common courteous usage) **2.** to forgive, to pardon
¶ *smeḥ f-* **1.** to abandon, to forsake (s.o., doing s.th., etc.) **2.** to give up on (s.o., s.th.)
smeḥ comp. of *smiḥ*
smăʕ v.t. (v.n. *smiʕ, semʕ*) **1.** to hear **2.** to listen to
¶ *smăʕ klam* (plus n. or pron.) to obey, to do as one says *smăʕ klami!* Do as I say!
semʕ v.n. of *smăʕ*
** *ʕănd s-semʕ u-ṭ-ṭaʕa, semʕăn wa-ṭaʕatăn.* expr. of willing obedience to s.o's wishes
sna isni v.t. to irrigate (garden, etc.)
sna pl. *sinin, snin* year, period of a year
snadef pl. of *sendaf*
snader pl. of *sendura*
snan pl. of *senna*
snasel pl. of *sensla* and *sensul*
snater pl. of *snitra*
snaḥ (sg.) arms, weapons
senbel (coll.) kind of hyacinth
sendaf pl. *snadef* busybody, shameless meddler
sendef v.i. to be a busybody, meddler
sendura pl. *-t, snader* bucktooth
snin pl. of *sana, sna,* and *ʕam*
snitra pl. *-t, snater* mandolin
senn (not very much used) age *šḥal f-sennek?* What's your age?
senna pl. *-t, snan, sennin* any of the four front upper or four front lower teeth
senned v.t. to rest, to lean *senned-lu ṛaṣu*

b-le-mxedda! Lean his head on the pillow! —*sennedt le-mkoḥla ʕăl l-ḥăyṭ.* I leaned the rifle against the wall.
sennin pl. of *senna*
sensel v.t. **1.** to fasten or bind with a chain *mʕa-š senselti l-kelb?* What did you chain the dog to? **2.** to dislocate (joint)
sensla pl. *-t, snasel* (link)chain
sensul pl. *snasel* vertebral or spinal column
senṭṛež same as *šenṭṛež*
sqa isqi v.t. (v.n. *sqi, seqyan*) **1.** to (go) get, to fetch (water, as from a well) **2.** to give (s.o.) to drink **3.** to water, to irrigate **4.** to cover, bathe or plate (with gold, silver)
¶ *sqa l-* to furnish or supply (s.o.) with (water, etc.) *l-gerrab huwa lli ka-isqi-lna l-ma.* The water carrier is the one who supplies us with water.
sqaqi pl. of *seqqaya*
sqaqeṭ pl. of *seqqaṭa*
sqaṭ pl. of *sqiṭ*
sqaṭa v.n. of *tseqqeṭ*
sqayeṭ pl. of *sqiṭa*
sqayṭi pl. *-ya* one who buys old things, refurbishes them, and resells them
sqef pl. *squfa* **1.** ceiling (room, etc.) **2.** roof (house)
sqi v.n. of *sqa*
sqiṭ pl. *-in, sqaṭ* unable to resist one's desires (usually eating)
sqiṭa pl. *sqayeṭ* portion of body including the upper leg and rump, and sometimes a part of the side (usually a butcher's term, but may refer to a person)
seqqa same as *segga*
seqqaṭ pl. *-a* ag. n. of *tseqqeṭ*
seqqaṭa pl. *sqaqeṭ* stick with a hooked or claw-like end used in shaking fruit (e.g., walnuts, olives) from the tree
seqqaya pl. *-t, sqaqi* kind of fountain where people may fill containers with water
seqqef v.t. to roof (house)
seqqem v.t. **1.** to do, to be engaged in **2.** to make (meal, bed, cabinet, etc.) **3.** to straighten (s.th. crooked, bent) **4.** to fix, to repair
¶ p.p. *mseqqem* very well, perfectly, to perfection *ka-yăʕmel dima š-šġol dyalu mseqqem.* He always does his work to perfection.
seqqeṭ v.t. **1.** to make fall, to knock down (from a high place, as fruit from a tree) **2.** to fail (s.o., in an exam or subject) **3.** to get done, to finish *men ṣ-ṣbaḥ meskin u-huwa ka-ixdem yaḷḷah seqqeṭ žuž d-le-fradi.* The poor guy's been working since morning and he's only got two pairs done.
seqṣa v.t. **1.** to ask or inquire of (s.o.) **2.** to interrogate
sqeṭ v.i. (v.n. *suquṭ*) **1.** to fall off or out of (as from a high place) **2.** to fail (in an exam or subject) **3.** to miscarry (woman) **4.** to become paralyzed
** *sqeṭ lunu.* He's become pale and wan. —*sqeṭ men ʕăyn ṣ-ṣeḷṭan.* He's fallen into disfavor.
squfa pl. of *sqef*
seqyan v.n. of *sqa*
sra isri v.i. (v.n. *seryan*) to spread (spot, spilled water, disease, etc.)
** *ʕad sra mʕah le-ḥdit.* It's finally sinking in (i.e., he's finally beginning to understand). —*sra mʕah d-dwa.* The medicine is beginning to take effect.
srab mirage
srabes pl. of *serbis*
srar pl. of *serr*
srareb pl. of *serraba*
sraref pl. of *serrifa*
sraser pl. of *sersar*
srawel pl. of *serwal*
srayer pl. of *srir*
srayri pl. *-ya* maker of beds (i.e. *srir*)
srayež pl. of *sriža*
sṛažem pl. of *seṛžem*
sraḥ freedom, liberty (as a result of being freed)
** *ṭḷeq ḷḷah sraḥkom.* You're free to go.
serba **1.** v.t. to serve (food) **2.** v.t. to wait on, to attend (s.o.) **3.** v.i. (often reflexive with *ṛaṣuᵠ*) to hurry up
serbay pl. *-a* waiter (as in a restaurant)
serbis pl. *srabes* line, file, queue (as in waiting for tickets)
¶ *ʕmel* (or *qbeḍ*) *s-serbis* to form a line, to get in line (waiting)
serbisa beer
sred v.i. (v.n. *srid*) to get wet, damp, humid
serdil, serdin n.u. *-a* sardine
serġina rue (plant)
srid v.n. of *sred*
sriksi pl. *-yat* (pair of) men's leather slippers
srim v.n. of *srem*
sṛiq, sṛiqa v.n. of *sṛeq*
srir pl. *srayer* **1.** scaffolding **2.** bed (sleeping)
sriža pl. *-t, srayež* saddle (especially for mules)
sriʕ pl. *-in* (comp. *srăʕ*) **1.** fast, rapid **2.** prompt, quick (s.o., in doing s.th.)
srem v.t. (v.n. *srim*) to take off, to remove (clothes)
sṛenbeq, sṛembeq n.u. *-a* mussel
sṛeq v.t. (v.n. *sṛiq, sṛiqa*) **1.** to steal (s.th.) **2.** to rob, to steal from (s.o.)
¶ *sṛeq ṭ-ṭṛiq* to take a short cut (e.g. in walking)

** *serqetni ṭ-ṭriq.* I lost my way. I took a wrong road.

¶ a.p. *sareq* pl. *sorraq* thief, robber

serqa pl. *-t* n.i. of *sreq*

¶ *be-s-serqa* furtively, without anyone knowing

serr pl. *srar* **1.** secret (n.) **2.** charm, attractiveness

¶ *be-s-serr* **1.** in secret, secretly **2.** in a very low voice (usually in praying)

serraba pl. *-t, srareb* track, trail (as in tracking water or mud into a house)

serraq pl. *-a* thief, robber

serraqa pl. *-t* **1.** f. of *serraq* **2.** dropper, syringe **3.** hypodermic syringe

sorraq pl. of *sareq* (a.p. of *sreq*)

serraž pl. *-a* saddler

sorraḥ pl. of *sareḥ* (a.p. of *sreḥ*)

serred v.t. **1.** to get wet, to wet, to dampen **2.** to humidify

serri pl. *-yen* secret (adj.)

serrifa pl. *-t, sraref* noose, running knot, slip knot

serrež v.t. to saddle (horse, etc.)

serreḥ v.t. **1.** to free, to liberate **2.** to permit, to authorize **3.** to lay or spread out (a rug, map, etc.)

¶ *serreḥ ʕăynuᵠ (f-)* to look closely (at), to "open one's eyes" (and look at)

sersar pl. *sraser* bell (as in a telephone, doorbell, clock, etc.)

serser v.t. and v.i. to ring (bell)

sertel v.t. to insert, to thread (thread through a needle)

sruž pl. of *serž*

serwal pl. *srawel* (pair of) pants, trousers

seryan v.n. of *sra*

serž pl. *sruž* saddle (horse, bicycle)

seržem pl. *sražem* window

sreḥ (v.n. *serḥa*) **1.** v.i. to graze (cattle, etc.) **2.** v.t. to graze, to put(out) to pasture

¶ a.p. *sareḥ* pl. *serraḥ, sorraḥ* one who tends grazing livestock

serḥa n.i. and v.n. of *sreḥ*

srăʕ comp. of *sriʕ*

sorʕa speed, velocity, rapidity

ˀesses v.t. to found, to establish, to institute

staden v.i. to ask permission

staġet b- to ask the help of (s.o.; for serious or dangerous situations)

stahel v.t. to deserve, to merit, to be worthy of

stanef v.t. to resume, to go on with

staqem v.i. (v.n. *stiqama*) **1.** to become straight, to straighten **2.** to line up, to get in line **3.** to straighten up, to reform oneself (morally)

¶ a.p. *mestaqem* pl. *-in* **1.** straight *had l-xeṭṭ ma-ši mestaqem.* This line isn't straight. **2.** upright, righteous **3.** well-behaved

staḥeq same as *stahel*

staʕed in *staʕed be-llah,* to call for God's forgiveness or protection, e.g. after uttering a fault in prayer or hearing a blasphemy

staʕen b- to make use of, to help oneself (out) with (s.th.) *staʕen be-l-flus lli dzadu-lu fe-l-ˀužra dyalu u-šra dar ždida.* He made use of the raise in salary they gave him to buy a new house.

stebrek b- to gain a (vicarious) blessing from (s.o. who has been to Mecca, or s.th. considered holy)

steˀden same as *staden*

stedʕa istedʕi v.t. **1.** to invite **2.** to summon **3.** to subpoena

stġell v.t. (v.n. *stiġlal*) **1.** to take advantage of (opportunity) **2.** to exploit (resources, people, etc.)

steġreb (*men*) v.i. to be surprised (at), to be astonished (by)

stehza b- to ridicule, to mock

stidʕa pl. *-ˀat* **1.** invitation **2.** summons **3.** subpoena

stiġlal v.n. of *stġell*

stinaf v.n. of *stanef*

stinṭaq v.n. of *stenṭeq*

stiqama **1.** v.n o.f *staqem* **2.** uprightness, righteousness **3.** good behavior

stir v.n. of *ster*

stitu f. *stitwa* pl. *stitwin* little, small (used primarily in northern Morocco)

stiʕmal v.n. of *stăʕmel*

stenbeṭ v.t. to invent, to devise

steˀnef same as *stanef*

stenfăʕ b- to make use of

stenna same as *tsenna*

stenṭeq v.t. (v.n. *stinṭaq*) to interrogate, to question

ster v.t. (v.n. *stir*) to hide, to cover, to conceal (nakedness, object, scandal, etc.)

** *ḷḷah isetrek!* God preserve you! (used in asking and thanking)

ster preservation, protection (God's)

sett, setta (former used with pl. of n. admitting du.) six

settar used in the expr. *ya ḥafiḍ u-ya settar* said as an invocation of God's protection

settef v.t. to put in order, to arrange (objects)

settin **1.** sixty **2.** sixtieth

stexber ʕla to inquire about (rather rare usage)

steḥla v.t. to enjoy or appreciate with pleasure

stḥăqq same as *stahel*

steḥsen v.t. to like, to approve of, to find good or acceptable

steḥya v.i. **1.** to become embarrassed, ashamed **2.** to be modest (as opposed to boastful) **3.** to be timid, shy

¶ *steḥya men* to become shy or embarrassed in the presence of (s.o.)
stăɛder v.i. to excuse oneself (as from a meeting), to make excuses *ma-žit-ši l-l-xedma l-bareḥ, la-bodda nestăɛder l-yum.* I didn't come to work yesterday and today I have to make my excuses.
stăɛfa (men) to resign (from)
stăɛmel v.t. to use, to employ, to utilize (s.th.)
stăɛmer v.t. **1.** to colonize **2.** to occupy (as troops)
stăɛžeb same as *tɛăžžeb*
ṣṭilaḥ pl. *-at* term, expression
ṣṭel, ṣeṭla same as *ṣṭel, ṣeṭla*
seṭrenz same as *šenṭrez*
seṭwan same as *ṣeṭwan*
*su*ˀ (no pl.) misfortune
¶ *su*ˀ *l-ḥăḍḍ* bad luck
¶ *mɛaref* (or *măɛrift*) *s-su*ˀ bad company, unsavory associations
*su*ˀ*al* pl. ˀ*as*ˀ*ila* question *šḥal men su*ˀ*al ɛṭawkom f-le-mtiḥan?* How many questions did they ask you in the exam?
¶ *ṣḥab s-su*ˀ*al* angels charged with questioning those who have died (preceding judgment)
subuɛ pl. *-at, sbaɛ,* ˀ*asbaɛ* seventh, seventh part
sud pl. of *swed*
suda **1.** f. of *swed* **2.** washing soda
sudan (with art.) Sudan
sudani pl. *-yen* (adj. and n.) Sudanese
sudin pl. of *swed*
sudud pl. of *sedd*
sudus pl. *-at, sdas,* ˀ*asdas* sixth, sixth part
sufaha pl. of *safih, sfih*
sufun pl. of *sfina*
suger v.t. **1.** to insure (car, house, etc.) **2.** to register (mail)
sukri same as *sokri*
sukun **1.** v.n. of sken 1 **2.** quiet, tranquillity **3.** diacritic indicating lack of vowelling (Arabic script)
sulu, suluw **1.** distraction, diversion (from boredom) **2.** lack of care and worry *ɛayša ġir f-sulu.* She lives a carefree life.
sum (no pl.) price, cost
¶ *sum-aš* at what price or cost
sumer pl. of *smer*
sunan pl. of *sunna*
sunna pl. *sunan* tradition or teaching of the Prophet Mohammed (often regarded as valid as Koranic law), orthodox Islam
sunni pl. *-yen* of or pertaining to *sunna,* orthodox Muslim
suq pl. *swaq* **1.** market, marketplace (usually open-air) **2.** section of city where one particular sort of product is made and/or sold
** *dxel suq ṛaṣek!* Mind your own business! —*ma-ši suqek!* None of your business! —*ma-ɛăndi suq, or ma-ɛăndi fih suq.* I don't care one way or the other.
¶ *suq ɛamm* fair, exposition (usually international)
suqan v.n. of *saq*
suqi pl. *-yen* ready-made (clothing, etc.)
suquṭ v.n. of *sqeṭ*
susa pl. *-t* decayed or rotted area (tree, tooth, etc.)
susan **1.** v.n. of *sas* **2.** n.u. *-a* lily
susdi gauze, muslin
suwwaq pl. *-a* **1.** same as *ṣuwwag* **2.** one who frequents the country markets either for buying or selling
suwwaqi pl. *-yen* ordinary, common, run-of-the-mill
suwwas pl. *-a* ag. n. of *sas*
suwwasa pl. *-t* long pole or stick used in knocking fruits, nuts, etc., from trees
suwwek **1.** v.t. to clean or treat with the bark of the walnut tree (teeth and gums) **2.** v.i. to use walnut bark for cleaning one's teeth
suwwel v.t. to ask, to put a question to
suwwes v.t. and v.i. to rot, to decay
sužud v.n. of *sžed*
sužun v.n. *of sžen*
suɛada pl. of *saɛid*
swa iswa to be worth, to cost *l-liṣanṣ fe-l-meġṛib ka-iswa tmanin fṛenk l-litru.* In Morocco gasoline costs eighty francs a liter.
swa . . . swa (second *swa* often omitted) whether . . . or *swa glesna l-qoddam swa l-luṛ, bḥal bḥal.* It makes no difference whether we sit in front or in back.
swagi pl. of *sagya* (same as *saqya*)
swak bark of the walnut tree (used in cleaning teeth)
swalef pl. of *salef*
swani pl. of *sanya*
swaq pl. of *suq*
swaqi pl. of *saqya*
swaqeṭ pl. of *saqṭa*
swari pl. of *sarya*
swaret pl. of *sarut*
swarež pl. of *sariž*
swayni pl. *-a* gardener (in charge of the *sanya*)
swayeɛ pl. of *saɛa*
swaḥel pl. of *saḥil*
swed f. *suda* pl. *sud, sudin* black (things, people)
swihel dim. of *sahel*
swiqa pl. *-t* kind of market dealing primarily in foodstuffs
swirti **1.** luck, good fortune **2.** luck, chance **3.** lottery, raffle **4.** pl. *-yat* amusement park having games for winning prizes, etc.
** *swirti!* Maybe! Could be!

—*swirti u-zheṛ.* Well, that's the way it goes. That's life.
swiɛa pl. *-t* (dim. of *saɛa*) a little while, a moment (or two)
sxa isxa b- (v.n. *sxi*) to want to give up or abandon (usually used with *ma-* in its opposite meaning) *ma-sxa-š be-bladu.* He didn't want to leave his country.
—*ma-sxa-š biha* (or *ifṛeqha*). He didn't want to be separated from her.
¶ *men ṣ-ṣbaḥ u-huwa gales, ɛad sxa ixrož.* He finally left after sitting around here since morning. —*bḥal le-ɛsel ma-tesxa-š mennu* (or *bih*). You're really going to like him.
sxan pl. of *sxun*
sxana pl. (of intensity) *sxayen* **1.** heat, warmth **2.** fever *žatu s-sxana.* He's got a fever.
sxaṛi pl. of *sexṛa, soxṛa*
sxawa generosity, largess
sxayen pl. of *sxana* and *sxina*
sxef v.i. (v.n. *sexfa*) **1.** to become exhausted (physically) *b-quwt ž-žri sxef.* He's exhausted from running. **2.** to faint, to pass out (from weakness, exhaustion)
sexfa **1.** v.n. of *sxef* **2.** exhaustion (from exertion) **3.** unconsciousness, fainting spell, faint *ɛli dima ka-tqebṭu s-sexfa mnin ka-išuf d-demm.* Ali always faints when he sees blood.
sexfan pl. *-in* **1.** exhausted (from exertion) **2.** faint, dizzy **3.** unconscious, fainted (passed) out
sxi **1.** v.n. of *sxa* **2.** pl. *-yen* generous, openhanded
sxina pl. *sxayen* kind of Jewish stew eaten on Saturdays
sxir v.n. of *sxeṛ*
sxiṭ v.n. of *sxeṭ*
sxen isxon v.i. (v.n. *sxuniya*) to get warm or hot
sxen comp. of *sxun*
sxeṛ v.i. (v.n. *sxir*) to turn out well, to be successful *sxeṛ-lu hadak l-mešruɛ.* That project turned out well for him.
sexṛa, soxṛa pl. *-t sxaṛi* **1.** commission, errand **2.** salary, pay **3.** tip, gratuity
sxeṭ ɛla (v.n. *sxiṭ*) same as *sexxeṭ ɛla*
sexṭ **1.** curse, malediction **2.** catastrophe, disaster
¶ *sexṭ ḷḷah* enormous, huge, monstrous *had r-rtila sexṭ ḷḷah!* This spider is enormous!
sxun pl. *-in, sxan* (comp. *sxen*) **1.** hot, warm **2.** hottest room of the public bath
sxuniya **1.** v.n. of *sxen* **2.** heat, warmth
sexxef v.t. **1.** to fatigue, to exhaust (s.o.) **2.** to make or cause to be faint
sexxen v.t. to warm (up), to heat (up)
sexxeṛ v.t. to commission, to give an errand to (s.o.)
¶ *ḷḷah isexxeṛ* . . . good luck . . . *ḷḷah isexxeṛ-lek f-had l-biɛa u-š-šeṛya.* Good luck in your business deal.
sexxeṭ (*ɛla*) v.i. to utter insults and curses (against)
syad pl. of *sid*
syasa used in *be-s-syasa* slowly, easily
syaž (no pl.) enclosure, enclosing fence, hedge, or line of trees (around a field)
syef pl. of *sifa*
seyl same as *sil*
syuf pl. of *sif* and *sifa*
syul pl. of *sil*
syur pl. of *sir*
soyyab pl. of *sayeb* (a.p. of *sab*)
soyyal pl. of *saᵓil*
soyyaḥ pl. of *sayeḥ* (a.p. of *saḥ*)
sžed v.i. (v.n. *sužud*) to prostrate oneself (in prayer)
sežda pl. *-t* n.i. of *sžed*
sžin v.n. of *sžen*
sžen v.t. (v.n. *sžin, sužun*) **1.** to close in, to keep in (person, chickens, etc.) **2.** to imprison, to lock up
¶ p.p. *mesžun* adj. pl. *-in* n.pl. *msažen* prisoner
sžen pl. *sžun* prison
sežna pl. *-t* coop, hut (chickens, rabbits, pigeons, etc.)
sžun pl. of *sžen*
sežžada pl. *-t* prayer rug
sežžel v.t. **1.** to register, to have recorded (name, documents, etc.) **2.** to record, to note, to keep a record of (minutes, etc.) **3.** to record (music, etc.)
sḥa isḥa (v.n. *sḥu*) to clear up (sky, weather)
sḥab v.t. or v.i. to seem (often used in the perfect as "think") *sḥabni* (or *sḥab-li*) *žiti l-bareḥ.* I thought you came yesterday.
sḥab n.u. *-a* cloud
sḥaq powdered charcoal or carbon (i.e., the powder which comes from larger chunks)
sḥari pl. of *ṣeḥra*
sḥaseḥ (no sing.) dim *sḥisḥat* lies, trickery *had š-ši ġir kdub u-sḥaseḥ.* That's just lies and trickery.
sḥăb same as *sḥab* (v.)
sḥiq v.n. of *sḥeq*
sḥir v.n. of *sḥeṛ*
sḥen pl. *sḥuna* mosque courtyard
sḥeq v.t. (v.n. *sḥiq*) **1.** to powder, to pulverize **2.** to crumble, to make into crumbs (as bread) **3.** to annihilate, to exterminate
** *ž-žuɛ sḥeq-li žufi.* I'm starving (i.e., very hungry).
sḥer v.t. (v.n. *sḥir*) to bewitch, to enchant, to put under a spell (person)

¶ *sḥer ɛla* same as *sḥer* (things and animals)
seḥseḥ ɛla **1.** to try to persuade (s.o.) **2.** to fib to, to lie to (s.o.)
sḥu **1.** v.n. of *sḥa* **2.** fair or clear weather
sḥuna pl. of *sḥen*
sḥur **1.** sorcery, magic (including prestidigitation, etc.) **2.** fascination, enchantment (i.e., through spells, etc.)
seḥḥar pl. *-a* magician, sorcerer (including prestidigitators, etc.)
seḥḥeb v.i. to get cloudy or overcast
sɛa isɛa v.i. (v.n. *sɛaya*) to beg (beggar)
¶ a.p. *saɛi* pl. *soɛyan* beggar
sɛad pl. of *sɛid* (same as *saɛid*)
sɛaya v.n. of *sɛa*
sɛăd v.i. (v.n. *saɛada*) to be (or become) happy
** *ḷḷah isɛăd ṣbaḥek, msak!* Good morning, evening!
¶ p.p.*mesɛud* used in the expr.
** *mbaṛek mesɛud!* congratulations! (said to s.o. who gains possession of s.th. new) —*mbaṛek mesɛud s-siyaṛa ž-ždida!* Congratulations on the new car!
sɛăd comp. of *sɛid, saɛid*
sɛid pl. *sɛad* same as *saɛid*
sɛil v.n. of *sɛăl*
sɛăl v.i. (v.n. *sɛil*) to cough (person)
soɛla, seɛla **1.** n.i. of *sɛăl* **2.** coughing, cough
sɛăṛ same as *ṣɛăṛ*
sɛăr, săɛr pl. *ʔasɛaṛ, ʔasɛar* official price, cost
soɛyan pl. of *saɛi* (a.p. of *sɛa*)
săɛɛăd v.t. to make happy
săɛɛăṛ v.t. to price (officially), to put an official price on (government authority)

ṣ

ṣab iṣib v.t. (v.n. *ṣiban*) **1.** to find *fayn ṣebti le-ktab?* Where did you find the book? **2.** to run across or into, to come across or upon (s.o., s.th.) **3.** to meet *iwa nṣibek ġedda f-bab l-bạnka.* Then I'll meet you tomorrow in front of the bank.
¶ *ṣabet l-muṣiba* to happen (s.th. bad or unfortunate) to *ṣabettu meskin waḥed l-muṣiba kbira.* He's had a terrible misfortune.
ṣaba **1.** pl. *-t* good harvest, crop **2.** pl. *-t, ṣyeb* kind of covered street or alley, sometimes dead-end
ṣabi, ṣabiy pl. *ṣebyan,* f. *ṣabiya* pl. *-t* child, little kid
ṣabṛa **1.** aloe(s) **2.** kind of artificial silk
ṣabun n.u. *-a* soap, or similar substance for washing
¶ *ṣabun beldi* kind of soft soap (used primarily in washing clothes)
¶ *ṣabuna* (n.u.) *de-r-riḥa* (cake of) perfumed or scented toilet soap
ṣadaqa pl. *-t* alms, charity
ṣaḍef v.t. to run or come across by chance, to chance upon (s.o., s.th.)
ṣaḍiq same as *ṣḍiq*
ṣaḍeq v.t. to tell the truth to, to be sincere with
ṣaḍeq a.p. of *ṣḍeq*
ṣafef, ṣaff v.t. to put or arrange in a line or file, to line up
ṣafi a.p. of *ṣfa*
ṣafeṛ v.i. **1.** to travel, to journey **2.** to leave or go on a trip or voyage
ṣafăṛ **1.** pl. *ʔaṣfaṛ* trip, voyage, journey **2.** second month of the Muslim lunar calendar
ṣafeṭ iṣifeṭ same as *ṣifeṭ*
ṣafeḥ v.t. to shake the hand of (s.o., in greeting)
ṣag iṣug v.t. (v.n. *ṣugan*) **1.** to drive, to operate (vehicle) **2.** to drive, to herd (livestock)
ṣag pl. *ṣigan* **1.** calf (leg) **2.** trunk (tree)
ṣaġ iṣuġ v.t. (v.n. *syaġa*) to make into jewelry (precious metal)
ṣaka pl. *-t* tobacco shop
¶ *mul ṣ-ṣaka* tobacconist
ṣal iṣul v.i. (v.n. *ṣewla*) to be strong, powerful, mighty
** *baqi ka-iṣul w-igul.* Don't count him out yet (i.e., he's still got plenty of fight or potential).
ṣaḷa pl. *-t, ṣyeḷ* **1.** living room **2.** large room (usually on the upper floor of a house)
ṣalat same as *ṣḷa*
ṣalawat pl. of *ṣḷa*
ṣalib pl. *ṣoḷbaw* cross, crucifix
ṣaliḥ pl. *-in* **1.** saint **2.** sanctuary **3.** saintly
ṣaleḥ v.t. to bring back harmony, to reconcile (persons)
ṣaleḥ a.p. of *ṣḷeḥ*
ṣam iṣum v.i. (v.n. *ṣum, ṣyam*) **1.** to fast (usually entails sexual and other abstinences) **2.** not to eat (voluntarily or as result of famine, etc.)
ṣan iṣun v.t. (v.n. *ṣun, ṣyana*) to protect, to safeguard (honor, reputation; not greatly used)

ṣanam pl. *ˀaṣnam, ˀeṣnam, ṣnam* idol, graven image
ṣaneɛ a.p. of *ṣnăɛ*
ṣaq same as *saq*
ṣaqṭa same *saqṭa*
ṣaṛ iṣiṛ **1.** to become (not too common usage) **2.** to start, to begin (doing s.th.) *ġir semɛu le-fqi daxel ṣaṛu iqṛaw.* As soon as they heard the teacher come in they started studying.
** *ṣaṛ daba ka-nekdeb!* So, now I'm a liar, am I!
¶ *ṣaṛ men* to become of *šnu ṣaṛ mennu?* What ever became of him?
ṣaṛaḥa frankness, candidness
ṣaṭ iṣuṭ v.i. to blow (wind, with mouth) *ila bġiti dik n-naṛ tezher, ṣuṭ ɛliha!* If you want that fire to get going, blow on it!
** *ṣaṭ fih b-waḥed ḍ-ḍeṛba l-wežhu.* He gave him a punch in the nose.
ṣaṭ imp, rascal, scoundrel (somewhat affectionate)
** *bqa ɛlih ṣ-ṣaṭ mmaṭ ḥetta žabu ṣafi.* He beat on him and beat on him until he laid him out flat.
ṣaweb same as *ṣuwweb*
ṣayeṛ pl. *ṣwayeṛ* expenses, what is spent
ṣaḥ iṣiḥ v.i. (v.n. *ṣyaḥ*) **1.** to cry, to wail (baby, mourner, etc.) **2.** to howl (dog, wolf)
ṣaḥabi pl. *ṣuḥaba* disciple (of the Prophet Mohammed)
ṣaḥeb v.t. **1.** to associate with, to become friendly with **2.** to accompany (s.o., as on a trip)
ṣaḥeb pl. *ṣḥab,* f. *ṣaḥba* pl. *-t, ṣḥabat* **1.** friend, (an) intimate **2.** companion (i.e., one who accompanies) **3.** partner (as in a card game) **4.** accomplice **5.** partisan follower (in same cause) **6.** lover (illicit) **7.** owner, proprietor
¶ *ṣaḥeb dɛăwti* **1.** (my) opponent (in a lawsuit) **2.** enemy (personal)
¶ *ṣaḥeb n-nešwa* one addicted to intoxicating or narcotizing habits (drinking, dope, etc.)
ṣaɛ pl. *ṣiɛan* dry measure approximately equal to a bushel
ṣbabeṭ pl. of *ṣebbaṭ*
ṣbabṭi pl. *-ya* shoemaker
ṣbaġa **1.** paint (not artist's) **2.** dye, tint
ṣbanya Spain
ṣbaḥ pl. *-at* morning
** *ṣbaḥek!* or *ṣbaḥ l-xir!* Good morning! —*ṣ-ṣbaḥ l-llah!* said when one is irked by s.th. s.o. does (only in the morning)
ṣbaɛ pl. of *ṣbăɛ*
ṣebb (v.n. *ṣebban*) **1.** v.t. to pour (liquids) **2.** v.i. to serve (up) food, to portion out food (at the table) **3.** v.i. to fall (rain, waterfall)
** *ṣebb!* scat! (to cat)
ṣebbab **1.** pl. *-in* ag. adj. of *ṣebb* **2.** waterfall
ṣebbaġ pl. *-a* **1.** painter (houses, etc.) **2.** dyer, tinter (cloth, etc.)
ṣebban v.n. of *ṣebb*
ṣebbana pl. *-t* laundry woman, washer woman
ṣebbaṛ pl. *-in* ag. adj. of *ṣbeṛ*
ṣebbaṭ pl. *ṣbabeṭ* pair of shoes (usually leather; one shoe, *ferda de-ṣ-ṣebbaṭ*)
ṣebbaɛa, ṣebbaɛiya pl. *-t* glove, mitten
ṣebben **1.** v.t. to wash, to launder **2.** v.i. to do the wash or the laundry
ṣebbeṛ v.t. **1.** to get or attempt to get (s.o.) to be patient **2.** to comfort, to console
ṣebbeḥ v.t. to cause to be, to make (the following morning) *l-lăɛb de-l-bareḥ fe-l-lil ṣebbeḥni mṛiḍ.* The game last night made me sick this morning.
** *ḷḷah iṣebbḥek ɛla xir!* Good night! —*ṣebbeḥna ɛăl ḷḷah.* same as *ṣ-ṣbaḥ l-llah* (see *ṣbaḥ*) —*ṛah ṣebbeḥ!* It's time for the morning prayer! (used often simply as a time reference)
¶ *ṣebbeḥ ɛla* **1.** to give a morning greeting to (s.o.) **2.** to start the day off with or by (drinking, shouting, etc.) *dima ka-iṣebbeḥ ɛăl š-šṛab.* He always starts the day off by drinking.
ṣbeġ v.t. (v.n. *ṣbiġ*) **1.** to paint (houses, etc.) **2.** to dye, to tint
¶ *ṣbeġ* (s.th.) *l-* (s.o.) to switch (s.th.) on (s.o.; usually in selling) *ṣebġu-li ṣ-ṣebbaṭ.* They switched shoes on me (i.e., gave me an inferior item).
ṣbiġ v.n. of *ṣbeġ*
ṣbiṭaṛ pl. *-at* hospital, dispensary
ṣbeḷyuni, ṣbenyuli adj. pl. *-yen* n.pl. *ṣbenyul* **1.** Spanish (n.sg. Spaniard) **2.** (f.) Spanish language
ṣbenyul n.pl. of *ṣbenyuli*
ṣbeṛ v.i. (v.n. *ṣbeṛ*) **1.** to be patient **2.** to be tolerant, forbearing **3.** to wait, to hold on **4.** to be resigned, to accept things as they are **5.** to control oneself (emotions and feelings) **6.** to last, to wear (shirt, shoes, etc.)
¶ *ṣbeṛ ɛla* **1.** to tolerate, to stand (one's actions, nature, etc.) **2.** to give (more time) to (s.o.) *ṣbeṛ ɛliya waḥed š-šheṛ.* Give me another month.
ṣbeṛ v.n. of *ṣbeṛ*
¶ *fihφ ṣ-ṣbeṛ* to be patient ≠
¶ *qellet ṣ-ṣbeṛ* impatience
ṣebyan pl. of *ṣabi, ṣabiy*
ṣbăḥ to be . . . in the morning, this morning *ṣbăḥ mṛiḍ.* He was sick this morning.

—*ṣbăḥ f-fas.* He was in Fez this morning. He arrived in Fez in the morning.

** *kif ṣbăḥti?* How are (were) you this morning? (e.g. to s.o. who has been sick)

—*ṣbăḥ ṣ-ṣbaḥ* (or *l-ḥal*). The dawn is breaking.

ṣbăḥ same as *ṣbaḥ*

ṣobḥ, ṣebḥ first daily prayer (early morning)

ṣebḥiya pl. *-t* early morning hours

ṣbăɛ pl. *ṣebɛan, ṣbaɛ* digit (toe or finger)

** *qṭăɛ-lhom ṣbaɛhom.* He swindled them.

¶ *ṣbăɛ kbir* thumb, big toe

¶ *ṣbăɛ ṣġir* little finger, little toe

¶ *ṣbăɛ weṣṭi* middle finger, middle toe

ṣebɛan pl. of *ṣbăɛ*

ṣḍa (m.) corrosion (metals)

ṣḍaf n.u. *-a* 1. button (clothing) 2. mother-of-pearl

ṣḍaq pl. *-at* 1. marriage certificate 2. dowry

¶ *dfăɛ ṣ-ṣḍaq* to give or pay a dowry

¶ *ḍreb ṣ-ṣḍaq* to sign a marriage contract, to marry or get married legally

ṣdaɛ noise, racket

ṣeḍḍa v.t. and v.i. to corrode (metals)

ṣeḍḍeq v.t. 1. to give as charity, to donate 2. to believe, to accept as true or truthful (s.o., s.th.)

¶ *ṣeḍḍeq ɛla* to give charity to

ṣeddăɛ v.t. to annoy with noise or chatter

ṣeḍfa 1. chance, coincidence 2. pl. *-t* button (clothing)

¶ *ġir ṣeḍfa* by chance, by coincidence

ṣḍim v.n. of *ṣḍem*

ṣḍiq pl. *aṣḍiqa, ˀaṣḍiqaˀ* friend

ṣḍem v.t. (v.n. *ṣḍim*) to run over or down (as a car)

ṣeḍma pl. *-t* shock, trauma (mental)

ṣḍeq v.i. 1. to be right, to guess right 2. to turn out well, to turn out to be good (usually foods) 3. to find oneself, to end up (somewhere)

¶ a.p. *ṣaḍeq* pl. *-in* honest, trustworthy

ṣeḍq 1. truth 2. honesty, trustworthiness

ṣdeṛ men to come from, to emanate from

** *ṣdeṛ mennu waḥed l-ġaḷăṭ kbir.* He made a big mistake.

ṣdeṛ same as *sder*

ṣeḍṛiya pl. *-t* 1. kind of jacket buttoned from the neck down 2. apron 3. bib

ṣdăɛ same as *ṣḍaɛ*

ṣfa iṣfa v.i. 1. to clear up (sky, water) 2. to be settled or cleared up (matter, business)

** *qelbu ṣfa.* He's lost all his rancor (for s.o.).

¶ *žab* (s.o.) *ṣafi* 1. to knock (s.o.) out cold 2. to kill

¶ a.p. *ṣafi* pl. *ṣafyen* (comp. *ṣfa*) 1. clear (sky, water) 2. pure (gold, heart) 3. exactly, perfectly (syntactically adjectival) *l-keswa žatu ṣafya.* The suit fits him perfectly.

** *ṣafi!* At last it's over, done! That's enough! That's all!

ṣfa comp. of *ṣafi* (a.p. of *ṣfa*)

ṣfaṛ v.i. 1. to yellow, to get or turn yellow 2. to pale, to get or become pale or pallid

ṣfaṣef pl. of *ṣefṣaf*

ṣfawa 1. purity (of gold, heart) 2. clearness, limpidness (water, sky)

ṣfayeḥ pl. of *ṣfiḥa*

ṣeff pl. *ṣfuf* 1. row, rank 2. line, file

¶ *dar* (or *ɛmel*) *ṣ-ṣeff* to form a line, to line up

¶ *šedd ṣ-ṣeff* to get in line

ṣeffa v.t. 1. to purify, to filter (water) 2. to strain (e.g. juices) 3. to refine (oil, metals) 4. to separate, to skim ≠ (milk from its cream, soup from its oil, etc.) *ṣeffi had le-mṛeq men z-zit.* Separate this gravy from the oil (i.e., it's too oily). 5. to settle (matter, business) 6. to finish, to end *mnin tṣeffi šġalek, xḷeṭ ɛliya.* When you finish work, join me.

¶ *ṣeffa mɛa* to kill (person, animal)

ṣeffaṛ pl. *-a* coppersmith

ṣeffaṛa pl. *-t* whistle (instrument or sound)

ṣeffaya pl. *-t* 1. filter (liquids) 2. strainer (juices)

ṣeffef same as *ṣaff, ṣafef*

ṣeffir see *bu-ṣeffaṛ*

ṣeffeq v.i. to clap, to applaud

ṣeffeṛ 1. v.i. to whistle 2. v.t. to yellow, to make yellow

¶ *xawi ka-iṣeffeṛ* completely deserted or empty (room, house, etc.)

ṣeffeḥ v.t. 1. to leaf through (as a book) 2. to press into sheets (metal, etc.) 3. to shoe (horse) 4. v.i. to die, to "kick the bucket"

ṣfeg v.i. (v.n. *ṣfig*) to tremble, to shiver (from cold, fear)

ṣefga pl. *-t* 1. n.i. of *ṣfeg* 2. chill, shiver

ṣfig v.n. of *ṣfeg*

ṣfiq v.n. of *ṣfeq* (same as *ṣfeg*)

ṣfiḥa pl. *-t, ṣfayeḥ* 1. horseshoe 2. tap (for shoes) 3. flat stone (for milling, manhole covers)

ṣfeq same as *ṣfeg*

ṣefqa same as *ṣefga*

ṣfeṛ 1. copper (metal) 2. copperware 3. travel, traveling

ṣfeṛ f. *ṣefṛa* pl. *ṣufeṛ* 1. yellow, yellowish 2. pale, pallid

ṣefṛa pl. *-t* trip, journey

ṣfeṛžel n.u. *-a* same as *sfeṛžel*

ṣefṣaf n.u. *-a* pl. *ṣfaṣef* poplar

ṣfuf pl. of *ṣeff*

ṣfuṛa, ṣfuriya **1.** yellowness, yellow **2.** paleness (skin, face)
ṣefḥa pl. *-t* page (book, etc.)
ṣguɛiya bad luck, misfortune
ṣgăɛ pl. *ṣugeɛ* ill-fated, unfortunate (person)
ṣġa iṣġa l- to listen to, to take the advice of (s.o.)
ṣġaṛ v.i. **1.** to get small(er), to shrink **2.** to become short(er) (in stature) **3.** to get or become young(er)
ṣġaṛ pl. of *ṣġiṛ*
ṣeġġeṛ v.t. **1.** to make small(er), to shrink **2.** to shorten (physically) **3.** to make young(er), to make look young(er)
ṣġiṛ pl. *ṣġaṛ* (dim. *ṣġiweṛ, ṣġeyyeṛ;* comp. *ṣġeṛ*) **1.** little, small **2.** young
ṣġiweṛ dim. of *ṣġiṛ*
ṣġeṛ comp. of *ṣġiṛ*
ṣġoṛ, ṣġeṛ **1.** youth, youthfulness **2.** early years, childhood **3.** smallness **4.** shortness (in stature)
ṣhil v.n. of *ṣheḷ*
ṣhiṛ v.n. of *ṣheṛ*
ṣheḷ v.i. (v.n. *ṣhil*) to neigh, to whinny (horse)
ṣheṛ v.i. (v.n. *ṣhiṛ*) **1.** to stay up (i.e., not sleep) **2.** to pass the evening or night
ṣehṛan pl. *-in* **1.** up, awake (not asleep) **2.** staying up, sitting up (all or part of the night)
ṣib n.u. *-a* nit or egg of the louse
ṣiban v.n. of *ṣab*
ṣiḍ v.n. of *ṣiyyeḍ*
ṣiḍa catch, (caught) game, what is caught in hunting
ṣiḍq same as *ṣeḍq*
ṣif pl. *ṣyuf* summer
ṣifa pl. *-t, ṣyef* description (of s.o., s.th.)
ṣifi pl. *-yen* summer (adj.), summery, pertaining to summer
ṣifeṭ v.t. to send (s.th., s.o.)
¶ *ṣifeṭ ɛla* (or *muṛa*) to send for (s.th., s.o.)
ṣigan pl. of *ṣag*
ṣikuk couscous served with buttermilk
ṣiniya pl. *ṣwani* (dim. *ṣwinya*) metal tray (primarily used for utensils used in making tea)
¶ *ɛmaṛa de-ṣ-ṣiniya* set of utensils, etc., used in making tea
ṣiyyeḍ v.t. (v.n. *ṣiḍ*) **1.** to hunt, to hunt for (game) **2.** to fish for (literal sense) **3.** to catch (fish, game)
ṣiyyeṛ v.t. **1.** to spend (money) *šḥal ṣiyyeṛti ɛla režlek lli kanet mṛiḍa?* How much did you spend on your bad leg? **2.** to separate the dirt from (wheat, with a *bu-ṣiyyaṛ*)
ṣiyyeḥ v.i. **1.** to scream, to cry out **2.** to howl (dog, etc.)
ṣiḥa pl. *-t* n.i. of *ṣaḥ*
ṣiɛan pl. of *ṣaɛ*
ʔṣel same as *ʔaṣel*
ṣḷa iṣḷi v.t. to hit, to strike (with open hand, whip, etc.)
ṣḷa (cons. *ṣḷat*) pl. *ṣḷawat, ṣalawat* prayer (usually ritualistic)
** *ṣ-ṣḷa ɛăl n-nbi!* Let's quit! I'm quitting! (some activity). It's over. It's all over with.
ṣḷab pl. of *ṣḷib*
ṣḷaba **1.** reckless courage or intrepidity, boldness **2.** insolence, impudence
ṣḷageṭ pl. of *ṣelguṭ*
ṣḷaṭa pl. *ṣḷayeṭ* undesirable or unjust situation or occurrence (e.g., a relative living off the family; also, applied to one who does this)
ṣḷaṭen pl. of *ṣeḷṭan*
ṣḷawat pl. of *ṣḷa*
ṣḷayeṭ pl. of *ṣḷaṭa*
ṣḷaḥ v.i. (v.n. *ṣḷaḥ*) to be usable or serviceable *ma-ṣḷaḥ-li-š.* I couldn't use it.
ṣḷaḥ v.n. of *ṣḷaḥ* and *ṣḷeḥ*
ṣoḷban pl. of *ṣalib*
ṣelguṭ pl. *ṣḷageṭ* coarse, ill-mannered bum (wide epithetical usage)
ṣḷib pl. *ṣḷab* recklessly intrepid or bold
ṣḷiḥ v.n. of *ṣḷeḥ*
ṣeḷḷa v.i. to pray
¶ *ṣeḷḷa b-* to lead in prayer
¶ *ṣeḷḷa ɛăl n-nbi* to say *ṣeḷḷa ḷḷah ɛlih wa-sellem* or *ḷḷahom ṣeḷḷi ɛăl n-nbi* after mention of the Prophet Mohammed
ṣeḷḷeb v.t. to crucify
ṣeḷḷeṭ (*ɛla*) to wish off (on), to burden or saddle (s.o.) with (s.th.) *ḅḅa ṣeḷḷeṭ ɛliya xay.* My father has saddled me with (e.g., the responsibility of watching) my brother.
ṣeḷḷeḥ v.t. **1.** to repair, to fix **2.** to use (to fix or mend) *ġadi nṣeḷḷeḥ had ṣ-ṣḍafa l-l-qamižža dyali.* I'm going to use this button for my shirt.
ṣoḷṭa pl. *ṣulaṭ* power, domination *ma-ɛăndu ṣoḷṭa ɛla mṛatu.* His wife does whatever she wants (i.e., he has no power over her).
ṣeḷṭan pl. *ṣḷaṭen* sultan, king
ṣeḷṭen v.t. to crown (s.o.)
ṣeḷṭna sultanate, kingship
ṣluɛiya baldness
ṣelya pl. *-t* n.i. of *ṣḷa*
ṣḷeḥ v.t. (v.n. *ṣḷiḥ, ṣḷaḥ, ʔiṣḷaḥ*) **1.** to correct (exam, a delinquent, etc.) **2.** to fix, to repair **3.** to iron, to press (clothes)
¶ a.p. *ṣaḷeḥ* pl. *-in* saint
** *ma-ɛăndi fih ṣaḷḥa.* I don't need it.
¶ p.p. *meṣḷuḥ* pl. *mṣaḷeḥ* iron (for pressing clothes)

ṣolḥ **1.** reconciliation (between two persons) **2.** peace (between countries)

ṣḷăɛ f. *ṣeḷɛa* pl. *ṣuḷeɛ* bald (head)

ṣeḷɛa pl. *-t* bald head or pate

ṣmaṛ (coll.) rush(es)

ṣmaṣṛiya pl. of *ṣemṣaṛ* (same as *semsaṛ*)

ṣmaṭi pl. of *ṣemṭa*

ṣmayem (f.) forty-day period of hot weather (from July 11 to August 21)

ṣmaɛi pl. of *ṣemɛa*

ṣmek f. *ṣemka* pl. *ṣumek* deaf (also, hard of hearing)

ṣemm **1.** n.u. *-a* rock, stone (usually preceded by *ḥăžṛa* e.g. *ḥăžṛa ṣemma,* etc.) **2.** pl. *ṣmum, ṣmuma* rounded, smooth stone

ṣemmaṛ pl. *-a* shoeing smith, horseshoer, farrier

ṣemmek v.t. to deafen, to cause to become deaf (or hard of hearing)

ṣemmeṛ v.t. to nail; to nail on, down, or up (door, box, etc.) *ḷḷah ixellik, ṣemmeṛ had l-luḥa fe-l-ḥiṭ.* Please nail this board on the wall.

ṣmeṛ f. *ṣemṛa* pl. *ṣumeṛ* same as *smeṛ*

ṣemṛa cold (of a clear night)

** *ḍeṛbettu ṣ-ṣemṛa.* He caught a cold as a result of staying up under the sky of a clear night)

ṣemṣaṛ same as *semsaṛ*

ṣemṣeṛ v.i. to deal in real estate (as a broker)

ṣemṣṛa **1.** pl. of *ṣemṣaṛ* (same as *semsaṛ*) **2.** auction

ṣmet v.i. (v.n. *ṣmut, ṣmutiya*) **1.** to quiet down, to become silent **2.** to get hard, to solidify

¶ a.p. *ṣamet* pl. *-in* **1.** solid, firm **2.** kind of hard food made of raisins, sugar and spices

ṣemt silence, taciturnity

¶ *qṭăɛ ṣ-ṣemt* to be quiet, to stop talking (no impv. use)

ṣemṭa pl. *-t, ṣmaṭi* **1.** belt (waist, machinery) **2.** razor strop

ṣmukiya deafness

ṣmum, ṣmuma pl. of *ṣemm* **2**

ṣmut, ṣmutiya v.n. of *ṣmet*

ṣemɛa pl. *-t, ṣmaɛi, ṣmăɛ, ṣwameɛ* minaret

ṣmăɛ pl. of *ṣemɛa*

ṣnaḍeḍ pl. of *ṣenḍiḍ*

ṣnaḍeq pl. of *ṣenḍuq*

ṣnaf pl. of *ṣenf*

ṣnam, ʔeṣnam pl. of *ṣanam*

ṣnan unpleasant odor from the armpit or mouth

ṣnaneṛ pl. of *ṣennaṛa*

ṣnaṭeḥ pl. of *ṣenṭiḥa*

ṣnayeɛ pl. of *ṣenɛa*

ṣnayɛi pl. *-ya* craftsman, artisan

ṣenḍiḍ pl. *ṣnaḍeḍ* (n. and adj.) brave, courageous, heroic

ṣenḍuq pl. *ṣnaḍeq* **1.** box (or similar object) **2.** chest, trunk, footlocker **3.** cash register **4.** safe, strong box

¶ *mul ṣ-ṣenḍuq* cashier (bank)

ṣenf pl. *ṣnaf* kind, sort, type (usually of foods) *š-men ṣenf had t-teffaḥ hada?* What kind of apples are these?

ṣniɛ v.n. of *ṣnăɛ*

ṣennaṛa pl. *-t, ṣnaneṛ* (fish)hook

ṣonnaɛ pl. of *ṣaneɛ* (a.p. of *ṣnăɛ*)

ṣenṣaḷ kind of white clay used on writing boards (Koranic school)

ṣenṭiḥa pl. *-t, ṣnaṭeḥ* **1.** forehead (implies a strong or hard head) **2.** audacity, effrontery, cheek

¶ *fihɸ ṣ-ṣenṭiḥa* to be cheeky, impertinent ≠

ṣenṭṛez same as *šenṭṛez*

ṣnubeṛ n.u. *-a* pine tree (also the wood)

ṣnăɛ v.t. (v.n. *ṣniɛ*) to make, to manufacture (cars, washers, etc.)

** *aš-ka-teṣnăɛ?* What are you doing, anyway? (implies annoyance)

¶ *ṣnăɛ le-klam* to speak eloquently

¶ a.p. *ṣaneɛ* pl. *ṣonnaɛ* craftsman or artisan

ṣenɛa pl. *-t, ṣnayeɛ* **1.** profession, job, craft **2.** workmanship (quality) *ṣenɛa mezyana hadi!* This is good workmanship! **3.** skill, dexterity **4.** ruse, artifice, clever trick

ṣqil v.n. of *ṣqel*

ṣqiṛ v.n. of *ṣqeṛ*

ṣqel v.t. (v.n. *ṣqil*) **1.** to polish, to shine, to burnish (metal) **2.** to hit, to strike, to slap

ṣeqla **1.** polishing powder (for polishing metals) **2.** pl. *-t* slap, blow (with the open hand)

ṣqelli kind of golden or silver thread (embroidery)

ṣeqqal adj. pl. *-in* n.pl. *-a* ag. adj. and n. of *ṣqel*

ṣeqqaṭ same as *seqqaṭ*

ṣeqqem same as *seqqem*

ṣeqqeṭ same as *seqqeṭ*

ṣqeṛ v.i. (v.n. *ṣqiṛ*) to be quiet, still (neither making noise nor moving)

ṣeqṛa pl. *-t* n.i. of *ṣqeṛ*

¶ *ḍṛebha b-ṣeqṛa* to keep quiet, to keep mum

ṣqeṭ, ṣeqṭ same as *sqeṭ, seqṭ*

ṣṛaṛfi pl. *-ya* money-changer

ṣṛaṣeṛ pl. of *ṣeṛṣaṛ*

ṣṛayem pl. of *ṣṛima*

ṣṛef v.t. (v.n. *ṣṛif*) to spend (money)

¶ *ṣṛef ɛla* to support (i.e., pay s.o's subsistence)

¶ p.p. *meṣruf* pl. *mṣaṛef* expense money
ṣeṛf **1.** change (money) **2.** behavior or manner of dealing (with others) **3.** pl. *ṣṛuf* weight (as used in weighing on a balance)
ṣeṛfeq v.t. to slap, to strike (open-handed)
ṣṛima pl. *-t, ṣṛayem* bridle (horse)
ṣṛiṛ v.n. of *ṣeṛṛ*
ṣṛiṭ v.n. of *ṣṛeṭ*
ṣeṛṛ v.t. (v.n. *ṣṛiṛ*) to tie or bundle up into a knotted cloth (e.g., money in a handkerchief)
ṣṛeṛ pl. of *ṣeṛṛa*
ṣeṛṛa pl. *-t, ṣṛeṛ* navel, umbilicus
ṣoṛṛa pl. *-t* bag, pouch (as for money; includes makeshift sacks, as one made of a knotted handerchief, etc.)
ṣeṛṛaxa whooping cough *fih ṣ-ṣeṛṛaxa.* He has the whooping cough.
ṣeṛṛed v.t. **1.** to send *ṣeṛṛed had r-risalat le-s-si aḥmed.* Send these letters to Mr. Ahmed. **2.** to count, to enumerate *ṣeṛṛed t-tnaber, waqila xaṣṣ waḥed wella žuž.* Count the stamps; there may be one or two missing. **3.** to review, to check *ḍ-ḍabiṭ ka-iṣeṛṛed l-ɛăskeṛ qbel-ma ixeržu.* The officer reviews the soldiers before they go out. **4.** to pick over and clean (grains, kernels) *ṣeṛṛed l-ful u-š-šɛir u-ddihom le-ṭ-ṭaḥuna.* Pick over and clean the beans and the barley and take them to the mill.
ṣeṛṛef v.t. to change (money, e.g. five ones for a five) *ṣeṛṛef-li had l-weṛqa drahem!* Change this bill into dirhams!
ṣeṛṛeṭ v.t. **1.** to review, to check, to go over (again) **2.** to review (troops)
ṣeṛṣaṛ pl. *ṣṛaṣeṛ* cricket (insect)
ṣeṛṣeṛ v.i. to scream, to cry out (person)
ṣṛeṭ v.t. (v.n. *ṣṛiṭ*) to swallow whole
ṣṛuf pl. of *ṣeṛf* **3**
ṣeṛžem same as *šeṛžem*
ṣṭab v.t. to enjoy (food, movie, swim, etc.)
¶ *ṣṭab ṛaṣu*ᶲ to enjoy oneself, to have fun
ṣṭaṛem pl. of *ṣṭeṛmiya*
ṣṭawem pl. of *ṣeṭwan*
ṣṭaḥ same as *ṣṭăḥ*
ṣṭila dim. of *ṣeṭḷa*
ṣṭiḥa dim. of *ṣṭăḥ*
ṣṭel pl. *ṣṭula* **1.** bucket, pail (metal) **2.** dunce, ignoramus
ṣeṭḷa pl. *-t* (dim. *ṣṭila*) same as *ṣṭeḷ* **1**
ṣṭeṛmiya pl. *-t, ṣṭaṛem* **1.** kind of throw-pillow or cushion **2.** hassock
ṣeṭṭa v.t. to drive crazy (literally and figuratively)
ṣeṭṭeṛ v.t. **1.** to draw (a straight line) **2.** to line, to put lines on (sheet of paper) **3.** to line up, to align (in single line)
¶ *ṣeṭṭeṛ ɛla* **1.** to cross out or off (as a name on a list) **2.** to count out, to exclude, to not count on *hi ṣeṭṭeṛ ɛla ḥmed!* Don't count on Ahmed (to be here, e.g.).
ṣṭula pl. of *ṣṭeḷ*
ṣṭuḥa pl. of *ṣṭaḥ*
ṣeṭwa power, influence
ṣeṭwan pl. *ṣṭawen* vestibule, hallway (at the entrance of a house)
ṣṭăḥ pl. *ṣṭuḥa* (dim. *ṣṭiyyeḥ, ṣṭiḥa*) flat roof (usually used as a terrace)
ṣubba pl. *-t* soup (usually with vegetables)
ṣuf pl. *ṣwaf, ṣwef* wool
ṣufa pl. *-t* **1.** same as *ṣuf* **2.** mold (as on old bread)
ṣufi pl. *-yen* excessively religious
ṣufeṛ pl. of *ṣfeṛ*
ṣuga pl. *-t* n.i. of *ṣag*
ṣugan v.n. of *ṣag*
ṣugeɛ pl. of *ṣgăɛ*
ṣuḷa **1.** power, strength (physical) **2.** power, authority
ṣulaṭ pl. of *ṣolṭa*
ṣulḍi pl. *ṣwaleḍ, ṣwalḍa* old coin minted with a hole in the center
¶ pl. *ṣwaleḍ* money
ṣuleɛ pl. of *ṣlăɛ*
ṣum v.n. of *ṣam*
ṣumek pl. of *ṣmek*
ṣumeṛ pl. of *ṣmeṛ* (same as *smeṛ*)
ṣun v.n. of *ṣan*
ṣuṛ pl. *ṣwaṛ* **1.** wall (as around a yard, city), rampart **2.** trumpet
ṣuṛa pl. *-t* **1.** picture, photograph **2.** painting, picture (wall) **3.** appearance, looks (face) **4.** pl. *-t, ṣwaṛ* chapter of the Koran **5.** flunky, puppet
** *ma-bqat fih ġir ṣ-ṣuṛa.* He's gotten to be as thin as a shadow.
ṣuṛḍi pl. *ṣwaṛḍa* same as *ṣulḍi*
ṣuṛṛa same as *ṣoṛṛa*
ṣut pl. *ṣwat* voice
ṣuṭi pl. *-yen* crazy (non-literal usage)
ṣuwwaf pl. *-a, -in* wool dealer
ṣuwwag pl. *-a* driver, operator (car, carriage, train, etc.)
ṣuwwaṛ pl. *-a* photographer
ṣuwwaṛa pl. *-t* camera (not movie)
ṣuwweb v.t. **1.** to make (meal, bed, chair, etc.) **2.** to make, to manufacture **3.** to fix, to repair **4.** to arrange, to put in order (as a messy room)
¶ *ṣuwweb* (s.th.) *ma bin* to settle (s.th.) between, to reconcile (s.th.) between
ṣuwwef v.i. to get moldy
ṣuwwem v.t. to make (s.o.) fast (in Ramadan)
ṣuwweṛ v.t. **1.** to draw, to paint (pictures) **2.** to take a picture of, to photograph **3.** to describe **4.** to earn (money)
¶ *ṣuwweṛ f-ɛăqlu*ᶲ to imagine

ṣuwweṭ v.t. **1.** to whip, to lash, to flog (extended to sticks)
ṣuḥaba pl. of *ṣaḥabi*
ṣuعuba same as *ṣعuba*
ṣwab good manners, courtesy
** *žiti fe-ṣ-ṣwab.* You came just at the right time.
ṣwabni pl. *-ya* soap dealer
ṣwaf pl. of *ṣuf*
ṣwaḷeḍ, ṣwaḷḍa pl. of *ṣuḷḍi*
ṣwameع pl. of *ṣemعa*
ṣwani pl. of *ṣiniya*
ṣwaṛ pl. of *ṣuṛ* and *ṣuṛa* 4
ṣwaṛḍa pl. of *ṣuṛḍi* (same as *ṣuḷḍi*)
ṣwat pl. of *ṣut*
ṣwayeṛ pl. of *ṣayeṛ*
ṣwef pl. of *ṣuf*
ṣwinya dim. of *ṣiniya*
ṣwiṛa (with art.) Mogador
ṣwiṛi pl. *-yen* of or from *ṣwiṛa*
ṣewla v.n. of *ṣal*
ṣxeṛ n.u. *ṣexṛa* pl. *-t, ṣxuṛ* rock, boulder (too big to lift)
ṣxeṭ, ṣexṭ same as *sxeṭ, sexṭ*
ṣxuṛ pl. of *ṣxeṛ*
ṣexxeṭ same as *sexxeṭ*
ṣyaḍa same as *ṣiḍa*
ṣyaġa v.n. of *ṣaġ*
ṣyam v.n. of *ṣam*
ṣyana v.n. of *ṣan*
ṣyaḥ v.n. of *ṣaḥ*
ṣyeb pl. of *ṣaba* 2
ṣyef pl. of *ṣifa*
ṣyeḷ pl. of *ṣaḷa*
ṣyuf pl. of *ṣif*
ṣeyyaḍ pl. *-a* **1.** hunter **2.** fisherman **3.** Casanova, ladies' man
ṣeyyaġ pl. *-a* jeweller (i.e., makes jewelry)
ṣeyyaḥ pl. *-in* ag. adj. of *ṣaḥ*
ṣḥa iṣḥa v.i. (v.n. *ṣḥu*) **1.** to come to, to regain consciousness **2.** to clear up (sky) **3.** to sober up (from drunkenness)
ṣḥab pl. of *ṣaḥeb*
ṣḥabat f. pl. of *ṣaḥeb*
ṣḥaṛi pl. of *ṣeḥṛa*
ṣḥaḥ v.i. to become strong (person)
ṣḥaḥ pl. of *ṣḥiḥ*
ṣḥăb same as *ṣaḥeb*
¶ *ṣḥăb mعa* to take with *ṣḥăb mعak le-bṛa!* Take the letter with you!
ṣeḥba, ṣoḥba friendship
ṣeḥfa pl. *-t* kind of large earthen dish used in preparing and kneading bread dough
ṣḥiḥ pl. *ṣḥaḥ* **1.** strong, powerful (person, animal) **2.** strong, solid (chair, piece of wood, etc.) **3.** healthy, in good health, fit **4.** true (not a lie) **5.** correct, right
** *ma-عăndi ġir flus ṣḥaḥ.* I don't have any change.
ṣḥiḥa dim. of *ṣeḥḥa*
ṣḥen pl. *ṣḥuna* same as *sḥen*
ṣeḥṛa pl. *ṣḥaṛi, sḥari* **1.** (barren) desert **2.** (with art.) Sahara desert
ṣeḥṛawa n.pl. of *ṣeḥṛawi*
ṣeḥṛawi adj. pl. *-yen* n.pl. *ṣeḥṛawa* desert dweller
ṣḥu v.n. of *ṣḥa*
ṣḥuna pl. of *ṣḥen* (same as *sḥen*)
ṣḥuṛ **1.** meal eaten during Ramadan before dawn **2.** time of the meal in 1 during Ramadan
ṣeḥḥ v.i. **1.** to get well, to recover **2.** to become strong
ṣeḥḥ **1.** truth **2.** strength (of wood, cloth, chair, etc.)
** *be-ṣ-ṣeḥḥ?* Really?
¶ *be-ṣ-ṣeḥḥ* is it true (that), really *waš be-ṣ-ṣeḥḥ ġadi tṣafeṛ?* Is it true you're going to take a trip?
ṣeḥḥa (dim. *ṣḥiḥa*) **1.** health **2.** strength (physical)
** *b-ṣeḥḥtek!* said to one who has just had a haircut, bath, or is wearing a new shirt, suit, etc. *—ḷḷah yăعṭik ṣ-ṣeḥḥa!* reply to *b-ṣeḥḥtek.*
ṣeḥḥaf pl. *-a* pallbearer, bier bearer
ṣeḥḥaqiya pl. *-t* **1.** colic, violent stomach ache **2.** action of tripping s.o.
ṣeḥḥeḥ v.t. **1.** to strengthen, to give strength to, to make strong(er) (s.o.) **2.** to verify, to get (s.th.) straight, to check **3.** to correct (exam, paper, etc.)
ṣعab v.i. **1.** to get or become hard or difficult (s.th.) **2.** to become hard or strict (person)
ṣعab pl. of *ṣعib*
ṣعăb comp. of *ṣعib*
ṣعib pl. *-in, ṣعab* (comp. *ṣعăb*) **1.** hard, difficult (to do) *had š-ši ṣعib ittăعmel.* This is hard to do. **2.** hard, strict (person) **3.** rough, difficult (as a road)
ṣعăṛ v.i. **1.** to become rabid (dog, etc.) **2.** to get furious (person)
ṣعăṛ rabies, hydrophobia
ṣعuba pl. *-t* difficulty
ṣăععăb v.t. to make hard(er) or (more) difficult

Š

š abbreviated form of *aš* and the *ši* of negation
ša, šaʔ used in the expr. **1.** *in ša ḷḷah* God willing **2.** *ma šaʔ ḷḷah.* That's the way it goes. That's life.
ša pl. *šyah* (not too common usage) sheep

šab išib v.i. **1.** to grey, to get grey (hair) **2.** to get old, to become aged (person)
¶ a.p. *šayeb* pl. *-in* old and grey
šabab pl. of *šabb*
šabb pl. *šabab, šobban* young man
šabba pl. *-t* young woman
šobban pl. of *šabb*
šabeh v.t. same as *šbeh l-*
šabel n.u. *-a* (dim. *šwibla*) shad
šadd a.p. of *šedd*
šaf išuf (v.n. *šufan, šuf*) **1.** v.t. to see *kif bġitini nšufha f-had ḍ-ḍlem?* How do you expect me to see it in this darkness? —*bġa išufek ع la waح ed l-qaḍiya.* He wants to see you about something. **2.** v.i. to look (mostly impv. usage) *šuf a hya!* Hey, look!
** *šuf ح dak!* Watch where you're going!
¶ *šaf f-* to look at
** *šuf fiya l-llah!* Have pity on me!
¶ *šaf l-* **1.** to find (s.th.) for (s.o.), to look for (s.th.) for (s.o.) *šuf-li ši-xedma, baṛek ḷḷahu fik.* Please find some work for me. **2.** to tell the fortune of (s.o., as a fortune teller)
šafa v.t. to heal, to cure (subject is usually God)
šafaqa pity, compassion (for one's fellow man)
šahada **1.** v.n. of *šhed* **2.** profession of basic Muslim faith (i.e., "there is no god but God and Mohammed is His prophet") **3.** pl. *-t* certificate, certification **4.** diploma
šahed **1.** pl. *šhud, šuhud* witness **2.** pl. *šwahed* index finger **3.** pl. *šwahed* tombstone
¶ *šahed ž-žuṛ* false witness (person)
šahiya appetite (food)
šakešmir **1.** cashmere (cloth) **2.** pl. *-at* turban **3.** pl. *-at* man's hat (felt)
šal išil v.t. to take or bring, to transport (by carrying)
šal pl. *šilan* **1.** (neck) scarf **2.** shawl
šala ع la (v.n. *šilan*) to hit, to strike *šalat ع lih be-l-beqrež.* She hit him with the tea kettle.
šam (with art.) Syria
šami adj. pl. *-yen* n.pl. *šwama* Syrian
šamex pl. *-in* **1.** busy, bustling (as a market) **2.** old and wise (person)
šan importance, significance (personal) *ma-ع ăndu šan.* He isn't very important (e.g., socially).
** *ṛžăع ح aža u-šan.* He's gotten to be somebody (i.e., important).
¶ *f-šan, ع la šan,* or *f-šeʔn, ع la šeʔn* about, concerning *ṛahom žtamع u băع da ع la šeʔnek.* They've already met together concerning you (i.e., your case or problem).
šanṭa pl. *šwaneṭ* **1.** bag, suitcase (travel) **2.** briefcase
šaqq a.p. of *šeqq*
šaquṛ pl. *šwaqeṛ* hatchet
šaṛ išiṛ v.i. **1.** to signal, to make a sign, to give a signal *mnin nšiṛ-lek aži!* Come when I give the signal. **2.** to hint, to infer
¶ *šaṛ l-* to refer to, to mention
šaṛa pl. *-t* target
¶ *ḍṛeb š-šaṛa* to target practice
šaṛeb a.p. of *šṛeb*
šareb pl. *šwareb* **1.** lip (mouth) **2.** rim, edge, lip (of a glass, bowl, etc.) **3.** mustache (short)
šaref a.p. of *šref*
šaṛăf **1.** honor, esteem **2.** state of being a descendant of the Prophet (i.e., *šrif*)
šarga woolen serge
šari a.p. of *šra*
šarik same as *šrik*
šarika pl. *-t* company, corporation
šariع a law, jurisprudence (Islamic)
šarek v.t. to participate with, to join (s.o.)
¶ *šarek f-* to take part in, to participate in
šariع pl. *šawariع* avenue, boulevard
šašiya pl. *šwaši* **1.** kind of conical hat with a tassel **2.** Jewish skull-cap
šati pl. *šatyen* rainy (day, weather)
šaṭ išiṭ v.i. to be left (over), to remain
¶ *šaṭ-luφ* to have left ≠ *šaṭu-li le-flus bezzaf.* I have a lot of money left.
šawariع pl. of *šariع*
šawen city in northern Morocco
šawni **1.** pl. *-yen* of or pertaining to the city of *šawen* **2.** pl. *-ya* inhabitant of *šawen*
šawniya pl. *-t* red pepper
šaweṛ v.t. (v.n. *šwaṛ*) to consult, to consult with
¶ *šaweṛ ع la* to announce (s.o. who has arrived to see s.o. else)
šaweš pl. *šuwwaš* kind of page or messenger (as between offices)
šay **1.** nothing, anything (with negative) *ma-šeft šay.* I didn't see anything. **2.** emphatic form of negative particle (*š, ši*) *ma-ža-šay.* He didn't come (at all).
¶ *šay llah* expr. of respect used at the mention of a saint
šayaṭin pl. of *šiṭan*
šayeb a.p. of *šab*
šayeع used in the names of the months *šayeع ع ašuṛ, šayeع mulud* second and fourth months of the Muslim calendar
šažaṛa pl. *-t* family tree, genealogy
šaح et pl. *-in* **1.** dry *ṣqi l-weṛd, ṛah šaح et.* Water the roses; they're dry. —*ع ṭini šṛiba, ح ălqi šaح et.* Give me a little drink, my throat's dry. **2.** stingy, miserly *šح al šaح et! ma-ixerrež le-fṛenk.* How stingy he is! Not a franc gets away from him.
šaع išiع v.i. to spread, to circulate (news)

šaɛir pl. *šuɛara* poet
šbab **1.** youth, youthfulness **2.** pl. *šobban* same as *šabb*
¶ *ḥăbb š-šbab* acne, pimples
šbabek pl. of *šebbak*
šbaki pl. of *šebka*
šbar pl. of *šber*
šebb, šebba alum
šebbak pl. *šbabek* window (originally iron grillwork on a window)
šebbakiya (coll. and sg.) pl. *-t* kind of cake made with honey
šobban pl. of *šabb* and *šbab* **2**
šebbeh v.t. **1.** to take or mistake (s.o. for s.o. else) *šebbehtini mɛa ši-waḥed axor.* You've mistaken me for someone else. **2.** to compare
** *šebbeh nebbeh.* There's no comparison; they're not at all alike. —*mɛa men šeftek šebbehtek.* A man is known by the company he keeps.
šebbek v.t. **1.** to interlace (slats in a trellis, fingers, etc.) **2.** to tangle, to get tangled up (thread, etc.) **3.** to make decorative openings in (a piece of cloth, by removing the threads of the woof or the warp)
šebber v.t. to measure in or by spans of the hand
šebbeṛ v.t. **1.** to hold (in the hands) **2.** to grab onto, to grasp, to take hold of **3.** to catch (s.th. thrown)
¶ *šebbeṛ f-* to get hold of, to hold onto (s.o., s.th.)
** *ḷḷah išebbeṛ fik.* May God preserve you.
šebbăɛ v.t. **1.** to be enough for, to satisfy, to satiate (s.o.) *had l-makla ma-tšebbăɛni-š.* This isn't enough food for me. **2.** to give a lot of (s.th.) to (s.o.) *ḅḅa šebbăɛni flus l-ɛam lli daz.* My father gave me a lot of money last year. —*šebbăɛha ɛṣa* (or *ḥṛawa*). He really beat her hard.
šbeh l- (v.n. *šbih*) to resemble, to look like
šbih v.n. of *šbeh*
šbiha resemblance, similarity
šbika dim. of *šebka*
šbiṭ v.n. of *šbeṭ*
šbiḥ v.n. of *šbeḥ*
šbek pl. of *šebka*
šebka pl. *-t, šbaki, šbek* (dim. *šbika*) **1.** net (fishing, hair, tennis, etc.) **2.** kind of sieve (for gravel)
šber pl. *šbar, šbura* span (of the hand; used as a measure)
šebšub pl. *šbašeb* same as *sebsub*
šbeṭ v.i. (v.n. *šbiṭ*) to reach its hottest point (battle, war, fire, etc.)
¶ *šbeṭ f-* to flare up at (s.o.) (in anger)
¶ *šbeṭ fihᶲ* to catch ≠, to catch on ≠ (fire) *šebṭet n-naṛ fe-ḍ-ḍaṛ.* The house caught on fire.
šbubiya youth, adolescence
šbura pl. of *šber*
šbeḥ v.t. (v.n. *šbiḥ*) to lay out, to knock flat (s.o., as with a blow)
šbăɛ **1.** v.i. to become full or satisfied (with food) **2.** v.t. to get or acquire a lot of (s.th.)
¶ *šbăɛ men* to get tired of, to get fed up with
šebɛa **1.** n.i. of *šbăɛ* **2.** abundance **3.** quality of being enough, sufficiency
šebɛan pl. *-in* **1.** full, satisfied (after eating) **2.** used as a.p. of *šbăɛ* —*šebɛan ṭ-ṭumubilat.* He has a lot of cars.
šdad pl. of *šdid*
šedd v.t. (v.n. *šeddan*) **1.** to close *šedd š-šeṛžem baš ma-idxol-š l-berd!* Close the window so the cold won't come in! —*šedd had l-meṭṛeb!* Close this bottle! —*šedd fommek!* Shut your mouth! Shut up! **2.** to button or zip up **3.** (*mɛa*) to tie, to fasten (to) (shoes, s.th. to s.th.) **4.** to hold, to hold onto *šedd-lha yeddiha* (or *f-yeddiha*)! Hold onto her hand! **5.** to catch (s.th. thrown) **6.** to catch, to apprehend (thief, etc.) **7.** to take, to grab **8.** to get, to obtain *ɛam luwwel šeddet š-šahada dyalha.* She got her degree last year.
** *iwa šedd ṛaṣek!* Keep your wits about you and do a good job.
¶ *šedd f-* to hold onto, to grab hold of
** *šedd fe-lḥăytek!* Watch it! Be careful (said to s.o. who has slipped and almost fallen) —*kan ġad-imut ġir ṛebbi šedd fih.* He's still alive only through the grace of God. —*šedd fe-l-hedṛa* (or *f-le-ḥdit*) *u-ma-bġa-š iṭleq.* He got to talking and wouldn't stop.
¶ *šedd ɛla* **1.** to keep (s.th., s.o.) away from *šedd ɛliya kelbek wella nqetlu!* Keep your dog away from me or I'll kill him! **2.** to lock up (s.o.) *šedd ɛliha fe-ḍ-ḍaṛ.* He locked her (up) in the house.
¶ a.p. *šadd* pl. *-in* different, peculiar, unlike the general run of things or people
šedd pl. *šdud, šduda* kind of brimless hat with a turban wrapped around it
šedda **1.** n.i. of *šedd* **2.** position of being faced with myriad problems, bind
šeddan v.n. of *šedd*
šdeg same as *šdeq*
šdid pl. *-in, šdad* **1.** strong (person physically) **2.** strict, hard (person) **3.** intense (heat, cold, hatred, etc.) **4.** skilled, expert (in some activity)
šdeq pl. *šduq, šduqa* **1.** cheek (internal) **2.** piece, morsel (bread)

** *šحal fih de-š-šdeq!* He's full of baloney! (i.e., doesn't know what he's talking about)

¶ *ḍṛeb š-šdeq* to "feed one's face"

¶ *عṭa* (s.o.) *be-š-šdeq* to make a sound similar to a "raspberry" at (s.o.; actually a bilabial trill; used to indicate one's incredulity in what s.o. says)

šdud, šduda pl. of *šedd*

šduq, šduqa pl. of *šdeq*

šfaq pl. of *šfiq*

šfaṛ pl. of *šfeṛ*

šfaṛi pl. of *šefṛa*

šfayef pl. of *šeffa*

šeffa v.t. to cause or make (s.o.) feel pity *ṣeححtu ka-tšeffini.* The condition of his health makes me feel sorry for him.

šeffa pl. *-t, šfayef* lip (of the mouth)

šeffaṛ pl. *-a* thief, robber, anyone who steals or robs

šeffeṛ v.t. **1.** to steal (s.th.) *šeffṛu-lha le-flus kollhom.* They stole all her money. **2.** to cut into strips (leather, in leathercraft) **3.** to trim (edge of a sole of an unfinished shoe)

šeffăع v.i. to say the optional prayer called *š-šfăع* or *š-šfaع*

šfiq pl. *-in, šfaq* humane and philanthropic

šfiع **1.** v.n. of *šfăع* **2.** Intercessor, Mediator (i.e., the Prophet Mohammed)

šfenž n.u. *-a* doughnut

šfeq *عla* to be compassionate or humane toward

¶ *šfeq men* to have mercy or pity on

šefqa n.i. of *šfeq*

šfeṛ pl. *šfaṛ* **1.** eyelash (single hair) **2.** slice (bread) **3.** fragment (usually glass)

šefṛa pl. *-t, šfaṛi* kind of knife (used primarily by leather craftsmen)

šfeṛžel n.u. *-a* same as *sfeṛžel*

šfăع v.t. (v.n. *šfiع*) to buy out (some other's share of s.th.)

šegg (*men*) more (than) *šegg men عamayn hadi ma-šeftu.* I haven't seen him for more than a year. —*mša šegg men myat kiluṃiteṛ.* He went more than a hundred kilometers.

šgeṛ f. *šegṛa* pl. *šugeṛ* blond(e)

šġal **1.** pl. *-at* same as *šġol* (in Fez) **2.** pl. of *šġol*

šġalat pl. of *šġol* and *šġal*

šeġġal pl. *-in* hard working, productive

šeġġef b- to fatigue, to tire out (s.o., physically and mentally)

šeġġel v.t. to hire, to employ, to give a job to

¶ *šeġġel ṛaṣuφ* (*b-*) to busy oneself (with)

šġel v.t. **1.** to occupy, to preoccupy (mind) **2.** to entertain, to keep company *šġelha عla-ma neṛžăع.* Keep her company until I arrive.

¶ *šġel عla* to distract from, to take the mind of (s.o.) off (s.th.) *dak l-bent kanet šaġlah* (a.p.) *عăl le-qṛaya.* That girl distracted him from his studies.

šġol pl. *šġal, šġalat* **1.** job, occupation **2.** task, job **3.** work *عăndi š-šġol bezzaf had le-عšiya.* I've got a lot of work this evening. **4.** business *عăndi waحed š-šġol temma.* I have some business there.

** *ma-ši šoġlek!* None of your business!

¶ *ḍaṛ š-šġol* shop, workshop (place of work of an artisan)

šhada **1.** same as *šahada* 1 and 2 **2.** pl. *-t, šhayed* same as *šahada* 3

** *šhadtek l-llah!* an entreaty to s.o. to testify about s.th. he has witnessed.

¶ *šhadti biha l-llah ila . . .* used to intensify a statement *šhadti biha l-llah ila xedma hadi!* This is (really rough) work!

šhawi pl. of *šehwa*

šhayed pl. of *šhada* 2 (same as *šahada* 3)

šheb f. *šehba* pl. *šuheb* **1.** albino (person, animal) **2.** light gray (horse, dog, etc.)

šhed (v.i. *šhada, šahada*) to be a witness, to testify

¶ *šhed f-* to testify against (s.o.)

¶ *šhed l-* to testify in behalf of, to be a witness for

¶ *šhed عla* **1.** to be a witness against **2.** to contract or set up an agreement with (s.o.) through the *عdul* (notaries) *عṭahom ḍ-ḍaṛ u-qal-lhom išehduha عlih* (*b-le-عdul*). He gave them the house and told them to draw up a notarized agreement with him.

¶ *šhed ẓ-ẓuṛ* (*f-*) to bear false witness (against)

šehda pl. *-t* honeycomb

šehha v.t. to excite the appetite or desire of (s.o., usually for food) *bqa ka-iعawed-li عla seksu حetta šehhani fih.* He kept talking about couscous until he aroused my appetite for some.

šehhed **1.** v.i. to say the *šahada* (see same, 2) **2.** v.t. to call as a witness, to have testify

šehheṛ v.t. **1.** to make become known or famous (s.o.) **2.** to advertise (s.th.)

šhiq v.n. of *šheq*

šhiwa dim. of *šehwa*

šheq v.i. (v.n. *šhiq*) **1.** to bray (donkey) **2.** to sob

šehqa n.i. of *šheq*

šheṛ same as *šehheṛ*

¶ p.p. *mešhuṛ* pl. *-in* famous, well-known, celebrated

šheṛ pl. *šhuṛ, šhuṛa* **1.** month **2.** crescent moon (after new moon)

šohṛa (no pl.) **1.** fame, renown **2.** reputation

šehṛi pl. *-yen* monthly

šehṛiya pl. *-t* 1. monthly pay or salary 2. monthly payment or installment
šhud pl. of *šahed* 1
šhuṛ, šhuṛa pl. of *šheṛ*
šehwa pl. *-t, šhawi* (dim. *šhiwa*) 1. appetite (food) 2. s.th. particularly desired (by s.o.) to eat
** *šehwa mennu.* He's a very charming fellow.
¶ *fteḥ š-šehwa* to be appetizing (food)
¶ *šhewtu*φ (with *-f* before n.) to want ≠, to desire ≠ *šhewti f-dak t-teffaḥa.* I want that apple.
** *šhewtek takol le-ɛṣa!* You're just asking for a licking! (to a child)
šehwani pl. *-yen* voluptuary, sybaritic
ši 1. some *sellefni ši-flus!* Lend me some money! 2. about, around, some (with quantity) *žaw ši ɛăšṛa de-n-nas.* About ten people came. —*aži mɛa ši-ɛăšṛa!* Come around ten o'clock! 3. anything, a thing *ṛažel meskin, ši ma-ɛăndu.* Poor man, he hasn't got a thing. 4. negative correlative of *ma-* (often abbreviated to *š*) *meskin ma-ɛăndu-š ḅḅah.* The poor boy hasn't any father. —*ma-ža-š fe-l-weqt.* He didn't come on time.—*ma-ši hna,* or *ma-huwa-š hna.* He's not here.
** *ši-bas ma-kan.* No harm done. That's all right.
¶ *dak š-ši* that *šnu dak š-ši?* What's that? —*ma-teqna-š b-dak š-ši lli qal-lna men ṭabiɛt l-ḥal.* Naturally we didn't believe what (that which) he told us.
¶ *had š-ši* this *šnu had š-ši?* What's this?
¶ *koll-ši* 1. everything 2. everyone, everybody *koll-ši xrež.* Everybody's gone out.
¶ *ši . . . ši* each other, one another (with continuous or repetitious action) *bqaw ġir ši ka-išuf f-ši,* or *bqaw ġir ka-išufu ši f-ši.* They just stood (or sat) there looking at each other.
¶ *ši b-ši* little by little, in small amounts, a few at a time (used with numbered items) *dexxelhom ši b-ši!* Have them come in a few at a time.
¶ *ši-ḥaža* something
¶ *š-ši l-axoṛ* the other (one) *ɛṭini š-ši l-axoṛ!* Give me the other one!
¶ *ši-šwiya* a little while *ṣbeṛ ši-šwiya!* Wait a little while!
¶ *ši-šwiya d-* a little (bit of) *ɛṭini ši-šwiya d-atay.* Give me a little tea.
¶ *ši-waḥed* f. *ši-weḥda* pl. *ši-weḥdin* see *waḥed*
¶ *ɛla had š-ši* that's why, (it's) for that reason *ɛla had š-ši žit.* That's why I came.
šib n.u. *-a* gray hair
šiba absinthe
šibani pl. *-yen* (adj. and n.) old, aged (person)
šibi pl. *-yen* absinthe green (color)
šifa healing, cure *ḷḷah yăɛṭik š-šifa.* May God make you well (heal you, cure you).
šifluṛ n.u. *-a, ṛaṣ de-š-šifluṛ* cauliflower
šifuṛ pl. *-at* 1. chauffeur 2. driver (truck, bus, etc.)
šikaya same as *škaya*
šiki 1. f. *-ya* pl. *-yen* smart or elegant dresser (person) 2. elegance, smartness (in dress) 3. conceit, arrogance
šilan 1. pl. of *šal* 2. v.n. of *šala*
šin pl. *-in* ugly
šiša pl. *-t* narguile, hookah, hubble-bubble
šit cretonne (material)
šita, šiṭa pl. *-t, šyet, šyeṭ* brush (shoe, hair, tooth, paint, etc.)
šiṭan pl. *šyaṭen, šayaṭin* 1. Satan, the Devil 2. devil, demon 3. (dim. *šwiṭen*) mischievous person, imp (child) 4. (dim. *šwiṭen*) cunning, clever person
šiṭana pl. *-t* f. of *šiṭan*
šiṭani pl. *-yen* 1. satanic, pertaining to Satan 2. diabolical
šiṭen (*bin*) to cause bad blood (between), to sow dissension (among)
šix 1. pl. *šyux* Arab chief (tribe), sheik 2. pl. *šyux* leader of a family group 3. pl. *šyax* kind of Moroccan folk-singer
¶ *šyux n-nḍeṛ* real estate experts or appraisers (usually court-appointed)
šixa pl. *-t* kind of female Moroccan folk-singer and dancer
šiyy 1. v.n. of *šwa* 2. broiled meat
šiyyeb v.t. 1. to make or cause to get gray-haired (as worry) 2. to cause to age or get old (especially before one's time)
šiyyek v.i. to dress up (sometimes implying in good taste)
šiyyer 1. to signal, to gesture, to motion (with the hand) *šiyyer-lu iži!* Motion for him to come! 2. to wave *šiyyer le-ḅḅak!* Wave to your father!
** *šiyyer be-l-ġoṛṛaf.* He's off his rocker, he's lost his marbles.
¶ *šiyyer b-* to throw *šiyyret ɛliya b-beqṛež.* She threw a tea kettle at me.
šiyyeṭ 1. v.t. to brush, to brush off (clothes, etc.) 2. v.t. to not spend, to have left (after some expenditure) *šiyyeṭ ši-flus men le-flus lli ka-teqbeṭ!* Don't spend all the money you get! 3. v.i. to burn (food) *ka-nšemm ši-tɛam ka-išiyyeṭ.* I smell something (food) burning.
šiyyex v.t. 1. to appoint as *šix* 2. to initiate into a brotherhood (by going through the proper rituals)
šiyyăɛ v.t. to announce, to make public

šiẓ artemisia

ška iški v.i. (v.n. *ška*) to complain (i.e., giving vent to grievances, discontent, etc.)
¶ *ška b-* to complain about or against (s.o.)

ška v.n. of *ška*

škal **1.** pl. of *škel* **2.** pl. *-at* leg irons
** *ka-imši be-š-škalat.* He struts around like a peacock (i.e., conceited, arrogant).

škaṛa pl. *škayeṛ* **1.** satchel **2.** bag, (men's) purse with shoulder strap
** *huwa be-škaṛtu.* He's got (the) money.

škawi pl. of *šekwa* **2**

škaya pl. *-t* n.i. and v.n. of *ška*

škayem pl. of *škima*

škayeṛ pl. of *škaṛa*

škayṛi pl. *-ya* one who makes satchels or purses (called *škaṛa*)

škima pl. *škayem* bridle (horse, etc.)

škiṛ v.n. of *škeṛ*

škiwa dim. of *šekwa* **2**

šekk (v.n. *šekk, šekkan*) to suspect *ka-nšekk* (or *šekkit*) *ṛah maži.* I suspect he's on his way.
¶ *šekk f-* **1.** to doubt (s.th.) **2.** to suspect (s.o.)

šekk **1.** v.n. of *šekk* **2.** suspicion *ʕăndu š-šekk fe-mṛatu.* He suspects his wife (e.g., of infidelity).
¶ *bla šekk* undoubtedly, without (a) doubt *bla šekk ġadi-ṭṭiẓ š-šta had l-lila.* It's undoubtedly going to rain tonight.
¶ *fihφ š-šekk* to be suspicious ≠
¶ *qṭăʕ š-šekk* to make sure, to remove all doubt

šekkam pl. *-a* **1.** tattletale **2.** informer, stool-pigeon

šekkaṛ pl. *-in* used in the expr. *šekkaṛ ṛaṣuφ* conceited person, braggart

šekkaṛa same as *škaṛa*

šekkel **1.** v.t. to hobble (horse, etc., by tying front foot to hind foot) **2.** v.i. to use variation or variety *šekkel, ma-tebqa-š dima ka-telbes ġir le-kẓăl.* Use a little variety; don't dress in black all the time.
¶ *šekkel l-* to trip (s.o.) (making him fall)

šekkem v.t. to bridle, to put a bridle on (horse, etc.)
¶ *šekkem b-* to tattle on, to inform against (s.o.)

škel pl. *škal* (art. for pl. *le-* in certain expr.) **1.** kind, sort, type **2.** category, class **3.** way, manner
** *ʕla škel!* What kind of person are you (is he, is she, etc.), anyway? (expr. of disgust and/or disappointment)
¶ *ʕăl le-škal* of all kinds *ʕăndu ṭ-ṭumubilat ʕăl le-škal.* He's got cars of all kinds.

šekḷaṭ chocolate (candy, etc.)

šekḷaṭi pl. *-yen* chocolate (colored)

šekma (often preceded by *ma-* and usually followed by pron. endings) *ma-šekmani fih.* I don't concern myself with him. I don't meddle in his affairs. —(*ma-*) *šekmak fiya?* What business is it of yours? (i.e., what are my affairs to you?)

škeṛ v.t. (v.n. *šokṛ, škiṛ*) **1.** to thank *ka-nšekṛek ʕla dak l-hadiya.* (I) thank you for that gift. **2.** to praise, to speak favorably of (s.o., s.th.)
¶ *škeṛ f-* same as **2**
¶ *škeṛ l-xir* to be grateful

šokṛ v.n. of *škeṛ*

škun who (interrogative) *škun ža ʕăndek l-bareẓ fe-l-lil?* Who came to your place last night?

šekwa pl. *-t* **1.** complaint, grievance *ila ḍeḷmek, ʕmel ʕlih šekwa.* If he treats you unjustly, make a complaint against him. **2.** pl. also *škawi* (dim. *škiwa*) goatskin bottle (for milk)

šḷaḍa pl. *-t, šḷayeḍ* salad

šlaġem (pl.) large moustache (handle-bar, etc.)

šlala rinsing or washing (of tea before brewing)

šlaqem pl. of *šelquma*

šlaxi pl. of *šelxa*

šḷayeḍ pl. of *šḷaḍa*

šelguma same as *šelquma*

šli pl. of *šelya*

šliman kind of poison

šella **1.** a lot, much *kanu bihom šella de-n-nas.* There were a lot of people. **2.** a long time *šella hadi ma-šeftek.* I haven't seen you for a long time.

šeḷḷeḍ v.t. **1.** to chop up, to chop fine (onions, radishes, etc.) **2.** to make into a salad, to make a salad out of

šellel v.t. to rinse, to rinse out or off (tea, dishes, clothes, etc.)
¶ *šellel b-* to plate or wash with (gold, silver, etc.)
¶ *šellel yedduφ men* to wash (one's) hands of, to be through with, to give up on (s.o., affair)
¶ p.p. *mšellel* pl. *-in* lacking in knowledge, ignorant

šellex v.t. to chip, to take a chip or chips out of (usually s.th. of wood)

šelquma pl. *šlaqem* lip (of donkey, horse, dog, etc.; extended to large human lips)

šluẓ pl. of *šelẓ*

šelweš v.t. and v.i. **1.** to swing or sling in the air *daz ka-išelweš be-l-mbexṛa.* He passed by, swinging the censer (in the air). **2.** to shake (s.o. or s.th.) at arm's length. *qebṭu men yeddu u-šelwšu.* He grabbed him by the hand and shook him. **3.** to hang up or stretch out (a garment or linen, etc.) without permitting it to dry completely, to leave (s.th.) damp *la-tyebbes l-qamižža bezzaf, ġir šelwešha.* Don't dry the shirt completely, just leave it damp.

šelweɛ same as *šelweš*

šelxa pl. *-t, šlaxi* chip, splinter (wood)

šelya pl. *-t, šli* chair (excluding the easy chair type)

šelɛ pl. *šluɛ* Berber (person of the southern Berber group)

šelɛa **1.** Berber language (southern) **2.** pl. *-t* f. of *šelɛ*

šmal left, left side *ka-yăɛrež men režlih de-š-šmal.* He limps with his left leg.

¶ *ɛăl š-šmal!* left, to the left *ḍuṛ ɛăl š-šmal!* Turn left!

šmarer pl. of *šemrir*

šmata pl. *šmayet* **1.** good-for-nothing (person) **2.** easily duped person (especially in business)

šmayet pl. of *šmata*

šmaɛ **1.** wax (candle, bees) **2.** n.u. *-a, šemɛa* pl. *-t* candle

¶ *šmaɛ l-xemm* beeswax

šmisa, šmiša dim. of *šems, šemš*

šmit v.n. of *šmet*

šmel family, family group (clan)

** *ḷḷah ibedded* (or *šettet*) *šemlek!* May God scatter your family! (strong insult)

šemla pl. *-t* front bottom section of a garment which can be gathered up to form a pouch

šemm v.t. (v.n. *šemman*) **1.** to smell **2.** same as *šemmem*

¶ p.p. *mešmum* pl. *mšamem* bouquet, bunch (flowers)

šemman **1.** v.n. of *šemm* **2.** (sense of) smell

šemmat pl. *-in* ag. adj. of *šmet*

šemmaɛ pl. *-a* chandler, seller of candles (not manufacturer)

šemmem v.t. to make or cause (s.th.) to be smelled (by s.o.) *šemmem-lha had l-beṣla!* Have her smell these onions!

šemmeṛ v.i. **1.** to roll one's sleeves up **2.** to get ready, to prepare oneself (literally, to roll up one's sleeves) *yaḷḷah nšemmṛu l-l-xedma!* Let's get to work (on this)!

šemmes, šemmeš v.t. to put in or expose to the sun, to sun, to solarize

šemmăɛ v.t. to rub wax (*šmaɛ*) on, to wax (as string, piece of paper)

¶ p.p. *mšemmăɛ* pl. *-in* dense, dull-witted, of low mental ability

šmen same as *aš-men* (see *aš*)

šemrir pl. *šmarer* hat (conventional or European type)

šems, šemš (f.) pl. *šmus, šmuš, šmusa* (dim. *šmisa, šmiša*) sun

** *šmuš hadi!* **1.** what a beautiful sunny day! **2.** That sun sure is hot! —*dexlet ɛlih š-šmuš.* He was practically overcome by the heat of the sun.

šemšem v.i. to sniff (as in trying to identify or follow an odor or scent)

šmet v.t. (v.n. *šmit*) **1.** to cheat, to gyp (s.o.) **2.** to play a joke or trick on (s.o.)

¶ *šmet f-* same as *šmet* above

šemta pl. *-t* **1.** n.i. of *šmet* **1 2.** (practical) joke, (dirty) trick

šmus, šmusa, šmuš pl. of *šems, šemš*

šmutiya dishonest, abusive behavior (as befitting one who cheats, takes advantage, etc.)

šmăɛ same as *šmaɛ*

šemɛa n.u. of *šmaɛ* **2**

šemɛi pl. *-yen* of or resembling the color of beeswax or candle wax

šeʔn same as *šan*

šnanef pl. of *šennuf*

šnaq pl. *-at* rope tied between the tops of the two sides of the *šwari* (to prevent spilling contents)

šnaqeṛ pl. of *šenquṛ*

šnatef pl. of *šentufa*

šendgura, šentgura germander, a type of herb with small blue flowers, used by some people in cooking

šenḍiḍ same as *ṣenḍiḍ*

šengiṭ same as *šenqiṭ*

šni, sniya (f.) what (interrogative) *šniya hadi?* What's this?

šniq v.n. of *šneq*

šnit v.n. of *šnet*

šniya same as *šni*

šennafa pl. *-t* lip (of donkey, etc.; extended to large human lips)

šennaqa pl. hangman's rope

šennef v.t. to to cut or separate into wedges (melon, orange, etc.)

šenneq v.t. to tie the rope *šnaq* on (the *šwari*)

¶ *šenneq ɛla* same as *šneq ɛla*

šennuf pl. *šnanef* wedge (of orange, melon, etc.)

šneq v.t. (v.n. *šniq*) to hang (s.o.)

¶ *šneq ɛla* **1.** to grab (s.o.) by the collar **2.** to pester, to "get on (one's) back"

šenqiṭ, šengiṭ Mauretania

šenqiṭi, šengiṭi pl. *šnaqṭa, šnagṭa* Mauretanian

šenquṛ pl. *šnaqeṛ* s.th. sharp and capable of injuring (e.g., thorn, piece of glass, splinter)

šnet v.i. (v.n. *šnit*) to get angry or upset

šenta n.i. of *šnet*

šentufa pl. *šnatef* small piece, crumb (food)

šenṭrež chess
šnu, šnuwa what (interrogative) *šnu ʕṭak?* What did he give you?
šenwila pl. *-t* gnat, midge (usually referring to one which has entered s.o.'s eye, ear, nose, or throat)
šqa išqa v.i. (v.n. *šqa*) **1.** to get tired, to become fatigued **2.** to take the trouble, to bother *ma-tešqa-š!* Don't bother!
šqa išqi v.t. **1.** to tire, to fatigue (s.o.) **2.** to cause (s.o.) some trouble or bother
šqa (m.) **1.** v.n. of *šqa išqa* **2.** tiredness, fatigue
šqaf pl. of *šqef*
šqaq pl. of *šqiq*
šqayeq pl. of *šqiqa* **2** and *šqiq* and *šeqq*
šqef pl. *šqaf, šquf, šqufa* **1.** fragment, broken piece (glass, pottery, china) **2.** bowl (of smoking pipe, usually of clay) **3.** old man (somewhat derogatory)
šeqfa pl. *-t* old woman (somewhat derogatory)
šqiq pl. *šqaq, šqayeq* brother of the same father and mother, brother-german
šqiqa **1.** migraine (headache) **2.** pl. *šqayeq* sister of the same father and mother, sister-german
šeqlayba pl. *-t* somersault, flip
šeqleb v.t. **1.** to mess up, to put in disorder (room, bookkeeping, etc.) **2.** to knock over, to upset (chair, glass, etc.) **3.** to flip (s.o.) (as in gymnastics)
¶ *šeqleb d-dmaġ l-* to get (s.o.) mixed up, confused *šeqlebti-li dmaġi.* You've got me all confused.
šeqq (v.n. *šeqqan*) **1.** v.t. to cut open (melon, boil, etc.) **2.** v.t. to penetrate, to go through (bullet, knife, etc.) **3.** v.t. to crack (glass, wood, wall, etc.) **4.** v.i. to be operated on *l-bareḥ šeqqet ʕăl l-meṣrana z-zayda.* She was operated on for appendicitis yesterday.
¶ *šeqq l-* to operate on (surgery)
¶ a.p. *šaqq* pl. *-in* fatiguing, tiring (e.g., work)
šeqq n.u. *-a* pl. *-at, šqayeq* (dim. *šqiqa*) **1.** crack (in wall, glass, wood, etc.) **2.** slit, slot **3.** cut (in skin)
šeqqan v.n. of *šeqq*
šeqqeq v.t. **1.** to crack (glass, wood, etc.) **2.** to leave ajar, to crack (door, window)
šqeṛ same as *šqeṛ*
šquf, šqufa pl. of *šqef*
šra išri v.t. (v.n. *šra, šeryan*) **1.** to buy **2.** to buy off (s.o.)
¶ a.p. *šari* pl. *šorray* buyer
šra v.n. of *šra*
šṛab alcohol (as a drink, usually wine)
šrabel pl. of *šerbil*
šrabli pl. *-ya* maker and seller of women's footwear called *šerbil*
šragi pl. of *šerga* **2**
šṛameṭ pl. of *šeṛmuṭa*
šṛaṛ pl. of *šrir*
šṛaref pl. of *šeṛṛafa*
šṛašeṛ pl. of *šeṛšaṛ* and *šeṛšuṛ*
šratel pl. of *šertla*
šṛaṭi pl. of *šeṛṭa*
šṛaweṭ pl. of *šeṛwiṭa*
šrayek pl. of *šrika*
šṛažem pl. of *šeṛžem*
šṛeb išṛob, išṛeb (v.n. *šṛib, šeṛb*) **1.** v.t. to drink **2.** v.i. to drink (alcoholic beverages) **3.** v.t. to absorb (blotter, dry earth, etc.) **4.** v.i. to get infected (wound, sore)
¶ *šaṛeb* (a.p.) *ʕăqluᵠ* not given to snap decisions, exercising wisdom
¶ p.p. *mešṛub* pl. *-at* refreshment, refreshing drink (as a soft drink)
šeṛb v.n. of *šṛeb*
šeṛba pl. *-t* **1.** n.i. of *šṛeb* **2.** drink *ʕṭini ši-šeṛba de-l-ma.* Give me a drink of water.
šoṛba, šeṛba pl. *-t* any kind of thin soup
šerbil pl. *šrabel* (sg. *ferda de-š-šerbil*) (pair of) a kind of woman's embroidered shoes or slippers
šeṛbiya pl. *-t* **1.** wedding veil **2.** brocaded, fringed headscarf or shawl
šref v.i. to get old, to age (person, animal, fruit on the plant, etc.)
¶ a.p. *šaref* pl. *šorraf* old person
šoṛfa pl. of *šrif*
šreg v.i. to eat or drink s.th. so as to choke on it (as down the windpipe)
šerga pl. *-t* **1.** n.i. of *šreg* **2.** (pl. also *šragi*) tear, rip (in cloth)
šergi (the) hot east summer wind, sirocco
šṛib v.n. of *šṛeb*
šrif (adj. and n.) pl. *šoṛfa* descendant of the Prophet Mohammed, sherif
šrik pl. *šerkan, šorkan* **1.** partner, associate (business) **2.** accomplice
šrika pl. *-t, šrayek* co-partner in marriage (i.e., one of the wives of a polygynous marriage)
šṛiq v.n. of *šṛeq*
šrir pl. *-in, šṛaṛ* cruel, mean
¶ *šrir mrir* pl. *šṛaṛ mṛaṛ* emphatic of *šrir*
šṛiṭ **1.** v.n. of *šṛeṭ* **2.** pl. *šeṛṭan* kind of cord made from the leaves of the dwarf palm
šriḥa (coll.) dried fig(s)
šrek (*mʕa*) (v.n. *šerk*) to join, to connect (to) (as one letter to another in script)
¶ *šrek be-llah* to believe in some god other than, or in addition to God
¶ *šrek* or *šrek f-* **1.** to be co-owner of *waš ka-tešrek mʕaya ḍaṛi?* Do you think this is your house too? (sarcastic) **2.** to be a partner in, to go into partnership in *škun lli ibġi išrek mʕaya f-had l-biʕa*

u-š-šerya? Who wants to go in with me in this deal?
šerk v.n. of *šrek*
šṛek n.u. *šeṛka* leaf of a palm frond
šerka n.i. of *šrek*
šeṛka n.u. of *šṛek*
** *xeṣṣatu šeṛka.* He's nuts. He doesn't have all his marbles.
šerkan, šorkan pl. of *šrik*
šeṛma pl. *-t* 1. n.i. of *šṛem* 2. tear, rip (in cloth; in ear or nose, as caused by an earring or nose ring)
šeṛmel v.t. to treat with *šeṛmula* before cooking
šeṛmula kind of sauce or dressing either stuffed into fish, put on meat preserves, or used to cook chicken (each meat has its own kind of dressing)
šeṛmuṭa pl. *-t, šṛameṭ* prostitute, whore
šṛenbeq, šṛembeq same as *sṛenbeq*
šṛeq v.i. (v.n. *šṛiq, šṛuq*) 1. to come up, to rise (sun) 2. to shine (a polished surface)
šeṛq 1. east (adv. and n.) *sir žuž de-l-ʔamyal šeṛq!* Go two miles east! 2. (with art.) Middle East (generally) 3. (with art.) Mecca
šeṛqi pl. *-yen* 1. eastern, of or on the east side *n-naḥiya š-šeṛqiya d-le-mdina kollha naḍet fiha l-ɛafya.* The whole eastern section of town caught on fire. 2. eastern, of or from the (Middle) East
šeṛṛ evil or bad deeds and actions (often implying cruelty)
šeṛṛafa pl. *šṛaref* kind of skylight (in ceiling)
šeṛṛaṭ pl. *-a* maker of cords and brooms (made from the dwarf palm)
šerray pl. *-a* buyer
šeṛṛeb 1. v.t. to give to drink (specifically water or alcohol) *šeṛṛebni ḷḷah ixellik!* Please give me a drink! 2. v.t. to water (animals) 3. v.i. to leak (ceiling, container)
šeṛṛef v.t. to honor *waš imken-lek tšeṛṛefna be-l-ḥuḍuṛ dyalek had l-lila?* Can you honor us with your presence this evening?
šerreg v.t. 1. to rip or tear (up) *ɛlaš šerregti dak l-žarida?* What did you tear up that (news)paper for? 2. to cause (s.o.) to choke while drinking or eating
šeṛṛeq used in expr. such as *ana ka-nšeṛṛeq u-huwa ka-iġeṛṛeb!* I talk about one thing and he talks about something else!
šeṛṛeqṛaq kind of ratchet-type noisemaker
šeṛṛeṭ 1. v.t. to mark or scratch (up) *l-qeṭṭa šeṛṛṭet-lu wežhu.* The cat scratched his face. 2. v.i. to have one's blood let (a folk remedy) 3. (*ɛla*) to be vaccinated (for smallpox)
¶ *šeṛṛeṭ l-* 1. to bleed (s.o.), to let the blood of (s.o.) 2. (*ɛla*) to vaccinate (for)
¶ *šeṛṛeṭ ɛla* 1. to cross off or out the name of (s.o., as from a list) 2. to exclude, to not count on (s.o.)
šeṛṛeḥ v.t. to slit, to slash, to make a gash in
šerrăɛ v.t. to open wide (door, window)
šeṛšaṛ pl. *šṛašeṛ* waterfall, cascade
šeṛšeṛ v.i. 1. to rush, to gush (water) 2. to fall, to cascade (water)
šeṛšuṛ pl. *šṛašeṛ* falling stream (of water, as from a pipe, a urinating boy)
šertel same as *sertel*
šertla pl. *-t, šratel* set of gold bracelets
šṛeṭ v.i. (v.n. *šṛiṭ*) to impose, make, or give (s.th.) as a condition, to stipulate *ila bġiti dži ɛăndi ka-nešṛeṭ ɛlik tkun ɛăndi fe-t-tmenya.* If you want to come over to my place I'm going to make the condition that you come at eight o'clock.
šeṛṭ pl. *šṛuṭ, šuṛuṭ, šuṛuṭat* condition, stipulation *kayen bezzaf de-š-šuṛuṭ f-had l-ɛoqda.* There are too many conditions in this contract.
¶ *b-šeṛṭ, bi-šeṛṭ,* or *ɛla šeṛṭ* on condition (that), only if *imken-lek dži b-šeṛṭ džib mɛak faṭima.* You can come only if you bring Fatima with you.
šeṛṭa pl. *-t, šṛaṭi* 1. stripe (denoting rank) 2. mark, scratch (as on a table, wall) 3. line, mark (as made with a pencil) 4. scar
šeṛṭan pl. of *šṛiṭ* 2
šṛuq 1. v.n. of *šṛeq* 2. sunrise
šṛuṭ pl. of *šeṛṭ*
šeṛwiṭa pl. *šṛaweṭ* 1. piece of cloth, rag (may be said sarcastically in reference to clothing) 2. (pl.) rags; old, worn-out clothes
šerya pl. *-t* 1. n.i. of *šra* 2. purchase, buy
šeryan v.n. of *šra*
šeṛžeb, šeṛžem pl. *šṛažeb, šṛažem* same as *seṛžem*
šṛeḥ v.t. (v.n. *šeṛḥ*) to explain
¶ *šṛeḥ l-xaṭeṛ l-* to cheer up *dak le-xbaṛ šṛeḥ-li xaṭri* (or *l-xaṭeṛ*). The news has cheered me up.
¶ p.p. *mešṛuḥ* pl. *-in* jovial, gay
šeṛḥ pl. *šuṛuḥ* 1. v.n. of *šṛeḥ* 2. explanation
šṛăɛ (with art.) Islamic law or justice
šta (dim. *štiwa*) 1. rain 2. winter
¶ *ṭaḥet* (or *hebṭet* or *nezlet* or *ṣebbet*) *š-šta* to rain
štaq v.t. (some speakers with *l-*) to miss, to yearn for (home, s.o., some food, etc.)
štarek, štaṛek 1. to join *aži štarekna f-le-ɛša.* Come join us for dinner. —*ġadi-neštarku u-nqimu ḥefla.* We're going to join together and give a party. —*ɛlaš ma-teštarek fe-n-nadi l-fenni?* Why don't you join the art club? 2. to subscribe *štarek fe-tlata de-l-mažellat.* He has subscribed to three magazines.
štawi pl. of *šetwa*

šṭebb kind of grass made into cords or rope
šṭef *ɛla* (v.n. *šṭif*) to stamp on (s.th.) repetitively with the feet
šṭif v.n. of *šṭef*
šṭim v.n. of *šṭem*
šṭiṛak **1.** v.n. of *šṭarek* **2.** participation, taking part **3.** subscription
šṭiwa dim. of *šṭa*
šṭem f- to speak ill of, to backbite
šetta v.i. to pass or spend the winter
šettaf pl. *-a* one employed in a tannery whose job it is to stamp on the hides with his feet while they are in certain solutions
šettam pl. *-in* ag. adj of *šṭem*
šettat pl. *-a* big money-spender
šettet v.t. **1.** to scatter, to strew (e.g., chicken feed) **2.** to disperse, to break up (crowd)
** *ḷḷah išettet šemlek!* May God disperse your family! (strong insult)
¶ *šettet le-flus* to squander money
šetwa pl. *šṭawi* **1.** winter **2.** (pl. for intensity) rain
šetwi pl. *-yen* winter, wintry, of or pertaining to winter
šṭaṛa haggling, bargaining (to buy)
šṭaṭa used in the expr. *šṭaṭa d-ɛibad ḷḷah* (or *de-n-nas*) said as an insult to indicate s.o.'s uselessness or worthlessness
šṭaṭeb pl. of *šeṭṭaba*
šṭaṭbi pl. *-ya* maker of brooms called *šeṭṭaba*
šṭaṭṭu pl. *-wat* sifter with a very fine mesh
šṭayen pl. of *šeṭna*
šṭayṛi pl. *-ya* one who bargains a great deal before buying
šṭeb n.u. *šeṭba* twigs
šeṭba pl. *-t* **1.** n.u. of *šṭeb* **2.** branch of a thorny plant **3.** shrewish woman, termagant
šṭin v.n. of *šṭen*
šṭiɛ v.n. of *šṭeɛ*
šṭen v.t. (v.n. *šṭin*) **1.** to pester, to importune **2.** to preoccupy the mind of (s.o.), to worry
¶ *šṭen ṛaṣu*$^{\phi}$ to cause oneself a lot of trouble or grief
šeṭna pl. *-t, šṭayen* s.th. that is a lot of trouble or bother, not worth the trouble
šeṭṭ pl. *šṭuṭ* **1.** shore (sea, lake) **2.** bank, edge, side (of river)
šeṭṭab pl. *-a* street cleaner or sweeper
šeṭṭaba pl. *-t, šṭaṭeb* broom (usually made from the leaves of the dwarf palm)
šeṭṭaɛ pl. *-a* dancer (chiefly folk dances)
šeṭṭeb v.t. to sweep (with a broom)
¶ *šeṭṭeb ɛla* to cross out or off (name from a list, a sentence, word, etc.)
šeṭṭeṭ v.t. to sift (with a *šṭaṭṭu*)
šṭuṭ pl. of *šeṭṭ*
šṭeɛ v.i. (v.n. *šṭiɛ*) to dance
šuf v.n. of *šaf*
šufa pl. *-t* n.i. of *šaf*
¶ *b-šuft l-ɛäyn* by looking, judging by eye (rather than by exact measurement or investigation)
šufan **1.** v.n. of *šaf* **2.** fortune-telling
šugeṛ pl. of *šgeṛ*
šuha pl. *-t* **1.** indiscreet or imprudent act, indiscretion **2.** (n. and invariable adj.) one who does **1** above **3.** (adj. invariable) ugly, unsightly **4.** exaggeration
šuheb pl. of *šheb*
šuhud pl. of *šahed* **1**
šuk n.u. *-a* **1.** thorn, spine (plant) **2.** spine, needle (animal) **3.** fish bone
šuka pl. *-t, šwek* **1.** sting, stinger (bee, etc.) **2.** point of a top (toy) **3.** shot, hypodermic injection **4.** ampoule (of serum for injections)
šum kind of sirocco, hot summer wind (considered more local than the *šergi*)
šun (no pl.) **1.** area or space between the neck and waist enclosed between the clothing and the body (often used as a pocket) **2.** side (of s.o., usually in bed) *mnin kont ṣġiṛ kanet l-qeṭṭa ka-tḥebb tenɛäs f-šuni.* When I was small the cat used to like to sleep by my side.
¶ *hḍeṛ f-šunu*$^{\phi}$ to mumble in one's beard
šuq pl. *šwaq* (pl. for intensity) yearning, longing
šuqeṛ v.t. to chop (with a hatchet)
šuqeṛ pl. of *šqeṛ* (same as *šgeṛ*)
šuṛa pl. *-t* trousseau
šuṛuq same as *šṛuq*
šuṛuṭ, šuṛuṭat pl. of *šeṛṭ*
šuṛuḥ pl. of *šeṛḥ*
šuša pl. *-t* tassel
šutanbir September
šuwwaf pl. *-a* fortune-teller
šuwwal **1.** tenth month of the Muslim calendar **2.** pl. *šwawel* tail (animal, bird, airplane)
šuwwaš **1.** pl. of *šaweš* **2.** pl. *-in* ag. adj. of *šuwweš*
šuwwaṭ pl. *-a* one who cooks and sells the heads of lambs or sheep
šuwwaya pl. *-t* grill (for broiling meat)
šuwweh v.t. **1.** to deform, to render unsightly (face, body) **2.** to ruin the appearance of *ila ṣbeġti dak l-bab b-le-ḥmeṛ ġir ġadi tšuwwehha.* If you paint that door red you'll ruin it.
¶ *šuwweh b-* to ridicule, to make fun of (s.o.)
šuwwek v.t. to give goose pimples or flesh to, to cause (s.o.) to have goose flesh (object may be *lḥäm* or *dat*)
šuwweq v.t. to make homesick or nostalgic *šuwweqtini fe-l-musiqa l-meġṛibiya.* You've made me homesick for Moroccan music.
šuwweṛ **1.** v.t. to give a trousseau to (a bride) **2.** v.i. to go slowly

šuwweš v.t. to upset, to cause (s.o.) to worry
¶ *šuwweš ɛla* to bother, to disturb (s.o. trying to read, etc.)
šuwweṭ v.t. **1.** to burn (usually meat by over-cooking) **2.** to burn (alcohol in a wound, hot pepper, hot soup, etc.) **3.** to (sun)burn
šuyan v.n. of *šwa*
šuyuɛi pl. *-yen* communist
šuyuɛiya communism
šuɛaṛa pl. of *šaɛiṛ*
šuɛub pl. of *šăɛb*
šwa išwi v.t. (v.n. *šiyy, šuyan*) **1.** to broil, to grill **2.** to (sun)burn) **3.** to sting (bee, etc.) **4.** to hit or strike with a sharp, stinging action (as with a switch, towel)
¶ *šwa f-* to deprive of *šwatu l-mut f-bentu.* Death took his daughter.
** (*ḷḷah*) *išwini fik!* used as a disapproving criticism of s.o.'s action, accomplishment, etc.
¶ p.p. *mešwi* grilled or broiled meat
šwa (m.) steamed meat (usually lamb)
šwahed pl. of *šahed* 2 and 3
šwama n.pl. of *šami*
šwaneṭ pl. of *šanṭa*
šwaq pl. of *šuq*
šwaqeṛ pl. of *šaquṛ*
šwaṛ **1.** v.n. of *šaweṛ* **2.** consultation
¶ *be-š-šwaṛ* on trial (i.e., on condition of being able to get a refund for s.th. bought for oneself or a third party if rejected by the same) *ka-nšriha mennek be-š-šwaṛ.* I'm buying it from you on condition I can return it if my friend doesn't (or, I don't) like it.
¶ *bla šwaṛ* without consulting (anyone)
šwareb pl. of *šareb*
šwari pl. *-yat* kind of large saddle bags (made from dwarf palm leaves) used on beasts of burden for hauling
¶ *ɛămmeṛ š-šwari ɛla* to feed (s.o.) a cock-and-bull story or a lot of bull
šwaš anything from unrest, disquietude to civil upheaval, rioting
šwaši pl. of *šašiya*
šwawel pl. of *šuwwal*
šway **1.** a little, a little bit **2.** a little while, a minute
** *šway šway!* Take it easy! Go a little slower!
¶ (*u-*) *šway šway* a little while afterward or later *xrež šway šway ṛžăɛ.* He left and came back a little while later.
šwibla dim. of *šabel*
šwirdat pl. of *šwirdi*
šwirdi pl. *-yat, šwirdat* young Negro boy in the service of a sultan or king (e.g. a fan-bearer), commonly in fairy tales, etc.
šwiṭen dim. of *šiṭan* 3 and 4
šwiya **1.** a little, a little bit *ɛṭini šwiya d-atay!* Give me a little tea! **2.** a little while, a minute *tsenna šwiya!* Wait a minute! —*men daba šwiya iži.* He'll be here in a little while.
¶ *be-š-šwiya* **1.** slowly *xellef ġir be-š-šwiya!* Walk slow(er)! **2.** softly, in a low voice
¶ *šwiya be-šwiya* little by little, a little at a time
¶ *šwiya šwiya* a little while later or afterwards *xrež šwiya šwiya ṛžăɛ.* He left and came back a little while later.
¶ *waɛed š-šwiya* **1.** a little while **2.** a little bit
šwiyeš same as *šwiya* (especially in meanings 1 and 2)
šwek pl. of *šuka*
šxiṛ v.n. of *šxeṛ*
šxeṛ v.i. (v.n. *šxiṛ*) to snore
šexṣ **1.** pl. *ˀašxaṣ* person, individual **2.** pl. *šxuṣa* important person
šexṣiya pl. *-t* personality (implies pleasant or nice) *dak s-siyyed ɛăndu šexṣiya.* That gentleman has a pleasant personality. —*l-yum ġadi-dži dẓuṛna waɛed š-šexṣiya muhimma.* Today an important personality is going to come and visit us.
šxuṣa pl. of *šexṣ* 2
šexweš v.t. to frighten, to scare *šexwšatni ši-ɛaža fe-ḍ-ḍḷam.* Something in the dark scared me.
šyah pl. of *ša*
šyaṭ odor of burning meat, wool, hair, cloth, feathers, etc.
šyaṭa what is left over (usually food, thrown away or fed to the dog)
šyaṭen pl. of *šiṭan*
šyax pl. of *šix* 3
šyaxa function or position of a sheik
šyet, šyeṭ pl. of *šita, šiṭa*
šyux pl. of *šix* 1 and 2
ššaɛ pl. of *ššiɛ*
ššed same as *sžed*
ššin same as *sžin*
ššiṛa dim. of *šežṛa* (n.u. of *ššeṛ*)
ššiɛ pl. *-in, šežɛan, ššaɛ* courageous, brave, intrepid
ššen pl. of *sžen*
ššeṛ n.u. *šežṛa* (dim. *ššiṛa*) tree (plant)
šežžada same as *sežžada*
šežžăɛ v.t. to encourage, to hearten
šežɛan pl. of *ššiɛ*
šɛal **1.** how much, how many *šɛal mennhom ɛăndek?* How many of them do you have? —*šɛal mennha ɛăndkom?* How much of it do you have? **2.** how long *šɛal ġadi-tebqa hna?* How long are you going to stay here?
¶ *be-šɛal* **1.** for how much *be-šɛal šriti had l-magana?* How much did you buy the

clock for? 2. how much *be-šɣal xelləṣti?* How much did you pay?

¶ *šɣal d-* how many, how much *šɣal d-le-flus ɛăndek?* or *šɣal ɛăndek d-le-flus?* How much money do you have?

¶ *šɣal hadi* 1. for a long time *šɣal hadi ma-šeftu.* I haven't seen him for a long time. —*šɣal hadi w-ana ka-nexdem hna!* I've been working here for a long time. 2. how long (has it been, have you been, etc.) *šɣal hadi ma-šeftiha?* How long has it been since you saw her? —*šɣal hadi u-nta ka-texdem hna?* How long have you been working here?

** *šɣal hadi fe-s-saɛa?* What time is it?

¶ *šɣal-ma, sɣal-emma* 1. however many, no matter how many *šɣal-emma žaw de-n-nas, dexxelhom.* No matter how many people come, have them come in. 2. however long, no matter how long *šɣal-emma ṭal l-lil itebɛu n-nhaṛ.* No matter how long the night lasts, the day follows.

¶ *šɣal men* (with sg.) how much, how many *šɣal men ktab ɛăndna?* How many books do we have?

šɣayṭi pl. *-ya* one who sells s.th. for more than it's worth, profiteer, crook

šɣaɣa avarice, miserliness

šɣiṭ v.n. of *šɣeṭ*

šɣem, šeɣma pl. *šɣum* (of intensity) animal fat or grease (before cooking)

šɣeṭ v.t. (v.n. *šɣiṭ*) 1. to strike, to hit (with s.th., usually producing a noise 2. to eat all of (s.th.) 3. to gyp (in a sale)

šeɣṭ beating (as with a stick, whip, etc.)

** *ɛṭina š-šeɣṭ l-l-xedma.* We worked hard and fast (at a job). —*ɛṭina š-šeɣṭ l-seksu.* We ate every bit of the couscous.

¶ *tɛaṭaw š-šeɣṭ ɛla* to haggle or bargain over (pl. subject)

šeɣṭa pl. *-t* n.i. of *šɣeṭ*

šɣum pl. of *šɣem, šeɣma*

šeɣɣ v.i. to be miserly, avaricious

šeɣɣ, šeɣɣa same as *šɣaɣa*

šeɣɣem v.t. to grease (mechanical parts; also specifically a soccer ball to keep it in good shape)

¶ p.p. *mšeɣɣem* pl. *-in* fat, fattened (livestock)

šeɣɣeṛ v.t. 1. to brew (tea) on the fire until ready 2. to make too high (price of s.th.) *šeɣɣeṛti ɛliya t-taman!* Your price is too high for me. 3. to make hard, difficult *šeɣɣru ɛliya le-mtiɣan.* That exam was really rough.

šɛa reflection (of a light, s.th. shiny)

šɛabi pl. of *šăɛba*

šɛakek pl. of *šăɛkuka*

šɛaṭeṭ pl. of *šăɛṭaṭa*

šăɛb pl. *šuɛub* people, nation

šăɛba pl. *-t, šɛabi* valley

šăɛban eighth month of the Muslim lunar calendar

šăɛbana pre-Ramadan feast or celebration, starting on the 27th of *šăɛban,* and extending to the next new moon

šɛil v.n. of *šɛăl*

šɛir n.u. *-a* barley

šăɛkuka pl. *šɛakek* hair, mess of hair (usually in need of combing, cutting)

šɛăl (v.n. *šɛil*) 1. v.t. to light (fire, cigarette, match, etc.) 2. v.t. to turn on (light, radio, etc.) 3. v.i. to sparkle, to glitter 4. v.i. to shine (polished surface)

** *l-ɛafya šăɛlet f-dik ḍ-ḍaṛ.* That house has caught on fire.

šăɛla pl. *-t* flame (fire)

šɛăṛ b- 1. to feel, to sense, to perceive *šɛăṛt b-ši-waɣed muṛay.* I felt that someone was behind me. 2. to realize what the intentions of (s.o.) are, to catch on to what (s.o.) is really doing *daba šɛăṛt bik!* Now I know what you're up to!

** *škun lli šɛăṛ bik!* Who cares what you think! Who's going to listen to you!

šɛăṛ n.u. *šăɛra* pl. *šɛuṛat* (pl. for intensity) hair

šăɛra pl. *-t* 1. n.u. of *šɛăṛ* 2. hairspring (clock, watch)

šăɛriya (coll.) noodles, vermicelli

šăɛšăɛ v.i. to shine, to beam (sun)

šăɛṭaṭa pl. *šɛaṭeṭ* mess of hair, a lot of hair (implying the need of a haircut)

šɛuṛat pl. of *šɛăṛ*

T

ta?adamit courtesy, politeness (often implies a somewhat formal manner)

tab itub (*men*) (v.n. *tuban*) to repent (of)

** *tab ɛliha ḷḷah.* She's turned over a new leaf.

¶ *tab men* to abandon, to give up, to swear off (e.g., drinking, smoking)

tabaqi rest, remainder *năɛṭik ṭeṛf men le-flus lli ka-tsalni daba we-t-tabaqi men daba šheṛ.* I'll give you some of the money I owe you now and the rest within a month.

tabaṛaka used in the expr. *ḷḷah tabaṛaka wa taɛala* sometimes said when mentioning God in conversation

tabašawit, tabašawiyet office or position of *baša* (often used in a derogatory manner to connote pomposity, "stuffed-shirtedness")
tabat steadfastness, constancy, stick-to-itiveness (of character, purpose, mind)
tabennayet vocation of mason or bricklayer, masonry
tabeqqa same as *tabaqi*
tabeqqalet occupation of *beqqal*
tabramlit, tabramliyet vocation of barrel-making
tabeṛġazet occupation of second-hand dealer, i.e. *beṛġaz*
taberraꜥet occupation of town or public crier
tabet a.p. of *tbet*
tabut pl. *twabet* **1.** bier **2.** coffin
tabuwwabet occupation of doorkeeper, gatekeeper
tabeꜥ a.p. of *tbăꜥ*
tadebbaġet occupation of tanner; tanning
tadeggaget profession of jeweler
tadellalet occupation of auctioneer
tadeqqa fine, reddish clay (if *de-l-lwani,* used in polishing metals; if *d-le-bni,* used in constructing ovens, braziers)
taderrazet occupation of textile weaver
taderrit, taderriyet childishness
tafala pl. *-t, twafel* bayonet
tafasir pl. of *tefsir*
tafaṣil pl. of *tefṣil*
tafatiš pl. of *teftiš* 2
tafḍulit, tafḍuliyet nosiness, meddling interference
taflaykit, taflaykiyet boatmanship
tafeṛṛanet occupation of an oven attendant
tafexxaṛet ceramics
tafeꜥꜥamet occupation of charcoal or coal vendor
tagebbaṣet occupation of plasterer
tagra pl. *twager* small, unglazed earthen bowl (used for drinking)
tagerrabet occupation of water carrier
tagezzanet fortune-telling
tagezzaret occupation of butcher, butchery
taġṛablit, taġṛabliyet occupation of sifter or sieve-maker
taġeššašet **1.** cheating (n.) **2.** fraud **3.** shirking (at work, school)
taġeyyaṭet art and occupation of playing the *ġiṭa*
tah itih v.i. (v.n. *tihan, tih*) **1.** to roam or wander about (as if lost) **2.** to show conceit
** *tah f-ꜥobbha.* He's head over heels in love with her.
takafrit cunning, slyness
takawt gall (from which a black dye and tannic acid are derived)
takebbuṛ pride, haughtiness
takfaytit, takfaytiyet occupation of *kfayti*
takelluf v.n. of *kellef* and *tkellef*
takotbiyet bookselling (occupation)
takoꜥbiyet bad luck, misfortune (chronic)
talamid pl. of *telmid*
tal'amint position held by a syndic (trade, business)
taleddud v.n. of *tledded*
tali **1.** end, conclusion *ꜥetta le-t-tali de-l-muꜥaḍaṛa ꜥad ža.* He came toward the end of the lecture. **2.** pl. *talyen, twala* last, final
¶ *fe-t-tali* lastly, in the end
talet pl. *-in* third (adj.)
taluwwayet roguery, mischievousness
tamam, tamamen **1.** exactly, just *ža fe-t-tlata tamam.* He came at exactly three o'clock. —*dak ṣ-ši lli golt-lu tamamen.* That's just what I told him. **2.** at all *ma-šeftu-š tamamen had l-iyam.* I haven't seen him at all lately. **3.** completely, entirely *nta ꜥmeq tamamen!* You're completely out of your mind!
taman pl. *-at, ʔetmina* price, cost
tamara (no pl., no art.) troublesome difficulty, hardship
¶ *ḍṛeb tamara* (*baš*) **1.** to go to a lot of trouble (to) **2.** to work hard (at, to) *ḍeṛbu tamara fe-l-qaḍiya dyalek.* They worked hard on your case.
tamasiꜥ pl. of *temsaꜥ*
tameddun civilization
tamḍaymit, tamḍaymiyet occupation of making women's belts (i.e., *mḍemma*)
tamm pl. *-in* complete
tamen pl. *-in* eighth (adj.)
tamselmit behavior befitting a good Muslim
tamettuꜥ v.n. of *mettăꜥ* and *tmettăꜥ*
tamwagnit, tamwagniyet watch or clock-making and repairing
tamxaznit, tamxazniyet position or office of *mxazni*
tamexxaṛet larceny
tamxeznit, tamxezniyet same as *tamxaznit*
tamžadlit, tamžadliyet occupation of trimming and decorating with fancy borders, tassels, tinsel, etc. (e.g., done to hats, belts)
tamꜥăllmit, tamꜥăllmiyet mastery, skill
tanawi pl. *-yen* secondary
¶ *medṛaṣa tanawiya* high-school, secondary school
tani **1.** also, too; either (with negation) *waš mšaw tani l-ꜥăndha?* Did they go to her place too? —*u-huwa tani ma-bġa-š ixdem l-yum.* He doesn't want to work today either. **2.** again *mša tani le-s-sinima.* He went to the movies again. **3.** pl. *tanyen* second *hadi hiya mṛati t-tanya.* This is my second wife.
¶ *tani ꜥid* second day of a holiday or feast time

¶ *xelleṣ be-t-tani we-l-metni* to pay double or much more than its worth for (s.th.)
taniyen secondly, in the second place
taᵓenni v.n. of *tᵓenna*
taneqqašet sculpture, sculpturing (including carving and relief work)
taneṣṛanit, taneṣṛaniyet 1. behavior befitting a good Christian 2. behavior befitting a Western or non-Oriental individual
tanežžaṛet carpentry
taq itiq b- to believe *ma-ka-ntiq-š bik!* I don't believe you!
¶ *taq f-* 1. to trust *qolt-lek ġadi nṛeḍḍ-lek le-flus š-šheṛ l-maži—waš ma-ka-ttiq-š fiya?* I told you I'd return the money next month —Don't you trust me? 2. to trust in, to believe in
taqaṛiṛ pl. of *teqṛiṛ*
taqbaybit, taqbaybiyet occupation of bucket and tub making (wooden)
taqedda 1. amount, sum (usually of money) 2. size
taqehwayžit, taqehwažiyet occupation of operating a shop where coffee is served (often tea, soft drinks, also)
taqiy pl. *-en* 1. pious, religious 2. honest
taqemmaṛt 1. v.n. of *qemmeṛ* 2. gambling 3. dishonesty, shady behavior
taqṛašlit, taqṛašliyet occupation of carding wool or cotton
taqeṛṛanet cuckoldry
taqṭaṭƐiyet occupation of highwayman or bandit, brigandage
taqzadrit, taqzadriyet occupation of tin-smith, tin-smithery
taṛ vengeance, revenge
¶ *fda ifdi taṛ men,* or *fda t-taṛ f-* to get revenge on, to get even with (s.o.) *daba dži l-wežba u-nefdi fik t-taṛ.* I'll get even with you when the time comes.
taṛa used in the expr. *ya taṛa* perhaps, maybe *Ɛăyyeṭ-lu, ya taṛa ikun ṛžăƐ.* Call him, maybe he's back.
** *ya taṛa u-kan mšit mƐahom.* I wish I had gone with them.
taraza pl. *-t, twarez* kind of wide-brimmed straw hat
taṛažim pl. of *teṛžama*
taṛebbaƐet occupation of gardener (of edibles) (i.e., *ṛebbaƐ*)
taṛix pl. *tawaṛix* 1. history 2. date *šnu huwa t-taṛix de-l-yum?* What's today's date?
taṛeqqi v.n. of *tṛeqqa*
tarta pl. *-t* goiter *fih tarta fe-l-ḥăngura.* He has a goiter of the throat.
taṛwabzit, taṛwabziyet occupation of bellows maker
taṛxaymit, taṛxaymiyet occupation of marble-worker
taṛžulit, taṛžuliyet 1. courage, bravery, intrepidity (of men) 2. manhood, virility
tasbaybit, tasbaybiyet occupation of second-hand dealer (often selling certain things at retail)
taseffaret bookbinding
taseffažet occupation of doughnut-maker (i.e., *sfenž*)
tasiƐ same as *tisaƐ*
tasiƐa pl. *-t* 1. square, plaza 2. surface area
taskayrit, taskayriyet 1. drinking (alcohol) 2. drunkenness, inebriation 3. alcoholism
tasellalet basketry (art)
tasemṣaṛet occupation of real estate broker
taserražet saddle-making, saddlery
taṣebbaġet occupation of painter (houses, etc.)
taṣebbanet occupation of launderer or laundress
taṣeffaṛet occupation of coppersmith
taṣguƐiyet bad luck, misfortune
taṣiyyaġet jewelry-making
taṣemmaṛet occupation of shoe-smith (horses, mules)
taṣemṣaṛet brokerage, real estate business
taṣuwwuf v.n. of *tṣuwwef*
taṣwaynit, taṣwayniyet occupation of coppersmith (making primarily *ṣwani*)
taṣeḥḥafet occupation of pallbearer
tašeffaṛet occupation or activity of thief, i.e., *šeffaṛ*
tašiṭanet malicious troublemaking
tašelḥit Berber language (i.e., Shilha, south Berber)
tašuwwafet fortune-telling, divination
tata pl. *-t* chameleon
taᵓtir same as *teᵓtir*
taṭebbaxet cooking, culinary art
taṭellayt occupation of painter (houses, fences, etc.)
taṭufaylit, taṭufayliyet party-crashing
taṭyaṛu same as *teṭyaṛu*
taṭeḥḥanet occupation of miller (i.e., *ṭeḥḥan*)
tawaṛix pl. of *taṛix*
tawil (no pl.) agreement, settlement
** *daba ḷḷah idir tawil l-xir.* Everything's going to turn out all right.
¶ *be-t-tawil* slowly *hḍeṛ be-t-tawil ila bġitini nfehmek.* Speak slowly if you want me to understand you.
¶ *fihΦ t-tawil* to be formal ≠ (in one's manner)
¶ *Ɛmel t-tawil* (*mƐa*) to make a deal (with), to come to a compromise (with) *šrit had ṣ-ṣebbaṭ u-Ɛmel mƐaya t-tawil fih.* When I bought these shoes he made me a deal (on them). —*Ɛămlu šwiya de-t-tawil băƐḍiyatkom!* Come to some sort of compromise with each other!
tawekkalet gluttony

taweƐdanit, taweƐdaniyet solitariness, state of being alone (voluntary)
taweƐšiyet brutality, savagery
taxbaṛžiyet spying, espionage
taxebbazet occupation of bread-baker
taxelwiyet solitariness (voluntary) *fih taxelwiyet.* He's the solitary type, a loner.
taxṛifin same as *tixṛifin* (see also *gṛăƐ*)
taxeṛṛaṭet occupation of lathe-worker
taxerrazet occupation of shoemaker or cobbler
taxeṭṭafet occupation or avocation of being a thief (i.e., *xeṭṭaf*)
taxeyyaṭet occupation of tailor, tailoring
tazoġbiyet bad luck, ill fortune (chronic)
tazehriyet myopia, nearsightedness
tazellažet, tazlayžiyet occupation of tile-layer and mosaicist
tazṛaybiyet occupation of rug-maker
tazraydit, tazraydiyet gluttony, excessive eating
tazerzayet occupation of being a porter
tazufrit, tazufriyet coarseness of manner, unrefined behavior
tazuwwaqet coloring, painting, and design-making (for decorative purposes)
taž pl. *tižan* crown, coronet (also pope's tiara)
tažarib pl. of *težriba*
tažnaynit, tažnayniyet gardening
tažer 1. pl. *tožžaṛ, džaṛ* merchant, businessman 2. pl. *-in* rich, wealthy
taƐeddadet occupation of blacksmith, smithery
taƐdudit, taƐdudiyet reservedness
taƐălwiyet occupation of a pastry cook
taƐemmalet occupation of porter (i.e., *Ɛămmal*)
taƐṛamiyat, taƐṛamiyet cunning, slyness
taƐesbiyet simplicity, plainness (person)
taƐṣayṛiyet occupation of mat-maker (i.e., *Ɛṣayṛi*)
taƐežžamet occupation of barber
taƐala used in set expr. *ḷḷah tabaṛaka wa-taƐala* (see *tabaṛaka*)
taƐăb 1. v.n. of *tƐăb* 2. tiredness, fatigue
taƐăddi v.n. of *tƐădda*
taƐăṣṣub v.n. of *tƐăṣṣeb*
taƐăššabet occupation of herbalist
taƐăṭṭaṛet occupation of dealer in spices
taƐwatqiyet virginity, maidenhood
taƐwim v.n. of *Ɛăwwem*
taƐăwwadet 1. art of playing the lute 2. occupation of lute-maker
taƐăzrit celibacy, bachelorhood
taƐzubiyyet virginity, celibacy (both male and female)
tbabex pl. of *tebbaxa*
tbadel v.i. and v.t. 1. to exchange, to trade *tbadel mƐaya be-ṭ-ṭumubil!* Trade me cars! Trade cars with me! —*bġaw itbadlu ṭ-ṭumubilat.* They want to exchange cars. 2. to take turns, to alternate *ka-itbadlu Ɛăl l-Ɛăssa.* They take turns at guard duty.
tbaka v.i. to cry (group)
tbared coolness (e.g., in a shady spot)
tbarek v.i. 1. to wish one another a happy holiday or event 2. to fight, to have a fight ¶ *tbarek mƐa* to wish a happy holiday or event to (s.o.)
tbaṛek ḷḷah (lit., God be blest) 1. expr. of admiration, amazement *tbaṛek ḷḷah Ɛla dak l-bent!* Man, look at that girl! What a terrific girl she is! 2. expr. of irony, e.g., *tbaṛek ḷḷah Ɛlik!* Thanks a lot! (i.e., a sort of negative praise, e.g., for s.o.'s spilling ink on one's shirt) 3. kind of expletive with some meaning of "May God preserve . . ." (i.e., a kind of protection from the "evil eye") *weld Ɛămmi nžib u-ka-iqṛa mezyan, tbaṛek ḷḷah Ɛlih.* My cousin is pretty sharp and does well in school (God bless him).
tbas m.p. of *bas*
tbat, tbata 1. firmness (of belief, principle) 2. stick-to-itiveness, constancy
tbaṭen pl. of *tebṭin* 2
tbawes v.i. to kiss (each other)
tbaxeṛ pl. of *tebxiṛa*
tbayeƐ u-tšara v.i. to do business
tbaƐ m.p. of *baƐ*
ˀetbaƐ pl. of *tabeƐ* 1 (a.p. of *tbăƐ*)
tbaƐed v.i. to get separated or away from each other (physically)
tebbaxa pl. *-t, tbabex* (dim. *tbibixa*) 1. sheep bladder (used as a toy by children) 2. bubble (soap, etc.) 3. blister
tebbet v.t. 1. to fix, to immobilize, to make solid (e.g., a shaky table) 2. to flatter (with insincere compliments) 3. to check, to confirm
tebbăƐ v.t. 1. to follow, to pay attention to and understand *waš ka-ttebbăƐni?* Do you follow me? (i.e., what I'm saying) 2. to follow, to stay on (a straight line, road, etc.)
tebdal 1. v.n. of *beddel* 2. change, alteration, modification 3. exchange, trade
tebdar v.n. of *bedder*
tbeddel v.i. m.p. of *beddel*
tbeddeṛ m.p. of *beddeṛ*
tebdil same as *tebdal*
tebdir v.n. of *beddeṛ*
tbehdila pl. *-t* n.i. of *behdel* and *tbehdel*
tbehdel v.i. 1. to be shamefully humiliated (as when caught doing s.th. wrong) 2. to be embarrassed
tbehhet v.i. to speak nonsense, claptrap, "bull," as in *xlaṣ ma-ttbehhet Ɛliya!* Don't give me that! (you know better.)

tbibixa dim. of *tebbaxa*
tbixṛa dim. of *tebxiṛa*
tbiyyeḍ m.p. of *biyyeḍ* 1
¶ *tbiyyeḍ l-* to flabbergast, to nonplus (usually impersonal verb) *tbiyyeḍ-lu melli smăʕha ṛežʕăt.* He was flabbergasted when he heard she'd returned.
tbiyyen m.p. of *biyyen*
tebkira n.i. of *bekker*
teblaġ v.n. of *belleġ*
¶ *teblaġ l-heḍṛa* tale-bearing
teblal v.n. of *bellel*
tebḷiṭa n.i. of *beḷḷeṭ*
¶ *ḍreb tebḷiṭa* to get drunk
tbelled v.i. 1. to become adjusted or adapted to a country's customs 2. to become urbanized, to adapt oneself to city life 3. to lose one's mental adeptness, to become stupid (usually as a result of associating with stupid individuals)
tbeḷḷeṭ m.p. of *beḷḷeṭ* 1
tben n.u. *tebna* straw (hay)
tebnaž v.n. of *bennež*
tbendiq v.n. of *bendeq*
tbenned v.i. to be somewhat of a show-off (in an irritatingly interfering way)
tbennen v.i. to become tasty, to acquire a good flavor (e.g., a soup being prepared)
¶ *tbennen b-* to savor, to enjoy the flavor of (some food)
tbeqbiq v.n. of *beqbeq*
tebrad v.n. of berred
tebraḥ v.n. of *berreḥ*
tberda m.p. of *berda*
tbergim v.n. of *bergem*
tebrida pl. *-t* n.i. of *berred*
tebriru, tebruri hail (precipitation)
¶ *ḥăbba de-t-tebruri* hailstone
tebriya v.n. of *berra*
tebriḥ v.n. of *berreḥ*
tberra m.p. of *berra*
¶ *tberra men* 1. to warn (s.o.) 2. to disown (one's son, daughter)
tberred m.p. of *berred*
tbeṛṛek b- or *men* to receive the benediction of, to be blessed by (s.o., saint)
tbeṛṛem v.i. 1. to move over *qul-lu itbeṛṛem šwiya ʕăl š-šmal baš imken-lek tegles.* Tell him to move over a little to the left so you can sit down. 2. to turn around *tbeṛṛmet fih u-qalt-lu . . .* She turned around to him and said . . .
tbeṛṛăʕ b- (*ʕla*) to donate (to), to give away free (to) *ḅḅaha tbeṛṛăʕ ʕăl l-meḍṛaṣa b-xemsa d-le-mlayen.* Her father donated five million to the school.
tebruri same as *tebriru*
tberya n.i. and v.n. of *berra*
tebsima pl. *-t* 1. n.i. of *tbessem* 2. smile, grin
tbessem v.i. to smile, to grin
tbeššeṛ b- to receive good news about or of (s.th.) *tbeššeṛ be-ṛ-ṛžuʕ d-weldu men l-xaṛiž.* He received the good news of his son's return from abroad.
tbet v.i. (v.n. *itbat*) to be confirmed or authenticated *tbet daba billa huwa lli darha.* It's been confirmed now that he's the one who did it.
** *had š-ši ka-itbet fe-l-kerš.* This causes constipation.
¶ *tbet ʕla* to recall, to remember
¶ a.p. *tabet* pl. *-in* 1. firm, strict 2. in control of oneself 3. solid, firm (as a strong tree)
tebṭal v.n. of *beṭṭel*
tebṭan v.n. of *beṭṭen*
tebṭil v.n. of *beṭṭel*
tebṭin 1. v.n. of *beṭṭen* 2. pl. *tbaṭen* lining (of garment)
tbuhil v.n. of *tbuhel*
tbuhel v.i. to go insane, to go crazy
tbuṛeḍ v.i. (v.n. *tbuṛiḍ*) to fire muzzle-loading rifles (especially horsemen engaging in a *musem* festival)
tbuṛiḍ v.n. of *tbuṛeḍ*
tburiša pl. *-t* chill (usually accompanied by goose flesh)
tbureš v.i. to get chills (with goose flesh)
tbuwweṣ m.p. of *buwweṣ*
tebxaṛ v.n. of *bexxeṛ*
tebxiṛa pl. *tbaxeṛ* (dim. *tbixṛa*) incense (general term)
tbexteṛ v.i. to strut about (pompously)
tbexxeṛ v.i. m.p. of *bexxeṛ*
tebyaḍ v.n. of *biyyeḍ*
tebyan 1. v.n. of *biyyen* 2. explanation
tebyiḍ v.n. of *biyyeḍ*
tebyin v.n. of *biyyen*
tbežġiṭ v.n. of *bežġeṭ*
tbežmeṭ m.p. of *bežmeṭ*
tbeḥbiḥ v.n. of *beḥbeḥ* and *tbeḥbeḥ*
tbeḥbeḥ v.i. to become hoarse
tbeḥḥeṛ f- to increase one's knowledge of (s.th.)
tbăʕ v.t. 1. to follow (i.e., behind s.o. or s.th. in motion) *ġadi nexṛož daba be-l-ḥăqq ma-ttbăʕni-š!* I'm going to leave now, but don't you follow me! 2. to conform to (rules, laws, behavior)
¶ a.p. *tabeʕ* 1. pl. *ˀetbaʕ* follower, disciple 2. pl. *twabeʕ* tail (animal) 3. pl. *twabeʕ* handle(s) of a plow
tebʕad v.n. of *băʕʕăd*
tbăʕbiʕa n.i. of *băʕbăʕ*
tdar m.p. of *dar*
tedbir v.n. of *debbeṛ*
tedbira n.i. of *debbeṛ*
tˀeddeb v.i. to be or become well-mannered, polite, proper

¶ *tᵊeddeb mƐa* to be courteous toward, to be considerate of (s.o.)
tedfag v.n. of *deffeg*
tdeffeg m.p. of *deffeg*
tdegg m.p. of *degg*
tdeġdiġ v.n. of *deġdeġ*
tedhib v.n. of *dehheb*
tedkaṛ v.n. of *dekkeṛ*
tedkas v.n. of *dekkes*
tedkir v.n. of *dekkeṛ*
tedkira pl. *-t* souvenir, memento
tedkisa n.i. of *dekkes*
tdekk m.p. of *dekk* 1 and 2
tedlas, tedlis v.n. of *delles*
tdell m.p. of *dell* 2
tdella (*men*) **1.** to hang, to be suspended (from) **2.** m.p. of *della*
tedmaƐ v.n. of *demmăƐ*
tdemmen l- to beg (s.o.) grovelingly
tedqiq **1.** accuracy, precision **2.** pains, care (in doing s.th.)
¶ *be-t-tedqiq* **1.** accurately, precisely **2.** exactly **3.** carefully, painstakingly
tdeqq m.p. of *deqq*
tedrab, tedrib **1.** v.n. of *derreb* **2.** training
tedris v.n. of *derres*
tedriž v.n. of *derrež*
¶ *be-t-tedriž* **1.** little by little, a little at a time **2.** progressively
tderra m.p. of *derra*
tderreb m.p. of *derreb*
tderya v.n. of *tderra* (m.p. of *derra*)
tedsas v.n. of *desses*
tedšin **1.** v.n. of *deššen* **2.** inauguration
tedwab v.n. of *duwweb*
tedwaz v.n. of *duwwez*
tedwaζ v.n. of *duwweζ*
tedwixa **1.** dizziness **2.** absent-mindedness
tedwiza n.i. of *duwwez*
tedxal v.n. of *dexxel*
tedxaṛ v.n. of *dexxeṛ*
tedxim **1.** v.n. of *ddexxem* **2.** opulence, luxury, high living
tedyaƐ v.n. of *diyyăƐ*
tdezz m.p. of *dezz*
tedƐam v.n. of *dăƐƐăm*
tedƐima pl. *-t* n.i. of *dăƐƐăm*
teḍṛiqa **1.** n.i. of *ḍeṛṛeg, ḍeṛṛeq* **2.** pl. *-t* shelter
teḍwaṛ, teḍwiṛ v.n. of *ḍuwweṛ*
teḍyaq v.n. of *ḍiyyeq*
¶ *teḍyaq l-xaṭeṛ* annoyance, pest
teḍyaƐ v.n. of *ḍiyyăƐ*
teḍyiqa pl. *-t* n.i. of *ḍiyyeq*
teḍƐaf v.n. of *ḍăƐƐăf*
tfada v.i. to be or become even (i.e., reciprocally revenged) *tfadina daba!* Now we're even!
¶ *tfada mƐa* to get even with (s.o.)
tfafa v.i. **1.** to be rickety, loose, unstable (as an old chair, a loose tooth) **2.** to be disconcerted or shook up (by some bit of shocking news) **3.** to get nervous, to get "butterflies" in the stomach
tfafel pl. of *teffal*
tfahem v.i. **1.** to understand each other (in speech as well as psychologically) **2.** to come to an agreement, to have an understanding
¶ *tfahem mƐa* **1.** same as *tfahem* *ka-itfahem mƐaha.* He and she understand each other. **2.** to understand (s.o. psychologically) **3.** to give (s.o.) what he desires, to fulfill the desires of (s.o.) **4.** to bribe, to grease the palm of (s.o.)
tfakk same as *tfekk*
tfakeṛ pl. of *tefkiṛa*
tfala residue, dregs (of tea)
tfara v.i. **1.** to straighten out or settle differences or grievances **2.** to be straightened out or settled (some difference or grievance)
tfaṛeḍ (*f-*) to go in together (on), to share the expense or expenses (of)
tfaṛeq v.i. to separate (two men fighting, man and wife, etc.)
¶ *tfaṛeq mƐa* to separate or be separated from (man and wife, etc.)
tfares v.i. to bite and tear at each other (animals fighting, people)
tfaṣel v.i. to compromise, to come to a compromise
tfatef pl. of *teftifa*
tfaten v.i. to dispute or quarrel rather violently
tfaya kind of couscous garnish made of onions, cinnamon, and raisins
tfeḍḍa v.i. **1.** m.p. of *feḍḍa* **2.** to end, to conclude, to terminate **3.** to run out, to become exhausted **4.** to go broke or bankrupt **5.** to reach a stage (or age) of impending death
tfeḍḍel v.i. (usu. in impv. only) used as a polite expr. of allowing, permitting, inviting (s.o. to or to do s.th.), etc. *waš imken-li nšuf had le-ktab?—tfeḍḍel!* Can I look at this book?—Go right ahead! —*tfeḍḍel* (pl. *tfeḍḍlu*)*!* Please have (a seat, a cigaret, etc., etc.)!
tfeḍfiḍ v.n. of *feḍfeḍ*
tefḍil v.n. of *feḍḍel*
tfeḍya v.n. of *feḍḍa* and *tfeḍḍa*
teffal pl. *tfafel* mat placed under millingstones to collect the material which is ground
teffaζ n.u. *-a* apple
teffaζa pl. *-t* coll. *šžeṛ de-t-teffaζ* apple-tree
tfegged to recall, to remember, to dawn on one *tfeggedt* (*belli*) *le-ζlib fuq l-Ɛafya.* I remembered (that) the milk was on the fire.
tefgid v.n. of *fegged* and *tfegged*

tefgida pl. *-t* n.i. of *fegged* and *tfegged*
tfehheṛ *f-* to gape in amazement at (s.o., s.th.), to be stunned by, astonished at (s.o., s.th.)
¶ *tfehheṛ f-ṛaṣuᵠ* to be taken with oneself, to think oneself the "greatest"
tefkiṛa pl. *-t, tfakeṛ* gift given to one's fiancée (as a token of the engagement)
tfekk m.p. of *fekk*
¶ *tfekk men* **1.** to get out of, to avoid (e.g., work) **2.** to get rid or free of (s.th. or s.o. unwanted) **3.** to get loose from (bonds, fetters)
tfekkeṛ **1.** to remember, to recall *w-ana ntfekkeṛ bin-la xeṣṣni nɛăyyeṭ-lu* I just remember that I have to call him. **2.** to be reminded of *melli šeftu tfekkeṛt ḅḅa.* When I saw him I was reminded of my father.
teflas v.n. of *felles* and *tfelles*
teflat v.n. of *fellet*
teflisa pl. *-t* **1.** n.i. of *fles, felles,* and *tfelles* **2.** bankruptcy, ruin
** *ḍaṛbah teflisa* (or *t-teflisa*) He's extremely dense.
tfella (v.n. *tfelya*) to joke, to jest
¶ *tfella ɛla* to make fun of
tfelles v.i. **1.** m.p. of *felles* **2.** to become stupid, dense
tfelya v.n. of *tfella*
tfelɛiṣ v.n. of *felɛăṣ*
tfelɛiṣa n.i. of *felɛăṣ*
tfelɛăṣ m.p. of *felɛăṣ*
tfenneg, tfenneq (*ɛla*) to turn up one's nose (at) (in disapproval or dislike)
tfenṭeẓ v.i. to put on airs, to act important
tefqaṣ v.n. of *feqqeṣ*
tfeqqeh m.p. of *feqqeh*
tfeqqeṛ v.i. **1.** m.p. of *feqqeṛ* **2.** to pretend poverty, to give the impression of living in poverty
tefrad v.n. of *ferred*
tefṛaġ v.n. of *feṛṛeġ*
tefṛaq v.n. of *feṛṛeq*
tefṛaš v.n. of *feṛṛeš*
tefṛax v.n. of *feṛṛex*
tefraz v.n. of *ferrez*
tferfir v.n. of *ferfer*
tfeṛgiɛ v.n. of *feṛgăɛ* and *tfeṛgăɛ*
tfeṛgiɛa pl. *-t* **1.** n.i. of *tfeṛgăɛ* **2.** explosion, bursting
tfeṛgăɛ v.i. to explode, to blow up, to burst (e.g., bomb, balloon)
¶ *tfeṛgăɛ be-ḍ-ḍeḥk, b-le-bka,* etc. to burst into laughter, tears, etc.
tefṛiṭ v.n. of *feṛṛeṭ*
tferkil v.n. of *ferkel*
tferkit v.n. of *ferket*
tferket m.p. of *ferket*
tfernisa pl. *-t* (broad)grin
tfeṛqiɛ same as *tfeṛgiɛ* (v.n. of *feṛgăɛ* and *tfeṛgăɛ*)
tfeṛqăɛ same as *tfeṛgăɛ*
tfeṛṛeq m.p. of *feṛṛeq*
tfeṛṛeš m.p. of *feṛṛeš*
tfeṛṛež v.i. to enjoy looking (movie, game)
¶ *tfeṛṛež ɛla* to watch, to amuse oneself by watching (s.th. or s.o.)
tfeṛṛăɛ to branch off (branch, road, etc.)
tferšex m.p. of *feršex*
tfertina tempest, storm
tferten v.i. to get or become rough, choppy, stormy (sea)
tfeṛteq v.i. to rip or come apart at the seams (clothing)
tfeṛṭiṭ v.n. of *feṛṭeṭ*
tefsir pl. *tafasir* (pl. somewhat classical) explanation (often accompanied by a commentary)
tfesser m.p. of *fesser*
tfesseḥ v.i. to take a break, a rest period
tefṣal v.n. of *feṣṣel*
tefṣil pl. *tafaṣil* detail, small item
¶ *be-t-tefṣil* in detail *fesser-li had š-ši be-t-tefṣil.* Explain this to me in detail.
tfešš m.p. of *fešš*
tfeššeš v.i. **1.** m.p. of *feššeš* **2.** to turn up one's nose (in disapproval or dislike) **3.** to act spoiled, to be a spoiled brat **4.** to like to be coaxed
teftaf pl. *-in* **1.** (n.) jack-of-all-trades, general handy man **2.** (adj.) trembling, shaky (from old age, anticipatory fright, etc.)
teftaš v.n. of *fetteš*
teftat v.n. of *fettet*
teftef v.i. **1.** to do general handy work **2.** to shake, to tremble (from anticipatory fear, old age) **3.** to nibble, to pick(at) (food)
** *ɛad klit be-l-ḥăqq nteftef mɛakom.* I've just eaten, but I'll have a bite with you.
teftifa pl. *tfatef* **1.** chore, s.th. that has to be done **2.** odd job
teftiš **1.** v.n. of *fetteš* **2.** inspection, examination (not medical)
tfettet m.p. of *fettet*
tfubeṛ ɛla to tip, to give a tip or gratuity to
tfuwweh v.i. to yawn (as from sleepiness)
tfuwweṛ m.p. of *fuwweṛ* **1**
tfuwwež v.i. to go for a walk or drive (in the country, to the beach)
tefwah v.n. of *fuwweh* and *tfuwweh*
tefwaṛ v.n. of *fuwweṛ*
tefxim v.n. of *fexxem*
¶ *be-t-tefxim* with emphasis, emphatically
tefzag, tefzig v.n. of *fezzeg*
tefziga n.i. of *fezzeg*
tfezzeg m.p. of *fezzeg*
tefžaž v.n. of *fežžež*
tefžila pl. *-t* n.i. of *fežžel*

tefžiṛ v.n. of *fežžeṛ*
tefžiža pl. *-t* n.i. of *fežžež*
tfežžel m.p. of *fežžel*
tfežžež v.i. to go sightseeing *mnin konna fe-ṛ-ṛbaṭ konna ka-nxeṛžu ntfežžžu.* When we were in Rabat we used to go sightseeing.
¶ *tfežžež f-* to enjoy watching, to entertain oneself by watching *meṛṛa meṛṛa ka-nemši l-l-meṛṣa baš ntfežžež fe-l-bbabuṛat.* From time to time I go to the harbor to watch the ships.
tfăɛfiɛa pl. *-t* n.i. of *făɛfăɛ*
tfăɛfăɛ m.p. of *făɛfăɛ*
tgadd same as *tqadd*
tgaṭeɛ same as *tqaṭeɛ*
tgaḥer mɛa to struggle with, to have a hard time with (a heavy object, a job, etc.)
¶ *bqa ka-itgaḥer mɛa* to stick with *bqa ka-itgaḥer mɛa šoġlu ḥetta tɛăllmu.* He stuck with his job until he learned it.
tegdam v.n. of *geddem*
tegdima pl. *-t* n.i. of *geddem*
tgeḍḍeṛ v.i. **1.** to become or grow big and strong **2.** to put on airs as if one were big and strong
tegfaḍ v.n. of *geffeḍ*
teglab v.n. of *gelleb*
tgelgil v.n. of *gelgel* (same as *qelqel*)
tgelgila n.i. of *gelgel* (same as *qelqel*)
tgelleb v.i. **1.** m.p. of *gelleb* (same as *gleb*) **2.** to turn over (as in bed) **3.** to change one's attitude, mood, opinion, etc.
tgelles m.p. of *gelles*
tgellet same as *gellet*
tgellăɛ m.p. of *gellăɛ*
tegmaṭ v.n. of *gemmeṭ*
tgemgim v.n. of *gemgem*
tgemmeṭ m.p. of *gemmeṭ*
tgennef m.p. of *gennef*
tegṛaṣ v.n. of *geṛṛeṣ*
tegraž v.n. of *gerrež*
tgerdăɛ m.p. of *gerdăɛ*
tgergir v.n. of *gerger*
tegṛiṣ v.n. of *geṛṛeṣ* (same as *qeṛṛeṣ*)
tegriɛ v.n. of *gerrăɛ* and *tgerrăɛ*
tegriɛa pl. *-t* n.i. of *gerrăɛ* and *tgerrăɛ*
tgermel m.p. of *germel*
tgeṛṛeḍ m.p. of *geṛṛeḍ*
tgeṛṛes m.p. of *geṛṛeṣ*
tgerrăɛ v.i. **1.** to belch, to burp (usually accompanied by a bad odor) **2.** to explode, to let loose a fit of anger
tegšaṭ, tegšiṭ v.n. of *geššeṭ* (same as *keššeṭ*)
tegšiṭa **1.** n.i. of *geššeṭ* (same as *keššeṭ*) **2.** same as *tekšiṭa* **2**
tgusis v.n. of *guses*
tegwad v.n. of *guwwed*
tegwal v.n. of *guwwel*
tegyad v.n. of *giyyed*
tegyaḥ v.n. of *giyyeḥ*
tegyila same as *teqyila*
tegzan v.n. of *gezzen*
tgezzer m.p. of *gezzer*
** *ṛaṣi ka-itgezzer ɛliya.* I've got a splitting headache.
tgeždir v.n. of *gežder*
tgăɛɛăd v.i. **1.** m.p. of *găɛɛăd* **2.** to sit up straight (in bed, a chair)
tġafeṛ v.i. to pardon or forgive one another (in connection with certain religious occasions)
tġamez v.i. to wink at each other
tġanen, tġann v.i. (v.n. *ġnan*) to argue, to contradict one another
tġaša v.i. to faint, to pass out
tġawet v.i. to shout at one another, to argue loudly
teġbaṛ v.n. of *ġebbeṛ*
tġebben v.i. to get or become saddened, downhearted (usually shown by the face)
teġbiṛ v.n. of *ġebbeṛ*
tġedda v.i. to eat dinner (at midday), to lunch
tġedded m.p. of *ġedded*
tġiyyeḍ m.p. of *ġiyyeḍ*
tġiyyem same as *ġiyyem*
tġiyyeṛ m.p. of *ġiyyeṛ*
teġlaḍ v.n. of *ġelleḍ*
tġelleb ɛla **1.** to manage to beat, defeat, or triumph over (in a game, battle) **2.** to master, to tame (an animal, with some difficulty)
tġemm m.p. of *ġemm*
tġemmeḍ m.p. of *ġemmeḍ*
teġṛaq v.n. of *ġeṛṛeq*
teġraz v.n. of *ġerrez*
tġerbil v.n. of *ġerbel*
tġerbel m.p. of *ġerbel*
teġrid v.n. of *ġerred*
tġeṛṛ m.p. of *ġeṛṛ*
tġerreb v.i. **1.** m.p. of *ġerreb* **2.** to get some fresh air (i.e., go outside and enjoy the *ġerbi*)
teġsal v.n. of *ġessel*
tġessel m.p. of *ġessel*
teġšam v.n. of *ġeššem* and *tġeššem*
tġeššem **1.** m.p. of *ġeššem* **2.** to play dumb, stupid, ignorant
tġeṭṭa m.p. of *ġeṭṭa*
tġeṭya v.n. of *ġeṭṭa*
tġufila **1.** n.i. of *ġufel* **2.** hair or beard which has gotten too long and is in need of cutting or shaving
tġuwwel (*ɛla*) to become furious (with)
teġwaġ v.n. of *ġuwweġ*
teġwal v.n. of *ġuwwel*
teġwiġa pl. *-t* n.i .of *ġuwweġ*
tegyaṛ v.n. of *ġiyyeṛ* **3** (see *teġyiṛ*)

teġyaṣ v.n. of *ġiyyeṣ*
teġyiṛ pl. *-at* **1.** v.n. of *ġiyyeṛ* **1** and **2** (see *teġyaṛ*) **2.** change, modification
teġyiṣ v.n. of *ġiyyeṣ*
thada v.i. to exchange gifts or presents
thaẉed (*mʕa*) to bargain (with), to lower the price by bargaining (with)
thaẉeš ʕ*la* to have a penchant for, to like especially (usually a food)
thebbeṛ v.i. to get fat, to become fattened (person, animal)
tehdan v.n. of *hedden* and *thedden*
thedda v.i. **1.** to dawdle, to dally (usually in walking) **2.** to strut **3.** to prance (horse)
thedded m.p. of *hedded*
¶ *thedded* ʕ*la* to menace, to threaten (s.o.)
theddem m.p. of *heddem*
thedden m.p. of *hedden*
tehdin v.n. of *hedden*
thedya v.n. of *thedda*
thiyyef **1.** to be or get greedy, to be avaricious **2.** to be miserly, stingy
tehkam v.n. of *thekkem*
thekkem ʕ*la* to make fun of
tehlil v.n. of *hellel*
theḷḷa f- (v.n. *theḷya*) **1.** to take care of (also in the underworld usage) **2.** to take care of, to give special attention to (s.o.)
theḷya v.n. of *theḷḷa*
them v.t. to accuse *tehmuni be-qtil mṛati.* They've accused me of killing my wife.
tehma, tohma pl. *-t, tuhăm* accusation
themhim v.n. of *hemhem*
tehniya pl. *-t* v.n. and n.i. of *henna*
thenkiṛ dragging of one's feet (literal)
thenkeṛ v.i. to grow, to get big or large (a boy's feet; boy may also be subject)
thenna v.i. to get or become rid of one's problems, to be relieved of some burden or trouble
¶ *thenna men* to get rid of (s.o., s.th.)
thenya same as *tehniya* (v.n. and n.i. of *henna*)
tehras v.n. of *herres*
thernin v.n. of *hernen*
theṛniṭ v.n. of *heṛneṭ*
theṛṛeb (*men*) to shy away (from), to balk (at), to avoid (doing s.th., as from apprehension)
therres m.p. of *herres*
therẉil v.n. of *herẉel*
therẉila pl. *-t* n.i. of *herẉel*
thetrif v.n. of *hetref*
thuẉẉel m.p. of *huẉẉel*
tehẉad v.n. of *huẉẉed*
tehẉas v.n. of *huẉẉes*
tehyaž, tehyiž v.n. of *hiyyež*
thezz m.p. of *hezz*
thežya v.n. of *thežža*
thežža v.t. **1.** to read aloud slowly (practically by syllables) **2.** to spell out (letter by letter)
thežžel v.i. to become a widow or widower, to become widowed
tibas v.n. of *yebbes*
tiġrad pl. *-at* possession, asset, property
tiġešt soapwort
tih, tihan v.n. of *tah*
tikiḍa pl. *-t* **1.** carob tree **2.** carob bean
tiktik *neʗla* children's game, characterized by hopping and turning on one foot
tilifun pl. *-at* telephone
¶ *ḍreb t-tilifun l-* to telephone (s.o.)
tin n.u. *-a* dried fig
tiqa confidence, trust *ma-fih tiqa.* He doesn't trust anyone; (also:) He can't be trusted.
** *wžedtu ṛažel tiqa* I found that he could be trusted.
¶ *qellet t-tiqa* lack of trust or confidence *ma-dayer flus fe-l-ḅenk, fih qellet t-tiqa.* He never puts money in the bank; he doesn't trust them.
tiqal slowness, retardation (of a watch or clock) *maganti ka-tăʕmel qṣem dyal t-tiqal f-koll ṛebʕa u-ʕešrim saʕa.* My watch loses five minutes every twenty-four hours.
tiqaṛ self-respect *xad daʔimen qabeṭ t-tiqaṛ dyalu.* My brother always maintains his self-respect.
tiran pl. of *tuṛ*
tirs (usually said in *ʔeṛḍ tirs*) black, fertile earth
tis pl. *tyus, tyusa* billy goat
tisaʕ pl. *tẉaseʕ* (pl. of intensity) **1.** space, room **2.** time (to do something) *ʕṭini šwiya de-t-tisaʕ.* Give me a little time.
¶ *fe-t-tisaʕ* away, aside, out of the way *ʗoṭṭ had ṭ-ṭabla fe-t-tisaʕ baš nsiyyqu l-ʔeṛḍ.* Put this table out of the way so we can clean the floor.
¶ *men t-tisaʕ* from a distance, from afar *šeft xak l-bareʗ men t-tisaʕ.* I saw your brother from a distance yesterday.
¶ ʕ*la tisaʕ* in sufficient time, in plenty of time *mnin dži tsafeṛ wežžed ʗwayžek ʕla tisaʕ.* Whenever you travel, pack well ahead of time.
¶ ʕ*ṭa be-t-tisaʕ* to get away from, to leave alone *ʕṭini be-t-tisaʕ!* Get away from me!
tisir v.n. of *yesser*
** *ḷḷah ižib t-tisir.* May God give you success.
tišišint dried cow dung used to light fires
titan used in the expr. *kʗăl titan* a very deep black
tixṛifin (coll., said primarily in Fez) zucchini squash
tiyyeq same as *taq*
tizbibint type of black olive with large pit

tizra kind of sumac
tižan pl. of *taž*
tižaṛa trade, business, commerce
tižari pl. *-yen* commercial, business (adj.)
tkaber pl. of *tekbira*
tkadeb v.i. to lie to one another
tkaka v.i. to burst into (loud) laughter
tkameš v.i. to scratch or claw at each other (cats, people)
tkaṛeh v.i. to hate one another
tkateb v.i. to correspond, to carry on a correspondence
tkayes ʕla **1.** to take it easy on, to treat or use with moderation (s.o., s.th.) **2.** to manage well, to economize on (e.g., money)
tekbab v.n. of *kebbeb*
tkebb same as *ttkebb* (m.p. of *kebb*)
tkebbeb m.p. of *kebbeb*
tkebbed m.p. of *kebbed*
tkebbeṛ v.i. to be snobbish, to overrate one's station or importance
tekbiṛ v.n. of *kebbeṛ*
tekbira pl. *-t* **1.** gift given to one's fiancée **2.** pl. also *tkaber*, n.i. of *kebbeṛ*
tkebrit v.n. of *kebret*
tkebret m.p. of *kebret*
tekdab v.n. of *keddeb*
tekdas v.n. of *keddes*
tkeddeb m.p. of *keddeb*
tkeddeṛ m.p. of *keddeṛ*
tkeddes m.p. of *keddes*
tekdib v.n. of *keddeb*
tekdis v.n. of *keddes*
tekfaf v.n. of *keffef*
tekfan v.n. of *keffen*
tekfas v.n. of *keffes*
tkeffes m.p. of *keffes*
tekfifa pl. *-t* n.i. of *keffef*
tekfisa pl. *-t* n.i. of *keffes*
tkiyyef v.i. **1.** to smoke (not necessarily *kif*)
¶ *tkiyyef mʕa* to adjust to, to adapt oneself to
tkiyyel m.p. of *kiyyel*
tekk itokk v.t. (v.n. *tekkan*) to prick, to stick (as with a pin)
tkek pl. of *tekka*
tekka v.i. to take a nap or snooze
¶ *tekka ʕla* to lean on or against
tekka pl. *-t, tkek* **1.** n.i. of *tekk* **2.** drawstring (as in pajamas, laundry bag)
tekkan v.n. of *tekk*
tekkel ʕla to rely on, to count on (s.o., s.th.)
tekkem v.t. to deal a volley of punches to (s.o.), to beat with the fists
tkelfeṭ m.p. of *kelfeṭ*
teklif v.n. of *kellef* and *tkellef*
tkellef m.p. of *kellef*
tkellem v.i. **1.** to speak, to talk *ma-ttkellem-š be-ž-žehd!* Don't talk so loud! **2.** to converse, to have a conversation **3.** to speak, to give a speech or talk **4.** to sing (birds)
¶ *tkellem f-* to speak ill of, to talk derogatorily about (s.o.)
¶ *tkellem l-* to answer, to report to (s.o. who has called for you)
tekmad v.n. of *kemmed*
tekmal **1.** v.n. of *kemmel* **2.** completion
tekmaš, tekmiš v.n. of *kemmeš*
tekmiša pl. *-t, tkameš* **1.** n.i. of *kemmeš* **2.** wrinkle, fold (face, clothes) **3.** pleat
tkemma v.i. to smoke, to have a smoke (connotes enjoyment)
tkemmeš m.p. of *kemmeš*
tkenna m.p. of *kenna*
tekṛaṭ v.n. of *keṛṛeṭ*
tkerbil v.n. of *kerbel*
tkerded v.i. to get or become kinky (hair)
tkerdeġ m.p. of *kerdeġ*
tkerdiġ v.n. of *kerdeġ*
tkerdiġa n.i. of *kerdeġ*
tkeṛfiṣ v.n. of *keṛfeṣ*
tkeṛfeṣ m.p. of *keṛfeṣ*
tekṛiṭa pl. *-t* n.i. of *keṛṛeṭ*
tkerkeb m.p. of *kerkeb*
tkerkib v.n. of *tkerkeb*
tkeṛkeṛ m.p. of *keṛkeṛ*
tkeṛṛem (*ʕla*) to be generous (toward)
¶ *tkeṛṛem b-* to donate *tkeṛṛem b-xemsin ˀalef fṛenk ʕăl l-meytem.* He donated fifty thousand francs to the orphanage.
tkeṛṛeṭ m.p. of *keṛṛeṭ*
teksal v.n. of *kessel*
teksaṛ v.n. of *kesseṛ*
teksiṛa n.i. of *kesseṛ*
tkessel m.p. of *kessel*
tkesseṛ m.p. of *kesseṛ*
tekšaṭ, tekšiṭ v.n. of *keššeṭ*
tekšiṭa pl. *-t* **1.** n.i. of *keššeṭ* **2.** suit (men's clothing) **3.** a (complete) change of clothes, set of clothes (either clean or new; can include everything from underwear to topcoat)
tkeššeṭ m.p. of *keššeṭ*
tektaf v.n. of *kettef*
tektaṛ, tektiṛ v.n. of *ketteṛ*
tkettef m.p. of *kettef*
tkufiṛ v.n. of *kufeṛ*
tkuwwen m.p. of *kuwwen* **1**
tkuwweṛ m.p. of *kuwweṛ*
tekwan v.n. of *kuwwen*
tekwaṛ v.n. of *kuwweṛ*
tekwina pl. *tkawen* **1.** n.i. of *kuwwen*
¶ *ḍṛeb tekwina* to keep quiet
tekwiṛ v.n. of *kuwweṛ*
tekyal v.n. of *kiyyel*
tekyas v.n. of *kiyyes*
tekʕaz v.n. of *keʕʕez*
tekʕil v.n. of *keʕʕel*
tkăʕwiṛ v.n. of *kăʕweṛ*

tkăʕweṛ m.p. of *kăʕweṛ*
tla used in the expr. *ma-tla-š* to no longer (do s.th.) to not . . . any more *ma-tla-š išṛeb.* He doesn't drink any more.
tlafef pl. of *telfifa*
tlaha v.i. to amuse oneself, to kill time
tlales pl. of *tellis*
tlamed pl. of *telmid*
tlameṭ pl. of *telmiṭa*
tlaqa v.i. **1.** to meet (each other), to run across one another **2.** to meet, to come together (e.g., two connecting wires) **3.** to agree, to be of the same opinion
¶ *tlaqa mʕa* **1.** to meet, to run across, to run into (s.o.) **2.** to run into (a tree, door, etc.)
tlaqem pl. of *telqima*
tlaseq v.i. to get stuck together, to adhere to each other
tlat see *tlata*
tlata (*telt* before pl. of words admitting du.) three
¶ *nhaṛ t-tlat, nhaṛ t-tlata, t-tlat, t-tlata* Tuesday
tlatin **1.** thirty **2.** thirtieth *ṣafeṛ nhaṛ t-tlatin fe-š-šheṛ.* He left the thirtieth of the month.
tlaṭem v.i. to collide, to run into each other
tlawi pl. of *tluwya*
tlaxem pl. of *telxima*
telbaq v.n. of *lebbeq*
telbas v.n. of *lebbes*
tlebbeq m.p. of *lebbeq*
tledded b- to savor, to relish (food)
tlef v.i. (v.n. *tlif*) **1.** to get lost (physically, in a speech, etc.) **2.** to lose one's concentration, to be distracted **3.** to lose one's common sense, to act nonsensically
¶ *tlef l-* to lose (lit., to get lost) ≠ *tlef-li l-meftaḥ d-le-xzana.* I've lost the key to the closet.
telf used in the expr. *fels fe-l-keff ḥsen men ʕăšṛa fe-t-telf.* A bird in the hand is worth two in the bush.
telfa pl. *-t* n.i. of *tlef*
¶ *ḍeṛbettu*$^{\phi}$ *t-telfa* to be out of one's mind, to act in a nonsensical manner ≠ *bla šekk ḍeṛbethom t-telfa.* They must be out of their minds.
telfaf v.n. of *leffef*
tleffef m.p. of *leffef*
tleffet v.i. to turn around, to face the opposite direction
¶ *tleffet l-* to turn and face toward
telfifa pl. *-t, tlafef* n.i. of *leffef*
tlegga same as *tleqqa*
tlif v.n. of *tlef*
tliyyen m.p. of *liyyen*
¶ *tliyyen mʕa* to be nice to, to treat with kindness
tella v.t. **1.** to leave or put off (until later) **2.** to leave until last, to do or take care of last
** *leh la-itellik!* expr. said, usually to one's child, as a wish or hope that the child will be taken care of in the event of the parents' death
¶ *tella b-* same as *tella*
tellaf adj. pl. *-in* n.pl. *-a* (one) who is constantly losing things, or causing others to either get lost or lose things
tellaža pl. *-t* icebox, refrigerator
tellef v.t. **1.** to lose *telleft l-magana dyali!* I've lost my watch! **2.** to get (s.o.) lost, to cause to get lost **3.** to waste, to squander (e.g. money) **4.** to mislead, to lead astray (both physically and figuratively) **5.** to break the train of thought or concentration of (s.o.), to distract
¶ *tellef l-* to cause (s.th.) to get lost or become hard to find for (s.o.) *tellefti-lu le-qlam dyalu.* You've made it impossible for him to find his pen.
¶ *tellef l-weqt* to pass the time, to kill time
¶ *tellef ṭ-ṭṛiq* to make the trip or way seem short (by passing the time in an interesting manner) *tellefna ṭ-ṭṛiq be-l-heḍṛa.* Because we talked all the way the trip seemed **short.**
tellis pl. *tlales* burlap sack, bag (used in storing grain, etc.)
tellet v.t. **1.** to triple, to multiply by three **2.** to place or arrange in groups of three (usually strands to be braided) **3.** to be the third part or constituent of (s.th., in order to complete it) *aži telletna!* Come and be the third man! (as in a card game) **4.** to walk on three legs (dog, horse, etc.)
tellež v.t. **1.** to freeze (liquids) **2.** to ice, to chill (as a drink)
telmid pl. *tlamed, talamid* pupil, student (below college level)
telmiṭa pl. *ṭlameṭ* **1.** bedspread **2.** kind of decorative slipcover for a divan or *sedriya*
tlemm m.p. of *lemm*
tlemmes ʕla to caress, to fondle, to pet (person, animal)
tlemmăʕ m.p. of *lemmăʕ*
telqaf v.n. of *leqqef*
telqaṭ v.n. of *leqqeṭ*
telqaḥ v.n. of *leqqeḥ*
telqim v.n. of *leqqem*
telqima pl. *-t, tlaqem* **1.** n.i. of *leqqem* **2.** amount of tea added to a pot of used tea (to bring it up to strength)
tleqqa l- to meet (s.o. who has just arrived)
tleqqem m.p. of *leqqem*
telsaq, telsiq v.n. of *lesseq*
tlesseq m.p. of *lesseq*
telt see *tlata*

tcltiya pl. *-t* type of three-shot rifle

tlettem m.p. of *lettem*

tlettaš 1. thirteen 2. thirteenth

tlettef (*Ɛla*) to be courteous, polite, congenial (toward)

¶ *tlettef mƐa* to go easy on, to not give a hard time to (s.o.)

tluwwa v.i. 1. m.p. of *luwwa* 2. to wind, to zigzag (car, snake, river, etc.) 3. to tack (boat)

¶ *tluwwa f-le-klam* to beat around the bush

¶ *tluwwa Ɛla* to wind around, to entwine oneself around (snake, vine)

tluwwen m.p. of *luwwen*

tluwya pl. *-t, tlawi* 1. n.i. of *luwwa* 2. curve, bend, crook (road, tree, rod, etc.) 3. sprain (ankle, wrist) 4. pl. *tlawi* zigzag(s)

¶ *hder bla tlawi* not to beat around the bush, to get to the point

telwin v.n. of *luwwen*

telxima pl. *-t, tlaxem* (bit of) phlegm

tlexxem v.i. to cough up and spit out phlegm

telyin v.n. of *liyyen*

telzam v.n. of *lezzem*

tlezzem v.i. to be obliged, to have to, to be forced *tlezzem* (*baš*) *imši le-franṣa.* He had to go to France.

telž 1. ice 2. snow

telᴢam v.n. of *leᴢᴢem*

telᴢifa n.i. of *leᴢᴢef*

tleᴢliᴢ v.n. of *leᴢleᴢ*

tleᴢᴢef m.p. of *leᴢᴢef*

tleᴢᴢem v.i. 1. to gain (weight), to get fat(ter) 2. to heal, to close (an open wound) 3. to be welded or soldered together

tmag pl. *tmayeg* (sg. *ferda de-t-tmag*) 1. leggings (pair) 2. boots (pair)

tmam same as *tamamen*

tmamen pl. of *temmun*

tmanin 1. eighty 2. eightieth

tmaṛa seriousness, gravity, honesty (mostly used attributively) *smãƐt belli hadak l-qaḍi ṛažel ma-ši tmaṛa.* I've heard that judge is not an honest man. —*šwiya de-t-tmaṛa!* Seriously! Let's be serious!

tmaseᴢ m.p. of *temsaᴢ*

tmatel v.i. to resemble each other, to be similar (in symmetry) *had ž-žuž de-d-dyuṛ ka-itmatlu.* These two houses resemble each other. —*had ṣ-ṣenḍuq ka-itmatel be-n-nesba l-nefsu.* This box is symmetrical.

¶ *tmatel mƐa* to be similar to *had l-Ɛimaṛa ka-tmatel mƐa lli qoddamha.* This building is similar to the one in front of it.

tmawet v.i. to play dead, to pretend illness, to malinger *ma-weqƐăt-lu ᴢetta ᴢaža, ġir

ka-itmawet. Nothing happened to him, he's just pretending (injury, illness).

tmawež v.i. 1. to undulate, to wave, to ripple (water, flag, etc.) 2. to shimmer (in a varicolored manner, as some fabrics)

tmayeg pl. of *tmag*

tmayel v.i. 1. to lean, to list (i.e., be in a state of tilt or leaning) 2. to roll (plane, ship) 3. to walk with a nonchalant, rolling or balancing motion 4. to stagger, to reel (drunk)

tmayez (*Ɛla*) to differ (from), to be different (from)

tmazeᴢ v.i. to fool around, to joke

tmedd m.p. of *medd*

tmedden m.p. of *medden*

tmedya v.n. and n.i. of *medḍa*

tmeġġet v.i. m.p. of *meġġet*

temġita n.i. of *meġġet*

tmin pl. *-in* (comp. *tmen*) valuable, precious

ʔetmina pl. of *taman*

tmiyyez m.p. of *miyyez*

temkin v.n. of *mekken*

tmekken m.p. of *mekken*

tmekṛeh Ɛla to cause trouble to (s.o.), to give a hard time to (s.o.), to be hard on (s.o.)

temlas v.n. of *melles*

temlaᴢ v.n. of *melleᴢ*

temlis v.n. of *melles*

tmelleġ v.i. (v.n. *mlaġa*) to joke, to jest

¶ *tmelleġ mƐa* to tease

¶ *tmelleġ Ɛla* to make fun of

tmellek (*b-*) 1. to get engaged (to) 2. to become owner (of)

tmelleᴢ m.p. of *melleᴢ*

tmelmel m.p. of *melmel*

temm 1. v.t. and v.i. to end, to finish, to be ended, to be finished. 2. v.i. to be exhausted, to run out *temm s-sokkaṛ.* We're out of sugar, the sugar has run out. 3. used with a.p. to express the perfect (usually with verbs of motion) *temmet nayḍa u-xeržet.* She got up and went out. 4. to begin, to start (with durative tense) *ġir ḍrebni temmit ka-nebti.* When he hit me, I started crying.

temm, temma, temmak, temmaki, temmaya there, over there

¶ *l-temma* there, thither *sir l-temma u-iᴢănn llah.* Go over there and we'll see what we can do for you.

¶ *men temma* 1. from there, thence 2. from that time, since then *kan mƐaya n-nhaṛ ž-žemƐa lli dazet u-men temma ma-Ɛawedt šeftuh.* He was with me last Friday but I haven't seen him since then.

¶ *temm nnit* right there, on the spot, right away, right then and there *ttedṛeb f-ḍaṛu u-temm nnit mat.* He was shot in his house and died right there. —*ṭlebtu dak š-ši u-ɛṭah liya temm nnit.* I asked him for that and he gave it to me on the spot.

¶ *temm temm* immediately, right away. *qal-li ši-klam xayeb u-žawebtu temm temm.* He said something bad to me and I answered him back right away.

temmem v.t. to finish *waš temmemti šġalek?* Have you finished your work?

temmen v.t. **1.** to arrange in groups of eight **2.** to multiply by eight or eight times, to octuple

temmeṛ v.i. **1.** same as *tmeṛ* **2.** to get or become serious (-minded)

temmun pl. *tmamen* beam of a plow (including the handle)

tmen **1.** comp. of *tmin* **2.** pl. *tmuna* eighth, eighth part **3.** pl. *tmuna* eighth part or division of the Koranic *ḥizeb* **4.** see *tmenya*

tmenna v.t. **1.** to desire, to have a desire for *ka-ntmenna ši-ṭažin de-s-seksu.* I'd like to have a bowl of couscous. **2.** to hope *ka-ntmenna nduwwez d-dokturạ men daba ɛamayn.* I hope to get my doctorate in two years.

¶ *tmenna ɛla* to desire of (s.o.), to ask of (s.o.)

tmenṭaš **1.** eighteen **2.** eighteenth

tmenya (*temm, tmen* with pl. of words admitting du.) eight

tmeqqeṣ m.p. of *meqqeṣ*

tmeṛ v.i. to bear or produce fruit (tree, etc.)

tmeṛ n.u. *temṛa* date (fruit)

¶ n.u. *temṛa* pl. *-t* glans penis (said of children)

temran v.n. of *merren*

temṛaṛ v.n. of *meṛṛeṛ*

tmeṛḍin v.n. of *tmeṛḍen*

tmeṛḍen v.i. to fool or joke around

temṛiġa pl. *-t* n.i. of *meṛṛeġ* and *tmeṛṛeġ*

temrin v.n. of *merren*

temrita n.i. of *merret* and *tmerret*

tmermed m.p. of *mermed*

tmermid v.n. of *mermed*

tmeṛṛeḍ v.i. to pretend or feign illness

tmeṛṛeġ **1.** m.p. of *meṛṛeġ* **2.** v.i. to wallow, to sprawl on one's back (as a dog scratching its back)

tmerren m.p. of *merren*

tmerret m.p. of *merret*

tmeṛṛeḥ v.i. **1.** to make oneself comfortable (usually sitting) **2.** to go to the bathroom, powder room (polite expression)

tmeṛwăḥ v.i. to fan oneself, to be fanned (with a *meṛwaḥ*)

tmeṛḥib v.n. of *meṛḥăb*

temsaḥ pl. *tamasiḥ, tmaseḥ* alligator, crocodile

tmesken v.i. **1.** to feign poverty, to act broke *žibu ɛameṛ b-le-flus u-ža ka-itmesken ɛliya.* His pocket was full of money and he came to me acting as if he were broke. **2.** to feign innocence, to act innocent *lemma žaw istenṭquh l-bulis bda ka-itmesken ɛlihom.* When the police came to interrogate him, he began to feign innocence.

tmess m.p. of *mess*

tmesxeṛ same as *tmešxeṛ*

tmešša v.i. **1.** to walk, to take a walk, to go for a walk **2.** to function, to operate, to work, to go *siyaṛti qdima, be-l-ḥăqq ka-ttmešša mezyan.* My car is old but it runs well. **3.** to get along *benti u-ṣadiqtha ka-itmeššaw mezyan mɛa băɛḍhom.* My daughter and her friend get along well together. **4.** to sell, to go *had s-selɛa ka-ttmešša b-soṛɛa.* This merchandise sells fast. **5.** to spend *tmešša ɛla qedd ḥalek.* Spend according to what you make.

¶ *tmešša mɛa* **1.** to associate with, to go around with *hadi ġir žuž de-l-ʔasabiɛ baš bdit ka-ntmešša mɛah.* It's only been two weeks since I started going around with him. **2.** to match, to go well with (s.th.) *ž-žiyyafa l-kăḥla ka-ttmešša mɛa koll-ši.* A black tie goes well with everything.

¶ *tmešša ɛla* to follow, to act on, to conform to *tmešša ɛăl n-naṣiḥa lli qolt-lek.* Follow the advice I gave you.

tmešxiṛ v.n. of *tmešxeṛ*

tmešxeṛ ɛla to make fun of, to laugh in the face of, to ridicule *ṣaḥbu ma-ɛăndu ṭumubil u-huwa ka-itmešxeṛ ɛlih.* He makes fun of his friend because he doesn't have a car.

temtam adj. pl. *-in* n.pl. *-a* ag. adj. and ag. n. of *temtem*

temtil v.n. of *mettel*

temtim v.n. of *temtem* (see *ttemtim*)

temtem v.i. to stutter, to stammer

tmettăɛ b- or *f-* to enjoy, to get enjoyment from

tmuna pl. of *tmen* 2 and 3

tmuwwen m.p. of *muwwen*

temwin **1.** v.n. of *muwwen* **2.** provisions, supplies

tmexzen v.i. to act important, to act with an air of authority (that one does not have)

temyal v.n. of *miyyel*

temyaq v.n. of *miyyeq*

temyaz, temyiz v.n. of *miyyez*

tmezzeq m.p. of *mezzeq*

tmeḥḥen m.p. of *meḥḥen*

tmăɛwiq v.n. of *măɛweq*

tna itni v.t. (v.n. *tenyan, tni*) to fold, to pleat, to roll up (sleeves)

¶ *be-l-metni* (p.p.) denotes a doubling of some action *xda l-makla be-l-metni.* He took a double helping of food.

tnabeh (*l-*) to pay attention (to), to listen (to)

tnaber pl. of *tenber*
tnafes v.i. to compete, to be rivals
tnafes pl. of *tenfisa*
tnager v.i. to dispute, to quarrel *kanu ka-iḍeẓku ẓetta wellaw ka-itnagru.* They were just fooling around until they began to quarrel.
tnahed pl. of *tenhida*
tnaqer same as *tnager*
tnaqeš (*ɛla, f-*) to discuss, to have a discussion (about)
tnaqez pl. of *tenqiza*
tnaseb v.i. **1.** to become related (by marriage) *ṛaʔis l-ẓukuma tnaseb mɛa l-malik.* The premier married into the king's family. **2.** to go (well) with each other (colors, parts of a set, people)
tnaṭeẓ v.i. to butt heads
tnaweb v.i. to work by turns, to relieve each other *ka-itnawbu ɛăl l-ɛăssa.* They relieve each other on guard duty.
tnayn two (used mostly in compound numbers) *f-ɛămṛu tnayn u-ṛebɛin ɛam.* He is forty-two years old.
tnazeɛ v.i. to quarrel, to dispute
tenbal v.n. of *nebbel*
tenbat v.n. of *nebbet*
tenbaɛ v.n. of *nebbăɛ*
tenbih pl. *-at* **1.** v.n. of *nebbeh* **2.** remark, observation
tenber pl. *tnaber* stamp (with adhesive backing, e.g., postage, trading)
tneddem (*ɛla*) to suffer sorrow, anguish or grief (over)
tneḍḍef m.p. of *neḍḍef*
tneḍḍem m.p. of *neḍḍem*
tenḍif v.n. of *neḍḍef*
tenḍim **1.** v.n. of *neḍḍem* **2.** organization
tenfaṛ v.n. of *neffeṛ*
tenfas **1.** v.n. of *neffes* and *tneffes* **2.** respiration
tneffed m.p. of *neffed*
tneffes v.i. **1.** to breathe **2.** to catch one's breath, to rest **3.** to breathe hard, to pant **4.** to leak, to have a leak (of air, liquid) **5.** to break wind
tneffex v.i. **1.** m.p. of *neffex* **2.** to be or become haughtily proud or prideful **3.** to pout (from wounded pride)
tneffăɛ b- to make use of, to get benefit from, to get use out of
tenfisa pl. *-t, tnafes* **1.** n.i. of *neffes* and *tneffes* **2.** breath **3.** (air) vent **4.** flatus, flatulence **5.** space, blank (to be filled in) **6.** improvised irrigation gate (i.e., break in the ditch bank)
tenfiẓa snuff
¶ *ṣbiyyeɛ de-t-tenfiẓa* pinch of snuff
tnefnif v.n. of *nefnef*
tengal v.n. of *neggel*
tneggeb v.i. to put on the veil (*ngab*)
tengila n.i. of *neggel*
tengiṛa n.i. of *neggeṛ*
tnegriz v.n. of *negrez*
tneġniġ v.n. of *neġneġ*
tnehhed v.i. to sigh (person)
tenhida pl. *-t, tnahed* sigh
tni v.n. of *tna*
tnin same as *tnayn*
tenkis width, breadth
tnekked m.p. of *nekked*
tenmar v.n. of *nemmer*
tenna **1.** v.t. to double (in amount) **2.** v.t. to form a pair with (s.o. or s.th. else) **3.** v.i. to do s.th. again, to repeat some action *klit u-tennit.* I've eaten twice.
tʔenna v.i. to be patient, to have patience (as in waiting)
tʔenni v.n. of *tʔenna*
tenqal v.n. of *neqqel*
tenqaz v.n. of *neqqez*
tenqila n.i. of *neqqel*
tenqiṛ v.n. of *neqqeṛ*
tenqiza pl. *-t, tnaqez* jump, bound
tneqqa m.p. of *neqqa*
tneqqel m.p. of *neqqel*
tneqya v.n. of *neqqa*
tensil v.n. of *nessel*
tnessel m.p. of *nessel*
tnesya v.n. of *nessa*
tenšaf, tenšif v.n. of *neššef*
tnešša m.p. of *nešša*
tneššeṭ m.p. of *neššeṭ*
tnešwa v.i. to indulge in some minor sensual pleasure (usually smoking or having a drink)
tnešya v.n. of *nešša*
tnuġiš v.n. of *nugeš*
tnuwwa (*men*) to be or become suspicious (of)
tnuɛiṛa pl. *-t* trick, ruse, bit of cunning
tnuɛăṛ (*ɛla*) to use cunning (on), to use trickery (on)
tenwaẓ v.n. of *nuwweẓ*
tenwiṛ v.n. of *nuwweṛ*
tenxima same as *telxima*
tnexxem same as *tlexxem*
tenya pl. *-t* **1.** wrinkle (cloth, face) **2.** pleat, fold **3.** crease (as in pants)
tenyan v.n. of *tna*
tenzal v.n. of *nezzel*
tnezzeh v.i. to go on a picnic, to go picnicking
tnezzel m.p. of *nezzel*
tnežya **1.** v.n. and n.i. of *nežža* **2.** rescue, deliverance
tneẓya v.n. and n.i. of *neẓẓa*
tneẓẓa m.p. of *neẓẓa*
tnăɛɛăm v.i. **1.** to live in comfort, to be well-to-do **2.** to prosper, to be prosperous
¶ *tnăɛɛăm ɛla* (s.o.) *b-* (s.th.) to give

(s.th.) to (s.o.), to present (s.th.) as a gift to (s.o.), to donate (s.th.) to (s.o.)

tqabeḍ v.i. **1.** to hold hands, to take each other by the hand **2.** to fight, to have a fight (physical)

tqabi pl. of *teqba, toqba*

tqabel v.i. **1.** to face each other (in position) **2.** to confront or come up against one another **3.** to meet, to have a meeting

tqabeṭ same as *tqabeḍ*

tqadd v.i. expresses the concept of coming to be on an equal basis of some sort, e.g. *l-ɛam lli daz kan sabeqni f-le-qṛaya walakin had l-ɛam tqaddit mɛah.* Last year he was ahead of me in school, but this year I've caught up to him. —*ḍ-ḍabiṭ qal l-l-žunub dyalu itqaddu fe-ṣ-ṣeff.* The officer told his men (soldiers) to line up. —*waxxa lebset ṣ-ṣebbaṭ l-ɛali ma-tqaddet-š mɛa ṛaželha.* In spite of her wearing high-heeled shoes, she didn't come up to her husband's height. —*mnin tqadd mɛah, reklu.* When he came up to him, he kicked him. —*had ž-žuž de-l-ʔenwaɛ de-t-tub ma-ka-itqaddu-š fe-l-qima.* These two kinds of material differ in price. —*l-mizan tqadd.* The scale is balanced. ** *daba ɛad atay tqadd.* The tea is just right (for drinking).

tqaḍa v.i. **1.** to end, to conclude, to be finished **2.** to be exhausted, to run out (gas, sugar, etc.) **3.** to become invalid or physically inactive (usually from age)

tqaf v.n. of *teqqef*

tqal v.i. to get or become heavy

tqal pl. of *tqil*

tqala **1.** heaviness (weight) **2.** slowness (speed) **3.** lethargy **4.** obtrusiveness, obnoxiousness

tqaqel pl. of *teqqala*

tqasem, tqaṣem v.t. to share

tqaṣeṛ pl. of *teqṣiṛa*

tqaṣeṣ pl. of *teqṣiṣa*

tqašeṛ, tqašer socks, stockings (sg. *teqšiṛa* or *ferda de-t-tqašeṛ*)

tqatel v.i. **1.** to fight, to battle, to have a fight or battle **2.** to kill one another (rare usage)

tqaṭeɛ v.i. to come to an agreement, to agree

tqaṭeɛ pl. of *teqṭiɛa*

tqayel v.i. to reach an agreement after bargaining, to make a deal

tqaḥer same as *tgaḥer*

tqaɛed pl. of *teqɛida*

tqeb v.t. (v.n. *tqib*) **1.** to pierce, to go through, to perforate **2.** to go into, to enter (as a bullet, knife) **3.** to deflower, to deflorate **4.** to violate, to rape

teqba, toqba pl. *-t, tqabi* **1.** n.i. of *tqeb* **2.** hole, perforation

teqbab v.n. of *qebbeb*

teqbaṛ **1.** v.n. of *qebbeṛ* **2.** burial, interment

tqebbeb m.p. of *qebbeb*

tqebbeḍ b- to get back at, to get even with (s.o.)

tqebbel **1.** m.p. of *qebbel* **2.** v.i. to face toward Mecca **3.** v.t. to resign oneself to accepting, to face (e.g., some hard fact)

tqebbeṛ m.p. of *qebbeṛ*

tqebbeṭ same as *tqebbeḍ*

tqebbeḥ (*ɛla*) to be impertinent, insolent, disrespectful (toward)

teqbiba **1.** n.i. of *qebbeb* **2.** arc **3.** dome

teqdaḥ v.n. of *qeddeḥ*

tqedded m.p. of *qedded*

tqeddem **1.** m.p. of *qeddem* **2.** v.i. to progress, to advance

tqeddeḥ m.p. of *qeddeḥ*

teqdim **1.** v.n. of *qeddem* **2.** advance (of money)

teqdir v.n. of *qeddeṛ* (same as *qeḍḍeṛ*)

¶ *be-t-teqdir* **1.** approximately, about **2.** for example

teqdis v.n. of *qeddes*

teqdiḥa pl. *-t* **1.** n.i. of *qeddeḥ* **2.** slap with the hand (on top of the head)

tqeḍḍa v.i. to go shopping for groceries

tqeḍḍeṛ m.p. of *qeḍḍeṛ*

tqehwa v.i. to have a drink (usually of coffee or tea, but may mean any drink)

tqib v.n. of *tqeb*

tqil pl. *-in, tqal* (comp. *tqel*) **1.** heavy *had ž-žellaba tqila ɛliya bezzaf.* This jellaba is too heavy for me. —*had ṣ-ṣenduq ma-ši tqil bezzaf.* This box isn't very heavy. —*tɛăššina ɛša tqila l-bareḥ.* We had a heavy meal last night. **2.** slow *had ṭ-ṭumubil tqila, ila ṣafeṛna fiha ɛămmeṛna ma-nweṣlu.* This car is (too) slow; we'll never get there if we go in it. —*magantek tqila b-sebɛa de-d-dqayeq.* Your watch is slow by seven minutes. —*dak l-weld tqil fe-šġalu.* That boy is slow in his work. **3.** pl. *tuqala* bothersome, obnoxious, annoying (person) **4.** pl. *tuqala* snobbish, uppity

¶ *wednu*$^{\phi}$ *tqila* to be hard of hearing ≠ *wednu tqila.* He's hard of hearing.

tqin v.n. of *tqen*

tqiyya v.i. and v.t. to vomit, to regurgitate

tqiyyed m.p. of *qiyyed*

tqiyyes m.p. of *qiyyes*

tqel comp. of *tqil*

tqol **1.** weight **2.** heaviness

toqla pl. *-t* **1.** ballast, weight **2.** burden, heaviness (on the heart or soul, etc.)

teqlab v.n. of *qelleb*

teqlal v.n. of *qellel*

teqlaq v.n. of *qelleq*

teqlaɛ v.n. of *qellăɛ*

teqlil v.n. of *qellel*

teqliqa n.i. of *qelleq*

tqelleb m.p. of *qelleb*
tqelleq v.i. **1.** m.p. of *qelleq* **2.** to get mad or angry **3.** to become or get impatient
tqellăɛ m.p. of *qellăɛ*
tqelqil v.n. of *qelqel*
tqelqel m.p. of *qelqel*
tqen itqen, itqon (v.n. *tqin, ʔitqan*) to do perfectly, to excel in, to be a master of (job, language, etc.)
teqqaba pl. *-t* **1.** drill (for perforating) **2.** punch (for punching tickets)
teqqala pl. *-t, tqaqel* **1.** counterweight, ballast **2.** weight used for flattening or pressing
teqqeb same as *tqeb*
teqqef v.t. (v.n. *tqaf*) **1.** to stop, to hold up, to arrest (payment, disease) **2.** to stop, to prevent *teqqfu le-ɛṛuṣ mnin ža idxol.* They stopped the groom from going in to his bride. **3.** to board up, to nail shut (door, window) **4.** to confiscate, to seize (property, etc.) **5.** to kidnap
teqqel v.t. **1.** to make heavy or heavier **2.** to make go slow(er), to slow up
¶ *teqqel ɛla* **1.** to make heavy or too heavy, to load down **2.** to weigh down, to put weight or s.th. heavy on **3.** to demand too much from, to overwork, to wear out (s.th., s.o.) **4.** to annoy, to bother
¶ *teqqel režlihΦ* to slow down, to not walk so fast *teqqel režlik šwiya!* Don't walk so fast!
teqṛab v.n. of *qeṛṛeb*
teqrad v.n. of *qerred*
teqṛib v.n. of *qeṛṛeb*
¶ *be-t-teqṛib, teqṛiben* approximately, about
teqrid v.n. of *qerred*
teqṛiṛ pl. *taqaṛiṛ* report *men băɛd-ma sala l-beḥt dyalu qeddem teqṛiṛ l-l-mudir.* After he finished his investigation he presented a report to the director.
tqeṛqeb m.p. of *qeṛqeb*
tqeṛqib v.n. of *qeṛqeb*
tqeṛṛeṣ same as *tgeṛṛeṣ* (m.p. of *geṛṛeṣ*)
tqeršil v.n. of *qeršel*
tqeršel m.p. of *qeršel*
teqṣaṣ v.n. of *qeṣṣeṣ*
teqṣaḥ v.n. of *qeṣṣeḥ*
teqṣiṛ **1.** v.n. of *qeṣṣeṛ* **2.** pleasant conversation, company with friends
¶ *be-t-teqṣiṛ* in short, briefly
teqṣiṛa pl. *-t, tqaṣeṛ* **1.** n.i. of *qeṣṣeṛ* **2.** soiree, evening get-together, party
teqṣiṣ **1.** v.n. of *qeṣṣeṣ* **2.** kind of marriage celebration or reception
teqṣiṣa pl. *tqaṣeṣ* **1.** material, cloth (i.e., the cutting to be used in making a suit, dress, etc.) **2.** amount of prepared *kif* obtained from a bunch of the uncut material

teqṣiḥa pl. *-t* **1.** n.i. of *qeṣṣeḥ* **2.** bruise, contusion
tqeṣṣeṣ m.p. of *qeṣṣeṣ*
teqšaṛ, teqšir v.n. of *qeššeṛ*
teqšiṛa, teqšira pl. *tqašeṛ, tqašer* sock, stocking
tqeššeṛ m.p. of *qeššeṛ*
teqteq v.t. to (get) wet, to moisten
teqṭab v.n. of *qeṭṭeb*
teqṭaṛ v.n. of *qeṭṭeṛ*
teqṭaɛ v.n. of *qeṭṭăɛ*
tqeṭbina quality of being svelte, slenderness
teqṭiba n.i. of *qeṭṭeb*
teqṭiṛ v.n. of *qeṭṭeṛ*
teqṭiṛa (sg. and coll.) pl. *-t* **1.** n.i. of *qeṭṭeṛ* **2.** eye-drop(s)
teqṭiɛ v.n. of *qeṭṭăɛ*
teqṭiɛa pl. *-t, tqaṭeɛ* **1.** n.i. of *qeṭṭăɛ* **2.** tear, slash, gash, rip
tqeṭṭeb m.p. of *qeṭṭeb*
tqeṭṭeṛ m.p. of *qeṭṭeṛ*
tqeṭṭăɛ m.p. of *qeṭṭăɛ*
tqunis v.n. of *tquneṣ*
tquneṣ v.i. to put on airs, to act the big-shot
tquwwa m.p. of *quwwa*
tquwwem m.p. of *quwwem*
tquwwes m.p. of *quwwes*
tquwwet m.p. of *quwwet*
teqwa (usually with art.) fear of or strong belief in God *t-teqwa we-l-ʔiman huma ʔasas l-ʔislam.* Fear of God and faith are the foundation of Islam.
teqwam v.n. of *quwwem*
teqwas v.n. of *quwwes*
teqwim v.n. of *quwwem*
teqwis v.n. of *quwwes*
teqwisa n.i. of *quwwes*
teqwiya v.n. of *quwwa*
teqyad v.n. of *qiyyed*
teqyas v.n. of *qiyyes*
teqyid v.n. of *qiyyed*
teqyida pl. *-t* n.i. of *qiyyed*
teqyila n.i. of *qiyyel*
teqzab v.n. of *qezzeb*
tqezdir v.n. of *qezder*
tqezder m.p. of *qezder*
tqezqez m.p. of *qezqez*
teqɛad v.n. of *qăɛɛăd*
teqɛida pl. *-t, tqaɛed* a type of sieve or strainer with a wooden frame and a woven reed mesh
¶ *ɛăyn t-teqɛida* wheat that has been passed once through a *teqɛida,* remaining rather coarse, used for making *xobz l-ḥăṛš* (a kind of whole wheat bread)
tqăɛɛăd v.i. **1.** m.p. of *qăɛɛăd* **2.** to clear up (weather) **3.** to settle (as dregs in a liquid), to clarify (as sediment in wine) **4.** to sit or stand straight (with good posture)
ṭṛab earth, soil, dirt

trabi (good) manners, behavior, deportment *t-trabi ka-itɛällmu fe-ḍ-ḍaṛ bḥal fe-l-meḍṛaṣa.* Manners are learned at home as well as at school. —*dak d-derri ka-ikmi, ma hna trabi hadi.* That kid is smoking; that's bad behavior.

¶ *qell t-trabi* ill-mannered, rude *žat le-ḍ-ḍaṛ ka-tebki ḥit ɛayerha waḥed qell t-trabi.* She came home crying because some rude person insulted her.

tṛadd used in the expr. *tṛadd le-klam* to have words, to have a spat *ža mɛäṭṭel u-tṛaddu le-klam.* They had a spat when he turned up late.

tṛaḍa v.i. **1.** to agree, to reach an agreement **2.** to like each other

tṛafeg, tṛafeq v.i. to go (somewhere) together, to travel together *fe-ṣ-ṣif l-maži ġadi-ntṛafgu fe-ṣ-ṣfeṛ l-l-uṛuḅḅa.* Next summer we're going to travel together to Europe. —*koll ž-žemɛa f-le-ɛšiya ka-itṛafgu le-s-sinima.* Every Friday night they go to the movies together.

trakeb v.i. to overlap *snanu trakbu.* His teeth overlap.

trakeb **1.** pl. of *terkiba* (n.u. of *rekkeb*) **2.** (also *trakib*) paraphernalia of a tailor or seamstress

tṛama ɛla **1.** to throw oneself at or on (s.o. or s.th.), to jump on *txebbaw-lu muṛ l-bab, u-ġir huwa dxel tṛamaw ɛlih.* They hid from him behind the door, and as soon as he came in they jumped on him. **2.** to seize, to appropriate, to take possession of (s.th.) **3.** to pick a fight with (s.o.)

tṛaṛeb pl. of *teṛrabi* and *teṛrabiya*

trared pl. of *terrada*

trares pl. of *terras*

tṛawem v.i. **1.** to fit, to coincide *la-tlesseqhom ḥetta itṛawmu.* Don't glue them together until they fit (properly). **2.** to go (well) together *had ṭ-ṭabla u-had l-korsi ka-itṛawmu.* This table and chair go well together **3.** to get along well with each other, to be understanding of one another *huwa u-mṛatu ka-itṛawmu bezzaf ɛad.* He and his wife understand each other very well.

¶ *tṛawem mɛa* to deal with, to do business with

tṛaxa v.i. **1.** to get lazy, to become sluggish or listless **2.** to get discouraged **3.** to slacken, to become slack (person)

tṛaya mɛa to consult (s.o.), to talk with (s.o.) *tṛayit mɛa m̄m̄i baš nešri dak l-qefṭan.* I talked with my mother about buying this caftan.

trayek pl. of *trika*

tṛažeɛ v.i. **1.** to regain consciousness, to come to **2.** to calm down (person) **3.** to regain one's sanity

** *tṛazeɛ l-llah!* Calm down!

traɛi pl. of *terɛa*

tṛaḥem v.i. to see s.o. again after a period of separation, to have a reunion (especially with family or close friends) *fe-l-ɛid dima ka-nemši ntṛaḥem mɛa l-ʔahl dyali.* I always go to see my family on holidays.

tṛebba m.p. of *ṛebba*

teṛbiya **1.** v.n. of *ṛebba* **2.** pl. *-t* newborn child, infant, baby

teṛbiɛ v.n. of *ṛebbăɛ*

tṛebya pl. *-t* (dim. *tṛibya*) infant, baby, child (from birth to about two years of age)

tṛedd m.p. of *ṛedd*

tṛedded v.i. to hesitate

teṛdida n.i. of *tṛedded*

teṛdaɛ v.n. of *ṛeḍḍăɛ*

tṛeḍḍ m.p. of *ṛeḍḍ* (same as *ṛedd*)

terfas n.u. *-a* truffle

tergya pl. *-t* clavicle

tṛehheṭ v.i. **1.** to change frequently and/or rapidly, to show frequent or rapid change, to be changeable *tata ka-ttṛehheṭ.* A chameleon changes (color) often. —*l-mumettila xeṣṣha ttṛehheṭ b-suhula men waḥed ḍ-ḍewṛ l-l-axoṛ.* An actress must be able to switch easily from one role to another. (She must be able to change her acting according to the demands of her roles.) —*ka-itṛehheṭ be-l-ġodda.* When he gets mad he turns all different colors. **2.** to tell (untrue) stories, to make up excuses, to say one thing and mean another *ka-ttṛehheṭ ɛliya koll meṛṛa ka-tqul-li klam ɛlih.* She tells me a different story every time she talks to me about him. —*ma-ža-š l-l-meḍṛaṣa l-bareḥ u-fe-ṣ-ṣbaḥ bda ka-itṛehheṭ ɛăl l-muɛällima melli suwwlettu ɛlaš.* He didn't come to school yesterday, and this morning he started making up excuses to the teacher when she asked him why. —*dima ka-itṛehheṭ ɛliya.* He always says one thing to me and means another.

tṛibya pl. *-t* dim. of *tṛebya*

trid n.u. *-a* a kind of very thin pancake, served with a sweet topping (honey, etc.)

trika pl. *trayek* **1.** descendents, progeny **2.** inherited quality or characteristic *fih ḥobb l-musiqa trika.* In him, the love of music is an inherited characteristic.

trisinti electricity

tritil **1.** v.n. of *ritel* **2.** disorder, disarray **3.** vandalism

triya pl. *-t* ceiling light fixture, chandelier *ka-išteḥ bḥal t-triya.* He's shaking like a chandelier.

triyyeb m.p. of *riyyeb*

tṛiyyes m.p. of *ṛiyyes*
triyyeš m.p. of *riyyeš*
triyyeε m.p. of *riyyeε*
tṛek v.t. **1.** to leave, to abandon *teṛku ḍ-daṛ qbel-ma trib!* Abandon the house before it falls in! **2.** to give up (s.th.), to quit (doing s.th.) *tṛekt t-tedxin.* I quit smoking. —*tṛek l-meḍṛaṣa u-lqa xedma.* He gave up school and found a job.
terkab, terkib v.n. of *rekkeb*
torki **1.** pl. *-yen* Turkish **2.** pl. *ʔatṛak* Turk
terkiba pl. *-t, trakeb* n.i. of *rekkeb*
trekkeb m.p. of *rekkeb*
torkya Turkey
teṛmaš v.n. of *ṛemmeš*
teṛmiša n.i. of *ṛemmeš*
ternen v.i. **1.** to ring, to tinkle (small bells only) **2.** to jingle (coins) **3.** to clink (glasses)
¶ *ternen b-* to ring (s.th.) *l-gerraba dima ka-iternnu be-n-nwaqeṣ dyalhom.* The water carriers always ring their bells.
tṛenž, tṛonž n.u. *-a* **1.** sour orange **2.** sour orange tree
teṛqad v.n. of *ṛeqqed*
teṛqaq v.n. of *ṛeqqeq*
teṛqaε v.n. of *ṛeqqăε*
teṛqiq v.n. of *ṛeqqeq*
teṛqiε v.n. of *ṛeqqăε*
tṛeqqa m.p. of *ṛeqqa*
tṛeqqeq m.p. of *ṛeqqeq*
teṛṛabi pl. *tṛaṛeb* **1.** heavy cloth placed around the bottom of a tent to protect the tent cloth **2.** basement, cellar
teṛṛabiya pl. *-t, tṛaṛeb* large basket with handles, made of woven rushes
terrada pl. *-t, trared* **1.** a grill or flat utensil for preparing *trid* **2.** a woman who prepares *trid*
terras pl. *-a, trares* **1.** a man who threshes (wheat), a thresher **2.** artilleryman
terrasa pl. *-t* threshing machine
terred v.i. **1.** to tremble, to shake (people and animals) *ka-iterred be-l-berd.* He's trembling with cold. **2.** to make *trid*
¶ *terred εla* to tremble or shake with anger at (s.o. or s.th.) *terred εliya.* He was shaking with anger at me.
terrika **1.** inheritance, legacy *lemma mat ḅḅahom xella-lhom terrika kbira.* Their father left them a large inheritance when he died. **2.** descendents, posterity *terrikthom kollha xeržat fasda.* All their descendents turned out (to be) worthless.
terrek v.t. **1.** to confiscate *t-tuwwaṛ terrku-lu l-mumtalakat dyalu kollha.* The rebels have confiscated all his possessions. **2.** to despoil, to plunder *fe-l-lil dxel le-εdu le-d-dšeṛ u-terrku.* The enemy entered the village at night and plundered it.
terrăε v.t. **1.** to open wide (a door) *terrăε l-bab baš ixrož had d-doxxan.* Open the door wide so this smoke can get out. **2.** to make a passage, to make an opening (in s.th.) *terrăε s-syaž baš ixeržu le-bhayem.* Make an opening in the fence so the livestock can get out.
tṛeʔʔes v.i. **1.** to become president, to become the head (of a group or an organization) *melli tṛeʔʔes kanet εăndu xemsa u-ṛebεin εam.* He was forty-five when he became president. **2.** to preside *l-wazir l-luwwel tṛeʔʔes εăl le-žtimaε l-wizari.* The Prime Minister presided over the cabinet meeting.
teṛṣaf, teṛṣif v.n. of *ṛeṣṣef*
teṛṣiε v.n. of *ṛeṣṣăε*
tṛeṣṣeḍ l- **1.** to spy on, to watch *koll yum ka-itṛeṣṣdu-lu.* They spy on him every day. **2.** to lie in wait for, to watch for *l-qeṭṭ tṛeṣṣeḍ l-l-faṛ qeddam ġaṛu.* The cat lay in wait for the mouse in front of its hole. —*tṛeṣṣeḍ-lha qeddam l-ḅenk εetta xeržat u-qal-lha: ṛedd-li mali!* He watched for her in front of the bank until she came out and said to her, "Give me back my money!"
tṛeṣya v.n. of *ṛeṣṣa*
tṛešš m.p. of *ṛešš*
tṛeššed v.i. to act or behave as an adult, to show the (mental and emotional) characteristics of adulthood *tṛeššed mεa ṛaṣu had l-iyyam.* He acts like an adult these days (implying that he did not heretofore).
teṛtab v.n. of *ṛetteb*
teṛtib **1.** v.n. of *ṛetteb* **2.** tax paid by farmers on harvests and livestock
tertil v.n. of *rettel*
tṛetteb m.p. of *ṛetteb*
teṛṭab v.n. of *ṛeṭṭeb*
tṛeṭṭa **1.** m.p. of *ṛeṭṭa* **2.** to somersault, to do a flip
tṛeṭṭeb m.p. of *ṛeṭṭeb*
teṛṭuga pl. *-t* ashtray
tṛeṭya pl. *-t* v.n. and n.i. of *ṛeṭṭa*
teṛwa possessions, riches, fortune, goods
teṛwab v.n. of *ṛuwweb*
teṛwam v.n. of *ṛuwwem*
terwan v.n. of *ruwwen*
teṛwim v.n. of *ṛuwwem*
terwina n.i. of *ruwwen*
terwiεa n.i. of *ruwweε*
teṛwiεa n.i. of *ṛuwweε*
tṛuwweb m.p. of *ṛuwweb*
truwweε m.p. of *ruwweε*
tṛuwweε **1.** m.p. of *ṛuwweε* **2.** to go out for (fresh) air **3.** to urinate
tṛuwwăε m.p. of *ṛuwwăε*
¶ *tṛuwwăε-luφ qelbuφ* to be about to vomit
teṛxaṣ v.n. of *ṛexxeṣ*
teṛxwin, trexwin v.n. of *tteṛxa* (m.p. of *ṛxa*)

ṭṛexya v.n. of *ṭṛaxa*
teryab v.n. of *riyyeb*
teṛyaḍ v.n. of *ṛeyyeḍ*
teṛyaq v.n. of *ṛeyyeq*
teryaš v.n. of *riyyeš*
teṛyiqa antidote *šṛeb s-semm u-ʕătquh be-t-teṛyiqa.* He swallowed a poison, but they saved him with the antidote.
teryiš v.n. of *riyyeš*
teṛẓam, teṛẓim v.n. of *ṛeẓẓem*
teṛžama pl. *taṛažim* translation
teṛžaʕ, teṛžiʕ v.n. of *ṛežžăʕ*
teṛžem v.t. to translate, to interpret *teṛžem had le-bṛa men l-ʕăṛbiya l-l-ingliziya.* He translated this letter from Arabic into English.
toṛžman, teṛžman pl. *-at* 1. translator 2. interpreter
ṭṛežža v.t. to expect, to hope for *weṣlat-lu r-risala lli kan ka-iṭṛežža.* He received the letter he was expecting.
ṭṛežžel v.i. to show courage, to show virility, to act like a man.
teṛɛab v.n. of *ṛeɛɛeb*
ṭṛeɛɛem *ʕla* 1. to visit the grave of (s.o.) 2. to pray for (s.o. dead)
terʕa pl. *-t, traʕi* an opening (to permit passage) *fetɛu terʕa fe-s-syaž baš iduzu le-bhayem.* They made an opening in the fence so the livestock could go through.
trăʕʕăd m.p. of *răʕʕăd*
trăʕʕăš same as *trăʕʕăd* (m.p. of *răʕʕăd*)
tsabb v.i. to insult each other
tsabeg, tsabeq v.i. 1. to compete, to vie with each other 2. to race
tsabeɛ pl. of *tesbiɛ* 2
tsahel v.t. to deserve, to merit, to be worthy of *lli dar d-denb itsahel l-ʕuquba.* He who commits wrongs deserves punishment.
¶ *tsahel mʕa* to be easy on (s.o.), to be nice to (s.o.)
tsakef v.i. to stream, to run (down) (said only for perspiration on the face) *l-ʕăṛq ka-itsakef ʕla žbehtu.* The sweat is streaming down his forehead.
tsala m.p. of *sala*
tsalem v.i. to greet each other
tsama m.p. of *sama*
tsameɛ v.i. 1. m.p. of *sameɛ* 2. to pardon each other, to become reconciled, to have a reconciliation
tsaned v.i. to help each other, to give assistance to each other
¶ *tsaned ʕla* to lean on or against *tsandu ʕăl l-ɛiṭ u-weqfu ka-itfeṛṛžu fe-l-mewkib.* They leaned on the wall and stopped to watch the procession.
tsaqeṭ v.i. to fall slowly, to float down (snow, leaves, paper, etc.) *le-wṛaq de-š-šžeṛ ka-itsaqṭu fe-l-xrif.* The tree leaves fall in autumn.
tsara 1. m.p. of *sara* 2. to take a walk
¶ *tsara ʕla* 1. to look for, to search for 2. to visit, to go to see 3. to sample, to try *tsarit ʕăl r-rwayeɛ kollha u-lqit lli bġit.* I tried all the perfumes and found the one I wanted.
tsarr v.i. to tell secrets to each other, to confide in each other
tsareɛ pl. of *tesriɛ* 2 and 3
tsawa m.p. of *sawa*
¶ *tsawa mʕa ṛaṣuᵠ* to relax, to make oneself comfortable, to stretch out
tsaxen (pl. or f.sg.) 1. spices 2. a kind of drug used by some people in cold weather in order to warm themselves
tsebbeb v.i. 1. to make excuses *melli tkellemt mʕah ʕăl le-ktab lli selleft-lu bda ka-itsebbeb* (*ʕliya*). When I talked to him about the book I loaned to him, he began to make excuses (to me). 2. to use subterfuge *kun ma-tsebbebt ʕliha ɛetta ʕṭatni le-wṛaq lli bġit ʕămmeṛni ma-nšufhom.* If I had not used subterfuge on her to get her to give me the papers I wanted, I would never have seen them.
tsebbel m.p. of *sebbel*
tesbil v.n. of *sebbel*
tesbiq v.n. of *sebbeq*
¶ *be-t-tesbiq* in advance, ahead of time
tesbiɛ 1. v.n. of *sebbeɛ* 2. pl. *tsabeɛ* rosary
tsebra to urinate
tsebṛek same as *stebṛek*
tsedd m.p. of *sedd* (same as *šedd*)
tsedya v.n. of *sedda*
tesfal v.i. to make the first sale of the day (businessman) (a slow or difficult first sale is taken as a sign of a bad day for business) *had ṣ-ṣbaɛ ma-zal ma-tesfalit be-l-koll.* This morning I haven't yet made my first sale.
tesfal v.n. of *seffel*
tesfar, tesfir v.n. of *seffer*
tesfira pl. *-t* n.i. of *seffer*
tsefsa (*ʕla*) to break one's promise (to), not to keep one's word (to)
tsegged m.p. of *sėgged*
tseggem same as *tseqqem* (m.p. of *seqqem*)
tsegṭiʕ v.n. of *tsegṭăʕ*
tsegṭiʕa pl. *-t* n.i. of *tsegṭăʕ*
tsegṭăʕ v.i. to jump up, to leap up
tsegya v.n. and n.i. of *segga*
tesġell same as *stġell*
tseġṛeb same as *steġṛeb*
teshil v.n. of *sehhel*
teshila pl. *-at* n.i. of *sehhel*
teˀsis v.n. of *ˀesses*

tsiyyeb m.p .of *siyyeb*

¶ *tsiyyeb ɛla* 1. to jump on, to leap at, to throw oneself on 2. to seize

tsiyyef used in expr. *tsiyyef f-sift* to imitate, to act like *tsiyyef f-sift l-qerd!* Act like a monkey!

tsiyyeq m.p. of *siyyeq*

tsekken m.p. of *sekken*

teslak, teslik v.n. of *sellek*

teslim v.n. of *sellem*

tesliya v.n. of *sella*

tsella m.p. of *sella*

tsellef v.t. to borrow *tselleft ši-flus men ḅḅa l-xuya.* I borrowed some money from my father for my brother.

tsellem m.p. of *sellem*

tsellet v.i. to sneak off, to slip away

tselsil v.n. of *selsel* (same as *sensel*)

tselya v.n. and n.i. of *sella*

tesmam v.n. of *semmem*

tesman v.n. of *semmen*

tesmaṭ v.n. of *semmeṭ*

tsemma m.p. of *semma*

** *tsemma kla ɛăqqu!* said of s.o. who did not show up (usually at a meal or a party), meaning that it is his tough luck that he missed the fun, the food, etc. —*ma-imken-š ntsennaweh n-nhaṛ kollu, ila ma-ža-š tsemma kla ɛăqqu.* Well, we can't wait all day for him; it's just his tough luck he didn't make it.

tsemmeṭ m.p. of *semmeṭ*

tsemmăɛ l- to be or get insulted ≠, to be verbally abused ≠, to get cursed at ≠, to be railed at ≠ *tsemmăɛ-lu ɛla wednih ɛăl lli qal-lha.* He really got railed at for what he said to her. —*tsemmăɛ-lu ɛetta dab be-l-ɛešma.* He was so insulted he almost died of shame.

tsemya v.n. of *semma*

tsenna 1. v.i. to wait 2. v.t. to wait for, to await 3. v.t. to expect (s.o., at such-and-such a time, etc.)

tsenned ɛla to lean on, to rest on *tsenned ɛăl ṭ-ṭabla.* He leaned on the table.

tsenya pl. *-t* n.i. of *tsenna*

tesqaf v.n. of *seqqef*

tesqam v.n. of *seqqem*

tseqqef m.p. of *seqqef*

tseqqem m.p. of *seqqem*

tseqṣya pl. *-t* v.n. and n.i. of *seqṣa*

tesrad v.n. of *serred*

tesraž v.n. of *serrež*

tesraɛ v.n. of *serreɛ*

tesriɛ 1. v.n. of *serreɛ* 2. pl. *tsareɛ* permit, authorization 3. pl. *tsareɛ* rectangular mat (for prayer)

tserreɛ 1. m.p. of *serreɛ* 2. v.i. to stretch out, to spread out, to repose

tseṛẓeq v.i. to (try to) make or earn a living *ka-ttseṛẓeq baš tɛăyyeš wladha.* She's just trying to make a living for her children. —*ma-ṛaṣi ɛetta f-ši-xedma, ġir ka-itseṛẓeq.* He doesn't have a steady job; he just tries to make a living.

tseṛɛa men to warn, to give (s.o.) warning *tseṛɛit mennek, debbeṛ l-ṛaṣek!* I warned you, now it's up to you!

tʔessef (*ɛla*) v.i. to be sorry (about) *tʔesseft lemma smăɛtu dxel l-l-musteš̌fa.* I was sorry when I heard that he had entered the hospital. *tʔessef ɛăl l-ɛadita lli weqɛăt-lha.* He was sorry about the accident that happened to her.

tʔesses m.p. of *ʔesses*

tessăɛ v.i. to move aside, to step aside, to go aside

¶ *tessăɛ men* to leave (s.o.) alone, to go away from, to withdraw from *tessăɛ menni!* Leave me alone!

testaf, testif v.n. of *settef*

tsettef m.p. of *settef*

tsugira n.i. of *suger*

tsuger m.p. of *suger*

tsuxira n.i. of *tsuxer*

tsuxer v.i. 1. to draw back, to pull back, to retreat, to withdraw *tsuxer le-ɛdu lemma tteqtel ɛadad kbir mennhom.* The enemy retreated when a great number of them were killed. 2. to move backwards, to move in reverse (as a vehicle) 3. to recoil, to kick (firearm) 4. to recede, to ebb (water)

teswak v.n. of *suwwek*

teswal v.n. of *suwwel*

teswiqa 1. n.i. of *tsuwweq* 2. pl. *-t* purchase

tsuwweq v.i. to go shopping, to go to market, to make purchases

tsuwwes same as *suwwes*

tesxan v.n. of *sexxen*

tesxaṛ v.n. of *sexxeṛ*

tesxiṛ v.n. of *sexxeṛ*

** *t-tesxiṛ men ḷḷah!* The success (of some enterprise) depends on God. (approximately equivalent to "Good luck!"; said to s.o. to wish him success in some undertaking)

tsexxen m.p. of *sexxen*

tsexxeṛ m.p. of *sexxeṛ*

tesyab v.n. of *siyyeb*

tesyaq v.n. of *siyyeq*

tesyas v.n. of *siyyes*

tesyiq v.n. of *siyyeq*

tesyiqa pl. *-t* n.i. of *siyyeq*

tesžal, tesžil v.n. of *sežžel*

tsežžel m.p. of *sežžel*

tesɛab same as *ttesɛab*

tseɛfeḍ to protect oneself, to take care of oneself *ttermaw fe-s-sariž de-l-ma baš itseɛfḍu men n-naṛ.* They jumped into the swimming pool to protect themselves from the fire.

¶ *tseɛfeḍ ɛla* to protect, to take care of *xeṣṣek ttseɛfeḍ ɛăl s-siyaṛa dyalek ila bġitiha ṭṭul-lek.* You must take care of your car if you want it to last.

tseɛya same as *steɛya*

tseɛɛeb same as *seɛɛeb*

tesɛ see *tesɛud*

tesɛa same as *tesɛud*

tesɛad same as *staɛed*

tesɛan same as *staɛen*

tesɛaṛ v.n. of *săɛɛăṛ*

tsăɛdeṛ same as *stăɛdeṛ*

tesɛin 1. ninety 2. ninetieth

tsăɛtaš 1. nineteen 2. nineteenth

tesɛud (*tesɛ* when used with pl. of n. admitting du.) nine

tsăɛɛăṛ m.p. of *săɛɛăṛ*

tṣaḍef v.i. to happen to meet, to meet by chance

tṣaḍem v.i. to collide, to run into each other

tṣafa v.i. 1. to clear up, to become clear *l-ɛal tṣafa l-yum.* The weather has cleared up today. 2. to be quits, to be even or equal with each other (by repayment of a debt or obligation)

¶ *lunu*ᶲ *tṣafa* to return to normal color (after anger, sickness, sunburn, etc.) *bṛat u-lunha tṣafa.* When she got well, her color came back to normal.

¶ *tṣafa mɛa* to make a deal with, to come to an agreement with

tṣaff v.i. to line up, to fall in (military), to get into rows or columns

tṣafeṭ m.p. of *ṣafeṭ* (same as *ṣifeṭ*)

tṣafeɛ v.i. to shake hands

tṣaleɛ v.i. to make up (after a fight), to become reconciled, to make peace (after war)

tṣaqeṭ same as *tsaqeṭ*

tṣaṛef v.i. to do business, to deal with each other

tṣaṭeɛ v.i. to run into each other, to collide

tṣaweb m.p. of *ṣaweb* (same as *ṣuwweb*)

tṣaweṛ pl. of *teṣwiṛa*

tṣaɛeb v.i. 1. to become friends 2. to associate with each other

teṣbin v.n. of *ṣebben*

teṣbina pl. *-t* n.i. of *ṣebben*

tṣeḍḍa same as *ṣeḍḍa*

tṣeḍḍeq b- same as *ṣeḍḍeq*

teṣḍiq v.n. of *ṣeḍḍeq*

tṣeḍya v.n. and n.i. of *ṣeḍḍa*

teṣfaf v.n. of *ṣeffef* (same as *ṣaff, ṣafef*)

teṣfaq v.n. of *ṣeffeq*

teṣfaṛ v.n. of *ṣeffeṛ*

teṣfaɛ v.n. of *ṣeffeɛ*

tṣeffa m.p. of *ṣeffa*

tṣeffef same as *tṣaff*

teṣfif v.n. of *ṣeffef* (same as *ṣaff, ṣafef*)

teṣfiq v.n. of *ṣeffeq*

teṣfiṛ v.n. of *ṣeffeṛ*

tṣefya v.n. and n.i. of *ṣeffa*

teṣġaṛ 1. v.n. of *ṣeġġeṛ* 2. diminution, reduction

teṣġiṛ 1. v.n. of *ṣeġġeṛ* 2. diminutive *ṭwibla, huwa t-teṣġiṛ dyal ṭabla. ṭwibla* is the diminutive of *ṭabla.*

tṣehheḍ v.i. to get hot *tṣehheḍ be-s-sxana.* He got hot with fever. —*l-ɛal tṣehheḍ l-bareɛ.* It (the weather) got hot yesterday.

tṣifeṭ m.p. of *ṣifeṭ*

¶ *tṣifeṭ mɛa* to see (s.o.) off, to say good-bye to (s.o.) *melli kont žayya l-ʔamrika tṣifṭet mɛaya ɛaʔilti kollha.* When I was coming to America my whole family saw me off.

tṣiyyeḍ m.p. of *ṣiyyeḍ*

tṣiyyeṛ m.p. of *ṣiyyeṛ*

tṣelgiṭ v.n. of *tṣelgeṭ*

tṣelgeṭ v.i. to behave in a coarse, ill mannered way; to act in a crude or vulgar fashion

tṣelleb m.p. of *ṣelleb*

tṣelleṭ ɛla or *b-* 1. to intrude on, to attach oneself to (s.o.) without leave or welcome, to impose oneself on, to force oneself on *f-weqt le-ġda tṣelltu biya žuž de-l-ʔaṣdiqaʔ, ddithom itġeddaw mɛaya.* At lunchtime, two friends attached themselves to me, (so) I took them to lunch with me. —*tṣelleṭ ɛlina waɛed l-ɛakem ma-fih la-ṛeɛma wa-la-šafaqa.* A ruler who had neither compassion nor pity imposed himself on us. —*tṣelleṭ ɛliha waɛed xiyyna u-dzuwwež biha ɛăn ṭariq ɛaʔiltha f-ɛămṛu settin ɛam.* Some character who's sixty years old forced himself on her and married her through (the influence of) her family. 2. to descend on, to invade, to befall *tṣelleṭ ɛlihom ž-žṛaḍ u-kla-lhom z-zṛăɛ kollu.* The grasshoppers invaded them and ate all their wheat. —*tṣelleṭ ɛlihom waɛed z-zilzal u-qḍa-lhom ɛăl le-mdina kollha.* An earthquake befell them and destroyed the whole city. 3. to fall upon (s.o.), to attack *fe-l-lil lemma kont ṛažeɛ le-ḍ-ḍaṛ tṣelltu biya žuž de-l-qemmaṛa u-ddaw flusi kollhom.* When I was returning to the house at night, two thieves fell on me and took all my money.

tṣelṭin v.n. of *tṣelṭen*

tṣelṭina pl. *-t* n.i. of *ṣelṭen*

tṣelṭen v.i. m.p. of *ṣelṭen*

teṣmaṛ, teṣmiṛ v.n. of *ṣemmeṛ*

teṣmiṛa pl. *-t* n.i. of *ṣemmeṛ*

tṣemmeṛ m.p. of *ṣemmeṛ*

tṣemṣeṛ 1. to eavesdrop, to listen secretly *ɛna konna ka-netkellmu u-huwa ža ka-itṣemṣeṛ*

ɛlina. We were talking and he came (up) to eavesdrop on us. **2.** (ɛla) to watch surreptitiously, to spy on
tṣennet (ɛla, l-) to listen (to)
tṣennăɛ v.i. **1.** to be mannered, to act in an artificial manner, to behave affectedly **2.** to show off *tṣennăɛ qeddam le-bnat.* He showed off in front of the girls. —*tṣennɛat ɛla ṣḥabha b-siyaṛtha ž-ždida.* She showed off in front of her friends with her new car.
tṣenteḥ v.i. **1.** to speak or act in a falsely authoritative manner, to put up a big front *klamu kollu xawi, ṛah ġir ka-itṣenteḥ.* He doesn't know what he's talking about; he's just putting up a big front. **2.** to be cheeky, insolent, smart-alecky; to act smart *l-ʔustad ɛaqebhom ɛla wedd tṣentḥu ɛlih.* The teacher punished them because they acted smart with him. **3.** to be shameless, to behave shamelessly *had s-siyyda dima ka-ttṣenteḥ ɛăl n-nas.* That woman is always acting shamelessly in front of people.
teṣṛaf v.n. of *ṣeṛṛef*
tṣeṛfiqa pl. *-t* slap, open-handed blow to the face
teṣṛif v.n. of *ṣeṛṛef*
tṣeṛṛef m.p. of *ṣeṛṛef*
¶ *tṣeṛṛef f-* to make use of, to exploit *ḥṛam ɛlih itṣeṛṛef f-amwal l-itama.* It's wrong for him to exploit the orphans' money. —*ɛăndu kamel l-ḥoṛṛiya baš itṣeṛṛef f-le-flus lli xella-lu ḅḅah.* He has complete freedom to make use of the money his father left him.
tṣeṛṣiṛ v.n. of *ṣeṛṣeṛ*
teṣṭaṛ v.n. of *ṣeṭṭeṛ*
tṣeṭṭa m.p. of *ṣeṭṭa*
tṣuliḥ v.n. of *tṣuleḥ*
tṣuleḥ v.i. to be sanctimonious, to feign saintliness
tṣuwweb m.p. of *ṣuwweb*
tṣuwweṛ m.p. of *ṣuwweṛ*
** *ma-itṣuwweṛ-ši fe-l-bal* (or *f-le-ɛqel*)! It's unimaginable!
¶ *tṣuwweṛ-luᶲ* to seem to (s.o.)
teṣwab v.n. of *ṣuwweb*
teṣwaṛ v.n. of *ṣuwweṛ*
teṣwaṭ v.n. of *ṣuwweṭ*
teṣwiṛ v.n. of *ṣuwweṛ*
teṣwiṛa pl. *-t, tṣaweṛ* **1.** drawing, sketch **2.** painting, portrait **3.** picture, illustration **4.** photograph **5.** statue **6.** doll
teṣwiṭ v.n. of *ṣuwweṭ*
teṣyaṛ, teṣyiṛ v.n. of *ṣiyyeṛ*
teṣyaḥ v.n. of *ṣiyyeḥ*
teṣḥaḥ v.n. of *ṣeḥḥeḥ*
teṣḥiḥ v.n. of *ṣeḥḥeḥ*
tṣeḥḥeṛ v.i. to eat the *ṣḥuṛ* (pre-dawn meal during Ramadan)
tṣeḥḥeḥ m.p. of *ṣeḥḥeḥ*
tšabeh v.i. to be alike or similar, to resemble one another
tšabek v.i. **1.** to get (all) tangled up (thread, etc.) **2.** to scuffle, to have a scuffle
tšabek pl. of *tešbika* and *tešbak* **2**
tšafa v.i. **1.** to recover, to recuperate (from an illness) **2.** to get better, to improve, to show improvement (sick person)
tšamir pl. *-at* **1.** shirt **2.** kind of long men's shirt, now obsolescent
tšames pl. of *tešmisa*
tšaneq v.i. to grab each other by the collar or throat (with hands)
tšaqeṛ v.i. to fight or fence with swords or sticks
tšarek v.i. to be or go partners, to join together (in buying s.th., in business, etc.)
tšaṛeṭ v.i. to mutally agree on terms or conditions
tšaš same as *ṭšaš*
tšawef v.i. to see each other *ana u-ṣaḥbi ka-ntšawfu koll yum.* My friend and I see each other every day.
tšaweh pl. of *tešwiha*
tšaweṛ v.i. to consult (together), to have a consultation, to deliberate
tšaweṭ pl. of *tešwiṭa*
tešbak **1.** v.n. of *šebbek* **2.** pl. *tšabek* complication, embroilment
tšebbek m.p. of *šebbek*
tšebbeṭ f- **1.** to grab hold of, to hold on to, to grasp (rope, rung, etc.) **2.** to scale, to climb (wall, mountain, tree, etc.)
tešbih **1.** v.n. of *šebbeh* **2.** comparison **3.** resemblance, similarity
tešbik same as *tešbak*
tešbika pl. *-t, tšabek* **1.** n.i. of *šebbek* **2.** complication, difficulty
tešbiṛ v.n. of *šebbeṛ*
tešbiṛa n.i. of *šebbeṛ*
** *tešbiṛt le-ɛma fe-ḍ-ḍelma.* expr. used to describe or indicate how strongly s.o. has grabbed on to s.o. else, i.e., as a blind man in the dark
tšedd m.p. of *šedd*
tešfaṛ **1.** v.n. of *šeffeṛ* **2.** stealing, robbery, theft (not too common usage)
tešfaɛ **1.** v.n. of *šeffăɛ* **2.** optional or extra prayer, coming after the last regularly prescribed daily prayer
tšeffa f- to rejoice over or be glad of the misfortune or bad luck of (s.o.)
tšeffeṛ m.p. of *šeffeṛ*
tšeffăɛ f- to ask (s.o.) to intercede for one (for help, to pray for one)
tešfiṛ same as *tešfaṛ*

tešfiɛ same as *tešfaɛ*
tšin (art. *le-*) same as *letšin*
tšiṭin devilry, devilment, mischief (usually children)
tšiyyeṭ m.p. of *šiyyeṭ*
tšiyyex m.p. of *šiyyex*
teškal, teškil v.n. of *šekkel*
teškila pl. *-t* n.i. of *šekkel*
tšekka (*men*) to gripe, to complain (about) ¶ *tšekka l-* to complain to, to lodge a complaint with
tšekkel m.p. of *šekkel*
tešlal, tešlil v.n. of *šellel*
tešlila pl. *-t* n.i. of *šellel*
tšellel m.p. of *šellel*
tšelwiḥ v.n. of *šelweḥ*
tešmiṛ 1. v.n. of *šemmeṛ* 2. string or cord used to keep sleeves up (used by women)
tešmis v.n. of *šemmes*
tešmisa pl. *-t, tšames* 1. n.i. of *šemmes* 2. sunburn
tešmiš v.n. of *šemmeš* (same as *šemmes*)
tšemmes, tšemmeš m.p. of *šemmes, šemmeš*
tšemšim v.n. of *šemšem*
tšeqleb v.i. 1. m.p. of *šeqleb* 2. to capsize, to overturn 3. to turn somersaults
tšeqlib v.n. of *šeqleb* and *tšeqleb*
tšeqq m.p. of *šeqq*
tšeqqeq m.p. of *šeqqeq*
tešrag v.n. of *šerreg*
tešṛaṭ v.n. of *šeṛṛeṭ*
tešṛaḥ 1. v.n. of *šeṛṛeḥ* 2. dissection
tešrig v.n. of *šerreg*
tešriga pl. *-t* 1. n.i. of *šerreg* 2. rip, tear, gash 3. cut, incision
tešṛiṭ v.n. of *šeṛṛeṭ*
tšeṛmila 1. n.i. of *šeṛmel* and *tšeṛmel* 2. same as *šeṛmula*
tšeṛmel m.p. of *šeṛmel*
tšeṛṛef m.p. of *šeṛṛef*
** *ana metšeṛṛef!* I'm glad to meet you (i.e., honored)!
tšerreg m.p. of *šerreg*
tšeṛṛeḥ m.p. of *šeṛṛeḥ*
tšeṛṛăɛ m.p. of *šeṛṛăɛ*
tšeṛšiṛ v.n. of *šeṛšeṛ*
teštat, teštit v.n. of *šettet*
tešteš v.i. to sizzle, to sputter (e.g. a frying steak, water on a hot rock)
tšettet m.p. of *šettet*
tešṭab v.n. of *šeṭṭeb*
tešṭaṭ v.n. of *šeṭṭeṭ*
tešṭib v.n. of *šeṭṭeb*
tešṭiba pl. *-t* n.i. of *šeṭṭeb*
tešṭiṭ v.n. of *šeṭṭeṭ*
tšeṭṭeb m.p. of *šeṭṭeb*
tšeṭṭeṛ v.i. to bargain, to haggle
tšeṭṭeṭ m.p. of *šeṭṭeṭ*
tšuwwa v.i. to lose or give up hope, to despair *tšuwwa f-mut žeddah.* He lost hope at (the time of) his grandmother's death.
tšuwwek v.i. 1. m.p. of *šuwwek* 2. to get a chill, to have chills up and down the spine
** *tšuwwek leḥmu.* He's got goose pimples.
tšuwweš m.p. of *šuwweš*
tšuwweṭ m.p. of *šuwweṭ*
tešwaš 1. v.n. of *šuwweš* 2. worry, preoccupation, inquietude
tešwaṭ v.n. of *šuwweṭ*
tešwiha pl. *-t, tšaweh* indiscretion, faux pas, breach of etiquette or protocol
tešwiš same as *tešwaš* 2
tešwiṭa pl. *-t, tšaweṭ* 1. n.i. of *šuwweṭ* 2. burn (from fire, sun, etc.) 3. sharp pain, burning pain (not necessarily from heat)
tšexwiš v.n. of *šexweš*
tšexweš v.i. to get or become frightened *kont weḥdi fe-ḍ-ḍaṛ u-tšexwešt.* I was alone in the house and I got scared.
tešyar v.n. of *šiyyer*
tešyaɛ v.n. of *šiyyăɛ*
tešyir v.n. of *šiyyer*
tešyira pl. *-t* 1. n.i. of *šiyyer* 2. hand gesture or signal (for any purpose)
tešyiɛ v.n. of *šiyyăɛ*
teššaɛ, teššiɛ 1. v.n. of *šezzăɛ* 2. encouragement
tšežžăɛ v.i. 1. m.p. of *šežžăɛ* 2. to gain courage, to become bold(er)
tšeḥḥeṛ v.i. m.p. of *šeḥḥeṛ*
tšeḥḥeḥ v.i. to be stingy, a skinflint
tšăɛbeṭ f- same as *tšebbeṭ f-*
tšăɛšiɛ v.n. of *šăɛšăɛ*
ttabeɛ v.i. to come in succession, to follow or succeed one another
ttafeq v.i. 1. to agree, to come to an agreement *ttafeqt mɛah (baš) iži ɛăndna.* I agreed with him that he would come to our house. —*ttafeqna ɛla xemsin derhem.* We agreed on fifty dirhams. 2. to get along (together), to be compatible 3. to go well together (colors, etc.)
ttaqa ḷḷah 1. to fear God, to believe in the one and only God 2. to be honest, truthful *ttaqa ḷḷah u-qul-lna š-ka-tăɛṛef!* Stop lying and tell us what you know!
ttaṣeḷ b- 1. to communicate with, to get in touch or contact with (s.o.) 2. to meet with (s.o.)
ttawa v.i. 1. to bargain, to haggle 2. to agree, to be in agreement 3. to get along (together), to be compatible
ttažer v.i. to do business
ttaseɛ v.i. to withdraw, to go aside
ttbas same as *tbas* (m.p. *of bas*)
tetbat 1. v.n. of *tebbet* 2. confirmation, proof (of a fact, information, etc.)

ttebheḍ, ttebheṭ m.p. of *bheḍ*
tetbit same as *tetbat*
ttebla 1. m.p. of *bla* 2. to be or get upset by a misfortune *ttebla meskin ma-عṛef kif idir, waš imši عănd m̄m̄u mṛiḍa aw igles mعa mṛatu حemqa.* The poor fellow was so upset he didn't know what to do—go to his sick mother or stay with his wife, who is crazy. —*ma-عṛef b-aš ittebla melli qalu-lu ḅḅah mat.* He didn't realize how upset he was when they told him his father died.
¶ *ttebla b-* to fall in love with *ttebla b-bent عămmu.* He fell in love with his cousin.
ttbell m.p. of *bell*
ttebna m.p. of *bna*
ttebžeġ m.p. of *bžeġ*
ttebعăž m.p. of *bعăž*
ttedbeṛ same as *tteḍbeṛ* (m.p. of *ḍbeṛ*)
ttedbez m.p. of *dbez*
ttedbeح m.p. of *dbeح*
ttedfen m.p. of *dfen*
ttedfăع m.p. of *dfăع*
ttedha m.p. of *dha*
ttedhen m.p. of *dhen*
ttedlek m.p. of *dlek*
ttedres m.p. of *dres*
ttedحa m.p. of *dحa*
tteḍbeġ m.p. of *ḍbeġ*
tteḍbeṛ 1. m.p. of *ḍbeṛ* 2. to be fed up (with (s.th.), to have enough (of s.th.) *ana tteḍbeṛt men had-l-xedma!* I'm fed up with this job.
tteḍbăع v.i. 1. to become stupid, to lose one's common sense 2. to be bewitched or enchanted, to fall under a spell 3. to be stunned, speechless
tteḍṛeb m.p. of *ḍṛeb*
ttefda m.p. of *fda*
ttefdăع m.p. of *fdăع*
ttefḍeح m.p. of *fḍeح*
ttefges m.p. of *fges*
ttefgăع m.p. of *fgăع*
ttefhem m.p. of *fhem*
ttefqed v.i. 1. m.p. of *fqed* 2. to become hard to find or get (merchandise)
ttefqeṛ v.i. to become poor or impoverished
ttefṛeḍ m.p. of *fṛeḍ*
ttefrem m.p. of *frem*
ttefṛeq m.p. of *fṛeq*
¶ *ttefṛeq men* (or *mعa*) 1. to leave alone, to stop bothering (s.o.) 2. to become separated from (wife, husband)
ttefrez m.p. of *frez*
ttefṛăع m.p. of *fṛăع*
ttefsex m.p. of *fsex*
ttefṣel m.p. of *fṣel*
tteften m.p. of *ften*
ttefteq m.p. of *fteq*
ttefteح m.p. of *fteح*
tteftem m.p. of *fṭem*
ttfu expr. of complete disgust and/or dislike (often indicated by spitting)
¶ *ttfu عlihφ* same as *ttfu,* but said directly to or about s.o.
ttefzăع m.p. of *fzăع*
ttefžeṛ 1. to burst open (abscess) 2. to well up, to spring forth (water)
tteghem m.p. of *ghem*
ttegleb m.p. of *gleb*
tteglăع m.p. of *glăع* (same as *qellăع*)
ttegعăṛ m.p. of *gعăṛ*
tteġḍeṛ m.p. of *ġḍeṛ*
tteġleb m.p. of *ġleb*
tteġleq m.p. of *ġleq*
tteġna m.p. of *ġna*
tteġṛem m.p. of *ġṛem*
tteġres, tteġṛeṣ m.p. of *ġres, ġṛeṣ*
tteġsel m.p. of *ġsel*
tteġṣeb m.p. of *ġṣeb*
tteġzel m.p. of *ġzel*
ttehda m.p. of *hda ihdi*
ttehdem m.p. of *hdem*
ttehḍem m.p. of *hḍem*
ttehlek m.p. of *hlek*
ttehṛeq m.p. of *hṛeq*
ttifaq pl. *-at* (art. *le-*) 1. v.n. of *ttafeq* 2. agreement 3. rapport
teʔtir 1. v.n. of *ʔetteṛ* 2. influence 3. impression, effect
ttiحad (art. *le-*) 1. v.n. of *ttaحed* 2. union (political, labor, etc.) 3. unity
ttkebb m.p. of *kebb*
ttekka 1. m.p. of *tekka* v.t. 2. same as *tekka* v.i.
ttkel 1. same as *ttenkel* 2. (with *عla*) to rely on, to count on
ttekma m.p. of *kma*
ttekra m.p. of *kra*
tteksa m.p. of *ksa*
ttekseṛ, tteksẹṛ m.p. of *kseṛ, kṣeṛ*
ttekteb m.p. of *kteb*
ttekwa m.p. of *kwa*
tetlaf v.n. of *tellef*
ttlaح m.p. of *laح*
ttelbes m.p. of *lbes*
ttleff m.p. of *leff*
ttelha m.p. of *lha*
ttella v.i. to come last, to be the last one (to do s.th.) *xrežna men ḍ-ḍaṛ u-m̄m̄i ttellat baš tsedd l-bab.* We came out of the house and my mother came last so she could shut the door.
ttelqa m.p. of *lqa*
ttelqef m.p. of *lqef*
ttelحes m.p. of *lحes*
ttemlek m.p. of *mlek*
ttemḷeṣ m.p. of *mḷeṣ*

ttemnăع m.p. of *mnăع*
ttemsex m.p. of *msex*
ttemseح m.p. of *mseح*
ttemtim (with art. *t-temtim*) v.n. of *temtem*
ttemxeḍ m.p. of *mxeḍ*
ttemحa m.p. of *mحa*
ttemعăs m.p. of *mعăs*
ttenfa m.p. of *nfa*
ttenfex m.p. of *nfex*
ttenkel v.i. **1.** m.p. of *kla* **2.** to be edible **3.** to wear out (tire, shoe, etc.)
ttenkes m.p. of *nkes*
ttenqed m.p. of *nqed*
ttenqeṛ v.i. to get upset, vexed, or peeved
ttenqeš m.p. of *nqeš*
ttensa m.p. of *nsa*
ttensex m.p. of *nsex*
ttensež m.p. of *nsež*
ttenṣeb m.p. of *nṣeb*
ttenṣeṛ m.p. of *nṣeṛ*
ttenšeˀ m.p. of *nšeˀ*
ttenšeṛ m.p. of *nšeṛ*
ttentef m.p. of *ntef*
ttenحeṛ m.p. of *nحeṛ*
tetqaf v.n. of *teqqef*
ttqal m.p. of *qal*
tetqal v.n. of *teqqel*
ttqam m.p. of *qam iqim*
¶ *ttqam عla* to cost *ṣ-ṣefṛa ttqamet عliya be-myat derhem.* The trip cost me one hundred dirhams.
ttqas m.p. of *qas*
tteqbeḍ m.p. of *qbeḍ*
tteqbel m.p. of *qbel*
tteqbeṭ m.p. of *qbeṭ* (same as *qbeḍ*)
tteqḍa m.p. of *qḍa*
tteqfel m.p. of *qfel*
tetqila n.i. of *teqqel*
tteqla m.p. of *qla*
tteqleb m.p. of *qleb*
tteqqef m.p. of *teqqef*
tteqqel m.p. of *teqqel*
tteqṛa m.p. of *qṛa*
tteqṛen v.i. to get upset, to get irritated
tteqṛeṣ m.p. of *qṛeṣ*
tteqṛeṭ m.p. of *qṛeṭ*
tteqṣem m.p. of *qṣem*
tteqšăع m.p. of *qšăع*
tteqtel m.p. of *qtel*
tteqteq m.p. of *teqteq*
tteqṭăع m.p. of *qṭăع*
ˀetteṛ عla **1.** to influence **2.** to affect, to have an effect on **3.** to impress (s.o.)
tetrad v.n. of *terred*
tteṛbeṭ m.p. of *ṛbeṭ*
¶ *tteṛbeṭ f-* to fall in love with (s.o.)
tterdem m.p. of *rdem*
tteṛfa m.p. of *ṛfa*
tterfed m.p. of *rfed*
tteṛġeb m.p. of *ṛġeb*
tteṛheb m.p. of *ṛheb*
tetrida n.i. of *terred*
tterkez m.p. of *rkez*
tteṛma v.i. **1.** m.p. of *ṛma* **2.** to jump, to leap
tternin v.n. of *ternen*
tteṛqa m.p. of *ṛqa*
tteṛqem m.p. of *ṛqem*
tterred m.p. of *terred*
tteṛšem m.p. of *ṛšem*
tteṛxa m.p. of *ṛxa*
tteṛxef m.p. of *ṛxef*
tterza m.p. of *rza*
tteṛžem m.p. of *teṛžem*
ttsal **1.** m.p. of *sal* **2.** to owe (lit. be demanded of) *ka-ittsaluha bezzaf d-le-flus.* She owes a lot of money.
ttsaع v.i. **1.** to make oneself comfortable, to relax *ttsaعu mعa ṛaṣkom!* Make yourselves comfortable! **2.** to go to the bathroom, rest room, powder room **3.** to fit, to be able to be contained *dak le-ktab ma-ittsaع-š f-le-mžeṛ.* That book won't go (or fit) in the drawer.
¶ *ttsaع f-baluᶲ* to be able or willing to believe or accept ≠ *ma-ittsaع-š f-balu l-xabaṛ de-l-mut de-ḅḅah.* He can't believe the news of his father's death.
tteshet m.p. of *shet*
tteskef m.p. of *skef*
¶ *tteskef mennuᶲ d-demm* to become pale, anemic ≠ *tteskef mennek d-demm.* You look pale.
¶ *tteskef عla* to want or desire, to be crazy about (s.th.)
ttesken v.i. **1.** to be inhabited, to be lived in, to be occupied (house, etc.) **2.** to be inhabitable (house, etc.) **3.** to be haunted (with demons, ghosts)
ttsell v.i. **1.** m.p. of *sell* **2.** to sneak, to move (about) surreptitiously
ttesmăع m.p. of *smăع*
¶ *ttesmăع l-* to listen to (seriously), to mind *ma-ttesmăع-li حădd l-le-klam dyali.* No one paid any attention to what I said. —*dak l-weld ma-ttesmăع-š le-ḅḅah.* That boy didn't mind his father.
ttesqa m.p. of *sqa*
ttester m.p. of *ster*
tteszen m.p. of *sžen*
ttesحab l- to think, to believe ≠ *ttesحab-li l-bab kanet mešduda.* I thought the door was closed.
ttesحeq m.p. of *sحeq*
ttesحer m.p. of *sحer*
ttṣab m.p. of *ṣab*
tteṣbeġ m.p. of *ṣbeġ*
tteṣleح m.p. of *ṣleح*
tteṣnăع m.p. of *ṣnăع*
tteṣṛef m.p. of *ṣṛef*
ttṣeṛṛ m.p. of *ṣeṛṛ*

ttšaf v.i. **1.** m.p. of *šaf* **2.** to be visible
¶ *ma-fihφ ma ittšaf* to be a horrible sight ≠, to look horrible ≠ (expr. of repugnance and revulsion) *had l-bent ma-fiha ma ittšaf!* What a horrible sight she is!
tteššăɛ m.p. of *šfăɛ*
ttešġel m.p. of *šġel*
ttešha v.t. to want, to desire *tteshit ši-feṛṛuž mḥămmeṛ* I want some roast chicken. I feel like having some roast chicken.
ttešheṛ m.p. of *šheṛ* (same as *šehheṛ*)
ttešmet m.p. of *šmet*
ttešneq m.p. of *šneq*
ttešnăɛ v.i. to become famous
ttešra m.p. of *šra*
ttešṛeb v.i. **1.** m.p. of *šṛeb* **2.** to be potable, drinkable
ttešrek m.p. of *šrek*
ttešwa m.p. of *šwa*
** *ttešwat f-weldha.* She lost her son.
ttešžen same as *tteszen* (m.p. of *sžen*)
ttešɛăl m.p. of *šɛăl*
ttetna m.p. of *tna*
ttetqeb m.p. of *tqeb*
ttetṛek m.p. of *tṛek*
ttetxem m.p. of *txem*
tteṭbex m.p. of *ṭbex*
tteṭbăɛ m.p. of *ṭbăɛ*
tteṭla m.p. of *ṭla*
tteṭḷeq m.p. of *ṭḷeq*
tteṭṛeš m.p. of *ṭṛeš*
tteṭṛeḥ m.p. of *ṭṛeḥ*
tteṭwa m.p. of *ṭwa*
tteṭḥen m.p. of *ṭḥen*
ttuled m.p. of *wled*
tturet, ttuṛet m.p. of *wret, wṛet*
ttuseq m.p. of *wseq*
ttuwled same as *ttuled* (m.p. of *wled*)
ttuwseq same as *ttuseq* (m.p. of *wseq*)
ttuz cry used to chase away a dog
ttuzen m.p. of *wzen*
ttužed m.p. of *wžed*
tetwal, tetwil v.n. of *tuwwel*
tetwiž **1.** v.n. of *tuwwež* **2.** coronation
ttexbeṛ m.p. of *xbeṛ*
ttexbeš m.p. of *xbeš* (same as *xebbeš* 2)
ttexdem m.p. of *xdem*
ttexdăɛ m.p. of *xdăɛ*
ttexla m.p. of *xla*
ttexlef m.p. of *xlef*
ttexleq m.p. of *xleq*
ttexlăɛ m.p. of *xlăɛ*
ttexneg, ttexneq m.p. of *xneg, xneq*
ttexreg m.p. of *xreg*
ttexṛeṭ m.p. of *xṛeṭ*
ttexṭef m.p. of *xṭef*
ttexwa m.p. of *xwa*
ttexzen m.p. of *xzen*
ttzad same as *dzad*
ttezḷeṭ v.i. to become very poor, impoverished (i.e., completely without financial resource)
ttezreg v.i. **1.** to sneak (especially to avoid paying s.th.) *ttezreg fe-s-sinima.* He sneaked into the movie. **2.** to slip, to worm one's way (as through a crowd)
ttezṛăɛ m.p. of *zṛăɛ*
ttežwa v.i. **1.** m.p. of *žwa* **2.** to become speechless, stunned (at some shock)
ttežbed m.p. of *žbed*
ttežbeṛ m.p. of *žbeṛ*
ttežla m.p. of *žla*
ttežmăɛ v.i. **1.** m.p. of *žmăɛ* **2.** to meet, to hold a meeting
ttežṛed m.p. of *žṛed*
ttžeṛṛ m.p. of *žeṛṛ*
ttežṛeḥ m.p. of *žṛeḥ*
ttḥaz v.i. **1.** m.p. of *ḥaz* **2.** to move *ttḥaz mɛa l-qent šwiya!* Move a little closer to the corner!
¶ *ttḥaz l-* to back, to support, to be on the side of (s.o.)
tteḥder m.p. of *ḥder*
tteḥfeḍ m.p. of *ḥfeḍ*
tteḥfeṛ m.p. of *ḥfeṛ*
tteḥgeṛ m.p. of *ḥgeṛ*
tteḥleb m.p. of *ḥleb*
tteḥma m.p. of *ḥma yeḥmi*
tteḥmel m.p. of *ḥmel*
tteḥna m.p. of *ḥna*
tteḥqeṛ same as *tteḥgeṛ* (m.p. of *ḥgeṛ*)
tteḥṛem m.p. of *ḥṛem*
tteḥṛeq m.p. of *ḥṛeq*
tteḥṛet m.p. of *ḥṛet*
tteḥseb m.p. of *ḥseb*
tteḥṣa m.p. of *ḥṣa*
¶ *la-itteḥṣa* (adj. usage; pl. *la-itteḥṣaw*) innumerable, countless, incalculable *kayen ɛadad la-itteḥṣa de-n-nas temma.* There are countless people there.
tteḥṣeḍ m.p. of *ḥṣeḍ*
tteḥša m.p. of *ḥša*
tteḥtaž m.p. of *ḥtaž*
tteḥḥef m.p. of *teḥḥef*
ttăɛbeṛ m.p. of *ɛbeṛ*
ttăɛmel m.p. of *ɛmel*
ttăɛqed m.p. of *ɛqed*
ttăɛṛef m.p. of *ɛṛef*
ttăɛṛek m.p. of *ɛṛek*
ttăɛṣem m.p. of *ɛṣem*
ttăɛṣeṛ m.p. of *ɛṣeṛ*
ttăɛteq m.p. of *ɛteq*
ttăɛṭa m.p. of *ɛṭa*
ttăɛṭeb m.p. of *ɛṭeb*
ttăɛzel m.p. of *ɛzel*
ttăɛžen m.p. of *ɛžen*
ttabex same as *ṭṭabex*
ttaleɛ same as *ṭṭaleɛ*
teṭbal, teṭbaḷ v.n. of *ṭebbel, ṭebbeḷ*
ttebbeq same as *ṭṭebbeq* (m.p. of *ṭebbeq*)
ttehheṛ same as *ṭṭehheṛ* (m.p. of *ṭehheṛ*)

teṭhiṛ 1. v.n. of *ṭehheṛ* 2. circumcision
tṭiyyeṛ same as *ṭṭiyyeṛ* (m.p. of *ṭiyyeṛ*)
teṭlaε v.n. of *ṭeḷḷăε*
tṭeḷḷeq same as *ṭṭeḷḷeq* (m.p. of *ṭeḷḷeq*)
tṭeḷḷeṣ same as *ṭṭeḷḷeṣ* (m.p. of *ṭeḷḷeṣ*)
teṭmaṛ v.n. of *ṭemmeṛ*
tṭemmen same as *ṭṭemmen* (m.p. of *ṭemmen*)
tṭemmeṣ same as *ṭṭemmeṣ* (m.p. of *ṭemmeṣ*)
tṭemmăε same as *ṭṭemmăε* (m.p. of *ṭemmăε*)
tṭenneb same as *ṭṭenneb* (m.p. of *ṭenneb*)
tṭenṭina same as *ṭenṭina* (n.i. of *ṭenṭen*)
tṭeqṭiq same as *ṭeqṭiq* (v.n. of *ṭeqṭeq*)
teṭṛab v.n. of *ṭeṛṛeb*
teṭṛaq v.n. of *ṭeṛṛeq*
teṭṛiba n.i. of *ṭeṛṛeb*
tṭeṛṛeb same as *ṭṭeṛṛeb* (m.p. of *ṭeṛṛeb*)
tṭeṛṛef same as *ṭṭeṛṛef* (m.p. of *ṭeṛṛef*)
tṭeṛṛeq same as *ṭṭeṛṛeq* (m.p. of *ṭeṛṛeq*)
tṭeṛṛeḥ same as *ṭṭeṛṛeḥ* (m.p. of *ṭeṛṛeḥ*)
tṭeṛṭiq same as *ṭeṛṭiq* (v.n. of *ṭeṛṭeq*)
tṭeṛṭiqa same as *ṭeṛṭiqa* (n.i. of *ṭeṛṭeq*)
tṭeṛṭeq same as *ṭṭeṛṭeq*
teṭṭawen Tetuan
teṭṭwan same as *teṭṭawen*
tṭufel same as *ṭṭufel*
tṭuwweḷ same as *ṭṭuwweḷ* (m.p. of *ṭuwweḷ*)
tṭuwweṛ same as *ṭṭuwweṛ* (m.p. of *ṭuwweṛ*)
teṭwaf v.n. of *ṭuwwef*
teṭwal v.n. of *ṭuwwel*
teṭwaš v.n. of *ṭuwweš*
teṭwaḥ v.n. of *ṭuwweḥ*
teṭwaε v.n. of *ṭuwwăε*
teṭwil v.n. of *ṭuwwel*
¶ *be-t-teṭwil* at length, in detail (as in telling a story)
teṭwiša pl. *-t* 1. n.i. of *ṭuwweš* 2. jet, stream (of liquid)
teṭyab 1. v.n. of *ṭiyyeb* 2. cooking, culinary art
teṭyaṛ v.n. of *ṭiyyeṛ*
teṭyaṛu 1. anger, rage 2. discontent, dissatisfaction
teṭyaš v.n. of *ṭiyyeš*
teṭyaḥ v.n. of *ṭiyyeḥ*
tṭeẓṭiẓ *same as* *ṭṭeẓṭiz* (v.n. of *ṭeẓṭeẓ*)
tub pl. *tyab, twab* cloth, material, fabric
tuba n.i. of *tab*
tuban 1. v.n. of *tab* 2. repentance, penitence
tubita pl. *-t, twabet* sateen, or similar cloth (not necessarily cotton)
tubix v.n. of *webbex*
tufri pl. *twafer* 1. barn 2. cave, grotto 3. basement, cellar
tuhăm pl. of *tehma, tohma*
tukal v.n. of *wekkel*
tulal n.u. *-a* wart, verruca
tulut pl. *-at* 1. third, third part 2. twenty minutes *hadi l-εăšṛa u-tulut.* It's twenty after ten.
tum n.u. *-a* (may also be coll.) garlic
tumi sg. of *twam* (which see)
tumun pl. *-at* eighth, eighth part
tunas v.n. of *wennes*
tunes 1. Tunisia 2. Tunis (city)
tunsi adj. pl. *-yen* n.pl. *twansa* Tunisian
tunya (coll. or sg.) pl. *-t* moth
tuqaf v.n. of *weqqef*
tuqala pl. of *tqil* 3 and 4
tuqaṛ 1. v.n. of *weqqeṛ* 2. respect, esteem
tuqiε 1. v.n. of *weqqăε* 2. signature
tuṛ pl. *tiran* 1. bull (male bovine) 2. ox
turad, turid v.n. of *werred*
tusax v.n. of *wessex*
tusaε v.n. of *wessăε*
tusixa pl. *-t* n.i. of *wessex*
tusuε pl. *-at* ninth, ninth part
tuṣal v.n. of *weṣṣel*
tuṣil pl. *twaṣel* receipt
tut n.u. *-a* 1. mulberry 2. mulberry tree
tutad v.n. of *wetted*
tutiya kind of sulfate compound used primarily for treating certain disorders of the eye
¶ *tutiya biḍa* zinc sulfate
¶ *tutiya ẓeṛqa* copper sulfate
tuwbix same as *tubix* (v.n. of *webbex*)
tuwliya pl. *-t* 1. v.n. and n.i. of *wella* 2. assignment, appointment (to a position)
tuwwel v.t. to put in order, to organize (mostly used by women)
tuwwež v.t. to crown (king, etc.)
tuxaṛ 1. v.n. of *wexxeṛ* 2. delay 3. postponement
tuzaε, tuziε 1. v.n. *of* *wezzăε* 2. distribution (of mail, etc.)
tužad, tužid 1. v.n. of *wežžed* 2. preparation(s)
tužiha pl. *-t* 1. n.i. of *wežžeh* 2. direction(s) (for how to do s.th.)
tuḥăf pl. of *toḥfa*
tuḥima pl. *-t* 1. n.i. of *tweḥḥem* 2. kind of birthmark
twab pl. of *tub*
twabet pl. of *tabut* and *tubita*
twabeε pl. of *tabeε* 2 and 3 (a.p. of *tbăε*)
twadd v.i. to give gifts to one another, to exchange gifts
twadeε v.i. to say good-by (to each other), to bid each other farewell
¶ *twadeε mεa* to get leave or permission from (a king, president)
twaḍeε v.i. 1. (*l-*) to humble oneself (before) 2. to condescend, to come down to another's level (no snobbery implied) *twaḍeε mεaya u-bqa ka-išṛăḥ-li.* He condescended to explain to me.
twafel pl. of *tafala*
twafeq v.i. to agree, to be in agreement
twager pl. of *tagra*
twala pl. of *tali* 2

twalef v.i. to become accustomed or used to one another
twam (pl.) twins
twanes v.i. 1. to keep each other company (to avoid loneliness, fear, etc.) 2. to keep oneself occupied or busy *šăƹlet r̦-r̦adyu u-bqat ka-ttwanes bih ƹla-ma ir̦žăƹ r̦aželha.* She turned on the radio, and kept herself occupied (with it) until her husband came home.
twansa n.pl. of *tunsi*
twarez pl. of *taraza*
twaṣel pl. of *tuṣil*
twaṭa v.i. to be or become levelled, even, flattened
twažeb same as *džaweb*
twažeh v.i. to face or confront one another (in physical position as well as in a contest, court, battle, etc.)
twaƹa v.i. to come to, to regain consciousness
twaƹed v.i. 1. to vow or promise (each other), to make a vow or promise (to each other) *twaƹedna baš nṣafr̦u žmiƹ.* We promised we'd travel together. 2. to make an appointment or date
twebbex m.p. of *webbex*
tweḍḍa v.i. 1. to perform one's ablutions (in preparation for praying) 2. to relieve oneself, to void and evacuate (always involving excrement, but not necessarily urine)
tweḍḍer̦ m.p. of *weḍḍer̦*
tweḍḍeƺ m.p. of *weḍḍeƺ*
tweffa v.i. to die, to expire (person, animal)
tewfiq 1. v.n. of *weffeq* 2. success
twefya v.n. of *weffa*
twegged m.p. of *wegged*
tewgiḍ v.n. of *wegged*
twеġġel m.p. of *weġġel*
twekkel m.p. of *wekkel*
¶ *twekkel ƹla* to rely on, to depend on (usually God)
twella 1. m.p. of *wella* 2. v.t. to take charge of, to take over (job, position)
twellef m.p. of *wellef*
¶ *twellef b-* to become used or accustomed to
twellăƹ b- to become fond of, to become keenly interested in (s.o., s.th.)
twelwil v.n. of *welwel*
twelya same as *tuwliya*
twennes 1. m.p. of *wennes* 2. same as *twanes*
tewqif v.n. of *weqqef*
tewqir̦ same as *tuqar̦*
tewqiƹ same as *tuqiƹ*
tweqqef m.p. of *weqqef*
¶ *tweqqef ƹla* 1. to need, to be in need of 2. to depend on
tewr̦a pl. *-t* revolution, revolt, rebellion
twerra m.p. of *werra*
twer̦r̦eḍ v.i. 1. to flush, to get or become red (face) 2. to acquire a healthy glow (face)
twerya n.i. and v.n. of *werra*
tewsixa pl. *-t* n.i. of *wessex*
tewsiƹ v.n. of *wessăƹ*
twessel l- to beg, to implore (s.o.)
twesseṭ v.i. 1. m.p. of *wesseṭ* 2. to mediate, to act as intermediary or go-between
twessex m.p. of *wessex*
twessăƹ v.i. 1. m.p. of *wessăƹ* 2. to go to the bathroom, rest room (polite expr.)
tweswis 1. v.n. of *weswes* 2. meticulousness, finicky scrupulousness
tweswes v.i. to be meticulous, finicky
tewṣil same as *tuṣil*
tweṣṣel m.p. of *weṣṣel*
¶ *tweṣṣel b-* to receive, to get (as a letter)
¶ *tweṣṣel* (*baš*) to (finally) manage (to)
tweṣya 1. v.n. of *weṣṣa* 2. counsel, advice 3. recommendation
twetted m.p. of *wetted*
twetter̦ m.p. of *wetter̦*
twetteš m.p. of *wetteš*
tewxir same as *tuxar̦*
¶ *bla tewxir* without fail, not later (than) *ƹṭini le-flus nhar̦ l-ƺădd bla tewxir!* Give me the money no later than Sunday!
tewxir̦ v.n. of *wexxer̦*
twexxer̦ m.p. of *wexxer̦*
tewziƹ same as *tuzaƹ*
twezzăƹ m.p. of *wezzăƹ*
tewžid same as *tužad, tužid*
twežžed m.p. of *wežžed*
twežžeh l- 1. to face, to face toward 2. to go or head toward, in the direction of 3. to address, to address oneself to (audience, God) 4. to favor, to support, to choose the side of (s.o.) 5. to choose, to follow (course of study)
twežžăƹ v.i. 1. to ail, to suffer pain 2. to have labor pains (woman)
tewƺid 1. v.n. of *weƺƺed* 2. unification, union 3. Islamic belief in the "oneness" of God, rather than a Godhead
tewƺima same as *tuƺima*
tweƺƺem v.i. to have cravings and strange desires (due to pregnancy)
tweƺƺeš 1. v.t. to miss *tweƺƺešnak bezzaf!* We really missed you! 2. v.t. to get homesick, nostalgic for 3. v.i. to become wild, savage
txa (m.) same as *text*
txaber̦ v.i. to confer, to have a discussion
txabeš v.i. to scratch or claw each other
txabeṭ v.i. to hit or strike each other (playfully or seriously)
txabeƹ pl. of *texbiƹa* 2
txala v.i. to withdraw or go aside in order to talk privately *mša txala huwa wiyah*

u-weṣṣel-lu le-xbaṛ. He went aside with him and told him the news.

¶ *txala mƐa* to take aside (i.e., to talk)

txalef v.i. **1.** to disagree, to be in disagreement **2.** to miss each other *Ɛmelna baš ntlaqaw f-le-mḥäṭṭa walakin txalefna.* We arranged to meet at the train station, but we missed each other. **3.** to be or become crossed, tangled, entwined *dima ka-inƐäs b-režlih metxalfin.* He always sleeps with his legs crossed.

txaḷeṭ v.i. to associate, to go around together, to hang around with each other *kan weld mʔeddeb walakin lemma bda ka-itxaḷeṭ mƐa ṣ-ṣlageṭ fsed.* He was a nice boy but when he began to associate with good-for-nothings he got corrupted.

¶ *txaḷeṭ l-* to get (s.th.) confused, to mix (s.th.) up ≠ *txaḷeṭ-li l-qamus mƐa had le-ktab.* I got the dictionary confused with this book. —*txaḷṭu-li le-ḥkayat dyal duk ž-žuž ktub.* I got the stories of the two books mixed up (in my mind).

txaref pl. of *texrifa* (n.i. of *xerref*)

txaṣem v.i. **1.** to quarrel, to have a falling out **2.** to be involved in a lawsuit

txaṭa v.i. to insult each other

txaṭef Ɛla **1.** to snatch or grab (s.th.) from each other *txaṭef huwa u-xutu Ɛäl l-Ɛineb.* He and his brothers snatched the grapes from each other. **2.** to snap up, to grab in a hurry *n-nuƐ ž-ždid dyal s-siyaṛat had l-Ɛam txaṭfu Ɛlih n-nas.* People have snapped up the new model cars this year.

txaṭeṛ v.i. to make a bet, to wager *txaṭṛet mƐah b-Ɛešrin derhem.* She bet him twenty dirhams.

txawa v.i. **1.** to become close friends (implying past enmity) *fṛanṣa u-ʔaḷmanya kanu Ɛädyan walakin bäƐd l-ḥäṛb txawaw.* France and Germany were enemies but after the war they became close friends. **2.** to resemble, to be similar (in color, size, etc.)

texbal v.n. of *xebbel*

txebba same as *txebbäƐ*

txebbel v.i. m.p. of *xebbel*

txebbeṛ v.i. m.p. of *xebbeṛ*

txebbeṭ v.i. **1.** to thrash or flail about *bqa itxebbeṭ mƐa l-ma u-fe-l-lexxeṛ ġṛaq.* He thrashed about in the water for a while and then finally sank. **2.** to do one's best *txebbeṭ mƐa le-mtiḥan walakin ma-žab-šay ḷḷah.* He did his best with the exam, but he flunked it.

txebbäƐ v.i. **1.** to hide *txebbäƐ menni.* He hid from me. **2.** to take shelter

¶ *txebbäƐ l-* to lie in wait for

texbil v.n. of *xebbel*

texbila pl. *-t* **1.** n.i. of *xebbel* **2.** labyrinth **3.** imbroglio

texbiƐa **1.** n.i. of *xebbäƐ* **2.** pl. *-t, txabeƐ* (dim. *txibƐa*) hiding place

¶ *be-t-texbiƐa* secretly, furtively

txebya v.n. and n.i. of *txebba* and *xebba* (same as *txebbäƐ* and *xebbäƐ*)

texdam v.n. of *xeddem*

texfaf v.n. of *xeffef*

txeffef m.p. of *xeffef*

texfif v.n. of *xeffef*

txibƐa dim. of *texbiƐa* **2**

teʔxir same as *tuxaṛ* and *tewxiṛ*

texḷaṭ v.n. of *xeḷḷeṭ*

texḷiṭa n.i. of *xeḷḷeṭ*

txella Ɛla **1.** to renounce, to give up (throne, position) **2.** to abandon, to leave (i.e., no longer take the responsibility for)

txeḷḷeṣ m.p. of *xeḷḷeṣ*

¶ *txeḷḷeṣ men* **1.** to punish **2.** to get revenge on (s.o.), to get back at (s.o.)

txeḷḷeṭ m.p. of *xeḷḷeṭ*

¶ *txeḷḷeṭ l-* to confuse, to get (s.o.) all mixed up *s-swaret kollhom txeḷḷṭu-lu.* All those keys confused him (he didn't know which one to use).

txelläƐ m.p. of *xelläƐ*

txelwa v.i. to go somewhere to be alone (for any reason)

txelxil v.n. of *xelxel*

txelxel v.i. m.p. of *xelxel*

¶ *txelxel f-Ɛäqluᶲ* to lose one's mind, to become deranged

txelya v.n. and n.i. of *xella*

texma pl. *-t* (attack of) indigestion, gastritis

texmal v.n. of *xemmel*

texmam, texmim v.n. of *xemmem*

texmima n.i. of *xemmem*

texmisa pl. *-t* share-cropping job (on the basis of one-fifth of the crop)

txennet m.p. of *xennet*

txenxiṛ v.n. of *xenxeṛ*

texṛab v.n. of *xeṛṛeb*

texraf v.n. of *xerref*

texraž v.n. of *xerrež*

txeṛbiq v.n. of *xeṛbeq*

txerbiš v.n. of *xerbeš*

txerbeš m.p. of *xerbeš*

txerdil v.n. of *xerdel*

texrib v.n. of *xerreb*

texrifa pl. *txaref* n.i. of *xerref*

texriž v.n. of *xerrež*

texriža n.i. of *xerrež*

txermiz v.n. of *xermez*

txerreb **1.** m.p. of *xerreb* **2.** to fall into ruin, to deteriorate

txeṛṛeṣ m.p. of *xeṛṛeṣ*

txerrež **1.** m.p. of *xerrež* **2.** to graduate (from school)

txeṛxiṛ v.n. of *xeṛxeṛ*

texṣaṛ v.n. of *xeṣṣeṛ* and *txeṣṣeṛ*
texṣiṣ **1.** v.n. of *xeṣṣeṣ* and *txeṣṣeṣ* **2.** specialization
txeṣṣ men to need, to be in need of
txeṣṣeṛ m.p. of *xeṣṣeṛ*
txeṣṣeṣ v.i. **1.** m.p. of *xeṣṣeṣ* **2.** to specialize
txeššen v.i. **1.** to get or become big, large (i.e., *xšin*) **2.** to get or become rough, coarse (in texture)
¶ *txeššen ɛla* to bully, to treat roughly (by virtue of one's size)
txešxiš v.n. of *xešxeš*
text dregs, lees
txettel v.i. to sneak, to walk on tiptoe
¶ *txettel f-* (or *bin*) to weave in and out, to elbow through (a crowd)
¶ *txettlu režlih*$^{\phi}$ to stagger ≠, to reel ≠ (as a drunk)
txetten m.p. of *xetten*
textiṭ v.n. of *xeṭṭeṭ*
txeṭṭa v.t. to step over (as a sleeping dog)
¶ *txeṭṭa ɛla* same as *txeṭṭa*
txeṭṭeṛ v.i. to make an appearance, to show up, to drop in
texwaḍ v.n. of *xewweḍ*
texwaf v.n. of *xewwef*
texwaṛ v.n. of *xewweṛ*
texwiḍ v.n. of *xewweḍ*
txewweḍ v.i. m.p. of *xewweḍ*
txewwex v.i. **1.** same as *xewwex* **2.** m.p. of *xewwex*
texyam v.n. of *xiyyem*
texyaṛ v.n. of *xeyyeṛ*
txeyyel l- to imagine, to believe, to think ≠ *txeyyel-li belli ɛṭitu flus le-kra l-ʔusbuɛ lli daz.* I thought I gave him the rent money last week.
txeyyeṛ v.t. to choose, to pick, to select
¶ *txeyyeṛ f-* to choose between (or among)
txezzez v.i. **1.** to become covered with moss or lichen **2.** to become covered with patina or oxide (bronze, copper)
¶ *txezzez f-* to get or have command or mastery of (s.th.), to have or get a thorough knowledge of (s.th.) *ɛašet f-ʔamirika xmeṣṭašel ɛam u-txezzzet f-l-ingliza.* She lived in America fifteen years and got a thorough knowledge of English.
tyab pl. of *tub*
tyesser m.p. of *yesser*
¶ *tyesser l-* **1.** to be able, to be possible for (s.o.) **2.** to be obtainable or available *ila tyessru-li le-flus nešri siyaṛa ždida.* If I get the money I'll buy a new car.
tzad same as *dzad*
tezfat v.n. of *zeffet*
tezlaž, tezliž v.n. of *zellež*
tezmam v.n. of *zemmem*
teẓmaṛ, teẓmiṛ v.n. of *ẓemmeṛ*
teẓṭiṭ v.n. of *ẓeṭṭeṭ*
tezwag v.n. of *zuwweg*
tezwal v.n. of *zuwwel*
tezwaq **1.** v.n. of *zuwweq* **2.** design (artistic) **3.** decoration, ornamentation
tezwig v.n. of *zuwweg*
teẓwiṛ v.n. of *ẓuwweṛ*
tezyan **1.** v.n. of *ziyyen* **2.** decoration, ornamentation, embellishment **3.** improvement (in health)
teẓyaṛ v.n. of *ẓiyyeṛ*
tezyat **1.** v.n. of *ziyyet* **2.** lubrication
teẓyaṭ v.n. of *ẓiyyeṭ*
tezyin same as *tezyan*
teẓyiṛa pl. *-t* **1.** n.i. of *ẓiyyeṛ* **2.** financial strait(s)
tezzara pl. *-t, dzazer* **1.** apron (as for the kitchen) **2.** loincloth, or s.th. used as such
tezzer v.i. **1.** to put on an apron **2.** to put on a loincloth or s.th. used as such
¶ *tezzer b-* to use as an apron or loincloth
težbad v.n. of *žebbed*
težbaṛ v.n. of *žebbeṛ*
teždad, teždid **1.** v.n. of *žedded* **2.** renovation, restoration
težfaf, težfif v.n. of *žeffef*
težfifa pl. *-t* n.i. of *žeffef*
težlad v.n. of *želled*
težmad v.n. of *žemmed*
težnina n.i. of *džennen*
težnis **1.** v.n. of *žennes* **2.** naturalization (citizen)
težṛab, težṛib v.n. of *žeṛṛeb*
težriba pl. *-t, tažarib* **1.** attempt, try **2.** experiment
težwid v.n. of *žuwwed*
težyaf **1.** v.n. of *žiyyef* **2.** strangulation **3.** suffocation
težyar, težyir v.n. of *žiyyer*
tožžaṛ pl. of *tažer* **1**
tɛabb v.i. to love one another (usually in the non-romantic sense)
tɛada v.i. to get or be placed next to one another
tɛafeḍ ɛla **1.** to take care of *tɛafeḍ ɛla ṣeɛɛtek!* Take care of your health. **2.** to maintain (in good condition)
tɛaged same as *tɛaqed*
tɛaka v.i. to tell each other stories
tɛakem v.i. **1.** to participate in a lawsuit, to be involved in a legal action (in court) **2.** to be tried, to be on trial (perfect tense may imply only the passing of judgment)
tɛalef v.i. to become allied, to form an alliance
tɛama v.i. to join forces, to gang up *huwa u-xah tɛamaw ɛliya.* He and his brother ganged up on me.
tɛamel v.i. to be on good terms, to get along
tɛann v.i. to become close to one another (sympathetically)

tḥaqed v.i. to hate each other, to bear malice or ill will toward one another
tḥaṛeb v.i. **1.** to war, to be at war **2.** to engage in combat
tḥaseb v.i. to settle accounts (together, usually financial)
tḥata pl. of *teḥti* and *teḥtiya*
tḥaz same as *ttḥaz*
tḥaža v.i. **1.** to tell each other stories **2.** to propose riddles to one another
tḥăbbeb v.i. **1.** to become granular **2.** to break out (as with sores)
¶ *tḥăbbeb l-* to try to gain favor with, to attempt to ingratiate oneself with (s.o.)
teḥdad v.n. of *ḥădded*
tḥădd m.p. of *ḥădd*
tḥăddeq v.i. **1.** m.p. of *ḥăddeq* **2.** to acquire knowledge or ability through study or experience
tḥăddet v.i. to talk, to converse
teḥdid v.n. of *ḥădded*
teḥdiqa n.i. of *ḥăddeq*
teḥḍan **1.** v.n. of *ḥăḍḍen* **2.** incubation (of eggs)
tḥăḍḍeq same as *tḥăddeq*
tḥăḍḍeṛ v.i. **1.** m.p. of *ḥăḍḍeṛ* **2.** to move to the city (and consequently adopt city ways)
teḥḍiqa n.i. of *ḥăḍḍeq* (same as *ḥăddeq*)
teḥḍiṛa n.i. of *ḥăḍḍeṛ*
toḥfa pl. *-t, tuḥăf* precious; of rare quality, beauty or excellence (object, person) (n. used attributively) *šraw waḥed ḍ-ḍaṛ toḥfa.* They bought a precious house. —*le-ktab lli qṛit toḥfa.* The book I read was an excellent one. —*toḥfa l-bent be-mmen dzuwwež.* He got married to a jewel of a girl.
teḥfaf v.n. of *ḥăffef*
teḥfif v.n. of *ḥăffef*
tḥăfya v.n. of *ḥăffa*
tḥimeṛ v.i. to behave in a stupid or ignorant manner, to act like a jackass
tḥăkk m.p. of *ḥăkk*
tḥekkek v.i. to get nervously frustrated (due to one's inability to do s.th.)
¶ *tḥekkek* ʕ*la* to rub against (s.o., s.th.)
teḥlal, teḥlil v.n. of *ḥellel*
teḥliqa n.i. of *ḥălleq*
tḥăll v.i. **1.** m.p. of *ḥăll* **2.** to open **3.** to melt
tḥălla m.p. of *ḥălla*
tḥălya v.n. and n.i. of *ḥălla*
teḥmaṣ v.n. of *ḥămmeṣ*
teḥmila pl. *-t* n.i. of *ḥămmel*
teḥmima pl. *-t* n.i. of *ḥămmem*
teḥmiṛa mild red pepper, paprika (powdered)
tḥămmeḍ v.i. to get or become sour
¶ *tḥămmeḍ* ʕ*la* **1.** to pester, to bother **2.** to give a hard time to (s.o.)
tḥămmel **1.** m.p. of *ḥămmel* **2.** v.t. to tolerate, to stand for
¶ *tḥămmel b-* to take charge of (responsibility, work, problem, etc.)
¶ *tḥămmel l-mesʔuliya* (*dyal*) to take (the) responsibility (for)
¶ *tḥămmel ṣ-ṣayaṛ* (*d-*) to afford the expense (of), to be able to pay (for)
tḥămmem m.p. of *ḥămmem*
tḥămmeq v.i. **1.** to act stupid, to play the fool **2.** to play innocent
tḥămmeṛ m.p. of *ḥămmeṛ*
teḥnaṭ v.n. of *ḥănneṭ*
teḥniš v.n. of *ḥănneš*
tḥenya v.n. of *ḥănna*
tḥănẓiẓa pl. *-t* n.i. of *ḥănẓeẓ*
tḥănḥin v.n. of *ḥănḥen*
teḥqiq v.n. of *ḥăqqeq*
¶ *be-t-teḥqiq!* (?) Really! (?)
tḥăqqeq m.p. of *ḥăqqeq*
¶ *tḥăqqeq b-* (or *men*) to verify, to confirm
teḥṛab v.n. of *ḥăṛṛeb*
teḥraf v.n. of *ḥărref*
teḥrak v.n. of *ḥărrek*
teḥṛam v.n. of *ḥăṛṛem*
teḥṛaṛ v.n. of *ḥăṛṛeṛ*
teḥṛaš v.n. of *ḥăṛṛeš*
teḥṛiḍ v.n. of *ḥăṛṛeḍ*
teḥrifa pl. *-t* **1.** n.i. of *ḥărref* **2.** curve, turn (road)
teḥrik v.n. of *ḥărrek*
teḥrim, teḥṛim **1.** v.n. of *ḥăṛṛem* **2.** prohibition, interdiction, ban
teḥṛiṛ v.n. of *ḥăṛṛeṛ*
teḥṛiṛa pl. *-t* **1.** n.i. of *ḥăṛṛeṛ* **2.** vacation (from school)
teḥṛiš v.n. of *ḥăṛṛeš*
tḥăṛṛeb v.i. **1.** m.p. of *ḥăṛṛeb* **2.** to learn, to acquire experience
tḥărref m.p. of *ḥărref*
¶ *tḥărref be-l-xenžeṛ* to put on or don the *xenžeṛ*
tḥărrek v.i. **1.** m.p. of *ḥărrek* **2.** to move (right) along, to progress
tḥăṛṛeṛ m.p. of *ḥăṛṛeṛ*
teḥsin v.n. of *ḥessen*
teḥsina pl. *-t* **1.** n.i. of *ḥessen* **2.** haircut **3.** shave (beard)
tḥessen v.i. **1.** m.p. of *ḥessen* **2.** to improve, to get or become better
teḥṣil v.n. of *ḥeṣṣeḷ*
teḥṣin v.n. of *ḥeṣṣen*
teḥšaš v.n. of *tḥăššeš*
teḥšiša n.i. of *tḥăššeš*
tḥeššem m.p. of *ḥeššem* and *tḥeššem*
tḥăššeš v.i. to use hashish
teḥt **1.** under, beneath, underneath *xebbit l-beẓtam dyali teḥt le-mxedda.* I hid my wallet under the pillow. —*šeddha men*

teḥt. Hold it by the bottom (i.e., from underneath). 2. below *weṣlet ḍaṛažt l-ḥaṛaṛa l-xemsa teḥt ṣ-ṣifṛ.* The temperature has gone to five below zero.

¶ *l-teḥt* 1. underneath, down below (adv.) 2. downstairs *ṛah l-teḥt.* He's downstairs.

¶ *teḥt men* same as *teḥt*

teḥtani pl. *-yen* (adj.) 1. lower, bottom 2. downstairs *l-bareḥ bett fe-l-bit t-teḥtani.* I slept in the downstairs room last night.

teḥtat v.n. of *ḥettet*

teḥti pl. *-yen, tḥata* downstairs (adj.)

teḥtiya pl. *-t, tḥata* kind of gown-like women's undergarment

tḥeṭṭ m.p. of *ḥeṭṭ*

teḥwal v.n. of *ḥăwwel*

teḥwam v.n. of *ḥăwwem*

teḥwil v.n. of *ḥăwwel*

teḥwiṣa pl. *-t* n.i. of *ḥăwweṣ*

tḥăwwel m.p. of *ḥăwwel*

tḥăwwež l- to be in need of

teḥyad v.n. of *ḥăyyed*

teḥyaṛ v.n. *ḥeyyeṛ* and *tḥeyyeṛ*

teḥyaḥ v.n. of *ḥeyyeḥ*

teḥyiṛa n.i. of *ḥeyyeṛ*

tḥăyyed m.p. of *ḥăyyed*

tḥeyyel ɛla to use trickery on, to (attempt to) outfox (s.o., an animal)

¶ *tḥeyyel fe-l-mešya* to walk stealthily (so as not to be noticed)

tḥeyyeṛ v.i. 1. m.p. of *ḥeyyeṛ* 2. to be puzzled, perplexed 3. to become entranced, to go into a trance (especially in ecstatic dancing) 4. to be boiled (egg) 5. to be cooked rare (meat)

teḥẓiṛ v.n. of *ḥeẓẓeṛ*

tḥeẓẓem v.i. 1. m.p. of *ḥeẓẓem* 2. to prepare to do s.th., to "roll up one's sleeves" *tḥeẓẓem l-le-mši* or *tḥeẓẓem baš imši.* He prepared to go.

teḥžiṛ v.n. of *ḥežžeṛ*

tḥežžeb v.i. to go into seclusion

teḥḥef 1. v.t. to decorate 2. v.i. to dress up *teḥḥfet l-l-ɛeṛs.* She dressed up for the wedding.

teḥḥef l- to dress (s.o.) up *teḥḥef le-wladu nhaṛ l-ɛid u-xrež itsara huwa wiyahom.* He dressed up his boys for the holiday and they all went out for a stroll.

tɛaben pl. of *toɛban*

tɛabes pl. of *tăɛbisa*

tɛabeẓ v.i. 1. to have a fight (physical) 2. to wrestle (informally or professionally)

tɛada v.i. 1. m.p. of *ɛada* 2. to have a falling out, to stop speaking to one another

tɛadel v.i. 1. to balance, to become balanced or in equilibrium 2. to become equal, to come to be on an equal basis

tɛaḍḍ v.i. to bite each other, to snap at each other

tɛafa (*men*) to recover (from, to become cured (of)

tɛafer (*mɛa*) 1. to struggle (with), to have a hard time (of) (a problem, a difficult book, etc.) 2. to compete (against, with)

tɛahed v.i. to make an agreement or pact, to form an alliance

tɛala f. *tɛali* pl. *tɛalu* impv. of *ža* (primarily country usage)

tɛala ɛla to outbid (s.o.)

tɛaleb pl. of *tăɛleb*

tɛaleq pl. of *tăɛliq* 2

tɛalež v.i. 1. to recover, to become cured 2. to eat well or properly (i.e., healthful foods) 3. to eat elegantly, richly

tɛama v.i. 1. to feign blindness 2. to pretend not to have seen s.th.

¶ *tɛama ɛla* to pretend not to have seen (s.o., s.th.), to close one's eyes to (s.th.)

tɛaned mɛa 1. to try to finish or do all at one time (s.th. that should be done little by little) 2. to compete against or with (race, business)

tɛaneq v.i. to embrace or hug each other

tɛaqeb m.p. of *ɛaqeb*

tɛaqed v.i. 1. to make an agreement or pact 2. to enter into a contract 3. to conclude a deal or transaction

tɛaṛef v.i. 1. to meet or get acquainted 2. to know one another

tɛaṛek v.i. to have a fight

tɛaṛež pl. of *tăɛṛiža*

tɛašer v.i. 1. to associate with each other, to pal around 2. to live together

tɛaṭa 1. to give reciprocally to each other (e.g. gifts). 2. (*l-*) to give oneself up (to), to devote oneself (to) (some activity)

tɛawed m.p. of *ɛawed*

tɛawen v.i. to aid or help each other, to give one another assistance

tɛaweṭ v.i. 1. m.p. of *ɛaweṭ* 2. to sit up straight (in a chair)

tɛayen v.i. to seem (to think, to believe ≠) *tɛayen-li žat.* I believe (it seems to me) she has arrived.

tɛayer v.i. to insult one another, to hurl insults at one another

tɛayeṭ v.i. to play a card game called *ɛăyṭa*

tɛăb v.i. (v.n. *taɛăb*) to get tired, fatigued

tăɛban pl. *-in* tired, worn out, fatigued

toɛban pl. *tɛaben* venomous snake

tăɛbas, tăɛbis v.n. of *ɛăbbes*

tɛăbbed v.i. 1. to pray (implies more devotion than *ṣeḷḷa*) 2. to consecrate oneself to religious devotion

tăɛbisa pl. *-t, tɛabes* 1. n.i. of *ɛăbbes* 2. grimace

tăɛdab 1. v.n. of *ɛăddeb* 2. torture, torment 3. suffering
tɛădd m.p. of *ɛădd*
tɛădda v.t. to pass, to go beyond, to go over (limit, boundary)
¶ *tɛădda ɛla* 1. to attack (usually without warning and reason) 2. to persecute, to oppress 3. to violate, to infringe on the rights of 4. to trespass on (one's property) 5. to appropriate the property of (s.o.)
tɛăddeb v.i. 1. m.p. of *ɛăddeb* 2. to work hard, to drudge 3. to have difficulty, to have a hard time (in doing s.th.) 4. to suffer
tɛăddel m.p. of *ɛăddel*
tăɛdib same as *tăɛdab*
tăɛdil v.n. of *ɛăddel*
tɛădya n.i. of *tɛădda*
tăɛḍim 1. v.n. of *ɛăḍḍem* 2. praise, honor (of God) 3. veneration, glorification (of God)
tɛăfrit skill, exceptional ability, talent
tɛăfret v.i. 1. to become skillful, to gain ability 2. to put on a front or show (of great ability or intelligence actually nonexistent)
tɛăggez v.i. 1. to stretch (one's muscles) 2. to be lazy, indolent
tɛiṛža dim. of *tăɛṛiža*
tɛis pl. *-in* deadly, fatal
tăɛkal v.n. of *ɛăkkel*
tăɛkaṛ v.n. of *ɛăkkeṛ*
tăɛkila pl. *-t* n.i. of *ɛăkkel*
tɛăkkel m.p. of *ɛăkkel*
tɛăkkes 1. to be stubborn, to be contrary 2. to not work, to break down (car, pen, etc.)
tɛăkkez to walk with a crutch
tăɛlaf v.n. of *ɛăllef*
tăɛlaq v.n. of *ɛălleq*
tăɛleb pl. *tɛaleb* 1. fox 2. jackal
tăɛlim 1. v.n. of *ɛăllem* 2. teaching, instruction 3. education
¶ *wiẓaṛat t-tăɛlim* Ministry (Department) of Education
tăɛliq 1. v.n. of *ɛălleq* 2. pl. *tɛaleq* comment, commentary
tɛălla m.p. of *ɛălla*
tɛăllem v.t. to learn, to receive instruction in
tɛălleq m.p. of *ɛălleq*
¶ *tɛălleq b-* 1. to have a connection with, to concern, to be relative to 2. to appeal to (for assistance, intercession)
tɛălya v.n. of *ɛălla*
tăɛmaṛ, tăɛmiṛ v.n. of *ɛămmeṛ*
tăɛmiṛa n.i. of *ɛămmeṛ*
tɛămmed v.t. to do intentionally, on purpose, with premeditation *tɛămmed l-qetl dyalu.* He killed him on purpose.
tɛămmeṛ m.p. of *ɛămmeṛ*
tăɛnaq v.n. of *ɛănneq*
tɛănfiž v.n. of *ɛănfež* and *tɛănfež*
tɛănfež m.p. of *ɛănfež*
tɛăngiṛa n.i. of *ɛăngeṛ*
tɛăngeṛ v.i. 1. to cock one's headdress forward and to the side 2. to put on airs of importance
tăɛniq v.n. of *ɛănneq*
tăɛniqa pl. *-t* hug, embrace
tɛănṣeṛ m.p. of *ɛănṣeṛ*
tăɛqad, tăɛqid v.n. of *ɛăqqed*
tɛăqqed m.p. of *ɛăqqed*
tɛăqqel v.i. to become wise or wiser, (more) reasonable
tăɛṛam v.n. of *ɛăṛṛem*
tɛăṛbiṭ v.n. of *ɛăṛbeṭ*
tăɛṛif 1. v.n. of *ɛăṛṛef* 2. definition (of a word, etc.) 3. introduction, presentation (of s.o., s.th.) 4. identity
¶ *waṛaqat* (or *weṛqet*) *t-tăɛṛif* identification card
tăɛṛiqa n.i. of *ɛăṛṛeq*
tăɛṛiža pl. *tɛaṛež* (dim. *tɛṛža*) kind of long, clay drum of one head
tɛăṛra v.i. 1. m.p. of *ɛăṛra* 2. to undress, to strip 3. to become broke or penniless, to run out of funds
tɛăṛṛeḍ l- 1. to meet (s.o. in some way) 2. to go to meet or receive (s.o. at his arrival) 3. to stand in the way of (s.o.) 4. to oppose, to be against 5. to rob (s.o.) on the road or highway 6. to be exposed to (danger, etc.)
tɛăṛṛef m.p. of *ɛăṛṛef*
¶ *tɛăṛṛef ɛla* or *b-* 1. to meet, to be introduced to (s.o.) 2. to get to know, to become acquainted with
tɛăṛṛem v.i. m.p. of *ɛăṛṛem*
tɛăṛya v.n. of *ɛăṛra*
tɛăssel v.i. 1. m.p. of *ɛăssel* 2. to become (too) sweet 3. to get or become syrupy
¶ *tɛăssel fe-l-heḍṛa* 1. to speak very slowly (like pouring cold molasses) 2. to use highfalutin language (often to the unintended amusement of others)
tăɛṣaṛ v.n. of *ɛăṣṣeṛ*
tɛăṣṣeb v.i. 1. to become stiff, rigid 2. to be or become stubborn, unyielding, inflexible
tɛăṣṣeṛ v.i. 1. m.p. of *ɛăṣṣeṛ* 2. to act as if one has to go to the bathroom badly 3. to strain and grunt while evacuating (in the bathroom)
tăɛšiṛ 1. v.n. of *ɛăššeṛ* 2. tithing, tithes
tɛăšša v.i. to eat or have supper, dinner (evening meal)
tɛăttel m.p. of *ɛăttel*
tăɛṭal 1. v.n. of *ɛăṭṭeḷ* and *tɛăṭṭeḷ* 2. delay
tăɛṭaṛ v.n. of *ɛăṭṭeṛ*
tɛăṭṭeḷ v.i. 1. m.p. of *ɛăṭṭeḷ* 2. to be late
tɛăṭṭeṛ m.p. of *ɛăṭṭeṛ*
tɛuqeb v.i. to become (an) invalid, infirm
tɛušira pl. *-t* 1. vacation, holiday (from

school) **2.** amount paid to the instructor (Koranic school)
tƐušer v.i. to have or take a vacation or holiday (from school, work)
tăƐwaḍ v.n. of *Ɛăwweḍ*
tăƐwag v.n. of *Ɛăwweg*
tăƐwal v.n. of *Ɛăwwel*
tăƐwaṛ v.n. of *Ɛăwweṛ*
tăƐwaž v.n. of *Ɛăwwež*
tăƐwiḍ pl. *-at* compensation, reimbursement, indemnification
tăƐwiga pl. *-t* **1.** howl (wolf, etc.) **2.** crow (of rooster)
tăƐwiža pl. *-t* **1.** n.i. of *Ɛăwwež* **2.** curve, bend, turn
tƐăwwed v.i. **1.** m.p. of *Ɛăwwed* **2.** to get or become hard, stiff, brittle (usually wood, bread) **3.** to say the expr. *aƐudu bi-llah*
¶ *tƐăwwed Ɛla* to become accustomed or used to
tƐăwweḍ m.p. of *Ɛăwweḍ*
tƐăwwež **1.** m.p. of *Ɛăwwež* **2.** to bend, to flex
** *mṛati tƐăwwžet Ɛliya.* My wife has turned her back on me (i.e., become cold).
tăƐyab v.n. of *Ɛăyyeb*
tăƐyaṛ v.n. of *Ɛăyyeṛ*
tăƐyaṭ v.n. of *Ɛăyyeṭ*
tăƐyin **1.** v.n. of *Ɛăyyen* **2.** appointment, designation, assignment **3.** nomination
tƐăyyeb v.i. **1.** m.p. of *Ɛăyyeb* **2.** to become (an) invalid, infirm
tƐăyyen m.p. of *Ɛăyyen*
tăƐzam v.n. of *Ɛăzzem*
tăƐzaz v.n. of *tƐăzzez*
tăƐzim v.n. of *Ɛăzzem*
tăƐziz v.n. of *tƐăzzez*
tƐăzya pl. *-t* **1.** n.i. of *Ɛăzza* **2.** condolence(s)
tƐăzzez Ɛla to give a hard time to
tƐăžžeb (*f-*) **1.** to be shocked or stunned (at) **2.** to marvel or wonder (at)
tăƐƐăb v.t. to tire, to weary, to fatigue

Ṭ

ṭab iṭib v.i. (v.n. *ṭyab*) **1.** to cook *qeššeṛ le-bṭaṭa Ɛla-ma iṭib l-lḥăm.* Peel the potatoes while the meat is cooking. **2.** to ripen, to become ripe **3.** boil *had neṣṣ saƐa u-l-beqṛež ka-iṭib.* The kettle has been boiling for half an hour. **4.** to accept, to agree (after showing some opposition) *bqaw ixedmuh ḥetta ṭab baš išriha mennhom.* They worked on him until he (finally) agreed to buy it from them.
** *ma-qal-lhom la-ṭabet wa-la-ttḥeṛqet.* He didn't tell them a word (about it).
¶ *ṭab qelbu*$^{\phi}$ (*b-*) to be fed up (with) ≠, to be sick (of) ≠ *ṭab-li qelbi be-š-ška dyalha.* I'm sick of her complaining.
ṭaba tobacco (e.g. for a pipe)
ṭabaġa snuff
ṭabaˀiƐ pl. of *ṭabiƐa*
ṭabaqa pl. *-t* **1.** classroom *had l-medṛaṣa fiha xemsin ṭabaqa.* This school has fifty classrooms. **2.** grade (school) *š-men ṭabaqa ka-tqeṛṛi had l-Ɛam?* What grade are you teaching this year? **3.** class (social)
ṭabaqu snuff
ṭabašir chalk *had ṭ-ṭabašir ḥṛeš bezzaf f-le-ktaba.* This chalk is too hard to write with.
¶ *qṭib de-ṭ-ṭabašir* piece of chalk
ṭabayeƐ pl. of *ṭabiƐa*
ṭabiƐa pl. *-t, ṭabaˀiƐ, ṭabayeƐ* **1.** nature *Ɛadad de-l-Ɛulama Ɛămlu ḍiṛasat Ɛăl ṭ-ṭabiƐa.* Many scientists have made studies of nature. —*ġiṛ m̄m̄u lli Ɛaṛfa-lu ṭ-ṭabiƐa dyalu.* His mother is the only one who knows his nature. **2.** scenery, landscape
¶ *men ṭabiƐt l-ḥal, b-ṭabiƐt l-ḥal* naturally, of course
ṭabiƐi pl. *-yen* **1.** natural *had l-fakya de-š-šmaƐ tqul ṭabiƐiya.* This wax fruit looks natural. **2.** plain, simple *ka-išri ktir-ši l-lbas ṭ-ṭabiƐi.* He buys mostly plain clothes. —*ka-ibġiha li-ˀennaha bent ṭabiƐiya.* He likes her because she's a simple girl. **3.** naturally, of course *ṭabiƐi* (*baš*) *idafeƐ Ɛăl l-ḥuquq dyalu.* Of course he should stand up for his rights. **4.** naturally, without affection *ma-ka-nḍenn-š ka-itkellem ṭabiƐi.* I don't think he talks naturally. **5.** plainly, simply *dima ka-telbes ṭabiƐi.* She always dresses plainly.
¶ *men ṭ-ṭabiƐi* (*baš*) . . . it's natural (that) . . .
¶ (*Ɛilm*) *ṭ-ṭabiƐiyat* the natural sciences
ṭabla pl. *-t, ṭwabel* same as *ṭebla*
ṭabliya pl. *-t* apron
ṭablu pl. *-yat* **1.** blackboard **2.** switchboard (telephone, electric) **3.** panel, pegboard (as one for hanging tools or utensils)
ṭabeq v.t. to compare, to check, to match *men băƐd-ma ṭabeqt le-klam lli qal-li mƐa le-bṛa dyalu žbeṛt koll-ši kdub.* After I checked what he told me against his letter I found everything was a lie.
ṭabeq pl. *ṭwabeq* **1.** armpit **2.** forequarter, front part of a half of mutton, veal, etc.
ṭabăƐ pl. *ṭwabeƐ* (dim. *ṭwibeƐ*) **1.** stamp (e.g., rubber stamp) **2.** seal *le-bṛa Ɛliha*

ṭ-ṭabăʕ ṛ-ṛesmi. The letter bears the official seal. **3.** stamp (stamping mark)

ṭaf iṭuf v.i. (v.n. *ṭufan*) to walk around the Kaaba during the performance of the Pilgrimage at Mecca

¶ *ṭaf f-* to go around *n-nhaṛ kollu u-huwa ka-iṭuf f-le-mdina.* He's been going around town all day.

¶ *ṭaf ʕla* to circle *ʕăšṛa de-l-meṛṛat ṭafu ʕăl s-sehriž.* They circled the pool ten times.

ṭagiya pl. *-t, ṭwagi* (dim. *ṭwigya*) knit skull-cap (usually worn by men)

ṭaġi a.p. of *ṭġa*

ṭaheṛ pl. *-in* pure, virtuous (morally, spiritually)

ṭaʔifa same as *ṭayfa*

ṭal iṭul v.i. **1.** to last *s-sefṛa ṭalet telt iyam.* The trip lasted three days. **2.** to stay *ʕăṛdu ʕlih ʕla yumayn u-ṭal ʕăndhom šheṛ.* They invited him for two days and he stayed a month. **3.** to stretch out, to seem long, to drag *l-medṛaṣa ka-ṭṭul mnin ka-tqeṛṛeb l-ʕoṭla de-ṣ-ṣif.* School drags when the summer vacation approaches.

¶ *l-lil u-ma-ṭal* all night long

¶ *n-nhaṛ u-ma-ṭal* all day long

¶ *ṭal z-zman aw qṣaṛ* sooner or later

¶ a.p. *ṭayel* pl. *-in* **1.** stale *had l-xobz ṭayel.* This bread is stale. **2.** spoiled, not fresh *le-ḥlib lli žebti ṭayel.* The milk you brought is not fresh.

ṭalab pl. *-at* **1.** v.n. of *ṭleb* **2.** request **3.** application *ma-zal ma-ṣafṭet ṭ-ṭalab dyalha.* She hasn't sent in her application yet.

¶ *neffed ṭalab* to respond to a request *dima ka-ineffed-lna ṭalabatna.* He always responds to our requests.

¶ *qeddem ṭalab,* or *ʕmel ṭalab* to apply, to make an application *ġad-nqeddem ṭ-ṭalab ʕla ši-xedma.* I'm going to apply for a job.

ṭalaba pl. of *ṭaleb* 1 (a.p. of *ṭleb*)

ṭaleb a.p. of *ṭleb* **1.** to read *ma-zal ma-ṭaleʕt had le-ktab.* I haven't read this book yet. **2.** to study, to review (for exam) *ka-ixeṣṣni telt iyyam baš nṭaleʕ d-duṛuṣ dyali.* I need three days in order to review my lessons. **3.** to tell, to let know, to inform, to disclose to *škun ṭaleʕ l-bulis ʕla dak d-debza?* Who informed the police about that fight?

ṭanga pl. *ṭwaneg* earring

ṭanža Tangier

ṭanžawi adj. pl. *-yen* n.pl. *hel ṭanža* native to Tangier

ṭanži adj. pl. *-yen* same as *ṭanžawi*

ṭaq iṭiq b- to be able to stand *ma-ka-iṭiq-š be-l-xedma mʕahom.* He can't stand working with them. —*ma-ka-nebqa-š nṭiq b-had le-mdina mnayn ka-iṣxon l-ḥal.* I just can't stand this town when it gets hot.

ṭaqa pl. *-t, ṭyeq* (dim. *ṭwiqa*) **1.** hole *ṭ-ṭyeq lli fe-ṣ-ṣuṛ de-l-medṛaṣa kollhom mʕăšššin fihom ṭ-ṭyuṛ.* Birds have nested in all the holes in the school wall. **2.** box office, ticket window **3.** porthole **4.** ability, competence *ma-ʕăndu ṭaqa l-had l-xedma.* He has no competence in this work. **5.** means *u-kan žberṭ ṭ-ṭaqa u-kan šrit siyaṛa ždida.* If I had the means I would buy a new car.

¶ *ʕmel* (or *dar*) *lli f-ṭaqtu* to do all one can

¶ *ʕmel* (or *dar*) *fuq ṭ-ṭaqa* to do one's best *ʕmelt fuq ṭaqti mʕah baš iḥeṣṣel ʕăl l-xedma.* I did my best for him to get the job.

ṭaṛ iṭiṛ v.i. **1.** to fly *had-le-bṛiṭel ma-zal ma-bda iṭiṛ.* This little bird hasn't begun to fly yet. —*ṭaṛu fiya ṭ-ṭšayeš mnayn kont ka-nṣuṭ ʕăl l-ʕafya.* Sparks flew onto me when I was blowing on the fire. **2.** to disappear, to vanish *ma-žit nduṛ l-ʕăndu ḥetta lqitu ṭaṛ.* By the time I turned around (to talk) to him he had already disappeared. **3.** to get away, to be spent rapidly *ma-ʕṛeft kif ka-iṭiṛu-lha le-flus.* I don't know how her money gets away from her.

¶ *ṭaṛ be-l-feṛḥa* to jump with joy

¶ *ṭaṛ-luᶲ* **1.** to get angry ≠ **2.** to be offended ≠

¶ *ṭaṛ-luᶲ n-nʕas* to lose sleep ≠, not to be able to sleep ≠

¶ *ṭaṛ-luᶲ ʕăqluᶲ* to lose one's mind ≠ *ṭaṛ-lu ʕăqlu melli mšaw-lu flusu.* He lost his mind when he lost his money.

¶ *ṭaṛet xelʕa mennuᶲ* to get or be frightened ≠ *ṭaṛet mennha xelʕa melli zdeḥ l-bab.* She got frightened when he slammed the door.

¶ *ṭaṛ ʕla* to attack, to set upon *s-sbăʕ ṭaṛ ʕlih u-fersu.* The lion attacked him and devoured him.

ṭaṛa pl. *-t* tare (difference between gross weight and net weight)

** *ḥăyyed* (or *zuwwel*) *ṭ-ṭaṛa.* said to a person who exaggerates while talking

ṭaṛaqa pl. *-t* salvo (of guns)

ṭaṛăb music

ṭaṛăf same as *ṭeṛf*

ṭaṛfa pl. *ṭwaṛef* noose, running knot

ṭarifa pl. *-t* **1.** tariff **2.** price tag

ṭariqa pl. *-t, ṭuroq* **1.** method *š-men ṭariqa stăʕmelti baš ḥălliti had l-muškil?* What method did you use in solving this problem? **2.** religious sect

ṭaṛma pl. *-t, ṭwaṛem* (dim. *ṭwiṛma*) small closet

ṭaṛṛu pl. *-wat* container made of tin or tin plate (e.g. a jerry can)

ṭaṛuṣ pl. *ṭwaṛeṣ* hunting dog
ṭaṣ pl. *ṭiṣan* metal basin with handles used for washing hands before or after a meal
¶ *yedd ṭ-ṭaṣ* kettle used to form a set with *ṭaṣ* (*ṭaṣ u-yeddu*)
ṭaṣa pl. *-t, ṭyeṣ* small metal bowl or cup
¶ *ɛămmeṛ ṭ-ṭyeṣ* to bluff *bqa iɛămmeṛ ɛlina ṭ-ṭyeṣ ḥetta ḥeṣṣelnah.* He kept bluffing us till we caught him.
ṭaš iṭiš v.i. (v.n. *ṭišan*) **1.** to swing, to use a swing **2.** to be "up in the air," to be unsettled **3.** (v.n. also *ṭiš, ṭeyš*) to be dissipated
** *ɛăqlu ṭayeš* (a.p.) He's (still) sowing his wild oats.
ṭawa pl. *-t* saucepan
ṭawa'if, ṭawayef pl. of *ṭayfa*
ṭaweṣ pl. *ṭwaṣ* peacock
¶ *ġṭaṛ ṭ-ṭaweṣ* pl. *ġeṭṛan ṭ-ṭaweṣ* large, expensive china plate with elaborate design
ṭayfa pl. *ṭawayef, ṭawa'if, ṭwayef* **1.** group (people) **2.** religious sect
ṭayel a.p. of *ṭal*
ṭayla pl. *-t* **1.** use, utility *š-men ṭayla ġad-teqḍi b-had le-flus?* What use will this money be to you? **2.** result *defɛăt waḥed l-ɛadad d-leflus u-ši-ṭayla ma-ḥeṣṣlet ɛliha.* She spent a great deal of money without getting any result.
** *dak l-weld ma-fih ṭayla.* That boy is a good-for-nothing.
ṭayṭay in the set expr. *b-ṭayṭay* frankly, bluntly
ṭayeḥ a.p. of *ṭaḥ*
ṭažin pl. *ṭwažen* (dim. *ṭwižen*) **1.** kind of round, brown earthenware serving dish with lid **2.** food served in **1** above
ṭaḥ iṭiḥ v.i. (v.n. *ṭyuḥ*) **1.** to fall *ṭaḥet men s-sellum u-herrset ṛželha.* She fell from the ladder and broke her leg. —*ma-ža-š mɛana ḥit ṭaḥ mṛiḍ ɛla beġta.* He didn't come with us because he suddenly fell ill. —*fuq-aš bda t-telž iṭiḥ?* When did the snow start to fall? —*qalu bin-la ṭamanathom kollhom ġad-iṭiḥu f-'axiṛ š-šheṛ.* They said all their prices will fall at the end of the month. —*wṣelna le-ḍ-ḍaṛ qbel-ma iṭiḥ l-lil.* We got home before night fell. **2.** to cost *be-šḥal ṭaḥ le-bni kollu?* How much did the whole building cost? **3.** to depreciate (value)
¶ *ṭaḥ f-* to find, to come across, to happen onto *ṭaḥ f-waḥed s-siyaṛa mezyana u-ṛxiṣa.* He found a nice inexpensive automobile. —*ṭeḥt fe-tlata de-n-nas lli qeblu ixedmu mɛana.* I came across three people who agreed to work with us.
¶ *ṭaḥ-luᵠ* **1.** to lose ≠ *ṭaḥ-lu beẓṭamu.* He lost his wallet. **2.** to drop ≠ *ši-ḥaža ṭaḥet-lha f-l-'eṛḍ.* She dropped something on the floor.
¶ *ṭaḥ men ɛăyn* (plus pron., n.) to lose the respect of *bda iṭiḥ men ɛăyn ṭ-ṭalaba dyalu.* He's losing his students' respect.
¶ *ṭaḥet klemtuᵠ* to lose one's influence ≠ *ṭaḥet klemthom.* They're no longer influential.
¶ *ṭaḥet smăɛtuᵠ* to lose one's reputation ≠ *dak š-šarika ṭaḥet smăɛtha.* That company has lost its reputation.
¶ *ṭaḥet ṣeḥḥtuᵠ* to be exhausted ≠ *ṭaḥet ṣeḥḥthom be-ž-žri.* They're exhausted from running.
¶ *ṭaḥ ɛla* to cost *had ḍ-ḍaṛ ṭaḥet ɛlina b-ṛebɛin alef derhem.* This house cost us forty thousand dirhams.
¶ a.p. *ṭayeḥ* pl. *-in* **1.** low *baɛha-lu b-waḥed t-taman ṭayeḥ.* He sold it to him at a low price. —*dima ka-išedd nuqaṭ ṭayḥa f-le-ḥsab.* He always gets low marks in mathematics. —*qaḍiya ṭayḥa hadik daret.* That was a pretty low thing she pulled. **2.** contemptible
ṭaḥuna pl. *-t, ṭwaḥen* flour mill
ṭaɛ iṭiɛ **1.** v.t. (v.n. *ṭiɛan, ṭaɛa*) to obey *dak l-weld ma-bqa-š iṭiɛ waldih.* That boy doesn't obey his parents any longer. —*ma-ka-ibġi iṭiɛ l-'awamir d-ḥădd.* He doesn't like to obey anybody's orders. **2.** v.i. (v.n. *ṭuɛ*) to be docile, submissive
ṭaɛa **1.** v.n. of *ṭaɛ* 1 **2.** obedience **3.** submission, docility
ṭaɛun pl. *ṭwaɛen* (bubonic) plague
ṭbabeẓ pl. of *ṭebbuẓ*
ṭbali pl. of *ṭebla*
ṭbaqi pl. of *ṭebqa*
ṭbasi pl. of *ṭebsi* (same as *ṭebṣil*)
ṭbaṣel pl. of *ṭebṣil*
ṭbayeɛ pl. of *ṭbăɛ, ṭebɛa* 3 and *ṭbiɛa*
ṭebb v.t. (v.n. *ṭebban*) **1.** to cure, to heal (used proverbially)
** *ža iṭebbu ɛmah.* He came to cure him, but he blinded him. (said of s.o. who, trying to bring help, makes a situation worse) **2.** to spend completely and rapidly (money)
ṭebba, ṭobba pl. of *ṭbib*
ṭobba pl. *-t* rat
ṭebbal pl. *-a, -in* drummer
ṭebban v.n. of *ṭebb*
ṭebbax pl. *-a* cook
ṭebbaɛ pl. *-a* ag. n. of *ṭbăɛ*
ṭebbel v.i. **1.** to beat a drum
** *ṭebbel u-ġiyyeṭ!* I don't give a damn what you do or say!
ṭebbeq v.t. **1.** to apply, to follow *ṭebbeqt l-qaɛida ṛ-ṛabɛa.* I applied rule (number) four. **2.** to conform to, to abide by (law) **3.** to enforce *l-bulisi ṭebbeq l-qanun.* The policeman enforced the law.

ṭebbăε v.t. to stain, to spot *ṭebbεăt ksewtha b-l-idam.* She stained her dress with grease.
ṭbeg pl. *ṭbuga* same as *ṭbeq*
ṭbib pl. *ṭebba, ṭobba* medical doctor, physician
¶ *ṭbib le-bhayem, ṭbib le-ḥmir* veterinarian
¶ *ṭbib s-snan* pl. *ṭobba de-s-snan* dentist
ṭebbuẓ pl. *ṭbabeẓ* stout, corpulent
ṭobbẓi pl. *-ya* gunner, artilleryman
¶ *ṭbib žiṛaḥi* pl. *ṭebba žiṛaḥiyen* surgeon
ṭbiqa dim. of *ṭbeq*
ṭbix v.n. of *ṭbex*
ṭbiε v.n. of *ṭbăε*
ṭbiεa pl. *-t, ṭbayeε* 1. nature *ma-ši men ṭbiεtha ka-tekdeb.* It's not her nature to lie. 2. habit *fih waḥed ṭ-ṭbiεa qbiḥa bezzaf.* He has a very bad habit. 3. disposition *ṭbiεtha mqellqa.* She has an irascible disposition.
ṭbeḷ pl. *ṭbula* drum (musical instrument)
¶ *menfux kif ṭ-ṭbeḷ* 1. swollen, bloated (person) 2. as fat as a pig 3. stuck up, cocky
ṭebla pl. *-t, ṭbali* (dim. *ṭwibla*) 1. table *had ṭ-ṭebla εăndha ġir tlata de-r-režlin.* This table has only three legs. 2. bongo drum
¶ *wežžed ṭ-ṭebla* to set the table
¶ *xemmel ṭ-ṭebla* to clear the table
ṭbeq pl. *ṭbuqa* (dim. *ṭbiyyeq, ṭbiqa*) 1. round bread container made of straw 2. metal can or straw basket with conical lid for keeping bread or cookies (with handles when made of metal)
ṭebqa pl. *-t, ṭbaqi* 1. shelf *le-ktub kollhom εmelthom f-ṭebqa weḥda.* I put all the books on one shelf. 2. floor, story *ṭlăεna ḥetta le-ṭ-ṭebqa s-sabεa.* We went all the way up to the seventh floor. 3. layer, stratum
ṭebsi pl. *ṭbasi* same as *ṭebṣil*
ṭebṣil pl. *ṭbaṣel* 1. plate *imken-lek tsexxen l-makla f-had ṭ-ṭebṣil.* You can warm food in this plate. 2. record, disc *bġit nesmăε had ṭ-ṭebṣil.* I want to hear this record.
ṭbuga pl. of *ṭbeg* (same as *ṭbeq*)
ṭbula pl. of *ṭbeḷ*
ṭbuqa pl. of *ṭbeq*
ṭbex v.t. or v.i. (v.n. *ṭebx, ṭbix*) 1. to cook *u-kan ṭbexti l-lḥăm huwa l-luwwel.* You should've cooked the meat first. —*xelli l-lḥăm izid iṭbex swiya.* Let the meat cook a little longer. 2. to boil (water, food)
ṭebx v.n. of *ṭbex*
ṭbăε v.t. (v.n. *ṭbiε*) 1. to stamp *weqqăε r-risala εad ṭbăεha.* Sign the letter and then stamp it. 2. to print *fuq-aš ġad-iṭebεu had le-ktab?* When are they going to print this book? 3. to type 4. to plug (a melon)
ṭbăε pl. *ṭbayeε* 1. behavior, conduct 2. movement in Andalusian music

** *ṭebεu mezyan.* He's easy to get along with. —*ṭbăεhom qbiḥ.* They're hard to get along with.
ṭebεa 1. n.i. of *ṭbăε* 2. pl. *-t* edition 3. pl. *-t, ṭbayeε* spot, stain
ṭebεăn of course, naturally *ġad-temši l-l-εers dyalu?—ṭebεăn.* Are you going to his wedding?—Of course. —*ṭebεăn ma-ġad-naxod-ši l-εoṭla dyali bla-ma nεălmek.* Naturally I'm not going to take my vacation without letting you know.
ṭfa iṭfa v.i. (v.n. *ṭefyan*) to go out (light, fire)
ṭfa iṭfi v.t. (v.n. *ṭefyan*) 1. to turn off, turn out *nsiti ma-ṭfiti-š ḍ-ḍuw.* You forgot to turn off the light. 2. to put out, to extinguish (fire) 3. to satisfy, to quench *ma-žbeṛt-š baš nṭfi le-εṭeš.* I couldn't find anything to quench my thirst with. 4. to dip (hot pastry into honey)
ṭfeḷ pl. *ṭfuḷa* little boy
ṭefḷa pl. *-t* little girl
ṭfuḷa pl. of *ṭfeḷ*
ṭefyan v.n. of *ṭfa*
ṭġa iṭġa v.i. (v.n. *ṭoġyan*) to trespass
¶ *ṭġa εla* to tyrannize, to rule with unjust severity
¶ a.p. *ṭaġi* pl. *ṭuġat* oppressor, tyrant
ṭoġyan v.n. of *ṭġa*
ṭhaṛa 1. v.n. of *ṭehheṛ* 2. cleanliness, purity (mainly spiritual, religious) 3. circumcision
ṭehheṛ v.t. (v.n. *ṭhaṛa*) 1. to cleanse, to purify (e.g. religiously) 2. to circumcise
ṭib aroma, fragrance (perfume)
ṭiba pl. *-t* taste *had l-ḥălwa fiha ṭibt le-ḥmaḍ.* This cake has a sour taste. —*had l-makla ma-fiha ṭiba.* This food is tasteless.
** *l-fukahat dyalu kollhom ka-ixeṛžu bla ṭiba.* All his jokes fall flat.
¶ *be-ṭ-ṭiba* slowly, carefully, cautiously
¶ *b-ṭibt l-xaṭeṛ* willingly *εṭaha-lhom b-ṭibt l-xaṭeṛ.* He gave it to them willingly.
ṭifuṛ pl. *ṭyafeṛ* 1. large tray for serving food 2. round serving table with raised rim
ṭikuk kind of parasite which attacks cattle
ṭiligṛam pl. *-at* telegram
ṭin clay
ṭiṛ pl. *ṭyuṛ* 1. bird 2. cancer
¶ *ṭiṛ a-bgeṛ* type of white heron which associates with cattle
¶ *ṭiṛ l-lil* bat (mammal)
ṭiṛa 1. n.i. of *ṭaṛ* 2. ill omen
ṭiṣan pl. of *ṭaṣ*
ṭiš v.n. of *ṭaš* 3
ṭiša n.i. of *ṭaš*
ṭišan v.n. of *ṭaš*
ṭiy v.n. of *ṭwa*
ṭiya pl. *-t* n.i. of *ṭwa*
ṭiyyaba pl. *-t, ṭyayeb* attendant or masseuse in a steam bath for women

ṭiyyaṛ pl. *-in, -a* aviator, pilot
ṭiyyaṛa pl. *-t, ṭyayeṛ* airplane
ṭiyyeb v.t. (v.n. *ṭyab*) **1.** to cook, to make, to prepare *ṭiyybet l-lƹăm qbel l-xoḍṛa.* She cooked the meat before the vegetables. —*škun ġad-iṭiyyeb le-ƹša l-yum?* Who's going to prepare supper today? **2.** to boil *ka-ṭṭiyyeb had l-ma l-l-qehwa?* Are you boiling this water for coffee? **3.** to ripen, to make ripe **4.** to argue into, to talk into *bġa iṭiyyebni baš nešri mennu siyaṛa.* He tried to talk me into buying a car from him.
ṭiyyeb pl. *-in* nice, pleasant *ƹbabha kollhom nas ṭiyybin.* All her relatives are nice people. —*had š-šežṛa ka-ṭṭleq riƹa ṭiyyba.* This tree gives off a pleasant odor.
ṭiyyeṛ v.t. **1.** to cause to fly (away) *ḍ-ḍeṛba d-le-mkeƹla lli ṭiyyṛet le-ƹmam.* It was the rifle shot that caused the pigeons to fly away. **2.** to steal, to filch, to pilfer *ši-waƹed ṭiyyeṛ-lha beẓṭamha.* Somebody stole her purse.
¶ *ṭiyyeṛ d-duxa* to sober up
¶ *ṭiyyeṛ l-ma* to go to the bathroom (polite euphemism)
¶ *ṭiyyeṛ le-wqeṛ* to come out of mourning, to end the mourning period
¶ *ṭiyyeṛ n-nƹas* to keep awake (by the use of some stimulant) *šṛebt bṛiq kamel de-l-qehwa baš nṭiyyeṛ n-nƹas.* I drank a whole pot of coffee to keep awake. —*šeṛṛebnah bezzaf de-l-qehwa baš nṭiyyṛu-lu n-nƹas.* We gave him a lot of coffee to keep him awake.
¶ *ṭiyyeṛ s-sekra* to sober up
¶ *ṭiyyṛu~ l-* to upset, to make angry *ṛakom ġad-ṭṭiyyṛuh-lu ila ma-žitiw-š.* You'll make him angry if you don't come.
¶ *ṭiyyeṛ xelƹa men* to frighten, to scare
¶ *ṭiyyeṛ ƹla* to alleviate the troubles of (by means of some entertainment)
ṭiyyeš v.t. **1.** to swing, to make oscillate **2.** to dismiss, to fire *ṭiyyšuh men dak l-waḍifa.* They dismissed him from that job.
¶ *ṭiyyeš b-* to rock *ṭiyyšet be-ṭ-ṭeṛbya baš tenƹăs.* She rocked the baby so it would go to sleep.
ṭiyyeƹ v.t. (v.n. *ṭyuƹ*) **1.** to drop, to let fall *ṭiyyƹet ṣiniya ƹamṛa be-l-kisan.* She dropped a tray full of glasses. **2.** to make fall *ƹăṛṛeḍ-lu režlu u-ṭiyyƹu.* He tripped him and made him fall. **3.** to knock down *ṭiyyƹu l-l-eṛḍ u-bda iḍeṛbu.* He knocked him down on the floor and started beating him. **4.** to pull down *ƹlaš ṭiyyeƹti le-ġlaqat?* Why did you pull the shades down? **5.** to demolish, to tear down *le-bni lli qdim kollu bġaw iṭiyyƹuh.* They want to tear down all the old buildings. **6.** to lower, to bring down *men băƹd ṛaṣ l-ƹam kollhom ka-iṭiyyƹu l-ʔatmina dyalhom.* After New Year's they all bring their prices down. **7.** v.i. to go down, to drop (value, price) **8.** v.i. to lose weight *ṭiyyƹet melli ma-bqat-š takol bin le-wqat.* She's lost weight since she stopped eating between meals. **9.** v.i. to abort, to miscarry
¶ *ṭiyyeƹ be-klemt* (or *be-klam*) **1.** to disobey *ƹămmeṛha ma-ṭiyyƹet be-klam waldiha.* She's never disobeyed her parents. **2.** to disregard or ignore a request (offensively) *ṛeġbettu ibqa mƹana saƹa ṭiyyeƹ-lha be-klemtha.* She begged him to stay with us, but he ignored her request (so, she's offended).
¶ *ṭiyyeƹ be-qdeṛ* (or *b-šaṛăf*) to humiliate *dak š-ši lli ṭiyyeƹ-lu b-šaṛafu.* That was what humiliated him.
¶ *ṭiyyeƹ b-ṛaṣu* (or *b-nefsu*) to stoop, to condescend, to lower oneself
¶ *ṭiyyeƹ ṣ-ṣuq ƹla* to undersell *š-šarika l-oxṛa ka-ṭṭiyyeƹ ƹlihom ṣ-ṣuq.* The other firm is underselling them.
ṭiƹa pl. *-t* n.i. of *ṭaƹ*
ṭiƹan pl. *ṭyaƹen* spleen
ṭiƹan v.n. of *ṭaƹ* 1
ṭla iṭli v.t. (v.n. *ṭla*) **1.** to smear or cover (with s.th. oily or greasy) *ṭlat-li ƹwayži be-z-zit.* She smeared my clothes with oil. **2.** to paint *bġa iṭli l-bit b-le-xḍeṛ u-n-nbeƹ b-le-byeḍ.* He wants to paint the room green and the hall white.
ṭla v.n. of *ṭla*
ṭlaleƹ pl. of *ṭellaƹa*
ṭlaq **1.** v.n. of *ṭelleq* **2.** divorce
¶ *ṭlaq ṛežƹi* type of divorce which still leaves room for a reconciliation if requested by the husband
¶ *ṭlaq t-ṭalat* strict type of divorce which allows no reconciliation
¶ *ṭlaq xelƹi* divorce requested by the wife
ṭlayeq pl. of *ṭliq*
ṭleb (v.n. *ṭalab, ṭlib*) **1.** v.t. to ask for, to request *ƹămmeṛha ma-ṭelbet l-musaƹada men ši-waƹed.* She's never asked anybody for any help. **2.** v.i. to beg, to ask for charity
¶ *ṭleb ḷḷah* to pray (to God), to hope
¶ *ṭleb l-ƹilm* to seek education
¶ *ṭleb men* to ask *ṭelbet men ƹămmha isellefha ši-flus.* She asked her uncle to lend her some money.
** *ka-nṭleb men ḷḷah u-mennek tƹawenni f-had l-muškil.* Please help me with this problem.
¶ a.p. *ṭaleb* **1.** pl. *ṭeḷba, ṭoḷba, ṭalaba* student **2.** pl. *ṭoḷḷab* beggar
¶ *ṭaleb mƹašu* pl. *-yat* porter *šƹal xeṣṣni năƹṭi l-had ṭaleb mƹašu baš ihezz-li*

š-šwaneṭ? How much should I give this porter for carrying my luggage?

ṭeḷba, ṭoḷba pl. of *ṭaleb*

ṭlib v.n. of *ṭḷeb*

ṭḷiḷa dim. of *ṭeḷḷa* (n.i. of *ṭeḷḷ*)

ṭḷiq pl. *ṭḷayeq* runner, rug

ṭḷiq v.n. of *ṭḷeq*

ṭeḷḷ v.i. (v.n. *ṭeḷḷan*) to look out *kan ka-iṭeḷḷ men š-šeṛžem.* He was looking out from the window. —*l-bit dyali ka-iṭeḷḷ ɛăl l-ɛăṛṣa.* My room looks out on the garden.

¶ *ṭeḷḷ ɛla* to call on, to pay a visit to (s.o. ill only)

ṭeḷḷa pl. *-t* (dim. *ṭḷiḷa*) n.i. of *ṭeḷḷ*

ṭoḷḷab pl. of *ṭaleb* 2 (a.p. *ṭḷeb*)

ṭeḷḷan v.n. of *ṭeḷḷ*

ṭeḷḷay pl. *-a* (house) painter

ṭeḷḷaɛ pl. *-a, -in* ag.n. and adj. of *ṭeḷḷăɛ*

ṭeḷḷaɛa pl. *-t, ṭḷaleɛ* 1. shoe-horn 2. key (watch, clock)

ṭeḷḷaɛiya pl. *-t* type of lady's slipper

ṭeḷḷel same as *ṭeḷḷ*

ṭeḷḷeq v.t. (v.n. *ṭḷaq*) to divorce

ṭeḷḷeṣ v.t. to smear, to daub

ṭeḷḷăɛ v.t. 1. to take up, to bring up *mnayn konna l-teḥt ṛġebtu iṭeḷḷăɛ-lha l-ḥăddada.* When we were downstairs I asked him to take the iron up to her. —*ɛăyyṭet-lu men l-fuqi u-qalt-lu iṭeḷḷăɛ-lha t-teṣbin.* She called him from upstairs and asked him to bring the laundry up to her. 2. to roll up *ġir wṣeḷ ṭeḷḷăɛ kmamu u-bda ixdem.* As soon as he arrived he rolled up his sleeves and got down to work. —*ṭeḷḷăɛ ž-žaž qbel-ma tšedd l-biban.* Roll up the (car) windows before you lock the doors. 3. to raise *ṭeḷḷăɛt le-ġlaqat kollhom baš idxol ḍ-ḍuw l-kafi.* I've raised all the blinds so enough light can get in. 4. to raise, to increase *l-ʔuṭilat kollhom ṭeḷḷɛu t-tamanat dyalhom.* All the hotels have raised their rates. 5. to draw (water from a well) 6. to leaven, to make rise 7. to find, to restore, to retrieve *žazatu ɛla lli ṭeḷḷăɛ-lha beẓṭamha lli ttesṛeq-lha.* She thanked him for having found her stolen purse. 8. to promote, to elevate *bġaw iṭeḷḷɛuh le-r-rotba d-mudir.* They want to promote him to the rank of director. 9. to build, to erect (wall, partition) 10. to wind *xeṣṣni nṭeḷḷăɛ maganti.* I have to wind my watch. 11. to tune (musical instrument) 12. to pull on, to wear (pants, underwear, socks, shoes) 13. to come up with, to dig up *mnayn ṭeḷḷăɛti had le-xbaṛ?* Where did you dig up this news? 14. to question, to interrogate *hadi telt iyam u-l-bulis ka-iṭeḷḷɛu fihom.* The police have been questioning them for the past three days. 15. to add up, to figure up *ma-ɛṛeft-ši kif-aš ṭeḷḷăɛti had le-ḥsab.* I don't see how you added up this bill. 16. to get, to obtain *ġir qul-lhom ma-iɛăddbu-š ṛaṣhom, ṛahom ma-iṭeḷḷɛu mennu walu.* Just tell them not to trouble themselves, they won't get anything from him. 17. to finish, to do completely (work, task) *le-bnat ṭeḷḷɛu waḥed z-zeṛbiya haʔila.* The girls have finished a beautiful rug.

¶ *ṭeḷḷăɛ b-* to praise, to build up, to laud

¶ *ṭeḷḷăɛ u-hebbeṭ f-* to look (s.o., s.th.,) up and down, to measure with one's eye *bqa iṭeḷḷăɛ fiya w-ihebbeṭ bla-ma iqul-li ḥetta ḥaža.* He kept looking me up and down without saying anything.

¶ *ṭeḷḷăɛ ḥsab* (or *ḥesba* or *xbaṛ*) (*l-*) 1. to pay attention (to) *ana ka-nehḍeṛ mɛah u-huwa ma-ṭeḷḷăɛ-li ḥsab.* I was talking to him, but he wasn't paying any attention to me. 2. to show concern *d-dbaz qayem u-hiya ma-mṭeḷḷɛa xbaṛ.* She wasn't showing any concern while the fight was going on.

ṭḷeq v.t. (v.n. *ṭḷuq, ṭḷiq*) 1. to let go, to turn loose, to release *šḥal d-le-msažen ġad-iṭeḷqu?* How many prisoners are they going to turn loose? —*ṭḷeqni ḷḷah ixellik, ṛani mezrub.* Please let me go, I'm in a hurry. 2. (v.n. also *meṭḷaqa*) to let off, to give vacation or time off to *ṭeḷquna ʔusbuɛ kamel.* They let us off for a whole week. 3. to turn on *ṭḷeq l-ma l-bared.* Turn on the cold water. 4. to start *škun lli ṭḷeq had d-diɛaya ɛlih?* Who started this rumor about him? —*ṭḷeqt l-muṭuṛ baš isxon.* I started the motor so it would warm up. —*ṭḷeqna ɛafya mžehda baš nešwiw l-kebš.* We started a big fire so we could roast the lamb. 5. to drop, to let fall *ṭeḷqet l-magana l-l-erḍ u-herrsetha.* She dropped the watch on the floor and broke it. 6. to give off *l-beqṛež bda iṭḷeq le-fwar.* The kettle started giving off steam (steaming). —*l-feṛṛan ka-iṭḷeq d-doxxan.* The oven is giving off smoke (smoking). —*xellat l-lḥăm iṭuḷ ḥetta bda iṭḷeq riḥa qbiḥa.* She kept the meat so long it started giving off a bad smell. —*ma-zal ma-ɛṛeft-ši škun lli ṭḷeq ɛliha had d-diɛaya.* I still don't know who started this rumor about her. 7. to stick out, to extend *ṭḷeq yeddek baš nšuf ž-žeṛḥa.* Stick out your arm so I can see the wound. 8. to spread, to lay out. *nṭḷeq-lek l-beṭṭaniya ila bġiti tġeṭṭi.* I'll spread the blanket for you if you want to cover yourself. 9. (v.n. also *ṭeḷq*) to sell to (s.o.) on credit *ṭḷeqtha b-sett myat derhem de-s-selɛa.* I sold her six hundred dirhams worth of merchandise on credit. 10. v.i. to fade *had t-tub ka-iṭḷeq mnayn ka-iṭṣebben.* This cloth fades when it's washed.

¶ *ṭḷeq le-briẓ* (or *l-berraẓ*) *ɛla* **1.** to hire a town crier to announce *ṭelqu l-berraẓ ɛăl d-degg lli mša-lhom.* They've hired a town crier to announce the loss of their jewelry. **2.** (*b-*) to announce publicly (usually by a town crier) *ṛahom ṭalqin le-briẓ b-had le-xbaṛ.* This news is being announced to the public (by a town crier).

¶ *ṭḷeq le-ɛṛuq* to take root, to be firmly established *had t-teffaẓa bdat ṭṭḷeq le-ɛṛuq.* This apple tree is taking root. —*l-ẓizb l-ištiṛaki ṭaḷeq ɛṛuqu f-dak le-blad.* The Socialist Party is firmly established in that country.

¶ *ṭḷeq men* **1.** to let go, to turn loose *ma-ġad-nṭḷeq mennu ẓetta iṛedd-li flusi.* I'm not going to let him go until he gives me my money back. **2.** to leave alone *qolt-ha ṭṭḷeq mennu ẓit ma-ɛmel-šay.* I asked her to leave him alone because he didn't do anything.

** *a-sidi ṭḷeq menni xḷaṣ!* Get off my back, will you?

¶ *ṭḷeq ṛaṣuφ* to hurry up *qol-lhom iṭeḷqu ṛaṣhom, ṛa-l-ẓal ka-imši.* Tell them to hurry up, it's getting late.

¶ *ṭḷeq režluφ* to take a stroll

¶ *ṭḷeq* (*ɛmaṛa b-*) to fire (a shot with) *ṭḷeq fih tlata d-le-ɛmaṛat be-l-ferdi.* He fired the pistol at him three times.

ṭeḷq v.n. of *ṭḷeq* 9

¶ *be-ṭ-ṭeḷq* on credit *ma-ka-nebġi nešri ẓetta ẓaža be-ṭ-ṭeḷq.* I don't like to buy anything on credit.

ṭluq v.n. of *ṭḷeq*

ṭḷuɛ v.n. of *ṭḷăɛ*

ṭelẓ n.u. *-a* acacia

ṭḷăɛ v.i. (v.n. *ṭḷuɛ*) **1.** to go up, to rise, to come up *ṭḷăɛna ẓetta le-ṭ-ṭebqa l-ɛašṛa.* We went all the way up to the tenth floor. —*taman s-sokkaṛ ɛawed ṭḷăɛ.* The price of sugar has gone up again. —*ma-zala š-šems ma-ṭeḷɛet.* The sun hasn't risen yet. **2.** to break (dawn, day) **3.** to rise (dough) **4.** to climb, to climb up *ġir huwa smăɛ d-dib u-huwa iṭḷăɛ le-š-šežṛa.* As soon as he heard the wolf he climbed the tree. **5.** to be promoted, to advance (to) *ṭeḷɛăt xlifa de-l-mudir.* She's been promoted to assistant director. **6.** to sprout, to come up *ṛ-ṛbiɛ ġir ka-izid iṭḷăɛ f-ɛăṛṣetna.* Grass keeps coming up in our garden.

¶ *ṭḷăɛ-luφ f-ṛaṣuφ* to get on one's nerves *ṛah bda iṭḷăɛ-li f-ṛaṣi.* He's getting on my nerves.

¶ *ṭḷăɛ-luφ* to gain ≠ *šnu ṭḷăɛ-lek men dak s-sefṛa?* What did you gain from that trip?

ṭeḷɛa pl. *-t* **1.** n.i. of *ṭḷăɛ* **2.** uphill slope (on a street or road)

ṭemmaɛ adj. pl. *-in* n.pl. *-a* venal, unduly influenced by hope of gain, greedy

ṭemmen v.t. to give assurance to, to reassure *ṛžăɛ ɛăndhom u-ṭemmenhom bin-la ṛ-ana la-bas.* Go back and reassure them that I'm all right.

ṭemmeṛ v.t. **1.** to store in a silo (wheat, corn, etc.) **2.** to hide in a secret place (e.g. money)

ṭemmăɛ v.t. to lure, to entice *ṭemmăɛha be-z-zyada fe-l-ʔožṛa.* He lured her back with a higher salary.

ṭmăɛ f- (v.n. *ṭmăɛ*) to be greedy for, to be covetous of

ṭmăɛ v.n. of *ṭmăɛ*

ṭnabeṛ pl. of *ṭenbuṛ*

ṭnaš **1.** twelve **2.** twelfth *had le-qṣeṛ ttebna fe-l-qeṛn ṭ-ṭnaš.* This castle was built in the twelfth century.

¶ *ṭ-ṭnaš de-n-nhaṛ* noon

¶ *ṭ-ṭnaš de-l-lil* midnight

ṭnaži pl. of *ṭenžiya*

ṭnažeṛ pl. of *ṭenžṛa* and *ṭenžiṛ*

ṭenbuṛ pl. *ṭnabeṛ* steel drum

ṭeng pl. *ṭnuga* tank (weapon) *hežmu b-xemsa de-ṭ-ṭnuga.* They attacked with five tanks.

ṭniẓ v.n. of *ṭneẓ*

ṭnižṛa dim. of *ṭenžṛa*

ṭnižya dim. of *ṭenžiya*

ṭenneb v.t. **1.** to stretch, to pull *la-ṭṭenneb-š le-wtaṛat, daba tqeṭṭăɛhom.* Don't stretch the strings, you might break them. **2.** to gorge, to overstuff with food *ṭennbet-lu keršu be-l-ẓălwa.* She gorged him with cake. —*ṭenneb keršu be-ṛ-ṛuz.* He gorged himself with rice.

ṭenneš v.t. **1.** to stretch out, to stick out **2.** to prick up *le-ẓmaṛ bda iṭenneš wednih.* The donkey is pricking up his ears.

ṭenṭina n.i. of *ṭenṭen*

ṭenṭen v.i. **1.** to boom, to resound, to ring (loudly) *n-nwaqeṣ de-l-kanisa ka-iṭenṭnu.* The church bells are booming. —*ṛaṣi ṣbeẓ ka-iṭenṭen b-le-ẓṛiq.* My head is ringing with pain this morning. **2.** to get very hot *f-le-ɛšiya ka-iṭenṭen l-ẓal.* In the afternoon it gets very hot.

ṭnuga pl. of *ṭeng*

ṭneẓ v.i. (v.n. *ṭenẓ, ṭniẓ*) to joke, to jest

¶ *ṭneẓ ɛla* to tease, to make fun of

ṭenẓ v.n. of *ṭneẓ*

ṭenẓa pl. *-t* **1.** n.i. of *ṭneẓ* **2.** laughingstock (person)

ṭenžiṛ pl. *ṭnažeṛ* cauldron

ṭenžiya pl. *-t, ṭnaži* (dim. *ṭnižya*) **1.** small earthenware cooking pot with lid and handles (also used for keeping leaven) **2.** meal prepared in 1 above

ṭenžṛa pl. *-t, ṭnažeṛ* (dim. *ṭnižṛa*) cooking pot (metal)

ṭeqṭiq v.n. of *ṭeqṭeq*
ṭeqṭeq v.t. **1.** to soak, to saturate **2.** to put or use too much of (s.th., e.g. salt in food)
ṭṛa iṭṛa v.i. to happen, to take place *ṭṛat-lu waḥed l-qaḍiya min ˀeġrabi ma yakun.* The most unusual thing happened to him.
ṭṛabeš pl. of *ṭeṛbuš*
ṭṛaf pl. of *ṭeṛf*
ṭṛaṛeḥ pl. of *ṭeṛṛaḥ*
ṭṛawa freshness (of fruit, meat, etc.)
ṭṛayeḍ pl. of *ṭṛiḍ* 2
ṭṛayeḥ pl. of *ṭṛiḥa*
ṭeṛbuš pl. *ṭṛabeš* fez
ṭṛeḍ v.t. (v.n. *ṭeṛḍ, ṭṛiḍ*) **1.** to chase away, to drive away **2.** to fire, to discharge, to dismiss
ṭeṛḍ v.n. of *ṭṛeḍ*
ṭeṛf pl. *ṭṛaf* **1.** piece, fragment, part **2.** side, bank (river)
 ** *ḥellit ṛ-ṛadyu ṭṛaf.* I took the radio apart.
 ¶ *ḍṛeb ṭ-ṭeṛf* to steal, to pick from a pocket
 ¶ *ḍeṛṛab ṭ-ṭeṛf* pl. *ḍeṛṛabin ṭ-ṭeṛf* pickpocket
 ¶ *men ṭeṛf* **1.** at random *xdat ktab men ṭeṛf u-qṛatu.* She took a book at random and read it. **2.** without exception *t-tlamed dyalha kollhom mezyanin men ṭeṛf.* All her pupils are good without exception.
 ¶ *ṭṛaf* (no sg.) parts of body including hands, feet, and face
 ¶ *ṭṛaf ṭṛaf, ṭṛifat ṭṛifat* into pieces *debḥu l-begṛa u-qeṭṭɛuha ṭṛaf ṭṛaf.* They slaughtered the cow and cut it into pieces.
ṭeṛfani, ṭeṛfi pl. *-yen* final, last one, extreme *šritha men l-ḥanut ṭ-ṭeṛfaniya ɛăl š-šmal.* I bought it from the last shop on the left.
ṭṛi pl. *-yen* fresh (food, air)
ṭṛiḍ **1.** v.n. of *ṭṛeḍ* **2.** pl. *ṭṛayeḍ* younger brother (or sister) of same parents
ṭṛinbu pl. *-yat* top (toy)
ṭṛiq (f.) *ṭeṛqan, ṭoṛqan, ṭuṛoq* (dim. *ṭṛiyqa*) **1.** road, route **2.** way *hadi hiya ṭṛiq l-meḍṛaṣa?* Is this the way to school? —*ma-xellit-ši ši-ṭṛiq ma-žeṛṛebtha-š mɛah.* I've tried every possible way with him. **3.** course *l-wad ka-itbăɛ had ṭ-ṭṛiq.* The river follows this course. **4.** right path, straight and narrow
 ¶ *ḍṛeb ṭ-ṭṛiq* to walk or drive (a rather long distance)
 ¶ *qbeṭ ṭ-ṭṛiq* to set out, to hit the road
 ¶ *qeṭṭaɛ ṭ-ṭṛiq* pl. *qeṭṭaɛin ṭ-ṭṛiq* highwayman, highway robber
 ¶ *qeṭɛan ṭ-ṭṛiq* brigandage, plundering, highway robbery
 ¶ *qṭăɛ ṭ-ṭṛiq ɛla* to attack, to rob (highwayman) *ṛebɛa de-r-ṛžal qeṭɛu ɛlihom ṭ-ṭṛiq.* They were robbed by four highwaymen.
 ¶ *ṛžăɛ le-ṭ-ṭṛiq* to turn over a new leaf
 ¶ *ṣṛeq* (or *xṭef*) *ṭ-ṭṛiq* to take a short cut
 ¶ *ṭṛiq kbira* highway, main road
 ¶ *xoṛžan ṭ-ṭṛiq* trespassing
 ¶ *xṛež ɛăl ṭ-ṭṛiq* to deviate, to go astray
 ¶ *zad mɛa ṭ-ṭṛiq* to beat it, to scram
 ¶ *ža le-ṭ-ṭṛiq* to tell the truth, to talk frankly *ma-bġa-š ižini le-ṭ-ṭṛiq.* He didn't want to tell me the truth.
 ¶ *ɛmel* (or *dar*) *ṭ-ṭṛiq mɛa* to give fair treatment to *ma-bġa idir mɛaha ṭṛiq, žat hiya dɛatu.* He wouldn't give her fair treatment, so she sued him.
ṭṛiš v.n. of *ṭṛeš*
ṭṛiyqa dim. of *ṭṛiq*
ṭṛiz v.n. of *ṭṛez*
ṭṛiḥ v.n. of *ṭṛeḥ*
ṭṛiḥa pl. *-t, ṭṛayeḥ* **1.** flogging, hiding, beating **2.** work done by the piece
ṭromba pl. *-t* **1.** water pump (with handle) **2.** apparatus for administering enemas
ṭrombiya pl. *-t* same as *ṭrinbu*
ṭeṛqan, ṭoṛqan pl. of *ṭṛiq*
ṭeṛṛ pl. *ṭṛuṛ, ṭṛuṛa* tambourine
ṭeṛṛaḍa pl. *-t* standard, banner, flag
ṭeṛṛaf pl. *-a* shoe repairman
ṭeṛṛaq pl. *-a* ag.n. of *ṭeṛṛeq*
ṭeṛṛaṛ pl. *-a* tambourine player
ṭeṛṛaz pl. *-a* embroiderer
ṭeṛṛaḥ pl. *-a, ṭṛaṛeḥ* boy hired to carry bread to the public oven to be baked and then deliver it to the homes
ṭeṛṛeb v.t. **1.** to pin, to clip **2.** to sharpen (with strop or whetstone)
ṭeṛṛef v.t. to repair (shoes)
 ¶ *ṭeṛṛfu~ l-* to fire, to dismiss *ṭeṛṛfuh-lhom men l-măɛmel.* They were fired from the factory.
ṭeṛṛeq v.t. **1.** to hammer **2.** to nail shut, to nail up
 ¶ *ṭeṛṛeq meṣmaṛ* to take care of an errand or a problem *ɛăndi šḥal d-le-mṣameṛ xeṣṣni nṭeṛṛeqhom.* I have so many problems to take care of.
 ¶ a.p. *mṭeṛṛeq* pl. *-in* clever, cunning
ṭeṛṛeṛ v.i. to play the tambourine
 ¶ *ṭeṛṛeṛ l-* to hurl a string of insulting remarks at (s.o.)
ṭeṛṛeš v.t. **1.** to deafen (s.o.) **2.** to slap (face)
ṭeṛṛeḥ v.t. **1.** to attend (animal) during birth **2.** to give a beating to (by any means, for any purpose) **3.** to clobber, to defeat overwhelmingly
ṭṛeš v.t. (v.n. *ṭeṛš, ṭṛiš*) to slap (face, s.o.)
ṭṛeš f. *ṭeṛša* pl. *ṭuṛeš* deaf
ṭeṛš v.n. of *ṭṛeš*
ṭeṛša pl. *-t* slap (in the face)
ṭeṛṭaqa pl. *-t* type of popgun

ṭeṛṭiq v.n. of *ṭeṛṭeq*
ṭeṛṭeq v.t. 1. to pop (e.g. balloon) 2. to make blow out (e.g. tire) 3. to shoot off, to detonate
ṭṛuṛ, ṭṛuṛa pl. of *ṭeṛṛ*
ṭṛuša, ṭṛušiya deafness
ṭṛuʕ, ṭṛuʕa pl. of *ṭeṛʕ* 2
ṭṛez v.t. (v.n. *ṭeṛz, ṭṛiz*) to embroider
ṭeṛz 1. v.n. of *ṭṛez* 2. embroidery
ṭeṛžama same as *teṛžama*
ṭeṛžem same as *teṛžem*
ṭoṛžman same as *toṛžman*
ṭṛeʕ v.t. (v.n. *ṭṛiʕ*) 1. to put down (e.g. on the ground) 2. to put into an oven (bread, pastry), to bake 3. to give birth to (animal) 4. (v.n. also *ṭeṛʕ*) to subtract *had l-ʕadad ṭeṛʕu men l-žemʕ.* Subtract this figure from the total.
ṭeṛʕ 1. v.n. of *ṭṛeʕ* 4 2. pl. *ṭṛuʕ, ṭṛuʕa* game *lʕăbna ṛebʕa de-ṭ-ṭṛuʕ de-ṣ-ṣenṭṛež.* We played four games of chess.
ṭeṛʕa pl. *-t* n.i. of *ṭṛeʕ*
ṭšaš n.u. *-a* pl. *-t, ṭšayeš* spark (e.g. emitted by fire)
ṭšayeš pl. of *ṭšaš*
ṭešṭeš v.i. 1. to emit sparks (fire) 2. to emit successive spurts of liquid
ṭṭabex v.i. to fight or struggle (to get s.o. or s.th. to do s.th. desired) *ʕyit ma nṭṭabex mʕah wa-lakin ma-bġa-š iži.* I tried and tried to get him to come but he wouldn't.
ṭṭalăʕ ʕla 1. to find out, to learn, to be informed about 2. to study, to examine (s.th. before making a decision)
ṭṭebbeq m.p. of *ṭebbeq*
ṭṭehheṛ m.p. of *ṭehheṛ*
ṭṭeḷḷeq m.p. of *ṭeḷḷeq*
ṭṭeḷḷeṣ m.p. of *ṭeḷḷeṣ*
ṭṭemmen m.p. of *ṭemmen*
ṭṭemmeṣ v.i. 1. to close (eyes) 2. to fail to use one's head (on some occasion)
ṭṭemmăʕ m.p. of *ṭemmăʕ*
ṭṭenneb m.p. of *ṭenneb*
ṭṭeṛṛeb m.p. of *ṭeṛṛeb*
ṭṭeṛṛef m.p. of *ṭeṛṛef*
ṭṭeṛṛeq m.p. of *ṭeṛṛeq*
¶ *ṭṭeṛṛeq mʕa ṛaṣuφ* to learn from the experience of others, or by associating with those who know
ṭṭeṛṛăʕ m.p. of *ṭeṛṛăʕ*
ṭṭeṛṭeq v.i. 1. m.p. of *ṭeṛṭeq* 2. to explode (balloon, bomb, etc.)
ṭṭufel v.i. to crash a party or occasion (primarily to partake of the food offered)
ṭṭuwwel m.p. of *ṭuwwel*
ṭṭuwweṛ m.p. of *ṭuwweṛ*
ṭṭeyyeṛ m.p. of *ṭeyyeṛ*
ṭub n.u. *-a* pl. *-t, ṭweb* (dim. *ṭwiba*) 1. clod (earth) 2. adobe brick 3. lump (e.g., sugar)
ṭufan v.n. of *ṭaf*
ṭufayli pl. *-ya* sponge, parasitic person
ṭuḷ 1. length *had l-bit fih ʕăšṛa miter de-ṭ-ṭuḷ.* This room is ten meters long. —*had l-wad šʕal fih dyal de-ṭ-ṭuḷ?* How long is this river? 2. height *iṣlaʕ l-l-kuṛa de-s-sella ʕla wedd ṭ-ṭuḷ dyalu.* He'd be good for basketball because of his height. 3. straight, straight ahead *zid ṭuḷ u-lwi ʕăl š-šmal fe-ḍ-ḍuw le-ʕmeṛ.* Go straight ahead and make a left turn at the red light. 4. all, during *ṭuḷ ʕyatu u-huwa xeddam mʕa dak š-šarika.* He's been working all his life for that firm.
¶ *ṭuḷ u-ʕăṛḍ* all over, everywhere *qellebt ʕlihom f-le-mdina ṭuḷ u-ʕăṛḍ u-ma-lqithom-š.* I looked for them all over town and I couldn't find them.
¶ *ʕla ṭuḷ l-xeṭṭ* completely, a hundred percent *ana mettafeq mʕak ʕla ṭuḷ l-xeṭṭ.* I agree with you completely.
ṭuḷa pl. of *ṭwaḷ*
ṭulan v.n. of *ṭwal*
ṭumubil pl. *-at* (cons. *ṭumubilt*) automobile, car
ṭun 1. tuna (fish) 2. pl. *ṭwan* ton, thousand kilograms
ṭuq pl. *ṭwaq* collar (shirt, dress)
¶ *f-ṭuq* in the charge of *f-ṭuq men xelliti siyaṛtek?* In whose charge did you leave your car?
ṭureš pl. of *ṭreš*
ṭuṛuq pl. of *ṭṛiq* and *ṭaṛiqa*
ṭuṭ filth
ṭuwwef v.t. 1. to assist (s.o.) in walking around the Kaaba (during the Pilgrimage) 2. to parade (a criminal) through the streets as an object of public scorn
ṭuwwel 1. v.t. to lengthen, to make longer *xeṣṣek ṭṭuwwel had z-zenṭiṭa.* You'll have to make this skirt longer. 2. v.t. to prolong, to extend *ṭuwwlu-lha l-ʕoṭḷa dyalha ʕla wedd le-ʕbala.* They extended her leave because of pregnancy. 3. v.i. to stay or spend too long, to take a long time *ṭ-ṭbib qal-lu ma-iṭuwwel-š fe-l-ʕămmam.* The doctor told him not to stay too long in the bath.
ṭuwweṛ v.t. to train, to instruct (men, animals, etc.)
ṭuwweš v.t. or v.i. 1. to squirt out, to spurt 2. to urinate (of animals, and vulgarly of people)
ṭuwweʕ v.i. 1. to cry, to lament 2. to bellow (bull)
ṭuwwăʕ v.t. 1. to throw away, to fling, to hurl 2. to tame, to domesticate 3. to subjugate, to subdue 4. to make flexible
ṭuyan v.n. of *ṭwa*
ṭuʕ v.n. of *ṭaʕ* 2
ṭwa iṭwi v.t. (v.n. *ṭiy, ṭuyan*) 1. to fold *ṭwat*

li-ẓuṛ bla-ma tḥäddedhom. She folded the sheets without ironing them. 2. to close ṭwi ktubek u-dirhom fe-škaṛṭek. Close your books and put them in your bag. —mnayn šaf l-bulisi maži ṭwa l-mus u-daru f-žibu. When he saw the policeman coming he closed his knife and put it in his pocket. 3. to roll up ṭwi ẓ-ẓeṛbiya baš teġsel l-eṛḍ. Roll up the rug so you can wash the floor.

¶ ṭwa le-klam, ṭwa le-ḥdit, ṭwa l-heḍṛa to change the subject (in conversation)

ṭwabel pl. of ṭabla (same as ṭebla)

ṭwabeq pl. of ṭabeq

ṭwabeε pl. of ṭabăε

ṭwagi pl. of ṭagiya

ṭwal v.i. (v.n. ṭulan) 1. to get longer fe-ṣ-ṣif ka-iṭwal n-nhaṛ. The day gets longer in summer. 2. to grow up, to get taller xay ṭwal melli bda ilεăb l-kuṛa de-s-sella. My brother has gotten taller since he started playing basketball.

ṭwal pl. -at, ṭula rope

ṭwal pl. of ṭwil

ṭwan pl. of ṭun 2

ṭwaneg pl. of ṭanga

ṭwaq pl. of ṭuq

ṭwaṛef pl. of ṭaṛfa

ṭwaṛem pl. of ṭaṛma

ṭwaṛeṣ pl. of ṭaṛuṣ

ṭwaṣ pl. of ṭaweṣ

ṭwayef pl. of ṭayfa

ṭwažen pl. of ṭažin

ṭwaḥen pl. of ṭaḥuna

ṭwaεen pl. of ṭaεun

ṭweb pl. of ṭuba (n.u. of ṭub)

ṭwiba dim. of ṭuba (n.u. of ṭub)

ṭwibla dim. of ṭebla

ṭwibeε dim. of ṭabăε

ṭwigya dim. of ṭagiya

ṭwil pl. ṭwal (dim. ṭwiwel, comp. ṭwel) 1. long režlin had ṭ-ṭebla ṭwal. This table has long legs. —bqat mεana modda ṭwila. She stayed a long time with us. 2. tall, big xutu kollhom ṭwal u-huwa qṣiṛ. All his brothers are tall, but he's short.

ṭwiqa dim. of ṭaqa

ṭwiṛma dim. of ṭaṛma

ṭwiwel dim. of ṭwil

ṭwižen dim. of ṭažin

ṭwel comp. of ṭwil

ṭyab v.n. of ṭab and ṭiyyeb

ṭyafeṛ pl. of ṭifuṛ

ṭyayeb pl. of ṭiyyaba

ṭyayeṛ pl. of ṭiyyaṛa

ṭyaḥen pl. of ṭiḥan

ṭyeq pl. of ṭaqa

ṭyeṣ pl. of ṭaṣa

ṭeyš v.n. of ṭaš 3

ṭyuṛ pl. of ṭiṛ

ṭyuḥ v.n. of ṭaḥ and ṭiyyeḥ

ṭeyyeb same as ṭiyyeb

ṭeyyeṛ same as ṭiyyeṛ

ṭeyyeš same as ṭiyyeš

ṭeyyeḥ same as ṭiyyeḥ

ṭeẓṭiẓ v.n. of ṭeẓṭeẓ

ṭeẓṭeẓ v.i. to break wind, to fart

ṭeẓẓ, ṭoẓẓ 1. fart, act of breaking wind 2. exclamation expressing discouragement or disappointment

ṭḥin 1. v.n. of ṭḥăn 2. flour (wheat)

ṭḥăn v.t. (v.n. ṭḥin) 1. to grind nṭḥăn-lek had l-qehwa? Shall I grind this coffee for you? —ka-iṭḥăn snanu mnayn ka-ikun naεes. He grinds his teeth when he's asleep. 2. to grind, to sharpen (cutlery, scissors, etc.)

ṭeḥḥan pl. -a 1. miller 2. knife grinder, one who sharpens knives

ṭεam pl. -at (dim. ṭεiyma) 1. food 2. couscous

ṭεim v.n. of ṭεăm

ṭεiyma dim. of ṭεam

ṭεăm v.t. (v.n. ṭεim) 1. to feed, to give food to 2. to poison, to give (s.o.) poison

ṭoεm bait

ṭăεma, ṭoεma pl. -t woof, loose threads on the loom

ṭăεεăm v.t. 1. to feed, to give food to 2. to bait, to put bait on

U

u (w before vowels, we- before some consonant clusters) 1. and teṛžemt had l-žumla u-hadik. I translated both this sentence and that one. 2. introduces an independent clause which functions as circumstantial modifier of preceding clause. hadi modda u-huwa ġeḍban εlina. It's a long time now that he's been mad at us. —mšit neštaġel w-ana mṛiḍa. I went to work although I was sick. 3. used in distributive expressions introduced by koll, approximately equivalent to "everyone has his own (particular) . . .," "to each his own. . ." koll waḥed u-ḍuqu. To each his own taste. —koll waḥed u-ṭabiεtu. Everyone has his own nature. —koll telmid u-xdemtu! (Let) each student do his own work! —koll ḥaža u-maḥällha! (Put) everything in its own place!

¶ *we-ḷḷah u-* implies a threat or promise somewhat equivalent to "so help me, if . . ." or "I promise, if . . ." *we-ḷḷah u-žiti ma-nḍeṛbek.* If you come I promise I won't hit you. —*we-ḷḷah u-ma ṛedditi-li flusi ḥetta ndɛik!* So help me, if you don't give me back my money, I'll sue you!
u-la same as *aw-la*
ʔuluf, ʔulufat pl. of *ʔalef*
ʔumam pl. of *ʔomma*
ʔumana pl. of *amin*
ʔumaṛa pl. of *ʔamir*
ʔummi pl. *-yen* illiterate *n-nesba dyal lʔ-ummiyin f-d-denya kbeṛ men le-mteqqfin.* The proportion of illiterate people in the world is greater than the educated.
ʔumuṛ, ʔumuṛat pl. of *ʔamṛ* **1**
uṛ used in expr. *men l-uṛ* and *me-l-luṛ* from behind, from the rear *žat me-l-luṛ u-ṭeyyḥatu fe-l-ḥafa.* She came up from behind and pushed him in the hole. —*fe-s-sinima ma-ka-nšuf-ši me-l-luṛ.* In the movies I can't see (well) from the rear.
uṛubḅa Europe
uṛubḅawi pl. *-yen* European
ʔustad pl. *ʔasatida* **1.** professor, teacher *s-si yunes ʔustad de-t-tarix fe-l-žamiɛa.* Mr. Yunes is a history teacher at the University. **2.** used with s.o.'s name to indicate his profession as a lawyer *ʔustad sliman muḥami haʔil.* Mr. (lawyer) Sliman is an excellent attorney.
ʔuṣul pl. of *ʔaṣel*
ʔutil, util pl. *-at* hotel
uwwel same as *luwwel*
ʔuxṛa classicized f. form of *ʔaxoṛ*
ʔuxṛin classicized pl. form of *ʔaxoṛ*
užba same as *wežba*
užṛa same as *ižaṛa*

W

w, we- see *u*
wa conjunction used in certain expr.:
¶ *la . . . wa-la* neither . . . nor *ana la ṛaʔis wa-la meṛʔus.* I'm neither a ruler nor am I ruled.
¶ *wa-iyyahφ* (not used in first person) expr. of warning, admonishment *wa-iyyak l-kas l-luwwel!* Watch out for that first glass (of liquor)! —*wa-iyyaha (u-) temši dži lle-hna!* She'd better not come here!
¶ *wa-la* (rather) than *ḷḷahu-mma siyaṛa qdima wa-la bla-š.* Better to have an old car than none at all.
waba (m.), *wabaʔ* disaster, catastrophe, calamity (e.g., epidemic, plague, earthquake)
wad pl. *widan* **1.** river, creek, stream, etc. **2.** sewer
** *nta f-wad w-ana f-wad.* We're talking about two different things.
waḍaʔif pl. of *waḍif, waḍifa*
waḍif, waḍifa pl. *waḍaʔif* position, job, function
waḍeḥ pl. *-in* (comp. *wḍeḥ*) clear (explanation, water, sky, etc.)
wafaʔ fidelity, faithfulness *l-wafaʔ ka-itteɛtabeṛ men ʔaḥsen xiṣal l-ʔinsan* Fidelity is considered as one of the better characteristics of an individual.
wafat (f.) death *men băɛd l-wafat dyal ḅḅah, baɛ d-daṛ lli xella-lu.* After his father's death he sold the house that he (his father) left to him.
wafi pl. *wafyen* **1.** indicates a little more than the amount specified *ɛṭani kilu wafi.* He gave a kilogram, plus a little more. **2.** fat, fatted (animals) **3.** abundant, plenty of *z-zṛăɛ ža wafi had l-ɛam.* There's plenty of wheat this year. **4.** (too) big, large *had l-kebbuṭ lli ɛṭitini wafi ɛliya.* This jacket you gave me is (too) big for me.
wafeq v.t. **1.** to agree with, to go along with (s.o.) **2.** to go (well) with, to match (colors, furniture, etc.)
¶ *wafeq ɛla* **1.** to agree on (s.th.) **2.** to ratify (decision, bill, etc.)
¶ a.p. *mwafeq* pl. *-in* **1.** reasonable **2.** suitable
wafeṛ pl. *-in* a great deal of, much *ɛăndna măɛlumat wafṛa.* We have a great deal of information.
wakala pl. *wkayel* agency *ṣeṛṛḥat wakalat l-ʔanbaʔ dyal l-meġrib belli l-malik ġadi itqabel mɛa ṛaʔis l-žumhuṛiya de-fṛanṣa.* The Moroccan News Agency announced that the king will meet with the president of the French Republic.
wakel a.p. of *kla, kal*
wala v.t. to be next to *škun walak l-bareḥ fe-s-sinima?* Who was that next to you yesterday in the theater?
¶ *wala l-* to make come or get close to *wali-li dak ṣ-ṣenduq!* Shove that box over here (where I can see it)!
wa-la-inni same as *walayenni*
wa-lakin, wa-lakenni but, however
walayenni **1.** expr. of amazement, surprise, astonishment *walayenni ʔemṭaṛ nezlat had l-ɛam!* Man, have we had rain this year! —*walayenni nta ḥṛami!* Well! Aren't you clever! (not sarcastic) **2.** but, however *hiya*

bent žmila, walayenni qṣiṛa šwiya mʕa l-ʔasaf. She's a pretty girl, but unfortunately a little short.

waled a.p. of *wled*

walĭd f. *-a* pl. *-in, waldin* (*walĭdi-* or *waldi-* before pron. endings) parent (mother, father)

walda pl. *-t* womb, uterus

waldin pl. of *walĭd*

walef v.t. **1.** to get used to, to become accustomed to, to accustom oneself to *waleft n-nʕas f-had l-bit.* I've gotten used to sleeping in this room. **2.** to familiarize oneself with, to become familiar with

wali f. *-ya* pl. *awliya, ʔawliyaʔ* **1.** guardian (of person under age) **2.** (usually in pl.) saint(s)

** *ma-ʕăndu la-wali wa-la tali.* He doesn't have anyone at all (i.e., no family, close friends).

¶ *wali d-le-mdina* mayor

walima pl. *wlayem* feast, party, reception (usually with food)

walem v.t. **1.** to be convenient to or for (s.o.), to be o.k. with (s.o.), to suit (s.o.) *dak l-weqt ma-ka-iwalemni-š.* That time isn't convenient for me. **2.** to be appropriate, fitting, or proper for (s.th.) **3.** to go (well) with, to match (s.o., s.th.)

walu (used with negative *ma-*) **1.** nothing; not . . . anything, a thing *ma-qal-li walu.* He didn't tell me anything. **2.** at all *dik d-dwa ma-nefʕătni walu.* That medicine hasn't done me any good at all.

w-amma same as *amma*

waqaʔiʕ pl. of *waqiʕa*

waqayeʕ pl. of *waqiʕa*

waqaḥa audacity

waqef a.p. of *wqef*

waqfiya used in the expr. *be-l-waqfiya* standing (up), while standing *dima ka-yakol be-l-waqfiya.* He always eats standing up.

waqila **1.** maybe, perhaps, possibly **2.** probably, most likely

waqiʕa pl. *waqayeʕ, waqaʔiʕ* **1.** unfortunate incident or event **2.** disaster, catastrophe

warĭt pl. *warata* heir, inheritor

wasiṭa pl. *wasayeṭ* **1.** mediation, intervention **2.** mediator, intermediary **3.** means, way

¶ *b-wasiṭet* (cons.) by means of, through, by

waseʕ pl. *-in* **1.** wide, broad (road, room, meaning, usage, etc.) **2.** vast, spacious

waṣi, waṣiy pl. *ʔawṣiya* guardian (of person under age)

waṣiya pl. *-t, waṣaya* will, testament

waṣṭa **1.** n.pl. of *waṣṭi* **2.** (with art.) Algeria

waṣṭi adj. pl. *-yen* n.pl. *waṣṭa* Algerian (some slight archaic connotation)

waš **1.** used to introduce questions answerable in the affirmative or negative *waš nta ṣayem?* Are you fasting? —*waš ka-tăʕṛfha?* Do you know her? **2.** often correlative of *wella la* —*waš ġad-iži wella la?* Is he or is he not coming? **3.** whether, if *šuf waš žaw wella ma-zal.* See if they've come yet. —*ma-ʕṛeft waš žahla wella ġir balida.* I don't know whether she's ignorant or just stupid.

wata v.t. to go (well) with, to match

** *ma-xeṣṣha wa-la wataha ttʕăllem l-ʕăṛbiya!* She'll never learn Arabic in a million years!

wateṛni **1.** expr. of some surprise at s.th. unsuspected or unexpected *wateṛni nta ḥṛami!* Well, you're quite a little devil, aren't you? **2.** but, whereas *lemma šeft l-xeṭṭ ḥsab-li xeṭṭu, wateṛni fe-l-ḥaqiqa huwa xeṭṭ ḅḅah.* When I saw the handwriting I thought it was his, whereas it's really his father's.

waṭa v.t. to flatten, to level, to even (horizontally only)

waṭan same as *waṭăn*

waṭani same as *waṭăni*

waṭaniya **1.** nationalism **2.** patriotism

waṭăn **1.** nation **2.** country

waṭăni pl. *-yen* **1.** national **2.** nationalist, nationalistic **3.** patriotic

waxed (*ʕla*) to blame (for), to hold it against (s.o.) (for)

waxed a.p. of *xda, xad*

waxxa **1.** common expr. of agreement, assent *bġiti temši mʕaya le-s-sinima?—waxxa!* Do you want to go with me to the movies? —Yes, I do! —*qul le-mṃṃi ġadi-nži mʕăṭṭeḷ le-ḍ-ḍaṛ.—waxxa!* Tell my mother I'll be late getting home.—O.K.! —*waš imken-li nestăʕmel had le-qlam?—waxxa!* Can I use this pencil?—Of course! **2.** although, (even) though, (even) if *waxxa ṣbeḥt mṛiḍ mšit neštaġel.* I went to work even though I got up sick. —*waxxa tkun ntiya hiya malikat l-žamal, ma-ndzuwwež bik.* (Even) if you were the queen of beauty I wouldn't marry you.

wayn (not common Moroccan) same as *fayn*

wayenni same as *walayenni*

wazaṛa pl. of *wzir*

wazen v.t. **1.** to balance, to put in equilibrium **2.** to balance (books, accounts) **3.** to weigh, to consider **4.** to compare

wazzan city in Northern Morocco, famous for its olives

wazzani pl. *-yen* native of *wazzan*

wažeb same as *žaweb*

wažeb **1.** a.p. of *wžeb* **2.** same as *wažĭb*

wažĭb pl. *-at* duty, obligation *qum be-l-wažĭb*

dyalek ka-muwaṭin! Do your duty as a citizen!

¶ *be-l-wažib ʕla* (to be) incumbent upon, to be one's duty ≠, to be supposed ≠ *be-l-wažib ʕlina nxedmu f-had le-wṛaq.* We're supposed to work with these slips (of paper).

waḥed f. *weḥda* pl. *weḥdin* **1.** one *šṛebt kas waḥed dyal atay.* I drank one glass of tea. **2.** (with art.) one, a person, you (impersonal) *ma-kayen fayn iḍḍeṛṛeg l-waḥed.* There's no place where one can take shelter. **3.** a, an *šrit waḥed s-siyaṛa faʕla tarka.* I've bought a terrific car. **4.** some, a certain *waḥed s-siyyed ža ka-iseqṣi ʕlik l-bareḥ, ma-ʕṛeftu škun huwa.* Some gentleman was asking for you yesterday; I don't know who he was. **5.** some, about, around (before numbers) *ʕăndi l-ġaṛaḍ d-waḥed l-xems mya de-r-ryal.* I need about five hundred riyals. **6.** same *ṭ-ṭumubil dyalek we-ṭ-ṭumubil dyali meṣnuʕin f-măʕmel waḥed.* Your car and my car were made in the same factory. **7.** (invariable) alike, the same *le-ʕyalat gaʕ waḥed.* Women are all the same.

¶ *b-weḥduΦ, b-weḥdihΦ* **1.** by oneself, alone *waš rekkebti had l-mutur b-weḥdek?* Did you put this motor together by yourself? —*žat be-weḥdha.* She came by herself. **2.** the only one ≠ (*ġir*) *ana b-weḥdi lli žit.* I was the only one that came.

¶ *ši-waḥed* pl. *ši-weḥdin* somebody, someone (pl. some, some people) *had š-ši ma-ka-yăʕžeb-š l-ši-weḥdin.* Some people don't like this.

¶ *weḥduΦ, weḥdihΦ* same as *b-weḥduΦ, b-weḥdihΦ*

¶ *ḥetta waḥed* (f. *ḥetta weḥda*) nobody, no one; not . . . anyone *ḥetta waḥed ma-ka-ibġini.* Nobody likes me. —*ʕămmṛi ma-qtelt ḥetta waḥed.* I've never killed anyone. —*škun lli mša ištaġel nhaṛ l-ʔiḍṛab?—ḥetta waḥed.* Who went to work on the day of the strike?—Nobody.

waʕed v.t. to promise, to vow to (s.o.) *waʕedtini baš tešri-li ṭumubil.* You promised me you'd buy me a car.

waʕeḍ v.t. **1.** to exhort, to admonish **2.** to advise, to counsel

waʕer pl. *-in* (comp. *wʕăr*) **1.** hard, difficult **2.** hard, strict, severe (person) **3.** violent, strong (blow, hit, storm) **4.** dangerous, perilous (e.g., mountain, region full of bandits) **5.** serious, grave (illness)

webbex (*ʕla*) to scold (for), to reprimand (for)

wber **1.** camel hair **2.** cloth made from camel hair

wdaya pl. of *wdiyi*

wedd b- (v.n. *weddan*) to give (s.th.) to (s.o.), to make a present of (s.th.) to (s.o.) *ʕyit ma-nweddek b-le-flus, ṣ-ṣḷa ʕăl n-nbi!* Damn it! I'm tired of giving you money!

¶ *a weddi* **1.** introductory expr. referring to the listener (sometimes translatable with "by the way," "incidentally") —*a weddi, waš xditi le-ktab lli xellit-lek hna l-bareḥ wella la?* By the way, did you get the book I left here for you yesterday? **2.** term of address equivalent to "chum" or "pal" *a-weddi aži tqeṣṣeṛ mʕana šwiya fe-l-lil.* Say, pal, come visit us a little while tonight. —*a-weddi ḷḷah yehdik hennina šwiya u-baṛaka men ṣ-ṣḍaʕ.* Hey, chum, give us a little peace and stop the noise, please.

¶ *ʕla wedd* **1.** because **2.** because of, on account of, in view of **3.** for the sake of **4.** concerning, about, on

wedda **1.** v.t. to fulfill, to carry out (duty, obligation) **2.** v.i. to pay for one's sin(s) or crime(s) (by imprisonment, mental suffering, etc.) **3.** v.t. to suffer, to go through (difficulties, hard times, etc.)

wedden same as *dden*

weddăʕ v.t. to say good-by to, to bid farewell to

wdina pl. *-t* dim. of *wden*

wdiyi pl. *wdaya* member of the Wdaya tribe

wden, pl. *wednin,* (*wedni-* before pron. endings) **1.** ear (anatomy) **2.** handle (cup, etc.)

wedḥa suint

wdăʕ n.u. *-a* **1.** shell of a warm water gastropod mollusk (cowrie) with a smooth, highly polished surface **2.** porcelain, china

weḍḍef v.t. to employ, to hire (for white-collar job)

weḍḍeṛ v.t. **1.** to lose, to misplace, to mislay **2.** to get (s.o.) lost **3.** to lead astray

weḍḍeḥ v.t. **1.** to make clear, to clear up (water, etc.) **2.** to explain, to clarify

wḍu obligatory ritual ablutions performed by Muslims before prayer

wḍuḥ clarity, lucidity (of thought, words) *le-wḍuḥ ṣifa ḍaṛuṛiya l-l-kottab.* Clarity (of thought) is a necessary quality for writers.

wḍeḥ comp. of *wadeḥ*

wfa (v.n. *wafaʔ*) **1.** v.i. to end, to terminate, to expire *l-žawaz dyali ʔažalu qṛib iwfa.* My passport is about to expire. **2.** v.t. to pass, to exceed *šḥal mšina de-ṭ-ṭṛiq? wfina xemsin kilumiter.* How far have we come? We've passed fifty kilometers. —*šḥal de-l-flus xṣeṛna? wfina myatayn ḍulaṛ.* How much money have we spent? We've exceeded two hundred dollars.

¶ *wfa b-* to remain faithful to (s.th.) *wfa be-klemtu.* He kept his word.

wfa v.n. of *weffa*
  ** *ṭ-ṭula u-le-wfa* refers to the fact that someone is tall and well built; usually used alone *dzuwwžat ṛažel ġani w-zin we-ṭ-ṭula u-le-wfa.* She married a man who is rich and handsome, tall and well built. —*ɛaʔila žmila, kollhom fihom ṭ-ṭula u-le-wfa.* They're a handsome family, all tall and well built.

weffa f- to give (sell) in full measure, plus a little extra at no extra charge *weffa mɛaya fe-l-letšin.* He gave me the oranges I paid for, plus a little more.

weffeq v.t. to help, to favor (God only subject)
  ¶ *weffeq bin* to conciliate between

weffeṛ v.t. **1.** to save, to put aside (money, etc.) **2.** to economize on, to use sparingly or economically **3.** to provide with, to give *mṛati ka-tweffeṛ-li s-saɛada.* My wife gives me happiness.

wegged v.t. **1.** to wake up, to revive, to bring to (through some physical aid, as water in the face) **2.** to remind *weggeḍtu be-lli l-ɛers ġad-ikun nhaṛ s-sebt.* I reminded him that the wedding was going to be on Saturday.
  ¶ *wegged ṛaṣuφ (mɛa)* **1.** to be alert (to), to pay attention (to) **2.** to be careful (of), to watch out (for)

wgid same as *wqid*

weġġel v.t. to get (s.th., s.o.) stuck (e.g., s.o. in mud, a knife in a tree; also metaphorical)

wehheb v.t. to give (a gift), to present *l-ḥukuma wehhbat melyun fṛenk l-le-xriya.* The government presented a million francs to the orphanage.

wehli used to emphasize one's feeling that s.th. has occurred a relatively long time ago, or has been going on for some time *wehli, šḥal hadi baš mat!* But he's been dead for quite a while now!

whem pl. *wham, ʔawham* premonition, presentiment, foreboding *dima ka-ikun biya (fiya) le-whem qbel ma-tewqăɛ ši-ḥaža.* I always have a foreboding before something happens.
  ¶ *ɛănduφ whem* **1.** to be afraid, to be apprehensive, to be worried *ɛăndu whem kbir belli ɛămmṛu ma-ġad-inžeḥ f-ḥetta ḥaža.* He's terribly afraid that he'll never succeed in anything. **2.** to have a delusion, illusory idea or ambition *kan ɛăndha le-whem belli ġadya tkun ši-nhaṛ mumettila.* She had the (illusory) idea that she would be an actress some day.

widan pl. of *wad*

wifaq **1.** understanding, rapport **2.** agreement

wik, wik kind of woman's scream or squeal (uttered in various emotional situations)

wil **1.** woe, grief (rare usage) **2.** s.th. (or s.o.) unpleasant, repulsive, messed up, etc.
  ** *a wili!* Oh, woe is me! I've had it now!

win same as *fayn*

wisam pl. *ʔawsima* decoration, medal

wkil, wakil pl. *wkayel, wukalaʔ, weklan* **1.** agent **2.** lawyer, defender
  ¶ *wakil d-dewla* prosecuting attorney

wekkal adj. pl. *-in* n.pl. *-a* big eater, one who eats a lot

wekked same as *ʔekked*

wekkel v.t. **1.** to make (s.o.) eat (s.th.), to feed (s.th.) to (s.o.) *ka-nwekklu d-dra l-le-bhayem* (or *le-bhayem*) *dyalna kollhom.* We feed corn to all our animals. —*ka-nwekklu-lhom* (or *ka-nwekkluhom*) *d-dra.* We feed them corn.
  ** *had l-xedma ma-ɛămmeṛha ma-ġad-twekkel l-xobz.* This job will never provide enough to eat.
  ¶ *wekkel* (s.o.) *le-ɛṣa* to beat (s.o.), to give a beating to (s.o. as punishment)
2. to hire or employ as an agent or manager (i.e., *wakil*)

wekkeḥ v.t. **1.** to dry out (said of things depending on water to live or be useful, e.g., soil, food in the process of cooking) **2.** to cause (s.o.) to become dehydrated (by depriving him of water)

wkeṛ pl. *wkaṛ* nest

wkeḥ v.i. to dry up, to go dry, to evaporate *l-wad lli fe-ṣ-ṣeḥṛa wkăḥ.* The river in the desert dried up. —*l-ma wkăḥ men l-kas de-l-werḍ u-l-werḍat matu.* The water in the vase of roses evaporated and the roses died. —*hḍeṛt ḥetta wkăḥt.* I talked until I went dry. —*nsit l-meqṛaž fuq l-ɛafya ḥetta wkăḥ.* I forgot the kettle on the fire and it boiled dry. —*zid šwiya de-l-ma fe-ṭ-ṭažin, ṛah wkăḥ.* Add a little water to the casserole, it's gone dry.

wekḥa **1.** n.i. of *wkeḥ* **2.** dryness (soil, body)
  ¶ *bihφ l-wekḥa* to be very thirsty ≠

wla worthier, more deserving *huwa wla men l-axoṛ.* He is worthier than the other (man).
  ¶ *wla l-* better for (s.o.), preferable for (s.o.) *had l-meḍṛaṣa wla-lek men hadik.* This school is better for you than that one.

wlad pl. of *weld*

wlada v.r. of *wled*

wlases pl. of *welsis*

wlaya saintliness *iwa hadi wlaya!* That's real saintliness!

wlayem pl. of *walima*

wlaži pl. of *welža*

wlaɛa v.n. of *wellăɛ*

wled v.i. and v.t. **1.** to have a baby, to give birth, to bear *dik s-siyyda weldat t-twam.* That woman gave birth to twins. —*l-begṛa weldat ɛžel byeḍ.* The cow had a white calf. **2.** to bear, to produce *l-weṛda weldat bezzaf de-l-weṛd had l-ɛam.* The rosebush bore a lot of roses this year. —*had t-teffaẓa ma-weldat teffaẓ had l-ɛam.* This apple tree didn't produce any apples this year.

¶ a.p. *waled* pl. *-in* having children or a family *huwa mzuwwež u-waled.* He's married and has a family.

weld pl. *wlad* **1.** boy **2.** young animal (especially those that may be personified) **3.** (pl. and dim. pl. *wlidat*) family (often only the wife)

¶ *wlad sidi ẓmad u-musa* group of Berber gymnasts or acrobats (deriving from *ẓmad u-musa,* famous acrobat)

¶ *weld le-klab* son-of-a-bitch (similar to "son-of-a-gun" with friends)

¶ *weld le-ẓṛam* bastard

¶ *weld n-nas* well-bred, well-brought up boy (of good family)

¶ *weld s-suq* gamin, street urchin

welda pl. *-t, wladat* **1.** n.i. of *wled* **2.** birth

welf v.n. of *wellef* and *walef*

¶ *ṛebba l-welf ɛla* to become used or attached to

welha attention, application

** *ma-ɛăndu welha.* He's a little odd, queer.

¶ *ṛedd l-welha l-* to pay attention to

¶ *ṛedd l-welha ɛla* to watch over, to take care of

wlidat pl. of *wliyyed,* dim. of *weld*

wliya pl. *-t* woman (usually implying some weakness or helplessness because of her sex, or because of real poverty or physical disability) *ɛawen had le-wliya ṭṭlăɛ le-ṭ-ṭubis.* Help this (poor) woman get on the bus. —*le-mṛa ġir wliya kif-emma kanet.* A female is only a (poor feeble) woman, whatever she is.

wliyyed pl. *wlidat* dim. of *weld*

wliža pl. *-t* dim. of *welža*

wella v.i. **1.** to return (go back, come back) **2.** to become *s-si muẓămmed wella ɛamĭl de-ṛ-ṛbaṭ š-šheṛ lli fat.* Mohammed became mayor of Rabat last month. **3.** to end up *wella ka-yeẓki ši-xṛafa.* He ended up by telling a story. **4.** to finally (do s.th.), to finally get around to (doing s.th.) *wellina ka-nxedmu.* We finally got around to working. **5.** v.t. to make, to appoint *wellawni mudir ɛăl š-šarika.* They made me manager of the company.

** *fayn bġiti twelli u-kan?* What the hell are you trying to do, anyway?

¶ *wella ɛla ṛeyyuᵠ* to change one's mind

wella or, or else *bġa idṛes imma ṭ-ṭibb wella ṣ-ṣeydala.* He wants to study either medicine or pharmacy. —*waš ka-tăɛṛefha wella la?* Do you know her, or not? (does not necessarily imply the impatience usually felt in the English)

wellad pl. *-in* **1.** fruitful, prolific (person, plant, etc.) **2.** fertile, fecund (person, plant, earth)

wellay pl. *-in* ag. adj. of *wella* **1**

wel-l-bareẓ, wel-l-barẓayn see *bareẓ*

welled v.t. **1.** to cause (a female) to bear (young) (relatively rare in this double object usage) **2.** to fertilize, to fecundate (woman, plant, animal) **3.** to generate, to produce, to put out (e.g. a battery current, engine horsepower) **4.** to create, to produce (ideas, happiness, etc.)

wellef v.t. **1.** to become accustomed or used to (s.o., s.th.) **2.** to help (s.o.) become accustomed to (s.th.), to familiarize (s.o.) with (s.th.), to acquaint (s.o.) with (s.th.) *wellefnah ṣugan ṭ-ṭumubil.* We helped him get accustomed to driving a car.

welsis pl. *wlases* glandular swelling, swollen gland (e.g., bubo, adenoma)

welwel v.i. to howl or ululate (women on certain, usually joyous, occasions)

welža pl. *-t, wlaži* rich, alluvial plain, situated in a valley

welɛa pl. *wlaɛi* passion, special fondness *ɛăndhom l-welɛa de-l-musiqa.* They have a passion for music.

wnis pl. *wnayes* companion, friend

we-n-names day before yesterday (country usage)

wennes v.t. to keep (s.o.) company

wqaqef pl. of *weqqafa*

wqaṛ same as *wqeṛ*

wqat pl. of *weqt*

wqef v.i. **1.** to stand up, to rise *t-tlamed kollhom weqfu lemma dxel l-mudir l-l-qiṣm.* The pupils all stood up when the principal entered the classroom. **2.** to stop, to halt *wqef temm!* Stop right there! —*s-siyaṛa weqfat.* The car stopped.

¶ *wqef ɛla* **1.** to take care of (s.th.), to attend to (s.th.) *wqef ɛăl ɛers xtu.* He took care of his sister's wedding. **2.** to watch over, to oversee *wqef ɛăl l-katiba ẓetta ṭebɛat ṛ-ṛasaᵓil, ɛad xellaha temši.* He watched over the typist until she typed the letters, and only then let her go. **3.** to need *weqfat ɛăl s-si yunes iɛawenha.* She needs Mr. Yunes to help her. **4.** to find out (the truth about something) *mufettiš š-šoṛṭa wqef ɛla ẓaqiqat l-qatel.* The police inspector found out the truth about the murderer.

¶ *wqef mɛa* to help, to aid *mm̄u weqfat mɛah baš qdeṛ išri ḍ-ḍaṛ.* His mother helped him so that he could buy the house.

¶ a.p. *waqef* exactly, on the dot *weṣlet le-ḍ-ḍaṛ fe-t-tmenya waqfa.* She arrived home at exactly eight o-clock.

weqfa **1.** n.i. of *wqef* **2.** height (of person) *had š-šeṛžem ɛlad qedd l-weqfa dyali.* This window is as high as I am.

¶ *weqfa de-ḍ-ḍhuṛ, weqfa de-ṣ-ṣla* the noon prayer (also the time of the prayer)

¶ *žmăɛ l-weqfa* to stand up, to get up

wqid n.u. *-a* pl. *-t* match *ṭiyyḥu ṣ-ṣenduq d-le-wqid fe-l-ma.* They dropped the box of matches in the water.

wqita pl. *-t* moment, instant *ila ɛăndek ši-wqita daba, aži nehdeṛ mɛak.* If you have a moment now, come let me talk to you.

wqiya du. *wqiytayn* pl. *-t, aweq* measure of weight equal to $\frac{1}{16}$ of a kilo, 62.5 grams

wqiɛ v.n. of *wqăɛ*

weqqaf **1.** pl. *-in* capable or used to standing for long periods of time **2.** pl. *-a* foreman, supervisor

weqqafa pl. *-t, wqaqef* one of the vertical supports on either side of a loom

weqqef v.t. **1.** to stand up or upright (chair, book, person, etc.) **2.** to stop, to halt **3.** to park (car, etc.) **4.** to immobilize, to make immovable **5.** to repress, to quell **6.** to suspend (i.e., debar s.o., make s.th. temporarily inoperative, etc.) **7.** to baste, to stitch temporarily

weqqeṛ v.t. to respect, to have respect for (s.o.)

weqqăɛ v.t. to sign (either name or document)

wqeṛ respect *ɛṭini šwiya d-le-wqeṛ!* Show a little respect for me! *bda ka-yeɛṭiha le-wqeṛ men n-nhaṛ lli txaṣmu.* He began to respect her from the day when they quarreled.

weqt pl. (of intensity) *wqat* time (includes epoch, era, etc.) *fe-l-weqt lli kont f-ʔamirika tɛăllemt ntkellem b-l-ingliza.* During the time I was in America I learned to speak English. —*šḥal de-l-weqt ka-iṭṭeḷḷeb le-bni dyal had ḍ-ḍaṛ?* How much time does building this house require? —*ka-iqḍi weqtu kollu f-lăɛb l-kaṛṭa.* He spends all his time playing cards.

** *ma-ɛăndu weqt.* He has no sense of time.

¶ *bla weqt* **1.** without any time schedule, at any odd time **2.** (too much) ahead of time, (too) early *wṣelna bla weqt.* We arrived too early. **3.** at an inopportune or bad time

¶ *daz l-weqt* to get late

¶ *f-had l-weqt* at the present time, right now, at the moment

¶ *fe-l-weqt* on time *dima ka-nxeržu fe-l-weqt.* We always leave on time.

¶ *f-weqt, fe-l-weqt d-* during *f-weqt t-temtil ši-ḥădd ṭaḥ men ṭ-ṭebqa l-luwla.* During the play someone fell from the first balcony.

¶ *qtel l-weqt* to kill time, to pass the time

¶ *weqt-aš* when, at what time

¶ *weqt lli, weqt-emma* whenever, anytime (that)

weqti pl. *-yen* **1.** in style, vogue, fashion **2.** time-conscious, having a good sense of time

wquf **1.** v.n. of *wqef* **2.** stop *ḍuṛ ɛăl l-imin u-telqa maḥăll wquf ṭ-ṭubis.* Turn to the right and you'll find the bus stop. **3.** pause, break, recess *fe-l-măɛmel saɛat le-wquf kanet ma bin l-weḥda we-ž-žuž.* In the factory, break time was between one and two o'clock. **4.** parking *xellaw maḥăll wquf s-siyaṛat wṛa ṣ-ṣuq.* They left a parking place for cars behind the market.

wquɛ v.n. of *wqăɛ*

wqăɛ v.i. **1.** to happen, to occur, to take place *weqɛat-lu ḥadita fe-ṛ-ṛbaṭ.* He had an accident in Rabat. **2.** to fall down *wqăɛ ɛla ḥăžṛa u-ttherrsat-lu senntu.* He fell on a rock and broke his tooth.

wṛa same as *mmuṛ, mmuṛa*

wṛani (*luṛani* after art.) pl. *-yen* back, rear *ɛṭawna maḥăll fe-ṣ-ṣeff l-luṛani.* They gave us a place in the back row.

wṛaq pl. of *weṛqa*

wred v.i. to drink (animal) *ddi le-bgeṛ iwerdu fe-l-ɛin.* Take the cattle to the spring to drink.

weṛḍ n.u. *-a* **1.** rose **2.** rosebush

** *xeddha weṛḍa.* She has rosy cheeks.

weṛḍi pl. *-yen* rose, rose-colored (may approach bright red)

wṛiḍa pl. *-t* dim. of *weṛḍa*

wṛiqa pl. *-t* dim. of *weṛqa*

werk, weṛk pl. *wrak, wṛak* hip

wrem to swell (up), to be swollen *ḍeṛṛatni ḍ-ḍeṛṣa ḥetta wrem-li l-ḥănk.* My tooth hurt me so much that my cheek swelled up.

weṛqa pl. *-t, wṛaq* **1.** leaf (tree, book) **2.** (sheet of) paper **3.** card (generic term) **4.** bill (currency) **5.** ticket (admission, travel) **6.** record, disc (phonograph) **7.** kind of thin crust used in making various pastries and meat pies, e.g., *beṣṭila*

¶ *qṭăɛ l-weṛqa* to buy or get a ticket

werra v.t. **1.** to show *werrini kif-aš ka-tḥoll had l-leġz!* Show me how to solve this puzzle! —*werrini ši-ḥaža xṛa!* Show me something else! **2.** to point (s.th.) out to (s.o.), to indicate (s.th.) to (s.o.)

** *leh la-iwerrik bas!* I hope you get better. May God maintain your health!
werred v.t. to water (animals)
weṛṛek v.i. (*ʕla*) 1. to lean or support oneself (on, against) 2. to press or exert pressure (on) 3. to put one's weight (on, against) 4. to lie down (on)
werret v.t. to cause, to produce *l-gaṛṛu werret-lu s-saṛaṭan.* Cigarettes have produced cancer in him.
** *măʕrifat s-suˀ ka-twerret le-bla.* He who associates with evil, evil becomes.
wret, wṛet v.t. (p.p. *murut*) to inherit *ma-wret men ḅḅah ġir le-ġdayed.* He inherited nothing from his father but gnawing worries.
wert 1. inheritance *ṭaḥ-lu wert kbir.* He's come into a large inheritance. 2. heritage 3. heredity
wsada pl. *-t, wsayed* cushion, pillow
wsiseʕ pl. *-in* dim. of *waseʕ*
wseq v.t. (v.n. *wesq*) 1. to load (s.th. onto or into s.th.) 2. to export
wesq v.n. of *wseq*
wessaq pl. *-a* 1. ag. n. of *wseq* 2. stevedore
wessed (*ʕla*) 1. v.i. to lay or lean one's head (on s.th., as a pillow) 2. v.t. to lay, to lean (s.o.'s head on s.th. used as a pillow) *wessed-lha ṛaṣha ʕăl le-mxedda!* Lay her head on the pillow!
wesseṭ v.t. 1. to put or place (s.th.) in the middle or center 2. to choose or appoint as mediator or intermediary
wessex v.t. 1. to dirty, to soil, to get (s.th.) dirty 2. to soil, to smirch (reputation, honor)
wessăʕ v.t. to enlarge, to broaden, to widen (room, road, knowledge)
¶ *wessăʕ men* to get away from, to avoid (s.o., s.th.)
¶ *wessăʕ xaṭṛuφ* 1. to get a hold of oneself (usually in one's sadness or grief) 2. to take it easy, to try not to get excited
¶ *wessăʕ ʕla* to help (s.o.) out, to offer aid to
weswas 1. suspicious distrust 2. haunting obsession
¶ *fihφ l-weswas* 1. to be suspiciously distrustful ≠ 2. to be obsessed or haunted by s.th. ≠
¶ *mṛiḍ be-l-weswas* same as *fihφ l-weswas*
weswes v.t. 1. to cause to be suspiciously distrustful, to give reason to be suspiciously distrustful to (s.o. or s.o.'s mind) 2. to influence (s.o.) to do bad or improper things, to corrupt
¶ p.p. *mweswes* pl. *-in* haunted
wsex pl. *wsax, wsuxat* 1. dirt, filth *ġsel wežhek men le-wsex.* Wash the dirt off your face. 2. draft (of a letter, speech, etc.) *f-le-mtiḥan, ma-kan ʕăndu weqt baš inqol lli kteb u-ʕṭa le-wsex mʕa wṛeqtu.* In the examination he didn't have time to recopy what he had written so he handed in the draft with his paper.
¶ *wsex d-denya* property, worldly goods, material possessions *l-mal ġir wsex d-denya.* Money is only a material possession. —*ʕăndu ktir men wsex d-denya.* He's filthy rich.
wesʕa pl. *-t* clear, open space or area (e.g. a field)
wṣaf pl. of *weṣf*
wṣaḷi pl. of *weṣḷa*
wṣaya pl. *-t* n.i. of *weṣṣa*
wṣayef pl. of *wṣifa*
weṣf pl. *ˀawṣaf* 1. description 2. characteristic trait, distinctive characteristic
wṣiya pl. *-t* n.i. of *weṣṣa*
wṣel v.i. to arrive *l-yum wṣelt mʕăṭṭeḷ l-l-xedma.* I arrived late to work today. —*wṣel le-n-natiža lli bġa.* He arrived at the result he wanted.
weṣḷa pl. *-t, wṣaḷi* 1. n.i. of *wṣel* 2. arrival 3. board used for carrying bread to and from the ovens
weṣṣa v.t. 1. to advise, to counsel 2. to order, to command, to tell (s.o.)
¶ *weṣṣa ʕla* to order (s.th.) from (s.o.) ≠, to put an order in for (s.th.) from (s.o.) ≠ *weṣṣit šarikat fuṛd ʕla siyaṛa ždida l-l-ʕam l-maži.* I've ordered a new car from Ford for next year.
weṣṣel 1. v.t. to take *weṣṣel-lha had le-bṛa!* Take this letter to her!—*weṣṣelthom l-bareḥ fe-l-lil le-ḍ-ḍaṛ be-ṭ-ṭumubil dyali.* I took them home last night in my car. 2. same as *wṣel*
weṣṭ middle, center
¶ *weṣṭ ḍ-ḍaṛ* kind of central court or patio of a (Moroccan) house
weṣṭani pl. *-yen* (adj.) middle, center, in the middle
weṣṭi pl. *-in* 1. same as *weṣṭani* 2. pl. also *wṣaṭa* room between the hot and cold rooms of the public bath, having a medium temperature 3. pl. *wṣaṭa* caftan (worn between other garments)
wṣul v.n. of *wṣel*
wšam v.n. of *wšem*
wešk used in the expr. *ʕla wešk* (to be) about to *ʕla wešk nsaliw.* We're about to finish.
wšem v.t. (p.p. *mušum*) to tattoo *wšem yeddih u-sedru.* He tattooed his hands and his chest. —*ṣaḥbu mšem-lu yeddih u-sedru.* His friend tatooed his hands and chest for him. —*wšem nuwwaṛa fuq draʕu.* He tattooed

a flower on his arm. —*wšem-lu ṣaḥbu.* His friend tattooed him.

wešma pl. *-t* 1. n.i. of *wšem* 2. tattoo (skin)

weššam pl. *-a* tattooer

wešweš v.t. and v.i. to whisper, to speak in a low voice or whisper

wted pl. *wtad* peg or small stick, usually pointed (as a tent peg)

wter extra prayer, said after the *ʕša* (last prayer of the day)

wetṛa n.u. of *wtaṛ*

wetṛa pl. *-t* string of a stringed musical instrument

wetted v.t. 1. to drive into the ground (pegs, stakes, etc.) 2. to drive into the ground the pegs or stakes of (tent)

wetteṛ v.t. to stretch or pull tight, to make taut (strings, rope, etc.)

wetteš v.t. to make kneel (camel)

wṭa n.u. *weṭya* pl. *-t* prairie, plain, flatland

weṭya pl. *-t* flat, level spot or area

wužud presence, existence *wužud n-nas fe-ḍ-ḍaṛ ka-ižʕălni nkun dayman feṛḥana.* The presence of people in the house always makes me happy. —*wužud bezzaf de-l-mužrimin f-le-mdun le-kbira xaṭaṛ ʕăl s-sokkan.* The presence of many criminals in the large cities is a danger for the inhabitants.

¶ *b-wužud* by the grace of, with the help of, thanks to *ġir b-wužud ḷḷah baš xeržat men l-ḥadita be-s-salam.* It was just by the grace of God that she came out of the accident safely. —*b-wužud s-si muḥămmed ḥeṣṣeḷt ʕăl l-žawaz dyali.* Thanks to Mohammed, I got my passport.

wxid v.n. of *xda*

wxem humidity, moisture, dampness

wexxeṛ 1. v.t. to delay, to make late(r) (train, etc.) 2. v.t. to delay, to postpone 3. v.t. to back up, to make go back, to move back *wexxeṛ s-siyaṛa šwiya!* Back the car up a little! 4. v.i. to back up, to move back 5. v.t. to keep or save until last

wzir, wazir pl. *wazaṛa, wzaṛa* 1. minister (government) *s-si gdira wella wzir l-xarižiya.* Mr. Gdira became the Minister of Foreign Affairs. 2. groomsman, attendant of the groom at a wedding

wziʕa pl. *-t* n.i. of *wezzăʕ*

wzen v.i., v.t. (v.n. *wzin, wzen,* p.p. *muzun*) 1. to weigh *wzen-li ši-kilu d-le-bṭaṭa.* Weigh me a kilo of potatoes. —*ana ka-newzen kteṛ mennek.* I weigh more than you do. 2. to measure, to regulate *wzen klamek!* Watch what you say! (Measure your words!)

wzen v.n. of *wzen*

wezna pl. *-t* n.i. of *wzen*

wezz n.u. *-a* goose

wezzan pl. *-a* weigher, one who weighs

wezzaʕ pl. *-a* ag. n. of *wezzăʕ*

wezzăʕ v.t. 1. to distribute; to send, hand, or dole out *l-muʕăllim wezzăʕ ktub ʕăl t-tlamed l-bareḥ.* The teacher distributed books to the pupils yesterday. —*wezzăʕ ʔamwalu ʕla ḥbabu qbel-ma imut b-ʕam.* He distributed his possessions among the members of his family one year before he died. 2. to buy and divide up (an animal for meat; done by a group of people)

wžab pl. *-at* same as *žwab*

wžeb ʕlih$^{\phi}$ to have to, to be necessary to, to be obliged to ≠ *ka-iwžeb ʕlik texdem mʕaya.* You have to work with me. —*šḥal wžeb ʕliya năʕṭihom?* How much should I pay them?

wežba pl. *-t* 1. (proper) occasion, time, (more) opportune moment (used mostly in expr. *žabtu*$^{\phi}$ *l-wežba*) 2. meal, dinner

¶ *žabtu*$^{\phi}$ *l-wežba* to come or show up at an opportune moment, just in time ≠

wžed 1. to be ready, to get ready *had saʕtayn w-ana ka-ntsennah u-baqi ma-wžed.* I've been waiting for him for two hours and he's still not ready. 2. to find *wžedti le-ktab lli mša-lek?* Did you find the book you lost? —*ila wžedtiha qol-lha tʕăyyeṭ-li.* If you find her, tell her to call me.

wežda city of Northeast Morocco

weždi adj. pl. *-yen* n.pl. *wžada* native to *wežda*

wžeh pl. *wžuh* 1. face, visage *wžehha ʕlih n-nuṛ.* She has a radiant face. 2. mien, look *wežhek ṣafi l-yum.* You look well today. 3. front (of a book, box, coin, etc.) 4. right side (as opposed to back or wrong side of cloth, paper, etc.) *wžeh had t-tub ḥṛeš.* The right side of this cloth is rough. 5. vamp (of shoe) *wžeh ṣebbaṭu melf u-le-gdem želd.* The vamp of his shoe is felt and the heel is leather.

¶ *b-wežhu*$^{\phi}$ oneself, in person *ṛ-ṛaʔis ddaxel f-dik l-qaḍiya b-wežhu.* The president himself intervened in that matter.

¶ *della wežhu*$^{\phi}$ to pout, to sulk *mnin ma-ʕṭatu-š m̄m̄u le-flus ġḍeb u-della wežhu ʕliha.* When his mother didn't give him the money, he got mad and pouted.

¶ *ma-ʕăndu*$^{\phi}$ *wžeh baš* . . . to be ashamed to . . . *ma-ʕăndu wžeh baš itlaqa biya ʕla wedd baqi ka-nsalu ši-flus.* He's ashamed to meet me because he still owes me some money.

¶ *wežhu*$^{\phi}$ *mqezder* to be brazen, to be cheeky

¶ *ḥămmeṛ le-wžeh* to make (s.o.) proud *ḥămmeṛ-li wežhi b-nažaḥu fe-d-diṛasa.* He made me proud (of him) by his success in his studies. —*ḥămmeṛ le-wžeh de-mṛatu be-l-xiṭab lli ɛmel.* He made his wife proud (of him) by the speech he made.

¶ *ɛănduᵠ wežhayn* to be two-faced

¶ *ɛla wžeh* for the sake of, because of *sameḥtu ɛla wežhek.* I forgave him for your sake.

wežhiyat (f.) favoritism, partiality

¶ *ɛmel* (or *dar*) *l-wežhiyat* to show favoritism (object not expressed)

wžuh pl. of *wžeh*

wežžeb v.t. to force, to make *wežžbuni baš nxeḷḷeṣ le-flus.* They made me pay the money.

¶ *wežžeb ɛla* same as *wežžeb* above

wežžed v.t. to prepare, to get ready (lesson, dinner, etc.)

wežžeh l- 1. to face or make (s.th.) face (toward) 2. to direct (e.g. discourse) to 3. to aim at, to point at or toward

wžăɛ v.t. (v.n. *wžăɛ*) to hurt, to have (a) pain, to ache *ṛaṣi ka-iwžăɛni.* My head hurts. —*dert r-riyaḍa l-bareḥ u-ṣebḥet dati kollha ka-tewžăɛni.* Yesterday I did calisthenics and today my body aches all over.

wžăɛ n.i. *wežɛa* pl. *-t* 1. v.n. of *wžăɛ* 2. labor pains *fiha le-wžăɛ, qṛiba tewled.* She's having labor pains, she's about to give birth.

¶ *fihᵠ le-wžăɛ* to have a stomachache

wežɛa pl. *-t* n.i. of *wžăɛ*

wḥam state or condition of a pregnant woman during the 2d, 3d or 4th month when she may feel unusual cravings, especially for food *kan baqi fiha le-wḥam melli weṣlat m̄m̄aha me-l-meġṛib.* She was still in the early stages of her pregnancy when her mother arrived from Morocco.

wḥayel pl. of *weḥla*

weḥd, b-weḥd pl. *-in* see *waḥed*

weḥda f. of *waḥed*

weḥdani pl. *-yen* 1. solitary, living all alone 2. isolated, solitary

weḥdaniya 1. unity, singleness (of God) 2. solitude, state of being alone

weḥdin pl. of *waḥed*

wḥiḥed 1. dim. of *waḥed* 2. just one, only one *ɛṭini ġir qlam wḥiḥed.* Just give me one pencil.

wḥel v.i. 1. to be entangled, to get tangled up *weḥlat l-mešṭa f-šăɛṛu.* The comb got tangled in his hair. 2. to get caught, to get stuck *wḥel l-xatem f-ṣebɛu.* The ring got stuck on his finger. 3. to be (caught) in an embarrassing or difficult situation *xerržu mul ḍ-ḍaṛ ḥit ma-xeḷḷeṣ-š le-kra, u-wḥel meskin ma-ɛṛef layn imši.* The landlord threw him out because he didn't pay the rent, and the poor guy was in a bad situation (because) he didn't know where to go.

weḥla pl. *-t, wḥayel* 1. n.i. of *wḥel* 2. delicate or touchy situation, bind 3. difficulty, problem

weḥš 1. longing, yearning, nostalgia 2. pl. *wḥuš* (ferocious) wild animal, beast 3. pl. *wḥuš* animal, brute (person)

¶ *faq l-weḥš ɛla* to long, to yearn ≠ *faq ɛlihom l-weḥš dyal wladhom.* They long to see their children.

weḥši pl. *-yen* 1. wild (animal, person, plant, etc.) 2. bestial, brutish

wḥuš pl. of *wăḥš*

weḥḥed v.t. to unite, to unify

weḥḥel v.t. 1. to get (s.th.) stuck (e.g., in the mud) 2. to put into an embarrassing or difficult situation

¶ *weḥḥel ṛaṣuᵠ* (*f-*) to get or become involved or mixed up (in)

wɛar (v.n. *wɛara*) to become difficult, hard

wɛara v.n. of *wɛar*

wăɛd pl. *wɛud* 1. v.n. of *wɛăd, waɛed* 2. promise, vow

** *a wăɛdi!* Oh, no! Oh, my God! (said upon seeing or hearing of some terrible event or thing); What's all this! What the hell's going on here! (said on coming upon some unusual or shocking situation)

** *l-wăɛd din.* Promises are debts.

¶ *xalef wăɛduᵠ* to break one's promise or word

wɛi pus

wăɛɛăr v.t. 1. to make (more) difficult or hard 2. to make or cause to be difficult to deal with (e.g. training a dog to be rough on strangers)

wăɛɛăṛ v.t. 1. to get (s.th.) stuck or bogged down 2. to get (s.o.) involved or mixed up (in s.th.)

X

xa (m.) same as *xu*

xab ixib v.i. used in certain expr.: *xab ʔamali fih,* or *xab ḍenni fih.* I'm disappointed in him. —*ma-txib-š.* It's not bad. It's all right.

xabuṛi pl. *-yen* 1. light yellow (adj.) 2. pale *siftu xabuṛi.* His face looks pale.

xabya pl. *xwabi* large clay jar (usually for storing food; often glazed)

xad yaxod same as *xda*

xadir (with art.) Elijah the prophet

xadem (f.) pl. *xdem* (dim. *xwidma, xwidem*) negro woman servant

xaf ixaf v.i. to be afraid, to be scared *ka-txaf men le-bṛeq.* She's afraid of lightning.
¶ *xaf ʕla* to be afraid for, to worry about *ma-txaf-š ʕla weldek, ṛah ma-ši b-weḥdu.* Don't worry about your boy—He isn't alone.
xal 1. pl. *xwal* maternal uncle 2. pl. *xilan* beauty spot, nevus, mole
¶ *weld* (or *bent*) *xaluᵠ* (one's) cousin
xala pl. *-t* maternal aunt (see *xal*)
xalal (no pl.) disorder, derangement, something wrong *ʕăndu ši-xalal f-ʕăqlu.* He has some disorder of the mind. —*had l-magana fiha ši-xalal.* There's something wrong with this watch.
xaled pl. *-in* immortal *ḷḷah xaled.* God is immortal.
xalef v.t. 1. to cross (s.th. with s.th. else) *ka-iqul-li ʕăqli ila xalefti duk s-syufa ḥsen* (or *dak s-sif mʕa l-axoṛ ḥsen*). I think it would be better if you crossed the swords. (as for a wall ornament) 2. to exchange the places of, to change around *xalefhom!* Change them around! 3. to be contrary, to go against *ʕlaš ka-txalef klami?* Why are you going against what I told you? 4. to contradict *ma-txalef-š klami!*, or *ma-txalefni-š f-le-klam dyali!* Don't contradict what I say! 5. to disobey *ma-txalef-š ᵓawamiṛi!* Don't you disobey my orders! 6. to break, to infringe upon *lli ka-ixalef l-qanun ka-imši l-l-ḥăbs.* Whoever breaks the law goes to jail 7. to break, to not keep *xalef wăʕdu.* He broke his word.
** *xalef yeddu mʕa yeddha.* He put his arm in hers.
xalifa pl. *xulafa* 1. caliph, successor of Mohammed 2. same as *xlifa*
xaleq (with art.) Creator, God
xaleṣ flour (specifically the fine as separated from the coarse)
xaleṭ v.t. to keep company with, to associate with *dik l-bent ka-txaleṭ waḥed ṣ-ṣelguṭ.* That girl is keeping company with a real jerk.
xaluṭa 1. mess, muddle 2. conglomeration, mixture *šnu had l-xaluṭa!* What's this conglomeration (of food, etc.)!
xamiya pl. *xwami* curtain, drape (window, door)
xames pl. *-in* (adj.) fifth
xamež a.p. of *xmež*
xan ixun v.t. (v.n. *xiyana*) 1. to betray *lli ka-ixun bladu ka-itteḥkem ʕlih be-l-ᵓiʕdam.* He who betrays his country is sentenced to capital punishment. 2. to be unfaithful to *ṭelleq mṛatu ʕla wedd xantu.* He divorced his wife because she was unfaithful to him.
xaṛeq a.p. of *xṛeq*
xarež a.p. of *xrež*
xariž outside (of) *had ṣ-ṣdaʕ lli ka-nesmăʕ xariž ḍ-ḍaṛ.* The noise I hear is outside the house.
¶ *fe-l-xariž* abroad, overseas
xariži 1. pl. *-yen* off-campus (i.e., not boarding at the school, primary school) 2. pl. *xwarež* heretic
xaṣiya pl. *-t* characteristic, peculiarity
xaṣem v.t. 1. to have a quarrel or falling out with 2. to cause to quarrel *huwa lli xaṣemni mʕak.* He's the one that caused me to quarrel with you.
¶ *xaṣem ʕla* to scold, to reprimand
xaṣṣ a.p. of *xeṣṣ*
xatima pl. *-t* 1. conclusion, inference *xatimat l-qewl dyali huwa ṛažel mezyan.* The conclusion drawn from what I've said is that he's a good man. 2. end, conclusion *fe-l-xatima de-l-qeṣṣa rižal š-šoṛṭa lqaw l-qebḍ ʕăl l-mužrim.* At the end of the story the police caught the criminal. 3. closing prayer (said after a reading from the Koran)
xatem pl. *xwatem* (finger-) ring
xater a.p. of *xter*
xataᵓ pl. *ᵓextaᵓ* error, mistake
xaṭaṛ danger, risk *ila bġiti tʕăṛreḍ nefsek l-l-xaṭaṛ, ṣuq b-ṣoṛʕa kbira.* If you want to expose yourself to danger, drive at excessive speed.
** *ka-ḍḍenn ġadi terbeḥ?—fe-l-xaṭaṛ.* Do you think you'll win?—I might.
¶ *fihᵠ l-xaṭaṛ* to be dangerous, risky ≠
xaṭeb v.t. to address, to direct oneself to (in speaking)
xaṭeṛ b- (v.n. *mxaṭṛa*) to risk, to take risks with *lli ka-ilʕăb le-qmeṛ ka-ixaṭeṛ be-flusu.* Whoever gambles is risking his money.
¶ *xaṭeṛ b-ṛaṣuᵠ* to expose oneself to danger
xaṭeṛ pl. *xwaṭeṛ* used in various expr.
** *aš-bġa l-xaṭeṛ?* or *aš-ža ʕla xaṭṛek?* What would you like? What can I do for you? —*b-xaṭṛek!* As you wish! Suit yourself! —*dir-lu xaṭṛu!* Let him have his own way! —*lli ža ʕla xaṭṛek.* (Do) Whatever you want (i.e., it makes no difference to me). —*wessăʕ xaṭṛek!* Take it easy! Calm down! (as from anger) —*xaṭṛu ḍiyyeq.* He's the irritable type; he's always in a bad mood. —*xellih ʕla xaṭṛu!* Let him go ahead and have his own way! —*ʕṭini xaṭṛek!* Now, simmer down and listen to me!
¶ *bqa f-xaṭṛuᵠ* 1. to regret, to be sorry (for not doing s.th.) ≠ *bqa f-xaṭṛi ma-mšit-š l-dik l-muḥaḍaṛa.* I'm sorry I didn't go to that lecture. 2. to offend, to hurt (feelings) ≠ *bqa f-xaṭṛi dak le-klam lli*

qal-li. What he told me hurt me (deeply).

¶ *b-xaṭeṛ, be-l-xaṭeṛ* willingly, of one's own accord *ɛ̄äbbitek dži b-xaṭeṛ.* I want you to come of your own accord.

¶ *ḍiyyeq l-xaṭeṛ l-* to irk, to give a pain in the neck to *ka-iḍiyyeq-li xaṭṛi.* He gives me a pain in the neck.

¶ *wessăɛ xaṭeṛ* **1.** to console *sir wessăɛ xaṭeṛ xtek.* Go console your sister. **2.** to encourage, to give hope to (s.o.)

¶ *xda b-xaṭeṛ,* or *xda be-l-xaṭeṛ* to treat with tact or diplomacy, to be tactful or diplomatic with *xud b-xaṭeṛha!* or *xudha be-l-xaṭeṛ!* Be tactful with her!

¶ *ɛla xaṭeṛ* because *ma-mšit-š ntnezzeh ɛla xaṭeṛ š-šta kanet ka-ṭṭiɛ̄.* I didn't get out into the country because it was raining.

¶ *ɛla xaṭṛu*$^{\phi}$ (to be) in a good mood or humor, cheerful ≠ *xiyyna ɛla xaṭṛu l-yum.* Our buddy's in a good mood today.

xawa v.t. to sort out (in pairs), to pair, to match (s.th. with its mate) *weldek xelleṭ ṣ-ṣbabeṭ dyal ḍ-ḍyaf, xeṣṣek txawihom.* Your son has mixed up the guests' shoes; you'll have to sort them out.

xawa brotherhood, friendship

** *a l-xawa!* polite form of address for getting s.o.'s attention (males only)

xawi a.p. of *xwa*

xayeb pl. *-in* **1.** bad *nta weld xayeb!* You're a bad boy! —*băɛɛăd mennu ɛla wedd ṛažel xayeb.* Stay away from him because he's a bad man. —*l-ɛ̄al xayeb ɛăndna hna had l-iyyam.* We're having bad weather here these days. —*l-biɛ u-š-šra xayeb.* Business is bad (i.e., I'm not selling very well, etc.). **2.** not good, of poor quality, no good *had l-qamežža xayba.* This shirt is of poor quality.—*had l-banana xayba.* This banana is no good. **3.** ugly *dik l-bent siftha xayba.* That girl's ugly.

xbabeṭ pl. of *xebbaṭa*

xbaṛ pl. *-at* news, tidings

** *aš-xbaṛek?* or *še-xbaṛek?* How are you? —*ɛăndu le-xbaṛ.* He (already) knows.

¶ *bla xbaṛu*$^{\phi}$ without one's knowledge, without informing or telling s.o. *xrežti bla xbaṛi.* You went out without my knowledge.

¶ *be-xbaṛu*$^{\phi}$ *(bin), fe-xbaṛu*$^{\phi}$ *(bin)* to know that ≠, to be aware that ≠ *be-xbaṛek (bin) ɛăndna ɛ̄äfla had l-lila.* You're aware that we're having a party tonight (aren't you?).

¶ *ṛedd* (or *ṛeḍḍ*) *le-xbaṛ ɛla* to let know, to report to, to give a reply to *ṛedd ɛliya le-xbaṛ waš ḅḅak maži had l-lila wella la.* Let me know whether your father is coming tonight or not.

¶ *saq le-xbaṛ* to find out, to know (in perfect) *ṛani seqt le-xbaṛ.* I already know.

xbaṛži pl. *ya* informer, stool-pigeon

xbat pl. of *xbit*

xbayṭi pl. *-ya* drunkard

xbazat pl. of *xobz*

xebba same as *xebbăɛ*

xebbaṛ pl. *-a* informer, stool-pigeon

xebbaš nebbaš pl. *xebbašin nebbašin* overly curious and noisy person

xebbaša pl. *-t* rake (tool)

xebbaṭa pl. *-t, xbabeṭ* **1.** beater used in cleaning clothes or rugs, made from a stripped palm branch **2.** big hand or foot

xebbaz pl. *-a* baker and seller of bread

xebbel v.t. **1.** to tangle (up) (as thread) **2.** to dishevel, to tousle (hair)

xebbeṛ same as *xbeṛ*

xebbeš v.t. **1.** to scratch (with sharp instrument, etc.) **2.** to claw (as a cat or with fingernails)

¶ *xebbeš nebbeš, ka-ixebbeš w-inebbeš* to be overly curious and nosy

xebbăɛ v.t. **1.** to hide, to conceal (also metaphorical) **2.** to keep *xebbăɛ ɛăndek had le-ktab ɛ̄etta neṛžăɛ.* Keep this book with you until I return.

¶ *xebbăɛ ɛla* to keep or hide from (also metaphorical) *ka-txebbăɛ ɛliya ši-ɛ̄aža.* You're keeping something from me.

xbit pl. *-in, xbat* **1.** mean, cruel (person, animal) **2.** obnoxious (person)

xbiṭ v.n. of *xbeṭ*

xbiz v.n. of *xbez*

xbiza dim. of *xobza*

xbeṛ v.t. to tell, to inform, to let know *xbeṛthom bin ḅḅahom ža.* I informed them that their father has arrived.—*xbeṛni fuq-aš ġad-iži!* Let me know when he's coming!

xbeš v.t. same as *xebbeš* 2

** *xbeš hna!* expr. said (with the hand outstretched, palm up) to one who expects to receive s.th. from the speaker, who has decided not to give it to him, i.e., "Tough luck, kid (you're not going to get it)!"

xebša pl. *-t* **1.** scratch (i.e., the mark left) **2.** n.i. of *xbeš* and *xebbeš*

xbeṭ (v.n. *xbiṭ*) **1.** v.t. to beat (as a rug or person, with a stick) **2.** v.i. to speak incoherently, to talk nonsensically

¶ *xbeṭha~* to get drunk *xbeṭha l-bareɛ̄ fe-l-lil.* He got drunk last night.

¶ *xbeṭ ɛăl ḷ-ḷeṛḍ* (or *le-ḷ-ḷeṛḍ*) to throw violently to the floor or ground

xbez v.i. (v.n. *xbiz*) **1.** to make bread (i.e., everything but baking) **2.** to speak nonsensically **3.** to botch things up, to do things carelessly

xobz pl. (of intensity) *xbazat* bread

xobza pl. *-t* (dim. *xbiza*) loaf of bread
** *llah yăƐṭik ši-xobza kbira.* May God grant you good fortune.

xda yaxod v.t. (v.n. *wxid,* a.p. *waxed,* p.p. *muxud,* impv. *xud* f. *xudi* pl. *xudu*) **1.** to take (for oneself) *xda ktabi.* He's taken my book. —*škun lli xda l-žaʔiza l-luwwla?* Who took first prize? —*ši-waḥed xda-li beẓṭami.* Somebody's taken my wallet. —*ġadi naxod hada.* I'll take this one. —*xdatu l-mut u-huwa ma-zal ṣġiṛ.* Death took him at an early age. —*xdit l-qiṭaṛ men fas le-ḍ-ḍaṛ l-biḍa.* I took the train from Fez to Casablanca. —*ila qṛiti had le-ktab ġadi yaxod-lek weqt ṭwil.* If you read this book it'll take you a long time. —*xud mƐak xak!* Take your brother with you! —*xud menni waḥed n-naṣiḥa!* Take a tip from me! **2.** to get *sir taxod ši-flus men Ɛănd bbak.* Go get some money from your father. **3.** to marry *xda mṛa hežžala.* He married a widow. **4.** to buy, to get *mnayn xditi had l-qamižža?* Where did you buy this shirt?
** *yaxod ḥăqqna fihom!* May God take revenge on them for us!
¶ *xda b-yedd* to help, to aid, to go to the aid of *xud b-yeddi!* Help me!
¶ *xda ṣuṛa* to take a picture *xdat-li ṣuṛa mƐa xaha.* She took a picture of me with her brother.
¶ *xda t-taṛ* to take revenge *xdaw taṛhom mennu.* They took their revenge on him. —*xdit taṛ xay.* I've gotten revenge for my brother.
¶ *xud(-lek) men* such as *f-dik l-ḥanut kayen lli bġiti, xud-lek men ġella, lḥăm, xoḍṛa, u-sir u-sir.* There's anything you want in that store, such as fruit, meat, vegetables, and so forth.

xdadi pl. of *xeddiya*

xdayeƐ pl. of *xdiƐa*

xedd pl. *xdud* cheek (of face)
¶ *xedd de-l-ḥiṭ* wall, face of the wall *xeṣṣna ngebbṣu had l-xedd de-l-ḥiṭ.* We have to plaster this wall.

xeddam **1.** pl. *-in* working, occupied in doing work (i.e., employed or busy working) **2.** pl. *-in* auxiliary used similarly to English progressive tense *š-šta xeddama ka-ṭṭiḥ.* It's raining. —*huwa xeddam ka-yakol.* He's eating. **3.** pl. *-a* worker, laborer

xoddam pl. of *xdim*

xeddama pl. *-t* (house)maid

xeddaƐ adj. pl. *-in* n.pl. *-a* traitor, betrayer (of some trust or confidence)

xeddiya pl. *-t, xdadi* (dim. *xdidya, xdidiya*) pillow, cushion (sleeping and sitting)

xeddem v.t. **1.** to run, to operate (as a machine) **2.** to hire, to employ **3.** to give work to (person) **4.** to use, to make use of *xeddem l-ḥila mƐah.* Use trickery on him. —*dima ka-ixeddemni l-ġaṛaḍu.* He's always using me for his own purposes. —*xeddem Ɛăqlek!* Use your head!

xdidiya, xdidya dim. of *xeddiya*

xdim pl. *xoddam* one who voluntarily cares for a *zawya*

xdima pl. *-t* dim. of *xedma*

xdiƐ v.n. of *xdăƐ*

xdiƐa pl. *-t, xdayeƐ* betrayal, treachery

xdem **1.** v.i. to work, to labor **2.** v.t. to work on, to try to persuade *xedmu-li baš ibiƐ-li siyaṛtu b-taman ṛxiṣ.* Work on him for me so he'll sell me his car cheap. **3.** v.t. to make *ḥăbbitek texdem-li ši-beẓṭam mezyan.* I want you to make me a nice wallet. **4.** v.i. to work, to run, to be operable (as a machine) **5.** v.i. to run, to be on (machine, radio)

xdem pl. of *xadem*

xedma pl. *-t* (dim. *xdima*) **1.** work, employment **2.** job, profession **3.** job, task **4.** workmanship *xedma mezyana hadi.* This is good workmanship.
** *had ṛ-ṛadyu xdemtu qbiḥa.* This radio doesn't work right.

xdud pl. of *xedd*

xdăƐ v.t. (v.n. *xdiƐ*) **1.** to betray (country, friend) **2.** to lure (by deception)

xdăƐ perfidy, faithlessness
¶ *b-le-xdăƐ* unfaithfully, perfidiously

xḍaṛ v.i. to get or turn green

xḍaṛi pl. of *xeḍṛa, xoḍṛa*

xeḍḍaṛ pl. *-a* vegetable merchant

xeḍḍeṛ v.t. **1.** to make green(er) (as rain a desert, pigment in paint) **2.** to use vegetables with (a meal) *b-aš ġadi txeḍḍeṛ l-lḥăm had n-nhaṛ?* What vegetables are you going to use with the meat today?
** *ana ġadi-nxeḍḍeṛ Ɛăyniya.* I'm going out to take in some of Nature's greenery (as a drive in the country).

xḍeṛ f. *xeḍṛa* pl. *xuḍeṛ* **1.** green *ka-nḥebb le-Ɛyun l-xuḍeṛ.* I like green eyes. —*t-teffaḥ le-xḍeṛ ka-ideṛṛ l-kerš.* Green apples upset the stomach. **2.** raw, underdone (meat)

xeḍṛa, xoḍṛa (sg. and coll.) pl. *xḍaṛi* vegetable (pl. refers to a variety)

xḍuṛa, xḍuṛiya **1.** green(ness) (color) **2.** greenery, verdure

xfa ixfa v.i. to disappear, to be gone (somewhere) *fayn xfiti Ɛlina?* Where did you disappear to (from us)?
¶ *ma-xfa-š Ɛla* to know, to be aware *ma-ka-ixfa-š* or *ma-xfa-š Ɛlik biʔannahu ṛažel mṛiḍ u-šibani.* You're aware that he's a sick old man.

xfa ixfi v.t. to hide, to conceal (as information)

xfaf v.i. **1.** to get or become light(er), to lose weight (things, not persons) **2.** to be fast (watch, clock)

** *xfaf šăɛru.* His hair has thinned out. —*xfaf ɛăqlu.* He's become eccentric, senile, mentally disturbed.

xfaf pl. of *xfif*

xeff **1.** comp. of *xfif* **2.** quickness

¶ *be-l-xeff* quickly *be-l-xeff!* Make it fast! Hurry up!

xoff pl. *xfuf* type of under-slipper of thin, soft leather (morocco) worn inside of the *belġa*

xeffa rapidity, quickness

¶ *be-l-xeffa* quickly, fast, in a hurry

¶ *fihΦ l-xeffa* **1.** to do things always in a rush ≠ **2.** to be fast (clock) ≠ *maganti fiha sebɛa de-d-dqayeq de-l-xeffa.* My watch is seven minutes fast.

xeffef v.t. **1.** to lighten, to make light(er) (in weight) **2.** to thin (as hair, soup) **3.** to reduce, to lessen (pain) *had d-dwa xeffef ɛliya le-ḥriq.* This medicine had reduced my pain.

¶ *xeffef le-ḥmel ɛla* to lighten (s.o.'s) load (also figurative)

xfif pl. *xfaf* (comp. *xeff*) **1.** light (in weight; also used with foods) **2.** fast, speedy (as a runner) **3.** having the quality of doing things without delay; on the ball **4.** light-minded, not serious (when one should be)

** *xfif f-ɛăqlu.* He's eccentric, senile, mentally disturbed. —*yeddih xfifa.* He gets somewhat light-fingered at times (i.e., he steals things).

xfif lead (metal)

** n.u. *-a* bullet, slug

xfuf pl. of *xoff*

xefya used in the expr. *be-l-xefya* secretly, on the sly

xiba pl. *-t* disappointment, disillusionment

xil pl. of *ɛăwd* (sometimes syntactically treated as f. sg.)

xilaf pl. *-at* **1.** disagreement, difference (of opinion), falling out **2.** quarrel

¶ *b-xilaf* in contrast to *had l-weṛqa biḍa u-hadi b-xilafha keḥla.* This piece of paper is white, and this one, in contrast to it, is black.

xilafa caliphate

xilan pl. of *xal* 2

xima pl. *-t, xyam, xyem* tent

** *huwa ṛažel xima.* He's a generous man.

xiṛ pl. *-at* good, goodness (used principally in set expr.)

** *fih l-xir lilek.* It'll do you good. It's for your own good. —*nxeṛžu? fiha xiṛ.* Shall we leave? All right. —*tebqa ɛla xiṛ* or *xellitek ɛla xiṛ.* Good-by (expecting to meet again sometime). —*ɛmelti l-xiṛ f-ṛaṣek lli xṛežti.* You did well by leaving (i.e., you didn't miss a thing).

¶ *bi-xiṛ* or *bi-xiṛ u-ɛla xiṛ* **1.** well, fine, in good health *kif ḥalek?—bi-xiṛ u-ɛla xiṛ.* How are you?—Fine. **2.** safely, safe and sound *ṛžăɛ bi-xiṛ u-ɛla xiṛ men l-ḥăžž.* He returned safe and sound from the pilgrimage.

¶ *l-xiṛ u-le-xmir* wealth *žaṛna ɛăndu l-xiṛ u-le-xmir.* Our neighbor is wealthy (i.e., has wealth).

¶ *men l-xiṛ lli* it is fortunate that, thank heavens *men l-xiṛ lli žiti fe-l-weqt.* Thank heavens you came on time.

¶ *nkeṛ l-xiṛ* to be ungrateful, an ingrate

¶ *škeṛ l-xiṛ* to be appreciative, grateful

¶ *xiṛ l-* it's better that ≠, (you, etc.) had better . . . (in sense of warning) ≠ *xiṛ-lek temši wella ižiw iɛăbbiwek be-z-zez.* You'd better go or they'll come and take you by force.

¶ *xiṛ ḷḷah, xiṛ ṛebbi* **1.** a long time *hadi xiṛ ḷḷah ma-šeftek.* I haven't seen you for a long time. **2.** a lot, a great deal *ɛăndha xiṛ ḷḷah d-le-flus.* She has a lot of money.

¶ *xiṛ men* better than *had t-teffaḥa xiṛ men hadi.* This apple is better than that one.

¶ *ɛmel xiṛ f-* to do a favor for *ɛmel fiya waḥed l-xiṛ ḷḷah ixellik.* Do me a favor, please.

¶ *ɛănduΦ xiṛ men* to prefer ≠ *hadi ɛăndi xiṛ men hadik.* I prefer this one to that one.

xiš **1.** burlap **2.** (coll.) burlap sacks

xit dim. of *xet, oxt*

xiṭ pl. *xyuṭ* thread (a strand as well as in general)

¶ *xiṭ de-ṣ-ṣuf* (wool) yarn

xiṭab pl. *-at* speech, discourse, oration

xiyana v.n. of *xan*

xiyyi (inh. pos.) **1.** dim. of *xay, xuya* **2.** guy, individual (often pejorative) *šuf dak xiyyi š-ka-yăɛmel!* Look at what that guy is doing!

xiyyem v.i. **1.** to go camping, to camp **2.** to bivouac

xizrana pl. *-t* **1.** bamboo stick **2.** bamboo cane or walking stick

xizzu n.u. *-ya* (no art.) carrot

xla ixla v.i. to empty, to become empty, deserted (of people)

¶ *xla ḍaṛ bu* (plus pron. or n.) to beat up (s.o.) *xlaw ḍaṛ buh.* They beat him up.

xla ixli v.t. used in set expr. *ḷḷah ixli ḍaṛek!* (or *daṛ buk!*) May God desolate your house! (strong insult) —*xla ḍaṛek!* Now you're in for it! (i.e., in trouble)

¶ *xla f- to* fire on, to shoot at *xlaw fe-l-ɛădyan.* They fired on the enemy.
¶ *xlaha~ ɛla* to ruin (s.o.)
xla pl. *-wat* wilderness, country (in contrast to populated area)
** *imši le-xla ḍaṛ buh!* He can go to hell! —*a-xla ḍaṛi!* Oh, my gosh! Oh, no!
xlaq v.i. (v.n. *xluq*) to be born *fayn xlaqiti?* Where were you born?
xḷaṣ **1.** v.n. of *xeḷḷeṣ* and *txeḷḷeṣ* **2.** pay, salary (regular or occasional) **3.** afterbirth, placenta
** *xḷaṣ!* Stop it! That's enough (of that)! —*xḷaṣ men l-heḍṛa!* Let's stop the talk! That's enough talking! —*xḷaṣ ɛla waḥed l-filem šeft l-bareḥ!* Man, what a terrific movie I saw yesterday!
xlaxel pl. of *xelxal, xolxal*
xlayef pl. of *xlifa*
xlayeq pl. of *xliqa*
xlef v.t. (v.n. *xlif*) **1.** to replace, to succeed (as in office) **2.** to replace, to give in exchange
** *ḷḷah ixlef ɛlik!* May God reward you (for helping me). Thank you (for some monetary gift).
xelfa pl. *-t* step, pace *xellef ṛebɛa de-l-xelfat l-l-qeddam!* Take four steps forward!
¶ *zad xelfa* to go away, to leave
** *zid xelfa!* Scram! Beat it!
xelfan, xolfan pl. of *xlifa*
xlif v.n. of *xlef*
xlifa pl. *xlayef, xelfan, xolfan* **1.** administrator of a city district **2.** lieutenant, vice-official (i.e., acting for one's superior at times)
xliq v.n. of *xleq*
xliqa pl. *xlayeq* creature
** *ɛla xliqa!* Boy, you're (he's, she's) a queer duck! —*xliqa de-l-ʔilah* (or *de-ḷḷah*). said upon seeing a congenitally deformed person
** *mezyana fe-xliqt ḷḷah.* She's good-looking.
xliɛ **1.** v.n. of *xlăɛ* **2.** type of meat preserves
xell vinegar
xella v.t. **1.** to leave *xellit ktabi fe-ḍ-ḍaṛ.* I left my book home. —*xellawni b-weḥdi.* They left me alone. —*xelli ṛ-ṛadyu mešɛul.* Leave the radio on. **2.** to let, to allow *xellini nemši mɛah!* Let me go with him!
** *ma-xella fayn mša.* He's been everywhere. —*ma-xella ma dar baš idzuwwež biha.* He's done everything he could to marry her. —*ka-ixelli b-režlu.* He limps. —*ma-ɛṭani la-yeddik wa-la ixellik.* He didn't give me a thing. —*ma-ixelli-lek gana.* He won't give you a minute's peace.
¶ *ḷḷah ixellik* please *ḷḷah ixellik sellefni ši-flus.* Please loan me some money.
¶ *ma-xellaha~ f-* to get even with, to get (s.o.) *weḷḷah ma-nxelliha fik!* I'll get even with you! I'll get you yet!
¶ *xella fiha~* to pull a boner (and so miss out of s.th.) *weḷḷahila xelliti fiha mnin ma-žiti-š ɛăndna l-bareḥ.* You really pulled a boner in not coming to our place yesterday.
¶ *xella ɛlih*$^{\phi}$ to leave alone *xelliha ɛlik!* Leave her alone! (stop bothering her)
xelled v.t. to immortalize (as in literature)
xellef v.i. **1.** to walk (particularly the action of walking) *ma-txellef-š bezzaf!* Don't walk so fast! **2.** to walk faster, to quicken the step
¶ *xellef ɛla* **1.** to step over *xellef ɛăl l-kelb!* Step over the dog! **2.** to step on *ma-xelleft-š ɛliha be-l-ɛani.* I didn't mean to step on her.
xeḷḷeṣ (v.n. *xḷaṣ*) **1.** v.t. to pay *xeḷḷeṣni wella ndɛik!* Pay me or I'll sue you! —*xeḷḷeṣni f-dak ṛ-ṛebɛin derhem lli ka-nsalek.* Pay me the forty dirhams you owe me. **2.** v.i. to have a baby, to give birth
¶ *xeḷḷeṣ l-* to buy for (s.o.) *xeḷḷeṣha-li!* Buy it for me!
¶ *xeḷḷeṣ men* to take or get away from *xeḷḷeṣni mennha!* Get her away from me!
xeḷḷeṭ v.t. to mix (up) *la-txeḷḷeṭ-š le-byeḍ mɛa le-kḥăl!* Don't mix the white with the black! —*xeḷḷeṭ had ṣ-ṣbaġa lili!* Mix this paint for me! —*ma-txeḷḷeṭ had le-wṛaq!* Don't mix these cards up!
¶ *xeḷḷeṭ bin* to sow discord or cause trouble between or among *huwa ka-ixeḷḷeṭ bin n-nas dima.* He's always causing trouble among people.
xellăɛ v.t. to prepare as *xliɛ* (kind of preserved meat) *xellăɛna žmel.* We've prepared some camel meat as *xliɛ.*
xleq v.t. (v.n. *xliq*) to create (usually God)
¶ p.p. *mexluq* pl. *-at* creature
xelq (sg. m. or pl.) people *šuf šḥal de-l-xelq temma!* Look at all the people over there!
xḷeṭ ɛla **1.** to join *xḷeṭ ɛliya mnin tsali be-l-xedma.* Join me when you finish work. **2.** to come and see *xḷeṭ ɛliya ġedda le-ḍ-ḍaṛ.* Come and see me tomorrow at home.
xoḷṭa association, relationship *l-xoḷṭa de-s-skayriya ma-ši mezyana.* Association with drunkards is not good.
xluq v.n. of *xlaq*
¶ *ɛma* (*ɛweṛ, ṭṛeš,* etc.) *xluq* congenitally blind (one-eyed, deaf, etc.)
xelwa pl. *-t* solitary place, lonely spot
xelwi pl. *-yen* **1.** wild (in contrast to domestic or tame; almost exclusively said of pigeons) **2.** solitary, keeping to oneself **3.** solitary, lone, out-of-the-way (place)

xelxal, xolxal pl. *xlaxel* **1.** anklet, ankle ornament (usually of silver) **2.** stocking (on horse's foot)
xelxel v.t. to shake (a bottle)
¶ *xelxel ʕqel* (with pron. or n.) to drive (s.o.) crazy (usually not in literal sense)
xlăʕ v.t. (v.n. *xliʕ*) **1.** to scare, to frighten *txebbăʕ-li xay muṛ l-bab u-xlăʕni mnin dxelt.* My brother hid behind the door and scared me when I came in. **2.** to take off (clothes) **3.** to fire, to dismiss (especially from government job)
xelʕa scare, fright
¶ *ṭaṛet xelʕa men* to be scared or frightened ≠ *ṭaṛet xelʕa men d-derri mnin tkellem ṛ-ṛʕad.* The child was frightened when it thundered.
¶ *ṭiyyeṛ xelʕa men* to scare, to frighten *ṭiyyeṛti menni xelʕa!* You frightened me!
ᵖ exmas pl. of *xumus*
xmasi **1.** pl. of *xemsa* **2.** pl. *-yen* composed of five elements (angles, divisions, etc.) *n-nežma l-meġṛibiya xmasiya.* The Moroccan star has five points.
xmasiya pl. *-t* five-shot rifle
xmaž v.i. to rot, to decay (usually food, tooth, tree)
** *xmaž be-l-mal.* He's filthy rich.
xmaž rot, decay, putrefaction (decayed matter as well as the process)
xmed v.i. (v.n. *xmid*) **1.** to become calm, to calm down (as a volcano, fire, pain) **2.** to take a nap or a snooze **3.** to sleep (usually from fatigue, sickness, etc.) **4.** to remain quiet and inconspicuous (person)
xemda n.i. of *xmed*
xmid v.n. of *xmed*
xmir v.n. of *xmer*
** *ʕăndu l-xir u-le-xmir.* He's quite wealthy.
xmira leaven (for baking and making soup)
xmis pl. *-at* (with art.) Thursday
¶ *nhaṛ le-xmis* (on) Thursday
xmisa dim. of *xemsa*
xemm used in the expr.:
¶ *šmaʕ l-xemm* beeswax
¶ *šmaʕa de-l-xemm* candle of beeswax
¶ *ḥmeṛ xemm* a kind of brown color (similar to the color of honeycomb)
xommagi pl. *-yen* rustic, bumpkin
xemmaṛ adj. pl. *-in* n.pl. *-a* (one) who drinks (alcoholic beverages)
xemmas pl. *-a* sharecropper (sharing a fifth of the crop)
xemmel v.t. **1.** to clean (up) *xeṣṣni nxemmel biti l-yum.* I have to clean my room up today. **2.** to clean out (the sludge and deposit in a well, ditch, etc.) *ġadi-nxemmlu had l-bir ġedda.* We're going to clean out this well tomorrow. **3.** to clear, to clear out (a room)
xemmem (*f-*) to think (about, of), to reflect (on) *men qbel-ma džaweb, xemmem.* Think before you answer.
xemmer v.t. **1.** to let rise (bread before baking) **2.** to make, let, or cause to ferment
xemmeṛ v.i. to drink (alcoholic beverages)
xemmež v.t. to make, let, or cause to rot, spoil or decay
** *băʕʕăd menni wella nxemmež-lek wežhek!* Get away from me or I'll bash your face in!
xmer v.i. (v.n. *xmir*) **1.** to rise (bread before baking) **2.** to ferment
** *xmer fe-n-nʕas l-bareḥ fe-l-lil.* He slept soundly last night.
xemri, xomri pl. *-yen* brown-skinned (person)
xems, xemsa (former used with pl. of n. admitting du.) five *ʕṭini xemsa de-d-drahem.* Give me five dirhams. —*weldi ṣ-ṣġiṛ ʕăndu xems snin.* My son is five years old.
¶ *l-xemsa u-xemsin* **1.** Moroccan Royal Orchestra **2.** type of Moroccan music based on Andalusian form
xemsa pl. *-t, xmasi* (dim. *xmisa*) piece of jewelry in shape of a hand worn as a protection against the "evil eye"
** *ʕṭani be-l-xemsa.* He raised his hand (with fingers spread) to protect himself from me (as if I had the "evil eye").
xemsin **1.** fifty **2.** fiftieth
xmesṭaš **1.** fifteen **2.** fifteenth
xmež same as *xmaž*
¶ a.p. *xamež* pl. *-in* rotten, spoiled, decayed
** *huwa xamež be-l-mal.* He's filthy rich.
xnadeq pl. of *xendeq*
xnafeṛ pl. of *xenfṛa*
xnafes pl. of *xenfusa* (n.p. of *xenfus*)
xnag pl. *-at* necklace
xnaši pl. of *xenša*
xnašeš pl. of *xenšuš*
xnat state of being spoiled or in habitual comfort and ease (usually a wife)
¶ *weld le-xnat* spoiled boy
xnayen pl. of *xnuna*
xnazer pl. of *xenzir*
xnažeṛ pl. of *xenžaṛ*
xendeq v.i. to become badly infected (wound)
xendeq pl. *xnadeq* **1.** trench (warfare) **2.** moat **3.** temporary opening made in a sewer conduit (by digging; used for access in case of sewer trouble)
xenfṛa pl. *xnafeṛ* (dim. *xnifṛa*) **1.** muzzle, nose (dog, horse, etc.) **2.** snout (as a pig)
xenfes v.i. **1.** to sign one's *xenfusa* (notary) **2.** to scribble or make scribblings
xenfus n.u. *-a* pl. *xenfusat, xnafes* dung-beetle, scarab

xenfusa pl. *-t* a notary's special signature
xnifṛa dim. of *xenfṛa*
xnig, xniq v.n. of *xneg, xneq*
xniša dim. of *xenša*
xennet v.t. to spoil (a child, etc.)
xennez v.t. to make or cause to stink
¶ *xennezha~ ʕla* to make trouble for (s.o.)
xneg, xneq v.t. (v.n. *xnig, xniq*) **1.** to strangle, to choke **2.** to smother (person) **3.** to block (up), to choke (chimney, sewer, etc.)
xenqaṭiṛa same as *xenṭaqiṛa*
xenša pl. *xnaši* (dim. *xniša*) **1.** bag, sack **2.** dolt, idiot
¶ *xenša de-l-xeyš* burlap bag
xenšuš pl. *xnašeš* face (pejorative and complimentary) *ʕla xenšuš!* What a beautiful (or horrible) face!
** *ḍeṛṛeq ʕliya xenšušek!* Get out of here! Scram!
xnet v.i. to become or be spoiled (person)
xenṭaqiṛa pl. *-t* **1.** trick (sleight of hand) **2.** game played with a string and the hands (as cat's cradle)
xnuna pl. *-t* (of intensity) *xnayen* mucus, snot
xnuzat pl. of *xenz, xnez*
xnuziya same as *xenz, xnez*
xenxeṛ v.i. **1.** to snore (mostly animals) **2.** to snarl with a snoring sound (as in frightening children)
xnez v.i. to stink, to give off an offensive odor
xenz, xnez pl. (of intensity) *xnuzat* stench, offensive odor
¶ *xenz d-denya* money
xenzir pl. *xnazer;* f. *xenzira* pl. *-t* **1.** pig, hog **2.** scrofula
xenžaṛ, xenžeṛ pl. *xnažeṛ* curved dagger
xṛa pl. (of intensity) *-wat* feces, excrement (vulgar)
x̄ṛa, oxṛa f. of *axoṛ*
xṛab ruins (usually in non-historic sense)
xṛafa pl. *-t, xṛayef* **1.** story, tale, legend, myth *ʕăwwed-lna xṛafa!* Tell us a story! **2.** (pl.) lie, fib, fish story
xragi pl. of *xorga*
xṛaqi pl. of *xeṛqa*
xṛaṛeb, xrareb pl. of *xeṛṛuba, xerruba*
xṛaṣ, xṛaṣi pl. of *xoṛṣa, xeṛṣa*
xrašeš pl. of *xoršaša*
xṛaṭi pl. of *xeṛṭa*
xṛaṭem pl. of *xeṛṭum*
xṛaxeš pl. of *xeṛxaša*
xṛayef pl. of *xṛafa*
xṛayfi pl. *-ya* teller of "tall" tales
xṛeb v.t. to destroy, to ruin (God)
xṛeb pl. of *xeṛba*
xeṛba pl. *-t, xṛeb* **1.** building in ruins **2.** pantry, food cellar
xeṛbeq v.i. **1.** to talk nonsense **2.** to scribble, to make scribblings **3.** to do things all wrong, to mess things up
¶ *xeṛbeq f-* to fool or mess around with *ma-txeṛbeq-š fe-ṛ-ṛadyu!* Don't mess around with the radio!
xerbeš v.t. to scratch (with fingernails or sharp instrument)
xorda **1.** second-hand goods (usually clothes) **2.** pl. *-t* second-hand store (usually for clothes) **3.** a lot (of) *šrat xorda d-le-ktub.* She bought a lot of books.
xerdel v.i. to talk nonsense
xṛef v.i. to get old, to become aged (person)
xerfan pl. of *xṛuf*
xreg v.t. (v.n. *xrig*) **1.** to slash (with a knife) **2.** to pierce, to go through
xorga pl. *-t, xragi* **1.** slash, cut **2.** n.i. of *xreg* **2** **3.** hole (left when s.th. goes through s.th., as a bullet, knife)
xrif autumn, fall
xrifi pl. *-yen* of or pertaining to autumn, autumnal
xrig v.n. of *xreg*
x̄ṛin, oxṛin pl. of *axoṛ*
xṛiṣa dim. of *xoṛṣa, xeṛṣa*
xṛiṭ v.t. of *xṛeṭ*
xriz v.n. of *xrez*
xermez (*f-*) to scribble, to make scribblings (on)
xṛeq **1.** same as *xreg* **2.** to violate (law, border)
¶ a.p. *xaṛeq* pl. *-in* used in the expr. *xaṛeq l-ʕada* extraordinary, unusual
xeṛqa **1.** pl. *-t, xṛaqi* physical condition (usually of babies) *mnin ttewled kanet xeṛqtu ḍʕifa.* When he was born his physical condition was weak. **2.** pl. *xṛaqi, xṛuq* type of white cloth used in wrapping babies **3.** pl. *xṛaqi, xṛuq* piece of cloth, cloth
xeṛqum curcuma
xerrab adj. pl. *-in* n.pl. *-a* destructive person, vandal
xerraf adj. pl. *-in* n.pl. *-a* same as *xṛayfi*
xorrag pl. *-a* country bumpkin, rustic
xeṛṛaṭ pl. *-a* lathe operator
xerraz pl. *-a* **1.** maker and seller of *blaġi* **2.** shoemaker
xerraža pl. *-t* (back or side) exit, way out (other than main door)
xerreb v.t. **1.** to destroy, to ruin **2.** to devastate, to lay waste to
xerref v.t. **1.** to glean (vineyard, etc.) **2.** to tell stories (false or true)
xeṛṛeṣ v.t. to make into the shape of a ring
xerrub, xeṛṛub n.u. *-a* pl. *xrareb, xṛaṛeb* **1.** carob tree, locust **2.** carob bean
xerrubi, xeṛṛubi pl. *-yen* shade of dark brown
xerrež v.t. **1.** to make leave or go out, to expel (s.o. from room, city, etc.) **2.** to put out, to take outside **3.** to omit, to leave out, to

discard **4.** to extract, to get out *mnin ka-iṣeffiw l-biṭrul ka-ixerržu mennu ƹadad dyal l-ˀenwaƹ.* When they refine oil they extract many products. —*xerrež l-feršiya men ṛ-ṛḍuma!* Get the cork out of the bottle! **5.** to issue, to send out *ġedda l-ḥukuma ġadi-txerrež ši-qaṛaṛ.* Tomorrow the government will issue a decree. **6.** to lead, to conduct, to take *had ṭ-ṭṛiq txerržek l-le-mdina.* This road will take you to town. **7.** to fire, to discharge (a shot, bullet) **8.** to solve, to find the answer to (mathematical problem) **9.** to provide a profit for *had le-ktab b-xemsa de-d-dṛahem ixerrežni.* I'll settle for five dirhams for this book (I'm selling). **10.** v.i. to have or offer a way out, to have an exit *had d-derb ma-ixerrež-š.* This little street has a dead end.

¶ *xerrež le-d-dlala* to put up for auction *xerržu le-mtaƹ dyalhom le-d-dlala.* They've put their possessions up for auction.

¶ *xerrež s-solka* **1.** to finish one's study and memorization of the Koran **2.** to recite the entire Koran (from memory)

xṛeṣ **1.** pl. of *xoṛṣa, xeṛṣa* **2.** f. *xeṛṣa* pl. *xeṛṣin, xuṛeṣ* mute, dumb

xoṛṣa, xeṛṣa pl. *-t, xṛeṣ, xṛoṣ, xṛaṣ, xṛaṣi* (dim. *xṛiṣa*) **1.** ring (nose, ear, any ring-shaped object) **2.** door-knocker (not necessarily ring-shaped) **3.** link (chain)

xoršaša pl. *-t, xrašeš* **1.** rattle (toy) **2.** rattletrap (old car, etc.)

xeršuf n.u. *-a* artichoke stalk (used in cooking)

xṛeṭ v.t. (v.n. *xṛiṭ*) to turn (on a lathe)

xeṛṭa pl. *xṛaṭi* **1.** design cut into the wood by turning on a lathe **2.** stripe, striation (design, grain in wood, etc.)

xoṛṭal oats, oatmeal

xeṛṭum pl. *xṛaṭem* trunk (elephant)

xṛuf pl. *xerfan,* f. *xṛufa* pl. *-t* lamb

xṛuq pl. of *xeṛqa* 2 and 3

xṛuṣ pl. of *xeṛṣa, xoṛṣa*

xruž v.n. of *xrež*

xerwaƹ n.u. *-a* castor-oil plant

¶ *zit l-xerwaƹ* castor oil

xeṛxaša pl. *-t, xṛaxeš* any old broken-down machine that still works (as an old car)

xeṛxeṛ v.i. **1.** to rattle (s.th. loose) **2.** to make a clanking noise (as pieces of iron, an old machine) **3.** to make a boiling or gurgling sound (water, etc.) **4.** to make a snoring sound (person)

xrez v.t. (v.n. *xriz*) to sew, to stitch (leatherwork)

xrež ixrož v.i. (v.n. *xruž*) **1.** to leave, to go out of *ƹad kif xrež men ḍ-ḍaṛ.* He just left the house. —*yemmaha qalet-lha texrož men l-bit.* Her mother told her to leave the room. **2.** to come out of, to come from *kan l-ma ka-ixrož men dik l-ƹăyn be-l-ḥăqq tteqṭăƹ.* Water used to come out of this spring but it has stopped. —*ma-ḍennit-š ixrož mennha dak š-ši.* I never thought such a thing would come from her. —*xeržu n-nžum wella ma-zal?* Have the stars come out yet? **3.** to break out *xeržu-lu le-ḥbub f-wežhu.* Sores broke out on his face. **4.** to end (month, long holidays) *mnin ixrož had š-šheṛ nxeḷḷṣek.* I'll pay you when this month ends.

** *xeržu ƹăynih mnin šaf dik l-bent.* His eyes popped out when he saw that girl. —*xrož ƹliya!* Get out of here (i.e., leave the room, house, etc.)!

¶ *xrež f-* **1.** to win out over (in some competition, fight) **2.** to come upon by surprise, to take by surprise (i.e., encounter) *ana maši fe-l-lil u-žuž de-r-ržal xeržu fiya.* I was walking last night and a couple of men took me by surprise. **3.** to run into *kan xeṣṣu yewqef be-l-ḥăqq xrež fiya.* He should have stopped but he ran into me (driving cars).

¶ *xrež ƹla* (s.o.) **1.** to let (s.o.) down **2.** to break (law, one's word) **3.** to leave, to go off (of) *ṭ-ṭumubil xeržet ƹăl ṭ-ṭṛiq.* The car went off the road.

** *xrež ƹăl ṭ-ṭṛiq.* He's left the straight and narrow (path).

¶ *xrež ƹla ƹăqluφ* to go crazy (lit. and metaphorical)

¶ a.p. *xaṛež* pl. *-in* projecting, protruding *keršu xaṛža.* He has a protruding stomach.

** *ana xaṛež men had š-ši.* I wipe my hands of the whole affair. —*ƹăqlu xaṛež ƹăl l-musiqa l-ˀandalusiya.* He's crazy about Andalusian music.

xerža pl. *-t* **1.** n.i. of *xrež* **2.** exit (act of leaving)

xṣa ixṣi v.t. to castrate (sheep, cattle)

xṣali pl. of *xeṣla* 3 and 4

xṣam same as *xṣuma*

xṣaṛa pl. *-t, xṣayeṛ* **1.** v.n. of *xṣeṛ* **2.** used in certain expr.: *xṣaṛa!* or *ya xṣaṛa!* That's too bad! —*xṣaṛtha ƹăwṛa.* Too bad she's only got one eye. —*ḥmed, xṣaṛa fih dik le-flus.* What a pity Ahmed has all that money.

xṣaṣ pl. of *xṣiṣ*

xṣayel pl. of *xeṣla*

xṣayem pl. of *xṣuma*

xṣayeṛ pl. of *xṣaṛa*

xeṣb fertility (land)

xeṣba (*ˀeṛḍ*) fertile (land)

xṣim pl. *xoṣman* adversary, opponent

xṣiṛ v.n. of *xṣeṛ*

xṣiṣ pl. *-in, xṣaṣ* (comp. *xeṣṣ*) base, mean, not honorable *xṣiṣa* dim. of *xeṣṣa*

xeṣla 1. pl. *xṣayel* dirty trick 2. pl. *xṣayel* clumsy act (e.g., knocking over a glass) 3. pl. *-t, xṣali* forelock 4. pl. *-t, xṣali* any tuft or lock of hair

xoṣman pl. of *xṣim*

xṣeṛ (v.n. *xṣiṛ, xṣaṛa, xoṣṛan*) 1. v.t. to lose (a game, money in a game) 2. v.i. to fail (exam) *waš xṣeṛti f-le-mtiḥan?* Did you fail (in) the exam? 3. v.t. to squander (money, time) 4. v.i. to spoil (food) 5. v.i. to become inoperable or out of order, to not work or run *ma-imken-li-š nweṣṣlek ɛla wedd-aš ṭ-ṭumubil dyali xeṣṛet.* I can't take you because my car isn't running. 6. v.i. to be unsuccessful, to not work out (as plans)

** *ṭ-ṭbăɛ dyalu xṣeṛ.* He's gotten awfully hard to get along with.

xoṣṛan v.n. of *xṣeṛ*

xeṣṣ 1. v.i. to be lacking or missing *xeṣṣ ktab hnaya.* There's a book missing here. 2. v.t. to have to, should, must ≠ (used in perfect or durative tense, with pron. object endings) *xeṣṣni* (or *ka-ixeṣṣni*) *nemši le-ḍ-ḍaṛ.* I have to go home. —*kan xeṣṣni* (or *kan ka-ixeṣṣni*) *nekteb-lha.* I should have written her (but I didn't). 3. to need (i.e., to be necessary for one to have; same syntax as in 2 above) *xeṣṣni ṭumubil.* I need a car.

** *ma-xeṣṣ-šay.* I (he, she, etc.) don't need anything at all; It was all right (e.g., when asked how the party was). —*ma-xeṣṣ babah ġiṛ le-ɛṣa.* What he needs is a good licking.

¶ *ma-xeṣṣ-šay men* to need ≠, to have to have ≠ *ma-xeṣṣek-šay men le-flus.* You'll have to have money.

¶ a.p. *xaṣṣ* pl. *-in* special

¶ a.p. *xaṣṣ* (*b-*) pl. *-in* (to be) about, to concern *had le-ktab xaṣṣ be-l-mirikan.* This book is about Americans.

¶ *l-xaṣṣ u-l-ɛamm* everybody, the public

xeṣṣ comp. of *xṣiṣ*

xeṣṣ n.u. *-a* lettuce

xṣeṣ pl. of *xeṣṣa*

xeṣṣa pl. *-t, xṣeṣ* (dim. *xṣiṣa*) fountain (with water spout)

xeṣṣeṛ v.t. 1. to make or cause to lose (a game, etc.) *huwa lli xeṣṣeṛna l-maṭš.* He's the one that lost us the game. 2. to fail, to make or cause to fail (exam, subject) *le-ḥsab huwa lli xeṣṣeṛni f-le-mtiḥan.* The mathematical part is what made me fail the exam. 3. to render inoperable, to treat (s.th.) so that it does not run or work anymore, to break *bqa ka-xewweṛ fe-ṛ-ṛaḍyu ḥetta xeṣṣṛu.* He kept messing around with the radio until he broke it. 4. to cause to be lost through a miscarriage, abortion (baby; can be used for domestic mammals)

¶ *xeṣṣeṛ bin* to cause discord among or between

¶ *xeṣṣeṛ l-* to dissuade, to talk (s.o.) out of (s.th.) *xeṣṣeṛ-lha fe-ṣ-ṣfeṛ.* He talked her out of the trip.

¶ *xeṣṣeṛ l-xaṭeṛ l-* to upset (by going against one's desires) *xeṣṣeṛti-lu xaṭṛu.* You've upset him (by not doing what he wanted).

¶ *xeṣṣeṛ wežhu*$^{\phi}$ to make a face *ɛlaš ka-txeṣṣeṛ wežhek fiya?* Why are you making a face at me?

¶ *xeṣṣeṛ le-wžeh dyal* (s.o.) to ruin the reputation of (s.o.)

xeṣṣeṣ v.t. 1. to reserve *xeṣṣeṣt-lkom had l-maḥăll.* I've reserved this place for you. 2. to devote, to consecrate *xeṣṣeṣ weqtu kollu le-ṣ-ṣla.* He's devoted all his time to prayer.

xṣuma pl. *xṣayem* quarrel, dispute, disagreement

xšan v.i. 1. to gain weight, to get fat 2. to become rough, to lose softness (as cloth) 3. to acquire an unpleasant appearance, to be in poor taste (e.g. clothing) 4. to become rude and coarse (manners)

xšan pl. of *xšin*

xšana same as *xšuna, xšuniya*

xšaša pl. *-t* small piece of wood, leaf, straw, etc.

xšeb n.u. *xešba* 1. wood (dressed) 2. beam, board, plank, piece of wood, etc. 3. pole (utility, telephone)

xšin pl. *xšan* 1. rude, coarse, rough (manners, cloth, wood, etc.) 2. heavy, fat (person, animal)

xšuna, xšuniya 1. rudeness, coarseness, roughness (manners, cloth, wood, etc.) 2. heaviness, obesity 3. in poor taste, awkward, having an unpleasant appearance

xeškaša pl. *-t* same as *xeṛxaša*

xešxeš v.i. to crackle, to crunch (as dried leaves)

xet, oxt pl. *xwatat* (dim. *xit*) 1. sister 2. exactly like, same as (with f. n.) *ḍaṛna xet ḍaṛkom.* Our house is exactly like yours. —*kan ɛăndi xetha tamamen l-bareḥ.* I had one just like it yesterday.

xtabeṛ v.t. 1. to test, to put to the test 2. to examine, to give an exam or test to

xtam v.n. of *xtem*

xtana pl. *-t, xtayen* 1. v.n. of *xetten* 2. circumcision

xtaṛ v.t. to choose, to elect, to select

xtaṛeɛ v.t. (v.n. *xtiraɛ*) 1. to invent 2. to make up, to imagine

xtaṣeṛ v.t. 1. to make short, to make brief or

concise (one's words) **2.** to summarize, to give a resume of
¶ *xtaṣeṛ ṭ-ṭṛiq* to take a shortcut
xtayen pl. of *xtana*
xtim v.n. of *xtem*
xtir v.n. of *xter*
xtiraɛ pl. *-at* **1.** v.n. of *xtaṛeɛ* **2.** invention
xtiṣaṛ v.n. of *xtaṣeṛ*
¶ *b-le-xtiṣaṛ* briefly, in short
xtem v.t. (v.n. *xtim, xtam*) **1.** to seal (with a signet ring) **2.** to finish, to end, to complete
¶ *xtem s-solka* **1.** to complete one's study and memorization of the Koran **2.** to finish reading a group of verses called *solka,* to terminate a passage of the Koran (as at a grave)
xetma pl. *-t* **1.** n.i. of *xtem* **2.** completion (of one's memorization of the Koran)
xter v.i. (v.n. *xtir*) to get or become thick(er), to thicken (liquid)
¶ a.p. *xater* pl. *-in* **1.** thick (liquid) **2.** unwatered, undiluted (usually potable liquids)
xetten v.t. (v.n. *xtana*) to circumcise
xetter v.t. to thicken, to make thick(er) (liquid)
xṭeˀ same as *xṭa ixṭa* **3**
xṭa ixṭa **1.** v.t. to miss (a target) **2.** v.t. to lose (as money in a game) **3.** (also *xṭeˀ*) v.i. to make a mistake, to err
** *ma-ixṭa-š men ḍ-ḍaṛ daba.* He should be home now. —*ḷḷah ma-xṭani maži.* I'll come for sure. —*ma-xṭani-š mennha.* I can't get along without her. —*xṭat ṣlatek.* Your prayer is unacceptable. —*xaṭini.* It doesn't concern me.
¶ *ma-xṭa, la-xṭa* except, but *koll-ši ža ma-xṭa ḥmed.* Everyone came except Ahmed.
¶ *ma-xṭahφ-š* expresses some assurance or definiteness about a statement *ma-xṭahom-š ikunu mužudin.* I'm sure there must be some.
¶ *xṭa f-* to fail (an exam, course)
xṭa ixṭi v.t. to not speak to, to ignore (s.o., from anger, etc.)
¶ *xṭa f-* to swear or curse at
¶ *xṭa ɛla* to leave alone, to stop bothering *xṭini ɛlik!* Leave me alone!
¶ *weḷḷahi ma-xṭahφ* emphasizes the determination to do s.th., etc. *we-ḷḷahi ma-xṭani ġadi!* I don't care what anyone says, I'm going anyway!
xṭa (m., no pl.) (spoken) insult, cursing
¶ *meṛṛa fe-xṭa* (with durative tenses) once in a (great) while
ˀexṭaˀ pl. of *xaṭaˀ*
xṭaṛ (no pl.) bet, wager
** *b-le-xṭaṛ?* You want to bet? (also in less literal sense as in English)
xṭawi pl. of *xeṭwa*

xṭeb **1.** v.t. to ask for (one's) hand in marriage *xṭebtha men waldiha.* I asked her parents for her hand in marriage. **2.** v.i. to speak, to give a speech, to discourse **3.** v.i. to preach, to give a sermon
xoṭba pl. *-t* **1.** n.i. of *xṭeb* **2.** speech, discourse, oration **3.** sermon
xṭef v.t. (v.n. *xṭif*) **1.** to snatch or grab away *ma-ɛṭitu-lha-š, xeṭfettu menni.* I didn't give it to her, she grabbed it away from me. **2.** to swipe, to steal
¶ *xṭef ṭ-ṭṛiq* to take a shortcut
xeṭfa pl. *-t* n.i. of *xṭef*
** *hadi l-xeṭfa hadi!* This is highway robbery (i.e., too much to pay)!
¶ *be-l-xeṭfa* rapidly, fast
xṭib pl. *xuṭaba* preacher, speaker (in mosque)
xṭif v.n. of *xṭef*
xṭiya pl. *-t* **1.** loss (financial) *ɛmelt waḥed le-xṭiya kbira.* I took a big loss (in selling s.th.). **2.** fine (monetary punishment)
** *had š-ši ma-fih hi le-xṭiya.* It's just a waste of time and money.
¶ *b-le-xṭiya* at a loss, with a loss *băɛtha b-le-xṭiya.* I sold it at a loss.
xṭeṛ v.i. (v.n. *xeṭṛan*) used with *bal* in certain expr.
¶ *xṭeṛ ɛla bal* to occur to *ma-xṭeṛ-š ɛla bali.* It didn't occur to me.
¶ *xṭeṛ f-baluφ* to think possible ≠ *waš ixṭeṛ f-balek be-lli rbeḥ had le-flus kollhom?* Would you think it possible that he earned all that money?
xeṭṛa du. *xṭeṛtayn, xṭeṛtin* pl. *xeṭṛat* time *mšit le-s-sinima tlata de-l-xeṭṛat had l-ˀesbuɛ.* I've been to the movies three times this week.
xeṭṛan v.n. of *xṭeṛ*
xeṭṭ pl. *xṭuṭ* **1.** handwriting, hand *ɛăndek xeṭṭ mezyan.* You have a nice hand. **2.** line *ṣeṭṭeṛ waḥed l-xeṭṭ teḥt le-klam.* Draw a line under the words. —*ma-teqṭăɛ-š l-xeṭṭ le-byeḍ.* Don't cross over the white line. **3.** furrow (plowed ground)
¶ *ḍṛeb l-xeṭṭ l-* to tell (one's) fortune *mša l-ɛăndha baš ḍḍṛeb-lu l-xeṭṭ.* He went to her to have her tell his fortune.
¶ *ḍṛib l-xeṭṭ* fortunetelling
¶ *ḍeṛṛab l-xeṭṭ* fortune teller
¶ *xeṭṭ l-yedd* signature
¶ *xeṭṭ žewwi* air route
¶ *xṭuṭ žewwiya* airlines
xeṭṭa v.t. **1.** to make or cause to lose *xeṭṭani flusi.* He made me lose my money. —*xeṭṭatni fe-l-lăɛb.* She made me lose the game. **2.** to make or cause to miss *xeṭṭawni t-tran.* They made me miss the train.
xeṭṭab pl. *-a* person given the charge of asking a girl's hand in marriage, marriage broker

xeṭṭaf pl. *-a* thief (particularly one who snatches or swipes things)
xeṭṭaṭ 1. pl. *-a* professional calligrapher 2. pl. *-in* having beautiful handwriting
xoṭṭayfa pl. *-t* swallow (bird)
xeṭṭeṭ v.t. to write (as a professional calligrapher)
xṭuṭ pl. of *xeṭṭ*
xeṭwa pl. *-t, xṭawi* 1. pace, step 2. stage, phase
xeṭya pl. *-t* 1. n.i. of *xṭa* 2. insult
xu (also *xa,* but *xuya, xay* my brother) pl. *xut, xwan, ˀixwan* 1. brother *mšit mʕa xay le-s-sinima.* I went to the movies with my brother. —*waš xuk lli qalha-lek?* Was it your brother that told you? 2. like, similar to (for m. n.) *had le-qlam xa l-axuṛ.* This pen is like the other one.
¶ *hada xuya mġeṛbi.* This is a fellow Moroccan of mine.
xud impv. of *xda*
xuḍeṛ pl. of *xḍeṛ*
xuf 1. fear 2. apprehension, misgiving
¶ *fihᶲ l-xuf* 1. to be dangerous ≠ *had ṭ-ṭriq fiha l-xuf.* This road is dangerous. 2. (to be) scared *fih l-xuf, ma-iqḍeṛ-š imši b-weḥdu.* He's scared and won't go alone.
xulafa pl. of *xalifa*
xulud 1. immortality 2. eternity
xumus pl. *ˀexmas* fifth (fraction)
xuṛeṣ pl. of *xṛeṣ* 2
xuṣuṣ used in the expr. *be-l-xuṣuṣ, xuṣuṣen* especially, in particular
xuṣuṣi pl. *-yen* 1. private *had l-mekteb xuṣuṣi.* This office is private. 2. special (often translated by "especially" in English) *had n-nḍaḍeṛ xuṣuṣiyin le-š-šems.* These glasses are especially for sunlight.
xut pl. of *xu*
xuṭaba pl. of *xṭib*
xux n.u. *-a* 1. peach 2. peach tree
xuxi pl. *-yen* type of light green
xuyan 1. v.n. of *xwa* 2. evacuation, exodus 3. emptiness
xwa ixwa v.i. (v.n. *xuyan, xewyan, xwi*) 1. to empty, to become empty 2. to run down (clock, battery)
¶ *xwa b-* 1. to fall through with, to collapse under (as a weak floor) 2. to let (s.o.) down, to break one's word to, to not come through for
¶ a.p. *xawi* f. *xawya* pl. *xawyen* 1. empty, vacant 2. run down (clock, battery)
¶ *klam xawi* empty words, nonsense
xwa ixwi v.t. (v.n. *xuyan, xewyan, xwi*) 1. to empty 2. to vacate (room, house) 3. to evacuate (house, city) 4. to pour (from a glass, etc.) 5. to leave (a place)
¶ *xwa blad u-ʕămmeṛ blad* to go from country to country, or city to citv
xwa (m., no pl.) (dangerous) hole or pit
¶ *le-xwa l-xawi* nonsense
xwabi pl. of *xabya*
xwaḍ pl. (of intensity) *-at* 1. muddy or turbid water 2. disorder, confusion, turmoil
xwal pl. of *xal* 1
xwami pl. of *xamiya*
xwan pl. of *xu*
xwarež pl. of *xariži* 2
xwašem (no sg.) nostrils
xwatat pl. of *xet*
xwatem pl. of *xatem*
xwaṭeṛ pl. of *xaṭeṛ*
xwaža pl. of *xwaži*
xwaži pl. *-yen, xwaža* rich, wealthy
xwi v.n. of *xwa*
xwidem, xwidma pl. *xwidmat* dim. of *xadem*
xwen v.t. to steal, to rob (s.th.) *xewnat l-beẓṭam dyali!* She stole my wallet!
xewna pl. *-t* 1. n.i. of *xwen* 2. theft, robbery
xewwa v.t. 1. to evacuate from, to make (s.o.) evacuate (a place) *l-ʕăṣkeṛ xewwaw n-nas le-mdina.* The army evacuated the people from the city. 2. to evict (s.o.) from (house) *xewwaw xay ḍ-ḍaṛ.* They've evicted my brother from the house. 3. to deport (s.o.) from (a country) *ḥeṣṣḷuh ka-idžesses u-xewwaweh le-blad.* They caught him spying and deported him from the country. 4. to throw (s.o.) out of (a place)
xewwaḍ pl. *-a* trouble-maker
xewwaf adj. pl. *-in* n.pl. *-a* coward(ly)
xewwan pl. *-a* thief, robber
xewwaṛ pl. *-a* nosy person, meddler
xewweḍ v.t. 1. to make muddy or turbid (water, by stirring it up) 2. to cloud, to confuse (situation, issue)
¶ *xewweḍ bin* to cause trouble between or among
¶ *xewweḍ ḍmaġuᶲ* to worry
ma-txewweḍ-š ḍmaġek! Don't worry!
¶ *xewweḍ le-ʕqel* to confuse, to mix up
ma-txewweḍ-š ʕăqli! Don't confuse me!
xewwef v.t. to frighten, to scare, to cause to fear
xewweṛ 1. v.t. to clear, to unclog (as a drain, with a finger or some instrument) 2. v.t. to poke (one's eye) *kan ka-ilʕăb mʕah u-huwa ixewweṛ-lu ʕăynu.* He was playing with him and poked him in the eye. 3. v.i. to rummage around (looking for s.th.) *žbeṛtu ka-ixewweṛ-li fe-mkatbi.* I found him rummaging around in my pockets. 4. v.i. to speak incoherently
xewwex v.i. to become hollow or eaten out (as a rotten tree)
xewyan same as *xuyan* (v.n. of *xwa*)
xxi, xxi fik said to s.o. who has had a misfortune and probably deserved it, e.g.,

That'll teach you! Tough luck! (ironically)

xxeṛ **1.** end, extremity **2.** end, finish **3.** pl. *-in* last, last one *škun lli žaw le-xxṛin?* Who were the last ones to come?

¶ *f-le-xxeṛ* in or at the end, finally

xxṛani pl. *-yen* **1.** last (i.e., preceding) *ma-le-t-teffaɛa le-xxṛaniya lli kliti?* What was wrong with the last apple you ate? **2.** last, final *h-ana ka-nqulha-lek u-hadi l-meṛṛa le-xxṛaniya.* I'm telling you for the last time.

xyab v.i. **1.** to become ugly or unsightly *had l-kebbuṭ xyab men băɛd-ma tṣebben, ma-bqa fih ma ittelbes.* This coat came out of the wash looking bad; it's not worth wearing. **2.** to become or go bad (food, person)

xyal pl. *-at* **1.** shadow (usually of person) **2.** silhouette (either one's shadow or effect of backlighting) **3.** phantom, specter (i.e., an indistinct mysterious image)

** *ḍeṛṛeq ɛliya xyalek!* Get out of my sight!

xyam pl. of *xima*

xyaṛ all right, fine, O.K. *tebġi temši mɛaya le-s-sinima?—xyaṛ!* Do you want to go to the show with me?—All right!

¶ *xyaṛ n-nas, l-xil,* etc. the best of people, horses, etc.

xyaṭa **1.** v.n. of *xeyyeṭ* **2.** sewing, needlework

xeyl same as *xil*

xyem pl. of *xima*

xeyma same as *xima*

xyer, ˀăxyeṛ better *had l-magana xyer min hadik.* This watch is better than that one.

¶ *xyer-ma* rather than *ɛsen-lek tebqa hna xyer-ma temši l-temma.* You'd better stay here rather than go there.

xeyš same as *xiš*

xeyṭ same as *xiṭ*

xyuba ugliness, unsightliness (person, things, temperament, etc.)

xyuṭ pl. of *xiṭ*

xeyyal pl. *-a* cavalryman, horseman

xeyyaṭ pl. *-a* tailor

xeyyaṭa pl. *-t* seamstress

xeyyeb v.t. **1.** to make ugly, unsightly **2.** to corrupt (one's nature, mind)

¶ *xeyyeb ḍ-ḍenn* (or *n-niya*) *l-* to disappoint *xeyyebti-li ḍenni* (or *ḍ-ḍenn*). You've disappointed me.

¶ *xeyyeb f-* to disparage, to make seem bad or inferior, to speak ill of

¶ *xeyyeb fe-l-fikṛa l-* to make (s.o.) change his mind

¶ *xeyyeb l-* to change (s.o.'s) mind, to dissuade, to talk (s.o.) out (of) *ɛlaš xeyyebti-lu fe-s-siyaṛa?* Why did you talk him out of (buying) the car?

¶ *xeyyeb le-wžeh f-* to make a face at

xeyyeṛ v.t. to let or allow to choose, to give a choice to *xeyyeṛtu f-had ž-žuž de-ṣ-ṣbabeṭ.* I let him choose between these two pairs of shoes.

¶ part. *mxeyyeṛ* pl. *-in* good, excellent, choice, first-rate, best

xeyyeṛ pl. *-in* good, righteous

xeyyeṭ v.t. (v.n. *xyaṭa*) **1.** to sew, to stitch (also surgery) **2.** to have (s.th.) made (by a tailor)

xza ixzi v.t. to damn (God) *ḷḷah ixzik!* (May) God damn you!

xzana pl. *-t, xzayen* **1.** tent (with center pole) **2.** cupboard, buffet

¶ *xzana* (*d-le-ktub*) bookcase

¶ *xzana de-l-mal* treasury (building)

xzayen pl. of *xzana* and *xzin* **2**

xzin **1.** v.n. of *xzen* **2.** pl. *xzayen* place for storage

xzir v.n. of *xzer*

xzit expr. of disgust or regret *xzit!* or *a-xzit!* or *ya-xzit!* Damn! Rats!

** *xzit mennu!* I can't stand him!

xzen v.t. (v.n. *xzin*) **1.** to store **2.** to hide, to conceal **3.** to save (money)

xezna pl. *-t* place for keeping or storing

** *huwa xezna de-l-ɛilm.* He's a treasure of knowledge.

xzer f- (v.n. *xzir*) to look threateningly at (as to stop a child from doing s.th.)

xezra pl. *-t* n.i. of *xzer*

xezz moss, lichen

xezzan pl. *-at* dam, dike

xezzi pl. *-yen* moss green (very dark)

xezzez v.i. to become mossy or covered with moss

Y

ya vocative particle *ya ɛabiba, fayn ɛmelti le-flus lli ɛṭitek?* Habiba, where did you put the money I gave you?

¶ *ya . . . ya* either . . . or *ya dži mɛana ya tebqa hna.* Either you come with us or you stay here. —*ya bṛahim ya naɛima, waɛed fihom huwa lli imken herresha.* Either Abraham or Naima may have broken it.

yaban Japan

yabani pl. *-yen* Japanese

yabes a.p. of *ibes*

ya-delli (Marrakech usage) surely, certainly, of course *ɛlah, ya-delli ma-idirha!* I'm sure he'll do it!

yak kind of emphatic interrogative particle similar to English, "Didn't I?," "Isn't it?," "Haven't you?," etc.) *yak qoltha-lek?* I told you, didn't I? —*ma-mša-š, yak?* He hasn't gone, has he? —*yak ma-mša?* Has he left (already)?

ya-ḷḷah f. *ya-ḷḷahi* pl. *ya-ḷḷahu* (f. and pl. less common) let's . . . *ya-ḷḷahu* (or *ya-ḷḷah*) *nemšiw le-s-sinima!* Let's go to the movies!

yamam n.u. *-a* dove

yaman (with art.) Yemen

yamani pl. *-yen* **1.** Yemenite **2.** small white pigeon

yamin oath (of office, etc.)

¶ *ʔedda* (or *ɛṭa*) *l-yamin* to take the oath (of office, in court)

yames (country usage) yesterday

yanayer same as *yennayer*

yaqin **1.** certainty, certitude **2.** conviction

¶ *ɛănduφ l-yaqin* (*bin*) to be sure, certain, convinced (that)

yaqut n.u. *-a* precious stone (mainly opaque, but may be extended to others)

yasmin n.u. *-a* jasmine (tree or flower)

yaxod impf. of *xda*

yažuṛ n.u. *-a* brick (building)

yebbes v.t. to dry (out) (clothes, soil, puddle, etc.)

yebṛayeṛ February

yebril same as *ʔabril*

yedd (f.) pl. *-in* (*yeddi-* with pron. endings, dim. *idida*) **1.** hand *ka-ikteb b-yeddu de-š-šmal.* He writes with his left hand. —*ɛṭini yeddek!* Give me a hand (some help)! **2.** (entire) arm, upper limb (human) **3.** forepaw, front foot or hoof (animal) **4.** handle, grip (suitcase, pitcher, etc.) **5.** pestle **6.** coat, layer (of paint) **7.** piece of music (on some hand-played instrument, e.g., lute)

** *ma-b-yeddi ma ndir.* There's nothing I can do (about it). —*šebbeṛ* (or *ṛebbi*) *yeddek!* Keep your hands off!

¶ *b-yedduφ,* or *b-yeddihφ* by oneself, alone *bnaw ḍ-ḍaṛ b-yeddihom.* They built the house by themselves.

¶ *f-yedd* (plus n. or pron.) in the hands or possession of

¶ (*ma*) *bin yeddin* **1.** same as *f-yedd* **2.** before (prep.) *kan xeṣṣu imtel ma bin yeddin l-qaḍi.* He had to appear before the judge.

¶ *nezzel yedduφ ɛla* (s.th.) to keep (s.th.) for oneself, to retain

¶ *rfed l-yedd l-* to fire or dismiss (s.o.) *refdu-li yeddi l-bareḥ.* They fired me yesterday.

¶ *rfed yedduφ men* (plus n.) to abstain from, to cease indulgence in (e.g. work, eating)

¶ *yeddek~* five *šṛebt yeddek de-l-kisan de-l-qehwa.* I drank five glasses of coffee.

¶ *yedduφ ṭwila* to have a lot of influence≠

¶ *ɛla yedd* (plus n. or pron.) thanks to, with the help of

¶ *ɛṭa yedd ḷḷah* to lend a hand to, to help

yeddem v.t. **1.** to put a lot of fat, grease, or oil in (food) **2.** to spot or dirty (s.th.) with grease or fat (from foods)

yemma (inh. pos., declined like *baba*) **1.** (my) mother **2.** used as a derogatory vehicle for pron. *bqit ɛla yemmah b-le-ɛṣa ḥetta sxeft.* I beat the s.o.b. until I almost fainted.

** *sir l-yemmak ɛliya!* Get the hell out of here!

yemta same as *ʔimta*

yennayer January

yeʔs despair, hopelessness

¶ *qṭăɛ l-yeʔs* to give up or lose all hope

yesser v.t. (v.n. *tisir*) **1.** to make easy (test, work, etc.) **2.** to prepare, to get ready (s.th., s.o.)

¶ *yesser ɛla* to aid, to assist (subject often God)

yulyu, yulyuz July

yum du. *-ayn, -in* pl. *ʔeyyam, iyyam, iyyamat* day (24 hours)

¶ *f-iyyam* (plus n.) at the time of, during

¶ *had l-iyyam, f-had l-iyyam* **1.** these days, nowadays **2.** lately **3.** the other day, a few days ago

¶ *l-yum* today

yumi pl. *-yen* daily

yunyeh, yunyu June (month)

yexx same as *ya-xzit!* (see *xzit*)

ʔeyyam pl. of *yum*

yyeh yes

Z

ẓabuṛ Psalms of David, Book of Psalms

zad izid (v.n. *zyada*) **1.** v.t. to add *zedna tlata de-l-ʔaqṣam f-dak l-medṛaṣa.* We added three classrooms to that school. **2.** v.t. to give more, to give extra *xeḷḷṣu-lu s-sfeṛ u-zaduh ʔalfayn derhem.* They paid his transportation and gave him two thousand dirhams extra. **3.** v.t. to bid (at an auction) *zad ʕešrin derhem kif tbaʕet.* He bid twenty dirhams just when it was sold. **3.** v.i. to go on, to keep (doing s.th.) *ṭelbu mennha teskot u-hiya ġir zadet ka-tġuwwet.* They asked her to be quiet, but she just kept shouting. **4.** v.i. to move (up, over, on, etc.) *qol-lu izid l-l-qoddam baš tegles.* Tell him to move up to the front so you can sit down.

¶ *zad f-* **1.** to increase *ġad-iziduh fe-l-ʔužṛa dyalu.* They're going to increase his salary **2.** to extend *ṭelbet men mʕällemha izidha fe-l-ʕoṭla dyalha.* She asked her boss to extend her vacation. **3.** to bid on *ʕäžbetni had ḍ-ḍaṛ, ġad-nzid fiha.* I like this house, I'm going to bid on it. **4.** to exaggerate *ma-ka-yăʕṛef iʕăwwed ʕetta ʕaža bla-ma izid fiha.* He can't tell anything without exaggerating.

¶ *zad xelfa* to leave, to go away *qalu-lu izid xelfa.* They told him to go away. —*zid xelfa ʕliya!* Beat it!

¶ *zad ʕla* **1.** to bid against **2.** to overcharge, to charge too much *zad ʕliya xemsa u-ʕešrin derhem.* He charged me twenty-five dirhams too much.

¶ *zid ʕla had š-ši* besides, furthermore

¶ a.p. *zayed* pl. *-in* unnecessary, superfluous, extra

¶ *b-zayed* **1.** much, a great deal of *ʕăndhom le-flus b-zayed.* They've got a great deal of money. **2.** very much, a lot *ka-tebġih b-zayed.* She likes him very much.

¶ *zayed naqeṣ* more or less

** *ʕăndi zayed naqeṣ.* I don't care. It doesn't make any difference to me. I couldn't care less.

zad (no pl.) provisions (for a journey)

ẓaġ iẓiġ v.i. (v.n. *ẓiġa*) **1.** to get out of hand *had l-weld xeṣṣu le-ʕṣa, ṛah bda iẓiġ.* This child needs a beating, he's getting out of hand. **2.** to show insolence, to be insolent **3.** to show (unwarranted) dissatisfaction with what one has

zahed adj. pl. *-in* n.pl. *zohhad* ascetic, hermit

zal izul v.i. (v.n. *zwal*) **1.** to come out *had ṭ-ṭebʕa dzul b-l-ixiya?* Will this spot come out with bleach? **2.** to go out, to disappear *l-fekra kollha zalet men balu.* The very thought has gone out of his mind. **3.** to come off *kerʕan š-šelya kollhom zalu.* All the legs of the chair have come off. **4.** to be dismissed, to be removed *ʕadad de-l-kottab zalu men băʕd ntixab ṛ-ṛaʔis ž-ždid.* Many secretaries have been dismissed since the election of the new president. **5.** to be omitted, to be left out *had l-feqṛa ġir zayda, imken-lha dzul.* This paragraph is unnecessary; it could be omitted.

¶ *ma-zal* f. *-a* pl. *-in* **1.** still *ma-zala ʕăndu maganti.* He still has my watch. —*ma-zal ma-ʕṛefnah š-ġad-idir.* We still don't know what he's going to do. —*ma-zalin ka-ixedmu mʕana.* They're still working with us. —*ma-zal-lna l-weqt.* We still have time. **2.** not yet (in a reply) *weždet le-ġda?—ma-zala.* Is lunch ready? —Not yet.

¶ *aw ma-zal, wella ma-zal* yet (in interrogative) *feḍḍa šġalu aw ma-zal?* Has he finished his work yet?

zaman same as *zman*

zamil pl. *zumalaʔ* **1.** colleague, associate **2.** friend

zanadiq pl. of *zendiq*

ẓaṛ iẓuṛ v.t. (v.n. *ẓyaṛa, ẓuṛan*) to visit, to pay a visit to

** *ẓaṛetna l-baṛaka.* said upon welcoming a guest, expressing one's joy over his visit

zaṛafa pl. *-t* giraffe

zaweg f- **1.** to seek asylum in *zawget fe-s-sifaṛa s-swiṣṛiya.* She sought asylum at the Swiss Embassy. **2.** to ask (s.o.) to intercede **3.** to beg, to beseech

ẓaweq mercury, quicksilver

ẓawš n.u. *-a* sparrow

zawya pl. *-t, zwawi* center where members of a Muslim brotherhood gather (usually a mosque built around the tomb of a saint)

zayed a.p. of *zad*

zaydun besides, furthermore

ẓaẓa pl. *-t* **1.** wail, wailing (e.g. of mourning women, crying child) **2.** shouting, yelling

¶ *nuwwed ẓaẓa, ʕmel ẓaẓa* **1.** to wail (e.g. in mourning) **2.** to shout

zaž n.u. *-a* **1.** glass *had z-zlayef de-z-zaž.* These bowls are made of glass. **2.** (window) pane **3.** windshield

¶ *zaž ʕraqi* stained glass

zaʕem v.t. **1.** to jostle, to elbow **2.** to compete with

zbabel pl .of *zebbala*

zbal pl. of *zbel*

ẓbaṭi pl. of *ẓebṭa*

ẓbayel pl. of *ẓebla*

zebbal pl. *-a* garbage man

zebbala pl. *-t, zbabel* garbage dump

ẓebbaṛ ag. n. of *ẓbeṛ*

ẓebbaṛa pl. *-t* billhook

zebbel f- or *l-* to cuss out, to call names *ma-ḍeṛbettu ʕetta ma-xella ma zebbel fiha.* She didn't hit him until he called her all sorts of names.

zebda pl. *zbud* sweet butter

zbib n.u. *-a* **1.** raisin **2.** large mole (skin)

zbibi pl. *-yen* purplish red

ẓbiṛ v.n. of *ẓbeṛ*

ẓbiṭa dim. of *ẓebṭa*

zbel pl. *zbal* **1.** trash, garbage **2.** worthless article, piece of junk
ẓebḷa pl. *-t, ẓbayel* **1.** blunder **2.** misdeed, wrongful act
ẓbeṛ v.t. (v.n. *ẓbiṛ*) **1.** to hedge, to trim a hedge **2.** to break, to destroy, to ruin (s.o.)
ẓebṛa pl. *-t* (blacksmith's) anvil
ẓbeṭ f. *ẓebṭa* pl. *ẓubeṭ* naked, nude
¶ *εăryan ẓbeṭ* stark naked
ẓebṭa pl. *-t, ẓbaṭi, ẓbuṭ* (dim. *ẓbiṭa*) (naked) body *ġselt d-derri u-ġeṭṭat-lu ẓbeṭṭu b-iẓaṛ.* She washed the baby and covered his body with a sheet.
ẓebṭi pl. *-yen* flesh-colored
zbud pl. of *zebda*
ẓbuṭ pl. of *ẓebṭa*
zdiḥ v.n. of *zdeḥ*
zdeḥ v.t. (v.n. *zdiḥ*) to slam *ġeḍbet u-zedḥet l-bab u-xeṛžet.* She got mad, slammed the door and left. —*rfed ṣ-ṣenḍuq u-zedḥu εăl l-eṛḍ ḥetta therres.* He took the box and slammed it (down) on the floor so hard that it broke.
ẓdim v.n. of *ẓdem*
ẓdem v.i. (v.n. *ẓdim*) to step, to set one's foot *ila mšiti ḥetta ẓdemti temma ṛa-ḅḅak iḍeṛbek.* If you set your foot in there your father will beat you.
¶ *ẓdem f-, ẓdem εla* to walk all over
zeff v.i. (v.n. *zeffan*) **1.** to blow (e.g. wind) **2.** *zeff εla* to jump on, to take by surprise (aggressively)
zeffan v.n. of *zeff*
zeffet v.t. to asphalt (both to pave with asphalt and also more generally)
zfer f. *zefra* pl. *zufer* rancid, emitting an unpleasant smell (food)
zeft asphalt
zfula pl. of *azfel*
zfura, zfuriya rancid smell
zefzafi strong, cold wind
zefzuf n.u. *-a* edible fruit of the jujube family
zga izga v.i. to be quiet *qul le-d-drari izgaw.* Tell the children to be quiet.
ẓga iẓgi v.i. (v.n. *ẓga, ẓegyan*) to shout
¶ *ẓga εla* **1.** to call *ġir xellik f-bitek, mnayn tužed le-ġda neẓgiw εlik.* Just stay in your room, we'll call you when lunch is ready. **2.** to chide, to reprimand
ẓga v.n. of *ẓga*
zgaden pl. of *zegdun*
zgafi pl. of *zegfa*
zegdun pl. *zgaden* rag, worn piece of cloth
zgef v.t. (v.n. *zgif*) to sip (often noisily)
zegfa pl. *-t, zgafi* (dim. *zgifa*) sip
zgif v.n. of *zgef*
zgifa dim. of *zegfa*
zgil v.n. of *zgel*
zgel v.t. (v.n. *zgil*) to miss *niyyeš εăl ṭ-ṭiṛ saεa zeglu.* He shot at the bird but missed it.
ẓegya pl. *-t* n.i. of *ẓga*
ẓegyan v.n. of *ẓga*
ẓġaba pl. of *ẓoġbi*
zġaṛet pl. of *zeġṛata*
ẓġeb n.u. *ẓeġba* (body) hair
ẓoġbi adj. pl. *-yen* n.pl. *ẓġaba* **1.** ill-fated **2.** jinx, cause of bad luck
zoġlal n.u. *-a* type of small snail
zeġnen v.i. to hum *kanet ka-dzeġnen mεa ṛaṣha.* She was humming to herself. —*n-nḥăl bdaw izeġnnu fe-ṣ-ṣbaḥ bekri.* The bees started humming early in the morning.
zeġṛata pl. *-t, zġaṛet* n.i. of *zeġṛet*
zeġṛet v.i. (v.n. *dzeġṛit*) to ululate joyously (women)
zha izha v.i. (v.n. *zhu*) to have an enjoyable time (especially an amorous drinking session in a cozy atmosphere)
zohd asceticism
zehha v.t. to entertain (s.o.) in the way described under *zha*
zohhad n.pl. of *zahed*
zehhar pl. *-in* ag. adj. of *zher*
zehheq v.t. **1.** to slide, to cause to slide **2.** to lead astray
¶ *zehhqu~ l-, zehheq le-εqel l-* to bewilder *zehhquh-lu* or *zehhqu-lu εăqlu.* They bewildered him.
ẓehheṛ v.i. **1.** to bloom, to blossom **2.** to prosper
zhiq v.n. of *zheq*
zhir v.n. of *zher*
ẓheq v.i. (v.n. *ẓhiq*) **1.** to slip, to skid **2.** to be slippery **3.** to err, to go astray
** *ẓehqet ṛuḥu.* He's dead (breathed his last). —*ẓheq-lu εăqlu.* He's lost his mind.
ẓehqa n.i. of *ẓheq*
zher v.i. (v.n. *zhir*) **1.** to roar (lion) **2.** to moan, to groan
¶ *zher εla* to scold, to reprimand
ẓheṛ v.i. to prosper
ẓheṛ **1.** orange blossom **2.** luck
¶ *ḥekmuφ* (or *ṭlăε-luφ* or *εănduφ*) *ẓ-ẓheṛ* to be lucky ≠
** *ṭaḷeε-lha ẓ-ẓheṛ.* Everything's going her way.
¶ *ṭḷeb ẓehṛuφ* to try one's luck *ġad-ṭṭḷeb ẓheṛha f-le-mtiḥan.* She's going to try her luck at the exam.
zehri, zohri pl. *-yen* nearsighted
zhu v.n. of *zha*
zehwani pl. *-yen* one who frequents parties of the type described under *zha*
zif pl. *zyuf, zyufa* **1.** handkerchief **2.** scarf
ẓiġa v.n. of *ẓaġ*
zin beauty
¶ *z-zin u-le-bha* balsam

zina pl. *-t* 1. v.n. of *zna* 2. ornament, decoration 3. make-up (cosmetics)
ẓina pl. *-t, ẓyen* dozen
zit f. pl. *zyut* oil (cooking, mineral)
¶ *zit l-gaz* kerosene
¶ *zit l-xeṛwăʕ* castor oil
¶ *zit l-ʕud* olive oil
ziti pl. *-yen* forest green
zitun n.u. *-a* 1. olive 2. olive tree
¶ *kḥăl zituna* pl. *kuḥăl zitun* pitch black
zituni pl. *-yen* olive green
ziwani goatskin leather dyed yellow
ziy pl. *ʔezyaʔ* style, fashion *ʕămmṛu ma-lbes z-ziy l-ʔuṛebbi.* He's never dressed in European style.
ẓiy v.n. of *ẓwa*
¶ *qṭăʕ ẓ-ẓiy* to hush, to shut up
ẓiyyaṛ pl. *-a* 1. vise (tool) 2. severity, strictness *kan ẓiyyaṛ kbir f-le-mtiḥan.* The exam was very severe.
ziyyat pl. *-a* oil dealer
ziyyed v.t. 1. to move *ziyyedt šleyti l-l-qeddam baš nqeṛṛeb l-l-muḥaḍiṛ.* I moved my chair to the front so I would be near the lecturer. 2. to take *ziyyed n-nas le-mwaḍeʕhom.* Take the people to their seats. —*huwa qal-li nziyyed l-ʕăwd le-s-sehriž išṛob.* He told me to take the horse to the pond to drink. 3. to get into, to involve *škun ziyydek l-had l-muwqif?* Who got you into this situation?
ziyyen v.t. 1. to adorn, to decorate 2. to embellish 3. to make better, to ameliorate, to improve 4. v.i. to get spruced up, to doll up
¶ *ziyyen f-* to praise *bqaw ka-iziyynu-lu f-bent ʕămmhom ḥetta xdaha.* They kept praising their cousin to him till he married her.
ẓiyyeṛ v.t. 1. to tighten (e.g. a screw) 2. to crack down on, to be strict with *melli bda iẓiyyeṛhom ma-bqaw-š ižiw mʕăṭṭlin.* Since he cracked down on them they stopped coming late. 3. to embarrass *ẓiyyṛettu melli žebdet d-dbaz lli wqăʕ binathom.* She embarrassed him by mentioning the argument they had. 4. to constrain *ẓiyyṛuha ḥetta xeḷḷṣet lli kan ittsalha kollu.* They constrained her to pay everything she owed.
¶ *ẓiyyeṛ ʕla* to be hard on *l-feqya kollhom ẓiyyṛu ʕlina f-le-mtiḥanat.* All the teachers were hard on us during the exams.
ziyyet v.t. to oil, to grease
ẓiyyeṭ v.i. to grind, to creak *l-bab xeṣṣha z-zit baš ma-tebqa-ši dẓiyyeṭ.* The door needs oiling so it will stop creaking.
ẓiẓen v.t. 1. to make dumb, speechless 2. to make be quiet (by intimidation)
ẓiẓun pl. *ẓyaẓen* dumb, mute
zizwa pl. *-t* small aluminum cup with a long handle, used for making tea or coffee
zka izka v.i. to increase, to abound *sokkan had le-mdina ġir ka-izkaw.* The population of this city keeps increasing.
zka pl. *-wat* tithe, tithing (paid by Muslims to the needy)
ẓkaṛem pl. of *ẓekṛum*
zekka v.i. to pay the *zka*
** *ḷḷah izekki ʕămṛek!* May you have a long life!
zekri see *bu-zekri*
ẓekṛum pl. *ẓkaṛem* 1. sliding metal bolt for locking doors 2. sourpuss
zlafa pl. *zlayef* 1. bowl (vessel) 2. mug, face (pejorative)
zlag pl. *-at* string (e.g. of beads, doughnuts, figs)
ẓḷaḷeṭ pl. of *ẓeḷḷaṭ*
zlayef pl. of *zlafa*
zlazel pl. of *zelzal*
zḷiq v.n. of *zḷeq*
zella pl. *-t* 1. blunder, gross error 2. sin, misdeed
ẓeḷḷaḷ pl. *-a* woman-chaser
ẓeḷḷaṭ pl. *ẓḷaḷeṭ* cudgel, club
zellayži pl. *-ya* mosaicist, tile-setter
zellef v.t. and v.i. 1. to scorch, to burn *š-šems ka-dzellef l-yum.* The sun is scorching today. 2. to cause great grief to, to grieve a great deal *zellfethom l-mut d-weldhom ṣ-ṣġiṛ.* The death of their young son caused them great grief.
zelleg v.t. 1. to thread, to pass through the eye of a needle 2. to string (e.g. beads, doughnuts, figs)
zelliž n.u. *-a* ceramic tile
zellež v.t. to cover with mosaic, to tile
zellăʕ v.t. to spill, to scatter *žmăʕ ẓ-ẓṛăʕ lli zellăʕti.* Pick up the wheat you spilled.
zḷeq v.i. (v.n. *zḷiq*) 1. to slide, to slip *zeḷqet u-ṭaḥet.* She slipped and fell. 2. to skid *s-siyaṛa zelqet u-dexlet f-šežṛa.* The car skidded and went into a tree. 3. to be slippery *ṣug ġir be-š-šwiya ḥit ṭ-ṭṛiq ka-dzḷeq.* Drive slowly because the road is slippery.
zelqef v.t. to catch (in the air)
ẓeḷṭ penury, poverty, misery
** *ḍaṛbu ẓ-ẓeḷṭ.* He's broke.
zelzal pl. *zlazel* earthquake
zelzel v.t. to shake, to cause to move
zelzla n.i. of *zelzel*
zmam pl. *-at, zmayem* written record (general term)
ẓmameṛ pl. of *ẓemmaṛa*
zman 1. time *z-zman iwerrina škun mʕah l-ḥăqq.* Time will show us who's right. 2. formerly, in time past *zman ma-kanu-š n-nas iṣafṛu bezzaf.* Formerly, people didn't travel a lot.

** *qehṛu z-zman* or *ṭaζ bih z-zman.* He's had difficult moments.
¶ *dwayeb z-zman* contingency, any future difficulty
¶ *ḍṛeb l-ζesba le-z-zman* to think of the hardships of life (and therefore take one's precautions)
¶ *fe-z-zman z-zamani* a long time ago, way back in the old days
zmayem pl. of *zmam*
zemm v.t. to close tight, to shut *zemm fommek.* Shut your mouth.
ẓemmaṛa pl. *-t, ẓmameṛ* **1.** toy horn (type of noisemaker) **2.** horn (e.g., used by a referee)
¶ *ζălq ẓ-ẓemmaṛa* piercing, high-pitched voice *ζălqha bζal ζălq ẓ-ẓemmaṛa.* She has a high-pitched voice.
ẓemmita food prepared from grilled ground maize, oil, and sometimes honey
zemmem v.t. **1.** to record, to note down *xeṣṣek dzemmem hadi f-konnašek.* You should record this in your notebook. **2.** to register, to enroll *ġad-izemmen weldu fe-l-meḍṛaṣa gedda.* He's going to register his son in school tomorrow.
ẓemmeṛ v.i. to blow a horn
¶ *ẓemmeṛ f-* to blow (a horn)
zemmuri pl. *-yen* inhabitant of the Zemmour region
ẓmeṛ expr. used in mild swearing *aš ζmelti l-had ẓ-ẓmeṛ de-š-šelya?* What did you do to this darn chair?
** *ẓ-ẓmeṛ!* Aw, shucks! —*ṭḷăζ-lu ẓ-ẓmeṛ f-ṛaṣu.* He got fed up.
ẓmet v.i. (v.n. *ẓemt*) to be muggy (weather)
ẓemt v.n. of *ẓmet*
zmurrud n.u. *-a* emerald (stone)
zmurrudi pl. *-yen* emerald green
zemzem (also *bir zemzem*) name of the sacred well in Mecca
zna izni v.i. (v.n. *zina, zna*) **1.** to commit adultery **2.** to become a prostitute **3.** to be promiscuous (both male and female)
zna v.n. of *zna*
¶ *weld* (*bent*) *z-zna* **1.** illegitimate boy (girl) **2.** dishonest person, swindler
znabel pl. of *zenbil*
znad pl. *-at* hammer (of a firearm)
znafer pl. of *zenfara*
znaqi pl. of *zenqa*
ẓnaṭeṭ pl. of *ẓenṭiṭ*
znaydi pl. *-ya* gunsmith
zenbil pl. *znabel* canister used for keeping tea
zned v.i. (v.n. *znid*) to get hotter (fire, argument, weather, etc.)
zenḍiq pl. *zanaḍiq* rascal, worthless person
zenfara pl. *znafer* protruding lip (animal)
¶ pl. *znafer* muzzle, snout (animal)
ẓeng zinc
znid v.n. of *zned*
zniqa dim. of *zenqa*
zenned v.t. **1.** to make hotter, to fan *xdit l-kir baš nzenned l-ζafya.* I used the bellows to make the fire hotter. **2.** to rile (up) *zenndettu melli bdat texṭi fih.* She riled him (up) when she started calling him names.
¶ *zennedha~* to gorge oneself (with food)
zenqa pl. *-t, znaqi* (dim. *zniqa*) street
zenqawi pl. *-yen* **1.** colloquial (speech) **2.** vulgar, low, base
ẓenṭiṭ pl. *ẓnaṭeṭ* tail (animal)
zenzen v.i. to ring (e.g. a tuning fork)
zenžaṛ, zenžaṛ le-ζṛaqi verdigris
zenžaṛi pl. *-yen* turquoise blue
zenžlan sesame
zenžeṛ v.t. and v.i. to rust *le-bruda zenžṛet s-swaret.* The dampness has rusted the keys. —*le-mṣameṛ kollhom zenžṛu.* All the nails have rusted.
ẓeqq v.t. (v.n. *ẓeqqan*) to feed (bird feeding its young, person feeding a bird)
ẓeqqa pl. *-t* n.i. of *ẓeqq*
ẓeqqan v.n. of *ẓeqq*
ẓṛabi pl. of *ẓeṛbiya*
zradi pl. of *zerda*
ẓṛaq v.i. (v.n. *ẓṛuqa, ẓṛuqiya*) to turn blue *ġir š-šta ζeṣṛet u-s-sma ẓṛaqet.* As soon as it stopped raining the sky turned blue.
zrareζ pl. of *zerriζa*
ẓṛaweṭ pl. of *ẓeṛwaṭa*
zrayeb pl. of *zriba*
ẓṛaybi pl. *-ya* **1.** rug weaver **2.** rug dealer
zraydi pl. *-ya* **1.** party-goer **2.** glutton
ẓṛaẓeṛ pl. of *ẓeṛẓuṛ*
zreb **1.** v.t. to hurry, to rush *ila zrebti l-xedma ṛaha ma-ṭṭḷăζ-š mezyana.* If you hurry the work it won't be well done. —*la-dzrebha-ši baš tṣuwweb l-xedma mζăwwṭa.* Don't rush her so she can do the work right. **2.** v.i. to hurry, to be in a hurry, to hasten *xeṣṣek dzreb baš teqbeṭ bḷaṣa mezyana.* You'll have to hurry to get a good seat.
** *zreb tăζṭel.* Haste makes waste.
ẓeṛb pl. *ẓṛuba* **1.** hedge **2.** thicket
zerba haste, hurry
¶ *b-zerba, be-z-zerba* **1.** immediately *qol-lhom ixeržu be-z-zerba.* Tell them to go out immediately. **2.** quickly *qṛit had le-ktab b-zerba baš nebda waζed axoṛ.* I read this book quickly so I could start another one. **3.** in a hurry *ktebt-lu risala be-z-zerba qbel-ma nexrož.* I wrote him a letter in a hurry before I left.
zerban pl. *-in* in a hurry, rushing *huwa dima zerban.* He's always in a hurry.
ẓeṛbiya pl. *-t, ẓṛabi* (dim. *ẓṛibya*) rug
zred v.i. (v.n. *zrid*) **1.** to gorge oneself (with food) **2.** to offer an elaborate meal, to put

on a "feed" **3.** to partake of an elaborate meal
zerda pl. *-t, zradi, zrud* feast, party with elaborate meal
zreg v.t. (v.n. *zrig*) to sneak in *ġir l-buwwab ḍuwweṛ wežhu u-hiya zerget weldha.* The minute the doorman turned his back she sneaked her son in.
ẓṛeg pl. *ẓuṛeg* **1.** same as *ẓṛeq* **2.** green, inexperienced
zriba pl. *zrayeb* type of stable for cattle
ẓṛibya dim. of *ẓeṛbiya*
zrid v.n. of *zred*
zrig v.n. of *zreg*
zriqa pl. *-t* type of gold or silver-colored fish
ẓṛiwṭa dim. of *ẓeṛwaṭa*
zrizi dim. of *zerzay*
zriƹ v.n. of *zrăƹ*
zermumiya pl. *-t* type of lizard
ẓṛeq f. *ẓeṛqa* pl. *ẓuṛeq* **1.** blue (color) **2.** livid, ashy pale **3.** useless, unproductive *xrež-lu n-nhaṛ ẓṛeq.* He's had an unproductive (unlucky) day.
ẓeṛqṭun, ẓeṛqṭuna minium, red lead
ẓeṛṛadiya pl. *-t* (pair of) pliers
ẓeṛṛeb v.t. to hedge in
zerreg v.i. to pour *zerrgu d-dmuƹ men ƹăyniha.* Tears poured from her eyes.
zerriƹa pl. *-t, zrareƹ* grain, seed
¶ *zerriƹt l-kettan* **1.** linseed **2.** linseed oil
zerrer v.i. to make a gift to a new-born baby
ẓeṛṛuq pl. *-in* blue-eyed
ẓeṛṭa v.i. to run away, to desert *kan ka-iẓeṛṭi men l-medṛaṣa.* He used to run away from school. —*ẓeṛṭaw men l-ƹăskeṛ u-qeṭƹu le-ḥdada.* They deserted the army and crossed the border.
ẓṛuba pl. of *ẓeṛb*
zrud pl. of *zerda*
ẓṛuqa, ẓṛuqiya **1.** v.n. of *ẓṛaq* **2.** blue, blueness
ẓṛuƹat pl. of *ẓṛăƹ*
zeṛwal pl. *-in* blue-eyed
ẓeṛwaṭa pl. *ẓṛaweṭ* (dim. *ẓṛiwṭa*) club, cudgel
ẓeṛweṭ v.t. to beat with a club, to club
zerzay pl. *-a* (dim. *zrizi*) porter, person who carries things for hire
ẓeṛẓuṛ pl. *ẓṛaẓeṛ* starling (bird)
zrăƹ v.t. (v.n. *zriƹ*) **1.** to sow *fuq-aš ġad-nzerƹu had l-ʔeṛḍ?* When are we going to sow this field? —*l-ƹam l-maži nzerƹu ġir z-zṛăƹ.* Next year we'll sow only wheat.
¶ *zrăƹ le-klam* to make insinuations, to make insinuating remarks *fuq-emma ka-išufu ka-izrăƹ-lu le-klam.* Every time he sees him he makes insinuating remarks to him.
zṛăƹ pl. (of intensity) *zṛuƹat* hard wheat
ẓṭaṭa protective escort (provided when crossing dangerous country)
ẓṭim v.n. of *ẓṭem* (same as *ẓḍem*)
ẓṭem same as *ẓḍem*
ẓeṭṭaṭ pl. *-a* ag. n. of *ẓeṭṭeṭ*
ẓeṭṭeṭ v.t. **1.** to escort (s.o. crossing dangerous country) **2.** to help, to give assistance to (s.o. in dire circumstance)
¶ *ẓeṭṭeṭ ṛaṣuᶲ* to manage, to get by
ẓubeṭ pl. of *ẓbeṭ*
zubya pl. *-t, zwabi* **1.** pit used as an incinerator **2.** obnoxious, difficult person
zufer pl. of *zfer*
zufri pl. *-ya* ill-mannered, uncultured person; boor
zuhaga pl. *zwaheg* earring
ẓuṛ forgery
¶ *šahed ẓ-ẓuṛ* false witness, perjurer
¶ *šhadt ẓ-ẓuṛ* false testimony, perjury
ẓuṛan v.n. of *ẓaṛ*
ẓuṛeg pl. of *ẓṛeg* (same as *ẓṛeq*)
ẓuṛeq pl. of *ẓṛeq*
ẓuwwa v.t. to make squeak *ma-tăƹṛef-ši tšedd l-bab bla-ma dẓuwwiha?* Can't you close the door without making it squeak?
zuwwaga pl. *-t* siren
ẓuwwaq pl. *-a* painter (artist)
ẓuwway pl. *-a* ag. n. of *ẓwa*
zuwwed v.t. to provide *hiya lli zuwwdetni be-l-măƹlumat lli ḥtažit kollha.* She's the one who provided me with all the information I needed.
zuwweg v.i. **1.** to blow a horn **2.** to blow a siren
zuwwel v.t. **1.** to take off *zuwwlet ṣ-ṣebbaṭ u-lebset nƹaltha.* She took off her shoes and put on her sandals. **2.** to take out, to remove *zuwwelt z-zažat lli meḥṛuqin kollhom.* I took out all the burned out bulbs. —*zuwwelna tmenya de-n-nas men l-laʔiḥa.* We removed eight people from the list. **3.** to take away *qeṭṭaƹin ṭ-ṭṛiq zuwwlu-lu beẓṭamu.* The highwaymen took his wallet away from him.
ẓuwweq v.t. to decorate, to embellish
ẓuwweṛ v.t. **1.** to forge (money, document, etc.) **2.** to pray for (s.o.) during the Pilgrimage or the visit to a saint
zuwwež v.t. to marry *zuwwžu benthom b-waḥed l-muḥami.* They married their daughter to a lawyer. —*l-qaḍi zuwwežhom had ṣ-ṣbaḥ.* The judge married them this morning.
zuž **1.** two **2.** same as *zewž*
zuža **1.** same as *zewža* **2.** pl. *-t, zwaž* (dim. *zwiža*) pair *šrit sett zwaž de-t-tqašeṛ.* I bought six pairs of socks. **3.** team (animals)
zuƹama pl. of *zƹim*
ẓuƹăṛ pl. of *ẓƹăṛ*
zwa same as *ẓwa* **1** and **2**
ẓwa iẓwi (v.n. *ẓiy*) **1.** v.t. to hit in the stomach (e.g. with the fist) **2.** to cause pain in the

stomach (e.g. blow with the fist, improper food, etc.) **3.** v.i. to squeak (bird, child, mouse, musical instrument, door, etc.)
zwabi pl. of *zubya*
zwaheg pl. of *zuhaga*
zwal v.n. of *zal*
zwan n.u. *-a* birdseed
ẓwaq pl. *-at* **1.** design, ornamentation **2.** decorative style (architecture)
zwawi pl. of *zawya*
zwaž **1.** pl. of *zuža* 2 **2.** pl. *-at* marriage
zwin pl. *-in* (dim. *zwiwen*) beautiful, attractive
zwiwen pl. *-in* dim. of *zwin*
zwiža pl. *-t* **1.** dim. of *zuža* 2 **2.** double-barrelled shotgun (includes over-and-under type)
ʔezyaʔ pl. of *ziy*
zyada v.n. of *zad*
¶ *zyada ʕla had š-ši* moreover, furthermore
** *baṛaka men z-zyada!* or *xḷaṣ men z-zyada!* Oh come on! What are you trying to pull?
zyan v.i. **1.** to get better *ḥaltu bdat dzyan.* His condition is getting better. **2.** to become (more) beautiful *hiya ka-tekber u-hiya ka-dzyan.* She becomes more beautiful as she grows up.
zyaṛa pl. *-t* **1.** v.n. of *ẓaṛ* **2.** visit (to a person, saint, place) **3.** offering placed into a chest when visiting a saint
ẓyaẓen pl. of *ẓiẓun*
ẓyen pl. of *ẓina*
zyuf, zyufa pl. of *zif*
zyut pl. of *zit*
ẓeyyeṛ same as *ẓiyyeṛ*
zezz used in the expr. *be-z-zezz* by force, unwillingly *xerrežnah men ḍ-ḍaṛ be-z-zezz.* We took him out of the house by force.
¶ *be-z-zezz men* (or *ʕla*) against one's will *dzuwwež biha be-z-zezz ʕlih.* He married her against his (own) will.
** *ġad-nebqaw mʕahom be-z-zezz aw be-l-xaṭeṛ.* We're going to stay with them whether they like it or not.
zḥam crowd, mob *zḥam kbir kan fe-ṣ-ṣuq.* There was a big crowd at the market.
zḥaḥef pl. of *zeḥḥaf*
zḥef v.i. (v.n. *zḥef*) to become paralyzed from the waist down
zḥef v.n. of *zḥef*
zḥăf paralysis of the lower part of the body
zeḥma pl. *-t* **1.** same as *zḥam* **2.** dysentery
zeḥḥaf pl. *-a, zḥaḥef* person without legs
zeḥḥafa pl. *-t* tank (military)
zeḥḥăf to paralyze from the waist down (also metaphorical)
zʕaf v.n. of *zʕăf*
ẓʕafeṛ (pl.) mustache *ʕăndu ẓʕafeṛ kbaṛ.* He has a big mustache.
zʕalel pl. of *zăʕlula*
zʕama **1.** v.n. of *zʕăm* **2.** courage, bravery *n-nas kollhom ka-iqeḍḍṛuh ʕăl z-zʕama lli fih.* Everybody respects him for his courage.
ẓʕaṭeṭ pl. of *ẓăʕṭuṭ*
zăʕbul n.u. *-a* prickly pear (cactus or fruit)
zʕăf v.t. (v.n. *zʕaf, zʕăf*) to get angry *zʕăf ʕliha ʕla lli ma-ʕăṛḍet-š ʕla xaltu.* He got angry at her for not inviting his aunt.
zʕăf v.n. of *zʕăf*
¶ *ṭḷăʕ-luᶲ z-zʕăf* to get fed up ≠
zăʕfan pl. *-in* angry, irritated *kanet zăʕfana ʕlih.* She was angry with him.
ẓăʕfṛan saffron
ẓăʕfṛani pl. *-yen* saffron yellow
zʕim pl. *zuʕama* courageous, brave
ẓʕiʕăṛ dim. of *ẓʕăṛ*
zăʕluk pl. *zʕalek* purée of eggplant or carrots
zăʕlula pl. *zʕalel* Ferris wheel
zʕăm v.i. (v.n. *zʕama*) to gamble, to take a chance *waxxa ma-ʕăndu-š le-flus l-kafyen zʕăm u-ʕṭa t-tesbiq fe-ḍ-ḍaṛ.* Although he doesn't have enough money he gambled and put up a deposit on the house. —*ma-ka-tʕăṛfu-š bezzaf, be-l-ḥăqq zăʕmet u-dzuwwžet bih.* She doesn't know him very well, but she took a chance and married him.
zăʕma **1.** supposedly *zăʕma huma la-bas ʕlihom.* They're supposedly well off. **2.** used as an intensifying adverb *ġir bġit nfesser-lu zăʕma kif ixeddem l-makina ž-ždida.* I just wanted to explain to him how to operate the new machine. —*zăʕma ma-ʕṛeftiha-ši kanet hna?* You mean you didn't know she was here? —*ʕlaš zăʕma ma-tebqaw-š mʕana ḥetta nxeṛžu mežmuʕin?* Why don't you stay with us so we can all leave together? —*zăʕma ana ṣaḥbu, u-băʕd dak š-ši zad ʕliya fe-t-taman.* I'm supposedly his friend, but he still overcharged me. —*ʕṭitu le-flus zaydin baš zăʕma idir xedma mezyana.* I gave him some extra money so he would do a good job. —*ka-itkellem bḥal zăʕma ši-ʕalem.* He talks like a learned man. —*šafet fina bḥal ila zăʕma ma-kanet-š tăʕṛefna.* She looked at us as if she didn't know us.
ẓʕăṛ f. *ẓăʕṛa* pl. *ẓuʕăṛ* (dim. *ẓʕiʕăṛ*) blond
zăʕṛaṭ pl. *-in* ag. adj. of *zăʕṛeṭ*
zăʕṛeṭ v.i. to gallop
ẓăʕteṛ thyme
ẓăʕṭ used in the expr. *be-ẓ-ẓăʕṭ* So what! Who cares!

ẓăɛtuṭ pl. *ẓɛaṭeṭ* long trumpet-like horn (similar to *nfir*)

zăɛzăɛ v.t. **1.** to shake, to jolt *ka-izăɛzɛu l-ˀerḍ mnayn ka-ikunu ka-ilăɛbu.* They shake the ground when they play. **2.** to disturb *la-dzăɛzăɛ-š xak, ṛah naɛes.* Don't disturb your brother, he's asleep.

ẓăɛẓăɛ v.i. to shout, to yell

zăɛɛam, zeɛɛam pl. *-in* daring, brave

zăɛɛăf v.t. to irritate, to make angry *had l-weld ka-izăɛɛăfni b-le-bka dyalu.* This child irritates me with his crying. —*zăɛɛfetni mnin qalt-li ma-mažya-š.* She made me angry when she told me she wasn't coming.

zăɛɛăm v.t. to encourage, to urge *naṣaˀiḥ l-ˀustad dyali hiya lli zăɛɛmetni baš ndir l-ḥuquq.* It was my teacher's advice that encouraged me to study law. —*ṣḥabu kollhom zăɛɛmuh ɛăl z-zwaž biha.* All his friends urged him to marry her.

Ž

ža iži (v.n. *mži;* n.i. *mežya;* impv. *aži* pl. *ažiw;* a.p. *maži* f. *mažya* pl. *mažyen* or *žay* f. *žayya* pl. *žayyen*) **1.** to come *waš nta maži l-ɛăndna had l-lila?* Are you coming to our house tonight? —*mnayn ža dak ṣ-ṣdaɛ?* Where did that noise come from? —*waš ža xak wella ma-zal?* Has your brother come yet? **3.** to be about to *mnin žit nexrož šedd l-bab.* When I was just about to leave he shut the door. **4.** to be, to be located (in perfect tense) *fayn žat ḍaṛkom?* Where's your house? **5.** to please, to suit, etc. *had l-keswa žatni mezyana.* I like this suit. —*kif žak dak le-ktab?* How do you like that book? —*kif žatek faṭima?* What do you think of Fatima?

** *kif žitek?* How about that? What do you think of that? —*š-ka-ižik?* What relation is he to you? —*šḥal žatni?* How much did it come to (i.e., what do I owe)? —*ma-nži fayn nwelli ṛažel muhimm ḥetta neṛžăɛ šibani.* By the time I'm an important person I'll be an old man. —*žah ḥṛiq ṛ-ṛaṣ.* He has a headache.

¶ *ža mɛa* **1.** to suit, to become *had ṭ-ṭeṛbuš ža mɛak.* That fez becomes you. **2.** to match, to go with *had t-triya ma-žat-š mɛa had l-bit.* That chandelier doesn't go with this room.

¶ a.p. *maži* pl. *mažyen, žay* pl. *žayyen* coming, next *ġadi nṣafeṛ š-šheṛ l-maži.* I'm going to take a trip next month.

žab ižib v.t. **1.** to bring *ḅḅaha žab-lha hdiya had n-nhaṛ.* Her father brought her a present today. **2.** to import *l-meġrib ka-ižib le-mwaken men fṛanṣa.* Morocco imports machines from France. **3.** to cause *weldek ka-ižib-lek bezzaf de-ṣ-ṣdaɛ mɛa n-nas.* Your boy causes you a lot of trouble with people.

** *aš žabek f-had le-fḍuḷ?* or *aš žabek fiya?* What business is this of yours?

¶ *žab-luᶲ ṛebbi* to think ≠ *žab-li ṛebbi šeftha l-bareḥ.* I thought I saw her yesterday.

¶ *žab ṣ-ṣfa l-* to beat, to defeat, to outdo, to win out over (s.o.) *kont ka-nḍenn ġlebtu lakin lɛăb be-ḷ-ḷaṣ u-žab-li ṣ-ṣfa.* I thought I had him beat but he played an ace and defeated me.

žababira pl. of *žebbaṛ*

žaḅan **1.** kind of taffy **2.** kind of divinity (candy)

žabṛ (art. *l-*) algebra

žad ižud v.i. to be generous *ka-ižud ɛlina dima b-le-flus.* He's always generous toward us with his money.

žadawil pl. of *žedwel*

žadel v.t. to argue with (rare usage)

žadaṛmi pl. *-ya* (obsolescent) type of rural and highway policeman

žaf ižif v.i. **1.** to drown **2.** to choke, to suffocate (to death)

žah (art. *l-*) esteem, prestige

** *ya žah n-nbi!* All right, let's get at it! (said upon undertaking some task)

¶ *b-žah* through, thanks to, by the grace of *b-žah l-walidin kemmelt le-qṛaya dyali.* Thanks to my parents I finished my studies.

žahed f- **1.** to combat, to wage holy war against (infidels) **2.** to work zealously at (some job)

** *ka-ižahed f-nefsu.* He's killing himself (with work, drinking, etc.).

žahiliya (with art. *l-*) pre-Islamic time (characterized by idolatry)

žahel see *žhel*

žahennam (f.), *žahennama* (no art.) hell

** *žahennama hadi!* It sure is hot (in here, today, etc.)!

žal ižul v.i. **1.** to travel around, to tour (tourist, troupe) **2.** to wander, to roam

žalala pl. *-t* (art. *l-*) majesty (title)

¶ *žalat* (or *žalalăt*) *l-malĭk* His Majesty the King

žalid (art. *l-*) same as *žlid*

žalil pl. *-in* **1.** fine, excellent, of excellent

quality (person, animal) 2. noble, great (person)
žaluq (art. *l-*) n.u. *-a* 1. tin (metal) 2. tin can
žamed a.p. of *žmed*
žamiʕ (art. *l-*) same as *žmiʕ*
¶ *be-l-žamiʕ, fe-l-žamiʕ,* in all, all together *šḥal žatni be-l-žamiʕ?* How much do I owe in all?
žamuṛ pl. *žwameṛ* (art. often *l-*) type of ornamental ball used on spires of buildings
žameʕ pl. *žwameʕ* (art. often *l-*) 1. mosque 2. Koranic school (usage not prevalent)
¶ *žameʕ de-n-nṣaṛa* church (building)
¶ *žameʕ d-l-ihud* synagogue
žanab (usually no art.) excellency (title for ministers, ambassadors, etc.)
¶ *žanab le-xlifa* (or *l-xalifa*) His Excellency the Caliph
žaneb v.t. 1. to sit beside (s.o.) 2. to avoid (s.o.)
žanib pl. *žawanib* (art. *l-*) side, viewpoint
žanub (art. *l-*) south (n.)
¶ *l-l-žanub* south (adv.) *mšat l-l-žanub.* She went south.
žanubi pl. *-yen* southern, from the south, south (usually for things)
žaṛ ižuṛ v.i. to act unjustly, to be unfair or unjust
¶ *žaṛ ʕla* to oppress, to tyrannize over
¶ a.p. *žayeṛ* pl. *-in* unfair, unjust (person)
žaṛ pl. *žiran* (art. often *l-*) neighbor
žaṛdini pl. *-ya* gardener
žari a.p. of *žra*
žarima pl. *-t, žrayem* (art. *l-*) crime, felony
žariya pl. *-t, žawari* (art. *l-*) concubine
žasăd (no pl., art. *l-*) body (live human)
žawanib pl. of *žanib*
žawari pl. of *žariya*
žaweb v.t. to answer (s.o., phone, an accusation, etc.) *žawebni ʕăl s-suʔal dyali!* Answer my question! —*žawebni b-žuž de-ḍ-ḍeṛmat ʕăl l-bab.* He answered me with two knocks on the door.
žawi (art *l-*) benzoin
žaweṛ v.t. 1. to be the neighbor of, to live next door to 2. to neighbor, to be next to (as one house does another)
žaweš (sg. and coll., art. *l-*) sparrow
žay a.p. of *ža*
žayeṛ a.p. of *žaṛ*
žayḥa pl. *-t* (art. *l-*) misfortune, disaster, calamity *ḍeṛbettu l-žayḥa.* He's been struck by misfortune.
¶ *ḍaṛbahφ* (*ž-*)*žayḥa* (adj. usage) worthless, useless, good-for-nothing ≠ *had ḍ-ḍaṛ ḍaṛbaha žayḥa.* This house is no longer any good.
žaza v.t. to reward, to recompense
** *ḷḷah ižazik bi-xir.* Thank you.
¶ *ḷḷah ižazik bi-xir . . . ila ma* (impv.) please . . . (impv.)
žaž same as *zaž*
žaʕ ižuʕ v.i. to become or get hungry *ana žăʕt.* I'm hungry.
žbaḅen pl. of *žeḅḅana*
žbahi pl. of *žebha*
žbal pl. of *žbel*
žbala n.pl. of *žebli*
žbayer pl. of *žbira*
žebbada pl. *-t* slingshot (kind with a forked frame)
žeḅḅana pl. *-t, žḅaḅen; žeḅḅaniya* pl. *-t* large bowl (for serving soup, fruit, etc.)
žebbaṛ pl. *-a, žababira* (art *l-*) 1. tyrant, despot 2. one who splints broken arms, legs, etc.
žebbayda same as *žebbada*
žebbed v.t. 1. to stretch 2. to pull or draw tight 3. to lay out (s.o. on a bed, etc.) 4. to pull, to tug 5. to knock down (s.o. with a blow)
¶ part. *mžebbed* pl. *-in* clever, cunning, keen-minded
žebbeṛ v.t. to set and splint (a broken leg)
žbed (v.n. *žbid*) 1. v.t. to pull on, to tug on (as a rope) 2. v.t. to pull out, to draw out (as a drawer) 3. v.t. to take out, to remove (as from a pocket) 4. v.t. to provoke, to incite (s.o. to fight) *huwa lli žbedni!* He started it! (i.e., he incited me to fight him) 5. v.t. to raise, to bring up (question, point) 6. v.i. to run or go rapidly (car, horse, runner) 7. v.i. to last, to go on *ma-zal ižbed saʕtayn.* There are still two hours to go. —*ma-zal ižbed sinin.* He's still got years to go. He'll last for years now.
¶ *žbed mʕa* to hit, to strike *žbed mʕaha b-ṭeṛša.* He struck her with his hand.
žebda pl. *-t* 1. n.i. of *žbed* 2. stretch (distance, time) *walayenni žebda menn hna l-meṛṛakeš!* It's a heck of a long way from here to Marrakech.
žebha pl. *-t, žbahi* 1. forehead 2. nerve, audacity *fih ž-žebha bezzaf.* He's got a lot of nerve.
žbid v.n. of *žbed*
žbiṛ v.n. of *žbeṛ*
žbira pl. *-t, žbayer* splint (along with its bandaging)
žbel pl. *žbal* mountain
žebli 1. pl. *žbala* member of *žbala* tribe 2. adj. pl. *-yen* n.pl. *žbala* from the mountains, mountain (folk)
žḅen cheese (usually the indigenous Moroccan type)
žbeṛ v.t. (v.n. *žbiṛ*) 1. to find *žbeṛti le-flus lli mšaw-lek?* Have you found the money you lost? —*lemma wṣelt žbeṛtu naʕes.* When I arrived I found him sleeping. 2. to discover

žebril Gabriel (angel)
žbuɛ̄a pl. of *žbeɛ̄*
žebži (adj.) (very) black
žbeɛ̄ pl. *žbuɛ̄a* (bee)hive
ždad pl. of *ždid*
ždam leprosy
ždawel pl. of *žedwel*
ždeb v.i. (v.n. *ždib*) to abandon oneself to ecstatic excitation (as in an ecstatic dance)
¶ *ždeb ɛla* to fly into a rage at (s.o.)
žedba pl. *-t* **1.** n.i. of *ždeb* **2.** fit of rage or anger
žedban pl. *-in* **1.** furious, raging **2.** in ecstatic excitation (as in a dance)
žedd comp. of *ždid*
žedd (art. *l-*) **1.** seriousness, gravity **2.** pl. *ždud* grandfather **3.** pl. *ždud* ancestor
¶ *be-l-žedd* seriously, in earnest, in all seriousness *ka-ntkellem mɛak be-l-žedd.* I'm speaking to you seriously.
¶ *bin žedd u-mlaġa* half serious(ly) half joking(ly)
žedda **1.** (no pl.) anything new, novelty **2.** pl. *-t* grandmother
žedded v.t. **1.** to bring up to date, to change *ḥmed žedded n-naḍaṛiya dyalu.* Ahmed has brought his views up to date. **2.** to (ex)change for new, to replace (with new) *žeddet l-ˀatat dyal bitha.* She's changed the furniture of her room for new. **3.** to renew (visa, contract, etc.)
žeddi pl. *-yen* **1.** serious(-minded) **2.** conscientious
žedder **1.** v.t. to hide, to conceal **2.** v.i. to take root (plant) **3.** v.i. to stay too long, to overstay one's welcome
ždib v.n. of *ždeb*
ždid pl. *-in, ždad* (comp. *žedd*) **1.** new **2.** modern, recent
¶ *men ždid, men da u-ždid* again, anew, all over again *ɛawed-lhom men ždid.* Tell them again.
ždida Jadida, formerly Mazagan
ždidi pl. *-yen* of or pertaining to *ždida*
žder pl. *ždur, ždura* **1.** root (of plant) **2.** foot (of wall)
¶ *žder le-fxeḍ* groin
žedri **1.** small-pox **2.** small-pox vaccination scar
ždud **1.** pl. of *žedd* 2 and 3 **2.** grandparents
ždur, ždura pl. of *žder*
žduɛa pl. of *ždăɛ*
žedwel (art. *l-*) pl. *ždawel, žadawil* (art. assimilated) time-table, schedule
ždăɛ pl. *žduɛa,* foal, colt
žedɛa pl. *-t* filly
žfan pl. of *žfen*
žfani pl. of *žefna*
žfayef pl. of *žeffaf* 1
žfayni pl. *-ya* maker of *žfani*

žeff (v.n. *žfif*) **1.** v.t. to absorb (like a sponge) **2.** v.t. and v.i. to dry (up, off) **3.** v.t. to pump out or off, to drain (by pumping)
žeffaf **1.** pl. *žfayef* large piece of burlap-like cloth used in washing floors **2.** pl. *-a* ag. n. and adj. of *žeffef*
žeffafa pl. *-t* **1.** sponge (natural and artificial) **2.** mopping machine (i.e., any machine used to clean a floor in a wet manner)
žeffef v.t. **1.** to dry (off, up) **2.** to sponge (up, off)
žfif v.n. of *žeff*
žfil v.n. of *žfel*
žfel v.i. (v.n. *žfil*) **1.** to shy (as a horse) **2.** to become wild (from fear, anger) and struggle to get away
žfen pl. *žfan* **1.** region under the eye (which often darkens with illness) **2.** eyelid **3.** pl. of *žefna*
žefna pl. *-t, žfani, žfen* type of large tub (usually for washing)
žoġlal n.u. *-a* **1.** empty shell or cartridge **2.** (empty) shell (conch, snail, etc.)
žoġma, žeġma pl. *-t* swallow (of liquid) *ɛṭini žoġma de-l-ma!* Give me a swallow of water!
žoġṛafiya (art. *l-*) geography
žhad same as *žihad*
žhaṛ same as *žehṛ*
žhaz trousseau
žehd (no colloquial pl.) **1.** strength *fih ž-žehd bezzaf.* He has a lot of strength. **2.** about, aproximately, around *glest f-meṛṛakeš žehd ši-ɛăšṛ iyyam.* I stayed in Marrakech about ten days.
** *hada ž-žehd!* Time's up! That's enough! It's time to go!
** *žehdi huwa xemsin.* Fifty is the best I can do. —*kollha u-žehdu* or *koll waḥed ɛla qdeṛ žehdu.* Each does what he can with what he has.
¶ *be-ž-žehd* indicates some extreme of action: *ma-ḍḍṛeb-š ɛla ketfi be-ž-žehd!* Don't hit my shoulder so hard! —*ma-tsug-š be-ž-žehd!* Don't drive so fast! —*ka-yăɛmel koll-ši be-ž-žehd.* He does everything violently. —*ɛăyyeṭ-lu be-ž-žehd!* Yell (at him) louder)!
¶ *žehd-aš* **1.** (about) how much *žehd-aš ḥăbbiti d-atay?* How much tea would you like? **2.** about what time *žehd-aš ġad-dži?* About what time are you coming?
¶ *žehd-emma, žehd-ma* as much as *xud žehd-emma tḥebb!* Take as much as you like.
¶ *ɛmel žehdu*ᶲ to do one's best *ɛmel žehdu be-l-ḥăqq bla fayda.* He did his best, but in vain.
žehhed v.t. indicates a general reinforcement of some action or condition *žehhed ṛ-ṛadyu!*

Turn up the radio! —*žehhed l-ma!* Turn the water on harder!

žhel **1.** v.t. to not know anything about, to be unaware of *ana ka-nežhel had š-ši.* I don't know anything about this. **2.** v.i. to indulge in or utter profanity

¶ a.p. *žahel* pl. *-in* ignorant, uneducated

žehl (art. *l-*) ignorance *xeṣṣna nʕaṛbu l-žehl.* We must fight against ignorance.

žehṛ used in the expr. *be-ž-žehṛ, be-l-žehṛ,* or *be-l-žhaṛ*: **1.** openly (as opposed to secretly) **2.** aloud (as in praying)

žib pl. *žyub* pocket (as in clothing)

žifa pl. *-t* (animal) carcass, carrion

žiha pl. *-t, žwayeh* (art. often *l-*) **1.** direction *mn-ina žiha nemši?* Which direction shall I go? **2.** place, area, spot *f-ina žiha žat ḍaṛkom?* Where (in what place) is your house located? —*waš hiya sakna f-had ž-žiha?* Does she live in this area? —*sir l-dak ž-žiha!* Go over there (to that place)! —*xeṣṣna nṣebġu had ž-žiha.* We have to paint this area (here). **3.** side *ṣbeġ žihtek u-neṣbeġ žihti.* You paint your side and I'll paint my side.

¶ *men žiht* **1.** a relative of, related to *huwa men žihti.* He's a relative of mine. **2.** on the side of (i.e., supporting, backing s.o.)

¶ *žiht* in the area of, near, around *ḍaṛna žat žiht l-ḅanka.* Our house is near the bank.

¶ *fe-žwayeh* around, about *žaw fe-žwayeh l-ʕăšṛa.* They came around ten (o'clock).

¶ *ža men žiht* to take the side of, to side with *ža men žihtha fe-d-dăʕwa.* He took her side in the lawsuit.

žihad (no pl.) holy war

žinaʔi pl. *-yen* (art. *l-*) criminal *ma-ka-ntkellef-š l-qaḍaya l-žinaʔiya.* I don't handle criminal cases.

žinaya pl. *-t* (art. *l-*) crime, felony

žir **1.** lime, quick-lime **2.** whitewash

žiran pl. of *žaṛ*

žiš same as *žeyš*

žiyyar pl. *-a* whitewasher

žiyyed pl. *-in* **1.** excellent, very good **2.** cultured, gentlemanly, proper, etc.

žiyyef v.t. **1.** to strangle (but not necessarily kill) **2.** to suffocate

žiyyer v.t. to whitewash, to spread with whitewash

ʔežl same as *ʔažăl*

¶ *l-ʔežl, men ʔežl* on account of, because of, for the sake of *dert had š-ši l-ʔežlu.* I did it for his sake.

žla ižli v.t. **1.** to lose *žliti dak le-ktab?* Have you lost that book? **2.** to cause to end up in an inaccessible or unknown place (as hitting a golfball into the woods) *fayn žlit dik l-ibra?* Where did I put that needle? **3.** to take away, to remove *žliha ʕliya!* Take her away from me! **4.** to exile **5.** to deport **6.** to corrupt, to lead astray

ʔăžlaf pl. of *ʔăžlef*

žlaleb pl. of *žellab, žellaba*

žlayel (pl.) lower part of a dress, skirt, or robe

žlayži pl. *-ya* tile setter or layer (floors and walls)

žleb v.t. (v.n. *želb*) **1.** to attract (magnet, light with bugs) **2.** to entice, to lure *želbatu le-ḍ-ḍaṛ.* She lured him into the house. **3.** to import (s.th. from a country) **4.** v.i. to be vaccinated

¶ *žleb l-* to vaccinate

želb v.n. of *žleb*

želba pl. *-t* **1.** n.i. of *žleb* **2.** vaccination

želban, želbana n.u. *ḥăbba de-ž-želban* (green) peas

želd pl. *žlud* **1.** skin, hide (human, animal) **2.** leather

želda pl. *-t* **1.** skin, hide *šḥal men želda ʕănziya šriti?* How many goat skins did you buy? **2.** piece of leather **3.** lash (with a whip) **4.** skinflint, niggard

ʔăžlef pl. *ʔăžlaf* son of a bitch, bastard

želfa pl. *žluf* rind (melon, cactus)

žlib vaccination (v.n.)

žlid frost, hoar frost

žellab, žellaba, žellabiya pl. *-t, žlaleb* type of North African robe with a hood

žellayži same as *žlayži*

želled v.t. **1.** to cover with a skin (as a drum) **2.** to punish, to correct (by some sort of beating)

želliž same as *zelliž*

žellex v.t. to spot, to strain (as with ink, grease, paint, etc.)

želležž same as *zellež*

žles same as *gles*

želsa pl. *-t* (art. *l-*) session

žlud pl. of *želd*

žluf pl. of *želfa*

žmal pl. of *žmel*

žmažem pl. of *žemžma, žemžuma*

žmaʕa pl. *-t* group (people)

žmaʕi pl. of *žemʕa*

žmed v.i. (v.n. *žmid*) **1.** to freeze *l-bareḥ fe-l-lil l-ma žmed fe-l-wad.* The river froze yesterday. —*žmed fe-bḷaṣtu be-l-xewf.* He froze in his tracks from fright. **2.** to coagulate (blood) **3.** to become solid, to solidify

** *žmed-lu l-ma fe-rkabih b-le-xbaṛ.* The news stopped him dead in his tracks.

¶ a.p. *žamed* pl. *-in* **1.** frozen (solid) **2.** immobile, standing still

žmid v.n. of *žmed*

žmil **1.** service, favor *ʕămmṛek ʕmelti fiya*

ši-žmil? Have you ever done me a service? **2.** pl. *-in* (comp. *žmel*) beautiful, pretty **3.** pl. *-in* (comp. *žmel*) good, fine *had l-xedma žmila.* That's a fine job (you've done).

** *bla žmil!* You're welcome! (in answer to an expression of thanks, particularly to *baṛek ḷḷahu fik!* Thank you!)

žmila dim. of *žemla*

žmiɛ **1.** v.n. of *žmăɛ* **2.** all *žmiɛ s-sokkan xeṛžu men le-mdina.* All the people left the city.

¶ *žmiɛ lli* everyone (who) *žmiɛ lli tlaqitu l-bareḥ sellem ɛlik.* Everyone I met yesterday told me to say hello to you. —*žmiɛ lli ka-itkellem b-l-ingliza irfăɛ yeddu.* Everyone who speaks English, raise his hand.

žmel comp. of *žmil* 2 and 3

žmel pl. *žmal* camel

žemla pl. *-t* (dim. *žmila*) she-camel

žemla used in certain expr.

¶ *be-l-žemla* or *be-l-žumla* wholesale *ka-ibiɛ w-išri be-l-žemla.* He deals wholesale.

¶ *men žmelt* (from) among *men žmelt l-boldan lli-ẓeṛt f-ˀuṛuppa swisra w-alṃanya.* Among the European countries I've visited are Switzerland and Germany.

¶ *men žmelt š-ši* among other things *men žmelt š-ši qal-li nta ġad-ikun ɛăndek musteqbal mezyan.* Among other things, he told me you would have a bright future.

žemmal pl. *-a* **1.** camel driver, cameleer **2.** wholesale dealer

žemmaɛ adj. pl. *-in* n.pl. *-a* (one) who enjoys group company during his leisure time

žemmed v.t. **1.** to freeze (solid) **2.** to cause to coagulate (blood) **3.** to solidify (some liquid)

žemmeṛ v.t. to bake or roast (as to form a hard crust)

žemmăɛ v.i. to get together (as for cards, drinking, etc.)

žmeṛ n.u. *žemṛa* (hot) coal, ember

žemžama pl. *-t; žemžma, žemžuma* pl. *-t, žmažem* **1.** skull **2.** very intelligent person

žmăɛ v.t. (v.n. *žmiɛ*) **1.** to gather together or in a group (people, fruit, etc.) **2.** to pick up (from the ground, etc.) **3.** to collect (payments, stamps, etc.) **4.** to save (money) **5.** to add (up), to total *žmăɛ had l-ˀeṛqam men fedḷek!* Add up these figures, please!

¶ *žmăɛ bin* **1.** to reconcile *ṛažel u-mṛatu txaṣmu u-ža huwa u-žmăɛ binathom.* A man and his wife had a quarrel and he came and reconciled them. **2.** to reunite

¶ *žmăɛ ṭṛafu*ᶲ (or *ṛaṣu*ᶲ) to get ready *žmăɛ ṭṛafek baš nemšiw!* Get ready so we can go!

¶ p.p. *mežmuɛ* pl. *-in* **1.** total, sum *šḥal ža fe-l-mežmuɛ?* How much is the total? **2.** (pl.) all together *žaw mežmuɛin.* They all came together.

žemɛ (no pl., art. *l-*) **1.** assembly (of people) **2.** addition (math.) **3.** plural *šnu huwa l-žemɛ dyal "šekkaṛa"?* What's the plural of *"šekkaṛa"?*

žemɛa pl. *-t, žmaɛi* week

¶ *ž-žemɛa, nhaṛ* (or *yum*) *ž-žemɛa* Friday

žemɛiya pl. *-t* (art. *l-*) **1.** organization, society **2.** committee, board **3.** meeting, conference

žna ižni v.t. (v.n. *žni*) to pick, to collect (flowers, fruit)

žnab pl. of *ženb*

žnan pl. *-at* garden (basically vegetables)

žnawa, žnawi pl. of *ženwi*

žnaweḥ pl. of *žnaḥ*

žnayni pl. *-ya* gardener (private garden)

žnaḥ pl. *ženḥin, žnaweḥ* **1.** wing (bird, airplane, building) **2.** overhanging roof (as over a porch)

ženb pl. *žnab* **1.** side (body, house, river, etc.) **2.** edge (table, knife, river, etc.) **3.** margin (as on paper) **4.** (pl.) environs, suburbs

** *rgod ɛla ženb ṛ-ṛaḥa men žihtha.* Rest assured there's no reason to worry about her.

¶ *f-ženb* next to, at the side of *ka-neskon f-ženb l-ḅanka.* I live next to the bank.

žni v.n. of *žna*

ženn pl. *žnun,* f. *ženniya* pl. *-t* **1.** genie **2.** ghost, specter, spirit **3.** devil

** *ḍeṛbuh ž-žnun.* He had an epileptic attack. —*fih ž-žnun.* He's possessed of the devil.

ženna heaven, paradise

ženneb v.t. **1.** to pull, push, draw over (to the side) *ženneb siyaṛtek šwiya!* Pull your car over a little! **2.** to turn (as a car) to one side (to avoid s.th.)

ženniya pl. *-t* **1.** f. of *ženn* **2.** fairy

žennes v.t. to match *žennes hada mɛa hadak!* Match this one with that one!

¶ *žennes ṛaṣu*ᶲ to become naturalized ≠ *žennset ṛaṣha be-l-žensiya l-meġṛibiya.* She became naturalized as a Moroccan.

žens same as *gens*

žensiya pl. *-t* (art. *l-*) nationality

žnun pl. of *ženn*

ženwi pl. *žnawa, žnawi* knife (kitchen, hunting, dagger)

ženžlan n.u. *ḥăbba de-ž-ženžlan* sesame (seed)

ženžeṛ v.i. to rust (iron, steel)

ženḥin pl. of *žnaḥ*

ˀžeṛ v.t. to hire, to employ (for a temporary job)

žra ižri v.i. (v.n. *žri*) **1.** to run *ṭaḥ mnin kan ka-ižri.* He fell while he was running. —*had l-ɛăwd ka-ižri b-soṛɛa kbira.* This horse can run very fast. —*kayen ši-ma ka-ižri f-had ḍ-daṛ?* Is there any running water in this house? **2.** to pass quickly (time)
** *waš žrat keršek?* Have your bowels loosened up yet? —*žra biha l-wad.* There's a lot of it around.
¶ *keršuᶲ žarya* to have diarrhea ≠ *waš keršek žarya?* Do you still have diarrhea?
¶ *žra ɛla* **1.** to run after, to chase **2.** to work hard for *žrit ɛăl š-šahada ḥetta šedditha.* I worked hard for my degree until I got it. —*žrit ɛlih ḥetta wella ṛažel.* I worked hard for him until he grew up.
¶ a.p. *žari* pl. *žorray* (tax) collector

žṛa ižṛa to happen, to occur *kif žṛa ḥetta žiti?* How does it happen you're here? —*žṛat-lu ši-ḥaža f-režlih.* Something's happen to his leg.

žṛadi pl. of *žeṛda*

žṛaḍ n.u. *-a* grasshopper

žṛaf pl. of *žoṛf*

žṛan n.u. *-a* frog

žrayed pl. of *žrida* (n.u. of *žrid*)

žrayem pl. of *žarima*

žṛayeṛ pl. of *žeṛṛaṛa*

žeṛba mange, scabies

žeṛbuɛ kankaroo rat, jerboa

žṛed v.t. (v.n. *žṛid*) to scratch (with s.th. sharp)

žeṛda pl. *-t, žṛadi* **1.** scratch **2.** garden (flower)

žoṛf pl. *žṛaf, žṛufa* bank, slope (of a cut in the ground or side of a road)

žri v.n. of *žra*
¶ *be-ž-žri* quickly, in a hurry

žṛi pl. of *žṛu*

žrid n.u. *-a* pl. *žrayed* branches of the date-palm

žṛid v.n. of *žṛed*

žerr v.i. to chew the cud, to ruminate

žeṛṛ v.t. (v.n. *žeṛṛan*) **1.** to pull (up) *žeṛṛ š-šelya le-ṭ-ṭebḷa!* Pull the chair up to the table. **2.** to take or drag (off) *ma-bġa-š ixrož ḥetta žeṛṛitu men yeddih.* He wouldn't leave until I dragged him off by the hand.
¶ *žeṛṛ* (or *žeṛṛ mɛa*) *baš* to get (s.o.) to, to entice (s.o.) into *žeṛṛuh baš ilɛăb mɛahom.* They got him to play with them.

žerra v.t. **1.** to make or cause (s.o.) to run (as from fright, force) **2.** to let or cause to run or flow (water) **3.** to dilute, to add water to **4.** to melt, to liquefy

žeṛṛa used in the expr. *wayenni žeṛṛa hadi!* or *ɛla žeṛṛa!,* expresses deep disgust and general feeling of being fed up

žeṛṛan v.n. of *žeṛṛ*

žeṛṛaṛa pl. *-t, žṛayeṛ* **1.** pulley **2.** spool (usually of paper or wood, used for thread, yarn, etc.)

žerray pl. *-a* ag. n. of *žra*

žeṛṛeb v.t. **1.** to try (out) *ɛămmṛek žeṛṛebti ʔaġlal?* Have you ever tried snails? —*žeṛṛeb had ṣ-ṣebbaṭ!* Try these shoes! **2.** to test, to put to the test

žeṛṛed v.t. **1.** to strip, to take the clothes off (s.o.) **2.** to steal from, to rob (s.o.)

žṛu pl. *-wat, žṛi* puppy, pup (dog)

žṛufa pl. of *žoṛf*

žerya pl. *-t* **1.** n.i. of *žra* and *žerra* **2.** life, manner of living **3.** efforts *kun ma-ši ž-žerya lli žerrit-lu ɛăl l-xedma, kun ɛămmṛu ma-iḥeṣṣeḷ ɛliha.* If it hadn't been for the effort I put forth for him to get the job, he never would have gotten it.

žeṛžeṛ v.t. to drag (as along the ground)

žṛeḥ v.t. **1.** to cut *žṛeḥ ṣebɛu mnin kan ka-ilɛăb be-s-sekkin.* He cut his finger while playing with the knife. **2.** to hurt (feelings) *žṛeḥti-li l-ɛawaṭif dyali.* You've hurt my feelings.
¶ p.p. *mežruḥ* pl. *mžaṛeḥ* wounded person, casualty

žoṛḥ, žeṛḥ, žerḥ n.u. *-a* cut *ɛăndu ši-žerḥ fe-draɛu.* He has a cut on his arm.

žud (art. often *l-*) magnanimity

žuf **1.** abdomen, belly **2.** inside, interior

žuheṛ **1.** precious ornaments or jewelry worn by the (Moroccan) bride **2.** jewelry made of gold and diamonds **3.** n.u. *žuhṛa* cpl. *žwaheṛ* pearl
¶ *xiṭ de-ž-žuheṛ* pearl necklace

žula pl. *-t* tour, trip (pleasure)

žumad (f.) used in the names: *žumad l-luwwla,* fifth month of the Muslim calendar; *žumad t-tanya,* sixth month of the Muslim calendar

žumhuri pl. *-yen* (art. *l-*) republican (both in general and specifically the American political party)

žumhuriya pl. *-t* (art. *l-*) republic

žumuɛa, yum (or *nhaṛ*) *ž-žumuɛa* Friday

žuqa pl. *-t* crowd (usually gathered due to curiosity)

žuṛ (art. *l-*) **1.** injustice **2.** partiality **3.** oppression, tyranny

žuṛa neighborly friendship or relationship

žuṭiya pl. *-t* **1.** second-hand store (including pawn shop) **2.** racket, noise, din

žuwwed v.t. and v.i. to chant (the Koran)

žuwweq v.i. to crowd, to form into a crowd or group

žuwwež same as *zuwwež*

žuwwăɛ v.t. to starve, to not feed

žuyuš pl. of *žeyš*

žuž two *ʕăndi žuž de-s-siyaṛat.* I have two cars.
¶ *b-žuž* **1.** both *žibhom b-žuž mʕak!* Bring them both with you! **2.** together (two) *žaw b-žuž.* They came together.
žuža pl. *-t* (dim. *žwiža*) pair *šrit xemsa de-ž-žužat dyal t-tqašeṛ.* I bought five pairs of socks.
žuʕ hunger
¶ *bihφ* (or *žahφ*) *ž-žuʕ* to be hungry ≠ *biya* (or *žani*) *ž-žuʕ.* I'm hungry.
žwa pl. *-wat* **1.** envelope **2.** sheath, scabbard **3.** case, container (s.th. used for keeping s.th. else)
žwab pl. *-at* answer, reply
žwad (pl.; art. *le-*) philanthropic, magnanimous people (of the city)
žwaheṛ cpl. of *žuheṛ* 3
žwahṛi pl. *-ya* jeweler (only jewelry)
žwameṛ pl. of *žamuṛ*
žwameʕ pl. of *žameʕ*
žwan **1.** June (month) **2.** n.u. *-a* birdseed
žwaṛ same as *žuṛa*
žwayeh pl. of *žiha*
žwaž same as *zwaž*
žwed (comp., no absolute form) more generous, kind
žwiža pl. *-t* **1.** dim. of *žuža* **2.** double-barrelled shotgun (includes over-and-under type)
žăwq pl. *žwaq* orchestra
žeyš pl. *žuyuš, žyuš* **1.** army **2.** service, branch (of service)
žyub pl. of *žib*
žyuš pl. of *žeyš*
ʔežžel v.t. to postpone
žḥed (v.n. *žḥid*) to deny *žḥed bin ʕămmṛu ma-ža lle-hna.* He denied he'd ever been (come) here.
¶ *žḥed l-xir* to be an ingrate, to be ungrateful
žeḥžeḥ v.i. to cuddle or snuggle up to a fire
žeḥš pl. *žḥuša* young ass or donkey
žḥuša pl. of *žeḥš*
žʕab pl. of *žăʕba*
žʕafeṛ (pl.) mustache (usually large or bushy)
žăʕba pl. *-t, žʕab* **1.** tube, (piece of) pipe **2.** barrel (rifle)
žʕil v.n. of *žʕăl*
žʕăl v.t. (v.n. *žʕil*) to put, to place *žʕăl dak le-ktab fuq dak l-korsi!* Put that book on that chair!
** *ḷḷah ižʕăl fik l-baṛaka.* Please. Thank you. That's enough.—*ḷḷah ižăʕlek tenžeḥ!* Good luck!

ح

ḥabaš, ḥabaša n.pl. of *ḥabaši*
ḥabaši adj. pl. *-yen* n.pl. *ḥabaš, ḥabaša* Ethiopian
¶ *blad l-ḥabaš* (or *ḥabaša*) Ethiopia
ḥabla f. a.p. of *ḥbel*
ḥabus same as *ḥbus*
ḥad iḥid (v.n. *ḥiyad*) to be or remain neutral (on an issue)
ḥada v.t. (v.n. *mḥadya*) to touch, to bother, to disturb *xelli ḥwayžek ʕăndha ila bġiti ma-iḥadihom ḥădd.* Leave your things with her if you don't want anyone to touch them.
ḥadeg same as *ḥadeq*
ḥadit pl. *ʔaḥadit* tradition taken from the teachings of the Prophet Mohammed, but not considered law
¶ *ža fe-l-ḥadit* (or *f-le-ḥdit*) . . . it is found in the traditions of the Prophet . . ., the Prophet said . . .
ḥadeq pl. *-in* **1.** intelligent, smart, clever **2.** able, very capable **3.** diligent
ḥader a.p. of *ḥder*
ḥaḍaṛi pl. *ḥaḍăṛ* **1.** city-dweller, urbanite **2.** (pl.) city population
ḥaḍi a.p. of *ḥḍa*
ḥaḍiṛa pl. *ḥawaḍiṛ* city (in contrast to the country) *waš ka-iʕiš fe-l-badiya wella fe-l-ḥaḍiṛa?* Does he live in the country or in the city?
ḥaḍeṛ a.p. of *ḥḍeṛ*
ḥaḍăṛ pl. of *ḥaḍaṛi*
ḥaf iḥuf v.i. (v.n. *ḥăwf*) to descend, to go down, to come down *ġiṛ hiya semʕăt weldha ža u-hiya ḥafet ka-tesbeg men l-fuqi.* As soon as she heard that her son had arrived, she came running down from upstairs. —*ma-zal xeṣṣna nḥufu ṭebqa.* We have to go down one more floor.
¶ *ḥaf ʕla* **1.** to borrow from and not return (purposely) *ḥaf ʕliya f-flusi.* He borrowed some money from me and didn't return it. **2.** to beat *ḥafu ʕlih le-ṛ-ṛaṣ.* They beat him about the head.
** *ḥafu ʕlihom š-šeffaṛa.* Some thieves robbed their house.
ḥafa pl. *-t* **1.** cliff, precipice **2.** steep bank (on the side of a mountain road) **3.** habitual borrower who never returns what he has borrowed
ḥafalat pl. of *ḥăfla*
ḥafeḍ ʕla **1.** to take care of, to handle with care *xeṣṣek tḥafeḍ bezzaf ʕla had l-makina ḥit baqya ždida u-šritha*

be-t-taman. You'll have to take good care of this machine because it's still new and I paid a lot for it. **2.** to save, to put away, to keep *ma-bġa-š iṛedd-li le-flus ḥit ma-ḥafeḍt-š ʿal t-tuwṣil.* He didn't want to give me the money back because I didn't save the receipt. **3.** to observe, to respect (law, etc.)

ḥafi a.p. of ḥfa

ḥafiḍ (with art.) the Protector (God)

ḥafiḍa (good) memory *ʿăndu ḥafiḍa mezyana.* He has a good memory.

ḥafer pl. ḥwafer **1.** hoof (cow, horse, sheep, etc.) **2.** heavy foot traffic (people, animals) *dak ẓ-ẓenqa dima mhuṛža ʿla wedd fiha bezzaf de-l-ḥafer.* That street is always noisy because of the heavy traffic.
—*ẓeṛbiytek deġya ka-ttwessex ḥit ʿăndek l-ḥafer.* Your rug gets dirty quickly because so many people walk over it.
    ¶ *suq l-ḥafer* animal market (cows, sheep, horses, etc.)

ḥaguz, ḥaguza legendary character, similar to Santa Claus, appearing during the month of January

ḥaguza **1.** kind of hot porridge prepared with cracked wheat and milk **2.** period (in January) in which 1 above is made

ḥakem a.p. of ḥkem

ḥakăm pl. ḥokkam referee

ḥal iḥil v.i. (v.n. ḥyala) to boast, to brag
    ¶ ḥal f-le-mši to prance, to strut (s.o., horse)
    ¶ a.p. ḥayel pl. -in boastful, bragging

ḥal iḥul v.i. (no v.n.) to get old, to age (as food)
    ¶ a.p. ḥayel pl. -in old, aged (refers to foods that both improve or get worse with age) *z-zit l-ḥayla mezyana le-ṭ-ṭyab.* Aged oil is good for cooking. —*ma-ka-nqedd-š nakol l-xobz l-ḥayel.* I can't eat old bread.

ḥal pl. ḥwal, ʿeḥwal **1.** state, condition, situation *kif ḥalek?* or *aš ḥalek?* How are you? (i.e., how's your condition)
    2. weather *l-ḥal sxun l-yum.* It's (The weather is) hot today.
    ** *baqi l-ḥal* or *ma-zal l-ḥal.* There's still (plenty of) time. —*mša l-ḥal.* It's late. It's too late. —*dzad ʿlih l-ḥal.* His condition has gotten worse. —*žah l-ḥal* or *ṭlăʿ fih l-ḥal.* He went into a trance (as an entranced dancer).
    ¶ *mša f-ḥaluᵠ* to leave, to go away *sir f-ḥalek!* Go away!
    ¶ *ʿla kolli ḥal* in any case, anyway, anyhow *ʿla kolli ḥal la-bedd nemši.* I'm going anyway.

ḥala pl. -t state, condition, situation *kif ḥaltu?* How is he? (his condition)

    ¶ *mša f-ḥalatuᵠ* same as *mša f-ḥaluᵠ* (see ḥal)

ḥalaqa pl. -t earring

ḥama ʿla to defend (in a fight, in court), to support, to back up

ḥamalat l-qoṛʾan pl. of ḥamǐl l-qoṛʾan

ḥameḍ **1.** pl. -in sour, acid **2.** pickled **3.** n.u. ḥamḍa lemon, lime

ḥami a.p. of ḥma yeḥma

ḥamǐl l-qoṛʾan pl. ḥamalat l-qoṛʾan one who knows the Koran by heart

ḥamla f. a.p. of ḥmel

ḥanan v.n. of ḥănn

ḥanana **1.** tenderness, gentleness, loving care **2.** sympathy, compassion, pity

ḥanut pl. ḥwanet (dim. ḥwinta) shop, store
    ¶ *ṛaṣ l-ḥanut* a spice mixture

ḥaqiqa truth, reality
    ¶ *fe-l-ḥaqiqa* in reality, really

ḥaqiqi pl. -yen real, genuine, true

ḥar iḥir v.i. (v.n. ḥira) to be confused, perplexed, hesitant

ḥaṛa pl. -t an expansive, isolated, barren spot (in the country)

ḥaṛaka pl. -t **1.** movement *ana mṛiḍ u-ma-nqedd-š năʿmel ḥaṛaka weʿda.* I'm so sick I can't make a single movement. —*l-ḥaṛaka š-šuyuʿiya bdat ddiyyăʿ f-had le-blad.* The Communist movement has begun to spread in this country. **2.** activity *kayna ḥaṛaka ktira f-ḍar l-ʿers.* There's a lot of activity in that house where the wedding is. **3.** function, job *šniya l-ḥaṛaka lli ka-tqum biha fe-l-măʿmel?* What's your job in the factory?

ḥaṛam forbidden (by religion)
    ¶ *bit llah l-ḥaṛam* The Holy Temple of the Kaaba

ḥaṛaṛa **1.** heat, warmth **2.** vivacity, life *fih l-ḥaṛaṛa.* He's full of life. **3.** temperature (weather, fever)
    ¶ *mizan l-ḥaṛaṛa* pl. *myazen l-ḥaṛaṛa* thermometer

ḥaṛeb v.t. to fight, to fight against (disease, feelings, enemy, etc.)

ḥaṛṛ pl. -in (comp. ḥăṛṛ) **1.** hot (temperature) *had n-nhaṛ qiyyal ḥaṛṛ.* It's been hot all day. **2.** hot, spicy **3.** touchy, irascible **4.** energetic, zealous
    ¶ *ma ḥaṛṛ* undrinkable water (e.g. river water)

ḥasab same as ḥsab

ḥasana pl. -t good deed

ḥasani **1.** pl. -yat an old coin worth half a *beṣṣiṭa* **2.** pl. -yen of the time of *mulay ḥasăn.*

ḥaseb v.t. to demand an accounting from (s.o., in the financial sense, also an explanation for doing s.th.)

ḥasen v.t. to be good (kind, charitable) toward

ḥasăn (comp. *ḥsen*) **1.** good (adj., interjectional usage) **2.** proper name (usually with art.)

¶ *l-ḥasăn u-l-ḥusin* the sons of Ali, grandsons of the Prophet Mohammed

ḥasud same as *ḥsed* 2

ḥaṣil used in the expr. *l-ḥaṣil, ḥaṣilu,* or *ḥaṣiluhu* briefly, in short, to make a long story short

ḥaṣul same as *ḥaṣil*

ḥaša used in the following:

** *ḥaša ḷḷah* or *ḥaša maɛaḍ ḷḷah.* I don't believe it! Impossible! Never happen! (expresses complete incredulity or denial of an accusation) —*ḥašak!* Thank you, but you shouldn't have done it (i.e., it's below your station); also used as an apology for some faux pas

ḥašiya pl. *-t* entourage, retinue (particularly the king's)

ḥašya pl. *-t, ḥwaši* **1.** border, fringe (cloth, garment) **2.** hem **3.** heel or rounded edge of a loaf of bread (Moroccan type)

ḥwaḍiṛ pl. of *ḥaḍiṛa*

ḥawel (v.n. *mḥawla, muḥawala*) to try, to attempt *ḥawel tqum!* Try to get up! *ḥawel ɛla* to take care of, to be careful with (s.th., s.o.)

ḥayat (f.) **1.** life (as opposed to death) **2.** life, lifetime

¶ *be-l-ḥayat* alive, living

ḥayati batiste

¶ *kas de-l-ḥayati* type of thin, unornamented tea glass

ḥayawan (sg. or pl.) pl. *-at* animal(s)

ḥayek pl. *ḥoyyak, ḥiyyak* large piece of material, usually white, used as an exterior garment by Arab women (wrapped around body and head)

ḥayel a.p. of *ḥal*

ḥaz iḥuz v.t. **1.** to get, to acquire *sir ḥuz le-ktab men ɛăndha.* Go get the book from her. **2.** to occupy, to take (legal) possession of (as a house) **3.** to put aside or to one side *ḥuz had le-ktab ɛăl limin ḥetta neḥtažuh.* Put this book aside until we need it. **4.** to take in, to adopt (child)

ḥazen a.p. of *ḥzen*

ḥazeq a.p. of *ḥzeq*

ḥaža v.t. (v.n. *mḥažya*) to propose a riddle or puzzle to (riddle itself introduced by *ɛla*)

ḥaža pl. *-t, ḥwayež* **1.** thing, object *šnu dak l-ḥaža f-žibek?* What's that thing in your pocket? **2.** something, thing *xellini nqul-lek waḥed l-ḥaža.* Let me tell you something. **3.** need, necessity *ḥažtu bik.* He needs you (i.e., has need of you).

** *ḥažti mɛah* or *ɛăndi ḥaža mɛah.* I've got business with him.

¶ *fe-l-ḥaža f-* (things), *b-* (persons) (to be) in need of *ana fe-l-ḥaža bik.* I need you.

¶ *ma . . . ḥetta ḥaža* nothing; not . . . a thing, anything *ma-qolt-lu ḥetta ḥaža.* I didn't tell him a thing.

¶ *ši-ḥaža* something

¶ (*ši*) *ḥaža qlila* a little bit

¶ *ḥwayež* (pl.) **1.** things (may include clothing), effects (personal) *xeṣṣni nemši nžib ḥwayži mne-ḍ-ḍaṛ.* I have to get my things from the house. **2.** clothes, clothing **3.** eating utensils **4.** luggage, baggage **5.** furniture

ḥažeb pl. *ḥwažeb, ḥežban* eyebrow

ḥažib pl. *ḥožžab* **1.** steward, chamberlain (at royal palace) **2.** chancellor (diplomatic rank)

ḥažež v.t. to contradict, to challenge (in a discussion, an argument)

ḥažž a.p. of *ḥăžž*

ḥba yeḥbu v.i. (v.n. *ḥbu;* impf. pl. *neḥbiw, teḥbiw, yeḥbiw*) to crawl (baby)

ḥbab pl. of *ḥbib* 2 and 3

ḥbal pl. of *ḥbel*

ḥbas organization, subsidized by the government, which cares for the needs of the Islamic religion (e.g., building, maintaining mosques)

ʔeḥbas pl. of *ḥbus*

ḥbasat pl. of *ḥăbs*

ḥbayeb, ḥbaybat pl. of *ḥbib* 1

ḥbayeṛ pl. of *ḥbuṛa*

ḥăbb iḥebb v.t. (v.n. *ḥăbb*) **1.** to like (food, a car, etc.) **2.** to love (s.o.) **3.** to want (usually in perfect tense) *ḥăbbit nakol.* I want to eat. **4.** expresses "would like" (in impf. tense) *ka-nḥebb nakol.* I would like to eat.

ḥăbb v.n. of *ḥăbb*

ḥăbb n.u. *-a* (dim. *ḥbiyyba*) grain (wheat, corn, etc.)

¶ *ḥăbba* pl. *-t, ḥbub* **1.** grain, kernel **2.** pimple, sore **3.** pill, tablet, capsule

¶ *ḥăbb le-mluk* n.u. *ḥăbb le-mluka* **1.** cherry **2.** cherry tree

¶ *ḥăbb š-šbab* pimple

¶ *ḥăbbet ḥlawa* anise

ḥobb love (romantic)

¶ *ḥobbăn wa-kaṛama* very willingly

ḥăbbeb **1.** v.t. to cause to like *ɛămmṛu la-šra dak ḍ-ḍaṛ u-kan ma-ḥăbbebtiha-lu-š.* He would never have bought that house if you hadn't made him like it. **2.** v.t. or v.i. to form into grains, to become granulated **3.** v.i. to curdle (milk) **4.** v.i. to become covered or afflicted with sores, pimples, etc.

ḥăbbes v.t. **1.** to donate (s.th.) to the *ḥabus*

(usually buildings or property) 2. to give, to donate *qbel-ma tmut ḥăbbset tlata de-ḍ-ḍyaṛ ʕăl l-itama.* Before she died she donated three houses to the orphans.

ḥbib 1. pl. *ḥbayeb, ḥbaybat* maternal uncle 2. pl. *ḥbab* friend, buddy; (pl.) close friends, relatives 3. pl. *ḥbab* boy-friend, sweetheart

¶ f. *ḥbiba* pl. *-t* girl-friend, sweetheart

ḥbik v.n. of *ḥbek*

ḥbis v.n. of *ḥbes*

ḥbek v.t. (v.n. *ḥbik*) to hem (garment)

¶ *ḥbek ʕla* to go after (as an escapee)

¶ *ḥbek fe-l-xedma, f-le-qṛaya,* etc. to work hard, to study hard, etc.

ḥbel v.i. (v.n. *ḥbala*) to get or become pregnant

¶ f. a.p. *ḥabla* pregnant

ḥbel pl. *ḥbal* rope, cable

** *tqeṭṭăʕ bih le-ḥbel.* He lost every cent he had.

ḥbeq basil

ḥbes v.t. (v.n. *ḥbis*) 1. to imprison, to put in jail 2. to arrest (police) 3. to catch, to find *ḥbest l-qeṭṭ ka-yakol l-lḥăm.* I caught the cat eating the meat. 4. to hold *ḥebsu ši-šwiya!* Hold it (for me) a minute. 5. v.t. and v.i. to stop, to halt

p.p. *meḥbus* pl. *mḥabes* prisoner, arrestee

ḥăbs pl. *ḥbasat* prison, jail

ḥbu v.n. of *ḥba*

ḥbub 1. same as *ḥăbb* 2. pl. of *ḥăbba* (see *ḥăbb*)

ḥbuṛa pl. *ḥbayeṛ* unwanted (usually of merchandise but can be applied to people)

ḥbus, ḥabus pl. *ʔeḥbas* organization which receives donations and bequests left to Islam, which, in turn, are used to further the cause (e.g., a house left to the *ḥbus* may be rented and the money used to build a mosque)

ḥda next to, near, close to, beside *had ṣ-ṣbaḥ fe-ṭ-ṭubis gles ḥdaya waḥed ṛ-ṛažel šibani bezzaf.* A very old man sat down next to me in the bus this morning.

ḥdada pl. *ḥudud* boundary, frontier (between countries, etc.)

ḥdaga, ḥdaqa intelligence, astuteness, quick-wittedness

ḥdayer pl. of *ḥdura*

ḥdebba pl. *-t* hump (camel, man)

ḥădd v.t. 1. to limit, to put boundaries or limits to 2. to fence off 3. to stop, to ward off

ḥădd pl. *ḥdud, ḥudud* boundary, limit *men băʕd l-istiqlal l-ḥudud lli kanet qaṣma l-meġṛib zalet.* After independence came, the boundaries which divided Morocco were eliminated. —*le-mlaġa ʕăndha ḥudud.* There's a limit to joking.

¶ *daz l-ḥădd* to go too far, to pass the limit

¶ *ma-ḥădd* while *yallah nxeṛžu ma-ḥădd ʕăndna l-weqt.* Let's leave while there's still time.

¶ *ma-ḥădd . . . u-* 1. the more . . . the more . . . *ma-ḥăddni* (or *ma-ḥăddi*) *ka-nexdem w-ana ka-neqbeṭ le-flus.* The more I work the more money I make. 2. the longer . . . the better (the worse) *maḥăddha galsa fe-l-feṛš u-ḥaltha ġad-tăʕdem.* The longer she stays in bed the worse she'll get. 3. as long as, so long as *ma-ḥădd t-telž ma-zal ka-iṭiḥ u-ḥna galsin ʕăndek.* We'll stay with you as long at it's still snowing.

ḥădd anybody, anyone (with negative) *ma-šeft ḥădd.* I haven't seen anybody.

¶ *l-ḥădd, nhaṛ l-ḥădd* pl. *ḥduda* (on) Sunday —*l-metḥef ka-ikun meḥlul nhaṛ l-ḥădd.* The museum is open on Sunday. —*mšina l-le-bḥăṛ tlata d-le-ḥduda mettabʕin.* We have gone to the beach three consecutive Sundays.

¶ *ma . . . ḥetta ḥădd* nobody, no one; not . . . anyone *ma-šeft ḥetta ḥădd.* I didn't see anyone. —*ḥetta ḥădd ma-ža išufu.* Nobody came to see him. —*škun kan mʕak temma?* —*ḥetta ḥădd.* Who was with you there?—Nobody.

¶ *ši-ḥădd* anyone, someone *ža ši-ḥădd?* Did anyone come?

ḥăddad pl. *-a* blacksmith

ḥădded v.t. 1. to iron, to press (clothes) 2. to limit, to set a boundary to 3. to set, to fix (date, time)

ḥăddeq v.t. to trim (hedge, hair, rough edge, etc.)

ḥădder v.t. to warn (rare usage)

ḥdibbi pl. *-yen* hunchback

ḥdid iron (metal)

ḥdida pl. *-t* 1. piece of iron 2. iron (for pressing)

ḥdidi pl. *-yen* 1. iron grey 2. resembling iron 3. rust (color)

ḥdir v.n. of *ḥder*

ḥdit pl. *ʔaḥadit* 1. conversation, talk 2. talk, sermon 3. one or all of the traditional sayings and customs of the Prophet Mohammed, not considered actual Islamic law

ḥdiya pl. *-t* buzzard

ḥder (v.n. *ḥdir*) 1. v.i. to bend down or over *fuq-emma ka-nži ndxol men dak l-bab ka-ixeṣṣni neḥder ḥit meḥniya.* Every time I want to go through that door I have to bend over, because it's low. 2. v.i. to come or go down, to descend (as a plane, the sun, etc.) *ṭ-ṭiyaṛa ḥedret ḥetta ʕlayen šefna n-nas lli kanu fiha.* The plane flew so low that we could almost see the people in it. 3. v.t. to lower, to bring down

¶ a.p. *ḥader* pl. *-in* low *had ṭ-ṭebla lli ka-naklu ɛliha ḥadra bezzaf.* This table we're eating on is very low.

ḥdet v.i. (v.n. *ḥdut*) to happen, to occur, to take place

** *qolti-li huwa ġani men zaman u-huwa ɛad ḥdet.* You told me he's been rich all along but (I know) he just recently struck it rich. —*had le-ktab ɛad ḥdet.* This book has just come out.

ḥdud pl. of *ḥădd*

ḥduda (with art.) pl. of *l-ḥădd* (see *ḥădd*)

ḥdudi pl. *-yen* quiet, reserved, taciturn

ḥdura pl. *-t, ḥdayer* down-hill grade, slope

ḥdut v.n. of *ḥdet*

ḥdež n.u. *ḥădža* colocynth or its fruit

ḥḍa yeḥḍi v.t. (v.n. *ḥḍi*) 1. to take care of, to keep 2. to keep an eye on, to watch (over)

** *ḥḍi ṛaṣek!* Be careful! Take care of yourself!

¶ a.p. *ḥaḍi* pl. *ḥaḍyen, ḥoḍḍay* same as *ḥăḍḍay* pl. *-a*

** *ḥaḍi ṛaṣu.* He's on his guard.

ḥḍana 1. incubation or brooding (period) *le-ḥḍana dyal d-džaž ka-ṭṭul waḥed u-ɛešrin yum.* The chicken's incubation period is twenty-one days. 2. adoption, custody *mnin mat xay qemna b-le-ḥḍana d-weldu.* When my brother died we took custody of his son.

ḥḍaṛ city (as opposed to the country)

ḥḍaṛi pl. of *ḥăḍṛa*

ḥăḍḍ 1. luck *ɛăndek l-ḥăḍḍ.* You're lucky. 2. share, part *hada ḥăḍḍek.* This is your share.

ḥăḍḍana pl. *-t* 1. brooding or incubating bird 2. incubator (for eggs)

ḥoḍḍay pl. of *ḥaḍi* (a.p. of *ḥḍa*)

ḥăḍḍay pl. *-a* watchman, guard

ḥăḍḍen ɛla 1. to incubate (eggs) 2. to be stingy with, to keep (for oneself) 3. to keep until prices go up (and then sell for big profit)

ḥăḍḍeṛ v.t. 1. to make (s.o.) attend or be present (at some meeting, etc.), to summon *qal-lhom l-qaḍi iḥăḍḍṛu lli mesʔulin kollhom.* The judge asked them to summon all those who are responsible. —*a-men ḥăḍḍṛek f-dak l-ɛers!* I wish you had been at that wedding! 2. to prepare (s.th. that is usually written, e.g., a speech or lesson) 3. to civilize, to give culture to *waš l-ġeṛb huwa lli ḥăḍḍeṛ fṛiqya l-žanubiya?* Was it the West that civilized South Africa? 4. to give back, to return *bġithom daba iḥăḍḍṛu-li flusi.* I want them to give me my money back right now.

¶ *ḥăḍḍeṛ baluɸ* to pay attention

ḥḍi v.n. of *ḥḍa*

ḥḍin v.n. of *ḥḍen*

ḥḍen v.t. (v.n. *ḥḍin*) to adopt, to take in (child)

¶ *ḥḍen ɛla* to incubate (eggs)

ḥḍeṛ v.i. *ḥḍuṛ, ḥuḍuṛ*) to show up, to appear *ḥăḍṛet metʔexxṛa.* She showed up late.

¶ *ḥḍeṛ f-* to attend, to be at *be-l-ʔasăf ma-ġad-imken-li-š neḥḍeṛ fe-l-ɛers dyalek.* I'm sorry I'm not going to be able to attend your wedding.

¶ *ḥḍeṛ ɛla* to witness, to see *ḥḍeṛna ɛla waḥed le-mdabza kbira had ṣ-ṣbaḥ.* We saw a big fight this morning.

¶ a.p. *ḥaḍeṛ* pl. *-in* present, in attendance

ḥăḍṛa pl. *-t, ḥḍaṛi* type of instrumental get-together similar to the American "jam session," often carried out at weddings, parties, etc.

ḥḍuṛ v.n. of *ḥḍeṛ*

ḥfa yeḥfa v.i. 1. to get dull or blunt (as a knife) 2. to become weak, feeble (particularly the mind)

¶ a.p. *ḥafi* pl. *ḥafyen* 1. alone, with nothing else, straight *klit l-xobz ḥafi.* I ate the bread straight (i.e., with no other food). 2. dull *had s-skaken kollhom ḥafyen.* All these knives are dull.

ḥfa (m.) barefootedness, state of being barefooted

¶ *b-le-ḥfa* barefoot(ed)

ḥfaḍa v n. of *ḥfeḍ*

ḥfali pl. of *ḥăfla*

ḥfani pl. of *ḥăfna*

ḥfaṛi pl. of *ḥăfṛa, ḥofṛa*

ḥfayeḍ pl. of *ḥfiḍ*

ḥfeḍ v.t. (v.n. *ḥăfḍ, ḥfaḍa, ḥifḍ*) 1. to protect (s.o., s.th.) 2. to learn by heart

ḥăfḍ v.n. of *ḥfeḍ*

ḥăfḍa pl. *-t* n.i. of *ḥfeḍ*

** *žabettu l-ḥăfḍa dayez.* He happened to be passing by.

ḥăffa v.t. 1. to dull, to blunt (as a knife) 2. to weaken, to make feeble (particularly the mind)

ḥăffaḍ pl. *-in* having the ability to learn and remember things well

ḥăffaṛ pl. *-a* digger (of wells, holes, trenches, etc., for a living)

ḥăffeḍ v.t. to make learn by heart *le-fqiha režɛăt tḥăffeḍna d-duṛus kollha.* The teacher started making us learn all the lessons by heart.

ḥăffef v.t. and v.i. to shave (beard, head) *škun kan iḥăffef-lek mnayn konti mṛiḍ?* Who shaved you when you were sick? —*ma-zal ma-ḥăffeft had n-nhaṛ.* I haven't shaved yet today.

ḥfiḍ pl. *ḥfayeḍ* grandson
ḥfiṛ v.n. of *ḥfeṛ*
ḥfiṛa dim. of *ḥăfṛa, ḥofṛa*
ḥăfla pl. *-t, ḥafalat, ḥfali* **1.** ceremony (e.g., wedding) **2.** party *konti fe-l-ḥăfla l-bareḥ fe-l-lil?* Were you at the party last night?
ḥăfna pl. *-t, ḥfani* handful (also with both hands)
ḥfeṛ v.t. (v.n. *ḥfiṛ*) to dig, to excavate, to hollow out
¶ *ḥfeṛ l-* to plot against
¶ *ḥfeṛ ɛla* to uncover by digging
ḥăfṛa, ḥofṛa pl. *ḥfaṛi* (dim. *ḥfiṛa*) hole, hollow, excavation, cavity
¶ *ḥăfṛa de-l-ɛăyn* eyesocket
¶ *ḥăfṛa de-z-zin* dimple
¶ *ḥfeṛ ḥăfṛa l-* to set a trap for, to plot against
ḥefyan pl. *-in* barefoot(ed)
ḥqed same as *ḥqed*
ḥgiṛ v.n. of *ḥgeṛ*
ḥgeṛ v.t. (v.n. *ḥgiṛ*) to make fun of, to humiliate
ḥăgṛa pl. *-t* n.i. of *ḥgeṛ*
ḥifḍ v.n. of *ḥfeḍ*
ḥikăm pl. of *ḥekma*
ḥila pl. *-t* trick, ruse, wile
ḥili pl. *-yen* wily, tricky, sly
ḥima **1.** v.n. of *ḥma yeḥmi 2* **2.** protection
ḥimaya **1.** protectorate (of a country) **2.** protection
ḥin used in the expr. *fe-l-ḥin* immediately, as soon as possible
ḥinen immediately, at once
ḥiqd v.n. of *ḥqed*
ḥira v.n. of *ḥar*
ḥit **1.** since, because *ḥit l-ḥal bared ġadi nelbes kebbuṭi de-ṣ-ṣuf.* Since it's cold I'm going to wear my wool coat. **2.** when *ḥit texrož š-šems, nnšeṛ t-teṣbin.* When the sun comes out I'll hang the wash out.
¶ *men ḥit* same as *ḥit*
ḥiṭ pl. *ḥyuṭ* wall
ḥiṭi same as *ḥăyṭi*
ḥiwel pl. of *ḥwel*
ḥiyad **1.** v.n. of *ḥad* **2.** neutrality (on some issue)
ḥiyaza pl. *-t* n.i. of *ḥaz*
ḥiyyak pl. of *ḥayek*
ḥizeb pl. *ḥzab, ˀeḥzab* **1.** party (political) **2.** any one of the sixty parts of the Koran
** *beddel ɛliya had l-ḥizeb!* Will you quit telling me the same thing over and over again!
ḥižr same as *ḥzer* (often metaphorical)
ḥka yeḥki v.t. to tell, to relate (story, adventure, etc.)
ḥkak pl. of *ḥăkk, ḥokk*
ḥkam same as *ḥokm*
ḥkama used in expr. such as *baṛaka men le-ḥkama ɛlina!* We've had enough of your ordering us around!
ḥkaya pl. *-t* story, tale, anecdote
** *aži nqul-lek waḥed le-ḥkaya.* Let me tell you something (that happened to me on the way to the office, etc.)
ḥkim pl. *ḥukama* **1.** philosopher, sage **2.** magician
ḥăkk iḥekk, iḥokk v.t. (v.n. *ḥekkan*) **1.** to rub **2.** to massage **3.** (also v.i.) to scratch (an itch) **4.** to scrub, to scour (as in washing)
** *ma-tḥekk-š ɛăl ḍ-ḍebṛa ḥetta isil d-demm!* You keep at it and you'll get into trouble!
¶ *ḥăkk ɛla* to persist in doing or saying s.th. to (usually distasteful to the other) *ila ma-bġit-š nqul-lek ma-tḥekk-š ɛliya!* If I wanted to tell you I'd tell you, so stop insisting!
ḥăkk, ḥokk pl. *ḥkak, ḥkuka* small box (for pills, snuff, jewelry, etc.)
¶ *ḥăkk r-rokba* kneecap
ḥekka pl. *-t* **1.** n.i. of *ḥăkk* **2.** the itch, mange
ḥekkak pl. *-a* masseur of the public (Moorish) bath
ḥokkam pl. of *ḥakem* (a.p. of *ḥkem*) and *ḥakăm*
ḥekkan v.n. of *ḥăkk*
ḥekkem v.t. to have act as judge, to set up as a judge *mnin ka-yuqăɛ bini u-bin xay ši-ġnan ka-nḥekkmu ḅḅana ɛlina.* Whenever my brother and I have a disagreement we have our father act as judge.
ḥkem yeḥkem, yeḥkom v.t. and v.i. (v.n. *ḥkam, ḥokm*) **1.** to govern, to rule **2.** to give orders to
¶ *ḥkem f-* **1.** to order, to give an order to **2.** to dominate *kaynin ɛyalat lli ka-iḥekmu fe-ržalhom.* There are women who dominate their husbands.
¶ *ḥkem ɛla* **1.** to judge, to pass judgment on (s.o., as in court) **2.** to sentence (s.o.) (to) *ḥekmu ɛlih be-l-ˀiɛdam.* They sentenced him to death. **3.** to command, to have command over
¶ a.p. *ḥakem* pl. *ḥokkam* **1.** judge **2.** commanding officer
ḥokm **1.** v.n. of *ḥkem* **2.** judgment, verdict
ḥekma pl. *-t, ḥikăm* **1.** maxim, proverb, wise saying **2.** wisdom **3.** magic (e.g., involved in magic lamps, rings, etc.)
ḥkuka pl. of *ḥăkk, ḥokk*
ḥla yeḥla v.i. **1.** to become sweet (taste) **2.** to become nice(r) or (more) pleasant (as weather, season, scenery)
¶ *ma-ḥlah* (or *ḥlaha*)! How sweet it is! (said of food, girl, beautiful day, etc.)
ḥla comp. of *ḥlu*
ḥlafi pl. of *ḥălfa* 2

ḥlal (no pl.) permitted by religious law
** *hiya bent le-ḥlal.* She's well-bred, well brought up.
ḥlaleb pl. of *ḥellab* 2
ḥlalef pl. of *ḥelluf*
ḥlali pl. *-yen* **1.** legitimate (child) **2.** honest, truthful **3.** pure, genuine (of metals, money) **4.** fine, of fine quality *had s-selɛa ḥlaliya.* These goods are of fine quality.
ḥlaqi pl. of *ḥălqa*
ḥlaqem pl. of *ḥălqum, ḥălquma*
ḥlas pl. *ḥlayes, ḥlales* type of pad filled with straw which is placed beneath the *šwari* on beasts of burden.
ḥlasa pl. *-t, ḥlayes* **1.** lazy good-for-nothing **2.** slow-acting individual (i.e., does things at a snail's pace)
ḥlawa pl. *-t* **1.** sweetness (of taste and character; pl. used for intensifying meaning) **2.** sweets *ṭ-ṭbib qṭăɛ ɛlih le-ḥlawa.* The doctor told him to stop eating sweets. —*ɛăndhom waḥed le-bnita ḥlawat.* They have such a sweet little girl. **3.** tip, commission (e.g., for helping s.o. sell s.th.) **4.** hush money
ḥlawi pl. of *ḥălwa*
ḥlayes pl. of *ḥlas* and *ḥlasa*
ḥlaywi pl. *-ya* pastry-cook
ḥlaḥel pl. of *ḥelḥal*
ḥleb v.t. (v.n. *ḥlib*) **1.** to milk (cow, etc.) **2.** to milk, to take for *mṛatu ḥălbettu men flusu kollhom.* His wife milked him of all his money.
ḥălba **1.** n.i. of *ḥleb* **2.** fennel seed
ḥlef v.i. (v.n. *ḥlif, ḥluf*) to swear, to testify by oath *ḥălfet ḥetta tqul l-ḥăqq.* She swore to tell the truth.
¶ *ḥlef f-* to be determined to get even with
¶ *ḥlef l-* to adjure, to plead with
ḥleft-lha ɛăl d-doxxan. I adjured her to stop smoking.
ḥălfa **1.** n.i. of *ḥlef* **2.** pl. *ḥlafi* esparto grass
ḥli (sg.) jewelry
ḥlib **1.** v.n. of *ḥleb* **2.** milk **3.** milky sap (as of the fig tree)
ḥlif v.n. of *ḥlef*
ḥlim v.n. of *ḥlem*
ḥliwa dim. of *ḥălwa*
ḥăll iḥell v.t. (v.n. *ḥellan*) **1.** to open (book, door, bottle, etc.) **2.** to open, to start (as a new store) **3.** to undo, to untie (a knot, etc.) **4.** to unfold, to unroll **5.** to unbutton **6.** to solve (as a problem) **7.** v.i. to take place *ṛemḍan ġadi iḥell fe-š-šheṛ d-daxel.* Ramadan will take place next month.
** *ḥăllet ɛlihom krat had š-šheṛ.* It's time for them to pay this month's rent.
¶ p.p. *meḥlul* pl. *-in* indolent, lazy, without energy

ḥălla **1.** v.t. to sweeten (food) **2.** v.i. to eat s.th. sweet (as candy) *tebġi tḥălli?* Would you like something sweet?
ḥăllab **1.** pl. *-a* one who milks **2.** pl. *ḥlaleb* milk pail, or other receptacle used for milk
ḥăllaba pl. *-t* **1.** milking machine **2.** milkmaid **3.** good milker (cow, goat, sheep)
ḥellaf adj. pl. *-in* n.pl. *-a* one who swears or utters oaths a great deal
ḥellan v.n. of *ḥăll*
ḥellef v.t. to make or have (s.o.) swear or utter an oath (as in promising to do s.th. or tell the truth)
ḥellel v.t. **1.** to declare permissible (s.th. that is usually forbidden) *l-ʔislam ka-iḥellel ɛlina nfeṭṛu f-ṛemḍan ila konna mṛaḍ aw mṣafṛin.* Islam makes it permissible for us to break the fast during Ramadan when we are ill or on a journey. **2.** to wash (clothes, hands, floors, etc.) **3.** to dissolve (as in water)
ḥălleq v.i. **1.** to spruce up, to dress up, to "doll" up (hair, make-up, etc., as well as clothes) **2.** to get by, to be satisfied with s.th. (after trying one's best)
¶ *ḥălleq l-* to make beautiful, to give a nice appearance to
ḥelles v.t. to put the *ḥlas* on (a beast of burden)
ḥelluf pl. *ḥlalef* **1.** pig **2.** pork
¶ *ḥelluf l-ġaba* wild pig
¶ *lḥăm l-ḥelluf* pork (meat)
ḥellufa pl. *-t* sow
ḥlem (v.n. *ḥlim*) to dream *ḥlemtek mṛiḍ had l-lila.* I dreamed you were sick last night. —*xellik ka-teḥlem!* You're just dreaming! (castles in the air, etc.)
ḥălq pl. *ḥluq, ḥluqa* **1.** throat (internal) *dima ka-iserreḥ ḥălqu qbel l-heḍṛa.* He always clears his throat before he speaks. **2.** voice (singing, speaking) **3.** neck (of bottle)
** *hadi telt iyam ma-dazet fertuta de-l-xobz ɛla ḥălqi.* I haven't eaten a thing for three days.
ḥălqa pl. *-t, ḥlaqi* **1.** circle or ring of people (as gathered around a street entertainer) **2.** type of skylight in Moroccan houses over the center patio, often open to the sky, sometimes covered with glass **3.** thimble
ḥălqum, ḥălquma pl. *ḥlaqem* **1.** throat (external) **2.** (pl.) tonsilitis *žawha le-ḥlaqem.* She has tonsilitis.
ḥlu f. *ḥluwa* pl. *ḥluwin* (comp. *ḥla*) sweet (taste, character)
ḥluf v.n. of *ḥlef*
ḥluq, ḥluqa pl. of *ḥălq*
ḥluwa f. of *ḥlu*
ḥluwin pl. of *ḥlu*
ḥălwa pl. *-t, ḥlawi* (dim. *ḥliwa*) **1.** pas-

try (cake, cookie, etc.) **2.** piece of candy (sucker, bonbon, etc.) **3.** (sg. and pl.) sweets

ḥălwi pl. *-ya* **1.** confectioner **2.** pastry-cook

ḥelḥal pl. *ḥlaḥel* lavender (plant)

ḥma yeḥma v.i. **1.** to get very warm or very hot *ṣ-ṣbăḥ ka-ikun mberred u-f-le-ɛšiya ka-yeḥma l-ḥal.* It's cool in the morning, but in the afternoon it gets very warm. **2.** to go up, to go higher (price)

¶ *ḥma fihφ d-demm* to become raging mad ≠

¶ *ḥami* pl. *ḥamyen* (very) hot (water, a radiator, etc.)

ḥma yeḥmi v.t. **1.** to heat, to make hot (water, iron, etc.) **2.** (v.n. *ḥima*) to protect (s.o. from s.th.)

ḥma (cons. *ḥmat*) pl. *-wat* mother-in-law (husband's mother)

ḥmaḍ v.i. **1.** to get or become sour, to sour, to go sour (as milk) **2.** to become unbearable (because of objectionable behavior)

ḥmaḍa **1.** sourness **2.** pl. *-t* absurd, silly act; s.th. done in bad taste

ḥmal pl. of *ḥmel*

ḥmala pl. *-t, ḥmayel* **1.** bandolier **2.** shoulder belt or cord used in carrying a dagger, sword, or pocketbook; baldric

ḥmali pl. of *ḥămla*

ḥmam n.u. *-a* pigeon

¶ *ḥmam le-bḥăṛ* (sea)gull

ḥmameṛ pl. of *ḥămmaṛ* **2**

ḥmaq v.i. (v.n. *ḥmaq, ḥomq*) **1.** to go crazy or mad, to become insane **2.** to pretend to be mad or insane

ḥmaq **1.** v.n. of *ḥmaq* **2.** insanity, madness

ḥmaṛ v.i. **1.** to turn or become red **2.** to blush, to redden (skin)

ḥmaṛ pl. *ḥmir* **1.** donkey (male), jackass **2.** idiot, dolt, jerk

¶ *ḥmaṛ l-lil* sleep-walking, somnambulism
** *ḍeṛbu ḥmaṛ l-lil.* He had a nightmare.

ḥmaṛa pl. *-t* she-donkey, she-ass

ḥmat cons. of *ḥma*

ḥmaya same as *ḥimaya*

ḥmayel pl. of *ḥmala*

ḥmaymi pl. *-ya* **1.** one who buys, raises, and sells pigeons **2.** one who owns or runs a public bath

ḥmed v.t. (v.n. *ḥămd*) to praise, to glorify (God)

ḥămd **1.** v.n. of *ḥmed* **2.** used in the expr. *l-ḥămdu l-llah, l-ḥămdu li-llah, li-llahi l-ḥămd.* Praise be to God.

¶ *l-ḥămdu l-llah lli . . .* thank God (that) . . . *l-ḥămdu l-llah lli žiti!* Thank God you came!

ḥămdel v.i. to say the expr. *l-ḥămdu l-llah* (see *ḥămd*)

ḥmil v.n. of *ḥmel*

ḥmimeṛ dim. of *ḥmeṛ*

ḥmir pl. of *ḥmaṛ*

ḥmiyyeṛ pl. *ḥmiyṛat* dim. of *ḥmaṛ*

¶ *ḥmiyyeṛ šwari* type of bread pinched in the middle so as to resemble slightly a dumbbell.

¶ *ḥmiyyeṛ* (pl. *ḥmiyṛat*) *žedda* type of wood louse capable of rolling up into a ball when disturbed (as the pill bug)

ḥmel (v.n. *ḥmil*) **1.** v.t. to carry (usually on the back) **2.** v.t. to stand, to bear *ma-bqit-š nḥămlu.* I can't stand him any more. **3.** v.i. to rise, to swell (as a river) **4.** v.i. to become or get pregnant

¶ *ḥmel ɛla* to attack (verbally)

¶ f. a.p. *ḥamla* pl. *-t* pregnant

ḥmel pl. *ḥmal* **1.** load (usually carried on the back) **2.** baby, foetus (as carried in pregnancy) **3.** responsibility, charge (of a family group) *melli bda ixdem rfed le-ḥmel de-l-ɛaʔila kollha.* Since he started working he's taken full charge of the family.

ḥămla pl. *-t, ḥmali* **1.** n.i. of *ḥmel* **2.** toothache (with abscess and swelling of the jaw)

ḥomma fever

ḥămmal pl. *-a* one hired to carry or transport items, usually with the help of a pack animal

ḥămmam pl. *-at* **1.** public (Moorish) bath **2.** private bath (as in one's house)

ḥommaq pl. of *ḥmeq*

ḥămmaṛ **1.** pl. *-a* one hired along with his donkey to transport items **2.** donkey or mule driver, muleteer **3.** pl. *ḥmameṛ* bridge (of violin, guitar) **4.** anything (such as a beam) used as a prop

ḥămmaṣa pl. *-t* roaster (machine)

ḥămmed v.i. to say *l-ḥămdu l-llah*

¶ *ḥămmed fe-s-slama l-* to say the expr. *l-ḥămdu l-llah ɛăl s-slama* to (s.o. back safe and sound from a trip)

ḥămmeḍ v.t. to make sour, to let go sour (as milk)

ḥommiḍa same as *ḥămmăyḍa*

ḥămmel v.t. **1.** to have or make (s.o.) assume (responsibility) *ḥămmeltu l-mesʔuliya.* I made him assume the responsibility. **2.** to hold and raise the feet of (s.o. to be punished by beating the soles of his feet, i.e. the bastinado) *ḥămmlu baš năɛṭih le-ɛṣa!* Hold up his feet so I can beat them (with the stick)! **3.** (*ɛla*) to incite (against)

ḥămmem v.t. to bathe, to wash (s.o.)

ḥămmeq v.t. **1.** to drive mad or insane **2.** to drive crazy, to exasperate

ḥămmeṛ v.t. **1.** to fry (meat) **2.** to make red, to redden (as with a slap, sunburn)

** *weldi ka-iḥămmeṛ-li wežhi.* I'm very proud of my son.

¶ *ḥămmeṛ f-* **1.** to stare at, to look at **2.** to look daggers at, to scowl at (with anger)

ḥămmeṣ v.t. to roast (e.g. coffee beans)

¶ part. *mḥămmeṣ* pl. *-in* made with chick peas (food)

ḥămmeṣ, ḥămmuṣ n.u. *ḥămmuṣa* chick peas

ḥămmuṣa n.u. of *ḥămmeṣ, ḥămmuṣ*

ḥămmăyḍa, ḥommăyḍa pl. *-t* sorrel (plant)

ḥmeq f. *ḥămqa* pl. *ḥumeq, ḥommaq* **1.** crazy (literal and metaphorical sense) **2.** immature (in behavior)

ḥomq **1.** v.n. of *ḥmaq* **2.** insanity, madness (literal and metaphorical sense)

ḥmeṛ f. *ḥămṛa* pl. *ḥumeṛ* (dim. *ḥmimeṛ*) **1.** red **2.** rust-colored **3.** fawn, reddish brown (as for animals) **4.** tanned, sunburnt

¶ *ḍ-ḍolm le-ḥmeṛ* gross injustice

¶ *l-baṭel le-ḥmeṛ* accusatory, bare-faced lies

¶ *sokkaṛ ḥmeṛ* brown sugar

ḥomṛani pl. *-yen* reddish (tending to orange)

ḥămri a fine, reddish soil, considered very fertile

ḥmuḍa, ḥmuḍiya same as *ḥmaḍa* **1**

ḥmum (pl., no sg.) soot

ḥmuṛa, ḥmuṛiya red, redness

ḥna yeḥni (v.n. *ḥenyan, ḥni*) **1.** v.t. to bow, to hang (the head) **2.** v.i. to stoop (over), to bend (down) **3.** v.i. to squat (down) **4.** v.i. to lean (over to the side)

¶ *ḥna ṛaṣu*$^{\phi}$ to submit, to allow oneself to be "walked all over" *ka-yeḥni-lha ṛaṣu bezzaf.* He lets her walk all over him.

ḥna (pl. disjunctive pron.) we, us, our *ḥna dima naštin.* We're always having a good time. —*had ḍ-ḍaṛ dyalna ḥna!* This is our house (not yours)!—*šafna ḥna b-waḥedna.* He saw only us.

ḥnabel pl. of *ḥănbel*

ḥnader pl .of *ḥăndira*

ḥnak pl. of *ḥănk*

ḥnan pl. of *ḥnin*

ḥnani pl. of *ḥănna*

ḥnaš pl. of *ḥenš*

ḥnaṭi pl. of *ḥănṭa*

ḥnaya same as *ḥna*

ḥnažeṛ pl. of *ḥănžuṛa*

ḥănbel pl. *ḥnabel* type of thick, heavy, wool carpet (usually for tents)

ḥăndira pl. *ḥnader* kind of bedspread

ḥni v.n. of *ḥna*

ḥnin pl. *-in, ḥnan* (comp. *ḥănn*) **1.** kind, kindly, kind-hearted **2.** tender, compassionate

ḥnit v.n. of *ḥnet*

ḥănk pl. *ḥnak, ḥnuk, ḥnuka* **1.** cheek **2.** jaw (as in a "blow to the jaw")

ḥănn v.i. (v.n. *ḥanan, mḥănna*) to be kind, kind-hearted

¶ *ḥănn men* to have pity or mercy on (e.g., forbearing to kill s.o. for revenge)

¶ *ḥănn ɛla* **1.** to have pity on (as a beggar) **2.** to be kind-hearted toward

ḥănn comp. of *ḥnin*

ḥănna pl. *-t, -wat* **1.** (inh. pos.) grandmother **2.** midwife

ḥănna v.t. to apply henna to (in bodily ornamentation, shampoo, etc.) *ḥănnit le-xti yeddiha.* I've applied henna to my sister's hands.

ḥănna pl. *ḥnani* henna (pl. used in intensifying meaning)

ḥănnaṭ pl. *-a* dealer in grains (usually wheat)

ḥănnaya pl. *-t* woman specialized in applying henna (as bodily decoration)

ḥănneš v.t. to write (s.th.), usually with a dry pen (for a student to trace with ink; used in teaching to write)

¶ p.p. *mḥănneš* pl. *-in* sinuous, winding, serpentine

ḥănnet v.t. to ignore or not heed the adjuration or solemn appeal of (s.o., may or may not be deliberate)

ḥănneṭ v.t. to embalm (body)

ḥenš, ḥneš pl. *ḥnuša, ḥnaš* **1.** snake **2.** type of intestinal vermiform parasite

ḥnet v.i. (v.n. *ḥnut, ḥnit*) to go back on one's promise or sworn statement *ḥălfet ḥetta dži wa-lakin ḥăntet.* She swore she'd come but she didn't (i.e., went back on her word).

ḥănṭa pl. *ḥnaṭi* **1.** any kind of grain used in making bread-stuffs **2.** a great quantity, an enormous amount, a (whole) lot of *žab ḥănṭa de-z-zṛăɛ.* He brought an enormous amount of wheat.

ḥănṭel fruit of the colocynth

ḥnuk, ḥnuka pl. *of ḥănk*

ḥnuša pl. of *ḥenš, ḥneš*

ḥnut v.n. of *ḥnet*

ḥnuṭ the substances used in embalming

ḥenyan v.n. of *ḥna*

ḥănzeẓ f- to stare at, to gawk at

ḥănžuṛa pl. *ḥnažeṛ* throat (external aspect)

ḥănḥen v.i. **1.** to neigh, to whinny (horse) **2.** to clear the throat (to get one's attention)

ḥqed v.t. (v.n. *ḥqed, ḥqid, ḥiqd*) to detest, to loathe

¶ *ḥqed ɛla* to oppress

ḥqed v.n. of *ḥqed*

¶ *fih*$^{\phi}$ *le-ḥqed* to be vindictive, to hold a grudge ≠

ḥqid v.n. of *ḥqed*

ḥqiqa same as *ḥaqiqa*

ḥqiqi pl. *-yen* same as *ḥaqiqi*

ḥqir v.n. of *ḥqeṛ* (same as *ḥgeṛ*)

ḥqiṛ pl. *-in* (comp. *ḥqeṛ*) looked down on,

contemptible, despicable (at least so considered)

ḥăqq v.i. to be necessary, to be incumbent *ka-iḥăqq ɛlik temši le-ḍ-ḍaṛ.* You've got to go home. —*xti ṣ-ṣġiṛa ma-zal ma-ḥăqq ɛliha ṣ-ṣyam.* My younger sister can't fast yet.

ḥăqq pl. *ḥquq, ḥuquq* **1.** truth *qul-li l-ḥăqq!* Tell me the truth! **2.** justice *ḷḷah xda l-ḥăqq men ḍ-ḍalem.* God has exacted justice from the culprit. —*ma-kayen ḥăqq f-had le-blad.* There's no justice in this country. **3.** duty, obligation *kan men ḥăqqek temši le-ž-žameɛ.* It was your duty to go to the mosque. **4.** share, part *ɛṭini ḥăqqi men le-flus!* Give me my share of the money! **5.** right *ma-ɛăndek ḥăqq baš tăɛṭini l-ˀawamiṛ.* You don't have the right to give me orders. **6.** (pl.) law, jurisprudence

** *u-ḥăqq ḷḷah l-ɛaḍim!* (I swear) by God Almighty! (for emphasizing the truth of s.th.)

¶ *be-l-ḥăqq* **1.** really (interrogatively) **2.** but, however *xdit le-mḍeḷḷ dyali had ṣ-ṣbaḥ, be-l-ḥăqq š-šta ma-ṭaḥet-š.* I took my umbrella this morning, but it didn't rain.

¶ *fihᵠ l-ḥăqq* to be wrong ≠

¶ *kulliyăt l-ḥuquq* faculty or college of law

¶ *ḥăqq š-šheṛ* menses, menstruation, period

¶ *ɛla ḥăqq, ɛla ḥăqq-aš* because *ka-nḥăbbu ɛla ḥăqq-aš huwa ṛažel mezyan.* I like him because he's a good man.

¶ *ɛmel* (or *xda*) *l-ḥăqq f-* **1.** to make pay (monetarily for some minor wrong) *ila ma-žiti-š fe-l-weqt năɛmel fik l-ḥăqq.* If you don't come on time I'll make you pay (for the movie, meal, etc.). **2.** to make pay a fine, to fine

¶ *ɛănduᵠ l-ḥăqq, mɛahᵠ l-ḥăqq* to be right *ɛăndek l-ḥăqq f-had l-qaḍiya.* You're right in this matter.

¶ *ɛṭa ḥăqq ḷḷah* to swear by God, to take an oath

ḥăqqăn really, in reality, to tell the truth, as a matter of fact *ḥăqqăn ana metˀellem.* As a matter of fact, I'm rather hurt (feelings).

ḥăqqeq **1.** v.t. to set on the correct time (watch, clock) **2.** v.t. to verify *kaynin ši-qaḍiyat xessni nḥăqqeqhom qbel-ma nemši.* There are some matters I have to verify before I leave. **3.** v.i. to be sure, to make sure *ḥăqqeq bezzaf!* Make absolutely sure!

¶ *ḥăqqeq f-* to look at closely or carefully

ḥqeṛ **1.** same as *ḥgeṛ* **2.** comp. of *ḥqiṛ*

ḥquq pl. of *ḥăqq*

ḥrafi pl. of *ḥărfa*

ḥraki pl. of *ḥărka*

ḥṛam s.th. forbidden by religion

** *ḥṛam ɛlik!* You shouldn't have done that!

¶ *weld le-ḥṛam* bastard (literal, also invectively epithetic)

¶ *ḥlef b-le-ḥṛam* to utter *ɛliya b-le-ḥṛam* (as an appeal to s.o. not to do s.th., which, if done, would cause the speaker to divorce his wife)

ḥṛami pl. *-yen* **1.** clever, sly, cunning **2.** dishonest **3.** illegitimate (child) **4.** false, fake (gold, diamonds, etc.)

ḥṛaq v.n. of *ḥṛeq*

ḥṛaṛ v.i. **1.** to become hot, spicy (food) **2.** to become unbearable (life, person, etc.)

ḥṛaṛ pl. of *ḥoṛṛ*

ḥṛaṛa same as *ḥaṛaṛa*

ḥrarek pl. of *ḥărrak*

ḥṛaṭen pl. of *ḥăṛṭani*

ḥrayef pl. of *ḥărfa*

ḥrayfi pl. *-ya* **1.** (skilled) craftsman **2.** professional (n.)

ḥṛayeq pl. of *ḥṛiqa*

ḥrayer pl. of *ḥrira*

ḥăṛb (f.) pl. *ḥuṛub* war

¶ *šheṛ l-ḥăṛb ɛla* to declare war against

ḥăṛba pl. *-t* **1.** spear, lance **2.** type of crosier or staff borne by the Imam

ḥăṛbi pl. *-yen* **1.** ready, willing (to act, to do s.th.) **2.** war (adj.) pertaining to war **3.** military (person)

ḥăṛf pl. *ḥṛuf* **1.** letter (of alphabet) **2.** edge (of table, cliff, paper, etc.)

ḥărfa pl. *-t, ḥrafi, ḥrayef* profession, craft

ḥṛeg same as *ḥṛeq*

ḥrik v.n. of *ḥrek*

ḥṛim v.n. of *ḥṛem*

ḥrin v.n. of *ḥren*

ḥṛiq **1.** v.n. of *ḥṛeq* **2.** burn (on skin) **3.** pain, ache

ḥṛiqa pl. *ḥṛayeq* fire, conflagration (destructive)

ḥrir silk

ḥrira pl. *ḥrayer* kind of soup, usually of flour, lentils, chick-peas, and maybe rice

** *ḥrirtek ḥrira.* In your case the matter's worse.

¶ *ṭleq le-ḥrira* to whitewash

¶ *ḥrira de-ž-žir* whitewash

ḥṛit v.n. of *ḥṛet*

ḥṛiyta dim. of *ḥăṛt*

ḥrek v.i. (v.n. *ḥrik*) to go away to war (on horseback)

¶ *ḥrek ɛla* to run after, to chase down

ḥărka pl. *-t, ḥraki* military expedition or campaign (on horseback)

ǥṛem v.t. (v.n. *ǥărman, ǥṛim*) to deprive *ǥṛemtihom men yemmahom.* You've deprived them of their mother.

ǥoṛm, ǥăṛm pl. *ǥṛuma* 1. holy place 2. sanctuary, place of refuge

ǥoṛma 1. honor, esteem 2. wife *l-ǥoṛma dyali bqat fe-ḍ-ḍaṛ.* My wife stayed home.

¶ *ṭiyyeǥ l-ǥoṛma, ẓḍem ɛăl l-ǥoṛma* to disgrace, to dishonor *ẓeḍmu-lu ɛăl l-ǥoṛma dyalu ǥda ṣǥabu.* They disgraced him in front of his friends.

ǥṛen v.i. (v.n. *ǥṛin*) 1. to balk (as a horse) 2. to be stubborn

ǥṛeq v.t. (v.n. *ǥṛiq, ǥṛaq*) 1. to burn (including to scorch) *ǥṛeqt yeddi be-l-ǥăddada.* I burnt my hand with the iron. —*fuq-emma ka-nǥădded l-qamiẓẓat l-buyeḍ dyali ka-neǥṛeqhom.* Every time I iron my white shirts, I scorch them. 2. to burn (down, up) *ǥṛeqt ḍ-ḍaṛ be-l-ɛani.* I burned the house down on purpose. 3. to hurt, to pain

ǥăṛq (no pl.) a burned area that has healed

ǥăṛqa acid indigestion, gassy stomach

ǥăṛqeṣ v.t. 1. to put black make-up on (the eyes) 2. to put black (beauty) spots on (the face)

ǥăṛquṣ black make-up (used for eyes and beauty spots)

ǥăṛṛ 1. comp. of *ǥaṛṛ* 2. same as *ǥaṛṛ*

ǥoṛṛ pl. *-in, ǥṛaṛ* 1. free, at liberty 2. free man (not a slave) 3. genuine, real (gold, diamond, painting, etc.) 4. of good quality

ǥărrak pl. *ǥrarek* object used for stirring or mixing (as a stick)

ǥăṛṛaqiya pl. *-t* firework (fire cracker, etc.)

ǥăṛṛaṛ pl. *-a* 1. dealer in silk 2. maker of silk material

ǥăṛṛat pl. *-a* plowman

ǥăṛṛatiya (f. adj. used with *ḷeṛḍ*) arable

ǥăṛṛeb v.t. to train, to drill (especially military)

ǥăṛṛeḍ v.t. (*ɛla*) to incite (against), to sick (on) *ǥăṛṛeḍ ɛlihom l-kelb dyalu.* He sicked his dog on them.

ǥărref v.t. 1. to distort, to alter (s.th. said or written by s.o.) 2. to place diagonally, to change the attitude of (as from straight to crooked)

ǥorriga, ǥărriqa, ǥorriqa pl. *-t* (stinging) nettle

ǥoṛṛiya liberty, freedom

ǥărrek 1. v.t. to move, to shake 2. v.t. to stir, to mix 3. v.i. to go or run at a gallop, to gallop (either rider or horse)

ǥăṛṛem v.t. 1. to forbid, to proscribe, to prohibit the usage of *d-din ka-iǥăṛṛem ɛlina makelt l-xenzir.* Religion (Islam) forbids us to eat pork. 2. to make impossible *ǥăṛṛemti ɛliya le-xṛuž.* You've made it impossible for me to go out.

ǥăṛṛeṛ v.t. 1. to set free, to free 2. to give time off to, to give a vacation to 3. to review and correct, to edit 4. to make hot(ter) or (more) spicy 5. to make unbearably difficult *ǥăṛṛeṛti ɛliya l-ɛiša.* You've made my life unbearable.

ǥăṛṛeš v.t. 1. to incite, to sick 2. to make rough, to roughen (a surface)

ǥṛeš f. *ǥăṛša* pl. *ǥuṛeš* 1. rough, not smooth (surface) 2. coarse, not fine (as sand)

ǥṛet v.t. (v.n. *ǥṛit, ǥăṛt*) 1. to plow 2. to prepare for seeding or planting (land)

¶ *ǥṛet ɛla* to exploit (s.o.)

ǥăṛt (dim. *ǥṛiyta*) 1. v.n. of *ǥṛet* 2. cultivation 3. cultivated land

ǥăṛṭani pl. *ǥṛaṭen* mulatto

ǥṛuf pl. of *ǥăṛf*

ǥṛuma pl. of *ǥoṛm, ǥăṛm*

ǥṛuṛa spiciness, hotness (food)

ǥṛuša, ǥṛušiya 1. roughness (surface) 2. coarseness (as of sand)

ǥruz, ǥruza pl. of *ǥărz*

ǥărz pl. *ǥruz, ǥruza* kind of written amulet used as a protection

ǥsab v.t. or v.i. same as *sǥab*

ǥsab pl. *-at* 1. v.n. of *ǥseb* 2. mathematics 3. account (expense) 4. bookkeeping, accounting

¶ *ṭeḷḷăɛ le-ǥsab d-* to add up, to total (s.th.)

¶ *ǥsabu*[Φ]*, fe-ǥsabu*[Φ] to think, to have the idea ≠ *fe-ǥsabi ža l-bareǥ.* I thought he came yesterday.

¶ *ɛla ǥsab* (or *ǥasab*) according to *ɛla ǥsabu huwa had le-ktab ma-fih menfaɛa.* According to him this book isn't very useful.

¶ *ɛmel fe-ǥsab* (or *be-ǥsab*) to take into consideration, to take into account

ǥsabi pl. of *ǥsiba*

ǥsak, ǥsaki pl. of *ǥeska*

ˀ*eǥsan* v.n. of *ǥsen*

ǥsana pl. *-t* v.n. of *ǥessen*

¶ *ǥsana de-ṛ-ṛaṣ* haircut

¶ *ǥsana de-le-wžeh* shave

ˀ*eǥsas* v.n. of *ǥess*

ǥsaybi pl. *-ya* 1. accountant, bookkeeper 2. one good at figures

ǥsayef pl. of *ǥsifa*

ǥsayfi pl. *-ya* a vindictive, retaliatory person

ǥseb v.t. (v.n. *ǥsab*) 1. to count *ǥseb šǥal men weṛqa hna.* Count how many sheets of paper there are here. 2. to calculate, to figure out *ǥseb šǥal dfăɛti fe-š-šheṛ lli daz.* Figure out how much you spent last month. 3. to take for, to consider, to think of as *kont ka-nǥesbu ṛažel mezyan.* I used to think of him as a good man.

** *ḥseb ṛaṣu ši kbir.* He thought he was really something.

ḥseb used in the expr. *weld* (or *bent*) *le-ḥseb u-n-nseb* son (or daughter) of a respectable family

ḥăsb used in the expr. *wa-ḥăsb ḷḷah: žak l-berd u-hada ṣ-ṣif, wa-ḥăsb ḷḷah ila žat iyam š-šta!* You think you're cold now in summertime, wait till winter comes!

ḥăsba pl. *-t* same as *ḥsab* **2, 3, 4**

¶ *ḍṛeb l-ḥăsba* same as *ɛmel le-ḥsab* (see *ḥsab*)

ḥăsbi pl. *-yen* simple, plain (person)

ḥsed v.t. (v.n. *ḥsid, ḥsed*) to envy, to be jealous of (s.o.) *ḥesdethom ɛla ḍaṛhom.* She envied them their house.

ḥsed **1.** v.n. of *ḥsed* **2.** envy, jealousy

ḥsiba pl. *-t, ḥsabi* bill *xesskom txeḷḷṣuh f-dak le-ḥsiba lli ṣafeṭ-lkom.* You have to pay him for the bill he sent you.

ḥsid v.n. of *ḥsed*

ḥsifa pl. *ḥsayef* rancor, grudge, vindictiveness

¶ *rfed le-ḥsifa f-* to feel rancor toward, to have a grudge against

ḥsik v.n. of *ḥsek*

ḥsek pl. of *ḥeska*

ḥsek v.t. (v.n. *ḥsik*) **1.** to cut or chop off at the base (with one blow, as a small tree) **2.** to thwart or frustrate (plan, project, etc.) **3.** to kill (implies in prime of life)

ḥeska pl. *-t, ḥsak, ḥsaki, ḥsek* candlestick, candelabra

ḥsen b- or *mɛa* (v.n. *ˀeḥsan*) to be generous to, to be kind to, to be magnanimous toward (as the poor)

ḥsen **1.** comp. of *ḥasăn* and *mezyan* **2.** better *had le-ktab ḥsen men hada.* This book is better than this one. **3.** prettier, more beautiful *had l-bent ḥsen men xti.* This girl is prettier than my sister.

** *ḥsen-lek tšedd fommek!* You'd better shut up! —*ḥsen-li ikun ɛăndi weld.* I'd rather have a boy.

¶ *le-ḥsen u-l-ḥusin* see *ḥasăn*

ḥosn beauty

ḥess b- (v.n. *ˀeḥsas, ḥessan*) **1.** to feel *ka-nḥess b-yeddih ɛla ketfi.* I feel his hand on my shoulder. **2.** to feel, to perceive *ka-nḥess b-waḥed l-xaṭaṛ maži.* I feel some danger coming.

¶ *ḥess b-ṛaṣu*$^{\phi}$ to feel *waš ka-tḥess b-ṛaṣek ɛăyyan?* Do you feel tired?

ḥess sound, noise *smăɛt waḥed l-ḥess fe-ḍ-ḍḷem.* I heard a sound in the darkness.

** *ma-bqa-š ḥessu hnaya.* There's not a sign of him here.—*tteqṭăɛ ḥessu.* You just don't hear about him anymore.

¶ *be-l-ḥess* **1.** quietly, silently **2.** in a low voice

ḥessab pl. *-a* same as *ḥsaybi*

ḥessad pl. *-in, -a, ḥossad* envious, jealous

ḥossad pl. of *ḥessad*

ḥessan v.n. of *ḥess*

ḥessi messi quietly, without being heard or seen (also metaphorical)

ḥessen (v.n. *ḥsana, teḥsin*) **1.** v.t. and v.i. to shave (head, beard, etc.) **2.** v.t. to cut (hair) **3.** v.i. to get or have a haircut, shave **4.** v.t. to make more beautiful, to enhance **5.** v.t. to improve

¶ *ḥessen bla ma l-* to take, to cheat, to bilk

ḥsuwa watery soup (of lentils or onions, etc.)

ḥṣa yeḥṣi v.t. (v.n. *ḥṣa, ˀiḥṣaˀ*) to count *ḥṣa băɛda le-ġnem.* He's already counted the sheep.

ḥṣa (m.) gravel, rock (coll.)

ḥṣa v.n. of *ḥṣa*

ḥṣaḍ v.n. of *ḥṣeḍ*

ḥṣanbal (no art.) type of incense

ḥṣaṛ **1.** blockade **2.** siege

ḥṣaṣeṛ pl. of *ḥeṣṣaṛ*

ḥṣayeṛ pl. of *ḥṣiṛa*

ḥṣayṛi pl. *-ya* one who makes *ḥṣiṛa*

ḥṣeḍ v.t. (v.n. *ḥṣiḍ, ḥṣaḍ*) to harvest, to reap (grain, sugarbeets, corn, etc.)

ḥṣiḍ v.n. of *ḥṣeḍ*

ḥṣiḍa field covered with stubble, stubble-field (after the harvest)

ḥṣil v.n. of *ḥṣeḷ*

ḥṣiṛ v.n. of *ḥṣeṛ*

ḥṣiṛa pl. *ḥṣayeṛ* mat or matting made of rush or similar plant

ḥṣeḷ v.n. (v.n. *ḥṣil, ḥṣul*) **1.** to get trapped (in a room, pit, etc.), to get stuck (in mud, etc.) **2.** to be caught up (in a lie or mistake)

ḥeṣḷa pl. *-t* n.i. of *ḥṣeḷ*

ḥṣenbal same as *ḥṣanbal*

ḥṣeṛ v.t. (v.n. *ḥṣiṛ, ḥṣuṛ, ḥeṣṛan*) **1.** to keep, to hold (s.o. from getting away) **2.** v.t. and v.i. to stop, to halt

¶ *ḥṣeṛ nefsu*$^{\phi}$ to restrain oneself

ḥeṣṛa pl. *-t* n.i. of *ḥṣeṛ*

¶ *ya-ḥeṣṛa* even though *imken-lu irfed myat kilu hada ya-ḥeṣṛa ɛad mṛiḍ.* He can lift a couple of hundred pounds even though he's sick.

** *ya ḥeṣṛa!* If only I had done it! If only such and such were true! If only . . .!, etc.

ḥeṣṛan **1.** v.n. of *ḥṣeṛ* **2.** strangury

ḥeṣṣaḍ pl. *-a* harvester, reaper (person)

ḥeṣṣaḍa pl. *-t* harvesting machine (wheat, corn, etc.)

ḥeṣṣaṛ pl. *ḥṣaṣeṛ* **1.** brake (as in each wheel; also the pedal) **2.** sluice gate **3.** petcock, valve **3.** same as *ḥṣayṛi*

ḥeṣṣeḷ v.t. to catch (a ball, s.o. running away, s.o. lying, a thief red-handed, etc.)

¶ ḥeṣṣel ʕla to get, to obtain, to acquire
ḥeṣṣen v.t. to fortify (a place)
ḥṣul v.n. of ḥṣel
ḥṣuṛ v.n. of ḥṣeṛ
ḥša yeḥši v.t. (v.n. ḥešyan) to stick (in), to put (in), to insert
** ḥšaha-li. He gypped me.
ḥšayši pl. -ya hashish or marihuana addict (eater)
ḥšiṛ v.n. of ḥšeṛ
ḥšiš grass
ḥšiša narcotic made from the marihuana plant (usually eaten)
ḥšem v.i. (v.n. ḥšuma) 1. to be or become ashamed or embarrassed 2. to be or get shy or timid 3. to not dare ḥšemt ndxol. I didn't dare go in.
ḥešma 1. modesty (in dress, actions, etc.) 2. shyness, timidity
ḥešman pl. -in 1. ashamed 2. embarrassed 3. shy, timid
ḥšeṛ v.t. (v.n. ḥšiṛ) to bury (corpse)
¶ yum le-ḥšeṛ day of resurrection
¶ ḥšeṛ bu-ʕlam to crash the party (or any group activity)
ḥešš v.t. (v.n. ḥeššan) to cut or mow
** ġir ḥeššiti u-žebti! Looks to me like you just grabbed the first thing you saw (i.e., you didn't use any care in choosing).
ḥešša v.t. 1. to stuff (food) 2. to stick (in), to stuff (into) (as into a drawer)
ḥešša pl. -t 1. n.i. of ḥešš 2. handful, shock (of grass, grain, etc.)
ḥeššan v.n. of ḥešš
ḥeššaṛ pl. -a one in charge of burial (of a corpse)
¶ ḥeṣṣaṛ bu-ʕlam party-crasher, gate-crasher
ḥeššaš pl. -a ag. n. of ḥešš
ḥeššem v.t. to shame, to embarrass
¶ ḥeššem b- same as ḥeššem above
ḥeššumi pl. -yen shy, timid
ḥšuma v.n. of ḥšem
ḥšuma pl. ḥšayem 1. embarrassment 2. shame ḥšuma ʕlik! You ought to be ashamed! 3. shyness, timidity 4. modesty (as in dressing)
ḥšumiya 1. shyness 2. modesty (in dress, action, etc.)
ḥešyan v.n. of ḥša
ḥtal to make preparations, to get ready
¶ ḥtal ʕla to use trickery or wiles on, to try to trick (into doing s.th.)
ḥtaṛem v.t. to revere, to respect
ḥtaž v.t. to need ila ḥtažiti le-flus nsellefhom-lek b-koll faṛăḥ. If you need money I'll be glad to lend you some.
** ma-teḥtaž-š or ma-iḥtaž-š. Never mind. —ḍaṛu ʕlik mnayn kanu meḥtažin fik. They looked for you when they needed you.
ḥtiḍaṛ 1. v.n. of ḥtaḍeṛ 2. death throes
ḥtilal v.n. of ḥtell
ḥtiṛam v.n. of ḥtaṛem
ḥtell v.t. (v.n. ˀiḥtilal, ḥtilal) to occupy, to take over (country, government, s.o.'s seat, etc.)
ḥett ʕla to attempt to persuade insistently, to importune ma-tḥett-š ʕliya bezzaf! Stop insisting so much!
ḥetta 1. until (followed by verbs) ġadi-nebqa hna ḥetta iži. I'm staying here until he comes. 2. after ḥetta nfeṭṛu ʕad nxeṛžu. After we have breakfast we'll go. 3. when (connotes an element of surprise) kont naʕes ḥetta deqq ʕliya ši-waḥed. I was asleep when someone knocked at the door. 4. so much that, to the point that, until bqit nešṭeḥ nešṭeḥ ḥetta ma-bqit-š nqedd nxellef. I danced and danced until I couldn't take another step. 5. in order to, so that, to kif ġadi-ndir ḥetta nemnăʕ mennu? What am I going to do to get away from him? 6. too, also ḥett-ana ġadi-nṣafeṛ š-šher l-maži. I'm taking a trip next month too. —ṛaželha ḥetta-huwa ka-ixdem ʕăndi. Her husband works for me too. 7. even ḥetta š-šibani ka-iḥebb le-bnat. Even an old man (still) likes girls. 8. not . . . either, neither ḥna ma-xaṛžin-š.—ḥettana. We're not leaving.—I'm not either. 9. used for emphasis in oaths we-ḷḷah ḥetta nži ġedda! I swear I'll come tomorrow.
¶ ḥetta l- 1. until (in time expr.) ġadi-nebqa hna ḥetta l-l-xemsa. I'm staying here until five o'clock. 2. up to, as far as qṛit ḥetta le-ṣ-ṣefḥa ʕešrin. I read up to page twenty. —l-ʕam lli daz wṣelt ḥetta l-meṛṛakeš. Last year I got as far as Marrakech.
¶ ḥetta ši (or šay, or ḥaža) nothing, (not) anything ma-ʕăndi ḥetta ḥaža. I don't have anything.
¶ ḥetta ḥădd (or waḥed) nobody ḥetta waḥed ma-sqeṭ. Nobody failed (the exam).
ḥettet v.t. to break up into little pieces, to crumble (as bread)
ḥṭeb (v.n. ḥṭib) 1. v.i. to gather firewood (and bring back) 2. v.t. to gather (firewood)
ḥṭeb n.u. ḥeṭba (fire)wood
ḥṭib v.n. of ḥṭeb
ḥeṭṭ (v.n. ḥeṭṭan) 1. v.t. to put, to place (s.th. somewhere) 2. v.t. (or with men) to degrade, to bring down (s.o.'s reputation, value of s.th.) 3. v.i. to stay, to stop over
ḥeṭṭab pl. -a ag. n. of ḥṭeb
ḥeṭṭan v.n. of ḥeṭṭ
ḥṭuṭa pl. -t penis (child's term)

ḥubus same as *ḥbas*

ḥudud pl. of *ḥădd* and *ḥdada*

ḥuḍ pl. *ḥwaḍ* (with some speakers *ḥwaḍ* is sg. with pl. *ḥwaḍat*) **1.** small plot or garden **2.** ditch leading from the noria

ḥuḍuṛ v.n. of *ḥḍeṛ*

¶ *f-ḥuḍuṛ, b-ḥuḍuṛ* in the presence (of)

ḥukama pl. of *ḥkim*

ḥukuma pl. *-t* **1.** government *menɛăt l-ḥukuma tažemmuɛat n-nas.* The government has prohibited public assembly. **2.** administration (of government) **3.** cabinet (government)

ḥuma pl. *-t, ḥwem* quarter, section (of a city)

ḥumma fever (sickness)

ḥumeq pl. of *ḥmeq*

ḥumeṛ pl. of *ḥmeṛ*

ḥuquq pl. of *ḥăqq*

ḥuriya pl. *-t* houri

ḥuṛeš pl. of *ḥṛeš*

ḥuṛub pl. of *ḥăṛb*

ḥut n.u. *-a* fish

¶ *ḥut musa* sole (fish)

ḥuta pl. *-t, ḥwet* usually in the phrase *ḥuta de-r-ržel* calf (of the leg)

ḥuwwal pl. *ḥwawel* baker's spatula for placing in and taking out of the oven

ḥužăž pl. of *ḥužža*

ḥužža pl. *-t, ḥužăž* **1.** proof *ɛăndu ḥužža qwiya ɛla baṛaʔtu.* He has strong proof of his innocence. **2.** evidence

ḥwaḍ pl. of *ḥuḍ* (with some speakers same as *ḥuḍ*)

ḥwafer pl. of *ḥafer*

ḥwal, ʔeḥwal pl. of *ḥal*

ḥwala pl. of *ḥăwli*

ḥwanet pl. of *ḥanut*

ḥwanti pl. *-ya* shopkeeper, shop owner

ḥwaši pl. of *ḥašya*

ḥwawel pl. of *ḥuwwal*

ḥwayež **1.** pl. of *ḥaža* **2.** (pl.) clothes, clothing

ḥwaz, ʔeḥwaz pl. of *ḥăwz* **2**

ḥwažeb pl. of *ḥažeb*

ḥăwḍ same as *ḥuḍ*

ḥăwf v.n. of *ḥaf*

ḥwinta dim. of *ḥanut*

ḥwiyyža dim. of *ḥaža*

ḥwel f. *ḥăwla* pl. *ḥiwel* cross-eyed, wall-eyed

ḥăwl year (usually used with the verb *ḍaṛ*) *ḍaṛ l-ḥăwl u-huwa ma-ṛžăɛ-š men ṣ-ṣfeṛ.* It's been a year now, and he hasn't returned from his trip. —*had z-zṛăɛ ḍaṛ ɛlih l-ḥăwl.* This wheat is a year old.

ḥăwla **1.** f. of *ḥwel* **2.** strength, power; used only in the expr. *la-ḥăwla wa-la-quwwata illa be-llah.* There is no power or might save in God. (expr. of condolence or pity said upon hearing of the death of s.o. or on seeing a cripple, etc.)

ḥăwli pl. *ḥwala* male sheep (not young)

ḥwem pl. of *ḥuma*

ḥăwma same as *ḥuma*

ḥwet pl. of *ḥuta*

ḥăwwa Eve (Adam's mate)

ḥăwwat pl. *-a* **1.** fisherman **2.** fishmonger

ḥăwweḍ ɛla to dig a (small) ditch around or near (a plant, for watering)

ḥăwwef v.t. to bring down, to lower (a flag, a window, etc.)

ḥăwwel v.t. **1.** to move (from one place to another) **2.** to distort, to twist (what s.o. has said) **3.** to cross, to make cross (eyes)

¶ *ḥăwwel ṭ-ṭriq* to take another or different road (from the one you are already on)

¶ *ḥăwwel ɛla* to take it easy on, to go easy with (s.o.)

ḥăwwem v.i. **1.** to wander around, to roam around (walking) **2.** to hover or glide in circles

¶ *ḥăwwem ɛla* to look (around) for (some stealthiness implied)

ḥăwweṣ **1.** v.i. to take a walk or a drive (as on Sunday afternoon) **2.** v.t. to rob (s.o. or s.th.) (taking everything he has)

ḥăwz **1.** with art.) region near Marrakech **2.** pl. *ḥwaz, ʔeḥwaz* suburb, outskirts (pl.)

ḥăwzi pl. *-yen* native of *ḥăwz* (see *ḥăwz* **1**)

ḥăwwež used in the expr. *leh-la iḥăwwžek* I hope some day you won't have to depend on anybody for anything (said to s.o. who cannot now have s.th. he wants).

ḥya yeḥya v.i. **1.** to live *ḥya ḥyat ṭwila.* He lived a long life. **2.** to come back to life (as from a grave illness, or as a wilted flower)

¶ *yeḥya l-malĭk!* Long live the king!

ḥya yeḥyi v.t. (v.n. *ʔeḥyaʔ*) **1.** to bring back to life (as from a grave condition) **2.** to revive **3.** to resurrect **4.** to celebrate (anniversary, etc.)

ḥya **1.** (m.) modesty, decency **2.** (m.) shyness **3.** (f.) life

¶ *bent le-ḥya* decent, virtuous girl

¶ *qlil le-ḥya* indecent, immodest

¶ *qellet le-ḥya* indecency, immodesty

ʔeḥyaʔ v.n. of *ḥya yeḥyi*

ḥyal v.i. to get old, to age (foods; either a good thing or a bad, depending on the food)

ḥyala v.n. of *ḥal iḥil*

ḥyat same as *ḥayat*

ḥyaṭa pl. of *ḥăyṭi*

ḥăyṛan pl. *-in* perplexed, bewildered, puzzled

ḥăyṭ same as *ḥiṭ*

ḥăyṭi pl. *ḥyaṭi* type of tapestry (usually used for ceremonies, feasts, etc.)

ḥyuṭ pl. of *ḥiṭ*

ḥeyy pl. *-in* alive, living

ḥeyya pl. *-t* viper (poisonous)
ḥoyyak pl. of *ḥayek*
ḥeyyan used in the expr. *lyali ḥeyyan* coldest period of winter
ḥeyyana, a-ḥeyyana used in the expr. *ḥeyyana εlik!* (expresses an incredulity at s.o.'s excuse or answer) *waš herresti had z-zaž?—la!—a-ḥeyyana εlik!* Did you break this window?—No!—Well, I think you did.
ḥeyyaḥ pl. *-a* ag. n. of *ḥeyyeḥ*
ḥăyyed v.t. **1.** to take (off) *ḥăyyed magantek men yeddek!* Take your watch off (your wrist)! —*ḥăyyed ṣebbaṭek!* Take your shoes off! **2.** to take (out of) *ḥăyyed yeddek men žibek!* Take your hand out of your pocket! **3.** to take (away from) *xeṣṣek tḥăyyed l-weldek dak l-mess.* You'd better take that knife away from your boy. **4.** to put (in) *fe-l-berd ka-nḥăyyed yeddiya fe-žyabi ḥit ma-ka-ikunu εăndi ṣebbaεat.* In wintertime I usually put my hands in my pockets when I don't have gloves. **5.** to hide (with removal of the object in question) *ḥăyyed had le-ktab deġya!* Quick! Hide this book! **6.** to keep (for) *ḥăyyed had l-ḥălwa l-weldek!* Keep this candy for your boy! **7.** v.i. to move or get away, to move aside *ḥăyyed men temma!* Get away from there!
ḥăyyel v.t. to age, to allow to get old (i.e., either to improve or impair quality of foods)
ḥăyyer v.t. **1.** to puzzle, to perplex **2.** to cause a lot of trouble for, to give a lot of trouble to
ḥăyyeṛ v.t. to boil (an egg)
ḥăyyeḥ v.t. **1.** to frighten away, to run off **2.** to rouse (game animals, by beating) **3.** to weep and wail
ḥzab, ʔeḥzab pl. of *ḥizeb*
ḥzam pl. *-at, ḥzuma* **1.** belt *had le-ḥzam kbir εla kerši.* This belt is too big for my waist. **2.** girth
¶ *ḥzam lalla faṭima* (or *faṭim*) *z-zohṛa* rainbow
ḥzami pl. of *ḥezma*
ḥzan pl. of *ḥzin*
ḥzim v.n. of *ḥzem*
ḥzima dim. of *ḥezma*
ḥzin pl. *-in, ḥzan* sad, grief-stricken
ḥziq v.n. of *ḥzeq*
ḥzem v.t. (v.n. *ḥzim*) to tie up or together (in a bundle)
*** ḥzem ṛaṣek!* Pull yourself together! Get on the ball!
ḥăzm **1.** willingness, readiness **2.** resolution, tenacity
ḥezma pl. *-t, ḥzami* (dim. *ḥzima*) bundle (of books, sticks, etc.)
ḥzen v.i. (v.n. *ḥăzn, ḥozn*) to become sad, grief-stricken
¶ *ḥzen εla* to go into mourning, to mourn *ḥzen εla ḅḅah moddet εamayn.* He mourned his father for two years.
¶ a.p. *ḥazen* pl. *-in* in mourning (state of mind)
ḥozn, ḥăzn **1.** v.n. of *ḥzen* **2.** grief, sadness
ḥzeq v.i. (v.n. *ḥziq*) **1.** to fart **2.** to go broke, to go bankrupt **3.** to take off, to beat it, to scram
¶ a.p. *ḥazeq* pl. *-in* broke, bankrupt (person)
ḥezqa pl. *-t* **1.** fart **2.** bankruptcy, state of being broke (personal)
ḥzuma pl. of *ḥzam*
ḥezzab pl. *-a* one who reads (aloud) from the Koran (in the mosque)
ḥezzama pl. *-t* s.th. used as a belt
ḥezzan pl. *-a* rabbi
ḥezzaq pl. *-a, -in* ag. n. of *ḥzeq*
ḥeẓẓaṛ pl. *-a* ag. n. of *ḥeẓẓeṛ*
ḥezzem v.i. to put a belt on
ḥezzen v.t. to grieve, to sadden, to cause to mourn (subject is death, failure, etc.)
ḥezzeq v.t. to cause gas in the bowels (as beans) and, therefore, farting
ḥeẓẓeṛ v.t. to console, to calm the feelings of (usual object is a child)
ḥžab pl. *-at, ḥžuba* **1.** veil (as worn by Arab women) **2.** charm, amulet (worn as a protection against danger, sickness, etc.)
ḥžeb v.i. (v.n. *ḥžib*) to shut oneself in, to seclude oneself (for privacy), to remain in seclusion *men băεd mat ṛaželha ḥăžbet telt šhuṛ.* After her husband's death she remained in seclusion for three months.
ḥežban pl. of *ḥažeb*
ḥžib v.n. of *ḥžeb*
ḥžel (coll.) f. *ḥăžla* partridge
ḥežli pl. *-yen* hazel (of eyes)
ḥžer pl. *ḥžura* **1.** lap *d-derri gales fe-ḥžer ḅḅah.* The child is sitting in his father's lap. **2.** male genital area, crotch
ḥžeṛ n.u. *ḥežṛa* **1.** stone, rock, boulder **2.** lump (of sugar) **3.** battery (dry-cell, as for a flashlight)
*** ṛaṣu qaṣeḥ bḥal l-ḥežṛa.* **1.** He's as stubborn as a mule. **2.** He's rather dense.
ḥžuba pl. of *ḥžab*
ḥžura pl. of *ḥžer*
ḥăžž v.i. (v.n. *ḥăžž*) to make a pilgrimage to Mecca
¶ a.p. *ḥažž* pl. *ḥožžaž* one who has made at least one pilgrimage to Mecca, Pilgrim (used also as honorific title)
ḥăžž v.n. of *ḥăžž*
ḥežža pl. *-t* **1.** n.i. of *ḥăžž* **2.** same as *ḥožža*
ḥožža same as *ḥužža*
ḥožžab pl. of *ḥažib*

ḥežžam pl. *-a* barber
ḥežžami pl. *-yen* related to a barber's work (e.g. shop, tool, etc.)
¶ *mess ḥežžami* straight razor
ḥožžaž pl. of *ḥažž* (a.p. of *ḥăžž*)
ḥežžeb v.t. to seclude, to shut in, to keep (s.o.) in (the house, as some men do their wives)
ḥežžeṛ v.t. **1.** to cover with gravel, stones, or rocks (as a road) **2.** to pacify (as a crying child with candy)

ع

ɛab iɛib v.i. (v.n. *ɛăyb, ɛyuba*) **1.** to turn bad, to become corrupted or ruined (person) **2.** to become useless, to become ruined (part of the body, machine, etc.)
ɛad iɛud **1.** v.i. (v.n. *ɛăwda*) to return, to go or come back **2.** v.i. (v.n. *ɛăwda*) to become **3.** v.t. (v.n. *ɛyada*) to visit, to pay a visit to (s.o. sick)
ɛad **1.** only (in time expr.) *hadi ɛad ṛubuɛ saɛa baš šeftu mɛaha.* It's only been a quarter of an hour since I saw him with her. **2.** just *ɛad wṣelt!* I just got here! **3.** then *kla, ɛad mša inɛăs.* He ate, then went to bed.
¶ *bezzaf ɛad* **1.** very, very; extremely *hiya mezyana bezzaf ɛad.* She's very, very pretty. **2.** very, very much; an awful lot **3.** much too much
ɛada (v.n. *ɛdawa*) **1.** v.t. to be on unfriendly terms with (s.o.) (a.p. usually used in present) **2.** v.t. to treat in an unfriendly manner **3.** v.i. to be contagious **4.** v.t. to contaminate (s.o.) (with disease) *kan fih s-soll, u-ɛada bih xutu.* He had tuberculosis and gave it to his brother and sisters.
ɛada pl. *-t, ɛwaʔid* custom, habit, tradition *l-makla bekri ɛăndna ɛada.* We're in the habit of eating early.
¶ *fe-l-ɛada,* or *men l-ɛada* usually
¶ *ma-ɛada* except, but *kollhom qṣaṛ ma-ɛada ana.* They're all short except me.
¶ *men ɛadtu*$^{\phi}$ to be one's custom or habit ≠, to usually (do s.th.) ≠ *men ɛadti ka-nešṛeb l-qehwa mɛa le-fṭuṛ.* I usually drink coffee with my breakfast.
ɛadad **1.** number, quite a few *qṛit ɛadad d-le-ktub.* I've read quite a few books. **2.** (sg. also *ɛadăd*) pl. *ɛadad, ʔăɛdad* number *l-ɛadad xemsa ma-ka-iqbel-š l-qesma ɛla žuž.* The number five isn't divisible by two.
ɛadaṛ pl. of *ɛodṛ*
ɛadaw used in the expr. *ɛăyyeṭ be-l-ɛadaw* to call for help
** *l-ɛadaw, a ɛibad ḷḷah!* Help, someone!
ɛadăd same as *ɛadad* 2
ɛadi pl. *-yen* **1.** usual, normal **2.** habitual
ɛadid pl. *-in* numerous, quite a few
ɛadel v.t. **1.** to balance, to put in equilibrium **2.** to be equal or equivalent to
ɛadel a.p. of *ɛdel*
ɛadăm **1.** nothing, nothingness, void **2.** used in cons. with n. of action to negativize (often translatable by "lack of") *ɛadăm ḥtiṛam l-qanun ka-imken iʔeddi le-s-sižn.* Disrespect for the law can lead to prison.
ɛadem a.p. of *ɛdem*
ɛaduw pl. *ʔăɛdaʔ* enemy, adversary
ɛaḍama **1.** enormity, hugeness **2.** s.th. monstrous, huge **3.** grandeur, splendor, glory, majesty, etc. (mountains, person, etc.) **4.** greatness, importance
¶ *waḥed l-ɛaḍama d-* monstrous, enormous, huge *šeft had ṣ-ṣbaḥ waḥed l-ɛaḍama d-waḥed r-rtila.* I saw an enormous spider this morning.
ɛaḍim pl. *-in, ɛiḍam, ɛuḍama* (comp. *ɛḍem*) **1.** magnificent, splendid, excellent **2.** great, huge, enormous **3.** great, eminent, distinguished **4.** (with art.) epithet of God
ɛaḍuḍ used in the expr. *šedd l-ɛaḍuḍ l-* to help (out), to aid (other usage rare)
ɛaf iɛif v.t. to be disgusted with, to not be able to stand, to have revulsion for (s.th., s.o.)
ɛafa v.t. to heal, to restore the health of (subject usually God) *ḷḷah iɛafik!* May God restore you your health!
¶ *ɛafak* **1.** please *ɛṭini šwiya de-l-melḥa ɛafak!* Give me a little salt, please! **2.** expr. of approving admiration *ɛafak a weldi!* Very good, son!
ɛaffak same as *ɛafak,* see *ɛafa*
ɛafiya (usually used in conjunction with *ṣeḥḥa*) health
ɛafya pl. *ɛwafi* (dim. *ɛwifya*) fire
** *l-ɛafya hadi!* **1.** Man, is it hot! **2.** Boy, this is expensive!
ɛager a.p. of *ɛger*
ɛahed v.t. **1.** to promise, to vow to (s.o.) *ɛahedt mṛati baš ma-nxunha-š.* I promised my wife I'd be faithful to her. —*ɛahedt l-xaṭiba dyali b-waḥed l-ḥăfla mezyana.* I've promised my fiancee a nice party. **2.** to make a pact or agreement with
ɛahiṛa pl. *-t* prostitute
ɛaʔila pl. *-t* family

εakes v.t. to oppose, to object to, to be against
εalama pl. *-t* **1.** sign, indication **2.** symptom, indication **3.** signal, sign (gesture, etc.) **4.** sign (road, directions, etc.) **5.** mark (scar, scratch, pencil mark, etc.) **6.** mark, brand (e.g., cattle) **7.** print, track (foot, finger, animal, etc.) **8.** badge, insignia, emblem **9.** symbol
εalaqa pl. *-t* relation, relationship
εalawi pl. *-yen* Alawite, of or pertaining to the Moroccan royal family and dynasty
εali f. *εalya* pl. *εalyen* (comp. *εla*) high *l-urika žbel εali ḥda meṛṛakeš.* Ourika is a high mountain near Marrakesh. —*ṣewtha εali.* She has a high voice. —*fe-l-meġrib taman s-siyaṛat l-ʔamrikiya εali.* In Morocco, the price of American cars is high.
εali **1.** proper m. name **2.** (usually *sidna εali*) the fourth caliph and successor of the Prophet Mohammed (also the latter's son-in-law)
εalăm pl. *εawalim* world
εalem a.p. of *εlem*
εalež v.t. **1.** to take care of the health of (preventively) **2.** to treat, to take care of (s.o. sick)
εam iεum v.i. (v.n. *εum, εuman*) **1.** to swim **2.** to float (in liquid)
εam du. *-ayn, -in* pl. *ʔaεwam, snin, sinin* year
εamaliya (*žiraḥiya*) pl. *-t* (surgical) operation
εamal, εamăl pl. *ʔăεmal* **1.** v.n. of *εmel* **2.** act, action **3.** accomplishment **4.** procedure, course of action **5.** execution, doing **6.** conduct, behavior
¶ *žari bihφ l-εamăl* (to be) in effect, in force, in operation ≠ (e.g., a law)
εamil pl. *εumalaʔ* flunky, "puppet"
εamel v.t. to treat, to deal with, to handle (s.o.) *ka-iεamelni bḥal xah.* He treats me like a brother.
εamel a.p. of *εmel*
εamĭl pl. *εommal* governor (provincial, etc.)
εamm pl. *-in* general (in contrast to specific, etc.)
εamma (the) common people, (the) masses (generally uneducated, illiterate, etc.)
εammi adj. pl. *-yen* n.pl. *εwamm* ignorant, illiterate, uneducated
¶ *l-εammiya* the vernacular, colloquial language or speech (in contrast to the classical)
εameṛ a.p. of *εmeṛ*
εan iεin v.t. (v.n. *muεawana*) to help, to assist, to aid (usually financially)
** *εinna, εăl ḷḷah!* Help us, for the love of God! (expr. of beggars) —*ḷḷah iεin!* Good luck! May God help you!
εanaṣiṛ pl. of *εonṣoṛ*
εanawin pl. of *εonwan*
εaned v.t. **1.** to vie or compete with, to try to outdo (s.o.) **2.** to attempt to overcome the obstinacy or stubbornness of (s.o., donkey, etc.)
εani used in the expr. *be-l-εani* purposely, on purpose
¶ *ma-ši be-l-εani* involuntarily, accidentally
εaq iεiq b- (v.n. *εiqan*) to become aware of, to notice (s.o.) *mnin dexlet m̄m̄u εaqet bih ka-ikmi.* When his mother came in she noticed that he was smoking.
εaqaʔid pl. of *εaqida*
εaqaṛ pl. *-at* building
εaqaṛi pl. *-yen* real estate agent
εaqeb v.t. **1.** to punish, to chastise *εaqbuh εla lli šarek fe-l-muʔamaṛa.* He was punished for taking part in the plot. **2.** to sentence *εaqbuh b-telt snin de-l-ḥăbs.* They sentenced him to three years in prison.
εaqiba pl. *-t, εawaqib* consequence
** *ḷḷah ixerrež l-εaqiba bi-xir.* I hope everything turns out all right.
εaqida pl. *-t, εaqaʔid* **1.** belief, faith, doctrine **2.** school of thought, doctrine
εaqel a.p. of *εqel*
εaṛ pl. (of intensity) *-at* **1.** shame, dishonor, ignominy, opprobrium **2.** protection (heavenly)
** *εaṛ εlik!* Shame on you!
¶ *ana f-εaṛek* (or *ha l-εaṛ*) *ila ma* . . . could or would you please . . . *ana f-εaṛek* (or *ha l-εaṛ*) *ila ma tthelḷa-li fe-d-drari ḥetta neṛžăε.* Would you please watch the children for me until I get back?
¶ *klam l-εaṛ* insulting remarks, insults
εaṛabi pl. *-yen* **1.** Arabic (adj.) **2.** Arab
¶ *l-εaṛabiya* **1.** Arabic (classical language) **2.** royal carriage (horse-drawn)
εaṛaḍ **1.** honor, dignity **2.** virtue (moral)
εaṛafat (f.) (usually *žabăl εaṛafat*) mountain near Mecca where pilgrims (*ḥožžaž*) gather near the end of their pilgrimage, on the 9th of *du-l-ḥižža,* for certain culminating ceremonies called *l-weqfa*
¶ *nhaṛ εaṛafat* day on which the above takes place, 9th of *du-l-ḥižža*
εaṛeḍ v.t. to oppose, to be in opposition to, to object to (s.th., s.o.) *εaṛḍu l-fikra de-z-zwaž dyalu biha.* They objected to the idea of his marrying her.
εarĭf pl. *εuṛafa* kind of representative or spokesman chosen to represent a class in school
εaṣi a.p. of *εṣa yăεṣa* and *εṣa yăεṣi*
εaṣima pl. *-t, εawaṣim* capital *fas hiya l-εaṣima d-diniya de-l-meġṛib.* Fez is the religious capital of Morocco.
εaṣiṛ juice (orange, lemon, etc.)

ɛaṣeṛ (with art.) the afternoon prayer

ɛaš iɛiš v.i. (v.n. *ɛăyš, ɛiš*) to live
 ** *ɛaš l-malīk!* Long live the King! *ɛaš men ṛak!* It's good to see you!—*ɛiš nhaṛ tesmăɛ xbaṛ.* Another day, another dollar. (lit., live a day and learn s.th.; said to acknowledge that another day has gone by)
 ¶ a.p. *ɛayeš* pl. *-in* alive, living

ɛašeq a.p. of *ɛšeq*

ɛašer v.t. (v.n. of *ɛošra*) to associate with (s.o.)

ɛašeṛ tenth (adj.)

ɛašuṛ 1. first month of the Muslim lunar calendar 2. (also *ɛašuṛa*) feast or holiday characterized by paying a tithe to the needy
 ¶ *šayeɛ ɛašuṛ* second month of the Muslim lunar calendar

ɛateb v.t. to scold, to reprimand

ɛateq a.p. of *ɛteq*

ɛaṭifa pl. *ɛawaṭif* sympathetic feeling or sentiment

ɛawalim pl. of *ɛalăm*

ɛawaqib pl. of *ɛaqiba*

ɛawaṣim pl. of *ɛaṣima*

ɛawaṭif pl. of *ɛaṭifa*

ɛawed v.t. 1. to redo, to do over or again 2. to repeat, to say or tell again 3. to tell (a story) 4. used with verbs to denote repetition *ɛawdet basetni.* She kissed me again. —*ma-tɛawed-š tṣifṭu!* Don't send him any more!

ɛawed, ɛawed tani 1. again *ṣbeġha ɛawed tani!* Paint it again! 2. also, too, as well (usually also with *ƶetta*) *ɛawed tani ƶetta huma ɛăndhom had l-muškila.* They also have this problem.

ɛawen v.t. 1. to help, to aid, to assist 2. to rescue, to save

ɛawtani same as *ɛawed, ɛawed tani*

ɛaweṭ v.t. 1. to fix, to arrange, to put in (good or proper) order 2. to improve (e.g., s.o.'s health) 3. to cut, to prune, etc. (grass, trees, etc.)

ɛayel pl. *ɛyal,* f. *ɛayla* pl. *-t* (chiefly Northern Moroccan usage) child

ɛayen v.t. to wait for, to await

ɛayer v.t. to insult, to curse at (s.o.) *bda ka-iɛayerha b-xaha.* He began insulting her concerning her brother.

ɛayeš a.p. of *ɛaš*

ɛazaʔim pl. of *ɛazima*

ɛazba pl. *-t* virgin (often extended to mean young girl)

ɛazima pl. *-t, ɛazaʔim, ɛzayem* hocus pocus, incantation (often used in pl.)

ɛaž ivory

ɛažaʔib pl. of *ɛžuba*

ɛažami pl. *-yen* non-Arab, non-Arabic
 ¶ *t-tarix l-ɛažami* Christian calendar (in contrast to Muslim)

ɛažib pl. *-in* 1. extraordinary, amazing 2. marvelous, excellent 3. strange, unusual, weird 4. mysterious

ɛbana pl. *-t, ɛbayen* blanket (usually handwoven)

ɛbaṛ pl. *-at* (pl. rare) measurement (both dimensional and quantitative) *šnu huwa le-ɛbaṛ d-had ṭ-ṭebḷa?* What are the measurements of this table?

ɛbayen pl. of *ɛbana*

ɛăbba v.t. to take (s.th. or s.o. somewhere) *ɛăbbi xak mɛak!* Take your brother with you!
 ¶ *ɛăbba u-žab* to be getting old or along in years
 ** *ma-ɛăbba ma-žab.* He couldn't care less.

ɛăbbad adj. pl. *-in* n.pl. *-a* ag. adj. and n. of *ɛbed*
 ¶ *ɛăbbad š-šems* litmus paper (for testing acidity)

ɛăbbaṛ pl. *-a* weigher, one whose occupation is weighing goods

ɛăbbeṛ ɛla to express, to tell of (one's feelings, ideas, happiness, etc.)

ɛăbbes (usually used in the expr. *ɛăbbes wežhuφ*) to frown

ɛăbbu 1. proper m. name 2. (also *ɛăbbu we-r-riƶ* or *ɛăbbu u-giliz*) nonsense, "bull" 3. half-heartedness *l-mežhud dyalu ġir l-ɛăbbu.* His efforts are only half-hearted.

ɛbed v.t. (v.n. *ɛibada*) to worship (God, woman, money, etc.)

ɛăbd 1. pl. *ɛbid* (negro) slave, bond servant, bondman (increasing usage as "negro" in general) 2. pl. *ɛibad* man, creature of God
 ¶ *ɛibad ḷḷah* people (usually used vocatively with *ya*)

ɛbid pl. of *ɛăbd* 1

ɛbiṛ v.n. of *ɛbeṛ*

ɛbeṛ v.t. (v.n. *ɛbiṛ*) 1. to weigh (s.th., s.o.) 2. to measure
 ¶ *ɛbeṛ ɛla* to play a dirty trick on

ɛăbṛa pl. *-t* 1. n.i. of *ɛbeṛ* 2. dirty trick

ɛebrani pl. *-yen* Hebrew

ɛebraniya (with art.) Hebrew (language)

ɛda yăɛdi v.t. 1. to contaminate, to infect (s.o.) (subject is usually the disease) 2. to affect adversely, to corrupt (as a bad habit may a person)

ʔăɛdaʔ pl. of *ɛaduw*

ɛdab torture, torment, suffering

ʔăɛdad pl. of *ɛadad* 2

ɛdala 1. v.n. of *ɛdel* 2. same as *ɛădl* 2

ɛdam pl. of *ɛdim*

ɛdawa v.n. of *ɛada*

ɛdayez pl. of *ɛduza* (same as *ɛguza*)

ɛădd v.t. (v.n. *ɛăddan*) 1. to count *ɛăddu*

ẓetta le-mya! Count to a hundred! 2. to consider, to think of *kont dima ka-nƐǎddha ᵉefḍel ṣaḍiqa.* I always considered her my best friend.

¶ Ɛǎdd Ɛla to count on, to rely on

Ɛǎdda v.i. 1. to do the best one can with what one has, to get along on what one has, to manage 2. to pass on, to die

¶ Ɛǎdda b- to make do with, to get along on (s.th.) (until s.th. better comes) *ġad-nƐǎddiw be-lli kayen Ɛla-ma iẓellu le-ẓwanet.* We'll get along on what there is until the stores open.

Ɛedda 1. same as Ɛidda 2. allowed period of time, time-limit

Ɛǎdda pl. -t 1. arms, weapons 2. gear, equipment

Ɛǎddad pl. -a 1. counter, counting machine, meter 2. stop-watch

Ɛǎddan v.n. of Ɛǎdd

Ɛǎddawi pl. -yen (adj.) ordinary, nothing special

Ɛǎddeb v.t. 1. to torture, to torment, to make suffer (physically, mentally, spiritually) 2. to treat badly, to mistreat 3. to weary, to cause to become exhausted

Ɛǎdded same as Ɛǎdd

Ɛǎddel v.t. 1. to balance, to equilibrate (balance system) 2. to fix, to put in order, to set right, to rectify 3. to solve, to settle (problem, difficulty, etc.) 4. to improve, to better 5. to do (less common than Ɛmel or dar)

Ɛdid same as Ɛadid

Ɛdim pl. -in, Ɛdam 1. poor, indigent, needy 2. helpless (due either to lack of financial means or to poor health)

Ɛdiṛ v.n. of Ɛdeṛ

Ɛdel v.i. (v.n. Ɛǎdl, Ɛdala) to be just, fair, impartial

¶ Ɛdel Ɛla to change one's mind about, to decide against (doing s.th.)

¶ a.p. Ɛadel pl. Ɛdul notary (public)

Ɛǎdl 1. v.n. of Ɛdel 2. justice, fairness, impartiality

Ɛǎdli pl. -yen 1. of or pertaining to a notary, notarial 2. judicial, judiciary

Ɛdem (v.n. ᵉiƐdam) 1. v.t. to execute, to put to death 2. v.i. to go bankrupt, to go broke, to be (financially) ruined 3. v.i. to become seriously ill, to be on the verge of dying (usually of an aging person)

¶ a.p. Ɛadem pl. -in 1. broke, penniless, out of funds 2. invalid, laid up

Ɛdeṛ v.t. (v.n. Ɛdiṛ) to excuse, to not blame (s.o.)

Ɛoḍṛ pl. Ɛadaṛ excuse, justification

** me-Ɛdeṛhom (or men Ɛdeṛhom) ma-ttafqu-š mƐaha. It's no wonder they didn't agree with her. —šeft xak fe-ṭ-ṭriq, ᵉa, xtek, m-Ɛǎdri (or men Ɛǎdri). On the

way over, I saw your brother . . . I mean your sister.

Ɛdes n.u. Ɛǎdsa lentil(s)

Ɛǎdsi pl. -yen (adj.) kind of medium brown (theoretically the color of lentils)

Ɛdu pl. Ɛǎdyan same as Ɛaduw

Ɛdul pl. of Ɛadel (a.p. of Ɛdel)

Ɛduza pl. Ɛdayez same as Ɛguza

Ɛǎdyan pl. of Ɛdu (same as Ɛaduw)

Ɛdam pl. of Ɛdem

Ɛǎḍḍ v.t. (v.n. Ɛǎḍḍan) 1. to bite (with the mouth) 2. to take a bite of, or out of 3. to sting (bee, scorpion, etc.)

Ɛǎḍḍa pl. -t 1. n.i. of Ɛǎḍḍ 2. bite (of food, of dog, etc.) 3. sting (of bee, ant, etc.)

Ɛǎḍḍaḍ adj. pl. -in n.pl. -a 1. ag. adj. and ag. n. of Ɛǎḍḍ 2. given to biting (e.g., a certain dog, snapping turtle)

Ɛǎḍḍaḍa pl. -t clothespin

Ɛǎḍḍan v.n. of Ɛǎḍḍ

Ɛǎḍḍed v.t. to back, to support, to side with

Ɛǎḍḍem v.t. to build up, to glorify, to praise, to laud

Ɛḍim same as Ɛaḍim

Ɛḍem comp. of Ɛaḍim

Ɛḍem pl. Ɛḍam, Ɛḍuma 1. bone 2. seed, pit, stone (of fruit, etc.)

** Ɛǎḍmuᵠ faxeṛ He's bony. —ma-bqaw fih ġir le-Ɛḍam. He's lost all his strength and energy.

¶ mṛiḍ b-le-Ɛḍam epileptic

¶ taẓ b-le-Ɛḍam to have or suffer an epileptic fit or attack

¶ ṭiyyẓuhᵠ le-Ɛḍam to have an epileptic fit ≠

Ɛḍuma pl. of Ɛḍem

Ɛfa yǎƐfi v.t. (v.n. Ɛǎfyan, Ɛfu) to release, to let go (from job, responsibility, etc.)

Ɛfa yǎƐfu (pl. yǎƐfiw) Ɛla (v.n. Ɛǎfw, Ɛfu) to pardon, to give a pardon to

¶ Ɛfa Ɛlihᵠ ḷḷah men to (manage to) give up ≠, to abandon ≠, to "kick" ≠ (bad habit, sinful practice, etc.) Ɛfa Ɛlihom ḷḷah men š-šṛab. They've managed to give up drinking.

Ɛfaret pl. of Ɛǎfrit

Ɛǎff used in the expr. lli ġleb iƐǎff. Let the victor be merciful (i.e., once the enemy is beaten, don't rub his nose in the dirt).

Ɛǎffa, Ɛeffa 1. modesty (both in dress and in contrast to conceit) 2. virtuousness, uprightness 3. restraint, continence

¶ qlil l-Ɛǎffa 1. inconsiderate 2. immodest

¶ qellt l-Ɛǎffa lack of consideration (for others)

Ɛǎffen v.t. (v.n. Ɛfuniya) to dirty, to get filthy (with specific implications of some sort of natural filth, e.g., excrement, slaver, vomit, rotting carcass, etc.)

Ɛǎffeṛ v.i. to be or act snobbish, to have

delusions of being better than others (may imply a desire to be coaxed into things, i.e. a sort of false snobbery)

عfis v.n. of *عfes*

عfen pl. (of intensity) *عfunat* filthiness, repulsive or sickening filth (connotes strong revulsion)

عăfrit pl. *عfaret* **1.** devil, demon **2.** (also adj.) brilliant, exceptional, "whiz" **3.** (also adj.) charmingly mischievous, devilish

عfes عla (v.n. *عfis*) to step on *عfes عla ẓenṭiṭ l-qeṭṭa u-hiya txebšu.* He stepped on the cat's tail and it scratched him.

عăfsa pl. *-t* n.i. of *عfes*

عfeṭ عla same as *عfes عla*

عăfṭa pl. *-t* same as *عăfsa*

عfu v.n. of *عfa*

** *l-yum bdu عfu, ġedda qebṭu u-kettfu.* This time excuse him, next time bruise him.

عfunat pl. of *عfen*

عfuniya v.n. of *عăffen*

عăfw v.n. of *عfa yăعfu*

عăfyan v.n. of *عfa yăعfi*

عăfyun opium

عgabi pl. of *عăgba*

عgadi pl. of *عogda* (same as *عoqda*)

عgaged pl. of *عăggad*

عgaṛeb pl. of *عăgṛeb* (same as *عăqṛeb*)

عgayez pl. of *عguz* and *عguza*

عgeb v.i. (primarily country usage; v.n. *عgib*) to return (go or come back)

عăgba pl. *-t, عgabi* hill, slope, incline, grade *f-fas kayen bezzaf d-le-عgabi.* There are a lot of hills (grades) in Fez. —*ḥḍi ṛaṣek mnin tkun nazel fe-l-عăgba!* Be careful when you go down the hill!

عogda same as *عoqda*

عăggad pl. *عgaged* bat, club

عăgged same as *عăqqed*

عăggez v.t. **1.** to discourage, to dissuade (s.o.) **2.** to cause or inspire (s.o.) to become lax or lazy

عgib v.n. of *عgeb*

عgig same as *عqiq*

عgir v.n. of *عger*

عgiṛ v.n. of *عgeṛ*

عger v.i. (v.n. *عgir*) to become sterile (land, person, animal)

¶ a.p. *عager* pl. *-in* sterile

عger sterility (land, person, animal)

عgeṛ v.t. (country usage; v.n. *عgiṛ*) to hurt, to cause pain to (s.o.)

عăgṛeb pl. *عgaṛeb* same as *عăqṛeb*

عguz pl. *عgayez* old man

عguza pl. *-t, عgayez* **1.** old woman **2.** mother-in-law

عgez v.i. (v.n. *عgez*) **1.** to get or become lazy **2.** to become dissuaded, to decide against doing s.th. (usually because it is either futile or easier some other way) *عgezt neṛžăع عla režli u-xdit ṭ-ṭubis.* I decided against coming back on foot, so I took the bus. **3.** to lie dormant (e.g., seeds, certain diseases)

¶ *عgez عla* to decide against (s.th.) *f-ʔaxir daqiqa عgezna عăl ṣ-ṣfeṛ.* At the last minute we decided against the trip (too much trouble).

عgez **1.** v.n. of *عgez* **2.** laziness

** *llah yăعṭik le-عgez!* said reproachfully to s.o. who is apparently too lazy to do some particular thing

عăgzan pl. *-in* **1.** lazy, indolent **2.** tired, fatigued

عăhd pl. *عuhud* **1.** promise, vow **2.** time, period, epoch

** *عăhdi bih l-ʔusbuع lli daz.* Last week was the last time I saw him.

¶ *عăhduϕ b-* (s.o.) . . . to think (usually past tense) that (s.o.) . . . ≠ *عăhdi bik dki, s-saعa nta men ʔekbeṛ l-bulada.* I thought you were smart, but you're really very stupid.

عib pl. *عyub, عuyub* **1.** shameful act or thing, improper act or thing **2.** vice, degrading or vicious habit **3.** defect, s.th. wrong or defective **4.** defect, infirmity (physiological)

** *عib عlik!* Shame on you!

¶ *عib عlihϕ* . . . he shouldn't or shouldn't have ≠ . . . *عib عlik tعădda عliha!* You shouldn't have hurt her!

عibad pl. of *عăbd* 2

عibada **1.** v.n. of *عbed* **2.** worship

¶ *عibadăt l-ʔaṣnam* idolatry, idol worship

عibaṛa pl. *-t* **1.** expression, term *pripellu عibaṛa mestăعmla kteṛ fe-ṛ-ṛbaṭ.* "*pripellu*" is an expression used mostly in Rabat. **2.** indication, sign **3.** butt of joking or jest (person)

¶ *b-عibaṛa ẍṛa* . . . in other words . . .

عid pl. *عyad* **1.** feast, celebration, (traditional) holiday **2.** anniversary (as observed by a particular country, group, etc.)

¶ *l-عid le-kbir* Greater Bairam, feast or celebration on the tenth of *du l-ḥižža* characterized by the sacrifice of a lamb

¶ *l-عid ṣ-ṣġiṛ* Lesser Bairam, feast or celebration on the first of *šuwwal* when the fast of Ramadan is broken, characterized by the giving of alms, usually wheat, to the poor

¶ *عid l-mewlid* (or *l-mewlud, l-milud*) birthday of the Prophet Mohammed

عidan pl. of *عud*

عidda number, large number, quite a few *عăndna عidda de-l-mašakil.* We have a number of problems.

عiḍam pl. of *عaḍim*

عifa pl. *-t* (wide adj. usage) **1.** n.i. of *عaf* **2.** repugnant or disgusting act or thing

3. filth, filthiness (also moral) *had l-ʔinsan hada ﻉifa, ḥetta waḥed ma-ka-iḥămlu.* This guy is absolutely filthy; no one can stand him.

ﻉ*ilm* **1.** v.n. of ﻉ*lem* **2.** pl. ﻉ*ulum* knowledge **3.** science **4.** (often pl.) used in cons. with various words to designate certain sciences e.g. ﻉ*ilm n-nabat* botany, ﻉ*ilm n-nužum* astronomy

ﻉ*imaṛa* pl. *-t* building

ﻉ*in* same as ﻉ*ăyn*

ﻉ*inaya* n.i. and v.n. of ﻉ*na yă*ﻉ*na*

ﻉ*ineb* n.u. ﻉ*inba* grape

ﻉ*iqan* v.n. of ﻉ*aq*

ﻉ*isawa* pl. of ﻉ*isawi*

¶ ﻉ*isawa ġidawa* meal consisting of meat, onions, raisins, cinnamon, prepared during *l-*ﻉ*id le-kbir* (primarily for the children)

ﻉ*isawi* adj. pl. *-yen* n.pl. ﻉ*isawa* banned fraternity characterized by certain savage rites

ﻉ*iṣyan* **1.** v.n. of ﻉ*ṣa yă*ﻉ*ṣi* **2.** disobedience, insubordination

ﻉ*iš* v.n. of ﻉ*aš*

ﻉ*iša* pl. *-t* **1.** n.i. of ﻉ*aš* **2.** life *ka-n*ﻉ*iš* ﻉ*iša mezyana.* I live a good life. **3.** way of life, manner of living

ﻉ*iwăḍ* (with *-ma* before v.; often *f-*ﻉ*iwăḍ;* ﻉ*ăwḍ* used with pron. endings) **1.** in place of, instead of *sir f-*ﻉ*ăwḍi!* Go in my place! —ﻉ*ṭani* ﻉ*ăšṛa* ﻉ*iwăḍ žuž.* He gave me ten instead of two. —ﻉ*iwăḍ le-ḥmaṛ ka-nḍenn ḥsen-li ila rkebt* ﻉ*ăl l-*ﻉ*ăwd.* Instead of the donkey, I think I'd better ride the horse. —ﻉ*iwăḍ-ma nemši l-tunes, žit l-l-meġṛib.* Instead of going to Tunisia, I came to Morocco. —ﻉ*iwăḍ-ma tekteb be-qlam ḥmeṛ,* ﻉ*laš ma-tekteb-š b-le-kḥăl?* Instead of writing with a red pencil, why don't you write with a black one? **2.** in exchange for

ﻉ*iweṛ* pl. of ﻉ*weṛ*

ﻉ*iwež* pl. of ﻉ*wež*

ﻉ*izza* **1.** v.n. of ﻉ*ăzz* **2.** glory

ﻉ*kakeṛ* pl. of ﻉ*ăkkaṛ*

ﻉ*kakez* pl. of ﻉ*okkaz*

ﻉ*ăkkaṛ* pl. ﻉ*kakeṛ* lipstick

ﻉ*okkaz* pl. ﻉ*kakez* **1.** cane, walking stick, **2.** crutch

ﻉ*ăkkel* v.t. **1.** to trip (s.o.) **2.** to complicate, to make (more) complicated **3.** to leave or put in a difficult or embarrassing position, to leave in the lurch

ﻉ*ăkkeṛ* v.i. **1.** to put lipstick or rouge on **2.** v.t. to cloud, to muddy (usually water) **3.** v.t. to trouble, to disturb (water, relationship between two persons)

ﻉ*ăkkez* v.i. to walk with a cane or crutches

ﻉ*keṛ* same as ﻉ*ăkkaṛ*

ﻉ*ăkri* pl. *-yen* kind of slightly purplish red

ﻉ*ăks* **1.** opposite, contrary *l-*ﻉ*ăks dyal l-kasal huwa l-ʔižtihad.* The opposite of laziness is industriousness. **2.** contrary to ﻉ*ăks ma qal, . . .* Contrary to what he said, . . .

¶ *be-l-*ﻉ*ăks* **1.** on the contrary **2.** backwards, in reverse manner

¶ *u-be-l-*ﻉ*ăks* (and) vice-versa

ﻉ*la* (ﻉ*ăl* before article, sometimes ﻉ*le-* before forms of the article other than *l-, le-;* ﻉ*li-* before pronoun suffixes) **1.** upon, on, on top of ﻉ*mel režlih* ﻉ*ăl ṭ-ṭabla.* He put his feet on the table. —*senned* ﻉ*ăl l-bab.* He leaned on the door. —*ḍaṛ šwiya be-š-šežṛa u-zad* ﻉ*la ṭriqu.* He circled the tree a little (while), then continued on his way. —*dfaw ḍ-ḍuw* ﻉ*lina.* They turned out the light on us. —*le-ḥsab* ﻉ*liya.* The check's on me. (I'll pay the check.) **2.** over *neqqez* ﻉ*ăl l-ḥiṭ.* He jumped over the wall. **3.** by, through *qṣem* ﻉ*ăšṛa* ﻉ*la žuž.* Divide ten by two. —*žit* ﻉ*ăl ṭ-ṭriq le-qṣiṛa.* I came by the shortest way. —*lli bġa iṣuq men l-meġṛib le-fṛanṣa ka-ixeṣṣu iduz* ﻉ*la ṣbanya.* Whoever wants to drive from Morocco to France must pass through Spain. **4.** along *bqina ġadyin* ﻉ*ăl l-wad l-wad ḥetta l-le-bḥăṛ.* We walked along the river as far as the sea. **5.** to, at *kdeb* ﻉ*ăl l-ʔustad.* He lied to the professor. —*ka-nfeḍḍel t-tmeṛ* ﻉ*ăl le-*ﻉ*sel.* I prefer dates to honey.—*dexlu l-l-mekteb* ﻉ*ăl t-tlata.* They entered the office at three o'clock. —*kollhom klaw* ﻉ*la ṭebla weḥda.* They all ate at the same table. **6.** from *lhitu* ﻉ*la šoġlu.* I distracted him from his work. —ﻉ*la had n-namudaž imken-lek txeyyeṭ bezzaf d-le-ksawi.* From this pattern you can sew several dresses. —*nzel* ﻉ*ăl l-*ﻉ*ăwd.* He got down from the horse. **7.** away from *qul-lu iḍuwweṛ wežhu* ﻉ*liya.* Tell him to turn his face away from me. —*ma-bġa-š imši* ﻉ*lina.* He doesn't want to go away from us. **8.** about, concerning *ddakeṛt m*ﻉ*ah* ﻉ*ăl š-šak lli ṣifeṭ lihom.* I talked to him about the check he sent them. **9.** for —*huwa msemmi* ﻉ*la žeddu.* He's named for his grandfather. **10.** out of (with numbers) *l-ʔustad de-l-fṛanṣiya* ﻉ*ṭaha tsă*ﻉ*ṭaš* ﻉ*la* ﻉ*ešrin fe-t-teṛžama.* The French teacher gave her 19 out 20 in translation. **11.** between, among *qṣem had d-dellaḥa* ﻉ*la had l-xemsa de-n-nas.* Divide this watermelon among these five people. **12.** in, into *qṣem had-l-weṛqa* ﻉ*la setta.* Divide this sheet of paper in six. **13.** used with an adj. to form the comp. *le-qlam le-zṛeq ṭwil* ﻉ*ăl le-ḥmeṛ.* The blue pen is longer than the red one. **14.** used with adj. to indicate "too (s.th.) for (s.o.)" —*huwa qṣiṛ* ﻉ*liha.* He's too short for her.

—*had l-kebbuṭ kbir ʕliya.* This jacket is (too) big for me. —*had l-xedma bezzaf ʕlik.* This work is too much for you.

¶ *ma-ʕlihφ-š* not to matter (to s.o.) *ma-ʕliya-š.* It doesn't matter to me.

** *ma-ʕlik-š.* Never mind.

¶ *ʕla-ma* 1. according to *ʕla-ma qal ṛ-ṛadyu ġad-isxon l-ḥal.* According to what the radio said, the weather's going to get hot. —*ʕla-ma smeʕt, baqi mṛiḍ.* According to what I heard, he's still sick. 2. while, until (in waiting for) *ġir ṣbeṛ ši-šwiya ʕla-ma nnežžel š-šanṭa.* Just wait a minute while I bring the suitcase down.

¶ *ʕla qibal* 1. because, because of *ma-mken-lhom-š ixoržu ʕla qibal š-šta kanet ka-ṭṭiḥ bezzaf.* They couldn't leave because it was raining very hard. —*ʕla qibali xellaha temši mʕa xutha.* Because of me (my influence) he let her go with her brothers. 2. about *tkellemt mʕaha ʕla qibal l-ḥăfla dyal nhaṛ ž-žemʕa.* I talked to her about Friday's party.

¶ *ʕlihφ l-luma* to be s.o.'s fault ≠

ʕla comp. of *ʕali*

ʕlah same as *ʕlaš*

ʕlalef pl. of *ʕăllafa*

ʕlaleq pl. of *ʕăllaqa*

ʕlam pl. *-at* flag, banner, bunting

¶ *weqt le-ʕlam* from 10 a.m. to 12:00 noon, when the white flag is raised over the mosque as a first call to prayer

ʔăʕlam pl. of *ʕălăm*

ʕlaš why *ʕlaš ġadi u-mxellini weḥdi?* Why are you going away and leaving me alone? *tzehzitu fe-l-xedma, ha ʕlaš ma-feḍḍituha bekri.* You were too slow with your work; that's why you didn't finish it on time.

***ma-kayen ʕlaš.* Never mind. It's not worth the trouble.

ʕla wedd see *wedd*

ʕlayel pl. of *ʕălla*

ʕlayen, ʕlayen-ma 1. nearly, almost *feḍḍiti šoġlek? ʕlayen!* Have you finished your work? Almost! —*ʕlayen teqfel ʕešrin ʕam.* She's nearly twenty years old. 2. about to, on the verge of *kont ʕlayen-ma nexṛož.* I was about to leave. —*mṛeḍ ḥetta ʕlayen imut.* He got so sick he was on the verge of dying.

ʕlef v.i. to eat (said of animals)

ʕălf feed, food (esp. for livestock)

ʕălk, ʕlek 1. resin 2. glue

¶ *ʕălk ṭ-ṭelḥ* gum arabic

ʕălla 1. v.t. to raise, to make higher *ʕăllaw l-ḥiṭ be-tlata de-l-miter.* They made the wall three meters higher. —*ʕăllat yeddiha baš tšiyyer-lu.* She raised her hand to signal him. 2. v.t. to throw (into the air) *ʕălla l-kuṛa le-s-sma.* He threw the ball into the air. 3. v.i. to go up (higher), to rise (in altitude) *ṭ-ṭiyaṛa ʕăllat baš texrož men s-sḥab.* The airplane went up higher to get out of the clouds.

¶ *ʕălla . . . ʕla* to put (s.th.) up out of reach of (s.o.) *ʕăllat d-dwa ʕăl d-drari baš ma-yakluh-š.* She put the medicine up out of reach of the children so they wouldn't eat it.

ʕălla pl. *-t, ʕlayel* fault, defect (in a person) *huwa ṛažel mezyan, mʕa l-ʔasaf fih ʕălla: keddab.* He's a good man, but unfortunately he has a fault: he's a liar.

¶ *la-ʕălla wa-ʕasa* 1. hoping, in the hope that *qeddmet ṭ-ṭalab la-ʕălla wa-ʕasa iqebluha.* She put in a request in the hope that she would be accepted. 2. perhaps *ʕăyyeṭ-lu la-ʕălla wa-ʕasa ikun ṛžăʕ.* Call him, perhaps he's back.

ʕăllafa pl. *-t, ʕlalef* 1. manger, feeding trough 2. feed-bag (e.g. for horses)

ʕăllali used in the expr. *be-l-ʕăllali* publicly, openly, overtly

ʕăllama pl. *-t* master (of one's art or field, usually famous)

ʕăllaqa pl. *-t, ʕlaleq* 1. (clothes) hanger 2. hat and coat tree 3. hook (clothes, crane, etc.) 4. sling (for broken arm)

ʕăllef v.t. 1. to feed (cows, sheep, horses, etc.) 2. to fatten (animals for slaughtering)

ʕăllek v.t. to make or cause to be chewy (e.g., in making candy)

¶ part. *mʕăllek* pl. *-in* gooey, chewy (e.g., caramel candy)

ʕăllem v.t. 1. to teach, to instruct (in) *škun lli ʕăllmek dak š-ši?* Who taught you that? 2. to mark the limits or boundaries of (field, yard, etc.) 3. to mark, to put a mark on (including branding, stamping, etc.) 4. to sign, to put one's signature on

ʕălleq v.t. 1. to hang (up) (clothes, tools, curtains, etc.) 2. to hang (s.o.)

¶ *ʕălleq kraʕuφ* (or *režluφ*) to die, to "kick the bucket"

ʕlem (v.n. *ʕilm*) 1. v.i. to find out, to be informed *ʕlem belli bbah daxel men ṣ-ṣfeṛ.* He found out his father was returning from his trip. —*kif-aš ʕlemti ʕăl l-ḥăfla?* How did you find out about the party? 2. v.t. to inform, to let know

** *ḷḷahu ʔăʕlem!* God only knows!

¶ *ʕlem b-* to inform on, to tattle on (s.o.)

¶ a.p. *ʕalem* pl. *ʕulama* 1. scientist (including mathematicians) 2. official expert on Islamic law

** *ḷḷah ʕalem!* God only knows!

ʕlem, ʔăʕlem comp. of *ʕalem* (a.p. of *ʕlem*) *ana ʕlem mennek.* I know more than you do.

ʕălăm pl. *ʔăʕlam* flag, banner, standard
ʕălg, ʕălq n.u. *-a* 1. leech 2. persistently annoying person, one who is always hanging around bothering s.o.
ʕlu (no pl.) height, altitude
ʕma yăʕma v.i. (v.n. *ʕma, ʕmiya*) to go blind, to be blinded
ʕma yăʕmi v.t. (v.n. *ʕma, ʕmiya*) to blind (s.o.)
** *ʕmah ḷḷah!* said of s.o. who has done s.th. very stupid, but should have known better
ʕma (m.) 1. v.n. of *ʕma* 2. blindness 3. f. *ʕămya* pl. *ʕămyen, ʕumi* blind, sightless
¶ p.p. *măʕmi* pl. *-yen* unable to understand, dense
ʔăʕmal pl. of *ʕamal, ʕamăl*
ʕmam pl. of *ʕămm*
ʕmama pl. *-t, ʕmayem* turban
ʕmaṛa pl. *-t, ʕmayeṛ* 1. slug, ball (of bullet) 2. bullet, cartridge, shell (also the empty casing) 3. shot (of gun) *smăʕt tlata d-le-ʕmayeṛ.* I heard three shots. 4. content(s) (of a container)
¶ *ʕmaṛa d-atay* tray with all the accessories necessary for serving tea
¶ *ʕmaṛa de-l-musem* fair, exposition
ʕmaš matter, rheum (of the eye)
ʕmayel pl. of *ʕămla*
ʕmayem pl. of *ʕmama*
ʕmayeṛ pl. of *ʕmaṛa*
ʕmed, ʕămdan pl. of *ʕmud*
ʕămdăn on purpose, intentionally
ʕmiṛ v.n. of *ʕmeṛ*
ʕmiya v.n. of *ʕma*
ʕmel v.t. (v.n. *ʕamăl, ʕamal*) 1. to do, to perform *ʕlaš ʕmeltiha?* Why did you do it? —*waš ʕmelti l-xedma dyalek wella ma-zal?* Have you done your work yet? 2. to make *mn-aš ʕmelti had ṣ-ṣenduq?* What did you make this box out of? —*baṛaka ma-tăʕmel ṣ-ṣdaʕ!* Stop making so much noise! —*wladek daymen ka-iʕămlu-li l-mašakil.* Your children are always making a lot of problems for me. 3. to compose (music, poetry) 4. to organize, to set up 5. to put, to place *ʕmel le-ktub f-le-mžeṛ dyalek!* Put the books in your drawer!
** *ma-tăʕmel-š ʕlih!* Don't pay any attention to him!
¶ *ʕmel b-* to take into consideration, to consider (what s.o. says, advises, etc.) *ʕmel be-klami* (or *be-lli qolt-lek*)! Consider what I told you!
¶ *ʕmel be-ḥsab* to consider, to have some consideration for, to think of *xeṣṣna nʕămlu be-ḥsab ž-žiran.* We've got to have some consideration for our neighbors.
¶ *ʕmelha b-* to put one over on, to deceive
¶ *ʕmel mʕa* to agree with, to make an agreement with *ʕmelt mʕaha baš ntlaqaw fe-s-setta.* I agree with her that we would meet at six.
¶ *ʕmel xaṭeṛ* to please *mšit mʕahom ġiṛ baš năʕmel xaṭeṛ ḅḅa.* I went with them just to please my father.
¶ *ʕmel xaṭṛuᵠ* to be patient, to have patience (usually impv.)
¶ *ʕmel ʕăqluᵠ* to behave, to act properly
¶ a.p. *ʕamel* pl. *ʕommal* worker, laborer
** *kif ʕamla?* How is it (or she)? —*had le-byut ʕamlin bḥal le-bnayeq.* These rooms look like prison cells.
¶ *ʕid l-ʕommal, ʕid š-šoġl* Labor Day (on first of May)
ʕămla pl. *ʕmayel* (usu. used in pl.) bad deed, piece of roguery
¶ *ʕmayel š-šiṭan* mischief, mischievousness
ʕămm pl. *ʕmam* uncle (paternal)
¶ *weld* (or *bent*) *ʕămmuᵠ* 1. (one's) m. (or f.) cousin (i.e., son or daughter of a paternal uncle) 2. s.o. from the same country, compatriot
¶ *ʕămmi l-ḥažž* polite title used in addressing a *ḥažž* (extended to any older man, often a stranger)
ʕămma pl. *-t* aunt (paternal)
¶ *ʕămmti l-ḥažža* f. of *ʕămmi l-ḥažž* (see *ʕămm*)
ʕămmal adj. pl. *-in* n.pl. *-a* one given to committing *ʕmayel* (see *ʕămla*)
ʕommal 1. pl. of *ʕamil* 2. pl. of *ʕamel* (a.p. of *ʕmel*)
ʕămmaṛ pl. *-a* 1. one whose occupation is stuffing mattresses 2. one who keeps the water buckets full for the bathers at a steambath
¶ *ʕămmaṛ s-swarež* boaster, braggart
ʕămmariya pl. *-t* kind of covered seat carried on the back of a camel
ʕămmem 1. v.t. and v.i. to generalize (a fact, etc.) 2. v.i. to cover one's head with a turban
ʕămmeṛ v.t. 1. to fill (up) *ʕămmeṛ l-gerba be-l-ma!* Fill the goatskin with water! 2. to fill out (forms, clothes) 3. to load (guns, truck, etc.) 4. to wind (clock, etc.) 5. to open, to start (shop, store as a business) 6. v.i. to live long, to have a full life
** *ḷḷah iʕămmeṛha ḍaṛ.* expr. of high praise (of one's greatness, magnanimity, etc.)
ʕămmeṛ (used in cons. with n. or with pron. endings; does not admit *-ši* or *-š* of negation) ever, (with *ma-* or with negative v.

or both) never, not ever *waš ʕămmeṛha xedmet ʕănd ši-ʕădd?* Has she ever worked for anyone? (i.e., in their house as a maid) *ma-ʕămmeṛni* (or *ma-ʕămmṛi*) *šefthom.* I've never seen them. —*ʕămmṛu ma-baqi itxaṣem mʕak.* He'll never quarrel with you any more. —*ʕămmeṛ ḅḅa* (or *ḅḅa ʕămmṛu*) *ma-ka-išṛeb.* My father never drinks.

ʕmeṛ v.i. (v.n. *ʕmiṛ*) to fill (up), to become full or filled up *l-bit ʕmeṛ be-n-nas băʕda.* The room has already filled up with people.

¶ *ʕmeṛ le-bʕăṛ* to be high tide

¶ a.p. *ʕameṛ* pl. *-in* **1.** full **2.** high (tide) **3.** taken, occupied (seat, etc.)

ʕmeṛ, ʕomṛ **1.** life, lifetime **2.** age *šʕal f-ʕomṛek?* What's your age? How old are you?

ʕomṛa (no pl.) visit made to a certain chosen holy place during the pilgrimage in Mecca

¶ *ˀedda l-ʕomṛa* to make or accomplish the *ʕomṛa*

ʕmeš f. *ʕămša* pl. *ʕumeš* half-blind, afflicted with poor eyesight (usually affected with rheum)

ʕmud pl. *ʕmed, ʕămdan* **1.** stick, rod (not necessarily wooden) **2.** stake, peg **3.** pole, post (fence, for pole-vaulting, etc.)

ʕămya f. of *ʕma*

ʕna yăʕna b- (v.n. *ʕinaya*) to take care of, to treat with care

ʕna yăʕni (v.n. *măʕna*) to mean *š-ka-tăʕni?* What do you mean? —*had l-kelma ma-ka-tăʕni-š dak š-ši.* This word doesn't mean that.

¶ *yăʕni, . . .* that is, . . .; in other words, . . .

ʕnabeb pl. of *ʕănbub*

ʕnabeṛ pl. of *ʕănbeṛ*

ʕnad same as *mʕanda*

ʕnageṛ pl. of *ʕăngṛa*

ʕnaq pl. of *ʕonq, ʕănq*

ʕnaqed pl. of *ʕănqud*

ʕneb n.u. *ʕănba* same as *ʕineb*

ʕănbeṛ pl. *ʕnabeṛ* **1.** ambergris (pl. for intensity) **2.** dry dock, (shipbuilding) stocks

ʕănbub pl. *ʕnabeb* **1.** faucet, tap **2.** spout (e.g., of teakettle)

ʕănd **1.** under, with *ka-neqṛa ʕănd d-doktur le-ʕḅaḅi.* I'm studying under Doctor Lehbabi. **2.** at the place or house of *aži l-ʕăndi had l-lila!* Come over to my place tonight! —*l-bareʕ tʕăššina ʕănd bṛahim.* We ate supper at Abraham's (place) yesterday. **3.** near, close to, beside, by *waqfa ʕănd š-šeṛžem.* She's standing by the window. **4.** at (time) *ġad-nemšiw ʕănd l-ʕăšṛa.* We're going to go at ten. **5.** among, in the eyes of, as far as . . . is (are) concerned *s-slam de-l-yeddin ʕănd l-ˀamirikiyen ma-ʕăndu ˀahemmiya kbira.* As far as Americans are concerned, shaking hands isn't too important. —*had š-ši ʕăndi kif walu.* I couldn't care less. That doesn't make any difference to me. —*aš ʕăndi fih?* What do I care? What's it to me?

¶ *men ʕănd* from (derivation, origination) *had r-risala men ʕănd ḅḅak.* This letter is from your father.

¶ *ʕănduᶲ* to have ≠ *ʕăndna tlata de-l-xut.* We have three brothers. —*ḅḅa ʕăndu siyaṛa ždida.* My father has a new car.

ʕăndak watch out (for), be careful (of) *ʕăndak s-siyaṛa!* Watch out for the car! —*ʕăndak tqul-lha had š-ši!* You'd better not tell her this! Be careful you don't tell her this!

ʕănfež v.t. to squash, to mash (s.th. squashy, usually inadvertently)

ʕăngeṛ v.t. to place or wear at an angle or cocked (hat)

¶ *ʕăngeṛ* (*ʕla*) to be uppity or snobbish (toward)

ʕăngṛa pl. *-t, ʕnageṛ* **1.** neck (of cow, camel, etc.) **2.** bullneck; thick, stout neck (of person)

ʕănkbut (no pl.) (spider) web

ʕănnaqiya pl. *-t* pillory

ʕănneg, ʕănneq v.t. to hug, to embrace

ʕonq, ʕănq pl. *ʕnaq* **1.** neck (animal, person, bottle) **2.** collar (of shirt, etc.)

¶ *f-ʕonq* (plus n. or pron.) in the charge of, on the shoulders of

ʕănqud pl. *ʕnaqed* bunch, cluster (usually grapes)

ʕonṣel n.u. *ʕonṣla* squill

ʕănṣeṛ **1.** v.t. to spray, squirt, or throw (a liquid) on (s.o.) *kanu ka-iġuwwtu teʕt š-šeṛžem u-hiya tʕănṣeṛhom be-l-ma.* They were shouting under her window, and she threw some water on them. **2.** v.i. to celebrate *ʕănṣṛa*

ʕonṣoṛ pl. *ʕanaṣiṛ* **1.** element (chemical) **2.** component, element, fundamental part

ʕănṣṛa (no pl.) occasion, occurring at the time of the summer solstice, celebrated by squirting or throwing water on people, going to the beach, feasts, etc.

ʕănṭiẓ pl. *ʕanaṭiẓ* Negro

¶ *weld l-ʕănṭiẓa* mulatto

ʕonwan pl. *ʕanawin* **1.** address (home, etc.) **2.** title (book, subject, etc.)

ʕqabi pl. of *ʕăqba* (same as *ʕăgba*)

ʕqad, ʕqadi pl. of *ʕoqda, ʕăqda*

ʕqaṛeb pl. of *ʕăqṛeb*

ʕqaṛeš pl. of *ʕăqṛuša*

ɛqayeb pl. of *ɛquba*
ɛqayeq pl. of *ɛqiq* and *ɛqiqa* (n.u. of *ɛqiq*)
ɛăqba same as *ɛăgba*
ɛqed (v.n. *ɛoqdan, ɛqid*) **1.** v.t. to tie, to fasten (shoes, tie, knot, etc.) **2.** v.t. to button **3.** v.t. to make, to conclude (deal, agreement, appointment, etc.) **4.** v.i. to solidify, to harden, to coagulate (blood, jello, etc.)
¶ *ɛqed debza* to make a fist, to double up one's fist
¶ *ɛqed mɛa* to make an appointment or date with
¶ *ɛqed ɛăbsa* to frown
ɛqed, ɛăqd pl. *ɛqud, ɛquda* **1.** contract **2.** necklace
ɛoqda, ɛăqda pl. *-t, ɛqad, ɛqadi* **1.** n.i. of *ɛqed* **2.** knot (in rope, wood) **3.** button made of silk **4.** contract, agreement **5.** difficulty, trouble, tight spot, "bind" **6.** Adam's apple, larynx
ɛoqdan v.n. of *ɛqed*
ɛqid v.n. of *ɛqed*
ɛqiq **1.** pl. *ɛqayeq* bead necklace (see **2**) **2.** n.u. *-a* pl. *ɛqayeq* bead (actually includes things like pearls, small stones, pieces of glass, etc.)
ɛqel ɛla to be reminded of, to recall
¶ a.p. *ɛaqel* pl. *ɛuqala, ɛoqqal* intelligent, wise, sensible
ɛqel pl. *ɛqul* mind
** *le-ɛqel u-le-mmen ɛṭah ḷḷah.* expr. said of s.o. who displays a sensible and intelligent behavior
¶ *b-ɛăqluφ* (to be) sensible, intelligent, wise ≠
¶ *dar ɛăqluφ* to behave properly, to act one's age, to "straighten up" (usually said to children)
¶ *qal-luφ ɛăqluφ* to (suddenly) decide, to get the idea (to do s.th.) *kanet galsa u-qal-lha ɛqelha tqeṭṭăɛ šɛăṛha.* She was just sitting there when she got the idea of having her hair cut.
¶ *xrež-luφ ɛăqluφ* to go crazy, to go out of one's mind, to lose one's senses (lit. and figurative)
ɛănduφ ɛqel (or *le-ɛqel*) to be sensible, intelligent, wise
ɛăqli pl. *-yen* mental, of or pertaining to the mind
¶ *maṛăḍ ɛăqli* mental illness, psychopathy (broad sense)
ɛăqliya mentality, temperament
ɛoqqal pl. of *ɛaqel* (a.p. of *ɛqel*)
ɛăqqed v.t. **1.** to thicken, to make thick(er), to coagulate **2.** to complicate, to make (more) complicated or knotty
ɛăqqel ṛaṣuφ **1.** to get serious, to quit being silly **2.** to come to one's senses, to become sensible
ɛăqṛayša same as *ɛăqṛuša*
ɛăqṛeb pl. *ɛqaṛeb* **1.** scorpion **2.** hand (of clock, watch)
ɛăqṛuša pl. *-t, ɛqaṛeš* **1.** crab (crustacean) **2.** old, crotchety woman
ɛquba pl. *-t, ɛqayeb* **1.** deformation, physiological defect **2.** same as *ɛaqiba*
** *ḷḷah ixerrež ɛqaybek ɛla xir.* I hope everything turns out all right for you.
¶ *qṛa le-ɛqayeb* to consider the consequences
ɛqud, ɛquda pl. of *ɛqed, ɛăqd*
ɛqul pl. of *ɛqel*
ɛra (m.) nudity, nakedness (generally the state of anything uncovered that usually is covered)
ɛṛaben pl. of *ɛăṛbun*
ɛṛaḍ pl. of *ɛṛiḍ*
ɛṛaḍa pl. *-t, ɛṛayeḍ* **1.** v.n. of *ɛṛeḍ* **2.** recitation (of poem, lesson, etc.) **3.** invitation *waš weṣḷatek le-ɛṛaḍa l-l-ɛers wella ma-zal?* Have you received the invitation to the wedding yet?
ɛraki pl. of *ɛărka*
ɛraq v.n. of *ɛṛeq*
ɛṛaqi used in the expr. *zaž ɛṛaqi* stained glass
ɛṛaṛem pl. of *ɛăṛṛam*
ɛrasat pl. of *ɛers*
ɛṛaṣi pl. of *ɛăṛṣa*
ɛṛaš pl. of *ɛăṛš*
ɛṛayeḍ pl. of *ɛṛaḍa*
ɛṛayef pl. of *ɛrifa*
ɛṛayeṣ, ɛṛayṣat pl. of *ɛṛuṣa*
ɛṛeb n.pl. of *ɛăṛbi*
ɛăṛbi adj. pl. *-yen* n.pl. *ɛṛeb* **1.** Arab **2.** peasant, one living in the country (i.e., not in the city)
ɛăṛbiya (with art.) Arabic (language) (often in context specifically the Moroccan colloquial)
¶ *be-l-ɛăṛbiya d-taɛṛebt* in plain language, speaking as plainly as possible
ɛăṛben v.t. to put a deposit on (house, car, etc.)
ɛăṛbeṭ v.i. to be or act drunk
ɛăṛbun pl. *ɛṛaben* deposit, (partial) advance payment (on s.th.) *ɛṭitu fiha ɛešrin ḍuḷaṛ de-l-ɛăṛbun.* I gave him a twenty-dollar deposit on it.
ɛṛeḍ v.t. (v.n. *ɛṛaḍa*) **1.** to expound, to present *ɛṛeḍ ɛliya r-reʔy dyalu.* He presented his views to me. **2.** to recite (poem, etc.) **3.** to invite (s.o.)
¶ *ɛṛeḍ ɛla* same as **3**
ɛăṛḍ, ɛoṛḍ width, breadth
ɛṛeḍ comp. of *ɛṛiḍ*

ع̆ăṛḍa pl. *-t* 1. n.i. of *ع̆ṛeḍ* 2. kind of pole used in supporting the sides of the *šwari* to avoid spillage

ع̆ṛef v.t. (v.n. *măع̆rifa*) 1. to know (s.th., s.o.) *waš ka-tăع̆ṛef dik l-bent?* Do you know that girl? 2. to learn of, to find out about 3. to recognize 4. to tell, to distinguish *ma-bqa-š l-waḥed yăع̆ṛef băع̆d l-lbas d-le-wlad men l-lbas d-le-bnat.* One can no longer tell boys' clothes from girls'. 5. to know how (to do s.th.) *ma-ka-năع̆ṛef-š nع̆um.* I don't know how to swim.

ع̆ărf, ع̆erf know-how, knowledgeability
** *hada ع̆ărfi.* That's the best I can do. I've done my best.
¶ *be-l-ع̆ărf* 1. skillfully, adroitly (may imply cunning) 2. by force, forcefully

ع̆ărf, ع̆oṛf pl. *ع̆ṛuf, ع̆ṛufa* forelock (horse; may extend to person)

ع̆oṛf socially acceptable customs, standards, or behavior

ع̆oṛfi pl. *-yen* of or pertaining to *ع̆oṛf* (social behavior, etc.)

ع̆ărg same as *ع̆ăṛq*

ع̆reg same as *ع̆ṛeq*

ع̆ărg, ع̆ărga same as *ع̆ăṛq, ع̆ăṛqa*

ع̆ărgan same as *ع̆ăṛqan*

ع̆ărgeb v.t. to hobble and hold (a sheep) on its side with the hands (so it can be slaughtered)

ع̆ărguba pl. *-t, ع̆ṛăgeb* steep (up-hill) grade, (steeply ascending) hill

ع̆ṛiḍ pl. *-in, ع̆ṛaḍ* (comp. *ع̆ṛeḍ*) 1. wide, broad 2. vast, sprawling (plains, etc.)

ع̆rifa pl. *-t, ع̆rayef* kind of policewoman

ع̆rik v.n. of *ع̆rek*

ع̆ris pl. *ع̆ărsan* bridegroom

ع̆ṛiṣa dim. of *ع̆ăṛṣa*

ع̆ṛiwṣa dim. of *ع̆ṛuṣa*

ع̆rek v.t. (v.n. *ع̆rik*) 1. to knead (dough) 2. to treat or handle roughly, to be rough with (physically)

ع̆ărka pl. *-t, ع̆raki* 1. n.i. of *ع̆rek* 2. bundle or load of laundry

ع̆ăṛma pl. *-t* pile, heap

ع̆ṛeq v.i. (v.n. *ع̆ṛaq*) to sweat, to perspire

ع̆ăṛq, ع̆ṛeq pl. (of intensity) *ع̆ṛuqat* sweat, perspiration
¶ *ḥ̆ăbb l-ع̆ăṛq* kind of heat rash which occurs on the forehead

ع̆ăṛq pl. *ع̆ṛuq* 1. blood vessel (vein, artery) 2. tendon, sinew 3. root (tree, tooth) 4. origin, source (usually of some group, e.g., the Jews, Arabs)
¶ *ع̆ăṛq d-demm* vein in the arm commonly used in blood tests
¶ *ع̆ăṛq s-sus* licorice (plant, wood)

ع̆ăṛqa pl. *-t* n.i. of *ع̆ṛeq*

ع̆ăṛqan pl. *-in* sweaty, covered with sweat or perspiration (person, animal)

ع̆ărra v.t. 1. to uncover (bed, pot, etc.) 2. to strip, to denude (person, tree, etc.) 3. to rob (s.o.; may imply taking one's clothes and all)

ع̆ăṛṛam pl. *ع̆ṛaṛem* same as *ع̆ăṛma*

ع̆ăṛṛaq pl. *-in* tending to sweat or perspire easily

ع̆ăṛreb v.t. 1. to translate into Arabic 2. to arabicize (people, customs, etc.)

ع̆ăṛṛeḍ v.t. to put, place, hold, or stick (s.th. somewhere) *ع̆ăṛṛeḍ-lu le-mxedda teḥt ṛaṣu!* Put the pillow under his head! —*xeṣṣna nع̆ăṛṛḍu l-l-qeṭṛa ši-ṣṭel.* We've got to put a bucket under the leak. —*ع̆ăṛṛeḍ-li režlu.* He stuck his leg out in front of me.
¶ *ع̆ăṛṛeḍ ṛaṣuφ* (*l-*) 1. to get involved (in) (s.th.) 2. to expose oneself (to) (danger, etc.)

ع̆ăṛṛef v.t. 1. to define (word, term, etc.) 2. to inform, to let (s.o.) know *ع̆ăṛṛefni b-had š-ši băع̆da.* He's already informed me about this. 3. to introduce, to present *bġit nع̆ăṛṛfek ع̆la* (or *b-*) *ṣaḍiqi.* I'd like to introduce you to my friend.
¶ *ع̆ăṛṛef b-ṛaṣuφ* (*l-*) to introduce oneself (to)

ع̆ăṛṛem v.t. to pile or heap up, to put in a pile or heap

ع̆ăṛṛeq 1. v.t. to make or cause to sweat or perspire 2. v.i. to take root (plant) 3. v.t. to partially cook (meat, usually by steaming; cooking completed at some later time)
¶ *ع̆ăṛṛeq l-* to insult the origin or lineage of (s.o.)

ع̆ărreš v.i. 1. to stand on end, to bristle (hair, quills, etc.) 2. to put on airs (of importance), to act the "bigshot"

ع̆ăṛṛeš v.i. to sprout branches, to branch out (tree)

ع̆ăṛṛež v.t. 1. to cripple (s.o., leg or foot) 2. to delay, to (partially) sabotage, to "cripple" (project, etc.)

ع̆ers, ع̆ărs pl. *ع̆rasat* wedding

ع̆ărsan pl. of *ع̆ris*

ع̆oṛṣ same as *ع̆ers, ع̆ărs*

ع̆ăṛṣa pl. *-t, ع̆ṛaṣi* (dim. *ع̆ṛiṣa*) 1. garden 2. orchard

ع̆ăṛš pl. *ع̆ṛaš, ع̆ṛuš* 1. branch (tree) 2. throne

ع̆ṛubi pl. *-ya* peasant, one living in the country (not city)

ع̆ṛubiya country (in contrast to the city)

ع̆ṛuf, ع̆ṛufa pl. of *ع̆ărf, ع̆oṛf*

ع̆ṛuq pl. of *ع̆ăṛq*

ع̆ṛuqat pl. of *ع̆ăṛq, ع̆ṛeq*

ع̆ṛuṣ same as *ع̆ris*

ɛṛuṣa pl. *-t, ɛṛayeṣ, ɛṛayṣat* (dim. *ɛṛiwṣa*) 1. bride 2. doll (toy) 3. daughter-in-law
ɛṛuš pl. of *ɛăṛš*
ɛṛužiya lameness, limping
ɛăryan pl. *-in* uncovered, naked
ɛṛež v.i. to limp (with a game leg or foot)
ɛṛež f. *ɛăṛža* pl. *ɛuṛež* afflicted with a limp, crippled (leg or foot)
ɛăṛɛaṛ arborvitae
ɛsalež pl. of *ɛăsluž*
ɛsila dim. of *ɛsel*
ɛsel pl. (of intensity) *ɛsulat* (dim. *ɛsila*) 1. honey 2. pestering, importunity
ɛăsli pl. *-yen* honey-colored
ɛăsluž pl. *ɛsalež* artichoke stalk (cooked as a food)
ɛăsri pl. *-yen* 1. left (usually used only with hand or foot) 2. left-handed
ɛăss v.i. (v.n. *ɛăssan*) to have guard duty, to go on guard duty
¶ *ɛăss ɛla* 1. to guard, to watch over 2. to watch, to keep an eye on (s.th., s.o.)
ɛses pl. of *ɛăssa*
ɛăssa pl. *-t, ɛses* 1. n.i. of *ɛăss* 2. guard, guard duty 3. guard, guard force
ɛăssak 1. much less, let alone *l-luġa dyalu ma-ka-itkellem-š biha mezyan ɛăssak itkellem b-luġa ˀažnabiya.* He doesn't even speak his own language well, let alone (speak) a foreign language. 2. indicates a worse consequence in some other time or situation *ṣġiṛ u-ka-yăɛmel le-fɛayel ɛăssak mnin ikber!* You think he's bad now, wait till he grows up!
ɛăssan v.n. of *ɛăss*
ɛăssas adj. pl. *-in* n.pl. *-a* guard, sentinel, one on guard duty
ɛăssel v.t. to oversweeten, to make too sweet (coffee, etc.)
¶ p.p. *mɛăssel* pl. *-in* 1. too sweet (e.g. overripe fruit) 2. (coll.) kind of flat, laminated crust food, fried and covered with honey
ɛsulat pl. of *ɛsel*
ɛṣa yăɛṣa v.i. (v.n. *ɛṣawa, ɛăṣyan*) to get hard (bread, cake, etc.)
¶ a.p. *ɛaṣi* pl. *ɛaṣyen* (comp. *ɛṣa*) 1. hard, brittle 2. stiff, inflexible (rope, body, etc.) 3. tough (meat)
¶ *ṛaṣuɸ ɛaṣi* 1. to be difficult to get along with ≠ 2. to be dumb, dense ≠
ɛṣa yăɛṣi v.t. (v.n. *ɛiṣyan*) 1. to disobey 2. to rebel or revolt against
¶ a.p. *ɛaṣi* pl. *ɛaṣyen* (comp. *ɛṣa*) 1. disobedient 2. indocile, intractable 3. pl. *ɛuṣat* rebel, one in revolt
¶ *ɛaṣi ḷḷah* sinner, irreligious person
ɛṣa comp. of *ɛaṣi* (a.p. of *ɛṣa yăɛṣa* and *ɛṣa yăɛṣi*)

ɛṣa (cons. *ɛṣat*) pl. *ɛṣi* (dim. *ɛṣiwa*) stick, rod, staff (wooden)
¶ *kla* (or *qbeṭ,* or *xda*) *le-ɛṣa* to be beaten (up), to get a beating
¶ *ɛṭa le-ɛṣa* to beat (up), to give a beating to
ɛṣab pl. of *ɛăṣba*
ɛṣakeṛ, ɛṣakṛiya pl. of *ɛăṣkṛi*
ɛṣat cons. of *ɛṣa*
ɛṣawa v.n. of *ɛṣa yăɛṣa*
¶ *ɛṣawt ṛ-ṛaṣ* denseness, dumbness, stupidity
ɛṣayeb pl. of *ɛăṣṣaba*
ɛṣayeḍ pl. of *ɛṣiḍa* 2
ɛṣeb pl. of *ɛăṣba*
ɛăṣba pl. *ɛṣab, ɛṣeb* 1. muscle 2. kind of whip made of animal tendons
ɛṣi pl. of *ɛṣa*
ɛṣiḍa 1. pl. *-t* (of intensity) uncooked dough (connotes disgust) 2. pl. *ɛṣayeḍ* kind of wheat or corn mush served with butter and honey
ɛṣim v.n. of *ɛṣem*
ɛṣiṛ v.n. of *ɛṣeṛ*
ɛṣiwa dim. of *ɛṣa*
ɛăṣkeṛ army, military force, troops (may extend to navy, air force, etc.)
ɛăṣkṛi pl. *ɛṣakeṛ, ɛṣakṛiya* soldier, military man (may extend to navy, air force, etc.)
ɛṣem v.t. (v.n. *ɛṣim*) to cause to get constipated, to constipate (s.o.)
ɛṣeṛ v.t. (v.n. *ɛṣiṛ*) 1. to squeeze, to press (e.g. against a hard surface) 2. to tighten, to make tight (screw, vise, etc.) 3. to wring out (clothes, etc.) 4. to win out over, to beat (in some competition)
ɛăṣṛa pl. *-t* n.i. of *ɛṣeṛ*
ɛăṣṛi pl. *-yen* modern, up-to-date
ɛăṣṣa v.t. to beat (up), to give a beating to
ɛăṣṣaba pl. *-t, ɛṣayeb* scarf (for the head)
ɛăṣṣaṛa pl. *-t* squeezer (for juicing oranges, etc.)
ɛăṣṣeb v.t. 1. to stiffen, to make stiff (arm, leg, body; in contrast to relax) 2. to wrap with a strip of cloth, bandage, etc. (head, wrist, etc.)
ɛăṣṣeṛ v.t. 1. to squeeze (lemon, orange, etc.) 2. to wring (out) (wet clothing)
ɛăṣyan v.n. of *ɛṣa yăɛṣa*
ɛša pl. *-wat* (cons. *ɛšat;* dim. *ɛšiwa*) 1. evening meal, supper 2. (with art.) last prayer of the day (after sunset; also the time of this prayer)
ˀăɛšaṛ pl. of *ɛušuṛ*
ɛšari pl. *-yen* consisting of ten parts or elements (e.g., ten-gallon tank, ten-pointed star)
ɛšariya pl. *-t* ten-shot rifle
ɛšaš pl. of *ɛošš, ɛešš*

ʕšat cons. of *ʕša*

ʕăšba **1.** pl. *-t, ʕšeb* finely shredded palm leaves (used to stuff pillows, mattresses, etc.) **2.** pl. *ʕšub* type of medicinal herb (unknown to some speakers)

ʕšiq v.n. of *ʕšeq*

ʕšir pl. *ʕošran* close friend, companion, intimate

ʕšiwa dim. of *ʕša*

ʕšiya pl. *-t* evening (usually from late afternoon to sunset)

ʕšeq v.t. (v.n. *ʕšiq*) to like, to be fond of (s.o., food, movies, etc.)

¶ a.p. *ʕašeq* **1.** pl. *ʕoššaq* lover (of s.o., food, etc.) **2.** (also *ʕašqa*) pl. *ʕwašeq* spoon

ʕăšṛ, ʕšeṛ, ʕăšṛa (first two forms used with pl. of n. admitting du.) ten

ʕošra **1.** v.n. of *ʕašer* **2.** association, relationship (with s.o.)

ʕošran pl. of *ʕšir*

ʕešrin **1.** twenty **2.** twentieth

ʕošš, ʕešš pl. *ʕšaš* nest (bird; possible metaphor)

ʕășša **1.** v.t. to feed supper (the evening meal) to **2.** v.i. to pass or spend the evening (*ʕšiya*)

ʕošša pl. *ʕšes* kind of conical, thatched hut (similar to American teepee)

ʕăššab pl. *-a* herbalist, dealer in herbs

ʕăššaq pl. *-in* ag. adj. of *ʕšeq*

¶ *ʕăššaq mellal* blowing hot and cold, fickle, capricious

ʕoššaq pl. of *ʕašeq* **1** (a.p. of *ʕšeq*)

ʕăššeṛ ʕla to tithe or pay tithing on (one's properties) and give it to the poor (during *ʕašuṛa*)

ʕăššeš v.i. to nest, to make a nest (bird; possible metaphor)

ʕšub, ʕšubat (pl. or f. sg.) (see *ʕăšba*) herbs (medicinal)

ʕšuṛ tithe or tithing (given to the poor during *ʕašuṛa*)

ʕăšwa same as *ʕășša* **2**

ʕăšwi (the) late afternoon

¶ *qbeṭ l-ʕăšwi* to spend or pass the late afternoon

ʕta (*men*) bigger, larger (than)

ʕtabi pl. of *ʕătba, ʕotba*

ʕtabeṛ v.t. (v.n. *ʕtibaṛ*) **1.** to consider, to think of (s.o., s.th.) as *ka-năʕtabeṛha ˀeṛfăʕ mumettila.* I consider her the best actress. **2.** to take into consideration, to think about (implies subsequent action based thereon)

ʕtali pl. of *ʕătla*

ʕtamed ʕla **1.** to rest or lean on, to support oneself on or with **2.** to rely on, to count on (for support, etc.)

ʕtana yăʕtani b- (v.n. *ʕtina, ʕtinaˀ*) **1.** to take care of, to watch after (child, possession, etc.) **2.** to trouble oneself about, to worry about (implies unduly) **3.** to be interested in, to take an interest in (actively or passively)

ʕtaqed to think, to believe *ka-năʕtaqed belli l-makla bla qyas ka-ḍḍeṛṛ.* I believe that overeating is harmful.

ʕtaṛef b- **1.** to recognize, to acknowledge (e.g., a new government, s.o.'s merits) **2.** to admit, to confess (crime, sin, etc.)

¶ *ʕtaṛef l-xir* to be grateful

ʕtares pl. of *ʕătrus*

ʕtateg pl. of *ʕăttug*

ʕătba, ʕotba pl. *-t, ʕtabi* doorstep (at the entrance to a house)

ʕotbaṛ, ʕătbaṛ (divine) punishment

¶ *xerrež l-ʕotbaṛ f-* to mete out (divine) punishment to

ʕtibaṛ v.n. of *ʕtabeṛ*

ʕtina, ʕtinaˀ v.n. of *ʕtana*

ʕtiq v.n. of *ʕteq*

ʕtiṛ v.n. of *ʕteṛ*

ʕătla pl. *ʕtali* hoe

ʕteq v.t. (v.n. *ʕtiq*) **1.** to save, to rescue **2.** to set free, to liberate, to emancipate (slaves)

** *ʕătqu ṛ-ṛuʕ!* Help!

¶ a.p. *ʕateq* pl. *-in* (comp. *ʕteq*) **1.** old, aged (of alcoholic beverages) **2.** pl. *ʕwateq* (dim. *ʕwitqa*) young girl, virgin (pre-adolescent)

ʕteq comp. of *ʕateq* (a.p. of *ʕteq*)

ʕteṛ (*f-*) (v.n. *ʕtiṛ*) to stumble (on, over, in) (hole, rock, etc.)

¶ *ʕteṛ ʕla* to stumble across or onto, to come across, to hit on (idea, discovery, some object)

ʕătṛa pl. *-t* n.i. of *ʕteṛ*

ʕătrus pl. *ʕtares* billy goat

ʕătteb ʕla to step (up) onto (e.g., a platform to get into a boat)

¶ *ʕătteb ʕla ḍaṛ* (or *bab ḍaṛ*) to set one's foot in the house of, to darken the door of (s.o.) *ma-ʕămmṛek tʕawed tʕătteb ʕla bab ḍaṛi!* Don't you ever darken my door again!

ʕăttel v.t. **1.** to cultivate (a garden, plot) with the use of a hoe (*ʕătla*) **2.** to regulate the flow of irrigation water in (a ditch, etc.) with a hoe (*ʕătla*) **3.** to track up (a newly cleaned floor, with, e.g., muddy feet)

ʕăttug f. *-a* pl. *ʕtateg* young chicken (cockerel, pullet)

ʕṭa yăʕṭi v.t. (v.n. *ʕṭi*) **1.** to give *ʕṭini žuž kilu d-le-bṭaṭa!* Give me two kilos of potatoes! —*mšit l-ʕăndu baš yăʕṭini ši-măʕlumat ʕăl ṣ-ṣfeṛ.* I went to him so he could give me some information on travel. —tqebbṭu bih fe-z-zenqa u-Ɛṭaweh le-Ɛṣa. They grabbed him in the street and gave him a beating. —bḫaha Ɛṭaha-lu. Her father gave her to him (in marriage). —Ɛṭiha-li! Give it to me! 2. to produce, to yield, to give (fruit, crops, etc.)

¶ p.p. măƐṭi used in the expr. măƐṭi-luφ gifted, endowed, having a gift for ≠ măƐṭiya-lha l-musiqa. She has a gift for music.

Ɛṭeb v.t. (v.n. Ɛṭib) to hurt, to injure, to cripple (not necessarily permanently)

¶ p.p. măƐṭub pl. -in invalid, crippled (may be permanent)

Ɛṭef Ɛla (v.n. Ɛăṭf) to be benevolent or sympathetic toward; to treat with kindness, sympathy, consideration, etc.

Ɛăṭf 1. v.n. of Ɛṭef 2. sympathetic kindness, benevolence

Ɛăṭfa 1. n.i. of Ɛṭef 2. same as Ɛaṭifa

Ɛṭi v.n. of Ɛṭa

Ɛṭib v.n. of Ɛṭeb

Ɛṭiṣ v.n. of Ɛṭeṣ (same as Ɛṭeš 2)

Ɛṭiš v.n. of Ɛṭeš 2

Ɛṭiya (no pl.) gift, talent

Ɛoṭla pl. -t time off, holiday, vacation

Ɛṭer pl. Ɛṭur perfume

Ɛăṭriya 1. spice(s), condiment(s) 2. drug

Ɛṭerša (coll.) geranium

Ɛṭes same as Ɛṭeš 2

Ɛṭeš v.i. 1. (v.n. Ɛṭeš) to get thirsty 2. (v.n. Ɛṭiš) to sneeze

Ɛṭeš 1. v.n. of Ɛṭeš 1 2. thirst žani le-Ɛṭeš. I'm thirsty.

¶ b-le-Ɛṭeš by the job or contract (implies a time limit and no significant breaks or respites)

Ɛăṭšan pl. -in thirsty (person, animal, plant, soil)

Ɛăṭṭal pl. -in ag. adj. of Ɛăṭṭel (in the usage with Ɛla)

Ɛăṭṭar pl. -a dealer in herbs and spices

Ɛăṭṭef (Ɛla) to inspire or make (s.o.) feel sympathy or kindness (for) (e.g., the sight of s.o.'s abject poverty) waxxa ma-ka-nɛămlu-š Ɛăṭṭefni Ɛlih lemma šeftu f-dik l-ɛala. Even though I can't stand him, I felt sorry for him when I saw him in that condition.

Ɛăṭṭel v.t. 1. to delay, to make late 2. to postpone, to delay (until later) 3. to stop, to cease (work) 4. (also v.i.) to be absent from, to not show up for, to take time off from (school, work)

¶ Ɛăṭṭel l-xedma to close up shop, to shut down (usually temporarily)

¶ Ɛăṭṭel Ɛla to be in need of, to lack

¶ p.p. mƐăṭṭel pl. -in late, delayed

Ɛăṭṭer 1. v.t. to perfume 2. v.i. to put perfume on, to perfume oneself

Ɛăṭṭeṣ same as Ɛăṭṭeš 2

Ɛăṭṭeš v.t. 1. to make thirsty 2. to make or cause to sneeze

Ɛṭur 1. pl. of Ɛṭer 2. (pl.) herbs

Ɛubudiya slavery, bondage, servitude

Ɛud pl. Ɛwad 1. wood (material) 2. stick (wooden) 3. (pl.) firewood 4. (also Ɛud le-qmari) kind of incense

¶ dreb l-Ɛud to draw lots or straws

Ɛud pl. Ɛidan a kind of lute

Ɛudama pl. of Ɛadim

Ɛuhud pl. of Ɛăhd

Ɛulama pl. of Ɛalem (a.p. of Ɛlem)

Ɛulum pl. of Ɛilm 2

Ɛum, Ɛuman v.n. of Ɛam

Ɛumalaʔ pl. of Ɛamil

Ɛumar same as Ɛumăr

Ɛumi pl. of Ɛma

Ɛumăr m. proper name

¶ Ɛumăr ʔibn l-xeṭṭab second Caliph after the Prophet Mohammed

Ɛumeš pl. of Ɛmeš

Ɛumumi pl. -yen public, open to or used by the public

Ɛuqala pl. of Ɛaqel (a.p. of Ɛqel)

Ɛuqeb v.t. to cripple, to mutilate (permanently)

Ɛuquba pl. -t punishment, chastisement

Ɛurafa pl. of Ɛarif

Ɛureṭ (b- s.o. or f- some place) to ask asylum or sanctuary of (s.o. or some place)

Ɛurež pl. of Ɛrež

Ɛuṣat pl. of Ɛaṣi 3 (a.p. of Ɛṣa yăƐṣi)

Ɛušer v.i. to go on vacation or leave

Ɛušur pl. -at, ʔăƐšar tenth, tenth part

Ɛuyub pl. of Ɛib

Ɛwa yăƐwi v.i. (v.n. Ɛwa) to howl (wolf, coyote, etc.)

Ɛwa (m.) v.n. of Ɛwa

Ɛwad pl. of Ɛud

Ɛwafi pl. of Ɛafya

Ɛwaʔid pl. of Ɛada

Ɛwamm 1. pl. of Ɛammi 2. (pl.) people, populace

ʔăƐwan, Ɛwan pl. of Ɛăwn

Ɛwašeq pl. of Ɛašeq 2 (a.p. of Ɛšeq)

Ɛwašer (f.) 1. vacation, leave 2. complete cleaning or cleanup (of a house, e.g. "spring" cleaning)

Ɛwateq pl. of Ɛateq 2 (a.p. of Ɛteq)

Ɛwaž v.i. (v.n. Ɛwaž, Ɛwužiya) 1. to get bent or twisted 2. to get all fouled up, to get disorganized (said of s.th. or s.o. that is usually in fairly good shape) 3. to go back on one's word

Ɛwaž v.n. of Ɛwaž

ع*ăwd* pl. *xil* (pl. sometimes treated syntactically as f. sg.) horse (specifically male)
ع*ăwda* **1.** v.n. of ع*ad* 1 and 2 **2.** pl. *-t* mare, female horse
ع*ăwḍ* same as ع*iwăḍ*
ع*wifya* dim. of ع*afya*
ع*win* (no pl.) **1.** provisions for a trip **2.** helper, assistant (a personal, temporary sort)
** *ḷḷah* (or *ṛebbi*) ع*winek!* God help you!
ع*wina* dim. of ع*ăyn*
ع*witqa* dim. of ع*ateq*
ع*ăwla* provisions (food)
ع*ăwn* **1.** assistance, aid, help **2.** pl. *ʔă*ع*wan,* ع*wan* aide, assistant
** *ḷḷah ikun f-*ع*ăwnu!* God help him!
¶ *bi-*ع*ăwni llah* with the help of God
ع*weṛ* f. ع*ăwṛa* pl. ع*ăwṛin,* ع*iweṛ* one-eyed, blind in one eye
ع*ăwṛa* **1.** f. of ع*weṛ* **2.** that part of the (human) body which in all modesty should be covered (usually genitalia)
ع*ăwšer* same as ع*ušer*
ع*wužiya* v.n. of ع*waž*
ع*ăwwad* pl. *-a* **1.** lute player **2.** maker of lutes (may include similar instruments)
ع*ăwwag* pl. *-in* given to howling and baying (said of a dog; connotes that the dog is announcing an impending death and, therefore, must be killed to avoid it)
ع*ăwwal* pl. *-in* ag. adj. of ع*ăwwel*
ع*ăwwam* pl. *-a* (good) swimmer
ع*ăwwaq* same as ع*ăwwag*
ع*ăwwaqa* hiccups
¶ *fihᶲ l-*ع*ăwwaqa* to have the hiccups ≠
ع*ăwwed* v.t. **1.** same as ع*awed* **2.** to cause to get hard (usually said of cake, bread, etc., when overbaked) **3.** to accustom, to get (s.o.) accustomed or used (to) *ma-t*ع*ăwwed-š ṛaṣek* ع*ăl t-tedxin.* Don't get yourself accustomed to smoking. —ع*ăwwdet d-drari dyalha inuḍu bekri.* She got her children accustomed to getting up early.
¶ part. *m*ع*ăwwed* pl. *-in* **1.** tough, not tender or soft (food) **2.** hard and dry (bread) **3.** inflexible, stiff **4.** stubborn, unyielding
ع*ăwweḍ* v.t. **1.** to replace, to change **2.** to give recompense for, to indemnify (s.th.)
ع*ăwweg* v.i. **1.** to crow (rooster) **2.** to bawl, to cry (child)
ع*ăwwel* ع*la* **1.** to plan on or for **2.** to prepare for, to get ready for **3.** to count or rely on
ع*ăwwem* v.t. **1.** to take (s.o.) to or into the water (so he can swim or play in it; may connote teaching to swim) **2.** to put or get into the water (boat)
ع*ăwweq* same as ع*ăwweg*
ع*ăwweṛ* v.t. to blind (either temporarily or partially)
ع*ăwwež* **1.** v.t. to bend, to twist, (iron rod, s.o.'s words, etc.) **2.** v.t. to put or place crooked **3.** v.i. to turn (corner, to the left, etc.) *sir* ع*etta l-ṛaṣ l-qent u-*ع*ăwwež* ع*ăl l-imin!* Go to the corner and turn right! **4.** v.t. to make deviate or veer (road, missile, etc.) **5.** v.t. to corrupt, to influence adversely **6.** v.t. to dissuade, to change the way of thinking of **7.** v.t. to foul up, to put in disorder, to get or put out of order or place **8.** to ape, to mimic, to imitate
¶ ع*ăwwež wežhuᶲ* to make a face or faces
¶ ع*ăwwež* ع*ăl ṭ-ṭriq* to make a detour (v.i.)
¶ p.p. *m*ع*ăwwež* pl. *-in* crooked, not straight
ع*wež* f. ع*ăwža* pl. ع*ăwžin,* ع*iwež* **1.** bent, twisted, crooked **2.** all fouled up, disorganized, etc.
ع*ăwži* used in the expr. *be-l-*ع*ăwži.* **1.** (while) looking askance (implies disdain, disgust), disdainfully **2.** awkward, clumsy (also corresponding adv. usage) **3.** botched or all fouled up
ع*ya yă*ع*ya* (*men*) (v.n. ع*ya*) **1.** to get tired, fatigued (from) **2.** to get tired (of), to get fed up (with)
¶ ع*ya ma* to get tired of (doing s.th.) ع*yit ma nakol had š-ši!* I'm tired of eating this!
ع*ya* (m.) **1.** v.n. of ع*ya* **2.** fatigue, tiredness
ع*yad* pl. of ع*id*
ع*yada* v.n. of ع*ad* 3
ع*yadu* used in the expr. *le-*ع*yadu be-llah!* God help us (you, me, etc.)!
ع*yal* **1.** pl. of ع*ayel* **2.** group or family of wives (usually of the king)
ع*yalat* pl. of *mṛa*
ع*yaṭ* v.n. of ع*ăyyeṭ* in the expr. ع*ăyyeṭ f-* (see ع*ăyyeṭ*)
ع*ăyb* **1.** v.n. of ع*ab* **2.** same as ع*ib*
ع*ăyn* (f.) pl. ع*yun* (dim. ع*wina*) **1.** pl. also *-in* (*-n* dropped before pron. endings) eye (person, animal, needle) **2.** evil eye **3.** spring (water) **4.** buttonhole **5.** same *žbeṛtha f-*ع*ăyn l-makan.* I found her in the same place. —*had l-*ع*am* ع*ăndi* ع*ăyn l-ʔustad.* I have the same professor this year.
** *šaf* ع*ăynu fe-qfatu.* He went through a lot of trouble and grief before he got what he wanted.
¶ *ḍeṛbatuᶲ l-*ع*ăyn,* or *tṣemmṛat fihᶲ l-*ع*ăyn* to be struck or cursed by the evil eye ≠

¶ *f-ɛăyn l-mut* dying, near death, at the point of death or dying

¶ *nɛăs ɛla ɛăyn qfatuΦ* to sleep on one's back

¶ *sqeṭ men ɛăyn* (plus n. or pron. ending) to fall from the good graces of, to lose the favor of (s.o.)

¶ *ɛla ṛaṣuΦ u-ɛăynuΦ,* or *ɛăl ṛ-ṛaṣ we-l-ɛăyn* with pleasure, gladly

¶ *ɛmel ɛăyn u-wden* to be on the alert, to keep one's eyes and ears open

¶ *ɛmel ɛăynuΦ ɛla* to keep an eye or one's eye on

¶ *ɛăyn ḍ-ḍheṛ* anus

¶ *ɛăyn d-le-qfa* base of the skull (sensitive area)

¶ *ɛăyn l-luɛ* knot (also knothole)

¶ *ɛăyn l-ɛut* callus (foot)

¶ *ɛăyn š-šems* (the) sun

ɛăyna pl. *-t* **1.** kind, sort, type **2.** brand, make **3.** grade, quality

ɛăyš v.n. of *ɛaš*

ɛăyšuṛ, ɛăyšuṛa same as *ɛašuṛ, ɛašuṛa*

ɛăyṭa **1.** pl. *-t* n.i. of *ɛăyyeṭ* **2.** pl. *-t* shout, yell **3.** (no pl.) kind of gambling card game **4.** pl. *ɛyuṭ* kind of folk song or chant

ɛyub pl. of *ɛib*

ɛyuba v.n. of *ɛab*

ɛyun pl. of *ɛăyn*

ɛyuṭ pl. of *ɛăyṭa* 4

ɛăyya v.t. **1.** to tire, to weary, to fatigue **2.** to cause to be or feel fed up

ɛăyyaf adj. pl. *-in* n.pl. *-a* ag. adj. and n. of *ɛaf*

ɛăyyan pl. *-in* **1.** tired, fatigued, weary **2.** sick, ill **3.** no good, worthless, of no value

ɛăyyaṛ pl. *-a* official inspector of scales and balances (used in weighing out merchandise for the public)

ɛăyyaṭ **1.** pl. *-in* ag. adj. of *ɛăyyeṭ* **2.** singer of *ɛyuṭ* (pl. of *ɛăyṭa*)

ɛăyyeb v.t. to mimic, to ape, to imitate

¶ *ɛăyyeb ɛla* to blame

ɛăyyed v.i. to pass, spend, or celebrate a holiday or feast

ɛăyyef (*l-*) to be disgusting, sickening, or nauseating (to)

¶ *ɛăyyef l-qelb* (*l-*) same as *ɛăyyef* (*l-*) above

ɛăyyen v.t. **1.** to appoint, to designate, to name *mudir š-šarika ɛăyyen l-katib dyalu naʔib ɛlih.* The director of the company appointed his secretary as his vice executive. **2.** to point out, to indicate, to specify **3.** to give or curse with the "evil eye"

ɛăyyeṛ v.t. **1.** to verify the value of, to appraise (s.th. precious, e.g. diamonds, mink) **2.** to assay (gold, silver)

ɛăyyeš v.t. **1.** to support, to provide subsistence for (s.o.) **2.** to bring (back) to life

ɛăyyeṭ *ɛla* or *l-* **1.** to call (on telephone, with a shout, etc.) **2.** to summon

¶ *ɛăyyeṭ f-* (v.n. *ɛyaṭ*) same as *ɛăyyen* 3

ɛzafeṛ (pl.) mustache (usually large and dense)

ɛzara pl. of *ɛăzri*

ɛzayeb pl. of *ɛzib*

ɛzayem pl. of *ɛazima*

ɛzayez pl. of *ɛziz* 4 and 5

ɛzaz v.i. to become liked, dear, desirable (see *ɛziz*)

ɛzaz pl. of *ɛziz* 2 and 3

ɛzazef pl. of *ɛăzzafa*

ɛăzban pl. of *ɛzib*

ɛzef v.t. (v.n. *ɛăzf*) to play (music)

¶ *ɛzef ɛla* to play (instrument)

ɛăzf v.n. of *ɛzef*

ɛzib pl. *ɛzayeb, ɛăzban* farm

ɛzil v.n. of *ɛzel*

ɛziz (comp. *ɛăzz*) **1.** pl. *-in, ɛzaz* dear, liked, beloved **2.** pl. *-in. ɛzaz* agreeable, pleasant **3.** epithet of God **4.** pl. *ɛzayez* oldest brother, big brother **5.** pl. *ɛzayez* brother-in-law

ɛziza pl. *-t* (also *ṃṃuΦ le-ɛziza*) grandmother (paternal)

ɛzel v.t. (v.n. *ɛzil*) **1.** to pick out, to choose **2.** to put or set aside **3.** to separate (connotes: undesirable from the desirable) **4.** to isolate, to seclude

ɛzem (*ɛla*) v.n. *ɛăzm*) to decide (on)

ɛăzm v.n. of *ɛzem*

ɛăẓṛaʔil, ɛăẓṛayn Azrael (angel of death)

ɛăzri pl. *ɛzara* **1.** bachelor **2.** young man, adolescent boy

ɛăzz (v.n. *ɛizza, ɛăzz*) same as *ɛzaz*

** *ɛăzzek ḷḷah!* You're welcome! (reply to *ɛašak,* which see)

¶ *ɛăzz ɛla* to cause to feel pity, to provoke the pity of (s.o.)

¶ (s.th. or s.o.) *ɛăzz ɛlihΦ* to be reluctant to part with (s.th. or s.o.) ≠ *ka-iɛăzzu ɛlih flusu.* He doesn't want to spend his money. —*ɛăzzet ɛliya s-siyaṛa dyali.* I'd rather not part with (e.g., sell, lend) my car.

ɛăzz **1.** v.n. of *ɛăzz* (same as *ɛzaz*) **2.** comp. of *ɛziz*

ɛăzza v.t. to present one's condolences to (s.o.) *xeṣṣek tɛăzzih fe-ḅḅah.* You should present your condolences to him on his father's death.

ɛăzzab pl. *-a* farmer (working on or owning *ɛzib*)

ɛăzzafa pl. *-t, ɛzazef* long stick or pole used in cleaning high, inaccessible spots (e.g., ceiling corners)

ɛăzzay pl. *-a* ag. n. of *ɛăzza*
ɛăzzeb **1.** v.t. to hire or employ (for work on a farm or *ɛzib*) **2.** v.i. to be employed on or work on a farm (*ɛzib*)
ɛăzzef v.t. to clean (with *ɛăzzafa*)
ɛăzzi (no pl.; also *ɛăzzi balạla*) very black negro
ɛăzzem ɛla to cast a spell on or over, to bewitch (with purpose of changing into s.th. else)
ɛžayeb pl. of *ɛžuba*
ɛžaž **1.** dust, sand (in the air) **2.** n.u. *-a* dust or sand storm
ɛžeb v.t. to please, to like ≠ *ka-yăɛžebni nfiq ṣ-ṣbaɛ bekri.* I like to get up early in the morning. —*ka-tăɛžebni bezzaf ɛad.* I like her a lot. —*ɛayati f-ˀamirika ɛažbani bezzaf ɛad.* I'm enjoying my stay in America very much.
¶ *ɛažbuᶲ* (a.p.) *ṛaṣuᶲ* conceited, impressed with oneself
¶ *ɛăžbuᶲ l-ɛal* . . . to be pleased or glad ≠ *ɛžebhom l-ɛal lemma wqăɛ-li l-ɛadita.* They were pleased when I had the accident.
ɛžeb (no pl.) **1.** astonishment, amazement, surprise **2.** mystery
ɛžib same as *ɛažib*
ɛžin **1.** v.n. of *ɛžen* **2.** dough (bread, etc.)
ɛžina same as *ɛžin* **2**
ɛžel f. *ɛăžla* pl. *ɛžul, ɛžula* **1.** calf (bovine) **2.** (f.) girl with a good figure or build
¶ *lɛăm d-le-ɛžel* veal
ɛžen v.t. (v.n. *ɛžin*) to prepare dough for (bread, etc.)
ɛžuba pl. *-t, ɛžayeb, ɛažaˀib* **1.** extraordinary or amazing act or thing, marvel (also wide interjectional usage) **2.** mystery, enigma
ɛžul, ɛžula pl. of *ɛžel*
ɛăžžel **1.** v.t. or v.i. to rush, to hurry **2.** v.t. to move up the time of, to make earlier *ɛăžželna l-ɛăfla.* We've moved up the time of the party.
¶ *ɛăžžel b-* to rush, to hurry (work, building, etc.)
ɛăžžež v.t. to raise dust in (a room) or on (a road, etc.), to cloud the air of (some place) with dust

A Dictionary of Moroccan Arabic

English-Moroccan

Edited by
Harvey Sobelman
and Richard S. Harrell

Compiled by
Thomas Fox, Alan McAninch, Allal Chreibi,
Majid Soussane, and Mohamed Neheiri

THE ARABIC RESEARCH PROGRAM
INSTITUTE OF LANGUAGES AND LINGUISTICS
GEORGETOWN UNIVERSITY

The Arabic Research Program was established in June of 1960 as a contract between Georgetown University and the United States Office of Education under the provisions of the Language Development Program of the National Defense Education Act.

The first two years of the research program, 1960-1962 (Contract number SAE-8706), were devoted to the production of six books, a reference grammar and a conversational English-Arabic dictionary in the cultivated spoken forms of Moroccan, Syrian, and Iraqi Arabic. The second two years of the research program, 1962-1964 (Contract number OE-2-14-029), call for the further production of Arabic-English dictionaries in each of the three varieties of Arabic mentioned above, as well as comprehensive basic courses in the Moroccan and Iraqi varieties.

The eleven books of this series, of which the present volume is one, are designed to serve as practical tools for the increasing number of Americans whose lives bring them into contact with the Arab world. The dictionaries, the reference grammars, and the basic courses are oriented toward the educated American who is a layman in linguistic matters. Although it is hoped that the scientific linguist and the specialist in Arabic dialectology will find these books both of interest and of use, matters of purely scientific and theoretical importance have not been directly treated as such, and specialized scientific terminology has been avoided as much as possible.

As is usual, the authors or editors of the individual books bear final scholarly responsibility for the contents, but there has been a large amount of informal cooperation in our work. Criticism, consultation, and discussion have gone on constantly among the senior professional members of the staff. The contribution of more junior research assistants, both Arab and American, is also not to be underestimated. Their painstaking assembling and ordering of raw data, often in manners requiring considerable creative intelligence, has been the necessary prerequisite for further progress.

Staff work has been especially important in the preparation of the dictionaries. Although the contributing staff members are named on the title page of the individual dictionaries, special mention must be made of Mr. Karl Stowasser's work. His lexicographical experience, acquired in his work on the English version of Professor Wehr's *Arabisches Wörterbuch für die Schriftsprache der Gegenwart*,*

*Hans Wehr, *A Dictionary of Modern Written Arabic*, ed. J Milton Cowan (Ithaca, N. Y.: Cornell University Press, 1961).

along with his thorough knowledge of Arabic, has been critically important for all our lexicographical work, covering the entire range from typography to substantive entries in the dictionaries.

In most cases the books prepared by the Arabic Research Program are the first of their kind in English, and in some cases the first in any language. The preparation of them has been a rewarding experience. It is hoped that the public use of them will be equally so. The undersigned, on behalf of the entire staff, would like to ask the same indulgence of the reader as Samuel Johnson requested in his first English dictionary: To remember that although much has been left out, much has been included.

Richard S. Harrell
Associate Professor of Linguistics
Georgetown University

Director,
Arabic Research Program

PREFACE

The English entries in this dictionary are based on the English-German section of the bilingual German and English *Dictionary of Everyday Usage*.* A number of changes were of course necessary, both in form and content, to meet the requirements of the differences between American and Moroccan cultural and linguistic uses. Our aim has been to present the core vocabulary of everyday conversational usage. Technical and literary matters have been largely avoided.

The major part of the labor of compiling Moroccan equivalents for the English entries was done by Thomas Fox and Allal Chreibi under the editorial supervision of Dr. Harvey Sobelman. Alan McAninch, Majid Soussane, and Mohamed Neheiri also made substantial contributions. The contributions of Mohamed Benlemlih and Abdel Wahab El-Berday must also be mentioned, although they were able to give us only a limited amount of their time. After the completion of the first draft of the dictionary, the undersigned accepted the task of giving the material a final editorial reworking. In the course of this final revision the entire dictionary was reread and extensive additions, deletions, and corrections were made.

In the compilation of the dictionary, as great a contribution as that of any one individual was made by a Moroccan colleague who has requested that his name be withheld. A conscientious worker with a passion for accuracy, this colleague wished to reread all the material and make a final check on the accuracy of the Moroccan entries. When this proved impossible because of time limitations, he preferred to have his name withheld. Since it is impossible to spell out in detail exactly who wrote which entries, he scrupulously wished to refuse possible implicit responsibility for parts of the dictionary that were not his work. Since much of what is good and very little of the possibly bad which is to be found in this book is due to the work of this colleague, it is only fair to recognize the importance of his contribution in these general terms.

The composition of this first English-Moroccan dictionary proved unusually difficult, quite aside from the normal technical problems of dictionary making. The ideal compiler of a bilingual dictionary is a person with professional linguistic training and a comprehensive command of both languages involved. There exists not even one person who has such qualifications in English, Moroccan Arabic, and scientific linguistics. Our staff consisted of American linguists and assistants with a limited knowledge of Moroccan Arabic, and Moroccan informants with varying degrees of proficiency in English. Under such circumstances, the goal of technical

---

**German-English English-German Dictionary of Everyday Usage,* ed. by J. Alan Pfeffer (New York: Henry Holt and Company). Although the content of this dictionary is, in strictly legal terms, public domain since it was prepared as a part of the American war effort in World War II, we wish to express our thanks to the publishers for raising no copyright objections to our use of the material.

and idiomatic accuracy in the entries turned out to be a severe intellectual, emotional, and physical trial for the staff. These difficulties were compounded by a strict time limitation, and there were periods, one lasting some three months, when our work was broken by the absence of any Moroccan co-workers. As a final problem, the proofs arrived at a moment when no Moroccans were present. Since it was impossible to hold up printing, the proofreading had to be done entirely by Americans. The undersigned read the galley proofs, while Thomas Fox undertook the reading of the page proofs.

For those who have worked on the composition of a dictionary, the temptation to quote Dr. Johnson is always difficult to resist. When a "first" dictionary is involved and the authors have to make their own way without benefit of predecessors, the temptation becomes impossible to resist. One is reminded especially of Dr. Johnson's comparison of dictionaries and watches: That while the best is not completely true, the worst is better than none.

Richard S. Harrell
Washington, D. C.
September, 1963

TECHNICAL DATA

The transcription used is that explained in *A Short Reference Grammar of Moroccan Arabic*.* The use of the dictionary presupposes a familiarity with the basic grammatical structure of Moroccan Arabic.

In cases where several Moroccan words correspond to one English word (e.g. "ruler" as the head of a government or as a tool for measuring and drawing), the specific meanings of the Moroccan words are usually indicated by illustrative sentences rather than by parenthetical explanation. The same device of the illustrative sentence has also been widely used to clarify the syntactic and contextual function of the Moroccan entries.

Necessary grammatical information (e.g. irregular plurals, irregular gender) is given with the entries. Verbs are entered in the third person singular of the perfect. The imperfect form is written immediately after the perfect form in those verbs which have an unpredictable imperfect vowel. Where word for word equivalents do not exist, idiomatic entries are signalled by a double asterisk. The abbreviations used are as follows:

adj.	adjective
art.	definite article
coll.	collective
f.	feminine
m.	masculine
n.	noun
pl.	plural
sg.	singular

---

*Richard S. Harrel, *A Short Reference Grammar of Moroccan Arabic* (Washington: Georgetown University Press, Arabic Series: Number 1, 1962).

A

a – **1.** *ši.* Do you have a dog? *waš Ɛendek ši-kelb?* –Give me a pencil. *Ɛṭini ši-qlam.* **2.** *waḥed.* He bought a house and didn't like it. *šra waḥed ḍ-ḍaṛ u-ma-Ɛežbettu-š.* **3.** (no equivalent in English). He bought a house. *šra ḍaṛ.* **4.** (a form of the definite article). These are 20 ryals a dozen. *hadu b-Ɛešrin ryal le-ẓ-ẓina.*

to **abandon** – **1.** *smeḥ f-.* She abandoned her son. *semḥet f-weldha.* **2.** *ġader.* He abandoned the burning house. *ġader ḍ-ḍaṛ lli kanet ka-tteḥṛeq.*

to **abbreviate** – *xtaṣeṛ.* In English 'for example' is abbreviated 'e.g.' *fe-n-negliza* 'for example' *ka-ixtaṣṛuha* 'e.g.'.

ability – **1.** *qadaṛ* pl. *ˀaqdaṛ.* He has the ability to climb (to the top of) the mountain. *Ɛendu l-qadaṛ baš iṭlƐ l-ṛaṣ ž-žbel.* **2.** *meqduṛa.* His writing ability is good. *Ɛendu meqduṛa mezyana l-le-ktaba.* **3.** *ˀimkan.* He did it to the best of his ability. *daru b-ˀeḥsen ma fe-l-ˀimkan dyalu.* **4.** Does she have the ability to do the job? *waš fe-stiṭaƐtha ddir l-xedma?*

able – *qadeṛ.* We need an able maid. *xeṣṣna ši-metƐellma qadṛa.*

to be able – **1.** *qdeṛ.* I'm able to run. *ka-neqdeṛ nežri.* **2.** *mken-lu.* He was not able to pay his rent this month. *ma-mken-lu-š ixelleṣ kratu had š-šheṛ.* **How were you able to see the king? *kif-aš Ɛmelti baš tšuf l-malik?*

aboard – **1.** *f-.* He got aboard the plane that just left. *rkeb fe-ṭ-ṭiyaṛa lli Ɛad xeṛžet.* **2.** *l-.* The boy got aboard the train to give a newspaper to his father. *l-weld tleƐ l-l-qiṭaṛ baš yeƐṭi žarida le-ḅḅah.*

to **abolish** – **1.** *qṭeƐ.* He abolished the veil. *qṭeƐ l-ltam.* –The slave market has been abolished in Morocco. *qeṭƐu s-suq d-le-Ɛbid fe-l-meġṛib.* **2.** *lġa ilġa.* He abolished three of the old laws. *lġa tlata men l-qawanin le-qdima.*

abortion – *seqṭa* pl. *-t.* My wife almost died from the abortion. *Ɛlayen mṛati kanet ġadi tmut men s-seqṭa.*

about – **1.** *teqṛiben.* There are about ten pencils on the table. *kaynin teqṛiben Ɛešṛa d-le-qluma fuq ṭ-ṭebla.* **2.** *ši.* The house is about four kilometers from here. *ḍ-ḍaṛ bƐida ši-ṛebƐa de-l-kilumiter men hna.* **3.** *Ɛla.* He talked about his children. *hḍeṛ Ɛla wladu.* –He was mad about his brother not coming. *ṭaṛ-lu Ɛla lli xah ma-ža-š.* **4.** *Ɛlayen.* Dinner is about ready. *le-Ɛša Ɛlayen tewžed.* –He spent just about all of the money. *ḍiyyeƐ Ɛlayen le-flus kollhom.* **Look at this map, I live about here. *šuf f-had l-xariṭa, ka-neskon f-had ž-žiha.* –It's about time you got here! *l-ḥemdu llah Ɛel s-slama lli žiti daba!* –Come about five o'clock. *aži fe-žwayeh l-xemsa.* –There's something about him I don't like. *kayna fih ši-ḥaža ma-ka-teƐžebni-š.* –I was just about to call you. *ṣebtini yaḷḷah ġad ndṛeb-lek t-tilifun.* –How about going for a ride in the car? *še-ḍheṛ-lek f-ši-msarya fe-ṭ-ṭumubil?* –What's this book about? *šnu f-had le-ktab?*

above – *fuq.* The bridge is above us. *l-qenṭṛa fuq menna.* –Jamal is above average. *žamal fuq men l-muƐaddal.* –A stone fell from above. *waḥed l-ḥežṛa ṭaḥet men l-fuq.* **He is above stealing. *wežhu ma-ši wžeh l-xewna.* –He's above suspicion. *huwa xaṛež Ɛel š-šekk.* –Above all I want to see the king. *bġit ktiṛ š-ši nšuf l-malik.*

abroad – **1.** *fe-l-xariž.* He was born abroad. *xlaq fe-l-xariž.* **2.** *l-l-xariž.* We should send more food abroad. *xeṣṣna nzidu nṣifṭu l-makla l-l-xariž.*

abrupt – **1.** *xšin* pl. *xšan.* He has a very abrupt manner. *sirtu xšina bezzaf.* **2.** *kbir* pl. *kbaṛ.* We noticed an abrupt change in his attitude. *laḥeḍna f-sirtu waḥed t-tebdil kbir.*

abruptly – *f-deqqa weḥda.* He stopped the car abruptly. *ḥbes s-siyaṛa f-deqqa weḥda.* **He treated me rather abruptly. *tkeṛfeṣ Ɛliya.*

absence – *ġiba.* He returned to his country after an absence of ten years. *ṛžeƐ le-bladu men beƐd waḥed l-ġiba d-Ɛešṛ snin.*

to be absent – **1.** *ġab iġib, ġiyyeb.* He was absent for a long time. *ġab weqt ṭwil.* –Two people were absent yesterday. *žuž de-n-nas kanu ġaybin l-bareḥ.* **2.** *beṭṭeḷ.* He was absent from school. *beṭṭeḷ l-meḍṛaṣa.*

absent-minded – *mṭehweṛ.*

absolute – *tamm.* Suleiman had absolute power. *sulayman kanet Ɛendu ṣoḷṭa tamma.* –That's the absolute truth. *hadi hiya l-ḥaqiqa t-tamma.*

absolutely – *tamamen.* He is absolutely wrong. *huwa ġaḷeṭ tamamen.*

**He is absolutely right. *Ɛendu l-ḥeqq bezzaf.*

to **absorb** – **1.** *šṛeb.* The earth has absorbed the rain water. *l-ʔeṛḍ šeṛbet l-ma de-š-šta.* **2.** *seff.* The sponge absorbed the spilled milk. *ž-žeffafa seffet le-ḥlib lli ttehṛeq.*

**You cannot absorb all of that material in one lesson. *ma-yemken-š had l-madda kollha ddxol-lek f-ṛaṣek f-ḍeṛṣ waḥed.*

to be absorbed: **He was so absorbed in his prayers that he did not see the fire. *kan mebluƐ fe-ṣḷatu u-gaƐ ma-šaf le-ḥṛiqa.* –He was so absorbed in his play that he didn't hear his mother calling him. *fe-l-leƐb dyalu, gaƐ ma-smeƐ m̃m̃u ka-tƐeyyeṭ-lu.*

to **abuse** – **1.** *ḍḷem.* He abuses his wife. *ka-iḍḷem mṛatu.* **2.** *ġtanem.* Many teachers abuse their authority. *Ɛadad dyal l-ʔasatida ka-iġtanmu ṣ-ṣoḷṭa dyalhom.* **3.** *tƐedda Ɛla.* Why do you abuse your little brother? *Ɛlaš ka-ttƐedda Ɛla xak ṣ-ṣġiṛ?*

academic – *dirasi.*

to **accelerate** – **1.** *zad (izid) fe-s-soṛƐa.* Tell him to accelerate. *qul-lu izid fe-s-soṛƐa.* **2.** *qewwa iqewwi.* He will accelerate production. *ġad-iqewwi l-ʔintaž.*

accelerator – *ksiliṛaṭuṛ* pl. *-at, musriƐa* pl. *masariƐ.*

accent – *lehža* pl. *-t.* He speaks Arabic with an American accent. *ka-iḥḍeṛ be-l-Ɛeṛbiya b-lehža amirikiya.*

**You must accent the last part of the word. *xeṣṣek tebrek Ɛel t-tali de-l-kelma.*

to **accept** – *qbel.* He accepted the present from his uncle. *qbel le-hdiya lli Ɛṭah Ɛemmu.* –The lawyer did not want to accept the death sentence. *l-muḥami ma-bġa-š iqbel l-ḥukm be-l-ʔiƐdam.*

accident – *ḥadita* pl. *-t, ḥawadit.* There was an accident on that street yesterday. *weqƐet waḥed l-ḥadita l-bareḥ f-dak š-šariƐ.*

**I met them by accident in Paris two years ago. *ṣaḍefthom f-bariz hadi Ɛamayn.*

accidentally: **I accidentally heard your friends talking about you. *ġir ṣeḍfa smeƐt ṣḥabek ka-iheḍṛu Ɛlik.* --I accidentally broke the dish. *bla-ma ndirha be-l-Ɛani herrest ṭ-ṭebṣil.*

to **accomodate** – **1.** *rfed.* His hotel accomodates 200 people. *l-ʔuṭil dyalu ka-irfed myatayn de-n-nas.* **2.** *tkellef b-.* I will accomodate four of them. *ġad ntkellef b-ṛebƐa menhom.*

accomodating – **1.** *ḷṭif* pl. *ḷṭaf.* The man I worked for was very accomodating. *ṛ-ṛažel lli kont xeddam mƐah ḷṭif bezzaf.* **2.** *mmeṛṛeḥ.* The next time you go to the hotel Balima you will find it very accomodating. *l-meṛṛa ž-žayya lli tenzel f-l-uṭil balima ṛak tṣibu mmeṛṛeḥ.*

accompaniment – *muṛafaqa.* The accompaniment of the guests from the airport to the palace was necessary. *l-muṛafaqa dyal ḍ-ḍyaf men l-maṭaṛ l-le-qṣeṛ kanet wažba.*

to **accompany** – **1.** *ṛafeq.* He will accompany you home. *ṛah iṛafqek ḥetta l-ḍaṛek.* **2.** *wṣeḷ mƐa.* Rashid was the one who accompanied my grandfather to the car. *rašid huwa lli wṣeḷ mƐa ḅḅa sidi ḥetta le-ṭ-ṭumubil.* **3.** Who will accompany her when she is in France? *škun lli ġad ibqa mƐaha melli tkun f-fṛanṣa?* **4.** *mša (imši) tsara mƐa.* Her aunt wanted the girl to accompany her on a trip through Egypt. *had l-bent bġatha Ɛemmtha temši ttsara mƐaha f-maṣeṛ.*

to **accomplish** – **1.** *dar idir.* He accomplished a lot in a short time. *dar bezzaf f-weqt qṣiṛ.* **2.** *kemmel.* He accomplished what he set out to do. *kəmmel dak š-ši lli dar f-balu idiru.* **3.** *Ɛmel.* Did you accomplish anything in Casablanca? *waš Ɛmelti ši-ḥaža fe-ḍ-ḍaṛ l-biḍa?* **4.** *qḍa iqḍi.* It accomplishes what I want it to do. *ka-teqḍi dak š-ši lli baġiha teqḍih.*

accomplishment - **1.** *fiɛl* pl. *ʔafɛal.* His accomplishments pleased his friends. *ṣḥabu ɛežbuhom l-ʔafɛal dyalu.* **2.** *ɛamal* pl. *ʔaɛmal.* Building the pyramids was a great accomplishment. *le-bni dyal l-ʔahṛam kan ɛamal kbir.*

accord - *ttifaq.* There was complete accord between France and Morocco. *kan ma bin fṛanṣa u-l-meġṛib ttifaq tamm.*

of one's own accord - *men ṛaṣu, b-weḥdu.* Khalid entered the army of his own accord. *xalid l-ṛaṣu dxel l-l-žiš.*

according to - **1.** *ɛla ḥasab.* According to what Rashid said you were not coming today. *ɛla ḥasab ma qal rašid ma-konti-š ġad dži l-yum.* **2.** *bḥal.* Did she cook the food according to the written instructions? *waš ṭiybet l-makla bḥal lli fe-l-ʔiršadat?*

accordion - *kir* pl. *kyar.*

account - *ḥsab* pl. *-at.* What bank do you have your account in? *f-ina ḅenk ɛendek le-ḥsab dyalek?* —The company's accounts were all burned up. *le-ḥsabat dyal š-šarika kollhom ttḥeṛqu.*

on account of - *ɛla sabab.* The party was postponed on account of the rain. *l-ḥefla tʔežžlet ɛla sabab š-šta.*

to call to account - *xaṣem ɛla.* If she was rude I will call her to account. *ila kanet qbiḥa daba nxaṣem ɛliha.*

to give an account of - **1.** *ɛṭa yeɛṭi le-ḥsab d-.* The servant will give me an account of the food bill. *l-metɛellem ġad yeɛṭini le-ḥsab de-flus l-makla.* **2.** *ɛewwed.* Give me an account of what happened. *ɛewwed-li šnu wqeɛ.*

to take into account - *ɛtabeṛ.* You have to take into account all of the details of the case. *xeṣṣek teɛtabeṛ t-tafaṣil dyal l-qaḍiya kollhom.*

to account for - **1.** *kan ikun mesʔul.* The Prime Minister has to account for his actions only to the king. *l-wazir l-ʔewwel ma-mesʔul ɛel l-ʔaɛmal dyalu illa qeddam l-malik.* **2.** *fesser.* How are you going to account for this? *kif-aš ġad tfesser had š-ši?*

accountant - *ḥsaybi* pl. *-ya.*

accurate - **1.** *dqiq* pl. *dqaq.* This adding machine is very accurate. *had l-makina d-le-ḥsab dqiqa bezzaf.* **2.** *metqun.* Are they accurate in their work? *waš metqunin fe-xdemthom?*

accurately - *b-tedqiq.* This old clock seems to still run accurately. *had l-magana le-qdima ka-iḍheṛ ɛliha ma-zala ka-ttmešša b-tedqiq.*

**My secretary does her work accurately. *l-katiba dyali ka-ttqen xdemtha.*

to **accuse** *them.* I accused them of stealing the money. *themthom be-l-xewna d-le-flus.*

to **accustom** - *wellef.* She accustomed the children to getting up early. *wellfet d-drari inuḍu bekri men n-nɛas.*

accustomed - *mwellef.* I'm not accustomed to small cars yet. *ana ma-zal ma-mwellef-š ṭ-ṭumubilat ṣ-ṣġaṛ.*

to get accustomed to - *twellef.* He got accustomed to seeing tall buildings. *twellef išuf l-binayat l-ɛalya.*

to **ache** - *wžeɛ, ḍeṛṛ.* My stomach aches. *keṛši ka-ḍḍeṛṛni.*

to **achieve** - *ḥeṣṣel ɛla, wṣel l-.* He achieved the rank of ambassador in three years. *ḥeṣṣel ɛla meṛtabt safir f-telt snin.*

acid - *l-ma l-qaṭeɛ.*

to **acknowledge** - **1.** *ɛtaṛef.* Do you acknowledge that what you did was wrong? *waš ka-teɛtaṛef biʔenna dak š-ši lli ɛmelti ma-mezyan-š?* **2.** *ɛeṛṛef, ɛlem b-.* Did you acknowledge his letter? *waš ɛeṛṛeftih be-wṣuḷ r-risala dyalu?*

acorn - *belluṭa* pl. *-t,* coll. *belluṭ.*

to **acquaint** - **1.** *ɛeṛṛef.* I want you to acquaint him with the place and the workers. *bġitek tɛeṛṛfu ɛel l-maḥell u-ɛel l-xeddama.* **2.** *ɛlem.* He will acquaint you with what happened. *ġad iɛelmek be-šnu wqeɛ.*

to be acquainted: Are you two acquainted with each other? *waš ntuma b-žuž ka-ttɛaṛfu?*

to acquaint oneself - *tɛeṛṛef.* It'll take a week to acquaint myself with the problem. *xeṣṣni žemɛa baš ntɛeṛṛef ɛel l-muškila.*

to get, become acquainted with - *tɛeṛṛef mɛa.* I'd like to get acquainted with her. *bġit ntɛeṛṛef ɛliha.*

acquaintance - *meɛrifa,* pl. *-t, mɛaref.* He is an acquaintance of mine. *huwa waḥed men le-mɛaref dyali.* —I was happy to make his acquaintance. *fṛeḥt bezzaf* *b-meƐriftu.*

to **acquire** - 1. *žmeƐ.* He acquired many books in one year. *žmeƐ Ɛadad d-le-ktub f-Ɛam waḥed.* 2. *ḥeṣṣel Ɛla.* Do you think he will acquire a new position in the government? *waš ka-ḍḍennu ġad iḥeṣṣel Ɛla ši-menṣib ždid fe-l-ḥukuma?* 3. *kseb.* Does he acquire all of that money in business? *waš ka-ikseb duk le-flus kollhom men l-biƐ u-š-šra?* 4. *xda yaxod.* Did he acquire that house for his father? *waš xda dik ḍ-ḍaṛ le-ḅḅah?*

**We acquire bad habits easily. *l-Ɛadat le-qbiḥa ka-telṣeq fina deġya deġya.*

to **acquit** - *berreʔ.* Did they convict him or acquit him? *waš ḥekmu Ɛlih wella berrʔuh?*

across - 1. *mqabel.* The bank is across the street from the post-office. *l-ḅenk žat mqabla mƐa l-buṣṭa.* 2. *qbalt.* He sat across the table from me. *gles qbalti fe-ṭ-ṭebla.* 3. *men ž-žiha l-oxṛa d-.* A new hotel will be built across the river. *ġad ibniw waḥed l-uṭil ždid men ž-žiha l-oxṛa de-l-wad.*

**Can we go across the bridge today? *waš imken-lna nduzu Ɛel l-qenṭṛa l-yum?*

act - 1. *Ɛamal* pl. *ʔeƐmal.* That was a brave act. *kan Ɛamal šžiƐ.* 2. *feṣl* pl. *fṣul.* I don't want to miss the first act. *ma-baġi-š nfellet l-feṣl l-ʔewwel.*

in the act - *f-Ɛemla.* The burglar was caught in the act. *l-xewwan tteqbeṭ fe-Ɛmeltu.*

to act - 1. *Ɛmel.* Don't act like a child. *ma-teƐmel-š bḥal d-derri ṣ-ṣġiṛ.* -I'll act on your advice. *ġad-neƐmel be-n-naṣiḥa dyalek.* 2. *mettel.* I can't act very well. *ma-imken-li-š nmettel mezyan.*

**Now it's time to act. *hada huwa weqt l-Ɛamal.*

active - *našeṭ.* He's still very active for his age. *ma-zal našeṭ mƐa ṛaṣu be-n-nesba l-sennu.*

activity - 1. *našaṭ.* He has to give up all physical activity for a while. *lazmu ismeḥ f-koll našaṭ ṛiyaḍi waḥed l-modda.* -There's very little activity around here on Sundays. *n-našaṭ ka-ikun qlil bezzaf f-had ž-žiha nhaṛ l-ḥedd.* 2. *ḥaṛaka.* Why all the activity over there? *Ɛlaš dak l-ḥaṛaka kollha temma?*

actor - *mumettil* pl. *-in.*

actress - *mumettila* pl. *-t.*

actual - *ḥaqiqi.* The actual reason was something entirely different. *s-sabab l-ḥaqiqi kan ši-axoṛ tamamen.*

actually - 1. *fe-l-ḥaqiqa, fe-l-waqiƐ.* She works here but her office is actually on the second floor. *ka-texdem hna wa-lakin l-mekteb dyalha fe-l-ḥaqiqa fe-ṭ-ṭebqa t-tanya.* 2. *ḥaqqen.* Do you actually believe that story? *waš ḥaqqen ka-tṣeḍḍeq dik le-xṛafa?*

acute - 1. *kbir* pl. *kbaṛ.* He was stricken by an acute pain. *qebṭu waḥed le-ḥṛiq kbir.* 2. *dqiq* pl. *dqaq.* Dogs have an acute sense of smell. *le-klab Ɛendhom šemman dqiq bezzaf.* 3. *ḥadd.* This triangle has two acute angles. *had l-mutellat Ɛendu žuž zawiyat ḥadda.*

**She has acute appendicitis. *Ɛendha l-meṣṛana z-zayda mṛiḍa bezzaf.*

to adapt oneself - 1. *wellef.* He adapts himself easily. *deġya ka-iwellef.* 2. *ṭṭewweṛ.* He adapts himself to situations. *ka-iṭṭewweṛ mƐa l-ḥal.*

to **add** - *zad izid.* You'll have to add some sugar. *ġad ixeṣṣek dzid ši-šwiya de-s-sokkar.* --I have nothing to add to that. *ma-Ɛendi ma nzid Ɛla had š-ši.* -Add it to my bill. *zidha Ɛel le-ḥsab dyali.*

to add up - *žmeƐ.* Add up those figures. *žmeƐ duk ṛ-ṛqam.*

to add up to - *ṭleƐ l-.* How much does this bill add up to? *le-šḥal ka-iṭleƐ had le-ḥsab?*

**It all adds up to the same thing. *bḥal bḥal.*

addition - *ḥsab.* Is my addition correct? *waš le-ḥsab dyali huwa hadak?*

in addition to - *zyada Ɛla.* In addition to that, he asked for ten dollars. *u-zyada Ɛla dak š-ši ṭleb Ɛešṛa de-ḍ-ḍulaṛ.* -In addition to his regular salary he gets a commission on what he sells. *zyada Ɛel le-xlaṣ dyalu l-Ɛadi ka-iqbeṭ ḥeqqu f-dak š-ši lli baƐ.*

additional - *zayed.* He gave me an additional amount for incidentals. *Ɛṭani waḥed l-qeḍṛ d-le-flus zayed Ɛel l-meṣṛuf l-žari.* -For an additional dollar you'll get something better than this. *b-ḍulaṛ zayed taxod ḥaža ḥsen men had š-ši.*

address - 1. *Ɛonwan* pl. *Ɛnawen, drisa*

pl. *-t.* Would you like to write down my address? *tebġi tekteb l-ɛonwan dyali?* 2. *xeṭba* pl. *-t.* The president delivered an important address. *ṛ-ṛaʔis lqa xeṭba muhimma.*

to address - 1. *bɛet, ṛsel.* The letter is addressed to me. *le-bṛa mebɛuta liya.* 2. *xaṭeb.* How shall I address him? *kif-aš ġad nxaṭbu?* 3. *lqa ilqi.* I would like to address a question to the speaker. *nebġi nelqi suʔal ɛel l-xaṭib.*

adhesive tape - *tub de-l-lṣaq.*

adjacent to - *mžaneb mɛa* or *mžaweṛ.* My garden is adjacent to his. *ž-žeṛḍa dyali mžanba mɛa dyalu.*

adjective - *neɛt.*

to **adjourn** - *weqqef, ʔežžel.* They adjourned the meeting early. *ʔežžlu le-žtimaɛ bekri.*

to **adjust** - 1. *ɛeddel, ɛewweṭ.* Did you adjust the binoculars? *waš ɛeddelti le-mrayat de-l-hend?* —He only adjusted a screw. *ġir ɛewweṭ ši-luleb.* 2. *ṣleḥ.* The manager will adjust your bill. *daba l-mudir iṣleḥ-lek l-faṭuṛa dyalek.*

to adjust oneself - *wellef.* I can't adjust myself to the climate here. *ma-imken-li-š nwellef be-ṭ-ṭeqṣ hna.*

to **administer** - *qam iqum b-.* Who's administering his estate? *škun lli qayem-lu be-l-ʔamlak dyalu?*

administration - *idaṛa.*

admiral - *amir le-bḥeṛ* pl. *umaṛa le-bḥeṛ.*

admiration - *ʔiɛžab.*

to **admire** - *tɛežžeb f-.* I admired his patience. *tɛežžebt fe-ṣ-ṣbeṛ dyalu.*

admission - 1. *dxul.* How much is the admission? *be-šḥal d-dxul?* 2. *ɛtiṛaf* pl. *-at.* His admission proved my innocence. *le-ɛtiṛaf dyalu kan ḥužža ɛel l-baṛaʔa dyali.*

admission charge - *taman d-dxul* or *flus d-dxul.*

to **admit** - 1. *xella (ixelli) idxol.* Mention my name and they'll admit you. *dkeṛ-lhom smiyti u-ṛahom ixelliwek ddxol.* 2. *ɛtaṛef.* I admit that I was wrong. *ka-neɛtaṛef be-lli kont ġaleṭ.* 3. *qbel.* They admitted him into the club. *qebluh fe-n-nadi.*

to **adopt** - 1. *xda (yaxod) baš iṛebbi.* My aunt has adopted a little girl. *ɛemmti xdat bnita baš tṛebbiha.* 2. *ttaxed, xteṛ.* He adopted the new program. *ttaxed l-beṛnamež ž-ždid.*

adult - *kbir* pl. *kbaṛ.* There was milk for the children and coffee for the adults. *kan mužud le-ḥlib le-d-drari u-l-qehwa l-le-kbaṛ.*

advance - 1. *taqeddum* pl. *-at.* There's been a great advance in medicine this year. *wqeɛ taqeddum kbir fe-ṭ-ṭibb had l-ɛam.* 2. *teṣbiq* pl. *-at.* Can you give me an advance? *waš imken-lek teɛṭini ši-teṣbiq?* 3. *zyada.* There will be an advance in prices after six o'clock. *men beɛd s-setta ġad-tkun zyada fe-t-tamanat.*

in advance - *ɛla tisaɛ.* Let me know in advance if you're coming. *ɛlemni ɛla tisaɛ waš ġad-dži wella la.*

to advance - 1. *qeddem.* He was advanced rapidly in his work. *qeddmuh fe-xdemtu b-soṛɛa.* 2. *tqeddem.* We advanced thirty kilometers in one day. *tqeddemna tlatin kilumiṭeṛ fe-nhaṛ waḥed.* 3. *ṣebbeq.* Could you advance me some money? *waš imken-lek tṣebbeq-li ši-flus?*

advantage - *fayda* pl. *-t, fawaʔid.* This method has advantages and disadvantages. *had ṭ-ṭaṛiqa fiha l-fayda u-l-xeṣṛan.*

to one's advantage - *fe-l-meṣlaḥa dyal-.* This is to your advantage. *had š-ši fe-l-meṣlaḥa dyalek.*

to have an advantage over - *ɛendu mtiyaz ɛla.* You have an advantage over me. *ɛendek mtiyaz ɛliya.*

to take advantage of - *lɛeb ɛla* (people), *ġtanem* (people or things). Don't let people take advantage of you. *ma-txelli-š n-nas teġtanmek.* —He takes advantage of every opportunity. *ka-iġtanem koll foṛṣa.*

advantageous - 1. *mfeḍḍel* comp. *ʔefḍel.* He sold his house at the most advantageous time. *baɛ ḍaṛu f-ʔefḍel weqt.* 2. *mufid, mnaseb, mwafeq.* He found himself in an advantageous position. *žbeṛ ṛaṣu f-ḥala mufida.*

adventure - *muġamaṛa* pl. *-t.* He wrote a book about his adventures in Africa. *ʔellef ktab ɛel l-muġamaṛat dyalu f-fṛiqya.*

to **advertise** - 1. *šheṛ.* The store is advertising a sale. *l-ḥanut šahṛa ši-biɛ fe-ṛ-ṛiklam.* 2. *dar (idir) iɛlan.* They are advertising for a cook. *ṛahom dayrin iɛlan ɛla ši-ṭebbax.*

advertisement - *iɛlan* pl. *-at, išhaṛ* pl. *-at.* I saw your advertisement.

šeft l-iɛlan dyalek. –The clothes that she's wearing are a good advertisement for her dressmaker. *le-ḥwayež lli labsa išhaṛ moɛtabaṛ l-l-xeyyaṭ dyalha.*

advertising – *išhaṛ, iɛlan.* Our company spends a lot on advertising. *š-šarika dyalna ka-texṣeṛ zebbala d-le-flus f-l-išhaṛ.*

advice – *naṣiḥa* pl. *-t, naṣaʔiḥ.* My advice to you is to leave immediately. *naṣihti lilek hiya texṛož daba.*

to ask one's advice – *tšaweṛ mɛa.* I asked his advice. *tšaweṛt mɛah.*

advisable – *men l-ʔeḥsen.* I think it is advisable for us to stay home today. *ka-iḍheṛ-li men l-ʔeḥsen nebqaw fe-ḍ-ḍaṛ l-yum.*

to **advise** – *nṣeḥ, weṣṣa iweṣṣi.* What do you advise me to do? *š-ka-tenṣeḥni ndir?*

to advise against – *ḥeḍḍeṛ men.* He advised me against it. *ḥeḍḍerni menha.*

adviser – *mustašaṛ* pl. *-in.* Who is his adviser? *škun huwa l-mustašaṛ dyalu?*

aerial – *ɛmud* pl. *-at, anṭin* pl. *-at.* The aerial on our radio needs fixing. *le-ɛmud dyal ṛ-ṛadyu dyalna ka-ixeṣṣu itṣewweb.*

aerial warfare – *l-ḥeṛb l-žewwiya.*

affair – **1.** *šeʔn* pl. *šuʔun.* I don't meddle in his affairs. *ma-ka-ndxol-lu-š fe-š-šuʔun dyalu.* **2.** *suq, šġal.* That's your affair. *dak š-ši šġalek nta.* **3.** *ʔamṛ* pl. *ʔumuṛ.* He handled the affairs of the company badly. *tkellef b-ʔumuṛ š-šarika b-kifiya qbiḥa.* **4.** *fṛaža* pl. *-t.* That party was the most brilliant affair of the year. *dak l-ḥefla kanet ʔeḥsen fṛaža fe-l-ɛam.* **5.** *mesʔala ġaṛamiya* pl. *mesʔalat, masaʔil ġaṛamiya.* The cook had an affair with the chauffeur. *weqɛet bin ṭ-ṭebbaxa u-š-šifuṛ ši-mesʔala ġaṛamiya.*

to **affect** – *ʔetteṛ.* That damp climate affected his health. *dak l-žeww ṛ-ṛṭeb ʔetteṛ-lu ɛla sehhtu.* ––His wife's death affected him deeply. *l-mut de-mṛatu ʔettṛet fih bezzaf.*

to **afford** – *qḍeṛ ɛla.* I can't afford that. *ma-neqḍeṛ-š ɛla hadik.*

**You can afford to laugh. *ḍḥek a wlidi, ɛṭak ḷḷah mn-aš.*

to be **afraid** – *xaf ixaf.* I'm afraid it's too late. *xeft ikun mša l-ḥal.* –Don't be afraid! *ma-txaf-š!* –He's not afraid of anyone. *ma-ka-ixaf men ḥetta waḥed.*

after – **1.** *men beɛd.* Can you call me after supper? *waš imken-lek ḍḍreb-li t-tilifun men beɛd le-ɛša?* **2.** *muṛa.* They left one after the other. *mšaw waḥed muṛa l-axuṛ.* **3.** *men beɛd-ma.* I answered him immediately after I received his letter. *žawebtu ḥinan men beɛd-ma weṣḷetni risaltu.*

**The police are after him. *l-bulis ka-tqelleb ɛlih.*

after all – **1.** *weḷḷahila.* You were right after all. *weḷḷahila ɛendek l-ḥeqq.* **2.** *ɛla kolli ḥal.* What can I do? After all he's my son. *š-ġad-neɛmel? hadak weldi ɛla kolli ḥal.*

after this: After this, please let us know in advance. *had l-meṛṛa ɛlemna ɛla tisaɛ.*

day after tomorrow – *beɛd ġedda.*

to look after – *ḥḍa yeḥḍi.* Is there anyone to look after the children? *kayen ši-waḥed lli yeḥḍi d-drari?*

afternoon – *beɛd ḍ-ḍhuṛ, ɛšiya.* He goes home every afternoon at three. *ka-imši le-ḍ-ḍaṛ koll nhaṛ men beɛd ḍ-dhuṛ fe-t-tlata.*

this afternoon – *l-yum f-le-ɛšiya.* Can you come this afternoon? *waš imken-lek dži l-yum f-le-ɛšiya?*

afterward(s) – *men beɛd.* He came at ten and I left shortly afterwards. *huwa ža fe-l-ɛešṛa w-ana xrežt ši-šwiya men beɛd.*

again – *ɛawed, ɛawed tani, nuba x̂ṛa.* I'll tell him again. *ġad-nqulha-lu ɛawed tani.* –Try it again. *ḥawelha ɛawed.*

**That's another matter again. *hadik ḥaža x̂ṛa.*

again and again – *u-ɛawed, ma-hiya meṛṛa ma-hiya žuž.* I told him again and again. *qoltha-lu ma-hiya meṛṛa ma-hiya žuž.*

time and (time) again – *meṛṛa ɛla meṛṛa, u-ɛawed.* He tried it time and again. *ḥawelha meṛṛa ɛla meṛṛa.*

against – **1.** *ḍeḍḍ.* Are you for him or against him? *waš nta mɛah wella ḍeḍḍu?* **2.** *mɛa.* Put it against the wall. *diru mɛa l-ḥiṭ.* **3.** *ɛla.* He's leaning against the wall. *huwa mtekki ɛel l-ḥiṭ.*

**Are you for the idea or against it? *waš nta mettafeq mɛa l-fikṛa wella-la?*

age – **1.** *senn.* State your age and occupation. *dkeṛ s-senn u-l-ḥerfa dyalek.* ––He's about my age. *huwa teqṛiben qeddi fe-s-senn.* **2.** *ɛaṣṛ.* This is the age of invention. *hada* *ɛaṣṛ le-xtiraɛ.*

in ages – *hadi snin, šḥal hadi.* We haven't seen them in ages. *šḥal hadi ma-šefnahom.*

to age – *šref.* He's aged a great deal lately. *šref bezzaf ɛad had l-iyamat.*

agency – *wikala* pl. *-t.*

agent – *wakil, ukil* pl. *weklan.* Your agent has already called on me. *l-wakil dyalek daz l-ɛendi beɛda.*

to **aggravate** – **1.** *zad izid ɛla.* Don't aggravate the situation. *ma-dzid-š ɛla had l-ḥala.* **2.** *qelleq.* Sometimes you're awfully aggravating. *ši-nubat ka-tqelleqni bezzaf.*

aggravation – *teṭyaṛu, ġiḍ* I get nothing but aggravation from her. *ma-ka-nžbeṛ fiha ġir teṭyaṛu.*

ago – *hadi.* I was there two months ago. *kont temma hadi šehṛayn.* –How long ago was that? *šḥal hadi baš wqeɛ had š-ši?* –That was a long time ago. *had š-ši kan šḥal hadi.*

a while ago – *hadi ši-šwiya.* He left a while ago. *hadi ši-šwiya baš mša.*

(just) a moment ago – *yaḷḷah hadi ši-šwiya.* Wasn't he here just a moment ago? *ma-kan-š hna yaḷḷah hadi ši-šwiya?*

agony – *ɛadab, ʔalam.* It was agony just to watch him. *ġir š-šufa fih kanet ɛadab.* --You're just prolonging the agony. *ha-nta ġir ka-ṭṭewwel l-ɛadab.*

to **agree** – **1.** *ttafeq.* We agreed to take turns. *ttafeqna baš ndiru n-nuba.* –They agreed on everything. *ttafqu ɛla koll ši.* –That's not what the two of you agreed on. *ma-ši dak š-ši ɛla-š ttafeqtiw b-žuž.* Do you agree? *waš mettafeq?* –The two statements don't agree. *l-bayanat b-žuž ma-mettafqin-š.* **2.** *wafeq.* Do you agree to these terms? *waš ka-twafeq ɛla had š-šuṛuṭ?* –This food doesn't agree with me. *had l-makla ma-ka-twafeqni-š.*

agreeable – *mešṛuḥ.* She has an agreeable personality. *ɛendha šexṣiya mešṛuḥ.*

to be agreeable to – *qbel.* Is he agreeable to that? *waš qabel dak š-ši?*

agreement – **1.** *muwafaqa* pl. *-t.* The agreement has to be ratified by the senate. *l-muwafaqa xeṣṣha dduz f-mežlis š-šuyux.* **2.** *ttifaq* pl. *-at.* The contract was extended by mutual agreement. *zadu fe-l-ɛoqda men beɛd ttifaq binathom b-žuž.*

in agreement – *mettafeq.* We're all in agreement on that. *kollna mettafqin ɛla dak š-ši.*

agricultural – *filaḥi, ziṛaɛi.*

agriculture – *filaḥa.* There isn't much agriculture in this region. *ma-kayna filaḥa ktira f-had n-naḥiya.*

ahead – **1.** *metqeddem.* He's ahead of everybody. *huwa metqeddem ɛel n-nas kollhom.* **2.** *sabeq, ṣabeq.* Are you next? No, he's ahead of me. *waš nubtek nta? la, huwa ṣabeqni.* **3.** *luwwel, ṣabeq.* Who's ahead in the race? *škun l-luwwel f-le-msabqa?*

straight ahead – *ṭuḷ.* Go straight ahead. *sir ṭuḷ.*

way ahead – **1.** *layen u-layen.* I'm way ahead in my work. *ana wṣeḷt layen u-layen fe-xdemti.* **2.** *ṣabeq (bezzaf).* Hurry up, the others are way ahead of us already. *serbi ṛaṣek, l-oxrin ṣabqinna beɛda.*

to get ahead – *tqeddem.* He doesn't seem to get ahead at all. *ka-idheṛ ɛlih bḥal ila gaɛ ma-ka-itqeddem.*

**You just go ahead, I'll follow later. *ġir sir ṣbeq nta, daba nexḷeṭ ɛlik men beɛd.* --Go ahead and tell him. *ġir qulha-lu.*

aid – *musaɛada, muɛawana.*

to aid – *ɛawen, saɛed.* Can I aid you in any way? *waš imken-li nɛawnek f-ši-ḥaža?*

ailing – *ɛeyyan.* She's always ailing. *hiya dima ɛeyyana.*

aim – **1.** *tenyaš.* Is your aim good? *waš t-tenyaš dyalek mezyan?* **2.** *hadaf.* His aim is to become a good doctor. *l-hadaf dyalu huwa ikun ṭbib mezyan.*

to aim – **1.** *niyyeš.* Aim higher. *niyyeš ɛali šwiya.* **2.** *ɛewwel.* What do you aim to do? *š-ka-tɛewwel ddir?*

**You're aiming too high. *ka-tniyyeš ɛla men le-qyas.* --That was aimed at me. *hadik kanet mwežžha liya.*

air – **1.** *hawa* (m.). The air in this room isn't good. *l-hawa f-had* (m.) *l-bit ma-mezyan-š.* –I have to get some fresh air. *xeṣṣni nšemm šwiya de-l-hawa.* **2.** *žeww.* There's an air of mystery about the whole affair. *kayen ši-žeww ġrib fe-l-qaḍiya kollha.*

to put on airs – *tfexxem u-tɛeḍḍem.* He loves to put on airs. *ka-iɛežbu ṛaṣu itfexxem w-itɛeḍḍem.*

to air – *hewwa ihewwi.* Please air the room while I'm out. *ɛafak hewwi l-bit ɛla ma nži.*

airfield - *maṭaṛ* pl. *-at.*
airplane - *ṭiyaṛa* pl. *-t.*
airport - *maṭaṛ* pl. *-at;* (military) *ḷabaẓ* pl. *-at.*
aisle - *medwez* pl. *mdawez.*
ajar - *meḥlul šwiya.* The door was ajar. *l-bab kanet meḥlul šwiya.*
alarm - *zuwwaga, zuwwaka* pl. *-t.* **Set the alarm for six. *dir l-magana de-s-sersar fe-s-setta.*
to alarm - *zƐež, šewweš.* Her screams alarmed the whole building. *ġwatha zƐež l-Ɛimaṛa kollha.*
to be alarmed - *tšewweš.* Don't be alarmed. *ma-ttšewweš-š.*
alarm clock - *magana de-s-sersar* pl. *maganat, mwagen de-s-sersar.*
alcohol - **1.** *alkuḷ.* Put a little alcohol on the wound. *dir ši-šwiya d-l-alkuḷ Ɛel ž-žerḥa.* **2.** *šṛab.* Muslims do not drink alcohol. *le-mselmin ma-ka-išeṛbu-š š-šṛab.*
alert - *fayeq.* He's an alert fellow, *huwa ṛažel fayeq mƐa ṛaṣu.*
on the alert: Be on the alert for a call from me. *kun Ɛla bal ṛani daba nḍṛeb-lek t-tilifun.*
Algeciras - *l-xuzirat, l-žazira l-xeḍṛa.*
Algeria - *l-žaza?ir, dzayer.*
Algerian - *žaza?iri* adj. pl. *-yin,* n. pl. *hel l-žaza?ir; dziri* adj. pl. *-yin,* n. pl. *hel dzayer.*
alike - *bḥal bḥal, kif kif.* These seats are all alike. *had le-krasa kollhom bḥal bḥal.* -We treat all our customers alike. *š-šaryin dyalna kollhom ka-nḥesbuhom kif kif.*
alien - *ažnabi* pl. *-yin.*
alive - *ḥeyy.* Get him alive or dead. *qebṭuh ḥeyy wella miyyet.*
to be alive with - *ġla iġli.* The store is alive with ants. *ḷ-ḥanut ka-teġli be-n-nmel.*
all - *koll.* Did you all go? *waš mšitiw kollkom?* -I've been waiting all day. *n-nhaṛ kollu w-ana ka-ntsenna.* -That upsets all my plans. *had š-ši hdem le-bḷanat dyali kollhom.* -The bread's all gone. *l-xobz mša kollu.*
**That's all. *had š-ši lli kayen.* -He isn't all there. *xeṣṣu ši-žuž de-l-buḷunat.* -If that's all there is to it, I'll do it. *ila kan ġir hakda, neƐmelha.* --That's all the same to me. *ana ma-Ɛendi suq.*
all along - *men l-luwwel.* We've suspected him all along. *konna šakkin fih men l-luwwel.*
to be all in - *ṣxef, Ɛya yeƐya.*
all of a sudden - *fuž?a.* All of a sudden it got dark. *fuž?a ḍlam l-ḥal.*
all over - **1.** *koll žiha.* They came from all over. *žaw men koll žiha.* **2.** *f- .... kollu.* He traveled all over the country. *ṣafeṛ f-le-blad kollha.* **3.** *kollu.* He began to tremble all over. *bda kollu ka-iġzel.*
all right - **1.** *f-?aman llah.* Is everything all right? *koll-ši f-?aman llah?* **2.** *meƐlum.* I'd like to go all right, but it's impossible. *nebġi nemši, meƐlum, be-l-ḥeqq ma-imken-li-š.* **3.** *waxxa.* That's true all right, but nevertheless ... *waxxa dak š-ši ṣeḥḥ, be-l-ḥeqq ...* -All right, I'll do it. *waxxa daba ndirha.*
**Is that all right with you? *waš ma-Ɛendek maniƐ.*
all the better - *ḥsen.* If that is so, all the better. *ila had š-ši hakda ḥsen.*
all the time - *dima.*
above all - *ktirt š-ši, xuṣuṣen.* Above all, don't get discouraged. *u-ktirt š-ši ma-tebred-š.*
after all - *weḷḷahila.* He's right after all. *la, weḷḷahila Ɛendu ṣ-ṣeḥḥ.*
at all - *gaƐ, walu.* He has no patience at all. *ma-Ɛendu ṣbeṛ gaƐ.*
in all - *bin koll-ši.* How many of them are there in all? *šḥal kaynin mennhom bin koll-ši?*
once and for all - *f-meṛṛa.* Once and for all, let's get this over with. *yaḷḷah nthennaw men had l-qaḍiya f-meṛṛa.*
alley - *medwez* pl. *mdawez, driba* pl. *-t.*
alliance - *muḥalafa* pl. *-t.*
to allow - **1.** *smeḥ b-.* He won't allow that. *ma-ġad-ismeḥ-š b-dak š-ši.* **2.** *ḥseb.* How much should I allow for traveling expenses? *šḥal ixeṣṣni neḥseb Ɛla meṣṛuf de-ṣ-ṣfeṛ?*
ally - *ḥlif* pl. *hulafa?.*
almond - *luza* pl. *-t,* coll. *luz.*
almost - *Ɛlayen.* I'm almost finished. *Ɛlayen nfeḍḍi.*
alone - *b-weḥd-.* Do you live alone? *waš saken b-weḥdek.*
**Better leave it alone! *ḥsen-lek txellih Ɛlik!* -Leave me alone! *xellini Ɛlik!*
along - **1.** *mƐa.* We walked along the shore. *tmeššina mƐa šeṭṭ le-bḥeṛ.* **2.** *b-ženb.* The road runs along the river. *ṭ-ṭriq ġadya b-ženb l-wad.*
all along - *men l-luwwel.* I told them so all along. *men l-luwwel*

w-ana ka-nqul-lhom dak š-ši.
to take along - *dda iddi mεa.* How many things should I take along? *šhal d-le-ḥwayež ka-ixeṣṣni nddi mεaya?*
**Come along with me! *yaḷḷah mεaya!*
already - *beεda.* He already speaks a little Arabic. *ṛah ka-itkellem ši-šwiya de-l-εeṛbiya beεda.*
also - see **too.**
to **alter** - *beddel, ġeyyeṛ.* Who altered my speech? *škun lli beddel l-xeṭba dyali?*
**I'll have to have the suit altered to fit me. *xeṣṣni nddi had l-keswa tteṣleḥ baš dži qeddi.*
alteration - *ʔiṣḷaḥ* pl. *-at.* There is no charge for alterations. *l-ʔiṣḷaḥat bla flus.*
although - *waxxa.* I'll be there, although I have very little time. *daba nkun temma waxxa ma-εendi-š l-weqt bezzaf.*
altitude - *εlu.* The plane was flying at a very high altitude. *ṭ-ṭiyaṛa kanet ġadya fe-εlu kbir bezzaf.*
altogether - **1.** *tamamen.* You're altogether right. *εendek ṣ-ṣeḥḥ tamamen.* **2.** *bin l-žamiε, bin koll-ši.* Altogether there are thirty books. *kaynin tlatin ktab bin koll-ši.*
alum - *šebb.*
always - *dima.* I'm always at home. *ana dima fe-ḍ-ḍaṛ.* -She's always been rich. *hiya dima kanet tažra.*
amateur - *muluε.* Frequently amateurs play better than professionals. *εadad de-l-meṛṛat l-muluεin ka-ileεbu ḥsen men lli meḥtarfin.* -For an amateur he paints quite well. *huwa ġir muluε walakin ka-iṣbeġ mezyan.*
to **amaze** - *bheḍ.* I was amazed at his indifference. *behḍetni le-bruda dyalu.*
to be amazed - *tεežžeb.*
ambassador - *safir* pl. *sufaṛa.*
amber - *εenbeṛ.*
ambition - *ṭumuḥ.* He has no ambition. *ma-εendu ṭumuḥ.* -There's no limit to his ambition. *ṭ-ṭumuḥ dyalu ma-εendu ḥedd.*
ambitious - *(lli) εendu ṭumuḥ.*
ambulance - *siyaṛa d-l-isεaf* pl. *siyaṛat d-l-isεaf.*
to **ambush** - *xrež f-.* They ambushed him in the hills. *xeṛžu fih fe-ž-žbal.*
America - *ʔamrika, blad l-mirikan.*
American - *ʔamriki; mirikani* pl. *mirikan.* He's an American. *huwa mirikani.*
among - **1.** *ma bin, f-weṣṭ.* You're among friends. *ṛak f-weṣṭ le-ṣḥab.* --Look among the papers. *šuf ma bin le-kwaġeṭ.* **2.** *εend.* He's popular among the masses. *huwa mešhuṛ εend š-šeεb.* **3.** *f-,* He's the biggest one among them. *huwa le-kbir fihom.* --There were many nice people among them. *kanu fihom bezzaf de-n-nas ḍṛaf.*
among other things - *zaydun εla ḥwayež x̂ṛin.* Among other things he collects stamps. *ka-ižmeε zaydun t-tnaber εla hwayež x̂ṛin.*
among ourselves (yourselves, themselves) - *ma binatna (binatkom, binathom).* We decided it among ourselves. *qeṛṛeṛnaha ma binatna.*
amount - *εadad.* What's the amount? *šnu huwa l-εadad?*
to amount to - *ṭḷeε, ža iži f-.* How much does the bill amount? *le-šḥal ṭḷeε le-ḥsab?* or *šḥal ža fe-l-fakṭuṛa?*
**He doesn't amount to much. *ma-ka-iswa-š kteṛ men ṣuḷḍi.*
to **amputate** - *qeṭṭeε.* His leg was amputated.
to **amuse** - *ḍeḥḥek.* That amuses me very much. *dak š-ši ka-iḍeḥḥekni bezzaf.*
to amuse oneself - *lha ilhi ṛaṣu.* He amuses himself by reading. *ka-ilhi ṛaṣu b-le-qṛaya.*
amusement - *mlahya.* He did it only for amusement. *darha ġir mlahya.*
**What do you do for amusement? *aš ka-teεmel baš dduwwez l-weqt?*
amusing - *fih ḍ-ḍeḥk.* Did you find this play amusing? *waš žak had t-temtil fih ḍ-ḍeḥk?*
ancestors - *ždud, slaf* or *ʔeslaf.*
anchor - *mexṭaf* pl. *mxaṭef.* The boat lost its anchor in the storm. *l-baxiṛa mša-lha l-mexṭef fe-l-εaṣifa.*
to drop anchor - *ṭḷeq l-mexṭaf.* The ship dropped anchor in the bay. *l-baxiṛa ṭelqet mexṭafha fe-l-xaliž.*
to weigh anchor - *qelleε l-mexṭaf.* We weighed anchor after the sea had quieted down. *qelleεna l-mexṭaf men beεd-ma thedden le-bḥeṛ.*
to anchor - *ṛeṣṣa iṛeṣṣi.* They anchored the ship near the mouth of the river. *ṛeṣṣaw s-sfina ḥda fomm l-wad.*
**He stood there as if anchored to the spot. *bqa waqef temma bḥal l-ḥežṛa.*
anchovy - *šṭun.*
ancient - *qdim* pl. *qdam.* I'm very much interested in ancient art. *l-fenn le-qdim ka-ihemmni bezzaf εad.*

--Why did you invest so much money in that ancient building? *Ɛlaš Ɛmelti had le-flus kollhom f-dak l-Ɛimaṛa le-qdima?*
**Oh, that's ancient history! *dak š-ši men Ɛehd musa.*

and - **1.** *u* (before consonants), *w* (before vowels). **2.** *wiyya-* (preceded by *ana* or *ḥna* with some pronoun ending suffixed). Only he and I were there. *kont ġir ana wiyyah temma.*
**Wait and see! *ṣbeṛ u-daba tšuf.*

Andalusia - *l-ʔandalus.*

Andalusian - *ʔandalusi* adj. pl. *-yin,* n. pl. *hel l-ʔandalus.*

anesthetic - *benž.*

angel - *malak* pl. *malayka, mlayka.*

anger - *teṭyaṛu, ġaḍab, zƐaf.*

angle - **1.** *zawiya* pl. -t. Measure each angle of the triangle. *Ɛbeṛ z-zawiyat de-l-mutellat kollhom.* **2.** *wžeh* pl. *wžuh.* We considered the matter from all angles. *Ɛtabeṛna l-qaḍiya men žamiƐ le-wžuh.*

angry - *ġeḍban.* What are you angry about? *Ɛlaš nta ġeḍban?*
to be(come) angry - *ġḍeb, ṭaṛ-l-, iṭiṛ-l-.* Please don't be angry with me! *Ɛafak ma-teġḍeb-š Ɛliya!* --Are you angry at him? *waš ṭayeṛ-lek mƐah?*

animal - *ḥayawan* pl. *-at.*

aniseed - *nafeƐ.*

ankle - *keƐba* pl. *-t, kƐab.* Did she sprain her ankle, or what? *waš ttfekket-lha keƐbetha wella šnu?*

anniversary - *dikṛa* pl. *-t.* They are celebrating their thirtieth anniversary. *meḥtaflin be-d-dikṛa (de-z-zwaž) t-tlatin dyalhom.*

to **announce** - **1.** *Ɛlem b-.* They just announced it on the radio. *yaḷḷah Ɛelmu biha fe-ṛ-ṛadyu.* **2.** *Ɛlen Ɛla.* They announced their engagement last night. *Ɛelnu Ɛla mlakhom l-bareḥ fe-l-lil.*

announcement - *iƐlan* pl. *-at, nabaʔ* pl. *ʔanbaʔ, xbaṛ* pl. *ʔaxbaṛ.*

announcer - *mudiƐ, mudiyyiƐ.* The announcer has a pleasant voice. *l-mudiƐ Ɛendu ḥelq ḍṛiyyef.*

to **annoy** - *bessel Ɛla.* Is this man annoying you? *waš had ṛ-ṛažel ka-ibessel Ɛlik?* --Stop annoying that poor dog! *baṛaka ma tbessel Ɛla dak l-kelb l-meskin!*
annoyed with - *zeƐfan mƐa.*
**That's very annoying. *dak š-si ka-iṭelleƐ z-zƐaf.*

another - *axoṛ,* f. *x̂ṛa,* pl. *x̂ṛin.* Please give me another cup of coffee. *Ɛṭini ši-kas axoṛ de-l-qehwa men feḍlek.* --I'd like another pattern. *bġit ši-škel axoṛ.* --I won't hear another word about it! *ma-nebġi-š nesmeƐ kelma x̂ṛa Ɛliha!*
one another - *beƐḍ.* (plus pl. pronoun ending) *beƐḍ, beƐḍiyat* (plus pl. pronoun ending). They hit one another. *ḍḍaṛbu beƐḍhom beƐḍ* or *ḍḍaṛbu beƐḍiyathom.*

to **antagonize** - *ṭeyyṛu-l-.* I don't want to antagonize them. *ma-baġi-š nṭeyyṛu-lhom.*

to **anticipate** - tweqqeƐ, *nwa inwa.* The attendance was larger than we had anticipated. *ḥeḍṛu n-nas kteṛ men lli konna tweqqeƐna.*
**He anticipates her every wish. *ka-iḥeḍḍeṛ-lha šnu-ma bġat men qbel gaƐ ma ṭṭeḷbu.*

anxious - **1.** *mehmum.* He's anxious about his future. *huwa mehmum Ɛel l-musteqbal dyalu.* **2.** *metšuwweq.* I'm anxious to see the new book. *ṛani metšuwweq baš nšuf le-ktab ž-ždid.* --He was just too anxious to sell. *kan metšuwweq kteṛ men le-qyas baš ibiƐ.*

any - **1.** *ši.* Do you have any other question? *Ɛendek ši-suʔal axoṛ?* --Did you find any books there? *waš žbeṛti ši-ktuba temma?* **2.** *škun-emma kan.* Any mechanic can fix it. *l-mikanisyan škun-emma kan iqḍeṛ iṣuwwebha.* --Any child knows that. *koll derri škun-emma kan ka-yeƐṛef dak š-ši.* **3.** *kif-emma kan.* Any work is better than none. *xedma kif-emma kanet ḥsen men blaš.* **4.** *ši-ḥaža d-.* Do you have any money with you? *waš mƐak ši-ḥaža d-le-flus?* **5.** (Often no equivalent in negative expressions). I don't have any money. *ma-Ɛendi flus.*
**Buy them at any price! *šrihom b-aš-emma kan!*

anybody - **1.** *ši-waḥed.* Will anybody be at the station to meet me? *waš ġad-ikun ši-waḥed metleqqi-li f-le-mḥeṭṭa?* --Did you find anybody? *waš žbeṛti ši-waḥed?* **2.** *škun-emma kan.* Anybody can do that. *škun-emma kan iqḍeṛ yeƐmel dak š-ši.*
not...anybody - *ma...ḥetta waḥed, ma...ḥetta ḥedd.* I don't know anybody here. *ma-ka-neƐref ḥetta waḥed hna.*

anyhow - **1.** *waxxa hakdak.* I said no, but he did it anyhow. *qolt-lu lla u-waxxa hakdak Ɛmelha.* **2.** *men ṛ-ṛeġm men dak š-ši.* I would have gone anyhow. *kun ṛani mšit men ṛ-ṛegm men dak š-ši.*

**What's the use anyhow! *šnu hiya l-menfiƐa beƐda?*
anyone - see **anybody**.
anything - **1.** *ši-ḥaža.* Is there anything for me here? *waš kayna ši-ḥaža liya ḥna?* --Did he say anything? *waš qal ši-ḥaža?* **2.** *šnu-mma, aš-emma.* You can have anything you like. *imken-lek taxod šnu-mma bġiti.*
anything but - *ma...gaƐ, ma... walu.* I was anything but pleased. *ma-kont-š ferḥan gaƐ.*
anything else - *ši-ḥaža xṛa.* Would you like anything else? *bġiti ši-ḥaža xṛa?*
not ... anything - *ma ... ḥetta ḥaža.* I can't do anything in this case. *ma-imken-li ndir ḥetta ḥaža f-had l-qaḍiya.*
**I wouldn't do that for anything. *ma-ndir-š dak š-ši waxxa ikun lli kan.*
anyway - **1.** *Ɛla kolli ḥal.* Sooner or later you'll have to buy a car. *daba wella ma-ši daba, Ɛla kolli ḥal ġad ixeṣṣek tešri ṭumubil.* **2.** *u-waxxa hakdak.* I didn't want to, but I did it anyway. *ma-bġit-š neƐmelha, u-waxxa hakdak Ɛmeltha.*
anywhere - **1.** *l-ši maḥell.* Are you going anywhere today? *waš ġadi l-ši maḥell l-yum?* **2.** *fayn-emma.* Anywhere you look, there's dust. *fayn-emma šefti ka-džbeṛ l-ġebṛa.*
**He'll never get anywhere. *Ɛemmṛu ma-ġad-yewṣel l-ši-ḥaža.* --That won't get you anywhere. *dak š-ši ṛah ma-ġad-iqḍi-lek say.*
not...anywhere - *ma...layn.* I don't want to go anywhere tonight. *ma-bġit nemši layn had l-lila.*
apart - *mefṛuq.* The house stands apart from the others. *ḍ-ḍar žat mefṛuqa Ɛel le-xṛin.*
to take apart - *ḥell ṭṛaf ṭṛaf.* Take it apart if necessary. *ḥellha ṭṛaf ṭṛaf ila kan lazem.*
**How do you tell the two apart? *kif-aš ka-teƐṛef waḥed men l-axuṛ?*
apartment house - *Ɛimaṛa de-s-sokna* pl. *Ɛimaṛat de-s-sokna.*
ape - *qeṛd* pl. *qṛuda.*
apiece - *l-l-waḥed.* My brother and I earned six dollars apiece. *ana u-xay rbeḥna setta de-ḍ-dulaṛ l-l-waḥed.*
to **apologize** - *Ɛtadeṛ, ṭḷeb s-smaḥa.* I apologize for doing that. *ka-neƐtadeṛ lli dert dak š-ši.* --Did you apologize to her? *waš ṭḷebti mennha s-smaḥa?*
apparatus - *ʔala* pl. *-t, makina* pl. *-t, mwaken.*
apparent - *ḍaheṛ.* It's apparent that he didn't understand the question. *ḍaheṛ ma-fhem-š s-suʔal.*
apparently - *Ɛla ma ka-iḍheṛ.* He has apparently changed his mind. *ġeyyeṛ balu Ɛla ma ka-iḍheṛ.*
appeal - *istinaf* pl. *-at.* The appeal was denied. *ṭaḷab l-istinaf tteṛfeḍ.*
to appeal - **1.** *twežžeh.* Appeal to his conscience. *twežžeh le-ḍ-ḍamiṛ dyalu.* **2.** *deqq.* It doesn't appeal to me at all. *ma-ka-ideqq-li-š gaƐ.* **3.** *ṭḷeb l-istinaf.* The lawyer decided to appeal the case. *l-muḥami qeṛṛeṛ iṭḷeb l-istinaf l-l-qaḍiya.*
to **appear** - *ḍheṛ, ban.* He appeared at the last minute. *ḍheṛ fe-d-daqiqa l-lexxra.* --This paper appears every Thursday. *had l-žarida ka-ḍḍheṛ koll xmis.* --He appears to be very sick. *ka-iḍheṛ Ɛlih mṛiḍ bezzaf.*
appearance - **1.** *ḍuhuṛ.* It's his first appearance on the stage. *hada ʔewwel ḍuhuṛ Ɛendu fe-l-mesṛeḥ.* **2.** *hiʔa, heyʔa.* You have to pay more attention to your appearance. *xeṣṣek tṛedd balek kteṛ l-l-hiʔa dyalek.*
**At least put in an appearance. *Ɛel l-ʔaqell ḍheṛ.*
appearances - *meḍheṛ, hiʔa.* I never judge by appearances. *ma-Ɛemmṛi ma-ka-neḥkem men l-meḍheṛ.* --Appearances are deceiving. *l-meḍheṛ xeddaƐ.*
**To all appearances he is a foreigner. *l-hiʔa dyalu kollha d-ši-ʔažnabi.*
appendicitis - *l-meṛḍ dyal l-meṣṛana z-zayda.*
appendix 1. *meṣṛana zayda.* He had his appendix removed when he was five. *ḥeyydu-lu l-meṣṛana z-zayda men lli kanet Ɛendu xems snin.* **2.** *fehres, fihrisa,* pl. *fhares.* Maybe you'll find it in the appendix. *imken had š-ši tṣibu fe-l-fehres.*
appetite - *šehwa, šahiya.* Our boy has a good appetite. *weldna Ɛendu šehwa ktira.*
appetizing - *(lli) ka-iftеḥ š-šahiya, (lli) ka-išehhi.*
to **applaud** - *ṣeffeq.*
applause - *teṣfiq.*
apple - *teffaḥa* pl. *-t,* coll. *teffaḥ.*
appliance - *ʔala* pl. *-t, makina* pl. *-t, mwaken.* We carry all kinds of electrical appliances. *Ɛendna ʔalat*

de-ḍ-ḍu Ɛla koll škel.

application - *ṭaḷab* pl. *-at.* I mailed in my application too late. *rselt ṭ-ṭaḷab dyali mƐeṭṭeḷ.*

application blank - *weṛqa de-ṭ-ṭaḷab,* pl. *wṛaq de-ṭ-ṭaḷab.* Fill out this application blank. *Ɛemmeṛ had l-weṛqa de-ṭ-ṭaḷab.*

to **apply** - **1.** *qeddem ṭaḷab.* I'd like to apply for a job. *bġit nqeddem ṭ-ṭaḷab dyali l-ši-xedma.* **2.** *ṭebbeq.* You've applied this rule incorrectly. *ṭebbeqti had l-qaƐida ġalṭa.* **3.** *ṭṭebbeq.* The rule doesn't apply here. *l-qaƐida ma-ka-ṭṭebbeq-š hna.* **4.** *steƐmel.* I had to apply all my strength. *tlezzemt nesteƐmel quwwti kollha.* **5.** *ṭḷa iṭḷi.* Apply the paint evenly. *ṭḷi ṣ-ṣbaġa f-koll maḥell qedd-qedd.* **6.** *wežžeh.* This order applies to everybody. *had l-ʔamṛ mwežžeh l- koll waƐed.* **7.** *kemmed b-.* Apply a hot compress every two hours. *kemmed b-fuṭa sxuna meṛṛa fe-s-saƐtayn.*

to **appoint** - *Ɛeyyen, semma, neṣṣeb.* They appointed him judge. *Ɛeyynuh qaḍi.*

appointment - **1.** *miƐad* pl. *-at.* I had to cancel all my appointments for tomorrow. *kan lazem nelġi l-miƐadat lli kanet Ɛendi l-ġedda kollha.* --I have an appointment with him. *Ɛendi mƐah miƐad.* --Did you make an appointment with the doctor? *derti ši-miƐad mƐa ṭ-ṭbib?* **2.** *tenṣib* pl. *-at, teƐyin* pl. *-at, tesmiya* pl. *-t.* Congratulations on your appointment. *ka-nhennik Ɛel t-tenṣib dyalek.*

appreciation - *teqdiṛ.* She has no appreciation for art. *ma-Ɛendha teqdiṛ l-l-fenn walu.*

approach - *ʔuslub, ṭaṛiqa, waṣiḷa.* Am I using the right approach? *waš l-ʔuslub lli ana mesteƐmlu huwa hakdak?*

**The approaches to the bridge are under repair. *ṭ-ṭoṛqan lli ka-ddi l-l-qenṭṛa ka-ttṣewweb.*

to approach - **1.** *qeṛṛeb.* They approached cautiously. *qeṛṛbu be-t-tawil.* **2.** *twežžeh l-.* Who shall I approach about the matter? *le-mmen xeṣṣni ntwežžeh Ɛel l-qaḍiya?* **3.** *dxel Ɛla.* How would you approach the problem? *kif-aš ġad-ddxol Ɛel l-muškila nta?*

appropriate - *(lli) ža f-maḥellu.* The remark is quite appropriate. *l-mulaḥaḍa žat f-mahellha.*

to appropriate - **1.** *dar idir yeddu Ɛla, xda yaxod.* My son has appropriated all my ties. *weldi dar yeddu Ɛel le-kṛafaṭat dyali kollhom.* **2.** *xeṣṣeṣ, ṛfeƐ.* The city has appropriated fifty thousand dollars for a new library. *le-mdina xeṣṣṣet xemsin ʔalef ḍuḷaṛ l-mektaba ždida.*

approval - **1.** *ttifaq.* You'll need your parents' approval. *gad-ixeṣṣek ttifaq waldik.* **2.** *muwafaqa* pl. *-t.* You'll have to get his approval on it. *ġad-ixeṣṣek tḥeṣṣel Ɛel l-muwafaqa dyalu Ɛliha.*

**Does it meet with your approval? *waš had š-ši wafqek?*

to **approve** - *qbel.* Your application has been approved. *qeblu ṭ-ṭaḷab dyalek.*

to approve of - **1.** *wafeq Ɛla.* Do you approve of my suggestion? *waš (nta) mwafeq Ɛel le-qtiṛaḥ dyali?* --He approves of my plans. *huwa mwafeq Ɛel l-mešruƐat dyali.*

approximate - *zayed naqeṣ.* The approximate length of the room is eight meters. *dyal had l-bit huwa tmenya de-l-miṭeṛ ṭ-ṭul zayed naqeṣ.*

approximately - *teqṛiben.* He left approximately a month ago. *hadi teqṛiben šheṛ baš mša.*

apricot - *mešmaša* pl. *-t,* coll. *mešmaš.*

April - *ibril, abril.*

apron - *ṭabliya* pl. *-t.*

apt - **1.** *fe-l-muḍuƐ.* That was an apt remark. *l-mulaḥaḍa kanet fe-l-muḍuƐ.* **2.** *dki* pl. *-yin, fih l-qabiliya, fayeq.* He's a very apt pupil. *huwa telmid dki bezzaf.*

Arab - *Ɛeṛbi* pl. *Ɛaṛab.*

Arabic - **1.** *l-Ɛeṛbiya.* Do you speak Arabic? *waš ka-ttkellem l-Ɛeṛbiya?* **2.** *Ɛeṛbi.* Do you like Arabic music? *ka-tebġi l-musiqa l-Ɛeṛbiya?*

arch - *qewṣ* pl. *qwaṣ.* That bridge has a tremendous arch. *dik l-qenṭṛa Ɛendha qewṣ Ɛḍim.*

fallen arches - *režlin mfeṭṭḥin.*

arched - *mqewweṣ.* This room has an arched ceiling. *had l-bit s-sqef dyalu mqewweṣ.*

architect - *muhendis* pl. *-in.*

area - **1.** *masaḥa* pl. *-t.* The area of this garden isn't very large. *had ž-žnan l-masaḥa dyalu ma-ši kbira bezzaf.* **2.** *naḥiya* pl. *-t, nawaḥi.* Does he live in this area? *waš huwa saken f-had n-naḥiya?* --The area around Casablanca is densely populated. *n-naḥiya lli ḍayṛa be-ḍ-ḍaṛ l-biḍa saknin fiha n-nas bezzaf.*

to **argue** - **1.** *tnaqeš.* They argue all

the time. *dima ka-itnaqšu.* --I won't argue about that. *ma-ġadi-š ntnaqeš f- dak š-ši.* --Don't agrue with me. *ma-tnaqeš-š mƐaya.* 2. *biyyen.* I argued that it would save us a lot of time. *biyyent bin had š-ši kan ġad-irebbeḥ-lna weqt. bezzaf.*

**You can't argue me into going there again. *ġir la-tḥawel-ši teqneƐni baš nemši l-temma Ɛawed.*

argument - 1. *noqṭa* pl. *-t, nqaṭi.* That's an argument in his favor. *hadi noqṭa men žihtu.* 2. *ḥužža* pl. *-t.* I don't follow your argument. *ma-fhemt-š l-ḥužža dyalek.* 3. *mxaṣma* pl. *-t.* We had a violent argument. *weqƐet binatna mxaṣma Ɛnifa.* 4. *mnaqša* pl. *-t.* It was just a little argument. *kanet ġir mnaqša ṣġiṛa.*

to **arise** - 1. *naḍ inuḍ.* They arose at the same time. *naḍu f-weqt waḥed.* 2. *ḍheṛ, ban.* The problem arose some time ago. *l-muškila ḍehṛet hadi ši-modda.* --Buy them as soon as the opportunity arises. *šrihom ġir ḍḍher l-foṛṣa.*

arithmetic - *ḥsab.*

arm - 1. *draƐ, dreƐ* pl. *derƐan.* He's lost an arm. *mqeṭṭeƐ-lu derƐu.* 2. *yedd* pl. *-in.* The arms of this chair are too low. *had š-šelya yeddiha meḥdurin bezzaf.* 3. *baṭ* pl. *biṭan.* Can you carry the package under your arm? *waš teqdeṛ terfed l-bakit teḥt baṭek?*

arms - *slaḥ* (coll.). All arms have to be turned over to the police. *s-slaḥ kollu xeṣṣu itsellem le-š-šoṛṭa.*

to arm - *selleḥ.*

armistice - *hedna, hodna; tewqif l-ḥeṛb.*

armor - *qešṛa.* These shells can't penetrate the armor of a warship. *had l-kuṛ ma-iqedṛu-š idexlu fe-l-qešra d-baxira ḥeṛbiya.*

army - *žiš* pl. *žyuš, Ɛesker.*

to join the army - *dxel l-l-Ɛesker.*

around - 1. *hna.* Is there anybody around? *waš kayen ši-waḥed hna?* 2. *f-.* He drove around the park. *Ɛmel ḍ-ḍuṛa fe-l-Ɛeṛṣa be-ṭ-ṭumubil.* 3. *ši, teqṛiben.* I have around twenty dirhams. *Ɛendi ši-Ɛešrin derhem.*

**He lives somewhere around here. *saken f-ši-maḥell f-had ž-žwayeh.* --She lives right around the corner. *ka-teskon fe-d-ḍuṛa de-d-derb.*

to **arouse** - *fiyyeq.* I was aroused in the middle of the night by a terrible bang. *ši-deqqa ka-tṣemmek fiyyqetni f-neṣṣ l-lil.*

**Her strange behavior aroused my suspicion. *s-sira dyalha le-ġriba dexxlet fiya š-šekk.*

to **arrange** - 1. *retteb, neḍḍem.* Who arranged the books? *škun lli retteb le-ktub?* 2. *ḍebbeṛ.* Arrange it so that you'll be here tomorrow. *ḍebbeṛ kif-aš teƐmel baš tkun hna ġedda.*

arrangement - 1. *tenḍim* pl. *-at.* How do you like this arrangement? *kif-aš žak had t-tenḍim?* 2. *tehyiʔ* pl. *-at.* They made all the arrangements to leave the following morning. *Ɛemlu t-tehyiʔat kollhom baš iṣafṛu lla-ġedda fe-ṣ-ṣbaḥ.*

arrest - *qbiḍ.*

to arrest - *qbeṭ, qbeḍ.*

arrival - *wṣul.* His arrival caused a bit of excitement. *wṣulu hezz d-denya.*

to **arrive** - *wṣel.*

arrow - *nebla* pl. *-t,* coll. *nbel.*

art - *fenn* pl. *funun.*

art gallery - *metḥef l-fenn* pl. *mtaḥef l-fenn.*

arthritis - *mfaṣel.*

artichoke - *quqa* pl. *-t,* coll. *quq.*

article - 1. *maqala* pl. *-t.* There was an interesting article about it in the newspaper. *kanet waḥed l-maqala mufida Ɛlih fe-l-žarida.* 2. *feṣl* pl. *fṣul.* I'm not clear on Article 3. *l-feṣl t-talet ma-bġa-š ittefhem-li.* 3. *ḥaža* pl. *ḥwayež.* Many valuable articles were stolen. *Ɛadad d-le-ḥwayež tmina ttxewnet.*

artificial - 1. *ṣṭinaƐi.* Are those flowers artificial? *waš dak n-nuwwaṛ ṣṭinaƐi?* 2. *meṣnuƐ.* He has an artificial leg. *Ɛendu ržel meṣnuƐa.*

artillery - *medfaƐiya.*

artist - *fennan* pl. *-a.*

as - 1. *bḥal-ma, kif-ma.* Write the letter as you wish. *kteb le-bṛa kif-ma tebġi.* 2. *men lli, melli.* Did you see anyone as you came in? *waš šefti ši-waḥed men lli dxelti?* 3. *men lli, melli, ḥit.* As he is leaving tomorrow, we must hurry. *xeṣṣna nzerbu men lli ġa-iṣafeṛ ġedda.*

**Do as you wish. *dir lli Ɛežbek.* --I regard it as important. *kaneƐtabeṛha muhimma.*

as if - *bḥal ila.*

as soon as - *ġir.* As soon as he

comes, let me know. *ġir huwa iži, ƐLemni.*
as usual - *bḥal l-Ɛada.*
so as to - We'll have to start early so as to be on time. *xeṣṣna nxeṛžu bekri baš nweṣlu fe-l-weqt.*
Asafi - *asfi.*
native of Asafi - *sfiwi* adj. pl. *-yin,* n. pl. *hel asfi.*
ash(es) - *ṛmaḍ.*
to be **ashamed** - *ḥšem.* You have no reason to be ashamed of that. *ma-Ɛendek Ɛlaš teḥšem men dak š-ši.*
ash tray - *ḍeffaya* pl. *-t, ṣiniya de-d-dexxan* pl. *ṣiniyat de-d-dexxan.*
ash tree - *derdar.*
aside - *xelli Ɛlik ...* All joking aside, I want my money. *xelli Ɛlik le-mlaġa, bġit flusi.*
aside from - *men ġiṛ, waxxa.* Aside from that, he's a nice fellow. *men ġir dak š-ši, huwa ḍṛif.*
to put aside - **1.** *xebbeƐ, xella ixelli.* Can you put the ties aside for me until tomorrow? *waš imken-lek txebbeƐ-li le-kṛafaṭat ḥetta l-ġedda?* **2.** *weffeṛ.* I think we have enough money set aside for the trip. *ka-iḍheṛ-li Ɛendna le-flus l-kafyin mweffṛin le-ṣ-ṣefra.* **3.** *xebbeƐ.* Put the book aside now. *xebbeƐ le-ktab daba.*
to stand aside - *dženneb.* Stand aside a little please. *dženneb šwiya men feḍlek.*
to **ask** - **1.** *ṣeqṣa iṣeqṣi, suwwel.* He asked me whether I had been with them or not. *ṣeqṣani waš kont mƐahom wella la.* **2.** *ṭḷeb.* Did you ask him his name? *ṭḷebti-lu smiytu?* --He asked for permission. *ṭḷeb l-ʔadn.* --He was asked to leave the house. *ṭeḷbu mennu ixṛož men ḍ-ḍaṛ.* --How much did he ask for it? *šḥal ṭḷeb fih?*
**Ask him in. *qul-lu idxol.*
to ask a question - *lqa ilqi suʔal.*
asleep - *naƐes.*
**I simply couldn't fall asleep. *ma-bġa-š iddini n-nƐas tamamen.*
asparagus - *sekkum.*
asphalt - *zeft.*
aspect - *žiha* pl. *-t.* We've considered every aspect of the problem. *Ɛtabeṛna l-muškila f-koll sifa men s-sifat dyalha.*
aspirin - *asbirin.*
to **assassinate** - *qtel.*
assault - **1.** *hužum.* The assault was repulsed with heavy losses. *l-hužum tweqqef b-xaṣaṛat kbira.* **2.** *tehdid.* He was charged with assault. *tehmuh be-t-tehdid.*
to assault - *hžem Ɛla.*
to **assemble** - **1.** *ddžmeƐ, žtameƐ.* The pupils assembled in the auditorium. *t-tlamed ddžemƐu fe-l-qaƐa d-le-žtimaƐ.* **2.** *rekkeb.* He assembles airplane engines. *ka-irekkeb l-muṭuṛat de-ṭ-ṭiyaṛat.*
assembly - *žemƐiya* pl. *-t, žtimaƐ* pl. *-at.* He spoke before a large assembly of lawyers. *xṭeb Ɛla žemƐiya kbira de-l-muḥamiyin.*
to **assign** - **1.** *Ɛṭa yeƐṭi.* The teacher has assigned us two pieces of poetry for tomorrow. *l-ʔustad Ɛṭana žuž de-l-qiṭƐat šiƐriya l-ġedda.* **2.** *Ɛeyyen.* He assigned two men to guard the prisoner. *Ɛeyyen žuž de-n-nas baš yeḥḍiw l-meszun.*
assignment - **1.** *xedma* pl. *-t.* The boss gave me an interesting assignment. *le-mƐellem Ɛṭani xedma mufida.* **2.** *tewziƐ.* The assignment of the various jobs is taken care of by the foreman. *tewziƐ l-xedmat kollhom mkellef bih hadak lli mṛaqeb š-ši.*
to **assist** - *wqef mƐa, Ɛawen, saƐed.*
assistant - *musaƐid* pl. *-in, muƐawin* pl. *-in.*
assistance - *musaƐada, muƐawana.*
associate - *šrik* pl. *šorkan.*
to associate - *txaḷeṭ.* We never did associate with them very much. *Ɛemmeṛna ma-txaḷeṭna mƐahom bezzaf.*
association - **1.** *žemƐiya* pl. *-t.* I don't think I'll join the association. *ma-ka-nḍenn-š ġad-ntšarek fe-l-žemƐiya.* **2.** *Ɛalaqa* pl. *-t.* My association with these people is my business. *Ɛalaqti mƐa had n-nas suqi.*
to **assort** - *retteb.* Assort these buttons according to size. *retteb had ṣ-ṣḍaf Ɛla ḥasab le-qyaṣ dyalhom.*
assorted - *mnewweƐ, mšekkel.* I want a kilo of assorted chocolates. *bġit kilu de-š-šeklaṭ mnewweƐ.*
to **assume** - **1.** *ḍenn (bla šekk).* I assume that he'll be there too. *ka-nḍenn bla šekk ġad-ikun temma ḥetta-huwa.* **2.** *ḥmel.* I can't assume any responsibility for that. *ma-neqḍeṛ neḥmel ḥetta ši-mesʔuliya Ɛla dak š-ši.*
**Don't assume such an air of innocence. *ma-ddir-š messek ma-ka-teƐṛef šay.*
assurance - **1.** *ḍamana.* What assurance do I have that I'll get the job? *š-men ḍamana Ɛendi billa ġad-nšedd l-xedma?* **2.** *kelma, weƐd.* He gave me his assurance that he would pay

on time. *Ɛṭani klemtu billa ġad ixeḷḷeṣ fe-l-weqt.*
to **assure** - *ˀekked.* He assured us that he'd come. *ˀekked-lna bin ġa-iži.*
asthma - *ḍiqa.*
at - **1.** *f-.* The bus stops at the next corner. *ṭ-ṭubis ka-yewqef f-had l-qent.* --I'll wait for you at the door. *ntsennak fe-l-bab.* --I'll be at home. *ġad-nkun fe-ḍ-ḍaṛ.* --I met him at the airport. *tleqqit-lu fe-l-maṭaṛ.* --He came at three o'clock. *ža fe-t-tlata.* --The children are at school. *d-drari ṛahom fe-l-meḍṛaṣa.* --It happened at night. *had š-ši wqeƐ fe-l-lil.* --I was astonished at the size of the city. *tƐežžebt fe-l-qedd d-le-mdina.* **2.** *Ɛla.* I did it at his request. *Ɛmeltha Ɛel ṭ-ṭalab dyalu.* --What are you laughing at? *Ɛlaš ka-ḍḍḥek?* **3.** *Ɛend.* We were at the tailor's. *konna Ɛend l-xeyyaṭ.* --They saw him at the dentist's. *šafuh Ɛend ṭbib s-snan.* --He lives at my brother's. (house). *ka-iskon Ɛend xay.* **4.** *l-.* We still haven't arrived at a decision. *ma-zal ma-wṣeḷna l-ḥetta ši-ḥell.*
**He's hard at work. *ka-ixdem b-žehdu kollu.* --He could read and write at the age of four. *kan ka-yeƐṛef iqṛa w-ikteb melli kanet Ɛendu ṛbeƐ snin.*
at all - *gaƐ.* I don't like him at all. *ma-ka-nebġih-š gaƐ.*
at all costs - *waxxa iqleb s-sma u-l-ˀeṛḍ.* We must get it at all costs. *waxxa nqelbu s-sma u-l-ˀeṛḍ lazem nḥewwzu dak š-ši.*
at best - *waxxa izyan šḥal ma zyan.* At best it's an unpleasant job. *waxxa dzyan šḥal ma zyanet, had l-xedma ma-fiha ma ibġi l-waḥed.*
at first - *fe-l-luwwel.* At first we didn't like the town. *fe-l-luwwel ma-Ɛežbetna-š le-mdina.*
at last - *l-ḥemdu llah.* He's here at last. *l-ḥemdu llah ha-huwa ža.*
at least - *Ɛel l-ˀaqell.* There were at least a hundred people present. *kanu ḥaḍṛin Ɛel l-ˀaqell ši-mya de-n-nas.*
at most - *kteṛ ma.* At most the bill will come to twenty dirhams. *kteṛ ma iži fe-l-fakṭuṛa huwa Ɛešrin derhem.*
at once - **1.** *daba, fe-l-ḥin.* Do it at once. *dirha daba.* **2.** *f-meṛṛa weḥda, f-weqt waḥed.* I can't do everything at once. *ma-imken-li-š ndir koll-ši f-meṛṛa weḥda.*
at that - *hna.* Let's leave the matter at that. *xellina nḥebsu l-qaḍiya hna.*
at times - *f-beƐḍ l-ˀaḥyan, f-beƐḍ l-meṛṛat.* At times I'm doubtful. *f-beƐḍ l-ˀaḥyan ka-idxol-li š-šekk.*
at will - *kif-emma bġa.* They come and go at will. *ka-idexlu w-ixeṛžu kif-emma bġaw.*
even at that - *waxxa Ɛla dak š-ši, waxxa b-dak š-ši.* Even at that I wouldn't pay a bit more. *waxxa Ɛla dak š-ši ma-nzid-š ṣulḍi.*
to **attach** - **1.** *Ɛeẓẓa.* Did she attach the belt to the dress? *waš Ɛeẓẓat ṣ-ṣemṭa fe-l-keswa?* **2.** *teqqef.* We can attach his salary if he doesn't pay. *imken-lna nteqqfu š-šehṛiya dyalu ila ma-xelleṣ-š.* **3.** *Ɛṭa yeƐṭi.* You attach too much importance to that. *ka-teƐṭi ˀahemmiya kbira kteṛ men le-qyas Ɛla dak š-ši.*
**I've become very attached to that child. *wellit ka-nḥebb dak l-weld bezzaf.* --She is very much attached to her grandmother. *ka-tebġi žeddatha bezzaf Ɛad.*
attack - **1.** *hežma* pl. *-t.* The attack was beaten back. *l-ḥežma ttḥebset.* **2.** *ḥemla* pl. *-t, ḥmula, ḥmali.* He had another attack yesterday. *žatu ḥemla x̂ṛa l-bareḥ.*
to attack - *ḥmel Ɛla.* He was violently attacked in the newspapers. *l-žaraˀid ḥemlu Ɛlih ḥemla mžehda.*
attempt - *muḥawala* pl. *-t, težriba* pl. *-t.* At least make an attempt. *Ɛel l-ˀaqell Ɛmel ši-muḥawala.*
**An attempt was made on his life. *ḥawlu iqetlu.*
to attempt - *ḥawel.* Don't attempt to do too much at one time. *ma-t-ḥawel-š teƐmel f-deqqa weḥda kteṛ men le-qyas.*
to **attend** - **1.** *ḥḍeṛ.* Did you attend the meeting? *waš ḥḍeṛti f-le-žtimaƐ?* **2.** *mša imši l-.* I attended business school. *kont ka-nemši l-meḍṛaṣa tižariya.* **3.** *qabel.* What doctor attended you? *škun huwa ṭ-ṭbib lli kan mqablek?*
to attend to - *qḍa iqḍi.* I still have some things to attend to. *ma-zal Ɛendi ši-šġal xeṣṣni neqḍihom.*
attendance - *ḥuḍuṛ.* Attendance is compulsory. *l-ḥuḍuṛ wažeb.*
**The attendance at the last three meetings has been very poor. *n-nas lli ḥeḍṛu fe-t-tlata d-le-žtimaƐat t-talya, l-Ɛadad dyalhom kan dƐif*

bezzaf.

attention - *reddan l-bal.* The children listened with attention. *d-drari tṣenntu b-reddan l-bal.*

**Attention please! *šwiya d-le-ntibah men fḍeḷkem!* --Can you do it without attracting attention? *waš imken-lak teƐmelha bla-ma iredd-lek l-bal ḥetta-waḥed?*

to call attention - *nebbeh.* I've called their attention to that repeatedly. *sḥal men meṛṛa w-ana ka-nnebbehhom Ɛla dak š-ši.*

to pay attention - *redd l-bal.* Don't pay any attention to the matter. *ma-tredd-š balek l-l-qaḍiya.*

attentively - *b-intibah, b-ihtimam!*

attitude - *hey?a.* I don't like his attitude. *ma-ka-teƐžebni-š l-hey?a dyalu.*

attorney - *muḥami* pl. *-yin.*

to attract - *žab ižib, žleb, žbed.* What's attracting the flies here? *šnu huwa lli žayeb d-debban lle-hna?*

to attract attention - *nebbeh.* Be quiet, you're attracting people's attention to us. *skot men ṣ-ṣḍaƐ, ṛak ka-tnebbeh n-nas lina.*

attractive - **1.** *žmil, mezyan.* She is very attractive. *hiya mezyana bezzaf.* **2.** *muhimm.* He proposed an attractive price to me. *Ɛṛeḍ Ɛliya taman muhimm.*

auctioneer - *dellal* pl. *-a.*

audience - **1.** *ḥaḍṛin* (pl.). They asked the audience to remain seated. *ṭeḷbu men l-ḥaḍṛin ibqaw galsin f-maḥellathom.* 2. *muqabala* pl. *-t.* I would like an audience with the king. *bġit muqabala mƐa l-malik.*

aunt - *Ɛemma* pl. *-t.* (paternal), *xala* pl. *-t* (maternal).

august - *ġušt, ?ut.*

Austria - *namsa.*

author - *mu?ellif* pl. *-in.*

authority - **1.** *ṣoḷṭa, ṣeḷṭa.* He has no authority to do that. *ma-Ɛendu ṣoḷṭa baš idir dak š-ši.* --Do you have the authority to sign this contract for him? *waš Ɛendek ṣ-ṣoḷṭa baš tnezzel xeṭṭ iddek f-had l-Ɛoqda f-maḥellu?* **2.** *mxeṣṣeṣ.* He's an authority on labor problems. *huwa mxeṣṣeṣ f-mašakil l-Ɛommal.*

authorities - *ṣuḷuṭat.* Apply to the proper authorities. *qeddem ṭ-ṭaḷab dyalek le-ṣ-ṣuḷuṭat lli mkellfa b-dak š-ši.*

to **authorize** - *Ɛṭa yeƐṭi ṣ-ṣoḷṭa.* Who authorized you to spend that money? *škun lli Ɛṭak ṣ-ṣoḷṭa baš ddfeƐ duk le-flus?*

automobile - *ṭumubil* pl. *-at, siyaṛa* pl. *-t.*

autumn - *xrif.*

available - **1.** *mužud.* All available cars are being used. *ṭ-ṭumubilat lli mužudin kollhom mešġulin daba.* **2.** *faḍi.* When will the director be available? *fuq-aš ġad-ikun l-mudir faḍi?*

**These papers were not available to me. *duk le-wṛaq ma-kan-š mesmuḥ-li newṣel-lhom.*

avenue - *šariƐ* pl. *šawariƐ.*

average - **1.** *metweṣṣeṭ.* He's of average intelligence. *d-daka? dyalu metweṣṣeṭ.* **2.** *muƐeddal.* He's better than the average. *huwa fuq l-muƐeddal.*

**We averaged forty kilometers an hour. *tmeššina b-muƐeddal ṛebƐin kilumitru fe-s-saƐa.*

to **avoid** - *beƐƐed men, besseƐ men.* Avoid that by all means. *beƐƐed men dak š-ši kif-emma kan.*

to **await** - *tsenna, ntaḍeṛ, Ɛayen.*

awake - *fayeq.*

to awake - *faq ifiq.* I awoke at seven. *feqt (men n-nƐas) fe-s-sebƐa.*

to **awaken** - *fiyyeq.* Some noise awakened me. *fiyyeqni ši-ṣḍaƐ.*

aware - *fayeq.* We're aware of that. *ḥna fayqin b-dak š-ši.*

away - **1.** *bƐid* pl. *bƐad.* His house is far away from here. *ḍ-ḍaṛ dyalu bƐida bezzaf men hna.* **2.** *mṣafeṛ, ġayeb.* Have you been away? *waš konti mṣafeṛ?*

to go away - *ṣafeṛ, mša imši.* When did he go away? *fuq-aš ṣafeṛ?*

to take away - **1.** *beƐƐed, besseƐ.* I want you to take this chair away. *bġitek tbeƐƐed had š-šelya.* 2. *zuwwel.* Take it away from him. *zuwwelha-lu.*

to throw away - *siyyeb.* Don't throw anything away. *ma-tsiyyeb ḥetta-ḥaža.*

awhile - *ši-šwiya, ši-modda qṣiṛa.* He was here awhile this afternoon. *kan hna ši-šwiya l-yum men beƐd le-ġda.*

awkward - **1.** *debbaz.* Is he awkward in his work? *waš huwa debbaz fe-xdemtu?* **2.** *(lli) ka-iḥeyyer.* It's an awkward situation. *hadik ḥala ka-tḥeyyer.*

ax - *qadum* pl. *qwadem.*

axle - *meġzel* pl. *mġazel.* The axle of the car is broken. *therres l-meġzel de-s-siyaṛa.*

B

baby - **1.** *teṛbya* pl. *-t, derri ṣġiṛ* pl. *drari ṣġaṛ.* I won't let anyone treat me like a baby. *ma-ġad-nxelli ḥetta waḥed yeḥsebni bḥal ši-derri ṣġiṛ.*
**You baby your children too much. *ka-tfeššeš wladek bezzaf.*
baby carriage - *keṛṛusa de-d-drari* pl. *keṛṛuṣat de-d-drari.*
bachelor - *ɛezri* pl. *ɛzara.*
back - **1.** *ḍheṛ* pl. *ḍhuṛ, ḍhuṛa.* He was lying on his back. *kan memdud ɛla ḍeḥṛu.* --They did it behind my back. *ɛemluha muṛa ḍehṛi.* --This chair has a higher back. *ḍheṛ had š-šelya ɛla.* **2.** *de-ḷ-ḷuṛa.* The back rooms are dark. *le-byut de-ḷ-ḷura medḷamin.*
**He isn't back yet. *ma-zal ma-ṛžeɛ-š.*
back and forth - *maši maši.* He walked back and forth in the room. *bqa maši maši fe-l-bit.*
in back of - *wṛa, muṛ, muṛa.* There's a garden in back of the house. *kayna ɛeṛṣa muṛ ḍ-ḍaṛ.*
to come back, to go back - *ržeɛ.*
to step back - *ṛžeɛ ḷ-ḷuṛ, twexxeṛ.* Step back a little bit. *ṛžeɛ ḷ-ḷuṛ šwiya.*
to back - *ˀeyyed.* All parties are backing him. *l-ˀeḥzab kollhom mˀeyydinu.*
to back up - *ṛžeɛ l-luṛ.* I still can't back up. *ma-zal ma-ɛendi kif--aš neṛžeɛ ḷ-ḷuṛ.*
backbone - *sensul, selsul* pl. *snasel, slasel.* Her backbone was injured when she was a child. *therres-lha sensulha men lli kanet ṣġiṛa.*
**Have a little backbone! *kan ɛendek ž-žebha šwiya!*
background - **1.** *qaɛ.* The background is too dark. *l-qaɛ medḷam bezzaf.* **2.** *ˀeṛḍ.* The material has a black background with white dots. *t-tub l-ˀeṛḍ dyalu keḥla u-mneqqṭa b-le-byeḍ.*
backside - *qaɛ* pl. *qiɛan.*
backward - **1.** *mˀexxeṛ, mwexxeṛ.* The people there are very backward. *n-nas temma mˀexxṛin bezzaf.* **2.** *naqeṣ f-ɛeqlu.* Her child is a bit backward. *weldha naqeṣ f-ɛeqlu.*
backward(s) - **1.** *ḷ-ḷuṛ.* He fell backwards. *ṭaḥ ḷ-ḷuṛ.* **2.** *meqlub.* You've got the coat on backwards. *ṛak labes l-kebbuṭ meqlub.*
bad - **1.** *qbiḥ* pl. *qbaḥ.* That's not a bad idea. *hadi fikṛa ma-ši qbiḥa.* **2.** *ḍɛif* pl. *ḍɛaf.* He has bad eyes. *ɛeynih ḍɛaf.* **3.** *ɛeyyan* pl. *-in, mṛiḍ* pl. *mṛaḍ.* I feel bad today. *ka-nḥess b-ṛaṣi ɛeyyan l-yum.*
**His business is going from bad to worse. *tižaṛtu ġir ka-dzid tefles.*
**Things are getting worse instead of better. *š-ši ka-izid itfelles f-ɛewṭ ma itḥessen.*
**Now he feels very bad about it. *daba ɛad nadem ɛlih.*
too bad - *xṣaṛa.* Too bad you couldn't come. *xṣaṛa ma-qḍeṛti-š dži.*
bag - **1.** *beẓṭam* pl. *bẓaṭem.* She took some change out of her bag. *xdat ši-šwiya de-ṣ-ṣeṛf men beẓṭamha.* **2.** *šanṭa* pl. *šwaneṭ.* The porter took his bags. *ṭaleb-mɛašu dda-lu š-šwaneṭ dyalu.* **3.** *xenša* pl. *xnaši.* Put these apples in a bag. *dir had t-teffaḥat f-ši xenša.*
**He took the money and I'm left holding the bag. *ɛebba le-flus u-xellani ḥaṣeḷ.*
**Who let the cat out of the bag? *škun huwa lli fḍeḥ s-serr?*
baggage - *qšaweš* (pl.). I want to send my baggage on ahead. *bġit nṣifeṭ le-qšaweš dyali huma l-luwlin.*
bail - *ḍmana* pl. *-t.* The court fixed his bail at two thousand dirhams. *l-meḥkama ḥekmet ɛlih ḍmana dyal ˀalfayn derhem.*
to put up bail for - *ḍmen.* Who's going to put up bail for him? *škun lli ġad-iḍemnu?*
to bail - *xwa ixwı.* We used our helmets to bail water out of the boat. *steɛmelna ṭ-ṭaṣat dyalna baš nexwiw le-fluka men l-ma.*
bait - *ṭoɛm, ṭoɛma.*
baker - **1.** *xebbaz* pl. *-a.* This baker has good bread. *had l-xebbaz ɛenbu xobz mezyan.* **2.** *ḥelwi* pl. *-ya.* This baker has good pastries. *had l-ḥelwi ɛendu ḥelwat mezyanin.*

balance - **1.** *mizan* pl. *myazen.* I lost my balance. *sqeṭ-li l-mizan.* --The butcher's balance isn't working right. right. *l-mizan dyal l-gezzar ma-ka-ixdem-š mezyan.* **2.** *baqiya.* Pay one third down and pay the balance in monthly installments. *sebbeq t-tulut u-l-baqiya dfeƐha men š-šheṛ le-š-šheṛ.*
**His life hung in the balance. *kanet ḥayatu Ɛla ḥafa.*
to balance - *weqqef.* Can you balance a stick on your forehead? *waš teqḍeṛ tweqqef Ɛud Ɛla žbehtek?*
**Does the account balance? *waš le-ḥsab metwazen?*
balcony - *balkuṇ* pl. *-at.*
bald - *ṣḷeƐ* pl. *ṣuḷeƐ.* He was bald at thirty. *wella ṣḷeƐ men tlatin Ɛam.*
ball - **1.** *kuṛa* pl. *-t, kwaṛi.* They played ball all afternoon. *le-Ɛšiya kollha u-huma ka-ileƐbu l-kuṛa.* **2.** *kobba* pl. *-t, kbeb.* I'd like a ball of white wool. *bġit ši-kobba de-ṣ-ṣuf biḍa.*
balled up - *meqlub ṛaṣ Ɛla režlin.* He's all balled up. *koll-ši Ɛendu meqlub-lu ṛaṣ Ɛla režlin.*
balloon - *neffaxa* pl. *-t.*
ballot - *weṛqa de-t-teṣwit* pl. *wṛaq de-t-teṣwit.*
secret ballot - *teṣwit serri.*
ballroom - *qaƐa de-ššṭiḥ* pl. *qaƐat de-š-šṭiḥ.*
banana - *banana* pl. *-t,* coll. *banan.*
band - **1.** *rbaƐa* pl. *-t, rbayeƐ.* A band of robbers attacked them. *nezlet Ɛlihom waḥed r-rbaƐa d-le-qṭaṭƐiya.* **2.** *žewq* pl. *žwaq.* The band played dance music all evening. *l-lil kollu u-l-žewq ka-ilƐeb l-muṣiqa de-š-šṭiḥ.*
bandage - *faṣma* pl. *-t.*
to bandage - *dar idir faṣma Ɛla.* You'd better bandage the cut at once. *hsen-lek ddir faṣma Ɛel ž-žeṛḥa fe-l-ḥin.*
bandit - *banḍi* pl. *-ya, qṭaṭƐi* pl. *-ya.*
bang - *ṣḍaƐ.* She was frightened by the loud bang. *ṣ-ṣḍaƐ le-qwi xleƐha.*
to bang - *zdeḥ.* He banged the book down on the table. *zdeḥ le-ktab Ɛel ṭ-ṭebḷa.* --He banged his fist on the table. *zdeḥ dbeztu Ɛel ṭ-ṭebḷa.*
banister - *ḍeṛbuz* pl. *ḍṛabez.* Hold on to the banister. *qbeṭ fe-ḍ-ḍeṛbuz.*
bank - **1.** *ḅanka, ḅenk* pl. *ḅankat, ḅnak.* I keep my money in the bank. *ana ka-nnezzel flusi fe-l-ḅanka.* **2.** *ḥeṛf* pl. *ḥṛufa, šeṭṭ* pl. *šṭuṭ.* He swam to the nearest bank. *bqa iƐum ḥetta wṣeḷ l-ʔeqṛeb ḥeṛf.*
to bank on - *ttkel Ɛla.* You can bank on that. *imken-lek ttkel Ɛla dak š-ši.*
banker - *mul l-ḅanka* pl. *mwalin le-ḅnak.*
bankrupt - *fales.*
to go bankrupt - *fles.*
bankruptcy - *falas, teflis, teflisa.*
banner - *bendiṛa* pl. *-t, bnader, banadir; ṛaya* pl. *-t.*
banquet - *ḍyafa* pl. *-t.*
bar - **1.** *qeṭƐa* pl. *-t, qṭaƐi; baḷa* pl. *-t; ṭeṛf* pl. *ṭṛaf.* Here's a bar of soap. *ha qeṭƐa de-ṣ-ṣabun.* **2.** *luḥa* pl. *-t.* He bought a bar of chocolate. *šra luḥa de-š-šeklaṭ.* **3.** *baṛ.* Let's have a drink at the bar. *yaḷḷah nšeṛbu ši-ḥaža fe-l-baṛ.*
**When were you admitted to the bar? *fuq-aš tsemmiti muḥami?*
to bar - **1.** *Ɛeṛṛeḍ.* He forgot to bar the gate. *nsa ma-Ɛeṛṛeḍ-š l-bab.* **2.** *qṭeƐ.* A fallen tree barred our way. *waḥed š-šežṛa ṭayḥa qetƐet-lna ṭ-ṭṛiq.*
barbecue - *mešwi.*
barbed wire - *selk be-s-snan* pl. *sluk(a) be-s-snan.*
barber - *ḥežžam* pl. *-a, ḥeffaf* pl. *-a, ḥellaq* pl. *-a.*
barber shop - *ḥanut l-ḥežžam.*
bare - **1.** *Ɛeryan* pl. *-in.* The trees are still bare. *š-šžeṛ ma-zala Ɛeryanin.* --The walls look so bare. *le-ḥyuṭ ka-ibanu Ɛeryanin bezzaf.* **2.** *bla tezwaq.* These are the bare facts. *hada huwa l-waqiƐ bla tezwaq.*
to bare - *Ɛeṛṛa iƐeṛṛi.* When the flag passed, the men bared their heads. *ṛ-ṛžal Ɛeṛṛaw ṛyuṣhom men lli dazet ṛ-ṛaya.*
barefoot(ed) - *b-le-hfa, hefyan.*
barely - *yaḷḷah.* He's barely ten. *yaḷḷah Ɛendu Ɛešṛ snin.*
bargain - **1.** *ttifaq.* According to our bargain, you were to pay half. *Ɛla ḥasab le-ttifaq dyalna, kan lazmek txeḷḷeṣ n-neṣṣ.* **2.** *biƐa u-šerya mezyana.* This book was a bargain. *had le-ktab kanet fih biƐa u-šerya mezyana.*
**All right, it's a bargain! *waxxa, ḷḷah irebbeḥ!*
to bargain - *tšeṭṭeṛ.*
bark - *qešṛa.* Palm trees have thick bark. *n-nxel Ɛendu qešṛa ġḷiḍa.*
to bark - **1.** *nbeḥ.* The dog barked as loud as he could. *l-kelb nbeḥ*

ɛla ma fih men žehd. --The dog barked at the children. *l-kelb nbeḥ ɛel d-drari.* 2. *ġuwwet ɛla.* The foreman barked at everybody today. *l-yum le-mɛellem ġuwwet ɛla koll-ši.*

barley - *šɛir.*

barn - *kuri* pl. *kwari.*

barrack(s) - *berraka* pl. *-t.* Our barracks are built of concrete. *l-berrakat dyalna mebniyin men l-geṣṣ.*

barrel - **1.** *bermil* pl. *bramel.* We drank a whole barrel of beer. *šṛebna bermil de-l-biṛṛa kollu.* 2. *žeɛba* pl. *-t, žɛab.* This gun barrel is bent. *ž-žeɛba d-had le-mkoḥla mɛewwža.*

base - **1.** *qaɛ* pl. *qiɛan.* The base of the statute was still standing. *l-qaɛ de-t-timtal kan ma-zal waqef.* 2. *qaɛida* pl. *qawaɛid.* There were many American bases in Morocco. *kanu fe-l-meġṛib ɛadad de-l-qawaɛid amirikiya.*

to base - *ʔesses.* What is your calculation based on? *ɛlaš mʔesses le-ḥsab dyalek?*

basement - *lakab.*

bashful - *ḥešman.*

to be bashful - *ḥšem.*

basil - *ḥbeq.*

basis - *ʔasas.* We can't continue on this basis. *ma-imken-lna-š nkemmlu ɛla had l-ʔasas.*

basin - *ṭaṣ* pl. *ṭiṣan.*

basket - *sella* pl. *-t, slel, qoffa* pl. *qfef.*

basketball - *kuṛa de-s-sella.*

to **baste** - *ṣeqqa iṣeqqi.* Did you baste the meat? *waš ṣeqqiti l-lḥem?*

bat - **1.** *ṭiṛ l-lil* pl. *ṭyuṛ l-lil.* I'm afraid of bats. *ka-nxaf men ṭiṛ l-lil.* 2. *ɛṣa* pl. *ɛṣi, ẓerwaṭa* pl. *-t, ẓṛaweṭ.* He hit the ball so hard that the bat broke. *b-quwt ž-žehd baš ḍreb l-kuṛa therrset le-ɛṣa.*

to bat - **1.** *ḍreb.* He batted the ball over the fence. *ḍreb l-kuṛa ḥetta xeṛžet men ɛel ṣ-ṣuṛ.* 2. *ṛemmeš.* He's always batting his eyes. *dima ka-iṛemmeš ɛeynih.*

**He really went to bat for me. *huwa bġa iḥami ɛliya.*

batch - **1.** *ɛeṛṛam* pl. *ɛṛaṛem.* What happened to that batch of papers that were on my desk? *dak l-ɛeṛṛam d-le-wṛaq lli kan ɛel l-mekteb dyali, fayn mša?* 2. *žmaɛa* pl. *-t.* The patrol returned with a batch of prisoners. *l-ɛessasa režɛu be-žmaɛa d-le-msažen.*

bath - **1.** *ḥemmam* pl. *-at.* Do you have a room with bath? *ɛendek ši-bit fih ḥemmam?* 2. *teḥmima* pl. *-t.* I'd like a hot bath. *bġit ši-teḥmima sxuna.*

to **bathe** - **1.** *tḥemmem.* I want to bathe before supper. *bġit ntḥemmem qbel le-ɛša.* 2. *ḥemmem, ġsel.* Bathe the baby in warm water. *ḥemmem t-teṛbya fe-l-ma dafi.* 3. *ɛam iɛum.* We went bathing in the sea almost every day. *konna ka-nemšiw nɛumu f-le-bḥeṛ ɛlayen koll nnaṛ.*

bathing cap - *ṭagiya de-l-ɛewm* pl. *ṭagiyat de-l-ɛewm.*

bathing suit - *mayyu* pl. *-wat.*

bathing trunks - *serwal de-l-ɛewm,* pl. *srawel de-l-ɛewm.*

bathrobe - *binwaṛ* pl. *-at, keswa de-l-ḥemmam* pl. *ksawi de-l-ḥemmam.*

bathroom - **1.** *ḥemmam* (for bathing). 2. *miḍa* pl. *-t, bit l-ma* pl. *byut l-ma* (toilet).

bathtub - *banyu* pl. *-wat.*

batter - *ɛžina.* Is the batter for the bread mixed? *waš mxalṭa le-ɛžina de-l-xobz?*

battery - *baṭṛi* pl. *-yat.* My car has to have a new battery. *s-siyaṛa dyali ka-ixeṣṣha baṭṛi ždida.*

battle - *mɛeṛka* pl. *mɛaṛek.*

battlefield - *midan le-mɛeṛka.*

to **bawl** - *ṣeṛṣeṛ.* That child's been bawling for an hour. *hadi saɛa u-dak d-derri ka-iṣeṛṣeṛ.*

to bawl out - *ġuwwet ɛla.* Why did he bawl you out? *ɛlaš ġuwwet ɛlik?*

bayonet - *ḥeṛba* pl. *-t.*

to **be** - **1.** *kan ikun* (pf. *kont, konti,* etc.) He will be very happy. *ġad-ikun feṛḥan bezzaf.* --Were you at home at seven o'clock? *waš konti fe-ḍ-ḍaṛ fe-s-sebɛa.* 2. (usually no equivalent for English present tense). Where is he now? *fayn huwa daba?* --This is the house that we were talking about. *hadi hiya ḍ-ḍaṛ lli konna ka-ntkellmu ɛliha.*

**Have you been here for a long time? *waš hadi modda u-nta hna?* --I've been waiting for you since yesterday. *men l-bareḥ w-ana ka-ntsennak.*

**Here you are! *hak!*

**How are you? *še-xbaṛek?*

**How much will that be? *šḥal žat?*

**Where have you been! *fayn had le-ġwayeb!*

there is, are - *kayen* (m.), *kayna* (f.), *kaynin* (pl.). Ask him what there is. *ṣeqṣih š-kayen.* --There are twenty people here. *kaynin*

Ɛešrin de-n-nas hna.

beach - *šeṭṭ le-bḥeṛ.*

beam - *gayza* pl. *-t, gwayez.* The roof was supported by strong beams. *ṣ-ṣqef kan mehzuz be-gwayez ṣḥaḥ.*

bean - *fula* pl. *-t,* coll. *ful.*

bear - *ḍebb* pl. *ḍbuba.* Are there any bears in this forest? *waš kaynin ši-ḍbuba f-had l-ġaba?*

to bear - **1.** *ṣbeṛ Ɛla.* I can't bear that idiot any longer. *ma-neqḍeṛ-š nzid neṣbeṛ Ɛla dak le-ḥmeq.* **2.** *steḥmel.* He has to bear all the trouble by himself. *lazem Ɛlih isteḥmel l-mašeqqa kollha b-weḥdu.*

bearable - *(lli) itteḥmel.* The heat is still bearable. *ṣ-ṣehḍ ma-zal imken itteḥmel.*

beard - *leḥya* pl. *-t, lḥi.*

beast - *hiša* pl. *hyuš, ḥayawan* pl. *-at.*

to **beat** - **1.** *ḍreb.* He was beating the dog with a stick. *kan ka-iḍreb l-kelb b-waḥed le-Ɛṣa.* **2.** *ġleb.* We beat them in today's contest. *ġlebnahom fe-l-mubaṛa de-l-yum.* **3.** *xeḷḷeṭ.* Don't forget to beat the egg whites. *Ɛendek tensa ma-txeḷḷeṭ-š le-byeḍ de-l-biḍ.* **4.** *qeṭṭeb.* Did you beat the carpet? *waš qeṭṭebti ẓ-ẓeṛbiya?*

**He beat me to it. *ṣbeqni liha.* --They beat him up. *helkuh be-ḍ-ḍeṛb.*

beautiful - *mezyan, ġzal.* What a beautiful day! *walayenni nhaṛ ġzal hada!*

because - *Ɛla ḥeqq-aš, Ɛla qibal.* He didn't come because he was sick. *ma-ža-š Ɛla ḥeqq-aš kan mṛiḍ.*

because of - *Ɛla sabab, Ɛla qibal.* They went into the house because of the rain. *dexlu le-ḍ-ḍaṛ Ɛla qibal š-šta.*

to **become** - **1.** *ṛžeƐ.* He became famous overnight. *ṛžeƐ mešhuṛ f-ṛemša de-l-Ɛeyn.* **2.** *wqeƐ.* What has become of them? *šnu wqeƐ-lhom?*

**What has become of my purse? *fayn mša beẓṭami?* --That color is very becoming to you. *dak l-lun ža mƐak bezzaf.*

bed - *fṛaš* pl. *-at.* He still has to stay in bed. *ma-zal ka-ixeṣṣu ibqa f-le-fṛaš.*

to go to bed - *nƐes.*

bedbug - *beqqa* pl. *-t,* coll. *beqq.*

bedding - *iẓuṛ u-ġṭi* (pl.). Air the bedding today. *hewwi l-iẓuṛ u-le-ġṭi l-yum.*

bedroom - *bit n-nƐas* pl. *byut n-nƐas.*

bedspread - *mlaya* pl. *-t.*

bee - *neḥla* pl. *-t,* coll. *nḥel.*

beef - *begri.* Give me a little bit of ground beef. *Ɛṭini ši-šwiya de-l-kefta de-l-begri.*

beehive - *žbeḥ de-n-nḥel* pl. *žbuḥa de-n-nḥel.*

beer - *biṛṛa, serbisa.*

beet - *baṛba* pl.

beetle - *xenfusa* pl. *xnafes, bu-žeƐṛan.*

before - **1.** *qbel-ma.* Call me up before you come. *ḍreb-li t-tilifun qbel-ma dži.* **2.** *qbel men.* The telegram should be here before noon. *l-beṛqiya tkun hna qbel men ṭ-ṭnaš.* --Work before pleasure. *l-xedma qbel men le-mlahya.* **3.** *men qbel.* I hadn't known him before. *ma-kont-š ka-nƐeṛfu men qbel.* --I've never been there before. *Ɛemmeṛni ma-kont temma men qbel.*

before long - *men daba šwiya.*

the day before yesterday - *wel-l-bareḥ.*

beforehand - *Ɛla tisaƐ.* I knew it beforehand. *kont Ɛaṛefha Ɛla tisaƐ.*

to **beg** - **1.** *sƐa isƐa.* The children begged for money. *d-drari sƐaw Ɛel le-flus.* --I saw him begging at the door of the hotel. *šeftu ka-isƐa fe-l-bab d-l-uṭil.* **2.** *ṛġeb.* They begged us to help them. *ṛeġbuna nƐawnuhom.*

**I beg your pardon! *smeḥ-li!*

beggar - *saƐi* pl. *seƐƐay.*

to **begin** - *bda ibda.* The show begins at half past eight. *le-fṛaža ġa-tebda fe-t-tmenya u-neṣṣ.* --It's beginning to rain. *bdat š-šta ka-ṭṭiḥ.* --He began his work yesterday. *bda l-xedma dyalu l-bareḥ.*

**To begin with, we haven't got enough money. *ʔewwalen ma-Ɛendna-š le-flus kafyin.*

beginning - *bdu.*

behind - **1.** *muṛ, muṛa.* There's a garage behind the house. *ṛah kayen waḥed l-gaṛaž muṛa ḍ-ḍaṛ.* **2.** *ḷ-ḷuṛ.* He was attacked from behind. *hežmu Ɛlih men ḷ-ḷuṛ.*

**My watch is always ten minutes behind. *l-magana dyali dima fiha qeṣmayn de-t-tiqal.*

to fall behind - *tʔexxeṛ.* He's fallen behind in his work. *tʔexxeṛ fe-xdemtu.*

to leave behind - *xella.* We had to leave our suitcases behind. *tlezzemna nxelliw šwaneṭna.*

to **belch** - *tgerreƐ.*

belief - **1.** *tiqa.* My belief in him is seriously shaken. *t-tiqa dyali fih tfeƐfƐet be-l-mufid.* **2.** *Ɛtiqad.* It is my firm belief that ...

fe-Ɛtiqadi t-tamm ...
to **believe** – **1.** *ḍenn.* I don't believe it's going to be possible for us to arrive on time. *ma-ka-nḍenn-š ġa-imken-lna nweṣlu fe-l-weqt.* **2.** *taq itiq b-.* Of course I believe him. *meƐlum ka-ntiq bih.*
to believe in – *ʔamen b-.* He doesn't believe in Christ. *ma-ka-iʔamen-š be-l-masiḥ.*
bell – *naquṣ* pl. *nwaqeṣ.*
belladonna – *ḥdež,' ḥedža.*
belly – *kerš* pl. *kruš, bṭen* pl. *bṭuna.*
to **belong** – **1.** *kan ikun dyal.* Does this book belong to you? *waš had le-ktab dyalek?* **2.** *kan ikun men.* He belongs to our club too. *ḥetta-huwa men n-nadi dyalna.*
belt – *ṣemṭa* pl. *-t, ṣmaṭi, ḥzam* pl. *-at, ḥzum.*
bench – *korsi* pl. *krasa.*
to **bend** – **1.** *Ɛewwež.* He bent the wire. *Ɛewwež s-selk.* **2.** *lwa ilwi.* The trees bend when the wind blows. *š-šžer ka-ilwiw melli ka-ihebb r-riḥ.*
to bend down – *ḥna yeḥni (l-l-ʔerḍ).* I can't bend down. *ma-ka-neqder-š neḥni l-l-ʔerḍ.*
beneath – *teḥt (men).*
**That's beneath him. *ma-huwa-š dyal dak š-ši.*
benefit – *rbeḥ.* I don't expect to get any benefit out of it. *ma-nawi iṭleƐ-li rbeḥ men had š-ši.*
bent – **1.** *metni.* He's bent with age. *ṛah metni b-le-kbeṛ.* **2.** *mƐewwež.* The nail is bent. *l-meṣmaṛ mƐewwež.*
Berber – *beṛbṛi* pl. *bṛabeṛ.*
berry – *tuta* pl. *-t* coll. *tut.*
beside – **1.** *f-ženb.* Please put this trunk beside that other one. *Ɛafak ḥeṭṭ had ṣ-ṣenduq f-ženb hadak l-axuṛ.* **2.** *ḥda.* Who's that standing beside your father? *škun huwa hadak lli waqef ḥda ḅḅak?*
**That's beside the point. *dak š-ši xaṛež Ɛel l-muḍuƐ.* --He was beside himself with rage. *kan ġa-imut b-le-ġdayed.*
besides – *zyada Ɛla dak š-ši.* He's a good worker, and besides, everybody likes him. *ka-ixdem mezyan, u-zyada Ɛla dak š-ši koll-ši ka-ibġih.*
best – **1.** *ḥsen, ʔeḥsen.* He's my best friend. *huwa ʔeḥsen ṣadiq Ɛendi.* **2.** *mxeyyeṛ.* Give me the best. *Ɛṭini le-mxeyyeṛ.* **3.** *mezyan.* It's the best in Rabat. *hiya l-mezyana fe-ṛ-ṛbaṭ.*
**I work best in the morning. *l-weqt lli ka-nexdem fih mezyan, huwa ṣ-ṣbaḥ.* --I like it best this way. *hakda ka-yeƐžebni kteṛ.* --Perhaps it's all for the best. *imken mketteb-lek fiha ḷḷah xir.* --We don't like our new house, but we'll have to make the best of it. *ḍ-ḍaṛ ž-ždida dyalna ma-Ɛažbana-š, be-l-ḥeqq ġa-ixeṣṣna neqḍiw biha.*
bet – *xṭaṛ* pl. *-at.*
to bet – *txaṭeṛ.*
to **betray** – *ġdeṛ, xan ixun.*
better – *ḥsen.* Do you have a better room? *waš Ɛendkom ši-bit ḥsen men hada?* --Do you feel better? *waš ka-tḥess b-ṛaṣek ḥsen?* --You'd better go. *ḥsen-lek temši.* --The longer the better. *koll-ma kan ṭwiḷ ḥsen.*
between – *bin* (takes the form *binat* before pl. pronoun endings). Between you and me, it's his own fault. *bini u-binek, l-faḷṭa dyalu.* --I want to sit between you. *bġit negles binatkom.*
to **beware** – *ṛeḍḍ balu.* Beware of the dog! *ṛeḍḍ balek men l-kelb!*
to **bewilder** – *ḥeyyer.*
to be bewildered – *ḥar.*
**I was completely bewildered. *kan Ɛeqli ṭayeḥ bezzaf.*
beyond – **1.** *men ... lhih.* The house is beyond the river. *ḍ-ḍaṛ men l-wad lhih.* **2.** *beƐd.* The school is right beyond the hospital. *s-sekwila beƐd ṣ-ṣbiṭaṛ šwiya.* **3.** *fuq.* She's living beyond her means. *Ɛayša fuq l-qedṛ dyalha.*
Bible – *inžil.*
bicycle – *beškliṭa* pl. *-t.* We went bicycle riding last Sunday. *l-ḥedd lli fat Ɛmelna waḥed ḍ-ḍuṛa Ɛel l-biškliṭat.*
big – *kbir* pl. *kbaṛ.*
bill – **1.** *ḥsab* pl. *-at.* I paid this bill yesterday. *xelleṣt had le-ḥsab l-bareḥ.* **2.** *menqaṛ* pl. *mnaqeṛ.* Storks have long bills. *bellarež Ɛendu l-menqaṛ ṭwiḷ.*
billfold – *bezṭam* pl. *bzaṭem.*
billion – *melyaṛ* pl. *mlayeṛ.*
to **bind** – *ḥzem.*
binoculars – *mraya de-l-hend.*
bird – *ṭiṛ* pl. *ṭyuṛ.*
birth – *zyada* pl. *-t, wlada.*
birthday – *dikṛa.*
bishop – *fil* pl. *fyal* (chess).
bit – **1.** *lezma* pl. *-t.* This bridle doesn't have a bit. *had l-lžam ma-Ɛendu lezma.* **2.** *šwiya.* Give me a little bit of butter. *Ɛṭini ši-šwiya de-s-smen.* --This tea is

a bit strong. *had atay qaṣeḥ šwiya.* --Can you wait a bit? *imken-lek ttsenna šwiya?* --We learned the story bit by bit. *le-ḥkaya tɛeṛṛefna ɛel šwiya be-šwiya.* **3.** *leqma.* There isn't a bit of bread in the house. *ma-kayna-š leqma de-l-xobz fe-ḍ-daṛ.*

to smash to bits - *herres ṭṛaf ṭṛaf.*

bite - 1. *leqma.* We haven't got a bite left. *ma-bqat-šay leqma lina.* **2.** *ɛeḍḍa.* The bite itches. *l-ɛeḍḍa ka-takolni.*

**Won't you have a bite with us? *ma-tebqa-ši ḥetta takol mɛana?*

to bite - *ɛeḍḍ.* Will the dog bite? *waš had l-kelb iɛeḍḍ?* --He bit into the apple. *ɛeḍḍ t-teffaḥa.*

bitter - 1. *merr.* This food is bitter. *had l-makla merra.* **2.** *ṣɛib* pl. *ṣɛab.* He's had some bitter experiences. *dazet ɛlih ši-tažarib ṣɛiba.*

**It was bitter cold. *l-ḥal kan bared bezzaf.* --They fought to the bitter end. *ḥaṛbu ḥetta le-t-tali.* --They're bitter enemies. *huma ɛedyan bḥal l-qeṭṭ u-l-faṛ.*

black - *kḥel* pl. *kuḥel.*

**He has a black eye. *ɛeynu mneffxa.*

blackboard - *ṣebbuṛa* pl. *-t.*

black-eyed pea - *ful gnawa* (coll.).

blacksmith - *ḥeddad* pl. *-a.*

bladder - *nbula* pl. *-t.*

blade - *neṣḷa* pl. *-t, nṣaḷi.* I need a knife with two blades. *xeṣṣni mus ɛendu žuž de-n-neṣḷat.*

blame - *lum.*

to blame - *lam ilum.* He blamed us for the accident. *lamna ɛel le-ksida.*

**Who's to blame for this? *škun lli fih l-lum ɛla had š-ši?*

blank - 1. *weṛqa* pl. *wṛaq.* Would you help me fill out this blank? *waš imken-lek tɛawenni baš nɛemmeṛ had l-weṛqa?* **2.** *maḥell xawi* pl. *maḥellat xawyin.* Fill in all the blanks. *ɛemmeṛ l-maḥellat l-xawyin kollhom.* **3.** *xawi.* There's only a blank sheet of paper in the envelope. *le-ġša ma-kayna fiha ġir weṛqa xawya ṣafi.* --My mind is blank. *ɛeqli xawi.*

blanket - *ġṭa* pl. *-wat.* Take another blanket and you won't be cold. *xud ġṭa axoṛ u-ma-iḍeṛṛek-š l-berd.*

to blanket - *ġeṭṭa.* A thick fog blanketed the airport. *waḥed ḍ-ḍbaba tqila ġeṭṭat l-maṭaṛ.*

blast - *tfeṛgiɛ.* People heard the blast from a long way off. *n-nas semɛu t-tfeṛgiɛ men bɛid.*

full blast - *ɛel ž-žehd.* The plant is going full blast. *l-meɛmel ka-itmešša ɛel ž-žehd.*

blaze - *ɛafya.*

blazing - *ḥaṛṛ.* We had to stand for a half hour in the blazing sun. *kan lazem ɛlina nweqfu neṣṣ saɛa f-šemš ḥaṛṛa.*

to **bleach** - *biyyeḍ.*

to **bleed** - *sal isil d-demm.* My hand is bleeding. *ka-isil d-demm men iddi.* --He nearly bled to death. *demmu sal ḥetta qeṛṛeb imut.*

blind - 1. *ɛma* f. *ɛemya* pl. *ɛumi; bṣiṛ* pl. *bṣaṛ.* He's been blind for a long time. *šhal hadi u-huwa ɛma.* **2.** *ḍeṛṛaqa* pl. *-t, ḍṛareq.* Shall I pull up the blinds? *nṭeḷḷeɛ ḍ-ḍeṛṛaqa?*

blind in one eye - *ɛweṛ* pl. *ɛewṛin, ɛiweṛ.*

to go blind - *tbeṣṣeṛ, ɛma yeɛma.* I hope he's not going blind. *ka-nṭḷeb ḷḷah ma-ikun-ši ġad-itbeṣṣeṛ.*

to blind - *ɛma yeɛmi.* The sun is blinding me. *š-šemš ka-teɛmini.*

blindman's buff - *ġommayḍa* (not used with art).

to **blink** - *ṛmeš.*

blister - *nebbala* pl. *-t, nbabel.*

to **block** - *ḥbes, qṭeɛ.* They blocked the road. *ḥebsu ṭ-ṭṛiq.*

blond - *ẓɛeṛ* pl. *ẓuɛeṛ.*

blood - *demm.*

blood pressure - *ḍeġṭ d-demm.*

bloom - *nuwwaṛa* pl. *-t* coll. *nuwwaṛ.*

in bloom - *mnuwweṛ.*

to bloom - *nuwweṛ.*

blot - *ṭebɛa* pl. *-t.* The page is full of blots. *l-weṛqa ɛamṛa b-ṭebɛat.*

to blot - *neššef.* Blot your signature before you fold the letter. *neššef xeṭṭ yeddek qbel-ma ṭṭwi le-bṛa.*

to blot out - *ḍeṛṛeq.* The trees blot out the view. *š-šžeṛ ka-iḍeṛṛeq l-menḍeṛ.*

to blot up - *neššef.* Take a blotter and blot up the ink. *xud neššafa u-neššef le-mdad.*

blotter - *neššafa* pl. *-t.*

blouse - *bḷuẓa* pl. *-t, bḷayeẓ.*

blow - *ḍeqqa* pl. *-t, ḍeṛba* pl. *-t.* He killed him with a single blow. *qetlu b-ḍeṛba weḥda.*

to blow - *ṣaṭ iṣuṭ.* A strong wind is blowing. *waḥed r-riḥ kbir ka-iṣuṭ.*

to blow away - *ddah iddih r-riḥ.* The wind blew the paper away. *l-weṛqa ddaha r-riḥ.*

to blow out - 1. *ḍfa iḍfi.*

Blow out the candle. *dfi š-šmaɛa.* **2.** *tferg̣eɛ.* The tire blew out. *le-bnu tferg̣eɛ.*

to blow up - 1. *neffex.* Blow up this balloon. *neffex had n-neffaxa.* **2.** *ferg̣eɛ.* The enemy has blown up all the bridges. *le-ɛdu ferg̣eɛ le-qnaṭeṛ kollhom.* **3.** *tferg̣eɛ.* The ship blew up. *l-baxira tferg̣ɛet.*

to blow the horn - *zuwweg.* We blew the horn three times. *zuwwegna tlata de-l-meṛṛat.*

blowtorch - *kuwwaya* pl. *-t.*

blue - *zṛeq* pl. *zuṛeq.*

blunder - *ġeḷṭa* pl. *-t.*

blunt - *ḥafi.* This knife is too blunt. *had l-mus ḥafi bezzaf.*

to **blush -** *ḥmaṛ.*

board - *luḥa* pl. *-t, lwaḥ* coll. *luḥ.* We need some large boards. *xeṣṣna ši-lwaḥ kbaṛ.*

to board - *rkeb f-.* We boarded the train in Tangier. *rkebna fe-l-mašina f-ṭanža.*

boarder - *daxili.* He's a boarder at this school. *huwa daxili f-had l-meḍṛaṣa.*

to **boast -** *ftaxeṛ.*

boat - 1. *fluka* pl. *-t, flayek* (small, rowing or sail). **2.** *ḅaḅ(ḅ)uṛ* pl. *-at* (large, steam).

body - 1. *dat, žasad.* He has a large body. *datu kbira.* **2.** *žetta* pl. *-t.* They took the body to the cemetary. *ddaw ž-žetta le-ṛ-ṛuḍa.*

**They left the room in a body. *xeṛžu men l-bit fe-žmaɛa.*

boil - *nefṭa* pl. *-t, nfaṭi.* He had a boil on his neck. *kanet ɛendu nefṭa f-ɛenqu.*

to boil - 1. *ṭab iṭib; ġla iġli.* The water is boiling. *l-ma ka-iṭib.* **2.** *ṭiyyeb, ġella.* Boil this water! *ṭiyyeb had l-ma.* **3.** *ṣḷeq.* Please boil the egg two minutes. *ṣḷeq l-biḍa žuž de-d-dqiqat ɛafak.*

boiler - *beṛma* pl. *-t, bṛem.* The boiler exploded. *l-beṛma tferg̣ɛet.*

bold - *zaɛem.*

bolt - 1. *buḷun* pl. *-at.* This bolt won't go into the nut. *had l-buḷun ma-bġa-š idxol fe-ṛ-ṛaṣ.* **2.** *ḥezma* pl. *-t, ḥzami.* There are ten meters of material left in this bolt. *baqyin ɛešṛa mitṛu de-l-kettan f-had l-ḥezma.* **3.** *ẓekṛum* pl. *ẓkaṛem.* Did you push the bolt shut? *waš šedditi ẓ-ẓekṛum?*

to bolt - *ẓekṛem.* You forgot to bolt the garage door. *nsiti ma-ẓekṛemti-š bab l-gaṛaž.*

bomb - *ḅumḅa* pl. *-t, qenbula* pl. *qanabil.*

bond - *ḅun* pl. *ḅwan.* He bought government bonds with his money. *šra ḅwan men l-ḥukuma b-le-flus dyalu.*

**There's a firm bond between the two friends. *kayna ṣoḥba kbira binathom b-žuž.*

bone - *ɛḍem* pl. *ɛḍam, ɛḍuma.* Give the dog a bone. *ɛṭi ɛḍem l-l-kelb.* --He's nothing but skin and bones. *huwa želdu ɛla ɛḍama.*

**He made no bones about his intentions. *ma-xzen-š lli f-niytu.* --I have a bone to pick with you. *ɛendi ši-ḥsiyyba mɛak.* --I have a bone to pick with you. *ɛendi ši-ḥsiyyba mɛak.*

book - *ktab* pl. *ktub.*

bookkeeper - *ḥsaybi* pl. *-ya.*

booklet - *ktiyyeb* pl. *ktiyybat.*

boom - 1. *deqq.* You could hear the boom of the cannon. *kan imken-lek tesmeɛ d-deqq d-le-mdafeɛ.* **2.** *weqt r-rwaž.* He made all his money in the boom. *rbeḥ flusu kollhom f-weqt r-rwaž.*

**He has a booming voice. *ɛendu ṣut ɛali.* --Our business is booming now. *l-biɛ u-š-šra dyalna fih r-rbeḥ bezzaf daba.*

to **boost -** *ṭeḷḷeɛ.* The drought has boosted the prices of corn. *qellet š-šta ṭeḷḷɛet t-taman de-ḍ-ḍṛa.*

boots - *ṣebbaṭ ṭaleɛ.*

border - 1. *ḥdada.* When do we cross the border? *weqt-aš ġadi nqeṭɛu le-ḥdada?* **2.** *ḥašya* pl. *-t, ḥwaši.* The border of this rug is a little frayed. *l-ḥašya d-had ẓ-ẓeṛbiya melḥusa šwiya.*

**Morocco is bordered on the east by Algeria. *l-žazaʔir mžawṛa l-meġṛib fe-ž-žiha š-šeṛqiya.* --That borders on the ridiculous. *had š-ši ɛlayen wṣeḷ l-le-bsala.*

to **bore - 1.** *ḥfeṛ.* We'll have to bore a hole through the wall. *lazemna nḥefṛu teqba fe-l-ḥiṭ.* **2.** *qenneṭ.* His talking bored me. *qenneṭni be-klamu.*

to be **born** → *xlaq, dzad.* Where were you born? *fayn xlaqiti?* --She was born blind. *xlaqet bṣiṛa.*

to **borrow -** *tsellef, sellef.* She borrowed the book from him. *tsellfet le-ktab men ɛendu.*

boss - *mɛellem.* Do you know my boss? *waš ka-teɛref le-mɛellem dyali?*

**Who wouldn't want to be his own boss? *škun lli kṛeh ikun d-ṛaṣu?*

to boss - *tḥekkem.* Who gave him

the right to boss me around? *škun lli Ɛṭah l-ḥeqq baš itḥekkem fiya?*
both - *b-žuž.* Both brothers are in the navy. *l-xut b-žuž fe-l-beḥriya.* --We both visited him. *ḥna b-žuž ẓeṛnah.* --I like to do them both equally well. *ana nebġi neƐmelhom b-žuž mliḥ.*
bother - **1.** *bas.* It's no bother at all. *ma-fiha ḥetta bas.* **2.** *basel.* He's a bother. *huwa basel.*
**Don't go to any bother on my account. *ma-tkellef-š nefsek Ɛla ḥsabi.*
to bother - **1.** *bessel Ɛla, ṣeḍḍeƐ.* Don't bother me! *ma-tbessel-š Ɛliya!* **2.** *ḍiyyeq Ɛla.* Does the smoke bother you? *waš d-dexxan ka-iḍiyyeq Ɛlik?*
**What's bothering you? *aš Ɛendek?* --I can't bother with that. *ma-baġi-š nḍiyyeƐ weqti mƐa had š-si.*
bottle - *qeṛƐa* pl. *-t, qṛaƐi, ṛḍuma* pl. *ṛḍayem.*
bottom - **1.** *qaƐ* pl. *qiƐan.* He found it in the bottom of the box. *lqaha f-qaƐ ṣ-ṣenḍuq.* **2.** *teḥt.* They searched the house from top to bottom. *fettšu ḍ-ḍaṛ men l-fuq l-l-teḥt.*
**We have to get to the bottom of this affair. *xeṣṣna nbeḥtu f-sabab had l-qaḍiya.* --We've reached bottom! *wṣelna l-lli qal žḥa.*
to **bounce** - **1.** *ḍṛeb mƐa.* This ball doesn't bounce. *had l-kuṛa ma-ka-ḍḍreb-š mƐa ḷ-ḷerḍ.* **2.** *neqqez.* The little boy bounced in the chair. *neqqez le-wliyyed Ɛel š-šelya.*
bound - **1.** *mwežžeh.* This boat is bound for Morocco. *had l-babuṛ mṣafeṛ /l-l-meġṛib.* **2.** *mektab.* It's bound to happen. *mektaba tewqeƐ.* **3.** *ḥedd* pl. *ḥdud.* His pride knows no bounds. *t-takebbuṛ dyalu ma-Ɛendu ḥedd.*
to bound - *ḥedd.* Algeria is bounded on the East by Tunisia. *l-žazaʔir ḥaddaha tunes fe-ž-žiha š-šeṛqiya.*
boundary - *ḥedd* pl. *ḥdud.*
bouquet - *mešmum* pl. *mšamem.*
bow - **1.** *qeddam.* I like to stand at the bow of the ship. *ka-nebġi newqef fe-l-qeddam de-l-babuṛ.* **2.** *tbendiqa* (as before a king).
to bow - **1.** *bendeq.* He bowed and left the stage. *bendeq u-xrež men l-mesreḥ* **2.** *Ɛmel xaṭeṛ.* He bowed to his father's wishes. *Ɛmel xaṭeṛ ḇḇah.*
bow - **1.** *qewṣ* pl. *qwaṣ.* Boys like to play with bows and arrows. *le-wlad ka-ibġiw ileƐbu be-l-qewṣ u-n-nbel.* **2.** *Ɛeqda* pl. *-t, Ɛqad.* She had a pretty bow in her hair. *kanet Ɛendha Ɛeqda zwina fe-šƐeṛha.*
bowl - *žebbaniya* pl. *-t, žbaben.*
bowlegged - *režlih mqewwṣin.* We're all bowlegged. *ḥna kollna režlina mqewwṣin.*
box - *ṣenḍuq* pl. *ṣnaḍeq.*
to **box** - *lakem,* (sport).
boxer - *mlakem.*
boxing - *mulakama.*
box office - *ṭaqa* pl. *-t, ṭyeq.*
boy - *weld* pl. *wlad.*
brace - *žbira* pl. *-t.* He's still wearing a brace on his left leg. *ma-zala režlu l-iṣṛa fe-ž-žbira.*
to brace oneself - *ttekka.* They both braced themselves against the door. *huma b-žuž ttekkaw Ɛel l-bab.*
bracelet - *demliž* pl. *dmalež, debliž* pl. *dbalež.*
to **brag** - *fšeṛ, faḥ ifuḥ.*
braid - *teḍfiṛa.*
to braid - *ḍeffeṛ.*
brain - *moxx* pl. *mxax, mxuxa; dmaġ* pl. *-at.* This brain tastes good. *had l-moxx fih maḍaq mezyan.*
**He hasn't a brain in his head. *huwa mfelles.*
brains - *Ɛqeḷ.* She hasn't got much brains. *ma-Ɛendha Ɛqel bezzaf.*
to rack one's brains - *herres ṛaṣu.* Don't rack your brains over that. *ma-therres-š ṛaṣek Ɛla had š-ši.*
to brain someone - *herres ṛ-ṛas l-.* If you do that again I'll brain you. *ila Ɛawed Ɛmeltiha ṛani nherres-lek ṛaṣek.*
brake - *ḥeṣṣaṛ* pl. *ḥṣaṣeṛ, fran* pl. *-at.* The brake doesn't work. *l-ḥeṣṣaṛ ma-xeddam-š.*
to put on the brakes - *brek Ɛel l-ḥeṣṣaṛ.*
branch - **1.** *Ɛeṛš* pl. *Ɛṛuš.* The wind broke off several branches. *ṛ-riḥ herres Ɛadad d-le-Ɛṛuš.* **2.** *feṛƐ* pl. *fuṛuƐ.* Our firm has a branch in Casablanca. *š-šarika dyalna Ɛendha feṛƐ fe-ḍ-ḍaṛ l-biḍa.*
to branch off - *ttefṛeq.* The road branches off here. *ṭ-ṭṛiq ka-ittefṛeq hna.*
brand - *nuƐ* pl. *nwaƐ, maṛka* pl. *-t.* What brand do you smoke? *aš-men maṛka ka-tekmi?*
to brand - *ṛšem.* He was branded as a traitor. *huwa ṛešmuh xaʔin.* --Have the new horses been branded? *waš ṛešmu l-xil ž-ždad?*
brand-new - *yaḷḷah ždid* pl. *yaḷḷah*

ždad.
brandy - *ma-ḥya.*
brass - *nḥas ṣfeṛ.*
brawl - *mdabza, mḍaṛba, mšabka.*
brave - *šžiƐ* pl. *šžaƐ.*
bread - *xobz.*
**How does he earn his bread? *kif ka-iṣuwweṛ meṣṛufu?*
loaf of bread - *xobza* pl. *-t, kesra de-l-xobz* pl. *kesrat de-l-xobz.*
breadth - *Ɛoṛḍ.*
break - *inqiṭaƐ.* A break between the two countries can no longer be avoided. *la-bodda yewqeƐ inqiṭaƐ bin l-beldan b-žuž.*
**Let's give him a break! *nṛexfu Ɛlih!*
bad, tough break - *meḥna* pl. *mḥayen.* He's had a lot of tough breaks. *huwa dazu Ɛlih le-mḥayen.*
**That's a tough break! *ya laṭif!*
to break - **1.** *herres.* I broke his leg. *herrest-lu režlu.* --Who broke the dish? *škun lli herres ṭ-ṭebṣil?* **2.** *ṛžeƐ Ɛla.* He won't break his word. *ma-gad-iṛžeƐ-š Ɛla klamu.* **3.** *qṭeƐ.* She broke her engagement with him. *qeṭƐet le-mlak mƐah.* **4.** *qeṭṭeƐ.* He broke the string. *qeṭṭeƐ l-qennba.* **5.** *tteqṭeƐ.* The string broke. *l-qennba ttqeṭƐet.* **6.** *tƐedda.* He has broken the law. *tƐedda l-qanun.* **7.** *belleġ.* We'll have to break the news to him gently. *xeṣṣna nbellġu-lu le-xbaṛ b-siyasa.*
to break down - **1.** *txeṣṣeṛ.* The machine broke down this morning. *l-makina txeṣṣṛet l-yum fe-ṣ-ṣbaḥ.* **2.** *rzem.* He broke down when he heard the news. *rzem melli smeƐ le-xbaṛ.*
to break in - **1.** *derreb.* I'll have to break in a new man. *xeṣṣni nderreb ṛažel ždid.* **2.** *dxel.* Thieves broke into our neighbor's house yesterday. *l-bareḥ l-xuwwana dexlu le-ḍ-ḍaṛ dyal žaṛna.*
to break off - **1.** *qṭeƐ.* They have broken off relations. *qeṭƐu l-muƐalaqat.* **2.** *therres.* Then the branch broke off. *u-men beƐd l-Ɛeṛš therres.*
to break out - **1.** *hṛeb.* He broke out of prison. *hṛeb men l-ḥebs.* **2.** *šƐel.* The fire broke out toward midnight. *l-Ɛafya šeƐlet fe-žwayeh neṣṣ l-lil.*
to break up - **1.** *feṛṛeq.* The meeting was broken up by the police. *š-šoṛṭa feṛṛqet l-mežmeƐ.* **2.** *therres.* The ice will break up soon. *ġadi t-telž itherres men beƐd ši-šwiya.* **3.** *tfeṛṛeq.* Break it up! *tfeṛṛqu!* or *siru f-ḥalkom! f-ḥalkom!*
to break someone of something - *qṭeƐ Ɛla.* I'll break him of that. *ġad-neqṭeƐha Ɛlih.*
breakfast - *fṭuṛ* pl. *-at.*
to breakfast, have breakfast - *fṭeṛ.*
breast - *bezzula* pl. *bzazel.*
breath - *nefs.*
out of breath - *sexfan.*
to catch one's breath - *tneffes.* I have to catch my breath first. *xeṣṣni ntneffes beƐda.*
**Don't breathe a word of this to anyone. *xelli hada bini n-binek.*
breeze - *riḥ xfif, ġerbi.*
bribe - *rešwa* pl. *-t.*
to bribe - *ṛša irši.*
brick - *yažuṛa* pl. *-t* coll. *yažuṛ.*
bricklayer - *bennay* pl. *-a.*
bride - *Ɛṛuṣa* pl. *-t, Ɛṛayeṣ, Ɛṛayṣat.*
bridge - *qenṭra* pl. *-t, qnaṭeṛ.*
bridle - *lžam* pl. *-at.*
brief - *qṣiṛ.* That was a very brief report. *had t-teqrir kan qṣiṛ bezzaf.*
in brief - *bla-ma iṭuwweḷ.* In brief, this is our plan. *bla-ma nṭuwwlu, hada huwa l-beṛnamež dyalna.*
to be brief - *qeṣṣeṛ.* Please be brief. *Ɛafak qeṣṣeṛ.*
bright - **1.** *naṣeḥ.* I like a bright fire. *ana ka-nebġi l-Ɛafya naṣḥa.* --She likes to wear bright colors. *hiya ka-tebġi telbes l-lwan naṣḥin.* **2.** *daki.* He's a bright boy. *huwa weld daki.* **3.** *Ɛažib.* That's a bright idea! *fikṛa Ɛažiba hadik!*
**She's always bright and cheerful. *hiya dima xfifa u-feṛḥana.* --We have to start out bright and early. *lazemna nebdaw fe-ṣ-ṣbaḥ bekri.*
brilliant - **1.** *lameƐ.* You can tell his paintings by the brilliant colors. *imken-lek teƐṛef tṣawṛu be-lwanhom l-lamƐin.* **2.** *mumtaz.* He's a brilliant speaker. *huwa xaṭib mumtaz.*
**He's the most brilliant man I know. *huwa ʔadka ṛažel ka-neƐṛef.*
brim - *fomm* pl. *fwam, fmam.* The glass is filled to the brim. *l-kas Ɛameṛ ḥetta l-l-fomm.*
to **bring** - *žab ižib.* Bring the children along. *žib d-drari mƐak.*
to bring back - *ṛežžeƐ.*
to bring down - *hebbeṭ, nezzel.* Did you bring down the big box? *waš*

hebbetti ṣ-ṣenduq le-kbir?
to bring in - 1. *rbeḥ.* We brought in fifty thousand francs with that sale. *rbeḥna xemsin alef frenk f-dik l-biɛa.* **2.** *ḥeḍḍeṛ.* The lawyer brought in a new piece of evidence. *l-muhami ḥeḍḍeṛ hužža ždida.* **3.** *dexxel.* Did you bring in all the suitcases? *waš dexxelti š-šwaneṭ kollhom?*
to bring out - 1. *xerrež.* They are bringing out a new edition of my book. *ġa-ixerržu ṭebɛa ždida dyal ktabi.* **2.** *fesser.* He brought out his point convincingly to them. *fesser-lhom l-fikṛa dyalu b-ʔiqnaɛ.*
to bring someone to - *fiyyeq.* Cold water will bring him to. *l-ma l-bared ifiyyqu.*
to bring up - 1. *ṛebba.* She was brought up by her aunt. *hiya ṛebbatha xaltha.* **2.** *qeddem.* I'll bring it up at the next meeting. *ġa-nqeddemha f-le-žtimaɛ ž-žay.*
British - *bṛiṭani.*
broad - *waseɛ.*
**It happened in broad daylight. *weqɛet f-weṣṭ n-nhaṛ.*
broadcast - *idaɛa* pl. *-t.*
to broadcast - 1. *nšeṛ idaɛa.* They'll broadcast directly from London. *ġadi inešṛu idaɛa qaṣda men London.* **2.** *diyyeɛ.* If you tell her, she'll broadcast it all over the neighborhood. *ila qoltiha-lha, ṛaha ddiyyeɛha fe-l-ḥuma kollha.*
broke - *ḥazeq.* I'm broke again. *ana ḥazeq tani.*
to go broke - *bqa ibqa bla flus.*
bronze - *nḥas ḥmeṛ.*
broom - *šeṭṭaba* pl. *-t, šṭaṭeb.*
brother - *ax* pl. *xut.* My brother *xay, xuya; xa-* or *xu-* before the other pronoun endings.
brow - *žebha* pl. *-t, žbeh.*
brown - *ṣmeṛ* pl. *ṣumeṛ, qehwi.*
to brown - *ḥemmeṛ.* Brown the potatoes first. *ḥemmeṛ le-bṭaṭa beɛda.*
bruise - *teqṣiḥa* pl. *-t.*
to bruise - *qeṣṣeḥ.*
brunette - *ṣemṛa* pl. *-t.*
brush - *šiṭa* pl. *-t, šyeṭ.*
to brush - *šiyyeṭ.*
brutal - *qaṣeḥ, weḥši.*
bubble - *buwwaqa* pl. *bwaweq.*
bucket - *ṣṭel* pl. *ṣṭuḷa* (metal); *qobb* pl. *qbab* (wood). *dlu* pl. *delwan, dlawi* (leather).
buckle - *bzim* pl. *bzayem.*
to buckle - *ḥzem.* I can't buckle the strap. *ma-imkenli-š neḥzem ṣ-ṣemṭa.*
bud - *zerriɛa* pl. *-t.* The frost killed all the buds. *t-telž keṛṛem z-zerriɛa kollha.*
**The uprising was nipped in the bud. *l-fetna ttḥeṣṛet f-le-bdu dyalu.*
budget - *mizaniya* pl. *-t.*
bug - *bexxuša* pl. *-t* coll. *bexxuš.*
to **build -** *bna ibni.*
building - *bni* pl. *binaʔat.*
bulb - *buḷa* pl. *-t.* This bulb is burned out. *had l-buḷa ttḥeṛqet.*
Bulgaria - *bulġarya.*
bulk - *ktir.* The bulk of my salary goes for food and rent. *ka-neṣṛef le-ktir f-l-ožṛa dyali fe-l-makla u-le-kra.*
bullet - *qeṛṭaṣa* pl. *-t, qṛaṭeṣ; ṛṣaṣa* pl. *-t* coll. *ṛṣaṣ.*
bump - 1. *beṛquqa* pl. *-t.* Where did you get that bump on your head? *mnin žatek hadik l-beṛquqa ɛla ṛasek?* **2.** *tqelqiza* pl. *-t.* The car went over a bump. *ṭ-ṭumubil dazet ɛla tqelqiza.*
to bump into - 1. *tlaqa.* Guess who I bumped into yesterday. *ila ɛṛefti škun lli tlaqit l-bareḥ.* **2.** *ɛteṛ f-.* He bumped into the chair in the dark. *ɛteṛ fe- š-šelya fe-ḍ-ḍlam.*
bumpy - *mqelqez.* We drove for an hour over a bumpy road. *ṣegna saɛa f-waḥed ṭ-ṭṛiq mqelqez.*
bunch - *ṛebṭa* pl. *-t.* Let me have a bunch of radishes please. *ɛṭini ṛebṭa d-le-fžel ɛafak.*
bundle - *ḥezma* pl. *-t, ḥzami; ṛezma* pl. *-t.*
burden - 1. *hemm* pl. *hmum, humum.* I don't want to be a burden to you. *ana ma-baġi nzid ɛla hemmek.* **2.** *ḥmel* pl. *ḥmal.* That's too heavy a burden for your donkey. *had le-ḥmel tqil bezzaf ɛel le-ḥmaṛ dyalek.*
bureau - 1. *maryu* pl. *-wat.* The bottom drawer of the bureau is stuck. *le-mžeṛṛ t-teḥtani de-l-maryu ḥaṣel.* **2.** *ʔidaṛa* (office, department).
burglar - *ṣeṛṛaq* pl. *-a.*
burglary - *xewna* pl. *-t.*
burial - *dfin, dfana, gnaza* pl. *gnayez.*
burn - *ḥeṛqa* pl. *-t.* This is a serious burn! *ḥeṛqa waɛṛa hadi!*
to burn - 1. *šɛel.* This wood burns well. *had l-ɛud ka-išɛel mezyan.* **2.** *ḥṛeq.* They burned their old papers. *ḥeṛqu wṛaqhom le-qdam.* **3.** *tteḥṛeq.* The building has burned (down). *le-bni tteḥṛeq (kollu).* --The lightbulb is burned out. *l-buḷa ttḥeṛqet.* --His books burned

up in the fire. *le-ktub dyalu ttḥerqu fe-l-ɛafya.*
**The rice tastes burnt. *ṭibt le-ḥṛaq fe-r-ruz.* --He's burned up because he can't come along. *ṭayeṛ-lu bezzaf ɛla ḥeqq-aš ma-imken-lu-š iži mɛana.*

to **burst - 1.** *tfeṛgeɛ.* The water pipe burst. *ž-žeɛba de-l-ma tfeṛgɛet.* --He burst into laughter. *tfeṛgeɛ be-ḍ-ḍeḥk.* --She burst into tears. *tfeṛgɛet b-le-bka.* **2.** *therres.* Last year the dam burst. *s-sedd therres l-ɛam lli fat.*

to **bury - 1.** *dfen.* She was buried yesterday. *defnuha l-bareḥ.* **2.** *ġeṭṭa.* My passport was buried under the other papers. *kan ž-žawaz dyali mġeṭṭi teḥt le-wṛaq le-xṛin.*

bus - *ṭubis* pl. *-at.*

bush - *šžiṛa* pl. *-t.*

business - 1. *tižaṛa, biɛ u-šra.* They do a lot of business. *ka-idiru l-biɛ u-š-šra bezzaf.* **2.** *qadiya.* Let's settle this business right now. *yaḷḷah nfeḍḍiw had l-qaḍiya daba.* **3.** *suq.* Don't meddle in other people's business. *ma-ddxol-š f-suq ġirek.* --Mind your own business! *dxol f-suq ṛaṣek.* --That's none of your business. *hada ma-ši suqek.* **4.** *šġol.* He knows his business. *ka-yeɛṛef šoġlu.* **5.** *ḥerfa* pl. *-t, ḥrayef* (profession). What business is he in? *aš-en hiya ḥfeftu?*
**You have no business around here. *ma-ɛendek ma teɛmel hnaya.* --Business comes before pleasure. *l-xedma qbel le-mlaġa.*

businessman - *biyyaɛ u-šerray* pl. *biyyaɛa u-šerraya.*

busy - *mešġul.* I'm busy and I don't have time to read the newspaper. *ana mešġul u-ma-ɛendi weqt baš neqṛa l-žarida.* --The line's busy. *xeṭṭ t-tilifun mešġul.*
**They live on a busy street. *ka-iseknu f-zenqa fiha l-maši u-l-maža.*

but - 1. *walakin, be-l-ḥeqq.* We can go with you but we'll have to come back early. *nqeḍṛu nemšiw mɛak walakin xeṣṣna nṛežɛu bekri.* --But you know that I can't go. *be-l-ḥeqq ka-teɛṛef ma-imken-li-š nemši.* **2.** *ġir, illa.* Nobody was there but me. *ḥetta waḥed ma-kan temma illa ana.* --All but one were saved. *nežžawhom kollhom ġir waḥed.*
all but - *ɛlayen.* He got very upset and all but wrecked the machine. *tqelleq bezzaf u-ɛlayen iherres l-makina.*
nothing but - *ġir.* Nothing but lies! *ġir le-kdub.*

butcher - *gezzar* pl. *-a.*

butt - 1. *qebḍa* pl. *-a, qbaḍi.* Take the pistol by the butt. *šebbeṛ l-ferdi men l-qebḍa.* **2.** *denba* pl. *dnabi.* The ash tray is full of butts. *ḍ-ḍeffaya ɛamṛa be-dnabi.*
to butt - *nṭeḥ.* The goat kept butting his head against the wall. *l-ɛetrus bqa inṭeḥ ṛaṣu fe- l-ḥiṭ.*
to butt in - *dexxel ṛaṣu f-.* That's none of your business, so don't butt in. *hada ma-ši suqek, ma-ddexxel-š ṛašek fih.*

butter - *zebda* (freshly made), *smen.*

butterfly - *bu-feṛṭiṭu* pl. *-yat.*

button - *ṣedfa* pl. *-t; ṣdafa* pl. *-t.* She sewed the button on for me. *xeyyṭet-li ṣ-ṣedfa.* --You have to press the button. *xeṣṣek twerṛek ɛel ṣ-ṣedfa.*

buttonhole - *ɛeyn ṣ-ṣdafa.*

buy - *šerya* pl. *-t.* That's a good buy. *hadik šerya mezyana.*
to buy - *šra išri.*

buzz - *dzenzin.*
to buzz - *zenzen, ṭenṭen.*

by - 1. *l-.* The house stands close by the river. *ḍ-ḍaṛ qṛiba l-l-wad.* **2.** *b-.* The store was closed by order of the police. *l-ḥanut ttšeddat b-ʔameṛ men š-šoṛṭa.* --Little by little he pushed his way out of the crowd. *šwiya be-šwiya xerrež ṛaṣu men l-ġaši.* --They make this by machine. *ka-iṣenɛu had š-ši be-l-makina.* --They sell apples by the kilo. *ka-ibiɛu t-teffaḥ be-l-kilu.* --One by one they left the room. *waḥed b-waḥed xeṛžu men l-bit.* **3.** *f-.* I'll send it to you by mail. *ġad nṣifetha-lek fe-l-barid.* --We came by car. *žina fe-ṭ-ṭumubil.* **4.** *qbel.* He'll be back by five o'clock. *ġadi iṛžeɛ qbel l-xemsa.*

C

cab - *ṭaksi* pl. *-yat.*
cabbage - *kṛomba* pl. *-t,* coll. *kṛomb.*
cabin - **1.** *beṛṛaka* pl. *-t, bṛaṛek.* We have a cabin in the mountains. *ɛendna beṛṛaka fe-ž-žbel.* **2.** *qamṛa* pl. *-t.* This steamer has a lot of cabins. *had l-babbuṛ fih bezzaf de-l-qamṛat.*
cabinet - **1.** *xzana* pl. *-t, xzayen.* We keep our good dishes in a small cabinet. *ka-nxebbɛu ṭbaṣeḷna l-mezyanin fe-xzana ṣġiṛa.* **2.** *mežlis l-wuẓaṛa.* The cabinet met yesterday with the king. *l-bareḥ ddžmeɛ mežlis l-wuzaṛa mɛa l-malik.*
cabinetmaker - *nežžaṛ* pl. *-a.*
cable - **1.** *selk* pl. *sluk, slukat.* Can they install the cable within ten days? *waš imken-lhom irekkbu s-selk f-ɛešṛ iyyam?* **2.** *ṭiḷigṛam* pl. *-at.* I want to send a cable to Casablanca. *ana baġi nṣifeṭ ṭiḷigṛam le-ḍ-ḍaṛ l-biḍa.*
cadet - *telmid ḥeṛbi* pl. *tlamed ḥeṛbiyin.*
cafe - *qehwa* pl. *qhawi.*
cage - *qfez* pl. *qfuza, qfaz.*
Cairo - *l-qahiṛa.*
cake - *ḥelwa* pl. *-t, ḥlawi.*
cake of soap - *ṣabuna* pl. *-t.*
to **calculate** - *ḥseb, ṭeḷḷeɛ.* It was difficult to calculate the cost. *kan ṣɛib iṭeḷḷeɛ t-taman.*
calendar - **1.** *yumiya* pl. *-t.* I need a good calendar. *xeṣṣni ši-yumiya mezyana.* **2.** *beṛnamež* pl. *baṛamiž.* What events are on the calendar this month? *aš men našaṭ kayen fe-l-beṛnamež had š-šheṛ?*
calf - **1.** *ɛžel* pl. *ɛžul, ɛžula.* Cows and calves were grazing in the field. *begṛat u-ɛžul kanu ka-iṛɛaw fe-l-meṛɛa.* **2.** *ɛanan.* This satchel is made of calf. *had š-škaṛa meṣnuɛa men l-ɛanan.* **3.** *ṣag* pl. *ṣigan.* The bullet struck him in the calf. *ḍeṛbatu ṛ-ṛṣaṣa fe-ṣ-ṣag.*
call - *ɛeyṭa* pl. *-t.* How much did the call to Tangier come to? *be-šḥal ṭaḥet l-ɛeyṭa l-ṭanža?*
to call - **1.** *ɛeyyeṭ ɛla.* I called him but he didn't hear me. *ɛeyyeṭt ɛlih be-l-ḥeqq ma-smeɛni-š.* --Shall I call a cab? *waš nɛeyyeṭ ɛla ṭaksi?* --Call a doctor! *ɛeyyeṭ ɛla ṭbib!* --I'll call for you (make the call for you) now, sir. *daba nɛeyyeṭ-lek a sidi.* **2.** *semma.* What do you call this thing in Arabic? *had š-ši š-ka-tsemmiweh be-l-ɛeṛbiya?* --Let's call him Ali. *aži nsemmiweh ɛli.*
to call attention to - *nebbeh ɛla.* I called his attention to it. *nebbehtu ɛliha.*
to call for - **1.** *ža iži muṛa.* Will you call for me at the hotel? *waš dži muṛaya l-l-uṭil?* **2.** *staḥeq.* This calls for a party. *hadi tstaḥeq ḥefla.*
to call in - *žab ižib.* We had to call in a specialist. *tlezzemna nžibu xtiṣaṣi.*
to call off - *lġa ilġi.* They called off the program because of the rain. *lġaw l-beṛnamež ɛla qibal š-šta.*
to call on - *ža iži išuf* or *mša imši išuf.* We'll call on you next Sunday. *ġad nžiw nšufuk l-ḥedd ž-žay.*
to call (out) - **1.** *ɛeyyeṭ ɛla.* Has my name been called out? *waš ɛeyyṭu ɛla smiyti?* **2.** *ɛlem b-.* The conductor calls out all the stops. *l-muṛaqib ka-yeɛlem be-l-maḥeṭṭat kollha.*
to call together - *žmeɛ.* He called us all together. *žmeɛna kollna.*
to call (up) - *ḍṛeb t-tilifun l-.* I'll call you up tomorrow. *ana nḍṛeb-lek t-tilifun ġedda.*
calm - *hani* pl. *hanyin.*
to be calm, to become calm - *thenna.*
to calm - **1.** *hedden.* We tried to calm the frightened animals. *ḥawelna nheddnu le-bhayem lli ttfezɛu.* --Try to calm him down. *ḥawel theddnu.* --Calm yourself! *hedden ṛaṣek!* **2.** *thedden, thenna.* It took her some time to calm down. *kan xeṣṣha ši-wqiyyet baš tthedden.* **3.** *hda ihda.* The wind has calmed down. *l-berd hda.*
camel - *žmel* pl. *žmal* (m.), *naga* pl. *-t, nyag* (f.).
camera - *ṣuwwaṛa* pl. *-t.*
camp - *mḥeṭṭa* pl. *-t.* What camp did you get your training in? *f-aš men*

mḥeṭṭa dderrebti?
to camp - *xeyyem.* We camped in the woods. *xeyyemna fe-l-ġaba.*
campaign - *ḥemla ɛeskaṛiya* pl. *ḥemlat ɛeskaṛiyin.*
camphor - *kafuṛ.*
can - *ḥokk* pl. *ḥkak.*
to can - *ṛeqqed.* Every summer my mother cans vegetables. *koll ṣif m̂m̂i ka-tṛeqqed l-xeḍṛa.*
can (to be able). **1.** *qḍeṛ.* Can we get there on time? *waš nqeḍṛu nweṣḷu fe-l-weqt?* **2.** *imken l-.* You can't go swimming in the lake. *ma-imken-lek-š temši tɛum fe-ḍ-ḍaya.* --Can I see the director? *waš imken-li nšuf l-mudir?* --He could have come. *kan imken-lu iži.*
**He did everything he could. *ɛmel mežhudu kollu.*
canary - *kalanyu* pl. *-wat, kalanya* pl. *-t, kanaṛ* pl. *-at.*
to **cancel** - **1.** *ḥdef.* This order has been canceled. *ḥedfu had ṭ-ṭalab.* --They canceled the meeting. *ḥedfu le-žtimaɛ.* **2.** *ṭḷeq.* I'd like to cancel my room reservation. *ana baġi nṭḷeq l-bit lli weṣṣit ɛlih.* **3.** *qṭeɛ, ḥṣeṛ.* I'd like to cancel my newspaper subscription. *ana baġi neqṭeɛ le-štiṛak dyali fe-l-žarida.* **4.** *ṭbeɛ.* These postage stamps are canceled. *had t-tnaber meṭbuɛin.* **5.** *smeḥ f-.* He canceled the rest of the debt I owed him. *smeḥ f-baqiyt d-din lli ka-isalni.* **6.** *beṭṭel.* I had to cancel my appointment with the doctor. *kan lazemni nbeṭṭel miɛadi mɛa ṭ-ṭbib.*
cancer - *saṛaṭan.*
candle - *šmaɛa* pl. *-t.*
candidate - *mreššeḥ* pl. *mreššḥin.*
candlestick - *ḥeska* pl. *-t, ḥsaki.*
candy - *fanida* pl. *-t,* coll. *fanid.*
cane - **1.** *ɛekkaz* pl. *ɛkakez, ɛṣa* pl. *ɛṣi.* He hit me with a cane. *ḍṛebni b-waḥeb lе-ɛṣa.* **2.** *qeṣba* pl. *-t,* coll. *qṣeb.* Do they grow much sugar cane in Morocco? *waš ka-iġeṛṣu sokkaṛ d-le-qṣeb bezzaf fe-l-meġrib?*
cannon - *medfeɛ* pl. *mdafeɛ.*
can opener - *sarut le-ḥkak* pl. *swaret le-ḥkak.*
cantaloupe - *beṭṭixa* pl. *-t,* coll. *beṭṭix.*
canvas - *kiṛiya.*
cap - **1.** *guṛṛa* pl. *-t.* He's wearing a cap. *labes guṛṛa.* **2.** *ġta* pl. *-wat.* I've lost the cap to my fountain pen. *ḍaɛet-li le-ġta dyal s-stilu dyali.* **3.** *ġeṭṭaya* pl. *-t.* Put the cap back on the bottle. *ṛežžeɛ l-ġeṭṭaya ɛel l-geṛɛa.* **4.** *ġlaf* pl. *ġlayef.* That tooth needs a cap. *dak s-senna xeṣṣha ġlaf.*
capable - *ḥadeq, ḥadeg.* She is a very capable woman. *hiya mṛa ḥadga.*
capacity - **1.** *ṣifa.* I'm here in the capacity of a guardian. *ana hnaya b-ṣifti waṣi.* **2.** *waḍifa.* What's his capacity, what does he do? *aš-en hiya waḍiftu w-aš ka-yeɛmel?*
**The tank has a capacity of one hundred liters. *had ṭ-ṭaṛṛu ka-irfed myat litra.*
capital - **1.** *ɛaṣima* pl. *-t.* Have you ever been in the capital? *waš ɛemmṛek konti fe-l-ɛaṣima?* **2.** *ṛaṣ-l-mal.* How much capital do you need to start your business? *šḥal xeṣṣek d-ṛaṣ-l-mal baš tebda l-ḥaṛaka dyalek?* --His capital is invested abroad. *ṛaṣ-malu mṛewwžu fe-l-xariž.*
capitalist - *ṛaṣ-mali* pl. *-yin.*
capital punishment - *ʔiɛdam.*
captain - *ṛaʔis* pl. *ṛuʔaṣa.* Who's the captain of the team? *škun huwa ṛaʔis l-feṛqa?*
captive - *meqbuṭ* pl. *-in.*
to **capture** - *šebbeṛ, qbeṭ.* They captured a general and his entire staff. *šebbṛu žiniṛal u-ṣḥabu kollhom.*
**The town was captured without a shot. *ṭaḥet le-mdina bla mɛeṛka.*
car - **1.** *siyaṛa* pl. *-t, ṭumubil* pl. *-at.* Would you like to ride in my new car? *waš tebġi terkeb fe-s-siyaṛa ž-ždida dyali?* **2.** *fagu* pl. *-wat.* How many cars are there in this train? *šḥal de-l-faguwat kaynin f-had l-qiṭaṛ? kaynin f-had l-qiṭaṛ?*
caraway - *keṛwiya.*
card - **1.** *kaṛṭa* pl. *-t, kwaṛeṭ.* They played cards all night. *leɛbu kaṛṭa l-lil kollu.* --Here's my card, come see me when you need me. *ha l-kaṛṭa dyali, aži tšufni weqt-ma bġitini.* **2.** *teṣwiṛa* pl. *-t, tṣaweṛ.* Did you get my card? *waš weṣḷatek t-teṣwiṛa dyali?*
**He's quite a card. *huwa ṛažel ḍeḥḥuki.*
cardboard - *kaṛṭun.*
care - *theḷya.* She took good care of him. *theḷḷat fih waḥed t-theḷya mezyana.*
**May I leave my things in your care? *imken-li nxelli ḥwayži ɛendek?* --Send me the letter in care of Allal Al-Mlih. *ṣifeṭ-li le-bṛa ɛend ɛellal le-mliḥ*
to take care of - **1.** *ḥda yeḥdi, theḷḷa itheḷḷa f-.* Don't worry,

I'll take care of your children. *ma-txaf-š, ana ġad-nthelḷa fe-wladek.* --Take care of my money for me. *ḥḍi-li flusi.* You'll have to take better care of yourself. *xeṣṣek tthelḷa f-ṛaṣek šwiya.* **2.** *feḍḍa ifeḍḍi.* I still have a few things to take care of. *baqi-li ši-šwiya d-le-ḥwayež nfeḍḍihom.*

to care - *bġa ibġi.* I don't care to go to the movies. *ana ma-baġi-š nemši le-s-sinima.*

**For all I care you can go. *ma-fiha bas, imken-lek temši.* --I don't care anything about that. *dak š-ši ma-ka-ihemmni-š.* --I don't care what he thinks. *ana ma-ihemmni-š aš xemmem huwa.* --What do I care! *ma-šekmani-š!*

carefully - **1.** *be-s-syasa.* They lifted the stretcher carefully. *hezzu l-meḥmel be-s-syasa.* **2.** *be-l-qaεida.* Check the figures carefully. *ṛažeε le-ḥsab be-l-qaεida.*

careless - *(lli) ma-ka-iḥawel-š εla.* He's careless with his money. *ma-ka-iḥawel-š εla flusu.*

cargo - *wesq.*

carnation - *qṛonfla* pl. *-t,* coll. *qṛonfel.*

carpenter - *nežžaṛ* pl. *-a.*

carpet - *ẓeṛbiya* pl. *-t, ẓṛabi.*

to carpet - *feṛṛeš be-ẓ-ẓṛabi.*

carrot - *xizzuya* pl*-t,* coll. *xizzu* (no def. art.).

to **carry** - **1.** *hezz, ḥmel.* He'll carry your bags for you. *huwa ġadi ihezz-lkom š-šwaneṭ.* **2.** *baε ibiε.* Do they carry socks in this shop? *waš ka-ibiεu t-tqašer f-had l-ḥanuṭ?*

to carry away - **1.** *ḥeyyed.* They carried away my chair. *ḥeyydu š-šelya dyali.* **2.** *žleb.* The crowd was carried away by his speech. *l-xeṭba dyalu žleb n-nas.*

to carry out - *ṭebbeq.* We'll try to carry out your plans. *nḥawlu nṭebbqu l-baṛamiž dyalkom.*

cart - *keṛṛusa* pl. *kṛaṛeṣ.*

cartridge - *qeṛṭaṣa* pl. *-t, qṛaṭeṣ,* coll. *qeṛṭaṣ.*

to **carve** - **1.** *nqeš.* They carved these figures out of wood. *neqšu had ṣ-ṣuṛat men l-εud.* --He carved his name on the tree. *nqeš smiytu εel š-šežṛa.* **2.** *qeṭṭeε.* Who's going to carve the meat? *škun ġa-iqeṭṭeε l-lḥem?*

carving knife - *ženwi* pl. *žnawi, žnawa.*

Casablanca - *ḍ-ḍar l-biḍa.*

native of Casablanca - *biḍawi* adj. pl. *-yin,* n. pl. *biḍawa.*

case - **1.** *ṣenduq* pl. *ṣnadeq.* Leave the bottles in the case. *xelli le-qṛaεi fe-ṣ-ṣenduq.* **2.** *ġša* pl. *-wat.* I need a case for my glasses. *xeṣṣni ġša le-n-nḍaḍeṛ dyali.* **3.** *qaḍiya* pl. *-t.* What did you do about the case of the trip? *aš derti f-qaḍiyt ṣ-ṣfeṛ?* --The judge refused to accept his case. *l-qaḍi ma-bġa-š iqbel l-qaḍiya dyalu.*

in any case - *εla kolli ḥal.* I'll drop by for you in any case. *εla kolli ḥal nduz εlik.*

in case - *ila.* In case he's late, give him this letter. *ila ža mεeṭṭel εṭih had le-bṛa.* --In case of some illness notify my home. *ila wqeε ši-maṛaḍ εlem ḍaṛi.*

cash - *flus.* I don't have any cash with me. *ma-hazz flus mεaya.*

to cash - *ṣeṛṛef.* Can you cash this check for me? *waš imken-lek tṣeṛṛef-li had š-šik?*

cashier - *mul ṣ-ṣenduq* pl. *mwalin ṣ-ṣnadeq.*

cast - **1.** *mumettilin* (pl.). The new play has an excellent cast. *ṛ-rwaya ž-ždida εendha mumettilin haʔilin.* **2.** *gebṣ; žbira* pl. *-t, žbayer.* How long will you be wearing the cast? *sḥal gadi tebqa εamel l-gebṣ?*

**The die is cast. *d-defla xeṛžet men l-fomm, ma-teṛžeε-š.*

Castile - *qeštala.*

castle - *qṣeṛ* pl. *qṣuṛa.*

castor oil - *zit l-xeṛwaε.*

cat - *mešš, mošš* pl. *mšaš; qeṭṭ* pl. *qṭuṭ.*

catalogue - *qayma* pl. *-t.*

catastrophe - *muṣiba* pl. *-t.*

catch - **1.** *saqṭa* pl. *-t, swaqeṭ.* The catch on the camera is broken. *s-saqṭa de-ṣ-ṣuwwwṛa mherrsa.* **2.** *teṣyiḍa* pl. *-t.* Ten fish is a good catch. *εešṛa de-l-ḥutat teṣyiḍa mezyana.*

to **catch** - **1.** *šebbeṛ.* We caught a lot of fish. *šebbeṛna bezzaf de-l-ḥut.* --Here, catch this! *hak, šebbeṛ hadi!* --They caught him just before he could get over the border. *šebbṛu šwiya qbel-ma iqṭeε le-ḥdada.* **2.** *qbeṭ, qbeḍ.* I have to catch the train at five o'clock. *xeṣṣni neqbeṭ l-qiṭaṛ fe-l-xemsa.* --The police caught the thief. *š-šoṛṭa qebḍet l-xuwwan.* **3.** *ḥeṣṣel.* The police caught him. *ḥeṣṣlettu š-šoṛṭa.* **4.** *tšebbeṛ.* My coat caught on a nail. *tšebbeṛ-li kebbuṭi f-meṣmaṛ.*

to catch cold - *ḍerbu l-berd, truwweḥ.* You'll catch cold. *ġa-iḍeṛbek l-berd,* or *ġadi ttruwweḥ.*
to catch fire - *qebḍet fih l-Ɛafya, šeƐlet fih l-Ɛafya.* The wood is so dry that it'll catch fire easily. *l-Ɛud našef bezzaf, teqbeḍ fih l-Ɛafya deġya.*
to catch hold - *šebbeṛ.* Catch hold of the other end. *šebbeṛ men ž-žiha le-x̂ṛa.*
to catch one's eye - *xṭef-lu Ɛeqlu.* The necktie in the window caught my eye. *le-gṛabaṭa lli fe-š-šeṛžem xeṭfet-li f-Ɛeqli.*
to catch the measles - *leṣṣeq fih bu-ḥemṛon.* I caught the measles. *leṣṣeq fiya bu-ḥemṛon.*
to catch up - *fda ifdi l-weqt lli ḍiyyeƐ.* Try to catch up in your work. *šuf waš tefdi l-weqt lli ḍiyyeƐti fe-l-xedma.*
to catch up with - *lḥeq Ɛla.* Go ahead, I'll catch up with you. *sir qeddami, daba nelḥeq Ɛlik.*
to be catching - *Ɛada iƐadi.* Measles are catching. *bu-ḥemṛon ka-iƐadi.*
caterpillar - *ḥessaka* pl. *-t.*
cattle - *bgeṛ, bqeṛ* (coll.).
cauliflower - *šifluṛ.*
cause - *sabab* pl. *sbab; sebba* pl. *-t, sbayeb.* What's the cause of the delay? *šnu huwa s-sabab de-t-teƐṭal?*
**What caused the accident? *šnu huwa sabab le-ksida?* --He caused her a lot of grief. *merretha.* --His answer caused surprise. *žwabu Ɛežžeb n-nas.*
caution - *iḥtiyaṭ.* Caution is needed with that dog. *xeṣṣek taxod l-iḥtiyaṭ mƐa dak l-kelb.*
cautious - *(lli) ka-iredd balu.*
cave - *ġaṛ* pl. *ġiran, ḥefṛa* pl. *-t, ḥfaṛi.*
to cave in - *ṭaḥ iṭiḥ.* I'm afraid the house is going to cave in. *ana xayef ḍ-ḍaṛ gadi ṭṭiḥ.*
cedar - *lerz.*
ceiling - *sqef* pl. *squfa.*
to **celebrate** - *ḥtafel b-.* We're celebrating independence day tomorrow. *ġadi neḥtaflu b-Ɛid l-istiqlal ġedda.*
celebration - **1.** *Ɛid* pl. *Ɛyad* (religious). **2.** *Ɛers* or *Ɛoṛṣ,* pl. *Ɛras, Ɛrasat* (wedding). **3.** *ḥefla* pl. *-t,* (party).
celery - *kṛafeṣ.*
cell - *bniqa* pl. *-t, bnayeq.* Take the prisoner to his cell. *ddi l-meszun le-bniqtu.*
cellar - *ḍehlis* pl. *ḍḥales.*
cement - *beṛṣlana.*
cemetary - *ṛuḍa* pl. *-t.*
censer - *mbexṛa* pl. *t, mbaxeṛ.*
censor - *muṛaqib* pl. *-in.*
to censor - *ṛaqeb.*
censorship - *muṛaqaba.*
census - *ḥsab de-s-sokkan.*
cent - **He doesn't have a cent. *ma-Ɛendu ḥetta gerš.* --I wouldn't give a cent for it. *ma-ka-teswa-š rbaƐiya.*
center - **1.** *weṣṭ.* The table is standing in the center of the room. *l-mida meḥṭuṭa f-weṣṭ l-bit.* **2.** **2.** *merkez.* Casablanca is a large commercial center. *ḍ-ḍaṛ l-biḍa merkez tižari kbir.*
**She's the center of attention. *gaƐ n-nas ka-itnabhu-lha.*
century - *qeṛn* pl. *quṛun.*
certain - *metyeqqen.* Are you certain? *waš nta metyeqqen?*
certainly - **1.** *bla šekk.* She's certainly right. *hiya Ɛendha l-ḥeqq bla šekk.* **2.** *meƐlum.* Why certainly, just go on in! *meƐlum, ġir dxol!*
certificate - *šahada, šhada* pl. *-t.*
Ceuta - *sebta.*
native of Ceuta - *sebti* adj. pl. *-yin,* n. pl. *sbata, hel sebta.*
chain - *sensla* pl. *-t, snasel; selsla* pl. *-t, slasel.*
to chain - *ṛbeṭ b-sensla.*
chair - *šelya* pl. *-t, šli, šwali.*
chalk - *ṭabašir.*
challenge - *mnahda* pl. *-t.*
**I challenge anybody else to do it. *lli kan ṣlib iži yeƐmelha.*
chamber of commerce - *l-ġoṛfa t-tižariya.*
champion - *baṭal* pl. *abṭal.*
chance - *foṛṣa* pl. *-t.* I had a chance to go to Egypt. *ana žani l-foṛṣa baš nemši l-maṣeṛ.*
**Is there any chance of us catching the train? *waš ġad-imken-lna nšebbṛu l-qiṭaṛ?* --Give me a chance! *mehhel Ɛliya!* --I met him by chance. *tlaqitu ṣoḍfa.*
chandelier - *triya* pl. *-t.*
change - **1.** *tebdil, tebdal.* This requires a change in our plans. *xeṣṣ tebdil fe-l-beṛnamež dyalna.* --I'm for a change in the government. *ana nfeḍḍel tebdil fe-l-ḥukuma.* **2.** *ṣeṛf.* Do you have any change? *waš Ɛendek ṣeṛf?*
**You need a change. *xeṣṣek tbeddel r-riḥ.* --For a change, I'd like to go to the movies today. *baš*

nbeddel šwiya ana baġi nemši le-s-sinima l-yum.

to change - 1. *ṣeṛṛef.* Can you change a ten thousand franc bill for me? *imken-lek tṣeṛṛef-li weṛqa dyal ʕešṛ alaf fṛenk?* **2.** *beddel.* I want five minutes so I can change my clothes. *bġit xemsa de-d-dqayeq baš nbeddel ḥwayži.* --They changed all the tires on my car for me. *beddlu-li le-bnuwat de-s-siyaṛa dyali kollhom.* **3.** *tbeddel.* The weather is going to change. *l-žuw ġadi itbeddel.* --I've changed my mind. *tbeddel-li n-naḍaṛ.*

channel - *mežṛa* pl. *mžaṛi.* The two lakes are joined by a narrow channel. *ḍ-ḍayat b-žuž mlaqyin b-waḥed l-mežṛa ḍiyyeq.*

chaos - *terwin, terwina.*

chapter - *feṣḷ* pl. *fṣuḷ.*

character - 1. *ṭbiʕa.* I've misjudged his character. *ana ġleṭṭ fe-ṭbiʕtu.* **2.** *šexṣ* pl. *ašxaṣ.* How many characters are there in the play? *šḥal men šexṣ kayen fe-r-riwaya?*
**That man is a familiar character here. *dak ṛ-ṛažel meʕṛuf hnaya.* --He's quite a character! *walayenni nuʕ mennu.*

characteristic - *xuṣuṣi.* That attitude is characteristic of her. *hadik l-ḥala xuṣuṣiya liha.*

charcoal - *faxeṛ.*

charge - 1. *ʕmaṛa* pl. *-t, ʕmayeṛ.* The charge is big enough to kill us all. *had le-ʕmaṛa mžehda imken-lha teqtelna kollna.* **2.** *xlaṣ.* There's no charge. *ma-kayen xlaṣ.* **3.** *tehma* pl. *-t.* What are the charges against this man? *šnu huma t-tehmat ḍeḍḍ had ṛ-ṛažel?*

free of charge - *bla flus, baṭeḷ.*

in charge - *mkellef.* Who's in charge of this work? *škun lli mkellef b-had l-xedma?*

to take charge - *tkellef.* My son is taking charge of the new branch. *weldi ġadi itkellef be-l-feṛʕ ž-ždid.*

to charge - 1. *ḥseb.* You've charged me very little. *ma-ḥsebti ġir šwiya.* --Charge it to my account. *ḥsebha ʕliya.* **2.** *them.* He was charged with theft. *tehmuh be-l-xewna.*
**You've charged me too much! *ġelliti ʕliya bezzaf.* --He gives all his money to charity. *ka-iṣeḍḍeq flusu kollhom.*

charming - *ḍṛif* pl. *ḍṛaf, ḍṛiyyef* pl. *ḍriyyfin.*

to **chase** - *žṛa iżri ʕla.*

chat - *muḥadata.*

to chat - *hḍeṛ, tḥeddet.*

chatter - *hḍuṛ.*

to chatter - 1. *hedhed.* They chatter incessantly. *ka-ihedhdu bla ḥbis.* **2.** *qeṛqeb.* My teeth are chattering. *snani ka-iqeṛqbu.*

chauffeur - *šifuṛ* pl. *-at, ṣiyyag* pl. *-a.*

cheap - 1. *ṛxiṣ* pl. *ṛxaṣ.* Fruit is very cheap here. *l-ġella ṛxiṣa bezzaf hna.* **2.** *ṭayeḥ.* She looked cheap in those clothes. *banet ṭayḥa f-dak le-ḥwayež.*
3. *basel.* That character played a cheap trick on me. *dak xiyyna lʕeb ʕliya leʕba basla.*
**That's cheap stuff. *hadi ferya.* --His kindness made me feel cheap. *ḍ-ḍṛafa dyalu ḥeššmetni.*

cheat - *ġeššaš* pl. *-a.* They all know he's a cheat. *huma kollhom ka-iʕeṛfu bin huwa ġeššaš.*

to cheat - *ġešš, šmet.* That shop keeper cheated me out of all my money. *dak mul l-ḥanut ġeššni f-flusi kollhom.*

check - 1. *šik* pl. *-at.* I'll send you a check tomorrow. *daba nṣifeṭ-lek šik ġedda.* **2.** *bṭaqa.* Give your check to the porter. *ʕṭi le-bṭaqa dyalek l-l-ḥemmal.*

to check - 1. *xella ixelli.* Check your hat and coat here. *xelli š-šemrir u-l-kebbuṭ dyalek hna.* **2.** *ṛšem.* Check the items you want. *ṛšem le-ḥwayež lli bġiti.* **3.** *qelleb.* Please check the oil. *qelleb z-zit ʕafak.* **4.** *ṛažeʕ.* Will you please check the bill once more? *ṛažeʕ le-ḥsab meṛṛa xṛa ḷḷah ixellik.*

to check off - *ḍṛeb ʕla.* Did you check this merchandise off the list? *waš ḍrebti ʕla had s-selʕa men l-qayma?*

checkers - *ḍama.* Let's play a game of checkers. *yaḷḷah nleʕbu ḍama.*

cheek - *xedd* pl. *xdud.*

cheerful - *ferḥan* pl. *-in.*

cheese - 1. *žḅen* (indigenous). **2.** *fṛumaž* (European).

chemist - *kimawi* pl. *-yin.*

cherry - *ḥebb le-mluk* (coll.).

chess - *šenṭṛež.*

chest - *sder* pl. *sdur, sdura.* He has a broad chest. *huwa ʕendu sder ʕṛiḍ.* **2.** *ṣenduq* pl. *ṣnadeq.* Put the tools in the chest. *ḥeṭṭ d-duzan fe-ṣ-ṣenduq.*
**That's a load off my chest. *hadik tneqqṣet men hemmi.*

chestnut - *qeṣṭaḷa* pl. *-t,* coll.

qeṣṭaḷ.
to **chew** – *mḍeġ.*
chewing gum – *meska.*
chicken – *džaža* pl. *-t,* coll. *džaž.*
chicken pox – *bu-šwika.*
chick-pea – *ḥemmuṣa* pl. *-t* coll. *ḥemmuṣ.*
chief – *ṛaʔis* pl. *ṛuʔasa.*
child – *derri* pl. *drari, ṭfeḷ* pl. *ṭfaḷ.*
 **I've been used to it ever since I was a child. *ana mwellefha men ṣoġṛi.*
childhood – *ṣġoṛ, ṣġeṛ.*
chill – *berd, bruda, brudiya.* I've got a chill. *ḍeṛṛni l-berd.* --Suddenly I felt a chill. *ana deġya ḥessit be-l-berd.*
 to chill – **1.** *berred.* Chill this beer for me please. *berred-li had s-serbisa baṛak ḷḷahu fik.*
chilly – *bared.* The weather's chilly. *l-ḥal bared.*
 **They gave us a chilly reception. *steqbluna be-l-brudiya.*
chimney – **1.** *mdexna* pl. *-t.* They're repairing the chimney. *ka-iṣelḥu le-mdexna.* **2.** *zaža* pl. *-t.* Where's the chimney for the lamp? *fayn hiya z-zaža de-ḷ-ḷamḅa?*
chin – *dqen* pl. *dquna.*
 **Chin up! *hezz ṛaṣek!*
China – **1.** *ṣ-ṣin* (country). **2.** *bdiƐ.* Germany is famous for its beautiful china. *almanya mešhuṛa b-le-bdiƐ dyalha l-mezyan.*
Chinese – *ṣini.*
chisel – *menqaš* pl. *mnaqeš* (stone); *menqaṛ* pl. *mnaqeṛ* (wood).
chocolate – *šekḷaṭ.*
choice – *texyiṛa.* This is a good choice. *texyiṛa mezyana hadi.*
choke – *žiyyaf* pl. *-a* (automobile).
 to choke – **1.** *žiyyef.* The little boy is choking the cat. *l-iššir ka-ižiyyef l-qeṭṭ.* **2.** *xneq.* The stovepipe was choked up. *d-deffaya kanet mexnuqa.*
 **I choked on a fishbone. *weḥlet-li šuka de-l-ḥut f-ḥelqi.*
cholera – *bu-glib.*
to **choose** – *xtaṛ.*
to **chop** – *šeqq.* Did you chop the wood? *waš šeqqiti le-Ɛwad?* --Chopped olives. *z-zitun l-mešquq.*
 to chop off – *qṭeƐ, qeṭṭeƐ, ḥsek.*
 to chop up – *qeṭṭeƐ, geṛṛeḍ.*
Christian – *masiḥi* pl. *-yin, neṣṛani* pl. *nṣaṛa.*
Christmas – *milad sidna Ɛisa.*
church – *knisa, knisiya* pl. *-t, knayes.*
cigar – *sigaṛ* pl. *-at.*
cigaret – *gaṛṛu* pl. *-wat.*
cigaret lighter – *briki* pl. *-yat.*
cigar store – *ṣaka* pl. *-t.*
cinder – *ṛmaḍ.* What's that pile of cinders for? *dyal-aš dak l-Ɛaṛam de-ṛ-ṛmaḍ?* --I've got a cinder in my eye. *dxel-li ṛmaḍ f-Ɛeyni.*
cinnamon – *qeṛfa.*
circle – **1.** *ḍuṛa* pl. *-t, ḍuṛ* pl. *ḍwaṛ.* We kept going around in a circle. *bqina ka-nƐemlu ḍuṛa.* **2.** *žmaƐa* pl. *-t.* He has a wide circle of friends. *Ɛendu žmaƐa kbira d-le-ṣḥab.*
 to circle – *ḍaṛ iḍuṛ.* The airplane is circling over the city. *ṭ-ṭiyaṛa ka-ḍḍuṛ fuq le-mdina.* --The wall circles the city. *ṣ-ṣur ḍayeṛ b-le-mdina.*
circumstance – *ḥala* pl. *-t, ḥal* pl. *ḥwal.*
city – *mdina* pl. *-t, mdun.*
civil – **1.** *ḷṭif* pl. *ḷṭaf, mʔeddeb* pl. *mʔeddbin.* At least he was civil to us. *be-l-qella kan ḷṭif mƐana.* **2.** *madani.* Civil authorities. *ṣ-ṣuḷat l-madaniya.*
civilization – *tameddun.*
civilized – *metmedden.*
claim – *ḥeqq* pl. *ḥquq.* I lay no claim to that. *ana ma-taleb-š l-ḥeqq f-had š-ši.*
 to claim – **1.** *ṭḷeb.* I claim my share. *ana ka-nṭḷeb ḥeqqi.* --Where do I claim my baggage? *fayn nṭleb le-qšaš dyali?* **2.** *ddaƐa iddaƐi.* She claims to know the man. *hiya ka-ddaƐi bin ka-teƐṛef ṛ-ṛažel.*
to **clap** – *ṣeffeq.*
class – **1.** *qiṣm* pl. *aqṣam, qṣam.* My first class starts at eight-thirty. *qiṣmi l-luwwel ka-ibda fe-t-tmenya u-neṣṣ.* **2.** *ḍeṛṣ* pl. *ḍuṛuṣ.* How many classes did you have last year? *šḥal de-ḍ-ḍuṛuṣ tebbeƐti Ɛam luwwel?*
to **classify** – *retteb.*
to **clatter** – *qeṛqeb.* The wagon clattered down the bumpy road. *l-keṛṛuṣa ġadya u-tqeṛqeb fe-ṭ-ṭriq le-mxeṣṣṛa.*
claw – *mexleb* pl. *mxaleb, ḍfeṛ* pl. *ḍfaṛ.*
clay – *ṭin.*
clean – *nqi* pl. *-yin.*
 to clean – **1.** *neḍḍef.* Hasn't the maid cleaned the room yet? *waš l-xeddama ma-zal ma-neḍḍfet l-bit?* **2.** *ġsel.* He went to clean his teeth. *mša iġsel snanu.*
 **I asked her to clean the chicken for me. *ṭḷebt mennha tentef d-džaža u-tḥeyyed-lha le-qšaweš.*

to clean out - **1.** *xwa ixwi.* This drawer has to be cleaned out. *xeṣṣna nexwiw had le-mžer.* **2.** *felles.* They really cleaned me out! *we-ḷḷah ila fellsuni!*

cleaning - *tenqiya.*

clear - *ṣafi.* The water is deep and clear. *l-ma ġareq u-ṣafi.* --His voice was very clear over the radio. *kan ḥelqu ṣafi bezzaf fe-ṛ-ṛadyu.* --We have had clear weather all week. *kan ɛendna žuw ṣafi ž-žemɛa kollha.* --Is the road clear up ahead? *waš ṭ-ṭriq ṣafya l-l-qeddam?* **It's clear from the letter that he isn't satisfied. *ḍaheṛ men had le-bṛa dyalu bin huwa ma-ši ferḥan.* --The news came out of the clear sky. *le-xbaṛ ža ɛla ġefla.*

to clear - **1.** *neqqa ineqqi, xwa ixwi.* Did you clear the table? *waš neqqiti l-mida?* **2.** *serreḥ* He cleared his throat. *serreḥ ḥelqu.*

to clear away, off - *zuwwel, ḥeyyed.* Ask her to clear away the dishes. *ṭḷeb mennha dzuwwel ṭbaṣel.*

to clear out - *xwa ixwi.* I'm going to clear out this closet tomorrow. *ġadi nexwi had le-xzana ġedda.*

to clear up - **1.** *fesser.* There are still a number of things we have to clear up. *ma-zal kayen ɛadad d-leḥwayež xeṣṣna nfessruhom.* **2.** *ṣfa iṣfa* The weather has cleared up. *ṣfa l-žuw.*

clerk - *ktatbi* pl. *-ya, kateb* pl. *kottab.* He's a clerk in my office. *huwa ktatbi fe-l-mekteb dyali.*

clever - **1.** *ḥadeq.* The candidate is a clever speaker. *le-mreššeḥ xaṭeb ḥadeq.* **2.** *ḥili.* This character is a clever businessman. *had xiyyna biyyaɛ šerray ḥili.*

cliff - *žeṛf* pl. *žṛaf, žṛufa.*

climate - *žuw* (def. art. *l-*).

to **climb** - **1.** *tšebbeṭ f-, ṭleɛ f-.* The children climbed a tree and their father yelled at them. *d-drari tšebbṭu f-waḥed š-šežṛa u-ḅḅahom ġuwwet ɛlihom.* **2.** *ṭleɛ.* I haven't climbed that mountain yet. *ma-zal ma-ṭleɛt l-dak ž-žbel.* --I don't like to climb stairs. *ana ma-nebġi-š nṭleɛ ḍ-ḍṛuž.*

to climb down - *hbeṭ.* Be careful as you're climbing down the ladder. *ṛeḍḍ balek u-nta habeṭ men s-sellum.*

to **cling** - *lṣeq.* The child is cling- to its mother. *d-derri laṣeq fe-m̂m̂u.*

clip - *filil* pl. *-at, fyalel.* She wore a golden clip on her dress. *hiya kan ɛendha filil de-d-dheb fe-ksuwtha.*

(paper) clip - *meqbeṭ* pl. *mqabeṭ.*

to clip - **1.** *qṭeɛ, meqqeṣ, qeṣṣeṣ.* Don't clip my hair too short. *ma-teqṭeɛ-š šeɛri qṣiṛ bezzaf.* --We have our dog clipped every summer. *ka-nqeṣṣṣu šɛeṛ kelbna koll ṣif.* --I clipped this article out of the magazine. *ana meqqeṣt had l-maqala men l-mažella.* **2.** *xellel.* Clip these papers together. *xellel had le-kwaġeṭ mežmuɛin.*

clipping - *qeṭɛa* pl. *-t.*

cloakroom - *bit le-ḥwayež* pl. *byut le-ḥwayež.*

clock - *magana* pl. *-t, mwagen.* We set our clock by the radio. *ka-nheqqqu l-magana dyalna ɛel ṛ-ṛadyu.*

to clock - *ḥseb l-weqt, ɛbeṛ l-weqt.*

to **clog** - *xneq.* The pipes are clogged. *le-qwades mexnuqin.*

close - **1.** *tali, nihaya.* I'll see you at the close of the meeting. *nšufek fe-t-tali d-le-žtimaɛ.* **2.** *qṛib* pl. *qṛab.* The hotel is close to the railroad station. *l-uṭil qṛib men lagaṛ.* **3.** *metqaṛeb.* We sat close together. *glesna metqaṛbin.* **4.** *tqil* pl. *tqal.* The air is very close in this room. *ṛ-ṛiḥ tqil bezzaf f-had l-bit.* **He's a close friend of mine. *huwa ṣaḥbi men ṛ-ṛuḥ le-ṛ-ṛuḥ.* --Pay close attention. *ṛeḍḍ balek bezzaf.* --He won by a close vote. *rbeḥ ġir b-si-ʔeṣwaṭ binu u-bin le-x̂ṛin.* --That was a close call for me. *felletni be-šwiya.*

close by - *qṛib men hna.* Is there a restaurant close by? *waš kayen ši-meṭɛem qṛib men hna?*

from close up - *men le-qṛib.* From close up the situation looks entirely different. *men le-qṛib l-ḥala ka-ḍḍheṛ gaɛ mextalfa.*

to close - **1.** *šedd, sedd.* Don't close the door before nine o'clock. *ma-tšedd-š l-bab qbel men t-tesɛud.* --They closed at six. *šeddu fe-s-setta.* **2.** *feḍḍa mɛa.* The deal was closed this morning. *feḍḍaw mɛa l-biɛa l-yum fe-ṣ-ṣbaḥ.*

closely - *be-t-tedqiq.* Examine it closely. *qellebha be-t-tedqiq.*

closet - *xzana* pl. *-t, xzayen.*

cloth - **1.** *tub* pl. *tyab.* Do you have this cloth in a different color? *waš ɛendkom had t-tub f-lun axoṛ?* **2.** *šeṛwiṭa* pl. *šṛawet.* Take a

clean cloth for dusting. *xud šerwiṭa nqiya baš tsus l-ġobṛa.*
clothes - *ḥwayež* (pl.).
clothes closet - *maryu* pl. *-wat.*
clothes hanger - *ƐellaqA* pl. *-t, Ɛlaleq.*
clothes hook - *mexṭaf* pl. *mxaṭef.*
cloud - *sḥaba* pl. *-t,* coll. *sḥab; ġmama* pl. *-t,* coll. *ġmam.* The sun has disappeared behind the clouds. *š-šemš ġebret muṛ s-sḥab.*
to cloud up - *ġiyyem.* The sky clouded up shortly after we left. *s-sma ġiyymet ši-šwiya men beƐd-ma mšina.*
cloudy - *mġiyyem.*
clove - *qṛonfla* pl *-t* coll. *qṛonfel.*
clover - *nefla.*
club - **1.** *Ɛṣa* (const. *Ɛṣat*) pl. *Ɛṣi.* The policeman had to use his club. *l-bulisi tlezzem isteƐmel le-Ɛṣa dyalu.* **2.** *nadi* pl. *-yat, nwadi.* Are you a member of the club? *waš nta men n-nadi?*
to club - *ẓeṛweṭ.*
clue - *dalil; imaṛa* pl. *-t, imayeṛ.*
clumsy - *keṛfaṣ.*
coach - **1.** *fagu* pl. *-wat.* Which coach would you like to sit in? *fe-š-men fagu tebġi tegles?* **2.** *muderrib.* He's the coach of our team. *huwa l-muderrib de-l-feṛqa dyalna.*
coal - *faxeṛ.*
coarse - **1.** *ḥreš* pl. *ḥeršin.* The cloth is too coarse for me. *t-tub ḥreš Ɛliya bezzaf.* **2.** *xšin* pl. *xšan.* His manners are coarse. *l-muƐamala dyalu xšina.*
coast - *šeṭṭ* pl. *šṭuṭ.*
**The coast is clear. *ṭ-ṭṛiq ṣafya.*
coat - **1.** *kebbuṭ* pl. *kbabeṭ.* You mustn't go out without a coat in this weather. *ma-lazmek-š texṛož f-had l-žuw bla kebbuṭ.* **2.** *šƐeṛ.* The foal has a beautiful coat. *had le-ždeƐ Ɛendu šƐer zwin.* **3.** *duza.* This door needs another coat of paint. *had l-bab xeṣṣha duza xṛa de-ṣ-ṣbaġa.*
to coat - *ṭla iṭli.* The car was coated with mud. *kanet ṭ-ṭumubil meṭliya be-l-ġis.*
coat hanger - *Ɛellaqa* pl. *-t, Ɛalaleq.*
cockroach - *ṣeṛṛaq z-zit, qeṛwaṭa* pl. *-t.*
coconut - *guz l-hend, kukuya.*
codfish - *beqlaw, lamuri.*
cod-liver oil - *zit l-beqlaw.*
coffee - *qehwa.*
coffee grinder - *ṭaḥuna* (pl. *-t, ṭwaḥen*) *de-l-qehwa.*
coffee grounds - *text de-l-qehwa.*
coffin - *tabut* pl. *twabet.*
coin - *sekka* pl. *skak.*
**Let's toss a coin to see who goes. *yaḷḷah nƐemlu ṣfeṛ wella kḥel baš nšufu škun lli imši.*
coincidence - *mṣaḍfa* pl. *-t.*
cold - **1.** *berd.* I can't stand this cold. *ana ma-imken-li-š neṣbeṛ Ɛla had l-berd.* **2.** *teṛwiḥa, rwaḥ.* He has a bad cold. *Ɛendu teṛwiḥa xayba.* **3.** *bared.* The water isn't cold enough. *l-ma ma-bared-š bezzaf.*

**The nights are getting colder. *l-lyali ka-iberdu.*
to catch cold - *tṛuwweḥ.*
to **collapse** - **1.** *rab irib.* The bridge suddenly collapsed. *l-qenṭṛa rabet Ɛla ġefla.* **2.** *ṭaḥ iṭiḥ.* He collapsed in the middle of the street. *ṭaḥ f-weṣṭ ṭ-ṭṛiq.*
collar - *reggabiya* pl. *-t.*
collar bone - *tergya* pl. *-t.*
to **collect** - **1.** *žmeƐ.* How much money has been collected so far? *šḥal d-le-flus žemƐu ḥetta l-daba?*
**Give me a chance to collect my thoughts. *xellini nxemmem šwiya.*
2. *ttežmeƐ.* A crowd collected in the square. *džemƐu n-nas fe-s-saḥa.*
collection - **1.** *mežmuƐa* pl. *-t.* The library has a famous collection of books on America. *l-xizana fiha mežmuƐa d-le-ktub mešhuṛa Ɛla amirika.* **2.** *žmiƐ.* When is the last collection? *fuq-aš ikun ž-žmiƐ t-tali?*
collision - *mṣaḍma* pl. *-t.*
colony - *musteƐmaṛa* pl. *-t.*
color - *lun* pl. *lwan.*
to color - *luwwen.*
colored - *mluwwen.*
colt - *ždeƐ* pl. *žduƐa.*
column - **1.** *sarya* pl. *-t, swari.* You can recognize the house by its white columns. *imken-lek teƐṛef ḍ-ḍaṛ be-swariha l-buyeḍ.* **2.** *deḷƐa* pl. *-t, ḍḷuƐ, ḍḷaƐi.* Write your name in the right-hand column. *kteb smiytek fe-ḍ-ḍeḷƐa l-imna.*
comb - *mešṭa* pl. *mšaṭi.*
to comb - *mšeṭ.*
**The police combed the whole city. *l-bulis fettšet le-mdina kollha.*
to **come** - *ža iži* (act. ptc. *maži, žay;* impv. *aži*). This cloth comes in only two colors. *had t-tub ka-iži ġir f-žuž de-l-lwan.* --I've come for my passport. *ana žit Ɛel t-tesriḥ dyali.*

**Come now, you don't really mean that. *xlaṣ, waš b-niytek?* --How did you come to think of that? *mnin ṭaḥet ɛlik had l-fikra?* --He comes from Rabat. *huwa men ṛ-ṛbaṭ.* --I don't know whether I'm coming or going.

ana ma-ɛaṛef ṛaṣi men režliya.

to come about - *ṭṛa iṭṛa, žṛa ižṛa.* How did all this come about? *kif-aš ṭṛa had š-ši?*

to come across - **1.** *ṭaḥ iṭiḥ f-.* He's the best professor I've ever come across. *ɛemmṛi ma-ṭeḥt f-ši-ʔustad ḥsen men hadak.*

to come along - **1.** *ža iži.* Do you want to come along? *waš baġi dži mɛana?* **2.** *tmešša.* Everything's coming along fine, *koll-ši ka-itmešša f-ġaya.*

to come apart - *tfekk.* This chair is coming apart already. *had š-šelya bdat ttfekk beɛda.*

to come by - **1.** *daz iduz men.* He's coming by here this afternoon. *ġa-iduz men hna f-le-ɛšiya.* **2.** *žah ižih.* How did he come by all that money? *u-mnin beɛda žaweh duk le-flus kollhom?*

to come down - **1.** *ḥaf iḥuf.* Can you come down here for a moment? *waš imken-lek tḥuf hnaya ši-šwiya?* **2.** *ṭiyyeḥ.* We can't come down a penny on this price. *ma-nqedṛu-š nṭiyyḥu ṣulḍi men had t-taman.*

to come in - *dxel idxol.* Please come in! *tfeḍḍel, dxol!*

to come in handy - *ṣlaḥ.* It'll come in very handy later. *ġa-iṣlaḥ bezzaf men beɛd.*

to come off - **1.** *tfekk.* One of the legs has come off the table. *waḥed le-kraɛ tfekk men ṭ-ṭebla.* **2.** *tqelleɛ, tḥeyyed.* The button has come off. *ṣ-ṣeḍfa tqellɛet.*

to come out - **1.** *xṛež, ixṛož.* My book has just come out. *le-ktab dyali yaḷḷah xṛež.* --The dirt won't come out. *le-wsex ma-bġa-š ixṛož.* --Who knows what will come out of all this? *škun lli ɛref aš ġadi ixṛož men had š-ši kollu?* **2.** *ban iban.* Now it comes out that I was right. *daba ban bin kan ɛendi l-ḥeqq.*
l-ḥeqq.

to come through - **1.** *daz iduz men.* You can't come through here. *ma-imken-lek-š dduz men hna.* **2.** *xṛež men.* He came through the operation nicely. *xṛež men le-ftiḥ b-xiṛ.*

to come to - **1.** *ža iži f-.* The bill comes to two dollars. *le-ḥsab žat fih žuž ḍuḷaṛ.* **2.** *faq ifiq.* After a few minutes she came to. *faqet men beɛd ši-šwiya.*

to come to pieces - *ža iži štat.* It'll come to pieces if you touch it. *ṛah iži štat ila messitih.*

to come up - **1.** *ṭḷeɛ.* Would you like to come up for a cup of coffee? *waš tebġi ṭṭleɛ baš tešṛeb ši-kas de-l-qehwa?* **2.** *ḥdet.* This problem comes up every day. *had l-muškila ka-teḥdet koll nhaṛ.* --Something has come up. *ši-ḥaža ḥedtet.*

to come upon - *ṭaḥ iṭiḥ ɛla.* I came upon the solution by accident. *ṭeḥt ɛel l-ḥell ġir ṣoḍfa.*

comedy - *riwaya hazliya.*
**Cut the comedy! *ḥṣeṛ had le-mlaġa!*

comfortable - *fih ṛ-ṛaḥa, mriyyeḥ.*

comical - *fih ḍ-ḍeḥk, muḍḥik.*

command - *amṛ* pl. *awamir.*

to command, be in command - *ḥkem.* Who's in command here? *škun lli ḥakem hnaya?* --Does he have a good command of English? *waš huwa ka-yeḥkem l-luġa l-ingliziya mezyan?*

commander - *ḥakem* pl. *ḥokkam.*

to **commend** - *škeṛ.* He was commended for his good behavior. *šekṛuh ɛla sirtu l-mezyana.*

comment - *mulaḥaḍa* pl. *-t; tenbih.*

commercial - *tižari.*

commission - **1.** *ležna* pl. *-t.* The commission has promised to investigate the matter. *l-žemɛiya qawlet baš tebḥet fe- l-qaḍiya.* **2.** *soxṛa* pl. *-t, sxaṛi.* I wouldn't take any commission on this sale. *ma-naxod f-had l-biɛa.*

to **commit** - **1.** *ɛmel.* Who committed the crime? *škun lli ɛmel l-žarima?* **2.** *dexxel.* They committed her to an asylum. *dexxluha l-l-meṛṣṭan.*
**He committed suicide. *qtel ṛaṣu.*

to commit oneself - *qawel ṛaṣu.*

committee - *ležna* pl. *-t.*

common - *ɛadi.* That's a common kind of shoe in this area. *had ṣ-ṣbabeṭ ɛadiyin f-had n-naḥiya.*
**It's common knowledge that he lies. *huwa meɛṛuf bin ka-ikdeb.*

commotion - *ḥaṛaž u-maṛaž.*

communist - *šuyuɛi.*

compact - *medkuk.* That's a compact package. *ṛezma medkuka hadik.*

company - **1.** *kubbaniya* pl. *-t, šarika*

pl. *-t.* Does he work for your company? *waš ka-ixdem fe-š-šarika dyalek?* **2.** *ṛfaqa, ṛfaga, ḍyaf* (pl.). We're having company this evening. *ɛendna ḍ-ḍyaf had le-ɛšiya.*
**A man is known by the company he keeps. *mɛa men šeftek šebbehtek.*

comparatively - *be-n-nesba.* It was comparatively easy. *be-n-nesba, kanet sahla.*

to **compare** - **1.** *qaṛen.* We compared the two methods. *qaṛenna ṭ-ṭaṛiqat b-žuž.* **2.** *tqedd.* I can't compare with you. *ana ma-ntqadd-š mɛak.*

comparison - *mušbiha, tešbih.* That's a lame comparison. *had l-mušbiha ɛewža.*

compartment - **1.** *qmaṛa* pl. *-t; bniqa* pl. *bnayeq.* All the compartments in this car are crowded. *gaɛ le-bnayeq f-had l-fagu ɛamṛin.* **2.** *xziyna* pl. *-t, mžiyyeṛ* pl. *mžiyṛat.* The document was hidden in a secret compartment. *l-watiqa kanet mxebbɛa f-waḥed le-xziyna mestura.*

compass - **1.** *buṣuḷa* pl. *-t.* Without the compass we would have been lost. *u-kan ma-kanet-š l-buṣuḷa u-kan tlefna.* **2.** *dabed* pl. *dwabed.* I can't draw a good circle without a compass. *ma-neqḍeṛ-š nxeṭṭeṭ ḍuṛ bla dabed.*

to **compel** - *lezzem ɛla.* I compelled him to go. *lezzemt ɛlih imši.*

compensation - *teɛwiḍ* pl. *-at.* I demand full compensation. *nṭḷeb t-teɛwiḍ t-tamm.*

to **compete** - **1.** *ḍaḍḍ.* Of course I can't compete with you. *meɛlum ana ma-neqḍeṛ-š nḍaḍḍek.* **2.** *šarek.* Are you competing in the contest? *waš nta mšarek fe-l-mubaṛa?*

competent - *qaḍeṛ.* He's competent in his work. *huwa qaḍeṛ ɛla xdemtu.*

competition - *msabqa, mubaṛa* (sport); *mzaḥma* (business).

competitor - *muzaḥim.*

to **complain** - *ška iški, tšekka.* Stop complaining! *baṛaka ma teški.* --We complained to the manager about the noise. *tšekkina l-l-mudir ɛel ṣ-ṣḍaɛ.*

complaint - *šekwa* pl. *-t.*

complete - **1.** *kamel.* Is your work complete? *waš l-xedma dyalek kamla?* **2.** *tamamen.* He's a complete fool. *huwa tamamen ḥmeq.*
**This volume makes my collection complete. *had le-ktab kemmel l-mežmuɛa dyali.*

to complete - *kemmel.* Did you complete your work? *waš kemmelti xdemtek.*

completely - *tamamen.* He convinced me completely. *qenneɛni tamamen.* --He's completely out of his mind. *huwa xaṛež-lu ɛeqlu tamamen.*
**I admit that I was completely wrong about him. *ana ka-neɛtaṛef bin kont ġeḷṭan bezzaf men žihtu.*

to **complicate** - *ṣeɛɛeb, ɛekkel.*

to **comply with** - *qbel.* We regret that we cannot comply with your request. *ḥna met?essfin bin ma-nqeḍṛu-š nqeblu ṭ-ṭalab dyalkom.*

to **compose** - *leḥḥen, kteb.* He composed that song during the war. *leḥḥen dik l-ġonya f-weqt l-ḥeṛb.*

to compose oneself - *žmeɛ ṛaṣu, ṣeffa xaṭṛu.*

composed - *mhedden.* His face remained composed during the entire trial. *wežhu bqa mhedden f-moddet d-deɛwa kollha.*

to be composed of - *meṣnuɛ men.* This fabric is composed of wool and cotton. *had t-tub meṣnuɛ men ṣ-ṣuf u-le-qṭen.*

composition - **1.** *telḥin* pl. *-at.* The orchestra is going to play his compositions tonight. *l-žewq ġadi ilɛeb t-telḥinat dyalu l-yum fe-l-lil.* **2.** *inša?* pl. *-at.* Have you done your English composition? *waš ɛmelti inša? de-n-negliza dyalek?*

compress - *tekmida* pl. *-t* (hot), *derra* pl. *-t.* A hot compress will relieve the pain. *waḥed t-tekmida ġa-txeffef-lek le-ḥriq.*

to compress - *ḍġeṭ, ɛṣeṛ.* The air is compressed by a pump. *ka-iḍeġṭu ṛ-riḥ be-l-ḅumḅa.*

compromise - *tawil.*

to compromise - *ttawa, tṣaleḥ, tfaṣel.* We compromised with him. *ttawina mɛah.*

to **conceal** - **1.** *xebba, xebbeɛ.* Are you concealing something from me? *waš nta mxebbeɛ ši-ḥaža ɛliya?* **2.** *xzen.* The paper was found concealed in the wall. *lqaw l-weṛqa mexzuna fe-l-ḥiṭ.*

conceited - *metkebber.*

to **concentrate** - **1.** *žmeɛ.* The most important industries are concentrated in the north. *ṣ-ṣnaɛi l-muhimmin mežmuɛin fe-š-šamal.* **2.** *ṛeḍḍ balu.* We'll have to concentrate on the first section. *xeṣṣna nṛeḍḍu balna l-l-feṣḷ l-luwwel.*

concern - **1.** *šarika* pl. *-t.* How long have you been with this concern?

šhal hadi u-nta mɛa had š-šarika? 2. *šġal.* She told me it was no concern of mine. *qalet-li ma-ši šgali hadak.* 3. *šwaš.* There's no cause for concern. *ma-kayen ɛla-š š-šwaš.*

to concern - 1. *tɛelleq b-.* This matter concerns you. *had l-qadiya ka-ttɛelleq bik.* 2. *ḥeyyer.* We're concerned about their safety. *ḥna mḥeyyrin ɛla slamthom.* 3. *hemm.* The details don't concern me. *ma-ka-ihemmuni-š t-tafaṣil.*

concert - *ṭarab* pl. *-at.*

to **conclude** - 1. *xtem, kemmel.* He concluded the investigation yesterday. *kemmel l-beḥt l-bareḥ.* 2. *fhem.* What did you conclude from that remark? *aš fhemti men dak l-mulaḥaḍa?*

concrete - 1. *geṣṣ.* The bridge is built of concrete. *l-qenṭra mebniya be-l-geṣṣ.* 2. *ṣḥiḥ* pl. *ṣḥaḥ.* Give me a concrete example. *ɛṭini ši-matal ṣḥiḥ.*

to **condemn** - 1. *ḥkem ɛla.* He was condemned to death. *ḥekmu ɛlih be-l-mut.* 2. *teqqef.* They've condemned this building. *teqqfu had le-bni.*

condition - 1. *ḥala* pl. *-t, ḥal* pl. *ḥwal.* You're in no condition to go out. *nta ḥaltek ma-ši d-le-xruž.* --The house is in poor condition. *ḍ-ḍar ḥaletha ḥala.* --The rug is in good condition. *ẓ-ẓerbiya f-ḥala mezyana.* 2. *šerṭ* pl. *šruṭ, šuruṭ.* I accept all your conditions for the sale. *ana qbelt š-šuruṭ dyalek kollhom fe-l-biɛa.*

**I won't go on any condition. *ɛla kolli ḥal ma-nemši-š.* --He keeps his things in good condition. *ka-itheḷḷa fe-ḥwayžu.*

conduct - *sira.* Your conduct is disgraceful. *sirtek tḥeššem.*

to conduct - 1. *siyyer.* Who's going to conduct the orchestra? *škun lli ġadi isiyyer l-žewq?* 2. *weṣṣel.* Metal conducts heat better than wood. *le-ḥdid ka-iweṣṣel le-ḥmaya ḥsen men l-ɛud.*

**She conducts herself like a lady. *sirtha sirt lallat le-ɛyalat.*

conductor - 1. *muraqib.* Did the conductor punch your ticket? *waš l-muraqib ɛellem n-nfula dyalek?* 2. *raʔiṣ* pl. *ruʔaṣa.* Where is the conductor of the orchestra? *fayn r-raʔiṣ de-l-žewq?*

conference - *moʔtamar* pl. *-at.*

to **confess** - 1. *ɛtaref.* I confess that I haven't read it yet. *ka-neɛtaref bin baqi ma-qritha-š.* 2. *gerr.* The defendant confessed. *l-medɛi gerr.*

confession - *gerran.*

confidence - *tiqa.* I have confidence in him. *ana ɛendi t-tiqa fih.*

**He told it to me in confidence. *qalha-li bini u-binu.*

confident - *myeqqen.* I'm confident that it will turn out all right. *ana myeqqen ikun f-ʔaman llah.*

to **confirm** - 1. *ḥeqqeq.* Hasn't the news been confirmed yet? *waš ma-zal ma-ḥeqqqu le-xbar?* 2. *tebbet.* That only confirms my faith in him. *had š-ši ġir ka-itebbet tiqti fih.*

conflict - *xilaf.*

to conflict - *txalef.* These two reports conflict. *had t-teqririat b-žuž ka-itxalfu.*

to **confuse** - 1. *ḥeyyer.* His talk confused me. *klamu ḥeyyerni.* 2. *tšebbeh-lu.* I confused you with someone else. *tšebbehti-li b-ši-waḥed axor.*

confusion - 1. *terwina.* That's going to cause a lot of confusion. *had š-ši ġa-yeɛmel bezzaf de-t-terwina.* 2. *rebla* pl. *-t, rbali.* He escaped in the confusion. *hṛeb men lli kanet r-rebla.*

to **congratulate** - *henna.* Let me congratulate you on your birthday. *ka-nhennik b-ɛid l-milad dyalek.*

congratulation - *tehniya* pl. *-t.*

**Congratulations! *mbarek mesɛud!*

to **connect** - *laqa.* Connect these wires to the battery. *laqi had s-sluka mɛa l-baṭariya.*

connection - 1. *mɛerfa* pl. *-t, mɛaref.* He has very good connections. *huwa ɛendu mɛaref mezyana.* 2. *munasaba.* In what connection did he mention it? *ɛla š-men munasaba qalha?* 3. *muwaṣala* pl. *-t.* The connections with that town are poor. *l-muwaṣalat mɛa dik le-mdina ṣɛab.* 4. *tebdil l-qiṭar.* I missed a train connection in Casablanca. *ana fellett tebdil l-qiṭar fe-ḍ-ḍar l-biḍa.*

to **conquer** - *fteḥ.*

conscience - *qelb.* I have a clear conscience. *ana qelbi ṣafi.*

conscientious - *b-niytu.* He's a conscientious worker. *huwa xeddam b-niytu.*

conscious - 1. *waɛi.* I wasn't conscious of it. *ma-kont-š waɛi biha.* 2. *fayeq.* Doctor, is he conscious? *ya doktur, waš huwa fayeq?*

consent - *qbul, qabul.* They sold the

house without my consent. *baɛu ḍ-ḍaṛ bla le-qbul dyali.*
to consent - *qbel.* He consented to stay. *qbel ibqa.*
consequence - *natiža* pl. *-t, nata?iž; ɛaqiba* pl *-t, ɛawaqib.* I'm afraid of the consequences. *ana xayef men l-ɛawaqib.*
conservative - *muḥafiḍ.*
to **consider** - **1.** *šaf išuf.* We have to consider the problem from every angle. *xeṣṣna nšufa l-muškila men koll žiha.* **2.** *xemmem f-.* I'll consider it. *qad-nxemmem fiha.* **3.** *ɛtabeṛ.* I consider him an able chemist. *ka-neɛtabṛu kimawi ɛendu meqduṛa.*
**He never considers other people. *huwa ma-ɛemmṛu ka-iddiha f-nas xṛin.*
considerable - *ɛḍim* pl. *ɛḍam.* That's a considerable sum. *hada mebleġ ɛḍim.*
to **consist** - *trekkeb.* That drug consisted of three poisonous substances. *dak d-dwa kan metrekkeb men tlata de-l-mawadd de-s-semm.*
consistent - *tabet.* He isn't very consistent in his work. *ma-huwa-ši tabet fe-xdemtu.*
conspiracy - *dasisa* pl. *-t, dasayes, dsayes.*
constant - *dayem.* He's in constant danger. *huwa f-xaṭaṛ dayem.*
constantly - *bla ḥbis, bla ḥṣiṛ, dima.*
constitution - **1.** *destur* pl. *-at.* The king signed a new constitution last year. *l-malik nezzel xeṭṭ yeddu ɛla waḥed d-destur ždid l-ɛam lli fat.* **2.** *xelqa.* He has a very strong constitution. *l-xelqa dyalu ṣḥiḥa bezzaf.*
to **construct** - *bna ibni.*
construction - *benyan.*
consul - *qunṣu* pl. *qwanṣa.*
consulate - *qunṣuliya.*
to **consult** - *šaweṛ.* You should have consulted us. *kan xeṣṣek tšaweṛna.*
to **consume** - **1.** *šṛeb.* My car consumes a lot of gas. *ṭ-ṭumubil dyali ka-tešṛeb bezzaf de-l-liṣanṣ.* **2.** *kla yakol.* How much meat do you consume a year? *šḥal de-l-lḥem ka-takol fe-l-ɛam?*
consumption - **1.** *stihlak.* Consumption has gone up fifty percent. *s-stihlak ṭleɛ xemsin f-le-mya.* **2.** *sell, meṛḍ s-sder.* He has consumption. *huwa fih s-sell.*
contact - *ttiṣal* pl. *-at.* I've made several new contacts. *ɛmelt ɛadad d-le-ttiṣalat ždad.*
**He's never been in contact with foreigners. *huwa ma-ɛemmṛu ttaṣel mɛa l-beṛṛaniyin.*
to contact - *ttaṣel b-.* I'll contact you as soon as I arrive. *ana ġir newṣel u-nttaṣel bik.*
to **contain** - *(kan ikun) fih, rfed.* That trunk contains only clothing. *had ṣṣenḍuq ma-fih ġir le-ḥwayež.*
container - *maɛun* pl. *mwaɛen.*
contempt - *ḥogṛa.*
content - **1.** *lli fih.* The alcholic content is small. *l-alkul lli fih ṣġiṛ.* **2.** *feṛḥan.* He was content with what we gave him. *kan feṛḥan b-dak š-ši lli ɛṭinah.*
contents - *lli fih.* Dissolve the contents of the package in one glass of water. *ḥell lli f-had l-bakit f-kas de-l-ma.*
table of contents - *fehrisa* pl. *fhares.*
contest - *mubaṛa* pl. *-t.*
to contest - *nazeɛ.* They're contesting the will. *ka-inazɛu l-waṣiya.*
continual - *mettabeɛ, dayem.*
continually - *dima.*
to continue - *zad izid.* Let's continue with our work. *yaḷḷah nzidu fe-xdemtna.* --We'll continue our discussion tomorrow. *ġedda nzidu fe-l-mudakaṛa dyalna.* --Continue, I'm listening to you. *zid, ana ka-ntṣennet-lek.* --I want to continue on to Fez. *baġi nzid ḥetta l-fas.*
contract - *ɛeqda* pl. *-t, ɛqad.*
to contract - **1.** *qeṣṣeṛ.* Heat expands, cold contracts. *le-ḥma ka-iṭuwwel u-l-brudiya ka-tqeṣṣeṛ.* **2.** *tqeṣṣeṛ.* The metal must have contracted. *ṛebbama l-meɛden tqeṣṣeṛ.* **3.** *tteɛqed.* They've contracted to put up the building in five months. *ttɛeqdu baš iṭellɛu le-bni f-xems šhuṛ.* **4.** *šebbeṛ.* I've contracted pneumonia. *šebbeṛt meṛḍ ž-ženb.*
contractor - *ṭašrun* pl. *-at.*
to **contradict** - *xalef, keddeb.*
contradictory - *mxalef.* We've heard the most contradictory talk about it. *smeɛna klam mxalef bezzaf ɛliha.*
contrary - *mɛekkes.* She's very contrary. *hiya mɛekksa bezzaf.*
contrary to - *ḍeḍḍ.* That's contrary to our agreement. *had š-ši ḍeḍḍ le-mwafqa dyalna.*
on the contrary - *be-l-ɛeks.*
contrast - *feṛq.* There's a big con-

trast between the two brothers.
kayen feṛq kbir bin l-xut b-žuž.
to contrast - *qabel.* He con-
trasted the programs of the two parties. *qabel baṛamiž le-ḥzab b-žuž.*
to contrast with - *xalef mƐa.*
These red flowers contrast well with
the white ones. *had n-nuwwaṛ le-
ḥmeṛ ka-ixalfu mezyan mƐa l-buyeḍ.*
to **contribute** - 1. *tberreƐ b-.* Have
you contributed anything to the
fund? *waš tberreƐti b-ši ḥaža Ɛel
le-friḍa?* 2. *zad izid f-.* This
noise just contributes to the confusion. *had ṣ-ṣḍaƐ ġir ka-izid fe-
l-haṛaž.*
control - *ḥokm, ḥkam.* The children
are getting beyond my control. *d-
drari xaṛžin Ɛla ḥkami.*
   **He lost control of the car.
ġelbet Ɛlih ṭ-ṭumubil. --He always
has himself under control. *huwa
dima ġaleb nefsu.* --Everything is
under control. *koll-ši fe-l-ġaya
u-n-nihaya.*
to control - *mlek, ṛaqeb.* He controls
sixty percent of the business. *ka-
imlek settin f-le-mya de-l-ḥaṛaka.*
   to control oneself - *ġleb nefsu,
šebber ṛaṣu.*
convenience - *suhula* pl. *-t.* Our new
apartment has every modern convenience. *s-sekna dyalna ž-ždida
Ɛendha gaƐ s-suhulat l-Ɛeṣṛiyin.*
   **Call me at your earliest con-
venience. *Ɛeyyeṭ-li f-ʔewwel weqt
mnaseb.*
convenient - *mwafeq, mnaseb.*
convention - *muž̌tamaƐ* pl. *-at.*
conventional - 1. *mtebbeƐ l-Ɛada.*
She's very conventional. *hiya
mtebbƐa l-Ɛada bezzaf.* 2. *Ɛadi.* I
prefer the conventional method.
ana ḥsen-li ṭ-ṭariqa l-Ɛadiya.
conversation - *mudakaṛa* pl. *-t.*
convict - *mesžun* pl. *msažen.*
   to convict - *tebbet.* He was con-
victed of murder. *tebbtu Ɛlih le-
qtila.*
to **convince** - *dexxel fe-ṛ-ṛaṣ.* You
can't convince me of that. *ma-
imken-lek-š ddexxel dak š-ši f-ṛaṣi.*
convinced - *myeqqen.* I'm convinced
she's innocent. *ana myeqqen bin
hiya barya.*
cook - *ṭebbax* pl. *-a* (m.); *ṭebbaxa
ṭebbaxa* p̄l. *-t* (f.). She's the
best cook we ever had. *hadi ʔeḥsen
ṭebbaxa lli ṭeḥna Ɛliha.*
   **Too many cooks spoil the broth.
*yeddi u-yedd l-qabla, ka-ixrež le-
ḥrami Ɛweṛ.*

to cook - *ṭiyyeb.*
cookie - *ḥelwa* pl. *ḥlawi, ḥlawat,
ḥalawat.*
cool - 1. *bared.* Keep it in a cool
place. *xelliha f-maḥell bared.*
2. *xfif* pl. *xfaf.* Wait until I get
into something cooler. *tsenna
ḥetta nelbes ši-ḥaža xfifa.*
   **It gets pretty cool here to-
wards evening. *l-ḥal ka-ibred
šwiya hnaya f-le-Ɛšiya.* --I tried
to keep cool. *ḥawelt nšebber ṛaṣi.*
   to cool - 1. *bred.* Don't let this
soup cool too much. *ma-txelli-š had
le-ḥrira tebred bezzaf.* 2. *berred.*
Take these bottles and cool them.
xud had ṛ-ṛḍayem u-berredhom.
coop - *qfez* pl. *qfaz, qfuza.*
   to coop up - *ḥbes.* I don't want to
keep the children cooped up in the
house all day long. *ana ma-baġi-š
neḥbes d-drari fe-ḍ-ḍaṛ n-nhaṛ
kollu.*
cooper - *qebbab* pl. *-a, qbaybi* pl.
-ya.
co-operation - *mƐawna.* Can we count
on your co-operation? *waš imken-
lna ntwekklu Ɛel le-mƐawna dyalkom?*
copper - *nḥas.*
coppersmith - *swayni* pl. *-ya*
copy - *nesxa* pl. *-t, nsaxi.* I made a
copy of the letter. *Ɛmelt nesxa
d-le-bṛa.*
   to copy - 1. *nsex.* Copy the letter carefully. *nsex le-bṛa be-t-
tedqiq.* 2. *neqqel.* She copies the
clothes that she sees in the movies.
*ka-tneqqel le-ḥwayež lli ka-tšuf
f-l-aflam.*
cord - 1. *qennba* pl. *-t* coll. *qenneb.*
The cord isn't long enough for me to
tie up the package with. *ma-ka-
tqeddni-š l-qennba baš neḥzem ṛ-
ṛezma.* 2. *xiṭ* pl. *xyuṭ.* We'll have
to get a new cord for the iron.
*xeṣṣna nḍebbru Ɛla xiṭ ždid l-le-
blanša.*
Cordova - *qoṛṭuba.*
coriander - *qeṣbuṛ, qeẓbuṛ.*
cork - *feršiya* pl. *-t* coll. *ferši.*
corn - 1. *ḍra* (grain). 2. *meṣmaṛ* pl.
mṣameṛ (on foot).
corner - 1. *qent* pl. *qnut* (internal or
external). 2. *ṛokna* pl. *ṛkani*
(internal).
corporal - *kabṛan* pl. *-at.*
corpse - *gnaza* pl. *gnayez; ž̌etta* pl. *-t;
miyyet* pl. *muta.*
correct - *ṣḥiḥ* pl. *ṣḥaḥ.*
   to correct - *ṣleḥ.*
correction - *iṣḷaḥ* pl. *-at.*
to **correspond** - 1. *naseb.* The trans-

lation doesn't correspond to the original. *t-ṭeṛžama ma-mnasba-š mƐa l-aṣili.* **2.** *tkateb.* We've been corresponding with each other for six years. *hadi sett snin u-ḥna ka-ntkatbu.*

correspondence – *murasala, mkatba.*

correspondent – *murasil* pl. *-in.*

corridor – *ṣeṭwan* pl. *ṣṭawen.*

cost – *taman* pl. *-at.*

at any cost – *baš-emma kan.*

to cost – **1.** *swa iswa.* How much does this one cost? *šḥal ka-teswa hadi?* **2.** *ṭaḥ iṭiḥ.* That will cost him dearly. *hadik ġadi ṭṭiḥ-lu ġalya.*

cottage – *dwira.*

cotton – *qṭen, qṭon.*

couch – *seddari* pl. *sdader.*

cough – *keḥba* pl. *-t; keḥḥa* pl. *-t; seƐla* pl. *-t.*

to cough – *kḥeb, keḥḥ, sƐel.*

counsel – **1.** *naṣiḥa* pl. *-t, naṣayeḥ.* Let me give you some good counsel. *xellini neƐṭik ši-naṣiḥa mezyana.* **2.** *muḥami* pl. *-yin.* Who is their counsel in the case? *škun huwa l-muḥami dyalhom fe-l-qaḍiya?*

count – *ḥsab* pl. *-at.* The count has not yet been made. *le-ḥsab ma-zal ma-tteƐmel.*

to count – *ḥseb.*

to count on – *Ɛewwel Ɛla.*

counter – *baṣeṭ* pl. *bwaṣeṭ.* Don't stand in front of the counter. *ma-tewqef-š qbalt l-baṣeṭ.*

counterfeit – *mẓuwweṛ.*

to counterfeit – *ẓuwweṛ.*

country – **1.** *blad* pl. *beldan, boldan.* I've seen many countries. *šeft bezzaf de-l-boldan.* **2.** *Ɛṛubiya, badiya.* They want to move to the country. *huma baġyin itḥewwlu l-le-Ɛṛubiya.* --That's beautiful country. *walayenni hadi badiya mezyana.*

courage – *ṛežla, ṛžuliya, šžaƐa.*

course – **1.** *ṭṛiq* pl. *ṭoṛqan.* The plane is holding a straight course. *ṭ-ṭiyaṛa tabƐa ṭṛiq mserrḥa* --The river has changed its course. *l-wad beddel ṭ-ṭṛiq dyalu.* **2.** *makla* pl. *-t.* The dinner had four courses. *kanu f-le-Ɛša ṛebƐa de-l-maklat.* **3.** *ḍeṛṣ* pl. *ḍuṛuṣ.* What courses did you take? *š-men ḍuṛuṣ xditi?*

of course – *meƐlum.*

court – **1.** *meḥkama* pl. *-t.* How many judges are there in this court? *šḥal de-l-qoḍya kaynin f-had l-meḥkama?* **2.** *mṛaḥ.* We have two rooms opening on the court. *Ɛendna žuž d-le-byut Ɛaṭyin Ɛel le-mṛaḥ.* **3.** *ḥašiya.* The ambassador has not yet been received at court. *s-safir ma-zal ma-tteqbel fe-l-ḥašiya.* **4.** *saḥa* pl. *-t.* The court is still too muddy for them to play in. *s-saḥa baqa mġiyyṣa u-ma-imken-lhom-š ileƐbu fiha.*

to court – *ẓeḷḷeḷ.* He's been courting her for quite some time. *šella hadi u-huwa ka-iẓeḷḷeḷha.*

courteous – *ḷṭif* pl. *ḷṭaf.*

courtesy – *ṣwab.*

cousin – *weld* (m.) or *bent* (f.) used in construct with *Ɛemm, Ɛemma, xal,* or *xala,* depending on the specific relationship (father's brother's son, etc.).

cover – **1.** *ġṭa* pl. *-wat.* I didn't have enough cover last night. *l-bareḥ ma-qeddetni-š le-ġṭa.* --Where are the covers for these boxes? *fayn le-ġṭawat dyal had ṣ-ṣnaḍeq?* **2.** *ġlaf* pl. *-at.* Who took the cover off this book? *škun lli ḥeyyed le-ġlaf men had le-ktab?*

**I read this book from cover to cover. *qrit had le-ktab men l-luwwel l-l-axir.* --Take cover! *xzen ṛaṣek!*

to cover – **1.** *ġeṭṭa.* They covered our roof with tile. *ġeṭṭaw ṣṭaḥna be-l-qermud.* --Everything is covered with snow. *koll-ši mġeṭṭi b-telž.* **2.** *ġellef.* We cov- the sofa with cretonne. *ġellefna s-seddari b-šit.* **3.** *ḍmen.* This check is covered. *had š-šik meḍmun.* **4.** *fesser.* I believe that you've covered all the questions. *nḍenn bin fesserti l-ʔasʔila kollhom.* **5.** *qṭeƐ.* We covered the distance in three hours. *qṭeƐna l-masaḥa f-felt swayeƐ.*

**Is your house covered by insurance? *waš ḍaṛek msugṛa?* --What territory do you cover? *f- aš men naḥiya ka-texdem?*

to cover up – *ġeṭṭa.* Cover me up! *ġeṭṭini!*

to cover up for – *ster.* Did you cover up for me? *waš stertini?*

cow – *begṛa* pl. *-t* coll. *bgeṛ.*

coward – *xuwwaf* pl. *-in.*

cozy – *mṛiyyeḥ.* What a cozy room! *walayenni bit mṛiyyeḥ hada!*

crab – *Ɛeqṛiša* pl. *-t, Ɛqaṛeš; bu-žniba* pl. *-t.*

**He's an old crab. *huwa bḥal l-Ɛetrus.*

crack – **1.** *šeqqa* pl. *-t, šqayeq,*

šqeq, šquq; coll. *šeqq.* The crack in the dam is getting wider. *š-šeqqa fe-s-sedd ka-tewsaƐ.* --There's a crack in the glass. *kayna waḥed š-šeqqa fe-z-zaž.* **2.** *ṭeqṭiq.* I thought I heard the crack of a rifle. *ḍheṛ-li smeƐt ṭ-ṭeqṭiq de-mkoḥla.*

at the crack of dawn - *f-le-fžer.*

to crack - **1.** *herres.* I'll crack the nuts. *ana ġad-nherres l-gergaƐ.* **2.** *ttšeqq.* The glass cracked when I poured the hot water in it. *l-kas ttseqq men-lli kebbit fih l-ma sxun.*

to crack jokes - *ṭḷeq xṛayef, tmelleġ.*

cradle - *kuna* pl. *-t.*

to **cram** - *xša ixši.* He crammed everything into one trunk. *xša koll-ši f-ṣenḍuq waḥed.*

cramp - *hebza* pl. *-t.* I have a cramp in my leg. *Ɛendi hebza f-ṣagi.*

cranky - *(lli) ka-itqelleq, ka-ithiyyež.*

crane - **1.** *ġeṛnuq* pl. *ġṛaneq* (bird). **2.** *buži* pl. *bwaža* (machine).

to **crash** - *ṭaḥ iṭiḥ* One of the planes crashed into the sea. *weḥda men ṭ-ṭiyaṛat ṭaḥet f-le-bḥeṛ.*

crawl - *ḥba yeḥbu.*

**The shop was crawling with ants. *l-ḥanut kan ka-iġli be-n-nmel.*

crayfish - *qemṛuna* pl. *-t* coll. *qemṛun.*

crazy - **1.** *ḥmeq* pl. *ḥumeq.* He was crazy, that's why they put him in the asylum. *kan ḥmeq, biha bas dexxluh fe-l-meṛṣṭan.* **2.** *mfelles.* That's a crazy ida! *fikra mfellsa hadi!*

to **creak** - *ẓwa iẓwi.* Shut the door so it won't creak. *sedd l-bab baš ma-dẓwi-ši.*

cream - **1.** *frara.* We make butter from from the cream. *ka-nṣawbu z-zebda men le-frara.* **2.** *dehna.* Put some of this cream on your hands and they won't hurt any more. *dir ši-šwiya d-had d-dehna Ɛla yeddik u-ma-ibqaw-š iḍeṛṛuk.* **3.** *semni.* The walls are cream colored. *lun le-ḥyuṭ semni.*

the cream of the crop - *xyaṛ ma fe-l-ġella.*

to **create** - **1.** *xleq.* God created the world. *xleq ḷḷah d-denya.* **2.** *xtaṛeƐ.* We have to create a new position for him. *xeṣṣna nextarƐu-lu bḷaṣa ždida.*

**The incident created a lot of excitement. *l-ḥadita kanet s-sabab d-bezzaf de-l-haṛaž.*

creature - *meẋluq* pl. *-at.*

credit - *ṭeḷq.* We can buy the furniture on credit. *imken-lna nešriw l-ʔatat be-ṭ-ṭeḷq.*

**He likes to take credit for what somebody else does. *huwa ka-iftaxeṛ be-dyal ġiru.* --I did the work and he got the credit. *ana Ɛmelt l-xedma u-huwa dda le-fḍeḷ.*

creditor - *mul d-din, ṣaḥeb d-din.*

crew - *feṛqa* pl. *-t.*

crib - **1.** *meƐlef* pl. *mƐalef.* Did you put hay in the crib? *waš ḥeṭṭiti t-tben fe-l-meƐlef?* **2.** *fṛaš* pl. *-at.* Our boy is getting too big for his crib. *weldna ma-bqa-š iži qeddu fṛašu.*

crime - *žarima* pl. *-t, žrayem.*

criminal - *mužrim* pl. *-in.*

cripple - *meƐṭub.*

to cripple - *Ɛeṭṭeb.*

crisis - **1.** *šedda* (physical). **2.** *azma* (political). **3.** *ksad* (commercial).

crisp - **1.** *mgermel.* The bread is fresh and crisp. *l-xobz ždid u-mgermel.* **2.** *bared šwiya.* The weather is a bit crisp tonight. *l-ḥal bared šwiya had l-lila.*

to **criticize** - *Ɛeyyeb Ɛla.*

to **crochet** - *ġzel be-l-mexṭaf.*

crockery - *bdiƐ.*

crocodile - *temsaḥ* pl. *-at, tmaseḥ.*

crocus - *ẓeƐfṛan.*

crooked - **1.** *mƐewwež.* This pin is crooked. *had le-fnita mƐewwža.* **2.** *xeṭṭaf* pl. *-a.* All those people are crooked. *duk n-nas kollhom xeṭṭafa.*

crop - *ṣaba.* The farmers expect a good crop this year. *l-fellaḥa mwekklin Ɛla ṣaba mezyana had l-Ɛam.*

cross - **1.** *ṣḷib* pl. *ṣoḷban.* Do you see the church with the big cross on the steeple? *waš ka-tšuf le-knisiya lli Ɛendha ṣ-ṣḷib le-kbir Ɛel l-borz?* **2.** *ġeḍban.* He's cross today. *huwa ġeḍban l-yum.*

to cross - **1.** *qṭeƐ.* Cross the street at the green light. *qṭeƐ ṭ-ṭṛiq fe-ḍ-ḍu le-xḍeṛ.* **2.** *tlaqa.* The two principal avenues cross in front of the post office. *ka-itlaqaw le-mḥažž le-kbaṛ b-žuž qbalt l-buṣṭa.*

to cross out - *ḍṛeb Ɛla.* Cross out the things you don't want. *ḍṛeb Ɛel le-ḥwayež lli ma-baġi-š*

to cross one's mind - *ža iži f-balu.* It never crossed my mind that he would oppose me. *Ɛemmeṛni ma-žani f-bali bin iƐaṛeḍni.*

crossed-eyed - *ḥwel* pl. *ḥiwel.*

crow – *ġṛab* pl. *-at, ġoṛban, ġṛobba.*
to crow – *wedden.* I woke up when the rooster crowed. *ana feqt men-lli wedden l-ferruž.*
crowd – *ġaši, zḥam.*
crown – *taž* pl. *tižan.*
crude – **1.** *xšin* pl. *xšan.* That man is just a bit crude! *ṛažel xšin šwiya hada!* **2.** *qbiḥ* pl. *qbaḥ.* That was a crude remark! *kanet mulaḥaḍa qbiḥa hadi!*
cruel – *qaṣeḥ.*
cruelty – *qṣuḥa, qṣuḥiya, qṣuḥiyt l-qelb.*
crumb – *tfertita.*
to **crush** – **1.** *ḍġeṭ.* You're crushing my hat. *nta ka-ḍḍġet š-šemrir dyali.* **2.** *mƐes.* Careful, you're crushing the eggs. *Ɛendak, nta ka-temƐes l-biḍ.* **3.** *ḥettem.* He was crushed by the news. *huwa ḥetmatu le-xbaṛ.*
crust – *qešṛa.*
crutch – *Ɛokkaz* pl. *Ɛkakez.*
cry – *ġuta* pl. *-t.* Then we heard a loud cry. *u-men beƐd smeƐna waḥed l-ġuta kbira.*
a far cry from – *bƐid men.* Your story is a far cry from the truth. *le-ḥkaya dyalek bƐida men l-ḥaqiqa.*
to cry – *bka ibki.*
cucumber – *feggusa* pl. *-t* coll. *feggus.*
culture – *tameddun.*
cultured – *mteqqef, qaṛi.* She's a cultured woman. *hiya mṛa mteqqfa.*
cunning – *ḥili, mṭuwweṛ.*
cup – **1.** *ṭaṣa* pl. *-t.* Is there any coffee left in your cup? *waš ma-zal kayna ši-qehwa fe-ṭ-ṭaṣa dyalek?* **2.** *kas* pl. *kisan.* Who won the cup? *škun lli rbeḥ l-kas?*
cupboard – *xzana* pl. *-t, xzayen.*
cure – *dwa* pl. *-yat, duyan, adwiya.* There is no cure for cancer. *ma-kayen-š dwa l-l-merḍ s-saṛaṭan.*
to cure – *dawa.* They cured him in two months. *dawaweh f-šehṛayn.*
curfew *menƐ t-tažewwol.*
curiosity – **1.** *ḥobb l-meƐrifa* (intellectual). **2.** *fḍuḷ* (indiscrete, prying).
curious – **1.** *fḍuli* (indiscrete, prying). **2.** *ġrib* pl. *ġribin, ġrab.* What a curious looking man! *walayenni ġrib had ṛ-ṛažel!*
currant – *zbiba ṛumya* pl. *zbibat ṛumyin* coll. *zbib ṛumi.*
current – **1.** *zerraf (de-l-ma).* He got caught in the current. *ḥṣel fe-z-zerraf.* **2.** *ḍu, kehṛaba.* The (electric) current has been turned off. *tteqṭeƐ ḍ-ḍu.* **3.** *žari.* Have you paid the bill for the current month yet? *waš xeḷḷeṣti le-ḥsab de-š-šheṛ ž-žari wella ma-zal?*
curry – *kerkub.*
curse – *leƐna* pl. *-t.*
to curse – *lƐen, xṭa ixṭi f-, dƐa idƐi Ɛla.*
curtain – *xamiya* pl. *xwami.*
curtain rod – *qṭib* (pl. *qeṭban, qṭayeb*) *de-l-xamiya.*
curve – *ḍuṛa* pl. *-t.* There are many curves in this road. *kaynin bezzaf de-ḍ-ḍuṛat f-had ṭ-ṭriq.*
to curve – *ḍuṛ iḍuṛ.* The road curves around the town. *ṭ-ṭriq ka-ḍḍuṛ Ɛel le-mdina.*
cushion – *mxedda* pl. *-t, mxadd, mxayed; xeddiya* pl. *-t, xdadi.*
custody – **1.** *ḥḍaya* (of children). **2.** *ḥebs* (arrest).
custom – *qaƐida* pl. *-t, qwaƐed, qawaƐid; Ɛada* pl. *-t, Ɛwayed.*
customary – *Ɛadi, fe-l-Ɛada.*
customs – *diwana* pl. *-t.* Do we have to pay customs on this? *waš lazemna nxeḷḷṣu ḥeqq d-diwana Ɛla hadi?*
customs inspection – *teftiš d-diwana.*
cut – *žeṛḥa* pl. *-t, žṛaḥi.* The cut is nearly healed. *ž-žeṛḥa qṛiba tebṛa.*
to cut – **1.** *qṭeƐ.* Cut the bread please. *qṭeƐ l-xobz Ɛafak.* **2.** *žṛeḥ.* I cut my finger. *žṛeḥt ṣbaƐi.* **3.** *ṭiyyeḥ.* We're going to cut these prices next month. *had t-tamanat ġad-nṭiyyḥuhom š-šheṛ ž-žay.* **4.** *nqeṣ men.* His salary was cut. *neqṣu men ižaṛtu.* **5.** *ḥsek.* Haven't you cut the grass yet? *waš baqi ma-ḥsekti-š ṛ-ṛbiƐ?*
**During the whole term he cut only two classes. *moddet l-fešḷ kollu huwa beṭṭel ġir žuž de-ḍ-ḍuṛuṣ.*
to cut across – *qṭeƐ.* He cut across the field. *qṭeƐ l-feddan.*
to cut down – **1.** *qṭeƐ.* These trees will have to be cut down. *had š-šžeṛ xeṣṣhom ittqeṭƐu.* **2.** *nqeṣ men.* We'll have to cut our expenses down. *xeṣṣna nneqṣu men ṣayeṛna.*
to cut off – *qṭeƐ.*
to cut out – *meqqeṣ.* I'm going to cut the picture out. *ġad-nmeqqeṣ t-teṣwiṛa.*
**Cut it out! *xḷaṣ men hadi!*
to cut short – *nqeṣ men.* We had to cut our trip short. *tlezzemna nneqṣu men ṣ-ṣfeṛ dyalna.*
**He cut me short. *xṭef menni le-klam.*
to cut through – *tqeb.* You've

cut through the lining. *tqebti t-tebṭin.*
to cut up – *qṣem.* Cut it up into four pieces. *qṣemha Ɛla ṛebƐa de-ṭ-ṭṛaf.*

cute – *ḍṛif* pl. *ḍṛaf, ḍṛiyyef.*

cutlet – *ḍeḷƐa* pl. *ḍḷuƐ.* I want the cutlet to be well done. *bġit ḍ-ḍeḷƐa tkun ṭayba šwiya.*

cylinder – *žeƐba* pl. *-t, žƐab.*

D

dad(dy) – *ḅḅa, baba.* Is your dad home, Ali? *ḅḅak fe-ḍḍaṛ a Ɛli?*

daffodil – *neṛžis.*

dagger – *xenžaṛ* pl. *xnažeṛ, kommiya* pl. *-t, kwami.*

daily – **1.** *fe-n-nhaṛ.* The mail is delivered twice daily. *le-bṛawat ka-itferṛqu meṛṛtayn fe-n-nhaṛ.* **2.** *koll nhaṛ.* That's a daily occurrence around here. *had š-ši ka-yuqeƐ hnaya koll nhaṛ.*
daily (paper) – *žarida yumiya.* Our town has only one daily paper. *mdintna ma-Ɛendha ġir žarida weḥda yumiya.*

dam – *sedd* pl. *sdud.* The dam is broken. *s-sedd metfeṛgeƐ.*

damage – *xaṣaṛa, ḍaṛaṛ.* How much damage has been done? *šḥal de-l-ʔxaṣaṛa weqƐet?*
damages – *xṣayeṛ.* He had to pay damages. *lezzmuh iƐewweḍ le-xṣayeṛ.*
to damage – *xeṣṣeṛ.* The storm damaged the roof. *l-ḥemla xeṣṣṛet ṣ-ṣṭeḥ.*

Damascene – *dimešqi.*

Damascus – *dimešq.*

damn – *meḷƐun.* Throw that damn cat out! *ṛmi dak l-qeṭṭ l-meḷƐun beṛṛa!*
**I don't give a damn what he says. *w-ana ka-nddiha fe-klamu?*
damn it! – *xzit! ixzit!* Damn(it), I have to go. *ixzit, xeṣṣni nemši.*
to damn – *sxeṭ.* I'll be damned if I do it! *ana mesxuṭ la dertha!*

damp – *mṭebbeb.* Don't lean against that wall, it's damp. *la-ttekka-š Ɛla dak l-ḥiṭ, ṛah mṭebbeb.*
to get damp – *fzeg.* Everything gets damp in the cellar. *koll ḥaža ka-tefzeg fe-d-dehliz.*

dampness – *ṛṭuba, bruda.*

dance – **1.** *šeṭḥa, šṭiḥ.* May I have the next dance? *waš tsemḥi-li be-š-šeṭḥa ž-žayya?* **2.** *šṭiḥ.* Are you going to the dance? *waš ġadi le-š-šṭiḥ?*
to dance – *šṭeḥ.* They danced until midnight. *bqaw ka-išeṭḥu ḥetta l-neṣṣ l-lil.*

dancer – *šeṭṭaḥ* pl. *-a.* The dancers will begin their performance at eight o'clock. *š-šeṭṭaḥa ġadi ibdaw fe-t-tmenya.*
**He's a good dancer. *ka-yeƐṛef išṭeḥ mezyan.*

dandelion – *asra.*

danger – *xaṭaṛ.* The doctor says she is out of danger now. *qal-lek ṭ-ṭbib daba menƐet men l-xaṭaṛ.* —He's in danger of losing his job. *xdemtu ṛaha f-xaṭaṛ.*

dangerous – *xaṭiṛ.* Is it dangerous to swim here? *waš l-Ɛewm hnaya xaṭiṛ?*

to **dare** – **1.** *qedd.* I didn't dare leave the baby alone. *ma-qeddit-š nxelli t-teṛbya wḥedha.* **2.** *zƐem.* I don't dare tell him. *ma-ka-nezƐem-š nqulha-lu.*
**Don't you dare! *Ɛendak!* —Don't you dare take it! *ila konti ṣḷib xudha!* —How dare you open my mail? *š-binek u-bin bṛawati tḥellhom?*

dark – **1.** *ḍḷem.* The road is hard to find in the dark. *ṣƐib ilqa l-waḥed ṭ-ṭṛiq fe-ḍ-ḍḷem.* **2.** *meḍḷam.* I couldn't find my seat because the room was dark. *ma-žbeṛt-ši ṛḥebti ḥit l-bit kan meḍḷam.* **3.** *meġluq.* I want a darker color. *bġit lun meġluq Ɛla hada.*
to get dark – *ḍḷam.* In summer it gets dark late. *fe-ṣ-ṣif l-ḥal ka-iḍḷam mƐeṭṭel.*
to keep (someone) in the dark – *xebbeƐ Ɛla.* Don't keep me in the dark! *la-txebbeƐ šay Ɛliya.*

darling – *Ɛziz bezzaf.* He's his mother's darling. *huwa Ɛziz Ɛla ṃṃu bezzaf.*

to **darn** – *ṛeqqeƐ.* Did you darn my socks? *waš ṛeqqeƐti tqašri?*
**He knew darn little about it. *xḷaṣ, ma-Ɛṛef ġir šwiya Ɛla dak š-ši.* —I'll be darned if that isn't Mustafa! *ṛani kafer ila ma-tṣab-ši hadak moṣṭafa!* —I don't give a

darn about it! *aš* *ɛendi fiha?* --Darn it! Where's my tie? *fayn le-xṣaṛa de-l-geṛfaṭa dyali?*

dash - **1.** *šeṛṭa* pl. *šṛaṭi.* Put a dash after the first word. *ḥeṭṭ šeṛṭa men beɛd l-kelma l-luwla.* **2.** *teftifa* pl. *tfatef.* All it needs is a dash of salt. *ma-xeṣṣha ġir ši-teftifa d-le-mleḥ.*

to dash - **1.** *neqqez.* He grabbed his coat and dashed for the door. *xṭef l-kebbuṭ dyalu u-neqqez l-l-bab.* **2.** *ṛma iṛmi.* He came right to when I dashed some water in his face. *faq değya değya melli ṛmit šwiya de-l-ma ɛla wežhu.*

to dash off - *mša imši be-z-zerba.* Before I could answer, he dashed off. *mša be-z-zerba qbel-ma mken-li nžaweb.*

dashboard - *ṭablu ṭ-ṭumubil* pl. *ṭabluyat ṭ-ṭumubil.*

date - **1.** *temṛa* pl. *tmeṛ.* How much are dates by the kilo? *be-šḥal t-tmeṛ l-kilu?* **2.** *tarix.* On what date did your brother leave for America? *fe-šmen tarix ṣafeṛ xak l-ʔamirika?* **3.** *miɛad* pl. *-at.* I have a date for lunch today. *ɛendi miɛad l-yum f-le-ġda.* **4.** *weqt* pl. *wqat.* You set the date! *nta ɛeyyen l-weqt.*

**What's the date today? *šḥal mɛana l-yum?*

out-of-date - *zemni.* These machines are out of date. *had l-makinat zemniyat.*

to date - *l-daba.* We haven't heard from him to date. *l-daba ma-wṣelna mennu ḥetta xbaṛ.*

up-to-date - **1.** *weqti.* Her clothes are always up-to-date. *ḥwayežha dima weqtiyen.* **2.** *mtebbeɛ.* I'm not up-to-date on this matter. *ana ma-mtebbeɛ-š had l-qaḍiya.*

to date - **1.** *tuṛex.* The letter is dated June 6th. *le-bṛa mtuṛxa nhaṛ setta yunyu.* **2.** *ṛžeɛ.* The oldest house in town dates from the 17th century. *ʔeqdem ḍaṛ f-le-mdina ka-teṛžeɛ l-l-qeṛn s-sbeɛṭaš.*

date-palm, date-tree - *nexla* pl. *nexlat* coll. *nxel.*

daughter - *bent* pl. *bnat.*

daughter-in-law - *meṛt l-weld* pl. *ɛyalat le-wlad, ɛyalat l-weld; ɛṛuṣa* pl. *ɛṛayeṣ.*

dawn - *fžer.* We had to get up at dawn. *konna melzumin baš nnuḍu fe-l-fžer.*

to dawn on - *ban iban l-.* It finally dawned on me what he meant. *f-l-axeṛ ɛad ban-li še-bġa iqul.*

day - **1.** *nhaṛ* pl. *-at, nhayeṛ.* He's been sleeping all day. *n-nhaṛ kollu u-huwa naɛes.* **2.** *yum* pl. *iyam, iyamat.* He's seen better days. *dazet ɛlih iyam ḥsen men hadi.* **3.** *weqt.* He's had his day. *fat weqtu.*

**Tuesday is my day off. *ana ka-nṛiyyeḥ nhaṛ tlata.*

a day - *fe-n-nhaṛ.* Three times a day. *tlata de-l-meṛṛat fe-n-nhaṛ.* --He earns forty dirhams a day. *ka-iṣewweṛ ṛebɛin derhem fe-n-nhaṛ.*

**Let's call it a day! *iwa nḥebsu hnaya l-yum.*

by the day - **1.** *koll nhaṛ.* He gets fresher by the day. *ka-dzid fih ḍ-ḍṣaṛa koll nhaṛ.* **2.** *be-n-nhaṛ.* You can rent this room by the day. *imken-lek tekri had l-bit be-n-nhaṛ.*

day after day - *nhaṛ ɛla nhaṛ.* Day after day he tells us the same old story. *nhaṛ ɛla nhaṛ ka-iɛawedna dak le-xṛafa l-bayta.* --Day after day his condition is improving. *ḥaltu ka-dzyan nhaṛ ɛla nhaṛ.*

day in, day out - *n-nhaṛ ɛla xah.* They fed us beans day in, day out. *kanu ka-iwekkluna l-lubya n-nhaṛ ɛla xah.*

every day - *koll nhaṛ.* He works every day except Sunday. *ka-ixdem koll nhaṛ men ġiṛ l-ḥedd.*

from day to day - *men nhaṛ le-nhaṛ.* It's getting worse from day to day. *ka-dzid tkeffes men nhaṛ le-nhaṛ.*

one of these days - **1.** *ši-nhaṛ.* I'll drop by your house one of these days. *ši-nhaṛ ġadi nži l-ɛendkom.* **2.** *ši-yum.* One of these days you'll be sorry. *ši-yum men l-iyam ġadi tendem.*

(the) day after tomorrow - *beɛd ġedda.* He's leaving the day after tomorrow. *ġadi imši beɛd ġedda.*

the other day - *dak n-nhaṛ.* I met him the other day. *tɛaṛeft mɛah dak n-nhaṛ.*

these days - *had l-iyam.* Prices are very high these days. *had l-iyam t-tamanat ṭelɛet.*

daybreak - *ṭluɛ n-nhaṛ.*

dazed - *dehšan.* He seemed completely dazed. *ḍheṛ dehšan tamamen.*

dead - *miyyet* adj. pl. *miyytin,* n. pl. *muta.* They buried their dead. *defnu l-muta dyalhom.* --His father is dead. *ḅḅah miyyet.*

**He brought the car to a dead stop. *ḥbes ṭ-ṭumubil tamamen.* --I'm in dead earnest about it. *hadi* *niyti be-l-mufid.* --It happened in the dead of night. *žṛat f-neṣṣ l-lil.* --That's been dead and buried a long time. *had š-ši tteqṭeƐ-lu ṛ-ṛaṣ šḥal hadi.* --The fire is dead. *l-Ɛafya ṭfat.*

dead broke - *mezluṭ.* I'm dead broke. *ṛ-ana mezluṭ.*

dead certain - *mḥeqqeq tamamen.* I'm dead certain I put it there. *ana mḥeqqeq tamamen billa ḥeṭṭitha temma.*

dead-end street - *derb ma-ka-ixeṛṛež-š* pl. *druba ma-ka-ixerrzu.* This is a dead-end street. *had d-derb ma-ka-ixerrež-š.*

deadly - *lli ka-iqtel.* This poison is deadly. *had s-semm ka-iqtel.*

deaf - *ṭṛeš* pl. *ṭuṛeš, ṭeṛšin; ṣmek* pl. *ṣumek.* He's completely deaf. *huwa ṭṛeš tamamen.*

**He's deaf to all requests. *ma-ka-iqbel ḥetta ṭalab.* --He can talk you deaf, dumb, and blind! *ṛah iṣeḍḍƐek.*

to deafen - *ṣemmek, ṭeṛṛeš.* The noise is deafening. *ṣ-ṣḍaƐ ka-iṭeṛṛeš.*

deal - **1.** *biƐa-u-šerya* pl. *biƐat-u-šeryat.* He made a lot of money on that deal. *walayenni šḥal de-l-flus Ɛmel f-dak l-biƐa-u-š-šerya.* **2.** *ḍemṣa.* Whose deal is it? *fe-mmen ḍ-ḍemṣa?*

**He got a raw deal. *tƐeddaw Ɛlih.* --All I want is a square deal. *ma-ka-nṭleb ġir ḥeqqi.*

a good deal - *bezzaf.* He smokes a good deal. *ka-ikmi bezzaf.*

a great deal - *qḍeṛ kbir, ši-kbir.* There's a great deal to be done yet. *ma-zal qḍeṛ kbir xeṣṣu itteƐmel.*

to deal - *feṛṛeq.* Who dealt (the cards)? *škun lli feṛṛeq l-kaṛṭa?*

to deal with - **1.** *tƐelleq b-.* The book deals with labor problems. *le-ktab ka-itƐelleq b-mašakil l-Ɛommal.* **2.** *tƐamel mƐa.* He deals directly with the company. *ka-itƐamel b-ṛaṣu mƐa š-šarika.*

to deal fairly with - *tṣewweb mƐa.* He dealt fairly with me. *tṣewweb mƐaya.*

dealer - **1.** *biyyaƐ-ušerray* pl. *biyyaƐa-u-šerraya, tažer* pl. *tožžaṛ, džaṛ* (merchant). **2.** *feṛṛaq l-kaṛṭa* pl. *feṛṛaqa l-kaṛṭa* (cards).

dear - *Ɛziz* pl. *Ɛzizin, Ɛzaz.* His sister is very dear to him. *xtu Ɛziza Ɛlih bezzaf.*

oh dear - *ya ḷaṭif.* Oh dear, we'll be late again! *ya ḷaṭif ġad nweṣlu mƐeṭṭḷin tani.*

death - *mut.* His death was announced in the newspapers. *l-žaridat xebbṛet be-l-mut dyalu.* --That carries the death penalty. *dak š-ši ka-itebƐu le-ḥkam be-l-mut.*

**You'll catch your death of cold. *mta ġad-tmut be-ṛ-ṛwaḥ.* --He'll be the death of me yet. *hada ġad-ihlekni.* --Don't work yourself to death. *ma-tehlek-š ṛaṣek be-l-xedma.*

debate - *mlažža* pl. *-t, munaqaša* pl. *-t, mužadala* pl. *-t, muḥažaža* pl. *-t, niqaš, židal.* The debate in the city council went on for hours. *l-munaqaša ṭalet swayeƐ fe-l-mežlis l-baladi.*

to debate - *lažež, naqeš, žadel.* The question was debated for a long time. *l-qaḍiya tnaqšet modda ṭwila. ṭwila.*

to debate with oneself - *tšaweṛ mƐa ṛaṣu.* I debated with myself whether or not to go. *tšaweṛt mƐa ṛaṣi waš nemši wella la.*

debt - *din* pl. *dyun.* This payment settles your debt. *had le-xḷaṣ ṣeffa d-din lli Ɛlik.*

in debt - *be-d-din, be-d-dyunat.* Is he still in debt? *waš huwa ma-zal be-d-din?* --He's up to his ears in debt. *huwa ġaṛeq fe-d-dyunat.* --They were always in debt. *dima kan Ɛlihom d-din.*

debtor - *medyun* pl. *-in, medyan* pl. *-in.* pl. *medyanin.*

decay - **1.** (physical) *susa.* Decay set in rapidly. *s-susa dexlet değya.* **2.** (social) *fsad, nḥilal.*

decayed - *msewwes, fased, menḥell.* The root is decayed. *ž-žder msewwes.*

deceit - *ġešš, xdiƐa* pl. *xdayeƐ, xdaƐ, šemta.*

deceitful - *ġeššaš.* He's very deceitful. *huwa ġeššaš kbir.*

to **deceive** - *xiyyeb ḍ-ḍenn, ġdeṛ, ġeṛṛ b-.* Appearances are deceiving. *ḍ-ḍwaheṛ ka-ixiyybu ḍ-ḍenn.* --His wife is deceiving him. *mṛatu ka-tġedṛu.* --He deceived us. *ġeṛṛ bina.*

December - *dužanbir.*

decency - *ṣwab.* It's common decency to answer letters promptly. *men ṣ-ṣwab l-waḥed ižaweb değya Ɛel le-bṛawat.*

decent - **1.** *fih le-ḥya, ḥeššumi, ka-iḥšem.* He's a decent fellow. *huwa waḥed ṛ-ṛažel ka-iḥšem.* **2.** *mwalem, mnaseb.* He makes a decent living. *ka-iṣewweṛ Ɛiša mwalma.*

to decide - **1.** *Ɛzem.* I decided to stay. *ana Ɛzemt baš nebqa.* **2.** *fṣeḷ.*

He's the one to decide the case between them. *huwa lli ifṣel l-qaḍiya binathom.* **3.** *feḍḍa b-.* What did you decide on? *b-aš feḍḍiti?* **4.** *qṭeƐ ṛ-ṛaṣ l-.* It isn't easy to decide that question. *dak l-qaḍiya ma-ši sahla itteqṭeƐ-lha ṛaṣha.*

decided - *bayen, waḍeḥ.* There's a decided difference between him and his brother. *kayen feṛq waḍeḥ binu u-bin xah.*

decidedly - *be-l-mufid.* He is decidedly worried about the exam. *huwa mšewweš Ɛel l-imtiḥan be-l-mufid.*

declaration - **1.** *teṣṛiḥ* pl. *-at.* *ʔiƐlam* pl. *-at,* *ʔiƐlan* pl. *-at.* Declaration of war. *ʔiƐlam be-l-ḥeṛb.* **2.** *bayan* pl. *-at.* He presented his declaration to the custom's inspector. *qeddem bayanu l-muṛaqib d-diwana.*

to **declare** - **1.** *šheṛ.* They declared war on us. *šehṛu l-ḥeṛb Ɛlina.* **2.** *biyyen.* Do I have to declare the tobacco at the customs? *waš lazem nbiyyen d-doxxan fe-d-diwana?*

decline - *neqṣan, seqṭ* pl. *squṭ.* There was a decline in exports. *kan neqṣan fe-l-wesq.*

to decline - **1.** *ṭaḥ itiḥ, nzel, qlal.* His strength is declining rapidly. *ṣeḥḥtu ka-teqlal deġya.* **2.** *ṛfeḍ.* They had to decline his invitation. *tṣabu melzumin baš iṛefḍu l-Ɛeṛḍa dyalu.*

to **decorate** - **1.** *ziyyen.* They decorated the streets for the king's visit. *ziyynu z-znaqi le-d-dexla de-l-malik.* **2.** *Ɛelleq wisam l-.* He was decorated for heroism. *Ɛellqu-lu wisam Ɛla šažaƐtu.*

decoration - **1.** *tezyina* pl. *-t; zina.* The decorations are in very bad taste. *ma-kayen ḥetta duq fe-z-zina.* **2.** *wisam* pl. *-at.* What did he get the decoration for? *še-Ɛmel baš xda l-wisam?*

decrease - *neqṣan.* Statistics show a decrease in the death rate in the last few years. *l-ʔiḥṣaʔat ka-tbiyyen neqṣan fe-n-nesba de-l-mut had s-snin t-talya.*

decree - *ḍahiṛ* pl. *ḍwaheṛ.* The decree goes into effect tomorrow. *ḍ-ḍahiṛ ġad-iṭṭebbeq ġedda.*

to decree - *ʔameṛ, ʔaden.* The government decreed a holiday. *l-ḥukuma ʔadnet be-nhaṛ de-l-Ɛoṭla.*

to **deduct** - *nqeṣ, zuwwel.* Deduct ten per cent. *zuwwel Ɛešṛa fe-l-mya.*

deed - **1.** *ṛṣem* pl. *ṛṣuma.* The deed to the house is at the lawyer's. *ṛ-ṛṣem de-ḍ-ḍaṛ Ɛend le-wkil.* **2.** *feƐla* pl. *fƐayel, fƐal; Ɛemla* pl. *Ɛmayel, Ɛmal.* There are good deeds and bad deeds. *kayna le-Ɛmal lli mezyana u-le-Ɛmal lli qbiḥa.*

to **deed** - *kteb f-esm-.* My father has deeded the house to me. *ḅḅa kteb-li ḍ-ḍaṛ f-esmi.*

deep - **1.** *ġaṛeq, Ɛmiq.* Is this lake very deep? *waš had ḍ-ḍaya ġaṛqa bezzaf?* **2.** *ġmiq, Ɛmiq.* That subject is too deep for me. *dak l-muḍuƐ ġmiq Ɛliya bla qyas.*

**How deep is the swimming pool? It's seven meters deep. *šḥal de-l-ġoṛq f-had s-sehriž? fih sebƐa miter de-l-ġoṛq.*

deeply - *bezzaf, bla qyas.* He was deeply affected by their story. *huwa tʔetteṛ bezzaf b-qeṣṣetham.*

defeat - **1.** *qehṛa* pl. *-t, nhizam* pl. *-at.* The enemy suffered a crushing defeat. *le-Ɛdu ṣabtu qehṛa qaṭƐa.* **2.** *ġelba* pl. *-at.* Our forces inflicted an unprecedented defeat on the enemy. *l-quwwat dyalna ġelbu le-Ɛdu waḥed l-ġelba Ɛemmeṛha ma-kanet.*

to defeat - *ġleb.* He's been defeated twice in the elections. *tteġleb meṛṛtayn f-l-intixabat.*

defect - *Ɛib* pl. *Ɛyub.* There must be a defect in the motor. *imken kayen ši-Ɛib fe-l-muṭuṛ.*

defective - *Ɛayeb.*

to **defend** - *dafeƐ Ɛla.* They decided not to defend the town. *qeṛṛṛu ma-idfaƐu-š Ɛel le-mdina.*

**You needn't defend yourself. *ma-kayen l-aš teƐtaḍeṛ.*

defense - **1.** *mdafƐa, difaƐ.* The defense was weak. *le-mdafƐa kanet ḍƐifa.* --What can you say in your defense? *aš imken-lek tqul fe-d-difaƐ Ɛla ṛaṣek?* **2.** *mḥamya* pl. *-t.* I didn't want him to come to my defense. *ma-bġit-š le-mḥamya dyalu.*

Ministry of Defense - *wiẓaṛat d-difaƐ.* He works for the Ministry of Defense. *huwa ka-ixdem f-wiẓaṛat d-difaƐ.*

to **define** - **1.** *ḥedded.* Can you define the word 'democracy'? *waš teqḍer tḥedded kelmet d-dimuqṛaṭiya?* **2.** *Ɛeyyen.* The boundaries were newly defined by the treaty. *l-ḥudud tƐeyynu Ɛewwed fe-l-muƐahada.*

definite - *mxeṭṭeṭ, mqeṛṛeṛ, mƐeyyen.* Do you have any definite plan? *waš Ɛendek ši-beṛnamež mxeṭṭeṭ?*

definitely - *bla ḥetta šekk.* I'm def-

initely coming. *ana žay bla ḥetta šekk.*
to **defy** - *tḥedda.* The deputy defied the Opposition to find a solution to the problem. *n-nayeb tḥedda l-muɛaṛaḍa baš ilqaw ḥell muškila.*
degree - **1.** *ḍaṛaža* pl. *-t.* Last night the temperature dropped ten degrees. *l-bareḥ fe-l-lil l-ḥaṛaṛa ṭaḥet b-ɛešṛa de-ḍ-ḍaṛažat.* **2.** *šahada* pl. *-t.* He received his degree last year. *šɛbbeṛ šahadtu l-ɛam lli fat.*
to a certain degree - *l-waḥed l-ḥedd, l-waḥed ḍ-ḍaṛaža.* To a certain degree he's responsible. *l-waḥed l-ḥedd, huwa mesʔul.*
delay - *teʔxiṛ, ažal.* What's causing the delay? *aš lli ɛamel had t-teʔxiṛ?*
to delay - *wexxeṛ.* We're going to delay the trip for a week. *ġad nwexxṛu ṣ-ṣafaṛ b-žemɛa.*
to be delayed - *tʔexxeṛ.* I was delayed on the way. *ana tʔexxeṛt fe-ṭ-ṭṛiq.*
delegate - **1.** *ɛuḍw wefd* pl. *ʔaɛḍaʔ wefd.* The delegates will arrive tomorrow. *ʔaɛḍaʔ l-wefd ġad iweṣlu ġedda.* **2.** *mumettil* pl. *-in.* Her uncle has been delegate to the U.N. for two years. *hadi ɛamayn u-ɛemmha mumettil f-hayʔat l-ʔumam.* **3.** *nayeb* pl. *nuwwab.* They've elected him to the House of Delegates. *ntaxbuh l-mežlis n-nuwwab.*
delegation - *wefd* pl. *wufud, beɛta* pl. *-t.* Will you receive this delegation? *waš imken-lek tqabel had l-wefd?*
deliberate - *mɛemmed, metɛemmed.* We caught him in a deliberate lie. *ḥeṣṣelnah f-kedba mɛemmda.*
deliberately - *be-l-ɛani.* I don't think he did it deliberately. *ma-ka-nḍenn-š darha be-l-ɛani.*
delicate - **1.** *raši.* Her health is very delicate. *ṣeḥḥtha rašya bla qyas.* **2.** *dqiq.* That's a delicate question. *qaḍiya dqiqa hadi.*
delicious - *ldid* pl. *ldad.* This is delicious candy. *had l-fanid ldid.*
delighted - *feṛḥan, mesrur.* I'm delighted to have seen him. *ana feṛḥan lli šeftu.*
delightful - *bahež, našeṭ.* We've had a delightful evening. *duwwezna teqṣiṛa bahža.*
to **deliver** - **1.** *dfeɛ.* They 'll deliver it to you there. *ġad idefɛu-lek dak š-ši temma.* **2.** *feṛṛeq.* How many times a day do they deliver the mail here? *šḥal men meṛṛa fe-n-nhaṛ ka-ifeṛṛqu l-barid hnaya?* **3.** *ṣifeṭ* or *ṣafeṭ iṣifeṭ.* We can deliver these purchases to you later. *imken-lna nṣifṭu-lek had s-selɛa men beɛd.*
to be delivered - **1.** *ttedfeɛ, tteɛṭa, tsellem.* The goods are to be delivered at the back door. *s-selɛa ka-ixeṣṣha ttedfeɛ men l-bab l-luṛani.* **2.** *wled.* His wife was delivered of a girl. *mṛatu weldet bnita.*
delivery - **1.** *dfuɛ.* The delivery of the merchandise was delayed. *tʔexxṛu be-dfuɛ s-selɛa.* **2.** *tefṛiqa* pl. *-t.* The letter came in the second delivery. *le-bṛa žat fe-t-tefṛiqa t-tanya.*
demand - *ṭaḷab* pl. *-at.* There's a big demand for fresh fruit. *l-ġella ṭ-ṭṛiyya ɛliha ṭaḷab kbir.* --The library can't supply the demand for books. *l-xizana ma-teqḍeṛ-š tneffed ṭ-ṭaḷabat lli kayna ɛel le-ktub.* --He makes no demands whatsoever. *ma-ka-yeɛmel ḥetta ši-ṭaḷab abadan.*
to make demands on - *ṭṭeḷḷeb men.* They make many demands on our time. *ka-iṭṭeḷḷbu mennna l-weqt bezzaf.*
in demand - *meṭḷub, ɛlih ṭ-ṭaḷab.* He was in great demand as a speaker. *kan meṭḷub bezzaf baš yeɛmel kalimat.*
to demand - *ṭaḷeb.* He's demanding more money. *ka-iṭaḷeb be-z-zyada fe-l-flus.*
democracy - *dimuqṛaṭiya.*
democratic - *dimuqṛaṭi.*
democratically - *be-d-dimuqṛaṭiya.*
demon - *ɛefrit* pl. *ɛfaret, ɛafarit; šiṭan* pl. *šyaṭen, šayaṭin.*
to **demonstrate** - **1.** *werra, biyyen.* I'll now demonstrate how the machine works. *daba ġad nbiyyen kif-aš l-makina ka-texdem.* **2.** *ḍḍaheṛ.* The students demonstrated against the new law. *ṭ-ṭaḷaba ḍḍahṛu ḍeḍḍ l-qanun ž-ždid.*
demonstration - **1.** *bayan.* He gave me a very clear demonstration of the problem. *ɛṭani bayan waḍeḥ l-l-muškila.* **2.** *muḍahaṛa* pl. *-t.* There was a demonstration yesterday in front of the Prime Minister's residence. *yames kanet muḍahaṛa qeddam ḍaṛ ṛaʔis l-wizaṛa.*
den - *ġaṛ* pl. *ġiṛan.* Why venture into the lion's den? *š-bini u-bin s-sbeɛ neɛmel ṛaṣi f-ġaṛu?*
dense - **1.** *mteqqel.* We drove through (a) dense fog. *segna f-waḥed ḍ-ḍbaba mteqqla.* **2.** *mkellex.* I've never seen anyone as dense as he is. *ɛemmṛi*

ma-šeft ši-waḥed mkeḷlex bḥalu.
3. *mzaḥem.* This area has a dense population. *had ž-žiha mzaḥma be-s-sokkan.*

dent - *tƐenfiža* pl. *-t.* Who put this dent in my car? *škun lli Ɛmel-li had t-tƐenfiža fe-ṭ-ṭumubil?*
to dent - *Ɛenfež, Ɛewwež.* The fender was badly dented. *d-dƐama de-ṭ-ṭumubil tƐenfžet bezzaf.*

dentist - *ṭbib de-s-snan* pl. *ṭobba de-s-snan.*

to **deny** - **1.** *nkeṛ.* He denies having been a member of that party. *ka-inkeṛ billa kan Ɛuḍw f-dak l-ḥizeb.* **2.** *redd fe-wžeh-.* I couldn't deny my uncle the favor. *ma-qḍeṛt-š nreddha fe-wžeh Ɛemmi.*
to deny oneself - *ḥṛem ṛaṣu men, qṭeƐ Ɛla ṛaṣu.* She never denies herself anything. *Ɛemmeṛha ma ka-teḥṛem ṛaṣha men ši-ḥaža.*

to **depart** - *ṣafeṛ, mša imši.* He departed for Beirut yesterday. *ṣafeṛ l-bayrut l-bareḥ.*

department - **1.** *qent* pl. *qnut; ṛeḥba* pl. *ṛḥabi; ṛekna* pl. *ṛkani; daʔira* pl. *-t.* In which department of the store does he work? *fe-š-men qent de-l-ḥanut ka-ixdem?* **2.** *xtiṣaṣ.* That sort of thing isn't in my department. *ḥaža bḥal dak š-ši ma-ši men xtiṣaṣi.*
Department - *wizaṛa* pl. *-at.* This matter is for the Department of State. *hadi qaḍiya xaṣṣa b-wizaṛt l-xarižiya.*

departure - *mši, ṣafaṛ.* The departure is scheduled for three o'clock. *le-mši ġad ʾikun fe-t-tlata.*

to **depend** - *Ɛtamed Ɛla, ttkel Ɛla, Ɛewwel Ɛla.* Can I depend on him? *waš imken-li neƐtamed Ɛlih?* --You can depend on that. *imken-lek ttkel Ɛla dak š-ši.* --I depend on him for support. *ṛ-ana mƐewwel Ɛlih iƐawenni.*
**That depends on the circumstances. *dak š-ši Ɛla ḥasab ḍ-ḍuṛuf.*

dependent on - *mettkel Ɛla, meƐtamed Ɛla.* I'm financially dependent on him. *ana mettkel Ɛlih fe-l-flus.*

to **depose** - *zuwwel, qelleƐ.* They want to depose the king. *bġaw izuwwlu l-malik.*

deposit - **1.** *flus.* I still have to make a deposit at the bank. *ma-zal ka-ixeṣṣni nnezzel le-flus fe-l-ḅenk.* **2.** *Ɛeṛbun* pl. *Ɛṛaben.* If you leave a deposit, we'll lay it aside for you. *ila xelliti l-Ɛeṛbun nxebbƐuha-lek.*
to deposit - *nezzel, ḥeṭṭ.* I'll have to deposit some money at the bank. *ġad ixeṣṣni nnezzel ši-flus fe-l-ḅenk.*

to **depress** - *keḍḍeṛ.* His letters always depress me. *bṛawatu dima ka-tkeḍḍeṛni.*

depressed - *mkeḍḍeṛ, ṭayeṛ-lu.* He's been very depressed lately. *huwa mkeḍḍeṛ bezzaf had l-iyam.*

depressing - *(lli) ka-ikeḍḍer, (lli) ka-iqbeṭ, (lli) ka-yeƐmel l-kaḍaṛ, (lli) ka-iqenneṭ.* His very presence is depressing. *ḥḍuṛu ka-iqenneṭ.*

depression - *iyam le-ksad, iyam l-ʔezma.* We lost all our money in the depression. *xṣeṛna flusna kollhom f-iyam le-ksad.*

to **deprive** - *ḥṛem, ġṣeb.* I wouldn't want to deprive you of your cigarettes. *ma-nebġi-ši nḥeṛmek men d-doxxan dyalek.* --He doesn't deprive himself of anything. *ma-ka-iḥṛem ṛaṣu ḥetta men ḥaža.*

depth - *ġoṛq, Ɛomq.*

deputy - *nayeb* pl. *nuwwab.* The deputy spoke before the council. *n-nayeb xṭeb Ɛel l-mežlis.*
Chamber of Deputies - *mežlis n-nuwwab* pl. *mažalis n-nuwwab.*

to be **derailed** - *xrež Ɛel ṭ-ṭriq, xrež Ɛel s-sekka.* The express was derailed near Tangiers. *l-qiṭaṛ s-sriƐ xrež Ɛel s-sekka ḥda ṭanža.*

Dervish - *derwiš* pl. *drawеš.*

to **descend** - **1.** *nzel, hḅeṭ.* The plane descended slowly. *ṭ-ṭiyyaṛa nezlet be-š-šwiya.* --All our relatives have descended upon us. *hbabna kollhom nezlu Ɛlina.*
2. *ṭiyyeḥ b-ṛaṣu.* I'd never have thought she'd descend so low. *Ɛemmeṛha ma-dži l-bali ṭṭiyyeḥ b-ṛaṣha l-had l-ḥedd.*
descended - *maži.* He's descended from an old Arab family. *huwa maži men waḥed l-Ɛaʔila Ɛaṛabiya qdima.*

descendant - *weld* pl. *wlad; men wlad.* He claims he's a descendant of Mulay Idris. *ka-iqul huwa men wlad mulay idris.*

to **describe** - *wṣef.* She described the scene accurately. *weṣfet l-menḍeṛ be-tedqiq.*

description - *weṣf* pl. *wṣaf.* Can you give me a detailed description? *waš teqḍeṛ teƐṭini weṣf mfeṣṣel?*

desert - *ṣeḥṛa* pl. *ṣḥaṛi.* They crossed the desert in twenty days. *qeṭƐu ṣ-ṣeḥṛa f-Ɛešrin yum.*
to desert - **1.** *hṛeb Ɛla.* Don't desert me now! *ma-teheṛeb-š Ɛliya daba.* **2.** *zeṛṭa.* The soldiers de-

serted in droves. *l-ɛesker ẓeṛṭaw žmaɛa žmaɛa.*

deserted - *xali.* After a long march they came to a deserted village. *beɛd modda ṭwila d-le-mši weṣḷu waḥed ḍ-ḍuwwaṛ xali.*

to **deserve** - *staḥeq, tteshel.* Such a good worker deserves better pay. *xeddam mezyan bḥal hada itteshel ʔužṛa ḥsen men hadi.*

design - 1. *texṭiṭ* pl. *-at.* He's working on the design for a new refrigerator. *huwa xeddam f-texṭiṭ tellaža ždida.* 2. *zwaq* pl. *zwaqat; zuwwaga* pl. *-t.* The tablecloth has a simple design. *l-mendil fih zwaq meṭluq.*

to **design** - *feṣṣel.* She designs her own clothes. *ka-tfeṣṣeḷ ḥwayežha l-ṛaṣha.*

desirable - 1. *meḥbub, meqbul.* A change would be very desirable. *ila wqeɛ ši-teġyiṛ ġad ikun meḥbub bezzaf.* 2. *f-ġaya.* This is a very desirable neighborhood for a hotel. *had l-ḥewma f-ġaya bezzaf l-ši-util.*

desire - *muṛaḍ* pl. *-at; ṛeġba* pl. *-t.* My desires are easily satisfied. *muṛaḍati ḍeġya ka-ttḥeqqeq.*

desk - *mekteb* pl. *makatib.* This desk is too small for me. *had l-mekteb ṣġiṛ ɛliya bezzaf.*

despair - *yaʔs, iyas.*

to despair of - *qṭeɛ l-iyas men.*

desperate - *yaʔes, myeʔʔes.* She was desperate. *kanet yaʔsa.*

desperate situation - *ḥala yaʔisa, ḥala baʔisa.* The failure of his business left him in a desperate situation. *xfuqu fe-l-ḥaraka dyalu xellah f-ḥala yaʔisa.*

to **despise** - *ḥgeṛ, ḥtaqeṛ.* They despise him because of his cowardice. *ka-iḥegṛuh ɛla iteṛ l-xewf dyalu.*

destination - *maḥell layn maši.* When do we reach our destination? *fuqaš ġad nweṣḷu l-l-maḥell layn mašyin?*

destiny - 1. *mektub* pl. *makatib.* It was his destiny to die in a foreign country. *kan mektubu imut fe-blad x̂ṛa.* 2. *maṣiṛ.* The Algerians want to decide their own destiny. *l-žazaʔiriyen bġaw iqeṛṛṛu maṣiṛhom b-iddhom.*

destroy - *heddem, heṭṭem.* The earthquake destroyed a third of the town. *z-zelzal heddem t-tulut f-le-mdina.*

to be destroyed - *theddem, tḥeṭṭem.* All my papers were destroyed in the fire. *wṛaqi kollhom tḥeṭṭmu fe-l-ɛafya.*

destroyer - 1. *heddam* pl. *-a.* 2. (ship) *mudemmira* pl. *-t.*

destruction - *tehdim, teḥṭim.* The fire caused a lot of destruction. *l-ɛafya ɛemlet bezzaf de-t-tehdim.*

to **detach** - *fṛeq.*

detail - *tefṣiḷ* pl. *tafaṣiḷ.* Today's paper gives further details. *žaridt l-yum ka-teɛṭi tafaṣiḷ x̂ṛa.*

in detail - *be-t-tefṣiḷ, koll-.* He described the incident in detail. *huwa wṣef l-waqiɛa be-t-tefṣiḷ.* --But I explained it to you in detail. *walakin fessertha-lek kollha.*

to go into detail(s) - *dxel fe-t-tafaṣiḷ.* I don't want to go into details. *ma-baġi-š ndxol fe-t-tafaṣiḷ.*

detailed - *mfeṣṣeḷ.* He gave a detailed report. *ɛṭa teqṛiṛ mfeṣṣeḷ.*

detective - *mufettiš š-šoṛṭa* pl. *mufettišin š-šoṛṭa.*

determination - *ɛezm, ɛazima* pl. *-t, ɛazayem.* He showed great determination. *ḍehheṛ ɛezm kbir.*

determined - *ɛazem.* She's determined to have her way. *hiya ɛazma ttbeɛ naḍaṛha.*

detour - *ḍuṛa* pl. *-t.* We made a long detour to see the lake. *ɛmelna ḍuṛa kbira baš nšufu ḍ-ḍaya.* 2. *teḥrif, teɛwiža.* There's a detour here because the road is under repair. *kayen teḥrif hnaya ḥit ṭ-ṭṛiq ka-tteṣḷeḥ.*

to detour - *ḥerref.* Traffic was detoured because of the automobile accident. *s-siyaṛat ḥerrfu ɛla-wedd l-ḥadita lli kanet.*

develop - 1. *xerrež.* Would you develop this film for me? *waš txerrež-li had l-qennuṭ?* 2. *ṭḷeɛ, kber, nḍež.* The boy's developing nicely. *l-weld ṭaḷeɛ f-ġaya, tbaṛek ḷḷah.* 3. *ṭṭuwweṛ.* His cough developed into a serious illness. *sɛeltu ṭṭuwwṛet l-waḥed l-merḍ ṣɛib.* 4. *ṛžeɛ, ṣaṛ iṣiṛ.* The plant developed into a big tree. *n-neqla ṛežɛet šežṛa kbira.*

development - *taṭewwuṛ* pl. *-at.* Do you know anything about the latest developments? *waš ɛaṛef ši-ḥaža ɛel t-taṭewwuṛat t-talya?*

device - *ʔala* pl. *-t.* That's an ingenious device. *dak l-ʔala bariɛa.*

devil - *šiṭan* pl. *šayaṭin, šyaṭen.*

to **devote** - *xeṣṣeṣ, sebbel, ɛṭa yeɛṭi.* He devoted all his time to his studies. *weqtu kollu xeṣṣṣu l-diṛastu.*

dew - *nda.*

diabetes - *merḍ s-sokkar.*
dial - **1.** *nmari* (pl.). Telephones with dials are a rather recent invention. *t-tilifunat lli be-n-nmari xtiraɛ qrib.* **2.** *rxama* pl. *-t.* The dial on my watch is dirty. *rxamt maganti mwossxa.*
to dial - *ḍuwwer.* She dialed the wrong number. *n-nemra lli ḍuwwret ġalṭa.*
dialect - *lehža* pl. *-t.* Many dialects are spoken here. *n-nas ka-itkellmu bezzaf de-l-lehžat hnaya.*
diamond - *žohra* pl. *-t* coll. *žuher, ḥežra* pl. *-t* coll *ḥžer.* He put his diamonds in the safe. *xzen ž-žuher dyalu fe-ṣ-ṣenduq.*
diarrhea - *džerya, kerš meṭluqa.* He had diarrhea. *l-kers kanet meṭluqa ɛlih.*
dice - *ḍwaḍeṣ* (pl.). sg. *ḍaḍus.* Let's play with my dice. *nleɛbu be-ḍwaḍeṣ dyali.*
**The die is cast. *lli ɛṭa ḷḷah ɛṭah.*
to **dictate** - *fta ifti.* He's dictating a letter. *ka-ifti waḥed le-bra.*
**I won't be dictated to. *ḥetta waḥed ma-ġad iqul-li š-ġad neɛmel.*
to take **dictation** - *kteb lli ttefta-lu.* Will you please take some dictation? *ɛafak kteb had š-ši lli ġad nefti-lek.*
die - see **dice.**
to **die** - **1.** *mat imut, tweffa.* He died this morning at two o'clock. *mat l-bareḥ fe-ž-žuž de-l-lil.* --The tree is dying. *š-šežra ka-tmut.* --I just about died laughing when I heard that. *kont ġad nmut be-ḍ-ḍeḥk melli smeɛt dak š-ši.* **2.** *wqef.* The motor died. *l-muṭur wqef.* **3.** *ḥmaq.* I'm dying to find out what he said. *ka-neḥmaq neɛref š-qaḷ.* **4.** *ġber, tqaḍa.* Old customs die hard. *l-ɛadat le-qdam ṣɛab baš iġebru.*
to die away - *ġab iġib.* The noise of the train died away in the distance. *haraž l-mašina ġab mɛa l-boɛd.*
to die down - **1.** *ṭfa iṭfa.* We let the fire die down. *xellina l-ɛafya ṭṭfa.* **2.** *bred, hmed.* The excitement will die down in a few days. *t-tehžiž ġad-ibred men daba ši-iyamat.*
to die off - *tqaḍa, tsala, mša imši.* The old inhabitants are dying off. *s-sokkan le-qdam ka-itqaḍaw.*
to die out - *mša imši, tqaḍa, tsala.* This old custom is gradually dying out. *had l-ɛada le-qdima ka-temši šwiya be-šwiya.*
diet - **1.** *makla* pl. *-t, mwakel.* The Moroccan diet is highly varied. *l-makla l-meġribiya matnuwwɛa bezzaf.* **2.** *qanun fe-l-makla.* An ailing person should follow a diet. *le-mriḍ ka-ixeṣṣu itebbeɛ l-qanun fe-l-makla.*
**I have to keep to a strict diet. *ka-ixeṣṣni neḥdi raṣi fe-l-makla.*
to diet - *kla yakol be-l-qanun.* I've been dieting for a month, but still I haven't lost any weight. *hadi šher w-ana ka-nakol be-l-qanun u-ma-zal ma-ṭiyyeḥt walu.*
to **differ** - **1.** *xtalef.* They differ in every respect. *ka-ixtalfu men koll žiha.* --Opinions differ here. *le-ryay ka-ixtalfu hnaya.* **2.** *xalef, xtalef mɛa.* I beg to differ with you this time. *smeḥ-li nxalfek had l-merra.*
difference - *ferq* pl. *fruqa.* Can you explain the difference to me? *waš teqḍer tfesser-li l-ferq?*
**Does it make any difference if I write in pencil? *waš kayen ši-bas ila ktebt b-le-qlam d-le-xfif?* --It makes no difference when you come. *weqt-aš-emma žiti huwa hadak.*
different - **1.** *mextalef.* The two brothers are very different. *l-xut b-žuž mextalfin bezzaf.* **2.** *axur* f. *x̂ra* pl. *x̂rin* f. pl. *x̂rat.* That's quite different. *hadak ši-axur.* --That's a different matter. *hadik ḥaža x̂ra.*
differently - *b-kifiya x̂ra, fe-škel axur.* I think differently about it. *ka-nfekker fiha b-kifiya x̂ra.*
difficult - *ṣɛib* pl. *ṣɛab, ṣɛibin.* It's difficult to understand what he means. *ṣɛib baš ittefhem š-ka-yeɛni.*
difficulty - *ṣuɛuba* pl. *-t, ṣiɛab.* He overcame all difficulties. *ṣ-ṣuɛubat kollha tġelleb ɛliha.*
to **dig** - *ḥfer.* Dig a hole here, please. *ḥfer ši-teqba hnaya ɛafak.*
to dig up - *žbed.* I don't know why he dug up that old story. *ma-ɛreft-ši ɛlaš žbed dak le-xrafa.*
**If you're hungry just dig in. *ila kan bik ž-žuɛ, kul ɛla raṣek.*
to **digest** - *hḍem.*
digestion - *hḍim.*
dignified - *(lli) ɛlih l-hemma.* His father was a dignified old gentleman. *ḅḅah kan ražel kbir u-ɛlih l-hemma.*
dim - *mdeɛmeš.* I couldn't see anything in that dim light. *ma-qdert nšuf ḥetta ḥaža f-hadak ḍ-ḍuw le-*

mdeƐmeš.

dimple – *ḥferṭ z-zin, ḥofṛa de-z-zin.*

to **dine** – **1.** (evening meal) *tƐešša.* **2.** (midday meal) *tġedda.* We always dine out on Sundays. *dima ka-ntġeddaw beṛṛa nhaṛ l-ḥedd.*

dining room – **1.** *bit l-makla* pl. *byut l-makla.* Bring another chair into the dining room. *žib šelya xṛa l-bit l-makla.* **2.** *ṣaḷa de-l-makla* pl. *-t de-l-makla, meṭƐem* pl. *maṭaƐim.* The hotel has two dining rooms. *l-util Ɛendu žuz de-ṣ-ṣaḷat de-l-makla.*

dinner – **1.** (evening meal) *Ɛša* pl. *-wat.* Dinner will be ready at six. *le-Ɛša tkun wažda fe-s-setta.* **2.** (midday meal) *ġda* pl. *-wat.* On Sundays we serve dinner at two o'clock. *nhaṛ l-ḥedd ka-nnezzlu le-ġda fe-ž-žuž.* **3.** *zerda* pl. *-t, zradi.* We're giving a dinner in his honor. *ġad ndiru-lu waḥed z-zerda.*

to have dinner – see **dine.**

dip – *Ɛewma* pl. *-t.* Shall we take a dip? *nƐemlu ši-Ɛewma?*

to dip – **1.** *hebbeṭ.* They dipped the flag in salute. *hebbṭu ṛ-ṛaya le-s-slam.* **2.** *ġṭeṣ.* I dipped my finger into the water. *ġṭeṣt ṣebƐi fe-l-ma.*

**I have to dip into my savings now. *xeṣṣni nežbed men le-ḥṣiyyṣa daba.*

direct – **1.** *qaṣeḍ.* There is no direct route. *ma-kayen-š ṭṛiq qaṣḍa.* **2.** *doġri.* I like his direct manners. *ka-yeƐžebni kif ka-itƐamel doġri.* **3.** *tamamen.* It's the direct opposite of what we expected. *had š-ši tamamen Ɛakes lli konna metweqqƐineh.*

to direct – **1.** *ʔameṛ.* We were directed to follow the old regulations. *ʔamṛuna baš ntebbƐu l-qawanin le-qdima.* **2.** *qabel.* A policeman is directing the traffic. *waḥed l-bulisi mqabel le-mši u-le-mži.* **3.** *werra.* Can you direct me to the post office? *waš imken-lek twerrini l-buṣṭa.* **4.** *siyyer.* Who directed the orchestra yesterday? *škun lli siyyer l-žuq l-bareḥ?* **5.** *wežžeh.* The speech was directed to the young people. *l-kalima kanet mwežžha le-š-šobban.* **6.** *meššа.* Who's directing the play? *škun lli ka-imešši r-riwaya?*

direction – *žiha* pl. *-t, žwayeh.* In which direction did he go? *le-š-men žiha mša?*

directly – **1.** *qaṣeḍ, doġri.* Let's go directly to the hotel. *yaḷḷah nemšiw qaṣḍin l-l-uṭiḷ.* **2.** *be-d-dat.* Our house is directly opposite the store. *ḍaṛna mqabla l-ḥanut be-d-dat.*

dirt – *tṛab* pl. *tṛabat, tṛubat.* My gloves fell in the dirt. *ṣebbaƐati ṭaḥu fe-t-tṛab.*

dirty – **1.** *mwossex.* The floor is dirty. *ḷ-ḷerḍ mwossxa.* **2.** *Ɛwež* pl. *Ɛiwež, mḥerref.* He gave us a dirty look. *šaf fina šufa Ɛewža.* **3.** *mbeṛṛeq.* That's a dirty lie. *hadik kedba mbeṛṛqa.* **4.** *mseffeh.* Most of his stories are pretty dirty. *xṛayfu ktir š-ši mseffha.*

**He played a dirty trick on us. *darha bina.* --That's a dirty shame! *ḥšuma kbira hadi!*

to dirty – *wessex.* Don't dirty your shoes. *ma-twessex-š ṣebbaṭek.*

disability – *Ɛaṭab* pl. *Ɛṭab, Ɛṭub.* He cannot play soccer because of a disability. *ma-ka-iqḍeṛ-š ilƐeb l-kuṛa Ɛla ḥeqq Ɛendu Ɛaṭab.*

to be **disabled** – *tƐeṭṭeb.* The soldier was disabled for life. *l-Ɛeskri tƐeṭṭeb Ɛla ṭul Ɛemṛu.*

disadvantage – *maḍeṛṛa* pl. *-t.* I'm at a disadvantage. *Ɛendi maḍeṛṛa.*

to **disagree** – **1.** *ma-ttafeq-š.* I disagree with you. *ana ma-mettafeq-š mƐak.* --I disagree with this method. *ana ma-mettafeq-š mƐa had ṭ-ṭaṛiqa.* **2.** *ma-wafeq-š.* Cucumbers disagree with me. *le-xyaṛ ma-ka-iwafeqni-š.*

to **disappear** – *ġber.* He disappeared in the crowd. *ġber fe-z-zḥam.*

to **disappoint** – *xiyyeb.*

to be disappointed – *xab ixib ḍennu.* I was very much disappointed. *xab ḍenni bezzaf.*

disappointment – *xiba, xayba* pl *-t.* It was a great disappointment *xayba kbira kanet.*

to **disapprove of** – *ma-wafeq-š Ɛla.* He disapproves of our plans. *ma-ka-iwafeq-š Ɛla mešṛuƐna.*

to **disarm** – **1.** *xda yaxod s-slaḥ men, žeṛṛed men s-slaḥ.* The prisoners were quickly disarmed. *deġya xdaw s-slaḥ men le-msažen.* **2.** *nzeƐ s-slaḥ* Do you think the great powers will ever disarm? *waš ka-ḍḍenn d-duwal le-kbira Ɛemmeṛha ġad tenzeƐ s-slah?*

disarmament – *nazƐ s-slaḥ.*

disaster – *muṣiba* pl. *-t, mṣayeb.* The airplane crash was a great disaster. *ḥaditat ṭ-ṭiyyaṛa kanet muṣiba kbira.*

disastrous – *muḍiṛṛ, muṣib.*

discharge - *tehrir (men l-žiš).* I got my discharge (from the army) in November. *šebbeṛt tehriri men l-žiš f-nuwanbir.*

to discharge - **1.** *dḥa idḥi.* Why was he discharged from that job? *Élaš dḥaweh men dik l-xedma?* **2.** *qam iqum b-.* He discharged his duties promptly. *qam b-wažibatu b-soṛÉa.*

discipline - *teṛbiya* pl. *-t; niḍam.* He insists on strict discipline. *ka-ileḥḥ Éla teṛbiya žiyyda.*

to **disclose** - *ḍehheṛ, biyyen.* The investigation disclosed new facts. *l-beḥt biyyen ḥqayeq xṛa.*

discount - *texfiḍ, ṭyuḥ, neqṣan.* Can you get a discount on these books? *waš imken-lek tḥeṣṣel Éla ši-texfiḍ f-had le-ktub?*

to **discourage** - *berred, ma-šežžeÉ-š.* It discouraged me completely. *had š-ši berredni tamamen.*

to discourage from - *redd.* He did everything he could to discourage me. *Émel koll-ma f-žehdu baš ireddni.*

to get discouraged - *mell, bred, Éya, fšel, qneṭ.* He gets discouraged easily. *deġya ka-imell.*

discouraging - *(lli) ma-ka-išežžeÉ-š, (lli) ma-ka-ibÉet-š Éel n-našaṭ.* The results are very discouraging. *n-nat?iž ma-ka-tšežžeÉ-š bezzaf.*

to **discover** - *ktašef, žbeṛ.* Columbus discovered America in 1492. *kuḷun ktašef ?amirika f-Éam ?alef u-ṛbeÉ mya u-tnayn u-tesÉin.*

discovery - *ktišaf* pl. *-at.* He made an important discovery. *Émel waḥed le-ktišaf muhimm.*

to **discuss** - *ddakeṛ, naqeš, žbed.* Discuss the matter with him. *ddakeṛ mÉah fe-l-qaḍiya.* --The question was discussed at length. *ṛa l-qaḍiya ddakṛu fiha b-teṭwil.*

discussion - *muḍakaṛa* pl. *-t, muḥadata* pl. *-t, munaqaša* pl. *-t.*

disease - *meṛḍ* pl. *?amṛaḍ.* This disease is contagious. *had l-meṛḍ ka-iÉadi.*

disfigure - *xeṣṣeṛ.* The scar disfigures his face. *?atar ž-žeṛḥ xeṣṣer-lu wežhu.*

disgrace - **1.** *Éaṛ* pl *-at, Éiṛan; ḥšuma* pl. *-t, ḥšayem.* Her behavior brought disgrace on her family. *sirtha žabet le-ḥšuma l-Éa?iltha.* **2.** *(lli) ka-ižib le-ḥšuma.* These pupils are a disgrace to the school. *had t-tlamed ka-ižibu le-ḥšayem l-l-meḍṛaṣa.*

to disgrace - *ḥeššem b-.*

disguise - *txefya* pl. *-t, texbiÉa* pl. *-t.* I didn't recognize him in his disguise. *ma-ÉṛeftU-š fe-t-txefya dyalu.*

to disguise - **1.** *beddel.* He disguised his handwriting. *beddel ktabtu.* **2.** *xebbeÉ.* They succeeded in disguising their feelings well. *Éeṛfu ixebbÉu Éawaṭifhom.*

to disguise oneself - *xfa ixfi ṛaṣu.* He disguised himself to avoid capture. *xfa ṛasu baš ma-itteqbeṭ-š.*

to disguise oneself as - *Émel ṛaṣu bḥal.* She had disguised herself as a man. *kanet Éamla ṛaṣha bḥal ṛ-ṛažel.*

disgust - *mellan.* He turned away in disgust. *ḍuwweṛ wežhu be-l-mellan.*

to disgust - *Éeyyef, ṭleÉ fe-ṛ-ṛaṣ l-.* His conduct disgusts me. *sirtu ka-ṭṭleÉ-li f-ṛaṣi.*

to be disgusted - *mell men.* I'm disgusted with everything. *ana mellit men koll-ši.*

disgusting - *(lli) ka-iÉeyyef ž-žeṛṛa.* This is disgusting! *had š-ši ka-iÉeyyef ž-žeṛṛa.*

dish - **1.** *ṭebṣiḷ* pl. *ṭbaṣeḷ.* How many dishes did your little sister break today? *xtek ṣ-ṣġiṛa, šḥal men ṭebṣil herrset l-yum?* **2.** *makla* pl. *-t, mwakel.* I have a recipe for a new dish. *Éendi l-iqama l-waḥed l-makla ždida.*

to **disinherit** - *berra f-, ḥṛem men l-weṛt.* His father threatened to disinherit him. *ḅḅah hedded billa ġad iberri fih.*

dislike - *keṛh, nfuṛ.* I couldn't conceal my dislike for him. *ma-qḍeṛt-š nexfi keṛhi lih.*

to dislike - *kṛeh, ma-bġa-s, ma-ḥmel-š.* I dislike that fellow. *ma-ka-neḥmel-š dak xiyyi.*

to **dislocate** - *fekk.* He dislocated his shoulder. *fekk ketfu.*

disloyal - *xeddaÉ* pl. *-a.*

dismal - *ḥazen, mkeddeṛ.* It's a dismal day today. *nhaṛ mkeddeṛ hada.*

to **dismiss** - **1.** *dḥa idḥi, ṣifeṭ* or *ṣafeṭ iṣifeṭ f-ḥalu, ṭṛed.* She was dismissed after two weeks. *ṣafṭuha f-ḥalha žmeÉtayn men beÉd.* The court dismissed the complaint. *l-meḥkama ṛefḍet š-šekwa.*

**He dismissed the matter with a shrug of the shoulder. *xṣeṛ Éel l-qaḍiya hezza d-ketfu.*

display - *testifa de-s-selÉa,* pl. *testifat s-slaÉi.* Did you see the beautiful displays on Mohammed V Avenue? *šefti testifat s-slaÉi*

l-mezyana f-šariε muḥemmed l-xamis?
on display – *meεṛuḍ, mεelleq.* The paintings are on display at the museum. *l-luḥat ṛahom meεṛuḍin fe-l-metḥef.*
to display – *ḍehheṛ, biyyen.* He displays great courage. *ka-iḍehheṛ ṛžuliya kbira.*

to **dispose of** – *tfekk men, thenna men, rtaḥ men.* They will leave as soon as they dispose of their furniture. *ġir itfekku men ḥwayežhom ġad imšiw f-ḥalhom.* --Because of the gasoline shortage, we had to dispose of our car. *εla qibal qellt l-iṣanṣ ṭṭeṛṛına nthennaw men s-siyaṛa.* --Where can I dispose of this? *fayn imken-li ntfekk men had š-ši?*

disposed – *mayel.* He is kindly disposed towards you. *huwa mayel-lek ši-šwiya.*

disposition – *ṭbiεa.* He has a mean disposition. *εendu ṭbiεa qbiḥa.*

to **disregard** – **1.** *ma-ddaha-š ma-iddiha-š f-.* If I were you, I'd simply disregard the letter. *la kont ana bḥalek gaε ma-nddiha f-le-bṛa.* **2.** *tεamaεla, hmel.* We can't disregard his objections. *ma-nqeḍṛu-š ntεamaw εel l-muεaṛaḍat dyalu.*

to **dissipate** – **1.** *dfeε, ṣṛef, bedder, xṣeṛ.* He dissipated his entire fortune. *maliytu kollha bedderha.* **2.** *ṭaš iṭiš.* If he continues to dissipate at this rate, he won't last long. *ila bqa ṭayeš εla had l-ḥala, ma-izid-ši men hna l-temma.*

dissipated – *ṭayeš.* He leads a dissipated life. *ka-iεiš εiša ṭayša.*
**He has a terribly dissipated look. *šuftu tamamen ma-ši hiya hadik.*

to **dissolve** – **1.** *duwweb.* Dissolve the tablet in a glass of water. *duwweb l-ḥebba f-kas de-l-ma.* **2.** *dab idub.* It dissolves in water. *ka-ddub fe-l-ma.* **3.** *zell.* The king dissolved the consultative assembly. *l-malik zell l-mežlis l-istišari.*

distance – *masafa* pl. *-t.* The distance between Rabat and Casablance is ninety-nine kilometers. *l-masafa ma bin ṛ-ṛbaṭ u-ḍ-ḍaṛ l-biḍa tesεud u-tesεin kilumiter.* --We can cover the distance in three hours. *nqeḍṛu nqeṭεu l-masafa fe-tlata de-s-swayeε.*
from a distance – *men bεid.* You can see the tower from a distance. *imken-lek tšuf l-boṛž men bεid.*
in the distance – *bεid, ṛa fayn.* You can see the village in the distance. *imken-lek tšuf ḍ-ḍuwaṛ bεid.*
to keep one's distance – *weqqeṛ ṛaṣu, šebbeṛ weqṛu.* He knows how to keep his distance. *ka-yeεṛef kif-aš išebbeṛ weqṛu.*

distant – *bεid.*

distinct – *waḍeḥ, bayen.* There's a distinct difference between the two. *kayen feṛq waḍeḥ binathom b-žuž.*

distinctly – *be-ṣ-ṣaṛaḥa, b-kifiya waḍḥa.* I told him distinctly not to come. *qolt-lu b-kifiya waḍḥa ma-iži-š.*

to **distinguish** – *fṛeq, miyyez.* I can't distinguish the colors. *ma-ka-neεṛef-š nmiyyez l-lwan.*
to distinguish between – *fṛeq bin, feṛṛeq bin, εṛef, frez.* Can you distinguish between the two? *waš teqḍeṛ tefṛeq bin hada u-hada?* --I could hardly distinguish one twin from the other. *ma-qḍeṛt-š ḥetta nefrez t-twam.*
to distinguish oneself – *tmiyyez, ban, tteεṛef.* He distinguished himself by his courage. *tmiyyez be-ṛ-ṛžuliya dyalu.*

distress – **1.** *šedda* pl. *-t, šdayed.* The Red Crescent did everything to relieve the distress. *l-hilal le-ḥmeṛ dar žehdu baš ixeffef š-šedda.* **2.** *xaṭaṛ.* The ship was in distress. *l-babbuṛ kan fe-l-xaṭaṛ.* **3.** *hemm* pl. *hmum.* He caused his mother much distress. *dar le-mmu bezzaf de-l-hemm.*

to **distribute** – *feṛṛeq, wezzeε.* What time do they distribute the mail? *fe-š-men saεa ka-ifeṛṛqu l-barid?*

district – **1.** *naḥiya* pl. *-t, nawaḥi.* This is a very poor district. *had n-naḥiya fqiṛa bezzaf.* **2.** *muqaṭaεa* pl. *-t.* The city is divided into ten districts. *le-mdina mqeṣṣma εla εešṛa de-l-muqaṭaεat.*

to **disturb** – **1.** *šuwweš εla.* Don't disturb the others. *ma-tšuwweš-š εel le-xṛin.* **2.** *ruwwen, xeḷḷeṭ.* Someone has disturbed my papers. *ši-waḥed ruwwen-li kwaġti.*
**This news disturbs me. *had le-xbaṛ qleb-li dmaġi.*

ditch – *ḥefṛa* pl. *-t, ḥfaṛi; ḥafa* pl. *-t.* The car got stuck in the ditch. *ṭ-ṭumubil ḥeṣlet fe-l-ḥefṛa.*

to **divide** – **1.** *qṣem, fṛeq, wezzeε.* My partner and I divided the profits. *ana u-šriki qṣemna le-fḍeḷ.* --The land was divided among the peasants. *ḷ-ḷeṛḍ twezzεet εel l-fellaḥa.* **2.** *xtalef.* Opinions are divided on that question. *le-ṛyay ka-textalef f-had l-qaḍiya.*
**The book is divided into two

parts. *le-ktab fih žuž d-le-qṣam.*
divorce - *ṭḷaq* pl. *-at.*
to get a divorce - *šebbeṛ ṭ-ṭḷaq, šedd ṭ-ṭḷaq, ṭṭeḷḷeq.* She wants to get a divorce. *hiya bağya tšebbeṛ ṭ-ṭlaq.*
to divorce - *ṭeḷḷeq.* She divorced her husband several years ago. *ṭeḷḷqet ṛaželha hadi snin.* --He's divorced from his wife. *huwa mṭeḷḷeq men mṛatu.*
dizzy - *dayex, bih d-duxa.* I feel dizzy and so does she. *ana dayex u-ḥetta hiya biha d-duxa.*
to **do** - **1.** *qam iqum b-.* He does his duty. *ka-iqum b-wažbu.* **2.** *ɛmel, dar idir.* I can't do more than forty kilometers an hour. *ma-neqḍeṛ-š neɛmel kteṛ men ṛebɛin kilumiter fe-s-saɛa.* --Do as I do. *dir bḥali.* --I'll do my best to have it ready on time. *ġad neɛmel žehdi baš tkun wažda fe-l-weqt.* **3.** *qḍa iqḍi.* What am I going to do with this hammer? *š-ġad neqḍi b-had le-mṭeṛqa?* **4.** *duwwez.* He did five years in jail. *duwwez xems snin fe-l-ḥebs.* **5.** *qedd, kfa ikfi.* This roast will do for four people. *had le-mḥemmeṛ ġad iqedd l-xemsa de-n-nas.* **6.** *walem.* This will do very nicely. *had š-ši iwalem f-ġaya.* **7.** *xemmel.* My room hasn't been done yet. *l-bit dyali ma-zal ma-txemmel.* **8.** *ṣuwweb.* It takes her an hour to do her hair. *ka-ixeṣṣha saɛa baš tṣuwweb ṛaṣha.*
**What's to be done with this? *l-aš ġad ixdem had-š-ši?* --That has nothing to do with this question. *dak š-ši ma-ɛendu ɛalaqa mɛa had l-mesʔala.* --They can't do a thing to him. *ma-ɛendhom-ši baš iʔadiweh.* --This won't do, my friend! *had š-ši ma-imken-š, a ṣaḥbi.*
to do away with - *feḍḍa men.* They plan to do away with all the requirements. *ka-ifekkṛu ifeḍḍiw men š-šuruṭ kollha.*
to do good - *nfeɛ, ɛewwen, ɛmel xiṛ f-.* It won't do you much good to complain. *ma-ġadi-š inefɛek teška.* --A vacation will do you lots of good. *ši-ɛoṭla. teɛmel fik l-xiṛ bezzaf.*
to do harm - *ḍeṛṛ.* Will it do harm if I leave it out? *waš iḍeṛṛ ila xellitha?*
to do out of - *ɛebba, ḍehmeṛ f-.* He did me out of all my money. *ɛebba-li flusi kollhom.*
to do the dishes - *ġsel l-lwani, ġsel le-mwaɛen.* We have to do the dishes now. *ka-ixeṣṣna nġeslu l-lwani daba.*
to do the laundry - *ṣebben, ġsel teṣbin.* Do you have to do the laundry tomorrow? *waš lazem tṣebben ġedda?* --Where can I have my laundry done? *fayn imken-li neɛṭi ḥwayži itṣebbnu?*
to do well - **1.** *ṭleɛ mezyan.* The wheat's doing well this year. *l-gemḥ ṭaleɛ mezyan had l-ɛam.* **2.** *tmešša mliḥ.* My sister is doing well at school. *xti ka-ttmešša mliḥ fe-l-medṛaṣa.*
to do with - *bġa ibġi, ma-kṛeh-š.* We could do with a little more help. *ma-nkeṛhu-š ši-maɛuna xṛa.*
to do without - *bqa ibqa bla, ttegna ɛla.* Can you do without this book for a while? *waš imken-lek tebqa bla had le-ktab ši-šwiya?*
dock - *mun* pl. *-a.* I nearly fell off the dock. *ġir šwiya kont ġad nṭiḥ men l-mun.*
to dock - *ṛeṣṣa.* Where does the boat dock? *fayn ka-iṛeṣṣi l-babuṛ?*
doctor - *ṭbib* pl. *ṭobba.* Please send for a doctor. *ɛafak ṣifeṭ ɛla ši-ṭbib.* **2.** *dokṭuṛ* pl. *dakatiṛa.* He's a Doctor of Philosophy. *huwa dokṭuṛ fe-l-felsafa.*
document - *watiqa* pl. *watayeq.* Do you have all the documents? *ɛendek l-watayeq kollha?*
dodge - *ḥila* pl. *-t, ḥiyal.* What sort of dodge has he thought of now? *š-men ḥila ɛawed ṭaḥet ɛlih?*
to dodge - **1.** *xwa ixwi.* If I hadn't dodged, he would have hit me. *kun ma-xwit-š, kan ġadi iḍṛebni.* **2.** *dženneb.* He tried to dodge the question. *ḥawel idženneb l-muḍuɛ.*
dog - *kelb* pl. *klab.* Please take the dog out for a walk. *ɛafak ddi l-kelb ittsara.*
to go to the dogs - *hlek ṛaṣu, qḍa ɛla ṛaṣu.* She's going to the dogs. *ka-teqḍi ɛla ṛaṣha.*
to dog - *tbeɛ.* He's been dogging my footsteps all day. *n-nhaṛ kollu u-huwa tbeɛni.*
dog tired - *miyyet b-le-ɛya.* They were dog tired after the excursion. *kanu miyytin b-le-ɛya men beɛd le-msarya.*
doing - *ɛamla, šġal, xedma.* That must be his doing. *bla šekk hadi xdemtu.*
doll - *munika* pl. *-t.* She likes to play with dolls. *ka-tebġi telɛeb be-l-munikat.*
dollar - *ḍuḷaṛ* pl. *-at.*

domestic – 1. *mwollef ḍ-ḍaṛ.* She's always been very domestic. *dima kanet mwollfa ḍ-ḍaṛ.* 2. *maḥelli.* Those are all domestic products. *hadik kollha mentužat maḥelliya.* 3. *daxili.* The government knew how to solve some domestic problems. *l-ḥukuma Ɛeṛfet tḥell beƐḍ l-mašakil d-daxiliya.*

domestic animal – *ḥayawan mṛebbi,* pl. *ḥayawanat mṛebbya.*

to **donate** – *Ɛṭa yeƐṭi, tbeṛṛeƐ, hda ihdi.* I donated five dirhams. *tbeṛṛeƐt b-xemsa de-d-drahem.*

donation – *hdiya* pl. *-t, tabeṛṛuƐ* pl. *-at.*

done – 1. *mhiyye?* pl. *mhiyy?in, mwežžed* pl. *mwežždin.* All my lessons are done. *ḍuṛuṣi kollha mhiyy?a.* 2. *ṭayeb* pl. *ṭaybin.* In ten minutes the meat will be done. *men daba Ɛešṛa de-d-dqayeq ikun l-lḥem ṭayeb.*

to be done – *kemmel, sala.* Are you done with the ironing? *waš kemmelti be-t-teḥdad?*

to be done for – 1. *tsala.* These tires are done for. *had le-bnuwat tsalaw.* 2. *mša f-ḥalu.* If the boss finds out, I'm done for. *ila saq le-mƐellem le-xbaṛ l-had š-ši, mšit f-ḥali.*

to be done in – *ttehlek, mat.* I'm done in from working in this heat. *ana ttehlekt be-l-xedma f-had ṣ-ṣehd.*

donkey – *ḥmaṛ* pl. *ḥmir.*

door – *bab* pl. *biban.*

**They live three doors down. *ḍaṛhom hiya t-talta men hna.*

out of doors – *beṛṛa.* Did you ever sleep out of doors? *waš Ɛemmṛek nƐesti beṛṛa?*

doorknob – *qebṭa* pl. *-t, qbaṭi.*

doorman – *buwwab* pl. *-a.*

dose – *meqdaṛ* pl. *-at, qyaṣ* pl. *-at.* That's too big a dose for a child. *had l-meqdaṛ kbir bezzaf Ɛel ḍ-derri.* —Take this medicine in small doses. *xud had d-dwa be-qyaṣ qlil.*

dossier – *mileff* pl. *-at.* Let me see Ali's dossier. *xellini nšuf l-mileff de-Ɛli.*

dot – *noqṭa* pl. *-t, nqaṭi.* Add three dots. *zid tlata d-noqṭat.*

with dots – *mneqqeṭ.* Wear your dress with the blue dots. *lebsi ksuwtek lli mneqqṭa b-lezṛeq.*

on the dot – *be-ḍ-ḍebṭ, tamam.* I'll see you at three on the dot. *nšufek fe-t-tlata tamam.*

double – 1. *twam.* He could be your double. *tqul twam nta wiyah.* 2. *žuž.* May I have a double portion of ice cream? *imken-li naxod žuž d-le-ḥquq de-l-basṭa?* 3. *Ɛla žuž de-l-meṛṛat.* Our house is double the size of theirs. *ḍaṛna kbeṛ men ḍaṛhom Ɛla žuž de-l-meṛṛat.*

to double – 1. *tna itni.* He's doubled his capital in two years. *tna ṛaṣmalu f-Ɛamayn.* 2. *zad izid qedd.* He doubled my bid. *zad Ɛliya qedd lli Ɛṭit.*

to double up – *luwwa, tna itni, ṭwa iṭwi.* He (was) doubled up with pain. *kan ka-itluwwa b-le-ḥṛiq.*

**We had to double up because there weren't enough beds to go around. *kan lazem neƐsu žuž ḥit le-fṛašat ma-qeddu-š.*

double-breasted – *mṛebbeƐ.* He wore a double-breasted suit. *kan labes keswa mṛebbƐa.*

doubles – *metgablin.* Let's play doubles. *ažiw nleƐbu metgablin.*

doubt – *šekk* pl. *škuk.* Do you have any doubts? *waš Ɛendek ši-šekk?* —No doubt the train will be late. *bla šekk ġad tkun l-mašina mƐeṭṭḷa.* —Without doubt he's the best man for this job. *ma-kayen šekk huwa ?eḥsen waḥed l-had l-Ɛamal.*

to doubt – *šekk, Ɛendu š-šekk.* I doubt if the story is true. *ka-nšekk waš had le-ḥkaya ṣḥiḥa.* —I don't doubt it the least. *ma-Ɛendi-ši š-šekk fiha ?abadan.*

doubtful – *šakk.* I'm still doubtful about it. *ana ma-zal šakk fiha.*

doubtless – *bla šekk.*

dough – *Ɛžina* pl. *-t, Ɛžayen.* The dough has to be allowed to rise first. *xeṣṣ le-Ɛžina tebqa beƐda texmeṛ.*

doughnut – *sfenža* pl. *-t* coll. *sfenž.*

down – *l-teḥt.* Did you look down there? *reggebti l-teḥt?*

**When you really get down to it the difference is insignificant. *mnayn ka-dži tšuf l-ḥaqiqa ka-tṣiḅ ši-ferq qlil.* —Why is he so down in the mouth? *ma-lu ṭayeṛ-lu?* —They're down and out now. *bqaw ḷḷah l-Ɛaṭi daba.*

to go up and down – *ṭḷeƐ hbeṭ, mša imši ṭuḷ u-Ɛeṛḍ.* He was walking up and down the room. *kan ṭaḷeƐ habeṭ fe-l-bit.*

to go down – *hbeṭ.* The elevator is going down. *l-miƐraž habeṭ.*

to down – *ṣṛeṭ, genṭeḥ.* He downed a glass of tea and ran outside. *ṣṛeṭ kas d-atay u-xrež ka-isbeg.*

downgrade – *hebṭa* pl. *-t*. The road has a steep downgrade. *ṭ-ṭṛiq fiha hebṭa mderdba.*
downhill – *habeṭ*. The road goes downhill. *ṭ-ṭṛiq žat habṭa.*
down payment – *tesbiq* pl. *-at*. How much will the down payment be? *šḥal ġad nƐemlu fe-t-tesbiq?*
downstairs – *l-teḥt*. I'll be waiting downstairs. *ġad ntsenna l-teḥt.*
to **doze** – *ġemmeḍ, Ɛmel ši-tġimḍa.* I've just been dozing. *Ɛad ġemmeḍt.* --She dozed off after supper. *Ɛemlet ši-tġimḍa beƐd le-Ɛša.*
dozen – *ẓina* pl. *-t, ẓyen* (with art. *l-ẓina*). Please give me a dozen eggs. *Ɛṭini ẓina de-l-biḍ men feḍlek.*
draft – **1.** *riḥ* pl. *ryaḥ, berd.* I can't stand the draft in this room. *ma-neqḍeṛ-š neṣbeṛ le-r-riḥ f-had l-bit.* --The fire went out because there wasn't enough draft. *l-Ɛafya tteṭfat men qellet r-riḥ.* **2.** *tenfisa* pl. *-t, tnafes.* Did you open the draft of the furnace? *ḥelliti t-tenfisa de-l-kanun?* **3.** *ṛṣem* pl. *ṛṣuma, mexṭuṭ* pl. *-at.* The first draft is ready. *ṛ-ṛṣem l-luwwel wažed.*
to draft – *xda yaxod l-l-žeyš, dexxel l-l-žeyš.* He was drafted last month. *dexxluh l-l-žeyš š-šheṛ lli fat.*
to **drag** – **1.** *žeṛṛ.* I had to drag the trunk into the house myself. *ma-fadni ġir nžeṛṛ ṣ-ṣenḍuq b-iddi le-ḍ-ḍaṛ.* --He could hardly drag himself to work. *yaḷḷah waš qedd ižeṛṛ ṛaṣu l-l-xedma.* **2.** *džeṛžeṛ.* Your coat is dragging on the floor. *baḷṭuk ka-idžeṛžeṛ fe-ḷ-ḷeṛḍ.* **3.** *džebbed, ṭwaḷ.* Time drags when you don't have anything to do. *l-weqt ka-idžebbed mnayn ma-ka-ikun Ɛendek ma teƐmel.* **4.** *xemmel, neqqa, xwa ixwi.* They dragged the river for the body. *xemmlu l-wad baš ilqaw l-kesda.*
to drag on – **1.** *ṭaḷ iṭuḷ.* The meeting dragged for three hours. *tlata de-s-saƐat ṭaḷ l-žemƐ.* **2.** *ṭwaḷ, džebbed.* The days just dragged on. *l-iyam ġir kanet ka-džebbed.*
drain – *qadus* pl. *qwades.* The drain has stopped up again. *l-qadus ttexneq tani.*
to drain – *neššef, ḥell.* They drained the swimming pool only yesterday. *ġir l-bareḥ neššfu s-sehriž.*
to drain off – *mša imši, tteqṭeƐ.* The water doesn't drain off. *l-ma ma-ka-itteqṭeƐ-š.*
drastic – *šdid* pl. *šdad, qwi* pl. *-yin.* The government took drastic measures. *l-ḥukuma xdat tadabir šdida.*
to **draw** – **1.** *ṣewweṛ, ṛṣem.* He draws best with crayons. *ka-iṣewweṛ ḥsen ktir š-ši b-le-qluma de-l-lwan.* **2.** *žbed.* He drew the winning number. *huwa žbed n-nemra r-rabḥa.* **3.** *žleb.* The film is sure to draw a big crowd. *bla šekk had l-film ġa-ižleb bezzaf de-n-nas.*
to draw into – **1.** *dxel.* The train is just drawing into the station. *l-mašina yaḷḷah daxla l-lagaṛ.* **2.** *dexxel, žeṛṛ.* I've been drawn into this argument against my will. *dexxluni l-had ṣ-ṣḍaƐ be-z-zez Ɛliya.*
to draw out – *xerrež men.* I'll have to draw out fifty dirhams from the bank. *ġad ixeṣṣni nxerrež xemsin derhem men l-ḅenk.*
to draw to a close – *qeṛṛeb ikmel.* This work is drawing to a close. *had l-xedma qeṛṛbet tekmel.*
to draw up – **1.** *xeṭṭeṭ, ṣewweb.* Who drew up the plan? *škun lli xeṭṭeṭ ṛ-ṛṣem?* **2.** *kteb.* I'll draw up the report. *ana ġad nekteb t-teqṛiṛ.* **3.** *qeṛṛeb.* Here's a taxi drawing up. *ha waḥed ṭ-ṭaksi ka-iqeṛṛeb.*
to draw breath – *ṭeḷḷeƐ n-nefs.*
to draw conclusions – *fhem, stentež.* Draw your own conclusions from that! *lli bġiti fehmu men dak š-ši.*
drawer – *mžeṛṛ* pl. *mžuṛa.* My passport is in the top drawer. *tesriḥi ṛaḥ f-le-mžeṛṛ l-fuqani.*
dread – *ṛehba.* I have a dread of doctors. *ka-džini ṛ-ṛehba men ṭ-ṭobba.*
to dread – **1.** *xaf ixaf men.* I dread the dark. *ana ka-nxaf men ḍ-ḍeḷma.* **2.** *rfed dbila l-, rfed dbayel l-.* I dread going to the dentist. *ka-nerfed dbila l-le-mši Ɛend ṭbib s-snan.*
**I dread the very thought of it. *ġir t-tefkir fiha ka-yeƐmel fiya ṛ-ṛehba.*
dream – *mnam, mnama* pl. *-t, mnayem.* I had a funny dream last night. *šeft mnama ġriba l-bareḥ fe-l-lil.*
to dream – **1.** *ḥlem.* Last night I dreamed that I was home. *l-bareḥ ḥlemt ṛaṣi f-daṛna.* **2.** *ža iži l-l-bal f-le-mnam.* I wouldn't dream of doing it. *ḥetta f-le-mnam ma-džini-š l-l-bal ndirha.*
dreary – *mbuʔes.* It was an awfully

dreary day. *nhaṛ mbuʔes kan bla qyaṣ.*

dress - *lebsa* pl. *-t, lbasi; keswa* pl. *ksawi.* She wants to buy a new dress. *bġat tešri keswa ždida.*

to dress - **1.** *lbes ḥwayež, lbes.* I'll dress quickly. *ġad nelbes ḥwayži b-z-zerba.* --His wife dresses in good taste. *mṛatu ka-telbes b-duq.* --He's always well dressed. *huwa dima labes mezyan.* **2.** *lebbes.* Mother is just dressing the baby. *mmi yallah ka-tlebbes le-t-teṛbya ḥwayežha.* **3.** *ziyyen.* They dress the store windows in the evening. *fe-l-lil ka-iziyynu z-zažat d-le-ḥwanet.*

**Look at him, all dressed up! *šuf Ɛla tešyika f-aš-en huwa!*

to dress a wound - *ṛbeṭ žeṛḥa.* Did you dress the wound? *ṛbeṭṭi ž-žeṛḥa?*

dressing - **1.** *mƐemmeṛ* pl. *mƐemmṛin.* They served roast turkey with a dressing of almonds and raisins. *nezzlu bibi mešwi b-le-mƐemmeṛ de-l-luz u-z-zbib.* **2.** *faṣma* pl. *-t, faṣmawat, ṛebṭ* pl. *ṛbaṭi.* The nurse changes his dressing every morning. *l-mumeṛṛiḍa ka-tbeddel-lu l-faṣma koll ṣbaḥ.*

dressing gown - *keswa de-ḍ-ḍaṛ* pl. *ksawi de-ḍ-ḍaṛ.*

dressmaker - *xeyyaṭa* pl. *-t.*

dried - *myebbes* pl. *myebbsin, yabes* pl. *yabsin, šaḥet* pl. *šaḥtin.* Buy me a kilogram of dried figs. *šri-li kilu de-l-keṛmuṣ yabsa.*

drill - **1.** *teqqaba* pl. *-t.* The mechanic needs another drill. *l-mikaniki xeṣṣu teqqaba xṛa.* **2.** *temrin* pl. *tamarin.* The soldiers went out for a rifle drill. *l-Ɛesker xeṛžu le-t-temrin d-le-mkaḥel.*

to drill - **1.** *tqeb, ḥfeṛ.* Drill a hole in this beam. *tqeb teqba f-had l-gayza.* **2.** *ḥfeṛ, xwa ixwi.* The dentist has to drill this tooth. *la-bodda ṭ-ṭbib ixwi had s-senna.* **3.** *derreb, merren.* Their teacher drills them in conversation a great deal. *ustadhom ka-iderrebhom ktir Ɛel l-muḥadata.* **4.** *dderreb, tmerren.* The soldiers drill every day. *l-Ɛesker ka-itmerṛnu koll nhaṛ.* --We were drilled in arithmetic. *tmerrenna f-le-ḥsab.*

drink - **1.** *mešṛub* pl. *-at, muberrid* pl. *-at.* What kind of drinks do you have? *š-men mešṛubat Ɛendek?* **2.** *šṛiba* pl. *-t, žġima* pl. *-t.* May I have a drink of water? *Ɛafak ši-šṛiba de-l-ma.* **3.** *kas* pl. *kisan.* He had only three drinks. *ma-xda ġir tlata de-l-kisan.*

to drink - *šṛeb.* Drink plenty of water! *šṛeb l-ma bezzaf.* --Let's drink to your return. *yallah nšeṛbu le-ṛžuƐek.*

to **drip** - *qeṭṭeṛ.* The faucet is dripping. *l-bezbuz ka-iqeṭṭeṛ.*

drive - **1.** *ṭṛiq* pl. *ṭoṛqan.* The drive goes around the lake. *ṭ-ṭṛiq ḍayṛa be-ḍ-ḍaya.* **2.** *ḥemla* pl. *-t.* In the last drive we raised five thousand dirhams. *fe-l-ḥemla t-talya žmeƐna xems alaf derhem.* **3.** *msarya be-ṭ-ṭumbil* pl. *msaryat be-ṭ-ṭumubil.* We took a nice drive. *Ɛmelna waḥed le-msarya haʔila be-ṭ-ṭumubil.*

to drive - **1.** *ṣag iṣug.* Can you drive his car? *teƐṛef tṣug siyaṛtu?* --Drive the horses over to the left. *ṣug l-xil Ɛel l-iṣeṛ.* **2.** *dfeƐ b-, ʔedda b-.* Hunger drove him to stealing. *ž-žuƐ dfeƐ bih le-s-sṛiqa.* **3.** *xeddem.* The foreman drives his workers continually. *l-weqqaf ka-ixeddem l-xeddama dyalu bla ṛaḥa.* **4.** *deqq.* Drive this nail into the wall. *deqq had l-meṣmaṛ fe-l-ḥeyṭ.*

**What are you driving at? *š-ka-tebġi teqṣeḍ?* --I'll drive you there. *nddik fe-s-siyaṛa l-temma.*

to drive away - **1.** *ṭṛeḍ, žra ižri Ɛla.* Drive the dog away. *žri Ɛla had l-kelb.* **2.** *zad izid be-ṭ-ṭumubil, mša imši be-ṭ-ṭumubil.* He just now drove away. *yallah kif zad be-ṭ-ṭumubil.*

to drive crazy, mad - *ḥemmeq.* You'll drive me crazy yet. *nta ṛak ġad tḥemmeqni.*

to drive off - *xerrež, Ɛewwež.* The wind drove the boat off its course. *r-riḥ xerrež le-fluka Ɛel ṭ-ṭṛiq.*

driver - **1.** *sayeq* pl. *suwaq.* He's the ambassador's driver. *huwa s-sayeq dyal s-safir.* **2.** *suwwaq* pl. *-a, guwwad* pl. *-a.* The driver lost control of the horses. *s-suwwaq ġelbet Ɛlih l-xil.*

**He's a good driver. *ka-iṣug mezyan.*

driver's license - *ṛexṣa de-s-siyaqa* pl. *ṛexṣat de-s-siyaqa.* Let me see your driver's license. *werrini ṛ-ṛexṣa de-s-siyaqa dyalek.*

to **drizzle** - *bexxet š-šta.* It's been drizzling all day. *n-nhaṛ kollu u-š-šta ka-tbexx.*

droop - *tteṛxa, tluwwa.* The flowers are beginning to droop. *n-nuwwaṛ* *bda itluwwa.*

drooping - *habeṭ.* He has drooping shoulders. *ktafu habṭin.*

drop - *qeṭṛa* pl. *-t, qṭaṛi; noqṭa* pl. *-t, nqaṭi.* Take three drops in a glass of water. *xud tlata de-n-nqaṭi f-kas de-l-ma.*

**He'll give you a lecture at the drop of a hat. *ġir lli žebdu ka-isemmeε-lu.*

to drop - **1.** *ṭaḥ iṭiḥ.* The box dropped out of the window. *ṣ-ṣenduq ṭaḥ men š-šeṛžem.* --The temperature dropped very rapidly. *mizan l-ḥaṛaṛa ṭaḥ deġya deġya.* --I dropped my billfold. *ṭaḥ-li l-beẓṭam dyali.* **2.** *ṭiyyeḥ.* He dropped the pistol when he saw the police coming. *ṭiyyeḥ l-ferdi mnin šaf l-bulis maži.* **3.** *nsa insa.* Let's drop the subject! *l-ḥaṣiḷ nnsaw l-muḍuε!* **4.** *nezzel.* Please drop me at the corner. *nezzelni fe-l-qent εafak.* **5.** *xerrež.* I'll be dropped by the club. *ġad ixerržuni men n-nadi.* **6.** *ṛma iṛmi.* Please drop this card in the (letter) box for me. *εafak ṛmi-li had ṣ-ṣuṛa f-ṣenduq l-barid.*

to drop a hint - *fehhem.* She dropped a hint that she wanted to go. *kanet fehhmet billa bġat temši.*

to drop in - *ža iži išuf.* Drop in to see me tomorrow. *aži šufni ġedda.*

to drop off - **1.** *nezzel, ḥeṭṭ.* Can you drop this off at the tailor's for me? *imken-lek tḥeṭṭ-li had š-ši εend l-xeyyaṭ?* **2.** *ṭaḥ iṭiḥ.* I dropped off to sleep immediately. *ṭeḥt be-n-nεas hiya hadik.*

drought - *keḥṭ.*

to **drown** - **1.** *ġṛeq.* He drowned in the river. *ġṛeq fe-l-wad.* **2.** *ġeṛṛeq.* She had to drown the kittens. *kan lazem baš tġeṛṛeq le-mšišat.*

to drown out - *ġeṭṭa.* The noise drowned out his remarks. *ṣ-ṣdaε ġeṭṭa mulaḥaḍatu.*

drowsy - *žah ižih n-nεas.* I'm getting drowsy. *bda ižini n-nεas.*

drug - **1.** *dwa* pl. *-yat, ʔadwiya.* This drug is sold only on prescription. *had d-dwa ka-ittbaε ġir b-ʔaden ṭ-ṭbib.* **2.** *εefyun* pl. *-at, muxeḍḍiṛ* pl. *-at.* He became addicted to drugs. *ttebla be-l-muxeḍḍiṛat.*

drugstore - *ṣeyḍaliya* pl. *-t.* Where is the nearest drugstore? I have to have a prescription filled. *fayn ʔeqṛeb seyḍaliya hnaya? xeṣṣni nešri ši-ʔadwiya ktebhom-li ṭ-ṭbib.*

drum - **1.** *ṭbeḷ* pl. *ṭbuḷa.* Can you hear the drums? *waš ka-tesmeε ṭ-ṭbuḷa?* **2.** *bermil* pl. *bramel.* They emptied six drums of gasoline. *xwaw setta d-le-bramel d-l-iṣanṣ.*

to drum - **1.** *ḍṛeb, ṭebbel, deqdeq.* Please don't drum on the table! *men feḍlek baṛaka u-ma-ttebbel εel ṭ-ṭabla!* **2.** *dexxel f-ṛaṣ-.* These rules have been drummed into me. *had l-qawaεid dexxluhom-li f-ṛaṣi.*

drunk - *sekran.*

to get drunk - *sker.*

dry - **1.** *yabes, našef.* The wash isn't dry yet. *ma-zal t-tesbin ma-ši yabes.* Let's gather some dry wood. *yaḷḷah nžemεu šwiya de-l-εud yabes.* --My throat is dry. *ḥelqi yabes.* --The well is dry. *l-bir našef.* **2.** *žaff.* The lecture was so dry, I walked out. *l-muḥaḍaṛa kanet žaffa l-ḥedd ʔannani xrežt f-ḥali.* **3.** *šahet.* It's been a dry summer. *had ṣ-ṣif kan šahet.*

dry land - *berr.* It's good to be on dry land again. *ṛ-ṛžuε l-l-berr u-ma-ḥlah!*

to dry - **1.** *ibes.* This paint dries in five hours. *had ṣ-ṣbaġa ka-tibes f-xems swayeε.* **2.** *neššef, mseḥ.* Who's going to dry the dishes? *škun ġad ineššef l-lwani?*

to dry oneself - Dry yourself well. *neššef ṛaṣek mezyan.*

to dry up - *nšef.* Every summer this stream dries up. *had l-wad koll šif ka-inšef.*

dual - *mutenna.* What's the dual of this word? *šnu huwa l-mutenna dyal had l-kelma?*

duck - *beṛka* pl. *-t* coll. *beṛk.*

to duck - *ḥna yeḥni, ḥder.* He ducked his head. *ḥna ṛaṣu.* --Duck! *ḥni ṛaṣek!*

to be **due** - *wžeb.* The rent is due next Monday. *le-kra ġad tužeb t-tnayen ž-žay.*

due to - *b-sabab.* Due to an oversight, she wasn't invited. *b-sabab l-ʔihmal ma-kanet-š meεṛuḍa.* --That's due to a mistake. *dak š-ši wqeε b-sabab ġelṭa.*

**He's due to arrive at ten. *muntaḍaṛ yuṣeḷ fe-l-εešṛa.*

dull - **1.** *ḥafi.* This knife is dull. *had l-mus ḥafi.* **2.** *(lli) ka-iqenneṭ.* He's terribly dull. *ka-iqenneṭ bla qyaṣ.* **3.** *mdehmes.* She likes dull colors. *hiya ka-tebġi l-lwan mdehmsin.* **4.** *balid* pl. *bulada.* I have seen dull students before, but not like him. *šeft t-tlamed l-bulada men qbel u-la-šeft bḥalu.*

dumb - **1.** *ẓiẓun* pl. *ẓyaẓen.* Can't you speak? You're not dumb, are you? *ma-teqḍer-š ttkellem? ma-ṛak-ši ẓiẓun?* **2.** *mṭemmeṣ.* Boy, that guy is dumb! *ya laṭif hadak xiyyna kif-aš mṭemmeṣ!* **3.** *basel, mebluẓ.* That was dumb of you. *ɛmeltiha basla.*
**We were struck dumb by the news. *le-xbaṛ zeggezna.*

dumfounded - *mešluṭ, mebhuṭ, mzeggez.* I was completely dumbfounded when I heard it. *bqit tamamen mešluṭ melli smeɛtha.*

dump - **1.** *zebbala* pl. *-t.* That empty lot is used as a dump. *dak s-saḥa l-xawya mṣeḷḷḥinha zebbala.* --Their house is an awful dump. *ḍaṛhom kollha bḥal z-zebbala.* **2.** *ḍiqa u-ġemma.* I've been down in the dumps all day. *n-nhaṛ kollu w-ana fe-ḍ-ḍiqa u-l-ġemma.*
to dump - **1.** *qleb, kebb.* They dumped the coal in front of the basement. *ṛahom kebbu l-faxeṛ qeddam d-dehlis.* **2.** *xwa ixwi, ferreġ.* He simply dumped all his packages on the floor. *ġir ža u-ferreġ ḥezmatu kollha ɛel ḷ-ḷeṛḍ.* **3.** *xwa ixwi, ṛma iṛmi.* Please don't dump the coffee grounds in the drain! *ɛafak ma-teṛmi-š t-text de-l-qehwa fe-l-qadus.*

dung - *ġbaṛ.*

duplicate - *nesxa* pl. *-t, nsaxi.* Is this an original or a duplicate? *waš hadi l-ʔaṣliya aw nesxa?*
to duplicate - *nsex, nqel.* That can't be duplicated. *dak š-ši ma-imken-lu-š ittensex.*

durable - **1.** *dayem.* The delegates to the United Nations are discussing the means to a durable peace. *l-mumettilin fe-l-ʔumam l-muttaḥida ka-itkellmu ɛel ṭ-ṭuṛuq lli tweṣṣel le-s-salam d-dayem.* **2.** *qaṣeḥ, ṣḥiḥ, de-ṣ-ṣeḥḥ.* Steel and cement are used for making durable goods. *l-henḍ u-l-beṛṣlaba ka-itṣuwwbu bihom ḥwayež de-ṣ-ṣeḥḥ.*

during - *f-weqt.* I met him during the war. *tɛaṛeft mɛah f-weqt l-ḥeṛb.*

dust - *ġobṛa* pl. *-t, ġbabeṛ.* There's a heavy layer of dust on the table. *kayna ṭebqa de-l-ġebṛa qedd-aš fuq ṭ-ṭebla.*
to dust - *mseḥ l-ġobṛa, nfeḍ l-ġobṛa.* Please dust my desk. *ɛafak mseḥ l-ġobṛa men l-mekteb dyali.*

duty - **1.** *wažeb, wažib* pl. *-at.* It was his duty to support his parents. *kan wažeb ɛlih irfed b-waldih.* **2.** *muhimma* pl. *-t.* Answering the phone is one of my duties. *men l-muhimmat dyali nžaweb t-tilifun.* **3.** *ḥeqq d-diwana* pl. *ḥquq d-diwana.* How much duty is there on this tobacco? *šḥal ḥeqq d-diwana ɛla had d-doxxan?*
to be off duty - *sala men l-xedma.* I'm off duty after five-thirty. *ka-nsali men l-xedma men beɛd l-xemsa u-neṣṣ.*

to **dwell** - **1.** *sken iskon.* They used to dwell outside the city. *kanu ka-iseknu xarež le-mdina.* **2.** *bqa ibqa.* There's no point in dwelling on this subject any longer. *ma-ɛendha meɛna nebqaw f-had l-muḍuɛ kteṛ men had š-ši.*

dye - *ṣbaġa* pl. *-t.* Please get me a package of blue dye. *ɛafak xud-li mɛak ṣenduq de-ṣ-ṣbaġa ẓeṛqa.*
to dye - *ṣbeġ.* I had my blue dress dyed black. *ksuwti ẓ-ẓeṛqa ṣbeġtha b-le-kḥel.*
dyed-in-the-wool - *xluq.* He's a dyed-in-the-wool conservative. *huwa muḥafiḍ xluq.*

dyeing - *taṣebbaġet.*

dyer - *ṣebbaġ* pl. *-a.*

dynamic - *našiṭ, ḥeyy.* He's dynamic in everything he does. *huwa našiṭ f-koll ḥaža ka-yeɛmelha.*

dysentery - *zeḥma.*

E

each - **1.** *koll waḥed.* Each of us received a pack of cigarettes. *koll waḥed menna ɛṭaweh bakiya de-l-gaṛṛu.* **2.** *koll.* He comes here each week. *ka-iži lle-hna koll ṣimana.* --Give one to each child. *ɛṭi weḥda l-koll derri.* **3.** *l-waḥed* f. *l-weḥda.* These apples are five francs each. *had t-teffaḥ ka-iswa xemsa fṛenk l-weḥda.*
**You can count on each and every one of us. *imken-lek twekkel ɛlina u-ɛla koll waḥed menna.*
each one - *koll waḥed.* Each one has to contribute his full share. *koll waḥed xeṣṣu yeɛṭi ḥeqqu kollu.*

each other - *beɛḍiyat* - (plus pl. pronoun ending.). They're hitting each other. *ka-iḍeṛbu beɛḍiyathom.*
**Do you see each other every day? *waš ntuma ka-tšawfu koll nhaṛ?* --We have to help each other. *xeṣṣna ntɛawnu.*

eager - **1.** *muštaq.* I'm eager to meet your friend. *ana muštaq ntlaqa b-ṣaḥbek.* **2.** *zerban.* He's eager to get started. *huwa zerban baš ibda.*

eagle - *ɛgab* pl. *-at, ɛogban.*

ear - *wden* pl. *wednin* (pl. *wedni-* before possessive endings, e.g., *wedniya* 'my ears', etc.) My ear hurts. *wedni ka-iḍeṛṛni.* --The walls have ears. *le-ḥyuṭ ɛendhom l-wednin.* --It goes in one ear and out the other. *ka-ddxol men wden u-texrož men l-oxṛa.* --He's up to his ears in debt. *huwa ġaṛeq ḥetta l-wednih fe-d-din.* --He has his ear to the ground. *huwa ṛaxi wednu.*

all ears - *wednin mɛa.* Go on with your story, I'm all ears. *ġir ɛewwed ḥkaytek, wedniya mɛak.*

ear of corn - *kbala* pl. *-t* coll. *kbal.*

ear of wheat - *sbula* (pl. *sbulat, sbayl*) *de-l-gemḥ.*

earlier - *qbel.* Come earlier than usual. *aži qbel men l-ɛada.*

early - **1.** *bekri.* Please wake me early. *fiyyeqni bekri ɛafak.* **2.** *ɛažel.* We expect an early reply. *ḥna ka-nntadru žwab ɛažel.*
**Tell me something about your early life. *tkellem-li ɛel l-iyam l-luwwla d-ḥayatek.*

to earn - **1.** *rbeḥ* How much do you earn a week? *šḥal ka-terbeḥ f-l-usbuɛ?* --She earns her living as a dressmaker. *ka-terbeḥ mɛaštha fe-l-xeyyaṭa.*

earring - *ḥalaqa* pl. *-t, ɛalaga* pl. *-t.*

earth - **1.** *denya.* Nothing on earth can save him. *ḥetta ḥaža f-had d-denya ma-teqḍeṛ tnežžih.* **2.** *tṛab.* This ditch has to be filled with earth. *had l-ḥefṛa xeṣṣha ttɛemmeṛ be-t-tṛab.* **3.** *ḷeṛḍ.* The earth is a sphere. *ḷ-ḷeṛḍ mkuwwṛa.*
**He has a down to earth attitude. *huwa ɛendu heyʔa ɛamaliya.*

earthquake - *zelzla* pl. *-t.*

ease - *suhula.* Did you notice the ease with which he does things? *waš laḥeḍti kif-aš ka-yeɛmel le-ḥwayež b-suhula?*

at ease - *(lli) ka-iḥess b-ṛaṣu mezyan.* I never feel quite at ease when I'm with her. *ɛemmeṛni ma-ka-nḥess b-ṛaṣi mezyan w-ana mɛaha.*

to ease - *xeffef.* This medicine will ease the pain. *had d-dwa ġadi ixeffef le-wžeɛ.*

easily - **1.** *b-suhula.* That's easily done. *had š-ši ka-itteɛmel b-suhula* or *hadi ḥaža qṛiba.* **2.** *men le-bɛid.* That's easily the best. *men le-bɛid hada huwa le-mxeyyeṛ.*

east - *šeṛq.* The wind's coming from the east. *l-berd žay men š-šeṛq.* --Our house is east of the railroad tracks. *ḍaṛna f-šeṛq sekket l-mašina.*

the Far East - *š-šeṛq l-ʔeqṣa.*

the Middle East - *š-šeṛq l-ʔewṣeṭ.*

east wind - *šergi.*

eastern - *šeṛqi.*

easy - *sahel.* That was an easy question. *kan suʔal sahel hada.*
**He's now living on Easy Street. *huwa ɛayeš fe-t-tebxiṛ.* --Take it easy! Why get excited? *be-šwiya ɛlik! ɛlaš ka-iṭiṛ-lek?*

to eat - *kla yakọl.* (a. p. *wakel,* p. p. *mukul*).
**She's eating her heart out. *hiya ka-tkemmed l-kuwya ɛla qelbha.*

echo - *ṣaḍa.*

economic - *qtiṣaḍi.* Their economic condition is bad because of the drought. *ḥalthom le-qtiṣaḍiya xayba men sabab l-keḥṭ.*

economical - **1.** *mḥawel.* She's very economical. *hiya mḥawla bezzaf.* **2.** *(lli) ka-iweffeṛ.* This type of heating is very economical. *had n-nuɛ de-t-tesxan ka-iweffeṛ bezzaf.*

economics - *iqtiṣaḍ.*

to economize - *ḥawel ɛla.* She economizes in household expenditures. *ka-tḥawel ɛel ṣ-ṣeṛf de-ḍ-ḍaṛ.*

edge - **1.** *ḥašiya* pl. *-t.* He lives at the edge of town. *ka-iskon f-ḥašiyt le-mdina.* --Don't put the glass too close to the edge. *ma-ddir-š l-kas qṛib bezzaf men l-ḥašiya.* **2.** *šefṛa* pl. *-t, šfaṛi.* The edge is dull. *š-šefṛa ḥafya.*

on edge - *mqelleq.* She's on edge today. *hiya mqellqa l-yum.*
**You have the edge on me. *nta fayetni be-šwiya.* --I could hardly edge my way through the crowd. *ana tsellett be-ṣ-ṣuɛuba men z-zḥam.*

edition - *ṭebɛa* pl. *-t.*

editor - *ṛaʔis t-teḥrir* pl. *ṛuʔasa t-teḥrir.*

to educate - *ɛellem.*

educated - *mteqqef, qaṛi.*

education - *teɛlim.*

Ministry of Education - wiẓaṛt t-teɛlim.

eel - nuna pl. -t coll. nun; ṣennuṛ.

effect - teʔtir.
**He just does it for effect. ka-yeɛmelha ɛla ɛeyn n-nas.
   to go into effect - ṭṭebbeq. This new law will go into effect next month. had l-qanun ž-ždid gadi iṭṭebbeq š-šheṛ ž-žay.
   to have an effect - ʔetter. Scolding has no effect on him. le-xṣam ma-ka-iʔettru-š.
   to put into effect - ṭebbeq. The new ruling was just put into effect. yaḷḷah ṭebbqu l-qaṛaṛ ž-ždid.
   to take effect - šebbeṛ. The injection is beginning to take effect. š-šuka bdat ka-tšebbeṛ.

effort - mežhud pl. -at, žehd pl. žhud. All his efforts were in vain. l-mežhudat lli ɛmel kollhom baṭlin. --That's a waste of effort. had š-ši teḍyaɛ ž-žehd.
   to make an effort - dar idir mežhud. Did he really make an effort? waš huwa dar mežhudu be-l-meɛqul?

egg - biḍa pl. -t coll. bid. How much is a dozen eggs? be-šhal ž-žina de-l-biḍ?
   to egg on - nǧez. His friends egged him on. ṣḥabu neǧzuh.

eggplant - denžala pl. -t coll. denžal; bu-denžala pl. -t coll. bu-denžal.

Egypt - maṣeṛ.

Egyptian - meṣṛi.

eight - tmenya, tmen, temn. Give me eight eggs. ɛṭini tmenya de-l-biḍ or tmen biḍat.

eighteen - tmenṭaš, tmenṭašeṛ. There are eighteen men. kaynin tmenṭaš de-r-ržal or tmenṭaseṛ ṛažel.

eighth - 1. tmen. He could only get an eighth of a kilo of butter. huwa ma-qḍeṛ yaxod ġir tmen kilu de-z-zebda. 2. tamen. That's his eighth book. hada huwa ktabu t-tamen.

eighty - tmanin.

either - amma. I leave either tonight or tomorrow morning. ġad nemši amma l-yum fe-l-lil wella ġedda fe-ṣ-ṣbaḥ. --Either I go or he goes. amma huwa imši walla ana nemši.
**He doesn't know it either. ḥetta huwa ma-ka-yeɛṛefha-š. --Either one is correct. lli kan fihom ṣḥiḥ.

elaborate - metqun, mdeqqeq. He gave us an elaborate description of the thief. ɛṭana neɛt mdeqqeq ɛel

ṣ-ṣeṛṛaq.

elastic - lastik. Do you need some elastic for the dress? waš xeṣṣek ši-lastik l-l-keswa?

elbow - meṛfeg, meṛfeq pl. mṛafeg, mṛafeq.

to elect - ntaxeb.

election - intixab pl. -at.

electric - kehṛabaʔi.
   electric bulb - buḷa pl. -t.

electrician - mul (pl. mwalin) ḍ-ḍu.

electricity - kehṛaba, trisinti, ḍu.

elementary - ʔasasi.

elementary school - medṛaṣa ibtidaʔiya.

elephant - fil pl. fyal.

elevation - ɛlu. The elevation of this village is six hundred meters above sea level. le-ɛlu d-had l-qeṛya sett myat mitru fuq le-bḥeṛ.

elevator - miɛṛaž pl. -at.

eleven - ḥḍaš, ḥḍašeṛ.

eleventh - ḥaḍeš.

to eliminate - 1. ḥdef. We can eliminate these difficulties easily. had ṣ-ṣuɛubat imken-lna nḥedfuhom b-suhula. 2. dḥa idḥi. He was eliminated in the third race. huwa dḥaweh f-le-msabqa t-talta.

else - axoṛ f. xṛa pl. xṛin. What else are we going to do? aš axoṛ gadi nɛemlu?
   anybody, somebody else - ši-waḥed axoṛ. Is anybody else here? waš kayen ši-waḥed axoṛ hna?
   anything, something else - ši-ḥaža xṛa. Do you have anything else? waš ɛendek ši-ḥaža xṛa?
   anywhere, somewhere else - ši-maḥell axoṛ. Can't we meet anywhere else? waš ma-imken-lna-š ntlaqaw f-ši-maḥell axoṛ?
   everybody, everyone else - le-xṛin. Everybody else has gone. le-xṛin kollhom mšaw.
   everything else - gaɛ š-ši l-axoṛ.

to embarrass - ḥeššem. That child is always embarrassing me. had d-derri dima ka-iḥeššemni.

to be embarrassed - ḥšem. I was terribly embarrassed. ḥšemt bezzaf.

embassy - sifaṛa pl. -t.

to embrace - ɛenneg, ɛenneq.

emigrant - mhažeṛ.

to emigrate - hžeṛ.

emir - ʔamir pl. ʔumaṛa.

emotion - dehša (surprise, etc.), xelɛa (fear), šafaqa (compassion, etc.).

to employ - xeddem. This factory employs a thousand workers. had l-meɛmel ka-imaddem ulef de-l-xeddama.

**Where are you employed? *fayn xeddam nta?*
employee – *xeddam* pl. *-a* (laborer), *mweḍḍef* pl. *mweḍḍfin* (white-collar).
employer – *mɛellem, baṭṛun.*
empty – *xawi.* Do you have an empty box? *waš ɛendek ṣenduq xawi?* --He made empty threats. *huwa ɛmel tehžimat xawya.*
**I wouldn't drink on an empty stomach. *ana ma-nešṛeb-š ɛel ṛ-ṛiq.*
to empty – **1.** *xwa ixwi, feṛṛeġ.* Please empty this barrel. *ɛafak xwi had l-bermil.* **2.** *xwa ixwa.* The hall emptied in five minutes. *ṣ-ṣala xwat fe-qṣem.* **3.** *kebb.* This river empties into the ocean. *had l-wad ka-ikebb f-le-bḥeṛ.*
to **enable** – *ɛṭa yeɛṭi l-kifiya.* This experience should enable you to get a good position. *had t-tedrib lazemha teɛṭik l-kifiya baš tṣib waḍifa mezyana.*
to **enclose** – *ṣifeṭ f-daxel.* I am enclosing the newspaper clipping. *ana ka-nṣifeṭ f-daxel l-qeṭɛa de-l-žarida.*
enclosed – *f-daxel.* Enclosed is the sum still due you. *f-daxel kayen l-mebleġ lli ka-tsal.*
to **encourage** – *šežžeɛ.* He encouraged me to stick it out. *šežžeɛni baš nšebbeṛ ḥetta l-l-axir.*
encouragement – *tešžiɛa, tešžaɛ.*
end – **1.** *axeṛ, ʔaxir.* I'll pay you the balance at the end of the month. *ana nxeḷḷeṣ-lek l-baqiya f-axeṛ š-šheṛ.* **2.** *ṛaṣ* pl. *ṛyuṣ.* Tie the two ends together. *ḥzem had ṛ-ṛyuṣ b-žuž.*
**He scolded him a bit and that was the end of it. *ġuwwet ɛlih u-ṣafi.* --You can't go to the movies, and that's the end of it! *ma-imken-lek-š temši le-s-sinima u-ṣafi.* --We had no end of trouble on the trip. *ḥna mṣafṛin u-l-mašakil ma-ḥeṣṛu-š bina.* --He gave us no end of trouble. *ma feḍḍa-š bina be-l-mašakil dyalu.*
odds and ends – *ḥwiyža* pl. *-t.* I still have some odds and ends to take care of. *bqaw-li ši-ḥwiyzat ma nfeḍḍi.*
to make (both) ends meet – *qadd ṭeṛf mɛa ṭeṛf.* He hardly earns enough to make both ends meet. *be-d-dreɛ baš ka-iqadd ṭeṛf mɛa ṭeṛf.*
to put an end to – *feḍḍa ifeḍḍi.* Can't you put an end to these squabbles? *waš ma-imken-lek tfeḍḍi had le-mdabza?*
to end – **1.** *feḍḍa ifeḍḍi.* He ended his speech with a quotation from the Koran. *feḍḍa l-xeṭba dyalu b-ʔaya de-l-qoṛʔan.* **2.** *tfeḍḍa.* Won't this gossip ever end? *was ġad itfeḍḍa had t-thedriz?* --When did the movie end? *fuq-aš tfeḍḍa l-film?*
endless – *ma-fih-š nihaya.*
to **endure** – *ṣbeṛ.* She endured the pain quietly. *ṣebṛet be-šwiya ɛla wžeɛha.*
enemy – *ɛdu* pl. *ɛedyan.*
**He's my worst enemy. *huwa demm snani.*
energy – *quwwa.* We need more electrical energy. *xeṣṣna kteṛ de-l-quwwa l-kehṛabiya.*
**He's full of energy. *huwa ḥeyy bezzaf.*
to **enforce** – *ṭebbeq.* They have never strictly enforced this law. *ɛemmeṛhom ma-ṭebbqu had l-qanun be-t-tedqiq.*
to **engage** – **1.** *xeddem.* We've just engaged a new maid. *ɛad xeddemna meṭɛellma ždida.* **2.** *ɛeṛben.* We engaged him for two concerts. *ɛeṛbennah l-žuž de-l-ḥeflat musiqiyin.* **3.** *dexxel ṛaṣu.* I don't engage in politics. *ma-ka-ndexxel-š ṛaṣi fe-s-siyasa.*
engaged – *mmellek.* How long have they been engaged? *šḥal hadi u-huma mmellkin?*
engagement – **1.** *miɛad* pl. *-at.* I have an engagement this evening. *ɛendi waḥed l-miɛad had le-ɛšiya.* **2.** *mlak.* She announced her engagement. *hiya ɛelmet b-le-mlak dyalha.*
engine – **1.** *muṭuṛ* pl. *-at.* You left the engine running. *xelliti l-muṭuṛ xeddam.* **2.** *makina* pl. *-t, mašina* pl. *-t.* The train has two engines. *had s-smandifiṛ ɛendu žuž de-l-makinat.*
engineer – **1.** *muhendis* pl. *-in.* I've asked the engineer to draw a new set of plans. *qolt l-l-muhendis iṣaweb ši-ṛsam ždad.* **2.** *ṣiyyag* (pl. *-a*) *l-qiṭaṛ.* The engineer was the only one hurt in the crash. *ṣiyyag l-qiṭaṛ b-weḥdu ttežṛeḥ fe-l-muṣiba.*
to engineer – *quwwed.* You engineered that affair rather well. *quwwedti dak-l-qaḍiya mezyan.*
engineering – *hendasa.*
English – **1.** *negliza, ingliziya.* He

speaks very good English. *ka-itkellem n-negliza mezyan bezzaf.* **2.** *neglizi.* That's an old English custom. *hadi Ɛada negliziya qdima.* --I'm English. *ana neglizi.*

Englishman - *neglizi.*

to **enjoy** - **1.** *ṣṭab.* He's enjoying life. *ka-iṣṭab l-ḥayat.* **2.** *žah ižih.* How did you enjoy the picture? *kif žak l-film?* **3.** *Ɛežbu.* Did you enjoy the swim? *waš Ɛezbek l-Ɛewm?* **He's enjoying excellent health. *huwa ṣeḥḥtu mezyana.* --Did you enjoy yourself at the party? *waš dazeṭ l-ḥefla mezyan?*

to **enlist** - *dxel, gaža igaži (f-).* He enlisted in the army two days ago. *hadi yumayn baš dxel l-l-žeyš.*

enormous - *kbir* pl. *kbaṛ (bezzaf).*

enormously - *bezzaf.* I liked the play enormously. *Ɛežbetni r-riwaya bezzaf.*

enough - *(lli) qadd, kafi.* Do you have enough money? *waš qadduk le-flus?* --Have you had enough to eat? *waš qaddettek l-makla?*

to be enough - *kfa ikfi.* Your answer isn't enough for me. *žwabek ma-kfani-š.* **He seemed glad enough to do it. *ban-li bin ṛšeq-lu idirha.* --Would you be good enough to hand me the paper? *medd-li ḷḷah ixellik l-žarida?* --Would you be kind enough to open the window? *waš imken-lek ḷḷah ixellik tḥell š-šeṛžem?*

to **enroll** - **1.** *qeyyed.* I'm going to enroll my son in first grade. *ġadi nqeyyed weldi fe-s-satta l-ibtidaʔiya.* **2.** *tqeyyed.* He's going to enroll in night school. *ġadi itqeyyed fe-ḍ-duṛus de-l-lil.*

to **enter** - **1.** *dxel.* Everyone rose when the judge entered. *kollhom weqfu men-lli l-ḥakem dxel.* --Enter the house by the rear door. *dxel le-ḍ-daṛ men l-bab ḷ-ḷuṛani.* **2.** *qeyyed, kteb.* Enter these names in the list. *qeyyed had s-smiyat fe-l-qayma.*

enterprise - *mešṛuƐ.* The enterprise was successful. *l-mešṛuƐ nžeḥ*

to **entertain** - **1.** *laha.* He entertained the guests with his amusing stories. *huwa laha ḍ-ḍyaf be-xṛafatu lli ka-iḍeḥḥku.* **2.** *qabel.* They entertain a great deal. *ka-iqablu bezzaf.*

entertainment - *fṛaža, tselya.* Who's going to provide the entertainment? *škun lli ġad iqabelna le-fṛaža?* **What do you do for entertainment around here? *kif-aš ka-dduwwzu l-weqt hna?*

enthusiasm - *ḥamasa.* He didn't show any enthusiasm. *ma-biyyen ḥetta ḥamasa.*

enthusiastic - *metḥemmes.* I'm quite enthusiastic about it. *ana metḥemmes bezzaf Ɛla dak š-ši.*

entire - *koll, gaƐ.* The entire amount has to be paid in cash. *ž-žemƐ kollu itxeḷḷeṣ Ɛel ṭ-ṭebla.*

entirely - **1.** *tamamen.* You're entirely right. *nta Ɛendek tamamen l-ḥeqq* or *Ɛendek l-ḥeqq t-tamm.* --The two are entirely different. *ž-žuž tamamen metxalfin.* **2.** He charged you entirely too much. *ḥsebha-lek bezzaf gaƐ.*

entrance - *dexla* pl. *-t.* Where is the entrance? *fayn hiya d-dexla?*

entry - *tesžil.* The last entry was five dollars. *t-tesžil t-tali kan xemsa de-ḍ-ḍulaṛ.*

envelope - *ġsa* pl. *-wat, ġešyan.* I need an envelope for this letter. *xeṣṣni ġša l-had le-bṛa.*

envy - *ḥsed.* He was green with envy. *huwa kan ka-imut b-le-ḥsed.* **You'll be the envy of all your friends. *ṣḥabek kollhom ġad iḥesduk.*

to envy - They envied him his success. *ḥesdu-lu n-nažaḥ dyalu.* **I envy you! *seƐdatek!*

epidemic - *meṛḍ sari.* An epidemic has broken out among the cattle. *waḥed l-meṛḍ sari wqeƐ Ɛend le-bgeṛ.*

Epsom salts - *melḥa Ɛeṛbiya.*

equal - *qedd-qedd.* Cut this bread into two equal parts. *qṭeƐ had l-xobz Ɛla žuž de-ṭ-ṭṛaf qedd-qedd.* **The two books are equally important. *dak le-ktub b-žuž Ɛendhom ahammiya weḥda.* --I liked his first play equally well. *Ɛežbetni riwayta l-luwwla qedd le-xṛa.*

to be equal to (something) - *qḍeṛ (idir).* I don't think I'm equal to that job. *ma-ban-li-š bin neqḍeṛ ndir had l-xedma.*

to equal - *qedd.* --The gains will never equal the losses. *r-rebḥ Ɛemmṛu ma-iqedd le-xṣeṛ.*

equality - *msawya.*

to **equip** - *rekkeb.* They've equipped the planes with the latest instruments. *rekkbu ṭ-ṭiyaṛat be-mwaƐen Ɛeṣṛiyin.*

to **erase** - **1.** *mḥa imḥi.* He erased the signature. *mḥa xeṭṭ l-yedd.* **2.** *mseḥ.* Will you please erase the board? *mseḥ ṣ-ṣebbuṛa Ɛafak.*

eraser - 1. *msaḥa* pl. *-t, guma* pl. *-t.* I bought two pencils and an eraser. *šrit žuž d-le-qluma u-msaḥa.* 2. *msaḥa* pl. *-t.* We need some chalk and an eraser. *xeṣṣna ši-tabašir u-msaḥa.*

errand - *sexṛa* pl. *-t, sxaṛi.* I have a few errands to do. *ʕendi ši-sexṛat ma neʕmel.*

error - 1. *ġaḷaṭ.* There must be some error. *la-bedd kayen ši-ġaḷaṭ.* 2. *ġeḷṭa* pl. *-t.* Did I make an error? *waš dert ši-ġeḷṭa?*

escape - *hṛib, heṛba* pl. *-t.* The prisoners' escape was cleverly planned. *le-hṛib d-le-msažen kan mneḍḍem mezyan.*
**We had a narrow escape. *felletnaha.*

to escape - 1. *hṛeb.* Two prisoners have escaped from the penitentiary. *žuž d-le-msažen heṛbu men l-ḥebs.* --The thief escaped. *l-xuwwan hṛeb.* --We escaped to France. *hṛebna le-fṛanṣa.* 2. *tlef-lu.* Her face is familiar but her name escapes me. *wežha ka-nʕeṛfu walayenni smiytha telfet-li.* --Nothing escapes her. *ma-ka-ttlef-lha ḥetta ḥaža.*

especially - *xuṣuṣen, be-l-xuṣuṣ.*

espionage - *tabiyyaʕet.*

essential - *ḍaṛuṛi.* Fresh vegetables are essential to good health. *l-xeḍṛa ṭ-ṭṛiya ḍaṛuṛiya le-ṣ-ṣeḥḥa.*

essentials - *l-muhimm.* You can learn the essentials in an hour. *imken-lek ttʕellem l-muhimm f-saʕa.*

to **establish** - 1. *ʔesses, qam iqum b-.* They established this firm in 1905. *ʔesssu had š-šarika f-sana tsʕeʕṭaš mya u-xemsa.* 2. *ʕmel.* He established a new record. *ʕmel ṛeqm qiyasi ždid.*

estate - *melk.* His entire estate went to his son. *l-melk dyalu kollu mša l-weldu.*

estimate - *teqdiṛ.* My estimate was pretty accurate. *t-teqdiṛ dyali kan ʕlayen ṣḥiḥ.*
**The painter made us an estimate. *ṣ-ṣebbaġ qeḍḍeṛ-lna t-taman.*

to estimate - *qeḍḍeṛ.* They estimated the flood damages at a million dollars. *l-muṣiba de-l-fiḍa qeḍḍṛuha b-melyun ḍuḷaṛ.*

eternal - *dayem.*

Ethiopia - *blad l-ḥabaša.*

Ethiopian - *ḥabaši* pl. *-yin, hel l-ḥabaša.*

Euphrates - *l-fuṛat.*

Europe - *uṛuḅḅa.*

European - *ṛumi, neṣṛani* (Christian). How can you tell that he's a European? *kif imken-lek teʕṛef bin huwa ṛumi?*
**Most European countries are thickly populated. *akteṛ boldan f-uṛubba fihom sokkan bezzaf.*

to **evade** - *tsellet men.* He evaded the question. *tsellet men l-ʔasʔila.*

to **evaporate** - *nšef, ṭaṛ iṭiṛ.* The alcohol has all evaporated. *l-alkuḷ kollu nšef.*

evaporated milk - *ḥlib d-le-ḥkak.*

even - 1. *zuži, zewži.* Two, four, and six are even numbers. *žuž, ṛebʕa u-setta huma ṛqam zužiyin.* 2. *waseʕ.* He has an even disposition. *huwa xaṭṛu waseʕ.* 3. *msawi, metfaḍi, qedd-qedd.* Now we are even. *daba ḥna msawyin.* 4. *ḥetta.* Even a moron can understand that. *ḥetta le-ḥmaṛ imken-lu ifhem had š-ši.*
**That's even better. *u-daba ʕad ḥsen.* --I have an even dozen left. *bqat-li tamamen ẓina.*

even so - *waxxa hakka, ṛeġma had š-ši.* Even so I can't agree with you. *waxxa hakka ma-imken-li-š nttafeq mʕak.*

even though - *waxxa.* Even though he succeeds in everything he's not satisfied. *waxxa ka-inžeḥ f-koll-ši ʕemmṛu ma-iqneʕ.*

not even - 1. *ma ... gaʕ.* I couldn't even see him. *ma-mken-li-š gaʕ nšufu.* 2. *ḥetta ... ma.* Not even he knows the truth. *ḥetta huwa ma-ka-yeʕṛef l-ḥaqiqa.*

to break even - *ža iži ʕel t-tmam.* He's just breaking even. *yaḷḷah ka-iži ʕel t-tmam.*

to get even with - *fdaha ifdiha f-.* Just wait, I'll get even with you! *tsenna, daba nefdiha fik!*

evening - *ʕšiya* pl. *-t.* The evenings here are cool. *le-ʕšiyat ka-ikunu bardin hna.* --Are they coming this evening? *waš ġad ižiw had le-ʕšiya?* --We take a walk every evening. *ka-ntmeššaw koll ʕšiya.*
**Good evening! *mse-l-xir!*

evenings - *f-le-ʕšiya.* Is this restaurant open evenings? *waš had l-meṭʕem ka-iḥell f-le-ʕšiya?*

evenly - 1. *msawi.* The paint isn't spread evenly. *had ṣ-ṣbaġa ma-meṭliya-š msawya.* 2. *metqadd.* Divide the apples evenly among you. *qṣem t-teffaḥ metqaddin.*

event - *ḥadita* pl. *ḥawadit.* It was the most important event of the year. *kan hadak ahemm ḥadita de-l-ʕam.*

in any event - *šnu-mma wqeƐ.* I'll be there in any event. *šnu-mma wqeƐ ġad nkun temma.*

in the event of - *ila wqeƐ ši ...* In the event of an accident, notify the police. *ila weqƐet ši-muṣiba Ɛlem š-šoṛṭa.*

ever - *Ɛemmeṛ* (plus pronoun endings). Have you ever been in the United States? *waš Ɛemmṛek mšiti l-ʔamirika?* --Who ever heard of such a thing! *škun lli Ɛemmṛu smeƐ men had š-ši!* --Haven't you ever been there? *waš Ɛemmṛek ma-žiti-š l-temma?*

ever since - *men ... u-.* Ever since the accident I've had pains in my leg. *men dak l-muṣiba w-ana mweƐƐet f-režli.*

hardly ever - *qlil fayn.* I hardly ever have a headache. *qlil fayn ka-ižini ḥṛiq ṛ-ṛaṣ.*

every - *koll.* He comes here every week. *ka-iži le-hna koll žemƐa.* --Give every child one. *Ɛṭi l-koll derri waḥed.* --I see him every day. *ka-nšufu koll nhaṛ.*

every now and then - *men meṛṛa l-meṛṛa, meṛṛa f-xṭa.* He takes a drink every now and then. *ka-yeƐmel ši-kwiyyes men meṛṛa l-meṛṛa.*

every one - *koll waḥed.* Every one of us received a pack of cigarettes. *Ɛṭaw l-koll waḥed menna bakit d-gaṛṛu.* --Every one of the children came. *ža koll waḥed men d-drari.*

every other day - *koll yumayn.* They have meat every other day. *ka-yaklu l-lḥem koll yumayn.*

every other week - *meṛṛa žmeƐtayn.* I see him every other week. *ka-nšufu meṛṛa fe-žmeƐtayn.*

every other month - *meṛṛa f-šehṛayn.* He comes to see us about every other month. *ka-izuṛna meṛṛa f-šehṛayn.*

every time - *fuq-emma.* It rains every time we want to go out. *ka-ṭṭiḥ š-šta fuq-emma ka-nebġiw nxeṛžu.*

everybody - *koll waḥed.* Everybody has to do his duty. *koll waḥed xeṣṣu yeƐmel šġalu.* --Everybody laughed. *koll waḥed ḍḥek.*

everybody else - *le-xṛin.* It's all right with me if it's all right with everybody else. *ana mettafeq ila kanu mettafqin le-xṛin.*

everything - **1.** *koll-ši.* He's mixed up everything. *xeṛbeq koll-ši.* **2.** *lli.* I'll do everything that's necessary. *ġadi neƐmel lli ḍaṛuṛi.*

everywhere - *f-koll muḍeƐ.* I've looked everywhere for that book. *qellebt f-koll muḍeƐ Ɛla had le-ktab.*

evidence - *ḥužža* pl. *-t, ḥužaž.* He was acquitted for lack of evidence. *ṭelquh Ɛla sabab qellt l-ḥužža.*

evident - *ḍaheṛ.* It was quite evident that she was sick. *ḍaheṛ Ɛliha bin kanet mṛiḍa.*

evil - *bla.* He chose the lesser evil. *xteṛ le-bla l-hiyyen.*

exact - *ṣḥiḥ* pl. *ṣḥaḥ.* Is this an exact copy? *waš had n-nesxa ṣḥiḥa?*

exactly - *tamamen.* That's exactly like the other one. *hadi tamamen bḥal le-xṛa.*

**That wasn't exactly nice of you. *ma-Ɛmeltiha-š mezyan.*

to **exaggerate** - *zad izid f-.* You're exaggerating as usual. *kama l-Ɛada ka-dzid fih.*

exaggeration - *zyada.* There's too much exaggeration in that story. *kayna zyada bezzaf f-dak le-xṛafa.*

examination - **1.** *imtiḥan* pl. *-at.* The examination was easy. *l-imtiḥan kan sahel.* **2.** *teqlab.* What did the examination show? *šnu ban fe-t-teqlab?* **3.** *(i)stinṭaq.* The examination of the witnesses lasted two hours. *ṭal l-istinṭaq de-š-šwahed saƐtayn.*

to **examine** - *qelleb.* The doctor examined me thoroughly. *qellebni ṭ-ṭbib men l-fuq ḥetta l-teḥt.* --I'm here to examine the books. *ana hna baš nqelleb le-ktuba.*

example - *mital.*

for example - *matalen.*

**We must make an example of this man. *xeṣṣna b-had ṛ-ražel nƐellmu n-nas.*

excavation - *ḥfir,* (action); *ḥefṛa* pl. *-t, ḥfaṛi* (hole).

excellent - *moƐtabaṛ.* This soup is excellent. *had ṣ-ṣubba moƐtabaṛa.*

except - *men ġir.* Everybody believed it except him. *koll waḥed taq b-dak-š-ši men ġir huwa.*

except for - *men ġir.* I like the book except for one chapter. *Ɛžebni le-ktab men ġir feṣl waḥed.*

exchange - *tebdil.* The Red Cross arranges for the exchange of prisoners. *ṣ-ṣalib le-ḥmeṛ ka-iḍebbeṛ Ɛla tebdil le-msažen.*

rate of exchange - *taman ṣ-ṣeṛf.* What's the rate of exchange today? *šnu huwa taman ṣ-ṣeṛf l-yum?*

stock exchange - *suq ṣ-ṣeṛf, burṣa.*

to exchange - *beddel.* I want to exchange this book for another one. *bġit nbeddel had le-ktab b-waḥed axoṛ.*

**I've been exchanging ideas with your friend. *ferreqt l-lġa mɛa ṣaḥbek.* *ṣaḥbek.*

to **excite** - **1.** *dda iddi l-ɛeql l-.* That was an exciting movie. *had l-film dda-li ɛeqli.* **2.** *hiyyež.* I'm so excited! *ana mhiyyež!*

**I'm not too excited about it. *ma-ka-ihemmni-š bezzaf.*

to get excited - *thiyyež.* Don't get excited. *ma-tthiyyež-š.*

excitement - *haraž.* Why the excitement? *ɛlaš dak l-haraž?*

exclusive - *xaṣṣ.* We have exclusive rights to this invention. *ɛendna ḥuquq xaṣṣa f-had le-xtiraɛ.* --This is quite an exclusive club. *hada nadi xaṣṣ.*

excuse - *ɛder* pl. *ɛdar.* That's no excuse! *hada ma-ši ɛder!*

to excuse - *smeḥ-l-.* Please excuse my bad Arabic. *smeḥ-li ɛafak l-ɛerbiya le-qbiḥa dyali.* --He was excused for the afternoon because of a headache. *semḥu-lu ɛel le-ɛšiya ɛla qibal kan ɛendu wžiɛ r-raṣ.* --Excuse me, please! *smeḥ-li ɛafak!*

to **execute** - **1.** *qtel.* The murderer was executed this morning. *qetlu l-qatel f-had ṣ-ṣbaḥ.* **2.** *neffed.* Have you executed my order yet? *waš neffedti š-šġal lli ɛṭitek wella ma-zal?*

execution - *qtila.*

exercise - **1.** *temrin.* Exercise ten is very difficult. *t-temrin l-ɛašer waɛer bezzaf.* **2.** *tedrab, tedrib.* I need more exercise. *xeṣṣni kter de-t-tedrab.*

to exercise - *dderreb.* You have to exercise every morning. *xeṣṣek tedderreb koll ṣbaḥ.*

exhausted - *mehluk.* I was completely exhausted after that long trip. *ana kont mehluk men beɛd had ṣ-ṣafar ṭ-ṭwil.*

exhibit - *fraža* pl. *-t.* Have you seen the exhibit? *waš šefti le-fraža?*

to exhibit - *werra.* His wife loves to exhibit her gold jewelry. *mratu ka-tebġi twerri le-qšawes de-d-dheb dyalha.*

exhibition - *meɛriḍ.*

exile - **1.** *nefyan* (action, state). **2.** *menfi* (person).

to **exist** - **1.** *kan ikun.* That exists only in your imagination. *had š-ši ma-kayen ġir fe-t-texyil dyalek.* --Such a thing doesn't exist. *had l-ḥaža ma-kayna-š.* **2.** *ɛas iɛiš.* How does he manage to exist on so little? *kif-aš ka-iḍebber iɛiš ġir b-had le-flus?*

**He doesn't exist, as far as I'm concerned. *ila žiti ɛliya, ma-ka-iswa ɛendi ḥetta ḥaža.*

existence - *ḥayat.* He's leading a miserable existence. *ɛayeš ḥayat baʔisa.*

**He's not even aware of my existence. *ma-šaɛer-š biya be-l-koll kayen.* --This business has been in existence for fifty years. *hadi xemsin ɛam u-had š-šarika xeddama.*

exit - *bab l-xuruž.* There's the exit. *ha bab l-xuruž.*

**He made a hasty exit. *xrež be-z-zerba.*

to expect - **1.** *tsenna.* I expect him at three o'clock. *ka-ntsennah iži fe-t-tlata.* **2.** *ɛewwel ɛla.* Does he expect a tip? *waš ka-iɛewwel ɛla ši-ižara.*

expectation - *intiḍar.* Contrary to my expectation, the experiment turned out well. *b-xalaf l-intiḍar dyali, t-težriba dazet mezyana.*

expedition - *beɛta* pl. *-t; ḥemla* pl. *-t* (military).

to **expel** - *dḥa idḥi.* The boy was expelled from school. *dḥaw l-weld men l-medraṣa.*

expense - *ṣayer* pl. *ṣwayer.* The expense is too much. *had ṣ-ṣayer bezzaf.*

at the expense - *b-meṣruf.* He made the trip at his company's expense. *ṣafer b-meṣruf š-šarika.*

expensive - *ġali.* This apartment is too expensive. *had s-sokna ġalya bezzaf.*

experience - *težriba* pl. *-t.* Have you any experience in such matters? *waš ɛendek ši-težribat f-had l-ʔumur?* --I had a strange experience last night. *kanet ɛendi težriba ġriba l-bareḥ fe-l-lil.*

to experience - *žerreb.* I never experienced anything like it. *ɛemmri ma-žerrebt ši-ḥaža bḥal hadi.*

experiment - *težriba* pl. *-t.* The experiment was successful. *had t-težriba nežḥet.*

to experiment - *žerreb.* I experimented with new colors. *žerrebt b-ʔalwan ždad.*

expert - **1.** *mxeṣṣeṣ.* The experts declared the document to be a forgery. *le-mxeṣṣṣin qal bin r-rṣem meṣnuɛ.* --We need an expert mechanic. *xeṣṣna makaniki mxeṣṣeṣ.* **2.** *d-le-mɛellmin.* I need some expert advice. *xeṣṣni ši-naṣiḥa d-le-mɛellmin.*

to **expire** - *fat ifut l-ʔažal d-.* His visa expired last week. *fat l-ʔažal de-l-biza dyalu ž-žemƐa lli fatet.*
to **explain** - *fesser.*
explanation - *tefsira.*
to **explode** - *tferge*Ɛ. The bomb didn't explode. *l-qenbula ma-tfergeƐ-š.*
exploit - *mziya* pl. *-t.* He never stops talking about his exploits. *huwa dima ka-iftaxeṛ b-le-mziyat dyalu.*
**He exploits his employees. *ka-ixeddem l-Ɛommala dyalu kif le-Ɛbid.*
to **explore** - **1.** *qelleb.* Let's explore that island. *yaḷḷah nqellbu l-žazira.* **2.** *bḥet.* We explored all the possibilities. *bḥetna l-imkaniyat kollhom.*
explosion - *tfeṛgiƐa* pl. *-t* coll. *tfeṛgiƐ.*
export - *ṣaḍiṛa* pl. *-t, biƐ l-l-xariž.* The country has no exports. *had le-blad ma-Ɛendha biƐ l-l-xariž.*
to export - *baƐ ibiƐ l-l-xariž.* Germany exports cameras. *aḷmanya ka-tbiƐ l-l-xariž makinat de-teṣwiṛ.*
to **expose** - **1.** *xella fe-ḍ-ḍu.* How long did you expose the film? *šḥal xelliti l-film fe-ḍ-ḍu?* **2.** *biyyen.* He was exposed as a spy. *biyynu bin huwa xaʔin.*
**He's exposed to constant danger. *huwa dima f-ḥala xaṭiṛa.*
express - **1.** *sariƐ.* Is the next train an express? *waš l-qiṭaṛ ž-žay sariƐ?* **2.** *waḍeḥ.* It was his express wish. *kan hadak ṭaḷabu l-waḍeḥ.*
(by) express - *mƐežžel.* We're sending your trunk by express. *ġad nṣifṭu-lek ṣ-ṣenḍuq dyalek mƐežžel.*
to express - **1.** *Ɛebbeṛ Ɛla.* He expressed his opinion freely. *Ɛebbeṛ Ɛel l-fikra dyalu be-ṣ-ṣaṛaḥa.* **2.** *dkeṛ.* Did he express any wish? *waš dkeṛ ši-muṛaḍ?*
expression - *Ɛibaṛa* pl. *-t.* There's no better expression for it. *ma-kayna ḥetta Ɛibaṛa ḥsen mennha.*
extension - **1.** *ʔažal.* He gave me another week's extension. *Ɛṭani ʔažaḷ axoṛ d-žemƐa.* **2.** *tusiƐ.* The extension to our house will soon be finished. *t-tusiƐ dyal ḍaṛna ġadi itfeḍḍa men daba šwiya.*
extensive - *waseƐ.*
extent - *ḥedd.* To a certain extent he is responsible for the disaster. *l-waḥed l-ḥedd huwa sabab l-musiba.*
extra - *zayed.* Do you have a few extra pencils? *waš Ɛendkom ši-qluma zaydin?* --Do I get extra pay for this job? *waš ġad yeƐṭiwni ižaṛa zayda l-had l-xedma?*
extraordinary - *Ɛžib* pl. *Ɛžab.* Only an extraordinary woman could accomplish all that. *ġir le-mṛa lli Ɛžiba imken-lha ddir had š-ši kollu.*
extreme - *šdid* pl. *šdad.* We had to resort to extreme measures. *tlezzemna naxdu tadabir šdida.*
**Their house is at the extreme end of the island. *ḍaṛhom f-qaƐ ž-žazira.*
extremely - *bezzaf (Ɛad).* This news is extremely sad. *had le-xbaṛ ḥzin bezzaf Ɛad.*
eye - *Ɛeyn* (f.) pl. *Ɛeynin (Ɛeyni-* before pronoun endings), *Ɛyun.* Her eyes are blue. *Ɛeyniha ẓuṛeq.* --I've had my eye on that for a long time. *šḥal hadi u-Ɛeyni f-dak š-ši.* --The eye of this needle is too small *l-Ɛeyn d-had l-ibra ṣġiṛa bezzaf.* --I never laid eyes on him. *Ɛemmeṛ Ɛeyniya ma-šafuh.*
**We just don't see eye to eye. *Ɛemmeṛna ma-ka-nttafqu.*
black eye - *Ɛeyn mneffxa.* Where did you get that black eye? *Ɛlaš Ɛeynek mneffxa?*
to keep an eye on - *redd l-bal l-.* Keep an eye on the children while I'm out. *redd l-bal le-d-drari melli nexṛož.*
to eye - *beḷḷeẓ Ɛeynu f-.* He eyed the chocolate longingly. *beḷḷeẓ Ɛeynu fe-š-šeklaṭ be-š-šehwa.*
eyebrow - *ḥažeb* pl. *ḥwažeb.*
eye glasses - *nḍaḍeṛ* (pl.).
eyelash - *šfeṛ* pl. *šfaṛ.*
eyelid - *žfen* pl. *žfan.*

F

fabric - *tub* pl. *twab.* What kind of fabric is this shirt made of? *be-š-men tub menṣuba had l-qamiža?*
face - **1.** *wžeh, wežh* pl. *wžuh; sifa* pl. *-t, syuf.* I'd tell him that right to his face. *nqulha-lu*

f-wežhu. --He tripped and fell on his face. *Ɛteṛ u-ṭaḥ Ɛla wežhu.* --She slammed the door in my face. *šeddet-li l-bab Ɛla wežhi.* **2.** *kemmara* pl. *kmamer.* He has a horrible face. *Ɛendu waḥed l-kemmara ka-texleƐ.*

face to face - 1. *metqablin.* They were sitting face to face. *kanu galsin metqablin.* **2.** *wžeh le-wžeh.* They discussed it face to face. *tkellmu Ɛliha wžeh le-wžeh.*

at face value - *men l-meḍheṛ.* She takes everything at face value. *koll ḥaža ka-tqeḍḍeṛha men l-meḍheṛ dyalha.*

on the face of it - *Ɛla ma ka-iḍheṛ.* On the face of it, it looks like a good idea. *Ɛla ma ka-iḍheṛ hadi fekra mezyana.*

in the face of danger - *qbalt l-xaṭaṛ.*

to lose face - *tḥeššem, tbehdel.*

to make (cause to) lose face - *ḥeššem, behdel b-.*

to make faces - *Ɛewwež wežhu.* Stop making faces. *xlaṣ u-ma-tƐewwež wežhek.*

to save face - *menneƐ ṛaṣu men t-tbehdila.*

to show one's face - *ḍehheṛ wežhu, biyyen wežhu.* He doesn't dare show his face around here again. *ma-ka-iqḍeṛ-š Ɛawed ibiyyen wežhu hna.*

to face - 1. *Ɛṭa yeƐṭi wežhu.* Face the wall! *Ɛṭi wežhek l-l-ḥiṭ!* **2.** *qabel.* My window faces south. *š-šeṛžem dyali mqabel l-žanub.* **3.** *wažeh, qabel.* Face the facts! *wažeh l-waqiƐ!* --I can't face him. *ma-neqḍeṛ-š nwažhu.*

face-powder - *buṛbu d-le-wžeh.*

facing - *mqabel.* He lives in the house facing the theater. *saken fe-ḍ-ḍaṛ lli mqabla s-sinima.*

fact - *waqiƐa* pl. *waqayeƐ, ḥaqiqa* pl. *ḥaqaʔeq.*

in fact - *fe-l-ḥaqiqa, fe-l-waqiƐ.*

factor - *ʔaṣel* pl. *ʔuṣul; sabab* pl. *ʔasbab.* His perseverance was the main factor of his success. *t-tbat dyalu kan ʔahemm sabab de-n-nažaḥ dyalu.*

factory - *meƐmel* pl. *maƐamil.*

to **fade - 1.** *kšef.* My socks faded in the wash. *tqašri kešfu fe-t-teṣbin.* **2.** *dbal.* These roses faded very quickly. *had l-weṛḍ deġya deġya dbal.*

to fade away - *ġab iġib šwiya be-šwiya.* The music faded away. *l-musiqa ġabet šwiya be-šwiya.*

to **fail - 1.** *ma-nžeḥ-š, xṣeṛ, xfeq.* His experiment failed. *t-težriba dyalu ma-nežḥet-š.* --All our efforts failed. *mežhudatna kollha xefqet.* **2.** *sqeṭ.* Five students failed the exam. *xemsa de-ṭ-ṭoḷḅa seqṭu f-le-mtiḥan.* **3.** *qlal, mša imši Ɛlih.* His eyesight is failing. *n-nḍeṛ dyalu ka-iqlal.* **4.** *ḍaƐ iḍiƐ.* The crops failed last year. *l-Ɛam lli fat ṣ-ṣaba ḍaƐet.* **5.** *smeḥ f-, daz iduz, xella.* I won't fail you. *ma-nesmeḥ-š fik* or *ma-nduzek-š.* **6.** *keddeb.* If my eyes don't fail me, it's him. *ila ma-keddbuni-š Ɛeyniya ṛah huwa hadak.* **7.** *Ɛendak ma, wiyyak ma.* Don't fail to go there. *Ɛendak ma-temši-š l-temma.*

without fail - *bla šekk.* I'll be there without fail. *bla šekk ġad nkun temma.*

failure - *suquṭ.* His failure in the exam made him sad. *s-suquṭ dyalu f-le-mtiḥan mṭiyyṛu-lu.*

faint - 1. *sexfan.* I feel faint. *ka-nḥess b-ṛaṣi sexfan.* **2.** *xfif.* pl. *xfaf.* I heard a faint noise. *smeƐt ši-ḥess xfif.*

**She lay in a dead faint. *kanet ġayba Ɛla Ɛqelha.* --I haven't the faintest idea. *ma-Ɛendi ḥetta fikra.* --There's only a faint hope left. *baqi ġir šwiya de-l-ʔamal.*

to faint - *sxef.* She fainted from fright. *sexfet be-l-xelƐa.*

fair - 1. *ḥeqq.* That wouldn't be fair! *ma-ši ḥeqq hadak.* **2.** *mnaseb, meƐqul.* That's a fair price. *had t-taman taman meƐqul.* **3.** *ẓƐeṛ* pl. *ẓuƐeṛ.* She has blue eyes and fair hair. *Ɛendha Ɛeynin ẓuṛeq u-šƐeṛ ẓƐeṛ.* **4.** *Ɛla qedd l-ḥal.* The work is only fair. *l-xedma Ɛla qedd l-ḥal.*

faith - 1. *iman, tiqa.* Do you have faith in God? *waš Ɛendek l-iman fe-ḷḷah?* --I lost faith in him. *ḍaƐet t-tiqa dyali fih.* **2.** *din* pl. *diyanat, dyun.* I don't know what his faith is. *ma-ka-neƐṛef-š šnu huwa d-din dyalu.*

to have faith in (God) - *amen be-ḷḷah, taq itiq fe-ḷḷah.*

to have faith in (someone) - *taq itiq b-.*

faithful - *xaleṣ, muxliṣ.* He's faithful to his wife. *huwa ṛažel xaleṣ le-mṛatu.* --She's very faithful in her work. *hiya muxliṣa fe-l-xedma dyalha.*

fake - 1. *mẓuwweṛ, ma-ši ḥaqiqi.* That picture is a fake. *dak t-teṣwiṛa* *mzuwwra.* **2.** *šharaṭ* pl. *šharṭiya.* He's not a real doctor, he's a fake. *ma-huwa-ši ṭbib ḥaqiqi, huwa ġir šharaṭ.*

to fake - 1. *zuwwer.* He faked the passport. *zuwwer l-žawaz.* **2.** *dar idir b-nefsu, dar idir b-ṛaṣu, dar idir b-ṛuḥu, Ɛmel messu.* I think you're just faking that you're tired. *ka-nḍenn ġir ka-ddir b-ṛaṣek Ɛeyyan.*

to fake poverty - *tmesken.*

to fake illness - *tmeṛṛeḍ.*

fall - 1. *ṭiḥa* pl. *-t.* He hasn't recovered from his fall yet. *ma-zal ma-bṛa-š men ṭ-ṭiḥa dyalu.* **2.** *xrif.* I'll be back next fall. *ġad neṛžeƐ le-xrif ž-žay.*

to fall - *ṭaḥ iṭiḥ.* He fell from the ladder. *ṭaḥ men s-sellum.* --He fell down the stairs. *ṭaḥ fe-ḍ-ḍruž.*

to fall apart - *ṭaḥ iṭiḥ be-ṭ-ṭraf.* The chair is falling apart. *š-šilya ka-ṭṭiḥ be-ṭ-ṭraf.*

to fall asleep - *nƐes, ṭaḥ iṭiḥ be-n-nƐas.* I fell asleep. *ṭeḥt be-n-nƐas.*

to fall back on - *ttkel Ɛla.* We can always fall back on our savings. *imken-lna daymen ntteklu Ɛel le-flus lli wefferna.*

to fall behind - *tʔexxeṛ, twexxeṛ.* We fell behind in the rent. *tʔexxeṛna b-le-kra.* --He fell behind the rest of them. *twexxeṛ muṛahom.*

to fall in love - *Ɛšeq.* She fell in love with him. *Ɛešqettu.*

to fall off - *qlal.* Profits have been falling off lately. *ṛ-ṛbeḥ ka-iqlal had l-iyam.*

to fall on - *ža iži, kan ikun.* New Year's falls on a Monday this year. *ṛaṣ l-Ɛam ġad iži n-nhaṛ t-tnin had l-Ɛam.*

to fall out - 1. *ṭaḥ iṭiḥ.* All his hair fell out. *šeƐṛu kollu ṭaḥ.* **2.** *txaṣem.* They've fallen out with each other since she wrecked the car. *txaṣmu beƐḍiyathom men beƐd-ma weqƐet-lha l-ḥadita be-s-siyaṛa.*

fallen arches - *režlin mgeṛṛṣin, režlin mbeššṭin.*

false - *ma-ši ṣḥiḥ* pl. *ma-si ṣḥaḥ.* Is this true or false? *waš had š-ši ṣḥiḥ wella la?*

false teeth - *snan ṛumiyin.*

familiar - 1. *metsanes.* I'm not familiar with that. *ana ma-metsanes-ši b-dak š-ši.* **2.** *ma-ši beṛṛani.* You have a familiar face. *wežhek ma-ši beṛṛani Ɛliya.*

to get familiar with - *ḍṣeṛ Ɛla.* Don't get too familiar! *ma-ḍḍšeṛ-š!*

to become familiar with - *tsanes b-, walef b-.*

family - *Ɛaʔila* pl. *-t.*

famine - *qeḥṭ, mžaƐa* pl. *-t.*

famous - *mešhuṛ.*

fan - 1. *ṛiyyaḥa* pl. *-t.* Turn on the fan. *ḍuwweṛ ṛ-ṛiyyaḥa.* **2.** *meṛweḥ* pl. *mṛaweḥ.* She has a fan from Spain. *Ɛendha meṛweḥ men ṣbanya.*

to fan - *ṛuwweḥ.* Fan yourself with the newspaper. *ṛuwweḥ ṛaṣek be-l-žarida.*

fancy - 1. *ṛšuq de-s-saƐa.* It's just a passing fancy with her. *hadak ġir ṛ-ṛšuq dyalha de-s-saƐa.* **2.** *de-š-šiki.* She doesn't like fancy clothes. *ma-ka-tebġi-š le-ḥwayež de-š-šiki.* **3.** *mšiyyek.* Don't you look fancy! *ka-ḍḍheṛ mšiyyek bezzaf!*

far - 1. *bƐid* pl. *bƐad.* People came from far and near. *n-nas žaw men qrib u-men bƐid.* **2.** *bezzaf.* That's not far wrong. *ma-fih-š l-ġalaṭ bezzaf.*

far be it - *ḥaša.* Far be it from me to criticize you. *ḥaša ḥetta nlaḥeḍ Ɛlik.*

to go far - 1. *tbeƐƐed.* Don't go far, children! *ma-tbeƐƐdu-š a d-drari!* **2.** *nžeḥ bezzaf.* He'll go far in this profession. *ġad inžeḥ bezzaf f-had l-mehna.*

to carry things too far - *zad izid fih, bessel.* At times he carries things too far. *beƐḍ l-meṛṛat ka-izid fih.*

far away - *bƐid* pl. *bƐad.* Is he far away? *was huwa bƐid?*

far off - *bƐid bezzaf.* The wedding is not far off. *z-zwaž ma-bƐid-š bezzaf.*

as far as - 1. *ḥetta l-.* We walked as far as the gate. *mšina ḥetta l-l-bab.* **2.** *Ɛla boƐd.* As far as you could see, everything was covered with snow. *Ɛla boƐd n-nḍeṛ kan t-telž mgeṭṭi koll-ši.* **3.** *Ɛla-ma.* As far as I know he's still alive. *Ɛla-ma ka-neƐṛef huwa baqi Ɛayeš.*

**The idea is good, as far as it goes. *hadi fekra mezyana, be-l-ḥeqq ma-ka-tḥell-š l-moškila kollha.*

as far as I'm concerned, etc. - *ila žiti Ɛliya,* etc. As far as he's concerned it's all right. *ila žiti Ɛlih huwa qabel.*

by far - *bezzaf Ɛad.* He is by far the most famous man in town. *huwa mešhuṛ kteṛ men koll waḥed f-*

f-had le-blad u-bezzaf ɛad.

few and far between - *qlal bezzaf ɛad.* Honest people are few and far between. *n-nas lli fihom l-aman qlal bezzaf ɛad.*

on the far side - *ɛel ž-žiha le-x̂ra.* Our house is on the far side of the river. *ḍarna žat ɛel ž-žiha le-x̂ra de-l-wad.*

so far - *ḥetta l-daba.* So far you've been pretty lucky. *ḥetta l-daba kan ɛendek z-zher bezzaf.*

Far East - *š-šerq l-ʔeqṣa.*

farewell party - *ḥefla de-l-wadaɛ* pl. *-t de-l-wadaɛ.*

far-fetched - *bɛid ɛel ḍ-ḍenn.* That's a bit far-fetched. *had š-ši bɛid ɛel ḍ-ḍenn ši-šwiya.*

farm - *ɛzib* pl. *ɛzayeb, firma* pl. *-t.*

farm hand - *xeddam d-le-ɛzib* pl. *xeddama d-le-ɛzib.*

farming - *flaḥa.* There isn't much farming in this region. *ma-kayna-š le-flaḥa bezzaf f-had ž-žiha. ž-žiha.*

to fascinate - *bhed.* The entire audience was fascinated by his story. *le-xṛafa dyalu behdet ž-žmaɛa kollha.*

fascinating - *ɛažib.* This is a fascinating book. *had le-ktab ɛažib.*

fashion - *muḍa* pl. *-t.* Green has gone out of fashion. *l-lun le-xḍeṛ ma-bqa-š muḍa.*

**She keeps house, after a fashion. *ka-theḷḷa f-ḍaṛha f-waḥed š-škel mɛaweṭ u-kan.*

fashionable - *muḍa, fe-l-muḍa.*

fast - **1.** *ṣyam.* One of the five pillars of Islam is the Fast. *ṣ-ṣyam huwa waḥed men l-xemsa de-r-rkayez lli ka-ittebna ɛlihom l-ʔislam.* **2.** *be-z-zerba.* Don't talk so fast. *ma-tehḍeṛ-š be-z-zerba.* **3.** *sriɛ* pl. *-in.* He has a fast car. *ɛendu siyaṛa sriɛa.* **4.** *aṣili.* Are these colors fast? *waš had ṣ-ṣbaġa aṣiliya?*

**My watch is ten minutes fast. *maganti fiha ɛešṛa de-d-dqayeq de-l-xeffa.* --He's fast asleep. *nɛasu tqil.*

fast company - *nas de-r-ršuq.* He travels in fast company. *ka-idžemmeɛ mɛa n-nas de-r-ršuq.*

to go fast - *sreɛ, žra ižri.* His new car will go very fast. *ṭumubiltu ž-ždida ka-tesreɛ bezzaf.*

to fast - *ṣam iṣum.*

to **fasten** - *ɛqed.*

fat - **1.** *šḥem* pl. *šeḥmat.* This meat has too much fat. *had l-lḥem fih šḥem bezzaf.* **2.** *smin* pl. *sman.* The woman is too fat. *had le-mṛa smina bezzaf.*

to get fat - *sman.* He's gotten fat this year. *sman had l-ɛam.*

fatal - **1.** *(lli) ka-iqtel, qatel, de-l-mut.* He received a fatal blow. *xda deqqa de-l-mut.* **2.** *muhlik, (lli) ka-ihlek, de-l-halak.* That was a fatal mistake. *kanet l-ġeḷṭa muhlika.*

fate - *l-mektab, l-mektub.*

father - *bu, ḅḅa.*

faucet - *ɛenbub* pl. *ɛnabeb, bezbuz* pl. *bzabez.* The faucet is dripping. *l-ɛenbub ka-iqeṭṭeṛ.*

fault - **1.** *ɛib* pl. *ɛyub.* We all have our faults. *koll waḥed fina ɛendu ɛyubu* or *ḥetta zin ma-xṭatu lula.* **2.** *ġalaṭ* pl. *ġlaṭi, ġeḷṭaṭ.* It's not his fault. *ma-ši l-ġalaṭ dyalu.*

to find fault - *laḥeḍ.* You're always finding fault. *daymen ka-tlaḥeḍ.*

faultless - *ṣḥiḥ* pl. *ṣḥaḥ, ma-fih ḥetta ġeḷṭa.*

faulty - *ɛayeb.*

fava bean - *fula* pl. *-t,* coll. *ful.*

favor - **1.** *mziya* pl. *-t.* I want to ask you a favor. *ḥebbit nṭḷeb mennek waḥed le-mziya.* **2.** *xir.* Don't do me any favors! *ma-ddir fiya ḥetta ši-xir!* or *xelli xirek f-ḍaṛek!*

to be in favor of - *mal imil l-.* I'm in favor of this party. *ana ka-nmil l-had l-ḥizeb.*

in one's favor - *men žiht-.* She spoke in my favor at the trial. *žat men žihti fe-l-muḥakama.*

to speak in one's favor - *škeṛ, tna itni ɛla.* She spoke to the boss in my favor. *šekṛetni l-le-mɛellem.* --That speaks in his favor. *had š-ši ka-itni ɛlih.*

to favor - **1.** *ža iži men žiht-.* He favors the youngest child. *ka-iži men žiht l-weld ṣ-ṣġiṛ.* **2.** *feḍḍel.* I favor black horses. *ka-nfeḍḍel l-xil l-kuḥel.*

favorable - *mnaseb.* He bought the house on very favorable terms. *šra ḍ-ḍaṛ b-taman mnaseb.*

favorably - *b-le-ɛtina.* The play was favorably received. *steqblu t-temtil b-le-ɛtina.*

fear - *xuf.* Your fears are unfounded. *l-xuf dyalek ma-ɛendu meɛna.* --He turned pale with fear. *ṛžeɛ ṣfeṛ be-l-xuf.*

for fear of - *ɛla wedd xaf ixaf.*

He took a taxi for fear of missing the train. *xda ṭaksi ʕla wedd xaf l-mašina temši ʕlih.*
to fear - *xaf ixaf.* You have nothing to fear. *ma-ʕendek-š mn-aš txaf.*
fearful - **1.** *xayef.* Mother is so fearful about my health. *m̃m̃i xayfa bezzaf ʕla ṣeḥḥti.* **2.** *(lli) ka-ixewwef.* He was a huge, fearful man. *kan ṛažel ṭwil u-ka-ixewwef.*
fearfully - *bla qyas, bezzaf ʕad.* I was fearfully seasick on the boat. *kont mṛiḍ bla qyas fe-l-babbuṛ.*
feast - *zerda* pl. *-t, zradi; ʕid* pl. *ʕyad.*
feather - *riša* pl. *-t* coll. *riš.*
feature - **1.** *ḥeṛf* pl. *ḥṛuf.* He has pleasant features. *ʕendu ḥṛuf mezyanin.* **2.** *xeṣṣiṣa* pl. *-t.* A feature of capitalism is free trade. *men xeṣṣiṣat ṛ-ṛaṣmaliya ḥoṛṛiyt t-tižaṛa.*
February - *febṛayer, ibṛayer.*
fee - *xḷaṣ* pl. *-at.* How much was the fee? *šḥal kan le-xḷaṣ?*
feeble - *ḍʕif* pl. *ḍʕaf.*
feed - *makla* pl. *-t.* Have you bought the feed for the chickens? *waš šriti l-makla le-d-džaž?*
to feed - *wekkel.* She's feeding the chickens. *ka-twekkel d-džaž.*
to be fed up with - *ʕya yeʕya, šbeʕ, ṭḷeʕ f-ṛaṣu.* I'm fed up with this whole business. *ana ʕyit men had š-ši* or *had š-ši kollu ṭaḷeʕ-li f-ṛaṣi.*
to **feel** - **1.** *qelleb.* The doctor felt my pulse. *ṭ-ṭbib qelleb n-neḥṭ dyali.* **2.** *ḥess b-.* He felt a strange hand on his shoulder. *ḥess b-ši-yedd ʕla ketfu.* --He doesn't feel well. *ma-ka-iḥess-š b-ṛaṣu la-bas.* **3.** *ḍenn, ḥess.* I feel she doesn't like me. *ka-nḥess biha ma-ka-tebġini-š.*
**We feel his loss keenly. *l-mut dyalu xellatha fina.* --I'll feel him out and let you know. *ġad nšuf šnu teḥt ṛaṣu u-nqul-lek.*
to feel about - *ḍenn f-.* How do you feel about this? *š-ka-ḍḍenn f-had š-ši?*
to feel for - *tʔessef ʕla, ʕezza.* I really feel for you. *ka-ntʔessef ʕlik bezzaf.*
to feel like - **1.** *bġa ibġi.* I feel like a cold drink. *baġi nešṛeb ši-ḥaža barda.* --I feel like dancing. *baġi nešṭeḥ.* **2.** *ḥess b-ṛaṣu bḥal.* I feel like a fool. *ka-nḥess b-ṛaṣi bḥal le-ḥmeq.*
to feel one's way - *desses.* He felt his way to the window. *desses ʕel ṭ-ṭṛiq le-š-šeṛžem.*
to feel up to - *ḥess b-qabiliya, ʕendu l-qabiliya.* I don't feel up to it right now. *ma-ʕendi-š l-qabiliya l-had š-ši daba.*
to get (used to) the feel of - *tsanes.* I haven't got the feel of the car yet. *ma-zal ma-tsanest-š be-ṭ-ṭumubil.*
feeling - *ʕaṭifa* pl. *ʕawaṭef.* I didn't mean to hurt your feelings. *ma-bġit-š nqeṣṣeḥ l-ʕawaṭef dyalek.*
**I have a feeling (that) he won't come. *ka-nšekk ma-ġad iži-š.*
to have a feeling for - *dduwweq.* He has no feeling for music. *ma-ka-idduwweq-š l-musiqa.*
to have feeling in - *ḥess iḥess b-.* I have no feeling in my right arm. *ma-ka-nḥess-š be-l-yedd l-imna.*
fellow - *ʔensan, ʔinsan* pl. *nas.* He's a nice fellow. *huwa waḥed l-ʔensan ḍṛif.*
the fellows - *d-drari.* Where are the fellows going to meet tonight? *fayn ġad itlaqaw d-drari had l-lila?*
**Poor fellow! *meskin!*
felt - *lbed, mlifa.*
female - *nta* pl. *-wat.* Is this animal a male or a female? *waš had l-ḥayawan dkeṛ wella nta?*
fence - *syaž* pl. *-at.*
wire fence - *ẓeṛb* pl. *ẓṛub.*
to fence (in) - *siyyež.* They fenced the house in. *siyyžu ḍ-ḍaṛ.*
to **ferment** - *xmeṛ, xellel.* The grapes are fermenting. *l-ʕineb ka-ixellel.*
fertile - **1.** *xeṣb.* This soil is very fertile. *had l-ʔeṛḍ xeṣba bezzaf.* **2.** *muntiž.* He has a very fertile mind. *ʕendu fikeṛ muntiž bezzaf.*
to **fester** - *qeyyeḥ.* Is the wound still festering? *waš ž-žeṛḥa baqya ka-tqeyyeḥ?*
festival - *musem* pl. *mwasem; feṛḥ* pl. *fṛaḥ, fṛaḥat, fṛuḥa.* The festival was canceled at the last minute. *ḥedfu l-musem f-ʔaxir saʕa.*
fever - *sxana.*
feverish - *fih sxana.* He's been feverish all day. *bqat fih s-sxana n-nhaṛ kollu.*
few - *qlil* pl. *qlal.* Few people come to see us in the summer. *ka-ižiw nas qlal išufuna fe-ṣ-ṣif.*
few and far between - *qlal bezzaf ʕad.* Honest people are few and far between. *n-nas ṣ-ṣadqin qlal bezzaf ʕad.*
a few - *ši.* May I ask a few ques-

tions? *waš imken-li newdeɛ ši-as?ila?*

a few things – *ši-ḥawyež.* There are a few things on the table. *kayen ši-ḥwayež ɛel ṭ-ṭabḷa.*

a few times – *beɛḍ l-meṛṛat.* I saw him only a few times. *šeftu ġir beɛḍ l-meṛṛat.*

quite a few – *ktaṛ šwiyeš, ɛadad ktir.* Quite a few people were present. *kanu n-nas ktaṛ šwiyeš ḥaḍṛin* or *kanu ɛadad de-n-nas ḥaḍṛin.*

Fez – *fas.*

native of Fez – *fasi* pl. *fasiyen, hel fas.*

fez – *ṭeṛbus* pl. *ṭrabeš.*

fickle – *ṭayeš.*

fiddle – *kamanža* pl. *-t.*

**He won't play second fiddle to anyone. *ma-ibġi-š ikun muṛa ḥetta ši-waḥed.*

to fiddle – *ḍṛeb l-kamanža, lɛeb l-kamanža.*

to fiddle (around) with – *xeṛbeq f-, lɛeb f-.* Don't fiddle (around) with the radio! *ma-txeṛbeq-š fe-ṛ-ṛadyu!*

to fiddle away – *ḍiyyeɛ.* He fiddled away the whole day doing absolutely nothing. *ḍiyyeɛ n-nhaṛ kollu bla-ma yeɛmel ḥetta ḥaža.*

field – **1.** *feddan* pl. *fdaden.* We walked across the fields. *qṭeɛna l-feddan.* **2.** *qeṭɛa de-l-?eṛḍ.* How much did you pay for that field? *be-šḥal šriti dak l-qeṭɛa de-l-?eṛḍ?* **3.** *midan* pl. *myaden, mihna* pl. *-t.* He's the best man in his field. *huwa ḥsen waḥed f-midanu.* **4.** *melɛeb* pl. *mlaɛeb.* The teams are coming onto the field. *l-feṛqat daxlin l-melɛeb.*

fierce – *ferras, hayež.* The lion I saw was very fierce. *s-sbeɛ lli šeft kan ferras bezzaf.*

fiery – *hayež.* He made a fiery speech. *dar xeṭba hayža.*

fifteen – *xemsṭaš, xmesṭaš.*

fifth – **1.** *xumus* pl. *xmas.* He got only a fifth of the estate. *žah ġir l-xumus de-l-melk.* **2.** *xames.* He was born on October fifth. *dzad nhaṛ l-xames fe-ktubeṛ.*

fifty – *xemsin.*

fight – **1.** *muḥaṛaba* pl. *-t.* He played an important part in the fight against tuberculosis. *šarek mušaraka muhemma f-muḥaṛabet meṛḍ s-sell.* **2.** *mdabza* pl. *-t.* It was a fight to the finish. *kanet mdabza dyal ṭyuḥ ṛ-ṛuḥ.* **3.** *mulakama* pl. *-t.* Were you at the fight last night? *waš tfeṛṛežti fe-l-mulakama l-bareḥ fe-l-lil?*

**He hasn't any fight left in him. *ma-bqa fih ma idabez.*

to have a fight – *ddabez.* He and his wife had a fight. *ddabez mɛa mṛatu* or *ddabez huwa u-mṛatu.*

to fight – **1.** *ḥaṛeb.* They fought bravely. *ḥaṛbu b-šažaɛa.* —You've got to fight that habit. *xeṣṣek tḥaṛeb had ṭ-ṭbiɛa.* **2.** *dafeɛ ɛla.* I'm going to fight this suit. *ġad ndafeɛ ɛla had l-qaḍiya.*

figure – **1.** *ṛeqm* pl. *ṛqam, ?eṛqam.* Add up these figures. *žmeɛ had l-?eṛqam.* **2.** *ṣuṛa* pl. *-t.* Figure seven shows the parts of the engine. *ṣ-ṣuṛa ṛeqm sebɛa ka-tbiyyen ṭ-ṭṛaf dyal l-makina.* **3.** *šexṣiya* pl. *-t.* He's a mighty important figure in this town. *huwa šexṣiya muhemma bezzaf f-had le-mdina.*

**Are you good at figures? *ka-teɛṛef teḥseb mezyan?*

to figure – *ḍenn.* I figure it's about five-thirty. *ka-nḍenn tkun teqṛiben l-xemsa u-neṣṣ.*

to figure out – **1.** *ḥell, xerrež.* Can you figure out this problem? *imken-lek tḥell had l-muškila?* **2.** *ḥseb.* Figure out how much it will cost. *ḥseb šḥal ġad iswa.* **3.** *fhem.* Can you figure out what he means? *waš imken-lek tefhem š-ka-ibġi iqul?* —I can't figure you out. *ma-neqdeṛ-š nfehmek.*

file – **1.** *mebṛeḍ* pl. *mbaṛeḍ.* You need a finer file than that. *xeṣṣek mebṛeḍ ṛeqq men hadak.* **2.** *mileff* pl. *-at.* This student's file must have been misplaced. *l-mileff dyal had ṭ-ṭaḷeb ma-huwa ġir talef.* —You'll find that in our files. *džbeṛ dak-š-ši ɛendna fe-l-mileffat.* **3.** *seff* pl. *ṣfuf.* Line up in single file! *diru ṣeff waḥed!*

on file – *mɛa l-mileffat.* Do we have his application on file? *waš ɛendna ṭ-ṭaḷab dyalu mɛa l-mileffat?*

to file – **1.** *bṛeḍ.* I have to file my nails. *ka-ixeṣṣni nebṛed ḍfaṛi.* **2.** *retteb.* The letters have not yet been filed. *ma-zal ma-rettbu-š le-bṛawat.* **3.** *qeddem.* I filed my application yesterday. *qeddemt ṭ-ṭaḷab dyali l-bareḥ.*

to fill – **1.** *ɛemmeṛ.* Fill this bottle with water. *ɛemmeṛ had l-qeṛɛa be-l-ma.* —The hall was filled to capacity. *ɛemmṛu l-qaɛa koḷlha.* —This tooth will have to be filled.

had ḍ-ḍeṛṣa ka-ixeṣṣha ttƐemmeṛ. **2.** *xda yaxod, šġel.* The bed just about fills half of the room. *le-fṛaš ka-yaxod Ɛlayen n-neṣṣ fe-l-bit.*

to fill in - 1. *Ɛemmeṛ.* The ditch has been filled in. *Ɛemmṛu l-ḥefṛa.* **2.** *kteb.* Fill your name in here. *kteb smek hna.* **3.** *nab inub.* I'm just filling in here. *ana ġir nayeb hna.*

to fill out - *Ɛemmeṛ.* Fill out this application. *Ɛemmeṛ had l-weṛqa.*

to fill up - *Ɛemmeṛ ḥetta l-l-fomm.* He filled up the glasses. *Ɛemmeṛ l-kisan ḥetta l-l-fomm.*

**I've had my fill of it! *šbeƐt mennu!*

film - 1. *beqƐa* pl. *-t, bqaƐi.* A thin film of oil formed on the water. *beqƐa de-z-zit ṭelƐet Ɛla wžeh l-ma.* **2.** *film* pl. *ʔeflam.* I don't particularly like funny films. *ma-ka-nebġi-š l-ʔeflam de-ḍ-ḍeḥk ḥetta l-temma.*

roll of film - *film* pl. *ʔeflam, qanuṭ (de-tṣaweṛ)* pl. *qnanet (de-tṣaweṛ).* I have to get another roll of film. *xeṣṣni naxod qanuṭ axuṛ de-tṣaweṛ.*

to film - *ṣuwweṛ.* They filmed the entire ceremony. *ṣuwwṛu l-ḥefla kollha.*

filter - *ṣeffaya* pl. *-t.*

to filter - *ṣeffa.*

final - 1. *ʔaxir.* Is that your final decision? *waš hada l-qaṛaṛ dyalek l-ʔaxir?* **2.** *mtiḥan ʔaxir.* How did you make out on your French final? *kif kan le-mtiḥan l-ʔaxir dyalek fe-l-fṛanṣawiya?*

finally - *fe-l-ʔaxir, fe-t-tali.*

financial - *maddi, mali.* For financial reasons I must say no. *Ɛla wedd ʔesbab maddiya ma-imken-li-š neqbel.*

to **find -** *žbeṛ, ṣab iṣib, lqa ilqa.* I found a coin in the street. *žbeṛt fels fe-ṭ-ṭṛiq.* --I found him at home. *lqitu fe-ḍ-ḍaṛ.*

a real find - *wežba* pl. *-t.* This book is a real find. *had le-ktab wežba mezyana.*

to find one's way around - *ṣab iṣib ṭṛiqu.* I never can find my way around here. *ma-Ɛemmṛi ma-ka-nṣib ṭṛiqi hnaya.*

to find out - 1. *Ɛṛef, ṭṭaleƐ.* I found it out just yesterday. *Ɛad l-bareḥ Ɛṛeftu.* **2.** *faq ifiq b-.* I found him out long ago. *feqt bih men hadi šḥal.*

fine - 1. *xṭiya* pl. *-t.* He had to pay a stiff fine. *tlezzem ixeḷḷeṣ xṭiya kbira.* **2.** *moƐtabaṛ.* Where did you get that fine material? *mnayn xditi dak t-tub l-moƐtabaṛ?* **3.** *ṣġiṛ* pl. *ṣġaṛ.* That's too fine a distinction. *hada feṛq ṣġiṛ bezzaf Ɛad.* **4.** *mezyan.* That's fine! *had š-ši mezyan!* **5.** *ḍṛif* pl. *ḍṛaf.* That was mighty fine of him. *kan ḍṛif bezzaf Ɛad.* **6.** *la-bas.* Thanks, I'm feeling fine. *baṛek ḷḷahu fik, ṛ-ana la-bas.* **7.** *ṛqiq* pl. *ṛqaq.* I'd like a pen with a fine point. *bġit qlam ṛaṣu ṛqiq.*

to fine - *ḍṛeb b-le-xṭiya.* The judge fined him five hundred dirhams. *l-qaḍi ḍeṛbu be-xṭiya d-xemsa myat deṛhem.*

finger - *ṣbeƐ* pl. *ṣebƐan.*

fingerprint - *xeṭṭ de-s-sbeƐ* pl. *xṭuṭ de-ṣ-ṣebƐan.*

finish - *tali.* I read the book from start to finish in one day. *qṛit le-ktab men l-ʔewwel ḥetta le-t-tali fe-nhaṛ waḥed.*

to finish - 1. *feḍḍa.* Have you finished the job? *waš feḍḍiti l-xedma?* **2.** *kmel, tsala, tqaḍa, tfeḍḍa.* The work is finished. *l-xedma kemlet.*

**It was a fight to the finish. *kanet mdabza dyal ṭyuḥ ṛ-ṛuḥ.* --If he does that once more, he'll be finished. *ila Ɛawed darha meṛṛa xṛa ġad tkun t-taliya Ɛlih.*

fire - 1. *Ɛafya* pl. *Ɛwafi, naṛ* pl. *niran.* --Has the fire gone out? *waš ṭfat l-Ɛafya?* **2.** *ḥṛiqa* pl. *-t, ḥṛayeq.* We had a big fire in town last year. *kanet ḥṛiqa kbira f-le-blad l-Ɛam lli fat.*

to be on fire - *tteḥṛeq, kan ikun nayḍa fih l-Ɛafya.* The house is on fire. *ḍ-ḍaṛ ka-tteḥṛeq* or *ḍ-ḍaṛ nayḍa fiha l-Ɛafya.*

to build a fire - *šƐel l-Ɛafya.* Let's build a fire. *aži nšeƐlu l-Ɛafya.*

to catch fire - *šeƐlet l-Ɛafya f-.* The hay caught fire. *t-tben šeƐlet fih l-Ɛafya.*

to light a fire - *šƐel l-Ɛafya.* Will you light the fire? *waš tebġi tešƐel l-Ɛafya?*

to set on fire - *šƐel l-Ɛafya f-.* He set the house on fire. *šƐel l-Ɛafya fe-ḍ-ḍaṛ.*

to fire - 1. *ḍṛeb (l-qeṛṭaṣ).* Why didn't you fire? *Ɛlaš ma-ḍṛebti-š l-qeṛṭaṣ?* **2.** *xerrež men l-xedma dḥa idḥi.* Why did the boss fire him? *Ɛlaš dḥah le-mƐellem?*

**I'm all ears, fire away! *h-ana*

ka-ntṣennet, ṭleq ma Ɛendek.
fire department - *l-ḅumḅiya.* Call the Fire Department! *Ɛeyyeṭ l-ḅumḅiya!*
fire escape - *ḍruž l-ʔiġata.*
fireman - *ḅumḅi* pl. *-ya.*
firm - **1.** *šarika* pl. *-at.* What firm do you represent? *š-men šarika katmettel?* **2.** *ṛaṣi, qaṣeḥ* The ground is firmer here than it is there. *l-ʔeṛḍ qaṣḥa hna kteṛ men temma.*
**I'm a firm believer in it. *ana mʔamen b-had š-ši bezzaf.*
first - **1.** *luwwel.* I get paid on the first. *ka-ixeḷḷṣuni l-luwwel fe-š-šheṛ.* --I wouldn't believe it at first. *ma-teqt-š fe-l-luwwel.* --I always travel first-class. *daymen ka-nṣafeṛ fe-ḍ-daṛaža l-luwla.* **2.** *ʔewwalen.* First let me ask you a question. *ʔewwelen xellini nsuwwlek.*
**He doesn't know the first thing about soccer. *ma ka-yeƐṛef ḥetta ḥaža f-leƐb l-kuṛa.*
first-class - *nimiru waḥed.* It's a first-class job. *hadi xedma nimiru waḥed.*
first of all - *beƐda, qbel koll-ši.* First of all, you misunderstood me. *qbel koll-ši, ṛak ma-fhemtini-š.*
in the first place - *ʔewwalen.* In the first place I have no money, and besides... *ʔewwalen, ma-Ɛendi flus, u-zaydun...*
fish - *ḥuta* pl. *-t* coll. *ḥut.*
to fish - **1.** *ṣiyyeḍ l-ḥut.* Do you want to go fishing? *waš tebġi temši tṣiyyeḍ l-ḥut?* **2.** *qelleb, ḍuwweṛ.* She's just fishing for compliments. *ġir ka-ḍḍuwweṛ Ɛel l-qobba.*
fist - *buniya* pl. *-t, Ɛeqda de-l-yedd.*
to **fit** - *ža iži qedd.* These shoes don't fit me. *had ṣ-ṣeḅḅaṭ ma-ka-iži-š qeddi.*
**I'm busy, but I'll try to fit you in somewhere. *ana mešġul, be-l-ḥeqq ndir žehdi baš nṣiḅ-lek ši-wqiyyeṭ.*
to fit together - *tlaqa.* These parts don't fit together. *had ṭ-ṭṛaf ma-ka-itlaqaw-š.*
to have a fit - *džennen.* Every time I mention it he has a fit. *fuq-emma ka-nžbedha-lu ka-idžennen.*
**This suit isn't a good fit. *had l-keswa ma-ši qeddi.*
to be fit - *ṣlaḥ.* What sort of work is he fit for? *le-š-men xedma iṣlaḥ?* --This meat isn't fit to eat. *had l-lḥem ma-iṣlaḥ-š l-l-makla.* --This water isn't fit to drink. *had l-ma ma-iṣlaḥ-š le-š-šṛib.*
**He's fit to be tied. *bezqu ṭayeṛ be-ž-žnun.*
to feel fit - *ḥess b-ṛaṣu mezyan.* He doesn't feel fit today. *ma-ka-iḥess-ši b-ṛaṣu mezyan l-yum.*
fitting - **1.** *qyaṣ* pl. *-at.* When will the suit be ready for a fitting? *mtaš tužed l-keswa l-le-qyaṣ?* **2.** *mnaseb.* Let's wait for a more fitting occasion. *xellina nsaynu weqt mnaseb kteṛ.*
five - *xemsa, xems.*
fix - *meʔzeq* pl. *mʔazeq.* He's in a terrible fix. *huwa f-waḥed l-meʔzeq ṣƐib.*
to fix - **1.** *dar idir, Ɛmel.* The price was fixed at one hundred dollars. *Ɛemlu t-taman myat derhem.* **2.** *Ɛewweṭ.* Fix your tie. *Ɛewweṭ le-gṛabaṭa dyalek.* **3.** *ṣleḥ.* Can you fix the typewriter for me? *waš imken-lek teṣleḥ-li l-makina d-le-ktaba?* **4.** *wežžed, ṣaweḅ.* I have to fix supper now. *ka-ixeṣṣni nwežžed le-Ɛša daba.* **5.** *Ɛaqeb.* I'll fix that swindler. *ġad nƐaqeb dak l-xeṭṭaf.*
to fix up - *ṣaweb, Ɛaweṭ.* They fixed everything up again. *ṣawbu koll-ši Ɛawed.*
flabby - *meṛxuf, meṛxi.* My muscles got all flabby when I was sick. *l-Ɛṣeb dyali wellaw meṛxiyin bezzaf melli kont mṛiḍ.*
flag - *Ɛlam* pl. *Ɛluma, Ɛalamat; bendiṛa* pl. *-t, bnadeṛ; ṛaya* pl. *-t.*
flake - *qešṛa* pl. *-t, qšuṛ.* The paint is coming off the wall in big flakes. *ka-iṭiḥu qšuṛ kbaṛ de-ṣ-ṣbaġa men l-ḥiṭ.*
flame - *šeƐƐala* pl. *-t.* The flame of the candle was red. *š-šeƐƐala de-š-šmaƐa kanet ḥemṛa.*
flap - *ġlaf* pl. *-at; ġṭa* pl. *-wat, ġṭi.* Do you want your pockets with or without flaps? *waš tebġi žyubek b-le-ġṭi wella blaš?*
to flap - *ferfer.* The bird flapped its wings and flew away. *l-beṛṭal ferfer be-žnawḥu u-ṭaṛ.*
to **flare up** - **1.** *lheb.* The fire flared up when I poured some gasoline on it. *l-Ɛafya lehbet mnin kebbit Ɛliha ḷ-ḷiṣanṣ.* **2.** *zƐef.* He flares up at the slightest provocation. *ġir ka-džebdu Ɛlik ka-izƐef.*
flash - *šƐa.* The flash of light blinded me. *š-šƐa de-ḍ-ḍuw Ɛemmani.*
in a flash - *bḥal le-bṛeq.* It was all over in a flash. *daz bḥal*

le-bṛeq.
flash of lightning - *beṛqa* pl. *-t* coll. *bṛeq.*
quick as a flash - *bḥal le-bṛeq.* He answered quick as a flash. *žaweb bḥal le-bṛeq.*
to flash - **1.** *bṛeq.* His eyes flashed with anger. *Ɛeynih beṛqu b-le-ġḍeb.* **2.** *šƐel.* He flashed the light right in my face. *šƐel-li ḍ-ḍuw f-wežhi.*
**Many thoughts flashed through my mind. *bezzaf de-l-fikrat žaw l-bali f-deqqa weḥda.*
to flash on - *šƐel.* I saw the light flash on. *šeft ḍ-ḍuw šƐel.*
flashlight - *fnaṛ* pl. *-at.*
flat - **1.** *ḍwiṛa* pl. *-t, sekna* pl. *-t.* I just moved into a new flat. *Ɛad rḥelt l-waḥed ḍ-ḍwiṛa ždida.* **2.** *ṛwiḍa mefšuša* pl. *ṛwayeḍ mefšušin.* You'll have to get the flat fixed. *xeṣṣek tṣaweḅ ṛ-ṛwiḍa l-mefšuša.* **3.** *mwaṭi.* All houses in Morocco have flat roofs. *fe-l-meġṛib ḍ-ḍyuṛ kollhom Ɛendhom ṣṭuḥa mwaṭyin.* **4.** *basel.* The food tastes flat. *l-makla basla.* **5.** *u-ṣafi, u-baṛaka, qeṭƐen.* His answer was a flat no. *žwabu kan la u-ṣafi.* **6.** *mbeẓẓeṭ.* He has a flat nose. *Ɛendu menxaṛ mbeẓẓeṭ.*
to have a flat - *ttfeššet ṛwiḍa l-.* On the way back we had a flat. *mnin konna ṛažƐin ttfeššet-lna ṛwiḍa.*
to **flatten** - *waṭa.*
to **flatter** - *leḥleḥ.*
to flatter oneself - *sḥab-lu ṛaṣu.* He flatters himself he's a good speaker. *ka-isḥab-lu ṛaṣu ka-ixṭeḅ mezyan.*
to feel flattered - *Ɛežbu ṛaṣu.* She felt flattered by his remarks. *Ɛžebha ṛaṣha be-l-mulaḥaḍat dyalu.*
flat tire - *ṛwiḍa mefšuša* pl. *ṛwayeḍ mefšušin.*
flavor - *madaq.* The coffee has lost all its flavor. *l-qehwa mša-lha l-madaq dyalha kollu.*
flavorless - *basel.*
flaw - *Ɛib* pl. *Ɛyub.*
flax - *kettan.*
flea - *beṛġuta* pl. *bṛaġet* coll. *beṛġut.*
to **flee** - *hṛeb.*
fleece - *gezza* pl. *gzez.*
fleet - *fṛageṭ, ʔusṭul.*
flesh - *lḥem* pl. *lḥum, lḥumat.*
to **flex** - *tna itni.*
flexibility - *lyana, lyuna.*
flexible - *liyyen.*
to **flicker** - *ġmez, ġzel, deƐmeš.* The light is flickering. *ḍ-ḍuw ka-iġmez.*
flight - **1.** *ṭayṛan.* The flight lasted four hours. *ṭ-ṭayṛan ṭal ṛebƐa de-s-saƐat.* **2.** *hežṛa* pl. *-t.* What do you know about the flight of the prophet? *š-ka-teƐṛef Ɛel l-hežṛa de-n-nbi?* **3.** *ṣeff* pl. *ṣfuf de-ḍ-ḍruž.* How many more flights do we have to climb? *šḥal men ṣeff de-ḍ-ḍruž ma-zal ka-ixeṣṣna nṭeḷƐu?*
flimsy - **1.** *raši, ma-ši ṣḥiḥ.* The flimsy house was destroyed by the wind. *ḍ-ḍaṛ r-rašya thedmet be-r-riḥ.* **2.** *xawi.* That was a flimsy excuse. *hadak kan Ɛdeṛ xawi.*
to **fling** - *laḥ iluḥ, ṛma iṛmi.*
flock - **1.** *qeṭƐa* pl. *-t.* They followed him like a flock of sheep. *tebƐuh bḥal qeṭƐa d-le-ġnem.* **2.** *qetta* pl. *-t.* We saw a flock of birds flying south. *šefna qetta de-ṭ-ṭyuṛ metwežžhin l-l-žanub.*
to flock - *dzaḥem.* The children flocked into the movie. *dzaḥmu d-drari fe-s-sinima.*
to flock around - *džuwwqu Ɛla, daru ž-žuqa Ɛla.* They flocked around the injured man. *džuwwqu Ɛel ṛ-ṛažel l-mežṛuḥ.*
flood - *fiḍa.*
to flood - **1.** *ḥmel, faḍ ifiḍ.* The river floods every year. *l-wad ka-yeḥmel koll Ɛam.* **2.** *ġeṛṛeq, ġeṭṭa (be-l-ma), faḍ ifiḍ Ɛla.* The high tide flooded the beach. *faḍ le-mlu Ɛel le-bḷaya.*
floor - **1.** *ḷeṛḍ.* My glasses fell on the floor. *n-nḍaḍeṛ dyali ṭaḥu fe-ḷ-ḷeṛḍ.* **2.** *ṭebqa* pl. *-t.* I live on the third floor. *ka-neskon fe-ṭ-ṭebqa t-talta.*
**May I have the floor? *waš imken-li ntkellem?*
first floor - *sefli.* We live on the first floor. *ka-nseknu fe-s-sefli.*
florist - *biyyaƐ n-nuwwaṛ.* Her brother is a florist. *xaha biyyaƐ n-nuwwaṛ.* florist. *xaha biyyaƐ n-nuwwar.*
to **flounder** - **1.** *xebbeṭ.* The horse floundered in the mud. *bqa l-Ɛewd ka-ixebbeṭ fe-l-ġis.* **2.** *tfafa.* He floundered a while before finding the right answer. *tfafa šwiya qbel-ma iṣiḅ ž-žwab.*
flour - *ṭḥin.*
to **flourish** **1.** *nbet mezyan.* The plants are flourishing here. *l-ġeṛṣ ka-inbet mezyan f-had l-muḍeƐ.* **2.** *tmešša mezyan.* His business is flourishing now. *daba t-tižaṛa dyalu metmešša mezyan.*

to **flow** - *sal isil.*
flower - *nuwwaṛa* pl. *-t, nwaweṛ* coll. *nuwwaṛ.*
to **fluctuate** - **1.** *ṭleƐ u-hbeṭ.* Prices fluctuate. *l-ʔetman ka-ṭṭleƐ u-tehbeṭ.* **2.** *tġeyyeṛ, tbeddel.* Around here the weather fluctuates a lot. *l-ḥal ka-tġeyyeṛ hna bezzaf.*
fluently - *belbel, be-ž-žri u-l-ma.* He speaks Arabic fluently. *ka-itkellem l-Ɛeṛbiya belbel.*
fluid - **1.** *ḥaža žarya, ši žari.* What is the fluid in this glass? *š-had š-ši žari f-had l-kas?* **2.** *žari.* I watched them pour the fluid metal into a mold. *šefthom ka-ikebbu l-meƐden žari fe-l-qaleb.*
to **flutter** - **1.** *ferfer, refref.* The scarf fluttered in the breeze. *d-derra kanet ka-trefref fe-r-riḥ.* **2.** *rdeḥ.* My heart fluttered when I saw her. *mnin šeftha qelbi bda irdeḥ.*
fly - *debbana* pl. *-t, dbaben;* coll. *debban.*
to fly - **1.** *ṭaṛ iṭiṛ.* The birds are flying south. *le-bṛaṭel ṭayṛin l-žiht l-žanub.* **2.** *xda yaxod ṭ-ṭiyaṛa.* We're flying to Paris tomorrow. *ġedda ġad naxdu ṭ-ṭiyaṛa l-bariz.* **3.** *ṣag iṣug.* Can you fly a plane? *waš ka-teƐṛef tṣug ṭ-ṭiyaṛa?*
**The ship was flying the Moroccan flag. *l-baxiṛa kanet mṭeḷḷƐa ṛ-ṛaya l-meġṛibiya.*
to fly into a rage - *ṭaṛ-lu, zƐef.* When I told my father he flew into a rage. *mnin qoltha le-ḅḅa ṭaṛ-lu.*
flyer - *ṭiyyaṛ* pl. *-in, -a.*
foal - *ždeƐ* pl. *žduƐa.*
foam - **1.** *ṛeġwa* pl. *-t, ṛġawi.* This soap doesn't produce much foam. *had ṣ-ṣabun ma-ka-ixerrež-š ṛ-ṛeġwa bezzaf.* **2.** *keškuša* pl. *-t.* There's more foam than beer in this glass. *kayen l-keškuša kteṛ men l-biṛa f-had l-kas.*
**He was foaming with rage. *kan ka-iġli be-l-ġedda.*
fog - *ḍbab, ḍbaba.*
fogged (up) - My glasses are fogged (up). *n-nḍadeṛ dyali mḍebbbin.*
foggy - *mḍebbeb.*
fold - *tenya* pl. *-t.* The curtains are faded at the folds. *t-tenyat d-le-xwami kašfin.*
to **fold** - **1.** *ṭwa iṭwi.* Help me fold the blanket. *Ɛawenni nṭwi le-ġṭa.* **2.** *tna itni.* Shall I fold the letter? *waš ntni le-bṛa?* **3.** *kemmes, ġeḷḷef, lemm, leff.* Fold the gloves in some paper. *kemmes ṣ-ṣebbaƐat fe-l-kaġiṭ.* **4.** *šebbek.* She sat there with folded hands. *kanet galsa ṣebƐan mšebbkin.* **5.** *ṛebbeƐ.* He folded his arms. *ṛebbeƐ iddih.*
to **fold in one's arms** - *Ɛenneq.* She folded the child in her arms. *Ɛennqet le-wliyed.*
to fold up - *fles.* That business folded up last year. *dak l-biƐ u-š-šra fles l-Ɛam lli fat.*
folder - *ġlaf* pl. *-at, mileff* pl. *-at.* The copies are in the blue folder. *ṛa n-nesxat fe-l-mileff le-zṛeq.*
to **follow** - **1.** *tbeƐ.* Somebody's following us. *ši-waḥed tabeƐna.* **2.** *tebbeƐ.* I think I'll follow your example. *ka-nḍenn ġad ntebbeƐ l-mital dyalek.* --Her eyes followed him sadly. *tebbƐettu b-Ɛeynin fihom l-ḥozn.* **3.** *xleṭ, tbeƐ.* We'll follow you in a little while. *nxeḷṭu Ɛlikom men daba šwiya.*
**From this it follows that ... *Ɛla had š-ši ...*
to follow up - *tebbeƐ.* We try to follow up every complaint. *ka-nḥawlu ntebbƐu koll šekwa.*
**The letter reads as follows ... *h-aš ka-tqul le-bṛa ...*
following - **1.** *ʔetbaƐ* (pl.). He has a very large following. *Ɛendu ʔetbaƐ bezzaf.* **2.** *(lli) men beƐd.* The following day it rained. *n-nhaṛ lli men beƐd ṭaḥet š-šta.*
**I need the following items ... *ha le-ḥwayež lli meḥtaž-lhom ...*
food - *makla* pl. *-t, mwakel; ṭƐam* pl. *-t.* Food got scarcer and scarcer. *l-makla qlalet šwiya be-šwiya.*
**This will give you food for thought. *had š-ši ġad yeƐṭik f-aš txemmem.*
fool - *buhali* pl. *-yin, buhala; ḥmeq* pl. *ḥumeq.* He's a fool if he believes that story. *ṛah ḥmeq ila taq b-dak le-ḥkaya.*
to make a fool of oneself - *ṛeḍḍ ṛaṣu ḍeḥka.* If you do that you'll make a fool of yourself. *ila ddir dak š-ši ġad tṛeḍḍ ṛaṣek ḍeḥka.*
to fool - **1.** *tmelleġ.* I was only fooling. *ġir kont ka-ntmelleġ.* **2.** *tfella Ɛla.* You can't fool me. *ma-imken-lek-š ttfella Ɛliya.*
to fool around - **1.** *xeṛbeq.* Don't fool around with that radio while I'm gone. *ma-txeṛbeq-š f-dak ṛ-ṛadyu melli nkun ġayeb.* **2.** *tlaha.* He just fools around. *ġir ka-itlaha.*
foot - *ṛžel* (f.) pl. *režlin.* (pl. *režli-* before pronoun endings).

--The chest of drawers stood at the foot of the bed. *le-xzana kanet* *Ɛend režlin le-fṛaš.*

on foot - *Ɛla režlin.* We had to cover the rest of the way on foot. *ṭṭeṛṛina nḍeṛbu ṭ-ṭṛiq lli bqat Ɛla režlina.*

to put one's foot down - *ẓiyyeṛ š-šġol.* Things won't improve until you put your foot down. *ila ma-ẓiyyeṛti-ši š-šġol ḥetta ḥaža ma-tthessen.*

to put one's foot in it - *keffesha.* I really put my foot in it that time! *walayenni keffestha dak n-nuba!*

to stand on one's own feet - *ttkel Ɛla ṛaṣu.* He's old enough to stand on his own feet. *huwa kbir daba iqdeṛ ittkel Ɛla raṣu.*

for - **1.** *l-.* Aspirin is good for headaches. *sbirin mezyan le-ḥṛiq ṛ-ṛaṣ.* --The train for Casablanca leaves in five minutes. *l-mašina lli ka-temši le-ḍ-ḍaṛ l-bida ġadi tqelleƐ men daba xemsa de-d-dqayeq.* --Is that for me? *waš hadak lili?* --What's that thing good for? *l-aš ka-iṣlaḥ dak š-ši?* **2.** *Ɛla.* Did anyone ask for me? *waš suwwel Ɛliya ši-waḥed?* **3.** *Ɛla wžeh.* She married him for his money. *xdatu Ɛla wžeh flusu.* --I did it for my mother. *dertha Ɛla wžeh ṃṃi.*

for a long time - *šḥal hadi.* I haven't heard from him for a long time. *šḥal hadi ma-smeƐt Ɛlih xbaṛ.*

force - *quwwa* pl. *-t.*

to force - *lezzem.*

to force open - *fṛeƐ.*

forehead - *žebha* pl. *-t.*

foreign - *ažnabi.*

foreigner - *ažnabi* pl. *-yin, ažaneb.*

forest - *ġaba* pl. *-t, ġyeb.*

forever - *daymen, dima.*

to **forget** - *nsa insa.*

to **forgive** - *smeḥ l-, sameḥ.*

fork - **1.** *mtekka* pl. *-t, mtekk; metšekka* pl. *-t.* Could I have a knife and fork please? *Ɛṭini sekkin u-mtekka baṛek ḷḷahu fik.* **2.** *mefṛeq* pl. *mfaṛeq.* Go until you reach the fork in the road. *sir ḥetta tuṣel l-mefṛeq ṭ-ṭoṛqan.*

to fork - *ttefṛeq.* The road forks beyond the village. *ṭ-ṭṛiq ka-ttefṛeq men muṛ l-qeṛya.*

form - **1.** *weṛqa* pl. *-t, wṛaq.* You'll have to fill out this form. *ka-ixeṣṣek tƐemmeṛ had l-weṛqa.* **2.** *qaleb* pl. *qwaleb.* They're pouring the molten iron into the form. *ka-ikebbu le-ḥdid le-mduwweb fe-l-qaleb.*

in good form - *našeṭ.* I'm in good form today. *ana našeṭ l-yum.*

to form - **1.** *ʔesses.* He formed a new cabinet. *ʔesses diwan ždid.* **2.** *ttaxed.* I haven't formed an opinion yet. *ma-zal ma-ttaxett ḥetta ši-naḍaṛ.*

formal - **1.** *metʔeddeb.* You needn't be that formal. *ma-tkun-š metʔeddeb bezzaf.* **2.** *resmi.* He paid him a formal visit. *ẓaṛu ziyaṛa resmiya.*

former - **1.** *ṣabeq, qdim.* The former owner of the shop has retired. *mul l-ḥanut le-qdim feḍḍa men l-biƐ u-š-šra f-nuba.* **2.** *luwwel.* I prefer the former suggestion. *ka-nfeḍḍeḷ l-fikra l-luwla.*

formerly - *men qbel.*

fort - *beṛž* pl. *bṛuž.*

fortunate - *saƐid* pl. *suƐada.* That was a fortunate coincidence. *kanet muṣadafa saƐida.*

to be fortunate - *Ɛendu s-seƐd.* He was very fortunate. *kan Ɛendu s-seƐd bezzaf.*

fortune - *teṛwa, mal.* She inherited a large fortune. *weṛtet teṛwa kbira.*

to tell someone's fortune - *ḍṛeb l-fal l-.* He told my fortune. *ḍṛeb-li l-fal.*

fortune teller - *ḍeṛṛab l-fal* pl. *ḍeṛṛabin l-fal.*

forty - *ṛebƐin.*

forward - *l-l-qeddam.*

to come, go forward - *tqeddem.*

to look forward to - *tṛežža.* I'm looking forward to your visit. *ka-ntṛežža z-ziyaṛa dyalek.*

foul - **1.** *ġeḷṭa* pl. *-t, ġḷaṭi.* A team member committed a foul. *waḥed men l-feṛqa dar ġeḷṭa.* **2.** *xanez, qbiḥ* pl. *qbaḥ.* Where does that foul smell come from? *mnin žayya had r-riḥa l-xanza?*

to foul up - *xeṣṣeṛ, keffes.* That mechanic fouled up my whole car! *dak mul l-gaṛaž xeṣṣeṛ-li ṭ-ṭumubil kollha.*

to **found** - *ʔesses.* Who founded this club? *škun ʔesses had n-nadi?*

foundation - **1.** *sas* pl. *-t, lsas* pl. *-at.* The earthquake shook the foundations of the building. *l-hezza l-ʔeṛḍiya zeƐzƐet l-lsas de-l-binaya.* **2.** *ʔasas* pl. *-at.* Your remarks are completely without foundation. *l-mulaḥaḍat dyalek ma-Ɛendhom ḥetta ʔasas.* **3.** *muʔessasa* pl. *-t, žemƐiya* pl. *-t.* Does the foundation for the blind have a branch in your city? *waš l-muʔessasa de l-Ɛumi Ɛendhu*

ši-ferᶜ fe-mdintkom?
fountain - *xoṣṣa* pl. *-t, xṣeṣ,* (wall fountain) *ṣeqqaya* pl. *-t.*
fountain pen - *stilu* pl. *-yat.*
four - *ṛebᶜa, ṛbeᶜ.*
fourteen - *ṛbeᶜṭaš.*
fourth - **1.** *ṛubuᶜ* pl. *-at; ṛbeᶜ* pl. *ṛbaᶜ.* Only one fourth of the students were listening. *ġir ṛbeᶜ de-t-tlamed kan ka-itṣenneṭ.* **2.** *ṛabeᶜ.* He died on the fourth. *mat n-nhaṛ ṛ-ṛabeᶜ fe-š-šheṛ.*
fox - *teᶜleb* pl. *tᶜaleb.*
fraction - **1.** *qesma* pl. *-t, qsam.* Leave out the fractions and just give me the round numbers. *ᶜṭini l-ʔerqam ṣ-ṣḥaḥ u-xelli le-qsam.* **2.** *ṭerf ṣġiṛ, qesma ṣġiṛa.* He got only a fraction of his father's fortune. *ma-žah ġir ṭerf ṣġiṛ men t-teṛwa de-ḅḅah.*
fracture - *tehrisa* pl. *-t, teksira* pl. *-t, gerḍa* pl. *-at.* The fracture is healing slowly. *t-tehrisa ka-tebṛa šwiyeš be-šwiyeš.*
to fracture - *kesser, herres, greḍ.* He fell off the bicycle and fractured his arm. *ṭaḥ men l-bisklit u-kesser yeddu.*
frame - *qžeṛ* pl. *qžuṛa.* I'd like to have a frame for this picture. *ḥebbit qžeṛ l-had t-teṣwiṛa.* --I've broken the frame of my glasses. *le-qžeṛ de-n-nḍaḍeṛ dyali therres.*
**He has a heavy frame. *ᶜeḍmu faxeṛ.*
to **frame** - *dar idir qžeṛ l-.* I'll have the picture framed. *ġad ndir qžeṛ le-t-teṣwiṛa.*
France - *fṛanṣa.*
frank - *ṣaṛiḥ* pl. *ṣṛaḥ, ṣṛiḥin.* Be frank with me! *kun ṣaṛiḥ mᶜaya.*
**Is that your frank opinion? *waš hada huwa n-naḍaṛ dyalek b-ṣaṛaḥa?*
frankly - *b-ṣaṛaḥa.* Why don't you tell me frankly what really happened? *ᶜlaš ma-tqul-li-š b-ṣaṛaḥa šnu wqeᶜ?*
fraud - **1.** *ġešš.* Fraud is a crime. *l-ġešš žarima.* **2.** *ġeššaš* pl. *-a, -in.* He was exposed as a fraud. *ḍheṛ bin huwa ġeššaš.*
freckle - *ḥebba de-n-nems* pl. *ḥebbat de-n-nems.*
freckles - *nems* (coll.).
freckles - *mnemmes.*
free - **1.** *msali.* Will you be free tomorrow? *waš ġad tkun msali ġedda?* **2.** *baṭel, bla flus.* Take one! It's free. *xud waḥed ṛah baṭel.* **3.** *ḥoṛṛ* pl. *ḥṛaṛ.* I prefer a free nation. *ka-nfeḍḍel d-dula tkun ḥoṛṛa.*
free and easy - *ṭabiᶜi mᶜa ṛaṣu.* He has a free and easy way about him. *huwa ṛažel ṭabiᶜi mᶜa ṛaṣu.*
free speech - *ḥoṛṛiyt t-teᶜbir.* Without free speech there is no real democracy. *ma-kayna dimuqṛaṭiya ḥaqiqiya bla ḥoṛṛiyt t-teᶜbir.*
to have a free hand - *ᶜendu ḥoṛṛiya tamma.* Can I have a free hand in this matter? *waš imken tkun ᶜendi ḥoṛṛiya tamma f-had l-qaḍiya?*
of one's own free will - *b-xaṭṛu.* Did you do it of your own free will? *waš dertih b-xaṭṛek?*
to free, to set free - *ḥeṛṛeṛ, ṭleq.* The prisoners were set free. *ṭelqu le-msažen.*
freedom - *ḥoṛṛiya* pl. *-t.*
freedom of speech - *ḥoṛṛiyt t-teᶜbir.*
freely - **1.** *mennu l-ṛaṣu, b-xaṭṛu.* He admitted freely that he had taken it. *mennu l-ṛaṣu ᶜtaṛef bin xdah.* **2.** *bla-ma ixaf.* You can speak freely. *hḍeṛ bla-ma txaf.* **3.** *bla ḥsab.* He spends his money freely. *ka-idfeᶜ flusu bla ḥsab.*
to **freeze** - **1.** *dxel ᶜlih l-berd, mat imut be-l-berd.* We froze all winter long. *dxel ᶜlina l-berd iyam š-šta kollha.* --I'm freezing. *ka-nmut be-l-berd.* **2.** *žmed, ttellež.* The water in the pitcher froze during the night. *l-ma žmed fe-l-ġoṛṛaf fe-l-lil.* **3.** *weqqef.* The government has frozen all foreign accounts. *l-ḥukuma weqqfet žmiᶜ le-ḥsabat l-ʔažnabiya.*
French - *fṛanṣawi.*
frequently - *bezzaf de-l-meṛṛat, meṛṛat mutaᶜeddida.* I see him frequently. *ka-nšufu bezzaf de-l-meṛṛat.*
fresh - **1.** *ṭṛi.* Are these eggs fresh? *waš had l-biḍ ṭṛi?* **2.** *nqi.* Let's go out for some fresh air. *yaḷḷah nxeṛžu nšemmu šwiya de-l-hawa nqi.* **3.** *mežhed.* A fresh wind was blowing. *kan riḥ mežhed ka-iṣuṭ.* **4.** *dṣuṛi.* I can't stand that fresh kid. *ma-ka-neḥmel-š dak l-weld d-dṣuṛi.*
friction - **1.** *ḥekkan.* There's too much friction in this wheel. *kayen ḥekkan bezzaf f-had ṛ-ṛwiḍa.* **2.** *mḥakka, ġnan.* There's friction between the two sisters. *kayen ġnan bin ž-žuž de-l-xwatat.*
Friday - *ž-žemᶜa, yum ž-žemᶜa.*
friend - *ṣaḥeb* pl. *ṣḥab, ṣadiq* pl. *ʔeṣdiqa?* He's a good friend of mine. *huwa ṣaḥbi bezzaf.* --We became fast friends. *ṛžeᶜna ṣḥab bezzaf.*

**Are we friends again? *waš tṣaleḥna?*

friendly - *ḍṛif* pl. *ḍṛaf*. She is friendly to everybody. *hiya ḍṛifa mƐa koll waḥed.*

**They came to a friendly agreement. *ttafqu be-l-xaṭeṛ.*

friendship - *ṣeḥba* pl. *-t, mṣeḥba* pl. *-t.*

fright - *xelƐa* pl. *xewwef.*

to **frighten** - *xleƐ, xewwef.*

to be frightened - *xaf ixaf, ttexleƐ.*

frog - *žṛana* pl. *-t žṛayen,* coll. *žṛan.*

from - **1.** *men Ɛend.* He just received a check from his father. *Ɛad weṣlu sik men Ɛend ḅḅah.* **2.** *men.* I've just come from the rehearsal. *Ɛad žit men t-temrin.* --I live ten kilometers from the city. *ka-nskon Ɛla boƐd Ɛešṛa de-l-kilumitṛat men le-mdina.* --He's from Rabat. *huwa men ṛ-ṛbaṭ.* --He was tired from overwork. *kan Ɛeyyan men l-xedma bezzaf.* --From now on I'll be on time. *men daba l-l-qeddam ġad nebda nži fe-l-weqt.* --The situation changes from day to day. *l-ḥala ka-tġeyyer men nhaṛ le-nhaṛ.* --Office hours are from eight to twelve. *l-mekteb meftuḥ men t-tmenya le-ṭ-ṭnaš.* --The situation went from bad to worse. *l-ḥala tġeyyret men kfes le-nḥes.* --The chair slipped out from under him. *š-šelya ẓehqet men teḥt mennu.* **3.** *Ɛla.* From what he says it must be very interesting. *Ɛla ma ka-iqul dak š-ši mufid.*

**He kept me from making a big mistake. *reddni men waḥed l-ġelṭa kbira.*

where ... from - *mnin, mnayn.* Where are you from? *mnin nta?*

**Where I come from it often rains for weeks. *fe-bladi ktir ma ka-ṭṭiḥ š-šta muddat ʔasabiƐ.*

front - **1.** *wžeh* pl. *wžuha.* The front of the house is painted white. *le-wžeh de-ḍ-ḍaṛ meṣbuġ be-l-byeḍ.* **2.** *qeddam.* The front of the room was all black with smoke. *l-qeddam de-l-bit kan kollu kḥel be-d-doxxan.* **3.** *qeddami.* We were sitting in the front row. *konna galsin fe-ṣ-ṣeff l-qeddami.* **4.** *luwwel.* The table of contents is in the front of the book. *l-fehṛes fe-l-luwwel d-le-ktab.*

in front of - **1.** *f-bab.* Let's meet in front of the post office. *ntlaqaw f-bab l-buṣṭa.* **2.** *qeddam.* I sit in front of him in school. *ka-negles qeddamu fe-l-meḍṛaṣa.* **3.** *qbalt.* He stopped the car in front of the building. *weqqef s-siyaṛa qbalt l-binaya.*

to **frown** - *Ɛebbes.*

to frown at - *xzer f-.*

**Her whole family frowned on the match. *kanet l-Ɛaʔila dyalha kollha ma-ṛaḍya-š be-z-zwaž dyalha.*

fruit - *fakya* pl. *-t; ġella* pl. *-t, ġlel.*

to **fry** - *qla iqli.*

fuel - *muqud* pl. *mwaqed.*

to **fulfill** - *Ɛmel, qam iqum b-.* He fulfilled his duty. *Ɛmel lli Ɛlih.*

to be fulfilled - *kmel.* Her wishes were fulfilled. *kmel-lha ržaha.*

full - **1.** *Ɛameṛ.* The glasses are full of oil. *l-kisan Ɛamṛin be-z-zit.* --The book is full of mistakes. *le-ktab Ɛameṛ be-l-ʔeġlaṭ.* **2.** *koll.* I paid the full price. *xeḷḷeṣt t-taman kollu.* **3.** *šebƐan.* I'm full. *ana šebƐan.* **4.** *kamel.* The papers carried a full account of the incident. *l-žaṛaʔed Ɛewwdu l-ḥadita kamla.*

fume - *buxaṛ, doxxan* pl. *dxaxen.* The escaping fumes are deadly. *d-dxaxen lli ṭalƐin ka-iqetlu.*

fully - **1.** *tamamen.* Are you fully aware of what is going on? *waš nta fayeq tamamen be-lli ka-iṛuž?* **2.** *kollu.* He described it fully. *weṣfu kollu.* **3.** *Ɛel l-ʔaqell.* There were fully two hundred people at the reception. *kanu Ɛel l-ʔaqell myatayn de-n-nas fe-l-ḥefla.*

fun - *našaṭ.* Fishing is a lot of fun. *ṣ-ṣyaḍa de-l-ḥut fiha n-našaṭ bezzaf.*

for fun - *baš itmelleġ, l-le-mlaġa.* I just did it for fun. *dertha ġir baš ntmelleġ.*

to make fun of - *tfella Ɛla.* Are you making fun of me? *waš ka-ttfella Ɛliya?*

function - *waḍif* pl. *wḍayef.* What is his function in the office? *šnu l-waḍif dyalu fe-l-mekteb?*

to function - *tmešša, xdem.* The radio doesn't function properly. *ṛ-ṛadyu ma-ka-ixdem-š mezyan.*

fundamental - *ʔasasi.*

funeral - *gnaza* pl. *-t, gnayez.*

funnel - **1.** *mdexna* pl. *-t.* The steamer has three funnels. *l-babbuṛ Ɛendu tlata d-le-mdexnat.* **2.** *meḥgen* pl. *mḥagen, duwwaz* pl. *-a.* The funnel is too big for the bottle. *l-meḥgen kbir Ɛla fomm l-qeṛƐa.*

funny - **1.** *(lli) ka-iḍeḥḥek, muḍḥik.* That's a very funny story. *hadi xṛafa ka-ḍḍeḥḥek.* **2.** *Ɛžuba.* Funny, I can't find my pen. *Ɛžuba, ma-žbeṛt-š qlami.*
funny bone - *qebṭal.*
furious - *mġuwwel.*
furnace - *kuša* pl. *-t.*
to **furnish** - **1.** *ʔettet.* I want a furnished room. *bġit bit mʔettet.* **2.** *Ɛṭa yeƐṭi, qeddem.* Can you furnish proof? *waš imken-lek teƐṭi ši-ḥožža?*
furniture - *ʔatat.* We still have to buy some furniture. *baqi ka-ixeṣṣna nešriw ši-ʔatat.*
furthermore - *u-zaydun.*
fuse - **1.** *rettaḥa de-ḍ-ḍuw.* The fuse blew out. *r-rettaḥa de-ḍ-ḍuw ttḥeṛqet.* **2.** *ftila* pl. *ftayel.* He lit the fuse and ran away as fast as he could. *šƐel le-ftila u-ḍṛebha b-sebga.*
fuss - *haṛaž, ṣdaƐ* pl. *-at.* Don't make such a fuss over him! *ma-ddir-š had l-haṛaž Ɛla weddu.*
fussy - *mzeƐlek.* He's very fussy about food. *huwa mzeƐlek fe-l-makla dyalu.*
future - *musteqbal.*
in the future - *men daba l-l-qeddam, men daba l-fuq.* In the future, come on time! *men daba l-l-qeddam aži fe-l-weqt.*
(sometime) in the future - *fe-l-musteqbal.* Sometime in the future I'm going to buy a car. *fe-l-musteqbal ġad nešri siyaṛa.*

G

gag - *lekkaka* pl. *-t, lekka* pl. *-t.* Take the gag out of his mouth. *zuwwel-lu l-lekkaka men fommu.*
to gag - **1.** *lekkek l-fomm l-.* They bound and gagged him. *kettfuh u-lekkku-lu fommu.* **2.** *muḍḥika* pl. *-t.* There are a few good gags in the new show. *kaynin ši-muḍḥikat mezyanin fe-l-fṛaža ž-ždida.* **3.** *žaf izif.* I almost gagged on the bone. *Ɛla šwiyeš kont ġad nžif b-le-Ɛḍem.* **4.** *žiyyef.* The shirt collar is gagging me. *l-Ɛenq de-l-qamiža mžiyyefni.*
to **gain** - **1.** *rbeḥ, ṭleƐ-lu.* What did he gain by that? *šnu rbeḥ men dak š-ši?* **2.** *mlek.* He has gained my confidence. *mlek t-tiqa dyali.* **3.** *lḥeq.* Can't you go faster? The car behind us is gaining. *waš ma-imken-lek-ši dzid dži? ṭ-ṭumubil lli wṛana Ɛlayen telḥeqna.*
**The patient is gaining rapidly. *le-mṛiḍ bdat ḥaltu ttḥessen b-soṛƐa.* --He couldn't gain a footing anywhere. *ma-ṣab fayn iḥeṭṭ režlih.* --She's gained a lot (of weight) recently. *zadet smanet bezzaf had l-iyam.*
gall - *mṛaṛ.*
gall bladder - *meṛṛaṛa* pl. *-t. mṛayeṛ.*
to **gallop** - *ḥerrek.* The horse began to gallop. *l-Ɛewd bda iḥerrek.*
galosh - *ġlaf ṣ-ṣebbaṭ.* pl. *ġlafat ṣ-ṣbabeṭ.*
gamble - *ẓheṛ* pl. *ẓhuṛ.* It was a pure gamble, but we had to risk it. *kan ġir ẓheṛ be-l-ḥeqq tlezzemna nxaṭṛu bih.*
to gamble - **1.** *qemmeṛ, lƐeb le-qmeṛ.* They were gambling for high stakes. *kanu ka-iqemmṛu b-le-flus bezzaf.* **2.** *xaṭeṛ b-.* He's gambling with his life. *ka-ixaṭeṛ b-ḥayatu.*
to gamble away - *xṣeṛ f-le-qmeṛ.* He gambled his whole salary away. *xṣeṛ le-xlaṣ dyalu kollu f-le-qmeṛ.*
gambling - *qmeṛ, taqemmaṛet.* Gambling is not allowed here. *taqemmaṛet. memnuƐa hnaya.*
game - **1.** *ṭeṛḥ* pl. *ṭṛuḥ, leƐba* pl. *-t.* Would you like to play a game of chess? *waš tebġi telƐeb ši-ṭeṛḥ dyal ṣ-ṣenṭṛež?* **2.** *ṣyaḍa, ṣiḍ, ṣyaḍ.* There's a lot of game in this region. *kayna ṣ-ṣyaḍa bezzaf f-had n-naḥiya.*
**I saw through his game. *Ɛeqt bih* or *feqt bih.* They realized that their game was up. *Ɛeṛfu ṛaṣhom bin ttfeḍḥu.*
gang - **1.** *Ɛiṣaba* pl. *-t.* The head of the gang was a notorious criminal. *kan ṛaʔis l-Ɛiṣaba mužrim mešhuṛ.* **2.** *zmaƐa* pl. *-t, rbaƐa* pl. *-t.* I can't stand the whole gang. *ma-ka-nehmel-š ž-žmaƐa kollha.* **3.** *feṛqa* pl. *-t.* Who's the foreman of your gang? *škun huwa ṛaʔis l-feṛqa dyalkom?*
gap - **1.** *xewya* pl. *-t, terƐa* pl. *-t.*

The gap has to be filled. *l-xewya ka-ixeṣṣha ttƐemmeṛ.* **2.** *noqṣan.* There are large gaps in his education. *Ɛendu noqṣan kbir fe-t-taqafa dyalu.*
garbage - *zbel.*
garden - *Ɛeṛṣa* pl. *-t, Ɛṛaṣi.*
to **gargle** - *ġeṛġeṛ.* Gargle with this medicine every three hours. *ġeṛġeṛ b-had d-dwa Ɛla ṛaṣ tlata de-ṣ-saƐat.*
garlic - *tuma* pl. *-t* coll. *tum.*
to **garnish** - *šeṛmel.* The fish was garnished with parsley and lemon. *l-ḥut kan mšeṛmel b-le-mƐednus u-l-limun.*
gas - **1.** *buṭagaz.* We cook with gas. *ka-nṭiyybu be-l-buṭagaz.* **2.** *ġaz.* Gas was used in the First World War. *fe-l-ḥeṛb l-Ɛalamiya l-luwla steƐmlu l-ġaz.* **3.** *liṣanṣ.* He had enough gas for ten kilometers. *kan Ɛendu l-liṣanṣ lli iqeddu l-Ɛešṛa de-l-kilumitṛat.* **4.** *benž.* Did the dentist give you gas? *dar-lek l-benž ṭ-ṭbib de-s-snan?*
gasoline - *liṣanṣ.*
gate - *bab* pl. *biban.*
to **gather** - **1.** *žmeƐ.* The children gathered wood in the forest. *d-drari žemƐu le-ḥṭeb fe-l-ġaba.* **2.** *ddžmeƐ.* A large crowd gathered in front of the courthouse. *ddžemƐet žuqa kbira qbalt l-meḥkama.* **3.** *fhem, ḍher-lu, ban-lu.* I gather from what you say that you don't like him. *men klamek ka-nefhem bin ma-ka-tebġih-š*
to **guage** - *qeḍḍeṛ.* I couldn't gauge the distance very well. *ma-mken-li-š nqeḍḍeṛ tamamen šḥal kayen de-l-boƐd.*
gay - **1.** *ṛaseq-lu, našeṭ.* He's in a gay mood today. *ka-iḍheṛ ṛašeq-lu l-yum.* **2.** *mluwwen.* The street was decorated with gay flags. *z-zenqa kanet mziyyna b-ṛayat mluwwna.*
gem - **1.** *ḥežṛa ḥoṛṛa* pl. *ḥežṛat ḥoṛṛat* coll. *ḥžeṛ ḥoṛṛ.* Those gems were invaluable. *dak le-ḥžeṛ l-ḥoṛṛ kan ma-Ɛendu taman.*
general - **1.** *žiniṛal* pl. *-at.* **2.** *Ɛumumi, Ɛamm.* A general election is held every year. *koll Ɛam ka-ikun ntixab Ɛamm.*
in general - *b-ṣifa Ɛamma.* In general, things are all right. *b-ṣifa Ɛamma, koll-ši ka-itmešša mezyan.*
general delivery - *barid Ɛumumi.* Write to me (in care of) general delivery. *kteb-li l-l-barid l-Ɛumumi.*
generally - **1.** *f-ġaleb l-ʔeḥyan.* He's generally on time. *f-ġaleb l-ʔeḥyan ka-iži fe-l-weqt.* **2.** *Ɛel l-Ɛumum.* That's generally known. *had š-ši meƐṛuf Ɛel l-Ɛumum.*
generally speaking - *b-ṣifa Ɛamma.*
generation - **1.** *žil* pl. *ʔežyal.* His family has been in America for four generations. *hadi ṛebƐa de-l-ʔežyal u-l-Ɛaʔila dyalu mužuda f-ʔamirika.* **2.** *težhiz.* The generation of electricity is inexpensive. *težhiz l-kehṛaba ma-ġali-š bezzaf.*
generous - *karim, krim* pl. *kuṛamaʔ, kṛam.* He's one of the most generous persons I ever met. *huwa ʔekṛem ṛažel tƐaṛeft bih.*
to be generous with - *sxa isxa b-.* He was very generous with his money. *kan ka-isxa be-flusu.*
**Don't be so generous with other people's things. *ma-tṣeḍḍeq-š men ḍaṛ žaṛtek.*
genius - **1.** *ṛažel Ɛebqaṛi* pl. *ržal Ɛebqaṛiyin.* Many people consider him a genius. *bezzaf de-n-nas ka-iḥesbuh ṛažel Ɛebqaṛi.* **2.** *Ɛebqaṛiya.* Someday my genius will be recognized. *waḥed n-nhaṛ ġad yeƐtaṛfu n-nas b-Ɛebqaṛiyti.*
gentle - **1.** *xfif* pl. *xfaf.* There was a gentle breeze coming from the sea. *kan hwa xfif maži men le-bḥeṛ.* **2.** *sahel.* This horse is very gentle. *had l-Ɛewd sahel bezzaf.* **3.** *ḍṛif* pl. *ḍṛaf.* He's always very gentle with his children. *huwa dima ḍṛif mƐa d-drari dyalu.*
gentleman - **1.** *siyyed* pl. *sadat.* Will you wait on this gentleman, please? *qabel had s-siyyed, baṛek ḷḷahu fik.* **2.** *mʔeddeb.* He's always a gentleman with me. *daymen mʔeddeb mƐaya.*
gently - **1.** *be-šwiyeš.* He knocked gently on the door. *deqq fe-l-bab be-šwiyeš.* **2.** *be-ḍ-ḍrafa, be-l-lṭafa.* You'll have to treat him gently. *ka-ixeṣṣek tƐamlu be-ḍ-ḍrafa.*
genuine - *ʔaṣili.*
geography - *žuġṛafiya* (with art. *l-žuġṛafiya*).
germ - *žurtuma* pl. *-t, žaratim.*
German - **1.** *aḷmani* noun pl. *aḷman.* Are there many Germans here? *waš kaynim ši-aḷman bezzaf hna?* **2.** *aḷmaniya.* He speaks good German. *ka-itkellem l-aḷmaniya mezyan.*
Germany - *aḷmanya.*
to **get** - **1.** *tweṣṣeḷ b-.* When did you get my letter? *mtaš tweṣṣeḷti b-le-bṛa dyali?* **2.** *žbeṛ.* Where did you get that book? *fayn žbeṛti dak le-ktab?* **3.** *xda yaxod.* Wait until I get my hat. *ṣbeṛ ḥetta naxod*

š-šemrir dyali. **4.** *ttaṣeḷ b-.* I couldn't get you on the phone. *ma-mken-li-š nttaṣeḷ bik fe-t-tilifun.* **5.** *ḥeṣṣeḷ Ɛla.* That's hard to get now. *dak š-ši ṣƐib tḥeṣṣeḷ Ɛlih daba.* --You can get the answer by Monday. *imken-lek tḥeṣṣeḷ Ɛel ž-žwab žwayeh t-tnayn.* **6.** *ṣab iṣib.* I have to get something for dinner. *xeṣṣni nṣib ši-ḥaža l-le-ġda.* **7.** *ṣdeq, dxel.* I got into the wrong room. *dxelt l-bit axuṛ ġaḷaṭ.* **8.** *redd, ṛežžeƐ.* The soot from the factory gets everything dirty. *d-doxxan de-l-meƐmel ka-iredd koll-ši mwessex.*

**Do you get the idea? *waš fhemti?* --I get it! *fhemt!* --I can't seem to get going today. *ma-imken-li ndir ḥetta haža l-yum.* --Let's get going! *ya be-smellah!* --What does it get me? *šnu fayda Ɛendi f-had š-ši?* --You've got me wrong. *ṛak ġaḷeṭ fiya.* --He gets about a great deal. *huwa ṛažel našeṭ bezzaf.*

to get across - *fehhem l-, fesser l-.* I wasn't able to get the idea across to him. *ma-mken-li-š nfehhem-lu l-fikra.*

to get a glimpse of - *šaf išuf be-z-zerba.* I just got a glimpse of him. *yaḷḷah šeftu be-z-zerba.*

to get along - **1.** *mša imši.* I'll have to be getting along now. *ka-ixeṣṣni nemši daba.* **2.** *ḍebbeṛ (Ɛla raṣu).* I'll get along somehow. *ġad ndebbeṛ (Ɛla raṣi) kif-emma kan.* **3.** *tƐašer.* I can't get along with him. *ma-neqdeṛ-š ntƐašer mƐah.* --We get along well with each other. *ka-ntƐašru mezyan.*

**He's getting along in years. *bda išref.* --How are you getting along? *še-xbaṛek mƐa d-denya?*

to get around - **1.** *tsara, ḍaṛ iḍuṛ.* Did you get around much when you were in Morocco? *waš tsariti bezzaf melli konti fe-l-meġṛib?* **2.** *šaƐ išiƐ.* The story got around quickly. *le-xbaṛ šaƐ b-soṛƐa.* **3.** *qneƐ.* You won't get around him. *ṛah ma-imken-lek-š tqenƐu.*

**She gets around pretty well for her age. *baqya ka-ddegg u-ddegdeg.*

to get at - **1.** *lḥeq.* I can't get at my luggage. *ma-imken-li-š nelḥeq l-bagaž dyali.* **2.** *žbeṛ, ṭeḷḷeƐ.* I'll get at the real reason yet. *daba nežbeṛ s-sabab l-ḥaqiqi.*

to get away - **1.** *beƐƐed.* I couldn't get her away from the window. *ma-mken-li-š nbeƐƐedha men š-šeṛžem.* **2.** *beƐƐed Ɛla, xrež men.* I want to get away from the city for awhile. *bġit nbeƐƐed Ɛel le-mdina ši-šwiya.* **3.** *flet.* If you think you can get away from me, you're mistaken. *ṛak ġaḷeṭ ila qal-lek Ɛeqlek ġad teflet.*

to get back - **1.** *ṛžeƐ.* When did you get back? *fuq-aš ṛžeƐti?* **2.** *ṛžeƐ-lu.* Did he get his money back? *waš ṛežƐu-lu flusu?*

to get by - **1.** *flet men.* How did you get by the guard? *kif-aš derti ḥetta fletti men l-Ɛessas?* **2.** *qḍa iqḍi.* I don't have much money, but I think I'll get by. *ma-Ɛendi flus bezzaf, be-l-ḥeqq ka-nḍenn ġad neqḍi.*

to get by with - *mneƐ b-.* Do you think you'll get by with that excuse? *sḥab-lek ġad temneƐ b-dak l-Ɛoḍṛ?*

to get even - *fdaha ifdiha.* I'll get even with him some day. *ġad nefdiha fih ši-nhaṛ.*

to get hungry - *žah ižih ž-žuƐ, žaƐ ižuƐ.* I got awfully hungry. *žani ž-žuƐ bezzaf.*

to get in - **1.** *dxel idxol.* How did he manage to get in here? *kif-aš dar ḥetta dxel le-hna?* **2.** *wṣeḷ.* What time did the train get in? *fuq-aš weṣḷeṭ l-mašina?* **3.** *ṭḷeƐ.* Get in, we'll take you down town. *ṭḷeƐ, nweṣṣḷuk le-mdina.* **4.** *dexxel.* Please get the clothes in before it rains. *ḷḷah ixellik dexxel le-ḥwayež qbel-ma ṭṭiḥ š-šta.*

**He doesn't let you get a word in edgewise. *ma-ka-ixellik tqul ḥetta kelma.*

to get in(to) - **1.** *dxel.* How did you get into the house? *kif-aš dxelti le-ḍ-ḍaṛ?* **2.** *ṭḷeƐ, dxel.* Then he got into the car and drove off. *u-men beƐd ṭḷeƐ fe-ṭ-ṭumubil u-zad.* **3.** *dexxel, Ɛmel, siyyeƐ.* How did you manage to get everything into one room? *kif mken-lek ddexxel koll-ši f-bit waḥed?* **4.** *ṭaḥ iṭiḥ f-.* He got into bad company. *ṭaḥ f-muxalaṭa qbiḥa.*

to get late - *bda imši l-ḥal.* It's getting late. *bda imši l-ḥal.*

to get off - **1.** *nzel, hbeṭ.* You have to get off in ten minutes. *xeṣṣek tenzel men daba Ɛešṛa de-d-dqayeq.* **2.** *zuwwel.* I can't get my shoes off. *ma-qdeṛt-š nzuwwel ṣebbaṭi.* **3.** *xrež, ṭḷeƐ-lu.* He got off with a light sentence. *xrež be-ḥkam mxeffef.* **4.** *mneƐ, flet.* This time you won't get off so easy.

had n-nuba ła-iqul-lek-ši ɛeqlek ġad temneɛ ġir hakdak.

to get old - *kber, šref.* He's getting old. *bda ikber.*

to get on - 1. *ṭleɛ, rkeb.* We got on in Rabat. *rkebna fe-ṛ-ṛbaṭ.* 2. *tɛašer.* The three of us get on very well. *ḥna be-tlata ka-ntɛašru mezyan.* 3. *tmešša.* How are you getting on in your work? *kif ka-ttmešša fe-l-xedma dyalek?*

**He's getting on in years. *bda ka-išref.* --How are you getting on? *še-xbaṛek mɛa d-denya?*

to get on with - *kemmel, tabeɛ.* Now let's get on with the discussion. *daba ažiw nkemmlu l-mudakaṛa dyalna.*

to get oneself something - *ḍebbeṛ ɛla ṛaṣu f-.* I got myself a radio. *ḍebbeṛt ɛla ṛaṣi f-ṛaḍyu.*

to get out - 1. *xerrež, zuwwel, qelleɛ.* I can't get the nail out. *ma-qḍeṛt-š nqelleɛ l-mesmaṛ.* --Get that out of your head. *zuwwel dak š-ši men balek.* 2. *xerrež, xrež b-.* They're getting out a new book. *ġad ixerržu ktab ždid.* --I was so frightened, I couldn't get a word out. *b-quwwet l-xelɛa ma-qdeṛt nxerrež ḥetta kelma.* 3. *ttefḍeḥ.* I don't know how the story got out. *ma-ɛṛeft-š kif ttfeḍḥet l-qaḍiya.* 4. *nzel, hbeṭ.* I'll have to get out at the next stop. *xeṣṣni nnzel f-le-mḥeṭṭa l-mažya.* 5. *šaɛ išiɛ, xrež.* We mustn't let this news get out. *ma-ka-ixeṣṣna-ši nxelliw had le-xbaṛ išiɛ.*

to get out of - 1. *žbed men.* You won't get anything out of him. *ma-imken-lek džbed mennu ḥetta ḥaža.* 2. *rbeḥ f-, ṭleɛ-lu.* How much did you get out of this sale? *šḥal ṭleɛ-lek men had l-biɛa?* 3. *xerrež.* Get the dog out of the house! *xerrež l-kelb men ḍ-ḍaṛ!* 4. *xrež men.* How did you get out of that room? *kif-aš xrežti men dak l-bit?* 5. *nzel men.* Get out of that car! *nzel men dak ṭ-ṭumubil!*

**Get out (of here)! *zid xelfa!* --Get out of his way! *zul men ṭṛiqu!* or *beɛɛed mennu!* --How did you ever get out of that mess? *kif-aš derti ḥetta selliti kerɛek men dak l-ḥeṣla?*

to get over - 1. *bṛa ibṛa men, rtaḥ men.* Has she gotten over that illness yet? *waš bṛat men dak l-meṛḍ wella ma-zal?* 2. *nsa insa, zal-lu izul-lu men balu, ttensa-lu.* He never has gotten over her. *ɛemmeṛha ma-zalet-lu men balu.*

**He certainly got over his wife's death quickly. *deġya deġya zalet-lu l-feqṣa de-l-mut de-mṛatu.*

to get ready - 1. *wežžed.* I have to get breakfast ready. *xeṣṣni nwežžed le-fṭuṛ.* 2. *wežžed ṛaṣu, wžed.* How long will it take you to get ready? *šḥal xeṣṣek de-l-weqt baš twežžed ṛaṣek?*

to get rid of - *thenna men.* How can I get rid of him? *kif-aš imken-li nthenna mennu?*

to get sick - *mṛeḍ, ṭaḥ iṭiḥ mṛiḍ.* I hope he doesn't get sick. *ka-ntmenna ma-imṛeḍ-š.*

to get someone to - *ḥṣeṛ f-, dfeɛ.* Can you get him to go there? *waš imken-lek teḥṣeṛ fih baš imši l-temma?*

to get something to someone - *weṣṣel l-.* Can you get this money to him? *waš imken-lek tweṣṣel-lu had le-flus?*

to get tired - *wella ɛeyyan, ɛya yeɛya.* He never gets tired. *ɛemmṛu ma-ka-yeɛya.*

to get to (someplace) - *wṣel, mša imši.* How can I get there? *kif imken-li nemši l-temma?* --I'll get there in an hour. *ġad nuwṣel men daba saɛa.*

to have got to - *xeṣṣu, la-bodda-lu.* I've got to go. *ka-ixeṣṣni nemši.*

to get through - 1. *daz iduz men.* You can't get through there. *ma-imken-lek-š dduz men temma.* 2. *kemmel.* I'll see you after I get through. *nšufek men beɛd-ma nkemmel.*

to get together - 1. *ttežmeɛ.* Let's get together tonight at my house. *nddžemɛu fe-ḍ-ḍaṛ dyali had l-lila.* 2. *ttafeq.* They never seem to get together on anything. *u-tqul ɛemmeṛhom ma-ittafqu ɛla ši-ḥaža.*

to get to work on - *bda ibda f-.* When are you going to get to work on the new house? *fuq-aš ġad tebdaw fe-ḍ-ḍaṛ ž-ždida?*

to get up - *naḍ inuḍ.* I get up at six every morning. *ka-nnuḍ koll ṣbaḥ fe-s-setta.*

to get well - *bṛa ibṛa.*

ghost - *ženn* pl. *žnun, xyal* pl. *-at.* I don't believe in ghosts. *ma-ka-namen-š be-ž-žnun.*

**He hasn't a ghost of a chance to escape. *u-tqul ɛendu kif yeɛmel ihṛeb.*

giant - **1.** *ɛemlaq* pl. *ɛamaliqa.* Compared to me, he's a giant. *be-n-nesba lili huwa ɛemlaq.* **2.** *qedd sexṭ ḷḷah.* There was a giant spider in my room. *f-biti kanet waḥed r-rtila qedd sexṭ ḷḷah.*
**He's no mental giant. *ma-ɛndu-ši ɛqel baheḍ.*

Gibraltar - *žbel ṭ-ṭeṛṛ, žabal ṭariq.*

gift - **1.** *hdiya* pl. *-t.* Thank you for your beautiful gift. *ka-neškṛek ɛla dak le-hdiya dyalek l-moɛtabaṛa.* **2.** *ɛṭiya* pl. *-t, muhiba* pl. *-t, mwaheb.* He has a gift for drawing. *t-tiṣwiṭ ɛendu ɛṭiya.*
**I wouldn't take that as a gift! *waxxa ittehda-li ma-naxdu-š!*

gifted - *muhub.* He's a gifted boy. *huwa weld muhub.*

to **giggle** - *qaqa.* The girls kept on giggling. *le-bnat bqaw ġir ka-iqaqiw.*

ginger - *skinžbir* (not used with art.).

giraffe - *ẓaṛafa* pl. *-t.*

girl - **1.** *bent* pl. *bnat, ṭefla* pl. *-t.* Isn't she a pretty girl! *walayenni bent ġzala!* **2.** *xeddama* pl. *-t, metɛellma* pl. *-t.* We pay our girl a hundred dirhams a month. *ka-nxeḷḷṣu l-xeddama dyalna myat derhem fe-š-šheṛ.*
little girl - *bniya* pl. *-t, bnita* pl. *-t, ṭfila* pl. *-t.* Your little girl has grown a lot. *bniytek kebret bezzaf.*

to **give** - **1.** *ɛṭa yeɛṭi.* Please give me the letter. *ɛṭini le-bṛa men feḍlek.* --I'll give you five dirhams for it. *neɛṭik fih xemsa de-d-drahem.* **2.** *hda ihdi, ɛṭa yeɛṭi.* What did he give you for your birthday? *šnu hda-lek f-ɛid l-milad dyalek?* **3.** *sellem.* Give the letter to him personally. *sellem-lu r-risala l-iddih.* **4.** *qal iqul, ɛṭa yeɛṭi.* Did he give a reason? *waš qal-lek ši-sabab?* **5.** *džebbed.* Does this belt give? *waš had le-ḥzam ka-idžebbed?* **6.** *ɛmel l-.* This noise gives me a headache. *ṣ-ṣdaɛ ka-yeɛmel-li ḥṛiq ṛ-ṛas.* **7.** *smeḥ b-.* Can you give me another hour to finish? *tesmeḥ-li b-waḥed s-swiɛa xṛa nkemmel?*
**I don't give a damn. *ma-ka-ihemmni-š be-l-koll.* --Why did you give him the gate? *ɛlaš dḥitih?* --Give him my regards. *sellem ɛlih men ɛendi.* --I have to finish in a given time. *ixeṣṣni nfeḍḍi f-waḥed l-weqt meḥdud.*
to give a speech - *xṭeb, lqa ilqi xoṭba, ɛmel kalima.* Who's giving the speech at the dinner? *škun ġad ixṭeb fe-l-ḥefla d-le-ɛša?*
to give away - **1.** *ṣeḍḍeq, ɛṭa yeɛṭi.* I gave my old clothes away. *ṣeḍḍeqt ḥwayži le-qdam.* **2.** *fḍeḥ.* Don't give my secret away! *ma-tefḍeḥ-š s-serr dyali!*
to give back - *ṛeḍḍ, ṛežžeɛ.* Please give me back my pen. *ṛeḍḍ-li rišti ḷḷah ixellik.*
to give in to - **1.** *traxa mɛa.* You give in to the child too much. *ka-ttraxa bezzaf mɛa had l-weld.* **2.** *qbel.* I wanted to borrow his car but he wouldn't give in. *bġitu isellefni ṭ-ṭumubil dyalu be-l-ḥeqq ma-bġa-š iqbel.*
to give off - *ṭḷeq.* This flower gives off a strange odor. *had n-nuwwaṛa ka-ṭṭleq ši-riḥa f-ši-škel.*
to give oneself up - *steslem, ɛṭa yeɛṭi ṛaṣu.* He gave himself up to the police. *steslem l-l-bulis.*
to give out - **1.** *feṛṛeq, tbeṛṛeɛ b-.* Who's giving out the candy? *škun lli ka-ifeṛṛeq l-fanid?* **2.** *tqaḍa.* My supply of ink is giving out. *le-mdad dyali ka-itqaḍa.*
to give service - *qḍa iqḍi ḥaža, ṣḷaḥ.* My old coat still gives me good service. *kebbuṭi le-qdim baqi ka-iqḍi ḥaža.*
to give time - *mehhel ɛla, ṣbeṛ ɛla.* You'll have to give me more time. *xeṣṣek tmehhel ɛliya.*
to give trouble - *šuwweš.* That fellow gives me a lot of trouble. *dak xiyna ka-išuwweš ɛliya bezzaf.*
to give up - **1.** *smeḥ f-, txella ɛla.* Joseph gave up his job. *yusef smeḥ fe-l-xedma dyalu.* **2.** *qṭeɛ, feḍḍa men, sala men.* I'm going to give up smoking. *ġadi neqṭeɛ d-doxxan.* **3.** *qṭeɛ l-iyyas, iʔes.* I don't give up easily. *ma-ka-neqṭeɛ l-iyyas deġya.*
to give way - *hwa ihwa.* The boards gave way under his weight. *le-xšeb hwa bih* or *le-xšeb hwa be-t-tqel dyalu.*

glad - *feṛḥan.* We're very glad about it. *ḥna feṛḥanin bezzaf b-had š-ši.*
**Glad to meet you! *metšeṛṛef!* --I'll be glad to do that for you. *ɛla ṛaṣi u-ɛeyniya* or *b-koll faṛaḥ.*

gladly - *ɛel ṛ-ṛas u-l-ɛeynin, b-koll faṛaḥ.* Would you do me a favor?

Gladly. *waš tebġi ddir fiya ši-mziya? ɛel ṛ-ṛaṣ u-l-ɛeynin.*

glance - *ṛemqa de-l-ɛeyn, šufa weḥda.* I could tell at a glance that something was wrong. *f-ṛemqa de-l-ɛeyn ɛṛeft ši-ḥaža ma-ka-ttmešša-š mezyan.*

to glance - *šaf išuf, ṛmeq.* He glanced at his watch. *šaf f-magantu.*

glare - *šɛa* (m.), *šɛaɛ.* The glare hurts my eyes. *š-šɛa ka-iqewqeš-li ɛeyniya.*

to glare at - *xzer f-.* Why are you glaring at me like that? *ɛlaš ka-texzer fiya hakdak?*

glaring - *(lli) ka-yeɛmi, mežhed.* How can you work in that glaring light? *kif ka-teqḍeṛ texdem f-dak ḍ-ḍuw ka-yeɛmi?*

glass - **1.** *zaž, žaž.* This pitcher is made of glass. *had l-ġoṛṛaf mṣuwweb men z-zaž.* **2.** *kas* pl. *kisan.* May I have a glass of water? *waš imken-lek teɛṭini ši-kas de-l-ma?*

glasses - *nḍaḍeṛ, neḍḍaṛat.* I can't read that without glasses. *ma-neqḍeṛ-š neqṛa had š-ši bla nḍaḍeṛ.*

magnifying glass - *beḷḷaṛa* pl. *-t.*

pane of glass - *zaža, žaža* pl. *-t.*

gleam - *šɛa, šɛaɛ.* There was still a faint gleam in the sky. *kan ma-zal waḥed š-šɛa qlil fe-s-sma.*

to **gleam** - *ḍwa iḍwi, lmeɛ.* His eyes were gleaming. *ɛeynih kanu ka-iḍwiw.*

to **glisten** - *ḍwa iḍwi, lmeɛ.* The tower was glistening in the sun. *ṣ-ṣemɛa kanet ka-ḍḍwi fe-š-šemš.*

to **glitter** - *bra ibri, lmeɛ.* The snow glittered in the sun. *t-telž kan ka-ibri fe-š-šemš.*

**All that glitters is not gold. *a le-mzuwweq mne-ɛ̄la beṛṛa, še-xbaṛek men daxel!*

gloomy - **1.** *meḍlam.* Yesterday was a very gloomy day. *l-baṛeḥ kan nhaṛ meḍlam bezzaf.* **2.** *mkeḍḍeṛ.* He looks gloomy. *ka-idheṛ mkeḍḍeṛ.*

glorify - *mežžed f-.* He may be good, but let's not glorify him. *imken ikun ṛažel mezyan be-l-ḥeqq ma-kayen ɛlaš nmežždu fih.*

glorious - **1.** *mažid* pl. *mžad, kbir* pl. *kbaṛ.* The day we won the war was a glorious day. *n-nhaṛ f-aš rbeḥna l-ḥeṛb kan nhaṛ mažid.* **2.** *ɛḍim* pl. *ɛḍam.* What a glorious day it is! *walayenni hada nhaṛ ɛḍim!*

glory - *mežd, ɛezz.*

glove - *ṣebbaɛiya* pl. *-t, ṣebbaɛa* pl. *-t.* I bought a pair of gloves yesterday. *šrit žuža de-ṣ-ṣebbaɛiyat l-bareḥ.*

**They worked hand in glove. *xedmu yedd f-yedd.* --This suit fits me like a glove. *had l-keswa ka-dži tamamen qeddi.*

glue - *lṣaq.* I bought a bottle of glue. *šrit meṭṛeb de-l-lṣaq.* --He stuck to me like glue. *lṣeq fiya bḥal l-leṣqa.*

to glue - *leṣṣeq.* They glued the picture to the wall. *leṣṣqu t-teṣwiṛa fe-l-ḥiṭ.*

**He stood as if glued to the spot. *bqa waqef tqul nabet fe-ḷ-ḷeṛḍ.* --He kept his eyes glued on her. *ma-zuwwel-š ɛeynih mennha.*

glutton - *bu-kerš; wekkal* pl. *-in, -a; keršawi* pl. *-yen.* Don't be such a glutton. *ma-tkun-š bu-kerš.*

to **go** - **1.** *mša imši* (imperative *sir*). I go to the movies once a week. *ka-nemši le-s-sinima meṛṛa fe-l-ʔusbuɛ.* --Go to the store. *sir l-l-ḥanut.* **2.** *ṭaḥ iṭiḥ, ža iži, mša imši.* --The old chair went to pieces when he touched it. *dak š-šelya le-qdima ġir qaṣha žat ṭṛaf.* **3.** *žra ižri, mša imši.* The train is going fast. *l-mašina ka-džri bezzaf.* **4.** *kan ikun.* This chair goes in the corner. *had š-šelya ka-tkun fe-r-rekna.* **5.** *ṭḷeɛ.* The wine has gone to his head. *le-xmeṛ ṭḷeɛ-lu le-ṛ-ṛaṣ.* **6.** *qedd l-, kfa ikfi l-.* There's enough cake to go around. *kayna l-ḥelwa lli tqedd l-koll-ši.* **7.** *bqa ibqa.* They went without food for three days. *bqaw telt iyam bla makla.* **8.** *daz iduz, kan ikun.* Whatever he says goes! *lli qalha huwa hiya lli dayza.*

**Go to the devil! *sir le-ž-žayḥa l-keḥla.* --Don't go to any trouble. *ma-tɛeddeb-š ṛaṣek.* --I don't know whether I'm coming or going! *ḥert ma-bqit neɛṛef ṛaṣi šnu ka-ndir.* --That goes without saying. *dak š-ši meɛṛuf.* --That's the way things go. *hadi hiya d-denya.* --We'll let it go at that. *aži nweqqfu l-qaḍiya hna.* --That's going a little too far! *iwa la! had š-ši tɛedda l-ḥudud.*

going to - *ġad* (+ imperfect). I'm going to do that work tomorrow. *ġad neɛmel had l-xedma ġedda.* --We're going to leave today. *ġad nemšiw l-yum.* --The roof is going to fall in. *s-sqef ġad iṭiḥ.*

to go ahead - *sbeq.* You go ahead,

I'll follow later. *sbeq, daba nexleṭ Ɛlik.*

**Just go ahead and finish. *ġir kemmel.* --Go ahead, take it! *ġir xudu!* --Go ahead, you tell him! *iwa qulha-lu nta!* or *zid, qulha-lu nta!*

to go at - **1.** *hžem Ɛla.* He went at him with a knife. *hžem Ɛlih b-sekkin.* **2.** *ṭaḥ iṭiḥ f-.* --They went at the food like wolves. *ṭaḥu fe-l-makla bḥal d-dyab.*

**You're not going at it right. *had š-ši lli ka-ddir ma-ši huwa hadak.*

to go back - *ṛžeƐ.* She went back home. *ṛežƐet l-daṛha.* --I never go back on my word. *Ɛemmṛi ma-ka-neṛžeƐ fe-klami.*

**I don't go back on my friends. *ma-ka-neġḍeṛ-š ṣḥabi* or *ma-ka-nḍuṛ-š Ɛla ṣḥabi.*

to go by - **1.** *daz iduz.* I wouldn't let that opportunity go by, if I were you. *u-kan kont mennek ma-nxelli-š had l-forṣa dduz.* **2.** *tebbeƐ.* Don't go by what he says. *ma-ttebbeƐ-š klamu.* **3.** *steƐmel.* He goes by an assumed name. *ka-isteƐmel smiya mzuwwṛa.*

to go down - **1.** *ṭaḥ iṭiḥ, nzel, hbeṭ.* Prices are going down. *l-ʔetman ka-ṭṭiḥ.* **2.** *hbeṭ, nzel.* Go downstairs and get my book. *hbeṭ l-teḥt u-žib-li le-ktab dyali.*

to go in - *dxel.* Has he gone in yet? *waš dxel wella ma-zal?*

to go in for - **1.** *htemm b-.* Do you go in for sports? *was ka-tehtemm be-ṛ-ṛiyaḍa?* **2.** *tƐaṭa l-.* I don't think he goes in for gambling. *ma-ka-nḍenn-š ka-itƐaṭa l-le-qmeṛ.*

to go in on - *šarek f-.* Would you like to go in with me on this deal? *waš tebġi tšarekni f-had l-biƐa u-š-šerya?*

to go into - **1.** *dxel l-.* Let's go into the house. *aži ndexlu le-ḍ-ḍaṛ.* **2.** *žbed.* There's no reason for us to go into that matter now. *ma-kayen Ɛlaš nžebdu dak l-qaḍiya daba.*

to go off - **1.** *ṭṭeṛṭeq.* Be careful, the revolver might go off! *ṛedd balek, daba l-ferdi iṭṭeṛteq!* **2.** *daz iduz.* The meeting went off without an incident. *le-žtimaƐ daz bla-ma tuqeƐ ḥetta ḥaža.*

to go on - **1.** *bqa ibqa, ṭal iṭul.* We mustn't let this lawsuit go on any longer. *had d-deƐwa ma-xeṣṣna-š nxelliwha ṭṭul kteṛ men had š-ši.* **2.** *bqa ibqa, zad izid.* He went on talking. *u-zad ka-itkellem.*

**Please go on! *zid kemmel, baṛak llahu fik.* --Go on! I don't believe that! *Ɛewwed le-s-seqqaya teddi-lek l-ġaya!*

to go on the road - **1.** *qbeṭ ṭ-ṭriq.* Our salesman is going on the road next week. *le-msuwweq dyalna ġadi iqbeṭ ṭ-ṭriq ž-žemƐa ž-žayya.* **2.** *Ɛmel waḥed l-žewla.* Is the whole cast going on the road? *waš l-feṛqa de-t-temtil kollha ġadi temši teƐmel waḥed l-žewla?*

to go out - **1.** *xṛež.* He just went out. *Ɛad xṛež.* --If you'd like, we'll go out for a little walk after dinner. *ila bġiti nxeṛžu ntsaraw ši-šwiya men beƐd le-Ɛša.* **2.** *ḍfa iḍfa.* Suddenly the lights went out. *ḍ-ḍuw ḍfa Ɛla beġta.*

**Sometimes we go out to dinner. *beƐḍ l-meṛṛat ka-nxeṛžu ntƐeššaw fe-l-meṭƐem.*

to go over - **1.** *mša imši l-.* I'm going over to his house for an hour. *ġad nemši l-ḍaṛu u-nebqa temmak ši-saƐa.* **2.** *nžeḥ.* Do you think my play will go over? *waš ka-ḍḍenn ʔenna t-temtil dyali ġad inžeḥ?* **3.** *ṛažeƐ.* Let's go over the details once more. *aži nṛažƐu t-tafaṣil kollha Ɛawed.* --I've gone over all the figures, but I can't find the mistake. *ṛžeƐt le-ḥsabat kollha u-ma-žbeṛt-š l-ġelṭa.*

to go through - **1.** *tteqbel.* Do you think my application will go through? *waš ka-ḍḍenn ṭ-ṭalab dyali ġad itteqbel?* **2.** *daz iduz f-, qṭeƐ f-.* He went through the red light. *daz ḍ-ḍuw le-ḥmer.*

**The poor woman has gone through a lot. *le-mṛa meskina duwwzet Ɛla qelbha.*

to go to - *tteƐṭa l-.* The first prize went to a young man. *l-žaʔiza l-luwwla tteƐṭat l-waḥed š-šabb.*

to go under - **1.** *steƐmel.* Although she is married, she goes under her family name. *waxxa mzuwwža ka-testeƐmel s-smiya de-l-Ɛaʔila dyalha.* **2.** *ġṛaq.* The ship went under at midnight. *l-baxiṛa ġṛaqet f-neṣṣ l-lil.*

to go unnoticed - *daz iduz f-xefya.* I hope the incident will go unnoticed. *ka-ntmenna l-mesʔala dduz f-xefya.*

to go up - **1.** *ṭleƐ.* Did you see him go up? *waš šeftih ṭleƐ?* **2.** *zad* *izid (fe-t-taman), ġla iġla.* Meat has gone up this week. *l-lḥem zad (fe-t-taman) had ž-žemɛa.*

to go with - *ža iži mɛa, walem.* This tie doesn't go with the suit. *had le-kṛavaṭa ma-žat-š mɛa had l-keswa.*

**The trip and everything that went with it cost me a hundred dollars. *ṭaḥ ɛliya ṣ-ṣfeṛ kollu be-myat ḍulaṛ.*

to let go (of) - *ṭḷeq (men).* Let go of my hand! *ṭḷeq men iddi!*

to let oneself go - **1.** *hmel ṛaṣu, smeḥ f-ṛaṣu.* Lately she's let herself go terribly. *f-had l-yam t-taliya hemlet ṛaṣha bezzaf.* **2.** *ttetḷeq mɛa ṛaṣu.* If you want to have fun, you'll have to let yourself go terribly. *f-had l-iyam t-taliya hemlet ṛaṣha bezzaf.*

to let someone go - *smeḥ l-.* This time we'll let you go. *had n-nuba ġad nsemḥu-lek.*

on the go - *ɛla kreɛ.* He's on the go day and night. *daymen ɛla kreɛ lil u-nhaṛ.*

goal - **1.** *hadaf* pl. *ˀehdaf, ġaya* pl. *-t.* He has set himself a very high goal. *dar qeddamu waḥed l-hadaf ɛali bezzaf.* **2.** *iṣaba* pl. *-t.* Our team made three goals in the first half. *l-feṛqa dyalna sežžlet tlata d-l-iṣabat fe-ṭ-ṭeṛḥ l-luwwel.*

goat - **1.** m. *ɛetrus* pl. *ɛtares,* f. *meɛza* pl. *-t, mɛiz.* How old do goats live to be? *šḥal men ɛam ka-iɛišu le-mɛiz?* **2.** *ḥmaṛ d-dbez.* He's always the goat. *huwa daymen ḥmaṛ d-dbez.*

**Don't let him get your goat. *ma-txellih-š ixerrež-lek ɛeqlek* or *ma-txellih-š yakol-lek moxxek.*

God - *ḷḷah* (in a certain number of fixed expressions, *llah*). God forbid! *ḷḷah yeḥfeḍ!* --Thank God! *l-ḥemdullah!* --God bless you! *iṛeḥmek ḷḷah!* --God willing! *ˀenšaˀ ḷḷah!*

god - *ilah* pl. *-at.*

go-getter - *(lli) ka-iḍebbeṛ ɛla ṛaṣu.* That boy is a go-getter. *dak l-weld ka-iḍebbeṛ ɛla ṛaṣu.*

goiter - *tarta.*

gold - **1.** *dheb* pl. *dhuba, dhubat.* Is that real gold? *waš hadak dheb ḥaqiqi?* **2.** *de-d-dheb.* I bought my wife a gold watch. *šrit le-mṛati magana de-d-dheb.*

goldsmith - *ṣiyyaġ* pl. *-a.*

goldsmith's craft - *taṣiyyaġet.*

good - **1.** *xir, meṣḷaḥa.* I'm only thinking of your good. *ka-nxemmem ġir fe-l-xir dyalek.* --He did it for the common good. *daru fe-l-meṣḷaḥa de-l-žamiɛ.* --The vacation has done him good. *l-ɛoṭḷa dyalu daret fih l-xir.*

good - **2.** *mezyan.* That was a good joke. *kanet mudḥika mezyana.* --This is a good piece of work! *xedma mezyana hadi!* --He's very good at figures. *huwa mezyan bezzaf f-le-ḥsab.* --Is this clay good for making pitchers? *waš had ṭ-ṭin mezyan l-le-ġṛaṛef?* **3.** *ḍrif* pl. *ḍraf.* They are good children. *huwa drari ḍraf.*

**At the end of the game he was fifty dirhams to the good. *f-ˀaxeṛ ṭ-ṭeṛḥ kan rabeḥ xemsin derhem.* --What good will it do him? *b-aš ġad inefɛu had š-ši?* --Good morning! *ṣbaḥ l-xir!* --Good evening! *mse-l-xir!* --Good night. *lila saɛida* or *ḷḷah imessik ɛla xir.* --He has a good head on his shoulders. *ɛendu ṛ-ṛaṣ.*

--These tires are good for another year. *had ṛ-ṛwayeḍ baqyin ižebdu ɛam axoṛ.*

good and - *bezzaf.* Make the tea good and strong. *ṣaweb atay mežhed bezzaf.*

good turn - *xir.* He did me a real good turn yesterday. *ɛmel fiya xir kbir l-bareḥ.*

a good deal of - *bezzaf d-, xir ḷḷah d-.* He spent a good deal of time on it. *duwwez fih bezzaf de-l-weqt.*

a good many - *ɛadad d-, ketṛa d-.* There were a good many foreigners in the hotel. *kanu ɛadad d-l-ažanib f-l-uṭil.*

for a good while - *hadi modda.* I haven't seen him for a good while. *hadi modda ma- šeftu.*

for good - *men daba l-qeddam.* I'm through with him for good. *men daba l-qeddam ma- bqa bini u-binu walu. walu.*

to be good - *ṣlaḥ, daz iduz.* The passport is good until the fifteenth. *l-žawaz baqi iṣlaḥ ḥetta l-l-xemsṭaš.*

to have a good time - *tsella mɛa ṛaṣu.* Did you have a good time? *tselliti mɛa ṛaṣek?*

to make good - **1.** *nžeḥ, tmešša mezyan.* I'm sure he'll make good. *ana metyeqqen bin ġad itmešša* *mezyan.* 2. *tkellef b-.* I'll make good the damage. *ana ntkellef be-l-xaṣa?ir.* 3. *wfa yufi b-.* He made good his promise. *wfa be-l-ɛehd dyalu.*

good-by - *ḷḷah ihennik* (sg.), *ḷḷah ihennikom* (pl.). Good-by, have a good trip! *ḷḷah ihennik, ṭṛiq s-slama!*

good-natured - *ṭiyyeb.* He's a good-natured fellow. *huwa ṛažel ṭiyyeb.*

goods - *selɛa, baḍa?eɛ.* We sent the goods yesterday. *ṣifeṭna s-selɛa l-bareḥ.*

goose - *wezza* pl. *-t* coll *wezz.* We had goose for dinner. *tɛeššina be-l-wezz.*

**I'll cook his goose! *daba nɛewwṭu mɛa ṛaṣu.*

gorgeous - *badiɛ* pl. *bdaɛ.* It was a gorgeous day. *kan nhaṛ badiɛ.*

gospel - *?inžil.*

gossip - 1. *heḍḍaṛ* pl. *-a, -in* f. *heḍḍaṛa* f. pl. *-t, (lli) fommu kbir (*or *waseɛ), kbir (*or *waseɛ) l-fomm.* His wife is an old gossip. *walayenni mṛatu waḥed kbirt l-fomm mennha.* 2. *hḍuṛ* pl. *-at, ?isaɛa* pl. *-t.* I wouldn't believe that gossip. *ma-ntiq-š b-dak le-hḍuṛ.*

to gossip - *hḍeṛ, kebbeṛ fommu, hḍeṛ fe-n-nas.* She gossips too much. *ka-tehḍeṛ bezzaf.*

to **gouge** - *ḥfeṛ.* He gouged a piece out of the new table. *ḥfeṛ ṭ-ṭabla ž-ždida.*

gourd - *qeṛɛa ḥeṛša* pl. *-t ḥeṛšat, -t hureš* coll. *qṛeɛ ḥeṛša.*

gourmand - *šehwani* pl. *-yin, keršawi* pl. *-yin.*

gourmet - *duqi* pl. *-yin, dwayqiya.*

to **govern** - *ḥkem (ɛla).*

government - *ḥukuma* a *-t.* Who heads the new government? *škun metre??es l-ḥukuma ž-ždida?*

governor - 1. *ḥakem* pl. *ḥokkam.* Who's the governor of this colony? *škun l-ḥakem d-had l-musteɛmaṛa?* 2. *ɛamel* pl. *ɛommal.* Who's the governor of this province? *škun l-ɛamel d-had l-?iqlim?*

to **grab** - 1. *qbeṭ, qbeḍ.* He grabbed her by the arm. *qbeṭha men draɛha.* 2. *xṭef.* Don't grab, you'll get your share all right. *ma-txeṭfu-š daba yuṣel-lkom ḥeqqkom.*

to grab (by the collar, etc.). - 1. *šneq ɛla, lgeṭ ɛla.* He grabbed the thief (by the collar). *šneq ɛel š-šeffaṛ.*

**I just want to grab a bite. *ġir bġit neɛmel ši-šdiyeq.*

gracious - *ḷṭif* pl. *ḷṭaf.* She's a very gracious queen. *hiya malika ḷṭifa bezzaf.*

**My gracious! What a mess! *walayenni txeṛwiḍa hadi!*

grade - 1. *neqṭa* pl. *nuqaṭ.* He received the highest grades in the class. *xda ?eḥsen nuqaṭ fe-l-qism.* 2. *qism* pl. *?eqṣam.* What grade is your boy in? *fe-š-men qism weldek?* 3. *ḍaṛaža* pl. *-t.* We buy the best grade of milk. *ka-nešriw le-ḥlib dyal ?eḥsen ḍaṛaža.* 4. *(upgrade) ɛeqba* pl. *-t, ɛqabi.* This old car won't make it up the grade. *had ṭ-ṭumubil l-balya ma-teqḍeṛ-š ṭṭleɛ fe-l-ɛeqba.* 5. *(downgrade) ḥdura* pl. *-t, ḥdayer.* Be careful going down the grade. *ṛedd balek melli tkun habeṭ f-le-ḥdura.*

**He'll never make the grade. *ɛemmṛu ma-yuṣeḷ.*

to grade - *ɛzel, xteṛ.* Oranges are graded according to size and quality. *ka-iɛezlu l-letšin (l-limun) ɛla ḥasab le-kbeṛ u-n-nuɛ.*

gradually - *šwiya be-šwiya, be-t-tedriž.* He's gradually getting better. *ṣeḥḥtu ka-dzyan šwiya be-šwiya.*

to **graduate** - *txerrež.* He graduated from the law school. *txerrež men l-kolliya de-l-ḥuquq.*

grain - 1. *ḥebb* pl. *ḥbub.* Canada exports meat and grain. *l-kanada ka-tuseq l-lḥem u-le-ḥbub.* 2. *terkib.* This wood has a beautiful grain. *had le-xšeb fih terkib žmil.*

**That goes against my grain. *dak š-ši ka-iqelleqni.* --There isn't a grain of truth in the matter. *gṛam de-ṣ-ṣeḍq ma-kayen-ši temma.*

grammar - 1. *neḥw.* I never really studied Arabic grammar. *ɛemmṛi fe-l-ḥaqiqa ma-qrit n-neḥw l-ɛaṛabi.* 2. *ktab de-n-neḥw* pl. *ktub de-n-neḥw.* Do you have a good Arabic grammar for beginners? *waš ɛendek ši-ktab de-n-neḥw dyal l-ɛeṛbiya iṣlaḥ l-lli ɛad bdaw?*

Granada - *ġeṛnaṭa.*

grandchild - m. *ḥfiḍ* pl. *ḥfayeḍ* f. *ḥfiḍa* f. pl. *-t.*

granddaughter - *ḥfiḍa* pl. *-t.*

grandfather - (with art *l-žedd*) *žedd* pl. *ždud, ḅḅa sid-.* That's his grandfather. *hadak ḅḅah sidu.*

grandmother - *žedda* (with art. *l-žedda*) pl. *-t, ṃṃ- lalla.* That's her grandmother. *hadik ṃṃha lallaha.*

grandparents - *ždud.*

grandson - *ḥfiḍ* pl. *ḥfayeḍ*.
to **grant** - **1.** *Eṭa yeEṭi*. We were granted the entire amount. *Eṭawna le-qḍeṛ kollu*. **2.** *Eṭaṛef*. I grant that I was wrong. *ka-neEṭaṛef ʔennani kont ġaḷeṭ*.
grape - *Einba* pl. *-t* coll. *Eineb*.
grapefruit - *letšina ṛumiya* pl. *-t ṛumiyat* coll. *letšin ṛumi*.
to **grasp** - **1.** *šedd f-*. She grasped the rope with both hands. *šeddet fe-ṭ-ṭwaḷ b-iddha b-žuž*. **2.** *fhem*. I don't quite grasp what you mean by that. *ma-fhemt-ši tamamen šnu bġiti tqul*.
to have a good grasp of - *Eendu meErifa kbira f-*. He has a good grasp of the subject. *Eendu meErifa kbira f-had l-muḍuE*.
grass - *ṛbiE*.
grasshopper - *bu-qeffaz* (sg. and pl.).
grate - *šebka* pl. *-t, šbek*. The furnace needs a new grate. *le-msexna xeṣṣha šebka ždida*.
to grate - *ḥekk*. Grate some cheese, please. *ḥekk šwiya de-ž-žḅen baṛek ḷḷahu fik*.
**This noise grates on my nerves. *had ṣ-ṣḍaE ka-yeEmel-li l-meEEak f-dati*.
grateful - *meEtaṛef*. I'm grateful to you for your help. *ana meEtaṛef-lek be-l-musaEada dyalek*.
to **gratify** - *lebba*. He gratified her every wish. *lebba žmiE ṛ-ṛeġbat dyalha*.
gratifying - *(lli) iferreḥ*. The news is very gratifying. *le-xbaṛ ka-iferreḥ bezzaf*.
gratitude - *Etiṛaf be-l-xir*. His gratitude knew no bounds. *Etiṛafu be-l-xir ma-kan Eendu ḥedd*.
**That's gratitude for you! *hakda ka-ireddu n-nas l-xir!*
grave - **1.** *qbuṛ* pl. *mqabeṛ*. The coffin was lowered into the grave. *hebbṭu t-tabut l-le-qbuṛ*. **2.** *mkeḍḍeṛ, waqef*. His face was very grave. *wežhu kan mkeḍḍeṛ bezzaf*. **3.** *xṭiṛ, f-xaṭaṛ*. His condition is grave. *ḥaltu xṭiṛa*. **4.** *kbir* pl. *kbaṛ*. That's a grave mistake. *hadi ġeḷṭa kbira*.
gravel - coll. *ḥeṣṣ* sg. *-a* pl. *-t*. The path is covered with gravel. *ṭ-ṭṛiq mġeṭṭya be-l-ḥeṣṣ*.
graveyard - *mqabeṛ* (sg. and pl.). *ṛuḍa* pl. *-t*.
gravy - *mṛeq, merqa* pl. *-t, mṛaqi*. Would you like a little gravy on your meat? *waš bġiti šwiya d-le-mṛeq mEa l-lḥem dyalek?*
gray - **1.** *rmadi*. Gray and red go together well. *r-rmadi u-le-ḥmeṛ ka-itwataw mezyan*. **2.** *byeḍ* f. *biḍa* pl. *buyeḍ*. He has a few gray hairs although he is very young. *waxxa ma-zal ṣġiṛ Eendu ši-šeEṛat buyeḍ*.
to gray - *byaḍ*. His hair is beginning to gray. *šeEṛu bda ibyaḍ*.
to **graze** - **1.** *ṛEa iṛEa*. The cows are grazing in the fields. *le-bgeṛ ka-iṛEaw f-le-mṛaEi*. **2.** *daz u-qaṣ, iduz w-iqiṣ*. The bullet just grazed his shoulder. *l-qeṛṭaṣa ġir dazet u-qaṣet ketfu*.
grease - *idam* pl. *idumat, idayem; šḥem, šeḥma* pl. *-t*. Don't leave the grease in the pan. *ma-txelli-š l-idam fe-l-meqla*.
to grease - **1.** *dhen b-l-idam, Emel l-idam*. Don't forget to grease the pan. *Eendak tensa ma-ddhen-š l-meqla b-l-idam*. **2.** *šeḥḥem*. They're greasing the car. *ka-išeḥḥmu ṭ-ṭumubil*.
to grease somebody's palm - *Eṭa yeEṭi r-rešwa l-, dhen ḥelq*. They had to grease somebody's palm to get these seats. *ḍṭeṛṛu yeEṭiw r-rešwa l-ši waḥed baš igelsu f-had le-krasa*.
greasy - **1.** *meṭḷi b-l-idam*. The dishes are still greasy. *had l-ġeṭran ma-zalin meṭḷiyin b-l-idam*. **2.** *midum, mšeḥḥem*. The soup is too greasy. *ṣ-ṣuḅḅa miduma bezzaf*.
great - **1.** *kbir* pl. *kbaṛ*. The risk would be too great. *l-xaṭaṛ ġad ikun kbir bezzaf*. --You'd be doing me a great favor. *ġad tkun Emelti fiya xir kbir*. **2.** *bezzaf*. He was in great pain. *kan fih bezzaf d-le-wžeE* or *kan fih le-wžeE bezzaf*. **3.** *mezyan, moEtabaṛ*. That's a great idea! *hadi fikra mezyana bezzaf!* **4.** *Eažib*. She's a great singer. *hiya muġenniya Eažiba*.
**It's a great pity! *xṣaṛa!*
great at - *Eefrit*. He's great at telling stories. *huwa Eefrit f-teEwid le-xṛayef*.
a great many - *waḥed l-Eadad kbir*. A great many books have been written on that subject. *waḥed l-Eadad kbir d-le-ktub tʔellfu f-dak l-muḍuE*.
greatly - *bezzaf*. She exaggerated greatly. *zadet fih bezzaf*.
Greece - *l-yunan*.
greed - *ṭmeE*.
greedy - *ṭemmaE*.
Greek - **1.** *yunani*. His father is a Greek. *ḅḅah yunani*. **2.** (language) *yunaniya*.

**That's all Greek to me. *ma-ka-nefhem-š ḥebba f-had š-ši.*
green - **1.** *xḍeṛ* pl. *xuḍeṛ.* What did you buy green apples for ? *ɛlaš šriti t-teffaḥ xḍeṛ?* --Give me that green book. *ɛṭini dak le-ktab le-xḍeṛ.* **2.** *ždid* pl. *ždad.* I'm still green at this job. *ana ma-zal ždid f-had l-xedma.*
**He turned green with envy. *žatu l-ġira bezzaf.*
greengrocer - *xeḍḍaṛ* pl. *-a.*
to **greet** - *sellem ɛla.*
greeting - *slam.* He didn't notice my greeting. *ma-dda-š l-ġaya le-s-slam dyali.*
grief - *ġbina* pl. *ġbayen.* She couldn't conceal her grief. *ma-qeḍret-š ḍḍeṛṛeq le-ġbina dyalha.*
grill - *šuwwaya* pl. *-t.* Broil the meat on the grill. *šwi l-lḥem ɛel š-šuwwaya.*
to grill - **1.** *šwa išwi.* Are you going to grill the meat? *waš ġadi tešwi l-lḥem?* **2.** *stenteq.* They grilled the prisoner for hours. *stentqu l-mesžun ɛadad de-s-saɛat.*
grim - *mɛebbes.* There was a grim look on his face. *kan wežhu mɛebbes.*
to **grind** - *ṭḥen.*
to **grip** - *qbeḍ, qbeṭ.*
to have a grip on - *ṛaqeb.* He has a good grip on the situation. *ka-iṛaqeb l-ḥala mezyan.*
to come to grips with - *wažeh.* They came to grips with the problem and solved it. *wažhu l-muškila u-ḥelluha.*
to **gripe** - *tšekka, ška iški.* Stop griping about everything! *feḍḍi u-ma-tšekka men koll-ši!*
grippe - *lagrip* (not used with art). Our whole family had the grippe. *l-ɛaˀila dyalna kollha žatha lagrip.*
groan - *tenwiḥ, tenwaḥ.* We hear his groans all night long. *ka-nsemɛu t-tenwiḥ dyalu l-lil u-ma ṭal.*
to groan - *nuwweḥ.* He groaned in his sleep. *nuwweḥ fe-n-nɛas dyalu.*
grocer - *beqqal* pl. *-a.* I bought the salt at the grocer's. *šrit le-mleḥ men ɛend l-beqqal.*
groceries - *temwin.* Send these groceries to my house. *ṣifeṭ had t-temwin le-ḍ-ḍaṛ dyali.*
grocery (store) - *ḥanut l-beqqal.*
to **grope** - *desses.* He groped for the switch in the dark. *desses ɛel ḍ-ḍeffaya fe-ḍ-ḍlem.*
grouchy - *mɛebbes.* Why is he so grouchy? *ɛlaš huwa mɛebbes bezzaf?*
ground - *ˀeṛḍ* f. pl. *aṛaḍi.* The ground is still wet. *ma-zala l-ˀeṛḍ fazga.* --How much ground goes with the house? *ṣḥal men mitru de-l-ˀeṛḍ ka-ttbaɛ mɛa ḍ-ḍaṛ?*
**The new method is rapidly gaining ground. *l-kifiya ž-ždida ɛliha le-qbal bezzaf.*
grounds - *tfel.* Throw the coffee grounds into the trash can. *siyyeb t-tfel de-l-qehwa fe-ṣ-ṣṭeḷ de-z-zbel.*
**The house is very small but the grounds are beautiful. *ḍ-ḍaṛ ṣġiṛa bezzaf lakin l-ˀeṛḍ lli ḍayṛa biha fiha menḍeṛ mezyan.*
groundfloor - *sefli.* Our apartment is on the ground floor. *l-mesken dyalna fe-s-sefli.*
group - *žmaɛa* pl. *-t.* The class is divided into three groups. *ṭ-ṭabaqa metqessma ɛla tlata de-ž-žmaɛat.*
to group - *žmeɛ.* Group the people according to age. *žmeɛ n-nas ɛla ḥasab s-senn dyalhom.*
to **grow** - **1.** *ṭwaḷ.* Your boy has grown a lot. *weldek ṭwal bezzaf.* **2.** *tquwwa, kber.* The crowd grew rapidly. *deġya kebret ž-žuqa.* **3.** *ẓṛeɛ.* They grow a lot of grain in this region. *ka-iẓeṛɛu le-ḥbub bezzaf f-had n-naḥiya.* **4.** *ġṛeṣ.* --I grow roses. *ka-neġṛeṣ l-woṛḍ.*
**She grows on you as you get to know her. *ma-ḥeddek ka-teɛṛef biha u-hiya ka-tɛežbek.* --He has grown away from his family. *tbeɛɛed ɛla ɛaˀiltu.* --The weather's growing colder (and colder). *l-ḥal ka-izid fe-l-bruda.* --The situation grew worse and worse. *tkeffset l-ḥala.* --My father's growing old. *ḅḅa bda išref.*
to grow up - **1.** *kber.* The children are growing up fast. *d-drari ka-ikebru deġya.* **2.** *tṛebba.* We grew up together. *tṛebbina b-žuž.*
to **growl** - *hernen.* The dog growled when he heard the noise. *l-kelb bda ihernen melli smeɛ ṣ-ṣdaɛ*
grown-up - *kbir* pl. *kbaṛ.* She has a grown-up daughter. *ɛendha bent kbira.* --Their children are already grown up. *wladhom ṛahom wellaw kbaṛ.*
grownups - *n-nas le-kbaṛ.* Children should keep quiet when grownups are talking. *ka-ixeṣṣ d-drari ṣ-ṣġaṛ isektu mnin ikunu n-nas le-kbaṛ ka-itkellmu.*
growth - *demmala* pl. *-t, dmamel.* That growth will have to be removed. *hadik d-demmala ka-ixeṣṣha ddzuwwel.*
**He has a two days' growth of

beard. *hadi yumayn ma-ḥessen lḥitu.*

grudge - *ḥsifa* pl. *ḥsayef.* She has a grudge against me. *rafda fiya le-ḥsifa.*

to hold (bear) a grudge - *rfed le-ḥsifa.* I don't bear a grudge against him. *ana ma-rafed-š fih le-ḥsifa.*

gruff - *ġliḍ* pl. *ġlaḍ.* He has a gruff voice. *ḥelqu ġliḍ.*

to **grumble** - *gemgem.* He grumbles each time we ask him for help. *ka-igemgem koll meṛṛa melli ka-nṭeḷbu mennu l-iƐana.*

guarantee - **1.** *gaṛanṭiya* pl. *-t; gaṛanṭi* pl. *-yat.* This watch has a five year guarantee. *had l-magana fiha xems snin gaṛanṭi.* **2.** *ḍamana* pl. *-t.* What guarantee do I have that he'll pay me? *š-men ḍamana Ɛendi baš ġad ixeḷḷeṣni?*

to guarantee - *ḍmen.* I guarantee that you'll like that movie. *nḍmen-lek bin l-film ġad iƐeƶbek.*

guard - **1.** *Ɛessas* pl. *-a.* The guard didn't let me pass. *ma-xellani-š l-Ɛessas nduz.* **2.** *Ɛessa.* The guard is changed at two o'clock. *ka-ibeddlu l-Ɛessa fe-ž-žuž.*

on one's guard - *Ɛla balu.* You have to be on your guard with her. *ka-ixeṣṣek tkun Ɛla balek mennha.*

to stand guard - *ḥḍa yeḥdi.* I'll stand guard for a couple of hours. *ġad neḥḍi saƐa wella žuž.*

to **guard** - *ḥḍa yeḥdi.* The building is guarded day and night. *dak le-bni meḥḍi lil u-nhaṛ.* --You can't guard against everything. *ma-imken-lek-š teḥdi ṛaṣek men koll-ši.*

guardian - *ḥaḍi* pl. *ḥoḍḍay.* I was appointed guardian of his son. *semmawni l-ḥaḍi d-weldu.*

to **guess** - **1.** *Ɛṛef.* If you guess what's in my pocket, I'll give it to you. *ila Ɛṛefti šnu f-žibi, neƐṭih-lek.* **2.** *ḍenn.* I guess he's sick. *ka-nḍenn bin huwa mṛiḍ.*

--Who would have guessed that! *škun lli imken-lu iḍenn had š-ši!*

guest - *ḍif* pl. *ḍyaf.*

guide - **1.** *dalil* pl. *-at.* All the theaters are listed in the guide. *s-sinimat kollhom medkuṛin fe-d-dalil.* **2.** *dalil* pl. *ʔadella.* The guide showed us the old mosque. *d-dalil werrana ž-žameƐ le-qdim.*

to guide - *guwwed.* Can you guide us there? *waš imken-lek tguwwedna l-temma?*

gull - *ḥamam* (coll.) *d-le-bḥeṛ.*

gum - *lḥem s-snan.* My gum is sore.

to **gum** - *ḥeṭṭ lṣaq Ɛla.* Did you gum the labels? *waš ḥeṭṭiti lṣaq Ɛel le-bṭayeq?*

gum Arabic - *Ɛelk ṭ-ṭeḷḥ.*

gun - *see* **rifle, pistol,** etc.

gutter - *mežṛa* pl. *mžaṛi.*

gym - **1.** *ṣaḷa de-ṛ-ṛiyaḍa* pl. *-t de-ṛ-ṛiyaḍa.* Our school has a large gym. *l-meḍṛaṣa dyalna Ɛendha ṣaḷa de-ṛ-ṛiyaḍa kbira.* **2.** *ṛiyaḍa.* We have gym three times a week. *Ɛendna ṛ-ṛiyaḍa tlata de-l-meṛṛat fe-ž-žemƐa.*

H

habit - *Ɛada* pl. *-t.* That's a bad habit. *Ɛada qbiḥa hadik.*

in the habit of - *metƐewwed.* I'm in the habit of sleeping late. *ana metƐewwed ka-nnƐes mƐeṭṭeḷ.*

to break oneself of a habit - *qṭeƐ Ɛada.* I'm trying to break myself of the habit of smoking. *ka-nƐawel neqṭeƐ l-Ɛada de-d-doxxan.*

to get in(to) the habit of - *bda ibda l-Ɛada dyal.* I got into the habit of smoking at college. *bdit l-Ɛada de-d-doxxan fe-l-žamiƐa.*

haggard - *mexṭuf.* His face looks haggard. *ka-iban wežhu mexṭuf.*

hail - **1.** *tebriru, tebruri.* That's not rain, that's hail. *hadik ma-ši š-šta, tebriru.* **2.** *ḥemla de-t-tebriru, ḥemla de-t-tebruri.* The hail destroyed the entire crop. *l-ḥemla de-t-tebriru xeṣṣṛet ṣ-ṣaḅa kollha.*

to hail - **1.** *ṭaḥ iṭiḥ tebriru* or *ṭaḥ iṭiḥ tebruri.* It's hailing. *tebriru ka-iṭiḥ.* **2.** *Ɛeyyeṭ l-.* The doorman hailed a cab. *l-buwwab Ɛeyyeṭ l-ṭaksi.* **3.** *htef b-.* Crowds hail him everywhere. *l-žamahir ka-tehtef bih f-koll maḥell.*

**His parents hail from Tetuan. *waldih ʔṣeḷhom men tiṭwan.*

hair - *seƐṛa* pl. *-t, šƐuṛat* coll.

šɛeṛ. What color is her hair? *š-men lun šɛeṛha?*

to get into one another's hair - *tġanen.* They're always getting into each other's hair. *dima ka-itġannu.*

**The stone missed me by a hair. *ɛla šwiya kanet ġad tqisni l-ḥežṛa.* --That's splitting hairs! *feṛq dqiq hada!*

haircut - *teḥsina* pl. *-t; ḥsana* pl. *-t, ḥsayen.* Where'd you get that funny haircut? *škun ɛmel-lek had le-ɛžuba men teḥsina?*

**Haircut, please. *ḥessen-li ṛaṣi men feḍlek.*

to get a haircut - *ḥessen ṛaṣu.* I have to get a haircut. *xeṣṣni nḥessen ṛaṣi.*

hair-dresser - *ḥežžam* pl. *-a.*

hair-raising - *(lli) ka-išuwwek d-dat.* That was a hair-raising experience. *težriba kanet ka-tšuwwek d-dat.*

half - *neṣṣ* pl. *nṣaṣ, nṣuṣa.* I'll give him half of my share. *daba neɛṭih n-neṣṣ f-ḥeqqi.*

to cut in half - *qṣem fe-n-neṣṣ.* Shall I cut it in half? *neqṣemha fe-n-neṣṣ?*

to go halves with - *ɛmel be-n-nṣiṣa.* Will you go halves with me? *teɛmel mɛaya be-n-nṣiṣa?*

half price - *neṣṣ taman.* I got it for half price at a sale. *xditha b-neṣṣ taman de-l-ʔišhar.*

half a kilo - *neṣṣ kilu.* Give me half a kilo of butter. *ɛṭini neṣṣ kilu de-s-smen.*

half an hour - *neṣṣ saɛa.* I'll be back in half an hour. *ġad neṛžeɛ men daba neṣṣ saɛa.*

half done - **1.** *mṣuwweb ḥedd n-neṣṣ.* This job is only half done. *had l-xedma mṣuwwba ġir ḥedd n-neṣṣ.* **2.** *neṣṣ ṭayeb.* The meat is only half done. *had l-lḥem ġir neṣṣ ṭayeb.*

half past - *u-neṣṣ.* We'll be there at half past eight. *nkunu temma fe-t-tmenya u-neṣṣ.*

**I've been listening with only half an ear. *kont ka-ntṣennet ġir b-ṭeṛf wedni.* --I've half a mind to go tomorrow. *ɛlayn qeṛṛeṛt nemši ġedda.* --That isn't half bad. *dak š-ši ma-ši qbiḥ be-l-koll.*

halfway - *f-neṣṣ ṭ-ṭriq.* We ran out of gas halfway to town. *f-neṣṣ ṭ-ṭriq l-le-mdina tqaḍa-lna l-iṣanṣ.*

hall - *nbeḥ* pl. *nbuḥa, nbayeḥ.* Mr. Ali lives down the other end of the hall. *s-si ɛli ka-iskon fe-l-qent l-axoṛ d-had n-nbeḥ.*

(meeting) hall - *qaɛa* pl. *-t.* We stood at the back of the hall. *wqefna fe-l-luṛ de-l-qaɛa.*

city hall - *baladiya* pl. *-t.* His office is in the City Hall. *l-mekteb dyalu fe-l-baladiya.*

to **halt** - *wqef.* Halt! Who's there? *wqef! škun hnak?*

halting - *mfafi, (lli) ka-ilhet.* He spoke in a halting voice. *kan ka-idwi u-ḥelqu mfafi.*

hammer - *mṭeṛqa* pl. *-t, mṭaṛeq.*

to hammer - *ṭeṛṛeq.* Our neighbor has been hammering all day long. *n-nhaṛ kollu u-žaṛna ka-iṭeṛṛeq.*

to hammer in - *ṭeṛṛeq, dexxel.* He can't even hammer in a nail. *ma-yeɛṛef-ši idexxel ḥetta meṣmaṛ.*

**The rules have been hammered into me. *l-qawaɛid dexxluhom-li be-d-draɛ f-ṛaṣi.*

hand - **1.** *idd, yedd* pl. *iddin (iddi-* before possessive endings). Where can I wash my hands? *fayn imken-li negsel iddiya?* --The matter is out of my hands. *l-mesʔala xeṛžet men iddi.* **2.** *muri* pl. *mwara.* The hour hand is broken. *l-muri le-kbir mherres.* --The minute hand doesn't work. *l-muri ṣ-ṣġiṛ ma-xeddam-š.*

hand in glove - *mettafeq.* They worked together hand in glove. *kanu ixedmu mežmuɛin mettafqin.*

at first hand - *men ṛaṣ l-ɛeyn.* I got this information at first hand. *xdit had le-xbaṛ men ṛas l-ɛeyn.*

by hand - *be-l-yedd.* This job has to be done by hand. *had l-xedma ka-ixeṣṣha ttṣuwweb be-l-yedd.*

on hand - *teḥt l-idd, qṛib* pl. *qṛab.* We don't have that size on hand. *ma-ɛendna-š dak le-qyaṣ teḥt iddna.* --He's always on hand when I want him. *weqt-aš ma bġitu ka-nṣibu qṛib.*

on the one hand ... on the other hand - *men žiha ... u-men žiha xṛa, la men ... la men.* On the one hand he wants it finished, but on the other hand he doesn't give us the material. *la mennu ka-ibġiha mkemmla, la mennu ma-ka-iyeɛṭina-š le-qwam.*

to get out of hand - *zaġ iziġ.* His students are getting out of hand. *ṭ-ṭalaba dyalu bdaw iziġu.*

to give a hand - *ɛawen, ɛewwen, ɛṭa yeɛṭi idd ḷḷah.* Can you give me a hand with this box? *ḷḷah* *ixellik waš ma-teɛṭini-š idd ḷḷah f-had ṣ-ṣenḍuq?*

to have in hand - *qbeṭ l-lžam.* He has the situation well in hand. *ṛah qabeṭ l-lžam de-l-weḍɛiya.*

to have a hand in - *ɛmel iddu, dexxel ṛaṣu f-.* He must have had a hand in that. *ma-huwa ġir kan ɛamel iddu temma.*

to keep (one's) hands off - *xella iddu ɛendu.* Just keep your hands off that! *ġir xelli iddik ɛendek!*

to lay hands on - *nezzel iddu ɛla, žbeṛ.* I can't lay my hands on it right now. *ma-neɛṛef-ši fayn nnezzel ɛliha iddi f-had s-saɛa.*

to shake hands - *tṣafeḥ.* They shook hands. *tṣafḥu.*

to take off someone's hands - *henna men, fekk men.* Can you take these tickets off my hands? *imken-lek tfekkni men had le-bṭayeq?*

to take into (one's) hands - *meššа b-iddih.* From now on I'll take things into my own hands again. *men daba l-fuq ġad nɛawed nebda nmešši l-ʔumuṛ b-iddiya.*

**Hands off! *zuwwel iddik!* --He's very clever with his hands. *iddih ka-iɛeṛfu ma iɛemlu.* --I've got a lot of work on my hands. *ɛendi bezzaf de-š-šġal.*

to hand - *mekkel, medd.* Will you hand me that pencil? *ɛafak medd-li dak le-qlam.*

to hand in - *qeddem, dfeɛ.* I'm going to hand in my application tomorrow. *ġad nqeddem ṭaḷabi ġedda.*

to hand out - *feṛṛeq.* Hand out these tickets. *hak feṛṛeq had le-bṭayeq.*

to hand over - **1.** *medd, mekkel.* Would you hand that book over, please? *b-le-fḍeḷ mennek medd-li dak le-ktab.* **2.** *dfeɛ, ḥeṭṭ, ɛṭa yeɛṭi.* They made us hand over all our money. *lezzmuna nḥeṭṭu-lhom flusna kollhom.*

handbag - *šekkaṛa* pl. *-t, škayeṛ.*

hand brake - *ḥeṣṣaṛ de-l-yedd* pl. *ḥeṣṣaṛa de-l-yedd.*

handcuff - *qṭina* pl. *-t.*

pair of handcuffs - *nimiru xemsa.* Here every policeman carries a pair of handcuffs with him. *koll šoṛṭi hnaya rafed mɛah nimiru xemsa dyalu.*

to handcuff - *ɛmel nimiru xemsa l-.* They handcuffed the prisoners. *ɛemlu nimiru xemsa l-le-msažen.*

handful - *kemša* pl. *-t, kmeš.* He took a handful of nuts. *xda kemša de-l-guz.*

to **handicap** - *xella ḷ-ḷuṛ.* He's been handicapped by poor eyesight all his life. *n-nḍeṛ le-qlil huwa lli xellah ḷ-ḷuṛ ḥyatu kollha.*

handkerchief - *derra* pl. *drer, zif* pl. *zyufa.*

handle - **1.** *qebṭa* pl. *-t, qbaṭi, qbeṭ.* My suitcase needs a new handle. *šaneṭti xeṣṣha qebṭa ždida.* **2.** *wden* pl. *wednin.* The handle of this cup is broken off. *wden had z-zlafa therrset.*

to fly off the handle - *dženneṇ.* At the slightest occasion he flies off the handle. *ɛlaš-emma kan ka-idžennen.*

to handle - **1.** *ɛamel, tmešša mɛa.* He knows how to handle people. *ka-yeɛṛef kif iɛamel n-nas.* --You have to handle him with kid gloves. *xeṣṣek ttmešša mɛah be-s-syasa.* **2.** *ruwwež, žab ižib.* We don't handle that brand. *ma-ka-nžibu-š dak l-ɛeyna.* **3.** *xeddem, qbeṭ.* Can you handle a gun? *ka-teɛṛef teqbeṭ mkoḥla?* --He knows how to handle your car. *ka-yeɛṛef ixeddem siyaṛtek.* **4.** *tsaɛ mɛa.* I can't handle him any more. *ma-bqit-š ntsaɛ mɛah.* **5.** *tḥemmel.* I simply can't handle all the work by myself. *ma-neqḍeṛ-š tamamen ntḥemmel l-xedma kollha weḥdi.* **6.** *rfed.* Please handle this box with care, it contains glass. *ɛafak rfed had ṣ-ṣenḍuq ġir be-š-šwiya, ṛah fih z-zaž.*

**Look at it all you want, but don't handle it. *šuf b-ɛeynik u-hda b-iddik.*

handmade - *meṣnuɛ be-l-yedd, mṣuwweb be-l-yedd.*

handsome - **1.** *žmil, menḍuṛ.* He's a handsome man. *ṛažel menḍuṛ hadak.* **2.** *kbir* pl. *kbaṛ.* That's a handsome sum of money. *qḍeṛ kbir d-le-flus hadak.*

handwriting - *xeṭṭ l-idd* pl. *xṭuṭ l-idd.* His handwriting is illegible. *xeṭṭ iddu ma-ka-itferrez-š.*

handy - **1.** *sahel le-t-texdam.* This tape recorder is very handy. *had l-museǧǧila sahla le-t-texdam.* **2.** *qṛib* pl. *qṛab.* Have you got a pencil handy? *ɛendek ši-qlam qṛib?* **3.** *ka-yeɛṛef ma yeɛmel b-ṣebɛanu.* He's a very handy fellow. *huwa ṛažel ka-yeɛṛef ma yeɛmel b-ṣebɛanu.*

to come in handy (to) - *nfeɛ.* Typing will come in handy to you some day. *le-ktaba ɛel le-mṭebɛa ġad tnefɛek ši-nhaṛ.*

hang - **1.** *šneq, šenneq.* He was

hanged yesterday. *l-bareḥ šennquh.* 2. *Ɛelleq.* Can't you hang the picture a little higher? *imken-lek tƐelleq t-teṣwiṛa l-fuq šwiya?* --His life hung by a thread. *Ɛemṛu kan mƐelleq b-šeƐṛa.*

to hang on - *qbeṭ, šedd.* I hung on as tight as I could. *qbeṭt ṣeḥḥ-ma imken.* **Hang on to my coat for a minute, will you? *b-le-fḍeḷ mennek kan ma-teḥḍi-li-š l-kebbuṭ dyali waḥed d-dqiqa.*

to hang out - *nšeṛ, Ɛelleq.* Did you hang the wash out? *nšeṛti t-teṣbin?*

to hang up - *Ɛelleq.* Hang up your hat and coat. *Ɛelleq šemrirek u-baḷṭuk.*

to hang one's head - *ḥna yeḥni ṛaṣu.* Why are you hanging your head? *l-aš ka-teḥni ṛaṣek?* **Now I'm getting the hang of it. *Ɛad bdit nefhem š-kayen.* **Hang it all, I've mislaid my glasses again. *xzit tani, Ɛawed telleft nḍaḍṛi.* --I don't give a hang any more. *llehla iqleb!*

hanger - *Ɛellaqa* pl. *-t.* Put your coat on a hanger. *Ɛmel baḷṭuk f-Ɛellaqa.*

hangover - *tuwgiḍa* pl. *-t.*

to **happen** - *wqeƐ, ḥdet, žṛa ižṛa.* When did that happen? *fuq-aš wqeƐ dak š-ši?*

happily - *fe-s-saƐada.* They are very happily married. *ṛahom mžuwwžin f-kamil s-saƐada.*

happiness - *saƐada* pl. *-t.* I wish you all the happiness in the world. *ka-ntmenna-lek saƐadat d-denya u-l-ʔaxiṛa.*

happy - 1. *sƐid* pl. *sƐad, saƐid* pl. *suƐada.* That was his happiest day. *hadak ʔesƐed nhaṛ kan Ɛendu.* 2. *meṣṛuṛ, feṛḥan.* I don't feel at all happy about it. *ma-ka-nešƐeṛ-š b-ṛaṣi be-l-koll meṣṛuṛ b-had š-ši.* **Happy New Year. *mebṛuk l-Ɛam ž-ždid.*

harbor - *meṛṣa* pl. *-t, mṛaṣi.* Casablanca has a good harbor. *ḍ-ḍaṛ l-biḍa Ɛendha meṛṣa mezyana.*

hard - 1. *qaṣeḥ.* I can't sleep on a hard mattress. *ma-neqdeṛ-š nnƐes Ɛla mṭeṛṛba qaṣḥa.* 2. *ṣƐib* pl. *ṣƐab.* Those were hard times. *iyyam ṣƐiba hadik kanet.* 3. *waƐer.* He's a hard man. *ṛažel waƐer hadak.* 4. *bezzaf.* He worked hard all day. *xdem bezzaf n-nhaṛ kollu.*

hard of hearing - *(lli) wednu tqila.* As he grew older, he became hard of hearing. *kif bda ikber wellat wednu tqila.*

to be hard up (for) - *xeṣṣu, lehhef Ɛla.* He's always hard up for money. *dima ka-ilehhef Ɛel le-flus.*

to have a hard time - *wžed ṣuƐuba.* I had a hard time getting here. *wžedt ṣuƐuba baš nuṣel lle-hna.*

to try hard - *Ɛmel žehdu.* He tried hard to do it right. *Ɛmel žehdu baš iṣuwwebha hiya hadik.* **He's a hard man to get along with. *ṛažel ṭebƐu maneƐ.*

hard-boiled - *mesluq.* All we got was some hard-boiled eggs. *ma-žawna ġir ši-biḍat mesluqin.*

hard-earned - *mṣuwweṛ b-tamara.* That was hard-earned money. *duk le-flus kanu mṣuwwṛin b-tamara.*

hardly - 1. *kif, yaḷḷah.* We had hardly begun to speak when ... *kif bdina ntkellmu u-* ... 2. *ġir ma.* You can hardly expect me to believe that. *ġir ma-ttkel-š Ɛliya ntiyyeq dak š-ši.* **I hardly think so. *muḥal, ma-ka-nḍenn-š.*

hardly ever - *qlil f-aš.* I hardly ever go out. *qlil f-aš ka-nexṛož.*

harm - 1. *šeṛṛ, munkaṛ* pl. *-at, manakir.* You can never undo the harm you've done. *Ɛemmṛek la-ṣḷeḥti š-šeṛṛ lli Ɛmelti.* 2. *bas.* No harm done! *ši-bas ma-kayen.* 3. *Ɛeyb, Ɛib* pl. *Ɛyub.* I meant no harm by it. *ma-qṣedt Ɛeyb biha.*

to harm - *qeṣṣeḥ.*

harmful - *muḍiṛṛ.* This drought is harmful for the crops. *had l-ibusa muḍiṛṛa le-ṣ-ṣaba.*

harmonica - *muziga* pl. *-t.*

harness - *Ɛedda* pl. *-t.* I just bought a new harness for my horse. *šrit Ɛedda ždida l-l-Ɛewd dyali.*

to harness - *serrež.* Has he harnessed the horses? *serrež l-xil?*

harrow - *hebbaša* pl. *-t.*

harsh - 1. *ṣƐib* pl. *ṣƐab.* Those are harsh terms. *šuṛuṭ ṣƐiba hadik.* 2. *ḥṛes* pl. *ḥuṛeš.* This soap contains no harsh ingredients. *had ṣ-ṣabun ma-fih mawadd ḥeṛša.*

harvest - *weqt le-ḥṣaḍ, ḥṣaḍ* pl. *ḥṣaḍat.* We had a good harvest. *weqt le-ḥṣaḍ daz-lna mezyan.*

to harvest - *ḥṣeḍ.* When do you harvest the wheat around here? *fuq-aš ka-tḥeṣḍu l-gemḥ hnaya?*

haste - *zerba* pl. *-t.*

hastily - *be-z-zerba.*

hasty - *mezrub.* You shouldn't have made a hasty decision. *ma-kan-š ka-ixeşşek taxod qaṛaṛ mezrub.*
to be hasty - *zreb, tqelleq, ddzreb.* There's no reason for us to be hasty. *ma-kayen l-aš nzerbu.*
hat - *šemrir* pl. *smarer.*
to **hatch (out)** - **1.** *feqqeş.* Three more chicks hatched today. *tlata d-le-flales xṛin feqqşu l-yum.* **2.** *tfeqqeş, sxeṛ.* Only seven of the eggs hatched out. *ġir sebɛa de-l-biḍat lli sexṛu.*
hatchet - *šaquṛ* pl. *šwaqeṛ, mqedda* pl. *-t.*
hate - *keṛh, koṛh.* His feeling of dislike gradually turned into hate. *qellt mḥebbtu šwiya be-šwiya wellat keṛh.*
to hate - *kṛeh.* I hate people who are selfish. *ka-nekṛeh n-nas lli ka-ibġiw ṛaşhom.*
**I hated to tell her that. *qolt-lha dak š-ši bezz menni.*
hatred - *keṛh, koṛh.*
haul - *şyaḍa* pl. *-t, teşyiḍa.* The hunters had a good haul today. *ş-şiyyaḍa qebṭu teşyiḍa haʔila l-yum.*
to haul - **1.** *žeṛṛ.* The horses were unable to haul the heavy load. *l-xil ma-qeddet-š džeṛṛ le-ḥmel t-tqil.* **2.** *žbed, xerrež.* They hauled me out of bed at six o'clock. *xerržuni men l-feṛš fe-s-setta de-ş-şbaḥ.*
to haul down - *hebbeṭ, nezzel.* Have they hauled the flag down yet? *hebbṭu ṛ-ṛaya wella ma-zal?*
to **have** - *kan ikun ɛendu.* I have two tickets for the movies. *ɛendi žuž d-le-bṭayeq le-s-sinima.*
**(often Measure II of the verb, in the sense of having another person do something). —Wouldn't it be better to have the tooth out right now? *ma-ši ḥsen tqelleɛ ḍ-ḍeṛsa fe-l-ḥin?* —I'll have to have my appendix out. *ka-ixeşşni nzuwwel l-meşṛana z-zayda.* —I'm having my teeth fixed. *ka-nşuwweb snani.* —I had my shoes soled. *ṭeṛṛeft şebbaṭi.*
**I haven't had a thing to eat today. *ma-klit walu had n-nhaṛ.* —Let's have the knife. *žbed l-mus lle-hnaya.*
to have a baby - *wled.* She's going to have a baby soon. *ġadya tuled qṛib.*
to have one's way - *ɛmel lli bġa, ɛmel naḍaṛu.* She has had her way. *ɛemlet lli bġat.*
to have to - *xeşş, lazem ɛla.* You have to buy some new shoes. *xeşşek tešri şebbaṭ ždid.*
**You don't have to do it. *nta ma-ši meṛġum teɛmelha.*
I had better, you had better, etc. - *ḥsen-li, hsen-lek,* etc. You'd better do it right away. *ḥsen-lek ddirha daba.*
hawk - *baz* pl. *bizan.*
hay - *goṛṭ.* The hay isn't dry yet. *l-goṛṭ ma-zal ma-ibes.*
**Let's make hay while the sun shines. *nḍeṛbu le-ḥdid ma-ḥeddu sxun.* —It's time to hit the hay. *hada weqt n-nɛas.*
hay fever - *nezla* pl. *-t, nzali.*
haystack - *nader de-l-goṛṭ* pl. *nwader de-l-goṛṭ; qetta de-l-goṛṭ* pl. *qtet de-l-goṛṭ.*
haze - *ḍbaba* pl. *-t* coll. *ḍbab.*
he - *huwa.*
head - **1.** *ṛaş* pl. *ṛyuş.* My head hurts. *ṛaşi ka-yužeɛni.* —Lettuce is half a dirham a head. *l-xeşş neşş derhem le-ṛ-ṛaş.* —He sold five head of cattle. *baɛ xemsa de-ṛ-ṛyuş men le-ksiba.* —Begin at the head of the page. *bda men ṛaş ş-şefḥa.* —We were sitting at the head of the table. *konna galsin f-ṛaş ṭ-ṭebḷa.* —Success has gone to his head. *n-nažaḥ sexxen-lu ṛaşu.* **2.** *mqeddem* pl. *mqeddmin, kbir* pl. *kbaṛ.* He's the head of the gang. *huwa mqeddem ž-žmaɛa.* **3.** *kbir* pl. *kbaṛ.* He's the head of the family. *huwa kbir l-ɛaʔila.* **4.** *ṛaʔis* pl. *ṛuʔasa, mudir* pl. *-in.* He's the head of the firm. *huwa ṛ-ṛaʔis de-š-šarika.* —Who is the new head of the school? *škun l-mudir ž-ždid de-l-meḍṛaşa?*
**My friend is head over heels in love. *şaḥbi meɛmi be-l-ḥobb.* —That's over my head. *dak š-ši bezzaf ɛliya.* —The man is positively out of his head. *ṛ-ṛažel bla šekk mša-lu ɛeqlu.* —Everyone kept his head. *koll-ši bqa mhedden.* —I can't keep everything in my head. *ma-imken-li-š neɛqel ɛla koll-ši.* —I can't make head or tail of the story. *had le-xṛafa ma-žbeṛt-lha ṛaş men režlin.* —I'm sure that if you put your heads together, you'll find a solution. *ana metyeqqen ila džmeɛtiw ši mɛa ši tşibu ši-ḥell.* —He just took it into his head that nobody likes him. *ġir huwa ɛmel f-balu ḥetta waḥed ma-ka-ibġih.* —Heads or tails? *kḥel wella byeḍ?*

to head - 1. *tṛe??es, siyyer.* He hopes to head his department some day. *ka-itmenna ši-nhaṛ itṛe??es l-feṛƐ dyalu.* 2. *ža iži l-luwwel.* My boy heads his class at school. *weldi ka-iži l-luwel f-ṭabaqtu.* —His name heads the list of candidates. *smiytu žat hiya l-luwla f-la?iḥat le-mṛeššḥin.*
**You're heading in the wrong direction. *ṛak maši xaṛež Ɛel ṭ-ṭṛiq.* —They're heading for Ujda. *huma mašyen l-wežda.*

headache - *ḥṛiq ṛ-ṛaṣ.*

heading - *Ɛunwan* pl. *Ɛanawin.*

headlight - *ḍuw de-l-qeddam* pl. *ḍwaw de-l-qeddam.*

head wind - *riḥ lli ka-iredd* pl. *ryaḥ lli ka-tredd.* We had a strong head wind all the way. *kan ireddna riḥ mežhed fe-ṭ-ṭṛiq kollha.*

to **heal** - *bṛa ibṛa.* The wound isn't healing properly. *ž-žeṛḥa ṛaha ma-ka-tebṛa-š hiya hadik.*

health - *ṣeḥḥa* pl. *-t.* How's his health? *kif dayra ṣeḥḥtu?*
in poor health - *mḍeƐḍeƐ f-ṣeḥḥtu.* He's been in poor health today. *had n-nhaṛ qiyyal mḍeƐḍeƐ f-ṣeḥḥtu.*

healthy - 1. *la-bas Ɛlih f-ṣeḥḥtu.* She looks very healthy. *ka-ḍḍheṛ la-bas Ɛliha f-ṣeḥḥtha.* 2. *ṣiḥḥi, mezyan le-ṣ-ṣeḥḥa.* This isn't a healthy climate. *had l-žuw ma-ši ṣiḥḥi.*

heap - *Ɛeṛma* pl. *-t, Ɛeṛṛam* pl. *Ɛṛaṛem.* That's a heap of money. *Ɛeṛma d-le-flus hadi.*

to **heap** - *Ɛeṛṛem, keṛkeṛ.* The table was heaped with all kinds of food. *ṭ-ṭebḷa kanet mƐeṛṛma b-le-mwakel kollha.*

to **hear** - *smeƐ.* I didn't hear anything. *ma-smeƐt walu.*
**We haven't heard from him since he left. *melli mša ma-wṣelna ḥetta xbaṛ men Ɛendu.*

hearing - *gelsa* pl. *-t, glasi.* The hearing was set for June sixth. *l-gelsa kanet mqeṛṛṛa nhaṛ setta yunyu.*
**His hearing is very poor. *wednu ma-ka-tesmeƐ-š mliḥ.*
hard of hearing - *(lli) wednu tqila.* My aunt is hard of hearing. *xalti wdenha tqila.*
to lose one's hearing - *ṭṛaš.* When did he lose his hearing? *fuq-aš ṭṛaš?*

heart - *qelb* pl. *qlub.* He has a weak heart. *Ɛendu l-qelb ḍƐif.*
by heart - *be-ž-žri u-l-ma.* I learned the poem by heart. *ḥfeḍt l-qiṭƐa de-š-šiƐr be-ž-žri u-l-ma.*
**It breaks my heart to let him go. *mqeṭṭeƐ men qelbi xellitu imši.* —At heart he's really a good fellow. *fe-l-ḥaqiqa ṛažel qelbu mezyan.* —She's in this work heart and soul. *Ɛamla qelbha u-žwareḥha f-had l-Ɛamal.* —He's a man after my own heart. *dak s-siyyed Ɛendi fuq qelbi.* —I intend to get to the heart of this matter. *baġi nšuf dwaxel had l-qaḍiya.*
to lose heart - *fšel, tterxa.* Don't lose heart. *Ɛendak tefšel!*
to take to heart - *Ɛmel f-qelbu.* He's taking it very much to heart. *Ɛamelha f-qelbu bezzaf.*

heart attack - *sekta qelbiya.*

heat - *ṣehd* pl. *ṣhud, ṣhudat; sxuniya* pl. *-t.* I can't stand the heat. *ma-ka-neḥmel-š ṣ-ṣehd.*
to heat - *sexxen.* The room is well heated. *l-bit msexxen mezyan.*
to heat (up) - 1. *sexxen.* I'll have to heat up some water first. *ka-ixeṣṣni beƐda nsexxen šwiya de-l-ma.* 2. *sxen isxon.* It'll be five minutes before the iron heats up. *xemsa de-d-dqayeq xeṣṣ baš tesxon le-ḥdida.*

heat-resistant - *(lli) ka-iṣbeṛ l-l-Ɛafya.* Is that glass heat-resistant? *dak z-zaž ka-iṣbeṛ l-l-Ɛafya?*

heaven - *ženna.* The person that does good goes to heaven. *lli Ɛmel l-xir ka-imši le-ž-ženna.*
**For heaven's sake, stop that noise! *le-wžeh ṛebbi ḥṣeṛ had ṣ-ṣḍaƐ.*

heavy - 1. *tqil* pl. *tqal.* Is that box too heavy for you? *tqil Ɛlik dak ṣ-ṣenḍuq?* —I can't take heavy fppd. *ma-ka-neqḍeṛ-š Ɛel l-makla tqila.* 2. *kbir* pl. *kbaṛ.* He had to pay a heavy fine. *tlezzem i?eddi xṭiya kbira.*
heavy rain - *mšati.* We can't leave in that heavy rain. *ma-ġadyen-š nemšiw f-had le-mšati.*

hedge - *ẓeṛb* pl. *ẓṛuba.* The two gardens are divided by a hedge. *ž-žnanat b-žuž qasemhom ẓ-ẓeṛb.*

heel - 1. *gdem* pl. *gdam, gdami.* I have a blister on my heel. *Ɛendi waḥed n-nefṭ f-gedmi.* 2. *gedmiya* pl. *-t.* These shoes need new heels. *had ṣ-ṣebbaṭ xeṣṣu gedmiyat ždad.*

height - 1. *rtifaƐ* pl. *-at.* How do you determine the height of a triangle? *kif ka-idžbeṛ rtifaƐ* *l-mutellat?* **2.** *ɛlu.* What is the height of this mountain? *šḥal f-had ž-žbel d-le-ɛlu?* **3.** *ṭul.* He's almost two meters in height. *fih ɛlayen žuž miter de-ṭ-ṭul.* **4.** *ṛaṣ* pl. *ṛyuṣ, qemma* pl. *-t.* He was then at the height of his power. *kan dak s-saɛa f-ṛaṣ ṣ-ṣuḷa dyalu.* **5.** *muntaha, ʔeqṣa ḥedd.* That's the height of stupidity. *hada ʔeqṣa ḥedd fe-t-teṭmiṣa*

heir - *waṛet* pl. *waṛata.* He's the sole heir. *huwa weḥdu waṛet.*

Hejira - *hižṛa.*

helicopter - *ferfara* pl. *-t.*

hell - *žahennam, žahennama* pl. *-t; n-naṛ* pl. *n-niran.*

hello - **1.** *ʔalu, ʔahlan.* Hello, operator! You've cut me off! *ʔalu l-buṣṭa, ḥṣeṛtiwni fe-l-heḍṛa.* **2.** *ʔahlan.* Hello! How are you? *ʔahlan, še-xbaṛek?*

helmet - *ṭaṣa* pl. *-t, ṭyeṣ.*

help - *musaɛada* pl. *-t, ɛwin, idd ḷḷah.* Do you need any help? *teḥtaž ši-musaɛada?*

to help - **1** *ɛawen, ɛewwen, saɛed, ɛṭa yeɛṭi idd ḷḷah.* I helped him as well as I could. *ɛawentu ɛla qedd žehdi.* **2.** *qḍa iqḍi.* Can I help you? *kayen ši ma neqḍi-lek?*

**Help! *ɛteq!* or *ɛetqu!* or *le-ɛtiqa l-llah!* --I can't help it. *ma-b-iddi šay.* --Sorry, that can't be helped. *metʔessef, dak š-ši ma-ɛendu dwa.* --Can I help you to something? *imken-li nmekkel-lek ši-ḥaža?* --I couldn't help but see it. *ma-fadni ġir nšufu.*

to help oneself - *tfeḍḍeḷ.* Please help yourself (sir)! *tfeḍḍeḷ a sidi!*

helper - *musaɛid* pl. *-in, muɛin* pl. *-in.* He has two helpers. *ɛendu žuž de-l-musaɛidin.*

helpless - *ɛagez, mɛeggez.*

hem - *teḥžiž* pl. *-at* coll. *teḥžiž, teḥžaž.* I'll have to let out the hem. *ka-ixeṣṣni nṭiyyeḥ t-teḥžaž.*

**The house is hemmed in between two tall buildings. *ḍ-ḍaṛ žat ḍayṛin biha žuž de-l-binayat kbaṛ.*

hen - *džaža* pl. *-t.*

henna - *ḥenna* pl. *ḥnani.*

herb - *ɛšeb* pl. *ɛšub, ɛešba* pl. *-t, ɛšub.* In Europe herbs are still widely used as home remedies. *f-ʔuṛubba ma-zalin ka-iṣeḷḷḥu le-ɛšub le-d-dwa.*

herd - *qeṭɛa* pl. *-t, qṭaɛi; ksiba* pl. *-t, ksayeb.* Who owns this herd? *de-mmen had le-ksiba?*

here - **1.** *hna, hnaya.* We can't stay here. *ma-imken-lna-š nebqaw hna.* **2.** *ha, hak.* Here's the book. *ha le-ktab.*

here and there - *f-beɛḍ l-maḥellat.* Here and there you can still see horse cabs. *f-beɛḍ l-maḥellat ma-zal telqa kṛareṣ de-l-xil.*

hereafter - *men daba l-fuq, men daba l-qeddam.* Hereafter I'll be more careful. *men daba l-fuq ġad neḥḍi ṛaṣi kteṛ men had š-ši.*

hernia - *fteq* pl. *ftuqa.*

herself - **1.** *ṛaṣha.* She fell on the stairs and hurt herself. *ṭaḥet fe-ḍ-ḍṛuž u-qeṣṣḥet ṛaṣha.* **2.** *b-iddha, b-iddiha, hiya lli.* She did it herself. *ɛemletha b-iddha* or *hiya lli ɛemletha.*

**She's not herself today. *ma-ši hiya hadik l-yum.*

to **hesitate** - **1.** *tredded.* He hesitated a moment before he answered. *tredded ši-šwiya qbel-ma ižaweb.* **2.** *tsaʔel, xemmem.* I'm still hesitating whether I should do it or not. *ma-zal ka-ntsaʔel waš ndirha wella la.*

hesitation - *tareddud.* He answered without hesitation. *žaweb bla tareddud.*

hey - *iwa.* Hey, what's the big idea? *iwa, še-mɛent had š-ši?*

**Hey you! Come over here! *ahya dak s-siyyed, aži lle-hna!*

hiccup - *fuwaqa* pl. *-t.* I have the hiccups again. *ɛawed qebṭetni l-fuwaqa.*

hide - *želd* pl. *žlud.* These hides still have to be tanned. *had ž-žlud ma-zal ka-ixeṣṣhom iddebġu.*

to **hide** - **1.** *xebbeɛ, xebba, ḥeyyed.* He hid the money in a drawer. *ṛah xebbeɛ le-flus f-waḥed le-mžeṛṛ.* **2.** *ḍeṛṛeq.* The trees hide the view. *š-ššeṛ ka-iḍeṛṛqu l-menḍeṛ.* **3.** *txebbeɛ, txebba.* Let's hide in the garage. *yaḷḷah ntxebbɛu fe-l-gaṛaž.*

high - **1.** *talta* (third gear); *ṛebɛa* (fourth gear). Now shift into high. *beddel le-t-talta daba.* **2.** *ɛali* pl. *ɛalyin.* This minaret is very high. *had ṣ-ṣemɛa ɛalya bezzaf.* **3.** *mezyan.* I have a high opinion of him. *ɛendi neḍṛa mezyana ɛlih.*

**That building is eight stories high. *dak l-binaya fiha tmenya de-ṭ-ṭebqat d-le-ɛlu.* --He's in high spirits today. *l-yum ṛašeq-lu mɛa ṛaṣu.* --There I was, left high and dry. *u-bqit gales meqṭuɛ ṛ-ṛaṣ.* --We searched for it high and low.

qellebna ɛliha s-sma u-l-ʔeṛḍ.
highly - *bezzaf.* She seemed highly pleased. *ḍehṛet našṭa bezzaf.*
to speak highly of - *mdeḥ, tna itni ɛla.* He spoke very highly of him. *tna ɛlih bezzaf.*
to think highly of - *ɛmel f-menzla ɛalya.* They think very highly of him. *ɛamlineh f-menzla ɛalya.*
high school - *meḍṛaṣa tanawiya* pl. *madaris tanawiya.*
high tide - *mlu.* Let's wait till high tide. *xellina ntsennaw ḥetta l-le-mlu.*
hike - *msarya* pl. *-t.* Let's go on a hike! *yaḷḷah nɛemlu ši-msarya.*
to hike - *mša imši, tsara, ɛmel msarya.* We hiked five kilometers. *ɛmelna xemsa kilumiter d-le-msarya.*
hill - *kodya* pl. *-t, kdi.* What's on the other side of the hill? *šnu fe-ž-žiha le-xṛa lli wṛa l-kodya?*
himself - **1.** *ṛaṣu.* He hurt himself badly. *qeṣṣeḥ ṛaṣu bezzaf.* **2.** *b-ṛaṣu, b-nefsu.* You'll have to see the director himself. *xeṣṣek tšuf l-mudir b-ṛaṣu.* **3.** *huwa lli, b-iddu, b-iddih.* Did he do it himself? *waš huwa lli darha?*
**He wasn't quite himself. *kan ma-ši tamamen huwa hadak.*
--He's himself again. *ɛad ṛžeɛ ɛla xaṭṛu ɛawed.*
to **hinder** - *ɛeṛqel, mneɛ, tɛeṛṛeḍ.*
hinge - *buz* pl. *bwaz.* One of the hinges of the trunk broke off. *buz dyal š-šanṭa therres.*
hint - *ʔišaṛa* pl. *-t.* Can't you give me a hint? *ma-teqḍeṛ-ši teɛṭini ši-ʔišaṛa?*
to hint - *šar išir.* He hinted that something was up. *šar billa ši-ḥaža kanet.*
to hint at - *bġa ibġi iqṣeḍ.* What are you hinting at? *š-ka-tebġi teqṣeḍ?*
hip - *weṛk* pl. *wṛak.*
hire - *kra* pl. *-wat.* These boats are for hire. *had le-flayek l-le-kra.*
to hire - **1.** *kra ikri.* We hired the boat for the whole day. *krina le-fluka n-nhaṛ kollu.* **2.** *xeddem, weḍḍef.* We have to hire more people. *ka-ixeṣṣna nzidu nxeddmu n-nas.*
hiss - *teṣfiṛa* pl. *-t.*
to hiss - **1.** *ṣeffeṛ.* Every time he mentioned her name the audience hissed. *ġir huwa kan idkeṛ smiytha u-l-metfeṛṛžin ka-iṣeffṛu.* **2.** *ṣeffeṛ ɛla.* He was hissed everywhere. *ṣeffṛu ɛlih f-koll muḍeɛ.*
historian - *muʔeṛṛix* pl. *-in.*
historic - *taṛixi.*
history - *taṛix* pl. *twaṛex.* Have you studied European history? *qṛiti taṛix ʔuṛubba?*
hit - **1.** *ḍeṛḅa* pl. *-t.* He made four hits. *ḍṛeb ṛebɛa de-ḍ-ḍeṛbat.* **2.** *(lli) meḥbub, mešhuṛ.* His song became a hit over night. *ʔoġniytu deġya deġya wellat mešhuṛa.*
to hit - **1.** *ḍṛeb.* I hit my knee against the door. *ḍṛebt ṛkebti mɛa l-bab.* **2.** *ḍṛeḅ, qaṣ iqiṣ.* The ball hit the wall. *l-kuṛa qaṣet l-ḥiṭ.* **3.** *ʔetteṛ ɛla, ʔetteṛ f-.* The news hit me very hard. *le-xbaṛ ʔetteṛ ɛliya bezzaf.*
to hit it off - *ttafeq, ttawa.* How do the two hit it off? *kif ka-ittawaw duk ž-žuž?*
to hit (up)on - *ṭaḥ iṭiḥ ɛla.* How did you hit on that? *kif ṭeḥti ɛla dak š-ši?*
hitch - **1.** *ḥaža ɛewža* pl. *ḥwayež ɛiwež.* I'm sure there's a hitch somewhere. *ana metyeqqen billa ši-ḥaža ɛewža f-ši-muḍeɛ.* **2.** *teɛqida* pl. *-t, tɛaqed.* Everything came off without a hitch. *koll-ši xrež huwa hadak bla teɛqida.*
**That's where the hitch comes in! *temma bqat.*
to hitch - *ṛbeṭ.* Hitch your horse to the post. *ṛbeṭ ɛewdek mɛa r-rkiza.*
hives - *lfafeṭ.*
to **hoard** - *ṭemm, žmeɛ.* They're hoarding sugar. *ka-iṭemmu s-sokkaṛ.*
hoarse - *mžebbeḥ.* He's shouted himself hoarse. *ṛžeɛ mžebbeḥ b-quwt le-ġwat.*
hoe - *ɛetla* pl. *-t, ɛtali.*
hobby - *hawaya* pl. *-t.* His latest hobby is collecting stamps. *l-hawaya dyalu ž-ždida hiya žmiɛ t-tnaber.*
hog - *ḥelluf* pl. *ḥlalef.*
to **hold** - **1.** *rfed.* She held the baby in her arms. *kanet rafda t-teṛbya f-iddha.* --The room holds twenty people. *l-bit ka-irfed ɛešrin de-n-nas.* **2.** *šedd, qbeṭ.* That knot will hold. *dak l-ɛeqda teqbeṭ.* --Hold your tongue! *qbeṭ lsanek ɛendek.* --Hold this box for me a minute. *qbeṭ-li had ṣ-ṣenduq waḥed š-šwiya.* **3.** *ɛmel.* The meetings are held once a week. *le-žtimaɛat ka-iɛemluha meṛṛa fe-ž-žemɛa.* **4.** *kan ikun ɛendu.* He holds a high position. *ɛendu mertaba ɛalya.* **5.** *ḥbes.* Hold him! *ḥebsu.* **6.** *žleb.* That speaker knows how to hold his audience. *dak le-xṭib ka-yeɛṛef kif*

ižleb n-nas lli ka-itṣenntu-lu.
7. *daz iduz, kan ikun.* When were the last elections held? *fuq-aš dazu l-intixabat t-talya?* 8. *kan ikun ṣḥiḥ, tbet.* This rule doesn't hold in every case. *had l-qaεida ma-ši ṣḥiḥa f-koll muqif.*

**Hold the wire. *ma-teqṭeε-š.*

to hold back – *ḥṣeṛ, redd.* I wanted to go, but he held me back. *kont bġit nemši, saεa ḥṣeṛni.*

to hold office – *xda yaxod menṣib.* He held office for a long time. *modda u-huwa waxed dak l-menṣib.*

to hold on – *ṣbeṛ.* Can you hold on for a minute? *imken-lek teṣbeṛ waḥed š-šwiya.*

to hold on to – **1.** *qbeṭ f-.* Hold on to me. *qbeṭ fiya.* **2.** *bqa ibqa f-.* Can you hold on to that job just a little longer? *imken-lek tebqa f-had l-xedma waxxa ġir ši-šwiya?*

to hold out – *ṣbeṛ, kaber, qbeṭ.* We would have held out for months, if we had had enough food. *konna ma-zalin nkabru šheṛ εla šheṛ u-kan kanet εendma l-makla l-kafya.*

to hold over – *ˀexxeṛ.* The movie was held over for another week. *l-film, ˀexxṛuh l-žemεa xṛa.*

to hold true – *kan ikun ṣḥiḥ.* That doesn't hold true in our case. *be-n-nesba lilna had š-ši ma-ši ṣḥiḥ.*

to hold under a lease – *εmel εoqda.* They held the land under a ten-year lease. *εemlu l-l-ˀeṛḍ εoqda d-εešṛ snin.*

to hold up – **1.** *εeṭṭel.* You're holding me up. *ṛak ka-tεeṭṭelni.* **2.** *ṣbeṛ.* Will these shoes hold up? *waš had ṣ-ṣebbaṭ iṣbeṛ?* **3.** *qṭeε ṭ-ṭṛiq εla.* I was held up by two men last night. *l-bareḥ fe-l-lil žuž de-r-ržal qeṭεu εliya ṭ-ṭṛiq.*

to get hold of – *ḥeṣṣel εla.* Where can I get hold of him? *fayn imken-li nheṣṣeḷ εlih?*

to take hold of – *qbeṭ f-.* Take hold of my arm. *qbeṭ fe-draεi.*

**How is he holding up under the pain? *kif-en huwa mεa le-ḥṛiq?*

holdup – *qeṭεan ṭ-ṭṛiq* pl. *qeṭεan ṭ-ṭoṛqan.* He has nothing to do with the holdup. *ma-kan-ši mšarek f-dak qeṭεan ṭ-ṭṛiq.*

hole – **1.** *teqba* pl. *-t, tqabi.* He has a hole in his pants. *εendu teqba f-serwalu.* **2.** *terεa* pl. *-t.* The trip made a big hole in my pocketbook. *ṣ-ṣefṛa xellat-li terεa kbira fe-l-beẓṭam.* **3.** *ḥefṛa* pl. *-t, ḥfaṛi.* He dug a hole and hid his money in it. *ḥfeṛ waḥed l-ḥofṛa u-xebbeε le-flus dyalu fiha.*

holiday – *εid* pl. *εyad.* Is today a holiday? *waš l-yum εid?*

hollow – **1.** *xawi* pl. *xawyin.* This wall seems to be hollow. *had l-ḥeyṭ ka-iḍheṛ bin lli qelbu xawi.* **2.** *ġaṛeq, daxel.* Her cheeks are hollow. *xdudha daxlin.*

holy – *mqeddes.*

home – **1.** *εaˀila* pl. *-t.* My home is in Casablanca. *εaˀilti fe-ḍ-ḍaṛ l-biḍa.* **2.** *le-ḍ-ḍaṛ.* I have to go home. *xeṣṣni nemši le-ḍ-ḍaṛ.* **3.** *maḥell.* There's no place like home. *ḥetta ši ma-kayen bḥal l-waḥed f-maḥellu.*

at home – **1.** *fe-ḍ-ḍaṛ.* I was (at) home all day yesterday. *l-bareḥ n-nhaṛ kollu w-ana fe-ḍ-ḍaṛ.* **2.** *f-maḥellu.* Make yourself at home. *ḥseb ṛaṣek f-maḥellek.* **3.** *fe-d-daxil.* At home and abroad... *fe-d-daxil u-fe-l-xariž ...*

house and home – *ḍaṛ u-ḥbab.* The war has driven many people out of house and home. *l-ḥeṛb xeṛržet εadad de-n-nas εla ḍyuṛhom u-ḥbabhom.*

homeless – *bla ḍaṛ* pl. *bla ḍyuṛ.* Thousands were made homeless by the flood. *l-ḥemla xellat l-ˀulufat bla ḍyuṛ.*

homemade – *mṣuwweb fe-ḍ-ḍaṛ.* This is a homemade cake. *had l-ḥelwa mṣuwwba fe-ḍ-ḍaṛ.*

to be **homesick** – *tweḥḥeš bladu.*

homework – *xedma de-l-meḍṛaṣa.* Have you done all your homework? *ṣuwwebti xḍemtek de-l-meḍṛaṣa kollha?*

honest – **1.** *(lli) fih ṣ-ṣeḍq.* Do you think he's honest? *ka-ḍḍenn billa fih ṣ-ṣeḍq?* **2.** *(lli) fih l-ˀaman.* He has an honest face. *wežhu bayen fih l-ˀaman.*

**An honest man is as good as his word. *ṛ-ṛažel ṛažel be-klemtu.*

honestly – **1.** *be-l-mufid.* I was honestly surprised. *ttebheḍt be-l-mufid.* **2.** *be-ṣ-ṣeḍq.* Tell me honestly... *tkellem mεaya be-ṣ-ṣeḍq* or *ažini le-ṣ-ṣeḍq.* **3.** *be-ṣ-ṣaṛaḥa.* To tell you honestly, I don't like it. *nqul-lek be-ṣ-ṣaṛaḥa, had š-ši ma-εažebni-š.*

honesty – *ṣedq, ṣaṛaḥa.* There's no question about his honesty. *ma-kayen šekk fe-ṣ-ṣeḍq dyalu.* --Honesty is the best policy. *ma-kayen ma-ḥsen men ṣ-ṣeḍq.*

honey – *εsel.*

honeymoon - *šehṛ l-ɛasal.*
to **honk the horn** - *zuwweg.* Honk the horn three times, and I'll come down. *zuwweg tlata de-l-meṛṛat u-nehbeṭ.*
honor - *šaṛaf.* We gave a banquet in his honor. *ɛmelna l-walima ɛla šaṛafu.* --I give you my word of honor! *ka-neɛṭik kalimat š-šaṛaf.*
**He's a man of honor. *ṛažel b-žudu u-ɛeṛḍu.*
to honor - **1.** *šeṛṛef, kebbeṛ b-.* I feel very much honored with your visit. *šeṛṛeftiwni b-ziyaṛtkom.* **2.** *qbel.* We can't honor this check. *ma-imken-lna-š nqeblu had š-šik.*
hood - *qobb* pl. *qbab.*
hoof - *ḥafer* pl. *ḥwafer, ferquš* pl. *fraqeš.* The horse got a nail in his hoof. *l-ɛewd dxel-lu meṣmaṛ f-ḥafru.*
to hoof (it) - *mša imši ɛel l-korraɛi.* We had to hoof it. *ma-fadna ġir mšina ɛel l-korraɛi.*
hook - *ɛellaqa* pl. *-t, ɛlaleq.* Hang your coat on the hook. *ɛmel balṭuk ɛel l-ɛellaqa.*
hook and eye - *dkeṛ u-nta* pl. *dkuṛa u-ntawat; ṭeṛṛašiya* pl. *-t.* Shall I put on a zipper or hooks and eyes? *neɛmel sensla wella d-dkuṛa u-n-ntawat?*
by hook or by crook - *be-d-draɛ aw be-l-xaṭeṛ.* He intends to get rich, by hook or by crook. *ġaṛuḍu itxuwwež be-d-draɛ aw be-l-xaṭeṛ.*
on one's own hook - *ɛla draɛu.* He did it on his own hook. *žabha ɛla draɛu.*
to hook - **1.** *qbeṭ, ṣiyyeḍ.* How many fish did you hook? *šhal de-l-ḥut ṣiyyeḍti?* **2.** *ṛbeṭ.* Help me hook this chain. *ṛbeṭ mɛaya had s-sensla.*
**She finally hooked him. *ma-mšat ḥetta kebblet-lu režlih.* --I haven't hooked up the new radio yet. *ma-zal ma-rekkebt-ši ṛ-ṛadyu ž-ždid.*
hookah - *rgila* pl. *rgayel.*
hop - *neqza* pl. *-t.* It's just a short hop by plane. *neqza weḥda fe-ṭ-ṭiyaṛa.*
to hop - **1.** *neqqez.* She hopped with joy. *neqqzet be-l-ferḥa.* **2.** *ḍaṛ iḍuṛ.* He was hopping around on one leg. *kan ka-iḍuṛ ɛla ržel weḥda.*
hope - **1.** *ṛža, yas, iyas.* Don't give up hope! *ma-teqṭeɛ-š l-yas.* **2.** *ʔamal.* I still have some hope of getting the job. *ma-zal ɛendi šwiya de-l-ʔamal nšedd dak l-xedma.*
to hope - **1.** *ʔemmel, tṛežža.* She had hoped to see you. *kanet ka-tʔemmel tšufek.* **2.** *ṭleb ɛel ḷḷah.* We hope he can come tomorrow. *ka-nṭeḷbu ɛel ḷḷah iži ġedda.*
let's hope - *meṣṣab.* Let's hope this weather keeps up. *meṣṣab ibqa had l-žuw hakda.*
to hope for - *ṭleb ṛebbi f-.* Let's hope for the best. *nṭeḷbu ṛebbi fe-l-xir.*
**I hope you didn't catch cold. *ɛendak tkun tṛuwweḥti?* --Will you be back by tomorrow night? I hope so. *ġedda fe-l-lil tkun ṛžeɛti? fi yadi llah.*
hopeful - *mʔemmel.*
hopeless - *(lli) ma-bqa fih ʔamal, (lli) ma-bqa fih dwa.* The situation is completely hopeless. *l-ḥala ma-bqa fiha ḥetta ši-ʔamal.*
hopscotch - *tšiktšika* (not used with art).
horizon - *ʔufuq* pl. *ʔafaq.*
horizontal - *wefqi.*
horn - **1.** *qeṛn* pl. *qṛun.* This bull's horns are very long. *le-qṛun d-had t-tuṛ ṭwal bezzaf.* **2.** *zuwaga* pl. *-t; kḷakṣun* pl. *-at.* The car's horn doesn't work. *z-zuwaga d-had ṭ-ṭumubil ma-xeddama-š.*
to blow the horn - *zuwweg.* Don't blow the horn so much. *ma-dzuwweg-š bezzaf.*
hornet - *zenbuṛ* pl. *znabeṛ; bu-rzizzi.*
horrible - *(lli) ka-ireɛɛeb.* It was a horrible sight. *menḍeṛ kan ka-ireɛɛeb.*
horrors - *fḍayeḥ.* The horrors of war are indescribable. *le-fḍayeḥ de-l-ḥeṛb ma-ka-ittweṣfu-š.*
horse - *ɛewd* pl. *xil, xeyl.*
**Now don't get on your high horse! *iwa la-tenfex-ši ɛlina!* --That's a horse of a different color. *iwa had š-ši ḥaža xṛa daba.* --A team of wild horses couldn't drag me there. *waxxa dželṛni l-temma nta u-ɛemmek ṣebbeḥ.*
horse race(s) - *mṣabqa de-l-xil* pl. *-t de-l-xil.* Let's go to the (horse) races. *yaḷḷah nemšiw l-le-mṣabqa de-l-xil.*
horse-radish - *fžel le-xla.*
hose - **1.** *žeɛba de-s-sqi* pl. *žɛeb s-sqi, kawatšu de-s-sqi.* The hose is still in the garden. *l-kawatšu de-s-sqi ma-zal fe-l-ɛeṛṣa.* **2.** *teqšira* pl. *tqašer.* We just got a new shipment of hose. *ɛad weṣḷetna neqla de-t-tqašer.*
hospitable - *krim, qelbu kbir.*

hospital - *musteša* pl. *-yat.* When did you get home from the hospital? *fuq-aš wṣelti men l-musteša le-ḍ-ḍar?*
hospitality - *karam, žud.*
host - *mul ḍ-ḍar* pl. *mmalin ḍ-ḍar.* Have you been introduced to the host? *qeddmuk l-mul ḍ-ḍar?*
hostess - *mulat ḍ-ḍar* pl. *mmalin ḍ-ḍar.*
hot - **1.** *sxun.* Do you have hot water? *ɛendek l-ma sxun?* **2.** *ḥarr.* This pepper is very hot. *had l-ibzar ḥarr bezzaf.*
**I made it hot for him. *ẓiyyerṭha ɛlih.* --He has a hot temper. *ṛaṣu sxun.* --We were hot on his trail. *konna tafrineh.*
hotel - *uṭil* pl. *-at.* I'm looking for a cheap hotel. *ka-nḍuṛ ɛla ši-uṭil ṛxiṣ.*
hour - *saɛa* pl. *-t, swayeɛ.* I'll be back in an hour. *ġad nwelli men daba saɛa.*
hour overtime - *saɛa zayda* pl. *swayeɛ zayda.* I worked five hours overtime. *xdemt xemsa de-s-swayeɛ zayda.*
after hours - *men beɛd l-xedma.* See me after hours. *šufni men beɛd l-xedma.*
at all hours - *f-ˀay weqt.* I can be reached at all hours. *f-ˀay weqt h-ana mužud.*
for hours - *saɛa ɛla saɛa, s-saɛa u-xetha.* She practices the piano for hours. *ka-ttmerren ɛel le-byanu s-saɛa u-xetha.*
a quarter of an hour - *ṛbeɛ saɛa, ṛubuɛ saɛa.*
**What are your working hours? *šnu huwa weqtek de-l-xedma?*
hour hand - *muri kbir* pl. *mwara kbaṛ.*
house - **1.** *ḍaṛ* pl. *ḍyaṛ, ḍyuṛ.* I want to rent a house. *baġi nekri ši-ḍaṛ.* **2.** *mežlis* pl. *mažalis.* Both houses are going to meet in a joint session. *l-mažalis b-žuž ġad idžemɛu f-gelsa weḥda.*
to keep house - *gabel ḍ-ḍaṛ.* She keeps house for her uncle. *ka-tgabel ḍ-ḍaṛ l-ɛemmha.*
**Where are they going to house the visitors? *fayn ġad iɛemlu ḍ-ḍyaf?*
housemaid - *metɛellma* pl. *-t, xeddama* pl. *-t.*
housework - *xedma de-ḍ-ḍaṛ.* Many girls prefer office work to housework. *bezzaf d-le-bnat ka-ifeḍḍlu l-xedma de-l-ˀiḍaṛa ɛel l-xedma de-ḍ-ḍaṛ.*
how - *kif.* How shall I do it? *kif ġad ndirha?* --How do you feel? *kif ka-tḥess b-ṛaṣek?*
**How come you're still here? *šniya qaḍiytek ma-zal hnaya?*
how many - *šḥal men* (followed by sg.), *šḥal de-* (followed by pl.). How many apples shall I take? *šḥal de-t-teffaḥat naxod?*
how much - *šḥal.* How much did he pay? *šḥal xeḷḷeṣ?*
however - *be-l-ḥeqq, walakin.* I'd like to do it; however, I have no time. *nebġi ndirha walakin ma-ɛendi-š l-weqt.*
howl - *teɛwiqa* pl. *-t* coll. *teɛwaq.* I thought I heard the howl of a wolf. *žab-li ḷḷah smeɛt teɛwaq d-dib.*
to howl - *ɛewweq.* The dog has been howling all night. *l-lil kollu we-l-kelb iɛewweq.*
to howl with laughter - *tferġeɛ be-ḍ-ḍeḥk.* The audience howled with laughter. *l-metferržin ttferġɛu be-ḍ-ḍeḥk.*
to **huddle** - *ɛeṛṛem, tɛeṛṛem, dzaḥem.* They were huddled in a corner. *kanu mɛeṛṛmin f-qent.*
to huddle together - *tkemmeš ši f-ši.* The sheep huddled close together. *le-kbaš tkemmšu metqaṛbin ši f-ši.*
to be in a huddle - *tqaṛa.* Those two are always in a huddle. *duk ž-žuž dima ka-itqaṛaw.*
hug - *teɛniqa* pl. *-t.*
to give a hug - *ḍṛeb teɛniqa, ɛenneq.* She gave me a big hug. *ḍeṛbet-li teɛniq qedd-aš.*
to hug - **1.** *ɛenneq.* She hugged her mother tightly. *ɛennqet mmha bezzaf.* **2.** *wqef qṛib l-.* Our boat hugged the coast line all day. *n-nhaṛ kollu u-l-baxiṛa dyalna waqfa qṛiba l-ṭeṛf le-bḥeṛ.*
huge - *ɛḍim* pl. *ɛḍam.*
hum - *dzeġnina* pl. *-t* coll. *dzeġnin.* What's that peculiar hum? *šni hiya dak d-dzeġnina le-ġṛiba?*
to hum - *zeġnen.* What's that tune you're humming? *šni hiya dak n-neġma lli ka-dzeġnen?*
human - *ˀinsan* pl. *nas.* I'm only human. *ma-ˀana ġir ˀinsan.*
human being - *ˀinsan, bnadem* pl. *nas.* He treats us like human beings. *ka-yeḥsebna bḥal n-nas.*
**It's only human to make mistakes. *subḥan men la-isha.*
humble - **1.** *metwaḍeɛ.* In the beginning he acted very humble. *fe-l-luwwel ban metwaḍeɛ bezzaf.* **2.** *ḍɛif*

pl. *ḍƐaf*. The president grew up in very humble circumstances. *ṛ-ṛaʔis kber f-waḥed ḍ-ḍuṛuf ḍƐifa.*
humidity - *bruda, ṛṭuḅa.*
to **humiliate** - *ḥeššem, ṭiyyeḥ b-.*
humor - *gana* pl. *-t*. Are you in a good humor? *nta Ɛla gantek?*
**Keep your sense of humor. *xellik fik l-beṣṭ.* --He has no sense of humor. *ma-ka-iqbel beṣṭ.*
hunch - *šuƐuṛ*. I have a hunch that something is wrong there. *Ɛendi šuƐuṛ billa ši-ḥaža ma-ši hiya hadik.*
hunchback - *ḥdibbi* pl. *-yin.*
hunched up - *meṭwi, metni*. Your back hurts because you're sitting hunched up. *ḍehṛek ka-iḥeṛqek ḥit gales metni.*
hundred - *mya* pl. *myawat, miʔin.* About a hundred people were present. *teqṛiben mya de-n-nas kanu ḥaḍṛin.*
hunger - *žuƐ*. I nearly died of hunger. *mšit nmut be-ž-žuƐ.*
hungry - *bih ž-žuƐ, žiƐan*. I'm hungry. *ana biya ž-žuƐ.*
to get hungry - *žaƐ izuƐ, žah ižih ž-žuƐ*. A lot of times I get hungry right in the middle of the night. *bezzaf de-l-meṛṛat ma-ka-ižini ž-žuƐ ġir f-neṣṣ l-lil.*
to go hungry - *bqa ibqa be-ž-žuƐ*. We didn't go hungry. *ma-bqina-š be-ž-žuƐ.*
to **hunt** - *ṣiyyeḍ*. They're hunting rabbits. *ṛahom ka-iṣiyyḍu le-qniya.*
to go hunting - *mša imši iṣiyyeḍ*. We're going hunting tomorrow. *ġad nemšiw nṣiyyḍu ġedda.*
to hunt for - *qelleb Ɛla*. We were hunting for a new house. *konna ka-nqellbu Ɛla ḍaṛ ždida.*
hunter - *ṣiyyaḍ* pl. *-a.*
hurry - 1. *zerba* pl. *-t*. There's no hurry. *ma-kayna zerba.* 2. *teqliqa* pl. *-t*. What's the hurry? *š-had t-teqliqa?*
in a hurry - 1. *mezrub*. I'm in a big hurry. *ṛ-ana mezrub bezzaf.* 2. *be-z-zerba*. He wrote the letter in a hurry and forgot to sign it. *kteb le-bṛa be-z-zerba u-nsa ma-weqqeƐha-š.*
to hurry *zreb*. You'll have to hurry to get a good seat. *xeṣṣek dzreb baš teqbeṭ bḷaṣa mezyana.* --Don't hurry! *ma-dzreb-š!* --Don't hurry me. *ma-dzrebni-š.*
**Hurry up! *deġya deġya!*
hurt - 1. *ḥṛeq, wžeƐ, ḍeṛṛ*. My arm hurts (me). *draƐi ka-yeḥṛeqni.* 2. *qeṣṣeḥ*. Where are you hurt? *fayn mqeṣṣeḥ?* 3. *ḍeṛṛ*. I didn't mean to hurt you. *ma-kanet-š niyti nḍeṛṛek.* 4. *qḍa iqḍi Ɛla, ḍeṛṛ*. This will hurt business. *had š-ši ġad iqḍi Ɛel t-tižaṛa.* 5. *žṛeḥ* I didn't want to hurt your feelings. *ma-bġit-š nežṛeḥ-lek Ɛawaṭifek.*
**Will it hurt if I'm late? *ma-kayen bas ila žit mƐeṭṭeḷ?*
husband - *ṛažel* pl. *ṛžal*. I'd like you to meet my husband. *smeḥ-li nqeddem-lek ṛažli.*
hush - *skat*. Hush! I can't hear a word. *s-skat! ma-ka-nesmeƐ-ši kelma.*
to hush up - *dfen*. They quickly hushed up the scandal. *deġya defnu le-fḍiḥa.*
husky - 1. *mžebbeḥ*. His voice sounds husky. *ḥelqu tqul mžebbeḥ.* 2. *ṣḥiyyeḥ, qelda*. He's such a husky fellow! *walayenni ṣḥiyyeḥ mƐa ṛaṣu!*
hut - *muwwala* pl. *-t, nwawel.*
hyena - *ḍbeƐ* pl. *ḍbuƐa.*

I

I - *ana.*
ice - *telž.*
to ice - *fenned*. Ice the cake as soon as it's cool. *fenned l-ḥelwa men ḥeddha barda.*
icebox - *tellaža* pl. *-t.*
ice cream - *baṣṭa.*
icy - *mtellež.*
idea - *fikra* pl. *-t, afkaṛ*. That's a good idea. *hadi fikra mezyana.* --What gives you that idea? *mnin žatek hadik l-fikra?*
**That's the idea! *hiya hadik!* --The idea! *walayenni ž-žebha!*
identification - *teƐrif.*
identification card - *weṛqa de-t-teƐrif.*
to **identify** - *Ɛeṛṛef*. The police identified him by his picture. *l-bulis Ɛeṛṛfuh be-ṣ-ṣuṛa dyalu.*
idle - 1. *ma-ši mešġul*. These men have been idle for quite a while. *hadi modda u-had ṛ-ṛžal*

ma-mešġulin-š. 2. *xawi.* That's just idle talk. *dak š-ši ġit klam xawi.*

**Her fingers are never idle. *dima ṣbaƐha ka-imelmlu.* The factory has lain idle for years. *hadi snin u-l-meƐmel ḥaṣeṛ l-xedma.*

if - 1. *ila* (for real conditions). If anyone asks for me, say I'll be right back. *ila suwwel Ɛliya ši-waḥed, qul-lu ana ġad neṛžƐ daba.* 2. *kun* (for contrary to fact conditions). If he had kept quiet, he would have gotten away. *kun sket, kun flet.* 3. *waš.* See if there's any mail for me. *šuf waš kayen ši-barid lili.*

as if - *bḥal ila.* He talks as if he had been there. *huwa ka-itkellem bḥal ila kan temma.*

even if - *waxxa.* I'll go even if it rains. *ana ġad nemši waxxa ṭṭiḥ š-šta.*

ignorance - *žehl.*

ignorant - *žahel.*

ill - *mṛiḍ* pl. *mṛaḍ.*

illness - *merḍ.*

to **imagine** - 1. *tṣuwweṛ.* I can't imagine what you mean. *ma-neqdeṛ-š ntṣuwweṛ aš bġiti tqul.* 2. *xtaṛeƐ, ḥlem.* He's just imagining it. *ġir ka-ixtaṛeƐ dak š-ši.* 3. *ḍenn.* I imagine he'll come. *ka-nḍenn billa ġa-iži.*

imam - *imam. ʔimam* pl. *ʔayemma.*

to **imitate** - *qelled.* He can imitate my voice. *huwa iqdeṛ iqelled ṣuti.*

imitation - *teqlid.* That's a poor imitation. *hadak teqlid ḍƐif.*

immediately - *fe-l-ḥin.*

immense - *waseƐ, kbir.*

immoral - *mxalef le-ḥya.*

impartial - *(lli) ka-yeƐdel be-l-ḥeqq.*

impatient - *qlil ṣ-ṣebṛ.*

impolite - *qlil l-ʔadab.*

import - *težlib* pl. *-at.* The government encouraged the import of raw materials. *l-ḥukuma seƐdet težlib l-mawadd l-luwwla.*

to import - *žleb.*

importance - *ʔahemmiya.*

important - *muhimm.*

impossible - *(lli) ma-imken-š, muḥal.* Why is it impossible? *Ɛlaš ma-imken-š?*

to **impress** - *ʔetter f-.*

impression - *teʔtir* pl. *-at.*

to **improve** - 1 *ḥessen.* I don't know how we can improve it. *ma-neƐṛef-š kif-aš imken-lna nḥessnu had š-ši.* 2. *tterxef, tḥessen.* His condition has improved. *tterxef Ɛlih l-ḥal.* 3. *tqeddem.* Ali is improving in school. *Ɛli ka-itqeddem fe-l-meḍṛaṣa.*

improvement - *teḥsin.*

**That's no improvement over what went before. *had š-ši ma-ḥsen-š men dak š-ši lli fat.*

impudence - *qellet le-ḥya, ḍṣaṛa.*

in - 1. *f-* (*fi-* before pronoun endings). There's no window in my room. *ma-kayen šeṛžem f-biti.* --He's in Casablanca now. *huwa fe-ḍ-daṛ l-biḍa daba.* --I can finish it in a week. *neqdeṛ nkemmelha f-žemƐa.* --If I were in your place I would go. *ila kont fe-bḷaṣtek, ana nemši.* --My family is in the country. *Ɛaʔilti f-le-Ɛṛubiya.* --We're three months behind in the rent. *ḥna mʔexxṛin b-telt šhuṛ f-le-kra.* --In my opinion... *f-ṛeyyi...* --Are you in on it, too? *waš fiha ḥetta nta?* --I'll see you in the morning. *nšufek fe-ṣ-ṣbaḥ.* 2. *men daba.* I'll be back in three days. *ġad neṛžeƐ men daba telt iyyam.* 3. *b-* (*bi-* before pronoun endings). Say it in English. *qulha be-n-negliza.* --Write in ink. *kteb b-le-mdad.*

**Come in! *dxol!* --He has it in for you. *huwa ḥalef fik.* --He's in poor health. *huwa ṣeḥḥtu ḍƐifa.* --I'm all in. *ana mehluk.* --Now we're in for it! *daba wḥelna!*

in behalf - *Ɛla ʔažel, li ʔazel.* His friends intervened in his behalf. *ṣḥabu tweṣṣṭu Ɛla ʔažlu.*

in half - *Ɛla žuž.* Cut the cake in half. *qsem l-ḥelwa Ɛla žuž.*

incense - *bxuṛ* pl. *-at.*

incense burner - *mbexṛa* pl. *-t, mbaxeṛ.*

incident - *ḥadita* pl. *-t; waqiƐa* pl. *-t, wqayeƐ.*

incidentally - 1. *bin u-bin.* He just said it incidentally. *huwa ġir qalha bin u-bin.* 2. *fekkeṛtini.* Incidentally, I saw our friend Ali the other day. *fekkeṛtini and šeft ṣaḥebna Ɛli dak n-nhar.*

to **include** - *kan ikun fih, žmeƐ.* The dictionary doesn't include technical expressions. *had l-qamus ma-fih-š l-Ɛibaṛat t-teqniya.*

**Include this is my bill. *ḥseb hadi fe-bṭaqti.*

income - *medxul.* How much of an income does he have? *šḥal l-medxul lli ka-ižih?*

to **inconvenience** – *bessel Ɛla,* I
don't want to inconvenience you.
ana ma-baği-š nbessel Ɛlik.
increase – *zyada.*
    to increase – 1. *zad izid f-.*
You'll have to increase the price.
xeṣṣek dzid fe-t-tamen. 2. *qwa
iqwi.* The population increased
greatly. *s-sokkan qwaw bezzaf.*
indeed – 1. *bla šekk.* That's very
good indeed! *dak š-ši mezyan
bezzaf bla šekk.* 2. *meƐlum.* Yes,
indeed! *meƐlum!* 3. *Ɛad.* He's
very strong indeed. *huwa qwi
bezzaf Ɛad.*
independent – *mustaqill.*
India – *hend, blad l-hend.*
Indian – 1. *hendi, hnud* (reference
to both America and India).
2. *de-l-hend, hendi.* Is that an
Indian turban? *waš hadik ṛeẓẓa
de-l-hend?*
to **indicate** – *biyyen.*
indifferent – *bared.*
individual – 1. (n.) *šexṣ.* pl. *šxaṣ,
šxuṣa.* 2. (adj.) *šexṣi.*
indoors – *l-daxel.* You'd better stay
indoors today. *ḥsen-lek tebqa
l-daxel l-yum.*
industry – *ṣenƐa* pl. *-t, ṣnayeƐ.*
infantile paralysis – *bu-kezzaz.* He
has infantile paralysis. *huwa fih
bu-kezzaz.*
infantry – *režliya.*
to **infect** – *Ɛeffem.* The wound is
infected. *l-žerḥa mƐeffna.*
inferior – *suluki.*
infinite – *bla ḥedd, (lli) ma
itḥedd-š.*
to **inflame** – **My eye is inflammed.
Ɛeyni ṭaleƐ fiha d-demm.
inflammation – *tenfixa.*
to **inform** – *Ɛlem.* I was not informed
in time. *ma-Ɛelmuni-š fe-l-weqt.*
information – *xbaṛ, meƐlumat* (pl.).
Where can I get some information
about that? *fayn imken-li nṣib
ši-xbaṛ Ɛla dak š-ši?*
information desk – *mekteb l-meƐlumat.*
infraction – *mxalfa* pl. *-t.*
to **inhabit** – *sken iskon f-.*
inhabitant – *saken* pl. *sokkan.*
to **inherit** – *wret.*
initial – *luwlani.* The initial
salary is small. *l-ʔižaṛa
l-luwlaniya ṣğiṛa.*
injection – *tedxal* pl. *-at.*
to **injure** – *žreḥ.*
ink – *mdad.*
inner – *dexlani.* The inner door is
locked. *l-bab d-dexlani meqful.*
innocence – *braya.*

innocent – *bari.*
    **It was just an innocent remark.
kanet ğir mulaḥaḍa bla Ɛaṛ.
innovation – *bedƐa* pl. *-t.*
to **inquire** – *suwwel.* Before we
rented the house, we inquired about
it. *qbel-ma nekriw d-ḍaṛ,
suwwelna Ɛliha.*
insane – *ḥmeq* pl. *ḥumeq.*
insane asylum – *merṣṭan* pl. *-at.*
inscription – *ketba* pl. *-t.*
insect – *ḥašaṛa* pl. *-t.*
inside – 1. *dexlani.* May I see the
inside of the house? *waš imken-li
nšuf d-dexlani de-ḍ-ḍaṛ?*
2. *l-daxel.* He left it inside.
xellaha l-daxel. 3. *f-.* Inside of
five minutes the building was
empty. *f-xemsa de-d-dqayeq
l-binaya xwat.*
    to come, go inside – *dxel.*
    to have on inside out – *lbes
meqlub.* He has his coat on inside
out. *huwa labes kebbuṭu meqlub.*
    to know inside out – 1. *ḥfeḍ.* He
knows his business inside out. *huwa
ḥafeḍ šoğlu.* 2. *Ɛref bḥal l-ma.* I
know the book inside out. *ana
neƐref le-ktab bḥal l-ma.* 3. *Ɛref
men l-fuq le-t-teḥt.* I know that
town inside out. *ana neƐref had
le-mdina men l-fuq le-t-teḥt.*
    to turn inside out – *qleb.* Some-
body turned my sleeve inside out.
ši-waḥed qleb kommi
    **The police turned the place in-
side out, but they couldn't find
anything. *š-šeṛṭa qellbet l-maḥell
kollu u-ma-lqat walu.*
insignia – *Ɛalama* pl. *-t.*
insomnia – *ṣmiṛ, ṭyaṛ n-nƐas.*
inspector – *muṛaqib, mufettiš.*
to **install** – *rekkeb.*
instead of – 1. *f-Ɛewḍ.* He gave me
lemons instead of oranges. *Ɛṭani
l-ḥameḍ f-Ɛewḍ l-limun.*
2. *f-Ɛewḍ-ma.* Why don't you do
something instead of complaining
all the time? *Ɛlaš ma-teƐmel-š
ši-ḥaža f-Ɛewḍ-ma ttšekka dima?*
instruction – *meƐluma* pl. *-t.*
instrument – *ʔala* pl. *-t.*
insult – *sebba* pl. *-t* coll. *sebb.*
    to insult – *Ɛayer, sebb.*
insurance – *teʔmin.*
to **insure** – *ṣugeṛ.*
intelligence – *Ɛqel.*
intelligent – *dki.*
to **intend** – *qṣeḍ, nwa inwi.*
intense – *šdid* pl. *šdad.*
intention – *ğaṛaḍ* pl. *ğraḍ, ğrayeḍ.*
interest – (money earned) *ṭaluƐ.*

to **interest** - *žleb*. Can't you interest him in the matter? *waš ma-teqdeṛ-š dželbu l-had l-qaḍiya?*

to **be interested in** - *tšuwweq l-*. I'm interested in sports. *ana metšuwweq le-ṛ-ṛiyaḍa.*

**He's only interested in her money. *huwa ma ɛeynu ġir f-le-flus dyalha.*

interesting - *mufid.*

to **interfere** - **1.** *tɛeṛṛeḍ*. He'll leave on Sunday if nothing interferes. *ġa-imši nhaṛ l-ḥedd ila ḥetta ḥaža ma-tɛeṛṛḍet-lu.* --You're interfering with my work. *nta ka-ttɛeṛṛeḍ-li fe-xdemti.* **2.** *dexxel ṛaṣu*. Don't interfere in other people's affairs. *ma-ddexxel-š ṛaṣek f-suq n-nas.*

intermission - *weqt ṛ-ṛaḥa.*

internal - *daxili.*

international - *duwali.*

to **interpret** - *ṭeṛžem.*

interpreter - *ṭeṛžman* pl. *-at.*

into - **1.** *b-*. Can you translate this into English? *waš teqdeṛ ṭṭeṛžem hadi be-n-negliza?* **2.** *f-*. Put my clothes into the box. *dir le-ḥwayež dyali fe-ṣ-ṣenḍuq.* **3.** *l-*. He just went into the house. *yaḷḷah dxel le-ḍ-ḍaṛ.*

**We'll have to take that into account too. *xeṣṣna nḥesbu dak š-ši ḥetta huwa.*

intoxicated - *sekran.*

to **introduce** - *qeddem.*

introduction - *muqeddima* pl. *-t.* It's mentioned in the introduction. *had š-ši medkuṛ fe-l-muqeddima.*

invalid - *baṭeḷ*. A will without a signature is invalid. *waṣiya bla xeṭṭ l-yedd baṭḷa.*

to **invent** - *xtaṛeɛ.*

invention - *xtiraɛ* pl. *-at.*

to **investigate** - *bḥet.*

investigation - *beḥt* pl. *bḥut.*

invitation - *ɛṛaḍa* pl. *-t.*

to **invite** - *ɛṛeḍ.*

to **involve** - *dexxel*. He was involved in it too. *ḥetta huwa kan mdexxel fiha.*

**The trip involved a lot of expense. *ṭaṛ ṣ-ṣafaṛ ġali.*

iodine - *naṛ barda, yud.*

Iran - *l-iran.*

Iraq - *l-ɛiṛaq.*

Iraqi - *ɛiṛaqi* pl. *-yin.*

iris - *beṣḷet d-dib* (flower), *kḥel de-l-ɛeyn* (eye).

iron - **1.** *ḥdid*. You have to be made out of iron to stand all that. *xeṣṣek tkun meṣnuɛ men le-ḥdid baš teṣbeṛ l-had š-ši kollu.* --Strike while the iron is hot! *ḍṛeb ma-ḥedd le-ḥdid sxun!* **2.** *meṣḷuḥ* pl. *mṣaḷeḥ, blanša* pl. *-t* (for pressing clothing).

to **iron** - *ḥedded, ḍṛeb le-blanša l-*. Did you iron my shirt? *waš ḥeddedti qamižti?*

irritable - *mqelleq.*

to **irritate** - **1.** *qelleq*. His remark irritated me. *l-mulaḥaḍa dyalu qellqetni.* **2.** *ḥṛeq*. This soap doesn't irritate the skin. *had ṣ-ṣabun ma-ka-yeḥṛeq-š ž-želd.*

Islam - *ʔislam.*

Islamic - *ʔislami.*

island - *žazira* pl. *-t* (no assimilation of art.).

to **isolate** - *ɛmel b-waḥed-, ɛzel*. The sick children were isolated. *d-drari le-mṛaḍ ɛemluhom b-waḥedhom.*

issue - **1.** *ɛadad, nešṛa* pl. *-t.* I haven't read the last issue. *ma-qṛit-š n-nešṛa t-talya.* **2.** *ġnan, muškila*. I don't want to make an issue of it. *ma-bġit-š nreddha ġnan.* You're trying to avoid the issue. *nta tḥawel dženneb l-muškila.*

Italian - **1.** *ṭaḷyani*. He's of Italian descent. *huwa aṣḷu ṭaḷyani.* **2.** *ṭaḷyaniya*. He speaks Italian well. *ka-itkellem ṭ-ṭaḷyaniya mezyan.*

Italy - *iṭaḷya, blad ṭ-ṭaḷyan.*

to **itch** - *kla yakol*. My wound itches. *ž-žeṛḥa ka-takolni.* --I itch all over. *leḥmi kollu ka-yakolni.*

**I'm itching to get started. *ana mšuwweq baš nebda.*

item - **1.** *selɛa* pl. *-t.* We don't have that item in our shop. *ma-ɛendna-š dik s-selɛa fe-l-ḥanut dyalna.* **2.** *maqala* pl. *-t.* Did you see the item in the paper? *waš qṛiti l-maqala fe-l-žarida?* **3.** *ḥaža* pl. *-t, ḥwayež*. How many items are there on that bill? *šḥal men ḥaža kayna f-dik le-bṭaqa?*

ivory - *ɛaž.*

J

jack - *krik* pl. *-at*. I left the jack in the garage. *xellit le-krik fe-l-garaž.*
  to jack up - **1.** *hezz (b-le-krik).* You'll have to jack up the car. *xeṣṣek thezz ṭ-ṭumubil (b-le-krik).* **2.** *zad izid f-.* They've jacked up the prices. *zadu fe-t-tamanat.*
jackass - *ḥmaṛ* pl. *ḥmir.* What a jackass! *walayenni ḥmaṛ hada!*
jacket - *kebbuṭ* pl. *kbabeṭ.*
jagged - *mšenqeṛ, mefṛum.*
jail - *ḥebs* pl. *ḥbas.*
  to jail - *sžen.*
jam - **1.** *meƐžun.* I prefer homemade jam. *ana ka-nebġi ḥsen l-meƐžun dyal ḍ-ḍaṛ.* **2.** *weḥla* pl. *wḥayel.* I'm in an awful jam. *ana f-weḥla qbiḥa.*
January - *yennayer.*
Japan - *yaban.*
Japanese - *yabani.*
jar - *tenžiya* pl. *-t, ṭnaži; qeṛƐa* pl. *-t, qṛaƐi.*
  to jar - *zeƐzeƐ.* Don't jar the table when you sit down. *ma-dzeƐzeƐ-š l-mida melli tegles.*
jaundice - *bu-ṣeffiṛ.*
jaw - *ḥenk* pl. *ḥnak, ḥnuk.*
jealous - *meġyaṛ.* Are you jealous of him? *waš nta meġyaṛ mennu.*
jealousy - *ġiṛa.*
jerk - *tehziza.* The train stopped with a jerk. *ḥṣeṛ l-qiṭaṛ b-tehziza.*
  **What a jerk he is! *walayenni Ɛla ḥmaṛ huwa!*
  to jerk - *xṭef.* She jerked the book out of his hand. *xeṭfet le-ktab men yeddu.*
jest - *mlaġa, tfėlya.*
  to jest - *tmelleġ.*
Jew - *ihudi* pl. *ihud.*
Jewish - *ihudi.*
jiffy - *dqiyqa.* It'll only take me a jiffy. *xeṣṣni ġir dqiyqa.*
  in a jiffy - **1.** *men daba šwiya.* I'll be back in a jiffy. *ġad nži men daba swiya.* **2.** *fisaƐ.* He was ready in a jiffy. *huwa kan fisaƐ wažed.*
job - **1.** *xedma* pl. *-t.* I'm looking for a job. *ana ka-nqelleb Ɛla xedma.* **2.** *šġol* pl. *šġal.* It isn't my job to tell him. *ma-ši šoġli baš nqulha-lu.*
to join - **1.** *dxel f-.* When did he join the party? *fuq-aš dxel fe-l-ḥizeb?* --He wants to join our club. *huwa baġi idxol fe-n-nadi dyalna.* **2.** *xḷeṭ Ɛla.* Would you like to join us? *waš tebġi texḷeṭ Ɛlina?* **3.** *laqa.* How do you join these two parts? *kif-aš tlaqi had ṭ-ṭṛaf b-žuž?* **4.** *tlaqa.* Where do these roads join? *fayn ka-itlaqaw had ṭ-ṭoṛqan?*
  **Won't you join us at the table? *waš bġiti tegles mƐana?*
joint - **1.** *mefṣeḷ* pl. *mfaṣeḷ.* All my joints ache. *gaƐ mfaṣḷi ka-iḍeṛṛuni.* **2.** *mešruk.* This is joint property. *had l-melk mešruk.*
  to come out of joint - *ttfekk.* My arm came out of joint. *ttfekk-li draƐi.*
joke - **1.** *mzaḥ* pl. *-at.* I've heard that joke before. *smeƐt b-had le-mzaḥ men qbel.* **2.** *mlaġa.* You've carried the joke too far. *zedti f-le-mlaġa bezzaf.* --He can't take a joke. *ma-ka-iqbel-š le-mlaġa.* **3.** *ḥila* pl. *-t.* I played a joke on him. *ana lƐebt Ɛlih ḥila.*
  to joke - *tmelleġ.* This time I'm not joking. *had l-meṛṛa ana ma-ka-ntmelleġ-š.*
  **You must be joking! *wa-la-bedd ka-ḍḍḥek!* **All joking aside! *nxelliw le-mlaġa fe-t-tisaƐ.*
jolly - *feṛḥan; xfif ṛ-ṛuḥ* pl. *xfaf ṛ-ṛuḥ.*
jolt - *hezza* pl. *-t.* The car stopped with a jolt. *s-siyaṛa ḥeṣṛet b-hezza.*
Jordan - *l-ʔoṛḍen.*
  Jordan River - *nehṛ l-ʔoṛḍen.*
Jordanian - *ʔoṛḍuni* adj. pl. *-yin,* n. pl. *hel l-ʔoṛḍen.*
journalist - *ṣaḥafi* (pl.). *-yin.*
journey - *ṣafaṛ, ṣfeṛ* pl. *ṣefṛat.*
joy - *feṛḥa.*
joyful - *bahež.*
judge - **1.** *qaḍi* pl. *qoḍya, quḍat.* When is the judge going to pass sentence on him? *fuq-aš ġa-yeḥkem Ɛlih l-qaḍi?* **2.** *muḥekkam.* The judges awarded his picture the first prize. *l-muḥekkamin Ɛṭaweh l-žaʔiza l-luwla Ɛel t-teṣwiṛa dyalu.* **3.** *ḥakem* pl. *ḥokkam.* The

judge says it's a net ball. *l-ḥakem qal bin l-kuṛa qaṣet š-šebka.*
**It was an awful job to convince her. *tamara ḥtažit baš nqenneɛha.*
to judge - *ḥkem ɛla.* Don't judge him too harshly. *ma-teḥkem-š ɛlih b-le-qṣuḥiya.*

judgment - *ṛeyy* pl. *ṛyay, ʔaṛa.* In my judgment this is a bad predicament. *f-ṛeyyi weḥla qbiḥa hadi.*

juice - *ma.* These oranges give very little juice. *had l-limunat fihom ġir šwiya de-l-ma.*

juicy - *mawi.*

July - *yulyu.*

jump - *tenqiza* pl. *-t.*
to get the jump on - *sbeq.* You don't want him to get the jump on you, do you? *ma-bġitih-š isebqek wella la?*
on the jump - *meštun.* She's constantly on the jump. *hiya dima meštuna.*
to jump - **1.** *neqqez.* How high can you jump? *šḥal teqdeṛ tneqqez?* --We jumped from page seven to page twelve. *neqqezna men l-weṛqa s-sabɛa le-ṭ-ṭanša.* **2.** *qfez.* He jumped when he heard the noise. *qfez melli smeɛ ṣ-ṣdaɛ.*
**The train jumped the track. *l-mašina xeṛžet ɛel ṭ-ṭriq.*

June - *yunyu.*

junk - *qžaqel* (pl.). Get all this junk out of here for me. *xerrež ɛliya had le-qžaqel kollhom men hna.*

just - **1.** *f-maḥellu.* That's a just punishment. *hadik ɛaquba f-maḥellha.* **2.** *ɛad.* They've just arrived in Morocco. *ɛad žaw l-l-meġrib.* **3.** *fe-l-ḥaqiqa.* Just what do you mean? *fe-l-ḥaqiqa aš ka-teɛni?* **4.** *ġir.* I'm just dead tired. *ana ġir miyyet b-le-ɛya.* --He's just a little boy. *huwa ġir weld ṣġiṛ.* **5.** *ma-mša ma-ža.* He's just like his father. *huwa bḥalu bḥal bbah ma-mša ma-ža.* **6.** *tamamen.* That's just what I wanted. *hadi tamamen aš bġit.* **7.** *beḥra.* You just made it. *beḥra deztiha.*
**That's just the way the world is! *d-denya hiya hadi.*

justice - **1.** *ɛedliya.* His father is the Minister of Justice. *bbah wzir l-ɛedliya.* **2.** *ḥeqq.* Don't expect justice from him. *ma-ttsenna-s l-ḥeqq mennu.*
to do justice - *ɛṭa yeɛṭi l-ḥeqq.* You're not doing him justice. *nta ma-ɛaṭih-š l-ḥeqq.*
**The picture doesn't do you justice. *t-teṣwiṛa ma-xerržettek-š mezyan.*

to **justify** - *ḥeqqeq.* She tried to justify her actions. *ḥawlet tḥeqqeq ɛamalatha.*
**I think you would be perfectly justified in doing that. *ana ka-ndenn belli ɛendek l-ḥeqq tamamen baš teɛmel dak š-ši.*

K

keen - **1.** *fayeq, nadež, maḍi.* He has a keen mind. *ɛeqlu fayeq.* --This blade is rather keen. *had l-mus maḍi bezzaf.* **2.** *mšuwweq.* I'm not so keen on that. *ana ma-mšuwweq-š l-had š-ši.*

to **keep** - **1.** *xella.* May I keep this picture? *waš imken-li nxelli ɛendi had t-teṣwiṛa?* --Do you want me to keep your dinner warm? *waš bġitini nxelli-lek ɛšatek sxuna?* --I'm sorry to have kept you waiting. *ana metʔessef ila xellitek ttsenna.* **2.** *qbeṭ. šebbeṛ.* I won't keep you long. *ma-ġadi-š nqebṭek-š bezzaf.* **3.** *ḥḍa yeḥḍi.* Please keep this money for me. *ɛafak ḥḍi-li had le-flus.* **4.** *ktem.* He kept the secret. *ktem s-serr.* **5.** *qbeṭ f-.* He kept his word. *qbeṭ fe-klemtu.* **6.** *ṣbeṛ.* This milk won't keep till tomorrow. *had le-ḥlib ma-iṣbeṛ-š l-ġedda.* **7.** *šedd.* Does your watch keep good time? *waš l-magana dyalek ka-tšedd l-weqt mezyan?* **8.** *beɛɛed.* Keep your hands off that! *beɛɛed yeddik men dak š-ši!* **9.** *bqa ibqa.* Keep to the right! *bqa ɛel l-imin.* --Can't you keep quiet? *waš ma-teqdeṛ-š tebqa hani?* --Keep calm! *bqa zagi!* --Keep trying! *bqa tḥawel!* --Keep out! *bqa beṛṛa!*
**Where have you been keeping yourself all this time? *fayn konti xazen ṛaṣek had š-ši kollu?* --Keep off the grass children! *beɛɛdu men*

ṛ-ṛbiƐ ad-drari! —I told him no a thousand times and he keeps coming back. *qolt-lu lla alef meṛṛa u-ma-zal ka-iži.*

to keep books – *žmeƐ ḥsabat.*

to keep from – 1. *mneƐ men.* No one can keep me from my sister's house. *ḥetta ši-waḥed ma-iqder imneƐni men ḍaṛ xti.* 2. *mneƐ baš.* Nobody can keep you from going there. *ḥetta ši-waḥed ma-iqder imenƐek baš temši l-temma.*

to keep house – *qabel ḍ-ḍaṛ.* She keeps house for her uncle. *hiya ka-tqabel ḍaṛ Ɛemmha.*

to keep in mind – *Ɛmel f-balu.* Let's keep that in mind. *daba nƐemluha f-balna.*

to keep one's temper – *mlek nefsu.*

to keep (on) talking – *zad izid fe-klamu.* Just keep on talking *ġir zid fe-klamek.*

to keep out – *ḥbes.* The curtain keeps the light out. *l-xamiya ka-teḥbes ḍ-ḍu.*

to keep out of – 1. *tbeƐƐed men.* It's his affair, you'd better keep out of it. *had š-ši šoġlu, ḥsen-lek ttbeƐƐed mennu.* 2. Keep him out of my way! *beƐƐdu men ṭriqi!*

to keep something from – *xzen ši-ḥaža Ɛla.* Are you keeping something from me? *waš nta xazen ši-ḥaža Ɛliya?*

Kenitra – *le-qniṭra.*

native of Kenitra – *qniṭri.* adj. pl. *-yin,* n. pl. *hel le-qniṭra.*

kerosene – *zit l-gaz.*

kettle – *moqṛaž* pl. *mqarež.*
That's a pretty kettle of fish! *walayenni xaluṭa hadi.*

key – 1. *sarut* pl. *swaret.* (to a lock). 2. *ḥerf* pl. *ḥṛuf* (of a typewriter).
He was all keyed up. *kan rafed d-dehša.*

kick – *rekla* pl. *-t, redḥa* pl *-t.* The horse nearly gave me a kick. *kan l-Ɛewd ġir šwiya u-yeƐṭini rekla.* —I felt like giving him a good hard kick. *kont baġi neƐṭih redḥa mezyana.*
He gets a kick out of sports. *ka-iṛšeq-lu Ɛel ṛ-ṛiyaḍa.*

to kick – *rkel, rdeḥ.*

to kick out – *ṛma iṛmi beṛṛa.*

kid – 1. *ždi* f. *ždya* pl. *ždyan.* The goat has two kids. *l-meƐza Ɛendha žuž de-ž-ždyan.* 2. *derri* pl. *drari.* The kids want to go to a movie. *d-drari bġaw imšiw le-s-sinima.*

kidney – *kelwa* pl. *-t, klawi.*

to kill – *qtel.*

kilogram – *kilu* pl. *-wat.*

kilometer – *kilumiter* pl. *kilumitrat.*

kind – 1. *škel* pl. *škal, nuƐ* pl. *nwaƐ.* This building is the only one of its kind. *had le-bni ma-Ɛendu-š xah f-had š-škel.* —We have only two kinds of coffee. *Ɛendna ġir žuž d-le-nwaƐ de-l-qehwa.* 2. *ḍṛiyyef, ḍṛif* pl. *ḍṛaf.* He's a very kind man. *ṛažel ḍṛiyyef bezzaf hada!*
I didn't say anything of the kind. *ana ma-qolt ḥetta kelma men had š-ši.*

kind of – *šwiya.* I felt kind of sorry for him. *ana tʔessft šwiya Ɛlih.*

all kinds of – *Ɛel le-škal.* I have all kinds of cloth. *Ɛendi t-tub Ɛel le-škal.*
What kind of car do they have? *š-men nuƐ s-siyaṛa lli Ɛendham?* —What kind of house do they have? *kif Ɛamla ḍ-ḍaṛ dyalhom?*

kindness – *ḷṭafa.*

king – *malik* pl. *muluk.*

kingdom – *memlaka* pl. *-t.*

kiss – *busa* pl. *-t.*

to kiss – *bas ibus.*

kitchen – *keššina* pl. *-t, kuzina* pl. *-t.*

kitten – *mšiša* pl. *-t, qṭiṭa* pl. *-t.*

to knead – *Ɛžen.*

knee – *rokba* pl. *-t, rkabi.*

to kneel – *rkeƐ.*

knife – *mus* pl. *mwas.*

knight – *faras* pl. *fras* (chess piece).

knock – *deqqa* pl. *-t* coll. *deqq.* Did you hear the knock on the door? *waš smeƐti d-deqqa Ɛel l-bab?*

to knock – 1. *deqq.* Someone knocked at the door. *ši-waḥed deqq Ɛel l-bab.* 2. *ṭiyyeḥ.* I knocked the knife out of his hand. *ṭiyyeḥt l-mus men yeddu.* 3. *ḍreb.* Don't knock against the table. *ma-ḍḍreb-š fe-ṭ-ṭabla.*

to be knocked around – *tmeḥḥen.* She's been knocked around a lot. *tmeḥḥnet bezzaf.*

to knock down – *ṭiyyeḥ.* The car knocked me down. *s-siyaṛa ṭiyyḥetni.*

to knock off – *ṭiyyeḥ, ṭiyyer.*

to knock out – *ṭiyyeḥ kaw.* He knocked him out in the tenth round. *huwa ṭiyyḥu kaw fe-ḍ-dewr l-Ɛašer.*

to knock over – *qleb.* Who knocked the pail over? *škun lli qleb ṣ-sṭel?*

(all) knocked out – *mehluk.* I was all knocked out after about an hour of work. *kont mehluk men beƐd ši-saƐa de-l-xedma.*

knot - **1.** *Ɛoqda* pl. *-t, Ɛqadi.* Can you untie this knot? *waš teqḍeṛ tḥell had l-Ɛoqda?* **2.** *mil beḥri* pl. *myal beḥriya.* The ship can make fifteen knots. *l-babuṛ ka-iqḍeṛ yeƐmel xemṣṭaš myal beḥriya fe-s-saƐa.* **3.** *meƐza* pl. *-t.* The board is full of knots. *l-luḥa Ɛamṛa be-l-meƐzat.*

to knot - *Ɛqed, Ɛeqqed.* Shall I knot the string? *waš neƐqed l-qennba?*

to **know** - *Ɛṛef.* Do you know Arabic? *waš ka-teƐṛef l-Ɛeṛbiya?* --I don't know how he did it. *ma-Ɛṛeft-š kif-aš Ɛmelha.*

to know how to - *Ɛṛef.* I don't know how to drive a car. *ma-ka-neƐṛef-š nṣug s-siyaṛa*

to let know - *Ɛlem.* I'll let you know tomorrow. *ana nƐelmek ġedda.*

knowledge - *meƐrifa* pl. *mƐaref, Ɛilm.* His knowledge of Arabic is weak. *meƐriftu fe-l-Ɛeṛbiya ḍƐifa.*

Koran - *qoṛʔan.*

koranic - *qoṛʔani, men l-qoṛʔan.*

L

label - *weṛqa* pl. *wṛaq; bṭaqa* pl. *-t, bṭayeq.* There's no label on this bottle. *had l-qeṛƐa ma-Ɛliha-š l-weṛqa.*

labor - **1.** *xedma.* Labor alone will cost three hundred dollars. *l-xedma b-waḥedha ṭṭiḥ Ɛlik b-telt myat ḍulaṛ.* --All our labor has been in vain. *l-xedma dyalna kollha ma-ṣlaḥet ḥetta ḥaža.* **2.** *wlada.* She was in labor nine hours. *le-wlada ṭalet tesƐud de-s-swayeƐ.*

hard labor - *l-ʔašġal š-šaqqa.* He was sentenced to five years at hard labor. *ḥekmu Ɛlih b-xems snin de-l-ʔašġal š-šaqqa.*

laborer - *xeddam* pl. *-a.*

labor movement - *ḥaṛaka de-l-Ɛommal.*

labor union - *niqaba* pl. *-t.* He's a member of our labor union. *huwa waḥed men n-niqaba dyalna.*

lace - *šebka* pl. *-t, šbaki.* I'd like five meters of that lace. *bġit xemsa mitru d-had š-šebka.*

shoe laces - *xiṭ ṣ-ṣebbaṭ.*

to lace - *šedd.* Wait till I lace my shoes. *tsennani nšedd ṣebbaṭi.*

lack - *qella.* There's a lack of trained personnel. *kayen qella de-l-xeddama le-mderrbin.*

for lack of - *men qella, b-qella.* He couldn't afford it for lack of money. *ma-qḍeṛ-š Ɛliha men qellt le-flus.* --For lack of something better to do I went to the movies. *b-qellt ḥaža xṛa ḥsen ma ndir mšit le-s-sinima.*

I lack, you lack, etc. - *ixeṣṣni, ixeṣṣek,* etc. I didn't lack anything there. *ma-kanet ka-txeṣṣni ḥetta ḥaža temma.*

lad - *weld* pl. *wlad.*

ladder - *sellum* pl. *slalem.*

ladle - *moġṛef* pl. *mġaṛef.*

lady - **1.** *mṛa* cons. *mṛat* pl. *Ɛyalat.* Is that lady his mother? *waš had le-mṛa yemmah?*

ladies room - *miḍa d-le-Ɛyalat.* Where's the ladies room? *fayn l-miḍa d-le-Ɛyalat?*

to **lag behind** - *tʔexxeṛ Ɛla.* Stop lagging behind! *baṛaka ma tʔexxeṛ Ɛel le-xṛin.*

lake - *ḍaya* pl. *-t; bḥiṛa* pl. *-t, bḥayeṛ.*

lamb - *xṛuf, xeṛf* pl. *xṛufa, xeṛfan.*

lame - **1.** *Ɛṛež* pl. *Ɛuṛež.* He can't run because he's lame. *ma-imken-lu-š ižri Ɛla qibal huwa Ɛṛež.* **2.** *ḍƐif* pl. *ḍƐaf.* That's a lame excuse. *hadi sebba ḍƐifa.*

lamp - *ḷamḅa* pl. *-t.*

lamp shade - *mkebb* pl. *mkabb, mkubba de-l-ḷamḅa; ġlaf* pl. *ġlafat de-l-ḅula.* I'll buy a new shade for this lamp. *ġad nešri mkebb ždid l-had ḷ-ḷamḅa.*

land - *ʔeṛḍ* (f.). We were glad to see land again. *fṛeḥna mnin Ɛawed šefna l-ʔeṛḍ.* The land here is very fertile. *l-ʔeṛḍ hna xeṣba bezzaf.*

to land - **1.** *nezzel (ṭ-ṭiyaṛa).* He had to land his plane in a field. *tlezzem inezzel ṭ-ṭiyaṛa dyalu f-waḥed l-feddan.* **2.** *nzel.* The plane landed smoothly. *ṭ-ṭiyaṛa nezlet be-ḥlawa.*

**We nearly landed in jail. *konna Ɛlayen gad ndexlu l-l-ḥebs.*

landlady - *mulat ḍ-ḍaṛ* or *mulat l-melk* pl. *mwalin ḍ-ḍaṛ* or *mwalin l-melk.*

landlord - *mul ḍ-ḍaṛ* or *mul l-melk* pl.

mwalin ḍ-ḍaṛ or *mwalin l-melk.*
language - *luġa* pl. *-t.*
lantern - *fnaṛ* pl. *-at.*
lap - **1.** *ḥžer* pl. *ḥžura.* She held the baby in her lap. *kanet hazza t-terbiya Ɛla ḥžerha.* **2.** *ḍuṛa* pl. *-t.* He was in the lead by five meters in the first lap. *huwa kan sabeqhom b-xemsa mitru fe-ḍ-ḍuṛa l-luwla.*
to lap up - *ṣṛeṭ.* The kitten lapped up the milk. *le-qṭiṭa ṣeṛṭet*
to **lapse** - *daz weqt.* If I don't pay this premium, my insurance policy will lapse. *ila ma-xeḷḷeṣt-š l-wažeb, daba iduz weqt le-msugra dyali.*
Larache - *le-Ɛrayeš.*
native of Larache - *Ɛrayši* pl. *Ɛrayšiyin, hel le-Ɛrayeš.*
large - *kbir* pl. *kbaṛ.*
at large - *ma-meqbuṭ-š.* The thief is still at large. *l-xuwwan ma-zal ma-meqbuṭ-š.*
largely - *le-ktir men.* Our group is made up largely of volunteers. *le-ktir men had n-nas de-ž-žmaƐa dyalna meṭṭuwƐin.*
large-scale - *waseƐ.* The city is considering a large-scale program. *ka-ixemmmu idiru f-le-mdine mešṛuƐ d-le-bni waseƐ.*
lark - *qubeƐ* pl. *qwabeƐ.*
last - **1.** *tali.* This is the last car to leave. *hadi ṭ-ṭumubil t-talya lli ġad temši.* --He came last. *huwa t-tali lli ža.* **2.** *luwwel, (lli) fat.* Last year I was in Europe. *Ɛam luwwel kont f-ʔurubba.*
**That's the last straw! *hadi l-muṣiba t-talya!*
last night - *l-bareḥ fe-l-lil.*
at last - *fe-l-ʔaxir.* Here we are at last! *ha-ḥna fe-l-ʔaxir!*
next to the last - *lli qbel t-tali.* You'll find it on the next to the last page. *ġad tṣibha fe-l-weṛqa lli qbel l-weṛqa t-talya.*
to last - **1.** *ṭal iṭul, dam idum.* The war lasted six years. *l-ḥeṛb ṭalet sett snin.* **2.** *bqa l-, ibqa l-.* I don't think my money will last. *ana ma-ka-nḍenn-š le-flus dyali ġad ibqaw-li kteṛ men had š-ši.* --This suit didn't last at all. *had l-keswa ma-bqat-li-š bezzaf.* **3.** *qḍeṛ imši.* Do you think you can last more than a kilometer? *waš ka-ḍdenn bin teqḍeṛ temši kteṛ men kilumitru?* **4.** *bqa ibqa.* I'm afraid he won't last much longer. *ka-nxaf Ɛlih ma-ibqa-š kteṛ men had š-ši.*
latch - *saqṭa* pl. *-t, žekṛum* pl. *žkaṛem.*
late - **1.** *ḷḷah iṛeḥmu.* Your late father was a friend of mine. *ḅḅak ḷḷah iṛeḥmu kan ṣaḥbi.* **2.** *mƐeṭṭeḷ.* I'll be home late in the afternoon. *ġad nži mƐeṭṭel le-ḍ-ḍaṛ f-le-Ɛšiya.*
lately - **1.** *(f-) had l-iyam.* I haven't been feeling so well lately. *ana Ɛeyyan had l-iyam.* **2.** *hadi modda qṛiba.* Have you seen her lately. *waš šeftiha hadi modda qṛiba?*
later - *men beƐd.* You'll see her later. *ġad tšufha men beƐd.* --One day later a letter came. *žat le-bṛa nhaṛ men beƐd.*
latest - *tali.* What's the latest news? *šnu huwa le-xbaṛ t-tali?* --That's the latest style. *hadi hiya l-muḍa t-talya.*
lather - *ṛeġwa* pl. *-t, ṛġawi.*
to lather - *Ɛmel ṛ-ṛeġwa.* This soap doesn't lather well *had ṣ-ṣabun ma-ka-yeƐmel-š ṛ-ṛeġwa mezyan.*
lattice - *mamuni* pl. *-yat.*
laugh - *ḍeḥka* pl. *-t, ḍḥayk.* What a dirty laugh! *walayenni Ɛla ḍeḥka ṣefṛa!*
to laugh - *ḍḥek.* Everybody laughed at him. *kollhom ḍeḥku Ɛlih.*
laughter - *ḍeḥk.*
to **launch** - *ṭḷeq.* Another ship was launched on Monday. *ṭeḷqu babbuṛ axoṛ nhaṛ t-tnin.*
laundry - **1.** *maḥell* (pl. *-at*) *ṣ-ṣebbana.* Where's the nearest laundry? *fayn huwa maḥell ṣ-ṣebbana lli qrib?* **2.** *teṣbin.* My laundry just came back. *Ɛad žabu-li t-teṣbin.*
law - **1.** *qanun* pl. *qwanen.* Is this a new law? *waš had l-qanun ždid?* **2.** *ḥuquq* (pl.). He's studying law. *ka-iqṛa l-ḥuquq.*
law school - *medṛaṣet l-ḥuquq* pl. *medṛaṣat l-ḥuquq.*
martial law - *ḥukuma ḥeṛbiya.* The city was placed under martial law. *le-mdina daruha teḥt ḥukuma ḥeṛbiya.*
lawsuit - *deƐwa* pl. *-t, dƐawi.*
lawyer - *ḅugaḍu* pl. *-wat, -yat; muḥami* pl. *-yin.*
lax - *merxi.* He's rather lax in his work. *huwa merxi fe-xdemtu ši-šwiya.*
**She's always been much too lax with her children. *hiya mwellfa ma-ka-tṛebbi-š wladha bezzaf.*
laxative - *sehla* pl. *-t.*
to **lay** - **1.** *ḥeṭṭ.* Lay the book on the table. *ḥeṭṭ le-ktab Ɛel ṭ-ṭabla.* **2.** *biyyeḍ.* Our hens are laying well. *d-džaž dyalna ka-ibiyyḍu*

bezzaf. **3.** *txaṭeṛ.* I'll lay ten to one that he does it. *ntxaṭeṛ mƐak b-Ɛešṛa Ɛla waḥed bin ġad yeƐmelha.*

**Don't lay the blame on me. *ma-tsleqha-š fiya.*

to lay aside - *xebba fe-l-qent.* He laid aside a pretty penny. *xebba fe-l-qent bezzaf d-le-flus.*

to lay claim to - *ṭḷeb.* A distant relative laid claim to the estate. *waḥed bƐid men l-Ɛaʔila ṭḷeb l-wert.*

to lay down - **1.** *ḥeṭṭ.* Lay him down gently. *ḥeṭṭu be-ḍṛafa.* **2.** *nezzel.* They were glad to lay down their arms. *kanu feṛḥanin melli nezzlu s-snaḥ dyalhom.*

to lay for - *txebbeƐ l-.* They laid for him at the corner. *txebbƐu-lu f-qent ẓ-ẓenqa.*

to lay it on thick - *šker bla qyaṣ.* He certainly laid it on thick! *šker fih bla qyaṣ.*

to lay off - *dḥa idḥi.* We have to lay off some people. *lazem ndḥiw ši-weḥdin.*

**Lay off me, will you! *xellini Ɛlik!*

to lay waste - *hdem.* The whole region was laid waste by the enemy. *n-naḥiya kollha hedmu Ɛliha le-Ɛdu.*

layer - **1.** *qešṛa* pl. *-t.* This cake has a thick layer of sugar on it. *had l-ḥelwa fiha qešṛa ġliḍa de-s-sokkaṛ.* **2.** *duza* pl. *-t.* This wall needs another layer of paint. *had l-ḥiṭ xeṣṣha duza xṛa de-s-sbaġa.*

laziness - *Ɛgez.*

lazy - *Ɛegzan, meƐgaz.*

lead - **1.** *xfif, ṛṣaṣ.* Is this made of lead? *waš had š-ši mṣuwweb men le-xfif?* **2.** *ḍuṛ muhemm* pl. *ḍuṛat muhemma.* Who's playing the lead? *škun Ɛendu ḍ-ḍuṛ l-muhemm?*

to lead - **1.** *guwwed.* The dog led the blind man across the street. *l-kelb guwwed le-Ɛma baš iqṭeƐ ṭ-ṭṛiq.* **2.** *tṛeʔʔeṣ.* The mayor led the parade. *l-Ɛamel tṛeʔʔeṣ le-steƐṛaḍ.*

**What do you think he was leading up to? *š-ka-ḍḍenn kan l-meqṣuḍ dyalu?* --That's just what I was leading up to. *dak š-ši lli kont ġad nqul.*

to lead to - *weṣṣeḷ l-, dda ddi l-.* Where will all this lead to? *fayn had š-ši ġad iweṣṣeḷna?* --That'll lead to nothing. *had š-ši ma-iddi layn.*

leader - *ṛaʔis* pl. *ṛuʔasa.*

leaf - *weṛqa* pl. *-t, wṛaq.* The leaf is still green. *l-weṛqa ma-zala xeḍṛa.* --The leaves are beginning to turn. *le-wṛaq bda lunhom ka-itbeddel.*

to turn over a new leaf - *tƐewweṭ.* He promised me to turn over a new leaf. *ṛah waƐedni baš itƐewweṭ.*

to leaf through - *ḍuwweṛ le-wṛaq.* I'm only leafing through the book. *ana ġir ka-nḍuwweṛ le-wṛaq d-le-ktab.*

to leak - **1.** *dxel fih l-ma.* The boat is leaking. *le-fluka ka-idxol fiha l-ma.* **2.** *sal isil.* This pot leaks. *had ṭ-ṭenžṛa ka-tsil.* --The faucet is leaking. *l-bezbuz ka-isil.*

to leak out - *sal isil.* All the water is leaking out. *l-ma kollu ka-isil.*

**The story has leaked out. *le-xbaṛ flet daba.*

lean - **1.** *hzil.* Do you want fat meat or lean? *waš bġiti l-lḥem smin wella hzil?* **2.** *sayeb, qaṣeḥ* It was a lean year for farmers. *kan Ɛam sayeb Ɛel l-fellaḥa.*

to lean - **1.** *ttekka.* There's nothing for me to lean on. *ma-kayen ḥetta ḥaža Ɛlaš nttekka.* **2.** *mal imil.* He leans toward the Istiqlal party. *ka-imil Ɛla ḥizeb l-istiqlal.* **3.** *tekka itekki.* Don't lean your chair against the wall. *ma-ttekki-š š-šilya dyalek Ɛel l-ḥiṭ.*

**Don't lean out of the window. *ma-txerrež-š ṛaṣek men š-šeṛžem.*

leap - *tenqiza* pl. *-t.* He cleared the ditch with one leap. *neqqez l-ḥefṛa b-tenqiza weḥda.*

leapfrog - *sebbsebbut* (not used with article).

leap year - *Ɛam kebsi.*

to **learn** - **1.** *tƐellem.* He hasn't learned a thing. *ma-tƐellem-š ḥetta ḥaža.* --He learns quickly. *ka-itƐellem be-z-zerba.* **2.** *Ɛṛef.* He learned the truth too late. *Ɛṛef l-ḥaqiqa mƐetteḷ bezzaf.*

to learn by heart - *ḥfeḍ be-ž-žri u-l-ma.* She learned the poem by heart. *ḥefḍet l-qaṣiḍa be-ž-žri u-l-ma.*

leash - *sensla* pl. *-t, snasel.* All dogs must be kept on the leash. *le-klab lazem ibqaw kollhom meṛbuṭin be-s-sensla.*

least - *ʔexxeṛ.* That's the least of my worries. *hada huwa ʔexxeṛ hmumi.*

least of all - *l-ḥaža t-talya.* Least of all I'd have expected it from you. *hadi l-ḥaža t-talya lli kont ka-ntsenna mennek.*

**She deserves it least of all.

ka-testahlu qell men le-x̂ṛin.

at least - *be-l-qella.* These shoes cost at least fifty dirhams. *had ṣ-ṣebbaṭ ka-iswa be-l-qella xemsin derhem.* --At least you might have written to me. *be-l-qella kan imken-lek tekteb-li.*

the least - *l-ḥaža t-talya.* That's the least you could do for him. *hadi l-ḥaža t-talya lli imken-lek tƐawnu fiha.*

leather - *želd* pl. *žlud.*

leave - *Ɛoṭla* pl. *-t.* He's taken a three months' leave. *xda telt šhuṛ de-l-Ɛoṭla.*

to leave - **1.** *mša imsi.* I have to leave now. *xeṣṣni nemši f-ḥali daba.* --The train leaves at two thirty. *l-mašina ġad temsi fe-ž-žuž u-neṣṣ.* **2.** *ṣafeṛ.* My father left yesterday for Europe. *ḅḅa ṣafeṛ l-bareḥ l-ʔuṛuḅḅa.* **3.** *smeḥ f-.* I'm leaving my job. *ġadi nesmeḥ fe-xdemti.* **4.** *xella.* He left a letter for you. *xella-lek bṛa.* --Where did you leave your suitcase? *fayn xelliti š-šanṭa dyalek?* --He left the door open. *xella l-bab meḥlula.* **5.** *xrež men.* I saw him leave the house. *šeftu ixṛož men ḍ-ḍaṛ.* --He left the country secretly. *xrež men le-blad be-t-texbiƐa.* --Where does that leave me? *šnu bqa-li ma neƐmel daba?*

to be left - *bqa.* Are there any tickets left for tonight? *waš bqaw ši-bṭaqat l-had l-lila?* --My brother got all the money, and I was left out in the cold. *xay xda le-flus kollhom w-ana bqit bla ḥetta ḥaža.*

to leave alone - **1.** *beƐƐed men.* You'd better leave that alone! *ḥsen-ḷek tbeƐƐed men dak š-ši.* **2.** *xella Ɛla.* Leave me alone! *xellini Ɛlik!*

to leave in the lurch - *xella waḥel.* He left us in the lurch. *xellana waḥlin.*

Lebanese - *lebnani* pl. *-yin.*

Lebanon - *lobnan.*

lecture - *muḥaḍaṛa* pl. *-t.* It was an interesting lecture. *kanet muḥaḍaṛa mezyana.*

to give a lecture - *Ɛmel muḥaḍaṛa.* He's giving a lecture on international trade. *ka-yeƐmel muḥaḍaṛa Ɛel t-tižaṛa bin d-dulat.*

**He always give us a lecture when we come in late. *fuq-emma žina mƐeṭṭlin ka-iƐeṣṣina.*

left - **1.** *iṣeṛ.* Take the other bag in your left hand. *qbeṭ l-xenša le-x̂ṛa b-yeddek l-iṣeṛ.* **2.** *yeṣṛi, iṣṛi.* Stand on the left side of the horse. *wqef fe-ž-žiha l-iṣṛiya de-l-Ɛewd.*

on the left - *Ɛel l-iṣeṛ.* You sit on the right, I'll sit on the left. *nta gles Ɛel l-imin w-ana ġadi negles Ɛel l-iṣeṛ.* --I sat on the speaker's left. *glest Ɛel l-iṣeṛ d-le-xṭib.*

(to the) left - *Ɛel š-šmal.* Turn left at the next corner. *ḍuṛ Ɛel š-šmal fe-l-qent ž-žay.*

left-handed - *yeṣṛi, iṣṛi, Ɛeṣṛi.*

leftist - *yasari.*

leg - *ṛžel* pl. *režlin* (pl. *režli-* before possessive endings).

to be on one's last legs - *tfeḍḍa-lu, tsala-lu.* They say he's on his last legs. *qalu bin tsala-lu.*

to pull someone's leg - *tmelleġ Ɛla.* Stop pulling my leg. *baṛaka u-ma-ttmelleġ Ɛliya.*

legal - *Ɛla ḥasab š-šṛeƐ* or *l-ḥuquq.* That's perfectly legal. *had š-ši fe-l-ġaya Ɛla ḥasab š-šṛeƐ.*

legal adviser - *mustašaṛ šeṛƐi.* He's her legal adviser. *huwa l-mustašaṛ š-šeṛƐi dyalha.*

leggings - *tmag* pl. *-at.*

legible - *(lli) ka-itteqṛa, ka-itferrez.* His handwriting is hardly legible. *l-xeṭṭ dyalu ma-ka-itteqṛa-š mezyan.*

lemon - *ḥamḍa* pl. *-t* coll. *ḥameḍ.*

lemonade - *munaḍa.*

to **lend** - *sellef l-.* Can you lend me fifty dirhams? *inken-lek tsellef-li xemsin derhem?*

to lend a hand - *Ɛṭa yeƐṭi yedd ḷḷah.* Lend me a hand, will you? *Ɛṭini yedd ḷḷah, Ɛafak.*

length - *ṭuḷ.*

at length - *be-t-tefṣil.* He discussed the plan at length. *bḥet Ɛel le-bḷan be-t-tefṣil.*

full length - *b-ṭuḷa.* He stretched full length on the bed. *džebbed b-ṭuḷtu kollha Ɛel le-fṛaš.*

to **lengthen** - *ṭuwweḷ.*

lengthwise - *men ṭ-ṭuḷ.* Cut the material lengthwise. *qṭeƐ t-tub men ṭ-ṭuḷ.*

lenient - *ḍṛiyyef.* You're too lenient with him. *nta ḍṛiyyef mƐah bezzaf.*

lens - *žaža* pl. *-t.* Your camera has a good lens. *ṣ-ṣuwwaṛa dyalek Ɛendha žaža mezyana.*

lentil - *Ɛedsa* pl. *-t* coll. *Ɛeds.*

less - *qell.* I have less money with

me than I thought. *Eendi le-flus qell men dak š-ši lli ḍennit.*

more or less - *be-t-teqḍiṛ.* He's more or less right. *huwa be-t-teqḍiṛ Eendu l-ḥeqq.*

lesson - *ḍeṛṣ* pl. *ḍuṛuṣ.*

to give lessons - *qeṛṛa, Eṭa yeEṭi ḍuṛuṣ.* She gives Arabic lessons. *ka-tqeṛṛi l-Eeṛbiya.*

to **let** - *xella.* He wouldn't let me do it. *ma-xellani-š neEmelha.* --I won't let you go so soon. *ma-bġit-š nxellik temši bekri daba.*

let's - *yaḷḷah.* Let's go home. *yaḷḷah nemšiw le-d-ḍaṛ.*

to let alone - *xella b-weḥdu.* Can't you let me alone for five minutes? *ma-imken-lek-š txellini b-weḥdi ši-xemsa de-d-dqayeq?*

to let down - **1.** *hebbeṭ.* Please let down the blinds. *Eafak hebbeṭ le-ġlaqat.* **2.** *xab ixib ḍennu f-.* His son let him down badly. *xab ḍennu f-weldu bezzaf.* **3.** *tkasetl.* He's beginning to let down in his work. *bda itkaṣel fe-xdemtu.*

to let go - *smeḥ f-, ṭleq men.* First I wanted to do it, but then I let it go. *l-meṛṛa l-luwla bġit neEmelha walayenni smeḥt fiha.*

to let go (of) - *ṭḷeq men.* Don't let go of the rope. *ma-ṭṭleq-š men le-ḥbel.*

to let have - *Eta yeEṭi.* Please let me have the menu. *Eṭini Eafak l-weṛqa de-l-makla.* --Can you let me have fifty dirhams? *waš imken-lek teEṭini xemsin derhem?*

**I really let him have it! *berredtha fih!*

to let in - *xella idxol.* Don't let anybody in. *ma-txelli ḥetta waḥed idxol.*

to let in on - *fḍeḥ l-.* Did you let him in on the secret, too? *waš fḍeḥti-lu s-serr ḥetta huwa?*

to let off - *xella iḥuf.* Please let me off at the next stop. *xellini nḥuf f-le-mḥeṭṭa ž-žayya.*

**I'll let you off easy this time. *ġaḍi nxeffef-lek le-Equba had n-nuba.*

to let out - **1.** *fteq.* I told the tailor to let out the seams of the pants. *qolt l-l-xeyyaṭ ifteq-li s-serwal.* **2.** *xella iḥuf.* Let the water out of the basin. *xelli l-ma iḥuf men s-sariž.* **3.** *xella ixṛož.* Let the dog out of the box! *xelli l-kelb ixṛož men ṣ-ṣenḍuq.*

to let stand - *xella iduz.* I can't let that objection stand. *ma-nxelli-š had le-mEeṛḍa dduz.*

to let up - *thedden.* The storm has let up. *thedden r-rEad.*

letter - **1.** *bṛa* pl. *-wat.* Are there any letters for me? *waš kaynin ši-bṛawat liya?* **2.** *ḥeṛf* pl. *ḥṛuf.* The word has five letters. *l-kelma fiha xemsa d-le-ḥṛuf.*

letter carrier - *feṛṛaq le-bṛawat* pl. *feṛṛaqin le-bṛawat, feṛṛaqa d-le-bṛawat.*

letter of introduction - *bṛa de-t-tedxal* pl. *bṛawat de-t-tedxal.*

level - **1.** *mwaṭi.* Is the country level or hilly? *waš l-ʔeṛḍ mwaṭya wella mkodya?* **2.** *mEaweṭ.* This floor is not level. *had l-ʔeṛḍ ma-ši mEawṭa.*

**He always keeps a level head. *huwa dima mṛeẓẓen.* --He did his level best. *dar l-mežhud dyalu.* --The water this year is at a very low level. *l-ma had l-Eam meḥdur bezzaf.*

liable - *mesʔul.* You will be liable for any damages. *ġad tkun mesʔul f-koll xṣaṛa.*

**You're liable to catch cold if you're not careful. *imken-lek iḍeṛbek l-berd ila ma-ḥḍiti-š ṛaṣek.*

liar - *keddab* pl. *-a.*

liberty - *ḥoṛṛiya.*

**You're at liberty to go at any time. *Eendek l-ḥeqq baš temši fuq-emma bġiti.*

library - *mektaba* pl. *-t.*

Libya - *libya.*

Libyan - *libi* pl. *-yin.*

license - *tesriḥ* pl. *tsareḥ.*

license plate - *bḷaka de-ṭ-ṭumubil* pl. *bḷayek de-ṭ-ṭumubil.*

to **lick** - **1.** *lḥes.* Just look at the cat licking her kitten. *šuf l-qeṭṭa ka-telḥes wliyyedha.* **2.** *Eeṣṣa.* I'm going to lick you if you don't stop. *daba nEeṣṣik ila ma-salititi-š.*

**All right, I'm licked. *waxxa, ana meġlub!*

lid - *ġṭa* pl. *-wat.*

lie - *kedba* pl. *-t, kdub.*

to lie - *kdeb.*

to **lie** - **1.** *kan meḥṭuṭ.* The book is lying on the table. *le-ktab meḥṭuṭ Eel-ṭ-ṭabla.* **2.** *kan mmeġġeṭ.* He's lying on the bed. *huwa mmeġġeṭ Eel le-fṛaš.* **3.** *ža* (no present form). Most of the town lies on the right bank of the river. *ṭṭeṛf le-kbir d-le-mdina ža Eel ššeṭṭ l-limin de-l-wad.*

to lie down - **1.** *ttmedd.* I want to lie down for a few minutes. *bġit nttmedd ši-dqiqat.* **2.** *kan merxi.*

He's lying down on the job. *huwa ṃerxi fe-xdemtu.*
to lie idle - *ḥṣeṛ l-ḥaṛaka.* The factory has been lying idle for a year. *hadi ɛam baš l-meɛmel ḥṣeṛ l-ḥaṛaka.*
lieutenant - *fesyan* pl. *-a.*
life - **1.** *ḥayat.* I've lived all my life in Morocco. *duwwezt ḥayati kullha fe-l-meġṛib.*
**He was the life of the party. *huwa lli ɛmel ṛšaq fe-l-ḥefla.* —I can't for the life of me remember where I put it. *weḷḷaḥ ma-ɛqelt-š fayn ɛmeltha.* —There he stood as big as life. *ya ɛažuba ha-huwa-da.*
life belt - *ɛewwama* pl. *-t.*
lifetime - *ḥayat.* A thing like that happens only once in a lifetime. *ḥaža bḥal hadi ma-ka-tuqeɛ ġir nuba weḥda fe-l-ḥayat.*
to **lift** - *hezz.*
ligament - *ṛbaṭ* pl. *-at.*
light - **1.** *ḍuw* pl. *ḍwaw* (with art. *le-ḍwaw*). The light is too glaring. *ḍ-ḍuw qwi bezzaf.* **2.** *meftuḥ.* She has a light complexion. *lunha meftuḥ.* —She prefers light colors. *ka-tebġi l-lwan meftuḥin.* **3.** *xfif* pl. *xfaf.* Why don't you take a light coat? *ɛlaš ma taxod-š kebbuṭ xfif?* —This weight is very light. *had l-wozn xfif bezzaf.*
**That throws quite a different light on the matter. *had š-ši žab-lna muškila ždida* or *had š-ši ka-ibeddel l-muškila.* —Do you have a light? *waš ɛendek baš nešɛel?* —It's staying light much longer nowadays. *n-nhaṛ ṭwil bezzaf had l-iyam.*
to light - *šɛel.* Wait till I light the fire. *tsenna ḥetta nešɛel l-ɛafya.* —Light a match. *šɛel wqida.* —I want to light my pipe first. *bġit nešɛel s-sebsi beɛda.* —Is your cigarette still lit? *waš l-gaṛṛu dyalek baqi mešɛul?*
to light up - *šɛel be-l-feṛḥa.* The children's eyes lit up. *l-ɛeynin d-le-wlad šeɛlu be-l-feṛḥa.*
light bulb - *ḅuḷa* pl. *-t.*
lighthouse - *ḍaṛ ḍ-ḍuw* pl. *ḍyuṛ ḍ-ḍuw*
lightning - *bṛeq.*
likable - *ḍṛif* pl. *ḍṛaf, ḷṭif* pl. *ḷṭaf.*
like - *bḥal.* You're just like my sister. *nti ɛlayen bḥal xti.* —Like father, like son. *bḥal l-bu bḥal weldu.*
**It looks like rain. *tqul bin š-šta ġad ṭṭiḥ.* —I don't feel like dancing. *ma-fiya ma nešṭeḥ.* —I feel like seeing a movie. *bġit nemši le-s-sinima.* —They're as like as two peas in a pod. *šbeh-lu qayem u-nayem.*
the like of it - *bḥalu.* Did you ever see the like of it? *waš ɛemmṛek šefti bḥalu?*
what ... like - *kif, kif-aš, kif-aš-en.* What's the weather like today? *kif huwa ṭ-ṭeqs l-yum?* —What's he like? *kif-aš-en huwa?*
to like - **1.** *bġa ibġi.* I don't like cats. *ma-ka-nebġi-š le-qṭuṭ.* —He never liked to do it. *ɛemmṛu ma-bġa yeɛmelha.* **2.** *ɛežbu.* He's never liked this car. *ma-ɛemmṛu ma-ɛežbettu had ṭ-ṭumubil.* —I like this kind of cake. *ka-yeɛžebni had š-škel de-l-ḥelwa.* —If you don't like it, you can leave! *ila ma-ɛežbek-š imken-lek temši!*
how do you like ... - *kif žatek.* How do you like this town? *kif žatek had le-mdina?*
to like to dance (smoke, eat, etc.) - *bġa išṭeḥ (ikmi, yakol,* etc.) Do you like to dance? *waš ka-tebġi tešṭeḥ?*
I would like, you would like, etc. - *ibġi* (imperfect tense only). Would you like another cup of coffee? *waš tebġi ši-kas axuṛ de-l-qehwa?*
lily - *susan* (no pl.).
limb - **1.** *ṭṛaf* (no sg.) I couldn't move my limbs. *ma-mken-li-š nḥerrek ṭṛafi.* **2.** *ġṣen* pl. *ġṣan.* One of the limbs of this tree is broken. *waḥed le-ġṣen dyal had š-šežṛa mherres.*
lime - *žir.* The soil doesn't contain enough lime. *ma-kafi-š ž-žir fe-l-ʔeṛḍ.*
limit - *ḥedd* pl. *ḥudud, ḥdud.* There's a limit to everything. *koll-ši fih l-ḥedd.*
**I've reached the limit of my patience. *ma-bqa-li ṣbeṛ.* —That's the limit! *hadi hiya kteṛ ṣ-ṣbeṛ!*
speed limit - *ḥedd s-soṛɛa.*
to limit - *ḥedded.* They've limited our time. *ḥedddu-lna l-weqt dyalna.*
limp - *merxi.*
to limp - *ɛṛež.*
linden (tree) - *zefzufa* pl. *-t,* coll. *zefzuf.*
line - **1.** *šeṛṭa* pl. *-t, šṛaṭi.* Draw a line between these two points. *šeṛṛeṭ šeṛṭa bin had ž-žuž de-n-nuqaṭ.* **2.** Last week they inaugurated a new

airline between Rabat and New York. *fe-l-ʔusbuƐ lli daz deššnu xeṭṭ žuwwi ždid ma bin ṛ-ṛbaṭ u New York.* —There are many telephone lines between Rabat and Casablanca. *kaynin bezzaf d-le-xṭuṭ dyal t-tilifun bin ṛ-ṛbaṭ u-ḍ-ḍaṛ l-biḍa.* **3.** *ḥeṛfa* pl. *-t, ḥṛayef.* What line is he in? *šnu hiya ḥṛeftu?* —That's not in my line. *hadi ma-ši ḥṛefti.* **4.** *tekmiša* pl. *-t, tkameš.* There were deep lines in his face. *kan Ɛendu tekmišat kbaṛ f-wežhu.* **5.** *ṣeff* pl. *ṣfuf.* There's a long line of cars ahead of us. *kayen ṣeff kbir de-ṭ-ṭumubilat qeddamna.* **6.** *ḥbel* pl. *ḥbal.* The wash is still hanging on the line. *ṣ-ṣabun ma-zal mƐelleq f-le-ḥbel.* **7.** *ṣṭeṛ* pl. *ṣṭuṛa.* I still have a few lines to write. *bqaw-li ši-ṣṭuṛa ma nekteb.* **It's along the line of what we discussed. *had š-ši ka-itwalem mƐa l-muḍakaṛa dyalna.* —Drop me a line. *ṣifeṭ-li ši-klima* or *kteb-li klima.*

to form a line – *tṣeffef, qbeṭ s-serbis.* Form a line in front of the window. *tṣefffu qeddam š-šubbak.* —Form a line double file. *tṣefffu žuž b-žuž.*

to have a smooth line – *Ɛṛef išeṛ mezyan.* Boy, does he have a smooth line! *ka-yeƐṛef iškeṛ mezyan*

to stand in line – *dar s-serbis, tṣeffef.* I had to stand in line for cigarettes. *xeṣṣni ndir s-serbis baš nešri l-gaṛṛu.*

to line – **1.** *beṭṭen.* Please line this coat with nylon. *beṭṭen-li Ɛafak had l-kebbuṭ be-n-nilun.* **2.** *tsettef f-.* People lined the streets to watch the parade. *n-nas tsettfu fe-ṭ-ṭriq baš išufu t-teṣṛaṭ.*

to line up – *tṣeffef.* Tell the boys to line up in front of the house. *qul le-d-drari itṣefffu qeddam ḍ-ḍaṛ.*

linen – *kettan.*

lining – *tebṭin* pl. *tbaṭen.* My coat needs a new lining. *l-kebbuṭ dyali xeṣṣu tebṭin ždid.*

link – *xoṛṣa* pl. *-t, xṛeṣ, xṛaṣ, xṛaṣi.* One link of the chain is broken. *xoṛṣa de-s-sensla mherrsa.*

lion – *sbeƐ* pl. *sbuƐa.*

lip – *šareb* pl. *šwareb.*

liquid – **1.** *lli mawi.* He's only allowed liquids. *ma-imken-lu-š išṛeb ġir lli mawi.* **2.** *mawi.* Do you have liquid soap? *was Ɛendek ṣabun mawi?*

liquor – *xemṛ.* The sale of liquor is prohibited here. *hna memnuƐ biƐ l-xemṛ.*

to **lisp** – *lesles.*

list – *qayma* pl. *-t.* His name is not on the list. *smiytu ma-kayna-š fe-l-qayma.*

to list – **1.** *dker.* Are you going to list these names? *waš ġad ddker had s-smiyat?* **2.** *mal imil.* The ship is listing badly. *l-baxiṛa ka-tmil bezzaf.*

to **listen** – **1.** *tṣenneṭ.* They listened intently. *kanu ka-itṣennṭu b-balhom bezzaf.* **2.** *smeƐ.* Listen! Somebody's coming. *smeƐ! ši-waḥed maži.*

to listen for – *tsenna u-smeƐ.* Listen for the sound of the bell. *tsenna u-smeƐ ḥess n-naquṣ.*

to listen in – *tṣenneṭ.* Somebody must be listening in. *ši-waḥed tƐayli ka-itṣenneṭ.*

to listen to – **1.** *smeƐ.* I like to listen to good music. *ka-nebġi nesmeƐ musiqa mezyana.* **2.** *tṣenneṭ.* They were sitting listening to the teacher. *kanu galsin ka-itṣennṭu le-fqi.* **3.** *ttesmeƐ l-.* The child doesn't listen to me. *d-derri ma-ka-ittesmeƐ-li-š.*

liter – *litru* (no pl.).

literal – *kelma b-kelma.* This is a literal translation. *hadi ṭeṛžama kelma b-kelma.*

literally – **1.** *kelma b-kelma.* Translate this literally. *ṭeṛžem had š-ši kelma b-kelma.* **2.** *tamamen.* She's literally penniless. *ma-Ɛendha tamamen ḥetta gerš.*

little – **1.** *ṣġiṛ* pl. *ṣġaṛ.* She has a little girl. *Ɛendha bent ṣġiṛa.* —That's of little value to me. *had l-ḥaža Ɛendha qima ṣġiṛa liya.* **2.** *ġir šwiya d-.* I have little money. *Ɛendi ġir šwiya d-le-flus.*

little by little – *šwiya be-šwiya.* Little by little he calmed down. *thedden šwiya be-šwiya.*

a little – *šwiya (d-).* I can speak a little French. *ka-ntkellem šwiya de-l-fṛanṣawiya.* —Do you have any money? Only a little! *waš Ɛendek d-le-flus? ġir šwiya!*

in a little while – *men daba šwiya.* I'll come back in a little while. *ġad neṛžeƐ men daba šwiya.*

little finger – *ṣbeƐ ṣġiṛ* pl. *ṣbuƐa ṣġaṛ.*

to **live** – **1.** *Ɛaš iƐis.* He lives like a pig. *ka-iƐiš bḥal l-xenzir.* —Before the war I lived in France. *qbel men l-giṛṛa Ɛešt f-fṛanṣa.*

2. *sken*. Does anyone live in this house? *waš ši-waḥed saken f-had d̦-dar̦?* 3. *ṣṭab ḥayatu*. He always worked hard and never really lived. *dima kan ka-ixdem bezzaf u-ɛemmr̦u ma-ṣṭab ḥayatu.*
**He didn't live up to my expectations. *xab d̦enni fih.*
to live a life - *duwewz ḥayat*. He lived a happy life. *duwwez ḥayat mezyana.*
to live on - *ɛaš iɛiš b-*. The people on this island live on nothing but fish. *s-sokkan dyal had l-žazira ma-ka-iɛisu ġir b-ʔekl l-ḥut.* --I couldn't live on so little. *ma-mken-li-š nɛiš ġir b-had š-ši.*
live - **1.** *ḥeyy*. There's a live snake in that box. *kayen waḥed l-ḥenš ḥeyy f-dak ṣ-ṣenduq.* **2.** *fih l-kehr̦aba*. Careful, that's a live wire. *ḥdi r̦aṣek had s-selk fih l-kehr̦aba.*
live coals - *žemr̦a* pl. *-t*. There are still live coals in the stove. *kaynin ma-zal ž-žemr̦at fe-l-kanun.*
lively - *našeṭ*.
liver - *kebda* pl. *-t*.
livestock - *ksiba*.
living - **1.** *mɛiša* pl. *-t*. Living is awfully expensive here. *le-mɛiša ġalya bezzaf hna.* --He'll have to earn his own living. *ġadi ixeṣṣu isuwwer̦ mɛištu b-weḥdu.* **2.** *ḥeyy*. Arabic is a living language. *l-ɛer̦biya luġa ḥeyya.*
**He's the living image of his father. *huwa ka-itšebbeh le-ḅḅah tamamen* or *huwa teṣwir̦t ḅḅah tamamen.*
to make a living - *rbeḥ ḥayatu*. He makes a living by selling shoes. *huwa ka-irbeḥ ḥayatu b-biɛ ṣ-ṣbabeṭ.*
load - *ḥmel* pl. *ḥmal*. The load is too heavy for him. *le-ḥmel tqil ɛlih bezzaf.*
**That's a load off my mind. *ɛla r̦aḥa.*
loads of - *bezzaf d-*. He has loads of money. *ɛendu bezzaf d-le-flus.*
to load - **1.** *ɛmel*. Load the boxes on the truck. *ɛmel ṣ-ṣnad̦eq fe-l-kamiyu.* **2.** *ɛemmer̦*. He loaded the truck in half an hour. *ɛemmer̦ l-kamiyu f-neṣṣ saɛa.* --Load the pistol for me. *ɛemmer̦-li l-ferdi.* --Do you know how to load a camera? *waš ka-teɛr̦ef tɛemmer̦ ṣuwwar̦a?* **3.** *ɛṭa yeɛṭi*. The boss loaded me with too much work. *l-mɛellem ɛṭani bezzaf de-š-šġal ma neɛmel.*
loaded down - *mteqqel*. She was loaded down with packages. *kanet mteqqla be-l-bwaket.*
loaf of bread - *xobza* pl. *-t*.
loan - *teslaf* pl. *tsalef*. I'd like to get a loan. *bġit teslaf.*
to loan - *sellef*. He loaned me an interesting book. *sellef-li ktab mezyan.*
to **loathe** - *kr̦eh*.
lobby - *ṣeṭwan* pl. *ṣṭawen*.
lobster - *bu-mqeṣṣ* (no pl.).
to **locate** - *ṣab iṣib, žber̦*. I couldn't locate him. *ma-mken-li-š nṣibu.*
to be located - *ža* (no present form). Where is your new store located? *fayn ža l-ḥanut ž-ždid dyalek?*
locality - *naḥiya* or *nawaḥi* (pl.). There's too much poor housing in this locality. *kaynin bezzaf de-s-soknat qbaḥ f-had n-nawaḥi.*
lock - *qfel* pl. *qfula, qful, qfal*. The lock needs oiling. *le-qfel xeṣṣu z-zit.*
to keep under lock and key - *šedd*. He keeps everything under lock and key. *ka-išedd ɛla koll-ši.*
to lock - **1.** *šedd*. Don't forget to lock the door when you leave. *ma-tensa-š tšedd l-bab ila xrežti.* --I locked it in the drawer. *šeddit ɛlih f-le-mžer̦r̦.* **2.** *tleṣṣeq*. The bumpers of the two cars locked together. *l-ḥeṣṣar̦at de-ṭ-ṭumubilat tleṣṣqu b-žuž.*
to lock up - **1.** *sežžen*. (to imprison). **2.** *šedd ɛla*. Lock up this pistol. *šedd ɛla had l-ferdi.*
locksmith - *mul* (pl. *mwalin*) *s-swaret*.
locomotive - *mašina* pl. *-t*.
locust - *žr̦ad̦a* pl. *-t*, coll. *žr̦ad̦*.
log - **1.** *gayza* pl. *-t, gwayez*. The logs floated down the river. *le-gwayez mšaw mɛa l-wad.* **2.** *xešba*. He sat there like a (bump on a) log. *gles bḥal l-xešba.* --I slept like a log. *nɛest bḥal l-xešba.*
logical - *mwafeq l-le-ɛqel*.
lonely - **1.** *weḥdani*. The lighthouse keeper lives a lonely life. *mul le-fnar̦ ɛayeš ḥayat weḥdaniya.* **2.** *xali*. This place is quite lonely in winter. *had l-maḥell xali bezzaf fe-l-berd.*
lonesome - *(lli) ka-iḥess b-r̦aṣu b-weḥdu*. She's very lonesome here. *ka-tḥess b-r̦aṣha b-waḥedha hna.*
to be lonesome for - *tweḥḥeš*. I'm very lonesome for you. *tweḥḥeštek bezzaf.*
long - **1.** *ṭwiḷ* pl. *ṭwaḷ*. My, that's a long snake! *waḷḷahi hada ḥenš*

twil! 2. *kbir* pl. *kbaṛ*. We had to make a long detour. *tlezzemna ndiru ḍuṛa kbira.* 3. *bƐid* pl. *bƐad*. It's a long way to the top of the mountain. *ṭ-ṭriq bƐida le-ṛ-ṛaṣ de-ž-žbel.*

**So long! *ḷḷah ihennik!* or *be-s-slama!*

**The room is ten meters long. *l-bit fih Ɛešṛa mitru de-ṭ-ṭuḷ.*

all night long, all day long, etc. - *l-lila kollha, n-nahaṛ kollu,* etc. The child cried all night long. *bka d-derri l-lila kollha.*

long after - *mƐeṭṭel bezzaf men beƐd.* He got there long after we did. *wṣel mƐeṭṭeḷ bezzaf men beƐdna.*

a long time - 1. *modda kbira.* The trip took a long time. *ṭaḷ ṣ-ṣafaṛ modda kbira.* 2. *bezzaf.* He stayed in our house a long time. *bqa Ɛendna bezzaf.*

(a) long (time) ago - *hadi modda kbira baš, šḥal hadi baš.* That happened a long time ago. *šḥal hadi baš wqeƐ had š-ši.*

as long as - 1. *šḥal-ma.* You can keep it as long as you wish. *imken-lek txellih Ɛendek šḥal-ma bġiti.* 2. *ma-ḥedd.* It doesn't bother me as long as you do your work. *ma-fiha bas men ḥeddek derti l-xedma dyalek.* 3. *melli.* As long as you're here, you might as well have dinner with us. *melli nta hna xeṣṣek ttƐešša mƐana.*

in the long run - *mƐa l-iyam.* It'll be best in the long run. *had š-ši ġad ikun ḥsen mƐa l-iyam.*

to long for - *tweḥḥeš.* He's longing for his family. *tweḥḥeš l-Ɛaʔila dyalu.* --He's longing for home. *tweḥḥeš ḍaṛu.*

to long to - *bṭa Ɛlih weqt-aš.* I'm longing to see my parents. *bṭa Ɛliya weqt-aš nšuf waldiya.*

longer - *kteṛ men had š-ši.* He wanted to stay longer, but I was sleepy. *kan bġa ibqa kteṛ men had š-ši walayenni kan žani n-nƐas.*

no longer, not any longer - *ma-bqa-š.* I can't stand him any longer. *ma-bqa-š imken-li nḥemlu.*

look - *sifa* pl. *-t, syef.* He has the look of a thief. *siftu sift l-xuwwan.*

take a look (at) - *šaf išuf.* Take a good look! *šuf mezyan!*

looks - *sifa* pl. *-t, syef.* To judge by his looks, he's a prize fighter. *b-siftu ḍaheṛ Ɛlih huwa mlakem.* --I don't like his looks. *ma-ka-teƐžebni-š siftu.*

to look - 1. *šaf išuf.* Look, a falling star! *šuf š-šihab!* 2. *ḍaheṛ Ɛlih.* You look sick. *ḍaheṛ Ɛlik mṛiḍ.*

to look after - *ḥḍa yeḥḍi.* Do you have someone to look after the child? *waš Ɛendek ši-waḥed lli yeḥḍi d-derri?*

to look alike - *tšabhu.* We look a lot alike. *ka-ntšabhu bezzaf.*

to look at - *šaf išuf.* I enjoy looking at pictures. *ka-iṛšeq-li nšuf t-tṣaweṛ.*

to look down - *ḥgeṛ.* You mustn't look down on people just because they're poor. *ma-xeṣṣek-š teḥgeṛ n-nas Ɛla qibal huma msaken.*

to look down one's nose at - *tquneṣ Ɛla.* She looks down her nose at everyone. *ka-ttquneṣ Ɛla koll waḥed.*

to look for - *qelleb Ɛla.* We're looking for rooms. *ka-nqellbu Ɛla ši-byut.* --He's always looking for trouble. *ka-iqelleb dima Ɛel ṣ-ṣḍaƐ.*

to look into - *bḥet Ɛla.* We'll have to look into the matter. *xeṣṣna nebḥet Ɛel l-qaḍiya.*

to look alike - *šbeh l-.* She looks like a boy. *ka-tešbeh l-l-weld.*

**It looks like rain. *tqul bin ġad ṭṭiḥ š-šta.*

to look out - 1. *ḥḍa yeḥḍi ṛaṣu.* Look out! *ḥḍi ṛaṣek!*

to look out on - 2. *Ɛṭa yeƐṭi Ɛla* The big window looks out on the garden. *š-šežṛa le-kbira ka-teƐṭi Ɛel l-Ɛeṛṣa.*

to look over - *ṭeḷḷeƐ Ɛeynu mƐa.* Will you look over these papers? *imken-lek ṭṭeḷḷeƐ Ɛeynek mƐa had le-wṛaq?*

to look up - 1. *hezz Ɛeynih.* He didn't even look up when I called him. *ma-ṛḍa-š ihezz Ɛeynih melli Ɛeyyeṭt-lu.* 2. *ḥtaṛem.* She looks up to him. *ka-teḥtaṛmu.* 3. *ẓaṛ iẓuṛ.* Look me up some time, won't you? *ma-tensa-š dẓuṛni ši-meṛṛa.* 4. *qelleb Ɛla.* I have to look up something. *xeṣṣni nqelleb Ɛla ši-ḥaža.* 5. *tteṣḷeḥ.* Things are beginning to look up. *l-ḥala bdat tteṣḷeḥ.*

lookout - *Ɛessas* pl. *-a.* A lookout was placed on every hill. *heṭṭu Ɛessas yeḥdi f-koll kodya.*

loose - 1. *merxi.* The button is loose. *ṣ-ṣḍafa merxiya.* 2. *ma-mrekkeb-š mezyan.* The nail is loose.

l-meṣmaṛ ma-mrekkeb-š mezyan. **3.** *meṭḷuq.* Is the dog allowed to run around loose? *waš l-kelb imken-lu itsara meṭḷuq?* **4.** *ṭwiḷ* pl. *ṭwaḷ.* She has a loose tongue. *isanha ṭwiḷ.*

**You must have a screw loose! *nta mselseɛ swiya!* --They cut loose the minute the teacher stepped out of the room. *ġir le-fqi xrež men l-bit u-huma ibdaw idiru l-haṛaž.*

to **loosen** – **1.** *ḥell.* Can you loosen this screw? *waš imken-lek tḥell had l-luleb?* **2.** *rxa irxi šwiya.* I want to loosen my shoelaces. *bġit nerxi šwiya š-šebbaṭ dyali.*

lopsided – *ma-mɛewweṭ-š, mɛewwež.* The picture's hanging lopsided. *teṣwiṛa ma-mɛewwṭa-š.*

to **lose** – **1.** *tellef.* I lost my pencil again. *telleft qlami ɛawed tani.* **2.** *ṭaḥ iṭiḥ l-.* I'm losing my hair. *ka-itiḥ-li šeɛṛi.* **3.** *mša imši l-.* He lost his entire fortune during the war. *mšat-lu malu kollu fe-l-ḥeṛb.*

**My watch loses three minutes a day. *maganti mɛeṭṭḷa be-tlata de-d-dqayeq koll nhaṛ.* --I lost sight of him after following him for two hours. *bqit ka-ntebɛu saɛtayn u-tlef ɛliya.*

to lose one's strength – *ḍaɛet ḍḍiɛ ṣeḥḥtu.* I've lost all my strength. *ḍaɛet-li ṣeḥḥti.*

to lose one's temper – *tqelleq, ṭaṛ iṭiṛ l-.* He loses his temper easily. *ka-itqelleq be-z-zerba.*

to lose one's way – *tlef.* Don't lose your way! *ma-ttlef-š!*

to be lost – *tweḍḍeṛ.* My shirt was lost in the laundry. *tweḍḍṛet qamižti ɛend ṣ-ṣebbana.*

**My things were lost in the fire. *ttḥeṛqu ḥwayži fe-l-ɛafya.* --Since his wife's death he's completely lost. *melli matet mṛatu huwa mtellef.*

loss – *xṣaṛa* pl. *-t, xṣayeṛ.*

lot – **1.** *qeṭɛa* pl. *qṭaɛi.* How big is your lot? *qedd-aš l-qeṭɛa dyalek?* **2.** *mektub.* I don't envy his lot. *ma-ka-neḥsed l-mektub dyalu.*

**I'll send you the books in three separate lots. *ġad nṣifeṭ-lek le-ktuba be-tlata de-l-meṛṛat mefṛuqin.*

lots of – *bezzaf d-.* She has lots of money. *ɛendha bezzaf d-le-flus.*

a lot – *bezzaf.* We like him a lot. *ka-nḥebbuh bezzaf.* --She's a lot better than people think. *hiya ḥsen bezzaf men dak š-ši lli ka-ixemmmu fiha n-nas.*

a lot of – *bezzaf d-.* I still have a lot of work. *ma-zal ɛendi bezzaf de-l-xedma.*

to draw lots – *ḍṛeb l-ɛud.* Let's draw lots. *yaḷḷah nḍeṛbu l-ɛud.*

loud – **1.** *mžehhed.* She has a loud, unpleasant voice. *ɛendha ḥelq mžehhed u-qbiḥ.* **2.** *be-ž-žehd.* Don't talk so loud! *ma-tkellem-š be-ž-žehd!* **3.** *bayen.* I don't like loud colors. *ma-ka-nebġi-š l-ʔelwan lli baynin bezzaf.*

loud-speaker – *buq* pl. *bwaq.*

louse – *qemla* pl. *qmul* coll. *qmel.*

love – *ḥobb.* Love is blind. *l-ḥobb ɛma.*

to fall in love (with) – *tteġṛem (f-).* He's fallen in love with her. *huwa tteġṛem fiha.*

in love (with) – *meġṛum (f-).*

to love – **1.** *ḥebb.* He loves her very much. *ka-iḥebbha bezzaf.* **2.** *ma-ɛendu ma ɛezz men.* I love apples. *ma-ɛendi ma ɛezz men t-teffaḥ.*

lovely – **1.** *ġzal* pl. *ġezlan.* They have a lovely home. *ɛendhom ḍaṛ ġzala.* **2.** *ɛžib.* It's a lovely evening. *le-ɛšiya ɛžiba.*

low – **1.** *qṣiṛ* pl. *qṣaṛ.* Do you want shoes with high or low heels? *waš bġiti ṣebbaṭ b-gdem qṣiṛ wella kbir?* **2.** *ḥader.* That plane is flying too low. *had ṭ-ṭiyaṛa ka-ṭṭir ḥadra bezzaf.* **3.** *dlil* pl. *dlal.* That was low of him. *had š-ši lli ɛmel dlil.* **4.** *meḥdur.* She spoke in a low voice. *tkellmet b-ṣuṭ meḥdur.* --He always gets low marks. *n-nuqaṭ dyalu dima meḥdurin.* **5.** *ḍɛif* pl. *ḍɛaf.* His pulse is low. *nfiḍu ḍɛif.* **6.** *luwla.* Put her in low (gear). *ɛmelha fe-l-luwla.*

**The sun is quite low. *š-šems ġeṛbet bezzaf.* --He made a low bow. *bendeq bezzaf.*

to get low – *qlal iqlal.* Our funds are getting low. *ṛaṣmalna ka-iqlal.*

lower – *teḥtani.* Put the boxes on the lower shelf. *dir ṣ-ṣnadeq fuq l-meṛfeɛ t-teḥtani.*

to lower – **1.** *ṛma iṛmi.* Lower the lifeboats. *ṛmiw le-flayek de-l-iġata.* **2.** *ḥder.* Lower the curtain. *ḥder l-xamiya.* **3.** *ḥuwwef.* Lower the bucket into the well. *ḥuwwef ṣ-ṣṭeḷ fe-l-bir.*

**He lowered his voice when he saw her come in. *tkellem be-šwiya melli* *šafha daxla.*

loyal - **1.** *ṣadiq.* You couldn't have a more loyal friend. *ma-imken-lek-š ikun ʕendek ṣaheb ṣaḍiq kteṛ men had š-ši.* **2.** *qelbu ṣafi (mʕa).* He has always been loyal to the government. *huwa dima qelbu ṣafi mʕa l-ḥukuma.*

loyalty - *ṣeḍq.*

luck - **1.** *ẓheṛ.* My luck has changed. *ẓ-ẓheṛ dyali tbeddel.* **2.** *seʕd.* Now you try your luck! *ṭḷeb seʕdek!* **3.** *swirti.* It's not merely a matter of luck. *ma-ši ġir mesʔala de-swirti.*

bad luck - *qellet s-seʕd.*

**You're in luck! *ʕendek swirti.* --You're out of luck! *ma-ʕendek-š swirti.*

luckily - *ʕla swirti.* Luckily she didn't see me. *ʕla swirti ma-šafni-š.*

lucky - *(lli) ʕendu seʕd.* You're a lucky fellow. *nta ʕendek seʕd.*

**It was a lucky coincidence. *kanet ṣeḍfa mezyana.* --You can consider yourself lucky. *imken-lek teḥmed ḷḷah.*

lukewarm - **1.** *dafi.* Take a lukewarm bath. *ġsel be-l-ma dafi.* **2.** *ma-mhiyyež-ž.* He's very lukewarm about that. *huwa ma-mhiyyež-š ʕla had l-ḥaža.*

lumber - *ʕwad* (pl.), *xšeb.* How much lumber will be needed for the book shelves? *šḥal de-le-ʕwad xeṣṣna baš nṣawbu le-xzana d-le-ktub?*

lump - **1.** *ṭub.* What are you going to do with that lump of clay? *aš ġad ddir b-had ṭ-ṭub de-ṭ-ṭin?* **2.** *beṛquqa* pl. *-t.* He has a big lump on his forehead. *ʕendu beṛquqa kbira fe-zbehtu.* **3.** *qaleb* pl. *qwaleb.* He took ten lumps of sugar. *xda ʕešṛa d-le-qwaleb de-s-sokkaṛ.*

lunatic - *ḥmeq* pl. *ḥumeq.*

lunch - *ġda* pl. *-wat.*

to lunch - *tġedda.*

lung - *riya* pl. *-t.*

**The little fellow yelled at the top of his lungs. *d-derri ṭḷeq ḥelqu kollu.*

luxury - *tedxim.*

lye - *lyan.*

M

macaroon - *ġṛiyba* pl. *-t.*

machine - *ʔala* pl. *-t.* The machine is working again. *ha l-ʔala xeddama ʕewtani.*

machine gun - *ṛeššaša* pl. *-t.*

machinery - *ʔalat* (pl.).

mad - **1.** *ḥmeq* pl. *ḥumeq.* They took him to the asylum because he was mad. *ddaweh l-l-meṛṣṭan ʕla ḥeqq-aš kan ḥmeq.* **2.** *mqelleq, zeʕfan, ṭayeṛ-lu.* I was mad when I didn't find him there. *kan ṭayeṛ-li melli ma-ṣebtu-š temma.* **3.** *mxaṣem.* He's mad at his brother. *huwa mxaṣem mʕa xah.* **4.** *meṣʕuṛ.* He was bitten by a mad dog. *ʕeḍḍu kelb meṣʕuṛ.*

to be mad, to go mad - *ḥmaq.* My son is mad about ice cream. *weldi ka-iḥmaq ʕel l-baṣṭa.* --The poor fellow went mad and they took him to the asylum. *ḥmaq meskin u-ddaweh l-l-meṛṣṭan.*

madam - *lalla.* Is somebody waiting on you, Madam? *waš ši-waḥed ka-iserbik a lalla?*

madhouse - *meṛṣṭan* pl. *-at.*

madman - *ḥmeq* pl. *ḥumeq.*

magazine - *mažella* pl. *-t.* Where can I buy that magazine? *fayn imken-li nṣib dak l-mažella?*

magnificent - *ʕažib, moʕtabaṛ, mumtaz.*

to **magnify** - *kebber.* This lens magnifies six times. *had l-ʕadasa ka-tkebber setta de-l-meṛṛat.*

magnifying glass - *mukebbara* pl. *-t.*

maid - *metʕellma* pl. *-t, xeddama* pl. *-t.* We let our maid go. *dḥina l-metʕellma dyalna.*

old maid - *ʕateq bayṛa* pl. *ʕawateq bayṛin.*

mail - *barid.* The mail is delivered at four o'clock. *ka-iferṛqu l-barid fe-ṛ-ṛebʕa.*

**Is there any mail for me? *waš kayna ši-bṛa liya?*

by mail - *mʕa l-buṣṭa.* We'll send you the package by mail. *ġadi nṣifṭu-lek l-bakit mʕa l-buṣṭa.*

to mail - **1.** *ṣifeṭ, ṣafeṭ iṣifeṭ.* Did you mail that package? *waš ṣifeṭṭi dak l-bakit?* **2.** *ṛma iṛmi.* Please mail the letter for me. *ṛmi-li had le-bṛa ḷḷah ixellik.*

mailbox - *ṣenḍuq de-l-briyat* pl. *ṣnaḍeq de-l-briyat.*

mailman - *feṛṛaq le-bṛawat* pl. *feṛṛaqin*

le-bṛawat.

main - *muhimm, kbir.* This is the main problem. *hadi hiya l-muškila l-muhimma.*

   in the main - *Ɛlayen dima.* The discussion revolved in the main around those two questions. *ḍaṛet l-mudakaṛa Ɛlayen dima Ɛla dak š-žuž de-l-masaʔil.*

   **I agree with him in the main. *ana mettafeq mƐah Ɛlayen f-koll-ši.*

   main office - *merkez* pl. *mrakez.*

to **maintain** - *ʔekked.* He maintains that he was there. *huwa ka-iʔekked bin kan temma.*

majority - 1. *ʔeġlabiya* pl. -*t.* The majority was against it. *l-ʔeġlabiya kanet ḍedd dak š-ši.* 2. *ʔektariya* pl. -*t.* The majority of the students were sick. *l-ʔektariya de-ṭ-ṭalaba kanu mṛaḍ.*

make - *maṛka* pl. -*t.* What make is your radio? *šnu hiya l-maṛka de-ṛ-ṛadyu dyalek?*

   to make - 1. *ṣeqqem, ṣaweb.* Did you make the chair yourself? *waš ṣeqqemti š-šelya b-yeddek?* —What shall I make for you, tea or coffee? *šnu nṣeqqem-lkom, atay wella l-qehwa?* —I've just had a suit made for myself. *Ɛad ṣeqqemt keswa l-ṛaṣi.* 2. *ṣneƐ, ṣeqqem.* Does this factory make watches? *waš had l-meƐmel ka-iṣneƐ l-maganat?* 3. *dar idir.* What are you going to do tomorrow? *š-ġadi ddir ġedda?* 4. *semma.* They made him chairman. *semmaweh ṛaʔis.* 5. *Ɛmel.* I made a long speech. *Ɛmelt xoṭba kbira.* —He made a terrible mistake. *Ɛmel ġaḷaṭ kbir.* —You made a good choice. *Ɛmelti xtiyaṛ mezyan.* 6. *ṛežžeƐ.* He has made himself very famous. *huwa ṛežžeƐ ṛaṣu mešhuṛ bezzaf.* 7. *xda yaxod fe-l-weqt.* Can we make the train? *waš imken-lna naxdu l-qiṭaṛ fe-l-weqt?* 8. *wṣel l-.* If we start out early, we can make Fez by evening. *ila ṣafeṛna bekri, imken-lna nweṣlu l-fas mƐa l-lil.* 9. *qbeṭ.* How much do you make a week? *šḥal ka-teqbeṭ fe-š-žemƐa?* 10. *lezzem.* Nobody made you do it. *ḥetta waḥed ma-lezzmek teƐmelha.* 11. *dfeƐ.* He made me spill the ink. *huwa lli dfeƐni baš nehṛeq le-mdad.*

   **Five times four makes twenty. *xemsa (ḍrebha) Ɛla ṛebƐa hiya ƐešRin.*

   to make a confession - *gerr.* He made a complete confession to them. *gerr-lhom koll-ši.*

   to make a fool of oneself -

tbehdel. If you do that, you'll make a fool of yourself. *ila Ɛmeltiha, ġadi ttbehdel.*

   to make a fuss - *dar idir haṛaž.* Don't make such a fuss! *ma-Ɛendek Ɛlaš ddir had l-haraž kollu.*

   to make a fuss over - *qleb d-denya Ɛla.* There's no reason for you to make a fuss over that. *ma-Ɛendek Ɛlaš teqleb d-denya Ɛla had š-ši.*

   to make a go of - *nžeḥ f-.* He'll never make a go of it. *Ɛemmṛu ma-inžeḥ fiha.*

   to make believe - *Ɛmel messu.* She is only making believe that she doesn't know it. *hiya ġir ka-teƐmel messha bin ma-ka-teƐṛefha-š.*

   to make good - *nžeḥ fe-šġalu.* They made good. *nežḥu fe-šġalhom.*

   to make good - *ġṛem.* You have to make good the damages you've done. *xeṣṣek teġṛem le-xṣayeṛ lli Ɛmelti.*

   to make off with - *ḥṛeb b-.* They've made off with our car. *ḥeṛbu-lna b-siyaṛtna.*

   to make out - 1. *qṛa iqṛa.* Can you make out the date on this postmark? *waš imken-lek teqṛa t-tarix d-had ṭ-ṭabeƐ?* 2. *fhem.* Can you make out what he means? *waš imken-lek tefhem aš ka-yeƐni?* 3. *Ɛemmeṛ.* Have you made out the application blank? *waš Ɛemmeṛti l-weṛqa de-ṭ-ṭalab?* 4. *wežžed.* Please make out our bill. *wežžed-lna l-weṛqa de-l-xlaṣ Ɛafak.* 5. *xeṛžet-lu l-qaḍiya.* How did you make out yesterday? *kif-aš xeṛžet-lek l-qaḍiya l-bareḥ?*

   to make peace - *tṣaleḥ.* The two countries have made peace. *tṣalḥu d-duwlat b-žuž.*

   to make sense - *Ɛendu ši-meƐna.* Does this make sense to you? *waš had š-ši Ɛendu ši-meƐna lilek?*

   to make up - 1. *qeyyed.* Make up a list of all the things you need. *qeyyed f-weṛqa lli xeṣṣek kollu.* 2. *ṣaweb.* Can you make up a bouquet of roses for me? *imken-lek tṣaweb-li ši-mešmum de-l-woṛd?* 3. *dar idir.* Make up a sentence with the word 'no'. *dir ši-žumla be-l-Ɛibara "lla".* 4. *xtareƐ.* Did he make up the story? *waš xtareƐ dak le-xṛafa?* 5. *ṣeqqem.* Did he make up the speech himself? *waš huwa lli ṣeqqem l-xoṭba?* 6. *tṣaleḥ.* They've made up again. *tṣalḥu Ɛewtani.* 7. *Ɛekker.* It takes her a year to make up. *xeṣṣha Ɛam baš tƐekker.* 8. *qbeṭ.* I'll make up tomorrow the hour I lost. *ġadi neqbeṭ ġedda s-saɛa lli ḍiyyeɛt.* --I'll have to make up for lost time. *ixeṣṣni neqbeṭ l-weqt lli ḍiyyeɛt.*

to make up one's mind - *qeṛṛeṛ, fṣeḷ.* I haven't yet made up my mind. *ma-zal ma-qeṛṛeṛt.*

make-up - **1.** *zwaq le-wžeh.* She uses a lot of make-up. *ka-tketter men z-zwaq d-le-wžeh.* **2.** *ṭabiɛa* pl. *-t.* It's not in his make-up to lie. *ma-ši men ṭabiɛtu ikdeb.*

makings - **1.** *hiʔa* pl. *-t; škel* pl. *škal.* This boy has the makings of a good actor. *had l-weld fih l-hiʔa d-ši-mumettil mezyan.* **2.** *qwam* pl. *-at; iqama* pl. *-t, iqayem.* We have all the makings for a good stew. *ɛendma le-qwam kollu dyal waḥed ṭ-ṭažin moɛtabaṛ.*

Malaga - *maḷqa.*

male - *dkeṛ.* Is that bird male or female? *waš hadak ṭ-ṭiṛ dkeṛ wella nta?*

malicious - *qbiḥ* pl. *qbaḥ.*

man - *ṛažel* pl. *ṛžal.*

to **manage** - **1.** *tkellef b-.* Who is managing your farm? *škun lli mkellef-lek b-le-ɛzib?* **2.** *treʔʔes ɛla.* He's been managing this bank for two years. *hadi ɛamayn u-huwa metreʔʔes ɛla had l-ḅenk.* **3.** *ṭuwweɛ.* That teacher just couldn't manage the children. *had le-fqi gaɛ ma-qḍeṛ-š iṭuwweɛ le-wlad.*

**Did you manage to get the tickets? *waš ḍebbeṛti f-le-wṛaq?* --How did you manage to find her? *kif-aš derti ḥetta žbeṛtiha?* --How do you manage on this salary? *kif-aš ka-teɛmel baš tɛiš b-had š-šehriya?* --I manage on what God has given. *ka-neqḍi ḥaža b-dak š-ši lli ɛṭa ḷḷah.*

manager - *mudir* pl. *-in.*

mankind - *l-bašariya, l-žens l-bašari.*

manner - *kifiya.* I liked the manner in which he went about the job. *ɛežbetni l-kifiya baš tkellef be-l-ɛamal.*

manners - *ʔaxlaq, ʔadab.* She has no manners. *ma-ɛendha ʔaxlaq* or *ma-fiha ʔadab.*

to **manufacture** - *ṣneɛ, ṣuwweb.*

manure - *ġbaṛ.*

many - *bezzaf d-, ɛadad d-.* I have many reasons. *ɛendi bezzaf de-l-ʔasbab.*

many a - *šḥal men.* Many a man owes his success to his wife. *šḥal men ṛažel kan n-nažaḥ dyalu ɛla yedd mṛatu.* I've passed here many a time. *dezt men hna šḥal men meṛṛa.*

a good many - *ɛadad kbir d-.* He knows a good many people there. *ka-yeɛṛef ɛadad kbir de-n-nas temma.*

how many - *šḥal men* (followed by sg.), *šḥal d-.* How many tickets do you want? *šḥal men bṭaqa bġiti?* or *šḥal d-le-bṭayeq bġiti?*

map - *xaṛiṭa* pl. *-t.*

marble - *ṛxam.*

March - *maṛeṣ.*

march - *mešya* pl. *-t.*

**He stole a march on all of us. *darha bina kollna.*

to march - *tmešša.*

mare - *ɛewda* pl. *-t.*

margin - **1.** *ḥašya* pl. *ḥwaši, ženb* pl. *žnab.* Leave a wider margin on the left side. *xelli ḥašya wseɛ men hadi ɛel l-iṣaṛ.* **2.** *rbeḥ.* pl. *rbaḥ.* We're operating on a very small margin. *ka-nxedmu b-waḥed r-rbeḥ ṣġiṛ bezzaf.* **3.** *feṛq.* We won by a narrow margin. *rbeḥna b-waḥed l-feṛq ṣġiṛ.*

marjoram - *merdeddu š.*

mark - **1.** *ɛalama* pl. *-t, ṛešma* pl. *-t.* Make a mark after the names of those present. *dir ši-ɛalama ḥda s-smiyat dyal n-nas lli ḥaḍṛin.* **2.** *neqṭ* pl. *nuqaṭ.* He always got good marks in mathematics. *kan dima ka-yaxod nuqaṭ mezyanin f-le-ḥsab.*

**I don't feel quite up to the mark today. *ma-ka-nḥess-š b-ṛaṣi huwa hadak l-yum.*

to mark - **1.** *ṛšem.* I've marked the important parts of the article. *ṛšemt l-maḥellat l-muhimmin de-l-maqala.* **2.** *ṛšem, biyyen.* The road is well marked. *ṭ-ṭṛiq mbiyyna mezyan.* **3.** *ṣeḥḥeḥ, ṣḷeḥ.* When are you going to mark the examinations? *fuq-aš ġad tṣeḥḥeḥ le-mtiḥanat.*

to mark down - **1.** *qeyyed, kteb, sežžel.* I've marked down the things I want. *ṛani qeyyedt le-ḥwayež lli baġi.* **2.** *hebbeṭ t-taman d-.* The suits have been marked down from 150 dollars to 100 dollars. *hebbṭu t-taman d-le-ksawi men mya u-xemsin duḷaṛ le-myat duḷaṛ.*

market - *ṣuq* pl. *ṣwaq.*

Marrakesh - *meṛṛakeš.*

native of Marrakesh - *meṛṛakši* adj. pl. *-yin,* n. pl. *hel meṛṛakeš.*

marriage - *žwaž* pl. *-at.*

to **marry** - **1.** *džuwwež b-, xda yaxod.* Is she going to marry him? *waš ġad taxdu?* **2.** *žuwwež.* He married his daughter to a man from Casablanca.

žuwwež bentu l-ṛažel men ḍ-ḍaṛ l-biḍa.

married – *mžuwwež.* They've been married for over a year. *hadi kteṛ men ɛam u-huma mžuwwžin.*

to get married – *džuwwež, žwež.*

Marseilles – *mersilya.*

marsh – *meṛža* pl. *-t.*

marvelous – *ɛžib, ɛažib.*

mass – **1.** *žemhur* pl. *žamahir; nas.* He has all the masses behind him. *l-žamahir kollha tabɛah.* **2.** *ɛeṛṛam* pl. *ɛṛaṛem.* He's collected a mass of information about that. *ṛah žmeɛ ɛeṛṛam de-l-meɛlumat ɛla dak š-ši.*

mat – *ḥṣiṛa* pl. *-t, ḥṣayeṛ.*

match – **1.** *wqida* pl. *-t* coll. *wqid.* Give me a box of matches please. *ɛafak ɛṭini ši-ṣenduq d-le-wqid.* **2.** *leɛba* pl. *-t.* Who won the match? *škun lli rbeḥ l-leɛba?* **3.** *žwaž* pl. *-at.* Her parents don't approve of the match. *waldiha ma-mwafqin-š ɛla žwažha.*

to be a match for – *qedd ɛla.* He's a match for anybody. *huwa iqedd ɛla men-ma kan.*

**I'm no match for him. *m-ana-š qṛinu.*

to match – **1.** *wafeq, naseb.* These colors don't match well. *had l-lwan ma-mnasbin-š mezyan.* **2.** *matel, dar idir bḥal.* I can match him any time. *neqḍeṛ ndir bḥalu weqt-emma kan.* **3.** *žbeṛ bḥal.* You'll never be able to match this color. *ma-ɛemmṛek ġad džbeṛ ši-lun bḥal hada.*

material – **1.** *madda* pl. *mawadd.* We use only the best materials. *ma-ka-nsteɛmlu ġir l-mawadd le-mxiyyra.* **2.** *meɛlumat* (pl.). He's collecting material for a book. *ka-ižmeɛ meɛlumat l-waḥed le-ktab.* **3.** *tub* pl. *tyab.* Is this material washable? *waš had t-tub ka-itsebben?* **4.** *muhimm.* There's no material difference between the two. *ma-kayen-š ši-feṛq muhimm binathom b-žuž.*

matter – *qaḍiya* pl. *-t; mesʔala* pl. *-t, masaʔil.* I'll look into the matter. *daba nšuf l-qaḍiya šnu hiya.*

**It's not a matter of price. *ma-bqat-š fe-t-taman.* --Something's the matter with his heart. *ši-ḥaža ɛendu f-qelbu.* --That doesn't matter. *ma-ka-ihemm-š.* --This is no laughing matter . *had š-ši ma-fih-š ḍ-ḍeḥk.* --What's the matter? *š-kayen?* --What's the matter with you? *yak la-bas?* or *š-ɛendek?* or *ma-lek?*

mattress – *feṛš* pl. *fṛuša; mtellta* pl. *-t; mṭeṛṛba* pl. *-t, mṭaṛeb.*

May – *mayu.*

may – **1.** *imken-l-.* May I have this pencil? *imken-li naxod had le-qlam?* **2.** *imken, ṛobbama.* I may go tomorrow night. *ṛobbama nemši ġedda fe-l-lil.*

mayor – *ɛamel* pl. *ɛommal.*

meadow – *meṛɛa* pl. *mṛaɛi.*

meal – *makla* pl. *-t, mwakel.* Three meals a day aren't enough for him. *tlata de-l-maklat fe-n-nhaṛ ma-ka-iqedduh-š.*

mean – *ḥqiṛ* pl. *-in; qbiḥ* pl. *qbaḥ.*

to **mean** – **1.** *ɛna yeɛni.* What do you mean by that? *š-ka-teɛni b-dak š-ši?* **2.** *nwa inwi.* I mean to go tomorrow. *ana nawi nemši ġedda.* --I meant to tell you but I forgot. *kont nawi nqul-lek be-l-ḥeqq nsit.* **3.** *qṣeḍ.* I didn't mean any harm. *ma-qṣeḍt walu.*

**I know he means well. *ka-neɛṛef niytu mezyana.* --That doesn't mean much. *dak š-ši ma-ɛendu ʔahemmiya.* --It means a lot to me to see him tonight. *muhimm bezzaf baš nšufu l-yum fe-l-lil.*

meaning – *meɛna* pl. *-t, mɛani.*

measles – *bu-ḥemṛun.*

to **measure** – *ɛbeṛ.* I measured the height of the windows carefully. *ɛbeṛt le-ɛlu dyal š-šṛažem b-tedqiq.* —Measure me two kilos of ground beef. *ɛbeṛ-li žuž kilu de-l-kefta de-l-begri.*

**How much does he measure around the waist? *šḥal ɛendu fe-ḍ-ḍuṛa de-l-keṛš?* --All necessary measures have been taken. *l-lazem kollu tteɛmel.*

measurement – *ɛbaṛ* pl. *-at.*

meat – *lḥem* pl. *lḥum, lḥumat.*

meat grinder – *ṭeḥḥana de-l-kefta.*

medal – *wisam* pl. *-at.*

to **meddle** – *dexxel ṛaṣu f-.* He likes to meddle in other people's business. *ka-ibġi idexxel ṛaṣu f-ṣuq n-nas.*

medical – *ṭibbi.*

medicine – **1.** *dwa* pl. *-yat, ʔedwiya.* This medicine tastes bitter. *had d-dwa madaqu meṛṛ.* **2.** *ṭibb.* My daughter is studying medicine. *benti ka-teqṛa ṭ-ṭibb.*

medium – *metweṣṣeṭ.* He's of medium height. *ṭulu metweṣṣeṭ.*

Mediterranean Sea – *le-bḥeṛ l-metweṣṣeṭ.*

to **meet** – **1.** *tlaqa.* Did you meet him on the street? *waš tlaqitih* *fe-ẓ-ẓenqa?* --Let's meet in front of the school. *iwa ntlaqaw qbalt l-medṛaṣa.* **2.** *tƐeṛṛef Ɛla, tƐaṛef mƐa.* I've known his father for a long time but I've just met his mother. *hadi modda ṭwila w-ana ka-neƐṛef ḅḅah be-l-ḥeqq Ɛad tƐaṛeft mƐa ṃṃu.* **3.** *tƐeṛṛeḍ l-.* We'll meet them at the railroad station. *ġad ntƐeṛṛḍu-lhom f-ḷagaṛ.* **4.** *tteǯmeƐ.* We used to meet once a week. *konna ka-nttǯemƐu meṛṛa fe-ǯ-ǯemƐa.*

**Pleased to meet you! *metšeṛṛef!* or *metšeṛṛfin!* --Will he meet the deadline? *waš ġad ikun waǯed fe-l-weqt?*

meeting - **1.** *ǯtimaƐ* pl. *-at* (art. *le-*). There were five hundred people at the meeting. *kanu xems mya de-n-nas f-le-ǯtimaƐ.* **2.** *mlaqya* pl. *-t.* I arranged for a meeting of the two. *ṛani ḍebbeṛt-ḷhom waḥed le-mlaqya lilhom b-ǯuǯ.*

Meknes - *meknas.*

native of Meknes - *meknasi* adj. pl. *-yin,* n. pl. *hel meknas.*

Melilla - *mlilya.*

native of Melilla - *mlili* adj. pl. *-yin,* n. pl. *hel mlilya.*

melody - *neġma* pl. *-t.*

to **melt** - **1.** *dab idub.* The ice has all melted. *t-telǯ kollu dab.* **2.** *duwweb.* The sun melted the ice. *š-šemš duwwbet t-telǯ.*

memory - **1.** *dakira* pl. *-t, Ɛqel* pl. *Ɛqul.* My memory is not what it used tp be. *Ɛeqli ma-bqa-š kif kan.* **2.** *tidkar* pl. *tadakir, dikṛa* pl. *-yat.* I have pleasant memories of that country. *Ɛendi dikṛayat mezyana Ɛla dak le-blad.*

menace - *tehdid, xaṭaṛ* pl. *ʔexṭaṛ.*

to **mend** - *ṛeqqeƐ.* When are you going to ment my shirts? *fuq-aš ġadi tṛeqqeƐ-li le-qwameǯ dyali?*

to **mention** - *dkeṛ.* He didn't mention the price. *ma-dkeṛ-š t-taman.*

merchandise - *selƐa* pl. *-t, sluƐ.*

merchant - *biyyaƐ-šeṛṛay* pl. *biyyaƐa-šeṛṛaya, taǯer* pl. *toǯǯaṛ.*

mercury - *zaweq.*

mercy - **1.** *ṛeḥma, šafaqa.* He has no mercy. *ma-fih ṛeḥma.* **2.** *smaḥa.* They pleaded for mercy. *ṭeḷbu s-smaḥa.*

to **merit** - *staḥel, staḥeqq.*

mess - *xebla* pl. *-t, qeṛbala* pl. *-t, tqeṛbila* pl. *-t.* Did you see the mess the painters left? *waš šefti l-xebla lli xellaw ṣ-ṣebbaġa?*

**The house is in an awful mess. *ḍ-ḍaṛ ma-fiha ma-ittšaf.* --You certainly got yourself into a nice mess! *walayenni f-aš ǯriti l-ṛaṣek!*

to **mess up** - **1.** *wessex.* Don't mess up the floor with your wet feet. *ma-twessex-š ḷerḍ u-reǯlik fazgin.* **2.** *xeṛbeq.* Who messed up the papers on my desk? *škun lli xeṛbeq-li le-kwaġeṭ lli fuq ṭ-ṭabla dyali?*

metal - *meƐden* pl. *mƐaden.*

method - *kifiya* pl. *-t, ṭaṛiqa* pl. *-t, ṭuṛuq.*

middle - **1.** *wesṭ.* I'm leaving the middle of next week. *ġad nemši. f-wesṭ ǯ-ǯemƐa ǯ-ǯayya.* --He was standing in the middle of the road. *kan waqef f-wesṭ ṭ-ṭriq.* **2.** *wesṭani, wesṭi.* Open the middle window. *ḥell š-šeṛǯem l-wesṭani.* **3.** *metwesṣeṭ.* He's a man of middle height. *huwa ṛaǯel qamtu metwesṣṭa.* **4.** *kerš* pl. *kruš.* He's put on weight around the middle. *kebret-lu l-kerš.*

**I'm in the middle of packing. *ṛ-ana xayed fe-ǯmiƐ ḥwayǯi.*

midnight - *neṣṣ l-lil.*

might - *quwwa* pl. *-t, ǯehd* pl. *ǯhud.* They're working with all their might. *ṛahom xeddamin b-quwwthom kollha.*

mile - *mil* pl. *myal.*

military - *Ɛeskari.*

milk - *ḥlib.*

to **milk** - *ḥleb.*

milkman, milk vendor - *lebban* pl. *-a, mul le-ḥlib* pl. *mwalin le-ḥlib.*

mill - *ṭaḥuna* pl. *-t, ṭwaḥen.* When are you going to take the grain to the mill? *fuq-aš ġadi teddi z-zṛeƐ le-ṭ-ṭaḥuna?*

miller - *ṭeḥḥan* pl. *-a.*

million - *melyun* pl. *mlayen.*

minaret - *ṣemƐa* pl. *-t, ṣmeƐ, ṣmaƐi.*

mind - **1.** *Ɛqel, fikr* pl. *fkaṛ.* He has a keen mind. *Ɛendu Ɛqel madi.* **2.** *bal.* That idea came to my mind as I was on my way home. *ǯatni had l-fikra l-l-bal melli kont ġadi le-ḍ-ḍaṛ.* --I have something else in mind. *ši-ḥaǯa x̂ṛa f-bali.*

**He doesn't know his own mind. *huwa b-ṛaṣu ma-ka-yeƐṛef-š š-baġi.* --Keep your mind on your work. *dir ṛaṣek fe-xdemtek.* --My mind still isn't clear on what happened. *dak š-ši lli wqeƐ ma-zal ma-bġa-š ittefhem-li.* --What's on your mind? *š-ṭeḥtek?* --Are you out of your mind? *waš xreǯ-lek le-Ɛqel?*

to **my mind** - *f-nadaṛi.* To my mind she's the right person for the job. *f-nadaṛi hiya lli tesḷaḥ l-had l-xedma.*

to change one's mind - *tbeddel-lu n-naḍaṛ.* I've changed my mind. *tbeddel-li n-naḍaṛ.*

to mind - 1. *ddaha iddiha f-.* Don't mind what he says. *la-ddiha-š fe-klamu.* 2. *ḥda yeḥdi.* Who's going to mind the children? *škun lli ġadi yeḥdi d-drari?* 3. *ttesmeɛ l-.* This little girl doesn't mind her mother any more. *had le-bnita ma-bqat-š ka-ttesmeɛ l-ommha.* 4. *ɛendu maniɛ.* You don't mind if I leave now? *yak ma-ɛendek maniɛ nemši daba?* **Mind your own business. *dxol suq ṛasek.*

mine - 1. *meqteɛ* pl. *mqateɛ.* He works in a mine. *ka-ixdem f-wahed l-meqteɛ.* 2. *mina* pl. *-t.* Their ship ran into a mine. *l-baxira dyalhom xeṛžet f-wahed l-mina.*

mine - *dyali.* Your room is to the right, mine is to the left. *l-bit dyalek ɛel l-imin u-dyali ɛel š-šmal.*

minister - *wazir, uzir* pl. *wuẓaṛa.* Three ministers have resigned. *tlata de-l-wuẓaṛa qeddmu stiqalthom.*

miniority - *ʔaqelliya* pl. *-t.*

mint - *neɛnaɛ* pl. *nɛaneɛ, iqama* pl. *iqayem,* We never drink tea without mint. *ɛemmeṛna ma-ka-nšeṛbu ʔatay bla neɛnaɛ.*

minute - 1. *dqiqa* pl. *dqayeq.* I'll be back in five minutes. *ġad neṛžeɛ men daba xemsa de-d-dqayeq.* 2. *sġiwer, dqiweq, stiwet.* It was so small you could hardly see it. *kan sġiwer l-hedd ʔennu kan sɛib baš ittšaf.* **I'll call you the minute I know. *ġir nsuq le-xbaṛ ndreb-lek t-tilifun.*

minute hand - *muri kbir* pl. *mwara kbaṛ.* The minute hand of my watch came off. *l-muri le-kbir d-maganti tqelleɛ.*

miracle - *muɛžiza* pl. *-t, ɛžuba* pl. *-t, ɛžayeb.*

mirror - *mraya* pl. *-t.*

miscarriage - *ṣqiṭ, ṣeqṭan.*

mischief - *tašiṭanet, štun.* That boy is always up to some mischief. *dak l-weld dima ka-iḍur ɛla ši-štun ma yeɛmel.*

miser - *bxil* pl. *bxal.*

miserable - 1. *mfelles.* What miserable weather! *walayenni hal mfelles hada!* 2. *mbuʔes, mɛenfeš.* I feel miserable today. *ka-nhess b-ṛaṣi mɛenfeš had n-nhaṛ.*

misery - *buʔs, šaqaʔ.* They lived in utter misery. *kanu ɛeyšin fe-l-buʔs t-tamm.*

misfortune - *muṣiba* pl. *-t, mṣayeb.*

to mislay - *tellef, wedder.*

to mislead - *xdeɛ, ġelleṭ.* The description is misleading. *had l-weṣf ka-ixdeɛ.*

misprint - *ġelṭa d-le-mṭebɛa* pl. *ġelṭat d-le-mṭebɛa.*

to miss - 1. *fellet.* I missed the first train. *fellett l-qiṭaṛ l-luwwel* or *mša ɛliya l-qiṭaṛ l-luwwel.* 2. *twehheš.* I'll miss you terribly. *ġad ntwehhšek bezzaf* or *ġad txelli fiya ṭ-ṭayla.* 3. *menneɛ.* Don't miss this movie. *ɛendek tmenneɛ had l-film.* **You haven't missed anything. *ma-fatek walu.* --You've missed the point. *ma-fhemti-š.* --Our house is so easy to find you can't miss it. *d-daṛ dyalna waṛya bezzaf, ma-imken-š texfa ɛlik.* --The child has been missing for three days. *hadi telt iyam u-l-weld ġayeb.* --One suitcase is missing. *šanṭa wehda ka-txess.*

mist - *dbaba.*

mistake - *ġalaṭ, ġelṭa* pl. *-t, ġlaṭi.* How could I make such a mistake? *kif imken hetta neɛmel ġelṭa bhal hadi?* --I took it by mistake. *xditu ġalaṭ.* **There is no mistaking his intentions. *niytu ma-fiha ma-iġleṭ l-wahed.* --Please don't mistake me. *llah ixellik ma-tefhemni-š ɛweš.* --Sorry, I mistook you for someone else. *smeh-li, šebbehtek l-ši-wahed axor.*

to be mistaken, to make a mistake - *ġleṭ.* you're mistaken! *ġletti!* or *ṛak ġalet!*

to mistreat - *tɛedda ɛla.*

to misunderstand - *fhem mɛewwež, fhem ɛweš.*

to mix - 1. *xelleṭ.* I mixed yellow and red. *xelleṭt le-ṣfeṛ u-le-hmeṛ.* 2. *ṣuwweb.* Shall I mix some paste? *nṣuwweb ši-šwiya de-l-leṣqa?* 3. *xaleṭ, txaleṭ mɛa.* We don't mix much with our neighbors. *ma-ka-ntxalṭu-š bezzaf mɛa žiranna.* 4. *txelleṭ.* Oil and honey don't mix. *z-zit u-le-ɛsel ma-ka-itxellṭu-š.*

to mix in - *dexxel ṛaṣu.* Don't mix in, this is none of your business. *la-ddexxel-š ṛasek, had š-ši ma-ši suqek.*

to mix up - 1. *tellef, duwwex, dehšer.* Don't mix me up!

la-dduwwexni-š! 2. *xeḷḷeṭ.* Don't mix up the cards. *la-txeḷḷeṭ-š l-kaṛṭa.*

mixture - *texḷiṭa* pl. *-t.* coll. *texḷaṭ, texḷiṭ.*

to **moan** - *naḥ inuḥ.*

model - 1. *namudaž.* pl. *namadiž.* He's working on the model of a bridge. *huwa xeddam fe-n-namudaž d-waḥed l-qenṭṛa.* 2. *nuɛ* pl. *mwaɛ, škel* pl. *škal.* This is a 1940 model. *hada n-nuɛ d-ɛam ʔalf u-tesɛa mya u-ṛebɛin.* 3. *miṭal.* She's a model wife. *hiya tbaṛek ḷḷah miṭal z-zužat.*

moderate - *moɛtadel, mweṣṣeṭ, mɛewweṭ.*

modern - *ɛeṣṛi.*

modest - *metwadeɛ, bṣiṭ* pl. *bṣaṭ.*

moist - *mbellel, fazeg, mneddi.*

moisture - *nda, blal, fzag.*

mold - 1. *ġmal.* There's a layer of mold on the cheese. *kayna qešṛa d-le-ġmal ɛla wžeh ž-žben.* 2. *qaleb* pl. *qwaleb.* Pour the plaster into the mold. *kebb l-gebṣ fe-l-qaleb.*

moldy - *ġamel, mṭebbeb.* This bread is moldy. *had l-xobz mṭebbeb.*

moment - *wqiyet.* Could you spare a moment? *ɛendek ši-wqiyyet?*
**Just a moment! *bellati šwiya!* —At the moment, I can't give you any further information. *f-had l-leḥda ma-imken-li nzid neɛṭik ḥeṭṭa ši-meɛlumat x̂ṛa.*

in a moment - *men daba waḥed d-dqiqa.* I'll give you your change in a moment. *daba nṛedd-lek ṣ-ṣeṛf dyalek men daba waḥed d-dqiqa.*

Monday - *t-tnayn, nhaṛ t-tnayn.*

money - *flus* (pl.)

to make money - *rbeḥ le-flus.*

monk - *ṛhib* pl. *ṛohban.*

monkey - *qeṛḍ* pl. *qṛuḍ, qṛuḍa.*

month - *šheṛ* pl. *šhuṛ, šhuṛa.*

monthly - *šehṛi.*

mood - *gana* pl. *-t, xaṭeṛ* pl. *xwaṭeṛ.* He's in a good mood this morning. *huwa ɛla gantu had ṣ-ṣbaḥ* or *huwa ṛašeq-lu had ṣ-ṣbaḥ* —I'm not in the mood for that now. *ma-ɛendi gana l-dak š-ši daba.*

moon - *gemṛa* pl. *gmaṛi.*

more - 1. *axoṛ* f. *x̂ṛa* pl. *x̂ṛin.* I want two more bottles of vinegar. *bġit žuž d-le-qṛaɛi x̂ṛin de-l-xell.* 2. *kteṛ.* They've sold more trucks than cars this year. *baɛu l-kamiyuwat kteṛ men s-siyaṛat had l-ɛam.* —You should study more. *xeṣṣek teqra kteṛ men had š-ši.* 3. *zyada.* He's asking for more money. *ka-iṭleb z-zyada f-le-flus.*

more and more - **This work is getting more and more difficult. *had š-šoġl ġir ka-izid yewɛar.* —Everything is getting more and more expensive. *koll-ši ġir ka-izid iġla.*

not any more - **Don't do that any more! *ma-tebqa-š teɛmel dak š-ši!* —I don't care any more. *ma-bqit-š mehtemm.*

the more...the more - *ma-ḥedd... u-, koll-ma.* The more I give him, the more he wants. *ma-ḥeddni ka-neɛṭih u-huwa ka-ibġi ši-axoṛ.* —The more I see him, the more I like him. *koll-ma šeftu ka-nzid nebġih.*

morning - *ṣbaḥ* pl. *-at, ṣbuḥa.* Good morning! *ṣbaḥ l-xir!*

in the morning - 1. *fe-ṣ-ṣbaḥ.* She's here only in the morning. *ka-tkun hna ġir fe-ṣ-ṣbaḥ.* 2. *(ġedda) fe-ṣ-ṣbaḥ.* I'll see you in the morning. *nšufek (ġedda) fe-ṣ-ṣbaḥ.*

mortar - 1. *beġli.* Mortar is made of lime and sand. *l-beġli mṣuwweb men ž-žir u-ṛ-ṛemla.* 2. *mehraz* pl. *mharez.* Mortar and pestle. *l-mehraz w-iddu.*

mortgage - *ṛhen* pl. *ṛhuna, ṛehniya* pl. *-t.*

to mortgage - *ṛhen, ɛmel fe-ṛ-ṛhen, xella fe-ṛ-ṛhen.*

mosaic - *zelliž* (coll). The mosaic in this mosque is ancient. *z-zelliž f-had ž-žameɛ qdim.*

mosque - *žameɛ* pl. *žwameɛ.*

mosque courtyard - *ṣḥen* pl. *ṣḥuna.*

mosquito - *namusa* pl. *-t.* coll. *namus.*

moss - *xezz.*

most - 1. *ʔekteṛ-ma, žehd-ma, qedd-ma.* That's the most I can pay. *hada ʔekteṛ-ma imken-li nxeḷḷṣu.* 2. *l-žoll f-, l-ʔektariya d-.* Most people left early. *l-žoll fe-n-nas mšaw f-ḥalhom bekri.* 3. What did you like most? *šnu lli ɛežbek kteṛ?* 4. *bezzaf ɛad.* The talk was most interesting. *l-xoṭba kanet mufida bezzaf ɛad.*
**I can pay fifty dirhams at the most. *ila kettert imken-li neɛṭi xemsin derhem.* —At most it's worth ten dirhams. *tamanha ma-itɛedda-š ɛešṛa de-d-drahem.* —For the most part I agree with him on that. *ana mettafeq mɛah f-žoll dak š-ši.* —We'd better make the most of our time. *ḥsen-lna nsġtanmu ma*

imken l-weqt lli f-iddna.
most of - *l-žoll f-, l-ʔektariya d-.* Most of those present were against it. *l-žoll fe-n-nas lli kanu ḥaḍṛin kanu ḍeḍḍha.* --He's the one that did most of the work. *huwa lli dar l-ʔektariya de-l-xedma.* --He's on the road most of the time. *l-žoll fe-l-weqt ka-ikun qabeṭ ṭ-ṭṛiq.*
**Most of the day I'm at the office. *ka-nkun fe-l-mekteb Ɛlayen n-nhaṛ kollu.*

moth - *tunya* pl. *-t.*

mother - *ʔomm* pl. *-ahat, -awat;* my mother *m̃m̃i,* form *m̃m̃-* before other possessive endings.

mother-in-law - **1.** (wife's mother) *nsiba* pl. *-t.* **2.** (husband's mother) *ḥma* pl. *-wat.*

motion - **1.** *ḥaṛaka* pl. *-t.* Did you watch her motions? *dditi l-ġaya l-l-ḥaṛakat dyalha?* **2.** *qtiraḥ* pl. *-at, multamas* pl. *-at.* I'd like to make a motion. *bġit nqeddem waḥed l-multamas.*
**The train was still in motion. *l-qiṭaṛ kan ma-zal ka-itḥerrek.*

motive - *sabab* pl. *sbab.*

motor - *muṭuṛ* pl. *-at.*

motorcycle - *ḍeṛṛaža nariya* pl. *ḍeṛṛažat nariya, muṭuṛ* pl. *-at.*

to **mount** - **1.** *rkeb Ɛla.* He mounted the horse and rode away. *rkeb Ɛel l-Ɛewd u-zad xelfa.* **2.** *rekkeb.* They mounted the new doors day before yesterday. *rekkbu l-biban ž-ždad wel-l-bareḥ.*

mountain - *žbel* pl. *žbal* coll. *žbel.*

mountaineer - *žebli* pl. *žbala, rifi* pl. *ryafa.*

to **mourn** - *ḥzen.* They all mourned their uncle's death. *kollhom ḥeznu Ɛel l-mut d-Ɛemmhom.* --The entire country mourned over the king. *le-blad kollha ḥeznet Ɛel l-malik.*

mourning - *ḥozn, ḥzen.*

mouse - *faṛ* pl. *firan.*

mouth - *fomm* pl. *fmam.*

move - **1.** *ḥaṛaka* pl. *-t.* Every move I make hurts. *koll ḥaṛaka Ɛmeltha ka-ḍḍeṛṛni.* **2.** *nuba* pl. *-t.* It's your move. *nubtek hadi.* **3.** *xelfa* pl. *-t.* He can't make a move without asking his wife. *ma-ka-iqdeṛ-š yeƐmel xelfa weḥda bla-ma išaweṛ mṛatu.*
to make a move - *tḥerrek.* Don't make a move or I'll kill you. *ma-tḥerrek-š wella ṛani nqetlek.*
on the move - *Ɛla gdem.* They're always on the move. *huma dima Ɛla gdem.*
to move - **1.** *ḥerrek.* She can't move her foot. *ma-ka-teqḍeṛ-š tḥerrek ṛželha.* **2.** *tḥerrek.* I can't move. *ma-ka-neqḍeṛ-š ntḥerrek.* **3.** *qtaṛeḥ.* I move we adjourn the session. *ka-neqtaṛeḥ nweqqfu l-želsa.* **4.** *ṛḥel.* We're moving on October first. *ġad nṛeḥlu fe-l-luwwel fe-ktubeṛ.* **5.** *lƐeb.* I just moved, it's your turn. *Ɛad lƐebt, nubtek.*

movie - *film* pl. *ʔeflam.*
movies - *sinima* pl. *-t.* We rarely go to the movies. *qlil f-aš ka-nemšiw le-s-sinima.*

to **mow** - *ḥešš.*

much - *bezzaf.* I haven't much time. *ma-Ɛendi-š l-weqt bezzaf.* --We like her very much. *ka-nebġiwha bezzaf Ɛad.* --I feel very much better today. *l-yum ka-nḥess b-ṛaṣi ḥsen bezzaf Ɛad.*
how much - *be-šḥal.* How much will it cost me? *be-šḥal ġad ṭṭiḥ Ɛliya?*
**We don't care for it very much. *ma-ka-nebġiweh-š ḥetta l-temma.*

mucus - *tenxima* pl. *-t, tnaxem.*

mud - *ġis* pl. *ġyusat.* All the roads were covered with mud after the rain. *ṭ-ṭoṛqan kollhom kanu Ɛamṛin be-l-ġis men beƐd-ma ṭaḥet š-šta.*

muddy - *mġiyyes.* Your shoes are muddy. *ṣebbaṭek mġiyyes.*
**This water is muddy. *had l-ma mƐemmeṛ be-l-ġis.*

muezzin - *mwodden* pl. *mwoddnin.*

mug - *ġoṛraf* pl. *ġṛaṛef.*

muggy - *mẓemmeṭ.* The weather's awfully muggy today. *l-yum l-ḥal mẓemmeṭ bezzaf.*

mule - *beġla* pl. *bġal,* f. *beġla* pl. *-t.*

to **multiply** - **1.** *ḍreb.* Multiply three by four! *ḍreb tlata f-ṛebƐa.* **2.** *kteṛ.* Rabbits multiply very quickly. *le-rneb ka-ikteṛ b-soṛƐa kbira.*

to **mumble** - *bergem.* I wish he wouldn't mumble that way. *tmennitu ma-ikun-š ka-ibergem hakdak.*

mumps - *ḥlaqem.*

municipal - *baladi, d-le-mdina.* He works in the municipal power plant. *ka-ixdem f-ḍaṛ ḍ-ḍuw l-baladiya.*

murder - *qtila.*
to murder - *qtel.*

murderer - *qatel.*

muscle - *Ɛeṣba* pl. *-t, Ɛṣab,* coll. *Ɛṣeb.*

museum - *metḥef* pl. *mtaḥef.*

mushroom - *feggiƐa* pl. *-t.* coll.

feggiƐ, feggaƐ.
music - 1. *musiqa.* Where is that music coming from? *mnayn žayya had l-musiqa?*
2. *weṛqa de-l-musiqa,* pl. *wṛaq de-l-musiqa.* I didn't bring the music with me. *ma-žebt-š le-wṛaq de-l-musiqa mƐaya.*
musical - *musiqi.* Do you play any musical instrument? *waš ka-ḍḍṛeb ši-ʔala musiqiya?*
musician - *musiqi* pl. *-yin.*
must - 1. *xeṣṣ* plus object pronoun endings. I mustn't be late. *ma-xeṣṣni-š nkun mƐeṭṭel.*
2. *lazem.* He must be sick. *lazem ikun mṛiḍ.*
mustache - *šareb* pl. *šwareb, ẓƐafeṛ* pl. *ẓƐafṛat.*
mustard - *ṣnab.*
to **mutilate** - *fṛem.*
mutiny - *tuṛa* pl. *-t.*
to **mutter** - *bergem.*
mutton - *ġelmi, ġenmi.*
muzzle - *kmama* pl. *-t, kmayem.* You ought to put a muzzle on that dog. *dak l-kelb xeṣṣek ddir-lu kmama.*

N

nag - *kiḍaṛ* pl. *kyaḍeṛ.*
nail - 1. *meṣmaṛ* pl. *mṣameṛ.* Don't hammer the nail in too far. *la-ddeqq-š l-meṣmaṛ bezzaf.*
2. *ḍfeṛ* pl. *ḍfaṛ.* I just broke my nail. *yaḷḷah herrest ḍefṛi.*
**He always hits the nail on the head. *dima ka-ižibha fe-t-tmam.*
to nail - *ṣemmeṛ.* Please nail the picture to the wall. *Ɛafak ṣemmeṛ t-teṣwiṛa fe-l-ḥiṭ.*
naked - *Ɛeryan.*
**On a clear day you can see the town from here with the naked eye. *mnin ka-ikun n-nhaṛ ḍawi ka-imken-lek tšuf le-mdina men hna ġir be-l-Ɛeyn.*
name - *sem, sm-; smiya* pl. *-t.* What is your father's name? *sem ḅḅak?* --What's your name, please? *smiytek men fedḷek?*
**What's your name? *š-semmak ḷḷah?*
first name - *smiya šexṣiya.*
last name - *smiya de-l-ƐaʔiIa.*
to name - 1. *semma.* He named his son Ahmed. *semma weldu ḥmed.* --They named the boy after his father. *semmaw l-weld Ɛla ḅḅah.*
2. *dkeṛ.* Can you name all the planets? *waš imken-lek ddkeṛ l-kawakib kollhom?*
**Name your own price. *Ɛṭi t-taman dyalek.*
napkin - *mendil* pl. *mnadel.*
narrow - *ḍiyyeq.* This street is very narrow. *had d-derb ḍiyyeq bezzaf.* --His views on education are very narrow. *n-naḍaṛiyat dyalu Ɛel t-teƐlim ḍiyyqa bezzaf.*
**He had a narrow excape. *yaḷḷah mneƐ b-ṛaṣu.*
to become narrow - *ḍyaq.*
to make narrow - *ḍiyyeq.*
nasty - 1. *qbiḥ.* pl. *qbaḥ.* Don't be so nasty! *ma-tkun-š qbiḥ bezzaf!* 2. *qbiḥ, mfelles.* Do you always have such nasty weather? *waš dima Ɛendkom l-žuw mfelles bḥal hakda?*
nation - 1. *ʔumma* pl. *ʔumam.* The whole nation mourned his death. *l-ʔumma kollha ḥeznet Ɛel l-mut dyalu.* 2. *dula* pl. *duwal* How many nations were there at the conference? *šḥal de-d-duwal kanu fe-l-muʔtamaṛ?*
national - 1. *qewmi.* He's no longer in the national assembly. *ma-bqa-š fe-l-mežlis l-qewmi.* 2. *Ɛamm.* When are the national elections going to be? *fuq-aš ġa-tkun l-intixabat l-Ɛamma?*
nationality - *žensiya* pl. *-t.*
natural - *ṭabiƐi.*
nature - 1. *ṭabiƐa, ṭbiƐa.* It's not his nature to lie. *ma-ši men tbiƐtu ka-ikdeb.* 2. *nuƐ.* I can't tell you anything about the nature of my job. *ma-imken-li nqul-lek ḥetta ḥaža Ɛla nuƐ l-xedma dyali.*
navy - *beḥriya.*
near - 1. *ḥda.* They're standing near each other. *ṛahom waqfin waḥed ḥda waḥed.* 2. *qṛib.* My house is near the bank. *ḍ-ḍaṛ dyali qṛib men l-ḅenk.*
near by - *f-had ž-žwayeh.* Is there a restaurant near by? *waš kayen ši-meṭƐam f-had ž-žwayeh?*
nearly - *Ɛlayen.* I'm nearly finished. *Ɛlayen nsali.*

neat - 1. *mretteb.* His desk is always neat. *le-mketba dyalu dima mrettba.* 2. *ʔaniq.* She always looks neat. *dima tšufha ʔaniqa.* 3. *mṣeqqem.* That was a neat trick you played on him. *leɛba mṣeqqma lɛebti ɛlih.*

necessary - 1. *lazem.* I'll stay if it's necessary. *nebqa ila kan lazem.* 2. *lli ka-ixeṣṣ, lazem.* Can you raise the necessary funds? *waš imken-lek džmeɛ le-qḍeṛ lli ka-ixeṣṣ?*

neck - 1. *ɛenq* pl. *ɛnuq, ɛnaq.* He fell down the stairs and broke his neck. *ṭaḥ fe-ḍ-ḍṛuž u-therres-lu ɛenqu.* --The bottle has a very narrow neck. *ɛenq l-qerɛa ḍiyyeq bezzaf.* 2. *ṭuq* pl. *ṭwaq.* My dress has an open neck. *ksuwti ṭuqha meftuḥ.*
  **Why are you always sticking your neck out? *ɛlaš dima ka-džib l-ṛaṣek le-bla?*

necklace - *xeyṭ* pl. *xyuṭ, xnag* pl. *-at.*

necktie - *gṛabaṭa* pl. *-t, žiyyafa* pl. *-t.*

need - *ḥtiyaž.* There's a great need for heavy clothes. *kayen ḥtiyaž kbir ɛel le-ḥwayež t-tqal.*
  if need be - *ila kan lazem.* I'll go myself if need be. *nemši ana b-nefsi ila kan lazem.*
  in need of - *meḥtaž l-.* He's badly in need of a vacation. *huwa meḥtaž bezzaf l-ši-ṛoxṣa.*
  to need - *ḥtaž, ɛendu l-ḥaža b-.* We have all we need. *lli meḥtažin bih kollu ɛendna.* --I need some rest badly. *ana meḥtaž bezzaf le-šwiya de-ṛ-ṛaḥa.*

needle - *ibra* pl. *ibari.* I can't thread the needle. *ma-bġa-š idzelleg-li xeyṭ f-l-ibra.*
  **I'm on pins and needles. *ana tqul gales ɛel š-šuk.*

negative - 1. *bḷaka* pl. *-t, bḷayek.* The negative is much clearer than the print. *le-bḷaka žat wḍeḥ men t-teṣwiṛa.* 2. *selbi.* The result of the test was negative. *n-natiža dyal le-mtiḥan kanet selbiya.*
  **I expected a negative answer. *kont mentaḍeṛ ṛefḍ* or *kont nawi ž-žwab ġad ikun la.*

to **neglect** - *ġfel ɛla, feṛṛeṭ f-.* He's been neglecting his work lately. *bda ifeṛṛeṭ fe-xdemtu had l-iyamat.*

negro - *ḍṛawi* pl. *ḍṛawa, ɛebd* pl. *ɛbid, kḥel* pl. *kuḥel.*

neighbor - *žaṛ* pl. *žiran.*

neighborhood - 1. *žiran, mmalin l-ḥewma.* The whole neighborhood was there. *ž-žiran kollhom kanu temma.* 2. *naḥiya* pl. *-t, nawaḥi; žiha* pl. *žwayeh.* Many artists live in our neighborhood. *ɛadad de-l-fennana saknin f-žihtna.*

neither - *la.* Neither he nor I will be there. *ma-ġad-nkunu temma la-ana la-huwa.*

nephew 1. (brother's son) *weld l-xa.* 2. (sister's son) *weld l-xet.*

nerve - *ɛeṛq* pl. *ɛṛuq.*
  **That noise is getting on my nerves. *dak ṣ-ṣḍaɛ bda iṭḷeɛ-li f-ṛaṣi.* --Some nerve! *žebha!*

nervous - *mqelleq.*

nest - *ɛešš* pl. *ɛšaš, ɛšuš.*

net - *šebka* pl. *-t, šbaki, šbek.*

never - *ɛemmeṛ ma-.* I never work. *ɛemmeṛni ma-ka-nexdem.*
  **Now or never! *daba wella b-naqeṣ!* --Never! *abaden!*

nevertheless - *waxxa hakdak.* Nevertheless I still can't believe it. *waxxa hakdak ma-zal ma-imken-li-š ntiyyeq dak š-ši.*

new - *ždid* pl. *ždad.*

news - *xbaṛ* pl. *-at.* The news came entirely unexpectedly. *le-xbaṛ ža tamamen ɛla ġefla.*

newspaper - *žarida* pl. *-t, žaṛaʔid.*

next - 1. *mazi, zay.* We're coming next month. *ġad nžiw š-šheṛ ž-žay.* --Next time do it right. *l-meṛṛa ž-žayya dirha mṣeqqma.* 2. *tabeɛ.* Who's next? *škun lli tabeɛ?* 3. *men beɛd.* What shall I do next? *aš xeṣṣni neɛmel men beɛd?*
  next to - *geddam, ḥda, b-ženb.* Sit down next to me. *gles qeddami.* --They live next to the church. *ka-iseknu ḥda le-knisiya.*
  the next day - *lla-ġedda.* The next day he got sick. *lla-ġedda ṭaḥ mṛiḍ.*

nice - 1. *mliḥ* pl. *mlaḥ, mezyan.* She wears nice clothes. *ka-telbes ḥwayež mezyanin.* 2. *ḷṭiyyef, ḍṛiyyef.* He was very nice to us. *kan ḍṛiyyef mɛana bezzaf.*
  **Did you have a nice time? *tselliti mɛa ṛaṣek?*

nickname - *laqab* pl. *ʔalqab.*

niece - 1. (brother's daughter) *bent l-xa.* 2. (sister's daughter) *bent l-xet.*

night - 1. *lila* pl. *-t, lyali.* I stayed there only one night. *bqit temma ġir lila weḥda.* 2. *lil.* The night was quiet. *l-lil kan hadeʔ.*
  nights - *fe-l-lil.* He works

nights. *ka-ixdem fe-l-lil.*
last night - 1. *l-bareḥ fe-l-lil.* We had unexpected company last night. *l-bareḥ fe-l-lil žaw ƐEendna ši-ḍyaf Ɛla ġefla.* 2. *l-bareḥ.* Did you sleep well last night? *nƐesti mezyan l-bareḥ?*
tomorrow night - *ġedda fe-l-lil.*
night watchman - *biyyat* pl. *-a.*
nine - *tesƐud.*
nineteen - *tseƐṭaš.*
ninety - *tesƐin.*
ninth - 1. (ordinal) *taseƐ.* 2. (fraction) *tusuƐ* pl. *-at, tsaƐ.*
no - *la, lla.* Do you always have to say no? *waš lazem dima tqul lla?*
**No smoking! *memnuƐ t-tedxin!*
nobody - *ḥetta waḥed, ḥetta ḥedd.* Nobody may leave this room. *ḥetta waḥed ma-ixṛož men had l-bit.* --Nobody saw him. *ma-šafu ḥetta ḥedd.*
noise - *ṣḍaƐ* pl. *-at.*
noisy - *(lli) fih ṣ-ṣḍaƐ, (lli) fih l-haṛaž, mhuṛež.* That's a noisy office. *hadak l-mekteb fih ṣ-ṣḍaƐ.* --What a noisy boy! *Ɛla weld u-ma mhuṛež.*
none - *ḥetta waḥed, u-tqul ši-waḥed.* None of my friends would help me. *u-tqul ši-waḥed men ṣḥabi bġa iƐawenni.* --None of the women knew anything about it. *ḥetta weḥda men le-Ɛyalat ma-kanet Ɛaṛfa ši-ḥaža Ɛla dak š-ši.*
**That's none of your business. *dak š-ši ma-ši ṣuqek.*
nonsense - *txerdil, klam fareġ, klam xawi.*
noodles - *fdaweš* (pl.), *šeƐriya.*
noon - *ġda, ḍhuṛ.* The weather cleared up some around noon. *l-žuw tṣeffa šwiya fe-žwayeh le-ġda.*
nor - *wala.* This shop-keeper has neither goods nor money left. *had mul l-ḥanut ma-bqa-lu la-selƐa wala flus.*
normal - *Ɛadi.*
normally - *fe-l-Ɛada.*
north - *šamal.* Rabat is north of Casablanca. *ṛ-ṛbaṭ žat f-šamal ḍ-ḍaṛ l-biḍa.*
northern - *šamali.* The northern part of the island was flooded. *ž-žiha š-šamaliya de-l-žazira kan fayeḍ Ɛliha l-ma.*
nose - *nif* pl. *nyaf, menxaṛ* pl. *mnaxeṛ.*
nosebleed - *tfenžira* pl. *-t.*
not - 1. *ma, ma- ...-š.* I didn't see him yesterday. *ma-šeftu-š l-bareḥ.* --He still hasn't done his work. *ma-zal ma-dar l-xedma dyalu.* 2. *ma-ši.* This house isn't good. *had ḍ-ḍaṛ ma-ši mezyana.*
note - 1. *teƐliq* pl. *taƐaliq, mulaḥaḍa* pl. *-t.* Look at the note at the bottom of the page. *šuf l-mulaḥaḍa lli l-teḥt fe-l-weṛqa.* 2. *šhada* pl. *-t.* He gave me a note for what he still owes me. *Ɛṭani šhada b-dak š-ši lli ma-zal ka-nsalu.*
to take note of - *laḥeḍ, dda iddi l-bal l-.* Haven't you taken note of that? *ma-laḥedti-š dak š-ši?*
to note - *redd l-bal l-, šaf išuf.* Note the difference between the two. *šuf l-feṛq binathom b-žuž.*
notebook - *konnaš* pl. *knaneš.*
nothing - *walu, ḥetta ḥaža.* There's nothing more for me to do here. *ma-bqa Ɛendi walu ma ndir hna.*
nothing but - *ma ... ġir.* They got nothing but bread and water. *ma-wṣelhom ġir l-xobz u-l-ma.*
to **notify** - *Ɛlem, suwweq le-xbaṛ l-.*
November - *nuwambir, nuwanbir.*
now - *daba.* I have to leave now. *xeṣṣni nemši daba.* --Are you satisfied now? *Ɛla xaṭṛek daba?*
now and then - *saƐa saƐa.* I hear from him now and then. *ka-yewṣelni ši-xbaṛ men Ɛendu saƐa saƐa.*
by now - *f-had s-saƐa hadi.* He really ought to be here by now. *f-had s-saƐa hadi ṛah kan lazmu ikun hna.*
from now on - *men daba l-fuq.* From now on, I'll be more careful. *men daba l-fuq ġad nebda nredd bali šwiya kteṛ.*
just now - *Ɛad daba.* I talked to him just now. *Ɛad daba tkellemt mƐah.*
up to now - *ḥetta l-daba.* I hadn't noticed it until now. *Ɛemmṛi ma-ddit-lha l-ġaya ḥetta l-daba.*
nowadays - *had l-iyamat.*
nude - *Ɛeryan.*
nuisance - *muṣiba* pl. *-t, mṣayeb.* The flies are a real nuisance this summer. *d-debban muṣiba had ṣ-ṣif.*
numb - *žamed.* My fingers are numb with cold. *ṣebƐani žamdin be-l-berd.*
number - *nemra* pl. *-t, nmari.*
to number - *nemmer.*
nurse - 1. *fermliya* pl. *-t.* This nurse works in the hospital that's near our house. *had l-fermliya ka-texdem fe-ṣ-ṣbiṭaṛ lli qṛib men ḍaṛna.* 2. *muṛebbiya* pl. *-t.* The children are in the park with the

nurse. *d-drari ṛahom fe-l-ɛeṛṣa mɛa l-muṛebbiya.*

to nurse - **1.** *qabel.* She nursed him back to health. *qablettu ḥetta ṛežɛet-lu ṣeḥḥtu.* **2.** *ṛeḍḍeɛ.* Does she nurse the baby herself? *waš hiya lli ka-tṛeḍḍeɛ t-terbya?*

nut - **1.** *guza* pl. *-t* coll. *guz; gergaɛa* pl. *-t* coll. *gergaɛ.* He's not allowed to eat nuts. *qaṭɛin ɛlih makelt l-guz.* **2.** *wšek* pl. *wšak.* This nut doesn't fit the bolt. *had le-wšek ma-ža-š qedd l-luleb.*

**He's nuts. *xaṣṣu buḷun.*

to go nuts - *xrez-lu le-ɛqel.* If this keeps up, I'll go nuts. *had š-ši ila zad ṭal, ġad ixṛož-li le-ɛqel.*

O

oak - *šežṛa de-l-beḷḷuṭ* pl. *šežṛat de-l-beḷḷuṭ, šžaṛ de-l-beḷḷuṭ.*

oar - *meqdaf* pl. *mqadef.*

oats - *xoṛṭaḷ.*

obedience - *ṭaɛa, ṭuɛ.*

obedient - *muṭiɛ, ṭayeɛ.*

to **obey** - *ṭaɛ iṭiɛ, ttesmeɛ l-.*

object - **1.** *ḥaža* pl. *ḥwayež.* He was struck on the head with a heavy object. *ḍeṛbuh f-ṛaṣu b-ši-ḥaža tqila.* **2.** *qeṣḍ* pl. *qṣuḍ.* What's the object of that? *šnu huwa l-qeṣḍ dyal dak š-ši?* **3.** *muṛaḍ* pl. *-at.* What do you suppose is his object in doing that? *š-ka-ḍḍenn imken ikun muṛaḍu men dak š-ši lli ɛmel?*

to **object to** - *ɛaṛeḍ.*

objection - *muɛaṛaḍa* pl. *-t; maniɛ.* He raised no objection. *ma-ɛmel ḥetta muɛaṛaḍa.* --Do you have any objections? *ɛendek ši-maniɛ?*

obligation - *wažib* pl. *-at.*

observation - **1.** *teqliba* pl. *-t* coll. *teqlab.* He was taken to the hospital for observation. *ddaweh le-ṣ-ṣbiṭaṛ baš iduwwzuh fe-t-teqlab.* **2.** *mulaḥaḍa* pl. *-t.* What did you gather from his observations? *šnu fhemti men l-mulaḥaḍat dyalu?*

to **observe** - **1.** *ḷaḥeḍ.* Did you observe how she reacted? *waš ḷaḥeḍti kif-aš ɛemlet?* **2.** *tebbeɛ.* Everybody must observe these rules. *koll-ši ka-ixeṣṣu itebbeɛ had l-qawanin.* **3.** *raɛa.* What holidays do you observe? *š-men ɛyad ka-traɛiw?*

obstinate - *(lli) ṛaṣu qaṣeḥ.* She's very obstinate. *ṛaṣha qaṣeḥ bezzaf.*

occupation - **1.** *xedma* pl. *-t; ṣenɛa* pl. *-t, ṣnaɛi, ṣnayeɛ.* What's your occupation? *šnu hiya ṣneɛtek?* **2.** *ḥtilal* pl. *-at.* Where were you during the occupation? *fayn konti f-weqt le-ḥtilal?*

to **occupy** - **1.** *ḥtell.* Later on the Americans occupied the town. *men beɛd l-mirikan ḥtellu le-mdina.* **2.** *sken f-.* The house hasn't been occupied for years. *snin hadi ma-sken ḥedd f-had ḍ-ḍaṛ.* **3.** *dda iddi, xda yaxod.* School occupies all of my time. *l-meḍṛaṣa ka-taxod-li weqti kollu.* --Is this seat occupied? *waš had l-korsi muxud?*

to **occur** - *wqeɛ, ḥdet.* When did the accident occur? *fuq-aš weqɛet l-ḥadita?*

**The name occurs twice in this chapter. *l-ʔism mežbud žuž de-l-meṛṛat f-had l-feṣḷ.* --It just didn't occur to me. *ma-ṭahet-li-š f-bali u-kan.* --That would never have occurred to me. *ɛemmeṛha ma-kanet džini l-l-bal.*

ocean - *bḥeṛ* pl. *bḥuṛ, muḥiṭ* pl. *-at.*

o'clock - *fe-l-magana.* The train leaves at seven (o'clock). *l-qiṭaṛ ka-ixṛož fe-s-sebɛa (fe-l-magana).*

October - *ktubeṛ.*

oculist - *ṭbib de-l-ɛeynin.*

odd - **1.** *f-ši-škel.* He's an odd person. *huwa ṛažel f-ši-škel.* --His behavior struck me as being odd. *dak š-ši lli kan ka-yeɛmel žani f-ši-škel.* **2.** *ferda* pl. *fradi.* Have you seen an odd glove anywhere? *waš šefti ši-ferda de-ṣ-ṣebbaɛat f-ši-maḥell?* **3.** *ferdi.* Pick an odd number. *xtaṛ ši-nemra ferdiya.*

odds and ends - *ḥwiyžat, tfitfat.* I still have some odds and ends to take care of. *ma-zal ɛendi ši-ḥwiyžat xeṣṣni nkemmelhom.*

of - **1.** *d-, dyal.* He's the manager of a big firm. *huwa mudir d-waḥed š-šarika kbira.* --It still tastes of it. *ma-zal fih ṭ-ṭiba dyal dak š-ši.* --The sleeves of my coat are wider. *le-kmam d-kebbuṭi ɛṛiḍin.* --Who's the driver of that car? *škun huwa s-suwwag dyal dak ṭ-ṭumubil?* **2.** *men.* The watch is made of gold. *l-magana mṣuwwba men d-dheb.* --She's afraid of him. *ka-txaf mennu.* --Nothing came of it. *ma-ṭelɛet mennha ḥetta ḥaža.* --He's one of us. *huwa waḥed mennna.* **3.** *f-.* I often think of her. *ka-nfekkeṛ fiha šḥal men meṛṛa.* --We lost half of our money. *ḍiyyeɛna n-neṣṣ f-flusna.* --He's very tall compared to the other children of his age. *huwa ṭwil bezzaf be-n-nesba le-d-drari le-x̂ṛin f-sennu.* --What does that remind you of? *f-aš ka-ifekkṛek dak š-ši?* **4.** *b-.* His father died of a heart attack. *ḅḅah mat b-sekta qelbiya.* --Can you take care of it? *waš imken-lek ttkellef biha?* --I've never heard of him. *ɛemmṛi ma-smeɛt bih.* --What is he accused of? *b-aš methum?* **5.** (Often translated by the construct state.) And now we're going to enter the gates of the city. *u-daba ġad ndexlu ɛla biban le-mdina.*

**What became of them? *šnu žṛa-lhom?* --It's five of eight. *hadi t-tmenya ġir qṣem.* --It's a quarter of eight. *hadi t-tmenya llaṛeb.*

off - *men.* The ship anchored three kilometers off shore. *l-baxiṛa weqfet si-tlata de-l-kilumitṛat men š-šeṭṭ.* --He knocked the bottle off the table. *ṭiyyeḥ l-qeṛɛa men ṭ-ṭabḷa.* --The color came off these gloves. *had ṣ-ṣebbaɛat mša mennhom lunhom.*

**She works off and on. *meṛṛa ha-hiya xeddama, meṛṛa ha-hiya galsa.* --June is still three months off. *yunyu ma-zal-lu telt šhuṛ.* --They're very well off. *la-bas ɛlihom* or *huma mxuwwžin mɛa ṛaṣhom.* --Our maid is off today. *l-metɛellma mriyyḥa l-yum.* --The power is off. *tteqṭeɛ ḍ-ḍuw.* --This item has been off the market for a year. *had s-selɛa hadi ɛam ma-ɛawed ḍehṛet fe-ṣ-ṣuq.* --I'm going to have a week off soon. *ġad nɛeṭṭel žemɛa men daba šwiya.*

--The post office isn't far off. *l-bușṭa ma-bɛida-š bezzaf.*

to **offend** - *žṛeḥ, ṭiyyṛu-lu.* I hope I haven't offended you. *ka-ntmenna ma-nkun-š ṭiyyeṛtu-lek.*

offer - *ɛeṛḍ* pl. *ɛṛaḍi.* He made me a good offer. *qeddem-li ɛeṛḍ mezyan.*

to offer - *qeddem l-, ɛṛeḍ ɛla.* He was offered an excellent position. *ɛeṛdu ɛlih mertaba mezyana.*

office - **1.** *mektab* pl. *mkateb.* You can see me in my office. *imken-lek tšufni fe-l-mekteb dyali.* **2.** *ʔidaṛa* pl. *-t; biru* pl. *-wat.* The offices close at five o'clock. *l-ʔidaṛat ka-išeddu fe-l-xemsa.*

**The whole office was invited. *kanu meɛṛuḍin l-muweḍḍafin kollhom.*

officer - *ḍabeṭ* pl. *ḍobbaṭ.* He was an officer during the war. *kan ḍabeṭ f-weqt l-ḥerb.*

official - *ṛeṣmi.* He paid me an official visit. *ẓaṛni ẓyaṛa ṛeṣmiya.*

often - *bezzaf.* Do you see him often? *waš ka-tšufu bezzaf?*

how often - *šḥal men meṛṛa.* How often do you go to the movies? *šḥal men meṛṛa ka-temši le-s-sinima?*

oil - *zit* pl. *zyut.*

to oil - *ziyyet.*

ointment - *dehna* pl. *-t.*

O.K. - **1.** *waxxa.* O.K., I'll come tomorrow. *waxxa, daba nži ġedda.* **2.** *muwafaqa* pl. *-t.* I need his O.K. *xeṣṣni l-muwafaqa dyalu.* **3.** *f-ʔaman llah.* Everything is O.K. now. *koll-ši f-ʔaman llah daba.*

**I'll go along if it's O.K. with you. *nemši mɛakom ila ža ɛla xaṭeṛkom.*

to O.K. - *wafeq ɛla.* He has to O.K. it first. *xeṣṣu iwafeq ɛliha beɛda.*

okra - *mluxiyya.*

old - **1.** *qdim* pl. *qdam.* Is this an old model? *waš hada škel qdim?* **2.** *bali.* I've given away all my clothes. *ḥwayži l-balyin ṣeḍḍeqthom.* **3.** *kbir* pl. *kbaṛ.* She is older than her brother. *hiya kbeṛ men xaha.*

**How old are you? *šḥal f-ɛemṛek?* or *šḥal ɛendek men ɛam?* --He's as old as the hills. *ka-yeɛqel ɛla žedd n-nmel.* --That boy has an old head on his shoulder. *dak l-weld ɛendu ṛ-ṛaṣ.*

to get old - *šref.* He's begun to

get old. *bda išref.*
old man - *Ɛguz* pl. *Ɛgayez.*
old woman - *Ɛguza* pl. *Ɛgayez.*
oleander - *defla.*
to **omit** - *ḥeyyed, ḥdef, zuwwel.*
on - **1.** *Ɛla, fuq.* Put this on the table. *nezzel had š-ši fuq ṭ-ṭabla.* **2.** *Ɛla.* It's a book on animals. *hada ktab Ɛel l-ḥayawanat.* --This is on me. *hadi Ɛliya.* **3.** *b-.* Do you sell on credit? *ka-tbiƐ be-ṭ-ṭelq?* **4.** *f-.* He's on vacation now. *huwa fe-l-Ɛoṭla daba.* --On what day? *fe-š-men nhaṛ?* --Who's on the team? *škun fe-l-feṛqa?* --I live on Mohamed V Avenue. *ka-neskon f-šariƐ muḥemmed l-xamis.* --Is there anything interesting on the radio? *kayna ši-ḥaža muhimma fe-l-ˀidaƐa?* **5.** *Ɛla, f-.* What are your ideas on this subject? *šni hiya ˀafkaṛek f-had l-muḍuƐ?* **6.** *men.* What do they live on? *mn-aš ka-iƐišu?* **7.** *mešƐul.* Is the light on? *waš ḍ-ḍuw mešƐul?*
**Are you open on Friday? *waš ka-tḥell nhaṛ ž-žemƐa?* --I got this on good authority. *had š-ši smeƐtu men meṣdeṛ ṣḥiḥ.* --The house is on fire. *ḍ-ḍaṛ šaƐla fiha l-Ɛafya.* --The race is already on. *le-msabqa bdat beƐda.* --What's on for tonight? *šnu huwa l-beṛnamež l-yum fe-l-lil?* --When do you start on your trip? *fuq-aš ġad tsafeṛ?*
on and on - *bla ḥsuṛ, bla wquf.* That woman talks on and on. *dak le-mṛa ka-tehdeṛ bla wquf.*
once - **1.** *meṛṛa (weḥda), xeṭṛa (weḥda).* I've seen him only once. *šeftu ġir meṛṛa weḥda.* --He feeds the dog once a day. *ka-iwekkel l-kelb meṛṛa fe-n-nhaṛ.* **2.** *hadi šḥal.* This was once the business section. *hadi šḥal had l-maḥell kan huwa l-ḥeyy t-tižari.*
once before - *men qbel, ši-meṛṛa men qbel.* I've been here once before. *kont žit lle-hna ši-meṛṛa men qbel.*
once in a while - *meṛṛa fe-xṭa.* Once in a while I like to take a long trip. *ka-yeƐžebni meṛṛa fe-xṭa neƐmel ši-ṣefṛa ṭwila.*
once more - *Ɛawed, meṛṛa xṛa.*
at once - **1.** *f-meṛṛa.* Everything happened at once. *koll-ši wqeƐ f-meṛṛa.* **2.** *daba, fe-l-ḥin.* Give it to me at once! *Ɛṭih-li fe-l-ḥin!*
one - **1.** *waḥed* f. *weḥda* pl. *weḥdin.* One of us can buy the tickets. *waḥed fina imken-lu iqeṭṭeƐ le-wṛaq.* --I have only one question. *ma-Ɛendi ġir suˀal waḥed.* **2.** *l-waḥed, bnadem.* One can never know. *l-waḥed Ɛemmṛu ma-iqdeṛ yeƐṛef.* **3.** *l-weḥda.* It's almost one (o'clock). *hadi Ɛlayen l-weḥda.*
**That's a tough one! *hadak waḥed men duk ṣ-ṣƐab.* --I prefer the expensive one. *nfeḍḍel l-ġali fihom.* --You're a fine one! *walayenni f-ši-škel nta!*
one at a time - *waḥed b-waḥed* f. *weḥda b-weḥda.*
one of these days - *ši-nhaṛ.* I'll see him one of these days. *daba nšufu ši-nhaṛ.*
that one - *hadak* f. *hadik* pl. *haduk.*
this one - *hada* f. *hadi* pl. *hadu.*
onion - *beṣla* pl. *-t* coll. *bṣeḷ.*
only - **1.** *b-weḥdu.* Am I the only woman here? *waš ana b-weḥdi lli mṛa hna?* **2.** *be-l-ḥeqq.* I was going to buy it, only he wouldn't let me. *kont ġad nešrih be-l-ḥeqq ma-xellani-š.* **3.** *ġir.* If you could only help me! *kun ġir mken-lek tƐawenni!* **4.** *ġir, ma-Ɛada.* This is only for you. *had š-ši ġir lilek b-weḥdek.* --We have only two left. *ma-bqaw-lna ma-Ɛada žuž.* **5.** *ġir yaḷḷah.* I got here only a moment ago. *yaḷḷah hadi ši-šwiya baš wṣeḷt.*
**He's our only child. *huwa l-weld lli Ɛendna.* --She's not only pretty but she's also intelligent. *ma-Ɛendha-š ġir z-zin, zayda Ɛlih ḥetta d-daka.*
open - **1.** *meḥlul, meftuḥ.* He must have come in through the open window. *ma-ikun dxel illa men š-šeṛžem l-meḥlul.* **2.** *waqef, meṭṛuḥ.* That's still an open question. *had s-suˀal ma-zal meṭṛuḥ.* **3.** *mužud.* Is the job still open? *waš dik l-xedma ma-zala mužuda?* **4.** *ḥall.* They're open from nine to six. *huma ḥallin men t-tesƐud le-s-setta.* **5.** *meftuq.* The seam is open. *l-ḥašya meftuqa.*
**We're open all day Sunday. *ka-nḥellu nhaṛ l-ḥedd kollu.* --Why don't you come out in the open and say it? *Ɛlaš ma-tqulha-š b-ṭaytay?* --He's always open to reasonable suggestions. *huwa dima ka-iḥell*

wednih l-le-qtiṛaḥat l-meƐqula.

to open – 1. *ḥell, fteḥ.* Open the door please. *ḥell l-bab Ɛafak.* 2. *bda ibda.* When does the season open? *fuq-aš ġad tebda l-menzla?* 3. *ttḥell.* The door opens easily now. *l-bab ka-ttḥell deġya deġya daba.*

to open onto – *ṭeḷḷ Ɛla, ṭeḷḷeḷ Ɛla.* Our bedroom opens onto the garden. *bit n-nƐas dyalna ka-iṭeḷḷeḷ Ɛel l-Ɛeṛṣa.*

to open wide – *terreƐ.* Open the windows wide! *terreƐ š-šṛažem!*

opening – 1. *teqba* pl. *tqabi.* The opening isn't big enough. *t-teqba ma-kafya-š.* 2. *ftitaḥ* Were you at the opening of the exhibition? *waš konti f-le-ftitaḥ de-l-meƐṛiḍ?* 3. *muḍeƐ xawya* pl. *mwaḍeƐ xawyin.* We'll call you as soon as we have an opening. *ġir tkun Ɛendna muḍeƐ xawya nƐeyyṭu-lek.*

to **operate** – 1. *šeqq, Ɛmel Ɛamaliya (žiṛaḥiya), fteḥ.* The doctor says he'll have to operate. *ṭ-ṭbib qal-lek lazem yeƐmel Ɛamaliya žiṛaḥiya.* 2. *xeddem, meššа.* How do you operate this machine? *kif-aš ka-txeddem had l-makina?*

to operate on – *fteḥ l-, šeqq l-, Ɛmel Ɛamaliya (žiṛaḥiya) l-.* The doctor says he'll have to operate on her. *ṭ-ṭbib qal-lek lazem ifteḥ-lha.*

operation – 1. *fetḥa* pl. *-t, Ɛamaliya* pl. *-t.* That's her third operation. *hadi l-fetḥa dyalha t-talta.* 2. *deqqa* pl. *-t.* One machine does the whole process in a single operation. *makina weḥda ka-teƐmel koll-ši f-deqqa weḥda.* 3. *xedma.* This line was only recently put into operation. *had l-xeṭṭ Ɛad qṛib hadi baš daruh l-l-xedma.*

opinion – 1. *naḍaṛ, naḍaṛiya.* In my opinion it was a waste of time. *f-naḍaṛi dak š-ši kan teḍyiƐ l-weqt u-xḷaṣ.* --I'm of another opinion. *Ɛendi naḍaṛiya xṛa.* 2. *naṣiḥa* pl. *-t, naṣaʔiḥ.* We'll have to get the opinion of an expert. *ġad ixeṣṣna naxdu naṣiḥt ši-waḥed mƐellem.*

opponent – *mḍaḍḍ* pl. *-in, xṣim* pl. *xoṣman.*

opportunity – 1. *furṣa* pl. *-t, furaṣ.* When will you have an opportunity to see him? *fuq-aš ġad tkun Ɛendek ši-furṣa baš tšufu?* 2. *munasaba* pl. *-t.* This is a big opportunity for you. *hadi munasaba Ɛendek haʔila.*

opposite – 1. *Ɛeks.* That's just the opposite of what I meant. *dak š-ši tamam Ɛeks ma bġit nqul.* 2. *axoṛ* f. *xṛa* pl. *xṛin.* He came from the opposite direction. *ža men ž-žiha le-xṛa.* 3. *qbalt.* We live opposite the library. *ka-nseknu qbalt l-mektaba.*

opposition – *muƐaṛaḍa* pl. *-t, muqawama* pl. *-t.* He's joined the opposition. *dxel fe-l-muƐaṛaḍa.* --The proposal met with unexpected opposition. *le-qtiṛaḥ žbeṛ muƐaṛaḍa ḥetta waḥed ma-kan nawi biha.*

or – *wla, wella, aw.* He's coming today or tomorrow. *ġa-iži l-yum wella ġedda.*

**Hurry up or you'll be late. *ṭḷeq ṛaṣek la-imši Ɛlik l-ḥal.*

either ... or – *ʔimma ... ʔimma, ʔimma ... wella.* I'll come either today or tomorrow. *daba nži ʔimma l-yum ʔimma ġedda.*

Oran – *wehṛan.*

native of Oran – *wihṛani, wehṛani* adj. pl. *-yen,* n. pl. *hel wehṛan.*

orange – 1. *limuna* pl. *-t* coll. *limun; letšina* pl. *-t* coll. *letšin.* How much are the oranges? *be-šḥal l-letšin?* 2. *renži.* She bought an orange dress. *šrat keswa renži.*

orchard – *Ɛeṛṣa* pl. *-t, Ɛṛaṣi.*

orchestra – 1. *žewq* pl. *žwaq.* Our orchestra is giving twelve concerts this summer. *l-žewq dyalna ġad yeƐmel ṭnašeṛ ḥefla had ṣ-ṣif.* 2. *sefli* pl. *sfali.* Are there any seats left in the orchestra? *ma-zalin ši-mwaḍeƐ xawyin fe-s-sefli?*

order – 1. *ʔamṛ* pl. *ʔawamir.* Is this a request or an order? *waš hada ṭaḷab wella ʔamṛ?* --I'm just following orders. *ma-ana ġir mtebbeƐ l-ʔawamir.* 2. *ṭaḷab* pl. *-at.* They gave me an order for twelve dozen eggs. *Ɛemlu-li ṭaḷab Ɛla ṭnaš-el ẓina de-l-biḍ.* 3. *niḍam.* Order was quickly restored. *deġya ṛžeƐ n-niḍam.* 4. *tertib.* Please put these papers back in their proper order. *Ɛafak ṛežžeƐ had le-wṛaq fe-t-tertib lli kanu fih.* 5. *gṭaṛ* pl. *goṭṛan.* Three orders of fish please. *tlata de-l-goṭṛan de-l-ḥut men feḍḷek.*

**Line up in order of height. *trettbu Ɛla ḥsab ṭuḷkom.* --I disposed of it in short order. *feḍḍitha f-ṛemša de-l-Ɛeyn.*

in order – 1. *f-maḥellu.* Your

remark is quite in order.
l-mulaḥaḍa dyalek ẓat f-maḥellha.
2. *mneḍḍem.* His papers are in
order. *le-wṛaq dyalu mneḍḍmin.*
   in order to - *baš.* I've come
from Fez in order to see you. *ǧit
men fas baš nšufek.*
   to be out of order - **1.** *xṣeṛ.*
The fan is out of order. *ṛ-ṛuwaḥa
xaṣra.* **2.** *fsed n-niḍam.* You're
out of order. *ṛak fased n-niḍam.*
   to put in order - *neḍḍem, Ɛewweṭ,
retteb.* I've put everything in
order. *ṛani neḍḍemt koll-ši.*
   to order - **1.** *ʔameṛ.* Who ordered
you to do this? *škun lli ʔamṛek
teƐmel had š-ši?* **2.** *ṭ̣leb, Ɛeyyeṭ
Ɛla.* Order the taxi for six o'clock.
Ɛeyyeṭ Ɛel ṭ-ṭaksi le-s-setta.
--This is not what I ordered. *had
š-ši ma-ši huwa lli ṭlebt.*
   to order around - *thekkem f-,
Ɛebba u-ǧab f-.* Stop ordering me
around. *baṛaka u-ma nta tƐebbi
u-dǧib fiya.*
ordinary - *Ɛadi, meṭluq.* He's just
an ordinary craftsman. *huwa ġir
ṣnayƐi Ɛadi.*
   out of the ordinary - *xaṛeq l-Ɛada.*
His competence is quite out of the
ordinary. *l-qabiliya dyalu xaṛeq
l-Ɛada bezzaf.*
ore - *meƐden* pl. *mƐaden, maƐadin.*
to organize - *neḍḍem, Ɛewweṭ.* The
whole thing was poorly organized.
*š-ši kollu kan mneḍḍem men ʔaflas
ma ikun.*
   **I'll have to get my work better
organized. *ka-ixeṣṣni nzid nneḍḍem
xdemti šwiya.* --We'll call you up
as soon as we get ourselves organized. *ġir nneḍḍem ṛyuṣna nḍeṛbu-lek
t-tilifun.*
original - **1.** *ʔeṣli.* The original of
this picture doesn't exist any more.
*t-teṣwiṛa l-ʔeṣliya Ɛla-š muxuda.
hadi ma-bqat-š mužuda.* **2.** *luwwel.*
The original plan was altogether
different. *l-mešṛuƐ l-luwwel kan
fe-škel axor tamamen.*
originally - *fe-l-luwwel.*
orphan - *itim* pl. *itama.*
other - *axoṛ* f. *x̂ṛa* pl. *x̂ṛin.* How
do I get to the other side of the
river? *kif-aš nduz le-ǧ-ǧiha le-x̂ṛa
de-l-wad?* --Do you have any other
books? *waš Ɛendek ši-ktuba
x̂ṛin?*
   **I can't tell one from the other.
ma-ka-neƐṛef-š hada men hadak.
--Do you see each other every day?

waš ka-ttšawfu koll nhaṛ? --They
have to help each other. *xeṣṣhom
itƐawnu.* --The meetings are held
every other Sunday. *le-štimaƐat ka-
ikunu ḥedd iyeh u-ḥedd la.* --They
have nothing to do with each other.
ma-binathom walu. --I saw your
friend the other day. *šeft ṣaḥbek
dak n-nhaṛ.*
ought - *xeṣṣ.* You ought to tell him.
xeṣṣek tqulha-lu. --He ought to
have written to us. *kan xeṣṣu
ikteb-lna.* --You ought to be
ashamed of yourself. *xeṣṣek teḥfeṛ
ḥefṛa u-tteṛma fiha.*
ounce - *neṣṣ wqiya.*
out - **1.** *meḍfi, ḍafi.* The lights are
out. *le-ḍwaw meḍfiyin.* **2.** *xaṛez.*
They were out when we called them.
*kanu xaṛžin melli ḍrebna-lhom
t-tilifun.*
   **The raise is definitely out.
*z-zyada ma-bqat ka-ittesmeƐ Ɛliha
ḥess tamamen.* --We send our laundry
out. *ka-ndefƐu le-ḥwayež dyalna
itṣebbnu Ɛla beṛṛa.* --The new edition isn't out yet. *ma-zala
ma-xeṛžet ṭ-ṭebƐa ž-ždida.* --I've
added it twice and I'm still out
three dirhams. *hadi t-tanya men
meṛṛa w-ana ka-nžmeƐ le-ḥsab
u-ma-zal xaṣṣani tlata de-d-drahem.*
--She's only out for a good time.
ma-Ɛeyniha ġir f-le-mlahya.
--You're an out and out liar. *nta
keddab ma-f-wežh-ek ḥ-ya.*
   out of - *men.* He came out of the
house. *xrež men ḍ-ḍaṛ.* --I did it
out of pity. *Ɛmeltha men le-mḥenna.*
   **We're out of this brand.
tqaḍat-lna had l-Ɛeyna. --It's too
cold to sit out of doors. *l-ḥal
bared bezzaf Ɛel le-glas Ɛla beṛṛa.*
to outgrow - *kber Ɛla.* The children
have outgrown their clothes.
d-drari kebru Ɛla ḥwayežhom.
outlet - *mešṛeb* pl. *mšaṛeb.* The lake
has two outlets. *ḍ-ḍaya Ɛendha žuž
d-le-mšaṛeb.*
   **Children must have some outlet
for their energies. *d-drari
la-bodda-lhom men ši-kifiya baš
ižahdu.*
outline - **1.** *xeṭṭ* pl. *xṭuṭ.* We could
see the outlines of the mountains
in spite of the mist. *waxxa kanet
ḍ-ḍbaba konna ka-nšufu xṭuṭ ž-žbal.*
2. *mulexxaṣ* pl. *-at.* Have you made
an outline of what you're going to
say yet? *ktebti beƐda ši-mulexxaṣ
d-dak š-ši lli ġad tqul wella
ma-zal?*

outrageous - *ḍalem, metƐeddi.*
outside - **1.** *beṛṛa.* It's cold outside. *kayen l-berd beṛṛa.* **2.** *xaṛež Ɛla.* He lives outside the city. *ka-iskon xaṛež Ɛel le-mdina.* **3.** *xaṛiž.* The house looks very pretty from the outside. *ḍ-ḍaṛ ka-tban mezyana bezzaf men l-xaṛiž.*
**I wouldn't trust anyone here outside of you. *ma-neƐmel t-tiqa ḥetta f-ši-waḥed men ġirek hna.*
oven - *feṛṛan* pl. *-at, fṛaṛen.*
over - **1.** *fuq.* Your jacket is hanging over the chair. *kebbuṭek mƐelleq fuq š-šelya.* --His office is located over mine. *l-mekteb dyalu ža fuq dyali.* **2.** *Ɛla.* Don't pull the cover over your head. *ma-džbed-š le-ġṭa Ɛla ṛaṣek.*
**When is the show over? *fuq-aš ġad ifeḍḍi l-ḥefla.* --Is it over three kilometers? *waš zayed Ɛla tlata de-l-kilumitṛat?* --The lecture was over my head. *l-muḥaḍaṛa kanet Ɛalya Ɛliya bezzaf.* --I've looked all over. *qellebt f-koll mudeƐ* or *ma-xellit fayn ma-qellebt.* --She blushed all over. *ḥmaṛet men ṛaṣha ḥetta l-režliha.*
over and over again - *meṛṛa Ɛla xetha.* He asked the same question over and over again. *nefs s-suʔal Ɛṭah u-Ɛawdu meṛṛa Ɛla xetha.*
to get over - *nsa insa.* He certainly got over his wife's death quickly. *deġya deġya nsa mut mṛatu.*
to go over - **1.** *mša imši.* I'm going over to his house for an hour or so. *ġad nemši nduwwez Ɛendu ši-saƐa fe-ḍ-ḍaṛ.* **2.** *nžeḥ.* Do you think my play will go over? *waš ka-ḍḍenn t-temtiliya dyali ġa-tenžeḥ?* **3.** *ṛažeƐ.* Let's go over the details once more. *yaḷḷah Ɛawed nṛažƐu t-tafaṣil.*
overcoat - *baḷṭu* pl. *-yat.*
to **overcome** - *tġelleb Ɛla.* She had many difficulties to overcome. *kanu Ɛendha Ɛadad de-ṣ-ṣuƐubat ka-ixeṣṣha ttġelleb Ɛlihom.*
to **overdo** - *ketter men.* I'm allowed to play tennis as long as I don't overdo it. *mesmuḥ-li nelƐeb t-tinis ila ma-kettert-š mennu bezzaf.*
**He always overdoes it. *dima ka-ibaleġ.*
overnight - *f-lila, deġya deġya.* He got rich overnight. *ṛžeƐ tažer f-lila.*
to stay overnight - *bat ibat, duwwez l-lil.* I intend to stay there overnight. *mƐewwel ġad nduwwez l-lil temma.*
oversight - *nesya* pl. *-t; shu.* That must have been an oversight. *hada ma-huwa ġir shu.*
to **oversleep** - *xmer be-n-nƐas, ṭal iṭul fe-n-nƐas.*
to **owe** - (the creditor is the subject and the debtor the object of the verb *sal isal*). How much do I owe you? *šḥal ka-tsalni?* --You owe me five dirhams. *ka-nsalek xemsa de-d-drahem.*
**She owes everything to him. *dak š-ši lli Ɛendha kollu b-feḍḷu huwa.*
owl - *muka* pl. *-t.*
own - (additional personal pronoun for emphasis). Are these your own things? *waš had le-ḥwayež dyalek nta?*
**Can I have a room of my own? *waš imken-li ikun Ɛendi bit liya weḥdi?* --Then I'll do it on my own hook. *Ɛla had l-qibal ġad ndebbeṛ l-ṛaṣi.*
on one's own - *qadd b-ṛaṣu, qayem b-ṛaṣu.* He's been on his own ever since he was sixteen. *melli kanet Ɛendu setṭaš-el Ɛam u-huwa qayem b-ṛaṣu.*
to own - *mlek, ksab.* Who owns this property? *škun lli malek had l-ʔeṛḍ?*
owner - *mul* pl. *mwalin.*
ox - *tuṛ* pl. *tiran.*
oyster - *meḥḥaṛa* pl. *-t* coll. *meḥḥaṛ.*

P

pace - *mši.* I can't keep pace with him. *ma-ka-neqḍeṛ-š ntqadd mƐah f-le-mši.*
to set the pace - *mešša.* He sets the pace. *huwa lli ka-imešši.*
to pace up and down - *ṭḷeƐ u-hbeṭ, mša u-ža.* He paced up and down the room. *kan fe-l-bit ṭaḷeƐ habeṭ.*
Pacific (Ocean) - *l-muḥiṭ l-hadi.*
pack - **1.** *ḥezma* pl. *-t, ḥzami.* The donkeys were loaded down with heavy packs. *Ɛemlu ḥezmat tqila l-le ḥmiṛ*

Ɛla ḍheṛhom. **2.** *rbaƐa* pl. *-t.* They went at the food like a pack of hungry wolves. *ṭaḥu fe-l-makla bḥal rbaƐa de-d-dyab.* **3.** *Ɛeṛma* pl. *-t, Ɛṛaṛem, belƐa* pl. *-t.* That's a pack of lies! *Ɛeṛma d-le-kdub hadi.*

pack of cards - *kaṛṭa* pl. *-t, kwaṛeṭ.* Where is the new pack of cards? *fayn l-kaṛṭa ž-ždida?*

to pack - **1.** *žmeƐ.* Have you packed your trunk yet? *žmeƐti šaneṭṭek wella ma-zal?* --My things are all packed. *ḥwayži mežmuƐin.* **2.** *šedd.* These dates were packed in Iraq. *had t-tmeṛ mešdud fe-l-Ɛiṛaq.* **3.** *ṛeqqed.* This fish is packed in oil. *had l-ḥut mṛeqqed fe-z-zit.* **4.** *dḥes.* The station was packed this morning. *le-mḥeṭṭa kanet medḥusa had ṣ-ṣbaḥ.*

to pack in - *ddaḥes.* We were packed in like sardines. *konna meddaḥsin bḥal l-ḥut.*

to pack into - *Ɛeṛṛem.* They shouldn't pack us into the train this way. *ma-Ɛendha meƐna iƐeṛṛmuna fe-l-mašina hakda.*

to pack up - *žmeƐ qžaqlu.* He packed up his things and left. *žmeƐ qžaqlu u-mša.*

package - **1.** *ṛezma* pl. *-t, ṛzem, ṛzami.* The mailman brought a package for you. *l-feṛṛaq žab-lek waḥed ṛ-ṛezma.* **2.** *xenša* pl. *-t, xnaši.* Do you sell the coffee loose or in packages? *ka-tbiƐu l-qehwa meḥlula aw f-le-xnaši?*

page - *ṣefḥa* pl. *-t.* The book is two hundred pages long. *le-ktab fih myatayn ṣefḥa.*

pail - *ṣṭeḷ* pl. *ṣṭuḷa.* Get a pail of water! *hezz ṣṭeḷ de-l-ma.*

pain - *ḥṛiq, wžeƐ.* I feel a sharp pain in my back. *biya ḥṛiq kbir f-ḍehṛi.*

to take pains - *tƐeddeb, tmerret.* She takes great pains with her work. *ka-tƐeddeb bezzaf fe-xdemtha.*

painful - **1.** *(lli) ka-iqeṣṣeḥ.* Was the operation very painful? *waš l-Ɛamaliya kanet ka-tqeṣṣeḥ?* **2.** *(lli) ka-iqeṭṭeƐ l-qelb, (lli) ka-iʔellem.* It's painful to watch him. *š-šufa fih ka-tqeṭṭeƐ l-qelb.*

painfully - *b-tamara, be-d-dreƐ.* Our progress was painfully slow. *konna yaḷḷah ka-nkeḥzu b-tamara.*

paint - *ṣbaġa* pl. *-t, ṣbayeġ.* The paint is still wet. *ṣ-ṣbaġa ma-zala xeḍṛa.*

to paint - **1.** *ṣbeġ.* They painted their house white. *ṣebġu ḍaṛhom biḍa.* **2.** *rsem.* She paints in oil. *ka-tersem be-z-zit.*

painter - **1.** *ressam* pl. *-a.* He's a famous painter. *ressam mešhuṛ hadak.* **2.** *ṣebbaġ* pl. *-a.* The painters will be through with the kitchen by tomorrow. *ṣ-ṣebbaġa ġedda ġad ikunu salaw l-meṭbex.*

painting - *resm.* That's a beautiful painting. *resm mezyan hadak.*

pair - *zuža* pl. *-t, zwež.* I bought myself a pair of gloves. *šrit l-ṛaṣi zuža de-ṣ-ṣebbeƐat.*

pair of scissors - *mqeṣṣ,* pl. *mquṣa.*

palace - *qṣeṛ* pl. *qṣuṛa.*

pale - **1.** *ṣfeṛ.* Did you notice his pale complexion? *šefti lunu kif ṣfeṛ?* **2.** *meftuḥ.* It's a pale blue. *ẓṛeq meftuḥ.*

to turn pale - *ṣfaṛ, ṛžeƐ ṣfeṛ.* When he heard that, he turned pale. *mnayn smeƐ dak š-ši ṛžeƐ ṣfeṛ.*

Palestine - *fiḷeṣṭin.*

Palestinian - *fiḷeṣṭini.*

palm - **1.** *nexla* pl. *-t* coll. *nxel.* These palms grow as high as thirty meters. *had n-nxel ka-yuṣeḷ ḥetta le-tlatin miter d-le-Ɛlu.* **2.** *keff l-idd* pl. *kfuf l-iddin.* My palm is all calloused. *keff iddi kollu ḥṛeš.*

to palm off - *zreƐ.* He palmed off his old books on me. *zreƐ-li duk le-ktuba l-balyen dyalu.*

pan - *meqla* pl. *mqali.* Did you wash the pots and pans too? *ġselti ḥetta ṭ-ṭnažeṛ u-le-mqali?*

pane - *zaža* pl. *-t* coll. *zaž.*

panic - *reƐba* pl. *-t.*

to **pant** - *lhet.* He came panting up the stairs. *ṭḷeƐ fe-ḍ-ḍṛuž ka-ilhet.*

pantry - *bit l-Ɛewla* pl. *byut l-Ɛewla.*

pants - *serwal* pl. *srawel.* I have to have my pants pressed. *ka-ixeṣṣni neƐṭi serwali itḥedded.*

paper - **1.** *kaġiṭ* pl. *kwaġeṭ.* Do you have a sheet of paper? *Ɛendek ši-weṛqa de-l-kaġiṭ?* **2.** *weṛqa* pl. *-t, wṛaq.* Some important papers are missing. *ši-wṛaq muhimma ka-ixeṣṣu.* **3.** *žarida* pl. *-t, žaraʔid.* Where is today's paper? *fayn l-žarida de-l-yum?*

paperweight - *qebbaṭa* pl. *-t.*

parachute - *mḍeḷḷ* pl. *mḍuḷa.*

parade - *stiƐṛaḍ* pl. *-at.*

paradise - *ženna* pl. *-t.*

paragraph - *feqṛa* pl. *-t.*

parallel - **1.** *xeṭṭ metsawi* pl. *xṭuṭ metsawyen.* Draw a parallel to this line. *ṣeṭṭeṛ xeṭṭ metsawi mƐa hada.* 2. *metsawi.* The road runs parallel to the river. *ṭ-ṭṛiq mašya metsawya mƐa l-wad.*

paralysis - *bṭeḷ, zḥef.*

to **paralyze** - **1.** *rezzem, beṭṭeḷ, qeƐƐed.* She's been paralyzed ever since she's had that stroke. *men lli nezlet Ɛliha dak l-madda u-hiya mrezzma.* **2.** *ḥṣeṛ, weqqef.* Traffic was completely paralyzed. *tteḥṣeṛ d-dwaz u-ṛ-ṛžuƐ tamamen.*

to be paralyzed - *rzem, tqeƐƐed.* I was paralyzed with fear. *rzemt be-l-xewf.*

parasol - *mḍeḷḷ* pl. *mḍuḷa.*

parcel - *ṛeẓma* pl. *ṛẓem, ṛẓami.* You forgot your parcels. *rak nsiti ṛẓamik.*

parcel post - *ṛeẓma baridiya, ḥezma baridiya.* I'm sending it by parcel post. *ṛ-ana mṣifeṭha-lek f-ḥezma baridiya.*

parcel-post window - *maḥell l-ḥezmat l-baridiya.* Where is the parcel-post window? *fayn maḥell l-ḥezmat l-baridiya?*

pardon - *smaḥa* pl. *-t.* He was refused a pardon. *ma-ttqeblet-ši smaḥtu.*

**I beg your pardon. *smeḥ-li a sidi.*

to pardon - **1.** *smeḥ, Ɛfa yeƐfi.* The president pardoned him at the last moment. *ṛ-ṛaʔis Ɛfah f-ʔaxir saƐa.* **2.** *smeḥ.* Pardon me! What time is it, please? *smeḥ-li b-le-fḍel mennek, šḥal hadi fe-s-saƐa?*

to **pare** - *qeššeṛ.* Shall I pare an apple for you? *nqeššeṛ-lek ši-teffaḥa?*

parents - *waldin,* (*waldi-* before possessive pronoun endings).

Paris - *bariz.*

park - *Ɛeṛṣa* pl. *-t, Ɛṛaṣi.*

to park - *ḥṣeṛ, weqqef.* You can park your car here. *imken-lek tweqqef siyaṛtek hnaya.*

parlor - *ṣaḷun* pl. *-at.*

parrot - *babġiyu* pl. *babġiyat.*

parsley - *mƐednus.*

part - *ṭeṛf* pl. *ṭṛaf.* This little screw is a very important part of the machine. *had l-lwileb ṭeṛf muhimm bezzaf f-had l-makina.*

parts - *žwayeh.* I haven't traveled much in these parts. *ma-ṣafeṛt-ši bezzaf f-had ž-žwayeh.*

for my part, for your part, etc. *men žihti, men žihtek,* etc. I for my part have no objection. *men žihti ana ma-Ɛendi maniƐ.*

for the most part - *ktir-ši.*

in part - *ši-šwiya.* I agree with you in part. *ana mettafeq mƐak ši-šwiya.*

part of the country - *žiha d-le-blad* pl. *žwayeh d-le-blad.* What part of the country do you come from? *mnayna žiha d-le-blad nta?*

spare part - *ṭeṛf ḥtiyaṭi* pl. *ṭṛaf ḥtiyaṭiya.* Can you get spare parts for your car? *imken-lek tḥeṣṣeḷ Ɛla ṭṛaf ḥtiyaṭiya siyaṛtek?*

to take part - *šarek.* Are you going to take part in the discussion? *ġadi tšarek fe-l-munaqaša?*

to take someone's part - *xda yaxod rḥebt ši-waḥed.* He always takes his brother's part. *dima ka-yaxod rḥebt xah.*

to part - *ttefṛeq.* They parted as friends. *ttfeṛqu ṣḥab.*

to part one's hair - *qṣem šeƐṛu, fṛeq šeƐṛu.* He parts his hair on the left side. *ha-ifṛeq šeƐṛu Ɛel l-iṣeṛ.*

to part with - *ṭḷeq men.* I wouldn't part with that book for any price. *ma-nṭḷeq-ši men dak le-ktab b-ʔeyy taman.*

partial - (*lli*) *ka-ifṛeq,* (*lli*) *ka-yeƐmel l-ferz,* (*lli*) *ka-yeƐmel l-wežhiyat.* He tries not to be partial. *ka-iḥawel ma-yeƐmel-ši l-wežhiyat.*

to be partial to - *feḍḍeḷ.* He's always been partial to his youngest daughter. *dima kan ka-ifeḍḍeḷ bentu ṣ-ṣġiṛa.*

partially - *ši-šwiya.* You're partially right. *mƐak l-ḥeqq ši-šwiya.*

particle - *ḥebba* pl. *-t, ḥbub.* There is not a particle of truth in that story. *ḥebba de-l-ḥaqiqa ma-kayna-ši f-dak le-ḥkaya.*

particular - **1.** *tefṣiḷ* pl. *tafaṣiḷ.* For further particulars write to the publishers. *ila bġiti tafaṣiḷ kteṛ men had š-ši kteb le-ṣḥab le-mṭebƐa.* **2.** *xaṣṣ, xuṣuṣi.* Is he a particular friend of yours? *waš hada ṣaḥbek xuṣuṣi?* **3.** *be-l-xuṣuṣ.* This particular dress costs more. *had l-lebsa be-l-xuṣuṣ ka-teswa kteṛ.* **4.** *mbeƐkek.* My husband is very particular about his food. *ṛažli mbeƐkek bezzaf fe-l-makla.*

in particular - *be-l-xuṣuṣ.* I remember one man in particular. *ka-neƐqel Ɛla waḥed ṛ-ṛažel be-l-xuṣuṣ.*

particularly - *be-l-xuṣuṣ, be-l-ʔaxeṣṣ.*

He's particularly interested in science. *huwa ka-ihtemm be-l-ʔaxeṣṣ be-l-ɛilm.*

partner – **1.** *šrik* pl. *šerkan.* My partner is coming back tomorrow. *šriki ṛažeɛ ġedda.* **2.** *ṣaḥeb* pl. *ṣḥab.* My partner and I have been winning every game. *ana u-ṣaḥbi rbeḥna f-koll ṭeṛḥ.*

partridge – *ḥežla* pl. *-t* coll *ḥžel.*

party – **1.** *ḥizeb* pl. *ʔeḥzab.* What party do you belong to? *fe-š-men ḥizeb nta?* **2.** *meddaɛi* pl. *meddaɛyen.* Neither of the two parties appeared at the session. *ma-ḍheṛ fe-l-gelsa la-l-meddaɛi l-luwel wala t-tani.* **3.** *ḥefla* pl. *-t, ḥfali.* She likes to give parties. *ka-yeɛžebha teɛmel l-ḥeflat.*

**I won't be a party to that. *š-bini u-bin dak š-ši?*

pass – **1.** *ṭṛiyqa* pl. *-t.* The pass is snowed under in winter. *ṭ-ṭṛiyqa ka-tkun mġeṭṭya be-t-telž fe-l-berd.* **2.** *tesriḥ* pl. *tsareḥ.* You'll need a pass to get by the gate. *ka-ixeṣṣek tesriḥ baš dduz fe-l-bab.*

to pass – **1.** *qbel.* The bill was passed unanimously. *qeblu ḍ-ḍahiṛ be-l-ʔižmaɛ.* **2.** *nžeḥ f-.* Did you pass your examination? *waš nžeḥti fe-mtiḥanek?* **3.** *daz iduz.* The exam was hard, but almost all of us passed. *le-mtiḥan kan ṣɛib, be-l-ḥeqq ɛlayen koll-ši daz.* **4.** *duwwez, mekkel.* Will you please pass the bread? *men fedḷek mekkel-li l-xobz.* **5.** *qal iqul la.* It's your turn, I passed. *nubtek, ana qolt la.* **6.** *qteɛ f-.* You passed the red light. *ṛak qteɛti fe-ḍ-ḍuw le-hmeṛ.* **7.** *daz iduz ɛla.* I pass this bank every day. *koll nhaṛ ka-nduz ɛla had l-ḅenk.*

to pass around – *ḍuwweṛ.* They passed the tea-pot around. *ḍuwwṛu l-berrad.*

to pass away – *mat imut.* Her mother passed away last week. *immaha matet ž-žemɛa l-fayta.*

to pass by – *daz iduz ḥda.* He passed right by me without seeing me. *daz ḥdaya u-ma-šafni-š.*

to pass judgment on – *ḥkem ɛla.* Don't pass judgment too quickly on him. *ma-teḥkem-ši ɛlih deġya.*

to pass out – *sxef.* A lot of people passed out from the heat. *bezzaf de-n-nas sexfu be-ṣ-ṣehd.*

to pass sentence – *ḥkem, qeṛṛeṛ le-ḥkam.* The court will pass sentence today. *l-meḥkama ġad teḥkem l-yum.*

to pass through – **1.** *qṭeɛ men.* You can't pass through here. *ma-imken-lkom-š tqeṭɛu men hna.* **2.** *duwwez men.* Pass the rope through here. *duwwez ṭ-ṭwal men hna.*

to pass up – *menneɛ.* You ought not to pass up an opportunity like that. *ma-xeṣṣek-ši tmenneɛ furṣa hakdak.*

to be passed – *daz iduz.* The buckets were passed from man to man *ṣ-ṣṭuḷa dazu men ṛažel l-ṛažel.*

passable – *dayez.* This work is passable. *had l-xedma dayza.*

passage – **1.** *medwez* pl. *mdawez, nbeḥ* pl. *nbuḥa.* He had to go through a dark passage. *la-bodda kan baš iduz men waḥed n-nbeḥ meḍlam.* **2.** *qeṭɛa* pl. *-t, qṭaɛi.* He read us an interesting passage from his book. *qṛa ɛlina waḥed l-qeṭɛa muhimma men ktabu.* **3.** *ṣefṛa* pl. *-t.* I've made the passage eight times. *ɛmelt dak ṣ-ṣefṛa tmenya de-l-meṛṛat.*

passenger – *mṣafeṛ* pl. *mṣafṛin.*

passer-by – *waḥed dayez* pl. *dayzin.* A passer-by must have picked it up. *ši-waḥed dayez ṛah rfedha.*

passing – **1.** *mut.* The whole nation mourned his passing. *le-blad kollha ḥeznet l-mutu.* **2.** *(lli) ka-iduz, dayez.* That's just a passing fancy with her. *hada ġir ḥal ka-iduz ɛliha.* **3.** *metweṣṣeṭ.* I got passing grades in all my subjects. *qbeṭṭ nuqaṭ metweṣṣṭa fe-l-mawadd kollha.*

in passing – *ʔiyyeh beɛda.* In passing I'd like to say that ... *ʔiyyeh beɛda, bġit nqul-lek billa...*

passion – *wlaɛa* pl. *-t.* He has a passion for music. *ɛendu wlaɛa de-l-musiqa.*

past – **1.** *maḍi, zman.* That's a thing of the past. *had š-ši dyal l-maḍi.* **2.** *fayet, lli daz, lli fat.* Where were you this past week? *fayn konti ž-žemɛa l-fayta?* **3.** *(lli) daz.* The worst part of the trip is past. *ʔafles ṭaṛaf de-ṣ-ṣfeṛ daz.*

**It's five minutes past twelve. *hadi ṭ-ṭnaš u-qṣem.* --It's twenty minutes past twelve. *hadi ṭ-ṭnaš u-tulut.* --I wouldn't put it past him. *ma-nkeddbu-š.* --It's way past bedtime. *tɛeddina weqt n-nɛas lhih.*

in the past – *men qbel, bekri.* That has often happened in the past.

dak š-ši kan saƐa saƐa ka-yuqeƐ men qbel.

to walk past - *daz iduz ḥda, daz iduz qeddam.* He walked right past me without seeing me. *daz qeddami u-ma-šafni-š.*

paste - *ġṛa* pl. *-t, leṣqa* pl. *-t.* I'll have to buy some paper and paste. *ġad ixeṣṣni nešri l-kaġiṭ u-le-ġṛa.*

to paste - *leṣṣeq.* Paste these labels on the jars. *leṣṣeq had le-bṭayeq Ɛel l-Ɛelbat.*

pastime - *mlahya* pl. *-t, mlahi.*

pastry - *ḥelwa* pl. *-t, ḥlawi.*

pasture - *meṛƐa* pl. *mṛaƐi, meṛteƐ* pl. *mṛateƐ.* Are the cows still in the pasture? *ma-zalin le-bgeṛ fe-l-meṛƐa?*

to **pat** - **1.** *ṭebbel.* He patted him encouragingly on the shoulder. *ṭebbel-lu Ɛla ketfu u-šežžƐu.* **2.** *melles Ɛla.* She patted the dog. *mellset Ɛel l-kelb.*

patch - *ṛeqƐa* pl. *-t, ṛqaƐi.* I'll have to put a new patch on. *xeṣṣni neƐmel ṛeqƐa xṛa.* **2.** *želda* pl. *-t, žlud.* He wore a patch over his eye for days. *modda u-huwa Ɛamel želda Ɛla Ɛeynih.*

to patch - *ṛeqqeƐ.* Mother patched my trousers. *mmi ṛeqqƐet-li serwali.*

**Have they patched up their quarrel yet? *tṣalḥu wella ma-zalin?*

patent - *ṛoxṣa* pl. *-t.* I've applied for a patent on my invention. *qeddemt ṭalab l-ṛoxṣa l-le-ktišaf dyali.*

path - *ṭṛiyqa* pl. *-t.* A narrow path leads to the river. *waḥed ṭ-ṭṛiyqa ḍwiyqa ka-teddi l-l-wad.*

patience - *ṣbeṛ.*

patient - **1.** *mṛiḍ* pl. *meṛḍa.* How's the patient today? *kif-en huwa le-mṛiḍ l-yum?* --There were two hundred patients in the hospital at that time. *kanu myatayn de-l-meṛḍa fe-l-mustešfa f-dak l-weqt.* **2.** *ṣebbaṛ.* He's very patient. *huwa ṣebbaṛ bezzaf.*

patriot - *waṭani* pl. *-yin.*

patrol - *Ɛessa* pl. *-t.* We sent a patrol to reconnoiter. *ṣifeṭna l-Ɛessa l-temma le-t-teḥqiq.*

to patrol - *Ɛess, ḥḍa yeḥḍi.* A policeman patrols these streets all night long. *kayen šoṛṭi ka-iƐess Ɛla had z-znaqi l-lil kollu.*

pattern - **1.** *škel* pl. *škal, škula; zuwaqa* pl. *-t.* This rug has a pretty pattern. *had ẓ-ẓeṛbiya fiha zuwaqa mezyana.* **2.** *fṣaḷa* pl. *-t.* Where did you get the pattern for your dress? *mnayn xditi le-fṣaḷa de-ksuwtek?*

pause - *ṛaḥa* pl. *-t, modda de-ṛ-ṛaḥa* pl. *moddat de-ṛ-ṛaḥa.* After a short pause the speaker continued. *men beƐd waḥed l-modda qṣiṛa de-ṛ-ṛaḥa, naḍ l-muḥaḍiṛ ikemmel.*

to **pave** - *geṣṣeṣ.* Our street has been paved. *geṣṣṣu zenqetna.*

to pave the way - *fteḥ ṭ-ṭṛiq.* If you have somebody to pave the way for you, it's easy enough to get ahead. *ila žbeṛti lli ifteḥ-lek ṭ-ṭṛiq, ishal Ɛlik ttqeddem.*

pavement - *geṣṣ* pl. *gṣeṣ.* The pavement is very bumpy. *l-geṣṣ mḥeffeṛ bezzaf.*

paw - *kreƐ* pl. *kwareƐ, ržel* pl. *ręžlin.* The dog has hurt his paw. *l-kelb tqeṣṣeḥ f-kerƐu.*

pawn - *biḍeq* pl. *byaḍeq.* You've already lost four pawns. *mšaw-lek beƐda ṛebƐa d-le-byaḍeq.*

pay - *xḷaṣ* pl. *-at, ižaṛa* pl. *-t.* How is the pay on your new job? *kif-en huwa le-xḷaṣ fe-xdemtek ž-ždida?*

to pay - **1.** *dfeƐ.* How much did you pay for your car? *šḥal dfeƐti f-siyaṛtek?* **2.** *xeḷḷeṣ.* I would like to pay my bill. *bġit nxeḷḷeṣ ḥsabi.* **3.** *qḍa iqḍi, xerrež.* That doesn't pay. *dak š-ši ma-ka-iqḍi šay.*

**You couldn't pay me to do that. *waxxa tekrini ma-ndir-lek-ši dak š-ši.*

to pay back - *redd.* I'll pay you back the ten dirhams on Monday. *daba nredd-lek l-Ɛešṛa de-d-drahem nhaṛ t-tnayn.*

to pay for - **1.** *ʔedda Ɛla.* We had to pay for it dearly. *walayenni šnu ʔeddina Ɛliha.* **2.** *dfeƐ f-, šra išri.* How much did you pay for your car? *be-šḥal šriti siyaṛtek?*

to pay for itself - *xeḷḷeṣ ṛasu.* This machine will pay for itself in five months. *had l-makina f-xems šhuṛ txeḷḷeṣ ṛasha.*

to pay off - *kemmel b-le-xḷaṣ.* He paid off all his debts. *kemmel d-dyunat lli Ɛlih kollha b-le-xḷaṣ.*

to pay up - *kemmel b-le-xḷaṣ.* In a month I'll have it all paid up. *men daba šheṛ nkun kemmeltha kollha b-le-xḷaṣ.*

payment - **1.** *xḷaṣ* pl. *-at.* We request prompt payment. *ka-nṭeḷbu le-xḷaṣ ikun mƐežžel.* **2.** *iṭṛa* pl. *iṭaṛi.*

I still have three more payments to make on this car. *ma-zal xeṣṣni nxeḷḷeṣ tlata d-l-iṭaṛi f-had s-siyaṛa.*

pea - *želbana* pl. *-t* coll. *želban.*

peace - **1.** *salam.* Our goal is lasting peace. *ġaytna hiya s-salam d-dayem.* **2.** *ṛaḥa* pl. *-t.* He doesn't give me any peace. *ma-ka-yeƐṭini ḥetta ṛaḥa.*

peaceful - *mhedden.* Everything is so peaceful around here. *koll-ši mhedden hna.*

peach - *xuxa* pl. *-t* coll. *xux.*

peacock - *ṭaweṣ* pl. *ṭwaṣ.*

peak - *ṛaṣ* pl. *ṛyuṣ.* We climbed to the peak of the mountain. *ṭḷeƐna ḥetta l-ṛaṣ ž-žbel.*

peanut - *kawkawa* pl. *-t* coll. *kawkaw.*

pear - *ngaṣa* pl. *-t* coll. *ngaṣ.*

pearl - *žuhṛa* pl.*-t* coll *žuheṛ.*

peasant - *fellaḥ* pl. *-a.*

pebble - *ḥeṣwa* pl. *-t* coll. *ḥṣa, ḥžiṛa* pl. *-t.*

peculiar - *ġrib* pl. *ġṛab.* He's a peculiar fellow. *ṛažel ġrib hadak.*

peel - *qešṛa* pl. *-t, qšuṛ.* These oranges have a thick peel. *had l-letšin qšeṛtu ġḷiḍa.*

to peel - **1.** *qeššeṛ.* I have to peel the potatoes. *ka-ixeṣṣni nqeššeṛ le-bṭaṭa.* **2.** *tqeššeṛ, ṭaṛ iṭiṛ* My skin is peeling. *žledti ka-ttqeššeṛ.*

to peel off - *ṭaṛ iṭiṛ, tqelleƐ.* The whitewash is peeling off the ceiling. *l-gebṣ ka-itqelleƐ men s-sqef.*

peep - **1.** *ḥess.* I don't want to hear another peep out of you. *ma-nebġi-ši nƐawed nesmeƐ ḥessek.* **2.** *teṭḷila* pl. *-t.* Take a peep into the room. *Ɛmel ši-teṭḷila fe-l-bit.*

to peep - *ṭeḷḷeḷ.* He was peeping through the hole in the wall. *kan iṭeḷḷeḷ men ṭ-ṭaqa lli fe-l-ḥiṭ.*

peeved - *(lli) ṭaṛ-lu, (lli) ttenqeṛ.* She was peeved about the remark you made. *kanet ttneqṛet men l-mulaḥaḍa lli Ɛmelti.*

pen - **1.** *riša* pl. *-t.* This pen scratches. *had r-riša ka-tšentef.* **2.** *qfez* pl. *qfuza.* We'll have to build a larger pen for the chickens. *ġad ixeṣṣna nṣuwwbu qfez kbeṛ men hada le-d-džaž.*

penalty - *Ɛuquba* pl. *-t.* The penalty is ten years' imprisonment. *l-Ɛuquba Ɛešṛ snin de-l-ḥebs.*

pencil - *qlam (d-le-xfif)* pl. *qluma (d-le-xfif).*

pending - *mƐelleq.* The matter is still pending. *l-qaḍiya ma-zala mƐeḷḷqa.*

pennyroyal - *fliyu.*

pension - *ṣiḷa* pl. *-t; ʔiƐana* pl. *-t; ḥeqq t-taqaƐud.* He gets a pension from the government. *ka-iqbeṭ ṣiḷa men Ɛend l-ḥukuma.*

to pension - *qeƐƐed.* They pensioned him last year. *qeƐƐduh Ɛam luwel.*

people - **1.** *nas.* Were there many people at the meeting? *kanu bezzaf de-n-nas f-le-žtimaƐ?* **2.** *šeƐb* pl. *šuƐub.* Can you name the most important peoples of Asia? *teqḍeṛ tsemmi-li ʔahemm š-šuƐub d-ʔasya?*

pep - *quwa* pl. *-t; ḥamas.* Where do you get your pep? *mnayn ka-džik had l-quwa?* --He's full of pep today. *kollu ḥamas l-yum.*

to pep up - *sexxen, ḥemmes.* I need something to pep me up. *xeṣṣni ši-ḥaža tḥemmesni.*

pepper - *ibẓaṛ.*

per - *l-.* How much are these eggs per dozen? *be-šḥal had l-biḍ le-ẓ-ẓina?*

per cent - *f-le-mya.* The cost of living has risen ten per cent. *le-mƐiša zadet Ɛešṛa f-le-mya.*

perfect - **1.** *kamel.* Nothing is perfect. *ḥetta ḥaža ma-kamla.* **2.** *Ɛažib, mumtaz.* He speaks perfect French. *ka-itkellem fṛanṣawiya Ɛažiba.*

to perfect - *ḥessen, ziyyen.* They haven't perfected the method yet. *ma-zalin ma-ḥessnu ṭ-ṭaṛiqa.*

perfectly - **1.** *tamamen.* He was perfectly satisfied. *kan ferḥan tamamen.* **2.** *huwa hadak, hiya hadik.* He did it perfectly the first time. *Ɛmelha hiya hadik nub l-luwla.*

to **perform** - **1.** *qam iqum b-.* Who performed the operation? *škun lli qam be-l-Ɛamaliya?* **2.** *mettel, lƐeb, qam iqum b-.* The actors performed the most difficult roles. *l-mumettilin mettlu ʔeṣƐeb ʔeḍwaṛ kayna.*

performance - *temtil* pl. *tmatel.* Did you enjoy the performance? *Ɛežbek t-temtil?*

perfume - *Ɛṭeṛ* pl. *Ɛṭuṛ.*

perhaps - *imken.*

period - **1.** *modda* pl. *-t.* He worked here for a short period. *xdem hnaya waḥed l-modda qṣiṛa.* **2.** *fetṛa* pl. *-t.* It's the most interesting period in American history. *hadi ʔahemm fetṛa f-tarix ʔamirika.* **3.** *nuqṭa* pl. *-t, nuqaṭ;*

weqfa pl. *-t*. You forgot to put a period here. *nsiti ma-Ɛmelti-š nuqṭa hnaya*.

perjury - *ḥent*.

to commit perjury - *ḥennet ṛaṣu*. She committed perjury. *ḥenntet ṛaṣha*.

permission - *ṛoxṣa* pl. *-t, tesriḥ* pl. *tsareḥ*. Did you get his permission? *šedditi ṛ-ṛoxṣa men Ɛendu?*

permit - *ṛoxṣa* pl. *-t; tesriḥ* pl. *tsareḥ*. You need a permit to play tennis here. *ka-ixeṣṣek ṛoxṣa baš telƐab t-tinis hnaya*.

to permit - *smeḥ*. I can't permit that. *ma-neqḍeṛ-ši nesmeḥ b-had š-ši*. --No one is permitted to enter this building. *ḥetta waḥed ma-mesmuḥ-lu idxol l-had l-Ɛimaṛa*.

perpendicular - *Ɛmudi, waqef*.

Persia - *blad l-fors*.

Persian - *farisi* pl. *-yin, fors*.

person - **1.** *siyed* pl. *sadat, ṛažel* pl. *ṛžal, ʔinsan* pl. *nas*. What sort of person is he? *kif Ɛamel dak s-siyed?* **2.** *siyda* pl. *-t; ʔanisa* pl. *-t*. She's a nice person. *siyda mezyana hadik*.

**Please deliver this to him in person. *b-le-fḍeḷ mennek weṣṣeḷ-lu had š-ši l-iddih*. --The king was there in person. *l-malik b-ṛaṣu kan temma*.

per person - *le-ṛ-ṛaṣ*. They paid three dirhams per person. *xeḷḷṣu tlata de-d-drahem le-ṛ-ṛaṣ*.

personal - *šexṣi*. He would like to discuss a personal matter with you. *bġa itkellem mƐak Ɛla ši-qaḍiya šexṣiya*.

**He asks too many personal questions. *ka-idxol fe-d-dwaxel bezzaf*.

personality - *šexṣiya* pl. *-t*.

personnel - *xeddama, muweḍḍafin* (pl.). We don't have enough personnel. *ma-Ɛendna-š l-xeddama kafyen*.

to **persuade** - *qneƐ*. He persuaded me to go. *qneƐni baš nemši*.

pest - *ṭaƐun* pl. *ṭwaƐen*.

to **pester** - *bessel Ɛla, teqqel Ɛla*. He's pestering me with his questions! *ka-iteqqel Ɛliya be-l-ʔasʔila dyalu*.

pestle - *idd l-mehraz* pl. *iddin le-mharez*. Mortar and pestle. *l-mehraz w-iddu*.

pet - **1.** *ḥayawan* pl. *-at*. We're not allowed to keep pets in our apartment. *ma-mesmuḥ-lna-š ndexxlu l-ḥayawanat le-skentna*. **2.** *Ɛziz* pl. *Ɛzaz*. She's her mother's pet. *hiya le-Ɛziza Ɛend mmha*.

to pet - *feššeš*. She's always been petted by everyone. *koll-ši kan dima mfeššešha*.

pet name - *kenya* pl. *-t; kniya* pl. *-t*. Don't call me pet names. *ma-tƐeyyeṭ-li ḥetta b-kenya*.

petition - *Ɛaṛiḍa* pl. *-t*. Why don't you get up a petition? *Ɛlaš ma-tṣuwwbu-ši ši-Ɛaṛiḍa?*

to petition - *qeddem Ɛaṛiḍa*. We petitioned the mayor for a new school. *qeddemna Ɛaṛiḍa l-l-baša Ɛla meḍṛaṣa ždida*.

pharmacy - *ṣayḍaliya* pl. *-t*. Pharmacies in Morocco don't carry refreshments. *ṣ-ṣayḍaliyat fe-l-meġrib ma-ka-ibiƐu-š l-mešṛubat*.

phone - *tilifun* pl. *-at*.

to phone - *Ɛmel t-tilifun, Ɛeyyeṭ fe-t-tilifun*. Did anybody phone? *Ɛeyyeṭ ši-waḥed fe-t-tilifun?*

phonograph - *funu* pl. *-yat, makina de-ṭ-ṭbaṣeḷ* pl. *-t de-ṭ-ṭbaṣeḷ*.

photograph - *teṣwiṛa* pl. *-t, tṣaweṛ*. The wall was just covered with photographs and paintings. *l-ḥeyṭ kan mžeḷḷeṭ be-t-tṣaweṛ u-l-lwaḥ*.

to photograph - *ṣuwweṛ*. Have you photographed the statue? *ṣuwweṛti t-timtal?*

photographer - *muṣuwiṛ* pl. *-in*.

physical - *žismi, badani*. Avoid every physical exertion. *lli fiha t-taƐab l-žismi kollha beƐƐed mennha*.

physical exercise - *ḥaṛaka badaniya* pl. *-t badaniya*.

physician - *ṭbib* pl. *ṭebba*.

physics - *l-fiziyaʔ*. Nuclear physics has become very important since the war. *l-fiziyaʔ n-nawawiya ṛežƐet muhimma bezzaf men l-ḥeṛb l-le-hna*.

piano - *byanu* pl. *-yat*.

pick - *fas* pl. *fisan*. The men were carrying picks and shovels. *ṛ-ṛžal kanu rafdin l-fisan u-l-baḷat*.

**I have three apples, take your pick. *Ɛendi tlata de-t-teffaḥat, xud lli Ɛežbettek fihom*.

to pick - **1.** *žna ižni*. All the ripe grapes have been picked. *l-Ɛineb lli ṭab kollu žnaweh*. **2.** *xewweṛ*. Don't pick your teeth! *ma-txewweṛ-š fe-snanek!* **3.** *xteṛ*. I picked the one that pleased me. *xteṛt lli Ɛežbetni*. **4.** *ṭṛeš*. Someone has picked this lock. *ši-waḥed ṭṛeš had l-feṛxa*.

to pick to pieces - *ma-xella ma qal f-*. They picked him to pieces. *ma-xellaw ma qalu fih*.

to pick on - *žbed, žbed f-, neggeṛ Ɛla*. He's been picking on me all day. *n-nhaṛ kollu u-huwa ka-ineggeṛ Ɛliya.*

to pick out - *xteṛ.* He picked out a very nice gift for his wife. *xteṛ hdiya mezyana l-meṛtu.*

to pick up - **1.** *rfed, leqqeṭ.* Please pick up the paper from the floor. *Ɛafak rfed had l-kaġiṭ men l-ʔeṛḍ.* **2.** *hezz.* They picked up three girls on the road. *hezzu tlata d-le-bnat fe-ṭ-ṭṛiq.* **3.** *ḥeṣṣel, leqqeṭ.* The police picked up several suspects. *l-bulis ḥeṣṣlu Ɛadad de-l-methumin.* **4.** *tƐellem deġya.* I picked up quite a bit of Italian on my trip. *deġya tƐellemt xiṛ ḷḷah de-ṭ-ṭalyaniya fe-ṣ-ṣefṛa dyali.*

pickle - *xyaṛa mṛeqqda* pl. *xyaṛat mṛeqqdat* coll. *xyaṛ mṛeqqed.*

**He's in a pretty pickle now. *walayenni ṛah f-waḥed l-ḥeṣla.*

to pickle - *ṛeqqed, Ɛmel le-mṛeqqed.* Did you do any pickling this year? *ṛeqqedtiw had l-Ɛam?*

picnic - *nzaha* pl. *-t, nzayeh.*

picture - **1.** *teṣwiṛa* pl. *tṣaweṛ.* They have some beautiful pictures for sale. *Ɛendhom ši-tṣaweṛ mezyanin l-l-biƐ.* **2.** *ṣuṛa* pl. *ṣuwar, neḍṛa* pl. *-t.* I have to get a clear picture of it first. *ka-ixeṣṣni beƐda naxod neḍṛa waḍḥa Ɛliha.* —He gave you a false picture of it. *Ɛṭak neḍṛa qbiḥa Ɛliha.*

pictures - *sinima.* She's been in pictures since she was a child. *melli kanet ṣġiṛa u-hiya fe-s-sinima.*

to take a picture of - *ṣuwweṛ.*

to have one's picture taken - *tṣuwweṛ.* I haven't had my picture taken in years. *hadi sinin ma-tṣuwweṛt.*

to picture - **1.** *ṣuwweṛ, wṣef.* This book pictures life a thousand years ago. *had le-ktab ka-iṣuwweṛ l-ḥayat dyal hadi ʔalef Ɛam.* **2.** *txeyyel, tṣuwweṛ.* I can't quite picture you as a politician. *ma-neqḍeṛ-ši tamamen ntxeyylek siyasi.*

piece - **1.** *ṭeṛf* pl. *ṭṛaf.* May I have a piece of cake? *imken-li naxod ši-ṭeṛf de-l-ḥelwa?* **2.** *qeṭƐa* pl. *-t.* What is the name of the piece the orchestra is playing? *smiyt had l-qeṭƐa lli ka-iḍṛeb l-žewq?*

**I gave him a good piece of my mind. *lli Ɛṭa ḷḷah qoltu-lu.*

to fall to pieces - *ṭaḥ iṭiḥ be-ṭ-ṭṛaf.* The book is falling to pieces. *le-ktab ka-iṭiḥ be-ṭ-ṭṛaf.*

to go to pieces - *tqeṭṭeƐ ṭṛaf.* She went completely to pieces when she heard the news. *melli semƐet le-xbaṛ tqeṭṭƐet ṭṛaf tamamen.*

to do piecework - *xdem be-l-qeṭƐa.*

pier - **1.** *mun* pl. *mwan.* We were standing on the pier, waiting for the boat. *konna waqfin fe-l-mun ka-ntsennaw l-baxiṛa.* **2.** *sarya* pl. *-t, ṣwari.* The bridge rests on four piers. *l-qenṭṛa waqfa Ɛla ṛebƐa de-s-swari.*

pig - *ḥelluf* pl. *ḥlalef.*

pigeon - *ḥmama* pl. *-t* coll. *ḥmam.*

pile - **1.** *rkiza* pl. *-t, rkayez; sarya* pl. *-t, swari.* The bridge is built on piles. *l-qenṭṛa mebniya Ɛel r-rkayez.* **2.** *Ɛeṛma* pl. *-t, Ɛeṛṛam* pl. *Ɛṛaṛem.* What am I going to do with that pile of books? *š-ġad neƐmel b-dak l-Ɛeṛma d-le-ktub?* **3.** *qetta* pl. *qtet; zebbala* pl. *-t.* That's a pile of money! *zebbala d-le-flus hadi!*

to pile - *Ɛeṛṛem.* Pile these books on the desk until I come. *Ɛeṛṛem le-ktub Ɛel le-mketba ḥetta nži.*

to pile up - *tƐeṛṛem.* My debts are piling up. *d-dyanut ka-ttƐeṛṛem Ɛliya.*

pillar - *sarya* pl. *-t, swari.* A large pillar blocked my view of the stage. *sarya kbira žat mḍeṛṛqa-li l-mesṛeḥ.*

pillow - *mxedda* pl. *-t, mxadd; xeddiya* pl. *-t, xdadi.*

pillowcase - *ġlaf l-xeddiya* pl. *ġlafat le-xdadi.*

pilot - **1.** *ṭiyyaṛ* pl. *-a; (lli) ka-iṣug ṭ-ṭiyyaṛa.* He's the pilot of a mail plane. *huwa ka-iṣug waḥed ṭ-ṭiyyaṛa de-l-barid.* **2.** *ṛayes* pl. *ṛuyas.* That ship is waiting for the pilot. *had l-baxiṛa ka-ttsenna ṛayesha.*

pimple - *demmala* pl. *-t, dmamel.*

pin - *fenta* pl. *-t, fnati.* She stuck herself with a pin. *tekket ṛaṣha b-fenta.* **2.** *šuka* pl. *-t, šwek.* She wore a silver pin. *kanet mƐellqa šuka de-n-noqṛa.*

to pin - **1.** *lesseq.* The two men were pinned under the overturned auto. *ṛ-ṛžal b-žuž kanu mlessqin teḥt s-siyaṛa lli ttqelbet.* **2.** *ṭeṛṛeb.* She pinned a flower on her dress. *ṭeṛṛbet weṛḍa Ɛla ksuwtha.* Let me pin (up) the hem first. *xellini nṭeṛṛeb t-teḥziz beƐda.*

**We couldn't pin him down to anything definite. *ma-qderna nxerržu mennu ḥetta ḥaža bayna.*

pinch - *šwiya, ṣbiyeɛ.* Add a pinch of salt to the soup. *zid ši-ṣbiyeɛ d-le-mleḥ f-le-ḥrira.*

in a pinch - *f-saɛt l-ḥaža, f-saɛt z-ziyar.* You can always count on him in a pinch. *imken-lek tɛedd ɛlih f-saɛt z-ziyar.*

to pinch 1. *qreṣ.* Don't pinch! *ma-teqreṣ-š!* **2.** *ziyyer.* Where does the shoe pinch? *fayn mziyyer ṣ-ṣebbaṭ?* **3.** *sḥeq.* I got my finger pinched in the door. *sḥeqt ṣebɛi fe-l-bab.*

pineapple - *anana* pl. *-t.* (not used with art.).

pinetree - *ṣnubṛa* pl. *-t* coll. *ṣnubeṛ.* These pine trees are almost fifty years old. *had ṣ-ṣnubṛat ɛlayen fe-ɛmeṛhom xemsin ɛam.*

pink - *weṛdi, fanidi.*

pious - *meddiyyen.*

pipe - 1. *žeɛba* pl. *-t, žɛeb.* The pipe has burst. *ž-žeɛba tfeṛgɛet.* **2.** *sebsi* pl. *sbasa.* He smokes a pipe. *ka-ikmi s-sebsi.*

to pipe - *ṭelleɛ.* We pipe our water from a spring. *ka-nṭellɛu l-ma dyalna men waḥed l-ɛeyn.*

pistol - *ferdi* pl. *frada; kabus* pl. *kwabes.*

pit - 1. *ḥefṛa* pl. *-t, ḥfaṛi; huwta* pl. *-t, hwet.* Nobody was in the pit when the explosion occurred. *ḥetta waḥed ma-kan fe-l-ḥefṛa melli žat t-tfeṛgiɛa.* **2.** *ɛḍem* pl. *ɛḍam, ɛḍuma.* Don't swallow the pit. *ma-tebleɛ-š le-ɛḍem.*

pitch - *ɛelk* pl. *ɛluk; zeft, ṛzina.* Pitch is used for paving roads. *z-zeft ka-ixeddmuh fe-nžir ṭ-ṭeṛqan.*

to pitch - 1. *degg.* Where shall we pitch the tent? *fayn ġad ndeggu l-xeyma?* **2.** *siyyeb, laḥ iluḥ.* Pitch me the ball. *luḥ-li l-kuṛa.*

to pitch in - *ɛṭa d-derk.* We pitched right in. *deġya ɛṭina d-derk.*

pitch-dark - *medḷam bezzaf.* It was pitch-dark when we came home. *kan l-ḥal medḷam bezzaf mnayn wṣelna le-ḍ-ḍaṛ.*

pitcher - *ġorraf* pl. *ġṛaṛef.*

pitiable - *(lli) ka-išeffi.* He played a pitiable role. *lɛeb waḥed ḍ-ḍuṛ ka-išeffi.*

pitiful - *(lli) ka-išeffi, (lli) ka-iqeṭṭeɛ l-qelb.* That was a pitiful sight. *menḍeṛ kan ka-iqeṭṭeɛ l-qelb.*

pity - *mḥenna.* She took pity on him. *žatha le-mḥenna ɛlih.*

**It's a pity you can't come. *be-l-ʔasaf ma-imken-lek-š dži.*

to pity - *šfeq men ḥal.* She doesn't want to be pitied. *ma-ka-tebġi ḥedd išfeq men ḥalha.*

I pity you, I pity him, etc. - *ka-tɛezz ɛliya, ka-iɛezz ɛliya,* etc. I pity them. *ka-iɛezzu ɛliya.*

place - *muḍeɛ* pl. *mwaḍeɛ; maḥell* pl. *-at.* Please put it back in the same place. *ḷḷah ixellik reddu f-nefs l-maḥell.*

in place of - *f-ɛewḍ, fe-ɛwaḍ.* May I have another book in place of this one? *imken-li naxod ktab axoṛ f-ɛewḍ hada?*

in the first place - *ṛa beɛda.* In the first place we can't leave until tomorrow. *ṛa beɛda ma-nqeḍṛu nemšiw ḥetta l-ġedda.*

to be out of place - *men ġir maḥell, xaṛež l-muwḍuɛ.* Your remark was out of place. *l-mulaḥaḍa dyalek xaṛža l-muḍuɛ.*

to put in one's place - *werrah ḍaṛhom.* Somebody ought to put him in his place. *xeṣṣ lli ġad iwerrih ḍaṛhom.*

to place - 1. *nezzel, ɛmel.* They placed that table in the bedroom. *dak ṭ-ṭebla nezzluha f-bit n-nɛas.* **2.** *ɛqel ɛla.* I've met him before, but I can't place him. *tɛaṛeft mɛah men qbel, walakin ma-ka-neɛqel-š ɛlih.* **3.** *weḍḍef, žbeṛ xedma l-.* We have placed all of our graduates. *l-metxerržin dyalna kollhom žbeṛna-lhom xedma.*

plain - 1. *meṭḷuq.* They're plain people. *huma nas meṭḷuqin.* **2.** *mɛewweṭ.* We have a plain home. *ɛendna ḍaṛ mɛewwṭa.* **3.** *meṭḷuq mserreḥ.* To put it in plain language... *l-ḥaṣiḷ b-heḍṛa meṭḷuqa mserrḥa...* **4.** *ḍaheṛ.* It's quite plain that he's only after money. *ḍaheṛ daba ma-bih ġir le-flus.*

5. *tamm.* I told him the plain truth. *qolt-lu l-ḥaqiqa t-tamma.*

**It's as plain as the nose on your face. *had š-ši bayen ɛayen* or *had š-ši bḥalu bḥal t-tuṛ le-bleq.*

plain - *weṭya* pl. *-t.* Many people prefer the mountains to the plains. *bezzaf de-n-nas ka-ifeḍḍḷu l-weṭya ɛel le-ḥbal.*

plan - 1. *ṛṣem* pl. *ṛṣuma.* The plans for the new house are ready. *ṛ-ṛṣuma de-ḍ-ḍaṛ ž-ždida waždin.* **2.** *beṛnamež* pl. *baṛamiž; mešṛuɛ -at.* Have you made any plans yet for the future?

Ɛmelti ši-mešruƐat l-l-mesteqbal aw ma-zal?

to plan - 1. *heyye?, neḍḍem.* Our trip was carefully planned. *ṣferṭna kanet mheyy?a be-l-qaƐida.* 2. *?emmel, Ɛewwel.* Where do you plan to spend the summer? *fayn ka-tƐewwel dduwwez ṣ-ṣif?* 3. *neḍḍem.* He doesn't know how to plan his time. *ma-ka-yeƐṛef-š ineḍḍem weqtu.*

**On the salary I get, I have to plan very carefully. *xeṣṣni l-?užṛa lli ka-neqbeḍ nqadedha be-l-qaƐida.*

to plan on - *Ɛewwel Ɛla, Ɛedd Ɛla, ḥseb Ɛla.* You'd better not plan on that. *ġir ma-tƐewwel-š Ɛla dak š-ši.*

plane - 1. *ṭiyyaṛa* pl. *-t, ṭyayeṛ.* What sort of a plane is it? *kif Ɛamla hadik ṭ-ṭiyyaṛa?* 2. *mustawa* pl. *-yat, ḍaṛaža* pl. *-t.* The discussion was not on a very high plane. *l-mustawa de-l-mudakaṛa ma-kan-ši Ɛali bezzaf.* 3. *melsa* pl. *-t, mlasi.* I borrowed a plane from the carpenter. *selleft l-melsa men Ɛend n-nežžaṛ.*

to plane - *melles.* These boards have to be planed. *had l-xešbat ka-ixeṣṣhom itmellsu.*

plant - 1. *ġeṛs* (coll.); *nabat* pl. *-at.* I water the plants every day. *ka-nesqi l-ġeṛs koll nhaṛ.* 2. *meƐmel* pl. *mƐamel.* The manager showed me around the plant. *l-mudir sarani l-meƐmel.*

to plant - *ġṛeṣ.* We planted flowers in our garden. *ġṛeṣna l-weṛḍ fe-žnanna.*

plaster - *gebṣ.* The plaster on the wall is all cracked. *l-gebṣ de-l-ḥeyṭ kollu mešquq.*

plaster cast - *lbixa* pl. *-t, lbayex; melzem* pl. *mlazem.* Her arm still has a cast on it. *iddiha ma-zala fiha l-lbixa.*

to plaster - *gebbeṣ.* Have they finished plastering the walls yet? *gebbṣu le-ḥyuṭ wella ma-zalin?*

plasterer - *gebbaṣ* pl. *-a.*

plate - 1. *ġṭaṛ* pl. *ġeṭṛan, ġeṭṛa; ṭebṣil* pl. *ṭbaṣel.* There's a crack in the plate. *le-ġṭar fih šeqqa.* 2. *luḥa* pl. *-t, lweḥ.* The illustration is on Plate Three. *ṛa t-teṣwiṛa fe-l-luḥa ṛeqm tlata.* 3. *fomm ṛumi* pl. *fmam ṛumiyen.* I didn't know she wore a plate. *ma-kont-ši ka-neƐṛef billa Ɛendha fomm ṛumi.*

platform - 1. *nbeḥ (le-mḥeṭṭa)* pl. *nbuḥa (d-le-mḥeṭṭat).* Let's meet on the platform. *ntlaqaw fe-n-nbeḥ (d-le-mḥeṭṭa).* 2. *beṛnamež* pl. *baṛamiž.* The two parties agreed on a common platform. *l-?eḥzab b-žuž ttafqu Ɛla bernamež waḥed.* 3. *mineṣṣa* pl. *-t.* The speakers were seated on the platform. *l-muḥaḍiṛin kanu galsin Ɛel l-mineṣṣa.*

platter - *ġṭaṛ* pl. *ġeṭṛan, ġeṭṛa; ṭebṣil* pl. *ṭbaṣel.*

play - 1. *leƐb.* The children are completely absorbed in their play. *d-drari xaydin f-leƐbhom.* 2. *riwaya* pl. *-t.* Are there any good plays in town? *kaynin ši-riwayat mezyanin f-le-mdina?*

to play - 1. *lƐeb.* The children are playing in the garden. *d-drari ṛahom ka-ileƐbu fe-l-Ɛeṛṣa.* 2. *ḍṛeb.* He plays the violin very well. *ka-iḍṛeb kamanža mezyan bezzaf.* 3. *lƐeb ḍuṛ, qam b-ḍuṛ.* He played Hamlet last night. *qam b-ḍuṛ Hamlet l-bareḥ.*

to play a joke (or trick) - *lƐeb ḍuṛ, tlaha.* He played a joke on me. *lƐeb Ɛliya ḍuṛ.*

to play around - *tmelleġ.* You've been playing around long enough. *iwa tbaṛek ḷḷah u-ma nta ttmelleġ.*

to play fair with - *tƐamel mezyan mƐa, ṣṣenṣef mƐa.* He really didn't play fair with me. *ma-tƐamel-š mƐaya mezyan.*

played out - *mehdud, meshut.* After a hard day's work he's all played out. *men beƐd nhaṛ mežhed de-l-xedma ka-iṛuḥ mehdud.*

player - *leƐƐab* pl. *-a.* One of the players got hurt during the game. *waḥed men l-leƐƐaba ttqaṣ fe-l-leƐb.*

plea - *ṭalab* pl. *-at.* He ignored my plea. *ma-ddaha-š f-ṭalabi.*

plead - *twessel.* She pleaded with him not to go. *twesslet-lu baš ma-imši-š.*

to plead guilty - *gerr b-denbu.* Do you plead guilty? *ka-tgerr b-denbek?*

pleasant - 1. *ḷṭif* pl. *ḷṭaf.* She's a pleasant lady. *mṛa ḷṭifa hadik.* 2. *ḷṭif* pl. *ḷṭaf; ha?il.* We spent a rather pleasant evening there. *duwwezna teqṣiṛa ha?ila temma.*

**It isn't pleasant for me to have to do this. *ma-ši mezyan-li ndir had š-ši bezz menni.* —Good-by! Have a pleasant trip! *ḷḷah ihennik! u-ṭṛiq s-slama!*

please - *Ɛafak,* pl. *Ɛafakom; men feḍlek,* pl. *men fḍelkom.* Please shut the door. *Ɛafak šedd l-bab.*

to please - **1.** *Ɛžeb, ža iži.* How does this please you? *kif žak had š-ši?* or *waš Ɛežbek had š-ši?* **2.** *ṛḍa iṛḍi.* He's hard to please. *ṣƐib iṛḍih l-waḥed.* **3.** *xella Ɛla xaṭṛu.* You can't please everybody. *ma-imken-lek-š txelli koll waḥed Ɛla xaṭṛu.* **4.** *bġa ibġi.* Do as you please. *dir kif tebġi.*

**He was pleased with that. *kan ferḥan b-dak š-ši.*

pleasing - *ḷṭif* pl. *ḷṭaf.* She has a very pleasing voice. *Ɛendha ṣut ḷṭif.*

pleasure - **1.** *našaṭ, mlaġa.* He never combines business with pleasure. *Ɛemmṛu ma-ka-ixəḷḷeṭ l-xedma mƐa n-našaṭ.* **2.** *faṛaḥ, našaṭ.* It will be a pleasure to have you visit us. *ġad ikun Ɛendna faṛaḥ kbir ila žiti dẓuṛna.*

pleat - *tenya* pl. *-t.* Do you want the dress with or without pleats? *bġiti l-keswa be-t-tenyat aw blaš?*

to pledge - **1.** *ḥellef.* He pledged me to secrecy. *ṛah ḥellefni baš nxebbeƐ s-serr.* **2.** *waƐed, qawel.* I pledged fifty dirhams to the Red Crescent. *waƐedt l-hilal le-ḥmeṛ b-xemsin derhem.*

plenty - *bezzaf.* You have plenty of time. *Ɛendek bezzaf de-l-weqt.*

pliers - *leqqaṭ* pl. *lqaqeṭ.* I need a hammer and (a pair of) pliers. *xeṣṣni mṭeṛqa u-leqqaṭ.*

plot - **1.** *terkib* pl. *-at.* The story has an interesting plot. *l-qiṣṣa Ɛendha terkib muhimm.* **2.** *muʔamaṛa* pl. *-t.* The plot was discovered in time. *l-muʔamaṛa ḥeṣḷet fe-l-weqt.*

to plot - *tʔameṛ.* They plotted against the government. *tʔamṛu ḍeḍḍ l-ḥukuma.*

plow - *meḥṛat* pl. *mḥaṛet.* You need a heavier plow. *xeṣṣek meḥṛat tqel men hada.*

to plow - *ḥṛet.* I'll need all day to plow this field. *xeṣṣni n-nhaṛ kollu baš neḥṛet had l-feddan.*

to **pluck** - *ntef.* Have you plucked the chicken yet? *ntefti d-džaža wella ma-zal?*

plum - *beṛquqa* pl. *-t* coll. *beṛquq.*

plumber - *qzadri* pl. *-ya; qwadsi* pl. *-ya.*

plural - *žemƐ.*

plus - *u.* Five plus seven is twelve. *xemsa u-sebƐa, ṭnaš.*

pocket - *žib* pl. *žyub.* Put this in your pocket. *Ɛmel had š-ši f-žibek.*

to pocket - *Ɛmel f-žibu, ṭebb.* His partner pocketed all the profits. *ṣaḥbu ṭebb r-rbeḥ kollu.*

pocketbook - *beẓṭam* pl. *bẓaṭem.*

pocketknife - *msiyyes* pl. *msiyysat.*

poem - *qṣiḍa* pl. *-t, qṣayeḍ.*

poet - *šaƐir* pl. *šuƐaṛa.*

poetry - *šiƐr.*

point - **1.** *ṛaṣ* pl. *ṛyuṣ.* I broke the point of my knife. *herrest ṛaṣ l-mess dyali.* **2.** *ʔiṣaba* pl. *-t.* Our team scored 23 points. *l-feṛqa dyalna Ɛmelt tlata u-Ɛešrin ʔiṣaba.* **3.** *noqṭa* pl. *-t, nuqaṭ.* We've gone over the contract point by point. *ṛažeƐna l-Ɛoqda noqṭa b-noqṭa.* **4.** *meƐna* pl. *-t, mƐani.* You missed the point. *feltet-lek l-meƐna.* **5.** *muḍuƐ* pl. *mawaḍiƐ.* Let's stick to the point. *xellina fe-l-muḍuƐ.* **6.** *ḥedd* pl. *ḥdud.* I can understand it up to a certain point. *ka-imken-li nefhem had š-ši l-waḥed l-ḥedd.*

**I don't get the point. *ma-fhemt-š.*

point of view - **1.** *ṛiy* pl. *ṛyay; fekra* pl. *-t, ʔefkaṛ; naḍaṛiya* pl. *-t.* Our points of view differ. *ʔefkaṛna ka-textalef.* **2.** *žiha* pl. *-t, žwayeh.* From his point of view he's right. *men žihtu huwa mƐah l-ḥeqq.*

to the point - *fe-l-wežba, f-maḥellu.* His comments are always to the point. *t-tƐaliq dyalu dima ka-ižiw fe-l-wežba.*

to be on the point of - *kan Ɛlayen ġad.* We were on the point of leaving when company arrived. *konna Ɛlayen ġad nxeṛžu mnin žawna ḍ-ḍyaf.*

to stretch a point - *žebbed l-qala.* In this case we can stretch a point. *ila kan hakda ġad imken-lna nžebbdu l-qala.*

to point - *mša imši l-žiht.* The arrow points north. *l-Ɛalama mašya l-žiht š-šamal.*

**Point out the place you told me about. *werrini l-muḍeƐ lli qolti-li Ɛliha.* --Point to the man you mean. *werrini ṛ-ṛažel lli Ɛla balek.* --All signs point toward cold weather. *l-Ɛalamat kollha ka-tqul ġad ikun l-ḥal bared.*

pointed - **1.** *maḍi.* Be careful with that pointed stick. *redd balek men dak le-qṭib l-maḍi.* **2.** *qaṭeƐ.* She's always making pointed remarks. *hiya dima ka-teƐmel mulaḥaḍat qaṭƐin.*

poise - *hemma* pl. *-t; nexwa* pl. *-t, nxawi; ṛẓana* pl. *-t.* She never loses her poise. *Ɛemmeṛ ṛẓantha*

ma-ka-dzul mennha.
poison - *semm* pl. *smum; šliman.*
to poison - *semmem, šelmen.* Our dog has been poisoned. *kelbna mat msemmem.*
poisonous - *mesmum.*
poker - *qṭib* pl *qeṭban.* The poker is behind the furnace. *ṛa le-qṭib mmuṛ l-kanun.*
pole - **1.** *rkiza* pl. *-t, rkayez.* Will the pole be long enough? *waš r-rkiza ġad tekfi fe-ṭ-ṭul?* **2.** *quṭb* pl. *qṭab.* How cold does it get at the poles? *ḥedd-aš ka-ibred l-ḥal f-le-qṭab?*
Pole - *buluni* pl. *-yin.*
police - *bulis, šoṛṭa.*
**The streets are well policed. *z-znaqi mṛaqbinhom l-bulis f-ġaya.*
policeman - *bulisi* pl. *bulis; šoṛṭi* pl *-yin.*
police station - *mḥeṭṭa* (pl. *-t*) *de-l-bulis, mḥeṭṭa de-š-šoṛṭa.* Where is the nearest police station? *fayn hiya le-mḥeṭṭa de-l-bulis lli qṛiba?*
policy - *siyasa.* We can't support his policies. *ma-imken-lna-š ndeɛɛmu siyastu.*
Polish - *buluni* pl. *-yin.*
polish - **1.** *ṭḷa.* I need some brown polish for my new shoes. *ka-ixeṣṣni ṭḷa qehwi l-ṣebbaṭi ž-ždid.* **2.** *seqla* pl. *-t.* I gave the knobs a good polish. *ɛmelt l-l-qebṭat waḥed s-seqla haʔila.*
to polish - **1.** *mseḥ.* I didn't have time to polish my shoes. *ma-kan-š ɛendi l-weqt f-aš nemseḥ ṣebbaṭi.* **2.** *sqel, mseḥ.* She hasn't polished the trays yet. *ma-zala ma-seqlet ṣ-ṣwani.*
polite - *mʔeddeb, (lli) fih ṣ-ṣwab.* He's not very polite. *ma-fih ṣwab bezzaf.*
political - *siyasi.*
politician - *siyasi* pl. *-yin.*
politics - *siyasa.* I'm not interested in politics. *ma-ka-themmni-š s-siyasa.*
polls - *mekteb l-intixabat* pl. *makatib l-intixabat.* The polls close at 8 p.m. *mekteb l-intixabat ka-išedd fe-t-tmenya.*
pond - *gelta* pl. *-t, glati.*
pool - **1.** (game) *biyaṛ.* **2.** (swimming pool) - *sehriž* pl. *sharež.* They have a big pool. *ɛendhom sehriž kbir.*
to pool - *šrek, žmeɛ.* If we pool our money we may have enough to buy a car. *ila šrekna flusna imken iqedduna baš nešriw siyaṛa.*
poor - **1.** *meskin* pl. *msaken; derwiš* pl. *draweš.* Many poor people live in this neighborhood. *bezzaf de-n-nas msaken saknin f-had ž-žiha.* **2.** *qbiḥ* pl. *qbaḥ.* This is poor soil for wheat. *had l-ʔeṛḍ qbiḥa l-l-gemḥ.* **3.** *ḍɛif* pl. *ḍɛaf.* He's very poor in arithmetic. *huwa ḍɛif bezzaf f-le-ḥsab.*
poppy - *ben-neɛman.*
poplar - *ṣefṣaf* pl. *ṣfaṣef.*
poplar - **1.** *meshuṛ.* The orchestra played popular numbers. *l-žewq lɛeb qeṭɛat mešhuṛa.* **2.** *šeɛbi.* Popular prices. *ʔetman šeɛbiya.*
to **populate** - *sken, ɛemmeṛ be-s-sokkan.* The industrial area is thickly populated. *ž-žiha ṣ-ṣinaɛiya kollha mɛemmṛa be-s-sokkan.*
population - *sokkan, ɛadad s-sokkan.* The population has almost doubled in the last twenty years. *ɛadad s-sokkan ɛlayen tna ṛaṣu f-had l-ɛešrin ɛam t-talya.*
pork - *lḥem l-ḥelluf.*
pork chop - *ḍelɛa de-l-ḥelluf.*
port - *meṛṣa* pl. *-t, mṛaṣi.* The ship lay at anchor in the port. *l-baxiṛa weqfet fe-l-meṛṣa.*
porter - *ḥemmal* pl. *-a, zerzay* pl. *-a.* Shall I call a porter? *nɛeyyeṭ l-zerzay?*
portion - *qyaṣ* pl. *-at.* Do they always serve such small portions? *waš dima ka-yeɛṭiw qyaṣat ṣġaṛ hakda?*
Portugal - *blad l-beṛṭqiz.*
Portuguese - *beṛṭqizi* pl. *beṛṭqiz.*
position - **1.** *ʔimkan.* I'm not in a position to pay right away. *ṛah ma-ši fe-l-ʔimkan baš nxeḷḷeṣ deġya.* **2.** *muqif* pl. *mawaqif.* This places me in a very difficult position. *had š-ši ḥeṭṭni f-muqif ḥariž.* **3.** *menzla* pl. *-t, mnazel; mertaba* pl. *-t.* A man in your position has to be careful of his conduct. *ṛažel f-menzla bḥal dyalek ka-ixeṣṣu ikun ḥaḍi ṛaṣu.*
positive - **1.** *ʔižabi, b-iyyeh.* I expect a positive answer. *ka-ntsenna žwab b-iyyeh.* **2.** *mḥeqqeq, metyeqqen.* I'm positive that he was there. *ana mḥeqqeq billa kan temma.*
positively - *be-l-mufid, be-ṣ-ṣeḥḥ.* Do you know that positively? *waš ka-teɛṛef had š-ši be-ṣ-ṣeḥḥ?*
to **possess** - *ksab.* That's all I possess. *hadak š-ši ma ka-neksab.*
**What possessed you to do that? *aš wqeɛ-lek ḥetta ɛmelti dak š-ši?*

possession - *kesb, melk.*
to take possession of - *ḥewwez.* The new owner hasn't taken possession of the house yet. *mul š-ši ždid ma-zal ma-ḥewwez ḍ-ḍaṛ.*
possibility - *ʔimkaniya* pl. *-t; ḥell* pl. *ḥulul.* I see no other possibility. *ma-ka-nšuf ḥetta ši-ḥell axoṛ.*
possible - *mumkin.*
possibly - *imken.* He may possibly call you. *ġad imken iεeyyeṭ-lek.*
**He works as fast as he possibly can. *ka-ixdem εla qedd žehdu.*
post - 1. *εmud* pl. *εmayed.* We need new posts for our fence. *xeṣṣna εmayed ždad le-syažna.* 2. *maḥell* pl. *-at.* A good soldier never deserts his post. *l-žundi lli mezyan εemmṛu ma-ka-ihṛeb εla maḥellu.*
to post - 1. *εeyyen.* The officer will post some soldiers at the bridge. *ḍ-ḍabeṭ ṛah ġad iεeyyen l-εeskeṛ l-l-qenṭṛa.* 2. *εelleq.* The order has been posted since yesterday. *men l-bareḥ u-l-ʔemṛ mεelleq.*
**He's pretty well posted. *huwa εla bal ḷḷah ibarek.*
postage - *wažeb.* How much is the postage on a registered letter? *šḥal l-wažeb εla bṛiya meḥfuḍa?*
post(al) card - *teṣwiṛa* pl. *-t, tṣaweṛ.* Did you get my post card? *weṣlettek teṣwiṛa men εendi?*
postal rate - *ḥeqq l-barid* pl. *ḥquq l-barid.*
poster - *ʔiεlan* pl. *-at.* He draws very nice posters. *ka-iṣuwweb ʔiεlanat mezyanin.*
postman - *feṛṛaq* pl. *-a.*
postmark - *ṭabeε l-buṣṭa* pl. *ṭwabeε l-buṣṭa.* The postmark is illegible. *ṭabeε l-buṣṭa ma-bayen-š.*
to postmark - *ṭbeε.* The letter was postmarked May fifteenth. *had le-bṛa meṭbuεa nhaṛ xmeṣṭaš mayu.*
post office - *buṣṭa* pl. *-t.*
post-office box - *ṣenḍuq l-barid* pl. *ṣnaḍeq l-barid.*
to **postpone** - *ʔexxeṛ.* I can't postpone the appointment. *ma-imken-li-š nʔexxeṛ l-miεad.*
posture - *weqfa* pl. *-t.* She has poor posture. *εendha weqfa ma-mezyana-š.*
pot - 1. *ṭenžṛa* pl. *-t, ṭnažeṛ.* There is a pot of soup on the stove. *kayna ṭenžṛa d-le-ḥrira fuq l-εafya.* 2. *bṛiq* pl. *bṛayeq.* Our pot holds eight cups. *bṛiqna ka-irfed tmenya de-l-kisan.* 3. *berrad* pl. *brared.* One pot of tea, please. *waḥed l-berrad d-atay men feḍḷek.*
potato - *bṭaṭa* pl. *-t, bṭayeṭ* coll. *bṭaṭa.*
potter - *fexxaṛ* pl. *-a.*
pottery - 1. (craft) *tafexxaṛet.* 2. (pots) *fexxaṛ.*
pound - *ṛṭeḷ* pl. *ṛṭuḷa; neṣṣ kilu* pl. *nṣaṣ kilu.* How much is a pound of tea? *be-šḥal ṛ-ṛṭeḷ d-atay?*
pound (sterling) - *ibra* pl. *-t.* How much is an English pound in Moroccan money? *šḥal ka-teεmel l-ibra negliziya b-le-flus mġaṛba?*
to pound - 1. *fṛeε.* We pounded on the door for five minutes before they heard us. *bqina nfeṛεu fe-l-bab xemsa de-d-dqayeq baš εad semεuna.* 2. *rdeḥ, ṭleε u-hbeṭ.* His heart was pounding with excitement. *qelbu kan ka-irdeḥ be-d-dehša.*
to **pour** - *εemmeṛ, kebb.* Please pour me some coffee. *kebb-li ši-šwiya de-l-qehwa ḷḷah ixellik.*
**It's pouring rain. *š-šta ka-ṭṭiḥ be-l-ġaṛaq.* —The crowd was just then pouring out of the theater. *n-nas kanu εad bdaw izerru men s-sinima.* —She poured her troubles out to me. *fažat qelbha εliya.*
poverty - *feqṛ, tameskinet.* He's living in great poverty. *huwa εayeš f-waḥed l-feqṛ kbir.*
poverty-stricken - *mqeṭṭeε be-ṭ-ṭṛaf.*
powder - 1. *ġobṛa* pl. *-t.* Take one powder with a glass of water! *xud ši-ġobṛa f-kas de-l-ma.* 2. *buṛbu.* She's got too much powder on her face. *εamla bezzaf de-l-buṛbu fe-wžehha.*
(gun)-powder - *baṛuḍ.*
power - 1. *istiṭaεa* pl. *-t.* That's beyond my power. *dak š-ši xaṛez εel l-istiṭaεa dyali.* 2. *ṣuḷṭa* pl. *-t, ṣuḷat; ḥkam* pl. *-at.* He weilds a lot of power. *ka-itmetteε b-ṣuḷṭa kbira.* 3. *quwa* pl. *-t.* The machine is operated by electric power. *l-makina ka-texdem be-l-quwa de-ḍ-ḍuw.*
powerful - *qwi, mežhed.* He has a powerful voice. *εendu ṣut mežhed.*
powerless - *(lli) ma-εendu žehd, (lli) ma-εendu qaḍaṛ.* I'm sorry, I'm powerless in this matter. *be-l-ʔasaf, ma-εendi qaḍaṛ f-had l-qaḍiya.*
practical - *εamali.* That isn't very practical. *had š-ši ma-ši εamali.*
practically - 1. *b-kifiya εamaliya.* You have to look at things practically. *xeṣṣek tenḍeṛ l-l-ʔumuṛ*

b-kifiya ƐamaLiya. 2. *Ɛlayen, teqṛiben.* I'm practically done. *Ɛlayen salit.*
**We're practically there now. *ma-bqa-lna šay u-nkunu temma.*

practice - 1. *nfad.* Dr. 'Azzouz has a wide practice. *nfad kbir Ɛel d-duktur Ɛezzuz.* 2. *Ɛamal* pl. *Ɛmal.* It's easy in theory but not in practice. *sahla be-l-fomm ma-ši be-l-Ɛamal.* 3. *derba* pl *-t, težṛiba* pl. *-t, tažarib.* I'm a little out of practice. *ṛ-ana šwiya ma-Ɛendi derba.*
to make it a practice - *Ɛewwed nefsu, Ɛewwed ṛaṣu.* I've made it a practice to get to work on time. *Ɛewwedt ṛaṣi Ɛel le-wṣuḷ l-l-xedma fe-l-weqt.*
to practice - *tmerren.* He's practicing on the piano. *ṛah ka-itmerren Ɛel le-byanu.*
to practice law - *mares l-ḥuquq.* How long do you have to study before you can practice law? *šḥal xeṣṣek teqṛa qbel ma-tebda tmares l-ḥuquq?*
to practice (medicine) - *bašeṛ.* Where does he practice? *fayn ka-ibašeṛ?*

praise - *teƐḍima* pl. *-t* coll. *teƐḍim.* Your praise of him went to his head. *t-teƐḍima lli Ɛmelti-lu nefxettu.*
to praise - *šker, mdeḥ.* Everybody praises his work. *koll-ši ka-iškeṛ xdemtu.*

prank - *mlaġa* pl. *-t.* That's a silly prank. *mlaġa mfellsa hadi.*

to **pray** - *ṣeḷḷa.*

prayer - *ṣḷa* pl. *-wat.*

to **preach** - *xṭeb.*

preacher - *xṭib* pl. *xuṭaba.*

precious - *be-t-taman.* Time is precious. *l-weqt be-t-taman* or *l-weqt de-d-dheb.*
precious stone - *ḥežṛa ḥoṛṛa* pl. *ḥežṛat ḥoṛṛin* coll. *ḥžeṛ ḥoṛṛ.* Emeralds are precious stones. *z-zemred ḥžeṛ ḥoṛṛ.*

to **predict** - *tnebbeʔ.*

preface - *muqeddima* pl. *-t.*

to **prefer** - *feḍḍeḷ.*
to prefer to - *bġa ibġi ḥsen.* Would you prefer to go to the movies? *waš tebġi temši le-s-sinima ḥsen?*

preference - *ferz, feṛq.* I don't give preference to anyone. *ma-ka-neƐmel feṛq bin hada u-hada.*
**I have no preference. *Ɛendi bḥal bḥal.*

preparation - 1. *lli ka-ixeṣṣ.* I've made all the preparations for the trip. *hiyyeʔt lli ka-ixeṣṣ kollu le-ṣ-ṣfeṛ.* 2. *ṭṛiq* pl. *ṭoṛqan.* Plans are in preparation. *l-baṛamiž ṛaha fe-ṭ-ṭṛiq.*

to **prepare** - 1. *qal iqul men qbel, Ɛlem.* You'd better prepare him for it. *ḥsen tqulha-lu men qbel.* 2. *wežžed.* Who's going to prepare the meal? *škun lli ġad iwežžed l-makla?*
**Prepare for the worst. *ġir wežžed ṛaṣek* or *ġir Ɛewwel Ɛla xzit.*

to **prescribe** - *kteb, ʔameṛ.* The doctor prescribed these pills for me. *ṭ-ṭbib kteb-li had l-ḥebbat.*

prescription - *dwa* pl. *-yat.* Where can I get this prescription filled? *fayn imken-li nešri had d-dwa?*

presence - *ḥḍuṛ, meḥḍeṛ.* The document has to be signed in your presence. *l-watiqa ka-ixeṣṣha ttweqqeƐ be-ḥḍuṛek.*
presence of mind - *šahed le-Ɛqel.* I admire your presence of mind. *ana ka-nttebheḍ f-had šahed le-Ɛqel lli Ɛendek.*

present - 1. *hdiya* pl. *-t.* Did you give him a present for his birthday? *Ɛṭitih ši-hdiya f-Ɛid l-milad dyalu?* 2. *ḥaḍiṛ, saƐt daba, l-yum.* We live in the present, not in the past. *ḥna Ɛeyyšin l-yum, ma-l-bareḥ daz* or *ḥna wlad l-yum u-ḷḷah iṛeḥmu lli mat.* 3. *ḥaḍeṛ.* All his friends were present. *ṣḥabu kollhom kanu ḥaḍṛin.* 4. *d-had s-saƐa.* In my present position I can't do anything else. *f-ḥalti d-had s-saƐa ma-imken-li neƐmel ḥetta ḥaža xṛa.*
at present - *f-had s-saƐa.* He's too busy to see you at present. *huwa mešġul bezzaf f-had s-saƐa baš išufek.*
for the present - *f-had s-saƐa.* That will be enough for the present. *dak š-ši ikfi f-had s-saƐa.*
to present - 1. *xleq.* Each separate case presents new difficulties. *koll qaḍiya qaḍiya ka-texleq mašakil ždida.* 2. *qeddem, Ɛewwed.* Why don't you present the facts as they really are? *Ɛlaš ma-tƐewwed-ši l-waqiƐ kif kayen fe-l-ḥaqiqa.* 3. *qeddem, hda ihdi.* They presented him a gold watch. *hdaw-lu magana de-d-dheb.*

to **preside** - *tṛeʔʔeṣ.* Mr. Lwali presided. *s-si lwali tṛeʔʔeṣ.*

president - 1. *raʔis* pl. *ṛuʔasa.* Nagib was the first president of the Egyptian Republic. *nažib kan ʔewwel ṛaʔis l-žemhuriya l-meṣṛiya.*

2. *mudir* pl. *-in*. He was president of of the Bank of Morocco. *kan mudir l-ḅenk l-meġṛibi.*

press - 1. *ṣaḥafa*. The press carried big stories about the attack. *ṣ-ṣaḥafa nešret maqalat kbira ɛel le-hžum.* 2. *ṣaḥafiyen* (pl.). Will the press be admitted to the conference? *ġad ikunu ṣ-ṣaḥafiyen meqbulin fe-l-muḥaḍaṛa?* 3. *mṭebɛa* pl. *-t*. Can you operate a press? *ka-teɛṛef txeddem le-mṭebɛa?*

to press - 1. *ḥedded*. Where can I get my suit pressed? *fayn imken-li nḥedded ksuwti?* 2. *ẓiyyeṛ, zḥem*. His creditors are pressing him. *ṣḥab d-din ṛahom mẓiyyṛineh.* 3. *brek ɛla*. Press the button. *brek ɛel ṭ-ṭeffaya.*

pressing - *ʔakid*. I have a pressing engagement. *ɛendi miɛad ʔakid.*

pressure - *ḍeġṭ*. We work under constant pressure. *ka-nxedmu dima teḥt ḍ-ḍeġṭ.*

to put pressure on - *ḍġeṭ ɛla*. We'll have to put pressure on him. *ka-ixeṣṣna nḍeġṭu ɛlih.*

to **presume** - *ɛtaqed*. I presume he is at home. *ka-neɛtaqed ṛah f-ḍaṛhom.*

to **pretend** - 1. *ɛmel ṛaṣu*. He pretended that he was a doctor. *ɛmel ṛaṣu ṭbib.* 2. *ɛmel messu*. He pretended not to know a thing about it. *ɛmel messu ma-ɛṛef walu ɛliha.*

pretext - *msebba* pl. *-t* coll. *sbayeb*. He's just looking for a pretext. *ġir ka-iḍuṛ ɛla sbaybu.*

pretty - 1. *mziwen, ġzal* pl. *ġezlan*. She's a very pretty girl. *bnita mziwna hadik.* 2. *bezzaf*. It tastes pretty good. *had š-ši madaqu ldid bezzaf.* 3. *ɛžib*. That's a pretty mess! *xebla ɛžiba!*

**He's sitting pretty. *mbeṛmek-lek mɛa ṛaṣu.* --He eats pretty much everything. *ka-yakol koll-ši ɛlayen.*

to **prevail** - *nfeɛ*. Nothing prevailed. *ḥetta ḥaža ma-nefɛet.*

to prevail (up)on - *qneɛ*. Can't we prevail on you to come along? *ma-imken-lna-š nqenɛuk baš temši mɛana?*

to **prevent** - 1. *ḥṣeṛ*. I couldn't prevent it. *ma-qdeṛt-š neḥṣeṛ dak š-ši.* 2. *ḥṣeṛ, mneɛ, zuwwel l-*. Nobody is going to prevent you from doing it. *ḥetta ḥedd ma-ġad imenɛek baš teɛmelha.*

previous - 1. *qdim* pl. *qdam*. I met him on a previous visit. *tɛaṛeft mɛah f-waḥed ẓ-ẓyaṛa qdima.* 2. *tali*. I met him on his previous visit. *tɛaṛeft mɛah fe-ẓ-ẓyaṛa dyalu t-talya.*

price - *taman* pl. *-at, ʔetmina*. The prices are very high here. *t-tamanat ɛalya bezzaf hnaya.*

to price - *seqṣa ɛel t-taman*. I priced this radio in several stores. *seqṣit ɛla taman had ṛ-ṛaḍyu f-ɛadad d-le-ḥwanet.*

pride - *nefs*. Don't you have any pride? *waš ma-ɛendek nefs?*

to take pride in - *ftaxeṛ b-*. He takes great pride in his work. *ka-iftaxeṛ bezzaf be-xdemtu.*

to pride oneself - *fšeṛ*. She prides herself on her cooking. *ka-tefšeṛ be-ṭyabha.*

priest - *rhib* pl. *rehban*.

primarily - *men qbel koll-ši*. He's primarily interested in tennis. *huwa mehtemm men qbel koll-ši be-t-tinis.*

primary school - *meḍṛaṣa btidaʔiya* pl. *mḍaṛeṣ btidaʔiya*.

prime - *moɛtabaṛ*. That butcher sells only prime meat. *dak l-gezzar ka-ibiɛ ġir l-lḥem l-moɛtabaṛ.*

prime minister - *ṛaʔis l-ḥukuma* pl. *ṛuʔasaʔ l-ḥukumat; ṛaʔis l-wiẓaṛa* pl. *ṛuʔasaʔ l-wiẓaṛat*.

principal - 1. *mudir* pl. *-in*. The principal called the teachers into his office. *l-mudir ɛeyyeṭ l-l-feqya l-l-mekteb dyalu.* 2. *ṛaṣ l-mal* pl. *ṛuṣ le-mwal*. Have you paid anything on the principal? *xeḷḷeṣti ši-ḥaža ɛla ṛaṣ l-mal?*

principle - *mebdeʔ* pl. *mabadiʔ*. I make it a principle to save some money every month. *xdit waḥed l-mebdeʔ baš nwoffeṛ le-flus koll šheṛ.*

as a matter of principle - *mebdaʔiyan*. I don't do such things as a matter of principle. *mebdaʔiyan ma-ka-neɛmel-š bḥal had le-ḥwayež.*

print - 1. *ḥeṛf* pl. *ḥṛuf*. The print in this book is too small. *le-ḥṛuf f-had le-ktab ṣġaṛ bezzaf.* 2. *meṭbuɛa* pl. *-t*. The museum has a fine collection of prints. *ɛendhom waḥed l-mežmuɛa haʔila de-l-meṭbuɛat fe-l-metḥef.* 3. *nesxa* pl. *-t*. How many prints shall I make of each picture? *šḥal de-n-nesxat nxerrež ɛla koll teṣwiṛa?*

**That book is out of print. *dak le-ktab ma-bqa-š.*

to print - 1. *ṭbeɛ*. We still have to print the programs. *ma-zal*

xeṣṣna nṭebʕu l-baṛamiž. 2. *nšeṛ.* The letter was printed in yesterday's paper. *nešṛu le-bṛa fe-l-žarida de-l-bareḥ.*
printed matter - *meṭbuʕat* (pl.). What are the postage rates for printed matter? *šḥal ka-yužeb fe-l-buṣṭa ʕel l-meṭbuʕat?*
printer - *ṭebʕi* pl. *-yin.*
print shop - *mṭebʕa* pl. *-t.*
prison - *ḥebs* pl. *ḥbasat.*
prisoner - *mesžun* pl. *msažen.* A prisoner has just escaped. *waḥed l-mesžun ʕad hṛeb.*
prisoner of war - *mesžun l-ḥeṛb* pl. *msažen l-ḥeṛb.*
private - 1. *ʕeskṛi (meṭḷuq)* pl. *ʕsakṛiya (meṭḷuqin).* He was a private in the First World War. *kan ʕeskṛi meṭḷuq fe-l-ḥeṛb l-ʕalamiya l-luwla.* 2. *xaṣṣ.* This is my private property. *hada melki l-xaṣṣ.*
**I'd like to talk to you in private. *baġi ntkellem mʕak bini u-binek.*
privilege - *ḥeqq* pl. *ḥquq; mtiyaz* pl. *-at.* He was denied all privileges. *zuwwlu-lu le-ḥquq kollha.*
prize - *žaʔiza* pl. *-t, žawaʔiz.* Who won first prize? *škun lli rbeḥ l-žaʔiza l-luwla?*
problem - 1. *muškila* pl. *mašakil.* We all have our problems. *kollna ʕendna mašakilna.* 2. *muškil* pl. *mašakil.* I couldn't solve the second problem. *ma-qḍeṛt-š nxerrež l-muškil t-tani.*
**She's a problem child. *hadik bent waʕra.*
to **proceed** - *zad izid.*
proceeds - *medxul* pl. *-at.* The proceeds will go to charity. *l-medxul ġad imši f-ʕamal xiṛi.*
process - 1. *xtibaṛ* pl. *-at.* The process was worked out in our laboratory. *dak le-xtibar tṣuwweb ʕendna fe-l-muxtabaṛ.* 2. *ṭaṛiqa* pl. *-t.* That will be a long drawn-out process. *dak ṭ-ṭariqa ġad ikun ʔmeṛha ṭwil.*
procession - *stiʕṛaḍ* pl. *-at.*
to **proclaim** - *ʕlen.* The government proclaimed Nov. 18 a holiday. *l-ḥukuma ʕelnet be-nhaṛ tmenṭaš muwanbir nhaṛ ʕoṭḷa.*
proclamation - *ʔiʕlan* pl. *-at.*
to **produce** - 1. *ntež, xerrež.* How many cars do they produce a month? *šḥal de-s-siyaṛat ka-ixerržu fe-š-šheṛ?* 2. *qeddem, žab, ižib.* Can you produce any written proof? *imken-lek tqeddem ši-ḥežža mektuba?*
production - *ʔintaž* pl. *-at.*
productive - *muntiž.* He's a very productive writer. *hadak katib muntiž bezzaf.*
profit - *rbeḥ* pl. *rbaḥ.* I sold it at a profit. *beʕtu be-r-rbeḥ.*
**I don't expect to get any profit out of that. *ma-ʕendi ma iṭleʕ-li men dak š-ši.*
to profit - 1. *stafed, dda iddi fayda.* I didn't profit much by the lecture. *ma-ddit-ši ši-fayda kbira men l-muḥaḍaṛa.* 2. *tʕellem.* You profit from your mistakes. *men ẓbaylu l-waḥed ka-itʕellem.*
profitable - *(lli) ka-idexxel, (lli) fih r-rbeḥ, (lli) fih medxul.* Is it a profitable business? *had l-ḥaṛaka fiha ši-medxul?*
profiteer - *xezzan r-rxa* pl. *xezzanin r-rxa.*
program - *beṛnamež* pl. *baṛamiž.*
progress - *taqeddum.*
to progress - *tqeddem.* You've progressed a lot in the six weeks I've been away. *tqeddemti ḷḷah ibarek f-had s-setta de-ž-žemʕat lli ġebt fiha.*
progressive - *taqeddumi.* He's a progressive teacher. *hadak ʔustad taqeddumi.*
to **prohibit** - *mneʕ.* Have they prohibited smoking on the train again? *ʕawed menʕu d-doxxan fe-l-mašina?*
project - *mešṛuʕ* pl. *mšaṛeʕ.* We're working on a project together. *ṛa-ḥna xeddamin f-waḥed l-mešṛuʕ mežmuʕin.*
to project - *biyyen.* We projected the film on the wall. *biyyenna l-film ʕel l-ḥeyṭ.*
to **prolong** - *ṭuwwel, žebbed.*
prominent - 1. *mešhuṛ, barez.* He's a prominent artist. *huwa fennan mešhuṛ.* 2. *xaṛež.* He has a prominent chin. *ʕendu leḥya xaṛža.*
promise - *ʕahed* pl. *ʕhud.* You didn't keep your promise. *ma-wfiti-š b-ʕahdek.*
to promise - *waʕed, qawel.* We promised him a present. *waʕednah b-ši-hdiya.* 2. *ʕṭa klemtu.* Promise me that you won't do it again. *ʕṭini klemtek ma-tʕewwed-š ddirha.*
to **promote** - 1. *ṛeqqa, redd.* He was promoted to captain. *redduh qebṭan.* or *ṛeqqaweh l-meṛtabt qebṭan.* 2. *šežžeʕ.* Most countries promote their foreign trade. *žul l-boldan ka-išežžʕu tižaṛthom l-xaṛižiya.*
prompt - 1. *sriʕ* pl. *sraʕ.* I expect

a prompt reply. *ka-ntsenna žwab sriƐ.* 2. *doğri.* He's prompt in paying his debts. *huwa doğri fe-xḷaṣ d-din lli ka-ikun Ɛlih.*

to prompt - *dfeƐ.* What prompted you to say that? *šnu defƐek tqul dak š-ši?*

promptly - *be-ḍ-ḍebṭ, tamam.* We start promptly at five. *ka-nebdaw fe-l-xemsa be-ḍ-ḍebṭ.*

to **pronounce** - 1. *nṭeq b-.* Am I pronouncing the word correctly? *waš ka-nnṭeq b-had l-kelma hiya hadik?* 2. *ḍehheṛ.* The judge will pronounce sentence tomorrow. *l-qaḍi ġad iḍehheṛ le-ḥkam ġedda.*

pronounciation - *noṭq.* That's not the correct pronounciation. *ma-ši huwa hadak n-noṭq.*

proof - *ḥužža* pl. *-t, ḥužaž.* What proof do you have of that? *š-men ḥužža Ɛendek Ɛla dak š-ši?*

to furnish proof - *dla idli b-ḥužža.* Can you furnish any written proof? *imken-lek tedli b-ši ḥužža mektuba?*

proper - *mnaseb.* This isn't the proper time to ask questions. *had l-weqt ma-ši mnaseb l-l-ʔasʔila.*

**That isn't the proper way to handle people. *ma-ši hadi hiya ṭ-ṭariqa baš ka-ittƐemlu n-nas.* --In 1937 the Japanese invaded China proper. *f-tseƐṭaš le-mya u-sebƐa u-tlatin l-yabiniyen hežmu Ɛel ṣ-ṣin b-nefsha.* --Everything at the proper time. *koll ḥaža b-weqtha.*

properly - 1. *be-l-qaƐida.* I'll show you how to do it properly. *ġad nwerrik kif teƐmelha be-l-qaƐida.* 2. *mƐewweṭ.* Can't you behave properly? *ma-teqḍeṛ-š ttmešša mƐewweṭ?*

property - *mulk* pl. *ʔamlak.* All the furniture is my property. *l-ʔatat kollu mulki.*

proportion - *qyaṣ* pl. *-at, Ɛbaṛ* pl. *-at.* The proportions in that building are all wrong. *l-qyaṣat f-dak le-bni kollhom Ɛiwež.*

in proportion to - *Ɛla hasab, be-n-nasba l-, Ɛla qedd.* Everybody is paid in proportion to what he does. *koll waḥed ka-itxeḷḷeṣ Ɛla qedd ma ka-yeƐmel.*

out of proportion - *ma-metqadd-š.* His expenses are entirely out of proportion to his income. *meṣṛufu ma-metqadd-š be-l-koll mƐa medxulu.*

proposal - *Ɛeṛḍ* pl. *Ɛṛuḍ; qtiṛaḥ* pl. *-at.*

to make a proposal - *Ɛṛeḍ.*

to **propose** - *qtaṛeḥ.* I propose that we go to the movies. *ka-neqtaṛeḥ nemšiw le-s-sinima.*

to propose to - *Ɛṛeḍ z-zwaž Ɛla.* He proposed to her. *Ɛṛeḍ Ɛliha z-zwaž.*

proposition - *qtiṛaḥ* pl. *-at.* He made me an excellent proposition. *Ɛmel-li waḥed le-qtiṛaḥ haʔil.*

**Is it a paying proposition? *l-qaḍiya fiha ši-mƐaš?*

prospect - *ʔamal.* What are his prospects of getting the job? *temma ši-ʔamal baš išebbeṛ l-xedma?*

prospective - *(lli) ġad ikun.* He is my prospective son-in-law. *hada lli ġad ikun nsibi.*

to **protect** - 1. *ḥfeḍ.* I wear these glasses to protect my eyes. *ka-neƐmel had n-nḍaḍeṛ baš neḥfeḍ Ɛeyniya.* 2. *ḥma yeḥmi, dwa idwi Ɛla.* He'll protect your interests. *huwa daba yeḥmi-lek l-maṣaliḥ dyalek.*

protection - *fekkan, fkak.* There is no protection against that. *ma-kayen fekkan men dak š-ši.*

to **protest** - 1. *ḥtežž.* It won't do you any good to protest. *ma-Ɛendek ma teqḍi ila ḥtežžiti.* 2. *ʔekked.* He protested his innocense throughout the trial. *ʔekked baṛaʔtu fe-l-muḥakama kollha.*

proud - *meftaxeṛ.* I am proud of you. *ana meftaxeṛ bik.*

to **prove** - *biyyen.* I can prove I didn't do it. *imken-li nbiyyen bin ma-dertha-š.*

to prove to be - *ban iban, ṣḍeq.* The rumor proved to be false. *d-diƐaya ṣeḍqet xawya.*

proverb - *metla* pl. *-t.*

to **provide** - *qewwem.* They provided us with supplies to last two weeks. *qewwmuna b-le-Ɛwin de-žmeƐtayn.*

to provide for - 1. *xdem Ɛla.* He has to provide for the whole family. *ka-ixeṣṣu ixdem Ɛel l-Ɛaʔila kollha.* 2. *nḍeṛ l-.* The law provides for such special cases. *l-qanun ka-inḍeṛ l-qaḍiyat xaṣṣa bḥal hadi.*

provided, providing - *be-l-ḥeqq b-šeṛṭ, be-l-ḥeqq ila.* I'll go, provided you come with me. *nemši be-l-ḥeqq b-šeṛṭ dži mƐaya.*

province - *ʔiqlim* pl. *ʔaqalim.* Morocco is divided into several provinces. *l-meġṛib meqsum l-Ɛadad de-l-ʔaqalim.*

provisions - *Ɛewla, Ɛwil.* Our provisions are running low. *Ɛewletna bdat*

teqlal.
to **provoke** - **1.** *nuwweḍ.* His remark provoked a roar of laughter. *l-mulaḥaḍa dyalu nuwwḍet muža de-ḍ-ḍeḥk.* **2.** *qelleq.* He's provoked about it. *qellqu dak š-ši.*
provoking - *(lli) ka-iqelleq, (lli) ka-ižennen.* His behavior is provoking. *sirtu ka-tqelleq.*
prune - *berquqa yabsa* pl. *berquqat yabsat* coll. *berquq yabes.* I don't care much for prunes. *ma-ka-yeƐžebni-š l-berquq l-yabes ḥetta l-temma.*
to prune - *qezzeb.* You need to prune your rosebushes. *ka-ixeṣṣek tqezzeb l-werdat dyalek.*
public - **1.** *Ɛumum.* Is this park open to the public? *had l-Ɛerṣa meḥlula l-l-Ɛumum?* **2.** *Ɛumumi.* Do you have a public telephone here? *waš Ɛendkom tilifun Ɛumumi hna?* **3.** *žemhur* pl. *žamahir.* Such books will always find a public. *ktub bḥal hadu la-bodda ikun-lhom žemhur.* **4.** *Ɛamm.* Public opinion is against him. *r-raʔy l-Ɛamm ḍeḍḍu.*
in public - *qbalt n-nas.* That's no way to behave in public. *had š-ši ma-ka-iddar-ši qbalt n-nas.*
publicity - *štihar* pl. *-at.* That's what I call clever publicity. *iwa hada huwa le-štihar wella balak!*
to **publish** - *nšer.* He hopes to publish his new book very soon. *ka-iʔemmel inšer ktabu ž-ždid qrib.*
publisher - *ṭebbaƐ* pl. *-a.*
puddle - *gelta* pl. *-t, glati.* Careful, don't step into the puddle! *Ɛendak teẓḍem fe-l-gelta!*
puff - *žebda* pl. *-t* coll. *žbid.* I got sick after only one puff. *mreḍt ġir men žebda weḥda.*
pull - **1.** *žebda* pl. *-t.* One more pull, and we'll have it open. *žebda xra u-ḥna ḥellinaha.* **2.** *idd* pl. *-in; kelma* pl. *-t.* You need a lot of pull to get a job here. *xeṣṣ tkun Ɛendek idd ṣḥiḥa baš teqbeṭ xedma hnaya.*
to pull - **1.** *žbed.* Don't pull so hard. *ma-džbed-š bezzaf.* **2.** *qelleƐ, zuwwel.* This tooth must be pulled *had s-senna xeṣṣha ttqelleƐ.*
**Don't pull any funny stuff! *iwa bla teḥramiyat.* --Don't try to pull the wool over my eyes! *ġir ma-termi-li-š le-Ɛžaž Ɛla Ɛeyniya.* --He pulled a fast one on me. *darha biya.* --I pulled a (big) boner. *beƐžeqtha.* --Pull over to the side! *ženneb l-l-ḥerf.*
to pull down - **1.** *hebbeṭ.* Shall I pull down the shades? *nhebbeṭ ḍ-ḍerraqat?* **2.** *ṭiyyeḥ.* They're going to pull down all the houses. *ġadyen iṭiyyḥu ḍ-ḍyur le-qdam kollhom.*
to pull in - *dxel, wṣel.* When did your train pull in? *fuq-aš weṣlet mašintkom?*
to pull oneself together - *žmeƐ ṭrafu.*
to pull out - **1.** *qelleƐ.* The children pulled out all the weeds. *d-drari qellƐu r-rbiƐ l-xayeb kollu.* **2.** *žbed.* Pull out your notebooks and we'll begin. *žebdu le-knaneš dyalkom u-nebdaw.*
to pull through - *ẓeṭṭeṭ.* We were afraid she might not pull through. *konna xewfanin Ɛliha ma-dẓeṭṭeṭ-š.*
to pull up - **1.** *wqef, ḥser, ḥbes.* The car pulled up in front of the house. *s-siyara weqfet qeddam ḍ-ḍar.* **2.** *žerr.* Pull up a chair. *žerr ši-šelya.*
pulse - *nebḍ.* The doctor just took my pulse. *ṭ-ṭbib Ɛad qelleb-li n-nebḍ.*
pump - *ṭromba* pl. *-t.* We have a pump in the backyard. *Ɛendna ṭromba fe-l-Ɛerṣa.*
to pump - **1.** *ṭelleƐ.* Shall I pump some water? *nṭelleƐ ši-šwiya de-l-ma?* **2.** *qdef.* Don't let him pump you. *la-txellih-š iqedfek.*
to pump up - *neffex.* Will you please pump up the front tires? *Ɛafak neffex-liya le-bnuwat l-qeddamiyen.*
pumpkin - *qerƐa ḥemra* pl. *qerƐat ḥemrat* coll. *qreƐ ḥemra.*
punch - **1.** *bunya* pl. *-t.* The punch knocked him down. *l-bunya ṭiyyḥettu.* **2.** *mleḥ, ledda.* His speech lacked punch. *klamu ma-kan fih mleḥ.* **3.** *mƐeṣṣer.* Would you like some punch? *tešreb ši-swiya d-le-mƐeṣṣer?*
to punch - *tqeb, ršem.* The conductor punched our tickets. *l-muraqib ršem-lna le-bṭayeq.*
puncture - *teqba* pl. *-t, tqabi.* Is there a puncture in the tire? *le-bnu fih ši-teqba?*
to puncture - *tqeb, ḥeffer.*
to **punish** - *Ɛaqeb.* Violations will be severely punished. *koll mxalfa ttƐaqeb b-šedda.*
punishment - **1.** *Ɛuquba* pl. *-t.* The punishment was too severe. *l-Ɛuquba kanet mžehda bezzaf.* **2.** *deqq.* Our car has taken a lot

of punishment. *siyaṛtna klat bezzaf de-d-deqq.*

pupil - 1. *mḥeḍri* pl. *-ya; telmid* pl. *tlamed.* She has twenty pupils in her class. *Ɛendha Ɛešrin mḥeḍri f-ṭabaqetha.* 2. *mummu* pl. *-yat.* The pupil of the left eye is injured. *mummu de-l-Ɛeyn l-iṣṛiya mqeṣṣeḥ.*

puppy - *žṛu* pl. *žṛawi* f. *žeṛwa* f. pl. *-t, žṛa.*

pure - 1. *ṣafi* pl. *ṣafyen.* Is this milk pure? *had le-ḥlib ṣafi?* 2. *ḥoṛṛ.* The necktie is pure silk. *had le-kṛafaṭa d-le-ḥrir l-ḥoṛṛ.*

purple - *mniyel.*

purpose - 1. *ġaya* pl. *-t.* What's the purpose of all these plans? *šni hiya l-ġaya men had le-mšareƐ kollha?* 2. *niya* pl. *-t.* What purpose did he have in doing that? *š-kanet niytu b-dak š-ši lli dar?*

on purpose - *Ɛenwa, be-l-Ɛani.* Did you do that on purpose? *waš Ɛmelti dak š-ši be-l-Ɛani?*

purse - 1. *šekkaṛa* pl. *-t, škayeṛ.* This purse is made of genuine leather. *had š-šekkaṛa mṣuwwba men ž-želd l-ʔaṣili.* 2. *medxul.* The purse was divided among the winners. *l-medxul tteqṣem Ɛla lli rebḥu.*

(change) purse - *bẓiṭem* pl. *bẓiṭmat.* I have either mislaid or lost my change purse. *bẓiṭmi ʔimma telleftu ʔimma mša-li.*

to **pursue** - 1. *tbeƐ.* The police pursued the thief the whole night. *l-bulis tebƐu s-saṛeq l-lil kollu.* 2. *tebbeƐ, ṭal iṭul f-.* I don't want to pursue the subject any further. *ma-baġi-š nṭul fe-l-muḍuƐ kteṛ men had š-ši.*

push - *defƐa* pl. *-t.* He gave me such a push I nearly fell over. *dfeƐni waḥed d-defƐa ḥetta kont ġad nṭiḥ.*

to push - 1. *dfeƐ.* Push the table over by the window. *dfeƐ ṭ-ṭebḷa l-žiht š-šeṛžem.* 2. *xella.* He was pushed way back. *wehli fayn xellaweh!* 3. *derr.* The crowd pushed into the stadium. *n-nas derru l-qelb l-melƐeb.* 4. *brek Ɛla.* Did you push the button? *brekti Ɛel ṭ-ṭeffaya?* 5. *ṛma iṛmi.* He tried to push the blame on me. *bġa iṛmi l-lum Ɛliya.*

to push off - *qelleƐ, mša imši, bda ibda ṭ-ṭriq.* Right after we pushed off, the boat capsized. *ġir ḥna qelleƐna u-l-baxiṛa ttqelbet.*

to **put** - 1. *nezzel.* Put the table over there. *nezzel ṭ-ṭebḷa hnak.* 2. *Ɛmel.* Put an ad in the paper. *Ɛmel ʔiƐlan fe-l-žarida.* 3. *weṣṣeḷ.* I have to put the kids to bed. *xeṣṣni nweṣṣeḷ d-drari ineƐsu.*

**I wouldn't put any faith in that story. *ma-ntiyyeq-š dak š-ši lli kan f-dak le-xṛafa.* --Why don't you put it straight to him? *Ɛlaš ma-tqulha-lu-š b-ṭayṭay?* --You stay put until I get back. *xellik fe-ṛḥebtek ḥetta nwelli.*

to put across - 1. *fesser, biyyen.* I don't know how to put it across to him that... *ma-Ɛreft-ši kif nfesser-lu billa...* 2. *faz ifuz b-.* Did you put the deal across? *fezti b-dak l-qaḍiya?*

to put an end (stop) to - *Ɛmel ḥedd l-, ḥṣeṛ.* I'll have to put an end to that nonsense. *xeṣṣni neƐmel ḥedd l-dak le-ḥmaq.* --Can't you put a stop to that talk? *ma-teqḍeṛ-ši teḥṣeṛ dak l-hedṛa?*

to put aside (or away) - *xebbeƐ, ḥeyyed.* She's been putting aside a little money each month. *koll šheṛ ka-txebbeƐ šwiya d-le-flus.*

to put back - *redd.* Put the book back where you got it. *redd le-ktab fayn xditih.*

to put down - 1. *ḥeṭṭ, nezzel.* Do you want to put the box down here? *bġiti tḥeṭṭ ṣ-ṣenduq hnaya?* 2. *kteb.* Put down your name and address. *kteb smiytek u-Ɛenwanek.*

to put in - 1. *Ɛṭa yeƐṭi.* They put in a lot of time on that job. *Ɛṭaw bezzaf de-l-weqt l-dak l-xedma.* 2. *rekkeb.* Did they put in a new windowpane? *waš rekkbu zaža de-š-šeṛžem ždida?*

**Will you put in a word for me? *iwa ġad tgeƐƐedni b-ši klima?*

to put in order - *Ɛewweṭ.* He's been putting his affairs in order. *ṛah ka-iƐewweṭ šġalatu.*

to put off - 1. *ʔexxeṛ.* I can't put the matter off any longer. *ma-imken-li-š nʔexxeṛ l-qaḍiya kteṛ men had š-ši.* 2. *txella Ɛla.* I can't put off the appointment. *ma-imken-li-š ntxella Ɛel l-miƐad.* 3. *tʔexxeṛ Ɛla.* Can't you put him off for a while? *ma-teqḍer-ši ttʔexxeṛ Ɛlih ši-šwiya?*

to put on - 1. *Ɛmel, ṭḷeq.* Put on a clean tablecloth! *ṭḷeq mendil nqi.* 2. *lbes, Ɛmel.* Put your coat on! *lbes l-kebbuṭ dyalek!* 3. *lesseq.* Did you put stamps on all the letters? *lesseqti t-tnaber Ɛel le-bṛawat kollhom?* 4. *šƐel.*

Put on the light, please. *šεel ḍ-ḍuw εafak.* 5. *zad izid.* I've put on three kilos. *zedt tlata de-l-kilu.* 6. *ṣenneε.* Don't you think her accent is put on? *ma-ka-ḍḍenn billa lehžetha mṣennεa?*

to put oneself out - *tεeddeb, tεeb nefsu, tεeb ṛaṣu.* Don't put yourself out on my account. *ma-ttεeb-ši nefsek εla ʔežli.*

to put out - 1. *ṭfa iṭfi.* Put out the light before you leave. *ṭfi ḍ-ḍuw qbel ma-temši.* 2. *xerrež.* Put him out if he makes too much noise. *xerržu ila εmel ṣ-ṣḍeε bezzaf.* 3. *nšeṛ.* Who's putting out your book? *škun ġad inšeṛ-lek ktabek?*

**He felt quite put out about that. *kan bayen εlih mxewṭeṛ men dak š-ši.*

to put over on - *lεeb εla, duwwezha b-.* You can't put anything over on him. *ma-imken-š dduwwezha bih.*

to put through - *neffed.* He put his own plan through. *neffed mešṛuεu b-iddih.*

to put to good use - *xeddem l-l-meṣlaḥa.* We'll put the money to good use. *ġad nxeddmu le-flus l-l-meṣlaḥa.*

to put to death - *εdem.* They put the murderer to death this morning. *εedmu qettal ṛ-ṛuḥ had ṣ-ṣbaḥ.*

to put to expense - *ṭeḷḷeb ṣayeṛ.* This will put me to considerable expense. *had š-ši ġad iṭeḷḷeb-li ṣayeṛ kbir.*

to put up - 1. *rekkeb.* New telephone poles are being put up. *ṛahom ka-irekkbu rkayez de-t-tilifun ždad.* 2. *εṛeḍ.* The farm will be put up for sale this week. *had ž-žemεa ġad iεeṛḍu le-εzib l-l-biε.* 3. *nezzel.* Each of them put up a thousand dirhams. *koll waḥed mennhom nezzel ʔalef derhem.* 4. *wežžed, ṭeḷḷeε.* This building was put up in six months. *ṭeḷḷεu had l-binaya f-sett šhuṛ.* 5. *biyyet, gelles.* Can you put us up for the night? *imken-lek tgellesna had l-lila?* 6. *biyyen.* They didn't put up a fight. *ma-biyynu mεaṛḍa.*

to put up with - *ṣbeṛ l-.* I don't know why you put up with it. *ma-εṛeft-ši l-aš ka-teṣbeṛ l-dak š-ši.*

puzzle - 1. *muškila* pl. *-t, mašakil; xenṭaqiṛa* pl. *-t; weḥla* pl. *-t.* Can you solve that puzzle? *teεṛef txerrež dak l-xenṭaqiṛa?* 2. *ḥiṛa* pl. *-t.* That is a puzzle to me. *ḥiṛa hadik žatni.*

to puzzle - *ḥeyyer.* His letter had us puzzled. *bṛatu ḥeyyretni.*

to puzzle out - *fhem, fesser.* I can't puzzle it out. *ma-εṛeft-ši kif nfesserha.*

pyramid - *haṛam* pl. *ʔehṛam.*

Q

qualification - *qoḍṛa* pl. *-t.* Do you think she has the necessary qualifications for the job? *waš ban-lek bin εendha l-qoḍṛa lli wažba l-had l-xedma?*

qualified - 1. *(lli) εendu wṣaf.* He is not qualified for this job. *ma-εendu-š le-wṣaf l-had l-xedma.* 2. *be-š-šeṛṭ.* He gave a qualified answer. *žaweb be-š-šeṛṭ.*

quality - 1. *nuε* pl. *ʔenwaε.* Don't you have any better quality? *waš εendek ši-nuε axoṛ ḥsen?* --Our product is of high quality. *nuε s-selεa dyalna moεtabaṛa.* 2. *ḥsiniya* pl. *-t.* She has many good qualities. *εendha bezzaf d-le-ḥsiniyat.*

quantity - *qeḍṛ, qḍeṛ.* It's not the quantity but the quality that counts. *ma-ši l-qeḍṛ lli l-muhemm walayenni n-nuε.*

in large quantities - *b-εadad kbir.* Radios are now produced in large quantities. *ka-iṣawbu daba ṛ-ṛadyuwat b-εadad kbir.*

in quantity - *b-εadad kbir.* We buy in quantity. *ka-nešriw b-εadad kbir.*

quarrel - *mdabza* pl. *-t.* Who started the quarrel? *škun lli bda le-mdabza?*

to quarrel - *dabez.* One of these days we're going to quarrel. *ši-nhaṛ ġadi ndabzu.*

quarry - 1. *meεden d-le-ḥžeṛ* pl. *mεaden d-le-ḥžeṛ.* Did this stone come from the quarry? *waš had l-ḥežṛa žat men l-meεden d-le-ḥžeṛ?*

2. *ṣiḍ.* Mice become the quarry of various birds of prey. *l-firan huma ṣiḍ dyal ɛadad d-le-bṛaṭel d-le-frisa.*

quarter - *ṛbeɛ* pl. *ṛbuɛa.* Each partner received a quarter of the profits. *koll šarik xda ṛbeɛ dyal r-rbiḥ.* --It's a quarter after ten already. *hadi beɛda ɛešṛa u-ṛbeɛ.*

the Empty Quarter - *ṛ-ṛobɛ l-xali.*

(a) quarter to three, etc. - *fe-t-tlata llaṛeb,* etc. The train leaves at a quarter to three. *l-mašina ġad temši fe-t-tlata llaṛeb.*

quarterly - *koll telt šhuṛ.* I pay my insurance quarterly. *ka-nxeḷḷes s-sugṛa dyali koll telt šhuṛ.*

quarters - *sokna.* Did you find decent quarters? *waš žberti sokna mezyana?*

at close quarters - *mqeṛṛeb (bezzaf).* They fought at close quarters. *tḥaṛbu mqeṛṛbin bezzaf.*

queen - **1.** (person) *malika* pl. *-t.* **2.** (at chess) *wzir* pl. *wẓaṛa, waẓaṛa.*

queer - *f-ši-škel.* He's a queer person. *huwa ṛažel f-ši-škel.*

to **quench** - *berred.* I simply can't quench my thirst. *ma-imken-li-š nberred l-ɛeṭša dyali.*

question - **1.** *as?ila* pl. *-t, su?al* pl. *asa?il.* Have you any further questions? *waš ɛendek ši-as?ila xṛa?* **2.** *šekk* pl. *škuk.* There is no question about it. *had š-ši bla šekk.* **3.** *qaḍiya* pl. *-t.* It was a question of saving a human life. *hadi kanet qaḍiya dyal ɛteq ṛ-ṛuḥ.*

**That's completely out of the question. *ma-temken-š.* --The gentleman in question was not there. *ṛ-ṛažel ɛla men ka-ntkellmu ma-kan-š temma.*

beyond question - *ma-ɛlih ḥetta šekk.* His honesty is beyond question. *ṣ-ṣfawa dyalu ma-ɛliha ḥetta šekk.*

to ask a question - *s?el.* They asked a lot of questions. *se?lu bezzaf.*

to question - **1.** *suwwel.* The police questioned him all night long. *l-bulis bqaw ka-isuwwlu l-lila kollha.* **2.** *šekk f-.* I question his sincerity. *ka-nšekk ƒe-ṣ-ṣedq dyalu.*

quick - *mezrub.* That was a quick decision. *hada kan teɛwal mezrub.*

**Be quick about it! *serbi ṛaṣek!*

quickly - *be-z-zerba.* Come quickly! *aži be-z-zerba.*

quicksilver - *zawaq.*

quick-tempered - *(lli) ka-itqelleq be-z-zerba.* She is very quick-tempered. *hiya ka-ttqelleq be-z-zerba.*

quiet - **1.** *sukut.* I demand absolute quiet. *ka-nṭḷeb mennkom sukut tamm.* **2.** *mhedden.* I live in a quiet neighborhood. *ka-nɛiš f-naḥiya mheddna.*

**Quiet, please! *sektu ɛafakom!*

to keep quiet - *thedden.* Why didn't you keep quiet? *ɛlaš ma-theddenti-š?*

to quiet (down) - *hedden.* See if you can quiet her. *šuf waš imken-lek theddenha.*

to quiet down - **1.** *thedden.* She quieted down after a while. *theddnet men beɛḍ ši-šwiya.* **2.** *bred.* Let's wait till the excitement quiets down a bit. *ntsennaw ḥetta l-ḥaṛaka tebred šwiya.*

quince - *ṣfeṛžla* pl. *-t* coll. *ṣfeṛžel.*

to **quit** - **1.** *xrež men.* He quit his job yesterday. *xrež men xdemtu l-bareḥ.* **2.** *wqef, ḥṣeṛ.* He quit right in the middle. *wqef fe-l-woṣṭ.* --Quit it! *ḥṣeṛ!*

**It's time to quit (work). *hada l-weqt baš nemšiw.*

quite - **1.** *tamamen.* Are you quite sure that you can't go? *waš nta mḥeqqeq tamamen bin ma-imken-lek-š temši?* **2.** *bezzaf.* The house is quite far from here. *ḍ-ḍaṛ bɛida bezzaf men hna.*

**That's quite possible. *imken.*

quotation - *neṣṣ* pl. *nṣaṣ, nṣuṣ, nuṣuṣ.* His speech was full of quotations. *l-xeṭba dyalu kan ɛendha bezzaf de-n-nṣaṣ.*

to **quote** - *dkeṛ.* That's quoted on page ten. *hada medkuṛ fe-ṣ-ṣefḥa ɛešṛa.*

**Don't quote me! *ma-tɛewwed-š klami.* --What price did he quote you? *š-men taman ṭḷeb-lek?*

R

Rabat - *ṛ-ṛbaṭ*.
native of Rabat - *ṛbaṭi* adj. pl. *yen*, n. pl. *hel ṛ-ṛbaṭ*.
rabbit - *qniya* pl. *-t*.
race - **1.** *muṣabaqa* pl. *-t*, *mṣabqa* pl. *-t*. I'm going to the (horse) races. *ġad nemši l-l-muṣabaqa (de-l-xil)*. **2.** *žens* pl. *žnus*. There is no such thing as a pure race. *ž-žens ṣ-ṣafi ma-kayen-š*.
foot race - *žri*, *sbiq*.
to race - **1.** *žra ižri be-z-zerba*. The car raced through the streets. *ṭ-ṭumubila žrat be-z-zerba fe-z-zenqa*. **2.** *sabeq*. Let's race. *yaḷḷah nsabqu*.
**Don't race the engine. *ma-txeddem-š l-muṭuṛ be-z-zerba*.
rack - **1.** *meṛfeƐ* pl. *mṛafeƐ*. Put the books back on the rack. *ṛežžeƐ le-ktub l-l-meṛfeƐ*. **2.** *šebka* pl. *-t*, *šbayek*. Put your baggage up on the rack. *ḥeṭṭ ḥwayžek fe-š-šebka*. **3.** *meqbeṭ* pl. *mqabeṭ*. I hung my coat on the rack. *Ɛelleqt kebbuṭi fe-l-meqbeṭ*.
to rack one's brains - *herres ṛaṣu*. Don't rack your brains over it. *ma-therres-š ṛaṣek Ɛlih*.
racket - *ṣdaƐ*. The children are making an awful racket. *d-drari ka-iƐemlu ṣdaƐ kbir*.
(tennis) racket - *ṛakiṭa* pl. *-t*. Her racket is much too heavy for you. *ṛ-ṛakiṭa dyalha tqila Ɛlik bezzaf*.
radio - *ṛadyu* pl. *-wat*.
radio station - *idaƐa* pl. *-t*.
radish - *fežla* pl. *-t* coll. *fžel*.
raft - *mƐeddya* pl. *-t*.
rag - *zif* pl. *zyuf*, *zyufa*; *šeṛwiṭa* pl. *šṛaweṭ*. Do you have a rag to dust the table? *waš Ɛendek ši-zif baš nemseḥ ṭ-ṭebla?*
**They were dressed in rags. *kanu labsin ḥwayež mšeṛwṭin*.
rage - *tezƐifa* pl. *-t*. His rage made him tremble. *t-tezƐifa dyalu ġezzlettu*
to fly into a rage - *džennen*, *tqelleq*. My father flew into a rage when I told him. *ḅḅa džennen melli qoltha-lu*.
to rage - *tqelleq*. He raged like a bull. *tqelleq bḥal ṭ-ṭuṛ*.
**The storm raged all night long. *r-reƐda ṭaḷet l-lila kollha*.

rail - *ṣekka* pl. *skek*.
railing - *ḍeṛbuẓ* pl. *ḍṛabeẓ*. Hold on to the railing. *qbeṭ ḍ-ḍeṛbuẓ*.
railroad - *šmandifir*. I prefer to go by railroad. *ka-nfeḍḍeḷ ṣafaṛ š-šmandifir*.
railroad station - *lagaṛ* pl. *-at*, *maḥeṭṭa* (pl. *-t*) *de-š-šmandifir*.
rain - *šta*.
to rain - *ṭaḥ iṭiḥ š-šta*. It rained all morning. *ṭaḥet š-šta ṣ-ṣbaḥ kollu*.
rainbow - *Ɛṛuṣt s-sma* pl. *Ɛṛuṣat s-sma*, *qus n-nbi* pl. *qwas n-nbi*.
raise - *zyada* pl. *-t*. He got a raise. *xda zyada*.
to raise - **1.** *ḍebbeṛ Ɛla*. I can't raise the money. *ma-imken-li-š nḍebbeṛ Ɛel le-flus*. **2.** *ḥṣeḍ*. They raise a lot of wheat here. *ka-iḥeṣdu bezzaf de-l-gemḥ hna*. **3.** *hezz*. Raise your hands! *hezzu iddikom!* **4.** *zad izid f-*. They're going to raise the rent on October first. *ġad izidu f-le-kra f-ʔewwel ktubeṛ*. **5.** *ṛebba*. Most farmers here raise sheep. *ʔekteṛ l-fellaḥa hna ka-iṛebbiw le-ġnem*. --She has raised nine children. *ṛebbat tesƐud de-d-drari*.
to raise the roof - **1.** *džennen (bezzaf)*, *tqelleq (bezzaf)*. My father raised the roof because I took the car. *ḅḅa džennen bezzaf Ɛla qibal xdit ṭ-ṭumubil*. **2.** *fṛeƐ ḍ-ḍaṛ be-ṣ-ṣdaƐ*. The kids are raising the roof again. *d-drari ka-ifeṛƐu ḍ-ḍaṛ be-ṣ-ṣdaƐ Ɛewtani*.
to raise a question - *žbed suʔal*. Who raised the question? *škun lli žbed s-suʔal?*
rake - *xebbaša* pl. *-t*. We need a new rake for the garden. *xeṣṣna xebbaša ždida l-l-Ɛeṛṣa*.
to rake - *xebbeš*, *keṛṛeṭ*.
range - **1.** *ʔenwaƐ*, *anwaƐ* (pl.). These shirts come in a large range of colors. *had le-qwamež Ɛendhom bezzaf de-l-ʔenwaƐ de-l-lwan*. **2.** *kanun* pl. *kwanen*. We just bought a new range. *Ɛad šrina kanun ždid*.
out of range - *bƐid men* pl. *bƐad men*, *bƐid Ɛla* pl. *bƐad Ɛla*. The tanks were out of range of our guns. *ṭ-ṭnuga kanu bƐad men le-mdafeƐ dyalna*.

**Quiet! let's wait until he's out of range. *skot, tsenna ḥetta itbeƐƐed menna.*
**Prices range from one to five dollars. *t-tamanat bin ḍulaṛ ḥetta l-xemsa.*

rank - *rotba* pl. *-t, ḍaṛaža* pl. *-t.* What's that officer's rank? *šnu r-rotba dyal dak ḍ-ḍabiṭ?*
**That's rank ingratitude! *koll z-znan u-lƐen mula!* --He's worked his way up from the ranks. *dar teṛqiya Ɛla ktafu.*

rapid - *be-z-zerba.* His heartbeat was very rapid. *qelbu kan ka-iḍṛeb be-z-zerba.*

rapidly - *b-soṛƐa.* This man can run quite rapidly. *had ṛ-ṛažel imken-lu džri b-soṛƐa.*

rare - **1.** *qlil* pl. *qlal.* That's a rare flower. *had n-nuƐ de-n-nuwwaṛa qlil.* **2.** *ma-mešwi-š bezzaf, demmu sayel.* I'd like my steak rare. *bġit l-biftik dyali ma-mešwi-š bezzaf.*

rarely - *qlil.* That rarely happens. *had š-ši ka-yuqeƐ qlil.*

rascal - *ḥṛami, mṭeṛṛeq.*

rash - **1.** *ḥbub* (pl.), *xṛuž* (pl.). He has a rash on his face. *xeṛžu-lu ḥbub f-wežhu.* **2.** *bla texmima.* I won't make any rash promises. *ma-neƐṭik-š aman bla texmima.*

rat - *ṭobba* pl. *-t.*

rate - *taman* pl. *-at.* What are the rates for single rooms? *šnu huwa t-taman l-bit waḥed?* --What are the new rates for airmail? *šnu huwa t-taman ž-ždid de-l-barid l-žewwi?* --What's the rate of exchange today? *šnu huwa taman ṣ-ṣeṛf l-yum?* --The rate of interest is four per cent. *taman l-intiris huwa ṛebƐa f-le-mya.*
**At this rate we'll never get done. *ila mšina f-had l-ḥala Ɛemmeṛna ma-nfeḍḍiw.*
at any rate - *Ɛla kolli ḥal.* At any rate, I'd like to see you. *Ɛla kolli ḥal bġit nšufek.*
first-rate - *nimiru waḥed.* This is a first-rate hotel. *hada uṭil nimiru waḥed.*

rather - **1.** *bezzaf.* The play was rather long. *t-temtil kan ṭwiḷ bezzaf.* **2.** *ḥsen.* I would rather wait. *bġit ntsenna ḥsen.*
rather ... than - *waḷḷah u-ma- ... wella.* I'd rather die than surrender. *waḷḷah u-ma-nmut wella nsellem rași.*

to **rattle** - **1.** *qeṛqeb.* Do you have to rattle the dishes that way? *ma-Ɛendek Ɛlaš tqeṛqeb ṭ-ṭbaṣeḷ hakda.* **2.** *xeṛxeṛ.* Stop rattling the doorknob! *baṛaka ma-txeṛxeṛ-š l-luba!*
to rattle on - *hedrez.* She can rattle on like that for hours. *imken-lha thedrez hakda swayeƐ.*
to get someone rattled - *šuwweš.* Don't get me rattled. *ma-tšuwwešni-š.*

to **rave** - *hetref.* He was raving like a madman. *kan ka-ihetref bḥal le-ḥmeq.*
to rave about - *ttexṭef Ɛeqlu f-.* Everyone raves about his new book. *koll waḥed ttexṭef Ɛeqlu fe-ktabu ž-ždid.*

raw - **1.** *xḍeṛ* pl. *xuḍeṛ.* The meat is almost raw. *l-lḥem Ɛlayen xḍeṛ.* **2.** *mžellef.* My throat is raw. *ḥelqi mžellef.*

ray - *šƐa* pl. *ašƐiya.* A ray of light came through the window. *šƐa de-ḍ-ḍuw dxel men š-šeṛžem.*
**There's still a ray of hope. *kayen ma-zal šwiya de-ṛ-ṛaža.*

razor - *mess* pl. *msus, mus* pl. *mwas.* I have to strop my razor. *xeṣṣni nmeḍḍi l-mess d-le-ḥsana dyali.*
safety razor - *makina d-le-ḥsana* pl. *mwaken d-le-ḥsana.*

razor blade - *mess* pl. *msus, mus* pl. *mwas.* Please buy me a dozen razor blades. *šri-li baṛaka ḷḷahu fik ẓina d-le-msas d-le-ḥsana.*

to **reach** - **1.** *wṣeḷ l-.* Can you reach that shelf? *waš imken-lek tuṣeḷ l-dak l-meṛfeƐ?* --We reached the city at daybreak. *wṣeḷna l-le-mdina f-le-fžer.* --Our garden reaches all the way to the river. *l-Ɛeṛṣa dyalna ka-tuṣeḷ ḥetta l-l-wad.* --The rumor even reached us. *l-ḥess wṣeḷ ḥetta l-Ɛendna.* **2.** *ntaṣeḷ b-.* There was no way of reaching him. *ma-mken-lna-š nntaṣḷu bih.* **3.** *medd.* Please reach me the salt. *medd-li l-melḥa Ɛafak.*
to reach for - *medd iddu (iddih) Ɛla.* He reaches for everything he sees. *lli šafha ka-imedd Ɛliha iddih.*
**He reached into his pocket. *ḥša iddu f-mektubu.*

to **read** - *qṛa iqṛa.*
**The thermometer reads thirty-five degrees. *l-mizan de-s-sxana fih xemsa u-tlatin ḍeṛža.* --Was my name read? *waš dekṛu smiyti?* --This reads like a fairy tale. *ka-itšebbeh le-xṛafa.*
to read aloud - *qṛa iqṛa be-l-Ɛali.*

reading – *qṛaya.* He got a perfect score in reading. *Ɛṭaweh Ɛešrin Ɛla Ɛešrin f-le-qṛaya.*

ready – *wažed.* Dinner is ready. *l-makla wažda.* --I'm ready for anything. *ana wažed l-koll-ši.*

**I don't have much ready cash. *ma-Ɛendi ġir šwiya d-le-flus Ɛel ṭ-ṭabḷa.* --She's always ready with an answer. *Ɛendha dima ž-žwab fe-lsanha.*

ready-made – *mužud.* Do you buy your clothes ready-made? *waš ka-tešri ḥwayžek mužudin?*

real – **1.** *ḥqiq* pl. *ḥqaq.* That's not his real name. *hadi ma-ši smiytu le-ḥqiqa.* --What is the real reason? *šnu huwa s-sabab le-ḥqiq?* --That's what I call a real friend. *hada huwa ka-nsemmi ṣaḥeb ḥqiq.* **2.** *ḥoṛṛ.* Is this real silk? *waš had le-ḥrir ḥoṛṛ?*

**It was a real pleasure to listen to him. *kanet ḥlawa baš ntṣenntuh.* --That never happens in real life. *had š-ši ma-Ɛemmṛu ka-yuqeƐ fe-d-denya.*

real estate – *melk* pl. *mluk.*

reality – *ḥqiqa* pl. *-t.*

to **realize** – **1.** *kemmel.* He never realized his ambition to become a doctor. *Ɛemmṛu ma-kemmel ṭ-ṭmeƐ dyalu baš ikun ṭbib.* **2.** *ban-lu.* I didn't realize it was so late. *ma-ban-li-š bin mša l-ḥal.* --He never realized the danger. *Ɛemmṛu ma-ban-lu l-xaṭeṛ.* **3.** *Ɛṛef ṛaṣu.* Does he realize he's sick? *waš ka-yeƐṛef ṛaṣu bin mṛiḍ?*

to realize a profit – *rbeḥ.* He realized quite a profit on that sale. *rbeḥ bezzaf f-had l-biƐa.*

really – *ḥeqqen.* I really wanted to stay at home. *ḥeqqen kont baġi nebqa fe-ḍ-ḍaṛ.*

**Do you really mean it? *waš had š-ši b-ṣeḥḥ?* --It really isn't very far! *waḷḷah ma-bƐid!*

rear – **1.** *ḷuṛ.* The rear of the house is being painted. *ka-iṣebġu ḷ-ḷuṛ de-ḍ-ḍaṛ.* --The emergency exit is in the rear. *bab l-iġata fe-ḷ-ḷuṛ.* **2.** *wṛani.* The rear windows haven't been cleaned yet. *š-šṛažem le-wṛaniyin ma-zal ma-ttsemḥu.*

to **rearrange** – *neqqel.* You ought to rearrange the furniture. *u-kan neqqelti le-qšuša.*

reason – **1.** *ḥeqq* or *ḥquq.* She has no reason for acting like that. *ma-Ɛendha l-ḥeqq baš teƐmel hakda.* or *ma-Ɛendha Ɛlaš baš teƐmel hakda.* **2.** *sabab* pl. *sbayeb.* Is that the reason you didn't go? *waš ma-mšiti-š Ɛla yedd had s-sabab?* --He was dismissed without any reason. *dḥaweh bla ḥetta sabab.* **3.** *Ɛqel.* If this keeps up, I'll lose my reason. *ila had š-ši ṭaḷ, ġad ixṛož Ɛeqli.*

**He gave me no reason for complaint. *ma-xellani mnayn ntšekka mennu.*

to reason (with) – *tfahem (mƐa).* You can't reason with him. *ma-imken-lek-š ttfahem mƐah.*

reasonable – **1.** *Ɛaqel.* She's a very reasonable person. *hiya Ɛaqla bezzaf.* **2.** *meƐqul.* That's a reasonable price. *hada taman meƐqul.* --That's a reasonable fee. *hadi užṛa meƐqula.*

to **rebel** – **1.** *nuwweḍ l-fetna.* The prisoners rebelled at the poor living conditions. *l-ḥebbasa nuwwḍu l-fetna Ɛel l-ḥala s-siʔa.* **2.** *tṛuwweƐ.* My stomach simply rebelled. *kerši tṛuwweƐ.*

to **recall** – **1.** *ṛežžeƐ.* The ambassador has been recalled. *ṛežžƐu s-safir.* **2.** *Ɛqel.* Do you recall whether he was there? *waš ka-teƐqel bin kan temma?*

receipt – **1.** *wṣuḷ.* Please acknowledge receipt of the books. *Ɛlem baṛaka ḷḷahu fik be-wṣuḷ le-ktuba.* **2.** *medxul.* The receipts are low today. *ma-kayen-š medxul bezzaf l-yum.* **3.** *tuṣiḷ* pl. *twaṣeḷ.* Please give me a receipt. *Ɛṭini Ɛafak tuṣiḷ.*

to receipt – *sellem Ɛla.* Please receipt this bill. *sellem Ɛla had l-weṛqa d-le-xlaṣ.*

to **receive** – **1.** *wṣel-lu, weṣlu.* Did you receive my telegram? *waš weṣlek t-tiligṛam dyali?* **2.** *steqbel.* We were cordially received. *steqbluna b-kolli faṛaḥ.*

receiver – *semmaƐa* pl. *-t.* You left the receiver off the hook. *ma-xelliti-š s-semmaƐa f-maḥellha.*

recent – *ždid* pl. *ždad.* Do you have any recent magazines? *waš Ɛendek ši-mažellat ždad?*

recently – *Ɛad.* I heard it only recently. *Ɛad smeƐt biha.*

recess – *ṛaḥa* pl. *-t.* We have a short recess at ten in the morning. *Ɛendna ṛaḥa qṣiṛa fe-l-Ɛešṛa de-ṣ-ṣbaḥ.*

reckless – *(lli) ma-ka-iredd-š balu.* He's a reckless driver. *huwa ṣuwwag ma-ka-iredd-š balu.*

recognition - *Ɛtiṛaf.*
to **recognize** - **1.** *Ɛqel, Ɛṛef.* I recognized him by his voice. *Ɛṛeftu men ḥelqu.* --You've grown so much I didn't recognize you. *ṭwaḷiti ḥetta ma-Ɛqelt-š Ɛlik.* **2.** *Ɛtaṛef b-.* They have finally recognized his merits. *ma-mšaw ḥetta Ɛtaṛfu-lu b-meqḍuṛtu.*
to **recommend** - *weṣṣa Ɛla.* I recommended her highly to him. *weṣṣit Ɛliha bezzaf lilu.*
recommendation - *wṣiya* pl. *-t.* I did it on your recommendation. *dertha Ɛla qibal Ɛṭitini wṣiya Ɛliha.*
to **record** - *sežžel.*
to **recover** - *bṛa ibṛa.* He recovered from his illness. *bṛa men l-meṛḍ dyalu.*
**He recovered his balance immediately. *tƐewweṭ-lu l-mizan deġya* or *tgeƐƐed-lu l-mil deġya.* --He's on the road to recovery. *huwa ka-iqeddem ṛ-ṛaḥa* or *huwa Ɛlayen bṛa.*
red - *ḥmeṛ* pl. *ḥumeṛ.* I want to buy a red hat. *bġit nešri šemrir ḥmeṛ.* --Red is not becoming on her. *ma-ka-iwatiha-š le-ḥmeṛ.*
Red Crescent - *l-hilal le-ḥmeṛ.*
Red Cross - *ṣ-ṣḷib le-ḥmeṛ.*
to **reduce** - *nqeṣ, ṭiyyeḥ.* We've reduced the prices ten percent. *nqeṣna Ɛešṛa f-le-mya men t-tamanat.*
to **refer** - **1.** *ṣifeṭ* or *ṣafeṭ iṣifeṭ.* I was referred to the manager. *ṣifṭuni l-Ɛend l-mudiṛ* **2.** *tkellem.* I'm referring to your mother not your sister. *ka-ntkellem Ɛla yemmak ma-ši Ɛla xtek.* **3.** *dkeṛ.* She referred to it in her book. *dekṛetha fe-ktabha.*
reflection - *šƐa.* You can see your reflection in the water. *imken-lek tšuf š-šƐa dyalek fe-l-ma.*
reform - *iṣlaḥ* pl. *-at.* He introduced many reforms. *qeddem Ɛadad d-l-iṣlaḥat.*
to reform - **1.** *ṣḷeḥ.* He's always trying to reform the world. *ka-ibġi dima iṣḷeḥ koll-ši.* **2.** *tbeddel, tḥessen.* I'm sure he'll reform. *ana mḥeqqeq bin ġad itbeddel.*
refreshment - *mešṛuba* pl. *-t.* Refreshments were served during the intermission. *Ɛṭahom l-mešṛubat f-weqt l-inqitaƐ.*
refrigerator - *tellaža* pl. *-t.*
refugee - *muhažir* pl. *muhažrin.*
to **refund** - *redd.* I'll refund your money. *ġad nredd-lek flusek.*
refusal - *reddan.*
refuse - *zbel.* Place the refuse in the container. *Ɛmel z-zbel fe-ṭ-ṭaṛṛu.*
to refuse - **1.** *redd f-wezhu.* He doesn't refuse me anything. *ma-redd-li f-wežhi ḥetta ḥaža.* **2.** *ma-qbel-š.* He refused my resignation. *ma-qbel-š t-teslim dyali.* **3.** *ma-bġa-ši.* She refused to help me. *ma-bġat-š tƐawenni.*
**What'll happen if I refuse to let you take it? *š-ġad yuqeƐ ila ma-xellitek-š taxdu?*
regard - *naḥiya.* In that regard, I agree with you. *f-had n-naḥiya ana mettafeq mƐak.*
to give regards to - *sellem Ɛla.* Give my regards to the folks at home. *sellem-li Ɛla mwalin ḍ-ḍaṛ.*
to have regard for - *tnebbeh l-.* He has no regard at all for others. *ma-ka-itnebbeh-š gaƐ l-ḥetta waḥed.*
with (in) regard to - *amma.* With regard to that subject... *amma f-had l-muḍuƐ...*
to regard as - *ḥseb, Ɛtabeṛ, Ɛedd.* He is regarded as a specialist. *ka-iḥesbuh xtiṣaṣi.*
regarding - *amma.* Regarding your new house... *amma ḍ-ḍaṛ ž-ždida dyalkom...*
region - *naḥiya* or *nawaḥi.*
register - *konnaš t-tesžil* pl. *knaneš t-tesžil.* Did you sign the register? *waš nezzelt xeṭṭ iddik f-konnaš t-tesžil?*
(cash) register - *ṣenḍuq* pl. *ṣnaḍeq.* Did you take any money out of the register? *waš xditi ši-flus men ṣ-ṣenḍuq?*
to register - **1.** *sežžel.* We registered him in this hotel yesterday. *sežželnah l-bareḥ f-had l-uṭil.* **2.** *tsežžel.* Have you registered with the police? *waš tsežželti Ɛend l-bulis?* **3.** *tqeyyed.* Where do you register here? *fayn imken-lna ntqeyydu hna?* **4.** *suger.* Where do you register letters? *fayn imken-li nsuger le-bṛawat?*
to **regret** - *ndem.* I've always regretted not having traveled much. *dima nadem Ɛla lli ma-ṣafeṛt-š bezzaf.*
regrettable - *lli ndem Ɛliha l-waḥed.*
regular - **1.** *Ɛadi.* The regular price is five dollars. *t-taman l-Ɛadi xemsa de-ḍ-ḍuḷaṛ.* **2.** *hadak.* His pulse is regular. *n-nebḍ dyalu huwa hadak.* **3.** *mneḍḍem.* He lives a very regular life. *huwa Ɛayeš*

ḥayat mneḍḍma.
**This is our regular waiter. *hada huwa l-garṣun lli mwellfin bih.*
regularly – *ɛel l-qaɛida.* He pays regularly. *ka-ixelleṣ ɛel l-qaɛida.*
to **regulate** – *sawa.*
regulation – *qanun* pl. *qwanen.* That's against regulations. *had š-ši ḍeḍḍ l-qanun.*
rehearsal – *temrin* pl. *tmaren.*
rein – *lžam* pl. *-at.*
to **reject** – *ma-qbel-š.* They rejected my application. *ma-qeblu-š ṭ-ṭaləb dyali.*
related – *men ɛaʔila weḥda.* He and I are related. *ḥna men ɛaʔila weḥda.*
relation – *ɛalaqa* pl. *-t.* The relations between the two countries are strained. *l-ɛalaqat bin l-boldan b-žuž metwettrin.*
**I have a lot of relations there. *ɛendi bezzaf de-n-nas men ɛaʔilti temma.*
relationship – *ɛalaqa* pl. *-t.* What's the relationship between those two? *šniya l-ɛalaqa lli kayna bin had ž-žuž?*
to **relax** – **1.** *rxa irxi.* Relax your muscles. *rxi ɛaṣabek.* **2.** *triyyeḥ.* I can't relax until I finish. *ma-imken-li-š ntriyyeḥ qbel-ma nsali.*
release – *meṭlaqa* pl. *-t.* Her release was delayed a couple of days. *ɛeṭṭlu-lha l-meṭlaqa dyalha b-yumayn.*
to release – **1.** *ṭleq.* The police released him right away. *š-šorṭa ṭelqettu degya.* **2.** *ḥell.* He forgot to release the brake. *nsa ma-ḥell-š l-ḥeṣṣar.*
reliable – *(lli) fih tiqa.* That's a reliable firm. *hadi šarika fiha tiqa.*
**He's a very reliable person. *huwa ražel imken-lek ttwekkel ɛlih.*
relief – *raḥa.* Did the medicine give you any relief? *waš had d-dwa žab-lek raḥa?*
**I bet it's a relief to have it off your mind. *ban-li bin raḥa ɛlik baš tfekk raṣek mennha.* —No relief (from the heat) is in sight. *ḥetta bruda ma-bayna.*
to **relieve** – **1.** *xeffef.* This will relieve your headache. *had š-ši daba ixeffef-lek merḍ r-raṣ.* **2.** *berra.* Do you have anything that will relieve his pains? *waš ɛendek ši-ḥaža lli tberri-lu le-wžeɛ?* **3.** *beddel.* The guard is relieved at twelve o'clock. *ka-ibeddlu l-ɛessas fe-ṭ-ṭnaš.*
to be relieved – *rtaḥ.* I'm glad I've been relieved of that worry. *ana ferḥan lli rtaḥit men had l-hemm.*
to relieve one another – *tnawbu.* We relieve one another. *ka-ntnawbu.*
religion – *din* pl. *dyan.*
religious – *dini.*
to **rely** – *twekkel.* You can't rely on him. *ma-imken-lek-š ttwekkel ɛlih.*
to **remain** – *bqa ibqa.* Only five remain. *ma-bqaw ġir xemsa.* —There remains nothing else for us to do but to wait. *ma-bqa-lna ġir ntsennaw.*
**That remains to be seen. *daba nšufu* or *ɛlem ḷḷah.*
remaining – *(lli) bqa.* What did you do with the remaining apples? *šnu ɛmelti be-t-teffaḥ lli bqa?*
remark – *tenbih* pl. *-at.* That remark wasn't called for. *had t-tenbih ma-ši fe-bḷaṣtu.*
remarkable – *fih ɛžuba.* What's so remarkable about it? *fayn ɛžuba fiha?*
remedy – *dwa* pl. *ʔedwiya, duyan.* That's a good remedy for colds. *hada dwa mezyan le-r-rwaḥ.* —There's no remedy for that. *had š-ši ma-ɛendu dwa.*
to remedy – *ṣleḥ.* I don't know how that can be remedied. *ma-ɛreft-š kif-aš ġad nṣelḥu had š-ši.*
to **remember** – **1.** *ɛqel ɛla.* It was in May, as far as I remember. *had š-ši wqeɛ f-mayu ila ma-zal ɛaqel ɛliha.* —I simply can't remember his name. *ma-imken-li-š u-kan neɛqel ɛla smiytu.* **2.** *ma-nsa-š ma-insa-š.* Remember to turn out the light. *ma-tensa-š ḍḍfi ḍ-ḍuw.* **3.** *sellem.* Remember me to your mother. *sellem-li ɛla yemmak.*
to **remind** – *fekker.* He reminded me of my appointment. *fekkerni fe-l-miɛad lli ɛendi.* —Remind me about it later. *fekkerni fiha men beɛd.*
remnant – **1.** *šyaṭa.* I found a few remnants of food. *ṣebt ši-šyaṭa de-l-makla.* **2.** *ʔatar* pl. *-at.* Did you see the remnants of that old city? *waš šefti l-ʔatarat dyal dak le-blad le-qdima?*
remote – *mbeɛɛed.* Our house is somewhat remote. *ḍarna mbeɛɛda šwiya.*
**There's a remote possibility that... *bɛid baš imken...* —I haven't the remotest idea what you mean. *bɛid ɛliya baš nefhem šnu*

ka-tqul.

to **remove** – 1. *ḥeyyed.* Please remove your hat. *ḥeyyed š-šemrir dyalek ɛafak.* --This will remove all the stains. *had š-ši ġad iḥeyyed ṭ-ṭebɛat kollhom.* 2. *qṭeɛ.* This should remove all doubt. *had š-ši ġad iqṭeɛ š-šekk.* 3. *neqqel.* He was removed from office. *neqqluh men xdemtu.* 4. *hewwel.* Remove everything from the desk. *hewwel koll-ši men l-biru.*

to **renew** – *žedded.*

rent – *kra* pl. *-wat.* How much rent do you pay for your apartment? *šḥal ka-txelleṣ d-le-kra le-s-sokna dyalek?*

to rent – *kra ikri.* I rented a room for three months. *krit bit l-telt šhuṛ.* --I rented the house to him. *krit-lu ḍ-ḍaṛ.* --I rented the house from him. *krit ḍ-ḍaṛ mennu.*

repair – *iṣlaḥ* pl. *-at.* The car needs only minor repairs. *ṭ-ṭumubila ma-xeṣṣha ġir ši-iṣlaḥat ṣġiṛa.*

beyond repair – *ma-ka-itteṣleḥ-š.* The watch is beyond repair. *had l-magana ma-ka-tteṣleḥ-š.*

to repair – *ṣleḥ.* Can you repair these shoes? *waš imken-lek teṣleḥ had ṣ-ṣebbaṭ?*

to **repeat** – 1. *ɛawed.* Repeat what I just said! *ɛawed had š-ši lli ɛad qolt.* --Repeat these words after me. *ɛawed had le-klam men beɛdi.* 2. *belleġ.* They repeat everything they hear. *lli ka-isemɛu ka-ibellġu le-xbaṛ.*

to **repent** – *tab itub, ndem.*

to **replace** – *nab inub ɛla, ža iži f-bḷaṣt-.* We haven't been able to get anyone to replace her. *ma-qdeṛna-š nṣibu ši-wehda lli dži fe-bḷaṣtha.*

**These glasses can't be replaced. *had l-kisan ma-imken-lna-š nžebṛu xuthom.*

reply – *žwab* pl. *-at.*

to reply (to) – *žaweb.*

report – *teqrir* pl. *tqaṛeṛ.*

to make (give) a report – *ɛmel teqriṛ.* When will you make your report! *fuq-aš ġad teɛmel t-teqriṛ dyalek?*

to report – *qal iqul, ɛawed.* It is reported that... *ka-iɛawdu bin...*

to report to – 1. *qeddem ṛaṣi ɛend.* To whom do I report? *ɛend men xeṣṣni nqeddem ṛaṣi?* 2. *fḍeḥ b-.* Somebody reported him to the police. *ši-waḥed fḍeḥ bih le-š-šorṭa.*

reporter – *muxbir ž-žarida* pl. *muxbirin ž-žaṛaʔid.*

to **represent** – *mettel.* Who is representing the defendant? *škun lli ka-imettel d-difaɛ?*

**What does this symbol represent? *šniya l-meɛna d-had ṛ-ṛemz?*

representative – *nayeb* pl. *nuwwab.* He is the European representative of a big concern. *huwa nayeb f-ʔuṛuḅḅa dyal waḥed ḍ-ḍaṛ de-t-tižaṛa kbira.* --Who's the representative from your district? *škun huwa nayeb l-ḥeuma dyalek?*

reproach – *mɛatba* pl. *-t, luma.* That's not a reproach. *hadi ma-ši mɛatba.*

to reproach – *ɛateb, lam ilum.*

republic – *žemhuṛiya* pl. *-t* (art. *l-*).

reputation – *sumɛa* pl. *-t.* He has a good reputation. *ɛendu sumɛa mezyana.*

**He has a reputation for being a good worker. *huwa mešhuṛ bin ka-ixdem mezyan.*

request – *ṭaḷab* pl. *-at.* Your request was granted. *qeblu ṭ-ṭaḷab dyalek.* --I am writing you at the request of a friend. *ana ka-nekteb-lek b-ṭaḷab waḥed ṣadiqi.*

to request – *ṭḷeb.* I must request that you leave this place. *ana lazem ɛliya nṭḷeb mennek texṛož men had l-maḥell.*

to **require** – 1. *ḥtaž.* That requires no proof. *had š-ši ma-yeḥtaž-š šhud.* 2. *xeṣṣ.* How much time will that require? *šḥal ka-ixeṣṣ de-l-weqt l-had š-ši?* --How much money does that require? *šḥal d-le-flus ka-ixeṣṣ l-had š-ši?* --That will require some time. *had š-ši ka-ixeṣṣ l-weqt.* --Do you require a deposit? *ka-ixeṣṣkom ɛeṛbun?*

**A matter like this requires careful study. *qaḍiya bḥal hadi lazem ɛlina nḍeṛṣuha be-t-tedqiq.*

requirement – *šeṛṭ* pl. *šuṛuṭ.*

to **resemble** – *šbeh l-.* Do you think that he resembles his mother? *waš ka-ḍḍenn lli ka-išbeh l-yemmah?*

to resemble each other – *tšabhu.*

to **resign** – *qeddem istiqala.* He resigned as chairman. *qeddem l-istiqala dyalu men ṛ-ṛiʔaṣa.* --I've resigned from the club. *qeddemt l-istiqala dyali men ž-žemɛiya.*

resignation – *istiqala* pl. *-t.* We

demand his resignation. *ka-nṭeḷbu istiqalṭu.*

to hand in one's resignation - *qeddem l-istiqala dyalu.* He handed in his resignation today. *qeddem l-istiqala dyalu l-yum.*

with resignation - *be-t-teslim.*

to **resist** - **1.** *Ɛaṛeḍ.* I resisted his suggestions. *Ɛaṛeḍt le-qtiṛaḥat dyalu.* **2.** *qawem.* The Moroccans resisted the French occupation. *le-mġaṛba qawmu l-iḥtilal le-fṛanṣawi.* --The Prime Minister resisted the opposition party in parliament. *ṛaʔis l-ḥukuma qawem ḥizeb l-muƐaṛaḍa fe-l-mežlis.*

resistance - *mqawma.*

to **resole** - *ṭeṛṛef.* I'm having my shoes resoled. *ka-nṭeṛṛef ṣebbaṭi.*

respect - *iḥtiṛam* or *ḥtiṛam.* He has won the respect of everyone. *rbeḥ le-ḥtiṛam de-n-nas kollhom.*

in every respect - *men koll žiha.* We were satisfied in every respect. *Ɛžebna l-ḥal men koll žiha.*

in many respects - *f-bezzaf de-n-naḥiyat.* In many respects I agree with you. *mettafeq mƐak f-bezzaf de-n-naḥiyat.*

to respect - *ḥtaṛem.* I respect your opinion. *ka-neḥtaṛem ṛ-ṛaʔy dyalek.*

respected - *meḥtaṛem.* He is a respected businessman. *huwa tažer meḥtaṛem.*

responsibility - *mesʔuliya* pl. *-t.*

responsible - You are responsible for it. *nta mesʔul Ɛliha.*

**It's a very responsible job. *hadi xedma fiha mesʔuliya bezzaf.* --He was held responsible for the damage. *ṛmaw Ɛlih l-mesʔuliya de-l-xaṣaṛ.*

rest - **1.** *baqi.* Eat some now and save the rest. *kul šwiya daba, xelli l-baqi.* --You raise the money and I'll do the rest. *nta ḍebbeṛ Ɛel le-flus w-ana ndir l-baqi.* **2.** *ṛaḥa* pl. *-t.* The doctor told him he needed a month of rest. *ṭ-ṭbib qal-lu xeṣṣu šheṛ de-ṛ-ṛaḥa.*

**I went to the mountains for a rest. *mšit nertaḥ fe-ž-žbal.*

rest of - *axoṛ* pl. *x̂ṛin.* Where are the rest of the boys? *fayn huma le-wlad le-x̂ṛin?*

at rest - *waqef.* Is the pointer at rest? *waš l-muri waqef?*

to take a rest - *rtaḥ.* Let's take a short rest. *yaḷḷah nertaḥu šwiya.*

to rest - **1.** *rtaḥ.* Rest awhile. *rtaḥ šwiya.* **2.** *retteḥ, riyyeḥ.* Rest your eyes. *retteḥ Ɛeynik.* **3.** *bqa ibqa.* The whole responsibility rests on him. *l-mesʔuliya kollha bqat Ɛendu.* **4.** *ḥeṭṭ.* Rest your foot on this chair. *ḥeṭṭ rezlek fuq had š-šilya.* **5.** *tekka.* The ladder was resting against the wall. *s-sellum kan mtekki Ɛel l-ḥiṭ.*

restaurant -*meṭƐem* pl. *mṭaƐem.*

restless - *mšuwweš, meftun, meṣṭun.*

to **restore** - *ṛedd, ṛežžeƐ.* The police intervened to restore order. *š-šoṛṭa ddexxlet baš tṛedd n-niḍam.* --They restored his money to him. *ṛežžƐu-lu le-flus dyalu.*

to **restrain** - *ḥṣeṛ.* She couldn't restrain her curiousity. *ma-mken-lha-š teḥṣeṛ le-fḍuḷ dyalha.*

rest room - *miḍa* pl. *-t, myaḍi; mirḥaḍ* pl. *-at.*

result - *natiža* pl. *nataʔiž.* The results were excellent. *n-nataʔiž kanu moƐtabaṛin.* --The result was that... *natiža had-š-ši hiya...*

retail - *be-t-tefṛad.* He sells wholesale and retail. *ka-ibiƐ be-ž-žemla u-be-t-tefṛad.*

**This coat retails at about thirty dollars. *be-t-tefṛad had l-kebbuṭ ka-iswa ši-tlatin ḍuḷaṛ.*

retreat - *ṛžuƐ l-luṛ.*

to retreat - *ṛžeƐ l-luṛ.*

return - **1.** *rbeḥ.* How much of a return did you get on that sale? *šḥal žak de-r-rbeḥ f-dak l-biƐa?* **2.** *ṛžuƐ.* I found many things changed on my return. *žbeṛt bezzaf d-le-ḥwayež tbeddlu men beƐd ṛ-ṛžuƐ dyali.*

returns - *nataʔiž d-le-ntixabat.* Have the returns come in yet? *waš Ɛṭaw n-nataʔiž d-le-ntixabat wella ma-zal?*

to return - **1.** *ṛežžeƐ.* Don't forget to return the book. *ma-tensa-š tṛežžeƐ le-ktab.* **2.** *ṛžeƐ.* When did you return? *fuq-as ṛžeƐti?*

revenge - *taṛ.*

reverse side - *žiha luṛaniya.*

to **review** - *ṛažeƐ.* He should have reviewed his lessons. *kan xeṣṣu iṛažeƐ ḍ-ḍuruṣ dyalu.*

to **revolt** - *nuwweḍ l-fetna.* They had good reason to revolt. *kan Ɛendhom l-ḥeqq baš inuwwḍu l-fetna.*

revolution - **1.** *tuṛa* pl. *-t.* There was almost a revolution. *Ɛlayen kanet ġadi tuqeƐ t-tuṛa.* **2.** *ḍuṛa* pl. *-t.* How many revolutions does this motor make per minute? *šḥal*

men ḍuṛa had l-muṭuṛ ka-idir fe-d-dqiqa?
to **revolve** - *ḍaṛ iḍuṛ.* The earth revolves around the sun. *l-ʔerḍ ka-ḍḍur ɛel š-šems.*
reward - *mžazya* pl. *-t.*
to reward - *žaza.* They rewarded him well for his work. *žazaweh mezyan ɛel l-xedma dyalu.*
rhyme - *qafiya* pl. *qwafi.*
**His suggestion has neither rhyme nor reason. *t-tenbih dyalu ma-ɛendu la ṛaṣ la režlin.*
rib - *ḍeḷɛa* pl. *ḍḷuɛ.*
ribbon - **1.** *sfifa* pl. *-t, sfayef.* She was wearing a blue ribbon in her hair. *mḍuwwṛa šɛeṛha sfifa ẓeṛqa.* **2.** *sinta* pl. *-t.* I need a new ribbon for my typewriter. *xeṣṣni sinta ždida l-le-mṭebɛa dyali.*
rice - *ṛuẓ.* I'd like a half kilo of rice. *bġit neṣṣ kilu de-ṛ-ṛuẓ.*
rich - **1.** *ġani.* He comes from a very rich family. *huwa men ɛaʔila ġanya bezzaf.* **2.** *xṣeb.* It's a rice soil. *had l-ʔeṛḍ xeṣba.* **3.** *qwi.* The food is too rich for me. *had l-makla qwiya ɛliya.*
riddle - *mḥažya* pl. *-t.*
to **ride** - **1.** *ṣag iṣug.* Do you know how to ride a motorcycle? *waš ka-teɛṛef tṣug l-muṭuṛ?* **2.** *mša imši.* This car rides smoothly. *had s-siyaṛa ka-temši be-šwiya.* **3.** *rkeb.* We rode in a beautiful car. *rkebna f-waḥed s-siyaṛa mezyana.*
to give a ride to - *weṣṣeḷ, dda iddi.* He gave me a ride to the airport. *weṣṣelni l-l-maṭaṛ.*
**Stop riding me! *baṛaka ma therres-li ṛaṣi.* --He mounted his horse and rode away. *rkeb ɛla ɛewdu u-zad xelfa.*
to be, get **rid of** - *ttfekk men, fekk ṛaṣu men.* I'm glad I got rid of that problem. *ana feṛḥan lli fekkit ṛaṣi men had l-qaḍiya.*
Riff - *r-rif.*
native of the Riff - *rifi* pl. *-yen, ryaf, hel r-rif.*
rifle - *mkoḥla* pl. *-t, mkaḥel.*
right - **1.** *ḥeqq* pl. *ḥuquq.* I insist on my rights. *ka-nwekked ɛel l-ḥuquq dyali.* --I have as much a right to it as you do. *ḥett-ana ɛendi ḥeqqi fih bḥalek.* --You have no right to say that. *ma-ɛendek ḥetta ḥeqq baš tqul had š-ši.* **2.** *imni.* I've lost my right glove. *telfet-li ṣ-ṣebbaɛa l-imniya.* **3.** *mṛebbeɛ.* A right angle has ninety degrees. *qent mṛebbeɛ fih tesɛin ḍaṛaža.* **4.** *mnaseb.* He came just at the right time. *ža tamamen fe-l-weqt le-mnaseb.* **5.** *ṣḥiḥ.* That's the right answer. *hada huwa ž-žwab ṣ-ṣḥiḥ.* **6.** *qaṣeḍ.* I'm coming right home from the office. *ana maši qaṣeḍ men ḍ-ḍaṛ l-l-mekteb.* **7.** *tamamen.* The house is right next to the church. *ḍ-ḍaṛ hiya tamamen ḥda le-knisiya.* **8.** *mezyan.* We'll leave tomorrow if the weather is right. *ġad nemšiw ġedda ila kan ṭ-ṭeqs mezyan.*
**Are we going the right way? *waš hiya hadi ṭ-ṭriq f-aš ṛa-ḥna ġadyen?* --We're going right after dinner. *ḥna mašyin ġir nfeḍḍiw b-le-ɛša.* --They fought right to the bitter end. *qawmu ḥetta l-l-ʔaxir.* --I'll be right there. *ana maži daba.* --You can't be in your right mind. *ši-ḥaža ɛendek f-ɛeqlek!* --It serves him right! *xxi fih!*
right away - **1.** *daba.* Let's go right away or we'll be late. *yaḷḷah nemšiw daba wella ġad nuṣḷu mɛeṭṭḷin.* **2.** *fe-l-ḥin.* He left right away. *mša fe-l-ḥin.*
right now - *f-had s-saɛa.* I'm busy right now. *ana mešġul f-had s-saɛa.*
all right - **1.** *waxxa.* All right, I'll do it if you want me to. *waxxa, daba ndirha ila bġitini ndirha.* **2.** *la-bas.* Everything's all right now. *koll-ši la-bas daba.* **3.** *la-bas ɛlih.* She'll be all right again in a little while. *men daba šwiya tkun la-bas ɛliha.*
**Everything will turn out all right. *daba ṛebbi ixerrež koll-ši ɛla xir.*
on the right - *ɛel l-imin.* Look at the store on the right. *šuf l-ḥanut lli ɛel l-imin.*
to be right - *ɛendu l-ḥeqq.* You're right in this matter. *ɛendek l-ḥeqq f-had l-qaḍiya.*
rightful - *ḥqiqi* pl. *-yin.* He is the rightful owner of the house. *huwa mul ḍ-ḍaṛ le-ḥqiqi.*
rim - **1.** *kwadṛu, qžeṛ* pl. *qžuṛa* The rim of my glasses is broken. *le-qžeṛ de-nḍaḍṛi mherres.* **2.** *žanṭa* pl. *-t.* The rim has come off the wheel. *ž-žanṭa tqellɛet men ṛ-ṛwiḍa.*
ring - *xatem* pl. *xwatem.* She wears a ring on her right middle finger.

ᶓendha xatem fe-ṣ-ṣbeᶓ l-weṣṭani d-yeddha d-l-imin.
**Give me a ring tomorrow. *ᶓeyyeṭ-li fe-t-tilifun ġedda.*
to ring - 1. *zenzen.* The noise is still ringing in my ears. *dak ṣ-ṣdaᶓ ma-zal ka-izenzen f-wedni.* 2. *serser.* The phone rang. *t-tilifun serser.* --The bell just rang. *ᶓad serser n-naquṣ.* --Have you rung the bell? *waš serserti fe-n-naquṣ?*

rinse - *tešlila* pl. *-t.*
to rinse - 1. *meḍmeḍ.* Rinse out your mouth with a little salt and water. *meḍmeḍ fommek be-šwiya de-l-melḥa u-de-l-ma.* 2. *šellel.* I rinsed my wash twice. *šellelt t-teṣbin dyali žuž de-l-merrat.*

riot - *fetna* pl. *-t.* Two people were killed in the riot. *žuž de-n-nas matu f-l-iḍṛab.*
**He's a riot. *huwa ḍeḥḥuki.*

rip - *tešriga* pl. *-t.* You have a rip in your shirt. *ᶓendek tešriga f-qamižtek.*
to rip - 1. *qeṭṭeᶓ.* I ripped the towel down the middle. *qeṭṭeᶓt l-fuṭa men l-weṣṭ.* 2. *fteq.* I have to rip the seams. *xeṣṣni nefteq le-xyaṭa.*
to rip open - *felleḥ.* I nearly ripped my hand open. *ᶓlayen felleḥt yeddi.*

ripe - *ṭayeb.* This apple isn't ripe. *had t-teffaḥa ma-ṭayba-š.*
**She lived to a ripe old age. *matet šarfa bezzaf.*

to **rise** - 1. *šṛeq.* The sun rises early in the summer. *š-šems ka-tešṛeq bekri fe-ṣ-ṣif.* 2. *ṭleᶓ.* The cake is rising. *l-ḥelwa ka-ṭṭleᶓ.* --Prices are still rising. *t-tamanat ka-izidu iṭelᶓu.* --The river is rising fast. *l-wad be-z-zerba ka-iṭleᶓ.* 4. *naḍ inuḍ.* All rose from their seats. *kollhom naḍu men šilyathom.*

risk - *xaṭaṛ.*
to risk - *xaṭeṛ b-.* He risked his life to save her. *xaṭeṛ b-ᶓemṛu baš ifekkha.* --He's risked his entire fortune. *xaṭeṛ b-malu kollu.*

rival - *mḍadd* pl. *-in.*

river - *wad* pl. *widan.*

road - *ṭriq* pl. *ṭorqan.* Where does this road go to? *fayn ka-tᶓebbi had ṭ-ṭriq?*
**He's on the road to recovery. *bda išebbeh le-ṛ-ṛaḥa.*

roar - 1. *haṛaž.* We can hear the roar of the waterfall from here. *imken-lna nsemᶓu l-haṛaž dyal š-šṛašeṛ men hna.* 2. *zhir.* The voice we heard sounded like the roar of a lion. *dak ṣ-ṣut lli smeᶓna kan ka-išbeh le-z-zhir de-s-sbeᶓ.*
to roar - 1. *zher.* The lion roared when he saw us. *s-sbeᶓ zher melli šafna.* 2. *tfeṛgeᶓ.* They roared with laughter. *tfeṛgᶓu be-ḍ-ḍeḥk.*

roast - *mešwi.* The roast is tough today. *l-mešwi qaṣeḥ l-yum.* --Do you like roast chicken? *waš ka-tebġi d-džaž mešwi?*
to roast - *šwa išwi.* You didn't roast the meat long enough. *ma-šwiti-š l-lḥem bezzaf.*

to **rob** - 1. *xwen.* They robbed and pillaged. *xewnu u-ritlu.* 2. *šeffeṛ.* They robbed me. *šeffṛuni.* --They'll rob you of your last cent. *daba išeffṛuk ḥetta l-l-gerš t-tali.*

robbery - *xewna, sṛiqa.*
**That's highway robbery. *tešfiṛ hada!*

robin - *bwiqša* pl. *-t.*

rock - 1. *ṣexṛa* pl. *-t, ṣxuṛa* coll. *ṣxeṛ.* The rock is hard to drill. *waᶓer baš nteqbu had ṣ-ṣxeṛ.* 2. *ḥežṛa* pl. *-t* coll. *ḥzer.* He was throwing rocks. *kan ka-iluḥ le-ḥžeṛ.*
to rock - 1. *tthezz.* The floor rocked under my feet. *l-ʔeṛḍ tthezzet teḥt ṛežliya.* 2. *zeᶓzeᶓ.* The boat's rocking. *l-babuṛ ka-dzeᶓzeᶓ.* 3. *hezz.* The explosion rocked the whole house. *t-tfeṛgiᶓa hezzet ḍ-ḍaṛ kollha.* 4. *duwweḥ.* She rocked the cradle until the baby fell asleep. *duwwḥet l-kuna ḥetta t-teṛbiya žatha n-nᶓas.*

rod - *qṭib* pl. *qoṭban, qṭayeb.* The parts are connected by an iron rod. *ṭ-ṭraf mlaqyin be-qṭib d-le-ḥdid.*

role - *ḍuṛ* pl. *ḍwaṛ.*

roll - 1. *qayma* pl. *-t.* Am I on the roll this year? *waš ana medkuṛ fe-l-qayma had l-ᶓam?* 2. *geṛṣa* pl. *-t, gṛeṣ.* Shall I get bread or rolls? *nžib l-xobz aw le-gṛeṣ?* 3. *qennuṭ* pl. *qnaneṭ.* They used five rolls of wire to install these telephones. *xeddmu xemsa d-le-qnaneṭ de-s-selk baš irekkbu had t-tilifunat.* --Bring me a roll of film. *žib-li waḥed l-qennuṭ de-t-teṣwiṛ.*
--He should have bought four rolls of paper but he only bought three.

kan ka-ixeṣṣu išri ṛebƐa d-le-qnaneṭ de-l-kaġiṭ be-l-ḥeqq šra hi tlata.

to call the roll - *Ɛeyyeṭ l-ʔasmaʔ.* Have they called the roll yet? *waš Ɛeyyṭu l-ʔasmaʔ wella ma-zal?*

to roll - **1.** *kerkeb.* Don't roll the barrel. *ma-tkerkeb-š l-bermil.* **2.** *tkerkeb.* A rock rolled down from the mountain. *waḥed le-ḥžeṛ tkerkbet men ž-žbel.* **3.** *žra išri.* The ball rolled under the table. *l-kuṛa žrat teḥt ṭ-ṭabḷa.* **4.** *ftel.* I roll my own cigarettes. *ka-neftel l-gaṛṛu dyali.* **5.** *mal imil men žiha l-žiha.* The ship was rolling heavily. *l-babuṛ kan ka-imil men žiha l-žiha bezzaf.*

to roll in money - *Ɛam iƐum f-le-flus.* He's rolling in money. *ka-iƐum f-le-flus.*

to roll up - *luwwa.* We rolled up the rug. *luwwina ẓ-ẓeṛbiya.*

Rome - *ṛuma.*

roof - *sqef* pl. *squfa.*

flat roof - *ṣṭaḥ* pl. *-at, ṣṭuḥa, ṣṭiḥan, ṣṭuḥ.*

roof of the mouth - *sqef l-fomm.*

room - **1.** *bit* pl. *byut.* This is quite a large room. *hada bit kbir bezzaf.* **2.** *muḍeƐ.* Is there any room left for my baggage? *waš ma-zal ši-muḍeƐ fayn neƐmel ḥwayži?*

roomy - *waseƐ.*

rooster - *feṛṛuž* pl. *fṛaṛež.*

root - *žder* pl. *ždur.* The roots of this tree are very deep. *ž-ždura d-had š-šežṛa ġarqin bezzaf.* --His molar decayed all the way to the root. *ḍ-ḍeṛṣa xmažet-lu ḥetta le-ž-žder.*

to take root - *Ɛmel ž-ždur.* How can you tell whether the rose bush has taken root? *kif-aš imken-lek teƐṛef bin l-weṛḍ Ɛmel ž-ždur?*

**He stood there as if rooted to the spot. *bqa waqef temma bḥal ila kan laṣeq fe-l-ʔeṛḍ.*

rope - *ṭwal* pl. *-at, ṭuḷa; ḥbel* pl. *ḥbul.* He chewed the rope in two to get loose. *qeṭṭeƐ ṭ-ṭwaḷ be-snanu baš ifekk ṛaṣu.*

**I'm at the end of my rope. *ana qaṭeƐ l-iyyas men ṛaṣi.* --He knows all the ropes. *ka-yeƐṛef l-xenṭaqiṛat kollhom.* --They roped the street off today. *šeddu ṭ-ṭṛiq b-le-ḥbal l-yum.*

rose - **1.** (flower). *weṛḍa* pl. *-t* coll. *weṛḍ.* **2.** (color). *weṛḍi, fanidi.*

rosebush - *weṛḍ.*

to **rot** - *xmaž.* The fruit is rotting on the trees. *l-ġella ka-texmaž fe-š-šžeṛ.*

rotten - **1.** *xamež.* The peaches are rotton. *l-xux xamež.* **2.** *msuwwes.* The beam was rotten through and through. *l-gayza kanet msuwwsa kollha.* **3.** *qbiḥ* pl. *qbaḥ.* They played a rotten trick on us. *leƐbu Ɛlina waḥed l-leƐba qbiḥa*

rough - **1.** *ḥreš* pl. *ḥuṛeš.* Why are your hands so rough? *Ɛlaš yeddik ḥuṛeš?* --This piece of wood is still rough, smooth it down a little more. *had l-xešba ma-zala ḥeṛša, zid mellesha šwiyyeš.* **2.** *ġliḍ* pl. *ġlaḍ.* He has a rough voice. *ḥelqu ġliḍ.* **3.** *waƐer.* She isn't used to such rough work. *ma-mwellfa-š b-xedma waƐra bḥal hadi.* --You've got to treat him rough. *xeṣṣek tkun waƐer mƐah.* **4.** *hažem.* The sea's pretty rough today. *le-bḥeṛ hažem bezzaf l-yum.* **5.** *qaṣeḥ.* He's a mighty rough man! *ṛažel qaṣeḥ bezzaf hada!*

round - **1.** *ḍuṛa* pl. *-t.* He finished him off in the first round. *sala mƐah fe-ḍ-ḍuṛa l-luwwla.* **2.** *mḍuwweṛ.* They have a round table in the dining room. *Ɛendhom ṭabḷa mḍuwwṛa f-bit l-makla.*

**Is there enough coffee to go round? *waš kayen l-qehwa l-koll waḥed?* --He's just coming round the corner. *ha-huwa ka-iḍuṛ fe-l-qent.* --I live here all the year round. *ana saken hna l-Ɛam kollu.* --In round numbers there were two hundred present. *kanu teqṛiben myatayn waḥed ḥaḍṛin.* --The book is making the rounds. *le-ktab ka-imši men yedd l-yedd.*

to round out - *kemmel.* I need this to round out my collection. *xeṣṣni had š-ši baš nkemmel l-mežmuƐa dyali.*

round trip - *mši u-mži.* Give me a round trip ticket. *Ɛṭini bṭaqa mši u-mži.*

route - *ṭṛiq* pl. *ṭoṛqan.* Which route did you take? *š-men ṭṛiq xditi?*

row - **1.** *ṣdaƐ.* My neighbors made a terrible row last night. *ž-žiran dyali Ɛemlu waḥed ṣ-ṣdaƐ kbir l-bareḥ fe-l-lil.* **2.** *mdabza* pl. *-t.* I had a row with him. *weqƐet-li mdabza mƐah.* **3.** *ṣeff* pl. *ṣfuf.* We sat in the first row. *glesna fe-ṣ-ṣeff l-luwwel.*

in a row - *mtabeƐ.* We won three

times in a row. *rbeḥna tlata de-l-merrat mtabƐin.*

to row - *qeddef.* We rowed across the lake. *qeddefna u-qṭeƐna ḍ-ḍaya.*

rowboat - *fluka* pl. *flayek.*

royal - *malaki.*

to **rub** - **1.** *ḍbeṛ.* My shoes rub at the heel. *ṣebbaṭi ka-iḍbeṛni f-le-gdem.* **2.** *duwwez Ɛla.* Keep rubbing the tray until it shines. *xellik dduwwez Ɛel ṣ-ṣiniya ḥetta ddwi.* **3.** *frek, ḥekk.* He kept rubbing his hands together until he got them warm *bqa ifrek yedd f-yedd ḥetta sexxenhom.* **4.** *dlek.* Rub his back with alcohol. *dlek-lu ḍehṛu b-l-alkuḷ*

to rub against - *tḥelles Ɛla.* The cat rubbed against my leg. *l-qeṭṭa žat tḥelles Ɛla režli.*

to rub out - *mḥa imḥi.* You forgot to rub out the price. *nsiti ma-mḥiti-š t-taman.*

rubber - *kawetšu.*

rude - *xšin* pl. *xšan.* Don't be so rude! *ma-tkun-š xšin!*

rudeness - *xšuna.* We can't understand his rudeness. *ma-imken-lna nfehmu le-xšuna dyalu.*

rug - *zeṛbiya* pl. *zṛabi.*

ruin - *ʔataṛ* pl. *-at.* They discovered the ruins of an old church. *ṣabu l-ʔataṛ dyal waḥed le-knisiya qdima.*

to ruin - *hlek.* The frost will ruin the crop. *daba ž-žlid ihlek le-ḥṣaḍa.* --He's ruining his health. *ka-ihlek ṣeḥḥtu.* --They were ruined by the war. *hlekhom l-ḥeṛb.* **2.** *keṛfeṣ.* The paint ruined his new suit completely. *ṣ-ṣbaġa keṛfṣet ksuwtu ž-ždida kollha.*

rule - **1.** *ḥkuma.* They were under Spanish rule for three centuries. *kanu teḥt le-ḥkuma de-ṣ-ṣbanya tlata d-le-qṛun.* **2.** *qanun* pl. *qwanen.* That's against the rules. *had š-ši ḍeḍḍ l-qanun.* --I'm sticking to the rules. *ana ka-ntebbeƐ l-qawanin.*

as a rule - *mwellef.* As a rule I don't drink. *mwellef ma-ka-nešṛeb-š.*

to rule - *ḥkem Ɛla.* They wanted to rule the entire world. *bġaw iḥekmu Ɛel l-Ɛalem kollu.* --He ruled over them for nineteen years. *ḥkem Ɛlihom tseƐṭašer Ɛam.*

ruler - **1.** *ḥakem* pl. *ḥokkam.* He was a benevolent ruler. *kan ḥakem ṛḥim.* **2.** *meṣṭaṛa* pl. *-t.* The ruler is too short. *l-meṣṭara qṣiṛa bezzaf.*

rumor - *ḥess.* The rumor spread like wildfire. *l-ḥess šaƐ be-z-zerba.*

**It's rumored that she was kicked out. *ka-iqulu bin dḥawha.* --It's been rumored for quite some time. *hadi modda u-n-nas ka-itkellmu Ɛla had š-ši.*

rumpus - *haṛaž, ṣḍaƐ.*

run - *ṣefṛa* pl. *-t.* The run takes five hours. *ṣ-ṣefṛa ka-ṭṭul xemsa de-s-swayeƐ.*

**You've got a run in your stocking. *fetqu-lek tqašrek.* --He's above the average run. *huwa fuq l-wasaṭ.*

in the long run - *mƐa l-weqt.* In the long run you'll get tired of that. *daba teƐya men had š-ši mƐa l-weqt.*

to run - **1.** *žra ižri.* Don't run so fast. *baṛaka ma džri bḥal hakka.* --I ran after him, but I couldn't catch up to him. *žrit Ɛlih walayenni ma-qdeṛt nqebṭu.* **2.** *xdem.* Why do you keep the motor running? *Ɛlaš ka-txelli l-muṭuṛ xadem?* **3.** *ṭḷeq.* The color runs. *had l-lun ka-iṭḷeq.* **4.** *xeddem.* Do you know how to run this machine? *waš ka-teƐṛef txeddem had l-makina?* **5.** *meššа imešši, ḥkem f-.* He's been running this company for three years. *hadi telt snin u-huwa ka-imešši had š-šarika.* **6.** *duwwez.* Run the rope through this ring. *duwwez ṭ-ṭwaḷ f-had l-xoṛṣa.* **7.** *ža iži.* The road runs right by my house. *z-zenqa žat tamamen qbalt ḍaṛi.* **8.** *wṣeḷ.* My horse ran last. *l-Ɛewd dyali wṣeḷ t-tali.*

**He's running a high fever. *sexxantu ṭaḷƐa bezzaf.* --He's running around with a bad crowd. *ka-ixeḷḷeṭ nas qbaḥ* --They ran him out of town. *lezzmu Ɛlih ixṛož men le-mdina.*

to run across - *tlaqa mƐa.* Maybe I'll run across him someday. *imken-li ntlaqa mƐah ši-nhaṛ.*

to run aground - *ḥeṛṛet.* My boat ran aground. *le-fluka dyali ḥeṛṛtet.*

to run away - *hṛeb.* My dog ran away. *hṛeb-li kelbi.* --When he saw us, he ran away. *melli šafna hṛeb.*

to run down - **1.** *tkellem b-le-qbiḥ.* She's always running her friends down behind their backs. *hiya dima* *ka-ttkellem b-le-qbiḥ fe-ḍheṛ sḥabha.* 2. *geddem, dxel f-.* He was run down by a truck. *geddmu kamyu.*

to run into - 1. *dxel f-.* The car ran into a tree. *dexlet ṭ-ṭumubil f-waḥed š-šežṛa.* 2. *ġṛaq f-.* He's running into debt. *ka-iġṛaq fe-d-din.*

to run off - *hṛeb.* He ran off with the club's funds. *hṛeb b-le-flus dyal n-nadi.*

to run out - *tsala.* Our sugar has run out. *tsala-lna s-sokkaṛ.*

to run over - 1. *faḍ ifiḍ.* Watch out that the bathtub doesn't run over. *ma-txelli-š l-ma ifiḍ men l-banyu.* 2. *ṛažeε.* Run over your part before the rehearsal. *ṛažeε ḍ-ḍuṛ dyalek qbel t-temrin.* 3. *geddem.* He was run over by a truck. *geddmu kamyu.*

run down - 1. *mxerreb.* The house is run down. *ḍ-ḍaṛ mxerrba.* 2. *mehluk.* He's very much run-down. *ṣeḥḥtu mehluka.* 3. *εeyyan.* She looks terribly run-down. *ḍaheṛ εliha εeyyana bezzaf.*

rung - *ḍeṛža* pl. *-t, ḍṛuž.* The last rung of the ladder is broken. *ḍ-ḍeṛža t-talya de-s-sellum mherrsa.*

runner - *žerray* pl. *-a.* He's a famous runner. *huwa žerray mešhuṛ.*

rupture - *fteq.* He has a rupture. *εendu fteq.*

ruse - *ḥila* pl. *-t.*

rush - 1. *zerba.* What's the rush for? *εlaš had z-zerba?* 2. *dḥas.* Let's wait till the rush is over. *xellina ntsennaw ḥetta isali d-dḥas.*

to rush - *zerreb.* Don't rush me, I'll do it. *ma-dzerrebni-š, daba neεmel-ha.*

to rush oneself - *zreb.* Don't rush yourself. *ma-dzreb-š.*

**Rush him to the hospital. *εebbih deġya l-l-mestešfa.*

Russia - *rusya.*

Russian - *rusi.*

rust - *tṣeḍya.*

to rust - *tṣeḍḍa.* The machine rusted. *tṣeḍḍat l-mašina.*

rustle - *xeṛxeṛ.* I thought I heard something rustling. *ban-li bin smeεt ši-ḥaža ka-txeṛxeṛ.*

rusty - 1. *mṣeḍḍi.* He scratched his hand on a rusty nail. *žreḥ iddu f-waḥed l-meṣmaṛ mṣeḍḍi.* --The lock is all rusty. *le-qfel mṣeḍḍi kollu.*

**My French is a little rusty. *le-fṛanṣawiya dyali ḍεafet.*

ruthless - *bla ḥanana.*

rye - *šqiliya.*

S

sack - *xenša* pl. *-t, xnaši.*

sacred - *mqeddes.* Nothing is sacred to him. *ḥetta ḥaža ma-εendu mqeddsa.*

sacrifice - *teḍḥiya* pl. *-t.* They made many sacrifices for their children. *qeddmu bezzaf de-t-teḍḥiyat le-wladhom.*

at a sacrifice - *be-ṭ-ṭyuḥ, b-le-xṭiya.* I sold my car at a sacrifice. *beεt siyaṛti b-le-xṭiya.*

to sacrifice - *ḍeḥḥa b-, sebbel.* She sacrificed her life for him. *ḍeḥḥat be-εmeṛha εlih.*

sad - *(lli) ṭayeṛ-lu.* Why does he look so sad? *ma-lu ka-iban ṭayeṛ-lu?*

saddle - *serž* pl. *sruža.* Can you ride without a saddle? *tqedd terkeb bla serž?*

to saddle - *serrež, rekkeb s-serž, εmel s-serž.* Do you know how to saddle a horse? *ka-teεṛef tserrež l-εewd.*

**He saddled me with all his troubles. *nezzel εliya hmumu kollhom* or *teqqelni be-hmumu kǝllhom.*

saddle making, saddlery - *taserražet.*

saddler - *serraž* pl. *-a.*

safe - 1. *xzana d-le-flus* pl. *xzayen d-le-flus.* We keep our safe in the office. *ka-nxelliw le-xzana d-le-flus fe-l-mekteb.* 2. *salem.* You are safe now. *nta salem daba.* --This bridge is safe, we can cross it. *had l-qenṭṛa salma, imken-lna nqeṭεuha.* 3. *(lli) fih l-ˀaman.* This neighborhood isn't quite safe. *had l-ḥewma ma-fiha-š l-ˀaman bezzaf.* 4. *maneε, salem.* Their house was the only one that remained safe from the fire. *ḍaṛhom hiya lli bqat manεa men l-εafya.*

**He's back safe and sound. *ṛžeε ma-εendu ḥetta bas.* --To be on the

safe side, let's ask him again. *baš nebqaw mertaḥin yaḷḷah nseqṣiweh.*
safely - *b-xir, Ɛla xir.* They arrived safely. *ṛahom weṣḷu Ɛla xir.*
safety - *salama.* This is for your own safety. *had š-ši Ɛel s-salama dyalek.*
safety pin - *šuka* pl. *-t, šwek.*
safety razor - *makina d-le-ḥsana* pl. *-t d-le-ḥsana, mwaken d-le-ḥsana.*
to **sag** - *mal imil.* The bookshelf sags in the middle. *ṭ-ṭebqa d-le-ktub mayla fe-l-woṣṭ.*
sail - *qlaƐ* pl. *qluƐ, qluƐa.* The wind tore the sail. *r-riḥ qeṭṭeƐ le-qleƐ.*
to sail - **1.** *ttsara f-merkeb le-qlaƐ.* We go sailing every Sunday. *koll ḥedd ka-nemšiw nttsaraw f-merkeb le-qlaƐ.* **2.** *qelleƐ.* The boat sails at five. *l-baxiṛa ġad tqelleƐ fe-l-xemsa.*
**Do you know how to sail a boat? *ka-teƐṛef txeddem merkeb le-qlaƐ?*
sailboat - *merkeb le-qlaƐ* pl. *mrakeb le-qlaƐ.*
sailor - *beḥri* pl. *-ya.*
salad - *šḷaḍa* pl. *šḷayeḍ.*
salad dressing - *meṛqa de-š-šḷaḍa.*
salary - *ʔužṛa* pl. *-t.* How can you manage on that salary? *kif ka-tƐiš b-dak l-ʔužṛa?*
sale - *biƐ.* The sale of alcohol to Moslems is prohibited. *biƐ le-xmeṛ l-le-mselmin memnuƐ.*
for sale - *l-l-biƐ.* Our neighbor's house is for sale. *ḍ-ḍaṛ d-žaṛna ṛaha l-l-biƐ.*
salesclerk - *bayeƐ* pl. *bayƐin* f. *bayƐa* pl. *-t.* He's a salesclerk in a department store. *huwa bayeƐ f-waḥed ḍaṛ s-selƐa.*
Sale - *sla.*
native of Sale - *slawi* pl. *-yen, hel sla.*
salesman - *bayeƐ* pl. *bayƐin.* One of our salesmen will call on you tomorrow. *waḥed men l-bayƐin dyalna ġad iži Ɛendkom ġedda.*
salt - *mleḥ, melḥ.*
to salt - *melleḥ, Ɛmel le-mleḥ.* Did you salt the soup? *mellehti le-ḥrira?*
**He salted away a tidy sum. *žmeƐ waḥed d-dqiqa d-le-flus.*
salt shaker - *mellaḥa* pl. *-t.*
salty - *maleḥ.*
same - **1.** *nefs.* I can be back on the same day. *imken-li neṛžeƐ f-nefs n-nhaṛ.* **2.** *waḥed* f. *weḥda.* They live in the same house. *ka-iseknu f-ḍaṛ weḥda.* --They arrived at the same time. *weṣḷu f-weqt waḥed.* **3.** *qedd qedd.* We're the same age. *ḥna qedd qedd fe-s-senn.*
**He said exactly the same. *dak š-ši lli qal ḥetta huwa.*
all the same - **1.** *tamamen bḥal bḥal.* That's all the same to me. *Ɛendi tamamen bḥal bḥal.* **2.** *beƐdella.* All the same, I want to see it. *beƐdella, ana baġi nšufu.*
sample - *mšetra* pl. *-t, mšater.* Do you have a sample of the material with you? *mƐak ḷe-mšetra dyal dak t-tub?*
sand - *ṛemla* pl. *-t, ṛmali* coll. *ṛmel.* Let's lie in the sand. *aži ndžebbdu fuq ṛ-ṛemla.*
sandal - *nƐala* pl. *-t, nƐayel.*
sandwich - *sandwiš* pl. *-at.*
**He was sandwiched in between two stout women. *kan mbeẓẓeṭ bin zuž d-le-Ɛyalat sman.*
sanitary - *ṣiḥḥi.*
sardine - *serdin.*
satisfaction - **1.** *našaṭ.* I don't get any satisfaction out of that kind of work. *ma-ka-nežbeṛ ḥetta ši-našaṭ f-xedma bḥal hadik.* **2.** *xaṭeṛ.* Was everything settled to your satisfaction? *iwa koll-ši tṣuwweb Ɛel l-xaṭeṛ dyalek?*
satisfactory - **1.** *(lli) ka-inešše ṭ.* His condition is satisfactory. *ḥaltu ka-tneššeṭ.* **2.** *(lli) f-ġaya.* This room is satisfactory. *had l-bit f-ġaya.*
to **satisfy** - **1.** *neššeṭ, berred l-xaṭeṛ l-.* That answer doesn't satisfy me. *had ž-žwab ma-berred-li-š l-xaṭeṛ.* **2.** *xella Ɛla xaṭṛu.* You can't satisfy everybody. *ma-imken-lek-š txelli koll-si Ɛla xaṭṛu.* **3.** *ferḥan.* I am not satisfied with my new job. *ma-ṛani-š ferḥan be-xdemti ž-ždida.*
**We'll have to be satisfied with less. *l-ḥaṣil nḥemdu ḷḷah Ɛel le-qlil.*
Saturday - *sebt* pl. *sbuta.*
sauce - *meṛqa* pl. *-t, mṛuq.*
saucer - *ġṭiyeṛ* pl. *ġṭiyṛat.*
Saudi Arabia - *l-žazira s-saƐudiya.*
savage - *weḥši.*
to **save** - **1.** *sellek, nqed, fekk.* Who saved her life? *škun sellek-lha Ɛmeṛha?* **2.** *xella, xebbeƐ.* Could you save this for me until tomorrow? *imken-lek txelli-li had š-ši ḥetta l-ġedda?* **3.** *theḷḷa f-.* Why do you save these old newspapers? *Ɛlaš ka-ttheḷḷa f-had l-žaraʔid le-qdam?*

4. *xda yaxod, ḥaz iḥuz.* Have you saved a seat for her? *xditiw-lha ši-muḍeƐ?* 5. *žmeƐ, weffeṛ.* Did you save any money? *žmeƐti ši-flus?*
**You could have saved yourself the trouble. *u-kan ġir ma-šqiti-š.*

savings - *wfeṛ.* He has used up all his savings. *feḍḍa le-wfeṛ lli kan Ɛendu kollu.*

saw - *menšaṛ* pl. *mnašeṛ.* Could I borrow a saw? *imken-li nsellef waḥed l-menšar?*
to saw - *nšeṛ.* He's been sawing wood all morning. *had ṣ-ṣbaḥ kollu u-huwa ka-inšeṛ f-le-xšeb.*

to **say** - **1.** *qal iqul.* She left the room without saying a word. *xeṛžet men l-bit bla ma-tqul ḥetta kelma.* --They say he speaks many languages. *ka-iqulu billa ka-iḥḍeṛ bezzaf de-l-luġat.* --He's said to be rich. *ka-iqulu la-bas Ɛlih.* **2.** *laḥeḍ.* I would like to say something in that connection. *baġi nlaḥeḍ ši-ḥaža f-had l-mụḍuƐ.* **3.** *žbed, dkeṛ.* The papers didn't say a thing about it. *l-žaraʔid ma-žebdet ḥetta ḥaža Ɛla dak š-ši.* **4.** *xebbeṛ b-.* The paper says rain. *l-žarida xebbṛet be-š-šta.*
**What does that sign say? *šnu mektub f-dak l-luḥa?*
to say good-bye to - *sellem Ɛla, weddeƐ.* I said good-bye to him yesterday. *sellemt Ɛlih l-bareḥ.*

saying - *metla* pl. *-t, mtul.* That's a very common saying. *hadik metla meƐṛufa bezzaf.*
**That goes without saying. *dak š-ši ma-yeḥtaž tefsir.*

scaffold - *srir* pl. *srayer.* He fell from the scaffold. *ṭaḥ men fuq s-srir.*

scale - **1.** *mizan* pl. *myazen, mwazen.* She practices scales all day. *ṛaha ka-ttmerren Ɛel le-myazen n-nhaṛ kollu.* **2.** *qyas* pl. *-at.* The scale is one to one thousand. *le-qyas waḥed Ɛla ʔalef.* **3.** *qeṣṛa* pl. *qšuṛ* coll. *qšeṛ.* This fish has big scales. *had l-ḥut Ɛendu qšuṛ kbaṛ.*
scale(s) - *mizan* pl. *myazen.* Put the meat on the scales. *Ɛmel l-lḥem fe-l-mizan.*
to scale - **1.** *tšebbeṭ, ṭḷeƐ.* Ten of us scaled the cliff. *Ɛešṛa bina lli tšebbeṭna fe-l-žoṛf.* **2.** *qeššeṛ.* Has she scaled the fish yet? *qeššṛet l-ḥut wella ma-zala?*

scandal - *fḍiḥa* pl. *-t, fḍayeḥ.*

scar - *šeṛṭa* pl. *-t, šṛaṭi.* He has a scar on his right cheek. *Ɛendu šeṛṭa fe-l-ḥenk l-imni.*

scarce - *qlil* pl. *qlal.* Food has become scarce. *l-makla ṛežƐet qlila.*

scarcely - *ġir šwiya.* I scarcely knew him. *ma-Ɛṛeftu ġir šwiya.*

scare - *xelƐa* pl. *-t, xlaƐi.* You gave me an awful scare. *ṭiyyeṛti menni xelƐa qedd-aš.*
to scare - **1.** *xuwwef, xleƐ.* The dog scared me badly. *l-kelb xleƐni bezzaf.* **2.** *ttexleƐ.* I scare easily. *ana deġya ka-nttexleƐ.*
**Where did he scare up the money? *mnayn ṭelleƐ le-flus?*

scared stiff - *miyyet be-l-xelƐa.* We were scared stiff. *konna miyytin be-l-xelƐa.*

scarf - *šaraṣakel* pl. *šarašaklat; šal* pl. *šilan; rumiya* pl. *-at, rwama.*

scarlet - *Ɛekri.*

scarlet fever - *bu-šwika.*

to **scatter** - **1.** *tfeṛṛeq.* The crowd scattered when the police arrived. *n-nas tfeṛṛqet ġir žat š-šoṛṭa.* **2.** *šettet.* The books were scattered all over the floor. *le-ktub kanu mšetttin Ɛel l-ʔeṛḍ kollha.*

scenery - **1.** *zina* pl. *-t.* Who designed the scenery? *škun lli ṣuwweb z-zina?* **2.** *menḍeṛ* pl. *manaḍiṛ.* We didn't have time to look at the scenery. *ma-kan-š Ɛendna l-weqt baš ntfežžžu fe-l-manaḍiṛ.*

scent - *šemman.* Our dog has a keen scent. *kelbna Ɛendu šemman qwi.*
to scent - *šemm, šemm riḥa.* The dogs have scented the fox. *le-klab šemmu riḥt t-teƐleb.*

schedule - *beṛnamež* pl. *baṛamiž.* We'll have to work out a schedule if we're going to finish on time. *xeṣṣna nṣuwwbu waḥed l-beṛnamež ila konna ġad nfeḍḍiw fe-l-weqt.*
**The train arrived on schedule. *l-mašina weṣḷet fe-l-weqt.*

scheme - *mešruƐ* pl. *mašariƐ; beṛnamež* pl. *baṛamiž.* Has he thought up a new scheme? *waš fekkeṛ f-ši mešruƐ ždid?*
to scheme - *ḍebbeṛ.* They're always scheming. *dima ka-ideḅḅṛu.*

school - *meḍṛaṣa* pl. *mḍaṛeṣ.*

science - *Ɛilm* pl. *Ɛulum.* He is more interested in science than in literature. *huwa mehtemm be-l-Ɛulum kteṛ men l-ʔadab.*

scientific - *Ɛilmi.*

scissors - *mqeṣṣ* pl. *mquṣa.* The scissors are dull. *had le-mqeṣṣ ḥafi.*

to **scold** - *ġuwwet Ɛla.* My mother scolded me. *mmi ġuwwtet Ɛliya.*

to **scorch** - *ḥṛeq.* I nearly scorched my dress. *Ɛlayen ḥṛeqt ksuwti.*

**The sun is scorching hot. *š-šems sxuna ka-teḥṛeq.*

score - **1.** *ḥsab, ḥsiyba.* I have a score to settle with that fellow. *Ɛendi ši-ḥsiyba ġad nṣeffiha mƐa dak xiyyna.* **2.** *naḥiya.* You don't need to worry on that score. *ma-Ɛendek mn-aš ttšuwweš men dak n-naḥiya.*

**What's the score? *fayn wṣeḷ l-leƐb?* --The score is three to one. *l-leƐb waqef fe-tlata l-waḥed.* --The score is tied. *l-leƐb metqadd.* --The final score was five to nothing. *n-natiža de-l-leƐb kanet xemsa l-walu.*

to score - *dar idir, rbeḥ.* They scored five points. *rebḥu xemsa de-n-nqaṭ.*

scoundrel - *ṣelguṭ* pl. *ṣlageṭ.*

scrap - **1.** *šyaṭa* pl. *-t.* Give the scraps to the dogs. *Ɛṭi š-šyaṭa l-le-klab.* **2.** *ṭeṛf* pl. *ṭṛaf.* That' only a scrap of paper. *hadak ġir ṭeṛf de-l-kaġiṭ.* **3.** *ġnan* pl. *-at.* They had an awful scrap last night. *kan binathom ġnan kbir l-bareḥ fe-l-lil.*

scrap metal - *ḥdid bali.* He deals in scrap metal. *ka-ibiƐ w-išri f-le-ḥdid l-bali.*

to **scrape** - *keṛṛeṭ.* She scraped her hands on the rock. *keṛṛṭet iddiha mƐa l-ḥežṛa.*

to scrape off - *keṛṛeṭ.* Scrape the paint off first. *keṛṛeṭ s-sbaġa beƐda.*

to scrape together - *qaded.* I couldn't scrape the money together. *ma-qdeṛt-š nqaded le-flus.*

scratch - **1.** *xebša* pl. *-t* coll. *xbaš.* Where did you get that scratch on your cheek? *mnayn žatek dak l-xebša lli f-wežhek?* **2.** *mʔadya* pl. *-t.* We escaped without a scratch. *mneƐna bla mʔadya.*

from scratch - *men walu, men l-luwwel.* After the fire he had to start from scratch. *men beƐd l-Ɛafya ḍteṛṛ ibda men l-luwweḷ.*

to scratch - **1.** *xebbeš.* Be careful not to scratch the furniture. *Ɛendak txebbeš l-ʔatat.* **2.** *šenqeṛ.* This pen scratches. *had r-riša ka-tšenqeṛ.*

to scratch out - *ḍṛeb Ɛla.* Scratch out the last sentence. *ḍṛeb Ɛel l-žumla t-talya.*

scream - *ġuta* pl. *-t* coll. *ġwat.* I thought I heard a scream. *žab-li ḷḷah smeƐt ši-ġuta.*

to scream - *ġuwwet.* The child screamed with fright. *d-derri ġuwwet be-l-xewf.*

screen - **1.** *deṛṛaqa* pl. *-t, dṛaṛeq.* Undress behind the screen. *zuwwel ḥwayžek muṛ d-deṛṛaqa.* **2.** *izar* pl. *izur.* He looks older on the screen. *ka-iban kbeṛ men dak š-ši f-l-izar.* **3.** *šebka* pl. *-t, šbek.* We need new screens in the living room. *xeṣṣna šebkat ždad fe-l-bit le-kbir.*

screw - *luleb* pl. *lwaleb.* These screws need tightening. *had l-lwaleb xeṣṣhom itƐeẓẓaw.*

to screw - *ẓiyyeṛ, Ɛeẓẓa.* Don't forget to screw the cap on the bottle. *Ɛendak tensa ma-dẓiyyeṛ-š le-ġṭa de-l-qeṛƐa.*

**If I can screw up enough courage, I'll ask for a raise. *ila žbeṛt l-qoḍṛa ġad ntḷeb z-zyada.*

screw driver - *bu-lwaleb* pl. *bu-lwalbat.*

to **scribble** - *xenfeš.* It's terrible the way he scribbles. *walayenni kif ka-ixenfeš.*

**The wall is all scribbled up. *l-ḥeyṭ kollu mƐemmeṛ be-t-txenfiš.*

to **scrub** - *ḥekk.* She still has to scrub the floor. *ma-zal xeṣṣha tḥekk l-ʔeṛḍ.*

sculptor - *neqqaš* pl. *-a.*

scythe - *mḥešša* pl. *-t.*

sea - *bḥeṛ* pl. *bḥuṛ, bḥuṛa.* How far are we from the sea? *šḥal binna u-bin le-bḥeṛ?*

seal - **1.** *kelb le-bḥeṛ* pl. *klab le-bḥeṛ.* We watched them feed the seals. *šefnahom ka-iwekklu klab le-bḥeṛ.* **2.** *ṭabeƐ* pl. *ṭwabeƐ.* The papers bore the official seal. *le-wṛaq kan Ɛlihom ṭ-ṭabeƐ r-resmi.*

to seal - **1.** *šedd.* Have you sealed the letter yet? *šedditi le-bṛa wella ma-zal.* **2.** *lekkek.* You have to seal the jars while the fruit is still hot. *ka-ixeṣṣek tlekkek le-Ɛleb ma-ḥedd l-fakya*

seam - *xyaṭa* pl. *-t.* Rip open this seam. *fteq had le-xyaṭa.*

search - *teqlab, teqliba.* The police made a thorough search. *l-bulis daru teqliba men ṛ-ṛas le-r-režlin.*

to search - *qelleb.* I've searched the whole house. *qellebt ḍ-ḍaṛ kollha.* --We searched for him everywhere. *ma-xellina fayn* *qellebna Ělih.*

season - 1. *menzla* pl. *-t, mnazel; feșl* pl. *fșul.* Which season do you like best? *š-men menzla ka-tĚežbek ktir-ši?* 2. *weqt* pl. *wqat; fetra* pl. *-t.* The hotel had an excellent season this year. *l-ʔuṭil daz Ělih weqt haʔil had l-Ěam.*

to season - *Ěmel l-Ěeṭṛiya.* What did you season the meat with? *š-men Ěeṭṛiya Ěmelti fe-l-lḥem?*

seat - 1. *korsi* pl. *krasa; šelya* pl. *šli.* This seat needs fixing. *had l-korsi xeșșu itșuwweb.* 2. *mudeĚ* pl. *mwaḍeĚ.* There's still a free seat. *ma-zala muḍeĚ xawya.* 3. *meqĚed* pl. *mqaĚed.* The pants are too tight in the seat. *had s-serwal mẓiyyeṛ bezzaf fe-l-meqĚed.*

to have (take) a seat - *gles.* Please have a seat. *tfeḍḍeḷ, gles.*

to seat - 1. *gelles.* She seated the children in the front row. *gellset d-drari fe-ș-șeff l-luwwel.* 2. *rfed.* The theater seats five hundred people. *l-mesṛeḥ ka-irfed xems-mya de-n-nas.*

second - 1. *taniya* pl. *-t.* He ran a hundred meters in ten seconds. *žra myat miter f-Ěešṛa de-t-taniyat.* 2. *tani* pl. *tanyin.* Will you please give me the second book from the left? *men fedlek Ěṭini le-ktab t-tani Ěel l-ișeṛ.*

second-class - *t-tanya.* Give me one second-class ticket to Rabat, please. *Ěṭini bṭaqa fe-t-tanya le-ṛ-ṛbaṭ ḷḷah ibarek fik.*

second-hand - 1. *neșș lebsa.* He bought the book second-hand. *šra le-ktab neșș lebsa.* 2. *men Ěend xṛin.* I only know that story second-hand. *dak le-ḥkaya ma-ka-neĚṛefha ġir men Ěend xṛin.*

secret - 1. *sirr* pl. *sṛaṛ.* Let me in on the secret. *ʔemmenni be-s-sirr.* --Can you keep a secret? *ka-teĚṛef tektem s-sirr?* 2. *sirri.* He was elected by secret ballot. *șuwwtu-lu be-ntixab sirri.* 3. *mestur, mexfi.* They have a secret plan. *Ěendhom beṛnamež mestur.*

**She keeps no secrets from me. *ma-ka-txebbeĚ šay Ěliya.*

to keep secret - *xebbeĚ.* I don't know why they keep it secret. *ma-Ěṛeft-ši Ělaš ka-ixebbĚuha.*

secretary - 1. *katib, kateb* pl. *kottab;* f. *katiba* pl. *-t.* She's my secretary. *hadik l-katiba dyali.* 2. *wazir* pl. *wuẓaṛaʔ.* His father is the Secretary of the Interior. *ḅḅah wazir d-daxiliya.*

secretly - *sirriyan, f-xefya, men teḥt l-teḥt.* They met secretly. *ṛahom tlaqaw men teḥt l-teḥt.*

section - 1. *feqṛa* pl. *-t.* You'll find it in Chapter One, Section Three. *ġad tșibha fe-l-feqṛa t-talta de-l-feșl l-luwwel.* 2. *naḥiya* pl. *-t, nawaḥi.* I was brought up in this section. *kbert f-had n-naḥiya.* 3. *ḥewma* pl. *-t, ḥwem; naḥiya* pl. *-t, nawaḥi.* He lives in one of the nicest sections of the town. *ka-iskon f-ḥewma men ʔeḥsen ḥwem d-le-mdina.*

secure - 1. *fe-l-ʔaman.* Nobody feels secure these days. *ḥetta waḥed ma-ka-iḥess b-ṛașu fe-l-ʔaman had l-iyam.* 2. *qabeṭ.* Is this bolt secure? *waš had ẓ-ẓekṛum qabeṭ?*

to secure - *ḍmen.* His future is secured. *musteqbalu meḍmun.*

security - 1. *ʔaman.* It gives us a sense of security. *had š-ši ka-yuḍeĚna šwiyeš fe-l-ʔaman.* 2. *ḍamana* pl. *-t.* What security can you give me that he'll pay me? *š-men ḍamana imken-lek teĚṭini ʔannahu ġad-ixeḷḷeșni?* 3. *rhen* pl. *rhuna.* I had to leave my watch as security. *tlezzemt nxelli maganti fe-r-rhen.*

to **see** - 1. *šaf išuf.* We've just seen a good movie. *Ěad šefna waḥed l-film mezyan.* 2. *šaf išuf, tqabel.* I can't see him until tomorrow. *ma-ġad imken-li ntqabel mĚah ḥetta l-ġedda.* 3. *šaf išuf, fhem, qšeĚ.* Anybody should be able to see that. *men wala ifhem hadik.* 4. *šaf išuf, mša imši Ěend.* Why don't you see a lawyer about this matter? *Ělaš ma-temši-š Ěend ši-muḥami Ěla had l-qaḍiya?* 5. *tsara f-.* I would like to see the town. *baġi ntsara f-le-mdina.*

**Oh, I see! *xyaṛ! žitek.* --See you again! *iwa ntlaqaw!* or *ḷḷah ihennik!* --Wait and see. *daba tšuf.* --He has seen better days. *kan Ěayeš fe-l-xir u-le-xmir.* --I'd like to see more of you. *baġi ntmetteĚ be-š-šufa fik kteṛ men had š-ši.* --We saw them off to the boat. *mšina mĚahom l-l-baxiṛa.* --He makes me see red. *ka-iṭeḷḷeĚ-li z-zĚef.* --Anybody can see through that guy. *men wala iĚiq b-dak xiyna.*

seed - 1. *zerriĚa* pl. *-t.* Did you buy any seeds? *šriti ši-zerriĚa?* 2. *Ěḍem* pl. *Ěḍam, Ěḍuma.* Some types of oranges have no seeds. *ši-xeṛž*

de-l-letšin ma-fih Ɛḍam.
to **seem** - *ban iban, ḍheṛ.* That seems peculiar to me. *ka-iban-li ġṛib dak š-ši.*
seesaw - *mizan* pl. *myazen.*
to **seize** - **1.** *xṭef, ġnem.* If I don't seize this opportunity it may be too late. *ila ma-xṭeft-ši had l-wežba ġad imken iduz l-weqt.* **2.** *qbeḍ, šedd.* He seized the rope with both his hands. *qbeḍ ṭ-ṭwal b-zuž iddih.* **3.** *ṣlaṭ Ɛla, nzel Ɛla.* He was seized by fear. *l-xewf nzel Ɛlih.* **4.** *ḥṣeṛ, ḥbes.* They seized his papers. *ḥebsu-lu kwaġṭu.*
seldom - *qlil (f-as).* I seldom agree with him. *qlil f-aš ka-nttafeq mƐah.*
to **select** - *xteṛ.*
to **sell** - **1.** *baƐ ibiƐ.* Did you sell your old car? *beƐti siyaṛtek le-qdima?* --He sold us out to the enemy. *baƐ bina l-le-Ɛdu.* **2.** *ttbaƐ.* This suit usually sells for two hundred dirhams. *had l-keswa ka-ttbaƐ Ɛadiyen be-myatayn derhem.*
**Sorry, we're all sold out. *be-l-ʔasaf, xerrežna koll-ši.*
semiannual - *meṛṛtayn fe-l-Ɛam.*
semolina - *smid, smida.*
to **send** - *ṣifeṭ, ṣafeṭ iṣifeṭ.* I want to send him a telegram. *bġit nṣifeṭ-lu berqiya.* --Have you sent for the doctor? *ṣifeṭṭi muṛ ṭ-ṭbib?* --When did he send that package off? *fuq-aš ṣafeṭ dak ṛ-ṛeẓma?*
**Send him in. *qul-lu idxol.*
to send one's regards - *sellem Ɛla.* He sends his regards to everybody. *ka-isellem Ɛla koll-ši.*
sensation - **1.** *šuƐuṛ* pl. *-at.* It's a very pleasant sensation. *šuƐuṛ ḥlu bezzaf.* **2.** *fetna* pl. *-t.* His speech created a sensation. *l-kalima dyalu Ɛemlet fetna.*
sensational - *Ɛažib, haʔil, (lli) ka-ifṭen.*
sense - *Ɛqel, ṛaṣ.* I hope he has enough sense to take a taxi. *meṣṣab ġir ikun Ɛendu ṛ-ṛaṣ u-yaxod ṭakṣi.* --I must have been out of my senses. *waqila kont xaṛez Ɛla Ɛeqli.* **2.** *meƐna.* There's no sense in doing that. *dak š-ši ma-Ɛendu meƐna ikun.* **3.** *šuƐuṛ.* It gives me a sense of security. *had š-ši ka-ibƐet fiya šuƐuṛ de-l-ʔaman.*
**That's true, in a sense. *dak š-ši ṣḥiḥ men waḥed n-naḥiya.* --That doesn't make sense. *had š-ši ma-ši meƐqul.* --That doesn't make any sense to me. *ma-zal dak š-ši ma-bġa-ši ittefhem-li.*
to sense - *ḥess.* I sensed right away that something was wrong- *deġya ḥessit b-ši haža ma-ši hiya hadik.*
senseless - **1.** *(lli) ma-Ɛendu meƐna.* That's altogether senseless. *had š-ši kollu ma-Ɛendu meƐna.* **2.** *(lli) ma-Ɛendu Ɛqel.* Anyone that would go out in this rain is senseless. *ma-Ɛendu Ɛqel lli ixrož f-had š-šta.*
sensible - *mƐeqqel.*
sentence - **1.** *žumla* pl. *-t, žumal.* I didn't understand the last sentence. *ma-fhemt-š l-žumla t-talya.* **2.** *ḥkam* pl. *-at.* The judge has already pronounced sentence. *l-qaḍi ṣeḍḍeṛ ḥkamu.*
to sentence - *ḥkem Ɛla.* He was sentenced to five years. *ḥekmu Ɛlih b-xems snin.*
sentimental - *Ɛaṭifi, (lli) qelbu rhif.*
sentry - *Ɛessa* pl. *-t, Ɛses.* The sentry didn't let me pass. *l-Ɛessa ma-xellatni-š nduz.*
separate - *mefṛuq.* Could we have separate rooms? *imken-lna naxdu byut mefṛuqin?*
under separate cover - *b-weḥdu.* I'm sending you my application under separate cover. *ṛ-ana mṣifeṭ-lkom ṭ-ṭalab dyali b-weḥdu.*
to separate - **1.** *fṛeq.* I could hardly separate those two. *ma-stateƐt-š ḥetta nefṛeqhom b-zuž.* --My parents are separated. *waldiya mefṛuqin.* **2.** *qṣem.* Separate that group into five sections. *qṣem dak ž-žmaƐa Ɛla xemsa de-l-feṛqat.*
separately - *b-weḥdu.* I want to talk to each one of the boys separately. *ḥebbit nehḍeṛ mƐa koll waḥed men le-wlad b-weḥdu.*
September - *šutanbir, šutambir.*
series - *selsila* pl. *-t.* He's written a series of books about it. *huwa kteb waḥed s-selsila d-le-ktub Ɛla dak š-ši.*
serious - **1.** *doġri.* That man is very serious in his work. *had ṛ-ṛažel doġri bezzaf fe-l-xedma dyalu.* **2.** *xaṭiṛ.* His illness isn't very serious. *l-merḍ dyalu ma-ši xaṭiṛ bezzaf.* **3.** *kbir* pl. *kbaṛ.* That's a serious mistake. *ġelṭa kbira hadi.*
seriously - **1.** *bezzaf.* She is seriously ill. *hiya mṛiḍa bezzaf.* **2.** *be-n-niya.* I'm seriously considering getting married. *ka-nxemmem be-n-niya fe-z-zwaž.*

sermon - *xoṭba* pl. *-t.* Our preacher gave a good sermon on Friday. *le-xṭib dyalna Ɛmel waḥed l-xoṭba mezyana nhaṛ ž-žemƐa.*

servant - *metƐellem* pl. *metƐellmin, xeddam* pl. *-a.*

to **serve** - **1.** *Ɛṭa yeƐṭi, duwwez, feṛṛeq.* Shall I serve the drinks now? *nfeṛṛeq l-mešṛubat daba?* **2.** *ṣlaḥ, qḍa iqḍi.* This will serve its purpose. *had š-ši ġad iqḍi meṣlaḥtu.* **3.** *duwwez.* He's serving a four-year term in prison. *ṛah ka-iduwwez modda d-ṛebƐa snin fe-l-ḥebs.* **4.** *nezzel.* When do you serve supper? *fuq-aš ka-tnezzlu le-Ɛša?*

**That serves you right! *xxi fik!* or *iwa baš ttƐellem!*

service - **1.** *mqabla, mgabla.* The service is bad in this restaurant. *le-mqabla Ɛendhom qbiḥa f-had l-meṭƐem.* **2.** *xedma* pl. *-ṭ.* The maid is giving us good service. *l-metƐellma ka-teƐmel-lna xedma mezyana.*

**These buses have been in service for twenty years. *had ṭ-ṭubisat hadi Ɛešrin Ɛam u-huma xeddamin.* --How long have you been in the service? *šḥal hadi u-nta fe-l-žeyš?* --Can I be of service to you? *tebġini neqḍi-lek ši-ḥaža?*

service station - *mḥeṭṭa d-l-iṣanṣ* pl. *mḥeṭṭat d-l-iṣanṣ.* Let's stop at the next service station. *nweqfu f-le-mḥeṭṭa d-l-iṣanṣ l-mažya.*

Sesame - *zenžlan.*

set - **1.** *serbis* pl. *srabes.* We have a whole set of these ash trays. *Ɛendna serbis kamel men had l-qeṭṛan de-ḍ-ḍefya.* **2.** *mežmuƐa* pl. *-t.* There's only one stamp missing in that set. *ma-xaṣṣ f-dak l-mežmuƐa ġir tenber waḥed.* **3.** *ʔala* pl. *-t.* He sold his old radio and bought a new set. *baƐ ṛ-ṛadyu le-qdim dyalu u-šra ʔala ždida.*

to set - **1.** *nezzel, Ɛmel.* Set it on the desk. *nezzelha fuq ṭ-ṭebḷa.* **2.** *ḥeqqeq.* I set my watch by the station clock. *ḥeqqeqt maganti Ɛel l-magana d-le-mḥeṭṭa.* **3.** *Ɛeyyen.* Why don't you set the time? *Ɛlaš nta ma-tƐeyyen-ši l-weqt?* **4.** *qeṛṛeq, ḥeḍḍen.* Is the hen setting? *waš d-džaža mqeṛṛqa?* **5.** *rekkeb.* I'd like to have these stones set in gold. *nebġi had l-ḥežṛat mrekkbin Ɛel d-dheb.* **6.** *bda ibda.* He set to work immediately. *deġya bda fe-l-xedma.* **7.** *ġṛeb.* The sun had already set. *š-šems kanet ġeṛbet beƐda.* **8.** *Ɛṭa yeƐṭi.* You've set a good example. *nta Ɛṭiti mital mezyan.*

**I set my watch five minutes ahead. *zedt xemsa de-d-dqayeq f-maganti.* --He set the price at fifty dirhams. *xemsin derhem t-taman lli Ɛmel.* --Set the clock for seven. *ṭeḷḷeƐ l-magana fe-s-sebƐa.* --The meeting has been set for nine o'clock. *le-žtimaƐ daruh le-t-tesƐud.* --He set the dogs on me. *ṭḷeq Ɛliya le-klab.* --Can you set me straight on this? *imken-lek tbiyyen-li had š-ši?*

to set aside - *xebbeƐ, xella.* Set this one aside for me. *xebbeƐ-li hadi.*

to set down - *nezzel.* Set the box down gently. *nezzel ṣ-ṣenduq be-š-šwiya.*

to set in - *bda ibda, dxel idxol.* The rainy season set in early this year. *weqt š-šta bda bekri had l-Ɛam.*

to set off - *ṭerṭeq.* They didn't have time to set off the charge. *ma-kan-š f-iddhom l-weqt baš iṭerṭqu le-Ɛmaṛa*

to set out for - *šedd ṭ-ṭriq l-.* They set out for home on Monday. *nhaṛ t-tnayn šeddu ṭ-ṭriq l-ḍaṛhom.*

to set the table - *wežžed ṭ-ṭebla.* Quick, set the table! *deġya wežžed ṭ-ṭebla.*

to set up - *rekkeb.* The new machines have just been set up. *Ɛad rekkbu l-ʔalat ž-ždad.*

all set - *wažed.* Everything is all set. *koll-ši wažed.*

to be set on - *Ɛmel Ɛeynu f-.* I'm set on that. *Ɛmelt Ɛeyni f-dak š-ši.*

to **settle** - **1.** *ṣeffa, feḍḍa.* He settled with his creditors. *feḍḍa mƐa mmalin ṭ-ṭeḷq.* --We must settle our accounts today. *xeṣṣna l-yum nṣeffiw ḥsabatna.* **2.** *ṛeṣṣa, feḍḍa.* You must settle that between yourselves. *xeṣṣkom tṛeṣṣiw dak š-ši beƐḍiyatkom.* **3.** *ṣḷeḥ.* Can you settle their argument? *imken-lek teṣḷeḥ ma binathom?* **4.** *tṛeṣṣa.* The wall has settled a little. *l-ḥiṭ tṛeṣṣa ši-šwiya.* **5.** *qƐed, rqed.* Wait until the tea has settled. *ṣber ḥetta iqƐed ʔatay.*

to be settled - *fra ifra.* This question was settled some time ago. *had l-qaḍiya frat šḥal hadi.*

**Now settle down to work! *iwa*

gles texdem Ɛ*la* ṛ*aṣek daba.* --On Sunday I like to settle myself in a chair and smoke my pipe. *nhar l-ḥedd ka-iršeq-li nwerrek* Ɛ*la ši-šelya u-nekmi s-sbisi dyali.*

to settle down - *ṛeṣṣa ṛaṣu.* Hasn't he settled down yet? *ma-zal ma-ṛeṣṣa ṛaṣu?*

to settle for - *ttawa b-.* We settled for two hundred dirhams. *ttawina be-myatayn derhem.*

settlement - *ttifaqiya* pl. *-t.* They couldn't reach a settlement. *ma-weṣḷu ḥetta l-ši ttifaqiya.*

seven - *seb*Ɛ*a.*

seventeen - *sbe*Ɛ*ṭaš.*

seventh - **1.** (ordinal). *sabe*Ɛ pl. *sab*Ɛ*in.* **2.** (fraction). *subu*Ɛ pl. *-at.*

seventy - *seb*Ɛ*in.*

several - Ɛ*adad d-.* We passed several beautiful houses. *dezna* Ɛ*la* Ɛ*adad de-ḍ-ḍyaṛ mezyanin.*

several times - *ma-hiya xeṭṛa ma-hiya zuž.* I've been there several times. *kont temma ma-hiya xeṭṛa ma-hiya zuž.*

severe - **1.** *qaṣeḥ.* It was a very severe winter. *l-berd kan qaṣeḥ bezzaf.* **2.** *kbir.* The punishment was too severe. *l-*Ɛ*uquba kanet kbira bezzaf* Ɛ*ad.* **3.** *xṭiṛ.* He has a severe case of pneumonia. *ṃeṛḍ s-sder lli fih xṭiṛ.*

Seville - *šbilya.*

to **sew** - *xeyyeṭ.* She sews her own dresses. *ka-txeyyeṭ ksawiha b-iddha.*

**Please sew these buttons on for me. *ḷḷah ixellik rekkeb-li had ṣ-ṣḍaf.*

sewer - *qadus* Ɛ*eṭṭaṛa* pl. *qwades* Ɛ*eṭṭaṛa.*

sewing machine - *makina d-le-xyaṭa* pl. *-t d-le-xyaṭa.*

sex - *žins* pl. *žnas.* In your application state age and sex. *fe-l-weṛqa de-ṭ-ṭalab dkeṛ s-senn u-l-žins dyalek.*

the fair sex - *l-žins ḷ-ḷṭif.*

sexual - *žinsi.*

shabby - *mbehdel.* His suit looks shabby. *ksuwtu ka-tban mbehdla.*

**That was very shabby of him. *hadik darha ṭayḥa.*

shade - **1.** *ḍeḷḷ* pl. *ḍḷuḷ.* Let's stay in the shade. *xellina fe-ḍ-ḍeḷḷ.* **2.** *ġḷaq* pl. *-at.* Pull down the shades. *hebbeṭ le-ġḷaqat.*

shadow - **1.** *ḍeḷḷ* pl. *ḍḷuḷ.* The trees cast long shadows. *š-šžeṛ ka-ye*Ɛ*ṭiw ḍeḷḷ kbir.* **2.** *xyal* pl. *-at.* He's afraid of his own shadow. *men xyalu ka-ixaf.* **3.** *ḥebba* pl. *-at.* There is not a shadow of doubt about it. *dak š-ši ma-fih-ši ḥebba de-š-šekk.*

**They hired a detective to shadow him. *kellfu bulisi sirri iṭmi* Ɛ*lih l-*Ɛ*eyn.*

shady - **1.** *mḍeḷḷeḷ.* That place is shady and we can play there. *dak l-maḥell mḍeḷḷeḷ w-imken-lna nle*Ɛ*bu temma.* **2.** *mdebdeb.* That's a shady business. *had l-bi*Ɛ*a u-š-šerya mdebdba.*

shaft - *wted* pl. *wtad.* The shaft broke off. *le-wted therres.*

to **shake** - **1.** *hezz.* She shook her head. *hezzet ṛaṣha.* **2.** *mxeḍ.* You must shake it before using. *xeṣṣek tmexḍu qbel-ma txeddmu.* **3.** *ze*Ɛ*ze*Ɛ*.* The earthquake shook everything within a radius of three kilometers. *l-hezza l-ʔeṛḍiya ze*Ɛ*z*Ɛ*et lli ttṣab kollu* Ɛ*la tlata kilumiter men hna.*

shaky - *mfe*Ɛ*fe*Ɛ*.* I'm still shaky. *ṛani ma-zal mfe*Ɛ*fe*Ɛ*.*

shall - *ġad* (plus the imperfect). We shall see who's right. *ġad nšufu škun m*Ɛ*ah l-ḥeqq.*

shallow - **1.** *ma-ġaṛeq-š.* The lake is very shallow at this point. *ḍ-ḍaya ma-ġaṛqa-š bezzaf f-had l-muḍe*Ɛ*.* **2.** *mbesseṭ, mgeṛṛeṣ.* Put it in a shallow bowl. *diru fe-ġṭaṛ mbesseṭ.* **3.** *ma-ši doġri.* He's a very shallow person. *huwa ma-ši ṛažel doġri.*

shame - **1.** *ḥya.* Haven't you any shame? *ma-fik ḥya?* **2.** *ḥšuma* pl. *ḥšayem.* It's a shame the way he treats us. *ḥšuma kif ka-i*Ɛ*amelna.*

**Shame on you! *ḷḷah iqellel ḥyak!* or *ḷḷah in*Ɛ*el men lla-yeḥšem!* --What a shame you can't come. *be-l-ʔasaf ma-imken-lek-š dži.*

shape - **1.** *fṣala* pl. *-t, fṣayel.* The fez is all out of shape. *ṭ-ṭeṛbuš ma-bqa qabeṭ ḥetta fṣala.* **2.** *ḥala* pl. *-t, ḥwal.* I'm in bad shape. *ṛ-ana f-waḥed l-ḥala mfellsa.* **3.** *ġaya* pl. *-t.* Is everything in shape? *waš koll-ši f-ġaya?*

to shape - *feṣṣeḷ.* His head is shaped like a watermelon. *ṛaṣu mfeṣṣeḷ bḥal ši-dellaḥa.*

to shape up - *t*Ɛ*ewweṭ.* Things are gradually shaping up. *l-ʔumuṛ ṛaha ka-tt*Ɛ*ewweṭ šwiya be-šwiya.*

share - **1.** *ḥeqq* pl. *ḥquq.* Everybody has to pay his share. *koll waḥed ixeḷḷeṣ ḥeqqu.* **2.** *sehm* pl. *sham, shuma.* How many shares did you buy? *šḥal men sehm šriti?*

to share - *qşem.* Let's share the cake. *aži nqeşmu l-ḥelwa.*

shareholder - *shaymi* pl. *-yat, msahem* pl. *msahmin.*

shark - *maraxu* pl. *-yat.*

sharp - **1.** *maḍi.* Do you have a sharp knife? *Eendek ši-mess maḍi?* **2.** *qaṭeE, (lli) ka-idbeḥ.* She has a sharp tongue. *Eendha lsan ka-idbeḥ.* **3.** *tamam.* We have to be there at five o'clock sharp. *xeşşna nkunu temma fe-l-xemsa tamam.*

to **sharpen** - **1.** *meḍḍa.* You have to sharpen this knife. *xeşşek tmeḍḍi had l-mus.* **2.** *nžeṛ.* Sharpen this pencil for me, please. *Eafak nžeṛ-li had le-qlam.*

shave - *ḥsana d-le-wžeh, tekṛiṭa, teḥsina.* I want a shave and a haircut. *bġit ši-teḥsina d-le-wžeh u-de-š-šEeṛ.* --The barber gave me a good shave. *l-ḥežžam dar-li waḥed t-tekṛiṭa ha?ila.*

to shave - *ḥessen le-wžeh.* Who shaved you? *škun ḥessen-lek wežhek?*

she - *hiya.*

to **shed** - **1.** *xwa ixwi.* She shed bitter tears. *xwat dmuE d-demm.* **2.** *ṛma iṛmi.* That sheds some light on the matter. *had š-ši ka-iṛmi šwiyeš de-ḍ-ḍuw Eel l-qaḍiya.* **3.** *zuwwel.* As soon as I got into my room I shed all my clothes. *ġir wşelt l-biti zuwwelt ḥwayži kollhom.*

sheep - *kebš* pl. *kbaš.*

sheer - **1.** *tamm.* That would be sheer madness. *iwa hadak le-ḥmaq t-tamm.* **2.** *rhif* pl. *rhaf.* I'd like a sheer fabric. *ana baġi ši-tub rhif.*

sheet - **1.** *iẓaṛ* pl. *iẓuṛ.* Shall I change the sheets, too? *nbeddel ḥetta l-iẓuṛ?* **2.** *weṛqa* pl. *-t, wṛaq.* Please give me a sheet of paper. *Eafak Eṭini ši-weṛqa.*
**Her face turned as white as a sheet. *wžehha wella bḥal l-ḥiṭ.*

shelf - *ṭebqa* pl. *-t.* The shelves are empty. *ṭ-ṭebqat xawyen.*

shell - **1.** *qešṛa* pl. *-t, qšuṛ.* These walnuts have a hard shell. *had l-guz qšeṛtu qaşḥa.* **2.** *kuṛa* pl. *-t, kweṛ.* A shell exploded near our house. *waḥed l-kuṛa ṭṭeṛṭqet ḥda ḍaṛna.*

to shell - *qeššeṛ.* Do you want to shell the walnuts? *tebġi tqeššeṛ l-guz?*

shelter - *tedṛiqa* pl. *-t.* Some bus stops have no shelters. *beEḍ le-mḥeṭṭat de-ṭ-ṭubis ma-fihom tedṛiqat.*

to shelter - *sekken.* They sheltered and fed us. *huma sekknuna u-wekkluna.*

shepherd - *sareḥ* pl. *sorraḥ.*

to **shield** - **1.** *deṛṛeq, xebbeE, ḥfeḍ.* You ought to shield your eyes against the sun. *lazem ddeṛṛeq Eeynik men š-šems.* **2.** *ster.* He must be shielding somebody. *ma-huwa ġir ka-ister ši-waḥed.*

shift - **1.** *refga* pl. *-t, rfagi.* Our workers work in three shifts. *l-xeddama dyalna Eamlin tlata de-r-refgat.* **2.** *teġyir* pl. *-at.* This will mean a shift in my plans. *had š-ši meEnah ġad ikun teġyir fe-l-baṛamiž dyali.*

to shift - **1.** *beddel, qleb.* You ought to shift into second. *xeşşek tbeddel le-t-tanya.* **2.** *ġiyyer, ḥewwel.* We have to shift the meeting to Tuesday. *la-bodda nġiyyru le-žtimaE le-nhaṛ t-tlata.* **3.** *tteqleb.* The wind has shifted. *ṛ-ṛiḥ tteqleb.*

to shift for oneself - *ḍebbeṛ Ela ṛaşu.* I always shift for myself. *dima ka-nḍebbeṛ Ela ṛaşi.*

shin - *qeşba de-r-ržel* pl. *qşeb r-režlin.*

shine - **1.** *lmiE.* If you polish the tray, the shine will come back. *had ş-şiniya ila mseḥtiha iṛžeE-lha l-lmiE dyalha.* **2.** *mesḥa* pl. *-t* coll. *msiḥ.* A shoe shine costs half a dirham. *l-mesḥa de-ş-şebbaṭ ka-teswa neşş derhem.*
**We'll come, rain or shine. *ġad nžiw waxxa ikun l-ġaṛaq.*

to shine - **1.** *lmeE, bṛeq, ḍwa iḍwi.* The sun isn't shinning today. *š-šems ma-ka-telmeE-š l-yum.* --Her eyes were shining with joy. *Eeyniha kanu ka-ibeṛqu be-l-feṛḥa.* **2.** *ban iban, bṛez, bṛeE.* He's good in all his subjects, but mathematics is where he shines. *huwa mezyan fe-l-mawadd kollha be-l-ḥeqq le-ḥsab fih ka-iban.* **3.** *mseḥ.* I have to shine my shoes. *xeşşni nemseḥ şebbaṭi.*

to be **shiny** - *ḍwa iḍwi.* His pants are shiny. *serwalu ka-iḍwi.*

ship - *babuṛ* pl. *-at, baxiṛa* pl. *-t.* When does the ship leave? *fuq-aš ġad temši l-baxiṛa?*

to ship - *şifeṭ, şafeṭ işifeṭ.* They can ship these goods by rail. *imken-lhom işifṭu had s-selEa mEa l-mašina.*

shipment - *selEa* pl. *-t, sluE.* We've just received a new shipment of

shoes. *ɛad weşletna selɛa ždida de-ş-şbabeṭ.*
shipwreck - *ġerqan l-babuṛ.*
shirt - *qamežža* pl. *-t, qwamež.* Are my shirts back from the laundry? *qwamži žaw men ɛend ş-şebban?*
**Keep your shirt on, I'll be right there. *xellik temma, daba w-ana žit.*
to **shiver** - *ġzel, qefqef.* The child was shivering with cold. *d-derri kan ka-iġzel be-l-berd.*
shock - **1.** *ḍeṛba* pl. *-t, deqqa* pl. *-t.* His death was a great shock to us all. *l-mut dyalu žatna kollna ḍeṛba kbira.* **2.** *qetta* pl. *-t, qtet.* They stacked up the wheat in shocks. *ɛeṛṛmu l-gemḥ qtet qtet.*
to shock - *šleṭ.* We were shocked by the news. *šleṭna le-xbaṛ.*
shoe - **1.** *ferda de-ş-şebbaṭ* pl. *şebbaṭ, şbabeṭ.* Where are my new shoes? *fayn ş-şebbaṭ ž-ždid dyali?* **2.** *şfiḥa* pl. *-t, şfayeḥ.* The horse lost one shoe. *l-ɛewd mšat-lu şfiḥa.*
**I wouldn't want to be in his shoes. *lleh-la yeɛmel-ni fe-rḥebtu.*
to shoe - *rekkeb şfayeḥ l-.* He's going to shoe his horse. *ġad irekkeb ş-şfayeḥ l-l-ɛewd dyalu.*
shoehorn - *ṭeḷḷaɛa* pl. *-t.*
shoelace - *sir* pl. *syur.*
shoemaker - *xerraz* pl. *-a.*
shoe polish - *siraž.* I need some brown polish for my new shoes. *baġi siraž qehwi l-şebbaṭi ž-ždid.*
shoe repair man - *ṭeṛṛaf* pl. *-a.*
shoot - *fṛiyeɛ* pl. *fṛiyɛat.* Our rosebush has two new shoots. *l-weṛḍa dyalna ɛemlet zuž d-le-fṛiyɛat xṛin.*
to shoot - **1.** *ḍṛeb, ɛdem.* You'll be shot for that. *iɛedmuk ɛla hadik.* **2.** *şuwweṛ.* They're shooting in Studio Five. *ka-işuwwṛu fe-s-stidyu l-xames.*
**The car shot past us. *s-siyaṛa dazet ḥdana be-ž-žehd.* --How the child has shot up in the last year! *walayenni kif faḍ d-derri had l-ɛam lli daz.*
to shoot dead - *qtel mqeṛṭeş.* They shot him dead. *qetluh mqeṛṭeş.*
to shoot down - *ṭiyyeḥ.* Four of our airplanes have been shot down. *ṭiyyḥu-lna ṛebɛa de-ṭ-ṭyayeṛ.*
shop - *ḥanut* (m. or f.) pl. *ḥwanet.* There are many shops on this street. *kaynin bezzaf d-le-ḥwanet f-had z-zenqa.*
to talk shop - *ḥḍeṛ ɛel l-xedma.* Stop talking shop! *iwa xḷaş u-ma-tehḍer ɛel l-xedma!*
to shop - *tşuwweq.*
**I want to shop around before I buy the present. *baġi nḍuṛ hna u-hna, ɛad nešri le-hdiya.*
shore - *ṭeṛf le-bḥeṛ* pl. *ṭṛaf le-bḥeṛ.* How far is it to the shore? *šḥal men hna l-ṭeṛf le-bḥeṛ.*
short - **1.** *selk meḥṛuq.* There must be a short in the radio. *hada ši-selk meḥṛuq fe-ṛ-ṛadyu.* **2.** *qşiṛ* pl. *qşaṛ.* She wears her dresses too short. *ka-telbes ksawiha qşaṛ bezzaf.*
**I am three dirhams short. *baqi ka-ixeşşuni tlata de-d-drahem.* --Right now, I am short of money. *f-had s-saɛa ana mexşuş men le-flus.* --It fell short of my expectations. *dak š-ši xeyyeb-li ḍ-ḍenn.*
in short - *l-ḥaşil.* In short, I can't. *l-ḥaşiḷ ma-imken-li-š.*
to cut short - *nqeş men.* They had to cut their trip short. *kanu melzumin baš ineqşu men ş-şfeṛ dyalhom.*
to run short - *qlal.* Our supplies were running short. *le-qwam kan bda iqlal-lna.*
short cut - *ṭṛiq mexṭufa* pl. *ṭoṛqan mexṭufin.* He knows a short cut to the beach. *ka-yeɛṛef waḥed ṭ-ṭṛiq mexṭufa l-le-bḥeṛ.*
to **shorten** - *nqeş men ṭ-ṭuḷ.* Shorten the pants for me, please. *ḷḷah ixellik nqeş-li men ṭ-ṭuḷ d-had s-serwal.*
shortly - *men daba šwiya.* He'll be here shortly. *ġad ikun hnaya men daba šwiya.*
shorts - **1.** *serwal teḥtani* pl. *srawel tḥata.* He ordered six pairs of shorts. *huwa ṭḷeb setta de-s-srawel t-tḥata.* **2.** *serwal qşiṛ* pl. *srawel qşaṛ.* The girls were all wearing shorts. *le-bnat kollhom kanu labsin s-srawel qşaṛ.*
short wave - *muža qşiṛa* pl. *mwaž qşaṛ.* You can get short wave on this radio too. *imken-lek teqbeṭ ḥetta l-muža le-qşiṛa f-had ṛ-ṛadyu.*
shot - **1.** *qoṛṭaş* pl. *qṛaṭeş.* Did you hear (the sound of) a shot? *smeɛti ši-teklima de-l-qoṛṭas?* **2.** *ɛmaṛa* pl. *-t, ɛmayeṛ.* He fired three shots. *xerrež tlata d-le-ɛmaṛat.* --Somebody took a shot at him. *ši-waḥed xla fih ɛmaṛa.* **3.** *niyyaš* pl. *-a.* His brother is a good shot. *xah niyyaš mezyan.* **4.** *teşwiṛa* pl. *-t, tşaweṛ.* We got beautiful shots of the lake. *t-tşaweṛ de-ḍ-ḍaya xeṛžu-lna mezyanin.* **5.** *šuka* pl.

šwek; ibra pl. ibari. Have you
gotten all your shots yet? kemmelti
l-ibari kollhom wella ma-zal?
**He thinks he's a big shot.
ka-ižib-lu ṛebbi huwa ši-ḥaža.

shotgun - zwiža pl. -t.

should - xeṣṣ (plus the imperfect).
You should study harder. xeṣṣek
teqra kteṛ men had š-ši.
   should have - kan xeṣṣ (plus the
imperfect). You shouldn't have
believed it. ma-kan-š xeṣṣek
ttiyyeq dak š-ši. --He should
have written to them. kan xeṣṣu
ikteb-lhom.

shoulder - ktef pl. ktaf. He has
very broad shoulders. Ɛendu ktaf
wasƐin bezzaf.
   **He doesn't even know how to
shoulder a rifle. ma-ka-yeƐṛef-š
ḥetta iqbet le-mkoḥla f-ketfu.
--Why did you give him the cold
shoulder? Ɛlaš nexxeltih. --Why
should I shoulder the blame for it?
Ɛlaš ana ġad naxod l-luma Ɛla dak
š-ši?
   straight from the shoulder -
be-ṣ-ṣaṛaḥa. --I gave it to him
straight from the shoulder.
qoltha-lu be-ṣ-ṣaṛaḥa.

to **shout** - ġuwwet. You don't have
to shout! ma-kayen Ɛlaš tġuwwet.
   to shout down - ġuwwet Ɛla. The
speaker was shouted down by the
crowd. n-nas ġuwwtu Ɛel l-muḥadiṛ.

shouting - ġwat pl. -at. Your
shouting is getting on my nerves.
had le-ġwat dyalek ka-iqelleqni.

shove - defƐa pl. -t. He gave me
such a shove that I nearly fell
over. dfeƐni waḥed d-defƐa ḥetta
Ɛlayen ġad nṭiḥ.
   to shove - dfeƐ.

shovel - baḷa pl. -t. You'll need a
pickax and a shovel. ġad ixeṣṣek
fas u-baḷa.
   to shovel - ḥfeṛ be-l-baḷa. We
had to shovel a path through the
snow. ma-fadna ġir nḥefṛu ṭriq
be-l-baḷa fe-t-telž.

show - fṛaža pl. -t. Did you go to
the horse show? mšiti l-le-fṛaža
de-l-xil? --When does the first
show start at this theater? fuq-aš
ka-ibda le-fṛaža l-luwwla f-had
s-sinima?
   to show - 1. werra. Could you
show me the way? imken-lek twerrini
ṭ-ṭriq? 2. ban iban. Only his head
head showed above the water. ġir
ṛaṣu lli kan iban fuq l-ma. 3. lƐeb.
What are they showing at the theater

this evening? š-ġad ileƐbu fe-s-
sinima had l-lila? 4. biyyen,
ḍehheṛ. The investigation didn't
show a thing. l-beḥt ma-ḍehheṛ
ḥetta ḥaža. --He doesn't dare show
himself again around here. ma-bqa-š
iqedd ibiyyen wežhu hnaya.
   to show around - sara isari.
She's showing her guest around town.
ka-tsari ḍ-ḍifa lli Ɛendha f-le-mdina.
   to show off - fšeṛ, ḥal iḥil.
He's just showing off. xeddam ka-
ifšeṛ.
   to show up - 1. ža iži, ban iban.
Nobody showed up. ma-ža ḥedd.
2. twata. Yellow shows up well
against a black background. le-ṣfeṛ
ka-itwata mezyan Ɛel le-kḥel.

shower - 1. nezla de-š-šta pl. -t
de-š-šta. We were caught in a
shower. qebṭetna n-nezla de-š-šta.
2. duš pl. dwaš. Does your bathroom
have a shower? l-ḥemmam dyalek fih
d-duš?
   to take a shower - xda yaxod duš,
dduwweš. I just have to take a
shower and get dressed. maši ġir
naxod ši-duš u-nelbes ḥwayži.

show-off - ḥayel pl. ḥaylin, ḥuyal.
He's a big show-off. hadak ḥayel
bla qyas.

shrewd - maḍi pl. maḍyen. He's a
shrewd businessman. huwa biyyaƐ
šerray maḍi.

shrimp - qemṛuna pl. -t coll. qemṛun.
We're having shrimp for dinner.
ġad ntġeddaw be-l-qemṛun.
   **He's a little shrimp. dak
r-ṛažel qṣiweṛ u-mḥetnek.

to **shrink** - kref. Does this material
shrink? had t-tub ka-ikref?

shrub - šžiṛa pl. -t.

to **shut** - šedd. I shut the door
because of the cold. šeddit l-bab
Ɛla qibal l-berd.
   to shut down - ġleq. Why was the
factory shut down? Ɛlaš ġelqu
l-meƐmel?
   to shut off - ḥṣeṛ, qteƐ. Shut
off the water. ḥṣeṛ l-ma.
   to shut up - 1. šedd. They've
shut up their shop for the winter.
šeddu l-ḥanut dyalhom Ɛla wedd
l-berd ža. 2. šedd Ɛla. Who shut
the dog up in the garage? škun
šedd Ɛel l-kelb fe-l-garaž?
   **Shut up! šedd fommek!

shutter - ġlaq pl. -t. Open the
shutters, please. ḥell le-ġlaqat
Ɛafak.

shy - (lli) ka-yeḥšem, ḥešman.

to shy - *žfel.* The horse shied. *l-ɛewd žfel.*
**He shies away from hard work. *ka-iḥṛeb men l-xedma de-t-tamara.*
sick - *mṛiḍ* adj. pl. *mṛaḍ,* n. pl. *moṛḍa.*
to be taken sick - *mṛeḍ.*
**I'm getting sick and tired of this. *qelbi ṛah ka-iṭib men had š-ši.*
sickle - *menžel* pl. *mnažel.*
sickness - *meṛḍ* pl. *mṛaḍ.*
side - **1.** *žiha* pl. *-t, žwayeh.* On this side of the street there are only a few houses. *had ž-žiha d-had z-zenqa fiha ḍ-ḍyaṛ qlal.* --It's difficult to take sides on this question. *ṣɛib l-waḥed iži men ši-žiha f-had l-qaḍiya.* --You always take his side. *dima ka-dži men žihtu.* **2.** *ženb* pl. *žnab.* I nearly split my sides laughing. *mšit nefṛeɛ žnabi be-ḍ-ḍeḥk.* --They walked along silently side by side. *kanu mašyen sahtin ž-ženb le-ž-ženb.*
**To be on the safe side, I asked him again. *baš nkun mhenni ɛawed seqṣitu.* --He does something else on the side. *ka-yeɛmel ši-ḥaža x̂ṛa men l-fuq.*
sidewalk - *meššaya* pl. *-t.*
sieve - *ġerbal* pl. *ġrabel.*
to **sift** - *ġerbel.* I still haven't sifted the flour. *ma-zal ma-ġerbelt ṭ-ṭḥin.*
sigh - *tenhida* pl. *-t, tnahed.*
to sigh - *tnehhed.*
sight - **1.** *nḍeṛ, bṣeṛ.* He nearly lost his sight in the accident. *ɛlayen mša-lu n-nḍeṛ f -dak l-ḥadita.* **2.** *menḍeṛ* pl. *mnaḍeṛ.* The dead bodies were a terrible sight. *menḍeṛ l-muta kan ka-ixewwef.* **3.** *reḥba* pl. *rḥabi.* Have you seen the sights of the town? *tsariti r-rḥabi d-le-mdina?*
**They had orders to shoot him on sight. *kan ɛendhom ʔawamir ġir iqešɛuh iḍeṛbuh.*
at first sight - *fe-ṛ-ṛemqa l-luwla.* I recognized you at first sight. *fe-ṛ-ṛemqa l-luwla ɛṛeftek.*
by sight - *b-le-wžeh.* I know him only by sight. *ka-nɛeṛfu ġir b-le-wžeh.*
to be in sight - *bda ibda iban.* The end is not yet in sight. *t-tali ma-zal ma-bda iban.*
to catch sight of - *ṛmeq.* As soon as he caught sight of you, he vanished. *ġir ṛemqek ġṭeṣ.*
to lose sight of - *tlef-lu.* Don't lose sight of that man. *ɛendak itlef-lek dak ṛ-ṛažel.*
sign - **1.** *ɛalama* pl. *-t, ʔišaṛa* pl. *-t.* What does this sign mean? *šnu mɛent had l-ɛalama?* **2.** *imaṛa* pl. *-t, imayeṛ.* Is that a good sign? *imaṛa mezyana hadik?*
to give a sign - *šiyyer.* He gave us a sign to follow him. *šiyyer-lna baš ntebɛuh.*
to sign - *ɛellem, weqqeɛ.* He forgot to sign the letter. *nsa ma-ɛellem-š le-bṛa.*
**Don't forget to sign in. *ɛendak tensa ma-teɛlem-š be-d-dxul!* --I forgot to sign out last night. *nsit ma-ɛlemt-š b-le-xruž l-bareḥ.* --He signed over the business to his son. *smeḥ fe-l-biɛ u-š-šra dyalu l-weldu.*
signal - *ɛalama* pl. *-t, ʔisaṛa* pl. *-t.*
to signal - *šaṛ išir.* He signaled me to come over. *šaṛ-li nži.*
signalman - *dmanži* pl. *-ya.* The signalman stopped the train in time. *d-dmanži ḥṣeṛ l-mašina fe-l-weqt.*
signature - *tuwqiɛ* pl. *-at.* The letter has no signature. *le-bṛa ma-fiha tuwqiɛ.*
silence - *skat, shat.* There was a profound silence in the room. *kan shat kbir fe-l-bit.* --They listened in silence. *tṣenntu be-s-skat.*
to silence - *sekket, hedden.* I couldn't silence him. *ma-qdeṛt-š nsekktu.*
silent - **1.** *sekkuti.* He's a silent partner. *hadak ṣaḥeb sekkuti.* **2.** *lli bla klam.* She used to play in silent pictures. *kanet ka-telɛeb fe-s-sinima lli ḅla klam.*
to be silent - *kuwwen, sket.* Why are you so silent? *ma-lek mkuwwen hakda?*
**The newspapers were silent about the accident. *l-žaṛaʔid ḍeṛbuha b-tekwina ɛel l-ʔafat.*
silk - *ḥrir.* You simply can't get silk stockings. *ṛak ma-tṣib-š t-tqašer d-le-ḥrir.*
silly - *mṣeṭṭi, mehbul.*
**He's not so silly as he looks. *ṛah niya u-ḥramiya.*
silver - **1.** *feḍḍa.* This is sterling silver. *feḍḍa ṣafya hadi.* **2.** *neqṛa.* She's wearing a silver ring. *ɛamla xatem de-n-neqṛa.*
similar - *bḥal.* I know of a similar case. *ka-neɛṛef qaḍiya bḥal hadi.*
simple - **1.** *sahel.* That's quite a simple matter. *hadi mesʔala sahla.* **2.** *meṭluq.* She wears very simple

clothes. *hiya ka-telbes ḥwayež metḷuqin.* 3. *tamm.* That's the simple truth. *hadi l-ḥaqiqa t-tamma.*
simplicity - *suhula* pl. *-t.* For the sake of simplicity let's say that... *Ɛla wedd s-suhula ġad nqulu...*
simplification - *teshil* pl. *-at.*
to **simplify** - *sehhel.*
sin - *denb* pl. *dnub.*
since - **1.** *men.* He has not been here since Monday. *men nhaṛ t-tnayn ma-ža lle-hna.* **2.** *melli.* I haven't seen anybody since I got back. *ma-šeft ḥedd melli ṛžeƐt.* **3.** *ḥit.* Since I didn't have the money I couldn't go. *ḥit ma-kanu Ɛendi flus ma-mken-li-š nemši.*
ever since - *men dak l-Ɛahed, men temma.* I haven't talked to him ever since. *men temma ma-Ɛawed tkellemt mƐah.*
sincere - *(lli) qelbu ṣafi.* He's a sincere person. *hadak ṛažel qelbu ṣafi.*
to be sincere about - *tkellem b-niytu Ɛla, kan b-niytu f-.* I think he's sincere about it. *ka-nḍenn ila ka-itkellem b-niytu Ɛla had š-ši.*
sincerely - **1.** *be-n-niya, be-l-mufid.* You sincerely believe it? *waš be-n-niya ka-ḍḍenn had š-ši?* **2.** *l-ġaya.* I'm sincerely sorry that you can't come. *ana met?essef l-ġaya lli ma-imken-lek-š dži.*
**I sincerely hope you'll be able to come. *ka-nṭḷeb Ɛel ḷḷah imken-lek dži.*
to **sing** - *ġenna.* I don't sing very well. *ma-ka-nġenni-š mezyan bezzaf.*
singer - **1.** *muġenni* pl. *-yin* f. *muġenniya* pl. *-t.* He's a well-known singer. *huwa muġenni mešhuṛ.* --She's a singer, too. *ḥetta hiya muġenniya.*
single - **1.** *Ɛezri* pl. *Ɛzara.* Are you married or single? *nta mzuwwež wella Ɛezri?* **2.** *waḥed* f. *weḥda.* He didn't make a single mistake. *ma-Ɛmel-ši ġelṭa weḥda.* **3.** *weḥdu* f. *wḥedha.* I looked through every single drawer, but couldn't find it. *qellebt koll mžeṛ weḥdu u-ma-ṣebtu-š.*
to single out - *Ɛzel, xerrež.* Why did they single you out? *Ɛlaš Ɛezluk ġir nta?*
sink - **1.** *žfina* pl. *-t.* The dishes are still in the sink. *l-ġeṭṛan ma-zalin fe-ž-žfina.* **2.** *qadus* pl. *qwades.* Don't throw it into the sink. You'll stop it up. *la-termih-ši fe-l-qadus, daba txenqu.*
to sink - **1.** *ġṛaq.* The ship sank in ten minutes. *l-baxiṛa ġṛaqet f-qeṣmayn.* **2.** *neḥder.* The house has sunk ten inches. *ḍ-ḍar nḥedret ši-Ɛešṛa d-l-iṣabeƐ.* **3.** *ġeṛṛeq.* They sank three enemy ships. *ġeṛṛqu tlata de-l-baxiṛat d-le-Ɛdu.*
sip - *zgifa* pl. *-t.* I only had a sip of it. *ma-xdit ġir zgifa mennha.*
to sip - *zgef.*
sister - *xet* pl. *xwatat.* Do you have any sisters? *Ɛendek ši-xwatat?* --All my brothers and sisters are still alive. *xuti u-xwatati kollhom baqyen Ɛeyyšin.*
sister-in-law - **1.** (wife's sister) *xet le-mṛa* pl. *xwatat le-mṛa.* She's my sister-in-law. *hadik xet mṛati.* **2.** (husband's sister) *lusa* pl. *-t, lwayes.* She's my sister-in-law. *hadik lusti.*
sit - *gles.* We sat in the front row. *glesna fe-ṣ-ṣeff l-luwwel.* --Please sit down. *tfeḍḍel, gles.* --He walked in just as we sat down to eat. *ḥna kif glesna naklu u-huwa dxel.*
**You won't get anywhere sitting around the house. *ma-ġad teqḍi walu b-le-glas fe-ḍ-ḍar.* --I sat in on all conferences. *ḥḍeṛt Ɛel l-mu?tamaṛat kollha.*
to sit up - *sher, bqa ibqa fayeq.* We sat up all night waiting for him. *sherna l-lil kollu u-ḥna ka-ntsennaweh.* --I sat up with him all night. *bett fayeq mƐah l-lil kollu.*
situation - **1.** *muqif* pl. *mwaqef.* She saved the situation. *neqdet l-muqif.* **2.** *weḍƐiya* pl. *-t, wḍaƐ.* He wasn't equal to the situation. *l-weḍƐiya kanet bezzaf Ɛlih.*
six - *setta.*
**It's six of one and half a dozen of another. *ḥemmuṣ kamun.*
sixteen - *seṭṭaš.*
sixth - **1.** (ordinal) *sades.* **2.** (fraction) *sudus* pl. *-at.*
sixty - *settin.*
size - **1.** *qyaṣ* pl. *-at.* What size do you wear? *š-men qyaṣ ka-telbes?* **2.** *kbeṛ.* Everything is arranged according to size. *koll-ši mƐewweṭ Ɛla ḥasab kebṛu.* **3.** *taqedda* pl. *-t.* They are about the same size. *huma Ɛlayen taqedda weḥda.*
**What size book will it be? *qedd-aš ġad ikun le-ktab?* --How do you size up the situation. *š-ka-iḍheṛ-lek fe-l-weḍƐiya?*
skeleton - *Ɛḍam* (pl.).

skeptical - *metšaʔem.* Don't be so skeptical! *la-tkun-ši metšaʔem l-had l-ḥedd.*
to **skid** - *zleq.* The car started to skid. *s-siyaṛa bdat tezleq.*
skill - *tamƐellmit, mḍawa.*
skilled - *mƐellem.* He is a skilled cabinet-maker. *hadak niyyaṛ mƐellem.*
skillfully - *be-l-qaƐida, b-le-qwaƐed.* You got yourself out of that situation very skillfully. *selliti ṛaṣek men l-muqif ġir b-le-qwaƐed.*
to **skim** - **1.** *zuwwel l-ġelya men, ṣeffa.* Did you skim the soup? *ṣeffiti le-ḥrira?* **2.** *zuwwel le-frara men.* I skimmed the milk. *zuwwelt le-frara men le-ḥlib.*
to skim through - *daz iduz Ɛla, duwwez Ɛla.* I just skimmed through the book. *yaḷḷah duwwezt Ɛel le-ktab.*
skin - **1.** *želd* pl. *žlud.* She has a very sensitive skin. *želdha meƐlal.* **2.** *želda* pl. *-t, žlud.* How many skins will you need for the coat? *šḥal de-ž-želdat xeṣṣek l-l-baḷṭu?* **3.** *qešṛa* pl. *-t, qšuṛ.* These apples have a very thick skin. *had t-teffaḥ qšeṛtu ġḷiḍa.*
**He has a thick skin. *qeššabtu wasƐa.* --I made it by the skin of my teeth. *be-d-dreƐ baš menneƐt ṛaṣi.*
to **skip** - **1.** *neqqez Ɛla.* I skipped a few pages. *neqqezt Ɛla ši-ṣefḥat.* **2.** *xella.* Skip the hard words. *xelli l-kelmat ṣ-ṣƐab.* **3.** *hṛeb Ɛla, hṛeb men, xwa ixwi.* They skipped town. *ṛahom xwaw le-mdina.*
to skip rope - *neqqez* or *lƐeb be-ṭ-ṭwal.* Can you skip rope? *ka-teƐṛef telƐeb be-ṭ-ṭwal?*
skirt - *zenṭiṭa* pl. *-t.* Her skirt is too short. *z-zenṭiṭa dyalha qṣiṛa bezzaf Ɛad.*
skull - *žemžma* pl. *žmažem.*
sky - *sma* pl. *-wat.* How does the sky look today? *kif dayra s-sma l-yum?*
**The news came out of a clear sky. *le-xbaṛ ža u-nzel.* --He praised her to the skies. *ma-xella kif meššed u-Ɛeḍḍem fiha.*
slack - **1.** *qlil, Ɛeyyan.* Business is slack. *l-biƐ u-š-šra Ɛeyyan.* **2.** *merxuf.* His work has become very slack. *šġalu ṛžeƐ merxuf.*
slacks - *serwal* pl. *srawel.*
to **slap** - *ḍṛeb, ṣƐeṭ.* I'll slap your hand if you touch it. *ṛani nḍeṛbek Ɛla iddek ila qesti fiha.*
to slap one's face - *ṭṛeš, Ɛṭa yeƐṭi ṭ-ṭeṛš l-.* She slapped his face. *ṭeṛšettu.*
slate - *luḥa d-le-ḥžeṛ* pl. *-t d-le-ḥžeṛ, lweḥ d-le-ḥžeṛ.*
slaughter - *dbiḥa* pl. *-t, dbayeḥ.* The slaughter was terrific. *d-dbiḥa kanet ka-texleƐ.*
to slaughter - *dbeḥ.* We always slaughter a lamb for the Great Feast. *dima ka-ndebḥu kebš fe-l-Ɛid le-kbir.*
slave - *Ɛebd* pl. *Ɛbid.*
to slave - *kdeḥ.* I've slaved enough today. *kfa ma kdeḥt l-yum.*
sleep - *neƐsa* pl. *-t* coll. *nƐas.* It was like awaking from a deep sleep. *bḥal lli faq men ši-neƐsa ṭwila.*
to sleep - *nƐes.* Did you sleep well? *nƐesti mezyan?*
**I didn't sleep a wink. *ma-ġemmeḍt-ši Ɛeyn weḥda.*
to sleep on something - *xemmem f-š-i ḥaža.* Sleep on it before you decide. *xemmem fiha Ɛla-ma tqeṛṛeṛ š-ġad teƐmel.*
sleeping car - *fagu de-n-nƐas* pl. *faguyat de-n-nƐas.*
sleepy - *fih n-nƐas.* I'm still sleepy. *ma-zal fiya n-nƐas.*
to make sleepy - *žab ižib n-nƐas l-.* The heat is making me sleepy. *ṣ-ṣehd ka-ižib-li n-nƐas.*
sleeve - *kemm* pl. *kmam.* The sleeves are too short. *le-kmam qṣaṛ bezzaf Ɛad.*
**He laughed up his sleeve. *ttefṛeƐ qelbu be-ḍ-ḍeḥk.* --I don't know what he's got up his sleeve. *ma-Ɛṛeftu Ɛlaš meṭwi.*
slender - *ṛqiq* pl. *-in, ṛqaq.*
slice - *sir* pl. *syur.* How many slices of bread shall I cut? *šḥal de-s-syur de-l-xobz nqeṭṭeƐ?*
to slice - *qeṭṭeƐ.* Do you want to slice the roast? *tebġi tqeṭṭeƐ le-mḥemmeṛ?*
to **slide** - **1.** *zleq, zheq.* Did you slide on this street? *zleqti f-had ṭ-ṭriq?* --She slid down the banister. *zehqet mƐa ḍ-ḍeṛbuẓ.* **2.** *duwwez, siyyeƐ.* Maybe you can slide it in sideways. *waqila imken-lek dduwwezha be-ž-ženbiya.*
to let slide - *xella ixmed.* Let's let things slide awhile. *nxelliw l-ʔumuṛ texmed waḥed š-šwiya.*
slight - **1.** *qlil, qliwel, ṣġiṛ.* There's a slight difference. *kayen ši-feṛq qlil.* **2.** *xfif* pl. *xfaf.* He has a slight cold. *Ɛendu ṛwaḥ xfif.* **3.** *ṛqiq* pl. *-in, ṛqaq.* She's very slight. *hiya ṛqiqa bezzaf.*
to slight - *hmel, tšennek.* She felt slighted. *ḥesset b-ṛaṣha*

bḥal lli hemluha.

slim - *ṛqiq* pl. *-in, ṛqaq.* She's gotten very slim. *wellat ṛqiqa bezzaf.*

**His chances are very slim. *ma-šeft-lu šay!*

sling - *meqlaƐ* pl. *mqaleƐ.* He killed a bird with his sling. *qtel waḥed ṭ-ṭiṛ be-l-meqlaƐ dyalu.*

slingshot - *žebbada* pl. *-t, žbabed.*

slip - **1.** *ġelṭa* pl. *-t.* Did I make a slip? *Ɛmelt ši-ġelṭa?* **2.** *ġlaf* pl. *-at.* Our pillows need new slips. *le-xdadi dyalna xeṣṣhom ġlafat ždad.* **3.** *ṭeṛf* pl. *ṭṛaf.* She wrote it on a slip of paper. *ketbetha f-waḥed ṭ-ṭeṛf de-l-kaġiṭ.*

**It was just a slip of the tongue. *ġir feltet-li men lsani.* --He's given us the slip again. *tlef-lna Ɛewtani.*

to slip - **1.** *zleq.* I slipped on the ice. *zleqt fe-t-telž.* **2.** *flet.* It slipped out of my hand. *feltet-li men iddi.* --I really didn't want to tell him, but it just slipped out. *fe-l-ḥaqiqa ma-kont-š baġi nqulha-lu be-l-ḥeqq feltet-li*

**It slipped my mind completely. *ma-bqat-š Ɛla Ɛeqli tamamen.*

to slip away - *sellu.* Let's slip away. *yaḷḷah nselluh.*

to slip up - *fellesha.* I slipped up badly on the second question. *fellestha be-l-mufid fe-s-suʔal t-tani.*

to let slip - *xella iduz.* Don't let the chance slip. *la-txelli-š l-foṛṣa dduz.*

slippers (pair of) - *belġa* pl. *blaġi.* I can't find my slippers. *ma-žbeṛt-š bleġti.*

slit - *fetḥa* pl. *-t.* Make the slit a bit longer. *Ɛmel l-fetḥa šwiyeš kbeṛ men had š-ši.*

to slit - *fteḥ.*

to slit someone's throat - *šleṭ l-geṛžuṭa l-.* The criminals slit his throat. *l-qettala šelṭu-lu geṛžuṭtu.*

slope - *hebṭa* pl. *-t.* Is the slope very steep? *waš l-hebṭa qaṣḥa bezzaf?*

to slope - *zerdeb.* The floor slopes. *l-leṛḍ mzerdba.*

sloppy - **1.** *mruwwen.* Don't be so sloppy! *la-tkun-ši mruwwen bezzaf.* **2.** *mdebbez.* They always do sloppy work. *dima ka-iƐemlu xedma mdebbza.*

slot - *teqba* pl. *-t, tqabi; ḥefṛa* pl. *-t, ḥfaṛi.* Insert four ryals in the slot. *ṭleq ṛebƐa de-r-ryal fe-t-teqba.*

slow - **1.** *tqil* pl. *tqilin, tqal.* He's a slow worker. *huwa xeddam tqil.* --She's slow in catching on. *dmaġha tqil.* **2.** *be-š-šwiya.* Drive slow. *ṣug ġir be-š-šwiya.* **3.** *Ɛeyyan.* The market was slow. *ṣ-ṣuq kan Ɛeyyan.* **4.** *mhil* pl. *mhal.* Cook the soup over a slow fire. *ṭiyyeb le-ḥrira Ɛla Ɛafya tkun mhila.*

**Your watch is slow. *magantek fiha t-tiqal.* --He's a slow payer. *ka-itƐeṭṭel b-le-xlaṣ.*

to slow down - **1.** *mehhel.* Slow down when you come to an intersection. *mehhel mnayn tqeṛṛeb l-ši-mefṛeq ṭ-ṭoṛqan.* **2.** *ṭiyyeḥ, nqeṣ.* He's slowing down in his work. *bda inqeṣ fe-xdemtu.*

slowly - *be-š-šwiya.* Drive slowly. *ṣug ġir be-š-šwiya.*

sly - *ḥṛami, mṭeṛṛeq.*

small - **1.** *ṣġiṛ* pl. *ṣġaṛ.* The room is rather small. *l-bit ṣġiṛ ši-šwiya.* --I haven't anything smaller. *ma-Ɛendi-ši ši-ḥaža ṣġeṛ men had š-ši.* **2.** *qlil* pl. *qlilin, qlal.* The difference is very small. *l-feṛq qlil bezzaf.* **3.** *bṣiṭ* pl. *bṣaṭ.* That's no small matter. *ma-ši ḥaža bṣiṭa hadi.* **4.** *rdil* pl. *rdal.* That was a small thing for him to do. *qaḍiya rdila hadik Ɛmel.*

small change - *mferred, mferrda, ṣeṛf.* I haven't any small change. *ma-Ɛendi mferrda.*

smallpox - *žedri.* We have all been vaccinated against smallpox. *kollna xerrežna ž-žedri.*

smart - **1.** *mšiyyek.* That's a smart dress. *keswa mšiyyka hadik.* **2.** *dki* pl. *ʔedkiya.* He looks like a smart boy. *ka-iban Ɛlih weld dki.*

to **smash** - *herres.* The boys smashed the window. *d-drari herrsu z-zaža de-š-šeṛžem.* --I found the lamp on the floor smashed to bits. *žbeṛt z-zaža de-ḍ-ḍuw mherrsa štat fuq l-eṛḍ.*

smell - *riḥa* pl. *-t, rwayeḥ.* Where does that unpleasant smell come from? *mnayn mažya had r-riḥa le-qbiḥa?*

to smell - *šemm.* Do you smell gas? *ka-tšemm riḥt l-gaz?*

to smell a rat - *šƐeṛ b-ši ḥaža kayna.* He must have smelled a rat. *hada ma-huwa ġir šƐeṛ b-ši-ḥaža kayna.*

**The roses smell beautifully.

l-weṛḍ riḥtu ha?ila.

smile - *ḍḥika* pl. *-t, tebsima* pl. *-t.* She has a charming smile. *ɛendha ḍḥika dṛiyfa.*

to smile - *tbessem.* She is always smiling. *hiya da?imen ka-ttbessem.* --She smiled at you. *ṛaha tbessmet-lek.*

**She was all smiles. *kanet tedḥek men wedniha.*

smoke - *doxxan* pl. *dxaxen.* Where's that smoke coming from? *mnayn mažį dak d-doxxan?*

to smoke - **1.** *kma ikmi.* Do you smoke? *ka-tekmi?* **2.** *ṭḷeq d-doxxan, ṭḷeq d-dxaxen.* The stove is smoking again. *n-nafex ɛawed ka-iṭḷeq d-dxaxen.*

**No smoking! *memnuɛ d-doxxan.*

smooth - **1.** *mles, males.* The ice is very smooth today. *t-telž males bezzaf l-yum.* **2.** *hade?, mhedden.* The sea was very smooth. *le-nheṛ kan hade? bezzaf.* **3.** *ṛṭeb.* I can' get a smooth shave with this blade. *ma-ka-ṭṭleɛ-li-š le-ḥsana ṛeṭba b-had l-mess.*

**He's a smooth talker. *lehhab hadak.*

to smooth down - *ṛeṭṭeb.* Smooth down your hair. *ṛeṭṭeb šeɛṛek.*

to smooth out - *ɛewweṭ, žebbed, ṭḷeq.* Smooth out the tablecloth. *ɛewweṭ mendil ṭ-ṭebḷa.*

smoothly - *fi ?aman llah.* Everything went smoothly. *koll-ši tmešša fi ?aman llah.*

to **smother** - *xneq, žiyyef.* The smoke nearly smothered him. *d-doxxan ɛlayen xenqu.*

snail - *ġlala* pl. *-t* coll. *ġlal; bebbuša* pl. *-t* coll. *bebbuš.*

snake - *henš* pl. *ḥnuša ḥnaš.*

snap - **1.** *šeddada* pl. *-t.* I have to sew snaps on my dress. *xeṣṣni nrekkeb š-šeddadat fe-ksewti.* **2.** *teṣwiṛa* pl. *-t, tṣaweṛ.* I'd like to take a snap of you. *nebġi naxod-lek ši-teṣwiṛa.* **3.** *ḥamas.* There's no snap to that song. *ma-kayen ḥamas f-dak l-ġenya.*

**That's a snap for me. *dak š-ši bḥal l-ḥelwa ɛendi.* --The exam was a snap. *le-mtiḥan kan sahel.* --Don't make snap judgments. *ma-tkun-š teḥkem b-soṛɛa.*

to snap - *tqeṭṭeɛ.* That rope is sure to snap. *had ṭ-ṭwaḷ bla šekk itqeṭṭeɛ.*

**Snap out of it! *sebḥan ḷḷah!* or *redd balek!* --The lock snapped shut. *l-feṛxa deġya tšeddet.*

to snap at - **1.** *naḍ inuḍ l-, nṭḷeq ɛḷa.* The dog snapped at me. *l-kelb naḍ-li.* **2.** *nṭḷeq ɛla, nheḍ f-.* I don't know why he snapped at me that way. *ma-ɛṛeft-ši ɛlaš nheḍ fiya hakdak.*

to snap one's fingers - *ṭerṭeq ṣebɛanu, kellem ṣebɛanu.* She snapped her fingers. *ṭerṭqet ṣebɛanha.*

snapshot - *teṣwiṛa* pl. *-t, tṣaweṛ.* Where did you take these snapshots? *fayn xditi had t-tṣaweṛ?*

to **sneak** - *tteslet.* He must have sneaked into the house. *waqila tteslet l-qelb ḍ-ḍar.*

to sneak in - *tteslet, tteḥša ttezleg.* He must have sneaked in while I wasn't looking. *ma-huwa ġir ttezleg mnayn ma-kont-š ka-nšuf.*

to sneak out - *tsell, flet.* He sneaked out while I wasn't looking. *ma-huwa ġir tsell mnayn ma-kont-š ka-nšuf.*

sneeze - *ɛeṭṣa* pl. *-t.*

to sneeze - *ɛṭeṣ.* He's been sneezing all morning. *ṣ-ṣbeḥ kollu u-huwa ka-yeɛṭeṣ.*

to **snore** - *šxeṛ.*

snow - *telž* pl. *tluž, tlužat.* How deep is the snow? *ḥedd-aš ṭaleɛ t-telž?*

to snow - *ṭaḥ iṭiḥ t-telž.* It snowed all night. *t-telž ṭaḥ l-lil kollu.*

snowed in - *ḥaṣel fe-t-telž.* They were snowed in for a whole week. *kanu ḥaṣlin fe-t-telž žemɛa kollha.* We're snowed under with work. *ṛa-ḥna ġaṛqin be-l-xedma.*

snowdrop - *ben n-neɛman.*

snowflake - *liqa de-t-telž* pl. *lyeq de-t-telž.*

so - **1.** *hakda.* So they say. *hakda ka-iqulu.* **2.** *kif.* It's so hot today. *walayenni kif l-yum l-ḥal sxun.* **3.** *?iden.* So you think it's a good idea. *?iden ka-ḍḍenn fekṛa mezyana.* **4.** *ḥetta.* I'm leaving now, so is he. *ana ġadi daba, ḥetta huwa.*

**I suppose so. *ka-nḍenn.* --I told you so. *qoltha-lek.* --Is that so? *hakda?* or *xḷaṣ?* --So I see. *hakdak qul-li.* --So long. *iwa be-s-slama.* --So what? *iwa u-š-kayen?* or *u-u-men beɛd?* --So much the better. *iwa mezyan.*

so as to - *baš.* I did some of the work so as to make things easier for you. *ɛmelt-lek šwiya men dak l-xedma baš nsehhef ɛlik l-ʔumuṛ.

so far - *l-ḥedd s-saɛa, f-had s-saɛa.* I haven't had any news so far. *f-had s-saɛa ma-ɛendi xḅaṛ.* --So far you've been pretty lucky. *l-ḥedd s-saɛa ṛah ḥekmek z-zheṛ.*

so far as - *ɛla ma.* So far as I know he is still in Egypt. *ɛla-ma ka-neɛref ma-zal 'f-maṣeṛ.*

so much - *bezzaf.* Not so much pepper, please. *la-teɛmel-li-š bezzaf d-l-ibzaṛ ḷḷah ixellik.*

so so - *ka-nɛeddi, ka-tɛeddi,* etc... How are you? So so. *še-xbaṛek? ka-nɛeddi.*

so that - *baš.* I'm telling you so that you'll know. *h-ana ka-nqul-lek baš teɛref š-kayen.*

ever so much - *bezzaf ɛad.* Thanks ever so much. *ka-nšekṛek bezzaf ɛad.*

or so - *ši...hakdak.* I need ten dirhams or so. *xeṣṣni ši-ɛešṛa de-d-drahem hakdak.*

to **soak** - *fezzeg.* We soak the laundry overnight. *ka-nbiyytu t-teṣbin mfezzeg.*

soaked - *fazeg, (lli) ka-iqṭeṛ.* We came home soaked. *wṣelna le-ḍ-ḍar ka-nqeṭṛu.*

to get soaked - *fzeg.* I got soaked to the skin. *fzegt hetta l-l-daxel.*

soap - *ṣabuna* pl. *-t* coll. *ṣabun.* I want a cake of soap. *bġit ṣabuna.*

to soap - *ġsel be-ṣ-ṣabun.* Dad is soaping his face. *ḅḅa ṛah ka-iġsel weẓhu be-ṣ-ṣabun.*

to **sob** - *šheq.* The child was sobbing violently. *d-derri kan ka-išheq be-ž-žehd.*

sober - 1. *saḥi.* He is never quite sober. *ɛemmṛu ma-ka-ikun saḥi.* 2. *mhedden.* He's as sober as a judge. *mhedden bḥalu bḥal ši-qaḍi.*

to sober up - *ṣḥa isḥa, ṣḥa isḥa.* He sobered up quickly. *deġya ṣḥa.*

so-called - *(lli) ka-iqulu-lu, (lli) ka-isemmiweh.*

soccer - *kuṛat l-qadam, l-kuṛa.* Soccer is a very popular sport in Morocco. *kuṛat l-qadam mešhuṛa bezzaf fe-l-meġrib.*

social - *štimaɛi.*

socialism - *le-štiṛakiya.*

socialist - *štiṛaki.*

society - 1. *muštamaɛ* pl. *-at.* He doesn't feel at ease in society. *ma-ka-iḥess-ši b-ṛaṣu huwa hadak*

fe-l-muštamaɛ. 2. *žemɛiya* pl. *-t.* He's a member of many learned societies. *huwa ɛuḍw f-ɛadad de-l-žemɛiyat mteqqfa.* 3. *muʔessasa* pl. *-t.* The society was founded ten years ago. *l-muʔessasa ṭeḷɛet hadi ɛešṛ snin.*

sock - *teqšira qṣiṛa* pl. *tqašer qṣaṛ.* I want three pairs of socks. *bġit telt zwaž de-t-tqašer qṣaṛ.*

to sock - *ɛṭa yeɛṭi bunya.* **I'd give him a sock on the jaw. *ṛ-ana nkeḥšu.*

soda - 1. *suda* pl. *-t.* I put some soda in my wash. *ṛ-ana ɛmelt ši-šwiya de-s-suda fe-t-teṣbin.* 2. *munaḍa* pl. *-t.* Bring me a bottle of soda. *žib-li waḥed l-qerɛa de-l-munaḍa.*

baking soda - *xmira* pl. *-t, xmayer.* Use one teaspoon of baking soda. *ɛmel mɛelqa ṣġira d-le-xmira.*

soft - 1. *ṛteb.* Is the ground soft? *l-erḍ ṛetba?* --He's terribly soft with his employees. *huwa ṛteb bla qyas mɛa l-xeddama dyalu.* 2. *meḥni.* She sang in a soft voice. *ġennat b-waḥed ṣ-ṣut meḥni.* 3. *qlil* pl. *qlal.* A soft light would be better. *ši-ḍuw qlil ikun ḥsen.* 4. *sahel* pl. *sahlin.* He's got a soft job. *ɛendu xedma sahla.*

to get soft - 1. *ṭhell.* The butter got too soft. *s-smen ṭhell bezzaf.* 2. *ṛṭab.* You're getting soft. *ṛak bditi teṛṭab.* --The earth got soft after it rained. *l-leṛḍ ṛṭabet men beɛd ṭaḥet š-šta.*

soft drink - *mešṛub* pl. *-at, muberrid* pl. *-at.* Only soft drinks are served here. *ma-kayen ġir l-mešṛubat hnaya.*

to **soften** - *ṛeṭṭeb.*

soil - *ʔerḍ* pl. *ʔaraḍi.* The soil here is very fertile. *l-ʔerḍ de-hnaya xeṣba bezzaf.*

to soil - *wessex, ṭebbeɛ.* You soiled your suit. *ṭebbeɛti ksuwtek.* --Everything is soiled. *koll-ši mwessex.*

soldier - *ɛeskri* pl. *ɛeskriya, ɛsaker, ɛsakriya* coll. *ɛesker.*

sole - 1. *qaɛ* pl. *qiɛan.* I have a blister on the sole of my foot. *ɛendi felḥa fe-l-qaɛ d-režli.* 2. *mešṭa* pl. *mšaṭi.* The soles of the brown shoes are worn through. *le-mšaṭi de-ṣ-ṣebbaṭ l-qehwi tqeṭṭɛu.* 3. *waḥid.* He was the sole survivor. *huwa l-waḥid lli bqa ɛeyyeš.*

**He came here for the sole purpose of meeting you. *ža lle-hna ġir baš itƐaṛef mƐak.*

to sole – *rekkeb mšaṭi ždad l-, ṭeṛṛef.* I want to have my shoes soled. *xeṣṣni nrekkeb mšaṭi ždad l-ṣebbaṭi.*

solid – 1. *qaṣeḥ.* The lake is frozen solid. *ḍ-ḍaya qaṣḥa be-ž-žmudiya.* 2. *kamel.* She talked to me for a solid hour. *tkellmet mƐaya saƐa kamla.* 3. *qabeṭ, ṣḥiḥ* pl. *ṣḥaḥ.* This chair doesn't seem very solid to me. *had š-šelya ka-tban-li ma-qabṭa-š bezzaf.* 4. *xaḷeṣ.* The statue is made of solid gold. *t-temtal mṣuwweb men d-dheb l-xaḷeṣ.*

solution – *ḥell* pl. *ḥlul.* He wants to find a solution to the political problem. *bġa ižbeṛ ḥell l-l-muškila s-siyasiya.*

to **solve** – *ḥell.* I can't solve the problem. *ma-qdeṛt-š nḥell l-muškila.*

some – 1. *ši.* There must be some way for us to find out. *la-bodda kayna ši-wasila baš nƐeṛfu š-kayen.* —I've seen you some place before. *sbeq-li šeftek f-ši-muḍeƐ.* —You'll regret that some day. *ši-nhaṛ ġad tendem.* 2. *šwiya, ši-šwiya.* He lent me some money. *huwa sellefni šwiya d-le-flus.* 3. *beƐḍ.* Some people can't stand noise. *beƐḍ n-nas ma-ka-iḥemlu-š l-ḥaṛaž.* 4. *f-, l-beƐḍ men, l-beƐḍ f-.* Some of us are going by train and some by boat. *fina lli mašyen fe-l-qiṭaṛ u-fina lli mašyen fe-l-baxiṛa.* 5. *ši ... hakdak.* We stayed some two or three hours. *bqina ši-tlata de-s-saƐat hakdak.*

**Boy, that's some jalopy! *siyaṛa hadi qolt-lek!* —I need some stockings. *xeṣṣni tqašer ṭwaḷ.* It's in some book or other on that shelf. *ṛaha fe-ktab men le-ktub lli Ɛel ṭ-ṭebqa.*

somebody – *ši-waḥed, ši-ḥedd.* Somebody asked for you. *ši-waḥed seqṣa Ɛlik.*

somehow – 1. *kif-emma kan l-ḥal.* We'll do it somehow. *kif-emma kan l-ḥal ġad ndiruha.* 2. *yeƐlem ḷḷah kif-aš.* The letter got lost somehow. *le-bṛa ḍaƐet yeƐlem ḷḷah kif-aš.*

somehow or other – *la-bodda.* Somehow or other he always gets what he wants. *dima l-ḥaža lli bġaha la-bodda ka-ilqaha.*

someone – *ši-waḥed, ši-ḥedd.* Is there someone here who can play the lute? *hna ši-waḥed ka-yeƐṛef iḍṛeb Ɛel l-Ɛud?* —You have to talk with someone else. *xeṣṣek ttkellem mƐa ši-waḥed axoṛ.*

something – *ši-ḥaža.* Is something the matter? *ši-ḥaža ma-ši hiya hadik?* 2. *šwiya, ši-ḥaža.* He knows something about medicine. *ka-yeƐṛef šwiya fe-ṭ-ṭebb.* 3. *ši, š-ši.* That's something to think about. *hada ši ka-ixeṣṣ l-waḥed ixemmem fih.*

something or other – *ši-ḥaža ma-Ɛṛef.* Something or other reminded me of home. *ši-ḥaža ma-Ɛṛeft fekkṛetni f-ḍaṛna.*

sometime – 1. *ši-weqt, ši-saƐa.* She'll be here sometime today. *ṛaha ġad tkun hna ši-weqt l-yum.* 2. *ši-wqiyyet, ši-swiƐa.* Come and see me sometime. *aži šufni ši-wqiyyet.*

sometime or other – *ši-nubu, ši-meṛṛa.* I'd like to read it sometime or other. *nebġi neqṛah ši-nuba.*

sometimes – *beƐḍ l-meṛṛat, beƐḍ l-xeṭṛat.* Sometimes it gets very hot here. *beƐḍ l-xeṭṛat ka-isxon l-ḥal bezzaf hnaya.*

somewhat – *šwiya.* I feel somewhat tired. *ka-nḥess b-ṛaṣi šwiya Ɛeyyan.*

somewhere – *ši-muḍeƐ, ši-maḥell, ši-ṛeḥba.* I saw them somewhere but I don't remember where. *šefthom f-ši-muḍeƐ be-l-ḥeqq ma-bqit-š Ɛaqel fayn.* —Let's meet somewhere else. *ntlaqaw f-ši-ṛeḥba xṛa.*

son – *weld* pl. *wlad.* Does he have any sons? *waš Ɛendu ši-wlad?*

song – *ġonya* pl. *-t; ġonnaya* pl. *-t.*

for a song – *Ɛlayen baṭel.* We bought the chair for a song *šrina š-šelya Ɛlayen baṭel.*

son-in-law – *nsib* pl. *nsab.*

soon – 1. *deġya.* He soon went away. *deġya mša f-ḥalu.* 2. *bekri.* It's too soon to tell what's the matter with him. *l-ḥal bekri bezzaf daba baš nqulu š-Ɛendu.*

as soon as – *kif, ġir.* Let me know as soon as you get here. *ġir tuṣel lle-hna Ɛlemni.*

**I'd just as soon not go. *ḥsen ma-nemši-š.* —The sooner you come, the better. *koll-emma bekkerti ḥsen.* —He'd sooner die than give in. *ka-ifeḍḍel imut wala itnazel.* —He no sooner mentioned her name than she appeared. *yaḷḷah kif žbed smiyytha u-hiya banet.* —Sooner or later we'll have to make up our minds.

daba aw saɛa xṛa la-bodda xeṣṣna nqeṛṛṛu.

to **soothe** – *ṛeṭṭeb, hedden.* This salve will soothe the pain. *had d-dehna ṛaha tṛeṭṭeb-lek le-ḥṛiq.*

sore – **1.** *demmala* pl. *-t, dmamel.* The sore is pretty well healed up. *d-demmala bṛat kamla.* **2.** *mṛid* pl. *mṛaḍ, mqeṣṣeḥ.* I have a sore toe. *ɛendi benna mṛiḍa.* --Where's the sore spot? *fayn ṛ-ṛeḥba le-mqeṣṣha?* --He has a sore throat. *ḥelqu mṛiḍ.*

to get sore – *tʔellem.* You needn't get sore right away. *ma-kayen l-aš tebda ttʔellem men daba.*

to be sore at – *ṭaṛ-lu iṭiṛ-lu mɛa.* Are you sore at me? *waš ṭayeṛ-lek mɛaya?*

sorrow – *ʔalam, ḥzen.* She can't get over her sorrow. *ma-qeddet-š tensa ʔalamha.*

sorry – **1.** *meskin, mbuʔes.* He's a sorry-looking specimen. *ṛažel hadak mbuʔes f-ḥaltu.* **2.** *mʔessef, metʔessef.* I'm really sorry. *ḥaqiqatan ṛani metʔessef.*

**I'm sorry for her. *hiya ka-tɛezz ɛliya.* --I'm sorry to say that can't be done. *be-l-ʔasaf ġad nqul-lek bin dak š-ši ma-imken-š ikun.* --Sorry! Did I hurt you? *smeḥ-li! qeṣṣeḥtek?*

sort – *xerž* pl. *xruž; škel* pl. *škula, škal; nuɛ* pl. *nwaɛ.* I can't get along with that sort of person. *ma-ka-neqder-š nthamel mɛa dak š-škel de-bnadem.*

**He's a decent sort. *hadak ṛažel mezyan.* --She's not a bad sort. *mṛa ma-qbiḥa-š hadik.* --I sort of knew that it was going to happen. *bḥal ila ɛṛeftha kanet ġad tuqeɛ.* --I feel badly out of sorts today. *tamamen ma-ka-nḥess-š b-ṛaṣi huwa hadak l-yum.* --I said nothing of the sort. *ma-qolt ḥetta ḥaža men had š-ši.* --What sort of person was he? *kif kan dak s-siyyed?* --He promised me all sorts of things. *ma-xella baš waɛedni.*

to sort – *frez.* Have you sorted the stockings yet? *freztiw t-tqašer ṭ-ṭwaḷ wella ma-zal?*

soul – **1.** *nefs* pl. *nfus.* There wasn't a soul to be seen. *nefs weḥda ma-kanet-š ttšaf.* **2.** *ṛuḥ* pl. *ṛwaḥ.* He's in it heart and soul. *xeddam fiha b-qelbu u-ṛuḥu.*

sound – **1.** *ṣut* pl. *ṣwat.* Light travels faster than sound. *ḍ-ḍuw ka-isṛeɛ kteṛ men ṣ-ṣut.* **2.** *ṣḍaɛ* pl. *-at.* What was that sound? *dyal aš dak ṣ-ṣḍaɛ lli kan?* **3.** *ẓewya* pl. *-t.* She didn't utter a sound. *ẓewya weḥda ma-xerržetha-š.* **4.** *meɛqul, mezyan.* That's a sound bit of advice. *naṣiḥa meɛqula hadik.* **5.** *ṣḥiḥ* pl. *ṣḥaḥ.* The house is old but sound. *ḍ-ḍar qdima be-l-ḥeqq ṣḥiḥa.* **6.** *qabeṭ.* That's a sound argument. *ḥužža qabṭa hadik.*

**He's sound asleep. *xamed fe-n-nɛas.* --He has a sound constitution. *la-bas ɛlih f-ṣeḥḥtu.* --He's back, safe and sound. *ṛžeɛ ma-ɛendu ḥetta bas.*

to sound – **1.** *ḍheṛ, ban iban.* That sounds very strange. *had š-ši ka-iban ġrib.* --The report sounds good. *t-teqrir ka-iḍheṛ mezyan.* **2.** *ɛbeṛ.* The boatman sounded the depth of the river. *le-flayki ɛbeṛ l-ġoṛq de-l-wad.*

soup – *ḥrira* pl. *-t, ḥrayer; šoṛba* pl. *-t.*

sour – *ḥameḍ.* The milk has turned sour. *le-ḥlib ṛžeɛ ḥameḍ.*

**Don't make such a sour face. *ma-txeṣṣeṛ-š wežhek hakdak.*

source – **1.** *žiha* pl. *-t, žwayeh; meṣdeṛ* pl. *mṣaḍeṛ.* I have this news from a good source. *had le-xbaṛ ɛendi men meṣdeṛ ṣḥiḥ.* **2.** *ʔaṣḷ* pl. *ʔṣuḷ.* Have you found the source of the trouble? *žbeṛti l-ʔaṣl de-l-haṛaž?*

to have its source – *nbeɛ, nebbeɛ.* The Sebu River has its source near Taza. *wad sbu ka-inebbeɛ fe-žwayeh taza.*

Sous – *sus.*

native of Sous – *susi* adj. pl. *-yen;* n. pl. *swasa, hel sus.*

south – **1.** *žanub.* I want to go south for the winter. *bġit nemši l-l-žanub fe-l-berd.* **2.** *qebli.* This is a south wind. *had r-riḥ qebli.*

South America – *ʔamirika l-žanubiya.*

southern – *žanubi.* This plant is found only in southern regions. *had n-neqla ma-kayna ġir fe-ž-žihat l-žanubiya.*

souvenir – *tedkaṛ* pl. *tdaker; tefkiṛa* pl. *tefkiṛa* pl. *-t.* I want to buy some souvenirs here. *bġit nešri ši-tefkiṛat men hna.*

sow – *ḥellufa* pl. *-t.*

to **sow** – *zṛeɛ.*

**As ye sow, so shall ye reap.

lli Ɛmel ši išibu.
space – 1. *tisaƐ.* The desk takes up too much space. *le-mketba waxda bezzaf de-t-tisaƐ.* 2. *fḍa.* You must leave some space between the lines. *xeṣṣek txelli šwiya d-le-fḍa ma bin ṣ-ṣṭuṛ.*
in the space of – *f-moddet.* He did that work in the space of two weeks. *dak l-xedma darha f-moddet žmeƐtayn.*
**The posts are spaced a meter apart. *kayen bin r-rkiza u-r-rkiza miter.*
spade – *Ɛetla* pl. *-t, Ɛtali.* Grab a spade and start digging. *xud Ɛetla u-bda teḥfeṛ.*
**Why don't you call a spade a spade? *Ɛlaš ma-ka-tƐeyyeṭ-š l-l-ḥaža be-smiytha?*
Spain – *ṣbanya.*
Spaniard – *ṣbanyuḷi* adj. pl. *yin,* n. pl. *ṣbanyuḷ.*
Spanish – *ṣbanyuḷi.*
spare – *faṛeġ.* What do you do in your your spare time? *š-ka-teƐmel fe-l-weqt lli ka-ikun Ɛendek faṛeġ?*
spare part – *ṭeṛf zayed* pl. *ṭṛaf zayda.* Can you get spare parts for your radio? *teqḍeṛ tḥeṣṣel Ɛla ṭṛaf zayda le-ṛ-ṛaḍyu dyalek?*
spare room – *maḥell šayeṭ.* Is there any spare room in the car? *šayeṭ ši-maḥell fe-s-siyaṛa?*
spare (tire) – *ṛwiḍa zayda.* We never travel without a spare tire. *Ɛemmeṛna ma-ka-nṣafṛu bla ṛwiḍa zayda.*
to spare – 1. *henna.* You can spare yourself the trouble. *ġir henni ṛaṣek men had tamara.* 2. *mneƐ, ma-Ɛṭa-š ma-yeƐṭi-š.* Spare me the details. *mneƐni men t-tafaṣil.* 3. *xella.* He spared no expense. *ma-xella ma-dfeƐ.*
**Can you spare a minute? *Ɛendek ši-dqiqa de-l-magana?* --He was the only one whose life was spared. *huwa b-weḥdu lli bqa Ɛeyyeš.* --I'm sorry, but I don't have a minute to spare. *met'essef, walakin ma-Ɛendi-ši daqiqa weḥda.* --Nobody was spared. *ma-bqa ḥedd.*
sparingly – *be-s-siyasa.* Use it sparingly. *steƐmlu be-s-siyasa.*
spark – *ṭšaša* pl. *-t* coll. *ṭšaš.*
to **sparkle** – *ḍwa iḍwi, lmeƐ.*
spark plug – *buži* pl. *bwaža.* I need a new spark plug for my car. *xeṣṣni buži ždid l-siyaṛti.*
sparrow – *beṛṭal* pl. *bṛaṭel.*
to **speak** – *tkellem, ḥḍeṛ.* He doesn't speak English very well. *ma-ka-itkellem-š n-negliza mezyan bezzaf.*
**May I speak to you? *tesmeḥ-li ntkellem mƐak?*
to speak up – 1. *ġuwwet.* Speak up! We can't hear you. *ġuwwet, ṛa-ḥna ma-ka-nsemƐuk-š.* 2. *dwa idwi.* Why didn't you speak up? *Ɛlaš ma-dwiti-š?*
to speak up for – *ḍaṛeb Ɛla, dafeƐ Ɛla.* Nobody spoke up for him. *ma-ḍaṛeb Ɛlih ḥedd.*
speaker – *xṭib* pl. *xuṭaba, muḥaḍir* pl. *-in.* He's an excellent speaker. *hadak xṭib Ɛažib.*
speaking – *heḍṛa, klam.* I prefer speaking to writing. *ka-nfeḍḍel l-heḍṛa Ɛel le-ktaba.*
**We're not on speaking terms. *ma-ka-nthaḍṛu-š.*
special – *xaṣṣ.* I'm saving it for a special occasion. *ṛani metheḷḷi fiha l-waḥed l-munasaba xaṣṣa.*
specialty – *xtiṣaṣ.* Children's diseases are his specialty. *xtiṣaṣu fe-l-'emraḍ de-d-drari.*
spectator – *metferrež* pl. *metferržin.*
speech – 1. *heḍṛa, lsan.* He lost his speech after the accident. *mša-lu l-lsan men beƐd l-ḥadita.* 2. *kalima* pl. *-t; xeṭba* pl. *-t, xuṭab.* He gave a very good speech. *lqa waḥed l-xeṭba mezyana.*
**Weigh your speech! *wzen klamek!* or *Ɛṛef ṛaṣek š-ka-tqul!*
speed – *soṛƐa* pl. *-t.* The train was going at full speed. *l-qiṭaṛ kan maši b-soṛƐa kbira.* --We are moving at good speed now. *daba ḥna ġadyen b-soṛƐa hiya hadik.*
to put on speed – *zreb.* Let's put on a little speed. *iwa nzerbu šwiya.*
**Can you speed things up a little? *teqḍer tƐežžel be-l-'umuṛ ši-šwiya?*
speed limit – *ḥedd s-soṛƐa.* The speed limit here is thirty-five kilometers an hour. *l-ḥedd de-s-soṛƐa hnaya huwa xemsa u-tlatin kilumiter.*
spell – 1. *sḥur* pl. *-at.* She's completely under his spell. *waxedha tamamen be-sḥuru.* 2. *weqt* pl. *wqat; nezla* pl. *-t, nzali.* Does she often get spells like that? *ka-dduz Ɛliha wqat bḥal had š-ši saƐa saƐa?* 3. *modda* pl. *-t.* He worked for a short spell. *huwa xdem waḥed l-modda qṣiṛa.*
cold spell – *nezla de-l-berd.*
hot spell – *muža de-ṣ-ṣehd.* How long do you think this hot spell

will last? *šḥal ka-ḍḍenn ġad ṭṭul had l-muža de-ṣ-ṣehd.*
to spell – *kteb.* How do you spell your name? *kif ka-tekteb smiytek?*

to **spend** – **1.** *dfeƐ.* We spent a lot of money. *dfeƐna bezzaf d-le-flus.* **2.** *duwwez.* I'd like to spend my vacation here. *nebġi nduwwez l-Ɛoṭla dyali hnaya.* **3.** *ḍiyyeƐ.* I can't spend any more time on this. *ma-neqḍer-š nḍiyyeƐ ši-weqt axoṛ f-had š-ši.*

sphere – **1.** *kuṛa* pl. *-t, kweṛ, kwaṛi.* The shape of the earth is a sphere. *fṣalt l-eṛḍ bḥal ši-kuṛa.* **2.** *da⁹ira* pl. *-t.* Their sphere of influence is very large. *d-da⁹ira de-t-te⁹tir dyalhom wasƐa bezzaf.*

spice – *Ɛeṭṛiya* pl. *-t.* Do you use spices much in your cooking? *ka-tƐemlu bezzaf de-l-Ɛeṭṛiya fe-ṭyabkom?*
to spice – *Ɛmel l-Ɛeṭṛiya.*

spider – *ṛtila* pl. *-t, ṛtayel.*

to **spill** – *hṛeq, deffeg, qleb.* Who spilled the milk on the counter? *škun hṛeq le-ḥlib Ɛel l-baṣeṭ?*
**There's no use crying over spilt milk. *le-gnaza men beƐd l-miyyet xṣaṛa.*

to **spin** – **1.** *luwwa.* The thread is spun unevenly. *l-xeyṭ mluwwi Ɛwež.* **2.** *ḍaṛ iḍuṛ, dax idux.* My head is spinning. *ṛaṣi ka-idux.*
to spin around – *ḍuwweṛ.* She picked the child up and spun him around. *hezzet le-wliyyed u-ḍuwwṛettu.*

spinach – *beqqula.*

spirit – **1.** *bal.* I was with you in spirit. *bali kan mƐakom.* **2.** *Ɛqel* pl. *Ɛqul, Ɛqula.* The spirit is willing, but the flesh is weak. *le-Ɛqel lli qwi, ma d-dat ḍƐifa.*
evil spirit – *ženn* pl. *žnun.* Some people believe in evil spirits. *beƐḍ n-nas ka-i⁹amnu be-ž-žnun.*
**I hope you're in good spirits. *ka-ntmenna tkun Ɛla xaṭṛek.* ––She seemed to be in low spirits. *kanet bḥal lli ṭayeṛ-lha.*

spiritual – *ruḥi, ruḥani.* There's a spiritual bond between them. *ṛabṭahom ši-Ɛalaqa ruḥiya.*

spit – **1.** *qṭib* pl. *qeṭban.* We roasted the lamb on the spit. *šwina l-xriyyef f-le-qṭib.* **2.** (saliva) *bezqa* pl. *-t* coll. *bzeq.*
to spit – *bzeq, dfel.*

spite – *keṛh.* He did it just for spite. *Ɛmelha ġir keṛh.*
in spite of – *ṛeġm, ṛeġma.* I went in spite of the rain. *ṛeġma š-šta mšit.*
to spite – *qeṣṣeḥ, ḍeṛṛ.* Are you doing that just to spite me? *waš ka-ddir dak š-ši ġir baš ḍḍeṛṛni?*

to **splash** – **1.** *ṭaṛ iṭiṛ ṛšayeš.* The water splashes in all directions. *l-ma ka-iṭiṛ ṛšayeš f-koll žih.* **2.** *reššš, ṭiyyeṛ ṛšayeš.* The car splashed me. *s-siyaṛa reššetni.*

splendid – *ha⁹il, Ɛažib.* That was a splendid idea! *fekra ha⁹ila kanet.*

splint – *žbira* pl. *-t, žbayer.* His arm had to be put in splints. *yeƐmel ž-žbira l-iddih.*

splinter – *šenquṛ* pl. *šnaqeṛ.* I've got a splinter under my nail. *dxel-li ši-šenquṛ teḥt ḍ-ḍfeṛ.*

split – *tefṛiqa* pl. *-t.* There was a split in the party. *weqƐet tefṛiqa fe-l-ḥizeb.*
to split – **1.** *šeqq, felleḥ.* The lightning split the tree from top to bottom. *le-bṛeq šeqq š-šežṛa men l-fuq ḥetta l-l-teḥt.* **2.** *qṣem, fṛeq, tqaṣem.* We split the profit three ways. *tqaṣemna r-rbeh Ɛla tlatal.* **3.** *tteqṣem, ttefṛeq.* The party has split into three groups. *l-ḥizeb ttefṛeq Ɛla tlata de-l-fi⁹at.* **4.** *tšeqq, ttefteq.* Your pants have split at theseam. *serwalek ttefteq f-le-xyaṭa.* **5.** *fṛeƐ.* I nearly split my sides laughing. *mšit nefṛeƐ žnabi be-ḍ-ḍeḥk.*

to **spoil** – **1.** *xeṣṣeṛ.* She's spoiled my whole fun. *xeṣṣṛet-li n-našaṭ dyali kollu.* **2.** *fsed.* The meat will spoil. *l-lḥem ġad ifsed.* **3.** *xmaž.* The apples are beginning to spoil. *t-teffaḥat bdaw ixmažu.* **4.** *feššeš.* You're spoiling her. *nta ka-tfeššešha.*

spoke – *qṭib* pl. *qoṭban, qṭayeb.* I put two new spokes in the front wheel. *rekkebt zuž de-l-qeṭban ždad fe-ṛ-ṛwiḍa l-qeddamiya.*

sponge – *žeffafa* pl. *-t, žfayef.*

spoon – *mƐelqa* pl. *-t, mƐaleq.*

sport(s) – *riyaḍa.* Do you go in for sports? *ka-tebġi r-riyaḍa?*
**Be a sport. *kun meṭluq mƐa ṛaṣek* or *kun mesrar.*

spot – **1.** *ṭebƐa* pl. *-t, ṭbayeƐ.* You have a spot on your tie. *Ɛendek ṭebƐa f-žiyyaftek.* **2.** *reḥba* pl. *-t, rḥabi; mudeƐ* pl. *mwadeƐ; maḥell* pl. *-at.* I stood in the same spot for a solid hour. *saƐa kollha w-ana*

waqef f-nefs l-maḥell. --You've touched a sore spot. *ṛak qesti fe-l-mudeƐ lli medṛuṛa* or *qesti d-demmala.* 3. *naḥiya* pl. *-t.* That's a sore spot with him. *hadik n-naḥiya f-aš huwa mqeṣṣeḥ.*
**A cup of coffee would just hit the spot. *ġir kas de-l-qehwa huwa lli ka-ixeṣṣ.* --He stood there as if rooted to the spot. *kan waqef temma tqul bḥal š-šežṛa.* --I was right on the spot when it happened. *ana kont temma mnayn wqeƐ dak š-ši.* --Now I'm on the spot. *ḥṣelt daba.* --You put me on the spot. *ḥeṣṣeltini.*
on the spot - *fe-l-ḥin.* They fired him on the spot. *dḥaweh fe-l-ḥin.*
to spot - 1. *frez.* I spotted him in the crowd. *freztu ma-bin n-nas.* 2. *ṭelleƐ.* I could spot him anywhere. *imken-li nṭellƐu fayn-emma kan.*

to **sprain** - *fekk.* She sprained her ankle. *ttfekket-lha l-keƐba.*

to **spray** - *ṛešš.* We have to spray the peach trees. *xeṣṣna nṛeššu l-xuxat.*

spread - 1. *ntišaṛ.* They tried to check the spread of the disease. *ḥawlu baš iṛaqbu ntišaṛ l-meṛḍ.* 2. *mlaya* pl. *-t.* They put new spreads on the beds. *daru mlayat ždad Ɛel le-fṛašat.*
to spread - 1. *ntašeṛ, sreḥ.* The fire is spreading rapidly. *l-Ɛafya değya serḥet.* 2. *feṛṛeq.* The payments were spread over several years. *feṛṛqu l-iṭaṛi Ɛla modda men snin.*
**Spread some honey on the bread for me. *dhen-li l-xobz be-šwiya d-le-Ɛsel.*
to spread out - *serreḥ, feṛṛeš.* Spread the map out. *serreḥ l-xaṛiṭa.*

spring - 1. *rbiƐ, weqt r-rbiƐ.* We arrived in spring. *wṣelna f-weqt r-rbiƐ.* 2. *saqya* pl. *-t, swaqi; Ɛeyn* pl. *Ɛyun.* There's a spring behind our house. *kayna waḥed s-saqya muṛ ḍaṛna.* 3. *neqša* pl. *-t, nqaši.* The spring in my watch is broken. *n-neqša d-maganti therrset.*
to spring - 1. *qfez.* She sprang from her seat. *qefzet men rḥebtha.* 2. *ṭleƐ, xrež, ža iži.* All the rumors spring from one and the same source. *l-ʔišaƐat kollha ka-ṭṭleƐ men ʔṣel waḥed.*
**He sprang the news on us at dinner. *ṛma-lna had le-xbaṛ f-weqt le-ġda.*

to **sprinkle** - 1. *ṛešš.* Have the streets been sprinkled yet? *ṛeššu z-znaqi wella ma-zal?* 2. *ġebbeṛ.* Sprinkle the sugar on the cake. *ġebbeṛ s-sokkaṛ Ɛel l-ḥelwa.*

sprinkler - *mṛešša* pl. *-t, mṛašš.*

spy - *biyyaƐ* pl. *-a, žasus* pl. *žawasis.*

square - 1. *saḥa* pl. *-t.* Our windows look out on a large square. *s-sṛažem dyalna ka-išeṛfu Ɛla waḥed s-saḥa kbira.* 2. *muṛebbaƐ* pl. *-at.* That's not a square, that's a rectangle. *hadak ma-ši muṛebbaƐ, hadak mustaṭil.* 3. *mṛebbeƐ.* I'd like a square box. *bġit ši-ṣenduq mṛebbeƐ.* 4. *doġri.* He's a pretty square fellow. *ražel doġri hadak bezzaf.* 5. *metqadd, kamel.* I haven't eaten a square meal in days. *hadi modda ma-klit makla metqadda.*
to square - *ṣeffa, sawa.* This will square our accounts. *had š-ši ġad iṣeffi ḥsabatna.*

squash - *qeṛƐa* pl. *-t* coll. *qṛeƐ.*
to squash - 1. *Ɛenfež.* I squashed the cake. *Ɛenfežt l-ḥelwa.* 2. *beƐƐez, bƐez, sḥeq.* I squashed my finger in the door. *sḥeqt ṣebƐi mƐa l-bab.*

to **squeal** - *ġuwwet.* The child squealed with joy. *d-derri ġuwwet be-l-feṛḥa.*

to **squeeze** - 1. *Ɛeẓẓa.* Don't squeeze my hand hard. *ma-tƐeẓẓi-li-š Ɛla iddi bezzaf.* 2. *dḥes.* I can't squeeze another thing into the trunk. *ḥaža weḥda ma-Ɛendi-š kif nzid ndḥesha fe-š-šanṭa.*
to squeeze (out) - *Ɛeṣṣeṛ.* I'll squeeze the oranges. *ana daba nƐeṣṣeṛ l-letšin.*

squirrel - *senžab* pl. *snažeb.*

to **stab** - *ṭƐeẓ.* Someone stabbed him in the brawl. *ši-waḥed ṭeƐẓu fe-d-debza.*
**He's just waiting for a chance to stab me in the back. *ka-itsenna ġir l-wežba yeƐṭini fe-ḍ-ḍheṛ.*

stable - 1. *rwa* pl. *rwi.* Are the horses in the stable? *waš l-xeyl fe-r-rwa?* 2. *mestqerr, qabeṭ, metqaƐed.* They haven't had a stable government for years. *hadi sinin ma-kesbu ḥukuma metqaƐda.*

stack - *Ɛeṛma* pl. *-t, Ɛṛaṛem; qetta* pl. *qtet.* I looked through a whole stack of newspapers for the article. *qellebt f-Ɛeṛma de-l-žaraʔid kamla*

Eel l-maqal.

staff - 1. *rkiza* pl. *rkayez; Emud* pl. *Emayed.* The flag staff is broken. *le-Emud de-ṛ-ṛaya therres.* 2. *muweḍḍafin* (pl.). He dismissed part of his staff. *dḥa ṭeṛf men l-muweḍḍafin dyalu.*

stage - *ḥala* pl. *ḥwal; weḍEiya* pl. *-t, wḍaE.* That depends on the stage it's in. *Ela ḥasab l-ḥala f-aš-en huwa dak š-ši.*

to stage - *ṣuwweb, neḍḍem.* We staged a birthday party for him. *neḍḍemna-lu ḥefla l-Eid miladu.*

to **stagger** - 1. *txeṛweE, tEeṛbeṭ.* I saw him stagger out of the saloon. *šeftu xaṛež men l-qehwa ka-itxeṛweE.* 2. *dehšer.* The blow staggered him. *ḍ-ḍeṛba dehšrettu.* 3. *ḍḍeEḍeE.* Prices are staggering. *l-ʔatmina ka-ḍḍeEḍeE.*

stain - *ṭebEa* pl. *-t, ṭbayeE.* I can't get this stain out of my dress. *ma-bġat-ši dzul-li had ṭ-ṭebEa men ksuwti.*

to stain - *ṭebbeE, ṭla iṭli, wessex.* You've stained your trousers. *ṭebbeEti serwalek.* --The tablecloth is all stained. *l-mendil kollu mṭebbeE.*

stairs - *ḍṛuž* (pl.). Take the stairs to your right. *xud ḍ-ḍṛuž lli Ela iminek.*

stake - 1. *wted* pl. *wtad.* Did you drive the stakes into the ground? *deqqiti le-wtad f-l-eṛḍ?* 2. *xṭaṛ* pl. *-at.* They doubled the stakes. *tnaw le-xṭaṛ.*

to **stammer** - *qewqew.*

stamp - 1. *tenber* pl. *tnaber.* Five one-dirham stamps, please. *xemsa de-t-tnaber dyal derhem ḷḷah ixellik.* 2. *ṭabeE* pl. *ṭwabeE.* Where is the 'Payment received' stamp? *fayn ṭ-ṭabeE lli fih "mʔeddi"?*

to stamp - 1. *ṭbeE.* I stamped all the documents. *le-wṛaq kollhom ṭbeEthom.* 2. *zdeḥ.* She stamped her foot with anger. *zedḥet ṛželha be-z-zEef.*

to stamp out - 1. *ṭfa iṭfi be-ẓ-ẓḍim.* They stamped out the fire. *ṭfaw l-Eefya be-ẓ-ẓḍim.* 2. *ḥeṭṭem.* They stamped out all the opposition. *ḥeṭṭmu l-muEaṛaḍa kollha.*

stand - 1. *ṭebla* pl. *-t, ṭbali.* They have a stand in the market. *Eamlin ṭebla fe-ṣ-ṣuq.* 2. *muqif* pl. *mwaqef.* He's changed his stand on this matter several times. *ġiyyer muqifu Eadad men meṛṛa f-had l-qaḍiya.*

to stand - 1. *wqef.* Don't let him stand outside. *ma-txellih-š yuqef Ela berra.* 2. *ṣbeṛ.* I can't stand it any longer. *ma-neqḍeṛ-ši neṣbeṛ kteṛ men had š-ši.* 3. *ḥmel.* I can't stand him. *ma-ka-neqḍeṛ-š nḥemlu.* 4. *tḥamel mEa.* She can't stand the cold weather. *hiya ma-ka-tthamel-š mEa l-berd.* 5. *bqa ibqa.* Tell him to stand right where he is. *qul-lu ibqa tamam fe-l-maḥell fayn huwa.* 6. *weqqef.* Stand the ladder in this corner. *weqqef s-sellum f-had r-rekna.*

**What I said the other day still stands. *dak š-ši lli qolt dak n-nhaṛ ma-zal huwa hadak.* --I want to know how I stand. *nebġi neEṛef kif ana.*

to stand aside - *dženneb, wqef l-had ž-žih.* Stand aside for a moment, please. *b-le-fḍel mennkom džennbu ši-šwiya.*

to stand by - 1. *wqef.* He stood by, doing nothing. *kan waqef bla ma-idir walu.* 2. *wqef mEa.* You know that I'll stand by you in case of trouble. *ka-teEṛefni billa nuqef mEak ila kanet ši-ḥaža.* 3. *qbeṭ.* He is not standing by his decision. *ma-ka-iqbeṭ-š fe-klamu.*

to stand for - 1. *ʔeyyed.* He stands for equality. *huwa ka-iʔeyyed l-musawat.* 2. *qbel, smeḥ b-.* I won't stand for that! *ma-nesmeḥ-š b-dak š-ši ikun.*

to stand on - *šedd f-, qbeṭ f-.* I stand on my rights. *ana šadd fe-l-ḥuquq dyali.*

to stand out - 1. *mtaz, bṛez.* He stands out in mathematics. *ka-imtaz f-le-ḥsab.* 2. *ban iban.* She stands out in a crowd. *ka-tkun bayna f-wosṭ ž-žmaEa.*

to stand up - *wqef, naḍ inuḍ, qam iqum.* Do you want me to stand up? *tebġini nuqef?*

to stand up for - *dafeE Ela.* If we don't stand up for him, nobody will. *ila ma-dafeEna-š Elih, ḥetta waḥed ma-ġadi idirha.*

to stand up to - *Eṭa yeEṭi ž-žebha, twažeh mEa.* Why don't you stand up to your boss once in a while? *Elaš ma-teEṭi-ši ž-žebha le-mEellmek saEa saEa?*

standard - 1. *mustawa* pl. *-yat.* You can't judge him by ordinary standards. *ma-imken-lek-š teḥkem Elih Ela ḥsab l-mustawa l-Eadi.* Their standard of living is lower than ours. *l-mustawa de-l-maEiša dyalhom* *qell men dyalna.* **2.** *mebda* pl. *mabadi.* Their standards are very high. *l-mabadi dyalhom ɛalya bezzaf.* **3.** *ɛadi.* Is this a standard size? *waš had le-qyas ɛadi?*

standing - *retba* pl. *-t; menzla* pl. *-t, mnazel; sumɛa* pl. *-t.* He has a high standing in his community. *ɛendu sumɛa mezyana fe-l-wasaṭ dyalu.*

**They are friends of long standing. *huma ṣḥab men zman.*

star - *nežma* pl. *nžum.*

**You can thank your lucky stars that it wasn't worse. *ḥmed ḷḷah lli ma-ṣeḍqet-lek-ši ši-ḥaža kfes.*

starch - *nša.* Mix some starch for the shirts. *xeḷḷeṭ šwiya de-n-nša l-le-qwamež.*

to starch - *neššа, dar ʔidir n-nša.* Did you starch the shirts? *neššiti? le-qwamež?*

to **stare** - **1.** *šaf išuf.* He just stared into space. *bqa ġir ka-išuf fe-s-sma.* **2.** *beḷḷeẓ.* She just stood there and stared at me. *bqat ġir waqfa temma ka-tbeḷḷeẓ fiya.*

start - *bdu, luwwel.* I read the book from start to finish in one day. *qṛit le-ktab men bduh l-talih fe-nhaṛ waḥed.*

**You gave me quite a start. *walayenni kif xleɛtini.*

to start - **1.** *bda ibda.* The game has just started. *ɛad kif bda l-leɛb.* --She started out at a good pace. *bdat f-aman llah.* **2.** *ṭleq, nuwweḍ.* You can start the motor now. *imken-lek ṭṭleq l-muṭuṛ daba.* --Who started this rumor? *škun ṭleq had d-diɛaya?* **3.** *xeddem.* Start up this machine. *xeddem had l-ʔala.* **4.** *šɛel.* Let's start a fire. *ažiw nšeɛlu ši-ɛafya.*

**I'll start the ball rolling. *ana ġad nɛeyyeṭ ya-fettaḥ.* --Starting today the bus will stop here. *men had n-nhaṛ ġad ibda iḥṣeṛ ṭ-ṭubis hnaya.*

to **startle** - *xleɛ.* The noise startled me. *xleɛni ṣ-ṣḍaɛ.*

to be startled - *ttexleɛ.* I was startled by the shot. *ttexleɛt be-ḍ-ḍeṛba.*

to **starve** - *mat imut be-ž-žuɛ.* Thousands of people were starving. *l-ʔalaf de-n-nas kanu ka-imutu be-ž-žuɛ.*

to starve to death - *mat imut be-ž-žuɛ.* They almost starved to death. *ɛlayen kanu ġad imutu be-ž-žuɛ.*

starved - *miyyet be-ž-žuɛ, sexfan be-ž-žuɛ.* I'm completely starved. *ṛani tamamen miyyet be-ž-žuɛ.*

state - **1.** *wilaya* pl. *-t.* What is the largest state in the U.S.A.? *šni hiya ʔekbeṛ wilaya f-ʔamirika?* **2.** *ḥukuma* pl. *-t, dula* pl. *duwwal.* The heads of the states will meet next week. *ruʔasaʔ d-duwwal ġad ižtemɛu ž-žemɛa ž-žayya.* **3.** *ḥala* pl. *ḥwal.* I'm in a very bad state. *ṛani f-waḥed l-ḥala qbiḥa bezzaf.* **4.** *ḥukumi.* It's a state institution. *hadik muʔessasa ḥukumiya.*

state of affairs - *weḍɛiya* pl. *-t, wḍaɛ.* Anything is better than the present state of affairs. *dak š-ši lli kan ḥsen men l-weḍɛiya d-had s-saɛa.*

to state - **1.** *qal iqul.* You just stated that you were not there. *ɛad qolti bin ma-konti-š temma.* **2.** *ɛṭa yeɛṭi, ṣeṛṛeḥ b-.* I thought he stated the facts plainly. *kan isḥabni ɛṭa l-ḥaqaʔiq mbiyyna.*

static - *šwaš* pl. *-at.* There is so much static I can't get a single station. *ma-qdeṛt nšedd ḥetta nḥeṭṭa be-ktert š-šwaš lli kayen.*

station - **1.** *mḥeṭṭa* pl. *-t.* Get off at the next station. *nzel f-le-mḥeṭṭa l-mažya.* **2.** *ʔidaɛa* pl. *-t.* What station did you hear it on? *fe-š-men ʔidaɛa smeɛtiha?*

to station - *dar idir, weqqef.* The officer stationed a guard on the hill top. *ḍ-ḍabiṭ dar ɛessas f-ṛaṣ l-kodya.*

statue - *timtal* pl. *tmatel.*

stay - *glas.* Our stay in the mountains was very pleasant. *glasna fe-ž-žbel kan haʔil.*

to stay - **1.** *bqa ibqa.* How long will you stay? *šḥal ġad tebqa?* --Our children stay up until nine o'clock. *d-drari dyalna ka-ibqaw fayqin ḥetta le-t-tesɛud.* --He must stay in bed. *xeṣṣu ibqa fe-l-feṛš.* **2.** *gles, bqa ibqa.* I stayed there three months. *glest temma telt šhuṛ.* **3.** *nzel.* Are you staying at the hotel? *ṛak nazel fe-l-ʔuṭil?* --Are you staying with friends? *ṛak nazel ɛend ši-ṣḥabek?*

steady - **1.** *ṣḥiḥ, mẓiyyeṛ.* This needs a steady hand. *had š-ši ka-ixeṣṣu ši-idd mẓiyyṛa.* **2.** *qabeṭ, mɛeẓẓi.* The ladder isn't steady. *s-sellum ma-qabeṭ-š.* **3.** *mettabeɛ.* We kept up a good steady pace. *qbeṭna-lek soṛɛa* *mettabƐa.* 4. *mwabed.* He's making steady progress. *t-taqeddum lli ka-yeƐmel mwabed.* 5. *mdawem.* I'm looking for steady work. *ka-nḍuṛ Ɛla xedma mdawma.*

steak - *biftik.*

to **steal** - *sṛeq, šeffeṛ.* They stole all my money. *seṛqu-li flusi kollhom.*

to steal away - *tsell, sell ṛaṣu.* We stole away early because we had to go somewhere else. *tsellina bekri Ɛla wedd konna ġadyen l-maḥell axoṛ.*

steam - *fwaṛ* pl. *-at.* Steam is coming up from the kettle. *le-fwaṛ ṭaleƐ men l-beqrež.*

**Don't mind him, he's just letting off steam. *ma-teddiha-š fih, ṛa ġir ž-žnun ṭalƐin fih.*

to steam - 1. *fuwweṛ.* The kettle is steaming. *l-beqrež ka-ifuwweṛ.* 2. *bexxeṛ.* Why don't you like to steam your vegetables? *Ɛlaš ma-ka-tebġi-š tbexxeṛ xḍeṛtek?*

steamer - *baxiṛa* pl. *bawaxir.*

steel - *hend.* The bridge is built entirely of steel. *l-qenṭṛa mebniya kollha men l-hend.*

steep - 1. *waqef.* Be careful, the stairs are steep. *redd balek, ṛa ḍ-ḍṛuž waqfin.* 2. *Ɛali.* The price is too steep for me. *t-taman Ɛali Ɛliya bezzaf.*

to steep - *qƐed, tqeƐded.* Let the tea steep a little longer. *xelli atay izid itqeƐded šwiya.*

steeple - *ṣemƐa* pl. *-t, ṣmeƐ, ṣmaƐi.* The steeples of the church are visible from a long way off. *ṣ-ṣmaƐi d-le-knisiya ka-ittšafu men bƐid.*

steer - *tuṛ* pl. *tiran.* How many steers did they take to the slaughter-house? *šḥal de-t-tiran ddaw l-l-goṛna?*

to **steer** -*wežžeh, xeddem l-žiht, redd l-žiht.* He steered the boat to shore on time. *redd l-baxiṛa l-žiht ṭerf le-bḥeṛ fe-l-weqt.*

to steer clear of - *beƐƐed men.* You'd better steer clear of that fellow! *ḥsen-lek tbeƐƐed men dak xiyyi.*

steering wheel - *dman* pl. *-at.*

stem - *ṣag* pl. *ṣigan.*

step - 1. *ḍeṛža* pl. *-t, ḍṛuž.* The steps are carpeted. *ḍ-ḍṛuž mfeṛṛšin b-ẓeṛbiya.* 2. *xelfa* pl. *-t.* He took one step forward. *zad xelfa l-l-qeddam.*

**We built up our business step by step. *bnina l-ḥaṛaka dyalna šwiya be-šwiya.* --He's always out of step with the times. *huwa dima ma-metqadd-š mƐa l-weqt.*

to step - 1. *wqef, ṭleƐ fuq.* Perhaps if you step on a chair you might be able to reach the ceiling. *waqila ila ṭleƐti fuq ši-šelya ṛak teqḍeṛ telḥeq s-sqef.* 2. *ẓḍem.* I stepped into a puddle. *ẓḍemt f-gelta.*

**Step lively! *bṭeṛ b-ṛaṣek!*

to step aside - *zal izul men ṭ-ṭṛiq.*

to step in - *dxel.* They just stepped in for a moment. *yaḷḷah dexlu waḥed š-šwiya.*

to step into - 1. *dxel l-.* I saw him step into the store. *šeftu daxel l-l-ḥanut.* 2. *ddaxel.* The President himself may step into this. *ṛ-ṛaʔis b-ṛaṣu imken iddaxel f-had š-ši.*

to step off - *nzel, hbeṭ.* He just stepped off the train. *Ɛad kif nzel men l-qiṭaṛ.*

to step up - *zad izid f-, Ɛella.* We'll have to step up the pace a bit. *ka-ixeṣṣna nzidu fe-s-sorƐa šwiyeš.*

to step up to - *zad izid l-Ɛend.* A strange man stepped up to me on the street and asked about you. *waḥed ṛ-ṛažel beṛṛani zad l-Ɛendi fe-z-zenqa u-seqṣa Ɛlik.*

stepfather - *ṛažel l-yemm.*

stepmother - *mṛat l-bu.*

sterling - *ṣafi, xaḷeṣ.* That's sterling silver. *hadik feḍḍa xaḷṣa.*

stern - *doġri, qaṣeḥ.*

stick - *qṭib* pl. *qoṭban.* She hit me with a stick. *ḍeṛbetni be-qṭib.*

to stick - 1. *tekk.* Something is sticking me. *ši-ḥaža ka-ttekkni.* 2. *lṣeq.* This stamp doesn't stick. *had t-tenber ma-ka-ilṣeq-š.* 3. *tƐeẓẓa, ḥṣel.* The door always sticks in damp weather. *l-bab dima ka-ttƐeẓẓa f-weqt š-šta.* 4. *ṛṣa iṛṣa, rsex.* Nothing sticks in his mind. *ḥetta ḥaža ma-ka-tersex fe-dmaġu.* 5. *dḥa idḥi, dexxel, Ɛmel.* Stick your hands in your pockets. *dḥi iddik fe-žyabek.* --He sticks his nose into everything. *ka-idexxel ṛaṣu f-koll-ši.* --Don't stick your nose into other people's business. *ma-tkun-š ddexxel ṣuqek f-de-x̂ṛin.*

to stick it out - *kaber, ṣbeṛ.* Try and stick it out a little longer. *ḥawel dzid tkaber šwiya.*

to stick out - *xrež, ṭṭenneš.* Watch out! There's a nail sticking out there. *ɛendak! ṛa waḥed l-meṣmaṛ xaṛež temma.*

to stick to - *qbeṭ.* I still stick to my opinion. *ana ma-zal qabeṭ f-fkerti.* --He never sticks to anything. *ɛemmṛu ma-ka-iqbeṭ ḥetta f-ḥaža.*

to stick together - *bqa ibqa mežmuɛ, ttaḥed.* Let's stick together. *xellina nebqaw mežmuɛin.*

to stick up - *xrež, ṭṭenneš.* Watch out! There's a nail sticking up over there. *ɛendak! ṛa waḥed l-meṣmaṛ mṭenneš temma.*

to get stuck - *ḥṣel.* My car got stuck in the mud. *siyaṛti ḥeṣlet fe-l-ġis.* --Now I'm stuck. *daba ṛ-ana ḥaṣel.*

sticky - **1.** *(lli) ka-ilṣeq.* My fingers are all sticky from honey. *ṣebɛani kollhom ka-ileṣqu b-le-ɛsel.* **2.** *mẓemmet.* It's awfully sticky today. *walayenni kif mẓemmet l-ḥal had n-nhaṛ.*

stiff - **1.** *waqef.* He always wears stiff collars. *dima ka-ilbes le-ɛnuq waqfin.* **2.** *mteqqef.* He has a stiff neck. *ɛenqu mteqqef.* **3.** *qaṣeḥ, waɛer.* **4.** *ṣɛib* pl. *ṣɛibin, ṣɛab.* Was it a stiff examination? *kan mtiḥan ṣɛib?*

still - **1.** *mhedden, hade?, haden.* The children stayed still for a while. *d-drari bqaw mheddnin ši-šwiya.* **2.** *ma-zal, baqi.* He still believes you. *ma-zal ka-itiq bik.* **3.** *waxxa hakdak, ṛeġma dak š-ši.* Still, I think you did the right thing. *waxxa hakdak ka-nḍenn billa ɛmelti mziya.*

to keep still - *thedden, tṛeṣṣa.*

stingy - *mežḥaḥ, qemšiš, mqemšeš.* Have you ever seen such a stingy millionaire? *ɛemmṛek šefti ši-mlayni qemšiš bḥal hada?*

stir - *šwaš, ṛuɛa.* There was a stir in the crowd when he got up to speak. *kan š-šwaš f-weṣṭ n-nas mnayn wqef itkellem.*

to stir - **1.** *ḥerrek.* If you had stirred up the soup it wouldn't have burned. *u-kan ḥerrekti le-ḥrira u-kan ma-ttheṛqet-š.* **2.** *tḥerrek.* Look, he's stirring now. *šuf, haw ka-itḥerrek daba.*

stirring - *(lli) ka-ihiyyež.* It was a stirring speech. *kalima kanet ka-thiyyež.*

stitch - **1.** *ġerza, ġorza* pl. *-t, ġraz.* Don't make such big stitches. *la-teɛmel-ši l-ġorzat kbaṛ.* **2.** *ḍeṛba* pl. *-t.* I haven't done a stitch of work today. *ma-ḍṛebt-š ḍeṛba weḥda fe-l-xedma had n-nhaṛ.*

to stitch - *ġrez, xeyyeṭ.* Did you stitch the hem yet? *ġrezti t-teɛṭaf wella ma-zal?*

to stitch on - *rekkeb, xeyyeṭ.* Did you stitch on the pockets? *rekkebti ž-žyab?*

stock - **1.** *xzin* pl. *xzayen.* I'll look through my stock and see if I have it. *daba nqelleb f-le-xzin dyali u-nšuf waš ɛendi.* **2.** *sehm* pl. *sham.* I advise you not to buy these stocks. *ka-nneṣḥek ma-tešri-š had le-sham.*

in stock - *f-le-xzin, mexzun.* What do you have in stock? *šnu ɛendek f-le-xzin?*

to be out of stock - *tsala, tqaḍa, tfeḍḍa.* It's out of stock, but we have reordered it. *tqada-lna be-l-ḥeqq ṛa-ḥna ɛawed ṭḷebnah.*

to take stock - *ɛmel le-ḥsab, ṛažeɛ s-selɛa.* Next week we're going to take stock. *ž-žemɛa.*

to take (put) stock in - *ṣeḍḍeq, tiyyeq, qbeṭ.* I don't put much stock in what he says. *ma-ka-neqbeṭ-ši haža weḥda men dak š-ši lli ka-iqul.*

to stock - *xzen, žab, ižib.* We don't stock that brand. *ma-ka-nxeznu-š dak l-ɛeyna.*

to stock up on - *dar idir ɛewla, dar idir ɛwil, ɛmel ɛewla, ɛmel ɛwil.* Did you stock up on coal? *derti le-ɛwil de-l-faxeṛ?*

stockholder - *shaymi* pl. *-ya, msahem* pl. *msahmin.* I'm a stockholder in that company. *ana msahem f-dak š-šarika.*

stocking - *teqšira ṭwila* pl. *tqašer ṭwal.* I'd like three pairs of stockings. *bġit ši-telt zwaž de-t-tqašer ṭwal.*

stomach - *kerš* pl. *kruš.* He has an upset stomach. *keršu mṛuwwɛa.*

**I'm sick to my stomach. *qelbi mṛuwweɛ.*

to stomach - *hḍem, qbel.* I can't stomach that fellow. *dak xiyyi ma-ka-ibġi-š ittehḍem-li.*

stomach-ache - *ḥṛiq l-kerš.* I have a a stomach-ache. *qabeṭni ḥṛiq l-kerš.*

stone - **1.** *ḥežṛa* pl. *-t, ḥžeṛ.* Who threw that stone? *škun ṛma dak l-ḥežṛa?* --That hall has a stone floor. *l-erḍ de-n-nbeḥ d-le-ḥžeṛ.* 2. *šahed* pl. *šwahed.* We had a beautiful stone put on his grave. *Ɛmel-na-lu waḥed š-šahed mezyan Ɛla qbuṛu.* 3. *Ɛḍem* pl. *Ɛḍam, Ɛḍuma.* These plums have big stones. *had l-beṛquq Ɛeḍmu kbir.*

**He killed two birds with one stone. *Ɛmelha ḥežža u-zyaṛa.* --He left no stone unturned. *ma-xella ma-žeṛṛeb.*

stool - *korsi* pl. *krasa.* Put the stool back into the room. *redd l-korsi l-qelb l-bit.*

stool pigeon - *biyyaƐ* pl. *-a.* Be careful, he's a stool pigeon. *redd balek, ṛa hadak biyyaƐ.*

stoop - *teqwiṣa* pl. *-t, tqaweṣ.* The man with the stoop is the inspector. *dak ṛ-ṛažel lli be-t-teqwiṣa, huwa l-mufettiš.*

to stoop - 1. *ḥna yeḥni.* She stooped to pick up the newspaper. *ḥnat baš thezz l-žarida.* 2. *ṭiyyeḥ b-ṛaṣu, hebbeṭ b-ṛaṣu.* I don't think she'd stoop to anything like that. *ma-ka-nḍenn-š ṭṭiyyeḥ b-ṛaṣha l-ši-ḥaža bḥal hadi.*

stop - 1. *mḥeṭṭa* pl. *-t.* You have to get off at the next stop. *xeṣṣek tenzel f-le-mḥeṭṭa ž-žayya.* 2. *weqfa* pl. *-t* coll. *wquf.* We have a ten-minute stop in Rabat. *Ɛendna qeṣmayn d-le-wquf fe-ṛ-ṛbaṭ.*

to bring to a stop - *ḥbes, ḥṣeṛ, weqqef.* Why did you bring the car to a stop? *Ɛlas weqqefti s-siyaṛa?*

to put a stop to - *Ɛmel ḥedd l-.* We must put a stop to this practice. *la-bodda nƐemlu ḥedd l-had l-Ɛada.*

to stop - 1. *ḥṣeṛ, ḥbes.* Shall I stop the car at the next crossing? *waš neḥṣeṛ s-siyaṛa f-mefṛeq ṭ-ṭorqan ž-žay?* 2. *mneƐ, ḥṣeṛ.* I couldn't stop him from going there. *ma-mken-li-š nmenƐu men le-mši l-temma.* 3. *feḍḍa men.* Please stop that noise. *ḷḷah ixellik feḍḍi men dak ṣ-ṣḍaƐ.* 4. *bqa ibqa, gles, nzel.* We stopped at a farm for two days. *glesna yumayn f-waḥed le-Ɛzib.* --We stopped in Fez for a while. *nzelna f-fas ši-modda.* 5. *wqef.* Where are we going to stop? *fayn ġadyen nweqfu?* 6. *teqqef.* I instructed the bank to stop the check. *qolt le-m̃m̃alin l-ḅenk iteqqfu š-šak.* 7. *sket, wqef.* My watch has stopped. *maganti sektet.*

**He stops at nothing. *ma-ka-ixaf ḥetta men ḥaža* or *ka-iṣḍem f-koll-ši.*

to stop over - *daz iduz, ḥṣeṛ, nzel.* Why don't you stop over at my place on the way? *Ɛlaš ma-dduž-ši Ɛendi mnayn tkun šadd ṭ-ṭriq?*

to stop short - 1. *deġya wqef.* The car ahead of me stopped short. *s-siyaṛa lli kanet qeddami deġya weqfet.* 2. *deġya qṭeƐ, delqem, qṭeƐ l-heḍṛa f-.* I stopped him short before he could say too much. *deġya qṭeƐtu qbel-ma izid fe-l-heḍṛa.*

to stop up - *xneq.* You're going to stop the drain. *ṛak ġad texneq l-qadus.*

stopper - *ḥeṣṣaṛ* pl. *-a, ḥṣaṣeṛ.*

store - 1. *ḥanut* (m. or f.) pl. *ḥwanet.* I know a store where you can buy that. *ka-neƐṛef waḥed l-ḥanut fayn imken-lek tešri dak š-ši.* 2. *xzin* pl. *xzayen.* We have a store of food in the pantry. *Ɛendna xzin de-l-muna f-bit l-Ɛewla.*

in store - *mxebbeƐ, ka-itsenna.* Who knows what is in store for us? *škun Ɛaṛef aš mxebbeƐ-lna?*

to store - *xebbeƐ, xzen.* Where shall I store the onions? *fayn ġad nexzen l-beṣḷa?*

to store up - *žmeƐ.* I stored up a lot of energy during my vacation. *žmeƐt bezzaf de-l-quwwa fe-l-Ɛoṭla dyali.*

storm - *ḥemla* pl. *-t, ḥmali.* There was a big storm yesterday. *žat waḥed l-ḥemla kbira l-baṛeḥ.*

to storm - *ṛeƐƐed.* It is storming outside. *d-denya ka-tṛeƐƐed Ɛla beṛṛa.*

stormy - *mṛeƐƐed.*

story - 1. *ḥkaya* pl. *-t; xṛafa* pl. *-t, xṛayef; qeṣṣa* pl. *-t.* I wish I could tell you the whole story. *tmennit u-kan mken-li nƐewwed-lek le-xṛafa kollha.* 2. *ṭebqa* pl. *-t, ṭbeq.* The house has five stories. *ḍ-ḍar fiha xemsa de-ṭ-ṭebqat.*

stout - *smin* pl. *sman.* He's gotten very stout lately. *ṛžeƐ smin bezzaf had l-iyyam.*

stove - *mežmaṛ* pl. *mžameṛ, nafex* pl. *nwafex.* Put the peas on the stove. *Ɛmel ž-želbana Ɛel l-mežmaṛ.*

straight - 1. *mƐewweṭ.* Draw a straight line. *ṣeṭṭeṛ xeṭṭ mƐewweṭ.* 2. *doġri.* He's always been straight with me. *huwa kan dima doġri mƐaya.* 3. *tamamen, be-d-dat.* Our house is straight across from the mosque. *ḍaṛna žat mqabla ž-žameƐ be-d-dat.* 4. *qaṣeḍ, doġri.* Go straight to school. *sir qaṣeḍ l-l-meḍṛaṣa.* 5. *ṣafi.* He can't think straight, much less talk straight. *tefkiru ma-ši ṣafi, Ɛassak klamu.*

to go straight - *tmešša mƐewweṭ, Ɛewweṭ ṛaṣu.* He promised us to go straight. *ṛah waƐedna baš itmešša mƐewweṭ.*

to get straight - **1.** *fhem.* I think you didn't get her straight. *ka-nḍenn ma-fhemtiha-š.* **2.** *biyyen ṛ-ṛaṣ men r-režlin.* Now let's get this straight once and for all. *daba aži nbiyynu l-had š-ši ṛaṣu men režlih u-nthennaw.* **3.** *Ɛṛef l-ḥaqiqa.* See if you can get that story straight. *šuf kan teƐṛef l-ḥaqiqa d-dak l-qeṣṣa.*

straight ahead - *ṭul, gud.* Just keep straight ahead. *ġir xellik ġadi ṭul.*

to work straight - *xdem (xedma) mettabƐa.* I worked for fifteen hours straight yesterday. *l-bareḥ xdemt xemsṭašeṛ saƐa mettabƐa.*

to **straighten** - *Ɛewweṭ, qaded.* Straighten this wire for me please. *Ɛewweṭ-li had s-selk Ɛafak.*

to straighten out, up - *Ɛewweṭ, neḍḍem.* Did you tell them to straighten up their rooms? *qolti-lhom ineḍḍmu byuthom?*

strain - **1.** *taƐab, tamara, mašeqqa.* It's a strain to read this small print. *mašeqqa l-waḥed iqṛa had le-ktaba ṣ-ṣġiṛa.* **2.** *težbad, žehd.* I don't think the rope will stand the strain. *ma-ka-nḍenn-š ṭ-ṭwal itḥemmel t-težbad.*

to strain - **1.** *ṣeffa.* Did you strain the coffee? *ṣeffiti l-qehwa?* **2.** *tƐeb.* I strained my eyes from reading. *tƐebt Ɛeyniya b-le-qṛaya.* **3.** *Ɛafer, tƐafer, tgaḥer.* The dog was straining at the leash. *l-kelb kan ka-itƐafer mƐa ṛbaṭu.*

**We must strain every effort to finish on time. *xeṣṣna nƐemlu žehdna kollu baš nsaliw fe-l-weqt.*

to strain oneself - *tƐeddeb, tmerret, ḍreb tamara.*

strained - *mwetteṛ.* At the moment our relations are somewhat strained. *f-had s-saƐa l-Ɛalaqat dyalna ši-šwiya mwettṛin.*

strange - *ġrib* pl. *ġribin, ġṛab.* There is something strange about this house. *ši-ḥaža ġriba kayna f-qaḍiyt had ḍ-ḍaṛ.*

stranger - *beṛṛani* pl. *-yin.* He always welcomes strangers to his house. *dima ka-ireḥḥeb be-l-beṛṛani l-ḍaṛu.*

strap - *ṣemṭa* pl. *-t, ṣmeṭ.* Put the strap around the suitcase. *Ɛmel ṣ-ṣemṭa Ɛel š-šanṭa.*

straw - **1.** *tebna* pl. *-t* coll. *tben.* That's made of straw. *dak š-ši mṣuwweb men t-tben.* **2.** *žeƐba* pl. *-t, žƐeb; žƐiba* pl. *-t.* May I have a straw to drink my Coca-Cola with? *Ɛafak Ɛṭini ši-žƐiba baš nešṛob kuka kula dyali.*

**That's the last straw. *daba Ɛad kmel lli bqa.*

strawberry - *tuta l-eṛḍ* pl. *-t l-eṛḍ* coll. *tut l-eṛḍ.*

stray - *talef, metluf.* He keeps bringing stray kittens home. *ġir ka-ižib f-le-qṭiṭat t-talfin le-ḍ-ḍaṛ.*

stream - *wad* pl. *widan, zerraf* pl. *zraref.* Where can we cross the stream? *fayn imken-lna nqeṭƐu l-wad?* --Did you see the stream of cars? *šefti Ɛla zerraf de-s-siyaṛat?*

to stream - *huwwed, sal isil.* The sweat was just streaming on his forehead. *le-Ɛṛeq kan ġir huwwad Ɛla žbehtu.*

street - *zenqa* pl. *-t, znaqi; ṭṛiq* pl. *ṭeṛqan, ṭoṛqan.* I met him on the street where I used to live. *tlaqitu fe-z-zenqa fayn kont ka-neskon.* --This is a dead-end street. *had z-zenqa ma-ka-txerrež-š.*

strength - **1.** *qowwa* pl. *-t; žehd, qaḍaṛ.* I haven't the strength to do it. *ma-Ɛendi-š l-qowwa baš ndirha.* **2.** *meqḍuṛa* pl. *-t.* He doesn't know his own strength. *huwa b-ṛaṣu ma-ka-yeƐṛef-š meqḍuṛtu.*

to **strengthen** - *quwwa, žehhed.*

strenuous - *metƐub.* That's a strenuous job. *xedma metƐuba hadik.*

stretch - *ṣemṭa* pl. *-t, ṣmeṭ; ṣmiṭa* pl. *-t; žebda* pl. *-t.* We had to run the last stretch. *ṣ-ṣmiṭa lli bqat-lna ḍṛebnaha be-ž-žri.*

at a stretch - *težbida weḥda, bla wquf.* He works about ten hours at a stretch. *ka-ixdem ši-Ɛešṛa de-s-swayeƐ bla wquf.*

to stretch - **1.** *žebbed.* The rope is stretched too tight. *ṭ-ṭwal mžebbed bezzaf.* **2.** *džebbed, wsaƐ.* These gloves will stretch. *had ṣ-ṣebbaƐat ġad yewsaƐu.* --I just want to stretch a little bit. *ġir bġit ndžebbed ši-šwiya.* **3.** *dar idir* *fe-l-qaleb, wesseƐ.* Can you stretch my shoes for me? *imken-lek ddir-li had ṣ-ṣebbaṭ fe-l-qaleb?*

to stretch out - *sreḥ.* The wheat fields stretch out for kilometers. *l-ʔaṛaḍi de-l-gemḥ sarḥa kilumiter Ɛla kilumiter.*

stretcher - *nƐaš* pl. *-at.* They carried him out on a stretcher. *ddaweh mehzuz Ɛel n-nƐaš.*

strict - *(lli) ma-ka-yeƐṛef mzaḥ.* His father is very striet. *ḅḅah ma-ka-yeƐṛef mzaḥ be-l-koll.*

strike - *ʔiḍṛab* pl. *-at.* How long did the strike last? *šḥal ṭaḷ l-ʔiḍṛab?* --We're going on strike tomorrow. *ġedda ġad ndiru l-ʔiḍṛab.*

to strike - **1.** *ḍṛeb, Ɛmel l-ʔiḍṛab.* Why are the workers striking? *Ɛlaš l-xeddama Ɛamlin l-ʔiḍṛab?* **2.** *ḍṛeb.* The clock has just struck ten. *l-magana Ɛad ḍeṛbet l-Ɛešṛa.* --Who struck you? *škun ḍeṛbek?* **3.** *šƐel.* Strike a match. *šƐel ši-wqida.* **4.** *qaṣ iqiṣ.* The ship struck a rock. *l-baxiṛa qaṣet waḥed ṣ-ṣexṛa.* **5.** *tkellem.* Did the lightning strike anywhere? *ṣ-ṣaḥqa tkellmet f-ši-ṛeḥba?*

**He must have struck oil, the way he's throwing money away. *ma-huwa ġir ṭaḥ f-ši-kenz Ɛel l-kifiya lli ka-iṛmi biha le-flus.*

to strike off - *šeṭṭeb Ɛla, ḍreb Ɛla.* Just strike his name off the list. *ġir šeṭṭeb Ɛla smiytu men l-laʔiḥa.*

to strike out - *ḥdef, mḥa imḥi.* Did you strike the second paragraph out? *mḥiti l-feqṛa t-tanya?*

to strike up - *bda ibda.* The two of them struck up a friendship very quickly. *haduk z-zuž deġya deġya bdaw ṣ-ṣeḥba binathom.*

to strike a blow - *žmeƐ b-ḍeṛba mƐa.* He struck him a blow with his cane. *žmeƐ mƐah b-ḍeṛba be-Ɛṣatu.*

**That was the first thing that struck my eye. *hadik ʔewwel ḥaža Ɛlaš ṛmit Ɛeyni.*

striking - **1.** *barez, (lli) ka-ixṭef.* She likes to wear striking colors. *ka-iƐžebha telbes l-lwan lli ka-ixeṭfu.* **2.** *Ɛḍim* pl. *Ɛḍam.* There's a striking resemblance between them. *mošbiha Ɛḍima kayna binathom.*

string - **1.** *qennba* pl. *-t, qnaneb* coll. *qenneb.* Tie your books with this string. *Ɛqed ktubek b-had l-qennba.* **2.** *wetṛa* pl. *-t; wtaṛ* pl. *-at.* I have to buy a new string for my violin. *xeṣṣni nešri wetṛa ždida l-l-kamanža dyali.* **3.** *xiṭ.* She's wearing a beautiful string of pearls. *Ɛliha xiṭ ž-žuheṛ ġzal.*

**He's still attached to her apron strings. *ma-zal laṣeq-lha fe-žlayelha.*

to string - **1.** *zelleg.* Where can I have my beads strung? *fayn imken-li nzelḷeg Ɛqiqi?* **2.** *Ɛelleq.* How are you going to string this wire? *kif ġad tƐelleq had s-selk?*

string beans - *lubya xoḍṛa.*

strip - *sir* pl. *syur.* Cut the paper into strips. *qeṭṭeƐ l-kaġiṭ syur syur.*

stripe - *šeṛṭa* pl. *-t, šṛaṭi.* His tie has red and white stripes. *žiyyaftu fiha š-šṛaṭi ḥumeṛ u-buyeḍ.*

stroke - **1.** *ḍeṛba* pl. *-t.* I haven't done a stroke of work on my book for three weeks. *hadi tlata de-ž-žemƐat ma-Ɛmelt ḥetta ḍeṛba f-le-ktab dyali.* **2.** *noqṭa* pl. *nqaṭi.* Her father had another stroke yesterday. *ḅḅaha Ɛawed hebṭet-lu n-noqṭa l-bareḥ.* **4.** *deqqa* pl. *-t.* At one stroke everything was changed. *f-deqqa weḥda koll-š tbeddel.*

**It was a real stroke of luck to find that car. *weḷḷah men Ɛada ḥekma de-z-zheṛ lli tṣabet dak s-siyaṛa.*

at the stroke of - *fe-d-deqqa d-, fe-ḍ-ḍeṛba d-, fe-t-teklima d-.* She arrived at the stroke of four. *weṣlet fe-d-deqqa de-ṛ-ṛebƐa.*

to stroke - *melles.* Our cat loves to be stroked. *l-qeṭṭa dyalna ka-tebġi bezzaf lli imelles Ɛliha.*

stroll - *msarya (Ɛel r-ržel)* pl. *-t.* First I'd like to take a stroll through town. *baġi ndir waḥed le-msarya Ɛla režliya f-le-mdina hiya l-luwla.*

to stroll - *tmešša.* Let's stroll through the old city. *yaḷḷah ntmeššaw f-le-mdina.*

strong - *ṣḥiḥ* pl. *ṣḥaḥ.*

struggle - *mqatla* pl. *-t, mgarḥa* pl. *-t, mƐafra* pl. *-t.*

to struggle - *Ɛafer, qatel, tƐafer, tqatel.* I've been struggling with this problem for some time. *hadi modda w-ana ka-nƐafer mƐa had l-muškila.*

stubborn - *ṛaṣu qaṣeḥ.* He's terribly stubborn. *walayenni ṛaṣu qaṣeḥ.*

student - *ṭaḷib* pl. *ṭaḷaba, ṭoḷba,*

ṭoḷḷab. How many students are there at the medical school? *šḥal de-ṭ-ṭaḷaba kaynin f-kulliyat ṭ-ṭibb?*

study - **1.** *dirasa* pl. *-t, durus*. Has he finished his studies? *feḍḍa d-dirasa dyalu?* **2.** *beḥt* pl. *buḥut; dirasa* pl. *-t*. He has published several studies in that field. *nšer ɛadad de-d-dirasat f-dak l-midan.*

to study - **1.** *dres*. We studied the map before we started. *dresna l-xaṛiṭa qbel-ma nebdaw.* **2.** *tɛellem, dres, qṛa*. He's studying Chinese. *ka-itɛellem ṣ-ṣiniya.*

stuff - **1.** *madda*. What are you going to make out of this stuff? *š-ġa-tṣuwweb men had l-madda?* **2.** *ši*. Throw that stuff away. *ṛmi dak š-ši ɛlik xḷaṣ!*

**Now we'll see what stuff he's made of. *daba ɛad ġad nšufu ḥennt iddih.*

to stuff - **1.** *ɛemmeṛ*. We had stuffed turkey for dinner. *tġeddina b-bibi mɛemmeṛ.* **2.** *ɛmel*. Stuff cotton in your ears. *ɛmel le-qṭeṇ f-wednik.*

to stuff oneself - *dḥes ṛaṣu, dekken ṛaṣu*. Don't stuff yourself with food. *ma-ddḥes-š ṛaṣek be-l-makla.*

to stuff up - *xneq*. My nose is stuffed up. *menxari mexnuq.*

to **stumble** - *ɛteṛ*. I stumbled over a step. *ɛteṛt f-waḥed ḍ-ḍeṛža.*

stupid - *balid*. He isn't that stupid. *ma-huwa-ši balid ḥetta l-temma.*

sty - *nežma* pl. *-at*. I'm getting a sty on my left eye. *nežma ṭalɛa-li fe-l-ɛeyn de-š-šmål.*

style - **1.** *ʔuslub* pl. *ʔasalib*. He has a very poor style. *ɛendu ʔuslub qbiḥ bezzaf.* **2.** *ṣenɛa* pl. *-t, ṣnayeɛ*. It's the latest style. *hadi ʔaxir ṣenɛa* or *hadi ṣ-ṣenɛa ž-ždida.*

to be in style - *ṇaḍet-lu ṣ-ṣuḷa*. Combs are in style again. *le-mšaṭi ɛawed ṇaḍet-lhom ṣ-ṣuḷa.*

subject - **1.** *muḍuɛ* pl. *mawaḍiɛ*. I'm not familiar with that subject. *ma-ka-neɛṛef-šay f-dak l-muḍuɛ.* **2.** *muwaṭin* pl. *-in*. He's a British subject. *hadak muwaṭin bṛiṭani.*

**This schedule is subject to change. *had l-beṛnamež imken yeḥdet fih ši-teġyir.*

to **submit** - *sellem, dfeɛ, qeddem*. I'll submit my report on Monday. *ġad nsellem t-teqṛir dyali nhaṛ t-tnayn.*

to submit to - *ɛṭa yeɛṭi ṛaṣu l-*. His mother had to submit to an operation. *ṃṃu ma-fadha ġir teɛṭi ṛaṣha l-l-ɛamaliya.*

to **subscribe** - *štarek*. I subscribed to both newspapers this time. *štarekt fe-l-žaṛidat b-zuž had n-nuba.*

substantial - *muhimm*. He lost a substantial sum of money. *mša-lu qḍeṛ muhimm d-le-flus.*

substitute - *lli ka-ixlef, lli ka-iɛewweḍ, lli ka-inub ɛla*. If you can't come tomorrow, send a substitute. *ila ma-mken-lek-š dži ġedda ṣifeṭ lli inub ɛlik.*

to substitute - *ɛmel fe-ɛwaḍ*. I'll substitute red for green. *daba neɛmel le-hmeṛ fe-ɛwaḍ le-xḍeṛ.*

to substitute for - *xlef, ɛewweḍ, nab inub ɛla*. Can you substitute for me today? *imken-lek tɛewweḍni l-yum?*

to **succeed** - **1.** *xlef, ža iži men beɛd*. Who succeeded him in office? *škun ža men beɛdu l-l-menṣib?* **2.** *nžeḥ, tweffeq*. I think he will succeed in his profession. *ka-nḍenn ġad itweffeq fe-l-mihna dyalu.*

**He succeeds in everything he undertakes. *lli ɛmelha ka-tesxeṛ-lu.*

success - *nažaḥ*. Congratulations on your success! *ka-nhennik be-n-nažaḥ dyalek.*

**The play wasn't much of a success. *ṛ-ṛiwaya ma-kan-lha-ši ši-nažaḥ kbir.*

successful - *nažeḥ, mweffeq.*

successor - *xlifa* pl. *xlayef.*

such - *bḥal* (plus pronoun). I've never seen such a man. *ɛemmeṛni ma-šeft ṛažel bḥal hada.* --A car such as yours is very expensive. *siyaṛa bḥal dyalek ġalya bezzaf.*

**Why are you in such a hurry? *ɛlaš ɛlik had z-zerba?* --It's been such a long time that I can't remember any more. *modda ṭwila hadi dazet ḥetta ma-bqit ɛaqel ɛla walu.* --She would never say such a thing. *ɛemmeṛha ma-tqul had š-ši.* --I heard some such thing. *ana smeɛt ši-ḥaža f-had š-škel.*

sudden: **There's been a sudden change in the weather. *deġya l-žuw tteqleb.* --All of a sudden I remembered that I had to mail a letter. *ma-fṭent b-ṛaṣi ḥetta tfekkeṛt ɛendi bṛa ġad nṣifeṭha.*

suddenly - *deġya, f-ṛemša de-l-ɛeyn.*

Suddenly everything disappeared. *f-ṛemša de-l-Ɛeyn koll-ši ġab.*

to **sue** - **1.** *dƐa idƐi, tbeƐ fe-l-meḥkama.* We sued him for damages. *dƐinah Ɛel t-teƐwiḍat.* **2.** *dafeƐ Ɛla, ṭaleb b-.* They have always sued for peace. *dima kanu iṭalbu b-l-aman.*

to **suffer** - *tƐeddeb, tmeḥḥen.* Did she suffer much? *tƐeddbet ši?*

**They suffered heavy losses. *nezlet Ɛlihom xaṣaṛat kbira.*

sufficient - *kafi.*

to **suffocate** - **1.** *žaf ižif.* I nearly suffocated. *Ɛlayen kont ġad nžif.* **2.** *žiyyef.* He nearly suffocated the baby. *Ɛlayen kan ġad ižiyyef t-teṛbya.*

sugar - *sokkaṛ.*

to **suggest** - **1.** *qtareḥ.* I suggest that we go to the movies. *ka-neqtareḥ nemšiw le-s-sinima.* **2.** *Ɛna yeƐni.* Are you suggesting that I'm wrong? *waš ṛak ka-teƐni bin ma-mƐaya-š l-ḥeqq?* **3.** *fekkeṛ f-.* What does this suggest to you? *f-aš ka-ifekkṛek had š-ši?*

to commit **suicide** - *qtel ṛaṣu.*

suit - **1.** *keswa* pl. *ksawi; lebsa* pl. *-t, lbasi.* He needs a new suit. *xeṣṣu keswa ždida.* **2.** *deƐwa* pl. *-t, dƐawi.* If we do not hear from you by Monday, we shall bring suit. *ila men daba le-t-tnayn ma-Ɛṭitina xbaṛ ṛa-ḥna nqeyydu deƐwa.*

to follow suit - *Ɛmel bḥal, dar bḥal.* If you take one I'll follow suit. *ila xditi weḥda neƐmel bḥalek.*

to suit - **1.** *Ɛmel xaṭeṛ.* It's hard to suit everybody. *ṣƐib l-waḥed yeƐmel xaṭeṛ koll-ši.* **2.** *walem, naseb.* It's suited to the age of the children. *dak š-ši ka-iwalem senn d-drari.* **3.** *ža iži mƐa.* Red doesn't suit you. *le-ḥmeṛ ma-ka-iži-š mƐak.*

**Suit yourself. *Ɛmel lli ža Ɛla xaṭṛek.* --Is she suited for this kind of work? *waš hiya dyal had n-nuƐ de-l-xedma?*

suitable - *mnaseb, mwalem.* We can't find a suitable house. *ma-ṣebna-ši ši-ḍaṛ mwalma.*

sullen - *mkeddeṛ.*

sultry - *meẓmuṭ.* It's awfully sultry today. *walayenni l-ḥal kif meẓmuṭ l-yum.*

sum - *qḍeṛ* pl. *qḍaṛ, qḍuṛa.* I still owe him a small sum. *ma-zal ka-isal-ni waḥed le-qḍeṛ ṣġiṛ.*

to sum up - *lexxeṣ.* Let me sum it up for you. *xellini nlexxeṣha-lek.*

**To sum up, he's no good at all. *ġaytu ma-Ɛendu-ši l-aš iṣlaḥ.*

summer - *ṣif, weqt ṣ-ṣif.*

sun - *šems, šemš* (f.), pl. *šmus, šmuš.*

to sun oneself - *tšemmes.*

Sunday - *l-ḥedd, nhaṛ l-ḥedd.* He'll be back on Sunday. *ġad iṛžeƐ nhaṛ l-ḥedd.*

sundown - *ġrub š-šems, le-ġrub, moġṛeb.*

sunny - *mšemmes.* The front rooms are sunny. *le-byut l-qeddamiyen mšemmsin.*

sunrise - *šṛuq š-šems.*

sunset - *ġrub š-šems, le-ġrub, moġṛeb.*

superior - **1.** *Ɛla men.* Is he your superior? *waš huwa Ɛla mennek?* **2.** *ṛaqi.* This is of superior quality. *had š-ši Ɛeyna ṛaqya.*

superstition - *ʔaman b-le-xṛayef; ṭiṛa* pl. *-t.*

superstitious - *(lli) ka-itiq b-le-xṛayef.* Don't be so superstitious. *la-tkun-ši ka-ttiq b-le-xṛayef hakdak.*

supervision - *muṛaqaba* pl. *-t.* They are under constant supervision. *huma Ɛlihom muṛaqaba mdawma.*

supper - *Ɛša* pl. *-wat.* I've been invited for supper. *ana meƐṛuḍ l-le-Ɛša.*

supplement - *zyada* pl. *-t.*

supply - *xzin* pl. *xzayen.* We still have a big supply of vegetables. *ma-zal Ɛendna xzin kbir de-l-xoḍṛa.*

to supply - **1.** *ṛna iṛni.* Their store supplies all the big restaurants. *ḥanuthom ka-teṛni Ɛel l-maṭaƐim le-kbira kollha.* **2.** *Ɛṭa yeƐṭi, feṛṛeq Ɛla.* He always supplies us with cigarettes. *dima ka-ifeṛṛeq Ɛlina d-doxxan.* **3.** *quwwem b-.* We have enough shoes to supply the demand. *iqedduna ṣ-ṣbabeṭ baš nquwwmu be-ṭ-ṭalab.*

support - *tegƐida* pl. *-t.* You can count on support from me. *imken-lek ttkel Ɛla tegƐida men Ɛendi.*

**You must offer some evidence in support of your statement. *xeṣṣek tedli b-ši ḥužža teʔyid le-klamek.*

to support - **1.** *ʔeyyed, deƐƐem.* He's being supported by all parties. *l-ʔeḥzab kollha mʔeyydah.* **2.** *Ɛewwen, xdem Ɛla.* He has to support his parents. *melzum baš ixdem Ɛla waldih.*

to support oneself - *xdem Ɛla ṛaṣu.* I've supported myself ever since I was fifteen. *melli kanet Ɛendi xemsṭašel Ɛam w-ana ka-nexdem Ɛla ṛaṣi.*

to **suppose** - **1.** *fṛeḍ.* Let's suppose you're right. *nfeṛḍu mƐak l-ḥeqq.* **2.** *ḍenn.* I suppose so. *ka-nḍenn (ila hakdak).*
**Suppose you wait till tomorrow. *še-ḍheṛ-lek ttsenna ḥetta l-ġedda?*

to be supposed to - **1.** *lazem Ɛlih.* I'm supposed to go tonight, but I'm too tired. *lazem Ɛliya nemši l-yum fe-l-lil, be-l-ḥeqq Ɛeyyan bezzaf.* **2.** *qalu Ɛlih, ka-iqulu Ɛlih.* She is supposed to be very intelligent. *ka-iqulu Ɛliha dkiya bezzaf.*

sure - **1.** *myeqqen, metyeqqen.* That's a sure thing. *haža myeqqna hadi.* --Are you sure of that? *waš nta myeqqen b-dak š-ši?* **2.** *meƐlum.* Sure, I'll come. *meƐlum nži.* **3.** *be-l-mufid.* I'd sure like to see him again. *nebġi nƐawed nšufu be-l-mufid.*
**You thought it would rain, and sure enough it did. *qolti imken ṭṭiḥ š-šta u-be-l-fiƐl ṭaḥet.*

for sure - **1.** *bla mzaḥ.* You must be there at five o'clock for sure. *xeṣṣek tkun temma fe-l-xemsa bla mzaḥ.* **2.** *be-t-teṣḥiḥ.* I know that for sure. *ka-neƐṛef dak š-ši be-t-teṣḥiḥ.*

to make sure - **1.** *tyeqqen, tḥeqqeq.* I just wanted to be sure that she was there. *ġir bġit ntyeqqen bin kanet temma.* **2.** *ḥawel išuf.* Make sure that it doesn't happen again. *ḥawel tšuf ma-tƐawed-š tuqeƐ had l-qaḍiya.*

surely - **1.** *meƐlum.* Will you be there? -Surely. *ġad tkun nta temma? -meƐlum.* **2.** *ma ... ġir.* I surely thought you would do it. *ma-ḍennitek ġir teƐmelha.*

surface - *wžeh* pl. *wžuh.*

surgeon - *žiraḥi* pl. *-yin.*

surplus - *zyada* pl. *-t.*

surprise - *mfaž'a* pl. *-t, fuž'a* pl. *-t.* She gave us a big surprise. *Ɛmelt-lna mfaž'a kbira.*

by surprise - *Ɛla beġta, Ɛla ġefla.* The rain caught me by surprise. *qebṭetni š-šta Ɛla beġta.* --You took me completely by surprise. *žitini Ɛla ġefla tamamen.*

to surprise - **1.** *faže'.* I wanted to surprise you. *kont baġi nfaž'ek.* **2.** *bheḍ.* Nothing surprises me any more. *ḥetta ḥaža ma-bqat tebheḍni.*

to be surprised - *ttebheḍ, bqa ibqa mebhuḍ.* I was very much surprised when I heard that he came. *bqit mebhuḍ bezzaf mnin smeƐtu ža.*

to be surprised - *tseƐžeb, tseġṛeb.* I am not surprised at anything you do. *ma-ka-ntseġṛeb ḥetta f-ḥaža Ɛmeltiha.*

to **surrender** - *steslem, sellem ṛaṣu, nezzel s-snaḥ.* The enemy surrendered immediately. *le-Ɛdu deġya nezzel s-snaḥ.*

to **surround** - **1.** *ḍaṛ b-.* A high wall surrounds the old city. *ḥeyṭ kbir ḍayeṛ b-le-mdina le-qdima.* **2.** *ṭuwweq.* They were surrounded by soldiers. *kanu mṭuwwqinhom l-Ɛesker.*

to **suspect** - *Ɛendu š-šekk f-, šekk f-.* Do you suspect him? *ka-tšekk fih?*

to **suspend** - **1.** *ḥṣeṛ, teqqef.* The bank has suspended all payments. *l-ḅenk ḥṣeṛ le-xḷaṣat kollhom.* **2.** *weqqef.* He was suspended for a week. *weqqfuh l-moddet žemƐa.*

suspense - *tešniqa* pl. *-t.* He was waiting in great suspense. *kan itsenna b-waḥed t-tešniqa kbira.*

suspicion - *šekk* pl. *škuk.* What aroused your suspicion? *šnu dexxel-lek had š-šekk?*

suspicious - **1.** *lli fih š-šekk, lli ka-idexxel š-šekk.* That looks suspicious to me. *dak š-ši ka-idexxel-li š-šekk.* **2.** *meškak.* He immediately gets suspicious. *deġya ka-iṛžeƐ meškak.*

swallow - *xeṭṭifa* pl. *-t.* coll. *xeṭṭif.* There were many swallows here last summer. *kanu bezzaf de-l-xeṭṭifat hnaya fe-ṣ-ṣif d-Ɛam luwwel.*

to swallow - **1.** *bleƐ, ṣṛeṭ.* I can't swallow because I have a sore throat. *ma-ka-neqḍer-š nebleƐ Ɛla wedd ḥelqi mṛiḍ.* **2.** *kemmed.* She couldn't swallow the insult. *ma-qeddet-š tkemmed l-xeṭya.* **3.** *taq itiq b-.* He swallows everything he hears. *l-ḥaža lli smeƐha ka-itiq biha.*

swamp - *gelta* pl. *-t, glati.* How far does the swamp go? *ḥedd-aš mašya l-gelta?*

to swamp - *faḍ ifiḍ.* I was swamped with work last week. *faḍet Ɛliya l-xedma ž-žemƐa l-fayta.*

swarm - *gežž* pl. *gžež.* They followed him like a swarm of bees. *mšaw tabƐineh bḥal ši-gežž de-n-nḥel.*

to swarm - *ġla iġli.* The swamp swarms with mosquitoes. *l-gelta ka-teġli be-n-namus.*

to **swear** - **1.** *ḥlef, qsem be-ḷḷah.*

She swears she's telling the truth. *ka-teḥlef bin ka-tqul l-ḥeqq.* **2.** *sebb, qal iqul klam s-sebb.* That soldier is always swearing. *dak l-ɛeskri dima ka-isebb.* **3.** *šhed.* Can you swear to that? *imken-lek tešhed b-dak š-ši?*

to swear in – *ḥellef.* Has the witness been sworn in yet? *ḥellfu š-šahed wella ma-zal?*

sweat – *ɛṛeq* pl. *ɛṛuqat.* Wipe the sweat from your forehead. *mseḥ le-ɛṛeq men žbehtek.*

to sweat – *ɛṛeq.*

to **sweep** – **1.** *šeṭṭeb.* Did you sweep the bedroom? *šeṭṭebti bit n-nɛas?* **2.** *džeṛžeṛ.* Her dress sweeps the ground. *ksuwtha ka-ddžeṛžeṛ f-l-eṛḍ.*

sweet – **1.** *ḥlu* f. *-wa* pl. *-win.* These apples are very sweet. *had t-teffaḥat ḥluwin bezzaf.* **2.** *ḥlilu, ḷṭiyef.* She is a very sweet girl. *hiya bnita ḥlilwa bezzaf.*

sweets – *fanid* (sg.), *ḥlawi* (pl.). I don't care much for sweets. *ma-ɛendi-šay bezzaf mɛa le-ḥlawi.*

to **swell** – *ttenfex.* My ankle is all swollen. *kɛebti kollha ttnefxet.*

**Does he have a swelled head? *waš ṛaṣu kbir?* or *waš huwa menfux?*

swelling – *nefx.* Has the swelling gone down? *ṛžeɛ n-nefx?*

swim – *ɛewma* pl. *-t.* How about a swim now? *še-ḍher-lek f-ši-ɛewma daba?*

to take a swim – *ḍṛeb ši-ɛewma.* He takes a swim every morning. *ka-iḍṛeb ɛewma koll ṣbaḥ.*

to swim – **1.** *ɛam iɛum.* Do you know how to swim? *ka-teɛṛef tɛum?* **2.** *qṭeɛ be-l-ɛewm.* Are we going to swim the lake? *waš ġad nqeṭɛu ḍ-ḍaya be-l-ɛewm?*

swing – *maṭiša* pl. *-t.* We have a swing in our garden. *ɛendna maṭiša fe-l-ɛeṛṣa dyalna.*

in full swing – *fe-l-qemma.* The party was in full swing. *l-ḥefla kanet fe-l-qemma dyalha.*

to swing – **1.** *ṭaš iṭiš.* You'll fall off if you swing so high. *ila ṭešti ḥetta l-l-fuq ṛak ṭṭiḥ.* **2.** *ṭiyyeš.* She swings her arms when she walks. *ka-ṭṭiyyeš iddiha mnin ka-tkun mašya.*

to swing around – *ḍuwweṛ.* Swing the car around. *ḍuwweṛ s-siyaṛa.*

switch – *ṭeffaya* pl. *-t.* The switch is next to the door. *ṭ-ṭeffaya ṛaha ḥda l-bab.*

to switch – **1.** *duwwez, ḥewwel.* The train was switched to another track. *l-qiṭar tḥewwel l-sekka x̂ṛa.* **2.** *beddel.* Let's switch places. *aži nbeddlu le-mwaḍeɛ.* **3.** *tbadel.* I don't know how we switched umbrellas. *ma-ɛreft-ši kif tbadelna le-mḍuḷa.*

to switch off – *ṭfa iṭfi.* Did you switch the light off? *ṭfiti ḍ-ḍuw?*

to switch on – **1.** *šɛel.* Switch on the light. *šɛel ḍ-ḍuw.* **2.** *ḍuwweṛ.* Switch on the ignition. *ḍuwweṛ l-muṭuṛ.*

sword – *sif* pl. *syuf, syufa.*

symbol – *ṛemz* pl. *ṛmuz.*

to **sympathize** – *ḥenn.* I can sympathize with you. *ka-imken-li nḥenn mennek.*

sympathy – *mḥenna* pl. *-t.* He has no sympathy for her. *ma-ɛendu mḥenna ɛliha.*

**You have my sincere sympathy. *l-baṛaka f-ṛaṣek.*

Syria – *surya.*

Syrian – *suri* adj. pl. *-yin,* n. pl. *hel surya.*

system – **1.** *ṭaṛiqa* pl. *-t, ṭuṛuq.* I have a better system. *ɛendi ṭaṛiqa hsen men ḥadik.* **2.** *maɛida* pl. *-t.* My system can't take that. *maɛidti ma-tthemmel-ši dak š-ši.*

T

table – **1.** *ṭabḷa, ṭebḷa* pl. *ṭwabeḷ.* Put the table in the middle of the room. *ḥeṭṭ ṭ-ṭabḷa f-weṣṭ l-bit.* **2.** *mida* pl. *-t, myadi.* There isn't much food on the table. *ma-kayen-š makla bezzaf fuq l-mida.* **3.** *luḥa* pl. *-t, lwaḥ, lwaḥi.* The figures are given in the table on page 20. *imken-lek tṣib ṛ-ṛqam fe-l-luḥa f-ṣefḥa reqm ɛešṛin.*

tablecloth – *zif de-ṭ-ṭabḷa* pl. *zyaf, zyuf de-ṭ-ṭabḷa.*

tack – *mṣimeṛ* pl. *mṣimṛat, meṣmaṛ mgeṛṛeṣ* pl. *mṣameṛ mgeṛṛṣin.*

Tafilalet – *tafilalet.*

native of Tafilalet – *filali* adj. pl. *-yin,* n. pl. *filala.*

tail – *šuwwal* pl. *šwawel.* My dog has

a short tail. *l-kelb dyali Ɛendu šuwwal qṣiṛ.*

**Can you make head or tail of what he's saying? *waš imken-lek tefhem had š-ši lli ka-iqul?* —Head(s) or tail(s)? *ṣfeṛ wella khel?*

tail light - *ḍuw ḷuṛani* pl. *ḍwaw ḷuṛaniyin.*

tailor - *xeyyaṭ.* pl. *-a.*

take - *medxul.* The take at the game ran to fifty thousand dollars. *ṭaḥ l-medxul de-l-leƐba b-xemsin ʔalf ḍuḷar.*

to take - 1. *xda yaxod.* Who took my ties? *škun lli xda-li gṛabaṭati?* —Why don't you take the plane? *Ɛlaš ma-taxod-š ṭ-ṭiyaṛa?* —Take these pills three times daily after meals. *xud had l-ḥebbat tlata de-l-meṛṛat fe-n-nhaṛ men beƐd l-makla.* —What else do you want to take with you? *šnu axoṛ bġiti taxod mƐak?* 2. *qbeṭ, qbeḍ.* She took her child by the hand. *qebṭet weldha f-yeddu.* 3. *Ɛebba, dda iddi.* He wants to take me to dinner. *bġa iƐebbini ntƐešša.* 4. *qbel.* Take my advice. *qbel n-naṣaḥ dyali.* 5. *wessel, dda iddi.* Who's taking her to the station? *škun ġadi iwesselha l-lagaṛ?* 6. *xeṣṣ.* How long will it take you? *šḥal de-l-weqt ixeṣṣek?* 7. *Ɛmel.* All necessary measures were taken. *Ɛemlu l-iḥtiyaḍat lli lazmin.*

**That doesn't take much brains. *had š-ši ma ka-iherres šay ṛ-ṛaṣ.* —Let's take a quick dip. *yaḷḷah nġeṭṣu šwiya fe-l-ma.* —All seats are taken. *le-blaṣat kollhom mƐemmṛin.* —I'll take the responsibility. *ana nkun l-mesʔul.* —He took the town by storm. *Ɛmel ḍ-ḍešša f-le-mdina.* —I take it you don't like it. *bayen Ɛlik ma-bġitiha-š.* —Shall we take a chance? *nƐemlu Ɛla ḷḷah?* —Let's take a chance on him. *yaḷḷah nġeṛṛbuh.* —You'll have to take a firm hold of things. *xeṣṣek teƐmel muṛaqaba qwiya l-l-masaʔil.* —I take back what I said. *ka-ntṛažeƐ fe-klami.* —I'm taking it easy today. *ma-ġad nherres ṛaṣi bezzaf l-yum.* —Take it easy! *šwiya Ɛlik!* —He takes too many liberties. *huwa mserreḥ bezzaf.* —I don't know why she took offense. *ma-Ɛṛeft Ɛlaš ṭayeṛ-lha.* —Did the doctor take your

temperature this morning? *waš Ɛbeṛ-lek ṭ-ṭbib s-sxana l-yum fe-ṣ-ṣbaḥ?*

to take a nap - *tmedd.* We always take a nap after dinner. *dima ka-ntmeddu men beƐd le-ġda.*

to take a short cut - *qteƐ ṭ-ṭriq.* You can take a short cut here. *imken-lek teqteƐ ṭ-ṭriq men hna.*

to take a walk - *tsara.* Would you like for us to take a little walk? *waš bġiti ntsaraw šwiya?*

to take after - *Ɛmel bḥal.* He takes after his father. *ka-yeƐmel bḥal bbah.*

to take back - *ṛeššeƐ.* When are you going to take his car back to him? *fuq-aš ġad tṛeššeƐ-lu s-siyaṛa dyalu?*

to take care of - *theḷḷa f-, ṛedd l-bal Ɛla.* We'll take care of everything. *daba ntheḷḷaw f-koll ḥaža.* —He takes good care of his things. *ka-itheḷḷa fe-ḥwayžu bezzaf.* —You should take better care of yourself. *ḥsen-lek ttheḷḷa f-ṛasek.*

to take charge of - *tkellef b-.* Who will take charge of my work? *škun ġad itkellef be-l-xedma dyali?*

to take down - 1. *ḥeyyed.* Take the picture down from the wall. *ḥeyyed t-teṣwiṛa men l-ḥiṭ.* 2. *kteb.* Take down my address! *kteb l-Ɛonwan dyali.* 3. *sežžel.* Who's taking down the minutes? *škun lli ka-isežžel l-gelsa?*

**I took him down a peg or two. *ṭeyyeḥt-lu be-l-qobba dyalu.*

to take hold of - *qbeṭ.* Take hold of the ropes! *qbeṭ t-twaḷ.*

to take in - 1. *rbeḥ.* He doesn't take in much more than a few dollars per day. *ma-ka-irbeḥ-š kteṛ men ši-ḍuḷaṛat fe-n-nhaṛ.* 2. *nqeṣ.* Will you take this dress in at the waist for me? *waš bġiti tenqeṣ-li had l-keswa f-le-ḥzam?* 3. *ḍeyyef.* I took in a child for the winter. *ḍeyyeft waḥed d-derri f-weqt l-berd.* 4. *Ɛbeṛ Ɛla.* Have you been taken in again? *waš Ɛebṛu Ɛlik Ɛawtani?*

to take off - 1. *ḥeyyed, zuwwel.* —I'm taking off my coat. *ka-nḥeyyed l-kebbuṭ dyali.* 2. *qelleƐ.* When does the plane take off? *fuq-aš ġadi tqelleƐ ṭ-ṭiyaṛa?*

to take on - 1. *xeddem.* I hear the factory is taking on some new workers. *smeƐt bin l-meƐmel ġadi *ixeddem ši-xeddama ždad.* 2. *xda yaxod.* In Rabat we'll take on two more cars. *fe-ṛ-ṛbaṭ naxdu žuž de-l-faguwat x̂ṛin.* 3. *bda ibda.* I took on a new job yesterday. *bdit xedma ždida l-bareḥ.*

to take out - *ḥeyyed, zuwwel.* Did you take it out of the box? *waš zuwweltih men ṣ-ṣenduq?*

to take part in - *tšarek f-.* I didn't take part in the discussion. *ma-tšarekt-š fe-l-muḍakaṛa.*

to take revenge - *ntaqem.* She took revenge on him. *ntaqmet mennu.*

to take sick - *ṭaḥ iṭiḥ mṛiḍ.* When did you take sick? *fuq-aš ṭeḥti mṛiḍ?*

to take up with - *txaleṭ mƐa.* I wouldn't take up with those people if I were you. *ana fe-bḷastek ma-ntxaleṭ-š mƐa had n-nas.*

talk - 1. *xeṭba* pl. *-t.* His talk was much too long. *l-xeṭba dyalu kanet ṭwila bezzaf.* 2. *klam.* Oh that's just talk! *hada ġir klam!*

**I had a long talk with him. *bqit ntkellem mƐah bezzaf.* --Her marriage is the talk of the town. *Ɛersha f-fomm n-nas d-le-mdina kollha.* --I had a heart-to-heart talk with him. *ddakeṛt mƐah menni lilu.*

to talk - *tkellem, hḍeṛ.* Don't you think he talks too much? *waš ban-lek bin ka-yehḍeṛ bezzaf?* --Now you're talking sense. *daba ka-ttkellem b-Ɛeqlek.*

tall - 1. *ṭwiḷ* pl. *ṭwaḷ.* She's tall and thin. *hiya ṭwiḷa u-ṛqiqa.* 2. *Ɛali.* Have you ever seen such a tall building? *waš Ɛemmṛek šefti ši-bni Ɛali bḥal hada?*

**How tall are you? *šḥal Ɛendek fe-ṭ-ṭuḷ?* --You don't expect me to believe that tall story, do you? *waš itteḥsabek ġadi ntiq b-had le-xṛafa?*

to **tan** - *dbeġ.* What do you use in tanning hides? *š-ka-testeƐmel baš ddbeġ ž-žlud?*

tangerine - *menḍaṛina* pl. *-t* coll. *menḍaṛin.*

Tangier - *ṭanža.*

native of Tangier - *ṭanžawi* adj. pl. *-yin,* n.pl. *hel ṭanža.*

tank - 1. *sariž* pl. *swarež.* Look at those big oil tanks. *šuf duk s-swarež de-z-zit le-kbaṛ.* 2. *ṭeng* pl. *ṭnuga.* A column of tanks led the attack. *waḥed ṣeff ṭ-ṭnuga guwwed l-hežma.*

tanner - *debbaġ* pl. *-a.*

tannery - *ḍaṛ d-dbeġ* pl. *ḍyuṛ d-dbeġ.*

tanning - *tadebbaġet.*

tap - *bezbuz* pl. *bzabez.* I can't get the tap out of the barrel. *ma-qḍeṛt-š nzuwwel l-bezbuz men l-bermil.*

to tap - 1. *deqq be-šwiya.* He tapped on the window. *deqq fe-š-šeṛžem be-šwiya.* 2. *ṭebbeḷ l-.* She tapped me on the shoulder. *ṭebbḷet-li Ɛla ktafi.*

tape - *sfifa* pl. *-t, sfayef.* I'd like five meters of the white tape. *bġit xemsa mitru d-dak s-sfifa l-biḍa.*

tape recorder - *sežžala* pl. *-t.*

tapeworm - *sinta* pl. *-t.*

tar - *zeft, qeṭṛan.*

target - *šaṛa* pl. *-t.*

tart - *ḥameḍ.* The apples have a tart taste. *had t-teffaḥ ḥameḍ.*

taste - 1. *madaq* pl. *-at.* This meat has a peculiar taste. *had l-lḥem Ɛendu madaq f-ši-škel.* 2. *duq.* She has good taste. *Ɛendha duq mezyan.* --Suit your own taste. *tebbeƐ duqek.* --She is always dressed in good taste. *hiya dima labsa ḥwayež fihom d-duq.*

**I just want a taste of it. *bġit nduqha u-kan.* --That remark was really in bad taste. *dak l-mulaḥaḍa kanet basla.*

to taste - *daq iduq.* Taste this coffee. *duq had l-qehwa.*

**The soup tastes good. *ṣ-ṣubba ldida.*

to taste of - *fih d-duq d-.* It tastes of vinegar. *fih d-duq de-l-xell.*

tasteless - (*lli*) *ma-Ɛendu duq.* The food is tasteless. *l-makla ma-Ɛendha duq.*

tax - *ḍaṛiba* pl. *-t.* Have you paid your taxes yet? *waš xeḷḷeṣti ḍ-ḍaṛiba wella ma-zal?*

to tax - *Ɛmel ḍaṛiba Ɛla.* Everybody was taxed two dollars. *Ɛemlu Ɛla koll waḥed ḍaṛiba d-žuž ḍuḷaṛ.*

tax collector - *mul ḍ-ḍaṛiba* pl. *mwalin, ḍ-ḍaṛiba.*

taxi - *ṭaksi* pl. *-yat.* I took a taxi from the station. *xdit ṭaksi men l-lagaṛ.*

tea - *atay* (not used with art).

to **teach** - 1. *Ɛellem.* Who taught you

that? *škun lli ɛellmek had š-ši?* —I'll teach him! *daba nɛellmu!* —I'll teach him not to disturb me! *daba nɛellmu iɛawed ibessel ɛliya!* 2. *qeṛṛa.* He teaches in a boys' school. *ka-iqeṛṛi f-waḥed l-medṛaṣa d-le-wlad.*

teacher - *fqi* pl. *feqya* f. *fqiha* pl. *-t; muɛellim.* He always wanted to be a teacher. *dima kan ka-itmenna ikun fqi.*

teakettle - *beqraž* pl. *bqarež.*

team - *feṛqa* pl. *-t.* Our team has won every game this year. *l-feṛqa dyalna rebḥet l-leɛbat kollhom had l-ɛam.*

teamwork - *yedd ž-žmaɛa, xedma ž-žmaɛa.* Teamwork did it. *yedd ž-žmaɛa daretha.*

teapot - *berrad* pl. *brared.*

tear - *tešriga* pl. *-t, teqṭiɛa* pl. *-t.* Can you mend this tear? *waš imken-lek tṛeqqeɛ had t-tešriga?*

to tear - 1. *qelleɛ.* She tore the letter out of his hand. *qellɛet le-bṛa men yeddu.* 2. *tšerreg.* Careful, the rope is tearing! *be-šwiya l-qennba ka-tšerreg!* 3. *qeṭṭeɛ.* You tore my coat with that nail. *qeṭṭeɛti-li l-kebbuṭ dyali b-dak l-meṣmaṛ.*

to tear down - *hdem.* The house was torn down last year. *hedmu ḍ-ḍaṛ l-ɛam lli fat.*

to tear off - 1. *qeṭṭeɛ.* Tear me off a piece of paper. *qeṭṭeɛ-li wṛiqa.* 2. *ṭaḥ iṭiḥ.* One of my buttons tore off. *ṭaḥ-li waḥed ṣ-ṣḍafa.*

to tear up - *šerreg.* I hope you tore that letter up. *ka-ntmenna bin šerregti le-bṛa.*

tear - *demɛa* pl. *dmuɛ.* Tears won't help you. *d-dmuɛ ma-ġadi iɛawnuk l-ḥetta ḥaža.*

to **tease** - *tmelleġ mɛa, qelleq b-le-mzaḥ, qelleq b-le-mlaġa.* Everyone teases him. *koll waḥed ka-itmelleġ mɛah.*

telegram - *tiligṛam,* pl. *-at.*

telephone - *tilifun* pl. *-at.*

to telephone - *ḍṛeb t-tilifun l-.* Telephone me tomorrow at six. *ḍṛeb-li t-tilifun ġedda fe-s-setta.*

telescope - *tiliskup* pl. *-at; mṛayet l-hend.*

to **tell** - 1. *qal iqul.* Tell him your name. *qul-lu smiytek.* —He told me to give you this letter. *qal-li neɛṭik had le-bṛa.* 2. *ɛewwed.* I'll tell you the whole story. *daba nɛewwed-lek dak š-ši lli wqeɛ kollu.* 3. *ɛṛef.* I can't tell one from the other. *ma-ka-neɛṛef hada men hada.* —You can never tell what's going to happen. *ɛemmṛek ma-imken-lek teɛṛef š-ġad yuqeɛ.* —You can tell by his voice that he has a cold. *b-ḥelqu imken-lek teɛṛef bin mṛuwweḥ.*

**Has your little boy learned how to tell time yet? *waš weldek ṣ-ṣġiṛ bda yeɛṛef išuf s-saɛa?*

temper - *ṭbeɛ.* He has an even temper. *ṭebɛu mezyan.*

to lose one's temper - *ṭaṛ iṭiṛ-lu.* He loses his temper easily. *ka-iṭiṛ-lu be-z-zerba.*

temperature - *sxana.* Did you take his temperature? *waš ɛberti-lu s-sxana?*

temple - 1. *meɛbed* pl. *mɛabed.* Is this a temple or a church? *waš hada meɛbed wella knisiya?* 2. *meḍḍaġa* pl. *mḍaḍeġ.* He's getting gray at the temples already. *šab fe-mḍaḍġu beɛda.*

temporary - *muweqqat.* This is a temporary solution. *hada fṣal muweqqat..*

to **tempt** - *ġwa iġwi.* That doesn't tempt me. *had š-ši ma-ka-iġwini-š.*

**I was tempted to tell him the truth. *kont ṭayeb baš nqul-lu l-ḥeqq.*

ten - *ɛešṛa, ɛešṛ.*

to **tend** - 1. *qabel, gabel.* Who's going to tend to the furnace? *škun ġad igabel l-boṛma?* 2. *ḥḍa yeḥḍi.* Who's going to tend the children? *škun lli ġad yeḥḍi d-drari?*

**Tend to your own business. *ddiha f-ṣuq ṛaṣek.* —He tends to be partial. *ka-yeɛmel l-ferẓ.*

tender - *fti.* The meat is so tender you can cut it with a fork. *men kteṛ l-lḥem fti imken-lek tqeṭɛu be-l-foṛšiṭa.*

tent - *xima* pl. *xyem, xyam.*

tenth - 1. (ordinal) *ɛašeṛ.* 2. (fraction) *ɛušuṛ* pl. *-at.*

term - 1. *šeṛṭ* pl. *šuṛuṭ, šṛuṭ, šuṛuṭat.* The terms are hard. *š-šuṛuṭ waɛrin.* 2. *modda* pl. *-t.* His term will end in October. *l-modda dyalu ġad ttsala fe-ktubeṛ.*

**We're on bad terms. *ḥna mxaṣmin.* —We're on good terms. *l-ɛalaqat binatna mezyanin.*

terrace - *ṣṭaḥ* pl. *-at, ṣṭuḥ, ṣṭuḥa, ṣṭiḥan.*
to **terrify** - *qtel be-l-xelƐa.* He terrified me. *qtelni be-l-xelƐa.*
terror - *xelƐa.* We were speechless with terror. *ma-qdeṛna-š ntkellmu be-l-xelƐa lli weqƐet-lna.*
test - *mtiḥan* pl. *-t, xtibaṛ* pl. *-at.* You have to take a test before they give you a driver's license. *xeṣṣek dduwwez mtiḥan qbel-ma yeƐṭiwek tesriḥ de-ṣ-ṣugan.* --Did you take all your tests? *waš duwwezti le-mtiḥanat kollhom?*
to test - **1.** *duwwez lxtibaṛ, duwwez mtiḥan.* I was tested in arithmetic today. *duwwzu-li mtiḥan d-le-ḥsab l-yum.* **2.** *žeṛṛeb.* You better test the brakes. *ḥsen-lek džeṛṛeb le-ḥṣayeṛ.*
to **testify** - *šehhed.* Have you anything further to testify? *waš Ɛendek si-ḥaža xṛa Ɛlaš tšehhed?*
to testify to - *šhed l-.* Can you testify to that? *waš imken-lek tešhed l-had š-ši?*
Tetuan - *tiṭṭawen, tesṭawen, tiṭwan.*
native of Tetuan - *tiṭwani* adj. pl. *tiṭwaniyen; teṭṭawni* adj. pl. *teṭṭawniyen;* n. pl. *hel tiṭwan.*
text - *neṣṣ* pl. *nṣaṣ, nṣuṣ, nuṣuṣ.*
than - *men.* He's older than his brother. *huwa kbeṛ men xah.*
to **thank** - *škeṛ.* I can't thank you enough. *ma-kfawni-š klami baš nšekṛek.* --You have only yourself to thank for this mess. *škeṛ raṣek Ɛla had l-xaḷuṭa.*
**Thank God!, Thank goodness!, Thank heaven(s)! *l-ḥemdu l-llah!*
--Thank you. *baṛaka ḷḷahu fik.*
thankful - *(lli) ƐtaṛeF.* We are very thankful to you. *ḥna neƐtaṛfu be-l-xir dyalek.*
thanks - *škiṛ.* I don't expect any thanks from him. *ma-ka-ntsenna-š škiṛ mennu.*
**Many thanks - *baṛaka llahu fik.*
that - **1.** *dak š-ši.* What does that mean? *šnu meƐna dak š-ši?* **2.** (near) *had;* (far) *hadak* or *dak,* f. *hadik* or *dik,* pl. *haduk* or *duk.* Look at that magnificent view. *šuf had l-menḍeṛ l-Ɛažib.* --Would you like that little one? *waš tebġi hadak ṣ-ṣġiṛ?* **3.** *lli.* Who's the man that just came in? *škun ṛ-ṛažel lli Ɛad dxel?* --Do you know the story (that) he told us? *waš ka-teƐṛef le-xṛafa lli Ɛewwed-lna.* **4.** *aš.* Where's the ship that you were riding in? *fayn l-baxiṛa f-aš kontiw rakbin?* **5.** *bin, billa.* They told him that his brother had left. *xebṛuh bin xah mša.*
**It's pretty good at that. *moƐtabaṛ baṛaka.*
--We'll leave it at that. *nḥeṣṛuha hna.* --I'm sorry that this happened. *ana met?essef Ɛla had š-ši lli wqeƐ.* --I don't want that much milk. *ma-bġit-š had le-ḥlib kollu.* --He's not that tall. *ma-Ɛendu-š had ṭ-ṭuḷa.* --What will you get by that? *aš ġadi terbeḥ f-had š-ši?* --How about that? *šu ban-lek Ɛla dak š-ši?* --That's life! *hadi hiya d-denya!* --Well, that's that! *salina daba.*
that is - *yeƐni.* I'll come tomorrow, that is, if it doesn't rain. *ġadi nži ġedda, yeƐni ila ma-ṭaḥet š-šta.*
that (one) *hadak* f. *hadik* pl. *haduk.* Take that one that's on the table. *xud hadak lli fuq ṭ-ṭabḷa.*
that way - *hakka, hakda.* You can't do it that way. *ma-imken-lek-s teƐmelha hakka.*
thaw - *duban de-t-telž.* This year the thaw set in rather early. *had l-Ɛam d-duban de-t-telž wqeƐ bekri.*
to thaw - *dab idub.* The ice is thawing. *ka-idub t-telž.*
**He was very reserved at first, but after a while he began to thaw. *fe-l-luwwel kan meqbuṭ u-men beƐd waḥed š-šwiya bda nṭḷeq.*
the - *l-* (*le-* before consonant clusters; assimilated before *d, ḍ, n, r, s, ṣ, t, ṭ, z, ẓ, š, l,* and usually *ž*). Look at the bread. *šuf l-xobz.* --Look at the donkey. *šuf le-ḥmaṛ.* --The house is big, and the car is small. *ḍ-ḍaṛ kbira u-s-siyaṛa ṣġiṛa.* --The guests are all gone. *ḍ-ḍyaf xollhom mšaw.*
the...the - *ma-ḥedd... u-.* The more she studies, the worse she gets. *ma-ḥeddha ka-teqṛa u-hiya ttfelles.*
theater - *meṣṛeḥ* pl. *mṣaṛeḥ.*
theft - *ṣṛiqa* pl. *-t.*
their - *-hom, dyalhom.* Do you know their address? *waš ka-teƐṛef Ɛonwanhom?*
theirs - *dyalhom.* Our house isin't as big as theirs. *ḍaṛna ma-ši qedd dyalhom.*
them - **1.** *-hom.* We haven't seen them. *ma-šefnahom-š.* --Give them a car. *Ɛṭihom ṭumubil.* **2.** *-lhom.* I

brought them a book. *žebt-lhom ktab.*

themselves – 1. *ṛaṣhom.* They killed themselves. *qetlu ṛaṣhom.* 2. *b-yeddihom, b-ṛaṣhom.* They did it themselves. *Ɛemluha b-yeddihom.*

among themselves – *binathom.* They discussed the matter among themselves. *ddakṛu l-qaḍiya binathom.*

by themselves – *b-waḥedhom.* Did they really do all that work by themselves? *waš be-ṣ-ṣeḥḥ daru l-xedma kollha b-waḥedhom?*

then – 1. *men beƐd.* What did he do then? *šnu Ɛmel men beƐd?* —Then what happened? *šnu wqeƐ men beƐd?* 2. *iden.* Then everything is settled. *iden koll-ši mṛeṣṣi.*

then and there – *f-dik s-saƐa.* Why didn't you take it then and there? *Ɛlaš ma-xditiha f-dik s-saƐa?*

by then – *f-had l-weqt, f-dak l-weqt.* Call Tuesday. We'll know by then. *Ɛeyyeṭ fe-nhaṛ t-tlat, daba nšufu f-had l-weqt.*

(every) now and then – *saƐa saƐa, meṛṛa meṛṛa.* We go to the movies now and then. *ka-nemšiw le-s-sinima saƐa saƐa.*

there – 1. *temma, temmak, hnak, temmaya.* My father is there now. *ḅḅah temma daba.* 2. *l-temma, l-temmak, le-hnak, l-temmaya.* She went there yesterday. *mšat l-temma l-bareḥ.*

**There, that's enough for me. *waxxa, had š-ši baṛaka Ɛliya.* —I'm afraid he's not quite all there. *xeftu ikun ḥmeq šwiya.* —There you are! I was looking all over for you. *ha-nta! kont ka-nqelleb Ɛlik.* —There you are! It's all done. *ṣafi. salit koll-ši.* —There you are! Now you're sneezing! *iwa šefti! ha-nta ka-teƐṭes!*

here and there – *hna u-hna, f-ši-maḥellat.* You can still find a copy here and there. *imken-lek tṣib waḥed n-nesxa hna u-hna.*

there is, there are – *kayen* f. *kayna* pl. *kaynin.* There are a few good shops in town. *kaynin šwiya d-le-ḥwanet mezyanin f-le-mdina.*

therefore – *iden.* I therefore assume it is so. *iden ġadi nefṛeḍ had š-ši ikun.*

these – see 'this'.

they – *huma.* They're alive. *huma Ɛayšin.*

thick – 1. *qaṣeḥ.* The soup is too thick. *ṣ-ṣubba qaṣḥa bezzaf.* 2. *ġliḍ* pl. *ġlaḍ.* This board isn't very thick. *had l-luḥa ma-ġliḍa-š bezzaf.*

**I'll go through thick and thin for him. *ġadi neƐmel šnu-ma kan lilu.* —He's too thick to understand that. *huwa ḥmaṛ baš ifhem had š-ši.*

thief – *xuwwan* pl. *-a, seṛṛaq* pl. *-a.*

thigh – *fxed.* pl. *fxaḍ.*

thimble – *ḥelqa* pl. *-t, ḥlaqi.*

thin – 1. *rhif* pl. *rhaf.* The paper is too thin. *l-kaġiṭ rhif bezzaf.* 2. *ṛqiq* pl. *ṛqaq.* She got thin. *režƐet ṛqiqa.* 3. *ḍƐif* pl. *ḍƐaf.* Her face is very thin. *wžehha ḍƐif.*

**That's a pretty thin excuse. *hada Ɛḍeṛ qbiḥ.*

to (get) thin – 1. *rhaf.* His hair is thinning. *rhaf-lu šeƐṛu.* 2. *ṛqaq.* She got thin. *ṛqaqet.*

to thin out – *qlal.* Let's wait until the crowd thins out. *yaḷḷah ntsennaw ḥetta iqlal z-zḥam.*

thing – 1. *ḥaža* pl. *ḥwayež.* Have you packed all your things yet? *waš žmeƐti ḥwayžek kollhom fe-l-bakit wella ma-zal?* —I don't know a single thing about it. *ma-ka-neƐṛef ḥetta ḥaža mennu.* —We've heard a lot of nice things about you. *smeƐna bezzaf d-le-ḥwayež mezyanin Ɛlik.* 2. *ši.* There is no such thing. *had š-ši ma-kayen-š.*

**It all adds up to the same thing. *kif kif* or *bḥal bḥal.* —How are things? *še-xbaṛ koll-ši?* —You poor little thing! *meskin!* —Well, of all things, what are you doing here? *u-nta beƐda qul-li aš ka-teƐmel hna?*

not a thing – *ḥetta ḥaža.* We haven't done a thing all week. *ma-Ɛmelna ḥetta ḥaža ž-žemƐa kollha.*

to **think** – 1. *xemmem.* He's never really learned how to think. *Ɛemmṛu ma-tƐellem ixemmem.* —Now he thinks differently. *daba ka-ixemmem fe-škel axoṛ.* —What are you thinking about? *f-aš ka-txemmem?* —Think twice before you do it. *xemmem bezzaf qbel ma-ddirha.* 2. *ban-lu.* Don't you think it's too warm? *ma-ban-lek-š bin kayen ṣ-ṣehḍ bezzaf?* 3. *nwa inwi ṛaṣu.* She thinks she knows everything. *nawya ṛaṣha ka-teƐṛef koll-ši.* 4. *ḍenn.* We thought he was gone. *ḍennina bin mša.* 5. *Ɛqel.* I can't think of his address right now.

f-had s-saƐa ma-Ɛqelt-š Ɛel l-Ɛonwan dyalu.
**That's what you think! *hada klamek!* --I'll think about it. *ġadi nšuf.* --Think nothing of it (no harm done)! *ma-fiha bas!* --You're welcome, think nothing of it! *bla žmil!*
to think up - *xtaṛeƐ.* Who thought that up? *škun lli xtaṛeƐ had š-ši?*

third - **1.** *tulut* pl. *-at.* A third of that will be enough. *iqeddni tulut men had š-ši.* **2.** *talet.* We couldn't stay for the third game. *ma-mken-lna-š nḥeḍṛu fe-l-leƐba t-talta.* --Give me one third-class ticket to Casablanca. *Ɛṭini weṛqa de-ṭ-ṭabaqa t-talta le-ḍ-ḍaṛ l-biḍa.*

thirst - *Ɛṭeš.* I can't quench my thirst. *ma-imken-li-š nberred le-Ɛṭeš dyali.*

thirsty - *Ɛeṭšan.* I'm very thirsty. *ana Ɛeṭšan bezzaf.*

thirteen - *telṭaš.*

thirty - *tlatin.*

this - **1.** *had.* Do you know this man? *waš ka-teƐṛef had ṛ-ṛažel?* --Why did you buy this house? *Ɛlaš šriti had ḍ-ḍaṛ?* **2.** *hada* f. *hadi* pl. *hadu.* This is my house. *hadi ḍaṛi.* **3.** *had š-ši.* What's this? *šnu had š-ši?*
this far - **1.** *had ṭ-ṭṛiq kollha.* Do you always have to walk this far? *waš dima lazem Ɛlik ttmešša had ṭ-ṭṛiq kollha?* **2.** *ḥetta le-hna.* Did he come this far? *waš ža ḥetta le-hna?*
this minute - *daba daba.* Come here this minute! *ʔaži daba daba!*
this morning - *l-yum fe-ṣ-ṣbaḥ.* I met her on the street this morning. *tlaqitha fe-z-zenqa l-yum fe-ṣ-ṣbaḥ.*

thorn - *šuka* pl. *-t* coll. *šuk.* The tree is full of thorns. *š-šežṛa Ɛamṛa be-š-šuk.*

thorough - *ḥadeq.* He's very thorough in everything he does. *huwa ḥadeq bezzaf fe-šnu ka-yeƐmel.*

thoroughly - *men ṛ-ṛaṣ ḥetta le-r-režlin.* It's been thoroughly tested. *biyynuha-lhom men ṛ-ṛaṣ ḥetta le-r-režlin.*

those - see 'that'.

though - **1.** *waxxa.* Though he knew it he didn't tell me anything about it. *waxxa kan Ɛaṛefha ma-bġa-š iqulha-li.* **2.** *walayenni.* I'll do it! Not now, though. *ġad neƐmelha, walayenni ma-ši daba.*
as though - *bḥal ila.* He acted as though he were sick. *Ɛmel bḥal ila kan mṛiḍ.*
**It looks as though it may rain. *tqul Ɛliha ġad ṭṭiḥ š-šta.*
even though - *waxxa.* He went there even though I warned him against it. *mša l-temma waxxa weṣṣitu ma-imši.*

thought - *texmima* pl. *-t* coll. *texmim, texmam; tefkiṛa* pl. *-t.* The very thought of it makes me sick. *t-texmima fiha ka-tmeṛṛeḍni.*
**I'll have to give this matter some thought. *xeṣṣni mxemmem šwiya f-had l-qaḍiya.*

thousand - *ʔalef* pl. *ʔalaf, ʔuluf.*

thread - **1.** *xiṭ, xeyṭ* pl. *xyuṭ.* Do you have a needle and thread? *waš Ɛendek l-ibṛa u-l-xiṭ?* **2.** *ḥṛuf* (pl.). The thread on this screw is worn out. *le-ḥṛuf d-had-l-luleb sxaw.*
**His life hung by a thread. *ḥayatu kanet qabṭa be-xwiyyeṭ.*
to thread - *zelleg.* I'll thread the needle for you. *daba nzelleg l-xiṭ lilek.*

to **threaten** - *hedded.* He threatned to leave if he didn't get a raise. *hedded b-le-mši ila ma-Ɛṭaw-š z-zyada.* --The entire city is threatened by the disease. *le-mdina kollha mehduda be-l-meṛḍ.*
**It's threatening to rain. *tqul Ɛliha ġadi ṭṭiḥ š-šta.*

three - *tlata, telt.* I have three books. *Ɛendi tlata d-le-ktub* or *Ɛendi telt ktub.*

to **thresh** - *dres.* They're threshing the wheat now. *ka-idersu ẓ-ẓṛeƐ daba.*

thrifty - *mḥawel.* She's a thrifty woman. *hiya mṛa mḥawla.*

throat - **1.** *ḥelq* pl. *ḥluq, ḥluqa.* The doctor painted my throat. *ṭ-ṭbib dhen-li ḥelqi.* --I have a sore throat. *ka-ideṛṛni ḥelqi.* --He cleared his throat and continued. *serreḥ ḥelqu u-zad.* **2.** *geṛžuṭa* pl. *gṛažeṭ, geṛžuma* pl. *gṛažem.* They cut his throat. *qeṭƐu-lu l-geṛžuṭa.*
**She wanted to say something, but the words stuck in her throat. *bġat tqul ši-ḥaža walayenni weḥlu-lha le-klam.*

throne - *Ɛeṛš* pl. *Ɛṛuš, Ɛṛaš.*

through - **1.** *Ɛla sabab.* The work was held up two weeks through his negligence. *weqfet l-xedma žmeƐtayn Ɛla sabab t-taṛaxi dyalu.* **2.** *bin.* The bullet passed through the wall. *l-qeṛṭaṣa dazet bin l-ḥiṭ.* --That man can see through walls. *dak*

ṛ-ṛažel imken-lu išuf bin le-ḥyuṭ. 3. *men.* The ball came through the window. *dexlet l-kuṛa men š-šeṛžem.*
**He fell through the floor. *l-eṛḍ xwat bih.* --The deal fell through. *ma-xedmet-š l-qaḍiya.* --We went through the woods. *qṭeƐna l-ġaba.*
through and through - *men ṛ-ṛaṣ ḥetta le-r-režlin.* We were soaked through and through. *konna fazgin men ṛ-ṛaṣ ḥetta le-r-režlin.*
to be through - 1. *sala isali, feḍḍa ifeḍḍi.* I'll be through work at five o'clock. *ġadi nsali xdemti fe-l-xemsa.* 2. *feḍḍa ifeḍḍi.* I am through with him. *feḍḍit mƐah.*
**If you ever do that again, we're through. *ila Ɛawtani derti had š-ši nfeḍḍi mƐak.* --He's been through a lot. *dazu Ɛlih le-mḥayen bezzaf.*

throughout - *f-...kollu.* You can get these vegetables throughout the whole year. *imken-lek tṣib had l-xeḍṛa fe-l-Ɛam kollu.* --This hotel is famous throughout the world. *had l-uṭil mešhuṛ fe-d-denya kollha.*

throw - *ṛemya* pl. *-t.* That was some throw. *hadi ṛemya mezyana.*
**His house is only a stone's throw from the station. *ḍaṛu qṛiba (bezzaf) men lagaṛ.*
to throw - 1. *laḥ iluḥ, siyyeb.* Let's see how far you can throw the ball. *yaḷḷah nšufu ḥetta l-ayn ġad tluḥ l-kuṛa.* 2. *ṭiyyeḥ.* The horse threw him. *ṭiyyḥu l-Ɛewd.*
**Throw that light this way, please. *ḍuwwi had l-mudeƐ Ɛafak.*
to throw away - *laḥ iluḥ, siyyeb.* Throw the papers away. *luḥ le-kwaġeṭ.*
to throw in - *zad izid.* The baker threw in a few extra rolls for us. *zadna l-xebbaz ši-xbizat.*
to throw on - *lbes (deġya).* I'll just throw a coat on an we'll go. *ġadi nelbes (deġya) l-kebbuṭ u-nemšiw.*
to throw out - 1. *laḥ iluḥ, ṛma iṛmi.* I threw the old shoes out. *leḥt ṣ-ṣebbaṭ le-qdim.* 2. *dḥa idḥi.* She almost threw me out. *Ɛlayen dḥatni.*
**The case was thrown out of court for lack of evidence. *l-meḥkama ṛefḍet l-qaḍiya Ɛla wedd ma-kanet ḥožža kafya.*
to throw over - 1. *laḥ iluḥ.* Can you throw it over to me? *waš imken-lek tluḥha-li?* 2. *feḍḍa ifeḍḍi mƐa.* She threw him over for a sailor. *feḍḍat mƐah Ɛla wedd waḥed l-beḥri.*
to throw up - *gell, tqiyya.* I throw up every time I ride on the train. *fuq-emma ka-nerkeb feš-mandifir ka-ngell.*

thumb - *ṣbeƐ kbir* pl. *ṣebƐan kbaṛ.*
**I'm all thumbs today. *ma-qdeṛt neƐmel b-yeddi walu l-yum.* --He's too much under his wife's thumb. *žaṛṛah mṛatu men menxaṛu.*

thunder - *ṛƐad.* Did you hear the thunder last night? *waš smeƐti ṛ-ṛƐad l-bareḥ fe-l-lil?*
**A thunder of applause greeted the speaker. *ṛeḥbu l-muḥaḍir b-muža de-l-keffan.*
to thunder - *ṛƐed, tkellem ṛ-ṛƐad.* I'ts beginning to thunder. *bda iṛƐed.*

Thursday - *le-xmis.*

thyme - *zeƐṭeṛ.*

tick - *grada* pl. *-t* coll. *grad.* The woods are full of ticks and mosquitoes. *l-ġaba Ɛamṛa b-le-grad u-n-namus.*

ticket - *weṛqa* pl. *wṛaq; bṭaqa* pl. *-t, bṭayeq.* Can you get us three tickets for the play? *waš imken-lek tṣib-lna tlata d-le-wṛaq le-r-riwaya?* I want a round-trip ticket to Paris. *bġit weṛqa d-le-mši u-d-le-mži l-bariz.*

to **tickle** - *herr.* He won't laugh even if you tickle him. *ma-idḥek-lek-š waxxa therru.*

ticklish - 1. *(lli) žah ižih l-herr.* Are you ticklish? *waš ka-ižik l-herr?* 2. *waƐer, ṣƐib* pl. *ṣƐab.* That's a ticklish question. *mesʔala waƐra hadi.*

tide - *mariya* or *maṛiya.* The tide is coming in. *mažya l-mariya.*
high tide - *mlu.*
low tide - *ḥṣiṛ.*
**Twenty dollars will tide me over until Monday. *Ɛešrin ḍulaṛ ifekkuni ḥetta l-le-tnin.*

tie - *kṛavaṭa, kṛabaṭa* pl. *-t; žiyyafa* pl. *-t.* He wears loud ties. *ka-ilbes kṛavaṭat lunhom ka-ixṭef.*
to tie - *Ɛqed.* I have to tie my shoes. *xeṣṣni neƐqed ṣebbaṭi.*
**My hands are tied. *ana yeddiya mteqqfin.*
to tie up - 1. *Ɛqed.* Please tie this package up for me. *Ɛqed-li*

had l-bakit Ɛafak. 2. *rbeṭ.* Did you tie up the boat? *waš rbeṭṭi l-qennba d-le-fluka.*
**I'm terribly tied down all day long. *ana mešġul n-nhaṛ kollu.* --Are you tied up this evening? *waš Ɛendek ši-ḥaža ma teƐmel had l-lila?*

tiger - *nmer* pl. *nmura.*

tight - **1.** *mƐeẓẓi.* This coat is too tight for me. *had l-kebbuṭ mƐeẓẓi Ɛliya bezzaf.* **2.** *sekran.* Boy, was I tight last night! *iyyeh, kont sekran l-bareḥ fe-l-lil!.* **3.** *mṣeqṛem.* He's very tight with his money. *huwa mṣeqṛem bezzaf Ɛla flusu.* **4.** *mẓiyyeṛ.* I was in a tight spot. *Ɛad kont f-waḥed l-ḥala mẓiyyṛa.*
**Is the jar sealed tight? *waš l-gella mƐeẓẓya mezyan?* --Shut your eyes tight. *ġemmeḍ Ɛeynik.* --Hold me tight! *Ɛeẓẓini Ɛlik!*

to **tighten** - *Ɛeẓẓa.* Tighten the rope. *Ɛeẓẓi l-qennba.*

tile - **1.** *zelliža* pl. *-t* coll. *zelliž.* We don't have enough blue tiles to finish this pillar. *ma-bqaw-lnas-š z-zelližat ẓ-ẓuṛeq l-kafyen baš nkemmlu had s-sarya.* **2.** *qeṛmuda* pl. *-t, qṛamed* coll. *qeṛmud.* Many of the tiles on this roof are broken. *bezzaf d-le-qṛamed mherrsin f-had ṣ-ṣteḥ.*

tiler, tile worker - *zellayži* pl. *-ya.*

tile work - *tazellayžit.* Tile work used to be a very popular craft. *tazellayžit kanet ḥerfa mešhuṛa bezzaf.*

till - *ḥetta.* Wait till I come back. *tsennani ḥetta neṛžeƐ.* --I won't be able to see you till next week. *ma-imken-li-š nšufek ḥetta ž-žemƐa ž-žayya.*

to **tilt** - **1.** *miyyel.* If you tilt the bottle, you can get it out. *ila miyyelti l-qeṛƐa imken-lek txerrežha.* I can't tilt my head. *ma-qdeṛt-š nmiyyel ṛaṣi.* --Don't tilt your chair so far back. *ma-tmiyyel-š š-šilya dyalek bezzaf l-luṛ.*

timber - *xšeb.*

time - **1.** *weqt* pl. *wqat.* I don't have the time to go with you. *ma-Ɛendi-š l-weqt baš nemši mƐak.* --Time will tell. *had š-ši iban mƐa l-weqt.* --At the time I thought differently about it. *f-dak-l-weqt kont xemmemtha f-kifiya xṛa.* --We got there at the same time. *wṣelna l-temma f-weqt waḥed.* **2.** *meṛṛa* pl. *-t, nuba* pl. *-t.* This is my first time here. *hadi l-meṛṛa l-luwla baš žit le-hna.* --How many times have you visited Morocco? *šḥal men meṛṛa ẓeṛti l-meġrib?* --I've asked him time after time not to do it. *qolt-lu nuba muṛ nuba ma-yeƐmel-ha-š.* --At times I work fourteen hours at a stretch. *ši-nubat ka-nexdem ṛbeƐṭašer saƐa bla ḥṣiṛ.*
**These are hard times. *hadi iyam ṣƐiba.* --What time is it? *šḥal hadi fe-s-saƐa?* --The time is up tomorrow. *ġedda huwa l-ʔažal.* --I see him at times. *ka-nšufu saƐa saƐa.* --Does your watch keep good time? *waš l-magana dyalek dima mḥeqqqa?* --Can your little boy tell time yet? *waš weldek ṣ-ṣġiṛ bda yeƐṛef išuf s-saƐa?* --What time do we eat? *fuq-aš ġad naklu?*
in no time - *deġya deġya.* He finished in no time. *sala had š-ši deġya deġya.*
times - *f-.* Two times two equals four. *žuž f-žuž hiya ṛebƐa.*
all the time - *dima.*
for a long time - *šḥal hadi.* I haven't seen him for a long time. *šḥal hadi ma-šeftu.*
from time to time - *saƐa saƐa.* He comes to see us from time to time. *ka-iži saƐa saƐa išufna.*
on time - **1.** *fe-l-weqt.* Please be on time. *aži fe-l-weqt Ɛafak.* **2.** *be-ṭ-ṭelq.* He bought the car on time. *šra ṭ-ṭumubil be-ṭ-ṭelq.*
to have a good time - *nšeṭ.* Did you have a good time? *waš nšeṭṭi?* --Have a good time! *nšeṭ mƐa ṛaṣek!*

timely - *fe-l-wežba, f-weqtu.* That's a timely topic. *had l-mudud Ɛ fe-l-wežba.*

timetable - *beṛnamež* pl. *baṛamiž.* According to the timetable we should be in Oujda at five o'clock. *Ɛla ḥasab l-beṛnamež ġadi nkunu f-wožda fe-l-xemsa.*

timid - *ḥešman.*

tin - *qezdir.* The price of tin went up last week. *t-taman de-l-qezdir ṭleƐ ž-žemƐa lli fatet.*

tinsmith - *qzadri* pl. *-ya.*

tiny - *ṣġiweṛ.*

tip - **1.** *ṭeṛf* pl. *ṭṛaf.* They landed on the northern tip of the island. *weṣlu f-ṭ-ṭeṛf š-šamali de-l-žazira.*

2. *ṛaṣ* pl. *ṛyuṣ*. My shoes are worn at the tips. *ṣebbaṭi melḥus f-ṛaṣu.* 3. *xbaṛ*. Let me give you a tip. *xellini neƐṭik ši-xbaṛ.* 4. *fabuṛ* pl. *-at*. How much of a tip shall I give the waiter? *šḥal de-l-fabuṛ xeṣṣni neƐṭi l-l-gaṛṣun?*

to tip - *Ɛṭa yeƐṭi l-fabuṛ l-*. Did you tip the waiter? *waš Ɛṭiti l-fabuṛ l-l-gaṛṣun?*

to tip off - *Ɛṭa yeƐṭi le-xbaṛ*. Who tipped you off? *škun lli Ɛṭak le-xbaṛ?*

to tip over - 1. *tteqleb*. The boat tipped over. *le-fluka ttqelbet.* 2. *qleb*. A wave tipped the boat over. *waḥed l-muža qelbet le-fluka.*

tiptoe - *ṛaṣ le-bnan*. The children came in on tiptoe. *d-drari dexlu Ɛla ṛaṣ bnanhom.*

to tiptoe - *tmešša Ɛla ṛaṣ le-bnan*. You don't need to tiptoe. *ma-Ɛendek-š Ɛlaš ttmešša Ɛla ṛaṣ bnanek.*

tire - *bnu* pl. *-wat*. Did you put air in the tires? *waš neffexti le-bnuwat?*

to tire - *Ɛya yeƐya*. I tire very easily in this heat. *ka-neƐya b-suhula f-had ṣ-ṣehḍ.*

tired - *Ɛeyyan*. He looks tired. *ḍaheṛ Ɛlih Ɛeyyan.*

tired out - *mehluk*. I'm tired out from the trip. *ana mehluk bezzaf men beƐd had ṣ-ṣafaṛ.*

to be tired of - *Ɛya yeƐya ma*. I'm tired of doing this over and over again. *Ɛyit ma nƐawed ndir had l-ḥaža.*

title - *Ɛonwan* pl. *Ɛnawen*. Do you know the title of the book? *waš ka-teƐṛef l-Ɛonwan d-le-ktab?*

to - 1. *l-*. (*li-* or *lil-* when used independently before pronoun endings.) Let's go to the movies. *yaḷḷah nemšiw le-s-sinima.* --Explain that to me! *fesser-li dak š-ši!* --What did he do to you? *šnu Ɛmel-lek?* --Send it to me. *ṣifeṭha-li.* --He sent me to you. *ṣifeṭni lilkom.* 2. *f-*. Apply this ointment to your feet. *dhen had l-ḅumaḍa f-režlik.* 3. *ḥetta l-*. They killed them to the last man. *qetluhom ḥetta le-r-ṛažel t-tali.* --I'm in my office from nine to twelve. *ana ka-nkun fe-l-mekteb dyali men t-tesƐud ḥetta le-ṭ-ṭnaš.* 4. *l-Ɛend*. Why do you come to me? Go to him! *Ɛlaš žiti l-Ɛendi? sir l-Ɛendu!* 5. *mƐa*. Did you talk to him? *waš tkellemti mƐah?* --To me he's always polite. *huwa dima mʔeddeb mƐaya.* 6. *ġir*. It's three minutes to four. *hadi ṛ-ṛebƐa ġir tlata de-d-dqayeq.* 7. *baš*. I'm doing my best to help you. *ka-neƐmel žehdi baš nƐawnek.* 8. *Ɛla*. Take the first turn to your left. *ḍuṛ fe-z-zenqa l-luwla Ɛla yeddek l-iṣeṛ.*

**The dog tore the rug to pieces. *l-kelb qetteƐ ẓ-ẓeṛbiya ṭraf ṭraf.* --I must go to bed. *xeṣṣni nemši nnƐes.* --To our surprise he passed the exam. *tƐežžebna melli nžeḥ f-le-mtiḥan.* --To date I haven't heard a thing. *baqi ma-smeƐt ḥetta ḥaža men dak š-ši.* --What do you say to this? *šnu ban-lek f-had š-ši?*

toad - *žṛana* pl. *-t* coll. *žṛan, gṛana* pl. *-t* coll. *gṛan*.

toast - *xobz mgermel*. Who ate my toast? *škun lli kla l-xobz le-mgermel dyali?*

**Let's drink a toast to the man of the house. *yaḷḷah nšeṛbu Ɛla mul ḍ-ḍaṛ.*

to toast - 1. *germel*. Do you want me to toast the bread for you? *waš bġitini ngermel-lek l-xobz?* 2. *šṛeb Ɛla*. Let's toast the boss! *yaḷḷah nšeṛbu Ɛel le-mƐellem!*

tobacco - *doxxan*.

today - *l-yum*.

today's - *de-l-yum*. I haven't read today's paper yet. *ma-zal ma-qrit l-žarida de-l-yum.*

toe - *benna* pl. *bnan*.

on one's toes - *Ɛla balu*. I have to be on my toes all the time. *xeṣṣni nkun dima Ɛla bali.*

together - (pronoun plus *wiya* plus pronoun ending). We work very well together. *ana wiyahom ka-nxedmu mezyan.*

to get together - *džemmeƐ*. Can we get together some evening? *waš imken-lna ndžemmƐu ši-lila?*

toilet - *miḍa* pl. *-t, myaḍi; bit l-ma* pl. *byut l-ma*.

toilet paper - *kaġiṭ de-l-miḍa*.

token - *Ɛalama* pl. *-t*. He gave it to me as a token of his friendship. *Ɛṭah-li b-Ɛalamt ṣ-ṣeḥba dyalna.*

toll - *ḥeqq d-dwaz* pl. *ḥquq d-dwaz*. You have to pay a toll on this bridge. *xeṣṣek txeḷḷeṣ ḥeqq d-dwaz f-had l-qenṭṛa.*

**The crash took a heavy toll of

life. *matu fe-l-muṣiba ɛadad kbir de-n-nas.*
to toll - *ṭenṭen.* Church bells tolled. *n-nwaqeṣ d-le-knisiya ṭenṭnu.*
tomato - sg. and coll. *maṭiša* pl. *-t.*
tomb - *qbeṛ* pl. *qbuṛa, qbuṛ.*
tomcat - *qeṭṭ* pl. *qṭuṭ.*
tomorrow - *ġedda.* I won't see him till tomorrow morning. *ma-ġad nšufu ḥetta l-ġedda fe-ṣ-ṣbaḥ.*
tomorrow's - *d-ġedda.* It'll be in tomorrow's paper. *ġadi tkun fe-l-žarida d-ġedda.*
the day after tomorrow - *beɛd ġedda.* It will be ready the day after tomorrow. *ġad ikun wažed beɛd ġedda.*
tongue - *lsan* pl. *-at, lsun.*
**Hold your tongue! *skot!*
tonight - *l-yum fe-l-lil.* What shall we do tonight? *aš ġadi nɛemlu l-yum fe-l-lil?*
too - **1.** *ɛetta.* May I come too? *imken-li nži ḥetta ʔana* or *ḥett-ana?* **2.** *bezzaf.* It's too hot. *l-ḥal šxun bezzaf.*
too long - *bezzaf.* Don't stay away too long! *ma-tġiyyeb-š bezzaf!*
**That play was none too good. *dak t-temtiliya ma-kanet-š mezyana bezzaf.*
tool - **1.** *mwaɛen* (pl.; a single item is generally referred to by its name). **2.** *ʔala muṣxaṛa* pl. *ʔalat muṣxaṛa.* The mayor is just a tool of his party. *l-ɛamil ġir ʔala muṣxaṛa de-l-ḥizeb dyalu.*
tooth - *senna* pl. *-t, snan* (front six upper and lower; also saw-tooth); *ḍeṛṣa* pl. *-t, ḍṛuṣ* (bicuspids and molars).
**She has a sweeth tooth. *ka-tḥebb le-ḥlawa.* --We fought against it tooth and nail. *ḥaṛebnah be-ž-žmiɛ ma ɛendna men quwwa.*
toothache - *ḥriq ḍ-ḍeṛṣa, ḍeṛṣa* (literally just tooth).
toothbrush - *šiṭa* (pl. *-t, šyeṭ*) *de-s-snan.*
tooth paste - *dwa de-s-snan.*
top - **1.** *ṛaṣ* pl. *ṛyuṣ* (of tree, mountain, etc.) You'll find it at the top of page 32. *imken-lek džberha f-ṛaṣ ṣ-ṣefḥa tnayn u-tlatin.* **2.** *ṭrinbu* pl. *-yat* (toy). **3.** *ḍheṛ* pl. *ḍhuṛa* (convertible car). **4.** *lexxṛani* pl. *-yin, tali* pl. *talyin.* There's still one room vacant on the top floor. *ma-zal bit xawi fe-ṭ-ṭebqa l-lexxṛaniya.* **5.** *fuqani* pl. *-yin.* It's in the top drawer. *ṛaha f-le-mžeṛṛ l-fuqani.*
**I don't know why he blew his top. *ma-ɛṛeft-š ɛlaš. zɛel.* --He yelled at the top of his voice. *ġuwwet ɛla ma fih men žehd.* --That story tops everything! *hadi hiya ḥkaya wella balak!*
from top to bottom - *men ṛ-ṛaṣ ḥetta le-r-režlin.*
on top - *l-fuq.* It's on top. *ṛah l-fuq.*
on top of - *fuq, fuq men.* It's on top of the refrigerator. *ṛah fuq t-tellaža.*
**He's sitting on top of the world. *le-mwara ɛendu fe-ṭ-ṭnaš.*
to top it off - *zad kemmel.* To top if off he stole my wallet. *u-b-aš zad kemmelha ṣreq-li bezṭami.*
to top off - *kemmel.* Let's top off the evening with a game of cards. *aži nkemmlu l-lila b-waḥed ṭ-ṭeṛḥ de-l-kaṛṭa.*
topic - *muḍuɛ* pl. *mawaḍiɛ.*
topsy-turvy - *mšeqleb,* or *meqlub ṛaṣ ɛla režlin.*
torch - *mešɛel* pl. *mšaɛel* (fire), *fnaṛ* pl. *-t* (electric).
torture - *ɛadab* (mental, physical).
to torture - *ɛeddeb.*
total - *žamiɛ* (art. *l-*), *bin l-žamiɛ.* My total earnings are two thousand dollars. *l-medxul dyali bin l-žamiɛ ʔalfayn ḍulaṛ.*
**The evening was a total loss. *l-lila kollha ḍaɛet.*
to total up - *žmeɛ.* Let's total up our expenses for the month. *aži nžemɛu l-maṣaṛif d-had š-šheṛ.*
touch - **1.** *qiṣa* pl. *-t.* She wakes up at a single touch. *b-qiṣa weḥda ka-tfiq men n-nɛas.* **2.** *nġiza* (of salt, spice, etc.).
to get in touch with - *ttaṣel b-.*
to touch - **1.** *qaṣ iqiṣ f-.* (physically). **2.** *ʔetteṛ f-* (i.e., move emotions).
**He's a little touched. *falta-lu n-neqša.*
tough - **1.** *mɛezzef* (as meat). **2.** *ṣɛib* pl. *-in, ṣɛab* (difficult).
tough luck - *ḥeḍḍ qbiḥ.*
tour - *žula* pl. *-t, msarya* pl. *-t.*
tourist - *saʔiḥ* pl. *suwwaḥ.*
tourist guide (person) - *gid* pl. *gyad.*
toward(s) - **1.** *mɛa.* I'll be there towards evening. *nkun temma mɛa le-ɛšiya.* --He was nice towards

us. *kan dṛiyyef mɛana.* 2. *l-žiha.* The bull came running toward me. *t-tuṛ ža ka-isbeg l-žihti.*
towel - 1. *fuṭa* pl. *-t, fweṭ* (hand, bath). 2. *mendil* pl. *mnadel* (dish).
tower - *boṛž* pl. *bṛuža.*
town - *mdina* pl. *-t, mdun, mudun; blad* pl. *-at.*
town-crier - *berraḥ* pl. *-a.*
toy - *qešwaša* pl. *qšaweš.*
trace - *ˀataṛ* pl. *-at* (clue, indication).
track - 1. *ˀataṛ* pl. *-t, imaṛa* pl. *-t, imayeṛ* (animal, truck, etc.). 2. *sekka* pl. *skek* (train).
**Now you're on the right track. *ṛak fe-ṭ-ṭṛiq daba.* --I've lost track of him. *ma-bqa yewṣelni ḥetta xbaṛ ɛlih.*
tractor - *trakṭuṛ* pl. *-at.*
trade - 1. *tabadul tižari* (as between countries). 2. *xedma* pl. *-t, xdami; ḥerfa* pl. *-t, ḥrafi; ṣenɛa* pl. *-t, ṣnaɛi* (job, profession). 3. *mbadla* pl. *-t* (exchange).
to trade - *beddel.* I traded my typewriter for a bicycle. *beddelt l-makina d-le-ktaba dyali b-bešklit.*
tragedy - *muṣiba* pl. *mṣayeb* (unfortunate occurrence).
trail - *ṭṛiq* pl. *ṭoṛqan.*
to trail - *tbeɛ* (s.o.).
train - *mašina* pl. *-t, qiṭaṛ* pl. *-at.* He went by train. *ṣafeṛ fe-l-mašina.*
to train - 1. *derreb, ɛellem.* He's trained his dogs well. *derreb le-klab dyalu mezyan.* 2. *dderreb.* We trained a lot before the race. *dderrebna bezzaf qbel le-mṣabqa.*
training - *tedrib.*
traitor - *xaˀin* pl. *xawana.*
tramp - *msiyyeḥ* pl. *msiyyḥin.*
to **trample** - *ẓḍem ɛla, štef ɛla.*
to **translate** - *ṭeṛžem.*
transparent - *(lli) ka-ibiyyen.*
transport - *neql* (of troops, goods, etc.).
to transport - *neqqel.*
trap - *mṣiḍa* pl. *mṣayeḍ, fexx* pl. *fxax.*
trash - *zbel* (includes garbage).
to **travel** - *ṣafeṛ, žal ižul.*
tray - *ṣiniya* pl. *-t, ṣwani.*
treason - *xiyana.*
treasure - *kenz* pl. *knuza.*
treat - *šehwa fe-d-denya* (pleasure).
to treat - 1. *ɛamel.* He treats me like a child. *ka-iɛamelni bḥal ši-derri.* 3. *xeḷḷeṣ ɛla.* He's treating us to a movie. *ġad ixeḷḷeṣ ɛlina dexla le-s-sinima.* 2. *gabel* (a patient).
to treat lightly - *tṛaxa f-.* You shouldn't treat this matter lightly. *ma-xeṣṣek-š ttṛaxa f-had l-qaḍiya.*
treatment - 1. *muɛamala* (manner with s.o.). 2. *mgabla* (of a patient).
treaty - *ɛeqd* pl. *ɛuqud, muɛahada* pl. *-t.*
tree - *šežṛa* pl. *-t* coll. *šžeṛ.*
to **tremble** - *ġzel.*
trial - *muḥakama* pl. *-t, deɛwa* pl. *-t, dɛawi* (court).
on trial - *be-š-šwaṛ* (in buying s. th.).
to give a trial - *žeṛṛeb* (i.e., try out).
triangle - *mutellat* pl. *-at.*
tribe - *qbila* pl. *-t, qbayel* (Indian, Arab, of Israel, etc.).
trick - 1. *ḥila* pl. *-t* (ruse, deception). 2. *benṭaxa* pl. *-t* (cards, magic.).
mean, dirty trick - *xeṣla* pl. *-t, xṣayel.* He played a dirty trick on me. *ɛmel-li waḥed l-xeṣla.*
to trick - *ɛmelha b-.* She tricked me into marrying her. *ɛemletha biya u-dzuwwežt biha.*
to **trim** - *ḥeddeq* (hair, mustache).
trip - *ṣefṛa* pl. *-t, ṣafaṛ* pl. *ˀeṣfaṛ.*
**Have a nice trip! *ṭṛiq s-slama!*
to trip - 1. *ɛekkel l-.* I tripped him and he fell. *ɛekkelt-lu u-ṭaḥ.* 2. *ɛteṛ.* He tripped on the stairs and fell. *ɛteṛ fe-ḍ-ḍṛuz u-ṭaḥ.*
to trip up - *ġleṭ* (to err).
triumph - *neṣṛ.*
troops - *ɛesker.*
trouble - *muškila* pl. *mašakil.* We've had some trouble in the office. *kanet ɛendna ši-muškila* (or *mašakil*) *fe-l-mekteb.*
**What's the trouble? *aš-kayen?*
to be in trouble - *ɛendu muškila.*
to give trouble to - *ɛeddeb.*
to trouble - *ɛeddeb* (e.g., a sore leg).
**What's troubling you? *ma-lek?*
troubled - 1. *qbiḥ* pl. *qbaḥ.* We live in troubled times. *ka-nɛišu f-waḥed l-weqt qbiḥ.* 2. *mšuwweš.* Her mother is very troubled now. *m̂m̂ha mšuwwša bezzaf daba.*
trousers - *serwal* pl. *srawel.*
trout - *bu-ḍeṛṣ.*
truck - *kamiyu* pl. *-yat, kamyun* pl. *-at.*
true - *ḥaqiqi* pl. *-yin* (factual, genuine).
**He's always true to his principles. *dima qabeṭ fe-l-mabadiˀ*

dyalu.
truly - *fe-l-ḥaqiqa.*
trumpet - **1.** *nfir* pl. *nfayer* (for Ramadan). **2.** *korniṭa* pl. *-t* (bugle).
trunk - **1.** *ṣag* pl. *ṣigan* (of tree). **2.** *ṣenḍuq* pl. *ṣnaḍeq* (for clothes). **3.** *kesda* pl. *-t, ksadi* (body). **4.** *xeṛṭum* pl. *xṛaṭem* (elephant).
trunks - *serwal* (pl. *srawel*) *de-l-Ɛewm.*
trust - *tiqa.* I'm putting my trust in you. *ka-neƐmel fik t-tiqa.*
to trust - *taq itiq b-.*
truth - *ḥeqq, ṣeḥḥ.*
to **try** - **1.** *ḥawel.* They tried to kill us. *ḥawlu iqetluna.* **2.** *žeṛṛeb.* Try them before you buy them. *žeṛṛebhom qbel-ma tešrihom.*
to try on - *qeyyeṣ* (a suit).
tub - *žefna* pl. *-t, žfani* (primarily for washing).
tube - *žaža* pl. *-t* (radio, etc.).
tuck - *tenya* pl. *-t* (as in a dress).
to tuck in - *ḥša yeḥši* (as a shirt).
Tuesday - *nhaṛ t-tlata, t-tlata.*
tug - *ṛmuk* pl. *-at* (boat).
to tug - *nteṛ.*
to **tumble** - *tšeqleb.* He tumbled down the stairs. *tšeqleb fe-ḍ-ḍṛuž.*
tumor - *welsis* pl. *wlases.*
Tunis - *tunes.*
Tunisia - *tunes.*
Tunisian - *tunsi* adj. pl. *-yen,* n. pl. *twansa, hel tunes.*
tunnel - *ġaṛ* pl. *ġiṛan.*
turban - *ṛeẓẓa* pl. *-t, ṛẓeẓ.*
Turk - *toṛki* pl. *-yin, ʔatṛak.*
Turkey - *toṛkya.*
turkey - *bibi* (no art.) pl. *-yat.*
Turkish - **1.** *toṛki* pl. *-yin.* **2.** *toṛkiya* (language).
turn - **1.** *ḍuṛa* pl. *-t* (around a corner, a pivot). **2.** *nuba* pl. *-t.* It's my turn. *hadi nubti.*
**One good turn deserves another. *lli Ɛmel ši-xir ka-ilqah.* --You're talking out of turn. *ma-Ɛendek ḥeqq baš ttkellem.*
at every turn - *f-koll muḍeƐ, f-koll qent, fayn-emma mša.*
in turn - *b-nuba* (i.e., when your turn comes, etc.).
to take turns - *tnawbu* (pl.).
to turn - *ḍuwweṛ* (make go round).
**She turned her back on me. *Ɛṭatni be-ḍheṛha.* --He turned his ankle. *tfekket-lu režlu.* --Now the tables are turned! *ma-ši bnita, had l-meṛṛa wliyyed!* --I don't know who to turn to. *ma-Ɛṛeft le-mmen nemši.* --My stomach turns when I think of that scene. *ka-iqum qelbi mnin ka-nfekkeṛ f-dak l-menḍeṛ.*
to turn around - **1.** *ḍuwweṛ.* Turn the wheel around. *ḍuwweṛ ṛ-ṛwiḍa.* **2.** *ḍaṛ iḍuṛ.* The propeller is turning around very slowly. *l-ferfar ka-iḍuṛ ġir be-š-šwiya.*
to turn back - *ṛžeƐ.*
to turn down - **1.** *ma-qbel-š, ṛfeḍ* (reject). **2.** *xda yaxod* (a road). **3.** *nqeṣ men* (radio, light). Turn the radio down. *nqeṣ men ṛ-ṛaḍyu.*
to turn in - **1.** *ṛežžeƐ* (as s. th. lost). **2.** *qeddem* (application, resignation). **3.** *nƐes* (go to bed).
to turn into - *wella, ṛžeƐ* (to become).
to turn off - **1.** *ḍfa iḍfi* (radio, light). **2.** *šedd* (water, gas).
to turn on - **1.** *šƐel* (light, radio). **2.** *xeddem* (machine). **3.** *ṭḷeq, ḥell* (water, gas).
to turn out - **1.** *ḍfa iḍfi* (light). **2.** *ṭḷeƐ, ṣdeq.* The work turned out bad. *l-xedma ṭeḷƐet qbiḥa.* **3.** *ḥḍeṛ.* A lot of people turned out for the president's speech. *bezzaf de-n-nas ḥeḍṛu Ɛel l-xoṭba de-ṛ-ṛaʔis.* **4.** *xerrež* (i.e., evict). **5.** *ṣneƐ, wežžed* (manufacture).
to turn over - **1.** *dfeƐ* (to hand over). **2.** *qleb.* I turned the table over so I could fix the legs. *qlebt ṭ-ṭabḷa baš nṣuwweb-lha l-kerƐan dyalha.* **3.** *tteqleb.* The chair turned over when I sat down on it. *š-šelya ttqelbet mnin glest Ɛliha.*
**Turn it over in your mind before you give him an answer. *ḍuwweṛ lsanek f-fommek sebƐa de-l-meṛṛat, Ɛad wažbu.*
to turn up - *ḍheṛ* (appear).
to turn upside down - *qleb.*
turnip - *lefta* pl. *-t* coll. *left.*
turtle - *fekṛun* pl. *fkaṛen.*
twelfth - *ṭaneš* pl. *ṭanšin.*
twelve - *ṭnaš.*
twenty - *Ɛešrin.*
twice - *žuž de-l-meṛṛat, meṛṛtayn.*
**I paid twice as much as you. *xeḷḷeṣtha metniya Ɛlik.*
twig - *ġṣen* pl. *ġṣan.*
twins - *twam* (no sg.).
twine - *qennba* pl. *-t, qnaneb* coll. *qenneb.*
to **twist** - **1.** *ḍaṛ iḍuṛ* (road). **2.** *luwwa iluwwi* (s.o.'s arm, a

rag, etc.). **3.** *fekk* (ankle).

two – *žuž, zuž; tnin, tnayn* (used in combinations, e.g. 22, 32, 42, etc.) **She actually didn't tell me but I can put two and two together. *fe-l-ḥaqiqa ma-qalet-li šay, ġir ana kemmelt men Ɛeqli.*

in, by twos – *žuž b-žuž.*

to cut in two – *fṛeq* or *qṣem Ɛla žuž.*

type – **1.** *nuƐ* pl. *ʔenwaƐ, škel* pl. *škal, Ɛeyna* pl. *-t* (kind, sort). **2.** *ḥuṛuf* (letters).

to type – *ḍṛeb Ɛel-l-ʔala.* Do you know how to type? *ka-teƐṛef ḍḍṛeb Ɛel l-ʔala?*

typewriter – *ʔala katiba* pl. *ʔalat katiba, makina d-le-ktaba* pl. *makinat d-le-ktaba.*

typhus – *tifus.*

tyranny – *ḍoḷm, ṭoġyan.*

tyrant – *ḍaḷem* pl. *ḍoḷḷam.*

U

ugly – *xayeb, qbiḥ* pl. *qbaḥ.* That's an ugly picture. *hadi teṣwiṛa xayba.* **They're spreading ugly rumors about him. *ka-itkellmu muṛ ḍehṛu.*

Ujda – *wežda.*

native of Ujda – *weždi* pl. adj. *weždiyen,* n. pl. *wžada, hel wežda.*

umbrella – *mḍeḷḷ* pl. *mḍuḷa.*

umpire – *ḥakem* pl. *ḥokkam.* The umpire got hit by the ball. *l-ḥakem ḍeṛbettu l-kuṛa.*

to be **unable** – *ma-qḍeṛ-š, ma-mken-lu-š.* I'm sorry I'm unable to give you that information. *metʔessef ma-imken-li-š neƐṭik had le-xbaṛ.*

unbiased – *(lli) ka-yeḥkem mƐewweṭ.* On this subject he's quite unbiased. *ka-yeḥkem mƐewweṭ f-had l-muḍuƐ.*

uncertain – *fih š-šekk, ma-mḥeqqeq-š.* His trip is still uncertain. *ma-zal ṣ-ṣafaṛ dyalu fih š-šekk.* **2.** *Ɛendu š-šekk.* I'm still uncertain whether I'll go. *ma-zal Ɛendi š-šekk waš nemši wella la.*

in no uncertain terms – *b-ṣaṛaḥa.* I told him in no uncertain terms what I thought of him. *qolt-lu b-ṣaṛaḥa aš ka-iswa Ɛendi.*

uncle – **1.** (paternal) *Ɛemm* pl. *Ɛmam.* **2.** (maternal) *xal* pl. *xwal.*

uncomfortable – *qaṣeḥ.* That's an uncomfortable chair. *had š-šilya qaṣḥa.*

unconscious – *ġayeb.* He's still unconscious. *huwa ma-zal ġayeb.* **He was unconscious of the real danger. *ma-kan-š šaƐeṛ be-l-xaṭaṛ le-ḥqiqi.*

unconsciously – *bla-ma išƐeṛ.* He did it unconsciously. *Ɛmelha bla ma-išƐeṛ.*

undecided – *ma-mḥeqqeq-š.* I'm still undecided. *ana ma-zal ma-mḥeqqeq-š.*

under – **1.** *men teḥt.* Slip the letter under the door. *duwwez le-bṛa men teḥt l-bab.* **2.** *teḥt.* The slippers are under the bed. *l-belġa teḥt n-namušiya.* **3.** *Ɛla ḥsab.* Under the new law, taxes will be higher. *Ɛla ḥsab l-qanun ž-ždid, ḍ-ḍaṛibat ġad iṭeḷƐu.* **Is everything under control? *waš koll ḥaža mṛaqba?* --I was under the impression that he wanted to go. *kan ka-yeḥsab-li bin bġa imši.*

underbrush – *hišer.*

underneath – *teḥt, teḥt men.* I found the ball underneath the bed. *žbeṛt l-kuṛa teḥt men n-namusiya.*

to **understand** – *fhem.* He doesn't understand French. *ma-ka-ifhem-š le-fṛanṣawiya.* --It's understood that you will stay with us. *mefhum bin ġad tebqa mƐana.*

understanding – *mfahma.*

to **undertake** – *Ɛmel.* I hope you're not planning to undertake that trip alone. *ka-ntmenna bin ma-ka-tenwi-š teƐmel had ṣ-ṣafaṛ b-weḥdek.*

underwear – *ḥwayež teḥtiyin* (pl.).

to **undo** – **1.** *ḥell, fekk.* Help me undo this knot. *Ɛawenni baš nḥell had l-Ɛoqda.* **2.** *ṣḷeḥ.* I'll need a week to undo his work. *xeṣṣni žemƐa baš nesḷeḥ l-xedma dyalu.*

undoubtedly – *bla šekk.*

to **undress** – *zuwwel le-ḥwayež, ḥeyyed le-ḥwayež.* I'll undress the children. *ana ġad nzuwwel le-ḥwayež de-d-drari,* --I want to undress before I go to sleep. *bġit nzuwwel ḥwayži qbel-ma nnƐes.*

unemployed – *beṭṭal* pl. *-a.*

unemployment – *qellet l-xedma.*

ungrateful - *nekkaṛ l-xir* pl. *nekkaṛin l-xir.* He's an ungrateful person. *huwa nekkaṛ l-xir.*
unhappy - *ma-ši feṛḥan.*
unharmed - *bla žeṛḥa.* He escaped unharmed. *menneƐ bla žeṛḥa.*
unimportant - *ma-ši muhimm.*
union - 1. *ttiḥad* pl. *-at.* Union gives strength. *le-ttiḥad ka-yeƐṭi l-quwwa.* 2. *niqaba* pl. *-t.* How many workers are there in this union? *šḥal de-l-xeddama kaynin f-had n-niqaba.*
unique - *frid* pl. *frad.*
unit - 1. *bab* pl. *bwab, feṣḷ* pl. *fuṣuḷ.* There are twenty units in this book. *had le-ktab fih Ɛešrin bab.* 2. *feṛqa* pl. *-t.* They've transferred him to another unit. *ḥewwluh l-feṛqa xṛa.*
united - *mettaḥed.*
United Arab Republic - *l-žemhuṛiya l-Ɛaṛabiya l-muttaḥida.*
The United States - *l-wilayat l-muttaḥida.*
university - *žamiƐa* pl. *-t.*
unjust - 1. *mxalef l-ḥeqq.* This stipulation is unjust. *had š-šeṛṭ mxalef l-ḥeqq.* 2. *ḍalem.* He is an unjust man! *ṛažel ḍalem hada!*
unknown - *mežhul, ma-ši meƐṛuf.*
unless - *ila ma-.* We're coming unless it rains. *ġadi nžiw ila ma-ṭaḥet š-šta.*
unlike - *ma-ši bḥal.*
unlikely - *muḥal.* That's very unlikely. *had š-ši muḥal ikun.*
to **unload** - *xwa ixwi.* They haven't unloaded the truck yet. *baqi ma-xwaw l-kamiyu.*
to **unlock** - *ḥell le-qfel d-.* Unlock the door! *ḥell le-qfel de-l-bab!*
unlucky - 1. *qbiḥ* pl. *qbaḥ.* It was an unlucky coincidence. *kanet waḥed ṣ-ṣeḍfa qbiḥa.* 2. *zoġbi, ma-Ɛendu ẓheṛ.* I don't know why I'm always unlucky. *ma-Ɛreft-š ġir Ɛlaš ana dima ma-Ɛendi ẓheṛ.*
unnecessary - *ma-ši ḍaṛuṛi.* That's entirely unnecessary. *had š-ši ma-ši ḍaṛuṛi be-l-koll.*
to **unpack** - *žbed, xerrež.* I am just unpacking my things. *ana ġir ka-nežbed ḥwayži.*
unpleasant - *qbiḥ* pl. *qbaḥ.* I have some unpleasant news for you. *ana Ɛendi ši-xbaṛ qbiḥ lilek.*
unreasonable - *ma-ši meƐqul.*
to **untie** - *ḥell.* Can you untie this knot for me? *waš imken-lek tḥell-li had l-Ɛoqda?* --Wait till I untie the package. *tsenna ḥetta nḥell l-bakit.* --My shoe is untied. *ṣebbaṭi meḥlul.*
until - 1. *ḥetta l-.* Wait until tomorrow. *tsenna ḥetta l-ġedda.* 2. *ḥetta.* Wait until I come. *tsennani ḥetta nži.*
unusual - *ma-ši men l-Ɛada, ġrib* pl. *-in.*
unwise - *qlil le-mbalya* pl. *qlal le-mbalya.*
up - 1. *l-fuq.* Hands up! *hezz yeddik l-fuq!* 2. *fe-l-fuq.* I'm up here. *ana fe-l-fuq hna.*
**Is he up already? *waš huwa naḍ beƐda?* --Your time is up. *l-ʔažal dyalek tfeḍḍa.* --Shut up! *šedd fommek!* --We all have our ups and downs. *nhaṛ lilek u-nhaṛ Ɛlik.* --What's up? *aš kayen.* --He's up and around again. *huwa bṛa u-bda ka-ixṛož.* --He was walking up and down the room. *kan ka-imši w-iži fe-l-bit.* --The decision is up to you. *le-fṣaḷ dyalek.* --What's he up to this time? *aš ġad yeƐmel had n-nuba?* --Because of the windstorm trains were up to two hours late. *Ɛla qibal r-riḥ qwi l-mašinat tƐeṭṭlu ḥetta b-saƐtayn.* --She only comes up to my shoulder. *ma-ka-tewṣeḷ-li ġir l-ketfi.* --Up to now he hasn't answered. *ḥetta l-daba ma-zal ma-žaweb-š.*
uphill - *ṭaleƐ.* This road goes uphill. *had ṭ-ṭriq ṭaḷƐa.*
upkeep - *maṣaṛif.* The upkeep on my car is too expensive. *l-maṣaṛif dyal ṭ-ṭumubil dyali ġalyin bezzaf.*
upper - *fuqani.* The fire started on one of the upper floors. *l-Ɛafya bdat f-weḥda men ṭ-ṭabaqat l-fuqaniyin.*
**Write the page number in the upper right-hand corner. *kteb ṛ-reqm de-ṣ-ṣefḥa l-fuq u-fe-l-qent l-limni.*
upset - *mqelleq.* He was all upset. *kan mqelleq bezzaf.*
**I have an upset stomach. *Ɛendi le-wžeƐ f-keṛši.*
to upset - 1. *qleb.* Be careful or you'll upset the pitcher. *ṛeḍḍ balek wella ṛak ġadi teqleb l-ġeṛṛaf.* --You're upsetting the boat! *ṛak ġadi teqleb le-fluka.* --The rain upset our plans. *š-šta qelbet-lna l-beṛnamež.* 2. *qelleq.* Nothing upsets him. *ḥetta ḥaža ma-ka-tqellqu.*

upside down - *meqlub*.
upstairs - **1.** *fuqani*. --The upstairs apartment is vacant. *s-sokna l-fuqaniya xawya*. **2.** *fe-l-fuqi*. He's upstairs. *huwa fe-l-fuqi*.
urge - *ṛeġba* pl. *-t*. I felt the urge to tell him what I thought of him. *ḥessit b-waḥed ṛ-ṛeġba baš nqul-lu aš ka-iswa εendi*.
to urge - *ṛġeb iṛġob*. She urged us to stay longer. *ṛeġbetna baš nqeεdu kteṛ*.
urgent - *mezrub*. I have an urgent request. *ana εendi ṭalab mezrub*.
use - **1.** *fayda* pl. *-t*. What's the use of arguing? *šni hiya l-fayda dyal le-mžadla?* **2.** *ġaṛaḍ*. I have no use for two. *ma-εendi-š l-ġaṛaḍ b-žuž*.
**It's no use hurrying. *ma-kayen εlaš z-zerba*. --It's no use, we've got to do it. *ma-kayen walu, xeṣṣna nεemlu had š-ši*.
to be of use - *ṣlaḥ*. Will that be of any use to you? *waš had š-ši ġad iṣlaḥ-lek l-ḥetta ḥaža?*
to use - **1.** *steεmel*. I can't use these tickets. *ma-imken-li-š nesteεmel had le-bṭayeq*. **2.** *xeddem*. Please show me how to use this machine. *εafak werrini kif-aš nxeddem had l-ʔala*.
used to - **1.** *kan* (plus imperfect). I used eat in a restaurant before I got married. *kont ka-nakol fe-l-meṭεem qbel-ma ndžuwwež*. **2.** *mwalef*. She's used to getting up at seven o'clock. *hiya mwalfa tnuḍ fe-s-sebεa*.
to get used to - **1.** *wellef*. I've got my children used to eating at five o'clock. *welleft d-drari dyali yaklu fe-l-xemsa*. **2.** *twellef*. I can't get used to getting up at three in the morning. *ma-imken-li-š ntwellef nnuḍ fe-t-tlata de-ṣ-ṣbaḥ*. --He never got used to that custom. *εemmṛu ma-twellef b-had l-εada*.
useful - *mufid*. I've found this book very useful. *lqit had le-ktab mufid bezzaf*.
useless - *(lli) ma-ka-iṣlaḥ*. This map is useless to me. *had l-xaṛiṭa ma-ka-teṣlaḥ-li ḥetta ḥaža*.
ususal - *εadi*. The train arrived at the usual time. *l-mašina weṣlet fe-l-weqt l-εadi*.
**We'll see each other at the usual place. *ntšawfu fe-l-maḥell l-meεlum*.
as usual - *bḥal l-εada*. Everything went along as usual. *koll-ši bqa mmešši bḥal l-εada*.
usually - *men εadtu*. I usually go to see them twice a week. *men εadti ka-nemši nšufhom žuž de-l-meṛṛat fe-ž-žemεa*.

V

vacant - *xawi*. The house has been vacant for a week. *hadi žemεa u-ḍ-ḍaṛ xawya*.
to **vacate** - *xwa ixwi*. When are you going to vacate the house? *fuq-aš ġadi texwi ḍ-ḍaṛ?*
vacation - *εwašer, εoṭla* pl. *-t*. The children are looking forward to their vacation. *d-drari ka-itsennaw le-εwašer b-koll faṛaḥ*.
on vacation - *mεušer*. Ahmed is on vacation. *ḥmed ṛah mεušer*.
vain - *menfux*. That is a very vain man! *ṛažel menfux bezzaf hada!*
in vain - *bla fayda*. The doctor tried in vain to save the boy's life. *ṭ-ṭbib ḥawel bla fayda imenneε l-weld men l-mut*.
valuable - *(lli) εendu qima*. That's a valuable ring. *had l-xatem εendha qima*.
valuables - *ḥwayež lli εendhom l-qima*. You'd better lock your valuables in the safe. *ḥsen-lek tšedd εel le-ḥwayež lli εendhom l-qima fe-ṣ-ṣenduq*.
value - *qima*. This book has no value. *had le-ktab ma-εendu qima*.
to value - **1.** *εtabeṛ*. I value his friendship highly. *ka-neεtabeṛ ṣḥebtu bezzaf*. **2.** *qeḍḍeṛ*. What do you value your house at? *be-šḥal qeḍḍeṛti ḍaṛek?*
to **vanish** - *ġber*. My father vanished during the war. *bba ġber f-weqt l-ḥeṛb*.
vapor - *fwaṛ*.
variety - *škel* pl. *škal, nuε* pl. *nwaε*. We have a wide variety of shirts. *εendna bezzaf de-š-škal de-l-qamizat*. --How many varieties of apples do you have in your orch

orchard? *šḥal men nuƐ de-t-teffaḥ Ɛendek fe-l-Ɛerṣa?*

various – *mnuwweƐ*. I have various reasons. *Ɛendi sbab mnuwwƐin.*

**The table was decorated with various kinds of flowers. *ṭ-ṭabḷa kanet mziyyna b-belƐa de-l-ʔenwaƐ de-n-nuwwaṛ.*

varnish – *berniz*. How long does it take the varnish to dry? *šḥal xeṣṣu l-berniz ibqa baš iybes?*

to varnish – *bernez*. We just varnished the floor. *Ɛad bernezna l-eṛḍ.*

to **vary** – 1. *tġeyyeṛ*. The size varies in each case. *le-qyas ka-itġeyyeṛ. f-koll meṛṛa.* 2. *beddel*. You can vary the colors if you wish. *imken-lek tbeddel l-lwan ila bġiti.*

vase – *ġoṛṛaf* pl. *ġṛaṛef.*

veal – *lḥem d-le-Ɛžel.*

veal cutlet – *šekla d-le-Ɛžel* pl. *škali d-le-Ɛžel.*

vegetables – *xoḍṛa* (coll).

veil – *ltam* pl. *-at.*

vein – *Ɛeṛq* pl. *Ɛṛuq.*

velvet – *mwobbeṛ.*

venereal disease – *meṛḍ n-nuwwaṛ.*

vengeance – *taṛ.*

vent – *tenfisa* pl. *tnafes.*

venture – *mġamṛa* pl. *-t.* It was a dangerous venture. *kanet mġamṛa xṭiṛa.*

to venture – *xaṭeṛ*. I wouldn't venture to go out in this cold. *ma-nxaṭeṛ-š nexṛož f-had l-berd.* --Nothing ventured, nothing gained. *lli ma-ka-ixaṭer walu, ma-irbeḥ walu.*

on the **verge** of – *Ɛlayen*. She's on the verge of a breakdown. *hiya Ɛlayen ttxelxel.* --I was on the verge of telling him. *Ɛlayen kont ġadi nqulha-lu.*

versus – *ḍeḍḍ.*

vertical – *Ɛamudi.*

very – 1. *bezzaf*. The bank is not very far from here. *l-ḅenk ma-bƐida-š bezzaf men hna.* 2. *tamamen*. He's the very man you want. *hada huwa tamamen ṛ-ṛažel lli ka-ixeṣṣek.* --She left the very next day. *mšat tamamen n-nhaṛ lli men beƐd.*

very much – *bezzaf, bezzaf Ɛad.* I liked it very much. *Ɛžebni bezzaf Ɛad.*

vest – *žili* pl. *-yat, bedƐiya* pl. *-t.*

vicinity – *naḥiya* pl. *nawaḥi*. There are good restaurants in the vicinity of the railroad station. *kaynin maṭaƐim mezyanin f-naḥiyet ḷ-ḷagaṛ.*

vicious – *weḥši*. The dog is vicious. *l-kelb weḥši.*

victim – 1. *ḍḥiya* pl. *-t.* He was the third to fall victim to the killer. *kan huwa t-talet lli mša ḍḥiya de-l-qettal.* 2. *frisa* pl. *frayes.* He was the victim of a swindle. *kan frisa f-waḥed tašeffaṛet.*

victor – *rabeḥ* pl. *rabḥin.*

victory – *nṣeṛ.*

view – *menḍeṛ* pl. *manaḍiṛ*. You have a nice view from here. *Ɛendek menḍeṛ mezyan men hna.*

vile – 1. *qbiḥ* pl. *qbaḥ*. Where's that vile smell coming from? *mnayn žayya had r-riḥa le-qbiḥa?* 2. *xbit* pl. *xbat*. He's a vile man. *huwa ṛažel xbit.*

village – *qeṛya* pl. *-t, ḍuwwaṛ* pl. *ḍwaweṛ.*

vinegar – *xell.*

to **violate** – *xalef*. That's not the first time he's violated the law. *hadi ma-ši hiya l-meṛṛa l-luwwla lli xalef l-qanun.*

violation – *mxalfa* pl. *-t.*

violent – *mežhed.*

violin – *kamanža* pl. *-t.*

violinist – *kamanži* pl. *-ya.*

virtue – *faḍila* pl. *faḍaʔil*. Patience is a virtue. *ṣ-ṣbeṛ faḍila.*

vision – *nḍeṛ*. His vision is getting poor. *n-nḍeṛ dyalu bda ka-iḍƐaf.*

visit – *ẓyaṛa* pl. *-t.*

to **visit** – *ẓaṛ iẓuṛ.*

visitor – *ẓayer* pl. *ẓuwwaṛ.*

voice – *ḥelq* pl. *ḥluq*. He has a beautiful voice. *Ɛendu waḥed l-ḥelq mezyan.*

volume – *žozʔ* pl. *ʔažzaʔ*. Volume Fifteen of this magazine is missing. *ka-ixeṣṣ l-žozʔ l-xemṣṭaš dyal had l-mažella.*

volunteer – *mutaṭawiƐ* pl. *-in.*

to **vomit** – *gell, tqeyya.*

vote – 1. *ṣewt* pl. *ʔeṣwat*. How many votes did he get? *šḥal de-l-ʔeṣwat Ɛlaš ḥeṣṣel?* 2. *teṣwit*. He succeeded on the third vote. *nžeḥ fe-t-teṣwit t-talet.*

to vote – *ṣuwwet*. Who did you vote for? *le-mmen ṣuwwetti?* --I voted against the proposal. *ṣuwwett ḍeḍḍ had le-qtiṛaḥ.*

to **vouch for** – *ḍmen*. I vouch for him. *ana ḍamnu.*

voyage – *ṣfeṛ, ṣefṛa* pl. *-t.*

W

to **wage** - *dar idir.* They can't wage a long war. *ma-iqedṛu-š idiru ḥeṛb ṭwila.*
wages - *ʔožṛa* pl. *-t.* Are you satisfied with your wages? *waš feṛḥan be-ʔžoṛtek?*
wagon - *keṛṛuṣa* pl. *t, kṛaṛeṣ.* Hitch the horses to the new wagon. *ṛbeṭ l-xil l-l-keṛṛuṣa ž-ždida.*
waist - *ḥzam* pl. *ḥzamat, kerš* pl. *kruš, kruša.* I took the pants in at the waist. *nqeṣt men s-serwal f-le-ḥzam.*
wait - *msayna* pl. *-t.* We have an hour's wait before the train gets in. *ɛendna saɛa d-le-msayna qbel-ma iži l-qiṭaṛ.*
to lie in wait - *ttelles.* They were lying in wait for us. *kanu mtellsin-lna.*
to wait - **1.** *tsenna.* We found him waiting at the station. *žbeṛnah ka-itsenna f-le-mḥeṭṭa.* --He kept me waiting an hour. *xellani ka-ntsenna saɛa.* **2.** *ṣbeṛ.* I can't wait any longer. *ma-neqḍeṛ-š neṣbeṛ kteṛ men dak š-ši.* **3.** *bqa ibqa.* That can wait till tomorrow. *dak š-ši imken-lu ibqa ḥetta l-ġedda.*
**I can hardly wait to see him. *ma-nertaḥ ġir ila šeftu.* --Go to bed, don't wait up for me. *ġir sir teṇɛes, ma-tebqa-š fayeq ka-ttsennani.*
to wait for - *tsenna.* I'll wait for you until five o'clock. *ġadi ntsennak ḥetta l-xemsa.*
**I can hardly wait for the day. *lehla yeḥremni ġir ila šeft dak n-nhaṛ.*
to wait on - *serba iserbi.* Will you please wait on me now? *serbini ɛafak daba.*
waiter - *serbay* pl. *-a.*
waiting room - *qaɛa d-le-ntiḍaṛ.*
waitress - *serbaya* pl. *-t, xeddama* pl. *-t.*
to **wake** - *fiyyeq.* Please wake me at seven o'clock. *fiyyeqni fe-s-sebɛa ɛafak.*
to wake up - **1.** *faq ifiq, ḍeṛbettu l-fiqa.* I didn't wake up until eight this morning. *ma-ḍeṛbetni l-fiqa ḥetta le-t-tmenya had ṣ-ṣbaḥ.* **2.** *fiyyeq.* The noise woke me up. *l-haṛaž fiyyeqni.*
walk - **1.** *msarya* pl. *-t.* Did you have a nice walk? *waš ɛežbatek le-msarya?* **2.** *mešya* pl. *-t.* You can recognize him by his walk. *imken-lek tɛeqlu men mšiytu.*
to take a walk - *tsara.* Let's take a walk. *yaḷḷah nemšiw ntsaraw.*
to walk - **1.** *tmešša, mša imši ɛla režlih.* Shall we walk or take the bus? *nemšiw ɛla režlina wella nrekbu fe-ṭ-ṭubis?* **2.** *tmešša, ṭḷeq režlih.* Can the little boy walk yet? *waš bda le-wliyed iṭḷeq režlih?* --Our maid walked out on us. *l-metɛellma dyalna heṛbet ɛlina.*
to walk down - *nzel, hbeṭ.* We were walking down the stairs. *konna habṭin mɛa ḍ-ḍṛuž.*
to walk up - *ṭḷeɛ.* He can't walk up the stairs. *ma-iqḍeṛ-š iṭḷeɛ fe-ḍ-ḍṛuž.*
wall - **1.** *ḥeyṭ, ḥiṭ* pl. *ḥyuṭ, ḥiṭan.* Hang the picture on this wall. *ɛelleq t-teṣwiṛa f-had l-ḥiṭ.* --Only the walls are still standing. *ma-bqaw waqfin ġir le-ḥyuṭ.* **2.** *ṣuṛ* pl. *ṣwaṛ.* The old city is surrounded by walls. *le-mdina ḍayṛin biha ṣ-ṣwaṛ.*
**They've walled up that doorway. *bnaw ɛel l-bab.*
wallet - *beẓṭam* pl. *bẓaṭem.* I've lost my wallet. *mša-li beẓṭami.*
walnut - *gergaɛa* pl. *-t.* coll. *gergaɛ.*
walnut tree - *šežṛa de-l-gergaɛ* pl. *-t de-l-gergaɛ* coll. *šžeṛ de-l-gergaɛ.*
want - *ḥtiyaž* pl. *-at.* My wants are very modest. *le-ḥtiyažat dyali qṛiba bezzaf.*
**I'll take it for want of something better. *ġad naxdu ḥit ma-kayen ma ḥsen.*
to want - **1.** *bġa* (imperfect *ibġi* is not usually translatable as 'to want'). I want to go swimming. *bġit nemši nɛum.* **2.** *ṭḷeb, bġa ibġi.* How much do you want for those three sheep? *šḥal ka-ṭṭleb f-had t-tlata d-le-kbaš?*
**He is wanted by the police. *š-šoṛṭa ka-tfetteš ɛlih.*
war - *ḥeṛb* pl. *ḥṛub.*
wardrobe - *mariyu* pl. *-wat.* What are

your shoes doing in my wardrobe? *š-ka-idir ṣebbaṭek fe-l-mariyu dyali?*

warehouse - *hri* pl. *herya.*

warm - *dafi.* It's very warm today. *l-ḥal dafi bezzaf l-yum.*

to warm oneself - *sxen isxon.* Come in and warm yourself by the fire. *dxol tesxon qeddam l-Ɛafya.*

to warm up - *sexxen.* Please warm up the soup for me. *sexxen-li le-ḥrira Ɛafak.*

warmth - *sxuniya* pl. *-t.*

to **warn** - *nebbeh.* I was warned about him. *nebbhuni Ɛlih.*

warning - *tenbih* pl. *-at.* Let that be a warning to you! *ṛa hada tenbih lilek!* or *ṛedd balek had l-meṛṛa!*

to **warp** - *tƐewweẓ, tluwwa.* This wood will warp. *had l-Ɛud ġad itƐewweẓ.*

wash - *teṣbina* pl. *-t,* coll. *teṣbin.* The wash isn't finished yet. *t-teṣbin baqi ma-kmel.*

to wash - **1.** *ṣebben.* I didn't have time to wash my socks. *ma-žbeṛt-š l-weqt baš nṣebben tqašri.* **2.** *ġsel.* She hasn't washed the floor yet. *ma-zala ma-ġeslet l-eṛḍ.* --I'd like to wash (up) before supper. *ma-da biya neġsel qbel le-Ɛša.* **3.** *tṣebben.* Does this material wash? *waš had t-tub ka-itṣebben?*

**Last spring the flood washed away the dam. *ṛ-ṛbiƐ lli fat l-ḥemla ddat s-sedd.* --The sea washed a lot of dead fish up on the beach. *le-bḥeṛ lah bezzaf de-l-ḥut miyyet.*

washcloth - *kis de-l-ḥemmam* pl. *kyusa de-l-ḥemmam.*

waste - **1.** *teḍyaƐ.* It's just a waste of time and energy. *hada ġir teḍyaƐ l-weqt u-ž-žehd.*

**Haste makes waste. *l-faṛ le-mqelleq men seƐd l-qeṭṭ.*

to go to waste - *ḍaƐ iḍiƐ.* A good cook doesn't let anything go to waste. *ṭ-ṭebbaxa l-mezyana ma-ka-txelli ḥetta ši iḍiƐ.*

to lay waste - *heddem.* The earthquake has laid waste the entire city. *z-zelzal heddem le-blad kollha.*

to waste - *ḍiyyeƐ.* He wastes a lot of time talking. *ka-iḍiyyeƐ bezzaf de-l-weqt fe-l-klam.*

wastebasket - *sellat l-muhmalat.*

watch - *magana* pl. *-t, mwagen.* By my watch it's five o'clock. *hadi l-xemsa f-maganti.*

to watch - **1.** *miyyez f-.* I've been watching him for some time. *hadi modda w-ana ka-nmiyyez fih.* **2.** *šaf išuf.* Watch how I do it. *šuf kif ka-ndirha.* **3.** *ḥḍa yeḥḍi, gabel.* Who's going to watch the children? *škun lli ġadi yeḥḍi d-drari?* **4.** *ḥḍa yeḥḍi, Ɛess Ɛla.* That fellow needs close watching. *dak xiyyna xeṣṣ lli iƐess Ɛlih men qṛib.*

**Watch your step! *Ɛendak!* or *ṛedd balek!*

to watch out - *ṛedd balu.* Watch out when you cross the street. *ṛedd balek mnin teqteƐ ṭ-ṭṛiq.*

**Watch out for that fellow. *ḥḍi ṛaṣek men dak xiyyna.*

water - *ma* pl. *myah.* Please give me a glass of water. *Ɛṭini kas de-l-ma Ɛafak.*

to water - **1.** *sqa isqi.* I water the flowers every day. *koll nhaṛ ka-nesqi n-nuwwaṛ.* **2.** *dmeƐ.* My eyes are watering. *Ɛeyniya ka-idemƐu.* **3.** *šeṛṛeb.* Have you watered the horses yet? *waš šeṛṛebti l-xil wella ma-zal?*

**This cake makes my mouth water. *had l-ḥelwa ka-džerri-li l-ma f-fommi.*

watermelon - *dellaḥa* pl. *-t.* coll. *dellaḥ.*

waterproof - *(lli) ma-ka-idexxel-š l-ma.* Is this coat waterproof? *had l-balṭu ma-ka-idexxel-š l-ma?*

wave - *muža* pl. *-t, mwaž.* The waves are very high today. *l-mužat Ɛalyin bezzaf l-yum.*

to wave - **1.** *ferfer, ṛefṛef.* The flags were waving in the breeze. *ṛ-ṛayat kanu ka-iferfru mƐa r-riḥ.* **2.** *šiyyer b-.* Somebody was waving a handkerchief. *ši-waḥed kan ka-išiyyer b-derra.* **3.** *šiyyer b-iddu.* I waved to him. *šiyyert-lu b-iddi.*

wax - **1.** *šmaƐ.* Don't put this doll near the fire; it's only made of wax. *la-teƐmel-ši had t-teṣwiṛa ḥda l-Ɛafya, ṛaha ġir de-š-šmaƐ.* **2.** *dehna* pl. *-t, ṭla.* This furniture wax has a strange odor. *had ṭ-ṭla fih ši-riḥa f-ši-škel.*

to wax - *sqel, ṭla iṭli.* The furniture gets waxed once a month. *ka-nseqlu l-ʔatat meṛṛa fe-š-šheṛ.*

way - **1.** *ṭṛiq* pl. *ṭoṛqan.* Is this the way to town? *waš hadi hiya ṭ-ṭṛiq l-le-mdina?* --I don't want you to go out of your way for my sake. *ma-nebġik-ši tƐewweẓ ṭṛiqek Ɛla weddi.* --Make way for the doctor. *diru ṭ-ṭṛiq le-ṭ-ṭbib.* **2.** *ḥal* pl. *ḥwal.*

That's just his way. *hadak huwa ḥalu.* 3. *ḥala* pl. *-t.* I'm afraid he's in a bad way. *ka-nxaf ikun f-ši-ḥala qbiḥa.* 4. *žiha* pl. *-t, žwayeh.* Are you going my way? *waš ġadi men žihti?* 5. *kifiya.* Let's do this work in a different way. *aži ndiru had l-xedma b-ši-kifiya xṛa.*

**That's no way to treat people. *ma-ši hakda ka-itƐamlu n-nas.* —That's no way to behave. *hadik ma-ši sira.* —Do you know your way around here? *ka-teƐṛef ṭ-ṭoṛqan d-had ž-žiha?* —Everything is going along (in) the same old way. *koll-ši ṛah baqi kif kan bekri.* —Have it your own way. *dir lli bġiti.* —I paid my own way. *xelleṣt Ɛla ṛaṣi.* —That's the way he wants it. *hakdak ka-ibġi.* —What have you got in the way of radios? *š-men škula de-ṛ-ṛadyuwat Ɛendek?* —His house is just across the way. *ḍaṛu ṛaha ġir fe-ž-žiha le-xṛa de-ṭ-ṭṛiq.* —The school is a long way from our house. *l-meḍṛaṣa žat bƐida Ɛla ḍaṛna.* —Ramadan is still a long way off. *ṛemḍan baqi bƐid.* —I don't see any other way out. *ma-ka-nšuf-ši ši-ḥell axoṛ.* —Which is the way out? *fayn bab le-xṛuž?* —You'll have to make your way through this crowd with your elbows. *be-d-draƐ xeṣṣek tsellek ṛaṣek f-had z-zeḥma.* —He has a way with children. *ka-yeƐṛef le-d-drari.* —They have a farm way out in the country. *Ɛendhom waḥed le-Ɛzib wahli fayn f-beṛṛa.* —We went by way of Casablanca. *dezna Ɛel ḍ-ḍaṛ l-biḍa.* —He said it by way of a joke. *qalha ġir b-le-mzaḥ.* —This is in no way better than what you had before. *had š-ši ma-fih ma ḥsen men lli kan Ɛendek.* —In what way is that better? *b-aš hadak ši-ḥsen?* —You shouldn't do the work that way *ma-ši hakda xeṣṣek teƐmel had l-xedma.* —This place is somewhat out of the way. *had l-maḥell ža mxebbeƐ ši-swiya.* —We went out of our way to make him feel at home. *ma-xellina ma Ɛmelna baš išƐeṛ b-ṛaṣu bḥal lli f-maḥellu.* —Make way! *ḅalak!* (sg.), *balaku!* (pl.)

we – *ḥna, ḥnaya.*

weak – 1. *xfif* pl. *xfaf.* Do you like coffee strong or weak? *ka-tebġi l-qehwa qaṣḥa wella xfifa?* 2. *ḍƐif* pl. *ḍƐaf.* I feel a little weak. *ka-nḥess b-ṛaṣi ḍƐif šwiya.*

weakness – 1. *ḍoƐf.* The doctor told her that her weakness was due to undernourishment. *ṭ-ṭbib qal-lha ḍ-ḍoƐf dyalha sbabu qellt l-makla.* —You have to do something with your boy about his weakness in arithmetic. *xeṣṣek teƐmel ši-ḥaža l-weldek Ɛel ḍ-ḍoƐf dyalu f-le-ḥsab.* 2. *Ɛib* pl. *Ɛyub.* That's one of his weaknesses. *hadak Ɛib men le-Ɛyub lli fih.*

wealthy – *ġani, mreffeh.* He married a wealthy widow. *džuwwež b-hežžala mreffha.*

weapon – *slaḥ* (coll.). All weapons have to be turned over to the police. *s-slaḥ kollu ka-ixeṣṣu itsellem le-š-šoṛṭa.*

wear – *ma ittelbes.* There's still a lot of wear left in these shoes. *had ṣ-ṣebbaṭ ma-zal fih ma ittelbes.*

**The cuffs are showing signs of wear. *le-kmam bdaw itbalaw.*

to wear – 1. *lbes.* He never wears a fez. *Ɛemmṛu ma-ka-ilbes ṭ-ṭeṛbuš.* 2. *ṣbeṛ.* This coat didn't wear well. *had l-kebbuṭ ma-ṣbeṛ-š bezzaf.*

to wear down – 1. *ttkel.* These heels are all worn down. *had l-gedmiyat tteklu bezzaf.* 2. *ġleb.* We finally wore him down. *ma-mšina ḥetta ġlebnah.*

to wear out – 1. *hlek, sala mƐa.* He wears out his shoes very fast. *deġya deġya ka-ihlek ṣbabṭu.* —Just don't wear yourself out. *ġir ma-tehlek-š ṛaṣek.* 2. *ttkel, tbala.* Our furniture is worn out. *ʔatatna tbala.*

weary – *Ɛeyyan.* I get very weary at times. *beƐḍ l-meṛṛat ka-nkun Ɛeyyan bezzaf.*

weather – *ḥal.*

**I'm a little under the weather today. *ṛani šwiya ma-ši huwa hadak l-yum.*

to **weave** – *nsež.* The children wove this rug at school. *had ẓ-ẓeṛbiya nesžuha d-drari fe-l-meḍṛaṣa.*

weaver – *derraz* pl. *-a.*

weaving – *taderrazet.*

wedding – *Ɛers* pl. *Ɛrasat.*

Wednesday – *l-aṛbeƐ.*

weed – *ṛbiƐa qbiḥa* pl. *ṛbiƐat qbaḥ* coll. *ṛbiƐ qbiḥ.* The whole garden is full of weeds. *ž-žnan kollu Ɛameṛ be-ṛ-ṛbiƐ le-qbiḥ.*

to weed – *neqqa.* I've got to weed the garden. *xeṣṣni nneqqi ž-žnan.*

week – *žemƐa* pl. *-at, ʔusbuƐ* pl. *ʔasabiƐ.* I'll be back in three weeks. *ġad neṛžeƐ men daba tlata de-ž-žemƐat.*

a week from tomorrow - *bḥal ġedda.* He'll come a week from tomorrow. *ġad iži bḥal ġedda.*

weekend - *ʔaxir ž-žemɛa, ʔexxeṛ ž-žemɛa.* We decided to spend the weekend at the lake. *mɛewwlin baš nduwwzu ʔexxeṛ ž-žemɛa fe-ḍ-ḍaya.*

weekly - **1.** *žarida ʔusbuɛiya.* He publishes a weekly. *ka-inšeṛ žarida ʔusbuɛiya.* **2.** *ʔusbuɛi.* Is your weekly report ready? *waš t-teqrir l-ʔusbuɛi dyalek mwežžed?* **3.** *meṛṛa fe-ž-žemɛa.* This magazine appears weekly. *had l-mažella ka-texṛož meṛṛa fe-ž-žemɛa.*

to weep - *bka ibki.*

to weigh - *wzen.* Please weigh this package for me. *wzen-li had l-bakit ɛafak.* --He always weighs his words. *dima ka-yuzen klamu.*

**This piece of meat weighs two kilos. *had ṭ-ṭeṛf de-l-lḥem fih žuž kilu.*

weight - **1.** *ṣeṛf* pl. *ṣṛuf, ṣṛufa.* The weights are under the scale. *ṣ-ṣṛuf ṛahom teḥt l-mizan.* **2.** *mizan, tqol.* The weight of the box is a hundred kilos. *tqol ṣ-ṣenduq myat kilu.*

**Don't attach too much weight to what he says. *ma-teddiha-š bezzaf fe-klamu!* --His opinion carries great weight. *ṛ-ṛeyy dyalu ɛendu teʔtir kbir.*

to lose weight - *ḍɛaf, ṭiyyez.* When I was sick I lost a lot of weight. *l-weqt lli kont mṛiḍ ḍɛafit bezzaf.*

welcome - *mṛeḥba* (b-). Welcome, welcome, please come in. *mṛeḥba, mṛeḥba, tfeḍḍel zid.* --Welcome to our house! *mṛehba bik ɛendna.*

**You're welcome! (in response to thanks). *bla žmil!* --You're always welcome to use my car. *imken-lek taxod siyaṛti weqt-emma bġiti b-koll faṛaḥ.* --You're always welcome here. *ṛak dima bḥal lli f-maḥellek hnaya.* --That is the most welcome news I've heard in a long time. *hada ʔeḥsen xbaṛ smeɛtu men hadi modda.*

to welcome - **1.** *ṛeḥḥeb b-.* They welcomed us very warmly. *ṛeḥḥbu bina b-qelbhom u-žwareḥhom.* **2.** *qbel b-faṛaḥ.* He would welcome the opportunity to go abroad. *ġad iqbel l-mešya l-l-xariž b-faṛaḥ.*

well - **1.** *bir* pl. *byar.* They're digging a well back of the house. *ṛahom ka-iḥefṛu bir muṛ ḍ-daṛ.* **2.** *bezzaf.* Do you know him well? *ka-tɛeṛfu bezzaf?* **3.** *mezyan.* He works well. *ka-ixdem mezyan.* **4.** *iwa.* Well, just as you wish. *iwa kif tebġi.*

**He couldn't very well refuse to come. *ma-qdeṛ-š tamamen iṛfeḍ baš iži.* --The new business is doing very well. *l-ḥaṛaka ž-ždida ka-ttmešša f-ġaya.* --The patient is doing very well today. *le-mṛiḍ bdat dzyan ḥaltu l-yum.* --I'm not feeling well. *ma-ka-nḥess-š b-ṛaṣi huwa hadak.* --He is quite well off. *huwa la-bas ɛlih tbaṛek ḷḷah.* --He's well off there. *ma-xeṣṣu ḥetta haža temma.*

as well as - **1.** *u-kadalik.* He knows German as well as several other languages. *ka-yeɛṛef l-ʔalṃaniya u-kadalik ɛadad de-l-lugat xṛin.* **2.** *bḥal.* He talks Arabic as well as I do. *ka-itkellem l-ɛeṛbiya bḥali.*

to get well - *rtaḥ.* First I must get well again. *ka-ixeṣṣni nertaḥ huwa l-luwwel.* --I hope you get well soon! *ka-ntmenna-lek deġya tertaḥ.*

well-to-do - *la-bas ɛlih, xwaži* pl. *-yin, xwaža.* His parents are well-to-do. *waldih xwažiyin.*

west - *ġeṛb.*

western - *ġeṛbi.* They live in the western part of the state. *ka-iseknu fe-ž-žiha l-ġeṛbiya de-l-wilaya.*

wet - **1.** *fazeg.* My socks are wet. *tqašri fazgin.* **2.** *mṛewwi.* We had a wet summer. *daz ɛlina ṣif mṛewwi.* **3.** *ṭṛi, xḍeṛ.* The paint is still wet. *ṣ-ṣbaġa ma-zala ṭṛiya.*

what - **1.** *aš, š-, šnu.* What would you like to eat? *aš tebġi takol?* --What's the color of the gloves? *šnu huwa l-lun de-ṣ-ṣebbaɛat?* --What do you need this for? *l-aš ġad teḥtaž had š-ši?* --What are you doing here? *š-ka-ddir hna?* **2.** *š-men.* What things are missing? *š-men ḥwayež ka-ixeṣṣu?* --Do you know what train we're supposed to take? *ka-teɛṛef fe-š-men qiṭaṛ xeṣṣna nrekbu?* --What house are you living in? *fe-š-men ḍaṛ ka-teskon?*

**That's just what I wanted to avoid. *dak š-ši huwa lli bġit neḥdi ṛaṣi mennu.* --I don't know what's what any more. *ma-bqit-š neɛṛef ṛaṣi š-ka-neɛmel.* --What time is it? *šḥal hadi fe-s-saɛa?* --What nonsense! *ɛla ɛqel!* --What beautiful flowers you have in your garden! *walayenni weṛḍat mezyanin ɛendek fe-l-ɛeṛṣa!*

what about - *u-, w-*. What about me? *w-ana?* --What about the job you applied for? *u-l-xedma lli ṭḷebti?* --What about your appointment? *u-l-miɛad lli ɛendek?*

what ... for - *ɛlaš*. What did you do that for? *ɛlaš ɛmelti dak š-ši?*

what if - *w-ila*. What if your friends don't get here at all? *w-ila ṣḥabek be-l-koll ma-žaw-š?*

what is more - *u-zaydun, u-fuq had š-ši*. And what's more, he is very efficient. *u-zaydun ɛendu meqḍuṛa kbira.*

what of it - *u-men beɛd, u-š-kayen*. He didn't get there in time, but what of it? *ma-wṣeḷ-š l-temma fe-l-weqt, u-men beɛd?*

whatever - **1.** *(dak š-ši) lli*. Whatever he does is all right with me. *lli ɛmel ana mwafeq ɛlih.* **2.** *be-l-koll*. I have no money whatever. *ma-ɛendi flus be-l-koll.*

**Whatever made you do that? *š-men ɛqel qal-lek ddir dak š-ši?*

wheat - *gemḥ*.

wheel - *ṛwiḍa* pl. *-t., ṛwayeḍ*. This wheel needs to be tightened. *had ṛ-ṛwiḍa xeṣṣha ddẓiyyeṛ.*

**He wheeled around suddenly and fired. *ḍaṛ deġya u-xerrež le-ɛmaṛa.*

when - **1.** *fuq-aš, weqt-aš*. When can I see you again? *fuq-aš imken-li nšufek?* **2.** *mnayn, mnin, melli*. When you finish your work you can go. *mnayn tsali šġalek imken-lek temši.* --I wasn't home when he called. *ma-kont-š fe-ḍ-ḍaṛ melli ɛeyyeṭ.* **3.** *melli, ila*. When he calls up, tell him I'm not home. *ila ɛeyyeṭ qul-lu m-ana-š fe-ḍ-ḍaṛ.* **4.** *u*. You'd scarcely gone when he came. *yaḷḷah kif mšiti u-huwa ža.*

whenever - *fuq-emma*. Come to see us whenever you have time. *aži šufna fuq-emma kan ɛendek l-weqt.*

**Whenever did you find time to write? *ġir fuq-aš žberṭi l-weqt baš tekteb.*

where - **1.** *fayn, fin*. Where are they living now? *fayn ka-iseknu daba?* **2.** *layn, fayn, fin*. Where are you going? *layn ġadi nta?* **3.** *(fe-l-maḥell) fayn*. We found him just where we told him to wait for us. *žbeṛnah tamamen (fe-l-maḥell) fayn qolna-lu itsennana.*

**Is this the house where they live? *waš hadi ḍ-ḍaṛ lli saknin fiha?*

where ... from - **1.** *mnayn, mnin*. Where did all this money come from? *mnayn žaw had le-flus kollhom?* **2.** *mnina blad*. Where does your friend come from? *mnina blad ṣaḥbek?*

**Where I come from it often rains for weeks. *fe-bladi ktir-ma ka-ṭṭiḥ š-šta žemɛa ɛla žemɛa.*

wherever - **1.** *fayn-emma, fin-emma*. Wherever you are, don't forget to write me. *fayn-emma konti, ma-tensa-š tekteb-li.* **2.** *layn-emma, l-ʔeyy maḥell*. Wherever you go in this part of the country you'll find good roads. *layn-emma mšiti f-had ž-žiha d-le-blad ġadi tṣiḅ ṭoṛqan mezyana.*

whether - *waš, kan*. I'd like to know whether he's coming. *nebġi neɛṛef waš ġad iži.* --Let me see whether that rascal is still there. *xellini nšuf waš dak xiyyna baqi temma.*

which - **1.** *šmen*. Which bag did you pick out? *š-men šekkaṛa xteṛti?* --Which car did you put the food in? *fe-š-men siyaṛa derti l-makla?* **2.** *lli*. Please return the book (which) you borrowed. *men feḍḷek ṛedd le-ktab lli sellefti.*

whichever - *lli*. Take whichever (one) you want. *xud lli bġiti.*

while - **1.** *šwiya, šway*. You'll have to wait a while. *xeṣṣek ttsenna šwiya.* **2.** *mnayn, mnin*. He came while we were out. *ža mnin konna beṛṛa.* **3.** *ma-ḥedd*. I want to arrive while it's still light. *bġit nuṣeḷ ma-ḥedd ma-zal ḍ-ḍuw.* **4.** *u*. Some people live in luxury, while others starve. *ši ɛeyyeš fe-ṛ-ṛafahiya u-x̂ṛin ka-imutu be-ž-žuɛ.*

**It isn't worthwhile. *ma-temma fayda.*

to while away - *tellef*. I'm whiling away the time playing cards. *ka-ntellef l-weqt be-l-kaṛṭa.*

whip - *mṣuṭa* pl. *-at, mṣaweṭ*

to whip - *ṣewweṭ, ḍṛeb b-le-mṣuṭa*. He whipped the horse mercilessly. *ṣewweṭ l-ɛewd bla mḥenna.*

whisper - *tweswis, tweswisa* pl. *-t*. His throat was so sore that he could only talk in a whisper. *ḥelqu mṛeḍ-lu ḥetta ma-bqa iqdeṛ itkellem ġir be-t-tweswis.*

to whisper - *weswes*. She whispered it in my ear. *weswsetha-li f-wedni.*

whistle - **1.** *ṣeffaṛa* pl. *-t, ṣfafeṛ*. He signaled to us with his whistle. *ɛlemna b-ṣeffaṛtu.* **2.** *teṣfiṛa* pl. *-t*. The signal was one long and

one short whistle. *l-ɛalama kanet fiha teṣfiṛa ṭwiḷa u-teṣfiṛa qṣiṛa.*
to whistle - *ṣeffeṛ.* Who's whistling? *škun ka-iṣeffeṛ?*
white - *byeḍ* pl. *buyeḍ.* She was wearing a white dress. *kanet labsa keswa biḍa.*
white (of egg) - *byeḍ.* --I put in the whites of four eggs. *ɛmelt le-byeḍ d-ṛebɛa de-l-biḍat.*
whitewash - *žir* pl. *žyur.* The whitewash is peeling off the walls. *ž-žir d-le-ḥyuṭ bda itqeššeṛ.*
to whitewash - *žiyyer, biyyeḍ.* How long will it take you to whitewash the garage? *šḥal de-l-weqt xeṣṣek baš tbiyyeḍ l-gaṛaž?*
who - **1.** *škun.* Who was the last one to use this book? *škun t-tali lli steɛmel had le-ktab?* --Who do you want? *škun bġiti?* **2.** *men, -mmen.* Who are you looking for? *ɛla men ka-tfetteš?* --Who did you give the book to? *le-mmen ɛṭiti le-ktab?* **3.** *lli.* Do you know the child who's playing out there? *ka-teɛṛef dak d-derri lli ka-ilɛeb temma?*
whoever - *lli.* Whoever wants this apple may have it. *lli bġa had t-teffaḥa yaxodha.*
whole - *kamel, koll-.* He ate the whole cake by himself. *kla l-ḥelwa kamla b-weḥdu.*
on the whole - *fe-l-žomla.* On the whole, I agree with you. *fe-l-žomla ka-nttafeq mɛak.*
wholesale - *be-l-žomla.* They sell only wholesale. *ma-ka-ibiɛu ġir be-l-žomla.*
wholly - *tamamen.*
whooping cough - *ɛewwaqa.*
whose - **1.** *de-mmen, dyal men.* Whose watch is this? *de-mmen had l-magana?* **2.** *men* (in construct with a preceding noun). Whose house do you live in? *f-ḍaṛ men ka-teskon?* **3.** *lli ...* (plus noun with possessive ending). Mr. Tazi's the one whose house I live in. *s-si t-tazi huwa lli ka-nskon f-ḍaṛu.*
why - *ɛlaš.* Why didn't he come yesterday? *ɛlaš ma-ža-š l-bareḥ?*
that's why - *biha b-as, ɛla dak š-ši, hadak ɛlaš.* That's why I didn't call you. *biha b-aš ma-ɛeyyeṭt-lek-š.*
wide - **1.** *waseɛ.* This street is very wide. *had z-zenqa wasɛa bezzaf.* **2.** *kbir* pl. *kbaṛ.* They have a wide selection of shoes. *ɛendhom mežmuɛa kbira de-ṣ-ṣbabeṭ.*
**Is this jellaba wide enough for you? *had ž-žellaba qeddek fe-t-tisaɛ?*
to open wide - *terreɛ.* Open the windows wide. *terreɛ š-šṛažem.*
to widen - *wesseɛ.* They're going to widen our street. *ġad iwessɛu z-zenqa dyalna.*
widow - *hežžala* pl. *-t.*
widower - *hežžal* pl. *-in, hžažel.*
width - *ɛoṛḍ, tisaɛ.* The room is four meters in width. *l-bit fih ṛebɛa miter de-t-tisaɛ.*
wife - *mṛa* (construct form *mṛat*) pl. *ɛyal, ɛyalat; zewža* pl. *-t.* She's the wife of a famous actor. *hadik mṛat waḥed l-mumettil meshuṛ.*
wild - *weḥši.*
**My boy is wild about ice cream. *weldi·meślum ɛel l-basṭa.*
wild animal - *weḥš* pl. *wḥuš.* There are no wild animals in this forest. *ma-kaynin wḥuš f-had l-ġaba.*
wilderness - *xla.*
will - **1.** *ɛazima* pl. *-t, ɛazayem.* He has a strong will. *ɛendu ɛazima qwiyya.* **2.** *wṣiya* pl. *-t.* He died without leaving a will. *mat bla-ma ixelli wṣiya.*
to will - *kteb, xella, ḥebbes ɛla.* He willed all his property to the city. *ḥebbes melku kollu ɛel le-mdina.*
I will, you will, etc. - **1.** *ġadi, ġad, ġa-* (plus imperfect tense). I'll go tomorrow. *ġad nemši ġedda.* **2.** (imperfect tense). I'll see you at three o'clock. *nšufek fe-t-tlata.*
**Will you please reserve a room for me? *ḥbes-li ši-ṛeḥba ḷḷah ibarek fik.* --He won't get anywhere. *ma-ġad iqḍi-šay.*
would - **1.** (imperfect tense). He would never take the job. *ɛemmṛu ma-išedd l-xedma.* **2.** *bġa* (past negative only). She wouldn't take it. *ma-bġat-š taxodha.*
would have - **1.** *kan* (plus the imperfect tense). He would never have gotten that job if it hadn't been for his father. *ɛemmṛu ma-kan išedd dak l-xedma kun ma-kan-š bbah.* --I would've gone to the movies with you but I didn't have any money. *kont nemši mɛak le-s-sinima be-l-ḥeqq ma-kanu ɛendi flus.* **2.** (the imperfect tense). I did it, but if he hadn't hit me I wouldn't have done it. *ɛmeltha, be-l-ḥeqq kun ma-ḍṛebni-š ma-neɛmelha.*
I would like, you would like,

etc. - *nebġi, tebġi,* etc. What would you like to drink? *š-tebġi teš*ṛ*ob?* --We haven't seen you at all as much as we would like. *ga*Ɛ *ma-šefnak kif nebġiw.*

I would rather, you would rather, etc. - *nfeḍḍel, tfeḍḍel,* etc. We would rather live in the country. *nfeḍḍlu nseknu f-be*ṛṛ*a.*

willing - *qabel.* He's willing to help us. •*huwa qabel baš i*Ɛ*awenna.*

will power - Ɛ*azima.*

to **wilt** - *tte*ṛ*xa, dbal.*

to **win** - *rbeḥ.* I'm going to win this game. *ana ġad nerbeḥ f-had l-le*Ɛ*ba.*

**I've won him over to our side. *že*ṛṛ*itu l-žihetna.*

wind - *riḥ* pl. *ryaḥ.* There was a violent wind last night. *kan ši-riḥ mežhed l-bareḥ fe-l-lil.*

**There's something in the wind. *ši-ḥaža ka-truž.*

**I got wind of it yesterday. *l-bareḥ wṣeḷni xba*ṛ *had š-ši.*

to **wind** - **1.** *tluwwa,* Ɛ*waž.* The road winds through the mountains. *t-*ṭṛ*iq mluwwya ma bin le-žbal.* **2.** *ḍuwwe*ṛ. Wind it around my finger. *ḍuwwe*ṛ*ha-li* Ɛ*la ṣeb*Ɛ*i.* **3.** *ṭeḷḷe*Ɛ. I forgot to wind my watch. *nsit ma-ṭeḷḷe*Ɛ*t-š maganti.*

to wind up - **1.** *luwwa, qenneṭ.* Will you help me wind up this yarn? Ɛ*afak t*Ɛ*awenni nluwwi had l-xiṭ?* **2.** *sala, feḍḍa, ṣeffa.* They gave him two weeks' time in which to wind up his affairs. Ɛ*ṭaweh žme*Ɛ*tayn iṣeffi fiha ġ*ṛ*aḍu.*

winded - *meqduf.* At the end of the game they were all winded. *fe-t-tali de-l-le*Ɛ*b kanu kollhom meqdufin.*

to get winded - *tteqdef.* I get winded easily. *değya ka-ntteqdef.*

window - **1.** *še*ṛ*žem* pl. *š*ṛ*ažem.* Please open the windows wide. Ɛ*afak terre*Ɛ *š-š*ṛ*ažem.* **2.** *šebbak* pl. *šbabek.* Inquire at window number three. *ṣeqṣi fe-š-šebbak* ṛ*eqm tlata.*

windowpane - *zaža de-š-še*ṛ*žem* pl. *zažat de-š-š*ṛ*ažem* coll. *zaž de-š-š*ṛ*ažem.*

wine - *š*ṛ*ab* pl. *-at.*

wing - **1.** *ženḥ, žneḥ* pl. *žnuḥa, žwaneḥ.* The pigeon broke its wing. *le-ḥmama herrset žneḥha.* **2.** *žiha* pl. *-t.* The office is in the left wing of the building. *l-mekteb ža fe-ž-žiha l-iṣ*ṛ*iya de-l-binaya.*

**She took him under her wing. *xdatu fe-ḥḍenha.*

wink - *ġemza* pl. *-t* coll. *ġmiz.* She understood me at a single wink. *b-ġemza weḥda fehmetni.*

**I didn't sleep a wink. *ma-*Ɛ*melt-ši teġmiḍa.*

to wink at - *ġmez.* Did she wink at you? *waš ġemzettek?*

winter - *iyyam l-berd.*

wipe - *mseḥ, neššef.* I'll wash the dishes if you wipe them. *negsel l-lwani ila ġad tneššefhom nta.*

to wipe (off) - *mseḥ, zuwwel.* First let me wipe off the dust. *xellini nzuwwel l-ġob*ṛ*a be*Ɛ*da.*

to wipe out - *mḥa imḥi.* The earthquake wiped out the whole town. *z-zelzal mḥa le-mdina kollha.*

wire - **1.** *selk* pl. *sluka.* The wire isn't strong. *had s-selk ma-ši ṣḥiḥ.* **2.** *be*ṛ*qiya* pl. *-t, tiliġ*ṛ*am* pl. *-at.* Send him a wire. *ṣifeṭ-lu be*ṛ*qiya.* --I'll let you know by wire. *ġad nxeb*ṛ*ek b-be*ṛ*qiya.*

**Hold the wire, please! *ma-teqṭe*Ɛ*-š, men feḍlek.* --I had to pull a lot of wires to get it. *šḥal de-n-nwa*Ɛ*e*ṛ *ḍuwwe*ṛ*t f-le-xwa baš wṣeḷt-lha!*

to wire - Ɛ*mel tiliġ*ṛ*am,* Ɛ*mel be*ṛ*qiya.* He wired me to meet him at the station. Ɛ*mel-li be*ṛ*qiya baš nt*Ɛ*e*ṛ*ṛeḍ-lu f-le-mḥetta.*

wiring - *sluka de-ḍ-ḍuw.* The wiring in this house is dangerous. *s-sluka de-ḍ-ḍuw f-had ḍ-ḍar fihom xaṭa*ṛ.

to do the wiring - *rekkeb ḍ-ḍuw.* Who is doing the wiring in your house? *škun ka-irekkeb-lkom ḍ-ḍuw fe-ḍ-ḍar?*

wisdom - Ɛ*qel* pl. Ɛ*qul,* Ɛ*qula.*

wise - *me*Ɛ*qul.* You have made a very wise decision. *xditi waḥed l-qara*ṛ *me*Ɛ*qul.*

**When are you going to get wise to yourself? *fuq-aš ġad tfiq men glebtek?* --Don't you think we ought to put him wise? *ma-ka-iḍhe*ṛ*-lek-š billa xeṣṣna nḥellu-lu* Ɛ*eynih?*

wish - **1.** ʔ*umniya* pl. *-t,* ʔ*amani.* I'll be able to satisfy my wishes easily. *ġad imken-li nḥeqqeq l-*ʔ*umniyat dyali b-suhula.* **2.** *tehni*ʔ*a* pl. *-t, tahani.* Best wishes for the New Year! *t-tahani l-ḥa*ṛṛ*a b-munasabat l-*Ɛ*am ž-ždid!*

to wish - **1.** *tmenna.* We wished him luck on his trip. *tmennina-lu ṣef*ṛ*a s*Ɛ*ida.* --I wish I could stay here longer. *tmennit u-kan imken-li nebqa hna ši-modda x*ṛ*a.*

**I wouldn't wish it to my worst enemy. *ma-tmennaha-š ḥetta le-*Ɛ*duk.* --Did you wish that on me? *waš*

tmenniti-li dak š-ši? --I wish you many happy returns for your birthday. *ka-nhennik b-ɛid miladek.*
to wish for - *tmenna, bġa ibġi.* What do you wish for most? *š-ka-ttmenna ktir-ši?*

wit - *fyaqa* pl. *-t, ḥdaqa* pl. *-t, fṭana* pl. *-t.* What I like about him especially is his wit. *ka-yeɛžebni ktir-ši b-le-fyaqa dyalu.*
**He's no great wit. *ma-fih-ši ši-fyaqa kbira.* --I'm at my wit's end. *ma-bqit-š neɛqel š-ka-neɛmel.*
wits - *ɛqel* pl. *ɛqul, ɛqula; dmaġ* pl. *-at.* She was out of her wits with fright. *flet-lha d-dmaġ be-l-xewf.*

witch - *seḥḥara* pl. *-t.*

with - 1. *mɛa.* I'll have lunch with him today. *ġad ntġedda mɛah l-yum.* --Do you want something to drink with your meal? *baġi tešṛob ši-ḥaža mɛa l-makla dyalek?* 2. *b-* (*bi-* before pronoun endings). Did you write with this pen? *ktebti b-had r-riša?* --The place was crawling with ants. *dak ṛ-ṛeḥba kanet ka-teġli be-n-nmel.* With pleasure. *b-koll farah.* --She was green with envy. *matet b-le-ḥsed.* 3. *ɛla.* The responsibility rests with him. *l-mesʔuliya ɛlih.* 4. *ɛend.* He's staying with us. *huwa nazel ɛendna.* 5. *beɛd-emma.* With all the work he's done he still isn't finished. *beɛd-emma dak l-xedma kollha ḷḷi dar, ma-zal ma-sala-š.*

wither - *ybes.*

within - 1. *men daba.* I expect an answer within three days. *ka-ntsenna ž-žwab ižini men daba telt iyyam.* 2. *daxel, f-qelb.* Speeding is forbidden within the city limits. *memnuɛa s-soṛɛa daxel ḥudud le-mdina.*
**The letters came within a few days of each other. *le-bṛawat žaw b-ši-modda ma bin l-weḥda u-l-weḥda.* --We're within walking distance of the theater. *ka-imken-lna nemšiw ɛla režlina men ɛendna le-s-sinima.*

without - 1. *bla.* Can I get in without a ticket? *imken-li ndxol bla bṭaqa?* 2. *bla-ma.* I took it without anyone seeing me. *dditha bla-ma išufni ḥedd.*

witness - *šahed* pl. *šhud.*
to witness - 1. *šaf išuf, tfeṛṛež f-.* A huge crowd witnessed the game. *bezzaf de-n-nas tfeṛṛžu fe-l-leɛb.* 2. *ḥdeṛ ɛla.* Did you witness the accident? *ḥdeṛti ɛel l-ʔafat?*
to give witness - *šhed.* She gave witness that she had seen him enter the house. *šehdet billa šafettu daxel le-ḍ-ḍaṛ.*

witty - *qeẓẓam* pl. *-a.*

wolf - *dib* pl. *dyab.*

woman - *mṛa* pl. *ɛyal, ɛyalat, nsa; siyyda* pl. *-t.*
old woman - *ɛguza* pl. *ɛgayez.*

wonder - *ɛažab* pl. *ɛažayeb, ɛžeb* pl. *ɛžayeb.* --The medicine works wonders. *d-dwa ka-idir le-ɛžayeb.*
**No wonder it's cold, the window is open. *iwa ɛliha kayen l-berd, š-šeṛžem meḥlul.*
to wonder - 1. *tseġṛeb, tɛežžeb.* I shouldn't wonder if this were true. *ma-ntseġṛeb-š ila kan had š-ši ṣḥiḥ.* 2. *tsaʔel.* I wonder whether they're at home or not. *ka-ntsaʔel waš huma fe-ḍ-ḍaṛ wella la.* 3. *tsaʔel, xemmem.* I was just wondering what you were doing when you called me up. *kont tamamen ka-nxemmem š-konti ka-teɛmel mnin ɛeyyeṭti-li.*
**I wonder what he'll do now. *men qal-li š-ġad yeɛmel daba.* --I wonder if she has written him. *šuf waš ketbet-lu!* --I wonder whether they're still here. *yeɛlem ḷḷah waš ma-zalin hnaya.*

wonderful - *ɛažib.*

wood - *ɛud* pl. *ɛwad, xšeb* (coll.). What kind of wood is this? *š-men nuɛ de-l-ɛud hada?*
woods - *ġaba* pl. *ġyeb.* Is there a path through the woods? *kayna ši-ṭṛiq f-woṣṭ l-ġaba?*
**He isn't out of the woods yet. *ma-zal ma-xrež men dak l-weḥla.*

wood carver - *neqqaš* pl. *-a.*

wood carving - *taneqqašet.*

wooden - *d-le-xšeb.* The pan has a wooden handle. *l-meqla qbeṭtha d-le-xšeb.*

wool - *ṣuf* pl. *ṣwaf.* The blanket is made of pure wool. *l-beṭṭaniya ṣuf xaḷṣa.*

woolen - *de-ṣ-ṣuf.* I bought a woolen sweater. *šrit kebbuṭ de-ṣ-ṣuf.*

woolens - *ḥwayež de-ṣ-ṣuf.*

word - 1. *kelma* pl. *-t* coll. *klam.* How do you spell that word? *kif ka-tekteb had l-kelma?* --We have to learn fifty new words for tomorrow. *xeṣṣna nḥefḍu xemsin kelma xṛa l-ġedda.* 2. *kelma, kelma de-š-šaṛaf.* He gave us his word that he would finish the job. *ɛṭana klemtu de-š-šaṛaf billa ġad ikemmel l-xedma.*
to have a word - *tkellem.* May I have a word with you? *imken-li ntkellem mɛak?*
**You can take his word for it.

imken-lek ttiq bih. --I don't mince my words. *klami ma-fih zwaq.* --Have you had any word from your son lately. *weṣḷek ši-xbaṛ had l-iyyam men ɛend weldek?*

work - **1.** *xedma* pl. *-t, xdami.* This work isn't important. *had l-xedma ma-ši muhimma.* **2.** *tamara* pl. *-t.* It took a lot of work to convince him that we were right. *tamara ḥtažina mɛah baš nqenɛuh billa kan mɛana l-ḥeqq.*

out of work - *bla xedma, gales.* He's been out of work since the factory closed. *melli šedd l-meɛmel u-huwa bla xedma.*

to work - **1.** *xdem.* I work from eight to five. *ka-nexdem men t-tmenya l-l-xemsa.* --The mechanic is just working on your car now. *l-mikaniki ṛah ka-ixdem f-siyaṛtek daba.* --The motor isn't working. *l-muṭuṛ ma-xeddam-š.* **2.** *xeddem.* He works his employees very hard. *ka-ixeddem l-xeddama dyalu bezzaf.*

**We're working on him to give us the day off. *ṛa-ḥna ka-nhawdu fih baš yeɛṭina n-nhaṛ de-ṛ-ṛaḥa.* --The doctor worked over him for an hour. *saɛa u-ṭ-ṭbib xeddam fih.*

to work loose - *tterxef, sxa isxa.* We almost had an accident when the steering wheel worked loose. *ɛla šwiya konna ġad nɛemlu ḥadita mnin bda d-dman itterxef.*

to work out - **1.** *xrež, ṣdeq.* How do you think this idea would work out? *kif ka-ḍḍenn ġad teṣdeq had l-fikra?* **2.** *tmešša.* How did things work out? *kif tmeššat l-ˀumuṛ?*

**The plan is well worked out. *l-mešṛuɛ mneḍḍem f-ġaya.*

worker - *xeddam* pl. *-a.* Workers in this factory are well paid. *ka-ixeḷḷṣu l-xeddama d-had l-meɛmel mezyan.*

**She's a good worker. *hiya ka-texdem mezyan.*

working hours - *saɛt l-xedma, weqt l-xedma.* May I call you during working hours? *imken-li nɛeyyeṭ-lek f-weqt l-xedma.*

workman - *xeddam* pl. *-a.*

world - *denya* pl. *-t, ɛalam* pl. *ɛawalim.* He's traveled all over the world. *huwa ṣafeṛ fe-l-ɛalam kollu.*

**Where in the world have you been? *qul-li ġir fayn konti!* --I wouldn't hurt him for the world. *ma-nqeṣṣḥu-ši waxxa ikun lli kan.* --My father thinks the world of you. *nta qedd-aš ɛend ḅḅa.*

worm - *duda* pl. *-t* coll. *dud.*

worn - *bali.* This rug doesn't look worn at all. *had ẓ-ẓeṛbiya ma-bayen-š ɛliha balya be-l-koll.*

worry - *hemm* pl. *hmum, dbila* pl. *-t, dbayel.* Her son gives her a great deal of worry. *weldha ka-ixleq-lha belɛa de-l-hemm.*

to worry - **1.** *šuwweš.* His silence worries me. *skatu ka-išuwwešni.* --I'm worried because I haven't heard from him in a week. *ana mšuwweš ḥit hadi žemɛa ma-žani ɛlih xbaṛ.* **2.** *rfed dbila.* Don't worry! *ma-terfed dbila!* **3.** *xaf ixaf.* You have nothing to worry about. *ma-ɛendek mn-aš txaf.*

**The future doesn't worry him. *l-musteqbal ma-ka-ihezz-lu wden.*

worse - **1.** *kfes.* He's feeling worse this morning. *had ṣ-ṣbaḥ ka-iḥess b-ṛaṣu kfes.* --Her condition is getting worse and worse. *ḥaltha ka-dzid kfes u-kfes.* **2.** *kteṛ.* It's snowing worse than ever. *ɛemmeṛ t-telž ma-ṭaḥ kteṛ men had š-ši.*

from bad to worse - *men kfes le-kfes, men kfes le-ṭḷeṣ.* His business is going from bad to worse. *ḥaṛaktu mašya men kfes le-ṭḷeṣ.*

to be worse off - *zad tkeffes* impf. *izid itkeffes.* He's even worse off now. *daba ɛad zad tkeffes.*

to **worship** - *ɛbed.* Many people worshipped idols. *ɛadad de-n-nas kanu iɛebdu l-ˀaṣnam.*

worst - **1.** *kfes.* But wait, I haven't told you the worst. *bellati ɛlik, ma-zal ma-qolt-lek-ši lli kfes men had š-ši kollu.* **2.** *ˀefles, ˀekbeṛ, ˀeqbeḥ.* It's the worst accident I can remember. *ˀefles ḥadita ka-neɛqel ɛliha.*

**Of the three he's worst off. *huwa lli mayla-lu f-had t-tlata.* --The worst is yet to come. *ma-zal ɛad tšuf ma kteṛ men had š-ši.* --If worst comes to worst, we can always sell our property. *ila ɛedmet l-ḥala ġad imken-lna nbiɛu melkna.* --You got the worst of the argument. *dditi ma kfak men d-dbaz.*

worth - *qima* pl. *-t.* He didn't appreciate her true worth. *ma-qeddeṛ-š qimetha le-ḥqiqiya.*

**That horse is worth three thousand dirhams. *dak l-ɛewd tamanu telt alaf derhem.* --Give me two dirhams worth of peanuts. *ɛṭini žuž drahem d-kakaw.* --I think he's easily worth a million. *ka-nḍenn yeɛmel melyun mxiyyeṛ f-resmalu.*

--Did you get your money's worth last night? *yak ma-mšaw-lek-ši flusek xṣaṛa l-bareḥ?* --It's worth the trouble. *ḥetta ila šqa l-waḥed beƐda be-l-fayda.* --Was it worth your while? *fadek ši dak š-ši?* --Is the book worth reading? *had le-ktab fih ši ma itteqṛa?* --That's really worth seeing. *dak š-ši kayen fih ma ittšaf.*

worthless - *bla qima, bla fayda, baṭeḷ.*

would - see 'will'.

wound - *žeṛḥ, žeṛḥa* pl. *-t.* It will be a couple of months before the wound in his leg is healed. *men daba ši-šehṛayn Ɛad ibṛa-lu ž-žeṛḥ lli f-fexḍu.*

to wound - *žṛeḥ.* He wounded him in the shoulder with the sword. *žeṛḥu f-ketfu be-s-sif.* --Several men were wounded in the brawl. *Ɛadad lli džeṛḥu f-le-mdabza.*

to **wrap (up)** - *kemmes.* Shall I wrap it up for you? *nkemmsu-lek?*

**He's all wrapped up in his work. *medhi fe-šġalu tamamen.*

wreck - **1.** *ʔafat* pl. *-at, ḥadita* pl. *-at.* Were any killed in the wreck? *mat ši-waḥed fe-l-ḥadita?* **2.** *rdem* pl. *rduma.* The bodies are still buried in the wreck. *l-žettat baqyen medfunin teḥt r-rdem.*

**He's a complete wreck. *mehluk f-ṣeḥḥtu.*

to wreck - **1.** *Ɛenfež.* The car was completely wrecked. *s-siyaṛa tƐenfžet kollha.* **2.** *heddem.* The explosion wrecked the whole plant. *t-tfeṛgiƐa heddmet l-meƐmel kamel.*

wretched - **1.** *mdeqlel.* I still feel wretched. *ma-zal ka-nḥess b-ṛaṣi mdeqlel.* **2.** *mfeƐfeƐ.* We had a wretched weekend. *ʔexxeṛ l-ʔusbuƐ daz-lna mfeƐfeƐ.*

wrinkle - *tekmiša* pl. *-t* coll. *tekmaš.* Her face is full of wrinkles. *wžehha kollu tekmaš.*

to wrinkle - *tkemmeš.* This silk wrinkles easily. *had ṣ-ṣabṛa değya ka-ttkemmeš.*

wrist - *meƐṣem* pl. *mƐaṣem, qebṭa (de-l-yedd)* pl. *qbaṭi.*

wrist watch - *magana de-l-yedd.*

to **write** - *kteb.*

writing - **1.** *xeṭṭ* pl. *xṭuṭ.* I can't read his writing. *ma-ka-nferrez-š xeṭṭu.* **2.** *ktaba* pl. *-t, ktayeb.* I don't get around to writing. *ma-ka-nsali-š le-ktaba.*

**I'd like to have that in writing. *bġit dak š-ši mektub.*

wrong - **1.** *ġaḷaṭ.* He admitted that he was in the wrong. *ṛah Ɛtaṛef billa kan fe-l-ġaḷaṭ.* **2.** *ġaleṭ.* I'll admit that I was completely wrong about him. *ka-neƐtaṛef billa kont tamaman ġaḷeṭ fih.* **3.** *xaṣeṛ.* Something is wrong with the telephone. *ši-ḥaža xaṣṛa fe-t-tilifun.*

**I'm afraid you're wrong. *ka-nxaf ikun ma-mƐak ḥeqq.* --Is anything wrong with you? *Ɛendek ši-ḥaža?* --I must have added the figures up wrong. *waqila ṛ-ana ġaḷeṭ f-žemƐ le-ḥsabat.* --Everything went wrong yesterday. *ḥetta ḥaža ma-mšat mƐewwṭa l-bareḥ.* --You're heading in the wrong direction. *ṛak maši xarež Ɛel ṭ-ṭṛiq.*

to do wrong to - *ḍḷem.* I have done no wrong to anyone. *ma-ḍḷemt ḥetta waḥed.*

to do (something) wrong - *ġḷeṭ f-.* You did your work wrong again. *Ɛawed ġḷeṭṭi fe-l-xedma dyalek.*

to wrong - *ḍlem, tƐedda Ɛla.* He thinks they have wronged him. *ka-iḍenn ila tƐeddaw Ɛlih.*

X

X ray - *bḷaka (de-ṛ-ṛadyu)* pl. *-t.* I asked the doctor if I could see the X-ray. *suwwelt ṭ-ṭbib waš imken-li nšuf le-bḷaka.*

to X-ray - *duwwez fe-ṛ-ṛadyu.* The dentist X-rayed my hand. *ṭ-ṭbib duwwez yeddi fe-ṛ-ṛadyu.*

Y

yard - *tasiƐa* pl. *-t*, *saḥa* pl. *-t*. The children are playing in the yard. *d-drari ka-ileƐbu fe-t-tasiƐa.*
yarn - **1.** *xiṭ*. I'll take six balls of that green yarn. *Ɛṭini setta de-l-kobbat men dak l-xiṭ le-xḍeṛ.* **2.** *ḥkaya* pl. *-t; xṛafa* pl. *-t, xṛayef*. He's telling one of his yarns. *ka-iƐewwed ḥkaya men l-ḥkayat dyalu.*
to **yawn** - *tfuwweh*.
year - *Ɛam* pl. *snin*. He's thirty years old. *f-Ɛemṛu tlatin Ɛam.* --They live in the country all year round. *ka-iseknu f-beṛṛa l-Ɛam kollu.* --I haven't seen him for years. *hadi modda men s-snin ma-šeftu.*
yearly - **1.** *fe-l-Ɛam*. How much is it yearly? *be-šḥal fe-l-Ɛam?* **2.** *koll Ɛam*. My uncle pays us a yearly visit. *xali ka-iži išufna koll Ɛam.*
to **yell** - **1.** *Ɛeyyeṭ*. We heard someone yelling for help. *smeƐna ši-waḥed ka-iƐeyyet l-iġata l-llah.* **2.** *ġuwwet*. He yelled when the doctor stuck him with the needle. *ġuwwet mnin ḍreb-lu ṭ-ṭbib l-ibra.*
yellow - **1.** *ṣfeṛ* pl. *ṣufeṛ*. She's wearing a yellow dress. *labsa keswa ṣefṛa.* **2.** *xuwwaf, xayef*. He's yellow. *huwa xuwwaf.*
Yemen - *l-yaman*.
yes - *iyeh, ih, nƐam*. She answered yes. *žawbet b-iyeh.*
yesterday - *l-baṛeḥ, yames*. I saw him only yesterday. *Ɛad šeftu l-bareḥ.*
the day before yesterday - *wel-l-bareḥ*. He left the day before yesterday. *mša f-ḥalu wel-l-bareḥ.*
yet - **1.** *wella ma-zal*. Have you seen the movie yet? *waš šefti l-film wella ma-zal?* **2.** *baqi, ma-zal*. He hasn't come yet. *baqi ma-ža.* --I'll get him yet! *baqi nqebṭu!* or *ma-zal yeḥṣel.* **3.** *u-be-l-ḥeqq, lakin*. He didn't want to go, yet he had to. *ma-bġa-š imši u-be-l-ḥeqq tlezzem imši.*
to **yield** - **1.** *xella*. His business doesn't yield much profit. *l-biƐ u-š-šra dyalu ma-ka-ixelli-lu rbeḥ bezzaf.* **2.** *Ɛṭa yeƐṭi*. This bomb yields a lot of heat. *had l-qenbula ka-teƐṭi l-ḥaṛaṛa bezzaf.* --This land yields a lot of wheat. *had l-ʔeṛḍ ka-teƐṭi z-zṛeƐ bezzaf.* **3.** *steslem, Ɛṭa yeƐṭi ṛaṣu*. The city yielded to the enemy. *le-mdina steslmet l-le-Ɛdu.*
**I'll yield on this point. *qabel had n-noqṭa.*
yolk - *feṣṣ* pl. *fṣuṣ*, *meḥḥ* pl. *mḥaḥ*.
yoke - *nira* pl. *-t*.
you - m. sg. *nta*, f. sg. *nti, ntiya*, pl. *ntuma*.
**You never know what's going to happen. *ma-ka-yeƐṛef l-waḥed š-ġad yewqeƐ.*
young - *ṣġiṛ* pl. *ṣġaṛ*. She's still very young. *ma-zala ṣġiṛa.*
young lady - *šabba* pl. *-t*.
young man - *šabb* pl. *šobban*.
young people - *nas ṣġaṛ*. The young people had a lot of fun. *n-nas ṣ-ṣġaṛ tmellġu mƐa ṛaṣhom.*
**I never worked very hard in my younger days. *f-iyam ṣoġṛi Ɛemmṛi ma-xdemt bezzaf.* --The night is still young. *l-lil ṭwil.*
your - **1.** *-ek* pl. *-kom*. Your hair is black. *šeƐṛek kḥel.* --Children, your uncle is in the house. *a d-drari, Ɛemmkom fe-ḍ-ḍaṛ.* **2.** *dyalek* pl. *dyalkom, mtaƐek* pl. *mtaƐkom*. Your tree is blooming, Ahmed. *a ḥmed, š-šežṛa dyalek mnuwwṛa.*
**You've got to watch your car in this town. *f-had le-blad l-ʔinsan ka-ixeṣṣu yeḥḍi ṭumubiltu.*
yours - *dyalek* pl. *dyalkom*. Is this yours or ours? *waš hada dyalkom wella dyalna?*
yourself - **1.** *ṛaṣek* pl. *ṛaṣkom, nefsek* pl. *nfeskom*. Did you hurt yourself? *waš qeṣṣeḥti ṛaṣek?* --Keep it for yourself. *xelliha l-nefsek.* **2.** *b-ṛaṣek* pl. *b-ṛaṣkom, b-nefsek* pl. *be-nfeskom*. You must do it yourself. *nta b-ṛaṣek xeṣṣek teƐmelha.*
**You have to guard yourself against the cold here. *hna l-ʔinsan lazem yeḥḍi ṛaṣu men l-berd.*

youth - 1. *ṣġeṛ, ṣġoṛ*. He worked hard in his youth. *xdem bezzaf f-ṣoġṛu*. 2. *weld* pl. *wlad*. The youth struck the old man. *l-weld ḍṛeb ṛ-ṛažel le-kbir*.

Z

zero - *sfer* pl. *sfura*. Add another zero. *zid sfer axoṛ*.
zinc - *ẓeng*.
Zionist - *ṣehyuni* pl. *-yin*.
zipper - *sensla* pl. *-t*.
zone - *menṭaqa* pl. *-t*.
zoo - *ɛeṛṣa de-l-ḥayawan*.